The World Book Encyclopedia

T   Volume 19

World Book, Inc.

a Scott Fetzer company

Chicago London Sydney Toronto

The World Book Encyclopedia

Copyright © 1983, U.S.A.
by
World Book, Inc.

Tt

T is the 20th letter of our alphabet. It was also a letter in the alphabet of the Semites, who once lived in Syria and Palestine. They called the letter *taw*, their word for *mark*. They used a cross-shaped mark they may have borrowed from an Egyptian *hieroglyphic*, or picture symbol, used as a check mark. The Greeks borrowed the letter from the Phoenicians. However, when they adopted the letter, they moved the crossbar to the top of the vertical stroke. The Greeks called their letter *tau*. See ALPHABET.

Uses. *T* or *t* is about the second most frequently used letter in books, newspapers, and other printed material in English. As an abbreviation in geographic names, it may stand for *territory* or *township*. As a musical abbreviation, *t* may indicate *tenor*, *tempo*, or *time*. In grammars and dictionaries, it means *tense* or *transitive*. It may also stand for *ton*, *temperature*, or *Testament*, as in *O.T.*, or *Old Testament*.

Pronunciation. A person pronounces *t* by placing the point of his tongue on his upper teethridge, with his lips and vocal cords open, and expelling his breath between his teeth and tongue. In such words as *fasten* or *castle*, the *t* is silent. In the combination *tion*, *t* may be pronounced *sh* as in *nation*, or *ch* as in *question*. In the combination *th*, as in *thin*, a person pronounces *t* by placing his tongue blade below the points of his upper teeth and expelling his breath between his tongue and teeth, with his vocal cords relaxed. In words like *thine*, the process is the same, but the vocal cords vibrate. See PRONUNCIATION.

I. J. GELB and JAMES M. WELLS

Development of the Letter T

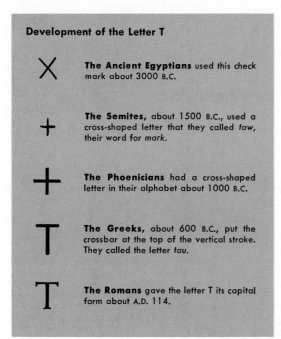

The Ancient Egyptians used this check mark about 3000 B.C.

The Semites, about 1500 B.C., used a cross-shaped letter that they called *taw*, their word for *mark*.

The Phoenicians had a cross-shaped letter in their alphabet about 1000 B.C.

The Greeks, about 600 B.C., put the crossbar at the top of the vertical stroke. They called the letter *tau*.

The Romans gave the letter T its capital form about A.D. 114.

The Small Letter t

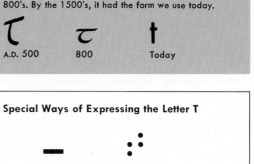

The Small Letter t developed during the A.D. 500's from Roman writing. The letter changed slightly in the 800's. By the 1500's, it had the form we use today.

A.D. 500   800   Today

Special Ways of Expressing the Letter T

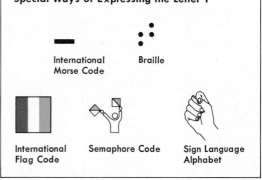

International Morse Code

Braille

International Flag Code

Semaphore Code

Sign Language Alphabet

Common Forms of the Letter T

Handwritten Letters vary from person to person. *Manuscript* (printed) letters, *left*, have simple curves and straight lines. Cursive letters, *right*, have flowing lines.

Roman Letters have small finishing strokes called *serifs* that extend from the main strokes. The type face shown above is Baskerville. The italic form appears at the right.

Sans-Serif Letters are also called *gothic letters*. They have no serifs. The type face shown above is called Futura. The italic form of Futura appears at the right.

Computer Letters have special shapes. Computers can "read" these letters either optically or by means of the magnetic ink with which the letters may be printed.

TAANIT ESTHER. See PURIM.

TAB. See AIRPLANE (The Wing).

TABASCO, *tuh BAS koh,* or *tah VAHS koh,* is a state of southeastern Mexico along the Bay of Campeche. For location, see MEXICO (political map). Tabasco has a population of 1,101,335, and covers an area of 9,522 square miles (24,661 square kilometers). It lies on a low, tropical plain, much of which is marshy. Tabasco is the largest source of petroleum in Mexico. The state's chief farm products include bananas, coconuts, cacao, and sugar cane. The large forests produce hardwoods, rubber, chicle, resins, and dyes. Tabasco was crossed by Hernando Cortés in 1524. It is one of the original states of Mexico. Villahermosa is the capital of Tabasco. See also OLMEC INDIANS.   CHARLES C. CUMBERLAND

TABBY. See CAT (Coat; picture).

TABERNACLE, *TAB er NAK'l,* or TENT OF MEETING, was the center of worship of the Israelites during early Biblical times. The Hebrews built it during their wanderings in the desert. While on Mount Sinai, Moses received instructions for building the Tabernacle. The materials were provided by the free offerings of the people. The Tabernacle was dedicated on the first day of the second year after the Israelites fled from Egypt on their way to Palestine.

According to the Bible, the place of worship was 45 feet (14 meters) long and had a height and width of 15 feet (4.6 meters). Its framework of acacia wood was overlaid with fine gold. The ceiling was of white linen with figures of blue, purple, and scarlet angels woven into it. The structure was covered with a curtain of goat's hair and a layer of skins. A veil of linen divided the inside into two sections, the *Holy of Holies* and the *Holy Place.* The Holy of Holies contained the Ark of the Covenant. The Ark held the Tables of the Law on which the Ten Commandments were written.

It was called Ark of the Covenant because it was a symbol of the Jews' *covenant* (agreement) with God. Above the Ark was the "mercy seat," a cover of gold with angels at each end. In the Holy Place were the table of *shewbread* (bread made without yeast), the altar of incense, and the candlestick, all made of gold.

The Tabernacle stood within a court, enclosed by rich curtains and brass pillars. It opened toward the east, and faced the altar where the people brought their sacrifices to be offered by the priests. The court also contained a laver where the priests washed their hands and feet before entering the Holy Place.

The Tabernacle and its furnishings could be carried from place to place. It was moved from the desert to Gilgal, then to Shiloh after the Israelites conquered Canaan. Later it was moved to Nob, then to Gibeon, and finally brought to Jerusalem, where its relics were preserved in Solomon's Temple. Other places of worship are sometimes called tabernacles.   LEONARD C. MISHKIN

See also ARK OF THE COVENANT; MORMONS (picture: The Mormon Tabernacle); TEMPLE.

TABERNACLES, FEAST OF. See SUKKOT.

TABES, *TAY beez,* means a wasting away of the body. It once was used to describe any condition that caused such wasting. But its modern usage is almost exclusively to describe the wasting caused by syphilis, one of the venereal diseases (see VENEREAL DISEASE). In this condition it is called *tabes dorsalis,* meaning a wasting away of the *dorsal* (back) part of the spinal cord. Persons with tabes dorsalis have difficulty coordinating their movements. They may lose all feeling in their arms and legs, and their leg muscles deteriorate. The *optic nerve,* an eye nerve, may be affected.   LOUIS D. BOSHES

TABLE MANNERS. See ETIQUETTE.

The Tabernacle was an ornate place of worship built by the Israelites during their wanderings in the desert. They could move it from place to place. The Israelites completed it in about six months.

A Formal Table Setting must follow traditional rules. A white tablecloth, a centerpiece, candles, and proper placement of dishes and silver are essential.

An Informal Table Setting for a buffet dinner can be arranged in various ways. The dinnerware, silver, and serving dishes are placed on the buffet.

TABLE SETTING is the art of providing an attractive background for a meal. Part of the pleasure in eating lies in the beauty of the dining table. Custom has long governed the proper setting of a table. Methods vary somewhat in different countries and among different peoples, but certain customs of table setting have become standard throughout the United States. These customs of table setting are much like those used in European countries.

Customs in table setting vary chiefly according to the formality of the meal, although variations for individual or family tastes are common. The main differences are in the number and types of dishes and pieces of silver used. There are also some differences in the placement of dishes and silver.

An important part of table setting is the tablecloth and decoration. For ordinary family meals, a cotton, rayon, or linen tablecloth is both customary and proper. It may be white or colored, or have a figured design. At more formal dinners a white damask or lace cloth is customary. At informal and semiformal meals, mats made of cloth, plastics, cork or light woods may be used.

The Centerpiece. No centerpiece is necessary for family meals, although many families keep a low bowl of flowers or a small centerpiece in the center of the table. But at a formal dinner party, a centerpiece of flowers or fruit, or some art object or even scattered leaves or flowers may be used. Candlesticks may be set in a group or arranged in pairs. Lighted candles are customary at formal dinners.

Serving silver is placed according to the manner in which the meal is to be served. If dishes are served family style, the serving silver lies in front of the host or hostess, to be placed in the different dishes as they are served. Carving tools are always placed in front of the person sitting at the head of the table. At a small table, the sugar bowl and cream pitcher are placed near the center of the table, along with the salt and pepper shakers and any relish dishes. If there are several sets of these condiment dishes, they are placed in groups along the center line.

At a Formal Dinner Party, nothing but salt and pepper shakers is ever placed on the table. All other seasonings and dishes are passed at the proper time. No serving silver is placed on the table.

The setting of the individual places follows a definite pattern, whether the meal is formal or informal. Forks are set to the left of the plate, and knives and spoons to the right. Knives have their cutting edges turned toward the plate. At dinners where a cocktail fork is to be used, it is placed to the right of the spoons. All silverware is arranged in the order of its use, with the first to be used laid on the outside, farthest from the plate. Only the silver needed for the courses and dishes being served is on the table. Dessert silver is brought on as the dessert is served.

Napkins may be placed to the left of the forks or on the service plate. A service plate is used at a formal dinner with a cocktail, soup, or fish course, or with a salad which is served as a separate course. The service plate is taken away at the end of the course for which it is used. A bread-and-butter plate is set in front of the forks. The bread-and-butter knife is laid on the bread-and-butter plate. A salad plate may be placed to the right or left, but is usually at the left. Glasses are set directly in front of the knives, and coffee cups are placed to the right of the spoons. Place cards and nut cups are customarily set on the left, just above the plate and the first fork. HELEN MARLEY CALAWAY

3

TABLE TENNIS

North Suburban YMCA (WORLD BOOK photo)

Table Tennis, also called *ping-pong*, provides lively indoor recreation for people of all ages. Many schools and youth clubs have ping-pong tables, which can be used by two or four players.

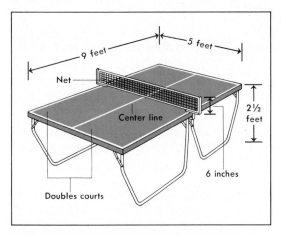

A Ping-Pong Table is divided into halves by a low net. A white center line further divides the surface of the table into four courts, which are used when playing doubles.

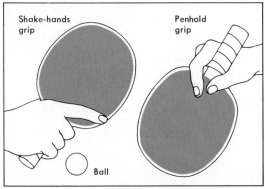

WORLD BOOK illustrations by Richard Fickle

Two Ways to Hold a Table-Tennis Racket are shown above. The *shake-hands grip* is used by most players in the United States and other Western countries.

TABLE TENNIS, or PING-PONG, is a lively indoor game that resembles a miniature version of tennis. The players use rackets, which are often called *paddles*, to hit a ball back and forth over a net that stretches across a table. They score points by hitting the ball so their opponent or opponents cannot return it. Table tennis may be played by two or four persons. If two persons play, the game is called *singles*. If four play, it is called *doubles*.

Table tennis developed in England during the late 1800's. Today, it is a popular form of recreation and an international sport. Players from more than 100 countries belong to the International Table Tennis Federation (ITTF). The ITTF holds a world championship tournament every two years. The United States Table Tennis Association sponsors several national tournaments, including the National Team Championships and the U.S. National Open.

Equipment for table tennis consists of a table, net, rackets, and ball. The table measures 9 feet (274 centimeters) long, 5 feet (152.5 centimeters) wide, and 30 inches (76 centimeters) high. Most tables are dark green with a white line along the edges. A white center line runs the length of the table. The center line divides the table into *courts* that are used for doubles. The net, which is suspended between two posts, extends across the width of the table at its center. The net measures 6 inches (15.25 centimeters) high.

The rackets may be any shape, size, or weight. Most are made of wood and are covered with rubber or sponge. The covering material cannot be more than $\frac{1}{6}$ inch (4 millimeters) thick on either side of the racket.

The ball is round and hollow and made of celluloid. It measures from 1.4 to 1.5 inches (37.2 to 38.2 millimeters) in diameter and weighs from $\frac{1}{12}$ ounce (2.4 grams) to $\frac{1}{11}$ ounce (2.53 grams).

How the Game Is Played. Table tennis players toss a coin to determine who serves first. The server places the ball on the palm of the hand, throws it up vertically, and hits it with the racket. When throwing the ball, the server must keep the fingers straight and together, and the thumb extended. The hand must be behind the end of the table when the server hits the ball. The ball must bounce on the server's side of the net, clear the net, and bounce on the opponent's side.

For a good return, a player must hit the ball after one bounce so that it clears the net and bounces on the opponent's court. *Volleying* (hitting the ball before it bounces) is not allowed. Play continues until one person misses the ball, hits it off the table, or hits it into the net. When a player fails to make a good serve or a good return, the opponent scores a point. After every five points, the other player serves.

The player who first scores 21 points wins the game. However, the winner must have at least a two-point lead. If both players score 20 points, they alternate serving after each point until one person leads by 2 points. A match consists of either two out of three games or three out of five games.

A few additional rules apply in table tennis for playing doubles. The server must serve from his or her right-hand court into the opponents' right-hand court. The teammates must alternate in hitting the ball on the returns.   LEAH NEUBERGER

TABLEAU, *TAB loh,* is a static scene composed of three-dimensional figures, either living or inanimate. Usually the scene represents a historical, legendary, or allegorical event.

A scene employing living figures is called a *tableau vivant* (living picture). Real persons assume poses on a stage or within some other framework, and maintain rigid, statuesque positions throughout the showing. Originally, in the 1500's, these living tableaux were used to make the visual art of the painter or sculptor more expressive. In the middle 1800's, tableaux were frequently used on the American stage to celebrate a striking historical scene. *The Signing of the Declaration of Independence* and Leonardo da Vinci's painting *The Last Supper* are frequently depicted in tableaux vivants.

A tableau may use figures of wax or other materials, as in Madame Tussaud's famous museum in London, or as in a department store display. One of the most familiar tableaux of this type is the *crèche*. During the Christmas season, figures representing the Holy Fam-

Arthur Gould

Living Tableau of a Painting called *Feeding Her Birds,* by Jean Millet, shows actors posing in the same position as the persons in Millet's painting. The frame and the painted backdrop behind the actors complete the illusion.

ily, the wise men, the shepherds, and their sheep are grouped around the Infant Jesus. This group is usually framed in a cutaway representation of the stable in Bethlehem.

Tableaux, whether composed of living or artificial figures, provide a simple and effective means to commemorate a special event. RICHARD MOODY

TABLELAND is similar to a plateau. See PLATEAU.

TABLEWARE. See KNIFE, FORK, AND SPOON; NICKEL SILVER; SILVER.

TABLOID. See NEWSPAPER (Kinds of Newspapers).

TABOO is an action, object, person, or place that is forbidden by law or culture. The word *taboo* comes from the Polynesian word *tapu,* or *tabu,* which means *something sacred, special, dangerous,* or *unclean.* Many societies believe that people who go to a taboo place or touch a taboo object will suffer serious injury. In addition, society may punish the offenders or consider them taboo.

Sacred objects or persons are taboo because they supposedly have a mysterious force that enables them to injure or kill a person. Unclean objects are taboo because they supposedly bring evil to a person or group.

People in many parts of the world avoid taboos. Until the 1900's, for example, Fiji Islanders could not touch any article that belonged to the tribal chief or priest. Australian Aborigines must not say the name of a dead person aloud. Muslims and Orthodox Jews must not eat pork or shellfish. Societies in many parts of the world consider *incest* taboo. These societies forbid marriage or sexual relations between closely related persons, such as a brother and sister. ALAN DUNDES

See also MAGIC (The Magician; Homeopathic Magic); MYTHOLOGY (Mythology of the Pacific Islands).

TABOR COLLEGE. See UNIVERSITIES AND COLLEGES (table).

TABRIZ, *tuh BREEZ* (pop. 571,000), is the fourth largest city in Iran. It is the capital of East Azerbaijan province, in the northwestern corner of the country. It lies about 35 miles (56 kilometers) from Lake Urmia, and is almost surrounded by mountains. For location, see IRAN (color map). Earthquakes have nearly destroyed the city several times.

Tabriz is famous for its fine Persian rugs, and has a large trade in dried fruits and leather goods. It also produces matches, flour, and textiles.

Historians do not know exactly when the city was founded, but it was probably before the A.D. 300's. It served as Iran's capital for a short time in the early 1500's. Russian troops occupied Tabriz in 1827, and again during World Wars I and II. RICHARD NELSON FRYE

TABULARIUM, *TAB yoo LAIR ee uhm,* was a magnificent library in which the ancient Romans stored their records. It stood on Capitoline Hill. The Romans built it in 73 B.C.

See also FORUM, ROMAN.

TACAMAHAC. See POPLAR.

TACHÉ, *tah SHAY,* **SIR ÉTIENNE-PASCHAL** (1795-1865), was a Canadian statesman. He served twice as prime minister of the Province of Canada, and presided over the Quebec Conference of 1864 that paved the way for the federation of the British North American colonies.

Taché was born in St. Thomas, Quebec. He was graduated from the Quebec Seminary. After serving in the British militia during the War of 1812, he practiced medicine. In 1841, Taché entered the Legislative Assembly of Canada. He later served as commissioner of public works, member of the legislative council, and receiver-general. He was knighted in 1858.

Taché formed a cabinet with John A. Macdonald in 1856, and became prime minister. In 1864, the two men again formed a cabinet with Taché as prime minister. But Macdonald was the real head of the government in both ministries. WILLIAM R. WILLOUGHBY

See also MACDONALD, SIR JOHN A.

TA-CH'EN ISLANDS, two islands off the China coast, lie 210 miles (338 kilometers) north of Taiwan. These islands served as Nationalist headquarters during the Chinese civil war until Communist planes bombed them in January, 1955. The Nationalists then left the islands and set up headquarters in Taiwan.

5

USDA
Red-Tailed Tachina Fly

TACHINA FLY, *TAK uh nuh,* is the name of a group of gray or black flies which have bristly bodies. They are helpful to people because their larvae eat many kinds of insects.

Scientific Classification. The tachina belongs to the tachinid fly family, *Tachinidae.* The red-tailed tachina fly is classified as genus *Winthemia,* species *W. quadripustulata.* DALE W. JENKINS

See also FLY.

TACHISTOSCOPE. See AUDIO-VISUAL MATERIALS (Programmed Instruction).

TACHOMETER, *tuh KAHM uh tuhr,* is a device that is used for measuring the speed of rotation of a spinning shaft or wheel, usually in terms of revolutions per minute (rpm).

The most common type of tachometer consists of a rubber cone that may be inserted in a hole in the center of the spinning shaft or wheel, a handle to hold it, and a speed-recording device. In some cases, this speed recorder resembles the parts of a speedometer. It has a rotating magnet that pulls on an armature restrained by a spring, and the movement of the armature gives the rotary speed in revolutions per minute. In other cases, the rubber cone sets in motion a train of wheels which has a centrifugal arm geared to it. The deflection of this arm under spin shows the number of revolutions per minute. In still other cases, a train of wheels merely reduces rotations from the rubber cone.

For some types of moderately high-speed machines, a tachometer consisting of a set of vibrating reeds may be used. These reeds resemble the teeth of a comb, and each tooth is cut to vibrate at just one frequency. By noting which tooth on the device is shaking, a person can tell how fast the machine is vibrating and, therefore, how fast it is turning. These reed tachometers are used on marine machines and on large steam turbines.

Electric tachometers are commonly used in airplanes. They consist of a voltage generator turned by the engine, and connected by electrical wires to an indicator which is a voltmeter. This shows the engine rpm on the dial face. E. A. FESSENDEN and H. S. STILLWELL

TACHYCARDIA, *TACK uh KAHR dee uh,* is an unusually fast heartbeat sometimes called "heart-hurry." The disorder is usually organic. The varieties of tachycardia depend upon the type of fast rhythm involved. For example, *paroxysmal* (spasmodic) tachycardia is a rapid heart action occurring at intervals.

TACHYLYTE, *TAK uh lyt,* is a glassy, basic igneous rock. Basalt is a tachylyte. These rocks are black, but seem brown in portions. Great masses are in Hawaiian lava flows. See also BASALT; IGNEOUS ROCK.

TACHYON, *TAK ee ahn,* is an atomic particle that exists only in theory. If tachyons exist in nature, they never stand still but always move at speeds greater than the speed of light. Light travels 186,282 miles (299,792 kilometers) per second. The name *tachyon* comes from the Greek word for *swift.*

According to the special theory of relativity, ordinary matter can move only at speeds less than the speed of light. The German-American physicist Albert Einstein published the special theory of relativity in 1905. But in 1962, several physicists discovered new solutions to the mathematical equations that make up Einstein's theory. These new solutions provided a mathematical description of the tachyon. No scientific experiment has ever found any evidence of a tachyon. FRANCIS T. COLE

TACITUS, *TAS ih tus,* **CORNELIUS** (about A.D. 55-about 120), was one of the world's greatest historians. His most important works were the *Histories,* which tell of the short reigns of the emperors Galba, Otho, and Vitellius; and the *Annals,* which describe Roman history from Augustus to Nero. Tacitus favored the republican form of government, and his *Histories* and *Annals* were extremely critical of the Roman emperors. He condemned them in sharp, unforgettable phrases, and overlooked any merits of the imperial system. The *Histories* and *Annals* cover periods for which our other sources are scanty. Another work, *Germania,* is important because it contains our first written account of the customs and habits of the Germanic peoples, who later spread over most of western Europe. He also wrote *Life of Agricola* and *Dialogue on Orators.*

Little is known of Tacitus' life except for a few references in his own works and letters written to him by his friend, Pliny the Younger. Tacitus rose to be a praetor (see PRAETOR). THOMAS A. BRADY

TACK. See HORSE (Riding Equipment).

TACKING. See SAILING (Trimming and Tacking).

TACKLE. See BLOCK AND TACKLE.

TACKLE. See FOOTBALL (pictures).

TACLOBAN, *tah KLOH bahn* (pop. 80,707), is the chief city of Leyte Island in the Philippines. It overlooks the San Juanico Strait that separates the northeast corner of Leyte from Samar Island. For location, see PHILIPPINES (color map). The city is the trading center and chief port for an area that produces abacá, rice, coconuts, and tobacco. Tacloban served as the temporary capital of the Philippine Islands in 1944 and 1945. RUSSELL H. FIFIELD and CARLOS P. ROMULO

TACNA-ARICA DISPUTE, *TAK nuh uh REE kuh.* Shortly after the middle of the 1800's, prospectors from Chile began to develop the guano and nitrate deposits of Antofagasta, a province belonging to Bolivia. In 1879, disputes between the two countries led to a war. The conflict soon spread into Tarapacá, a province of Peru. Chile won the war. In 1883, the Treaty of Ancón forced Peru and Bolivia to give up their claims to Tarapacá and Antofagasta. Chile also took control of two provinces of Peru, known as Tacna and Arica.

For the next 45 years, Peru and Chile disputed over the provinces. Finally, in 1928, the United States persuaded Chile and Peru to resume diplomatic relations. In 1929, the countries agreed to let Chile keep Arica while Peru took possession of Tacna. ISAAC J. COX

See also PERU (The War of the Pacific).

TACO. See MEXICO (Food).

TACOMA, *tuh KO muh,* Wash. (pop. 158,501; met. area pop. 485,643), is the third largest city in Washington. It serves as a seaport and industrial center. Tacoma grew up around a sawmill and today is the center of a large forest-products industry. The building of small ships and fishing boats is also a leading industry in Tacoma. Dur-

Richards Studio

Tacoma lies on an inlet of Puget Sound between the Olympic Mountains and the Cascade Range. Mount Rainier, *background*, rises about 55 miles (89 kilometers) southeast of the city.

cade Range to the east. The Tacoma Narrows Bridge, one of the world's longest suspension bridges, spans Puget Sound to connect Tacoma with the Olympic Peninsula.

The Puyallup River flows through Tacoma and empties into Commencement Bay. The shipyards, mills, and factories of the city stand along the narrow coastal plain. Residential districts lie on the rolling upland.

Fort Lewis, an army division post and training center, is about 15 miles (24 kilometers) south of Tacoma. McChord Air Force Base and Madigan Army Medical Center are nearby. Tacoma is the home of the University of Puget Sound and Pacific Lutheran University.

Industry. Surrounding forests supply lumber for Tacoma's woodworking and furniture industries. Copper and other ores are refined in Ruston, a town that lies within the limits of Tacoma. Other important industries in Tacoma include chemical and food-processing plants, and machine and railroad repair shops.

History. The first sawmill was built on the south shore of Commencement Bay in 1852. Pioneers soon erected other mills, and called the settlement *Old Tacoma*. In 1873, a site about 1½ miles (2.4 kilometers) south of the settlement was selected for the terminal of the Northern Pacific Railway. The site received the name *New Tacoma*. This town and Old Tacoma were consolidated as the city of Tacoma in 1884.

The seat of Pierce County, Tacoma has a council-manager type of government.   HOWARD J. CRITCHFIELD

TACONIC MOUNTAINS. See MASSACHUSETTS (Land Regions).

TACONITE, *TAK uh nyt*, is the name of a hard rock containing about 30 per cent iron in the form of fine specks of iron oxide. It is named for the Taconic Mountains of western Massachusetts and Vermont.

Taconite is found in large quantities in the Mesabi Range of Minnesota. It is the mother rock from which the great Mesabi iron-ore deposits were formed. These important iron-ore deposits lie like raisins in a great cake of taconite, 100 miles (160 kilometers) long and 1 to 2 miles (1.6 to 3.2 kilometers) wide. The iron in

ing World War II, the city's shipbuilding industry greatly aided the war effort. Tacoma also ranks high among the cities of the United States as a chemical and metallurgical center.

Location, Size, and Description. Tacoma lies on Commencement Bay, an inlet of Puget Sound (see WASHINGTON [political map]). The city is about 28 miles (45 kilometers) south of Seattle. Tacoma occupies a picturesque site on uneven ground that rises from the bay to a height of 300 feet (91 meters) above sea level. The Olympic Mountains lie to the west, and the Cas-

Steelways, published by American Iron and Steel Institute

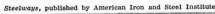

Patterson, Black Star

Taconite Pellets, *above*, produced from taconite rock in the Mesabi iron range of Minnesota, are stockpiled by the gigantic stacker, *left*, during the winter. They are shipped to steel mills when the Great Lakes open in the spring.

taconite occurs principally as the black oxide *magnetite*, or *loadstone*, and the red oxide *hematite*.

Taconite is so hard that ordinary drilling and blasting methods cannot be used to obtain it. In one widely used method of processing taconite, miners use a jet piercing machine, which shoots alternate streams of burning kerosene and cold water. The kerosene heats the taconite to about 4700° F. (2590° C), making it white hot. The cold water jet then cracks the rock by suddenly changing its temperature. Engineers can then blast the taconite into chunks.

Taconite next goes through several stages of crushing, until the pieces are less than $\frac{3}{4}$ inch (19 millimeters) in size. Large cylinders grind it down into even smaller pieces, and magnets separate the useful taconite from the waste sand. After the taconite has been ground almost to a powder and purified, it is fed into a steel barrel. The particles of taconite, when mixed with clay and heated, form marble-sized balls. When the clay burns away, the taconite marbles are strong enough to stand up well in shipment to the blast furnaces where they are used to make iron.

In 1955, the first large-scale taconite processing plant was opened by Reserve Mining Company in Silver Bay, Minn., near Lake Superior. In 1976, a federal court ordered the company to end water pollution and reduce air pollution caused by the plant's method of disposing of taconite waste materials. As a result, in 1980, the company stopped discharging waste materials into Lake Superior, and began depositing them in a special land-disposal basin. E. W. DAVIS

See also HEMATITE; IRON AND STEEL (Kinds of Iron Ore; Processing); LOADSTONE.

TACTILE SENSE. See TOUCH.

TADPOLE, or POLLIWOG, is a newly hatched frog or toad. It is a *larva* (early stage of growth). A frog or toad is a tadpole from the time it hatches until it has grown enough to be a land-living animal. The tadpole stage may last a few weeks, or even up to two years.

Tadpoles vary in color. For example, the tadpole of the common toad is black, but the bullfrog tadpole is green with a spotted tail and a yellow belly. The wood frog tadpole is olive with a pink belly. A tadpole may be from 1 to 6 inches (2.5 to 15 centimeters) long. Bullfrog tadpoles are the largest.

Tadpoles live in quiet pools and streams. The tadpole has a round head joined to the body in such a way that it is impossible to tell which is the head and which is the body. It has a long tail which it uses for swimming. The tadpole changes continuously, always looking more like the mature animal. Its head begins to take shape, it begins to grow back limbs and then front limbs, and its tail becomes shorter. Finally, the tadpole loses its gills and absorbs its tail into its body. The change from tadpole to land-living animal is a process called *metamorphosis*. W. FRANK BLAIR

See also FROG; TOAD.

TADZHIKISTAN, *tah JIK ih STAHN,* is a region that makes up the Tadzhik Soviet Socialist Republic, one of the 15 republics of the Soviet Union. It borders Afghanistan and China in a mountainous area of Central Asia (see RUSSIA [political map]). It covers 55,251 square miles (143,100 square kilometers), and has about 3,801,000 persons. Most of the people are Tadzhiks. Their language is much like the Iranian (Persian) language. Dushanbe (formerly Stalinabad) is the capital and largest city. Cotton is the chief crop. Other crops include rice, wheat, millet, and barley. Factories make cloth, leather goods, and flour. Tadzhikistan has rich deposits of lignite, lead, zinc, oil, and uranium. Exports include cotton, silk, and fruit. THEODORE SHABAD

TAEGU, *ty goo* (pop. 1,310,768), is a commercial city of South Korea. Taegu manufactures shoes and rice flour and serves as a distribution point for copper, tungsten, and various agricultural products. The city is the center of the South Korean textile industry.

Taegu is also an educational center. Kyongbuk National University, Yongnam University, Kyemyong College, and several technical training schools are in the city. Taegu lies on a plain surrounded by mountains. For location, see KOREA (map). WILLIAM E. HENTHORN

TAEJON, *tah jawn* (pop. 509,708), is a transportation center of South Korea. Taejon's location in west-central Korea makes it an important junction for air and railroad traffic. For location, see KOREA (map).

Most of the city's people supply farm products for Seoul, the capital. Industries produce textiles, knit goods, and processed foods. WILLIAM E. HENTHORN

TAEL, *tayl,* was a Chinese weight indicating a unit of value in silver. Although its worth often varied, the tael was the basis of value for Chinese money until 1935.

TAFARI, RAS. See HAILE SELASSIE I.

John H. Gerard; Field Museum of Natural History

A Leopard Frog Tadpole, *above,* looks somewhat like a fish and measures about $3\frac{3}{8}$ inches (8.6 centimeters) long. It has a translucent tail.

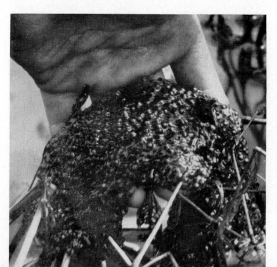

The Tadpoles Hatch and mature into small frogs many days after the leopard frog lays its mass of eggs, *left.*

TAFFETA, *TAF uh tuh,* is a smooth, rather stiff cloth of rayon, nylon, or silk. The name *taffeta* comes from the Persian word *taftah,* meaning *twisted* or *woven.* Taffeta has a plain, close weave. It comes in widths of 36 to 39 inches (91 to 99 centimeters) for dresses, bedspreads, and draperies, and in narrower widths for ribbon.

TAFT, LORADO (1860-1936), was an American sculptor, teacher, and lecturer on art. One of his most famous statues is a symbolic group called *The Spirit of the Great Lakes,* at the Art Institute of Chicago. Taft also designed the *Fountain of Time,* near the campus of the University of Chicago.

Taft was born at Elmwood, Ill., and was graduated from the University of Illinois. He studied art for three years at the École des Beaux Arts in Paris. He taught at the Art Institute of Chicago, and later at the universities of Chicago and Illinois. His major works include *Thatcher Memorial Fountain,* in Denver, Colo.; and *Black Hawk,* at Oregon, Ill.   JEAN LIPMAN

See also BLACK HAWK.

United Press Int.
Lorado Taft

TAFT, ROBERT AL-PHONSO (1889-1953), was an American political leader. He was often called *Mr. Republican,* because of his influence as a policymaker in his party.

Taft was born Sept. 8, 1889, in Cincinnati, Ohio, the son of William Howard Taft, the 27th President of the United States. He attended Yale University and Harvard Law School. He opened a law office in Cincinnati in 1922, and served in the Ohio legislature.

United Press Int.
Robert A. Taft

Taft was elected to the United States Senate in 1938, and was re-elected in 1944 and 1950. In the Senate, he argued for a balanced budget, and opposed most of President Franklin D. Roosevelt's proposals for domestic spending. He also objected to U.S. participation in international affairs before World War II. After the war, however, he worked for federal aid for housing, medical care, and education. He coauthored the Taft-Hartley Act of 1947, which set up controls over labor unions. He set forth his views on foreign affairs in his book *A Foreign Policy for Americans* (1951).

Taft was a candidate for the Republican nomination for President in 1940, 1948, and 1952. He was the leading opponent of Dwight D. Eisenhower for the presidential nomination in 1952. After Eisenhower's election, Taft became Senate floor leader and one of the President's most trusted advisers. He was one of the first five men elected to the U.S. Senate Hall of Fame in 1957. The Robert A. Taft Memorial Foundation was formed in his honor. From 1971 to 1977, his son Robert A. Taft, Jr., served as a U.S. senator from Ohio.   F. JAY TAYLOR

The Art Institute of Chicago
Lorado Taft's monumental fountain, *The Spirit of the Great Lakes,* shows his excellent talent for group sculpture.

The Robert A. Taft Memorial, a bell tower located near the U.S. Capitol in Washington, D.C., honors the Senator from Ohio.

WILLIAM HOWARD TAFT

McKINLEY
25th President
1897 — 1901

T. ROOSEVELT
26th President
1901 — 1909

WILSON
28th President
1913 — 1921

HARDING
29th President
1921 — 1923

Oil painting by Anders L. Zorn (1911), © White House
Historical Association (National Geographic Society)

27TH PRESIDENT OF THE UNITED STATES 1909-1913

TAFT, WILLIAM HOWARD (1857-1930), was the only man in the history of the United States who served first as President, then as Chief Justice. Taft did not want to be President. At heart, he was a judge and had little taste for politics. Above all, he wanted to be a justice of the Supreme Court of the United States.

Taft, a Republican, spent most of the first 20 years of his career as a lawyer and judge. His mother recognized his distaste for politics. "I do not want my son to be President," she said. "His is a judicial mind and he loves the law." But Taft's wife opposed his career as a judge because she felt it was a "fixed groove."

In the end, Taft's mother proved to be right. Hardly any other President has been so unhappy in office. When Taft moved out of the White House in 1913, he told incoming President Woodrow Wilson: "I'm glad to be going. This is the lonesomest place in the world." When he was appointed Chief Justice eight years later, Taft said it was the highest honor he ever received. He wrote: "The truth is that in my present life I don't remember that I ever was President."

Taft was the largest man ever to serve as President. He stood 6 feet (183 centimeters) tall and weighed more than 300 pounds (136 kilograms). A newspaperman wrote that he looked "like an American bison—a gentle, kind one." He had a mild, pleasant personality, but he clung firmly to what he considered the rugged virtues. He did not smoke or drink. He was honest by nature, plain of speech, and straightforward in action. He was completely, and sometimes blindly, loyal to his friends and to his political party.

The modest Taft felt he was not fully qualified for the presidency. He had no gift of showmanship like his predecessor, President Theodore Roosevelt. Taft gave the public an adequate administration, but a poor show. Partly because of this, he failed to capture popular imagination, and many persons called him a failure as President.

During Taft's administration, most of the world was at peace. In Europe, the leading nations lined up in a balance of power that later led to World War I. In China, a revolution overthrew the imperial government and set up a republic. Explorers reached both the North Pole and the South Pole.

In the United States, the pace of life was speeding up. A majority of the people still lived on farms, but more and more were moving to cities. Women had won the right to vote in 12 states. Amendment 16 to the Constitution allowed Congress to pass a federal income tax, although it did not do so until Wilson's administration. The United States grew to 48 states with the admission of Arizona and New Mexico.

Early Life

William Howard Taft was born in Cincinnati, Ohio, on Sept. 15, 1857. He was the second son of Alphonso Taft and his second wife, Louise Maria Torrey Taft. Alphonso Taft's ancestors had lived in Massachusetts and Vermont since emigrating from England in the 1600's. His wife was descended from an English family that helped settle Weymouth, Mass., in 1640.

The elder Taft, whose father was a Vermont judge,

moved to Cincinnati about 1838. He became a successful lawyer and a nationally prominent figure in the Republican party.

Will Taft was a large, fair, and attractive youth. He was brought up in the Unitarian faith. Two older half brothers, two younger brothers, and a younger sister were his playmates. They called Taft "Big Lub" because of his size. During the summers, the five Taft boys visited their Grandfather Torrey in Millbury, Mass. He

made them cut wood in his wood lot to pay for their vacations, and also to teach them the value of money.

When Taft was 13 years old, he entered Woodward High School in Cincinnati. At 17, he enrolled in Yale College. In 1878, Taft was graduated second in his class. He then studied law at the Cincinnati Law School. He received his law degree in 1880 and was admitted to the Ohio bar.

Political and Public Career

First Offices. During 1881 and 1882, Taft served as assistant prosecuting attorney of Hamilton County, Ohio. In March, 1882, President Chester A. Arthur appointed him collector of internal revenue for the first district, with headquarters at Cincinnati. Taft resigned a year later because he did not want to discharge good workers just to make jobs for deserving Republicans.

IMPORTANT DATES IN TAFT'S LIFE

1857 (Sept. 15) Born in Cincinnati, Ohio.
1886 (June 19) Married Helen Herron.
1892 Appointed judge of U.S. Circuit Court of Appeals.
1901 Appointed governor of the Philippines.
1904 Appointed Secretary of War.
1908 Elected President of the United States.
1912 Defeated for re-election by Woodrow Wilson.
1921 Appointed Chief Justice of the United States.
1930 (March 8) Died in Washington, D.C.

THE WORLD OF PRESIDENT TAFT

U.S. population was 97,200,000 in 1913, the year Taft left the presidency. New Mexico and Arizona joined the Union during Taft's term. They became the 47th and 48th states in 1912.

Admiral Peary

WORLD EVENTS

1909 Admiral Robert E. Peary discovered the North Pole.
1910 The Union of South Africa was founded.
1910 The Mexican Revolution began.
1911 Explorer Roald Amundsen discovered the South Pole.
1912 The Republic of China was established, with Sun Yat-sen as provisional president.

Sun Yat-sen

Amundsen

First Junior High School was established in Columbus, Ohio, in September, 1909, and the second in Berkeley, Calif., in January, 1910.

INCOME TAX

Amendment 16 to the Constitution, which gave Congress the legal power to levy income taxes, became law in 1913.

FOR PRESIDENT THEO. ROOSEVELT

Bull Moose Campaign for the presidency in 1912 pitted Theodore Roosevelt against President Taft and Woodrow Wilson.

POSTAL SAVINGS   PARCEL POST

Post Office Department established the Postal Savings System in 1910, and began parcel-post service in 1913.

Helen Herron Taft, the President's wife, was a gracious White House hostess.

Taft's Birthplace, in Cincinnati, Ohio, was photographed when the future President was 13 years old. He sat on top of the gatepost of the carriage entrance for this picture.

He then formed a successful law partnership.

Taft's Family. On June 19, 1886, Taft married Helen "Nellie" Herron (Jan. 2, 1861-May 22, 1943), the daughter of John W. Herron of Cincinnati. Herron had been a law partner of President Rutherford B. Hayes. Taft wrote that his wife was "a woman who is willing to take me as I am, for better or for worse." Mrs. Taft was both intelligent and ambitious. Throughout her husband's career, she encouraged him to seek public office.

The Tafts had three children. Robert Alphonso Taft (1889-1953) became a famous U.S. Senator from Ohio and a leader of the Republican party (see TAFT, ROBERT ALPHONSO). Helen Herron Taft Manning (1891-   ) served as professor of history and dean of Bryn Mawr College in Bryn Mawr, Pa. Charles Phelps Taft II (1897-   ), a lawyer, was mayor of Cincinnati from 1955 to 1957.

State Judge. Taft was happy as a lawyer, but his father's importance in the Republican party kept pushing him toward political life. Early in 1885, Taft was named assistant county solicitor for Hamilton County. In March, 1887, Governor J. B. Foraker of Ohio appointed him to a vacancy on the Cincinnati Superior Court. The next year, the voters elected Taft to the court for a five-year term. This was the only office except the presidency which Taft won by popular vote.

Solicitor General. Taft resigned from the Cincinnati Superior Court in 1890 to accept an appointment by President Benjamin Harrison as Solicitor General of the United States. During his first year, he won 15 of the 18 government cases that he argued before the Supreme Court.

Federal Judge. In March, 1892, President Harrison appointed Taft a judge of the sixth circuit of the newly established federal Circuit Court of Appeals. Taft spent the next eight years as a circuit judge. From 1896 to 1900, he also served as dean of the University of Cincinnati Law School.

Governor of the Philippines. In 1900, President William McKinley appointed Taft chairman of a civil commission to govern the newly acquired Philippines. The next year Taft was named the first civil governor of the islands.

Taft's career in the Philippines was an example of the best in colonial government. He established new systems of courts, land records, vital and social statistics, and sanitary regulations. He built roads and harbors, worked toward the establishment of limited self-government, and led a movement for land reform. Taft also established schools in many parts of the islands, and worked steadily to improve the economic status of the people.

Taft ardently desired to be a justice of the Supreme Court. But in 1902, he turned down his first chance for appointment to the court, because he felt he had not finished his work in the Philippines.

Secretary of War. Secretary of War Elihu Root resigned in January, 1904, and Taft returned to Washington to assume this post in President Theodore Roosevelt's Cabinet. Taft's appointment was good politics. The 1904 presidential campaign was approaching, and Taft had won great popularity for his work in the Philippines.

The President soon began using Taft as his unofficial trouble shooter, both at home and abroad. Taft's department supervised the construction of the Panama Canal and set up the government in the Canal Zone. Taft himself advanced Roosevelt's tariff policy and assisted the President in negotiating the Treaty of Portsmouth, which ended the Russo-Japanese War. Everything was all right in Washington, the President said, because Taft was "sitting on the lid."

Election of 1908. Roosevelt announced he would not seek re-election in 1908, and recommended Taft as the man who would follow his policies. At first, Taft objected, preferring to wait for possible appointment to the Supreme Court. But Mrs. Taft and his brothers helped change his mind. With Roosevelt's support, Taft won the nomination on the first ballot at the Republican national convention. Representative James S. Sherman of New York received the vice-presidential nomination. The voters gave Taft a plurality of more than a million votes over William Jennings Bryan, who suffered his third loss as Democratic nominee for President. Bryan shared the ticket with John W. Kern, a Democratic party leader of Indiana.

Taft's Administration (1909-1913)

"Even the elements do protest," said Taft unhappily when a blizzard swept Washington on the morning of his inauguration in March, 1909. From the start, Taft was filled with doubt about being President. He knew he could not be another Roosevelt. "There is no use trying to be William Howard Taft with Roosevelt's ways," he remarked. "Our ways are different." Taft decided to "complete and perfect the machinery" with which Roosevelt had tried to solve the nation's problems.

Legislative Defeats. Taft began his term with a divided party, although the Republicans controlled both houses of Congress. On the advice of Roosevelt, Taft refused to support the liberal Republicans in their fight to curb the almost unrestricted powers of the Speaker of the House, Joseph "Uncle Joe" Cannon of Illinois. But these Republicans, led by Representative George W. Norris of Nebraska, overthrew "Cannonism" (see NORRIS, GEORGE WILLIAM). Because of his political inexperience in this and other matters, Taft soon lost the support of most liberal Republicans.

Like many other Americans, Taft believed in tariff protection. But he also felt that somewhat lower tariffs would help control trusts (see TRUST). He called Congress into special session to pass a tariff-reduction law, but was reluctant to impose his ideas on Congress. The House passed a bill with big reductions. But in the Senate, Nelson W. Aldrich of Rhode Island, one of Taft's chief advisers, led the campaign to keep high tariffs. The resulting law, the Payne-Aldrich Act, lowered some tariff rates slightly, but left the general level of rates as high as they had been. Taft said he knew he "could make a lot of cheap popularity by vetoing the bill." Instead, he accepted it as better than nothing, defended it in public, and suffered from the great unpopularity it received.

Taft further antagonized the liberal Republicans by his stand in the Pinchot case. In late 1909, Chief Forester Gifford Pinchot made sensational charges that the Department of the Interior, and especially Secretary of the Interior Richard A. Ballinger, had abandoned the conservation policies of Theodore Roosevelt. He also accused the department of selling land concessions to water and power companies too cheaply, and of illegal transactions in the sale of Alaska coal lands. Taft upheld Ballinger who was later cleared by a congressional investigating committee. Taft then dismissed

Pinchot. Liberal Republicans became convinced that some of Pinchot's charges were true, and began turning to Roosevelt as their true leader.

Legislative Achievements of the Taft administration included the first scientific investigation of tariff rates, for which the President established the Tariff Board. Taft took the first steps toward establishing a federal budget by asking his Cabinet members and their staffs to submit detailed reports of their financial needs. Congress created the Postal Savings System in 1910, and parcel post in 1913. At Taft's request, Congress also organized a commerce court and enlarged the powers of the Interstate Commerce Commission. The President pushed a bill through Congress requiring that campaign expenses in federal elections be made public. During Taft's administration, Alaska received full territorial government, and the Federal Children's Bureau was established. The President took action against many trusts. Nearly twice as many "trust-busting" prosecutions for violation of the Sherman Antitrust Act took place during Taft's four years in office as had occurred during Roosevelt's administration of almost eight years.

Foreign Affairs. The Taft administration had an uneven record in international relations. During the late 1800's, nations customarily used diplomacy to expand their commercial interests. "Dollar diplomacy," as promoted by Secretary of State Philander C. Knox, had just the opposite purpose. To Knox, it meant the use of trade and commerce to increase a nation's diplomatic influence (see DOLLAR DIPLOMACY). The United States made loans to China, Nicaragua, Honduras, and other countries in order to encourage investments by bankers in loans to these nations. Taft ended the second American occupation of Cuba in 1909, and negotiated treaties of arbitration with England and France. These

Taft Threw Out the First "First Ball." He started a presidential custom by opening the 1910 major league season in a game between the Washington Senators and the Philadelphia Athletics.

The Bettmann Archive

TAFT'S ELECTION

Place of Nominating Convention...Chicago

Ballot on Which Nominated.......1st

Democratic Opponent...........William Jennings Bryan

Electoral Vote....................321 (Taft) to 162 (Bryan)

Popular Vote....................7,678,908 (Taft) to 6,409,104 (Bryan)

Age at Inauguration..............51

treaties ranked as landmarks in the effort of nations to settle their differences peacefully, but the Senate rejected them.

Life in the White House. Mrs. Taft, a skillful hostess, enjoyed presiding at state functions and entertaining friends at small teas. She hired a woman to replace the traditional male steward, because she thought the service would be improved. At Mrs. Taft's request, the mayor of Tokyo presented about 3,000 cherry trees to the American people. The trees were planted along the banks of the Potomac River. Mrs. Taft suffered a stroke in the winter of 1909. Thereafter, her daughter, Helen, or her sister, Mrs. Louis More, often acted as Taft's official hostess.

Mrs. Taft had a better head for politics than did her husband. He relied on her judgment, and missed her help after she became ill. Mrs. Taft might have controlled the President's fellow Republicans better than he did.

On summer evenings, the Tafts often sat on the south portico of the White House and listened to favorite phonograph recordings. Taft, although a large man, was an excellent dancer, and Mrs. Taft organized a small dancing class for his diversion. He played tennis and golf well, and often rode horseback.

Election of 1912. Theodore Roosevelt had returned in 1910 from an African hunting trip. He denied an interest in running for the presidency again, but began making speeches advocating a "New Nationalism." Under this slogan, Roosevelt included his old policies of honest government, checks on big business, and conservation, as well as demands for social justice, including old-age and unemployment insurance. Conservative Republicans lined up with Taft against Roosevelt.

Although Roosevelt won most of the primary elections, a majority of the delegates to the nominating convention were pledged to Taft. The President was renominated on the first ballot. James S. Sherman was renominated as Vice-President. Roosevelt and the progressive Republicans accused Taft of "stealing" the convention by recognizing the votes of pro-Taft delegations. They organized the Progressive party with Roosevelt as their nominee, and chose Senator Hiram W. Johnson of California as his running mate. The Democrats nominated Governor Woodrow Wilson of New Jersey for President and Governor Thomas R. Marshall of Indiana for Vice-President. Taft faced

inevitable defeat. He received only 8 electoral votes, against 88 for Roosevelt and 435 for Wilson.

Later Years

Law Professor. After Taft left the White House in March, 1913, he became professor of constitutional law at Yale University. That same year he was elected president of the American Bar Association. During World War I, President Wilson appointed Taft joint chairman of the National War Labor Board.

Chief Justice. In 1921, President Warren G. Harding appointed Taft Chief Justice of the United States. Taft regarded this appointment as the greatest honor of his life. His accomplishments as administrator of the nation's highest court were more important than his decisions. The Supreme Court had fallen far behind in its work. In 1925, Taft achieved passage of the Judiciary Act. This law gave the court greater control over the number and kinds of cases it would consider, and made it possible for the court to function effectively and get its work done. Taft was also instrumental in obtaining congressional approval for a new court building. See SUPREME COURT OF THE UNITED STATES.

Taft performed more than his share of the court's great work load, and often advised President Calvin Coolidge. He watched his health, and held his weight to about 300 pounds (136 kilograms). Taft became a familiar figure in Washington as he walked the 3 miles (5 kilometers) between his home and the court almost every morning and evening. But finally the strain of overwork became too great. Bad health, chiefly due to heart trouble, forced his retirement on Feb. 3, 1930. Taft died on March 8, and was buried in Arlington National Cemetery. Taft and President John F. Kennedy are the only Presidents buried there.

JOHN M. BLUM. Critically reviewed by ROBERT TAFT, JR.

Related Articles in WORLD BOOK include:

Outline

Questions

What were Taft's chief personal virtues?

What were the main legislative achievements of his administration?

What was Taft's lifelong ambition? Did he achieve it?

What was the Pinchot case? The Payne-Aldrich Act?

How did Taft lose the confidence of liberal Republicans during his term?

What was the only public office except the presidency to which Taft was elected?

What were Taft's main achievements as governor of the Philippines?

What was Taft's attitude toward the presidency?

What were some of Taft's accomplishments as Secretary of War?

VICE-PRESIDENT AND CABINET

Vice-President.................*James S. Sherman
Secretary of State.............*Philander C. Knox
Secretary of the Treasury........Franklin MacVeagh
Secretary of War...............Jacob M. Dickinson
                            *Henry L. Stimson (1911)
Attorney General...............*George W. Wickersham
Postmaster General.............Frank H. Hitchcock
Secretary of the Navy...........George von Lengerke Meyer
Secretary of the Interior........Richard A. Ballinger
                            Walter L. Fisher (1911)
Secretary of Agriculture.........James Wilson
Secretary of Commerce and
  Labor........................Charles Nagel
*Has a separate biography in WORLD BOOK.

ANDERSON, JUDITH I. *William Howard Taft: An Intimate History.* Norton, 1981.

MANNERS, WILLIAM. *TR and Will: A Friendship That Split the Republican Party.* Harcourt, 1969.

PRINGLE, HENRY F. *The Life and Times of William Howard Taft.* 2 vols. Farrar, 1939. The standard biography.

SEVERN, BILL. *William Howard Taft: The President Who Became Chief Justice.* McKay, 1970.

TAFT-HARTLEY ACT is the popular name for the federal *Labor-Management Relations Act of 1947.* The act was named for its main sponsors, Senator Robert A. Taft and Representative Fred Hartley. It was an amendment to the Wagner Act (National Labor Relations Act of 1935). It continued the Wagner Act's basic guarantees of workers' rights, and outlawed certain union practices. The Taft-Hartley Act provided that strikes which might cause a national emergency can be delayed for 80 days.

The act forbids unions to use force or discrimination against individuals during organizing campaigns. It also prohibits union political contributions in national elections. The act prohibits use of the *secondary boycott, sympathy strike,* and *jurisdictional strike.* A secondary boycott occurs when striking employees bring pressure on a party not involved in the dispute in hopes that the party will stop doing business with their employer. A sympathy strike is called by one union in support of another union striking against its employer. A jurisdictional strike is called by rival unions over which union has the right to work on a job.

The act outlaws the *closed shop,* the practice of hiring only union members, and gives the states power to restrict the *union shop,* in which employees have to join the union after being hired. It requires unions to file such information as constitutions and financial statements with the federal government.

Taft-Hartley supporters said the act equalized power between union and management. Unions called it a "slave labor law," and tried to repeal or amend it. The Landrum-Griffin Act of 1959, the first major amendment to Taft-Hartley, strengthened federal regulation of internal union affairs.   GERALD G. SOMERS

See also CLOSED SHOP; OPEN SHOP; UNION SHOP.

Additional Resources

LEE, R. ALTON. *Truman and Taft-Hartley: A Question of Mandate.* Greenwood, 1980. Reprint of 1966 ed.

McLAUGHLIN, DORIS B., and SCHOOMAKER, ANITA. *The Landrum-Griffin Act and Union Democracy.* Univ. of Michigan Press, 1979.

MILLIS, HARRY A., and BROWN, E. C. *From the Wagner Act to Taft-Hartley: A Study of National Labor Policy and Labor Relations.* Univ. of Chicago Press, 1950.

PATTERSON, JAMES T. *Mr. Republican: A Biography of Robert A. Taft.* Houghton, 1972.

TAGLIONI, *tahl YOH nee,* **MARIE** (1804-1884), was one of the most famous ballerinas of the early 1800's. She was the first ballerina to make toe-dancing beautiful. Her leaps are described as slow flights through the air. To audiences, the effortless grace of her movements made her appear weightless. Her dancing and her acting looked effortless and cool.

Taglioni was born in Stockholm, Sweden. She was rigorously trained by her father, Filippo Taglioni, an Italian dancer and *choreographer* (dance composer). Her dancing in his ballets, particularly in *La Sylphide* (1832), brought about the romantic period in ballet which lasted until the mid-1840's. Audiences all over Europe idolized her. She retired in 1848.   P. W. MANCHESTER

See also BALLET (Romantic Ballet; picture).

TAGORE, *tuh GAWR,* **SIR RABINDRANATH** (1861-1941), was an Indian poet, philosopher, and supporter of freedom for India. In his many poems and songs, he stirred pride among his fellow Hindus. He also had a strong influence on the West. Tagore was influenced by European models in his writings. He was a mystical and religious poet, and saw God in all beauties of nature. He wrote prose and poetry in the Bengali language. Tagore received the 1913 Nobel prize in literature.

Tagore was born in Calcutta, and went to England to study law. He returned to Bengal, a province of British India and the center of the Hindu cultural and spiritual revival in the 1800's. In 1901, he set up a school at Shantiniketan which tried to blend the best in Hindu and Western culture.   T. WALTER WALLBANK

TAGUS RIVER, *TAY gus,* also called *Tajo,* is the longest river of the Iberian Peninsula of southwest Europe. It rises in central Spain and flows west across Portugal to the Atlantic Ocean. The river is 626 miles (1,007 kilometers) long and drains an area of about 31,000 square miles (80,300 square kilometers). The mouth of the Tagus gives Lisbon, Portugal, one of the finest harbors in Europe.   GEORGE KISH

TAHITI, *tuh HEE tee,* an island in the South Pacific Ocean, is famous for its exotic beauty and tropical climate. It is the largest island in French Polynesia, a French overseas territory made up of several island groups. Tahiti is one of the 14 Society Islands. For location, see PACIFIC ISLANDS (map). Papeete is the largest city and chief port of Tahiti. The city is also the capital of French Polynesia.

Tahiti gained worldwide fame as a tropical paradise through the works of many artists and writers who visited the island or lived there. The French artist Paul Gauguin portrayed Tahiti's lush beauty and peaceful atmosphere in many paintings. Many authors, including Herman Melville and James Michener of the United States and Robert Louis Stevenson of Scotland, wrote glowing descriptions of the island. Such works have helped make Tahiti popular with tourists.

Tahiti covers 402 square miles (1,041 square kilometers). A broken coral reef surrounds the island. A strip of flat, fertile land lies along the coast, where most of the people live. The interior of the island is mountainous, and the land is so steep that it is almost entirely uninhabited. Heavy rainfall helps create many fast-flowing streams and spectacular waterfalls there. The island has much lush vegetation, including coconut palms and banana, orange, and papaya trees.

About 85,000 people live on Tahiti. Most of them are Polynesians or have mixed Polynesian and European ancestry. The population also includes a few thousand Chinese and a few hundred Europeans.

Many Tahitians live in or near Papeete and work in the tourist industry, which is the base of the island's economy. Tahiti's Chinese population controls much of the retail and shipping trade on the island. People in rural areas farm the land or work in the fishing industry. The farmers grow breadfruit, taro, and yams for their own use and produce small quantities of copra and vanilla for export.

The earliest inhabitants of Tahiti were Polynesians who came there from Asia hundreds of years ago. The first European to visit the island was the British sea captain Samuel Wallis in 1767. He claimed Tahiti for Great Britain. The next year, a French navigator named Louis Antoine de Bougainville landed on Tahiti and claimed it for France.

Tahiti became a French protectorate in 1842 and a colony of France in 1880. In 1946, France declared Tahiti and the other islands of French Polynesia to be a French overseas territory. Several independence movements developed in French Polynesia during the mid-1900's, but most of the people want to remain under French rule. PHILLIP BACON

See also GAUGUIN, PAUL; SOCIETY ISLANDS.

TAHOE, LAKE. See LAKE TAHOE.

TAIGA. See FOREST (Kinds of Forests).

TAIKA REFORM. See JAPAN (History).

TAIL is the part of the body of a vertebrate animal that extends backward beyond the pelvis. In animals without limbs, the tail is the part of the body that extends beyond the anus. The term *tail* includes both the fleshy portion and the outgrowths it may have, such as fins and feathers.

Animals use their tails in many ways. The tails of most water animals serve to move them and to steer them. Squirrels use their tails to keep their balance when they are leaping and climbing. Woodpeckers and kangaroos prop themselves up with their tails. Spider monkeys and opossums grasp things with their tails.

TAILORBIRD is a songbird of China, India, Malaya, and the Philippines. Its name comes from the way it builds its nest in a large folded leaf. It sews the edges of the leaf together with strips of silk or wool thread, or vegetable fiber, using its bill as a needle. The nest in-

Loke Wan Tho

The Tailorbird Uses Its Long Bill As a Needle.

side the leaves is made from plant down, fine grass, and hair. The female lays three or four eggs. They vary in color from reddish-white to bluish-green and are marked with brownish-red. Tailorbirds are 4 to $5\frac{1}{2}$ inches (10 to 14 centimeters) long.

Scientific Classification. Tailorbirds belong to the kinglet family, *Sylviidae*. They are classified as genus *Orthotomus*. ALBERT WOLFSON

See also BIRD (picture: Kinds of Bird Nests).

TAIN BO CUAILNGE. See CUCHULAINN.

TAINE, *tayn* or *ten*, **HIPPOLYTE ADOLPHE** (1828-1893), was a French critic. His application of the philosophy of *determinism* to art and literature did much to shape French intellectual attitudes in the 1800's.

To understand the origin and development of an artist's or writer's work, Taine said we must discover all the significant facts about the person's *race* (heredity), *milieu* (environment), and *moment* (state of the artistic tradition in which the person worked). Through this theory and through his emphasis on documentation, Taine greatly influenced the naturalist movement in literature (see NATURALISM). Taine's *History of English Literature* (1863) and *Philosophy of Art* (1865-1869) illustrate his deterministic philosophy.

Taine was born in Vouziers. He was a professor at the École des Beaux-Arts in Paris almost continuously from 1864 to 1883. ROBERT J. NIESS

TAIPEI, *TY PAY,* or *TY BAY* (pop. 2,220,427), is the capital and largest city of Taiwan and the seat of the Chinese Nationalist government. Mountains surround Taipei, which lies on the Hsintien, Keelung, and Tanshui rivers. The city's name is also spelled TAIPEH. For location, see TAIWAN (map).

Industries in Taipei manufacture electrical equipment, plastics, plywood, steel, textiles, and other products. Taiwan's west coast railroad and the Taipei International Airport serve the city. Taipei is the home of National Taiwan University. The Chungshan, National Central, and National Palace museums near Taipei feature some of the world's finest Chinese art.

The Chinese founded Taipei in 1708. The city grew from three separate settlements. The Wanhwa section, in the southwest, was the original city. In the mid-1800's, the Tataocheng district developed to the north. About 1885, settlers built up Chengnei to the southeast. The three districts merged in 1920.

The Chinese Nationalist government moved to Taipei in 1949 after the Chinese Communists conquered mainland China. Since then, the city and its suburbs have expanded rapidly in all directions. RALPH N. CLOUGH

TAIRA, *ty EE rah,* or **HEIKE,** was the name of a family that ruled Japan from about 1160 to 1185. After the emperor lost his political influence in the late 700's, powerful families fought for control of the government. The Taira family became a leader of this new warrior class that ruled the country until 1867.

Taira Kiyomori, the head of the family, seized control of the government about 1160. Through arranged marriages, Kiyomori's grandson became heir to the throne as Emperor Antoku.

After Kiyomori died in 1181, the Taira family's power declined rapidly. Taira rule ended in 1185, when the family was defeated in a sea battle by its main rival, the Minamoto family. The young Emperor Antoku drowned during the battle. TETSUO NAJITA

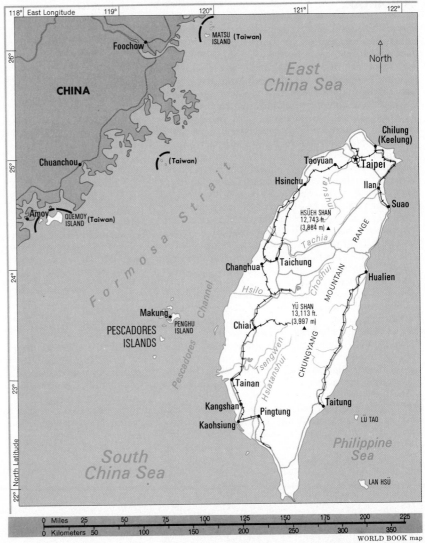

Legend:
* ⊛ National Capital
* • Other City or Town
* —— Road
* ⊢⊣⊢ Rail Line
* ∼ River
* ▲ MOUNTAIN

WORLD BOOK map

TAIWAN

TAIWAN, *ty wahn,* is a mountainous island in the South China Sea, about 90 miles (140 kilometers) off the Chinese coast. The Chinese call the island *Taiwan,* meaning *terraced bay.* The wild, forested beauty of the island led Portuguese sailors in 1590 to name it *Ilha Formosa,* meaning *beautiful island.*

After the Chinese Communists conquered mainland China in 1949, the Chinese Nationalist government moved to Taiwan. Generalissimo Chiang Kai-shek, the Nationalist president, made Taipei the capital of the Republic of China. The Nationalist government also controls several islands in the Formosa Strait. These islands include the Matsu, Pescadores, and Quemoy groups.

Government. The Chinese Nationalist government is based on a Constitution adopted in 1946 on the mainland. Taiwan's National Assembly has about 1,250 members. Its main functions are to elect the president and to amend the Constitution. The president is Tai-

wan's most powerful government official. The president appoints the prime minister and many other government officials.

The government has five branches—executive, judicial, legislative, control, and examination—each headed by a *yuan* (council). The executive, judicial, and legislative yuan resemble the three branches of the United States government. The control yuan watches over the activities of government officials and has the power of impeachment. The examination yuan gives tests that are used to hire and promote government workers.

Although Taiwan is the seat of the Chinese Nationalist government, it is administered as a province of China. The president appoints a provincial governor who serves an indefinite term. The people elect the members of a provincial Assembly to four-year terms. The provincial Assembly has duties that are similar to those of a state legislature in the United States. The

I 7

people also elect county and city government officials.

People. Almost all the people of Taiwan live on the coastal plain that makes up the western third of the island. Most Taiwanese are Chinese whose ancestors came to the island from Fukien and Kwangtung provinces on the mainland. Over $1\frac{1}{2}$ million more persons fled to Taiwan from the mainland after the Communist take-over in 1949. The population also includes about 150,000 persons who probably are related to peoples in the Philippines. Most of these Taiwanese live on reservations in the mountains.

About a third of the people of Taiwan farm the land. Farms on the island average only 2 or 3 acres (0.8 to 1.2 hectares) in size, but Taiwanese farmers live well by Asian standards. Power tillers are gradually replacing water buffaloes in the fields. Many farmers can afford bicycles, motorcycles, refrigerators, radios, and television sets. Most of the farmhouses are made of brick, with tile roofs and central courtyards of packed earth or cement. A typical Taiwanese meal includes rice, served with vegetables and chopped meat or fish.

Most city people in Taiwan wear Western-style clothing. Some workers go barefoot or wear wooden sandals. Farmers and others who work in the hot sun wear cone-shaped straw hats.

The Taiwanese speak various Chinese dialects, depending on their regional birthplace. But almost all the people also use Mandarin, the official Chinese dialect. The majority of Taiwanese are Buddhists or Taoists.

About 90 per cent of the population can read and write. The law requires children to have six years of elementary school and three years of high school. Taiwan has about 2,250 elementary schools; more than 800 high

Facts in Brief

Capital: Taipei.

Official Language: Chinese.

Form of Government: Republic.

Area: 13,885 sq. mi. (35,961 km²), including the Pescadores islands, but excluding Matsu and Quemoy. *Greatest Distances*—north-south, 235 mi. (378 km); east-west, 90 mi. (145 km). *Coastline*—555 mi. (893 km).

Elevation: *Highest*—Yü Shan (Mount Morrison), 13,113 ft. (3,997 m) above sea level. *Lowest*—sea level.

Population: *Estimated 1983 Population*—18,783,000; distribution, 66 per cent urban, 34 per cent rural; density, 1,352 persons per sq. mi. (522 per km²). *1980 Census*—17,805,067. *Estimated 1988 Population*—20,536,000.

Chief Products: *Agriculture*—asparagus, bananas, mushrooms, pineapples, rice, sugar cane, sweet potatoes, tea. *Fishing*—sardines, tuna. *Forestry*—bamboo, camphor, plywood. *Manufacturing*—cement, electrical machinery, fertilizer, plastics, television sets, textiles.

National Anthem: "Chung Hwa Min Kuo Kuo Ko" (The National Anthem of the Republic of China).

Flag: The flag has a red field. A white sun appears on a blue canton in the upper left-hand corner. Red stands for liberty and sacrifice, and white for fraternity and honesty. Adopted in 1928. See FLAG (color picture: Flags of Asia and the Pacific).

Money: *Basic Unit*—New Taiwan dollar or yuan. See MONEY (table: Exchange Rates). See also YUAN.

schools; and over 90 colleges, junior colleges, and universities. National Taiwan University in Taipei has the largest enrollment among Taiwan's universities.

Land and Climate. Taiwan, including the Pescadores islands, covers 13,885 square miles (35,961 square kilometers). This area does not include the Matsu and Quemoy island groups, which are part of Fukien province on the mainland.

Jack Fields, Photo Researchers

Taiwanese Farmers dry rice on cement terraces after harvesting it. About a third of the people of Taiwan work in agriculture, though most of the land is too mountainous for farming. Industrial plants, *background,* employ many Taiwanese and have helped develop the island's economy.

Thickly forested mountains run from north to south and cover about two-thirds of Taiwan. The highest peak, Yü Shan (Mount Morrison), rises 13,113 feet (3,997 meters) above sea level. At many places along the eastern coast, the mountains drop sharply to the sea. Short, swift rivers have cut gorges through the mountains. In the west, the mountains slope to gently rolling hills and level land. The farmers have terraced many hills to provide more fields for growing rice.

Taiwan has a subtropical climate, with hot, humid summers and an average annual rainfall of more than 100 inches (250 centimeters). Temperatures average about 80° F. (27° C) in summer and 65° F. (18° C) in winter. Summer monsoons bring strong winds and rain to Taiwan. In winter, monsoons bring rain and cooler weather to the north. Typhoons occur almost every year, with damaging rains and winds that sometimes exceed 100 miles (160 kilometers) per hour.

Economy. Taiwan has few natural resources except its mountain forests. But the island's economy has expanded steadily with the growth of manufacturing and foreign trade. Forest products include bamboo, camphor, lumber, paper, and plywood. Taiwanese factories make cement, fertilizer, plastics, television sets, and other products. Exports include bananas, canned foods, chemicals, electrical machinery, metals, plywood, sugar, and textiles. Most exports go to Hong Kong, Japan, the United States, and West Germany.

Only about a fourth of Taiwan's land can be farmed. The farmers use much fertilizer and harvest two or three crops a year from the same field. The chief crops include asparagus, bananas, citronella grass, mushrooms, pineapples, rice, sugar, sweet potatoes, and tea. The farmers raise hogs and poultry. Workers in the fishing industry catch such ocean fish as mackerel, sardines, and tuna. Inland ponds produce carp, eels, and other fish.

Coal is Taiwan's most important mineral, though the island has only small deposits. Copper, gold, limestone, salt, and sulfur are also mined. The government operates the natural gas and oil industries.

Taiwan has more than 10,500 miles (16,900 kilometers) of roads and over 3,400 miles (5,470 kilometers) of railroad track. Hualien, Kaohsiung, and Chilung (Keelung) are international ports. Taipei International Airport is the main air terminal.

Taiwan has over 80 radio stations and 3 television stations. More than 30 newspapers are published there.

History. Aborigines were the first inhabitants of Taiwan. Some Chinese came to the island from the mainland as early as the 500's, but large settlements did not begin until the 1600's. Dutch traders occupied a Taiwanese port from 1624 until 1661. Koxinga, a Chinese Ming dynasty official, drove them out. Manchu conquerors had overthrown the Ming dynasty in mainland China, and Koxinga hoped to restore the dynasty to power. He wanted to use Taiwan as a base from which to attack the Manchus. But the Manchus conquered Taiwan in 1683 and administered it as part of China.

In 1895, Japan gained control of Taiwan as a result of the first Chinese-Japanese War. The Japanese developed Taiwan's agriculture and industry and expanded its transportation networks. China regained Taiwan after World War II ended in 1945. In a peace treaty signed in 1951, Japan gave up all claims to Taiwan and the Pescadores islands.

In 1949, the Chinese Communists defeated Chiang Kai-shek's Nationalist forces and took control of the mainland. Chiang moved his government to Taiwan on Dec. 8, 1949. Both governments consider Taiwan a province of China. Each claims to be the legal ruler of all China, and each has declared its determination to take over the other's territory.

After the Korean War began in 1950, the United States said it would protect Taiwan against possible attack from mainland China. The U.S. and Chinese Nationalist governments signed a mutual defense treaty in 1954. The Chinese Communists repeatedly shelled Matsu and Quemoy during the 1950's. The shelling of Quemoy in 1958 led U.S. air and naval forces to patrol the Formosa Strait. Taiwan received about $1½ billion in U.S. economic and technical aid up to 1965. That year, Taiwan said its economy could stand on its own. But it continued to receive U.S. military aid.

In the early 1970's, Taiwan expressed concern over improved relations between the United States and Communist China. In 1971, the United States announced it favored United Nations (UN) membership for Communist China. But the United States also said that Nationalist China—a charter member of the UN—should retain its UN seat. In October 1971, the UN expelled the Nationalists and admitted Communist China. In 1972, President Richard M. Nixon visited Communist China and agreed to gradually withdraw U.S. military forces from Taiwan.

During the 1970's, a number of nations ended their diplomatic relations with Taiwan and established ties with Communist China. The United States ended its diplomatic relations with Taiwan at the end of 1978, and established diplomatic relations with Communist China at the start of 1979. In April 1979, the United States completed its military withdrawal from Taiwan. The mutual defense treaty between the two countries was ended on Dec. 31, 1979. But the U.S. agreed to continue to supply Taiwan with some military aid. Also, the two countries agreed to carry on unofficial relations through nongovernmental agencies.

President Chiang Kai-shek died in 1975. Chiang Ching-kuo, a son of Chiang Kai-shek, had become prime minister in 1972. He became the country's most powerful leader after his father died. In 1978, he was elected president of Taiwan.   RALPH N. CLOUGH

See also CHIANG KAI-SHEK; CHIANG SOONG MEI-LING; PESCADORES; QUEMOY; TAIPEI; CHIANG CHING-KUO.

TAJ MAHAL, *tahj muh HAHL,* is one of the most beautiful and costly tombs in the world. The Indian ruler Shah Jahan ordered it built in memory of his favorite wife. Her title, Mumtaz-i-Mahal, which means *pride of the palace,* gave the building its name. The tomb stands at Agra in northern India. About 20,000 workers built it between 1632 and 1653.

The Taj Mahal is made of white marble. It rests on an eight-sided platform of red sandstone. Each side is 130 feet (39.6 meters) long. At each corner of the platform stands a slender *minaret* (prayer tower). Each tower is 133 feet (40.5 meters) high. The building itself is 186 feet (56.7 meters) square. A dome covers the center part of the building. It is 70 feet (21.3 meters) in diameter and 120 feet (36.6 meters) high. Passages from the Moslem holy book, the *Koran*, decorate the outside. A central room contains two *cenotaphs* (monuments). Visitors can see the monuments through a screen of carved alabaster. The bodies of Shah Jahan and his wife lie in a vault below. The tomb stands in a garden, where pools reflect the building.   HOWARD M. DAVIS

See also INDIA (Arts [picture]).

TAJO RIVER. See TAGUS RIVER.

TAJUMULCO. See GUATEMALA (The Highlands).

TAKAKI, KANEHIRO. See VITAMIN (History).

TAKAKKAW FALLS, *TAK uh kaw,* consist of a series of waterfalls in the Canadian Rockies. The main falls drop 1,200 feet (366 meters). The Takakkaw Falls are near the eastern border of British Columbia, near the village of Field. They are on the Yoho River in Canada's Yoho National Park. See also WATERFALL (chart).

TAKLA MAKAN DESERT, *TAH klah mah KAHN,* lies in northwestern China between the Tien Shan and Kunlun mountains. Its small hills and shifting sand dunes cover about 125,000 square miles (323,700 square kilometers) in the Sinkiang region. For location, see CHINA (physical map).   THEODORE H. E. CHEN

TALBOTYPE is a picture made by an early photographic process. The name honors its inventor, W. H. Fox Talbot, an English scientist. He first described the process in 1839. He made a sheet of paper sensitive to light by putting it in a series of baths of sodium-chloride and silver-nitrate solutions. Then he exposed the paper to light, either in a camera, or in the sunshine. The silver salts formed a negative image by turning dark where light fell upon them. After Fox Talbot treated this master negative with salt solution, he could print an endless number of paper positives.

In 1841, Fox Talbot increased the sensitivity of the paper by developing it in gallo-nitrate of silver and treating it in sodium thiosulfate. He called the new process *calotype*. Later, he called it *talbotype*. Fox Talbot's work, however, did not make such a clear picture as the daguerreotype (see DAGUERREOTYPE). The talbotype process was the first negative-positive process. After 1851, the wet-collodion technique, which used glass for negative material, replaced it.   BEAUMONT NEWHALL

TALC (chemical formula, $Mg_3Si_4O_{10}(OH)_2$) is a soft mineral found in flat smooth layers of rock, and in compact masses. It is so soft that it can be scratched with the fingernail, and it feels soapy or greasy. Talc is translucent, which means that it will allow light to go through, yet is not transparent. Talc is white, greenish, or dark gray. *Steatite* (soapstone) is a compact talc.

Talc has many commercial uses. It is sold in slabs or in powdered form. Slabs are used to line furnaces and heating stoves, and for electric insulation, because talc is a poor conductor of heat and electricity. It is ground up to make talcum powder. Powdered talc is also used in crayons, paint, paper, and soap.

The leading talc-producing nations include Japan, Russia, South Korea, and the United States. Montana, New York, Texas, and Vermont are important talc-producing states.   CECIL J. SCHNEER

See also HARDNESS; SOAPSTONE; MINERAL (picture: Common Minerals with Nonmetallic Luster).

TALENT is a famous old unit of weight and value. The Hebrews, Babylonians, Greeks, and Romans used

it. No coin of this denomination was ever *struck* (made), because such a coin would be too large. Instead, a certain number of other coins equaled a talent. The Hebrew silver talent equaled 3,000 shekels in silver (about $1,800 in today's United States currency). A silver talent in Athens, Greece, was worth about $1,000. The gold talent had different weights and values in different places. The Roman *great talent* was worth about $480, and the *little talent* about $363. The present use of the word, meaning *special ability*, may come symbolically from a Bible story (Matthew 25:14-30). BURTON H. HOBSON

TALIPES. See CLUBFOOT.

TALK SHOW. See RADIO (Kinds of Programs); TELEVISION (Commercial Television; pictures).

TALKING BOOK. See HANDICAPPED (Special Education).

TALL OIL, or TALLOL, is a by-product of paper making. It is a blend of fatty and resin acids obtained from pine wood pulp. Crude tall oil is a black, frothy mass skimmed from the top of the cooking liquid of the pulp. When processed, it is a clear, yellow liquid. Tall oil has valuable commercial uses in the manufacture of hard and soft soaps, synthetic detergents, varnishes, and printer's ink.   RONALD G. MACDONALD

TALLAHASSEE, *TAL uh HASS ee,* Fla. (pop. 81,548; met. area pop. 159,542), is the state capital. It lies in northwestern Florida, about 15 miles (24 kilometers) from the Georgia border. For location, see FLORIDA (political map).

Tallahassee is primarily a seat of government. The old State Capitol, which was completed in 1845, and the one in Austin, Tex., were the only Confederate state capitols that Union troops did not capture. A new state Capitol opened in Tallahassee in 1977. Tallahassee is the trading center for a rich agricultural region that produces dairy foods, fruits and nuts, and lumber. It is the home of Florida State University and Florida Agricultural and Mechanical University. The seat of Leon County, Tallahassee has a council-manager government.   KATHRYN ABBEY HANNA

See also FLORIDA (pictures; Climate).

TALLCHIEF, MARIA (1925-   ), is an American ballerina often praised for her superb technical disci-

Fred Fehl

Maria Tallchief danced the role of the Sugarplum Fairy in *The Nutcracker* with the famous Danish ballet dancer, Erik Bruhn.

pline and command of style. As one of the first American ballerinas to gain international fame, she showed that American ballet dancing could equal European dancing in quality.

Maria Tallchief was born in Fairfax, Okla., the daughter of an Osage Indian father and a Scottish-Irish mother. She danced with the Ballet Russe de Monte Carlo from 1942 to 1947, but her career has been associated chiefly with the New York City Ballet. She danced with this company from 1947 to 1960. She was once married to New York City Ballet director George Balanchine. She created roles in many of Balanchine's ballets, including *Orpheus* (1948) and *Scotch Symphony* (1952). SELMA JEANNE COHEN

TALLEYRAND, *TAL ee rand,* or *TAH LAY RAHN* (1754-1838), CHARLES MAURICE DE TALLEYRAND-PÉRIGORD, PRINCE DE BÉNÉVENT, was a French statesman famous for his diplomatic achievements under Napoleon I and at the Congress of Vienna. He was born in Paris. A childhood accident made him lame, and he was educated for a religious career. He became a priest in 1775. In 1789, Talleyrand was appointed bishop of Autun, a high position in the church.

Supports State Above Church. Talleyrand was elected in 1789 to the States-General, the French parliament. He became a moderate leader of the French Revolution. He favored constitutional monarchy and signed the Declaration of the Rights of Man and of the Citizen. He was elected president of the National Assembly in 1790. Talleyrand won popularity for proposing that the government take church property to pay its debts. The Pope excommunicated him in 1791 for his part in giving control of the French Catholic Church to the state, and for taking an oath to the constitution.

Talleyrand was in England on a diplomatic mission when the Revolution took a radical turn in 1792, and he was exiled as a royalist sympathizer. After two years in England, he fled to America.

Joins Napoleon. Talleyrand was allowed to return to France in 1796. Through the influence of Madame de Staël, one of his friends, Talleyrand was made Minister of Foreign Affairs. While serving his nation, he decided to rebuild his fortune. In the famous XYZ Affair in 1797, he was accused of demanding bribes of the United States representatives (see XYZ AFFAIR).

Talleyrand also decided to build his political future by attaching himself to Napoleon. He helped Napoleon replace the Directory, first with the Consulate in 1799, and then with the Empire in 1804. As Napoleon's adviser and foreign minister, he conducted delicate negotiations such as those that produced the Peace of Tilsit with Russia in 1807. See NAPOLEON I.

Deserts Napoleon. Napoleon depended on Talleyrand, but distrusted him. Talleyrand came to oppose Napoleon's conquests as injurious to France and to European peace. After 1807, Talleyrand resigned from office and became the center of the growing opposition to the emperor. His leadership was decisive in securing Napoleon's abdication and the restoration of the Bourbon kings in 1814. His diplomatic skill at the Congress of Vienna of 1814 and 1815 gave defeated France a powerful voice there (see VIENNA, CONGRESS OF).

His Last Years. After 1815, the Bourbon court excluded Talleyrand from public affairs. But in 1830, when the Bourbons lost public confidence, Talleyrand

helped steer a revolution toward constitutional monarchy under Louis Philippe. He became ambassador to Great Britain, where he guided negotiations that made Belgium independent, and brought France and Britain into alliance. RAYMOND O. ROCKWOOD

See also FRENCH REVOLUTION.

TALLINN (pop. 371,000) is the capital and largest city of Estonia, one of the 15 republics of the Soviet Union. It lies on the northern coast of Estonia, along the Gulf of Finland. For location, see ESTONIA (map).

Tallinn is an important industrial and cultural center and seaport. Its products include industrial machinery, paper, and textiles. The city is best known for its many beautiful churches, castles, and other buildings that were erected from the 1200's to the 1500's. It also has many modern buildings constructed after World War II ended in 1945.

Tallinn existed before the mid-1100's, but its founding date is unknown. It was the capital of the independent nation of Estonia from 1918 to 1940. Russian troops occupied Estonia in 1940, and the country became part of the Soviet Union. V. STANLEY VARDYS

TALLIS, THOMAS (1505?-1585), was a prominent English composer. He was called the *Father of English Church Music.* He served as organist at the Abbey of the Holy Cross in Waltham, England, and wrote some of his most important music there. With William Byrd, he shared the post of organist at the Chapel Royal, and joined Byrd in publishing *Cantiones Sacrae,* or *Sacred Songs for Chorus,* a set of *motets,* in 1575. Tallis and Byrd were granted exclusive rights by Queen Elizabeth I to print and sell music for 21 years.

Tallis displayed skill in the use of counterpoint and an advance in style over the pre-Elizabethan composers. Most of his works were church pieces in Latin and English. He composed many anthems, and set others to English words. He composed many part songs in four, five, eight, and even more parts. WARREN S. FREEMAN

TALLMADGE AMENDMENT. See MISSOURI COMPROMISE.

TALLOW is a fatty substance used in many products. It is obtained by *rendering* (melting) the fat of cattle, goats, or sheep. Tallow is classified as *edible* or *inedible.* Edible tallow is used primarily as an ingredient in shortening for cooking and baking. Most of the inedible tallow produced in the United States is used in making animal feed, such as cattle feed and pet food. Inedible tallow is also treated with chemicals to make bar soap, soap flakes, and detergents (see DETERGENT AND SOAP [How Detergents Are Made]). Edible tallow is white and almost tasteless. Inedible tallow may be white, yellow, or brown.

Tallow is an important source of certain fatty acids that are used to make hundreds of everyday products. These products include automobile tires, cosmetics, detergents, lubricants, and plastics. Fatty acids obtained from tallow can do the job of many of the chemicals that are ordinarily manufactured from petroleum. Thus, tallow can help conserve the world's limited supply of petroleum.

The United States produces more than half the world's tallow. About 500 million pounds (230 million kilograms) of edible tallow and about 5 billion pounds

TALLOW TREE

(2,300,000,000 kilograms) of inedible tallow are manufactured annually in the United States.　　GERHARD MAERKER

TALLOW TREE is the name of various trees which produce a waxlike substance that may be used like tallow for making candles. The Chinese tallow tree grows more widely than other types. It has been introduced into North America, and is a familiar sight along the coasts of Georgia and the Carolinas. At the beginning of winter, the long, leathery leaves of the tallow tree turn a deep red. The seeds hang on waxlike threads among the leaves. To obtain tallow (wax), workers crush and boil both capsules and seeds, and skim off the tallow as it rises. They melt and refine this.

Tallow tree wax is used chiefly for making candles. Scented soap is also made from it. The leaves of the tree furnish a black dye, and the stem yields a resinous substance called *copal*. Copal is used in making varnish.

Scientific Classification. The tallow tree belongs to the spurge family, *Euphorbiaceae*. It is classified as genus *Sapium*, species *S. sebiferum*.　　HAROLD NORMAN MOLDENKE

TALMUD is a collection of Jewish religious and civil laws, together with scholarly interpretations of their meaning. It ranks second to the Bible as the most sacred and influential written work of the Jewish religion. Judaism considers the full-time study of the Talmud to be one of the most honorable occupations.

The Talmud consists of two parts, the *Mishnah* and the *Gemara*. The Mishnah is the written version of traditional Jewish oral law. Short passages of the Mishnah are followed by extremely thorough explanations, which make up the Gemara. The scholars who wrote the Gemara did not always agree in their interpretations of the Mishnah. As a result, the Gemara includes many debates on small details of Jewish law. It also discusses historical events and Jewish customs and includes Jewish folk tales.

The Talmud consists of 63 sections called *tractates*, which are divided into six *orders*. Each order deals with a different subject. For example, the order *Nashim* (Women) discusses marriage, divorce, and other matters that concern relationships between a man and a woman. Other orders cover such subjects as cleanliness, religious feasts, and civil and criminal law.

According to Jewish tradition, the Mishnah originated in the time of Moses during the 1200's B.C. and was memorized and handed down from generation to generation. Its contents were collected and written down from about A.D. 70 to 200. The Gemara, which has two versions, was written between about 200 and 500. The *Palestinian Gemara* was completed about 425 and the *Babylonian Gemara* about 500.　　JACOB NEUSNER

See also AKIBA BEN JOSEPH.

Additional Resources

ADLER, MORRIS. *The World of the Talmud.* 2nd ed. Schocken, 1963.
NEUSNER, JACOB. *Invitation to the Talmud: A Teaching Book.* Harper, 1975.
STEINSALTZ, ADIN. *The Essential Talmud.* Basic Books, 1976.

TALON, *tah LOHN,* **JEAN BAPTISTE** (1625-1694), a French official, served from 1665 to 1672 as Intendant of Justice and Finance in Canada, which was then called New France. He put the colony on a sound economic basis. He established a royal shipyard in Quebec, encouraged the search for iron, copper, and other minerals, and tried to make the colonists grow flax and weave their own linen and cloth. Talon was born in Châlons-sur-Marne, France.　　EDWARD R. ADAIR

TAMALES. See MEXICO (Food).

TAMARACK. See LARCH.

TAMARIN. See MARMOSET.

TAMARIND, *TAM uhr ihnd,* is an attractive evergreen tree that grows in the tropics. It may grow 75 feet (23 meters) high. It develops small pale green leaves and tiny yellow flowers. Pods about 3 to 4 inches (8 to 10 centimeters) long contain the seeds of the tree. These pods contain an acid brown pulp used to prepare refreshing drinks. In India and Arabia, the pulp is pressed into cakes and sold as a delicacy. Ornamental tamarinds are grown in warm parts of the United States.

Scientific Classification. The tamarind belongs to the pea family, *Leguminosae*. It is classified as genus *Tamarindus*, species *T. indica*.　　JULIAN C. CRANE

USDA
The Tamarind Pod contains several large flat seeds.

TAMAYO, *tah MAH yo,* **RUFINO,** *rew FEE no* (1899-), is one of Mexico's greatest artists. He is noted for small paintings of human figures and still life. Tamayo's paintings are profoundly Mexican in their brilliant color, gaunt Indian figures, and feeling of tragedy. Tamayo was born at Oaxaca, and studied art in Mexico City.　　ROBERT C. SMITH

TAMBOURINE, *TAM buh REEN,* is a percussion instrument that consists of a narrow wooden or metal hoop with a thin sheet of plastic or animal skin stretched across one side. All tambourines have small metal disks attached to the hoop. Performers hold the tambourine in one hand. They play it by striking it with the other hand, by hitting it against the knee or upper leg, and by shaking it. The tambourine was made popular by Turkish soldiers called Janissaries, who played the instrument in military bands from the 1400's to the early 1800's. Western musicians began using the tambourine during the 1700's.　　JOHN H. BECK

See also MUSIC (Percussion Instruments).

TAMERLANE (1336?-1405) was an Asian conqueror who created by the sword a vast but short-lived empire.

Press Syndicate
The Tambourine Adds Rhythm to Music.

Tamerlane was also referred to as Timur the Lame.

Tamerlane was a Tartar, a Mongol Turk descended from Genghis Khan, another Asian conqueror. He was born of a chief's family near Samarkand in Turkestan. He was a well-educated, devout Muslim. As a youth, Tamerlane became noted for his athletic prowess. After 1358 he engaged in numerous wars. He mounted the throne at Samarkand in 1369, and ruled an extensive central Asian kingdom. After 1369, his armies struck west and south into Afghanistan, Persia, India, and Asia Minor.

Tamerlane invaded India in 1398, sacked Delhi, and massacred most of its inhabitants. In 1401, he turned to Syria. He captured Baghdad, and in 1402 he completely destroyed the Turkish army that had been sent against him. He then captured Damascus and defeated Egyptian armies. Tamerlane was now the ruler of a vast empire with its heart in Turkestan. He next moved to conquer China. But before he could reach his objective, he died of fever in his camp. His empire soon fell apart.   T. WALTER WALLBANK

TAMING OF THE SHREW. See SHAKESPEARE, WILLIAM (Shakespeare's Plays).

TAMM, IGOR YEVGENEVICH (1895-1971), a Russian physicist, shared the 1958 Nobel physics prize with Pavel A. Cherenkov and Ilya M. Frank. Tamm and Frank explained theoretically the origin of the blue light, or radiation, which Cherenkov discovered and which is now named for him. See also CHERENKOV, PAVEL A.   R. T. ELLICKSON

TAMMANY, SOCIETY OF, also called the COLUMBIAN ORDER, was founded in New York City in 1789 by William Mooney. The organization took its name from the Sons of Saint Tammany. This colonial society was named after an early Delaware Indian chief known for his wisdom. Tammany began as a "fraternity of patriots solemnly consecrated to the independence, the popular liberty, and the federal union of the country."

But Tammany soon came to have a political purpose. For many years, it wielded vast powers as a Democratic political machine in New York and New York City. Its popular name, Tammany Hall, came from the name of its headquarters building, located at 331 Madison Avenue, New York City. Many scandals have darkened the organization's history. The most famous one was exposed in 1871, when Tammany boss William M. Tweed and others were arrested and charged with defrauding New York City of several million dollars. The organization soon regained its power and dominated much of the city's politics until 1933.   DONALD R. McCOY

See also BUCKTAILS; NAST, THOMAS; TWEED, WILLIAM M.; CLEVELAND, GROVER (Governor of New York).

TAMPA, Fla. (pop. 271,523), is a major United States seaport and an important industrial center of the state. Among the cities of Florida, only Jacksonville and Miami are larger. Tampa and its "twin city," St. Petersburg, lie on opposite sides of Tampa Bay. For location, see FLORIDA (political map). The metropolitan area of the two cities has a population of 1,569,492.

In 1824, the government moved many Seminole Indians to a reservation near Tampa Bay. The Indians had fought to keep their hunting grounds in northern Florida but had been defeated by the Army. That same year, the Army built Fort Brooke on Tampa Bay to supervise the Seminole. The Army chose this site be-

cause it included a harbor where troops and supplies could be landed. White settlers soon established a village near the fort and named it for the bay. Two centuries earlier, Spanish mapmakers had named the bay for an Indian village that once stood in the area.

Description. Tampa, the county seat of Hillsborough County, covers about 150 square miles (388 square kilometers). This area includes about 65 square miles (168 square kilometers) of inland water. Much of the city lies on islands and peninsulas. Downtown office buildings stand near Tampa Bay and the mouth of the Hillsborough River. Tampa has a large Spanish-speaking population, chiefly in a section known as Ybor City.

Tampa is the home of the University of South Florida and the University of Tampa. The city's public schools form part of the Hillsborough County school system. To achieve racial integration in the schools, the system buses some city students to suburban schools and some suburban children to city schools. The Tampa Public Library operates about 15 branch libraries.

Cultural attractions in Tampa include the Tampa Museum and the Hillsborough County Museum of Science and Industry. The San Carlo Opera Company and the Florida Gulf Coast Symphony perform in McKay Auditorium. Busch Gardens, a famous zoo, attracts more than 2 million visitors annually. Every February, the Florida State Fair and the Gasparilla Carnival are held in Tampa. The carnival features a "pirate attack" on the city. The Tampa Bay Buccaneers of the National Football League play in Tampa Stadium.

Economy. Tampa has about 750 manufacturing plants. They employ about 15 per cent of the city's workers. Processed foods are the chief product, and Tampa also makes chemicals, cigars, and machinery.

The Port of Tampa handles about 40 million short tons (36 million metric tons) of cargo yearly. Its annual exports include over 10 million short tons (9 million metric tons) of phosphate ore from nearby mines.

Fishing fleets based in Tampa catch large amounts of shrimp and other seafood. Tourism and trade also make important contributions to the economy. Nearby MacDill Air Force Base has about 8,000 civilian and military employees. Major airlines use Tampa International Airport. Passenger trains also serve Tampa.

Government and History. Tampa has a mayor-council form of government. The voters elect the mayor and the seven council members, all to four-year terms.

Calusa and Timucuan Indians lived near what is now Tampa Bay when white people first arrived. Several groups of Spanish explorers visited the area during the 1500's. One of these expeditions, led by Hernando de Soto, landed near the bay in 1539.

Robert J. Hackley of New York City became the first U.S. citizen to settle in the area. He built a plantation there in 1823. The Army built Fort Brooke the next year, and Tampa grew up around the fort. The city was incorporated in 1855 and had a population of 885 in 1860. Union troops occupied Tampa during the Civil War (1861-1865).

Henry B. Plant, an industrialist from Atlanta, Ga., spent millions of dollars during the 1880's and early 1890's to develop Tampa. He built a railroad that linked Tampa with the North and established the city's

Greater Tampa Chamber of Commerce

Tampa is one of Florida's chief commercial centers. The Hillsborough River flows through the city into Tampa Bay.

tourist industry. In 1886, a Florida tobacco processor named Vincente M. Ybor founded a cigar industry in what is now Ybor City. Phosphate mining began near Tampa in 1888. The city served as a military base during the Spanish-American War (1898) and as a shipbuilding center during World War I (1914-1918). By 1920, 51,608 people lived in Tampa.

Real estate speculation in Florida attracted thousands of persons to Tampa during the 1920's. The city had 101,161 people by 1930. For an account of the real estate boom, see FLORIDA (History [The Early 1900's]). Shipbuilding thrived in Tampa during World War II (1939-1945), and the Army Air Forces built three bases nearby. The 1950's brought industrial growth to the city. By 1960, Tampa's population had grown to 274,970.

In the 1960's and 1970's, Tampa undertook several urban renewal projects. One project eliminated some slums near the Hillsborough River. New construction on the site included apartment buildings, a convention hall, a new city library, and office towers.

By the early 1970's, the growth of Tampa had overloaded the city's waste disposal and water systems. Tampa Bay became polluted, and the city suffered several water shortages. In 1973, construction began on a plant designed to expand Tampa's waste-treatment system and produce pure drinking water from treated sewage. The plant opened in 1978.   THOMAS T. INGLIS

TAMPERE, *TAHM peh reh* (pop. 165,418; met. area pop. 239,940), is Finland's chief manufacturing center. It lies about 125 miles (201 kilometers) northwest of Helsinki. For location, see FINLAND (political map). Factories in Tampere produce furniture, leather goods,

machinery, paper, precision instruments, railway supplies, saws, and textiles. The city was founded in 1779.   PEKKA KALEVI HAMALAINEN

TAMPICO, *tahm PEE koh* (pop. 231,183; met. area pop. 359,008), is the second most important port in Mexico, after Veracruz. It stands 7 miles (11 kilometers) west of the Gulf of Mexico on the Pánuco River (see MEXICO [political map]). Tampico serves as a refining center for Mexico's petroleum industry and is the chief outlet for oil exports. A mild winter climate and good hunting and fishing make it a favorite resort center. Spaniards settled the city in the 1500's.   JOHN A. CROW

TANA, LAKE. See LAKE TANA.

TANAGER, *TAN uh jer*, is the common name given a family of American birds, many of which have brilliant red, blue, or green feathers. Tanagers are from 6 to 8 inches (15 to 20 centimeters) long, and are usually found in the forests, where they feed on insects, fruits, and flowers. There are more than 200 species of tanagers, most of which live in Central and South America. Only a few species of tanagers live in the United States.

The best known of this family are the *scarlet tanagers.* They have a loud, cheery song somewhat like that of the robin. They are sometimes called *firebirds.* They nest in the eastern United States and as far north as New Brunswick. The male has bright red feathers, with velvety black wings and tail. The female is dull yellow below and olive green above, with darker wings and tail. The tanager builds its frail, saucer-shaped nest near the end of a horizontal limb. The female lays three to five bluish-green eggs with reddish-brown markings.

In the Southern States, the *summer tanager* is a familiar bird. It has rosy-red feathers. Its nesting habits are much like those of its scarlet-coated relative. The *western tanager*, or *Louisiana tanager*, lives in summer from the Rockies to the Pacific Coast. The male has a black

Ron Austing

The Summer Tanager nests in the Southern United States. The male, *above*, is also called the *summer redbird.*

back, tail, and wings, red head, and yellow underparts.

The tanagers are helpful because they eat harmful insects. But the western tanager has a great fondness for cherries and may harm cherry orchards.

Scientific Classification. The tanagers make up the tanager family, *Thraupidae.* The scarlet tanager is genus *Piranga*, species *P. olivacea;* the summer tanager is *P. rubra;* the western tanager is *P. ludoviciana.*   LEONARD W. WING

See also BIRD (picture: Birds' Eggs).

TANAKA, *tah NAH kah*, **KAKUEI,** *KAH koo ay* (1918-   ), served as prime minister of Japan from 1972 to 1974. He resigned after being accused of using his political influence for financial gain. In 1976, he was charged with accepting bribes from Lockheed Aircraft Corporation, an American firm, while serving as prime minister. Unlike most Japanese leaders, Tanaka came from a poor family and had no college education. But he became a millionaire businessman and, at the age of 54, one of the youngest prime ministers in Japanese history.

Tanaka was born in Nishiyama, a small farming town about 200 miles (320 kilometers) northwest of Tokyo. He left home at the age of 16 and went to work in Tokyo. He held a variety of jobs and studied engineering at night. During World War II (1939-1945), Tanaka founded a construction company and earned a fortune.

Tanaka won election to the *Diet* (parliament) in 1947. Ten years later, he was named to the Cabinet office of minister of posts and telecommunications. He then held a series of Cabinet offices and important posts in the Liberal-Democratic Party. In 1976 and again in 1979, while still facing bribery charges, Tanaka won election to the Diet. LEWIS AUSTIN

TANANARIVE. See ANTANANARIVO.

TANDEM. See BICYCLE (Specialty Bicycles; picture).

TANEY, *TAW nee*, **ROGER BROOKE** (1777-1864), was one of the great chief justices of the United States. But the merit of his work is clouded by his decision in the Dred Scott case, which helped bring on the Civil War. Taney held that Congress had no power to abolish slavery in the territories.

Taney was born in Calvert County, Maryland, and was educated at Dickinson College. He began practicing law in Annapolis, Md., in 1799. He entered politics, and served several years in the state Senate. He also gained a high reputation as a lawyer. In 1831, President Andrew Jackson appointed him U.S. attorney general and made him a trusted adviser.

Brown Bros.
Roger B. Taney

Jackson was opposed to the United States Bank and decided to end its influence by withdrawing the government deposits over the opposition of Congress (see BANK OF THE UNITED STATES). In 1833, he appointed Taney secretary of the treasury to have him withdraw the funds. The Senate was so angered that it refused to confirm Taney's appointment, and he retired to private life.

In 1835, Jackson appointed Taney an associate justice of the Supreme Court, but the Senate refused to confirm the appointment. In 1836, the Senate majority changed. Jackson named Taney as chief justice, and the Senate approved. Taney favored states' rights but not at the expense of basic national powers. He kept most of John Marshall's broad interpretation of the Constitution. JERRE S. WILLIAMS

See also DRED SCOTT DECISION.

T'ANG DYNASTY, *tahng*, was a series of rulers who governed China from A.D. 618 to 907. Many historians consider the T'ang period the golden age of Chinese

civilization. The dynasty's capital city, Ch'ang-an (now Sian), became one of the great cultural centers of the world. Artists, poets, scholars, and government and religious leaders from many countries visited Ch'ang-an and the Chinese coastal trading centers.

The T'ang rulers united China and established a strong central government. They carefully hand-picked their chief officials. The T'ang emperors also set up a council of ministers to act as advisers. In addition, the emperors sent inspectors into the provinces of China to check on the activities of local governors.

The T'ang rulers also promoted trade, which became the basis of the empire's great prosperity. Jade, porcelain, rice, silks, spices, tea, and other Chinese products flowed to India, the Middle East, and Europe along trade routes opened by the T'ang emperors.

During the T'ang period, the Chinese invented block printing, which soon replaced the handwritten scriptures of the Chinese Buddhists. In 868, the Chinese produced the *Diamond Sutra*, the world's first block-printed book.

The Rise of the Dynasty. The T'ang dynasty followed the Sui dynasty, which had ruled China from A.D. 589 to 618. Li Yuan, an aristocrat, overthrew the Sui emperor and became the first T'ang ruler (see LI YUAN). He set up his capital at Ch'ang-an in northwestern China. *Ch'ang-an* meant *long peace*, but China was soon torn by civil war. In addition, a struggle for power developed among the nobility. In 627, Li Yuan turned the control of China over to his son, Li Shih-min, who took the name T'ang T'ai-tsung. T'ai-tsung ruled for 22 years and became one of the greatest emperors in Chinese history.

T'ai-tsung was a powerful leader. He destroyed his competitors for the throne, began an alliance with the Korean state of Silla, and forced Turkish nomads out of Northern China. His armies conquered parts of Tibet and Turkestan, opening overland trade routes from China to India and central Asia. The trade routes not only brought great wealth to the empire, but they also promoted religious and cultural exchange. The routes gave Christian and other foreign missionaries an overland entrance into China and allowed Chinese Buddhist pilgrims to visit India.

T'ai-tsung reorganized the administration of the empire. He built colleges to help select and train officials for government work. Although Buddhism was the country's main religion, T'ai-tsung knew that many Chinese who could help him carry out his programs followed Confucianism. As a result, he named many Confucians to high government posts.

In 649, T'ang Kao Tsung became emperor. But his wife, Empress Wu, soon took control of the government. Kao Tsung died in 683, and his son became emperor—but in name only. Empress Wu continued to control the government, and she became the second great leader of the T'ang dynasty.

Empress Wu governed China with great skill. She appointed able ministers to major government posts and had the complete loyalty of her advisers and officials. She maintained the high reputation of the T'ang dynasty abroad because of her political brilliance. The empress also showed great favoritism to Buddhism and

This map shows the land ruled by the T'ang emperors from their capital at Ch'ang-an. The T'ang Empire reached its greatest size under Emperor Hsüan Tsung. It controlled territory from eastern China to Persia. Arabs defeated the Chinese armies at Athlach in A.D. 751. This battle marked the end of T'ang power in Turkestan and the closing of overland trade routes to the west.

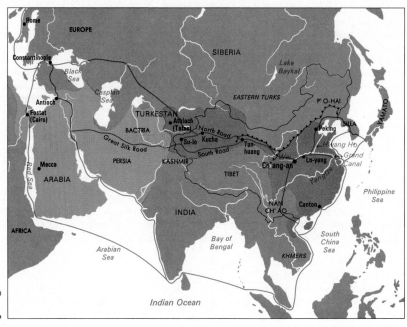

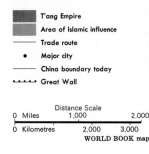

	T'ang Empire
	Area of Islamic influence
	Trade route
●	Major city
	China boundary today
	Great Wall

Distance Scale
0 Miles 1,000 2,000
0 Kilometres 2,000 3,000
WORLD BOOK map

promoted art and literature. In the late 600's, Tibet forced the Chinese out of Turkestan. To protect China's trade routes there, Empress Wu sent her armies into the region and recovered the T'ang territory.

The Middle Years. T'ang Hsüan Tsung, the grandson of Empress Wu, became emperor in 712. Hsüan Tsung, also known as Ming Huang, was the last of the three great T'ang rulers. During his reign, China produced some of its best artists and such great poets as Li Po and Tu Fu. Hsüan Tsung's economic programs, including the development of new farming regions in the Yangtze Valley, greatly increased China's wealth.

In 747, China reached its peak of influence in western Asia. T'ang armies invaded Bactria and Kashmir and defeated an Arab-Tibetan alliance that had been formed against China's allies in central Asia. But in 751, a revolt in Turkestan closed China's trade routes to the Middle East.

When Hsüan Tsung was more than 60 years old, he fell in love with his son's wife and took her as his mistress. She soon gained control over the emperor and made him appoint a cunning Manchurian military governor, An Lu-shan, to the royal court. In 755, An Lu-shan organized a rebellion against Hsüan Tsung and captured and briefly occupied the capital of Ch'ang-an. In 756, Hsüan Tsung turned the throne over to his son, Su Tsung. In 766, a combination of Chinese and foreign troops defeated the rebel armies of An Lu-shan. But during the rebellion, army generals and military governors in the provinces had increased their power, weakening the central government.

While Su Tsung was fighting An Lu-shan, Tibet had been united into a powerful kingdom. In 763, Tibetan forces invaded China. The T'ang rulers battled the Tibetans in northwestern China for about 80 years. This long conflict further weakened the T'ang dynasty.

The Fall of the Dynasty. Border wars and rebellions in the provinces troubled China between 766 and 868. Yet the T'ang dynasty remained prosperous, largely because of a new tax system. The Chinese had been required to pay their taxes with labor and goods. Under the new system, they could also pay with cash. This new system was more efficient than the older one and provided increased income.

In 868, a second long and powerful military revolt broke out against the T'ang dynasty. In 881, peasant rebels led by Huang Ch'ao captured the capital of Ch'ang-an. One by one, the governors of the provinces declared their independence from the central government. In 907, the T'ang dynasty finally came to an end. Until the Sung dynasty gained control of China in 960, the country was governed by a series of short-lived military dynasties.   EUGENE BOARDMAN

See also CHINA (The T'ang Dynasty; picture: Multicolor Ceramics).

TANGANYIKA. See TANZANIA.

TANGANYIKA, LAKE. See LAKE TANGANYIKA.

The Metropolitan Museum of Art, New York City

Figures of Four Female Musicians illustrate the simple charm of pottery figures of the T'ang dynasty. The figures were created to be placed in a tomb when a person was buried.

TANGELO, *TAN juh lo,* is any citrus fruit that results from cross-pollination between tangerine and *pomelo* (the old name for grapefruit) trees. Tangelos have thin peels and a delicious flavor. American tangelos include the Orlando, Minneola, Sampson, and Thornton. The Ugli is an important Jamaican tangelo that is widely grown in the West Indies.   WILLIAM GRIERSON

TANGENT, in geometry, is a straight line that touches a curve at only one point. Two circles are *externally tangent* when they lie on opposite sides of a line tangent to both of them. See also CIRCLE.

TANGERINE, *tan juh REEN,* is the popular name for a citrus fruit of the mandarin group. These fruits look like oranges, but are smaller and flatter, peel more easily, and the sections separate more readily. The tangerine is an orange-red mandarin fruit which originated in Southeast Asia. It has a thin, fragrant peel. The fruit is delicate. But the tree is more resistant to cold than is the orange tree. Varieties of tangerines include Dancy, Clementine or Algerian, Ponkan, and new hybrid varieties such as Kara, Kinnow, Wilking, and Paige. In the United States, tangerines are grown in Arizona, California, and Florida. They are also grown in Australia, Japan, and North Africa. See also TANGELO; TANGOR.

J. Horace McFarland
Tangerine

Scientific Classification. The tangerine belongs to the rue family, *Rutaceae*. It is classified as genus *Citrus*, species *C. reticulata*.   WILLIAM GRIERSON

TANGIER, *tan JEER,* also spelled TANGER, is a region on the Atlantic coast of Morocco (see MOROCCO [map]). It covers 135 square miles (350 square kilometers) between the sea and the Rif Mountains. It includes the city of Tangier (pop. 187,894).

Location and Description. The city of Tangier lies opposite Gibraltar at the western opening to the Mediterranean Sea. It ranks second to Casablanca among Morocco's seaports. From the sea, the city looks like an amphitheater, with rows of white houses lining the hills.

Most of the people of the Tangier region are Muslim Berbers or Arabs. Spanish, French, and Arabic are the official languages. The city of Tangier has few industries, but it ranks as an important shipping center.

History. Portugal, Spain, and England held Tangier at different times from the 1400's until the late 1600's, when the Moors gained control. The Moors held the city until 1924, but granted special privileges to several European countries. In 1925, an international zone was established in Tangier, under the control of leading world powers. Spanish forces occupied Tangier during World War II. In 1945, Tangier regained its international status. Tangier became a part of Morocco after Morocco gained its independence from France and Spain in 1956. That same year, the sultan of Morocco called a conference of the nine nations that formerly controlled Tangier. They voted to end Tangier's international status, and to give up most of their former rights in the area.   HIBBERD V. B. KLINE, JR.

TANGO, *TANG goh,* is a contemporary ballroom dance of South American origin. It has long, gliding steps and intricate poses. The *tango Argentina* became popular in the United States during the early 1900's. *Tango* is also the name of the music for this dance, written in $\frac{2}{4}$ or $\frac{4}{4}$ time. *El tango* is a Spanish dance of the flamenco type (see FLAMENCO). It has heavier and simpler steps than other types of flamenco, but resembles them in its elemental steps and poses.

TANGOR, *tan JOR,* is any citrus fruit produced by cross-pollination between tangerine and orange trees. Two natural tangors, called *Temple* and *Murcott*, have become major crops in Florida. A tangor called the *Umatilla* results from cross-pollination of the Satsuma mandarin and the Ruby orange.   WILLIAM GRIERSON

TANGUY, YVES (1900-1955), a surrealist artist, painted with exacting technique a strange world where objects like bones and rocks are grouped in fantastic structures. He decided to paint when he saw a Giorgio de Chirico painting in 1923. His first works were crude because he taught himself, but by 1927 he had developed his style. Tanguy was born in Paris, but moved to Connecticut in 1939.   GEORGE D. CULLER

TANIMBAR ISLANDS. See INDONESIA (The Moluccas; table).

TANK, MILITARY, is an armored combat vehicle. Most tanks travel on caterpillar tracks. They carry such weapons as cannons, machine guns, and missile launchers. In most tanks, these weapons are mounted in a revolving structure called a *turret*. A tank has a crew of three to five members.

Tanks are used to attack other armored vehicles, infantry, and various ground targets; and to fire on aircraft. Armies throughout the world have a total of about 100,000 tanks. Russia has about 40,000, and the United States has about 10,000.

Tanks are classified as *main battle tanks* or as *armored reconnaissance vehicles*. Main battle tanks weigh from 35 to 60 short tons (32 to 54 metric tons). Armored reconnaissance vehicles weigh from 10 to 25 short tons (9 to 23 metric tons).

Performance. Tanks travel as fast as 50 miles (80 kilometers) per hour on level ground. They average only 10 to 20 miles (16 to 32 kilometers) per hour on rough terrain. Tanks can climb and descend slopes as steep as 30 degrees, and can turn around within their own length. Some small tanks can travel in water.

The newest tanks have 100- to 120-millimeter guns, which can be combined with computer fire control systems. These guns can hit small targets 1 mile (1.6 kilometers) away, even if the tank is moving. The new tanks also have heavy armor that can withstand attack by conventional and nuclear weapons.

History. Tanks got their name from the British, who developed them during World War I (1914-1918). While the vehicles were being built, the British called them water tanks to conceal their real purpose. The British first used tanks against the Germans in the Battle of the Somme in 1916. The early tanks were slow and clumsy, but they were used successfully in the Battle of Cambrai in 1917.

During World War II (1939-1945), all the warring nations used tanks. German tank units won important

The Crew and Basic Parts of a Tank

This diagram of a U.S. Army M60A1 main battle tank shows the position of the crew members, plus some parts of the vehicle. The crew consists of a commander and three other persons. One crew member drives the tank, one loads the guns, and the other two fire the guns. The tank has a 105-mm gun and two machine guns.

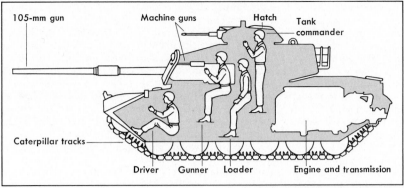

105-mm gun — Machine guns — Hatch — Tank commander — Caterpillar tracks — Driver — Gunner — Loader — Engine and transmission

WORLD BOOK illustration by Dick Fickle

U.S. Army

A Main Battle Tank, such as the U.S. Army's M60A1 shown above, is used to attack other armored vehicles, infantry, and various ground targets; and for defense against aircraft.

victories over Poland, France, and Russia. In 1943, the Russians defeated the Germans at Kursk, Russia, in the greatest tank battle in history. Thousands of tanks fought in this battle. In 1944, Allied tanks swept into Germany, helping to assure victory in Europe.

Since World War II, tanks have taken part in many regional wars, especially in the Middle East. More than 6,000 tanks were used in the Arab-Israeli war of 1973. Nearly half the tanks were destroyed in only 18 days of combat. During this war, precision-guided weapons were used against tanks for the first time. Despite the high tank losses, the vehicles were effective when given infantry and artillery support.   KENNETH S. BROWER

See also ARMY, U.S. (Armor); PERISCOPE.

TANK DESTROYER is a vehicle developed by the United States and British armies in World War II. Armored tanks became such powerful weapons during World War II that military experts were forced to seek new weapons to fight them. The experts produced these lightly armored vehicles. They were mounted on tank frames, but were much faster and more heavily armed than tanks. The U.S. M-3 tank destroyer carried a 105-mm gun which shot a shell 7 miles (11 kilometers). The M-3 traveled at a speed of 35 mph (56 kph). The M-10 tank destroyer had a 3-inch cannon mounted in a turret. Tank destroyers moved on wheels or on caterpillar tracks like tanks.

See also BAZOOKA.

TANKA. See JAPANESE LITERATURE.

TANKER is a ship designed to carry liquid cargo. Most tankers transport oil, but some carry such products as molasses, wine, and even dry cargoes, including coal, grain, and iron ore.

A tanker consists basically of a series of as many as 25 tanks, the walls of which are formed in part by the hull. A tanker has a crew of 25 to 40 persons. They live in the deckhouse, which forms part of an enclosed area called the *superstructure.* The superstructure is on the main deck, above the engines. The superstructure has five or six stories, with the ship's bridge on top. Some larger tankers have a second superstructure for the bridge halfway between the bow and the stern. Cargo pumps and piping line the main deck.

Kinds of Tankers. There are three chief kinds of tankers: (1) oil tankers, (2) ore-bulk-oil carriers, and (3) liquefied natural gas carriers.

Oil Tankers carry crude oil and refined petroleum products. The hull forms the outside of the tanks. *Bulkheads* (walls) run the length and width of the ship and divide the tanks into compartments. This type of construction strengthens the hull. It also enables an oil tanker to carry several products, such as diesel fuel, gasoline, and kerosene, at the same time.

An extra large type of oil tanker, called a *supertanker* or *very large crude carrier* (VLCC), was developed during the 1960's. The largest supertanker measures more than 1,300 feet (396 meters) long and 200 feet (61 meters) wide. It can hold over 500,000 short tons (450,000 metric tons) of oil. When filled, a supertanker's hull extends as much as 92 feet (28 meters) under the water line. Supertankers cruise at speeds of about 15 knots (nautical miles per hour) and are extremely difficult to maneuver. A VLCC with its engines off may travel over 3 miles (5 kilometers) before stopping completely.

Supertankers sail from Africa and the Middle East to Canada, the Caribbean, Europe, and Japan. In Europe, Japan, and the Persian Gulf, VLCC's load and unload their cargo through underwater pipelines provided by offshore ports. The Deepwater Port Act of 1974 authorized the construction of offshore ports for VLCC's in the United States. The first of these ports, located off the coast of Louisiana, opened in 1981. It has a capacity of 1.4 million barrels of oil a day.

Ore-Bulk-Oil Carriers (O/B/O's) carry such cargoes as bauxite, coal, grain, and iron, as well as oil. These tankers have tanks and pumps for storing and unloading liquids. But they also have large hatches on the main deck for loading and unloading dry cargo. Such ships

Tankers transport chiefly liquid cargo, but some carry such dry cargoes as coal, grain, and iron ore. The oil tanker shown above measures nearly 1,100 feet (335 meters) long and weighs more than 250,000 short tons (227,000 metric tons). It can carry about 2 million barrels of oil.

can carry oil in one direction and dry bulk cargo on the return voyage.

Liquefied Natural Gas (LNG) Carriers were developed in the 1960's. When natural gas is chilled to −260° F. (−162° C), it shrinks to about 1/600 of its volume and becomes liquid. Plants on shore liquefy natural gas and pump it into spherical insulated tanks on the tankers. These tanks rise high above the decks.

Water Pollution by Tankers ranks as one of the chief problems of the oil industry. Tankers spill more than 2 million short tons (1.8 million metric tons) of oil into the world's oceans annually. This pollution results from accidents and from normal ship operations.

The oil industry has taken various steps to reduce pollution. Some tankers have double hulls to minimize the loss of oil in accidents. Methods have been developed to keep spilled oil from spreading over the water and to remove spills from its surface.   JOSEPH E. KASPUTYS

See also SHIP (Tankers; pictures); PETROLEUM (diagram: How Oil Is Transported).

TANNER, BEATRICE. See CAMPBELL, MRS. PATRICK.

TANNER, HENRY OSSAWA (1859-1937), was an American painter. During the late 1880's, he studied under the noted artist Thomas Eakins at the Pennsylvania Academy of the Fine Arts in Philadelphia. Eakins encouraged Tanner to paint professionally.

Tanner's early works reflect the influence of Eakins' realistic style. Tanner, a black, first gained recognition for his pictures of black life on plantations. Perhaps his best-known early work is *The Banjo Lesson*.

In 1891, Tanner moved to Europe to continue his studies and to escape the racial prejudice he had experienced in the United States. He settled in Paris and began to paint pictures with religious themes. These works show the influence of the Dutch artist Rembrandt in their glowing, warm colors and dramatic contrasts between light and dark areas. Tanner was born in Pittsburgh and died in Paris.   ROBERT F. REIFF

TANNHÄUSER, *TAHN hoy zer*, was a German *minnesinger* (minstrel) of the 1200's. He led a very restless life and even went to the Holy Land on a crusade. A ballad of the 1500's tells the story that one evening, as he was riding by the Hörselberg in Thuringia, a beautiful woman appeared before him. He recognized her as the goddess Venus. He followed her to a palace inside the mountain and spent seven years there.

Finally, Tannhäuser left Venus and went on a pil-

grimage to Rome to seek forgiveness for his sins. The pope said that just as the staff he held in his hand could never blossom, so would Tannhäuser's sins never be forgiven. Tannhäuser went sorrowfully back to Germany. Three days later, the pope's staff miraculously bore flowers. Messengers hurried to seek out Tannhäuser, but he had gone back to Venus. Richard Wagner's opera *Tannhäuser* is based on this legend.   ARTHUR M. SELVI

TANNIC ACID, also called TANNIN, is an organic compound obtained chiefly from the *galls* (unnatural growths) of oak tree leaves. Most other trees also contain some tannin. The word tannin comes from the early French word *tan*, which meant *bark of an oak*.

Tanner's *The Banjo Lesson* shows the painter's sympathetic treatment of life among Southern blacks during the late 1800's.

23

TANNING

Tannins are used to tan animal hides. Hides contain gelatin that combines with the tannin, converting the hides to leather. Tannins are also used as *mordants* (dye-fixatives), and in manufacturing inks.

Tannins from different kinds of trees have various chemical formulas. The most important difference is the color produced in the tanned leather. Tannic acid is a bulky powder, ranging from light yellow to brown in color. It is soluble in water.　　　JOHN E. LEFFLER

See also GALL; LEATHER (Vegetable Tanning).

TANNING. See LEATHER; TANNIC ACID.

TANSY, *TAN zee*, is a plant related to the thistle. The tansy first grew in Europe, but is now found throughout North America. It is usually grown in gardens, but also grows wild. The leaves and flowers of the tansy have a bitter taste and a strong odor. The leaves were once used in flavoring. These dark green leaves give off an oil which is known as *oil of tansy*. This oil is poisonous, but is used to some extent in medicines. The flowers of the tansy are yellow.

Scientific Classification. Tansies are in the composite family, *Compositae*. They make up the genus *Tanacetum*. Common species are classified as *T. vulgare*, *T. capitatum*, and *T. huronense*.　　　HAROLD NORMAN MOLDENKE

TANTALUM, a chemical element, is a rare, gray metal with a high melting point. Tantalum resists attack by almost all chemicals at ordinary temperatures, because a thin layer of tantalum pentoxide (Ta_2O_5) forms and protects the metal's surface. For this reason, tantalum is used to make corrosion-resistant equipment, including industrial chemical apparatus, surgical instruments, and aircraft and missile parts. Mixtures of tantalum and other metals make strong, useful alloys.

Tantalum is not found as a metal. It occurs chiefly in the mineral tantalite. Tantalum is always found combined with a similar element called niobium. It is separated from niobium and converted into a metal by chemical processes.

Tantalum reacts with few elements. It combines with oxygen to form tantalum pentoxide. This compound is widely used to make *capacitors* (electronic devices for storing electricity). The compound is an important ingredient in camera lenses because it increases the *refracting* (light bending) power of glass.

Tantalum (symbol Ta) has the atomic number 73. Its atomic weight is 180.948. It melts at 2996° C and boils at 5425° C ($+100°$ C). It was discovered in 1802 by Anders Ekeberg of Sweden.　　　ALAN DAVISON

See also ELEMENT, CHEMICAL (tables).

TANTALUS was a king in Greek mythology. He was the son of Zeus and the sea nymph Pluto. Tantalus was punished because he killed his son Pelops and served him to the gods as food. Later, Pelops was restored to life. In the Lower World, Tantalus was forced to stand under threat of a hanging rock and up to his chin in water. When he tried to drink, the water always vanished. Fruit and grapes hung above him. When he tried to eat them, the winds whirled the branches out of reach. The word *tantalize*, which means to tease or torment by keeping something out of reach, is taken from his name.　　　JAMES F. CRONIN

TANZANIA, *TAN zuh NEE uh*, or *tan ZAN ee uh*, is a large country in East Africa. It consists of Tanganyika,

a large area on the African mainland; and Zanzibar, a group of several offshore islands in the Indian Ocean. The largest island is also called Zanzibar, and the second largest is called Pemba. Both Tanganyika and Zanzibar were British possessions until the early 1960's, when they became independent. In 1964, Tanganyika and Zanzibar united to form one nation, officially called the United Republic of Tanzania. Dar es Salaam is the capital and largest city (see DAR ES SALAAM).

Tanzania has much wildlife and beautiful scenery. The country is noted for its buffaloes, elephants, giraffes, leopards, lions, zebras, and many varieties of antelope. Game reserves on the Serengeti Plain and the Ngorongoro Crater have abundant animal life. Big-game *safaris* (hunting expeditions) attract many hunters to the country. Africa's highest mountain, Kilimanjaro, rises 19,340 feet (5,895 meters) in the north. Lake Victoria, Africa's largest lake, extends into northern Tanzania. Lake Tanganyika, the world's longest freshwater lake, forms part of the western border.

Government

Tanzania is a republic. A president serves as head of state, and heads the cabinet that governs the country. The president is assisted by two vice-presidents. The people elect the president and the members of the National Assembly, Tanzania's one-house legislature. The National Assembly has 189 members, including 41 from Zanzibar and 15 elected by national organizations. The mainland is divided into 20 regions, and the islands are divided into 4 regions.

People

Tanzania has a population of 20,629,000. About 20,086,000 people live on the mainland, and about 543,000 on the islands. Most of the people are Africans. The African people on the mainland are divided into about 120 ethnic groups. English and Swahili are the country's official languages (see SWAHILI).

About 75,000 Asians, most of them traders, shopkeepers, or skilled workers, live in Tanzania. Some Arabs work in Tanzania's wholesale and retail trades.

Facts in Brief

Capital: Dar es Salaam.

Official Languages: English and Swahili.

Form of Government: Republic. *Head of State*—President.

Area: 364,900 sq. mi. (945,087 km²).

Population: *Estimated 1983 Population*—20,629,000; distribution, 62 per cent rural, 38 per cent urban; density, 57 persons per sq. mi. (22 persons per km²). *1978 Census*—17,527,564. *Estimated 1988 Population*—24,850,000.

Chief Products: *Agriculture*—cassava, citrus fruits, cloves, coconuts, coffee, copra, corn, cotton, fibers, hides and skins, nuts, oilseeds, rice, sisal, sugar cane, tea, tobacco. *Manufacturing and Processing*—clove oil, coconut oil, lime juice and oil. *Mining*—diamonds, gold, lead, mica, salt, silver, tin.

National Anthem: "Mungo Ibariki Africa" ("God the Almighty Bless Africa").

Flag: The flag combines the old Tanganyika and Zanzibar flag colors in diagonal stripes. Green is for land, gold for mineral wealth, black for the people, and blue for the sea. See FLAG (picture: Flags of Africa).

Money: *Basic Unit*—shilling. See MONEY (table).

Tanzania

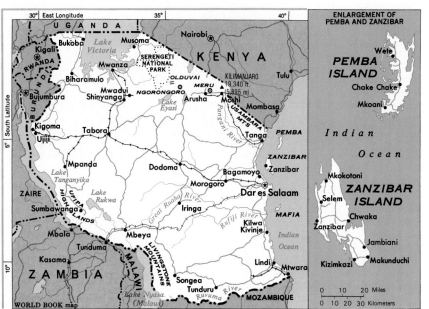

NATIONAL CAPITAL
OTHER CITY OR TOWN
ROAD
RAIL LINE
MOUNTAIN
CRATER
GORGE

0   50   100   200 Miles
0   100   200   300 Kilometers

Most Africans on the mainland follow traditional African religions. But some are Christians and others are Muslims. Most people on the islands are Sunni Muslims.

Many of the older Africans in Tanzania cannot read and write. But about half the school-age children attend school. Christian missionary societies operate most primary and some secondary schools in the country. The government supports mission schools and operates its own schools. The University of Dar es Salaam was founded in 1961.

Land

The mainland is part of the Great Rift Valley that crosses East Africa. The 500-mile (800-kilometer) coastal strip is covered with mangrove swamps and coconut palm groves. Temperatures there are always high. The land rises to plateaus about 4,000 feet (1,200 meters) above sea level behind the coast. This area is a hot, dry grassland with patches of thorn trees and open woodlands. Several mountains stand above the plateau, including Kilimanjaro, Meru, and Usambara in the northeast, and the Livingstone Mountains and Ufipa Highlands in the south and southwest.

The Zanzibar Channel, 22 miles (35 kilometers) wide, separates Zanzibar Island from the mainland. Pemba lies 25 miles (40 kilometers) northeast of Zanzibar Island. Zanzibar Island, the largest coral island off the African coast, covers 640 square miles (1,658 square kilometers). Pemba covers 380 square miles (984 square kilometers). The islands have a hot, tropical climate.

Economy

Tanzania is chiefly an agricultural country and most of the people are farmers. They raise crops on the coastal plain, along the lake shores, and in the highlands. Their most important food crops are cassava, corn, and beans. They also raise groundnuts, millet, rice, sugar cane, and tobacco. Cooperative farms and plantations produce coffee, cotton, sisal, and tea.

Zanzibar Island is noted for its cloves and coconuts. Farmers there also raise citrus and other fruits, tobacco, and chili peppers. Many of the people also fish for a living. Tanzania's most important exports are cloves, coffee, cotton, diamonds, and sisal fibers.

The country has one of the most important diamond deposits in the world. The Williamson diamond mines at Mwadui produce most of the diamonds. Miners also dig for gold, mica, salt, silver, and tin.

The country has about 2,200 miles (3,540 kilometers) of railroads, and about 30,000 miles (48,000 kilometers) of roads. Dar es Salaam, Tanga, and Mtwara are important seaports. Tanzania has over 50 airports and landing strips, including international airports in Dar es Salaam and near Arusha.

Tanzania has eight daily newspapers, about 20 other newspapers and magazines, and about 100,000 radios. The mainland has about 17,000 telephones.

History

Archaeologists have discovered the fossils of several types of manlike creatures called *australopithecines* (southern apes) in the Olduvai Gorge in northern Tanzania. Scientists believe these creatures lived as long as 2 million years ago (see AUSTRALOPITHECUS).

Historians believe that Greek explorers traveled down the east African coast in the first hundred years A.D. The Portuguese established settlements in the area in the 1500's, but were later forced out.

The Slave Trade. In the late 1700's and in the 1800's, the Arabs greatly expanded the slave trade. In 1832, the town of Zanzibar, on Zanzibar Island, became the capital of a large sultanate. It became the main town in eastern Africa. Many Africans from Tanganyika were sold in the Zanzibar slave market. The Arabs finally closed the market in 1873, and slavery was abolished on the mainland in 1876.

German and British Rule. The German Colonization Society made treaties in 1884 with African chiefs for

25

their lands. Germany gained the coastal area of the mainland from the Sultan of Zanzibar in 1890. At the same time, Zanzibar became a British protectorate. In 1891, Germany declared the mainland territory the Protectorate of German East Africa. After World War I, Britain received a League of Nations mandate over most of German East Africa and renamed it Tanganyika.

Independence. Tanganyika became a United Nations trust territory under British rule in 1946. Julius K. Nyerere, a nationalist leader, and his Tanganyika African National Union Party won the country's first general election in 1958. Tanganyika became an independent country on Dec. 9, 1961, and a republic in December, 1962. Nyerere became the first president, and a one-party system of government was adopted.

Great Britain granted Zanzibar internal self-government in early 1963. Sheik Muhammed Shamte Hamadi, leader of the Zanzibar and Pemba People's party, became the first prime minister. Zanzibar achieved full independence on Dec. 10, 1963.

The United Republic. In January, 1964, the Afro-Shirazi Party, representing the African majority in Zanzibar, ousted the Arab minority government. Abeid Karume became president, and the sultan fled the country. The country then became a one-party republic.

On April 23, 1964, Tanganyika and Zanzibar signed an Act of Union that made them one nation. Nyerere became the first president of the united republic. Karume became the vice-president. In 1965, Tanzania adopted a temporary constitution and Nyerere was elected as president. He was reelected in 1970, 1975, and 1980. Karume was assassinated in 1972. In 1977, Tanzania adopted its first permanent constitution.

In 1978, a border dispute led to fighting between Tanzania and Uganda, which was ruled by Idi Amin Dada. In 1979, Tanzanian troops, aided by Ugandans who opposed Amin, defeated Uganda's army and overthrew Amin's government. The Ugandans who opposed Amin then took control of the government.

In 1973, Tanzanians voted to move the capital from the coastal city of Dar es Salaam to Dodoma, near the country's center. The move was scheduled for completion by the 1990's. Critically reviewed by JANE SYMONDS

See also NYERERE, JULIUS KAMBARAGE; ZANZIBAR; KILIMANJARO; LAKE TANGANYIKA; LAKE VICTORIA.

TANZANITE is a rare gemstone that was discovered in Tanzania in 1967. It is a colored variety of *zoisite*, a mineral that consists of calcium-aluminum silicate. Most zoisite is grayish or white, but tanzanite ranges in color from yellowish-green to brown, blue, and violet. Geologists believe that tanzanite gets its color from small amounts of a chemical element called *vanadium*. The gemstone becomes sapphire-blue permanently if it is heated.   MARIA LUISA CRAWFORD

TAOISM, *TOW ihz uhm* or *DOW ihz uhm*, is a philosophy that began in China, probably during the 300's B.C. Taoism is also the name of a religion that began in about the 100's B.C. Through the centuries, the philosophy has influenced artists and writers in the East and West. The religion has about 29 million followers. The word *tao* originally meant *road* or *way*. The Tao (Way) represents the characteristics or behavior that makes each thing in the universe what it is. The word is also used to mean reality as a whole, which consists of all the individual "ways."

Taoism As a Philosophy. The beliefs of Taoism as a philosophy appear in two books, the *Lao Tzu* (later renamed the *Tao Te Ching, The Classic of the Way and the Virtue*) and the *Chuang Tzu*. The *Lao Tzu* is a collection from several sources and its authors and editors are unknown. The ideas were partly a reaction against *Confucianism*, a philosophy that developed in China beginning in about 500 B.C.

According to Confucianism, people can live a good life only in a well-disciplined society that stresses attention to ceremony, duty, and public service. The Taoist ideal, on the other hand, is a person who avoids conventional social obligations and leads a simple, spontaneous, and meditative life close to nature.

Taoist philosophy had a great influence on Chinese literature and art. For example, the poetry of T'ao Ch'ien (A.D. 365?-472?) expresses a distaste for worldly affairs and a yearning for a life in harmony with nature. During the early 1200's, Hsia Kuei painted landscapes that reflect the Taoist sensitivity to nature (see PAINTING [Oriental Painting]).

Taoism As a Religion was influenced by Chinese folk religion. In folk religion, most gods are human beings who displayed exceptional powers during their lives. For example, Kuan Ti, the protector of business people, was a general of the A.D. 200's.

Taoism has a hereditary priesthood. The priests con-

The Symbol of Taoism stands for what Taoists believe are the two basic forces in the universe—*yin* (female) and *yang* (male). The dark shape in the center and the broken lines represent yin. The white shape in the center and the solid lines symbolize yang.

duct public rituals, during which they submit the people's prayers to the gods of folk religion. The chief priest, who is in a trance, prays to other divinities on behalf of the worshipers. These divinities are not former human beings but represent aspects of the Tao.

The members of some Taoist groups have sought immortality through magic, meditation, special diets, breath control, or the recitation of scriptures. The Taoist search for knowledge of nature has led many believers to pursue various sciences, such as alchemy, astronomy, and medicine.   N. SIVIN

See also LAO TZU; CHUANG TZU; CONFUCIANISM; RELIGION (Taoism; picture: Taoist Deities).

Additional Resources

BYNNER, WITTER. *The Way of Life According to Lao Tzu.* Capricorn, 1962. A free translation of the *Tao te Ching.*

RAWSON, PHILIP, and LEGEZA, LAZSLO. *Tao: The Eastern Philosophy of Time and Change.* Crown, 1974.

WELCH, HOLMES. *Taoism: The Parting of the Way.* Beacon Press, 1966.

TAOS, *tows,* N. Mex. (pop. 3,369), is three communities in one. Taos proper serves as a trade center for the nearby farm and ranch region. The Pueblo Indian village of San Geronimo de Taos lies north of the town. To the south is the old Spanish farming center, Ranchos de Taos. All three communities lie near the base of the Sangre de Cristo Mountains in north-central New Mexico. Taos is 75 miles (121 kilometers) north of Santa Fe (see NEW MEXICO [political map]).

The well-known Taos "art colony" started in 1898. Sights of interest to tourists are the Plaza, the center of community life during the 1800's; the "Kit" Carson House, where the famous frontiersman lived from 1858 to 1866; and the Charles Bent House, where Governor

Bent was murdered during a Mexican revolt in 1847.

The pueblo village has adobe houses, four and five stories high, in which the Indians have lived since prehistoric times. White people first saw these when an expedition led by Francisco Vásquez de Coronado visited the region in 1540. The ruins of a Spanish mission, built in 1706, also stand there. Spanish colonists settled in the area in the early 1700's. Taos is the seat of Taos County.   FRANK D. REEVE

See also NEW MEXICO (picture: The Taos Rio Grande Gorge Bridge).

TAP. See PLUMBING.

TAP-DANCING. See DANCING (The Rise of Romanticism).

TAPE RECORDER is a device for recording sounds, pictures, and various kinds of information on magnetic tape. Most tape recorders can also play back tape recordings. The tape on which the recordings are made is a thin plastic ribbon. It is coated on one side with particles of iron oxide or some other substance that is easily magnetized. When electric waves are fed into a tape recorder, they magnetize the particles on the tape in varying patterns. The electric waves may come from a microphone, television camera, or computer. In fact, anything that can be changed into electric waves—as sound is by a microphone—can be recorded on magnetic tape. When the tape is played back, the magnetic patterns produce electric signals that are changed back into sounds, pictures, or information.

Tape recorders have many uses, and new uses are continually being found. Tape recorders provide home entertainment and are used by the radio, recording,

Motorola Inc.

Ampex Corporation

Ampex Corporation

Prerecorded Audio Tapes are made in three main forms. Cassettes, *left,* and cartridges, *upper right,* are the most popular forms because they are compact and easy to play. But reel-to-reel tapes, *lower right,* provide recordings of much higher quality.

TAPE RECORDER

and television industries. Scientists obtain information from tape recordings made on space flights. Tape recorders help students learn to speak a foreign language or to play a musical instrument. The uses of tape recorders in business and industry range from recording dictation to storing computer information.

Tape recordings have several advantages over phonograph recordings. They can be played back immediately after being made, and the same tape can be used to record again and again simply by erasing the previous recording. Changes can easily be made in tapes by cutting out unwanted sections and joining the ends of the tape together.

The most common use of tape recorders is to record sound, and this article deals chiefly with audio tape recorders. Much of the article also deals with other types of tape recorders because they all operate on the same basic principles.

How an Audio Tape Recorder Works

Basic Parts of an audio tape recorder are: (1) a supply reel, (2) a take-up reel, (3) a capstan, (4) a pinch roller, (5) an erase head, (6) a recording head, (7) a recording amplifier, (8) a playback head, and (9) a playback amplifier. These parts may differ slightly from one type of tape recorder to another.

Recording and Playing Back. To operate a tape recorder, one end of the tape from the *supply reel* is attached to the *take-up reel*. Between the two reels, a soft rubber roller called the *pinch roller* presses the tape tightly against a metal rod called the *capstan*. A motor turns the capstan. As the capstan turns, tape is pulled from the supply reel. On the other side of the capstan, the take-up reel pulls gently on the tape to wind it up. Before the tape reaches the capstan, it touches the *erase head*, which erases any previous recording, and then touches the *recording head*.

The recording head is an electromagnet. There is a small gap between the poles of the magnet. The electromagnet is magnetized by electric waves from a microphone. These waves have been strengthened by the *recording amplifier*. A magnetic field is created in the gap between the magnet's poles.

As the tape crosses the recording head, it touches the head at the gap. The changing magnetic field magnetizes the particles on the tape in a pattern like that of

A Tape Transport System. The capstan, aided by the pinch roller, pulls the tape from the supply reel, around an idler, and past the various heads. The tape winds onto the take-up reel.

WORLD BOOK diagram

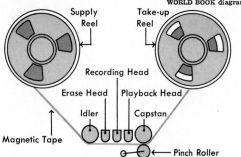

Supply Reel — Take-up Reel — Recording Head — Erase Head — Playback Head — Idler — Capstan — Magnetic Tape — Pinch Roller

Magnetic Tape is a thin strip of plastic coated with magnetic particles. The black areas in the greatly enlarged photograph below are iron oxide particles on a piece of unrecorded tape.

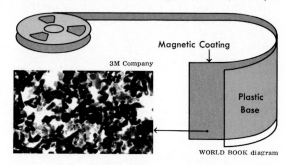

3M Company

Magnetic Coating — Plastic Base

WORLD BOOK diagram

Audio Tape Recordings. In recording, electric waves from a microphone create a magnetic field around a gap in the recording head. The field magnetizes the particles on the tape in patterns like the original sound waves. The photo below shows these patterns. During playback, the tape creates electric waves in the playback electromagnet. These waves are changed into sound.

3M Company · WORLD BOOK diagram

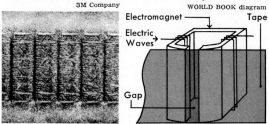

Electromagnet — Tape — Electric Waves — Gap

the sound waves entering the microphone. As soon as the recording is completed, it can be played back. The magnetic recording on the tape lasts until it is erased.

For playback, the tape is run through the recorder again. This time, the *playback head* is switched on. It picks up the tape's magnetic pattern, which creates electric waves in an electromagnet inside the head. The *playback amplifier* strengthens these waves enough to operate a loudspeaker, which changes them into sound.

Tape Widths and Playing Speeds. Different kinds of audio tape recorders use different widths of magnetic tape. The three most common widths are $\frac{1}{8}$, $\frac{1}{4}$, and $\frac{1}{2}$ inch (3.2, 6.4, and 12.7 millimeters). The wider the tape, the more *tracks* (separate recordings) that can be recorded on it. Most tape recorders can record more than one track on a tape. A tape recorder must be able to record two tracks at the same time to produce stereophonic (stereo) sound. Most stereo recorders can record at least four tracks on a tape, so that the tape carries two or more stereo recordings.

Different kinds of audio tape recorders move the tape through the recording and playback mechanisms at different speeds. The speeds are measured in *inches per second (ips)*. The speeds that are generally used are $\frac{15}{16}$, $1\frac{7}{8}$, $3\frac{3}{4}$, $7\frac{1}{2}$, 15, and 30 inches per second (2.4, 4.8, 9.5, 19, 38, and 76 centimeters per second). Speeds of $7\frac{1}{2}$, 15, and 30 ips produce sound recordings of the best quality, though recording at slower speeds adds to the playing time of a tape.

Kinds of Audio Tape Recorders

There are three main kinds of audio tape recorders: (1) *reel-to-reel*, (2) *cassette*, and (3) *cartridge*. A *stereophonic tape recorder* may be any one of the three. *Dictating machines* are a special kind of audio tape recorder.

Reel-to-Reel Tape Recorders are used by radio stations and recording studios and in many homes. To use a reel-to-reel recorder, the operator must unwind a piece of tape from the supply reel, thread it through the erase-record-playback mechanism, and attach it to the take-up reel. The recorder is then ready to operate.

In general, reel-to-reel recorders produce better-quality sound than do cassette or cartridge recorders. The tape moves faster and the width of each track is greater than in cassettes or cartridges. Reel-to-reel audio recorders for home use run at $1\frac{7}{8}$, $3\frac{3}{4}$, and $7\frac{1}{2}$ ips. Recording studios operate their recorders at 15 or 30 ips to make master tapes of music for phonograph records (see PHONOGRAPH [Making the Master Tape]). Professional tape recorders and many home tape recorders can record and play back sound with high fidelity (see HIGH FIDELITY).

Most home reel-to-reel audio recorders use quarter-inch tape, which has one, two, or four tracks. Many professional audio recorders use half-inch tape, which has up to eight tracks. Some recorders use 1- or 2-inch (2.5- or 5.1-centimeter) tape, which has as many as 24 tracks.

Cassette Tape Recorders are in most ways small copies of reel-to-reel recorders. But they are easier to operate because the tape does not have to be threaded through them. A cassette recorder uses a small plastic case called a *cassette*. Inside the cassette are a supply reel, which holds the tape, and a take-up reel. The cassette is simply snapped into the recorder and is ready to use. Cassette tape is only an eighth-inch wide, but it can carry four tracks. The recorders operate at only one speed—$1\frac{7}{8}$ ips.

Cartridge Tape Recorders, like cassette recorders, are smaller and easier to use than reel-to-reel types.

Four Tape Track Systems are shown below. The darker color indicates the placement of one of the tracks on monaural tapes and of one pair of stereo tracks on stereo tapes. The lighter color represents additional tracks. In most recorders, the tape is turned over to play additional tracks. But in cartridge recorders, the playback head can be aligned with each pair of stereo tracks.

WORLD BOOK diagram

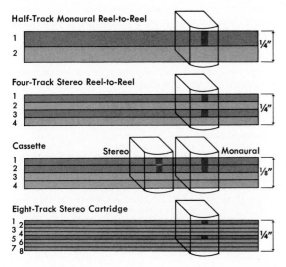

Half-Track Monaural Reel-to-Reel

Four-Track Stereo Reel-to-Reel

Cassette

Eight-Track Stereo Cartridge

Kinds of Tape Holders. Tape used in reel-to-reel recorders is wound on open reels and must be threaded through the recorder by hand. Cassette and cartridge tapes come in small plastic cases. They are simply snapped into the recorder and are ready to play.

WORLD BOOK diagram

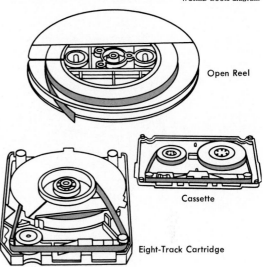

Open Reel

Cassette

Eight-Track Cartridge

However, the listener cannot quickly locate a given selection on the tape because the tape cannot be moved forward at high speed. The tape comes in a small plastic case called a *cartridge*, which is inserted into the recorder. The tape is wound in an endless loop on a single reel inside the cartridge. It unwinds from the center of the reel and rewinds around the outside. A recording made on cartridge tape plays until the recorder is turned off. Cartridge tape recorders use quarter-inch tape that carries either four or eight tracks. They are played at $3\frac{3}{4}$ ips.

Stereophonic Tape Recorders add to the realism of recordings by reproducing sound from different directions. To create this effect, two separate recordings are made of the same performance. For example, one microphone picks up the left section of an orchestra and another microphone the right section. When the tape is played back, one sound track is reproduced through the left speaker and the other track is reproduced through the right speaker. See HIGH FIDELITY (Stereophonic Hi-Fi).

Most reel-to-reel, cassette, and cartridge recorders are equipped for stereo. They have recording and playback heads that record and play back both stereo tracks at the same time. They also have two recording and two playback amplifiers and two speaker systems.

Dictating Machines make only voice recordings. The speeds at which they operate—usually less than $1\frac{7}{8}$ ips—are too slow to record music with high fidelity. Dictating machines may be reel-to-reel, cassette, or cartridge recorders. They are widely used in business offices for dictating letters.

Other Kinds of Tape Recording

Videotape is a special kind of magnetic tape used to record both the audio and the *video* (picture) portions

WORLD BOOK photo by Dan Miller

A Home Videotape Recorder records and plays back television programs, or plays prerecorded cassettes over a TV set.

of television programs. Videotape recordings are made in much the same way as audio tape recordings. The television camera changes patterns of light and shade into electric waves. The recording head of a videotape recorder, or VTR, is magnetized by these waves. The head creates a magnetic pattern on the videotape as the tape touches it. Videotape equipment can record both color and black-and-white pictures.

Most television programs are recorded on videotape. Professional videotape recorders generally use two-inch tape, which has separate tracks for the sound and for the picture. It also has a track for signals that control the set on which the picture appears. The sound and control tracks are recorded lengthwise on the tape. The video tracks are recorded crosswise, somewhat like railroad ties, and are called *channels*. Recording in channels increases the amount of picture information that can be recorded on a tape.

Videotape recorders are also used to record and play back programs received on television sets in the home. The earliest home videotape recorder was a reel-to-reel type. Engineers then developed a less expensive cassette videotape recorder. The tape is in a cassette similar to audio tape cassettes.

Computer Tape is used to record computer information. Devices called *tape units* put the information on the tape. The tape units operate in much the same way as audio and videotape recorders. In solving problems, many computers use electrical pulses to stand for letters and numbers. These pulses are recorded on the magnetic tape. The recorded information can be fed back into a computer when it is needed.

Tape units generally operate at 60 inches per second (152 centimeters per second) or faster. They record in channels and so can pack hundreds of *bits* (units of information) onto a short section of tape.

For more information on the use of magnetic tape in computers, see COMPUTER (The Input Equipment).

Instrumentation Tape Recorders have many scientific uses. Scientists and engineers use them to record readings from instruments in spacecraft and elsewhere. The readings may measure such data as heat, light, or temperature. The readings are changed into electric signals, which are recorded on the magnetic tape. Scientists and engineers play back the tapes to learn about outer space and the space flight itself.

Instrumentation tape recorders are also used to record readings from laboratory instruments. Such instruments may test the strength of metals or the performance of rockets and jet engines. In medical laboratories, heartbeats, brain waves, and similar information can be recorded on magnetic tape.

History

In the late 1800's, Valdemar Poulsen, a Danish engineer, invented the first machine for recording sound magnetically. Poulsen's machine made a magnetic recording on steel wire. However, phonograph recordings were more popular, and little use was made of magnetic recording for a number of years.

In the 1930's, German engineers found a more efficient and convenient substitute for the steel wire used in Poulsen's recorder. They worked out a method for using plastic tape coated with a magnetic material. During World War II (1939-1945), the Germans further developed the process of recording sound on magnetic tape.

After the war, engineers in the United States continued the German experiments. By 1950, tape had largely replaced phonograph records for radio recordings. Stereo tape recorders were introduced in the United States in 1955. About the same time, television networks began to record programs on videotape.

During the early 1960's, many radio stations began to use cartridge tape recorders for broadcasting music. Cartridge recorders were mass-produced for the first time in 1965, as equipment for some 1966-model automobiles. Also in the early 1960's, engineers in The Netherlands developed the cassette audio tape recorder. Cassettes were introduced in the United States in 1964 and soon became the most popular type of audio tape recorder. In the late 1960's, Ray Dolby, an American physicist, developed an electronic system to improve the quality of audio tape recordings. The Dolby system nearly eliminates the faint hissing sound made by tapes. Cassette videotape recorders, which had been developed in the late 1960's, became popular in the 1970's. Prerecorded tapes, both audio and video, also gained widespread use. ROBERT A. BERKOVITZ

Related Articles in WORLD BOOK include:

Computer	Electronic Music	Magnet and
Electro-	Headphones	Magnetism
magnet	High Fidelity	Microphone

Additional Resources

DOLAN, EDWARD F. *It Sounds Like Fun: How to Use and Enjoy Your Tape Recorder and Stereo.* Simon & Schuster, 1981. For younger readers.

JORGENSON, FINN. *The Complete Handbook of Magnetic Recording.* TAB, 1980.

TAPESTRY is a woven fabric made from threads of different colors to form a picture or design. Most tapestries serve as indoor wallhangings, but some are used as curtains or upholstery.

How Tapestries Are Made. Tapestries are woven on a loom. Like other woven fabrics, tapestries consist of horizontal threads, which form the *weft*, and vertical threads, which make up the *warp*. A tapestry weaver winds the threads of the weft around the threads of the warp, which are attached to the loom. In an ordinary woven fabric, the weft and the warp can both be seen. But in a tapestry, the weft completely conceals the warp. In addition, the back of a tapestry looks the same as the front, except that the design is reversed.

A tapestry weaver works from the back of the tapestry and follows a pattern called the *cartoon*, which indicates the thread colors to use on the tapestry. The weaver packs the threads tightly in place with a comblike tool called a *reed*.

History. The technique of making tapestries probably originated in prehistoric times. The craft was practiced during ancient times, but scholars know little about tapestry making before the Middle Ages.

Tapestry making first flourished in Europe from the 1300's to the 1500's. Professional workshops produced large tapestries for castles and churches. Most weavers worked from a full-scale cartoon painted by another artist. They wove many sets of three or more tapestries, which were hung on all sides of a room. Most tapestries were made of wool. They helped insulate rooms as well as decorate the walls.

Paris became the first major tapestry-making center. The *Apocalypse*, one of the oldest sets of tapestries in existence, was produced there during the 1370's or 1380's. Another set, the *Heroes Tapestries*, was also woven in Paris during the late 1300's. During the 1400's, Arras, France, and Brussels and Tournai, Belgium, became major tapestry-making centers.

Most tapestries from the Middle Ages picture scenes from history, legends, mythology, the Bible, or daily life. Many with scenes from daily life have a *millefleurs* design as a background. *Millefleurs* is a French word that means *a thousand flowers*. A millefleurs design consists of realistic flowers and leaves. One famous set of millefleurs tapestries is called *The Lady and the Unicorn*.

In the early 1500's, the great Italian painter Raphael designed cartoons for a set of tapestries called *Acts of the Apostles*. These tapestries greatly influenced tapestry weaving. Formerly, tapestry makers had concentrated on skillful weaving. But they now began to consider the design just as important and made tapestries that imitated paintings.

Tapestry weaving continued to thrive in Europe during the 1600's and 1700's. The Gobelin factory in Paris produced many fine tapestries. Such artists as Peter Paul Rubens, a Flemish painter, and François Boucher, a French painter, and Francisco Goya, a Spanish painter, designed cartoons.

The popularity of tapestry weaving declined during the 1800's, when wallpaper became widely used in

A French Tapestry woven during the late 1400's, *left*, has a *millefleurs* design in the background. Such a design consists of numerous flowers and leaves. A detail from the design appears below. This tapestry, called *The Unicorn at the Fountain*, is part of a famous series known as *The Hunt of the Unicorn*.

TAPEWORM

homes. In the 1900's, the French artist Jean Lurcat helped renew interest in the craft. Bonnie Young

See also Animal (picture: Animals That Hunt); Jesus Christ (picture: Jesus Was Brought Before Pilate).

Additional Resources

Ackerman, Phyllis. *Tapestry: The Mirror of Civilization*. AMS, 1974. Reprint of 1933 ed.

Gibbs-Smith, Charles H. *The Bayeux Tapestry*. Phaidon, 1973.

Thomson, Francis P. *Tapestry: Mirror of History*. Crown, 1980.

TAPEWORM is a parasite that feeds on and lives in the intestines of people and animals. It has a slender, flat body made up of blocklike *segments* (pieces). A tapeworm has no mouth. Its body walls absorb food from the *host* (the animal in which the worm lives). Some tapeworms are less than 1 inch (2.5 centimeters) long and have only three or four segments. Others may be 30 feet (9 meters) long and have thousands of segments.

A tapeworm has three body regions: a head or *scolex;* a neck; and a body or *strobila* made up of blocklike parts. The head is small and has suckers or hooks by which the worm attaches itself to the intestine. The neck is narrow. As the neck grows longer, the segments form in a row resembling a chain to form the body. The number of segments increases as the body of the tapeworm grows. The segments formed first are pushed backwards as the others form, so that the youngest segments are closest to the neck and the oldest are farthest away. The oldest segments often break off and are lost.

The Life Cycle. A tapeworm segment is mainly a machine of reproduction. A long tapeworm can produce millions of eggs in a single day. Each segment develops a complete set of male and female reproductive organs. Male cells *fertilize* (unite with) female cells to form thin-shelled eggs. The eggs pass into a sack called the *uterus.* In some tapeworms, the uterus has an opening through which the eggs can escape. But most kinds of tapeworms have no opening in the uterus. In these, the ripe eggs can escape only when the segments fall off the body and break up. Then the eggs pass out of the *primary host* (the animal in which the adult worm lives) with the body wastes.

Some eggs hatch in the water. Others hatch after they are eaten by another animal. The animals that house the *embryos* (newly hatched worms) are called *intermediate hosts.* The embryo burrows through the intestine of the intermediate host to muscle or other organs. The embryos are usually then called *larvae.* Tapeworms that attack human beings are carried by intermediate hosts, such as fish, hogs, and cattle. Diseased fish, pork, or beef must be completely cooked, or the tapeworm larvae may infect a person (primary host) who eats the diseased animal (intermediate host).

Kinds of Tapeworms. The broad tapeworm that infects human beings has two intermediate hosts, water

fleas and fish. The dwarf tapeworm, which is common in human beings, rats, and mice, grows from an egg to adult without an intermediate host. People become infected by eating food that contains eggs. People can also serve as an intermediate host for the huge *cysts* or sacs of tiny tapeworms found in dogs. These cysts, called *hydatids*, enclose the worm larvae.

The larvae of tapeworms are more dangerous to people than adult forms. In some cases, adult tapeworms produce no bad effects in human beings. Sometimes they cause irregular appetite, abdominal discomfort, *anemia* (lack of red blood cells), weakness, or nervousness. Drugs used to expel tapeworms include Atabrine, pelletierine, arecoline, and carbon tetrachloride. In most tapeworm treatment, the head of the worm must be expelled along with the body. If the hooks and suckers hold the head to the intestine, the neck can produce segments for a new body through regeneration.

Scientific Classification. The tapeworm belongs to the tapeworm class *Cestoda* of the phylum *Platyhelminthes.* The pork tapeworm belongs to the genus *Taenia,* species *T. solium;* the beef tapeworm is *Taenia saginata;* the broad tapeworm is *Dibothriocephalus latus;* and the tiny tapeworm found in dogs is *Echinococcus granulosus.* J. A. McLeod

TAPIOCA, *TAP ih O kuh,* is a food starch that is widely used in making puddings. It is taken from the root of the bitter manioc, or cassava, a tropical plant of the same family as the castor bean. Commercial tapioca comes chiefly from Brazil, Java, and the Malay Peninsula. A single plant may yield 10 pounds (5 kilograms) of starch. The roots are 2 to 8 inches (5 to 20 centimeters) thick, and 1 to 4 feet (30 to 120 centimeters) long. They are washed to remove prussic acid, and then reduced to a pulp. The pulp is strained until all the starchy particles are separated from the root fibers. The moist starchy mass is set on hot iron plates and left to dry. During the drying, the starch grains form the small, uneven, milky white balls known as *pearl tapioca.* A finer form, called *quick-cooking tapioca,* does not require soaking before cooking. Tapioca swells and thickens the liquid in which it is cooked.

Tapioca pudding is healthful and easily digested. Tapioca has a fuel value of 1,650 calories per pound (3,638 per kilogram) of dry tapioca. A flour made from cassava root is used as a thickening. This flour is one of the starches called *arrowroot.* Leone Rutledge Carroll

See also Cassava.

TAPIR, *TAY per,* is related to the horse and rhinoceros, though it looks more like a pig. The tapir has a short, heavy body, and a thick neck. Its nose is drawn out to form a movable, short trunk. Its front feet have four toes, and the hind feet have three toes. The tail is short. Tapirs are wary creatures. They live in the depths of the forests, and near water, in which they love to swim. Tapirs feed on the twigs and foliage of trees and shrubs, and on fruit and other vegetable food.

There are two kinds of tapirs in South America. The

The Long, Ribbonlike Tapeworm May Grow 30 Feet (9 Meters) Long in the Intestines of an Animal.

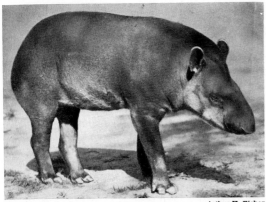
Arthur H. Fisher

The Brazilian Tapir looks much like a pig, except that it has a short movable trunk. Tapirs walk slowly, with their snouts close to the ground. Their keen senses of smell and hearing warn them of danger. They would rather run than fight.

most common one lives in the forest regions east of the Andes. The other makes its home high in these mountains. The two species of tapirs that live in Central America are the smallest of the family. All full-grown American tapirs are of a uniform dark-brown color, but the young are marked with yellowish streaks.

The Malayan tapir is found in Sumatra and the Malay Peninsula. It stands 3 to 3½ feet (91 to 107 centimeters) high at the shoulder. The back, rump, and sides are white while the rest of the thinly haired body is glossy black or dark brown.

Natives hunt tapirs for their flesh and thick hides. As a result of both hunting and the cutting of forests, tapirs have become rare in many areas.

Scientific Classification. Tapirs form the tapir family, *Tapiridae.* The South American tapir is genus *Tapirus*, species *T. terrestris.* Mountain tapir is *T. roulini.* The Central American tapir is *T. bairdi.* Malayan tapir is *T. indicus.*   THEODORE H. EATON, JR.

See also ANIMAL (color picture: Animals of the Tropical Forests); SOUTH AMERICA (Animals).

TAR is any of a group of thick, oily, dark-brown or black liquids. Most tars are by-products of the conversion of such organic matter as coal, petroleum, or wood into useful industrial products.

Coal Tar, also called *high-temperature coke-oven tar*, is the most important industrial tar. It is condensed from vapors given off during the manufacture of coke from bituminous coal (see COKE). This tar is used as a raw material for such products as disinfectants, dyes, perfumes, plastics, roofing and water-proofing materials, and synthetic drugs. See COAL TAR.

Coal Gasifier Tar is a by-product of certain manufacturing processes that convert coal into a high-energy gas. This gas can be used as a substitute for natural gas. The tar serves as a source of various organic chemicals.

Wood Tar is a by-product of the *destructive distillation* of wood in the production of charcoal (see DISTILLATION [Destructive Distillation]). The tar is condensed from vapors given off during the process. It is an important source of acetic acid, methyl alcohol, pine oil, and turpentine.

Oil-Gas Tar and Water-Gas Tar were once widely used in the manufacture of road-paving materials, wood

preservatives, and other products. These tars are by-products of the conversion of petroleum oils into gas used for heating and lighting. They are seldom produced today because other sources supply energy for those purposes.   FRANK A. SMITH

See also PITCH.

TAR HEEL STATE. See NORTH CAROLINA.

TAR SANDS. See BITUMINOUS SANDS.

TARABULUS, *tah RAH blus* (pop. 175,000), the second largest city in Lebanon, lies on the Mediterranean Sea about 40 miles (64 kilometers) north of Beirut. The city is also called TRIPOLI. It is at the end of an oil pipeline in Iraq. The city was probably founded about 700 B.C.

TARANTELLA, *TAR uhn TEHL uh*, is a lively Italian folk dance. The tarantella gets its name from the superstition that the dance is a cure for a bite by the tarantula.

TARANTULA, *tuh RAN chuh luh*, is the common name of any one of a group of mostly large, hairy spiders. Tarantulas are found in warm climates such as those of the southern and western United States, and in Central and South America. Some tarantulas live more than 20 years. Tarantulas get their name from a large wolf spider found around Taranto in southern Italy. People once believed this spider's bite caused a disease called *tarantism.* The victims supposedly leaped in the air and ran about making strange noises. According to superstition, the best cure was a lively Italian folk dance that became known as the *tarantella.*

One of the world's largest spiders, the *bird spider* of South America, is a tarantula. The bird spider has a body from 3 to 3½ inches (7.6 to 8.9 centimeters) long, and can spread its legs about 7 inches (18 centimeters). Some bird spiders live in trees and eat small birds.

Tarantulas found in the United States are quiet

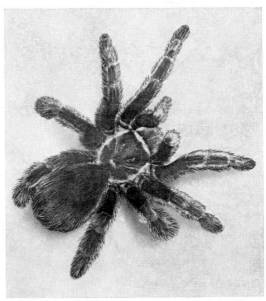
Lee Passmore

A Tarantula Looks Fierce, but its bite is usually no more dangerous than that of other spiders. It eats harmful insects.

creatures. Their bite is no more dangerous to man than the sting of a bee. The bite of some South American tarantulas may be serious. The *trap-door spider*, a tarantula found in the United States, grows about 1 inch (2.5 centimeters) long (see TRAP-DOOR SPIDER).

Scientific Classification. Tarantulas make up the suborder *Orthognatha*. Bird spiders form the bird spider family, *Theraphosidae*. Trap-door spiders form the trapdoor spider family, *Ctenizidae*.   H. K. WALLACE

See also SPIDER (Tarantulas; pictures); INSECT (pictures).

TARASCAN INDIANS, *tah RAHS kuhn*, were an important group in central Mexico. At the time of the Spanish Conquest in the 1500's, they controlled about the same area as the present state of Michoacán. The Tarascans developed an empire in a way similar to that of the Aztec, but on a smaller scale. Their capital, which was called Tzintzuntzan (*TSEENT soont SAHN*) or *place of the humming birds*, stood on the shore of Lake Pàtzcuaro.

The Tarascans were farmers, warriors, and craftsmen. They made copper tools, feather "paintings," and gold objects. They refused to join the Aztec against the Spanish, and were subjugated. Their descendants still live in the area. They farm, make fine lacquerware, fish from dugouts, and hunt.   GORDON F. EKHOLM

See also MEXICO (picture: Ancient Ways of Life).

TARAWA, *tah RAH wah* (pop. 20,000), is the capital of Kiribati, a country of many small islands in the southwest Pacific Ocean. Tarawa is an *atoll* (ring-shaped reef) composed of many coral islets that cover a total of 9 square miles (23 square kilometers).

The commercial and shipping center of Kiribati is Betio, a densely populated islet in the southwest area of Tarawa. Bairiki, east of Betio, is the government center. Bonriki, an islet in the southeast, has an international airport.

In 1788, the British explorer Captain Thomas Gilbert became the first European to sight Tarawa. The British took control of Tarawa in the 1890's. In 1942, during World War II, Japanese troops seized the atoll. American forces captured Tarawa from the Japanese in 1943 in one of the bloodiest battles of the war. Britain then ruled Tarawa until 1979, when it became part of the independent nation of Kiribati.   ROBERT LANGDON

See also KIRIBATI; WORLD WAR II (Tarawa; picture: U.S. Marines).

TARBELA DAM. See PAKISTAN (The Republic).

TARBELL, *TAHR bel,*
IDA MINERVA (1857-1944), an American author, led in the muckraking movement of the early 1900's which attacked dishonesty in politics and business. Her *History of the Standard Oil Company* (1904) exposed the practices of some great corporations, and strengthened the movement for outlawing monopolies. She also wrote biographies of Na-

Drake Well Museum, Titusville, Pa.
Ida M. Tarbell

poleon Bonaparte and Abraham Lincoln and an autobiography, *All in the Day's Work* (1929).

Ida Tarbell was born in Erie County, Pennsylvania. She was graduated from Allegheny College, and studied in Paris. Between 1883 and 1915, she was successively associate editor of *The Chautauquan, McClure's Magazine,* and *American Magazine.*   MERLE CURTI

TARBOOSH. See FEZ.

TARE. See VETCH.

TARGET. See ARCHERY.

TARGUM. See BIBLE (The First Translations).

TARHE. See OHIO (Exploration and Settlement).

TARIFF, *TAR ihf,* is a tax placed on goods that one nation imports from another. Many nations use tariffs to protect their own industries from foreign competition. Tariffs provide such protection by acting to raise the price of imported goods. Thus, tariffs encourage people to buy goods produced in their own country. Governments rarely place tariffs on exports because most nations want to sell as much as possible in other countries.

A nation also may use tariffs to influence the political and economic policies of other countries. For example, a nation may raise its tariffs to protest tariff increases by others.

Nations set their tariff rates in various ways. Two or more nations may sign a *reciprocal trade agreement* to set tariff rates for one another. Such an agreement may include a *most-favored-nation* clause. This clause requires the countries involved to use their lowest tariff rates on all products when dealing with one another. Nations also may set tariffs by forming a *free trade area,* a *customs union,* or a *common market.* The members of a free trade area have no tariffs among themselves, but each member may set its own tariffs on nonmembers. In a customs union, the members have no tariffs among themselves, but they establish a common set of tariffs for nonmembers. A common market has the same tariff policies as a customs union, but a common market provides for greater economic cooperation among its members.

Kinds of Tariffs

Economists classify tariffs according to (1) the purpose of the taxes and (2) how the taxes are levied. A tariff levied in order to restrict imports is called a *protective tariff.* A tariff levied simply to raise the income of a government without protecting any industry is known as a *revenue tariff.*

In some cases, a revenue tariff may also serve as a protective tariff. For example, if domestic and foreign companies both produce woolen sweaters, a revenue tariff might give the domestic firms an advantage. Such a tariff could raise the price of the imported sweaters enough to reduce their sale—and thus protect domestic firms.

Through the years, many governments have used revenue tariffs to increase their income. But protective tariffs usually play a more important role in a nation's economy than do revenue tariffs.

Protective tariffs or revenue tariffs may be levied in any of three ways—as (1) specific duties, (2) ad valorem duties, or (3) compound duties.

Specific Duties are placed on imported products according to a certain amount per unit of weight or volume. For example, a government might levy a specific duty of 10 cents per pound or 25 cents per liter of a product. Most specific duties are levied on raw materials, such as iron ore or rubber, or on bulk products, such as sugar or wheat.

Ad Valorem Duties are levied according to the value of a product. In most cases, governments levy ad valorem duties on manufactured goods. The rate may be as low as 5 per cent or less, or as high as 100 per cent or even higher.

Compound Duties are a combination of specific and ad valorem duties. They are levied on certain manufactured products according to the weight of the raw material used and the value of the finished article. For example, a government might impose a compound duty on copper pipe. This duty could consist of a specific duty on the weight of the copper, plus an ad valorem duty on the value of the pipe.

Disagreements About Tariffs

Many people believe that tariffs help a nation improve its economy. On the other hand, most economists argue that tariffs lower the standard of living in a country by forcing its citizens to pay higher prices for goods. Most economists also believe that tariffs lower the standard of living throughout the world by reducing trade.

Arguments for Tariffs. Supporters of tariffs claim these taxes help provide (1) domestic job protection, (2) an aid to industrial development, and (3) a strong national defense.

Domestic Job Protection. Many people believe the workers of any nation cannot compete successfully with those of other countries who earn lower wages or produce more. To protect domestic jobs and industries, business companies and worker organizations may form *special interest groups* that promote high tariffs. These

groups argue that tariffs make up for the lower wages in other nations and keep wages high at home.

Aid to Industrial Development. Tariffs can help a country develop and maintain a variety of industries. Without tariffs, a nation might be able to produce only a few kinds of goods profitably. In many cases, a new industry cannot compete successfully with established industries in other countries. A protective tariff may help new industries survive until they have developed completely.

Tariffs also may stop foreign competitors from putting established domestic industries out of business. Some foreign suppliers use a practice called *dumping* to win an unfair share of a nation's markets. Dumping involves selling certain products at different prices in different countries—sometimes even at a loss. For example, radio manufacturers in one country may sell their products so cheaply in another country that radio firms in the importing nation cannot compete successfully. As a result, those radio firms may go out of business. The importing nation would then have to depend completely on foreign manufacturers for radios. The foreign companies could then raise prices far above their original levels. Many countries use *antidumping duties* to protect their industries against unfair competition from foreign countries. A nation may impose antidumping duties against certain products from certain countries even though regular tariffs would not apply to those products.

Strong National Defense. Tariffs may help a nation develop industries needed for national defense. Many nations do not want to depend on other countries for such essential products as oil or steel. If a nation has no oil industry, an enemy might cut off its oil supply in time of war. Many economists believe a nation

WHAT PROTECTIVE TARIFFS DO   Nations levy protective tariffs to guard their industries from foreign competition. The tariffs make imported products more expensive and thus encourage people to buy goods produced in their own country. But most economists believe tariffs reduce world prosperity by discouraging trade.

With tariffs

Tariffs protect a nation's industries by increasing sales of domestic products. On the other hand, tariffs reduce international trade, raise prices to consumers, and deprive nations of the benefits of specialization.

Little international trade

PRICE PLUS TARIFF — High prices on imports

IMPORTS DOMESTIC — Large sales of domestic products

Without tariffs

Each country can specialize in making the goods it produces best and most economically. Nations exchange a large volume of goods, and consumers buy many imported products because they are better or cheaper.

Much international trade

PRICE — Low prices on imports

IMPORTS DOMESTIC — Large sales of imported products

WORLD BOOK illustration

should use tariffs to develop industries needed for national defense.

Arguments Against Tariffs include the belief that they result in (1) higher prices, (2) industrial inefficiency, and (3) unfair support for some industries. Tariffs may reduce trade, and so many economists believe they lower the standard of living in trading nations.

Higher Prices. Many people believe tariffs waste a nation's supply of labor and natural resources and thus raise prices. A country wastes money if it tries to produce everything it needs. Therefore, it should produce chiefly what it makes best and most economically. If a country has excellent factories but poor farmland, for example, it should export manufactured products and import most of its food. If such a nation tries to expand its farming by placing a tariff on imported food, its people will have to pay higher prices for food.

Industrial Inefficiency. Tariffs may encourage inefficiency by protecting industries from competition. Without competition, an industry has little need to become more efficient. If a nation's tariff policy encourages inefficiency, its industries will lose business to those of more efficient countries. Many economists claim that tariffs themselves cannot make—or keep—a nation prosperous by protecting inefficient industries.

Unfair Support for Some Industries. Tariffs may help some industries—but only at the expense of others. If a high tariff protects a nation's aluminum industry, for example, aluminum might cost more in that country than it would without a tariff. All domestic industries that use aluminum would save money if they could buy the imported product at a lower price. But the tariff forces those industries to pay the higher price.

History

Tariff policies reflect the economic and political conditions within various countries. Throughout history, nations have changed their tariff policies to keep in step with their economic and political goals.

The First Tariffs. In early times, nations did not have well organized foreign trade nor formal tariffs—but they did collect such taxes. Most tariff collectors simply charged merchants the highest duties they thought they could get.

From about 1100 to 1300, the Christian military campaigns called the Crusades brought increased trade between Europe and the Middle East. The rise in trade led to formal tariffs during this period. The first tariff agreements were made by Italian trading cities, such as Genoa and Venice, with various commercial partners in Africa and Asia. England levied a revenue tariff in 1303 that included an ad valorem duty on imported and exported goods. Collectors based this duty, called *poundage*, on the value in pounds of the goods.

Beginning in the 1490's, the explorations of Christopher Columbus, Vasco da Gama, and other Europeans resulted in a great increase in foreign trade. European trading nations began to follow an economic policy called *mercantilism*. This policy involved the use of high tariffs to limit imports, so that exports would exceed imports. An excess of exports over imports produced a *favorable balance of trade*—and boosted the size of a nation's treasury. Mercantilism flourished in Europe from the 1500's to the 1700's.

The Changing Role of Tariffs. During the late 1700's, the beginning of industrialization in Europe led to a major change in the role of tariffs. The production of goods increased in the industrial nations, such as Belgium and Great Britain. As a result, these nations wanted to sell more and more products to other countries. Many industrial nations, in an effort to increase trade, sought lower tariffs with their trade partners. But nations that were just beginning to industrialize kept tariffs high to protect their new industries. Efforts to reduce tariffs increased as industrialization progressed during the 1800's and 1900's.

Modern Tariff Policies. By the mid-1900's, three major trading groups had developed, each with its own tariff policies. These groups were: (1) the non-Communist industrial nations, (2) the underdeveloped countries, and (3) the Communist nations. The non-Communist industrial nations sought to increase their trade by reducing tariffs. For example, the Western European countries formed the European Economic Community to eliminate tariffs on one another's goods. Many developing nations in Africa, Asia, and Latin America continued to use high tariffs to protect their industries. The Communist nations worked toward removing tariffs on one another's products.

United States Tariffs have played a major role in the nation's history. The U.S. government has changed its tariff policies many times through the years.

The Revolutionary Period. Many people in the American Colonies resented the tariffs that Great Britain put on goods that they imported. They sought independence partly to free themselves from the British tariffs.

Soon after the Revolutionary War ended in 1783, many Americans demanded that the government establish a tariff. They argued that a tariff would (1) protect the nation's industries, (2) raise government revenue, and (3) encourage other nations to grant fair tariffs to the United States. The first Congress passed the Tariff Act of 1789, which set up U.S. tariffs.

The 1800's. The nation's first tariffs were low, but most of them rose during the early 1800's. People in various parts of the country called for different tariff policies. For example, people in the New England and Middle Atlantic states sought high tariffs to protect their manufacturing industries. But Southerners, whose income came chiefly from agriculture, demanded low tariffs. They wished to buy European products, which were better and cheaper than those made in the United States. Westerners, whose income also came mostly from agriculture, at first opposed high tariffs. But they came to accept a plan called the "American System" proposed by Representative Henry Clay of Kentucky. This plan included a protective tariff. Clay believed that Westerners would benefit by supporting such a tariff for Eastern manufacturers. He thought it would bring increased prosperity for the East, which in turn would create a larger market for Western farm products. In 1824, Congress boosted most tariffs as a result of Clay's proposals.

Many people, especially Southerners, protested the rising tariffs, particularly what they called the "Tariff of Abominations" of 1828. This tariff again increased the cost of foreign products needed by farmers. To satisfy those who wanted to eliminate all tariffs, Clay helped work out the Compromise Tariff of 1833. This law maintained some high duties but included a plan to reduce tariffs gradually until 1842. However, poor economic conditions resulted in a new and higher tariff in 1842. In 1846, after the economy had improved, Congress lowered tariffs with the Walker Tariff Act. Further reductions were made in 1857, but the Morrill Tariff Act of 1861 again raised tariffs because of poor economic conditions.

The tariff disagreement between the North and South helped cause the Civil War, which began in 1861. Southerners felt betrayed when the Westerners and Northerners joined in support of high tariffs.

During the Civil War, the government raised tariffs to new highs. Most tariffs remained high throughout the 1800's. Several attempts to lower them failed. For example, the Mills bill of 1888 included President Grover Cleveland's proposal to lower tariffs. The House of Representatives passed the bill, but the Senate never voted on it. The McKinley Tariff Act of 1890 raised the average level of tariffs to a new high.

The 1900's. During the early 1900's, many people in the United States wanted to increase the nation's trade by lowering tariffs. The Payne-Aldrich Tariff of 1909 changed many tariff rates but failed to lower the average level of tariffs. In 1913, the Underwood Tariff Act generally reduced tariffs. However, a decline in shipping during World War I (1914-1918) cut trade and limited the effects of the lower tariffs. In 1922, the Fordney-McCumber Tariff Act raised tariff rates sharply. United States tariffs reached an all-time high under the Smoot-Hawley Tariff Act of 1930.

In 1934, during the Great Depression, Congress passed the Reciprocal Trade Agreements Act in an effort to increase trade. This law made the most significant change in the history of the nation's tariffs. It authorized the President to cut tariffs for certain nations by as much as half. It also enabled him to make agreements setting the exact tariff rate for each product. Formerly, Congress had set the rates.

After World War II ended in 1945, a number of countries made further efforts to lower tariffs. In 1947, the United States and 22 other nations signed the General Agreement on Tariffs and Trade (GATT). This pact reduced tariffs and provided for the settlement of trade disputes. It also restricted its members from banning or limiting imports from other member nations. As a result of a series of meetings held under terms of the GATT, nations throughout the world lowered their tariffs. In 1967, more than 50 nations that had signed the GATT agreed on tariff concessions that covered more than $40 billion in world trade.

By the mid-1970's, about 85 nations had signed the GATT. In addition, Congress had passed several laws to help industries and labor unions adjust to increased competition attracted by lower tariffs. In 1955, an amendment to the Reciprocal Trade Agreements Act of 1934 provided for the gradual lowering of U.S. tariffs. Such action helps protected industries adjust to foreign competition. The Trade Expansion Act of 1962 provided financial and technical assistance to firms and workers harmed by the effects of lower tariffs. This law also gave the President authority to make trade agreements for lower tariffs without congressional approval.

The Trade Reform Act of 1974 made further efforts to lower tariffs and increase trade. It enlarged the President's authority to determine tariff rates within limits specified by Congress. The law also authorized the President to grant most-favored-nation benefits to Romania and Russia for the first time. In addition, the act increased financial assistance to U.S. workers, communities, and industries that suffered economic hardship caused by tariff reductions.   HAROLD J. HECK

Related Articles in WORLD BOOK include:

Balance of Payments	General Agreement on Tariffs
Customs Union	and Trade
Exports and Imports	International Trade
Free Trade	Reciprocal Trade Agreement

TARIFF ACT OF 1842. See OBSCENITY AND PORNOGRAPHY.

TARIFF COMMISSION, UNITED STATES. See INTERNATIONAL TRADE COMMISSION, UNITED STATES.

TARIFF OF ABOMINATIONS. See ADAMS, JOHN QUINCY (The "Tariff of Abominations").

TARKENTON, FRAN (1940-   ), was one of the top quarterbacks in National Football League (NFL) history. He was noted for his passing and his ability to scramble—that is, to avoid tacklers. Tarkenton holds several NFL regular season career records, including most passes attempted, most passes completed, most yards passing, and most touchdown passes. During his 18-year professional career, he attempted 6,467 passes and completed 3,686 for 47,003 yards and 342 touchdowns. He also gained 3,669 yards by running, more than any other NFL quarterback.

Tarkenton won all-America honors while playing at the University of Georgia from 1958 to

Minnesota Vikings
Fran Tarkenton

1960. He played for the Minnesota Vikings from 1961 to 1966 and was traded to the New York Giants in 1967. He returned to the Vikings in 1972. Tarkenton retired after the 1978-1979 season. Francis Asbury Tarkenton was born in Richmond, Va.   BOB WOLF

See also FOOTBALL (picture).

TARKINGTON, BOOTH (1869-1946), was an American novelist and dramatist. His writings are considered one of the best mirrors of the wholesome aspects of life in the Middle West. His works range from the sentimentally romantic *Monsieur Beaucaire* (1900) to the humor of *Penrod* (1914) and the realism of *Alice Adams* (1921). In the trilogy entitled *Growth* (1927), a collection of *The Turmoil* (1915), *The Magnificent Ambersons* (1918), and *The Midlander* (1923), he presented a cross section of city life such as it was in his home town, Indianapolis. *Penrod, Penrod and Sam* (1916), and *Seventeen* (1916) portray the joys and problems of young people.

Tarkington also published plays, short stories, and essays. He was amiable, optimistic, and somewhat passive in emphasizing the smiling aspects of life and the joys of boyhood. Tarkington was awarded two

TARN

Pulitzer prizes for literature, in 1919 and 1922, for *The Magnificent Ambersons* and *Alice Adams*.

Huston, Pix

Booth Tarkington

Tarkington was born on July 29, 1869, in Indianapolis, Ind. He was elected to the Indiana House of Representatives for the 1902-1903 term. He was a neighbor and admirer of the poet James Whitcomb Riley, and a devotee of William Dean Howells and Mark Twain. Tarkington also wrote some of the verses that were sung in the Ziegfeld Follies in the early 1900's.

Several of Tarkington's short stories dealing with political life were collected into one work entitled *In the Arena*. He also wrote *The Gentleman from Indiana* (1899), *The Beautiful Lady* (1905), *Beauty and the Jacobin, an Interlude of the French Revolution* (1912), and *The Plutocrat* (1927). HARRY H. CLARK

TARN is a name given to small mountain lakes with steep banks, formed by glaciers. There are a number in the western mountain region of Scotland. See also ICE AGE (picture).

TARNISH. When a metal rusts, or combines with oxygen, it is tarnished. When a metallic or mineral surface loses its luster, it is also tarnished. The word *tarnish* is used for rust formed on metals other than iron, or *nonferrous* metals.

See also RUST.

TARO is a tropical plant used as food. The edible portion of the plant consists of one or more large underground stems called *tubers*. The taro is grown mainly in Hawaii and on other Pacific Islands. It has several names. In the southern United States, it is called *dasheen*. In certain tropical countries, it is known by such names as *eddo*, *malanga*, and *yautia*. The taro is closely related to the ornamental plants called *elephant's-ear* and *caladium*.

Scientific Classification. The taro belongs to the arum family, *Araceae*. It is classified as genus *Colocasia*, species *C. esculenta*. JULIAN C. CRANE

See also ELEPHANT'S-EAR.

TAROT CARDS. See MAGIC (History; picture).

TARPAN, *TAR pan*, was a wild horse that lived in the forests of Europe. The tarpan has been extinct since the 1800's. However, scientists believe that they have bred a horse that is exactly like the original European forest horse. These scientists worked at the Hellabrunn Zoo in Munich, Germany. They developed a process of back-breeding which produced a small horse in the 1950's that looks like the ancient tarpan.

See also HORSE (Wild Horses); PRZEWALSKI'S HORSE.

TARPEIAN ROCK, *tahr PEE uhn*, was a rocky surface on the southwestern corner of the steep Capitoline Hill in Rome. According to the legend, this rock was named for Tarpeia, the daughter of the governor of the Roman citadel in the time of Romulus. The story says that Tarpeia wanted the golden bracelets worn by the Sabine enemies of Rome. She treacherously opened the gate of the fortress for them after they promised they would give her what they wore on their left arms. Once inside the citadel, they crushed and killed her when they threw upon her the shields they wore on their left arms. Tarpeia was buried at the foot of the rock, which ever afterward bore her name. In later times, the Romans killed traitors by hurling them down from the top of the Tarpeian Rock. WILLIAM SCOTT FERGUSON

TARPON is a large game fish related to the herring. It lives in the Atlantic Ocean from Long Island to Brazil, in the Gulf of Mexico, and in West Indian waters. It is abundant off the southern Atlantic Coast of the United States. The tarpon grows to a length of 8 feet (2.4 meters), and sometimes weighs 200 pounds (91 kilograms). Its flesh is coarse and not desirable for food. The large, tough, silvery scales are used in decorative designs. Tarpon fishing is one of the best American sports, because the fish is a strong, skillful fighter. Most fishing for tarpon is done off the south Atlantic Coast. Tarpon enter fresh waters and may be seen rolling, giving off bubbles of air as they dive. Sometimes they leap out of the water. Tarpon spawning grounds are unknown.

See also FISH (Fish of Coastal Waters).

Scientific Classification. Tarpons belong to the tarpon family, *Elopidae*. The tarpon found near Florida is genus *Megalops*, species *M. atlantica*. LEONARD P. SCHULTZ

TARPON SPRINGS, Fla. (pop. 13,251), is one of the world's largest sponge markets. It lies along the Gulf of Mexico on the western coast of Florida. For location, see FLORIDA (political map).

New York Botanical Garden

The Taro has a large underground stem with several side-stems. These underground stems are used as food on many Pacific Islands.

The sponge industry began in 1905, when Greek fishermen arrived in the area. It grew to a fleet of more than 100 deep-sea boats, manned by fishermen of Greek descent. By the 1950's, disease and overfishing had depleted the supply of sponges. But the situation improved in the 1960's, and fishing began again. Tarpon Springs was founded in 1876.   KATHRYN ABBEY HANNA

TARQUINIUS, *tahr QUIN ih us,* was the name of two of the seven legendary kings of Rome.

Lucius Tarquinius Priscus (reigned 616-578 B.C.) was the fifth king. According to legend, he was born in Etruria and was not of royal blood. He moved to Rome and became a good friend of the king, Ancus Marcius, who made him guardian for his children. When the king died, Priscus was elected to take his place. His reign was very prosperous and successful. He made many conquests, and built many monuments and public works, including the Circus Maximus and the Temple of Jupiter. Legends claim that either Priscus or his son Superbus acquired the Sibylline books. See SIBYL.

Lucius Tarquinius Superbus, the Proud (reigned 534-510 B.C.), was the son of Priscus, and the last of the seven legendary kings. He was the son-in-law of Servius Tullius, whom he murdered in order to gain the throne (see SERVIUS TULLIUS). Superbus was a tyrant and took away the rights of the lower classes. When his son, Sextus Tarquinius, committed a crime against Lucretia, the people revolted and drove Superbus from the throne (see LUCRETIA). Then the people established the Roman Republic. They also put down several attempts to bring Superbus back. The most famous attempt, by Lars Porsena, inspired Thomas Macaulay's poem "Horatius at the Bridge."   THOMAS A. BRADY

See also ROMAN EMPIRE (Legendary Rome; The Early Republic).

TARRAGON, *TAIR uh gahn,* is a plant that provides leaves used to flavor pickles, cookies, and vinegar, and to make a cooking oil. It is related to American sagebrushes and the absinthe plant.

Scientific Classification. The tarragon belongs to the composite family, *Compositae.* It is classified as genus *Artemisia,* species *A. dracunculus.* HAROLD NORMAN MOLDENKE

TARSAL BONES. See FOOT (in anatomy).

The Tarsier is a small Southwest Pacific animal with large eyes. Pads on its fingers and toes help it to grip branches.
Cy La Tour

TARSIER, *TAHR see uhr,* is a small mammal with a round head and unusually large owl-like eyes. Like man and apes, it belongs to the order *primates* (see PRIMATE). The tarsier lives in the East Indies and the Philippines. It has big ears and a long thin tail with a little tuft of fur on the end. Its fur is kinky and woolly. It has short front legs, and long hind legs that help it hop among the branches of its tree-home. All of its long fingers and most of its toes have nails, but the second and third toes have claws. The tarsier grows to be about as large as a rat. Its name comes from the long tarsal bones in the animal's feet. The tarsier moves through trees at night, feeding on insects, snails, and small lizards.

Scientific Classification. The tarsier belongs to the tarsier family, *Tarsiidae.* It is genus *Tarsius.* Species include *T. spectrum, T. bacanus,* and *T. syrichta.* GEORGE B. SCHALLER

TARSUS, *TAR sus* (pop. 78,033), a city in south-central Turkey, is an agricultural center. Tarsus was the birthplace of Saint Paul. Ancient Tarsus was an important trading center, surrounded by fertile land. The Cydnus River linked the city with a good harbor on the Mediterranean Sea, and an important trade road ran through Tarsus. For location, see TURKEY (political map).

Tarsus was first mentioned in the records of the Assyrians, a group of people from western Asia. The Assyrians probably seized control of the city about 850 B.C. from Greek colonists. After 104 B.C., the Romans took control of Tarsus, and the city was rich and prosperous while they controlled it.   MARY FRANCIS GYLES

TARTAN, *TAHR tun,* is a plaid cloth pattern that developed chiefly in Scotland. The design consists of stripes of various widths and colors. The stripes cross at right angles against a solid color background. The chief *clans* (tribes), families, and districts of Scotland have their own tartans. In the United States, the word *tartan* also means a cloth or a garment with a tartan design. The cloth is usually wool, but may be of other materials. A tartan design is called a *sett.* It may be made in any size, depending on the use of the cloth. Regardless of the size of the sett, the proportions of the stripes must be the same. The colors of a sett may vary in shade from pale to dark.

A Scottish Highlander wears a tartan *kilt* (a knee-length pleated skirt). The Highlander may carry a *plaid* over his left shoulder. A plaid is a blanketlike mantle fastened at the shoulder with a brooch. Other parts of the costume include a *sporran* (pouch) hanging in front of the kilt, a *doublet* (jacket), and a *bonnet* (cap). The stockings may be of tartan pattern, and the *brogues* (shoes) are low-cut.

The use of checkered garments dates back to ancient times. The Irish, the Britons, the Caledonians of Scotland, and the Celts in Europe wore them. Scottish literature first referred to the tartan in the 1200's. Originally, tartans in Scotland were associated with districts. Later, they were used to identify the chief clan or family of an area. Extra lines were added to some setts to show the wearer's rank. Early weavers colored the tartan with vegetable dyes. They kept a record of the exact design of a tartan by marking the number and color of every thread on a pattern stick.

TARTAN

Colorful Scottish Tartans are favorite designs in many countries. The tartan developed chiefly in the Highlands of Scotland, where each clan and family designed its own pattern. Some Scottish clans wear a bright tartan on formal occasions, and a more restrained hunting tartan for everyday wear. There are hundreds of different tartans. Some of the best-known clan tartans are illustrated in this article. Because of the problem of matching dyes, the colors of different samples of the same tartan may vary in shade. The uniform of the famous Black Watch Royal Highland Regiment, *right*, includes the government tartan. The soldier is a drum major in the regiment, which was organized in 1725.

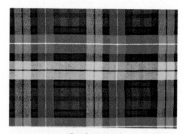

Buchanan

Exclusive WORLD BOOK photos by Sidney H. Siegel; tartans courtesy Kinloch Anderson, Ltd., Edinburgh, Scotland

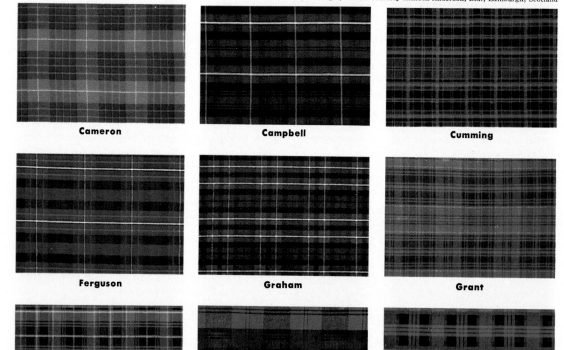

| **Cameron** | **Campbell** | **Cumming** |

| **Ferguson** | **Graham** | **Grant** |

| **Innes** | **Lindsay** | **MacDuff** |

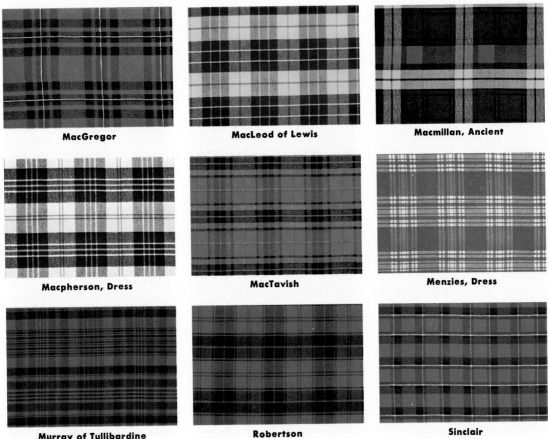

MacGregor

MacLeod of Lewis

Macmillan, Ancient

Macpherson, Dress

MacTavish

Menzies, Dress

Murray of Tullibardine

Robertson

Sinclair

The Tartan of the British Royal Family is called the Royal Stewart. The Stuarts, the royal family of Scotland from 1371 to 1714 and of England from 1603 to 1714, regarded it as their tartan. The Dress Stewart and Hunting Stewart tartans are also associated with the family. The name of the family was originally *Stewart*, but it later came to be spelled *Stuart*.

Stewart, Dress

Stewart, Royal

Stewart, Hunting

38a

Originally, the kilt and the plaid were part of a single large piece of tartan cloth. Wearers folded the tartan lengthwise and gathered it around the waist with a belt. They threw the rest over the shoulder and pinned it. In bad weather, they wore the tartan over the head and shoulders as a cloak. When sleeping outside, they used it as a blanket. Today, the kilt and the plaid are worn separately.

After the Jacobite Rebellion in 1745, the British Parliament banned the tartan and the use of Highland dress until 1782. Some old setts were lost, but many new ones were invented, especially about 1820. Today, the tartan is popular throughout the world, particularly in the United States, where many people have Scottish ancestors. There are no rigid rules for its use, but people usually wear tartans associated with their name or ancestry. For pictures of tartans, see the two preceding pages. W. J. KINLOCH ANDERSON

See also CLAN; SCOTLAND (Way of Life; Traditions; picture: Bagpipes and Kilts).

TARTAR. See TEETH (Dental Checkups; Periodontal Diseases).

TARTAR EMETIC is a medicinal preparation which people once used as an emetic. It is now used as an expectorant to make patients cough up phlegm and mucus. Tartar emetic is prepared from antimony oxide and potassium tartrate. In large doses, it is a violent, irritating poison. Because of its effect on the body, it should be taken only when prescribed by a physician.

TARTARIC ACID is an important industrial and household chemical. It occurs naturally in fruits, both as the acid and as the potassium salt, called *cream of tartar*. Carl Scheele, a Swedish chemist, first isolated the acid from its salt in 1770. Louis Pasteur did some of his pioneer research on the acid.

Cream of tartar is used in the manufacture of one kind of baking powder. In addition, it is treated with sodium hydroxide to give *Rochelle salts*. The acid is used in carbonated beverages, and as a *mordant* (dye-fixative).

Most commercial tartaric acid is obtained from the wine industry. As wine ferments, the salt crystallizes on the walls of wine casks.

Tartaric acid forms clear to white crystals, easily soluble in water. They melt at 170° C (338° F.). The chemical formula is $C_2H_2(OH)_2(COOH)_2$. JOHN E. LEFFLER

See also ACID; SCHEELE, CARL WILHELM.

TARTARS are Turkic peoples who live in central and southern Russia. Tartar is a form of the Turkic word *Tatar*, which is the Tartars' name for themselves.

All Tartars use some form of the Turkic language. Typical Tartar groups include the Crimean Tartars, the Siberian Tartars, and the Volga Tartars. Most Tartars are Muslims.

The Soviet Union consists of republics based on nationality groups, and the Tartars have their own republic, the Tatar Autonomous Soviet Socialist Republic. It is part of the Russian Soviet Federated Socialist Republic, the nation's largest republic. More than 1½ million Tartars live in the Tatar republic. Its capital, Kazan, is a center of Tartar culture.

During the Middle Ages, Mongol and Turkish warriors called Tartars invaded Europe from central Asia.

They were so fierce that people associated them with Tartarus, an ancient name for hell. But those medieval Tartars have little relation to the Tartars of modern Russia. JOHN R. KRUEGER

See also TARTARY; KAZAN.

TARTARUS, *TAHR tuh rus*, was a dark place below the earth in early Greek mythology. It was as far below Hades as earth is from heaven, and a falling stone would take nine days to reach it. A river of fire called Phlegethon circled Tartarus. Zeus put the rebelling Titans in Tartarus, and any god who swore a false oath was kept there for nine years. According to later belief, Tartarus was a place of punishment for the most wicked sinners, and was part of Hades. It corresponds in some ways to the Christian idea of hell. PADRAIC COLUM

See also HADES.

TARTARY was once the name of a vast region in Europe and Asia which was inhabited by tribes of Tartars. The region lay outside the Great Wall of China. It included present-day northern China, Mongolia, Sinkiang, and the southern parts of Russia in Europe and Asia.

Today, the name Tartary usually applies only to the area more commonly known as Sinkiang, or Chinese Turkestan, plus western Mongolia. This is a rugged mountain area north of Tibet. J. E. SPENCER

TARTINI, *tahr TEE nee,* **GIUSEPPE** (1692-1770), was a great Italian master of the violin, a noted composer, and a teacher. He influenced violin playing by introducing a system of violin bowing and fingering. He also started the use of thicker strings and lighter bows. In 1728, he founded a school of violin playing at Padua. His best-known composition for violin is the *Devil's Trill Sonata*. He also composed about 140 concertos, 40 trios, and 150 violin sonatas. Tartini was born in Pirano, Italy. DOROTHY DELAY

TARTU, *TAHR too* (pop. 104,000), is a city in southeastern Estonia. The first university in the Baltic states was founded in Tartu in 1632. The city long has been Estonia's cultural and religious center. For location, see ESTONIA (map).

TARTUFFE. See MOLIÈRE; DRAMA (picture).

TARZAN. See BURROUGHS, EDGAR RICE.

TASCHEREAU, *tash roh,* **SIR HENRI ELZÉAR** (1836-1911), served as chief justice of Canada from 1902 to 1906. He also served on the Superior Court of Quebec from 1871 to 1878, and he was associate justice on the Supreme Court of Canada from 1878 until he became chief justice. Born in Ste. Marie de la Beauce, Quebec, Taschereau came from a distinguished Canadian family of ecclesiastical and governmental servants. In the 1860's, he supported the confederation of Canada. He was knighted in 1902. J. E. HODGETTS

TASHKENT, *tash KENT* (pop. 1,779,000), is the capital of Uzbek Soviet Socialist Republic in Russia. The largest city in Soviet Asia, Tashkent lies north of Afghanistan, in the valley of the Chirchik River (see RUSSIA [political map]). The city is divided into two sections, the old Asiatic and the new Russian. The Russian section reflects modern city life, while the Asiatic section resembles a dusty caravan town. Tashkent has railroad connections with Krasnovodsk and with the railroad lines in Siberia. The city has machinery plants and a cotton-textile mill. For the monthly weather, see RUSSIA (Climate). THEODORE SHABAD

TASK FORCE is a temporary grouping of military units under a single commander. It is set up to perform a specific mission or operation. The three military branches of the armed forces often use task forces. When a task force contains units from more than one service, it is called a *joint task force*.

In the navy, a task force is a major subdivision of a fleet. It usually contains a variety of ships, some of them chosen for the specific task and others picked to provide security for the force as a whole.

In the air force and army, a task force may contain one or several types of units, large or small, depending on the mission it is set up to accomplish. An army task force usually takes its name from the last name of its commander. CHARLES B. MACDONALD

TASMAN, ABEL JANSZOON (1603-1659), a Dutch sea captain, explored the South Pacific. In 1642, he sailed southeast from Batavia, Java, and became the first European to reach the island now called Tasmania and to sight New Zealand. See TASMANIA (History).

On this famous voyage, which lasted 10 months, he sailed completely around Australia without sighting it. As a result, the question of whether Australia or New Zealand were parts of a great southern continent remained unanswered until the voyages of Captain James Cook (see COOK, JAMES). On his voyage in 1644, Tasman entered the Gulf of Carpentaria along northern Australia. Historians believe he was born at Hoorn (near Alkmaar), The Netherlands. JAMES G. ALLEN

TASMAN SEA is that part of the Pacific Ocean which lies between southeastern Australia, Tasmania, and New Zealand. It covers about 900,000 square miles (2,300,000 square kilometers). A submarine cable on the bed of the sea provides communication between Sydney, Australia, and Cape Farewell, New Zealand. The Dutch navigator, Abel Janszoon Tasman, reached the sea in the mid-1600's. BOSTWICK H. KETCHUM

TASMANIA, *taz MAY nee uh,* is the island state of the Australian Commonwealth. It is the smallest Australian state, and one of the most beautiful. Many Australians spend their vacations on the island.

Location, Size, and Description. Tasmania once formed the southeastern corner of the Australian mainland. But this heart-shaped chunk of land split off from the continent, and the rough waters of Bass Strait now separate Tasmania from the state of Victoria. For location, see AUSTRALIA (political map).

Tasmania administers several small islands, including Macquarie, Maria, and King islands. Tasmania and its islands cover an area of 26,200 square miles (67,800 square kilometers). The mountains in eastern Tasmania form part of the Great Dividing Range that runs down the eastern edge of the Australian mainland. Western Tasmania has steep jagged mountains. Mount Ossa (5,305 feet, or 1,617 meters) in western Tasmania is the highest point on the island.

Tasmania's lakes and rivers are the source of electricity for industry. Its swift rivers rise in the mountains of the central region. The chief rivers are the Derwent, Coal, Arthur, Pieman, Gordon, Spring, and Tamar. The lakes include Great Lake, St. Clair, Sorell, and Echo. The coastline has many capes and bays.

Climate. Tasmania's temperature averages 60° F. (16° C) in January and 50° F. (10° C) in July. The annual rainfall averages 20 to 40 inches (51 to 100 centimeters) in eastern Tasmania and 40 to 60 inches (100 to 150 centimeters) in the west.

Natural Resources. Many mineral deposits are found in the mountains of Tasmania. These minerals include coal, copper, gold, iridium, lead, osmium, silver, tin, and zinc. Large forests cover parts of the island. The seeds that produced California's first eucalyptus trees came from Tasmania. The Tasmanian wolf and a small bearlike beast called the Tasmanian devil live on the island, but not on the Australian mainland.

The People. Tasmania has a population of about 419,000. Most of the people are of British descent, and most of them were born in Australia. In the early 1800's, European settlers hunted down and killed most of the Aborigines who lived in Tasmania (see ABORIGINES). Those who remained were taken to Flinders Island in Bass Strait for protection. The last surviving Tasmanian Aborigine died in 1876.

Most of the important cities and towns of Tasmania lie on or near the coast. Tasmania has no large cities. Hobart is the capital and largest city, and Launceston ranks as the second largest city. Other important towns include Burnie-Somerset, Devonport, and Ulverstone.

Agriculture. Farmers cultivate scattered areas because of Tasmania's mountains and rugged landscape. But the soil is rich and farm products include apples, hay, oats, potatoes, wheat, and vegetables. The raising of sheep and dairy cattle is also important.

Mining and Manufacturing. Important minerals taken from Tasmania's mountains include coal, copper, lead, silver, and zinc. Hobart has great zinc works. Bell Bay is the site of an aluminum-processing plant. Other industries include metal-working and the processing of fruit, dairy products, and wool. During World War II, Tasmania's wood pulp and paper industry at Burnie was greatly enlarged. Australia's only newsprint mill operates at Boyer.

Transportation. Tasmania has about 700 miles (1,100 kilometers) of railroads. More than three-fourths of the rail lines belong to the state. The island has about 12,000 miles (19,300 kilometers) of roads, and is served by airlines and shipping companies.

Education. Children are required by law to attend school until they reach the age of 16. Education is free. The state has about 285 state schools and 60 private schools. The University of Tasmania is in Hobart.

Government. The British Crown appoints the governor of Tasmania. The voters elect a 19-member legislative council for six years, and a 35-member house of assembly for four years. Tasmania sends 10 senators and five representatives to the Australian parliament.

History. In 1642, the Dutch navigator Abel Janszoon Tasman became the first European to reach Tasmania. He called the island Van Diemen's Land, in honor of the governor of the Dutch East Indies (later Netherlands Indies). British convicts settled on the island in 1803. None were brought after 1853. Great Britain granted responsible government to the island in 1855, and its name was changed to Tasmania the following year. In 1901, it became part of the Commonwealth of Australia. C. M. H. CLARK

See also HOBART; TASMAN, ABEL J.; TASMANIAN DEVIL; TASMANIAN TIGER.

The Tasmanian Devil, a fierce animal of the Australian island of Tasmania, hunts small mammals and reptiles at night.

TASMANIAN DEVIL is a fierce animal that lives on the Australian island of Tasmania. It eats small mammals and reptiles, plus any dead animals it can find. It hunts mainly at night and spends the day in a cave, a hollow log, or some other shelter. Tasmanian devils measure from 3 to 4 feet (0.9 to 1.2 meters) long, including a tail of about 1 foot (30 centimeters). Most have black fur with white markings, but some are entirely black. Tasmanian devils are *marsupials*. Female marsupials give birth to tiny, poorly developed offspring. Like most marsupials, young Tasmanian devils are carried in a pouch on the mother's belly until they develop more completely.

Scientific Classification. Tasmanian devils belong to the marsupial family Dasyuridae. They are *Sarcophilus harrisii*.
MICHAEL L. AUGEE

TASMANIAN TIGER, or TASMANIAN WOLF, was a large animal of the Australian island of Tasmania. Most scientists believe it is extinct. The Tasmanian tiger measured about 5 feet (1.5 meters) long, including a tail of about 20 inches (51 centimeters). It had short brown fur and looked like a wolf. Dark stripes resembling those of a tiger crossed the rear part of its back. However, the animals were neither tigers nor wolves. Australians sometimes call them *thylacines*.

The Tasmanian tiger was a *marsupial*. Female marsupials give birth to tiny, poorly developed young. Like the offspring of most living marsupials, young Tasmanian tigers were carried in a pouch on the mother's belly until they developed more completely.

Tasmanian tigers were fairly common until the early 1900's. European settlers hunted them—and probably killed them off—because the animals preyed on sheep and poultry.

Scientific Classification. Tasmanian tigers make up the marsupial family Thylacinidae. They are *Thylacinus cynocephalus*.
MICHAEL L. AUGEE

TASS is an abbreviation for the name of the official news agency of Russia. Its full name is TELEGRAFNOE AGENTSVO SOVETSKOVO SOYUZA, or the TELEGRAPH AGENCY OF THE SOVIET UNION. The agency sends news throughout Russia and to other countries. It has representatives in many of these countries. In 1950, a coordinating group of state news agencies in several communist countries was linked with Tass. The Russians formed Tass in 1925. It is directly responsible to the highest executive body in Russia, the Council of Ministers. The agency grew from two press services. The first was the Czarist Petrograd News Agency. After the Russian Revolution, this organization became the Rosta Agency. See also NEWS SERVICE.
EARL F. ENGLISH

TASSO, TORQUATO (1544-1595), was an Italian poet of the late Renaissance period. He was long connected with the court of Alfonso II, Duke of Ferrara. Tasso was one of the greatest masters of Italian poetry. He took full advantage of the sonorous beauty of the language, and gave his poems a gently mournful mood that makes them unforgettable. His pastoral drama, *Aminta* (1573), concerns the victory of true love over base love in a make-believe world of loyal shepherds.

Tasso's masterpiece was his *Jerusalem Delivered* (1575), an epic about the first crusade and the delivery of the sacred tomb from the infidels. It is written, like Ludovico Ariosto's *Orlando Furioso*, in melodious, eight-line stanzas. It is more compact and regular than Ariosto's epic, though it is filled with valiant warriors, noble heroines, enchantresses, miracles, and dire dangers. But Tasso restrained his epic. He feared that the Roman Catholic Church might censor it because of its sensuousness and its evidence of pagan mythology.

Tasso's natural inclination toward morbidity finally induced him to rewrite his epic under the title of *Jerusalem Conquered*. During the last 20 years of his life, he became mentally ill and was in an insane asylum at times. Tasso was born in Sorrento.
WERNER P. FRIEDERICH

TASTE is an important sense in people and many animals. The taste of foods helps determine what and how much we eat. People may reject foods whose taste they dislike and so not have a proper diet. Our sense of flavor is affected by how things smell. When we have a cold and a stopped-up nose, some foods may taste alike (see SMELL). Food must be moist to be tasted. If the tongue and food are dry, there is no taste.

Many people believe that there are four kinds of taste—salt, sour, sweet, and bitter. But the *receptor cells* that make up our *taste buds* do not have structural or functional differences that correspond to these tastes. The idea of the four categories of taste seems to be something that is learned. Taste categories may be only easily identified characteristics of taste. They tell us little about how the taste sense functions.

Taste buds are grouped on the tongue into small

The Tasmanian Tiger, which most scientists believe is extinct, had stripes along its back like those of a tiger. The photo above, taken in 1933, shows the last Tasmanian tiger in captivity.

mounds called *papillae*. The papillae on the front part of the tongue have their taste buds connected to one nerve. The papillae on the edges of the tongue—about halfway between front and back—and those at the back of the tongue are connected to a second nerve.

When we take food into our mouth, the taste buds transmit information about the chemicals in the food to the nerves. The nerves may respond differently to the same chemicals in foods. In addition, small amounts of some chemicals are more easily tasted on the front of the tongue, and others are more easily tasted on the back or sides of the tongue. The taste of still other chemicals changes little over the entire tongue.

The nerves from the papillae come together at the back part of the brain stem. Here, some taste signals carried by the nerves are separated according to the different chemicals they respond to. The taste signals then travel to the front of the brain stem, the *thalamus*. From the thalamus, the signals move to the *cerebral cortex* of the brain. Here, the signals are interpreted, and we become aware of taste.

The receptor cells that make up the taste buds are continually being replaced. The receptor cells develop from skin cells that surround the taste buds. The skin cells slowly move into the area of the taste

HOW TASTE WORKS

The sense of taste is sent to the brain through taste buds located in the tongue. In the diagrams below, each boxed-in section is enlarged in the following drawing.

WORLD BOOK diagram by Lou Bory Associates

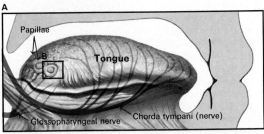

Brain

Taste center deep inside brain

Olfactory nerve

Aromas from food

Chorda tympani (nerve) to front of tongue

A

Tongue

Muscles

Glossopharyngeal nerve to back of tongue

A

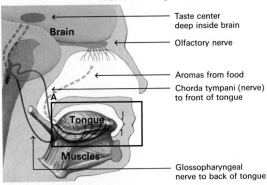

Papillae

B

Tongue

Glossopharyngeal nerve

Chorda tympani (nerve)

B

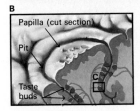

Papilla (cut section)

Pit

Taste buds

C

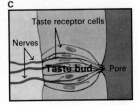

Taste receptor cells

Nerves

Taste bud

Pore

buds. As the skin cells move, they turn into receptor cells. About half the receptor cells are replaced every 10 days. BRUCE P. HALPERN

TATARS. See TARTARS.

TATE, ALLEN (1899-1979), was an American poet and critic. Tate's writing stresses links between the present and the past. A major theme is a yearning for the rural, aristocratic way of life that was common in the South before the Civil War. Many of Tate's writings express dislike for what he regarded as the crowded, dehumanizing way of life in modern industrial society.

Tate is best known for his poetry, much of which is powerful, intense, and written in violent language. His early poem "Ode to the Confederate Dead" (1930) shows the influence of the poet T. S. Eliot. Tate's conversion to Roman Catholicism in 1950 led to an increased concern with religion and ethics in his work. His *Collected Poems: 1919-1976* was published in 1977.

As a literary critic, Tate became noted for his essays on the nature of the imagination and the value of literature. He became known for his essays about literary figures and for detailed analyses of poems. Many of his critical works were published in *Essays of Four Decades* (1969). Tate included both critical and autobiographical essays in *Memoirs and Opinions* (1975).

John Orley Allen Tate was born in Winchester, Ky. As a student at Vanderbilt University, he helped found the Fugitives, a group of Southern writers who hoped to preserve the cultural heritage of the South. Tate's ties with the South can be seen in his novel *The Fathers* (1938) and in his biographies *Stonewall Jackson: The Good Soldier* (1928) and *Jefferson Davis: His Rise and Fall* (1929). JOHN B. VICKERY

TATE, NAHUM. See POET LAUREATE.

TATTOOING is the practice of making permanent colored designs on the body. It is done by pricking small, deep holes in the skin and placing coloring matter in them. Tattooing is a popular custom among soldiers and sailors of many countries.

No one knows when or where tattooing started, but some Egyptian mummies of 1300 B.C. show blue tattoo marks under the skin. The Japanese and the Burmese have done the most elaborate tattooing in the world. Many Burmese have their entire bodies covered with colorful pictures of plants, animals, and human faces. The people of southeastern New Guinea regard tattoo marks on girls as signs of beauty.

Tattooing is not the only way of marking the body. The Bambara, Bamiléké, Mossi, and some other African peoples cut scars into their skin in a process called *scarification*. Each group has its own design, which serves to identify group members. The Maori of New Zealand once rubbed blue coloring into deep grooves in their faces. WILFRID D. HAMBLY

See also MARQUESAS ISLANDS (picture).

TATUM, ART (1910-1956), ranks among the greatest piano soloists in the history of jazz improvisation. Tatum's light and delicate touch and swinging beat were perhaps unequaled among pianists of his time. His brilliant keyboard technique earned him the praise of many classical pianists.

Arthur Tatum was born in Toledo, Ohio. He was blind in one eye from birth and had only slight vision in the other eye. He arrived in New York City in 1932 as an accompanist for a singer. He soon became a favorite soloist in the small nightclubs along Manhattan's West 52nd Street, a hotbed of jazz during the 1930's and 1940's. Tatum led a trio for many years. However, he was one of the rare jazz pianists who needed no support from a rhythm section.   LEONARD FEATHER

TATUM, EDWARD LAWRIE (1909-1975), an American biochemist, shared the 1958 Nobel prize for physiology or medicine for discovering that genes regulate specific chemical processes. He and George W. Beadle found that mutations caused by X rays and biochemical processes are passed on to successive generations. Tatum was born in Boulder, Colo.   HENRY H. FERTIG

See also BEADLE, GEORGE W.; HEREDITY (The Study of the Chemistry of Genes).

TAUM SAUK PROJECT. See MISSOURI (Electric Power).

TAUNTON FLAG. See FLAG (color picture: Flags in American History).

TAURUS is the second sign of the zodiac. Taurus, an earth sign, is symbolized by a bull. Astrologers believe that the planet Venus, named for the ancient Roman goddess of love and beauty, rules Taurus.

According to astrologers, people born under the sign of Taurus, from April 20 to May 20, are loyal, patient, practical, and trustworthy. They appreciate beauty, comfort, and the countryside. Taureans move slowly

Taurus—The Bull

Symbol

Birth dates: April 20–May 20.
Group: Earth.
Characteristics: Affectionate, conservative, loyal, sensible, possessive, stubborn.

Signs of the Zodiac

Aries
Mar. 21–Apr. 19
Taurus
Apr. 20–May 20
Gemini
May 21–June 20
Cancer
June 21–July 22
Leo
July 23–Aug. 22
Virgo
Aug. 23–Sept. 22
Libra
Sept. 23–Oct. 22
Scorpio
Oct. 23–Nov. 21
Sagittarius
Nov. 22–Dec. 21
Capricorn
Dec. 22–Jan. 19
Aquarius
Jan. 20–Feb. 18
Pisces
Feb. 19–Mar. 20

and can be lazy, but they are determined to finish any task they begin. They have a down-to-earth personality and rely on their common sense.

Taureans, though not talkative, are affectionate, friendly, and warm-hearted. They are even-tempered but can become fierce when angered. They are stubborn, and tend to keep grudges.   CHRISTOPHER MCINTOSH

See also ASTROLOGY; HOROSCOPE; ZODIAC.

TAURUS MOUNTAINS. See TURKEY (The Land).

TAUSSIG, *TOU sig,* **FRANK WILLIAM** (1859-1940), was a leading American economist. In principle, he favored free trade, but in practice he accepted moderately protective tariffs. He served as the first chairman of the U.S. Tariff Commission (now the International Trade Commission) from 1917 to 1919. He taught economics at Harvard University from 1901 to 1935. His *Principles of Economics* was first published in 1911 and was a leading textbook on economics for nearly 25 years. Taussig was born in St. Louis, Mo.   DUDLEY DILLARD

TAUSSIG, HELEN BROOKE (1898-   ), is an American physician who specializes in children's heart diseases. She discovered the major defect that causes the bluish tinge in the skin of *blue babies* (see BLUE BABY).

From 1930 to 1963, Taussig served as chief of the Cardiac Clinic of the Harriet Lane Home, the children's section of the Johns Hopkins Hospital in Baltimore. She found that blue babies have a partial blockage of the pulmonary artery at birth. The heart pumps blood through this artery to the lungs, where oxygen enters the blood. A lack of oxygen in the blood gives the skin a bluish color. In 1944, Taussig and a surgeon, Alfred Blalock, developed an operation that enables the blood to bypass the faulty artery.

Taussig was born in Cambridge, Mass. She graduated from the University of California in 1921 and received her M.D. degree from the

WORLD BOOK photo by E. F. Hoppe
Helen Brooke Taussig

Johns Hopkins University School of Medicine in 1927.   MIRIAM SCHNEIR

TAUTOG. See BLACKFISH.

TAWNEY, RICHARD HENRY (1880-1962), was a noted British historian and social philosopher. His most famous work, *Religion and the Rise of Capitalism* (1926), related economic growth in the 1500's and 1600's to the spread of Protestantism. According to Tawney, such virtues as hard work and efficiency, stressed by the Protestants, contributed to the success of capitalism. In *The Acquisitive Society* (1920) and *Equality* (1931), Tawney argued for a more just and humane society based on the moderate and democratic socialism of the Fabian Socialists (see FABIAN SOCIETY). Tawney was born in Calcutta, India, and attended Oxford University. He was an expert on English history between 1485 and 1715. He was a professor of economic history at London University from 1931 to 1949.   ROLAND N. STROMBERG

TAX COURT, UNITED STATES, is a federal court that handles disputes involving income, estate, gift, and other taxes. Taxpayers who cannot reach an agreement with the Internal Revenue Service may appeal to the U.S. Tax Court. The court has offices in Washington, D.C., but it holds sessions at locations throughout the country for the convenience of taxpayers.

Taxpayers may choose to take a case involving $1,500 or less to the court's Small Tax Division. This division provides simplified procedures for handling cases, and its decisions are final. All other Tax Court rulings may be appealed to the U.S. Court of Appeals and then to the Supreme Court of the United States.

The Tax Court was established in 1924 as the U.S. Board of Tax Appeals. It received its present name in 1969.   Critically reviewed by the UNITED STATES TAX COURT

TAXATION is the process by which the people pay the expenses of carrying on the government. Taxation is as old as government. Even the earliest and simplest societies needed some method of maintaining order and providing for justice, and those services could not be provided without cost. So, early systems of public finance, or of collecting and spending taxes, developed. In earliest times taxes were paid in goods rather than money. This is called *payment in kind*.

Kinds of Taxes. Many kinds of taxes have been used and are being used throughout the world. One important way to classify these taxes is into *direct* and *indirect* taxes. A direct tax is one that the taxpayer pays directly to the government. The federal income tax is a direct tax. An indirect tax is one that is paid by a manufacturer or dealer, who then passes its cost on to the buyer. For example, the tax on cigarettes is an indirect tax. The manufacturer or dealer who pays this tax to the government passes its cost on to the consumer in the form of a higher price.

When the person who pays a tax passes the cost on to someone else, the tax is called a *shifted* tax. The problem of who finally pays the tax is the problem of *incidence*. It is not always easy to determine the incidence because many persons may pay part of a tax.

Another important way to classify taxes is according to the way the rates of the tax are varied. For example, a tax is called *proportional* if the rate of taxation remains the same, whether it is applied to a small sum or a very large one. The amount of tax paid is proportional to the sum to which the tax is applied, because the rate is a constant flat rate. The tax on houses and farms is an example of a proportional tax because the rate is the same whether the house or farm is large or small.

A tax is called *progressive* if the rate of the tax goes up as the sum to which it is applied increases. The federal income tax is the commonest progressive tax because its rates are higher for large incomes than for smaller ones. If the rates of a tax are lower when applied to a larger sum, the tax is called *regressive*.

Taxes are rarely meant to be regressive, but in practice they sometimes are. A general sales tax is usually regressive. The more wealthy a family is, the more of its income is saved, spent on travel, or used in other ways that are not subject to a sales tax. A low-income family spends most of its income in ways that are subject to the sales tax; for example, for food and clothing.

Bases for Taxes. Taxes also may be identified according to the base on which they are applied. One of the oldest taxes in the United States is the property tax. This tax has traditionally been the most important single source of revenue for state and local governments. The tax may be levied on such property as land, commercial buildings, homes, and automobiles. In Canada, the property tax is the chief source of revenue for municipal governments.

The tax on income is much newer than the property tax. But it has become the most important federal tax. It is also levied by almost all states and some cities.

Other taxes classified according to the base on which

Taxes in the United States

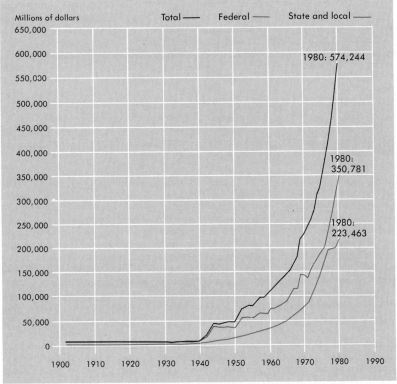

Year	Total Tax (Millions)	Total Tax Per Person
1902	$ 1,373	$ 17.34
1913	2,271	23.35
1922	7,387	67.12
1927	9,451	79.39
1932	7,977	63.89
1934	8,854	70.06
1936	10,583	82.64
1938	12,949	99.74
1940	12,688	95.78
1942	20,793	154.18
1944	49,095	366.61
1946	46,380	329.67
1948	51,218	349.06
1950	51,100	336.90
1952	79,066	503.49
1954	84,476	521.83
1956	91,593	547.61
1958	98,387	567.86
1960	113,120	628.47
1962	123,816	666.32
1964	138,292	722.78
1966	160,836	820.86
1968	185,126	926.27
1970	232,877	1,145.98
1972	262,534	1,260.78
1973	286,595	1,365.71
1974	314,785	1,489.12
1975	331,435	1,555.15
1976	358,227	1,668.82
1977	419,721	1,940.17
1978	468,161	2,146.89
1979	524,446	2,382.77
1980	574,244	2,535.24

Source: U.S. Bureau of the Census

The Federal Government Dollar

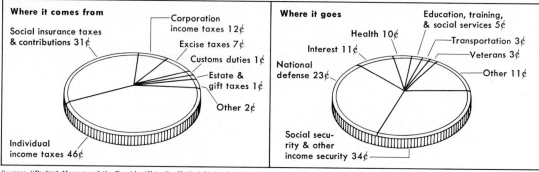

Source: "Budget Message of the President" to the United States Congress, Jan. 28, 1980, in *The U.S. Budget in Brief, 1981*, Office of Management and Budget. Estimates for fiscal year Oct. 1, 1980–Sept. 30, 1981.

they are levied include the following: The *inheritance tax* is placed on the value of property a person inherits. The *estate tax* is placed on an estate before it is divided among the heirs. Both inheritance and estate taxes are direct and progressive. *Sales taxes*, levied on sales, may apply either to all kinds of sales or only to certain kinds. Some sales-tax laws place taxes on services such as those of a barber, a repairman, or a doctor. Others exempt services. Sometimes sales taxes are placed on luxury goods. These are called *luxury taxes* and generally represent a high rate of taxation. The *value-added tax* is a form of sales tax that is assessed not only on retail sales, but also on production, distribution, and wholesaling. At each stage, a tax is paid on the value added at that stage.

Excise taxes are those placed on a specific commodity, or thing. Tobacco and liquor taxes are excise taxes. *Customs duties*, or *tariffs*, are taxes placed on imports or exports. A *license tax* is placed on the right to do something, such as to sell liquor or tobacco; to get married; to own a dog; or to go hunting or fishing. A *franchise tax* is a payment for a special privilege, such as the right to run a bus line or a public utility. A *severance tax* is levied on such products as timber, oil, or minerals when they are taken from the earth.

Principles of Taxation. The fundamental problem of a tax system is to make it produce enough money to pay government expenses. Even if the system provides enough revenue, that does not mean that it is perfect.

Most economists agree on certain desirable principles for taxation. It should be possible to expand the tax system to collect more money in periods of emergency, when the government must spend more money. It should also be possible to reduce the amount of taxes in normal times, when government expenditures are at a minimum. This is called the principle of *elasticity*. Unless the tax system is elastic, the government is likely to go into debt in periods of emergency and be forced to borrow money to meet current expenses.

Everyone agrees that the tax system should be simple. Those who pay taxes and those who collect them should be able to understand and easily obey the tax laws.

The tax system should be stable. If the taxpayer knows in advance that he must pay the tax, he will be able to save money to pay the tax. If the system is unstable, the taxpayer cannot make plans.

There are other common principles of taxation. These include the beliefs that taxes should be fair and just,

that they should be convenient as to the time and method of payment, and that they should be inexpensive to collect. There should be no favoritism in levying or collecting taxes. All citizens should be treated equally. Taxes also should come at times when taxpayers have the means of paying them. The sales tax is so convenient that it is used widely in spite of its other defects. The real-estate tax, if at very high rates, may be inconvenient, since property does not always yield an income with which to pay taxes. For example, land where timber is grown does not produce income until the timber is mature. The present federal income tax on the "pay-as-you-go" plan is much more convenient than the old system of annual or quarterly payments.

In the past, there has been considerable discussion of the following principles of taxation: ability to pay, benefit, cost of service, and sacrifice. Most people now recognize that each of these principles has its own argument. For example, the *cost of service*, or the closely related *benefit*, principle should be used to determine tax rates for cleaning streets. These principles are recognized as fair where persons or their property directly benefit by public services. The *sacrifice* that a taxpayer undergoes on account of a tax is so hard to measure that this principle is not of much practical use to the legislator, even though it seems reasonable. So, *ability to pay* is left as the most usable principle, although its application is not clear and simple. In general, this principle supports progressive taxes, rather than regressive taxes or proportional taxes.

Other Considerations in Taxation. Some economists consider the principles of taxation outlined above as too narrow to serve as guides to a proper tax policy. There are those who feel that the tax system should be used to reduce differences in individual incomes. These economists argue that the easiest way to accomplish this is to tax the rich at a much higher rate than the poor. They say that if the funds raised in this way are spent on social services which benefit the poor, the equalizing effect would be even greater.

Other economists insist that taxation must be guided by the desire to do minimum damage to the economic system of the country. These economists argue that *all* types of taxes, even the best, do some damage to a free-enterprise economic system. This, they say, is a strong argument for keeping government activities and expenses to a minimum in order to reduce the need for tax revenues. In particular, these economists argue

44

against taxes that tend to destroy the incentive system of a free-enterprise economy. "Double taxation" of income from corporations, excess-profits taxes, and steeply progressive income taxes are examples of the taxes which these economists say are undesirable.

Still other economists say that the tax program should be designed to accomplish the goal of economic stability, with full employment for all workers. These economists argue that taxes, but not government expenditures, should be reduced when depression threatens. This, they say, would leave more money for consumers and would help prevent a depression. If the threat is inflation, taxes, but not government expenditures, should be increased, they say, in order to leave less money for consumers to spend to send prices up.

Taxation in the United States. The founders of the United States were suspicious of a central government that was too powerful. Most citizens also felt the federal government was so far away that they were unwilling to pay taxes to support it. As a result, the United States Constitution required direct taxes to be *apportioned* (divided) among the states according to population.

In 1895, the Supreme Court of the United States ruled that an 1894 income tax law was unconstitutional because it was a direct tax not apportioned according to population. In 1913, the 16th Amendment removed this restriction. The first modern federal income tax in the United States went into effect that year. It is still in effect, but it has been changed greatly.

The income tax is levied on corporations, estates, trusts, and individuals. It provides most of the revenue for the federal government. Rates have varied, but they have always been progressive. Major reductions in the federal income tax rate were made in 1964, 1965, and 1975. In 1981, the government enacted one of the largest tax cuts in the nation's history.

As demands for government services have increased through the years, the federal tax system has usually provided sufficient revenue. But state and local governments have had trouble getting adequate revenue from their tax systems. There has been a growing tendency for the federal government to share its revenue with states and cities. This revenue sharing often takes the form of *grants-in-aid*. These special funds help finance such state and local projects as roadbuilding and housing projects. Usually, the states and cities must meet certain requirements to receive the aid. In 1972, Congress approved a new revenue-sharing program. This program provided billions of dollars with a minimum of restrictions for state and local governments. In 1980, state revenue sharing was discontinued for the period from Oct. 1, 1980, to Sept. 30, 1981.

Taxation in Canada. The Canadian government and most provincial governments levy income taxes on corporations and individuals. The federal government collects the income taxes for itself and also for provinces that request the service. Most of the provinces have gift and estate taxes as well. Some of them also levy taxes on logging, mining, sales, the transfer of securities, and other activities.   CHARLES J. GAA

Related Articles in WORLD BOOK include:

Assessment	Franchise	Inland Revenue
Capital Gains Tax	Gasoline Tax	Internal Revenue
Excess Profits Tax	Income Tax	License
Excise	Inheritance Tax	Poll Tax

Property Tax	Stamp
Revenue Sharing	Stamp Act
Roads and Highways	Tariff
(How Roads and Highways	Tithe
Are Paid For)	Trust Fund
Sales Tax	Turnpike
Single Tax	Value-Added Tax

See also *Taxation* in the RESEARCH GUIDE/INDEX, Volume 22, for a *Reading and Study Guide*.

Additional Resources

AARON, HENRY J., and BOSKIN, M. J., eds. *The Economics of Taxation*. Brookings Institute, 1980.

ASHWORTH, WILLIAM. *Pork Barreling: How the Government Rips Off the American Taxpayer*. Dutton, 1981.

SOBEL, LESTER A., ed. *The Great American Tax Revolt*. Facts on File, 1979.

TAXATION WITHOUT REPRESENTATION. See REVOLUTIONARY WAR IN AMERICA (Quartering and Stamp Acts); FRANKLIN, BENJAMIN (A Delegate in London).

TAXCO, *TAHS koh* (pop. 27,089), officially TAXCO DE ALARCÓN, *day AH lahr KOHN*, is a historic silvermining town 70 miles (113 kilometers) southwest of Mexico City. For location, see MEXICO (political map).

Taxco looks like an old Spanish town. Narrow cobblestone streets climb the steep hills on which it stands. In order to preserve the town's appearance, the Mexican government has made Taxco a national monument. It is illegal to erect buildings in the contemporary style. The town's beauty, charm, crafts, and mild climate attract tourists, artists, and writers. Taxco has served as a mining center since Hernando Cortés founded it in 1529 (see CORTÉS, HERNANDO). It is the center of Mexico's silverware industry today.   JOHN A. CROW

See also LATIN AMERICA (picture).

TAXICAB is an automobile for hire. It is an important part of the transportation system of a modern city. City law fixes the maximum rates for taxicabs. Almost all cabs have taximeters, which show the fare for the distance traveled. Some cities have zonal fares. Taxis charge additional fares when passing from one zone into another. About 260,000 taxis operate in the U.S.

The first motor-driven taxicab in the United States appeared about 1898. It had an electric motor. The first gasoline-engine taxicab and the first use of the taximeter came in 1907, in New York City. In 1914, the French Army organized the "taxicab army" to move troops from Paris to halt the Germans at the Marne (see AUTOMOBILE [World War I]).   FRANKLIN M. RECK

See also JINRIKISHA; PEDICAB.

TAXIDERMY, *TAK suh DUR mee*, is a technique for preserving animals and showing them as they looked when alive. The word taxidermy comes from two Greek words meaning *arrangement* and *skin*. Museums of natural history exhibit birds, fish, squirrels, antelope, tigers, and other wild animals in their natural settings.

Process of Mounting. The taxidermist first takes accurate measurements of the skin of the dead animal. The skin is carefully removed and treated with a preservative, such as arsenical soap. The taxidermist then makes a drawing of the muscles, ribs, and hollows. This copy becomes a guide. Next, the taxidermist makes a model of wire; shredded wood; and clay, plaster, or papier-mâché. This model must correspond accurately with the figure of the animal. Finally, the taxi-

Steps in Taxidermy

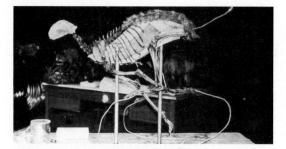

A Skeletal Framework Is Assembled First.

A Clay Model Is Sculpted on the Framework.

A Casting Is Made from a Mold of the Sculpture.

The Tanned Skin Is Placed on the Casting.

The Skin Is Carefully Sewed and Glued into Place.

Field Museum of Natural History, Chicago

The Finished Model Shows a Running Cheetah.

dermist places the skin on the model, and sews it together. Skins of large, heavy animals must be tanned before being mounted on the model.

Taxidermists must add many other body features, such as the eyes and tongue. They must also shape the ears. They use painted hollow globes instead of glass eyes to give the preserved animal a natural expression.

Some museums use a *freeze-drying* technique to preserve specimens. This method is used mainly for small animals, such as songbirds and squirrels.

Careers in Taxidermy. Taxidermy is a complicated art. It requires a knowledge of anatomy, natural history, drawing, sculpture, mechanics, tanning, and dyeing. At one time, many museums had taxidermy studios or departments. Today, most museums hire commercial studios to mount their specimens. The Natural History Museum of Los Angeles County is one of the few museums that have a taxidermy department. The Universi-

ty of Iowa has a museum training program that includes instruction in taxidermy.   HERBERT FRIEDMANN

Additional Resources

GRANTZ, GERALD J. *Home Book of Taxidermy and Tanning.* Stackpole, 1969.
McFALL, WADDY F. *Taxidermy Step By Step.* Winchester, 1975.

TAXONOMY. See CLASSIFICATION, SCIENTIFIC.

TAY-SACHS DISEASE is a hereditary disorder of the nervous system. It occurs chiefly among Jewish children of eastern European ancestry. Tay-Sachs disease causes severe brain damage, enlargement of the head, convulsions, blindness, deafness, lack of energy, and eventually death. Victims develop a reddish spot on the retina of the eye. They begin to have symptoms when they are about 6 months old. There is no treatment for the disease, and most victims live only three or four years.

46

Tay-Sachs Disease

Tay-Sachs disease is a hereditary brain disorder that occurs chiefly among Jews of eastern European ancestry. Individuals who inherit the Tay-Sachs gene from both parents have the disorder.

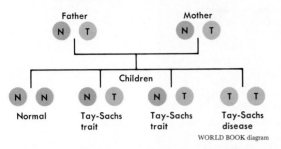

WORLD BOOK diagram

In the chart above, each parent carries one normal gene and one Tay-Sachs gene. A child of such parents has one chance in four of inheriting the Tay-Sachs gene from both parents—and thus having Tay-Sachs disease. People who inherit the Tay-Sachs gene from only one parent do not get the disease, but they may transmit the abnormal gene to their children. The magnified photographs below show a normal brain cell, *left,* and an abnormal cell from the brain of a Tay-Sachs victim, *right.* The many dark, round bodies in the diseased cell are characteristic of the disorder.

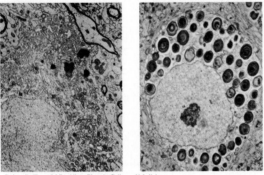

Robert D. Terry, M.D., Albert Einstein College of Medicine,
© *Journal of Neuropathology and Experimental Neurology*

Tay-Sachs disease occurs in children who have too little of the enzyme *hexosaminidase.* This enzyme controls the amount of *ganglioside* that accumulates in nerve cells. Ganglioside is a fat produced by normal cell growth. Nerve cells that store too much ganglioside become swollen and eventually die. A large number of damaged or dead nerve cells causes brain damage.

The symptoms of Tay-Sachs disease were first reported during the 1880's by two physicians, Waren Tay of Great Britain and Bernard Sachs of the United States. In 1969, researchers discovered that the lack of hexosaminidase caused the disease. Today, scientists use a variety of tests to determine the activity of hexosaminidase in samples of blood and various tissues. These tests can reveal whether unborn babies have Tay-Sachs disease. They also show whether adults are carriers of the disease. Carriers do not have the disease themselves. But if two carriers marry, their children may inherit it from them.   ROSCOE O. BRADY

TAYLOR, EDWARD (1644?-1729), was perhaps the greatest New England poet who lived before the 1800's. Taylor combined strong religious feeling with simple, commonplace language. He wrote in the *metaphysical* style of the British poet John Donne. This style made

use of fantastic comparisons and seeming contradictions. For instance, Taylor called the soul a "Bird of Paradise" in a "Wicker Cage," and humanity God's "Spinning Wheele." Taylor was born in England. He graduated from Harvard College. He asked that his works never be published. But his poems were found in 1937, and published as *Poetical Works* (1939).   PETER VIERECK

TAYLOR, FREDERICK WINSLOW (1856-1915), was an American engineer and efficiency expert. He joined Midvale Steel Works in Philadelphia in 1878 as a laborer, and left the company in 1890 as chief engineer. During this time, he conducted experiments to determine the maximum possible efficiency of people and machines. Taylor expanded his ideas into a detailed system for organizing and systematizing factory work. The best-known part of his system is the *time and motion study.* In this study an efficiency expert clocks each step in a job and looks for ways to reduce the time needed to do the job. Taylor's system was only one of many proposed in the early 1900's. However, the entire efficiency movement was often called *Taylorism* after 1910. Taylor was born in Germantown, Pa.   MONTE A. CALVERT

TAYLOR, GEORGE (1716-1781), was a Pennsylvania signer of the Declaration of Independence. He served in the provincial assembly from 1764 to 1769 and in 1775. He became a colonel in the Pennsylvania militia in 1775. He also served as a member of the Continental Congress. Elected a member of the First Supreme Executive Council of Pennsylvania in 1777, he soon retired because of illness. Taylor was born in Ireland and came to Pennsylvania about 1736.   RICHARD B. MORRIS

TAYLOR, MAXWELL DAVENPORT (1901-   ), won fame as a United States Army general in World War II and the Korean War. President John F. Kennedy called him out of retirement in 1961 to become his personal military adviser. Taylor served as chairman of the Joint Chiefs of Staff from 1962 to 1964. He was U.S. ambassador to South Vietnam in 1964 and 1965. Later in 1965, President Lyndon B. Johnson made Taylor a special consultant on diplomatic and military affairs.

Taylor was born in Keytesville, Mo. He graduated from the United States Military Academy in 1922. He helped organize the army's first airborne divisions, and commanded the 101st Airborne Division during World War II. He was the first general to land in Normandy on D-Day. After the war, Taylor served as chief of staff of the European Command Headquarters in Germany and also as U.S. commander in Berlin.

Taylor commanded the U.S. Eighth Army in Korea from early in 1953 until March 1955. Then he became commander in chief of the U.S. and United Nations Far East Commands. From 1955 to 1959, he served as army chief of staff. He retired in 1959.   MAURICE MATLOFF

TAYLOR, MILDRED, an American author of books for children, received the 1977 Newbery medal for *Roll of Thunder, Hear My Cry* (1976). This novel tells the story of a black family's struggle against racial prejudice and poverty during the Great Depression of the 1930's. The story is set in rural Mississippi. Taylor also wrote an earlier novel about the same family, *Song of the Trees* (1975). Both books are based partly on incidents from the author's family history. Taylor was born in Jackson, Miss.   ZENA SUTHERLAND

ZACHARY TAYLOR

Z. Taylor

The United States Flag had 30 stars throughout Taylor's term of office.

Oil painting by John Vanderlyn,
Corcoran Gallery of Art, Washington, D.C.

TYLER
10th President
1841 — 1845

POLK
11th President
1845 — 1849

FILLMORE
13th President
1850 — 1853

PIERCE
14th President
1853 — 1857

12TH PRESIDENT OF THE UNITED STATES   1849-1850

TAYLOR, ZACHARY (1784-1850), served his country for 40 years as a soldier and for 16 months as President. His courage and ability during the Mexican War made him a national hero. Taylor showed the same courage while he was President, but he died before he could prove his full abilities as a statesman. He was succeeded by Vice-President Millard Fillmore.

President Taylor was one of the large slaveowners of the South. But he did not oppose admitting California and New Mexico to the Union as free states. The South demanded that other slavery problems be settled before those territories became states, and threatened to secede. The President replied that he was ready to take his place at the head of the army to put down any such action. Taylor died at the height of this argument. Fillmore's policies delayed the Civil War for 10 years.

Taylor made his greatest contribution to his country as a soldier. This quiet, friendly man was no military genius. But he was a good leader. He never lost a battle. His troops nicknamed him "Old Rough and Ready."

Early Life

Childhood. Zachary Taylor was born near Barboursville, Va., on Nov. 24, 1784. He was the third son in a family of six boys and three girls. His parents, Richard and Sarah Strother Taylor, came from leading families of the Virginia plantation region. Richard Taylor served as an officer in the Revolutionary War. In 1783, he received a war bonus of 6,000 acres (2,400 hectares) of land near Louisville, Ky. He settled there in 1785.

Zachary grew up on "the dark and bloody ground" of Kentucky's frontier. There were no schools, but the boy studied for a while under tutors, and gained much practical knowledge by working on his father's farm.

Perhaps it was natural that Zachary should turn to a military career. He grew up in the midst of Indian warfare, and heard tales of the Revolutionary War from his father. In 1808, Taylor received an appointment as a first lieutenant in the U.S. Army. Two years later, he was promoted to captain.

Taylor's Family. Early in 1810, Taylor met Margaret Mackall Smith (Sept. 21, 1788-Aug. 14, 1852). She was the orphaned daughter of a Maryland planter. Taylor and Miss Smith were married on June 21, 1810. They had a son and five daughters, two of whom died as infants. Their daughter Sarah married Jefferson Davis, the future President of the Confederacy. She died three months after her wedding. The Taylors' son, Richard, served as a general in the Confederate Army.

Military Career

Indian Campaigns. During the War of 1812, Taylor won promotion to major for his defense of Fort Harrison in the Indiana Territory. He left the army briefly after the war, but returned and by 1829 had become a lieutenant colonel. He served in Wisconsin during the Black Hawk War, and received the surrender of Chief Black Hawk in 1832 (see BLACK HAWK).

Taylor was sent to Florida in 1837. There he defeated the Seminole Indians at Lake Okeechobee on Dec. 25,

48

1837. This victory brought him the honorary rank of brigadier general. In 1841, Taylor became commander of the second department of the western division of the U.S. Army, with headquarters at Fort Smith, Ark.

Mexican War. In 1846, Mexico threatened war with the United States over the annexation of Texas. Taylor was ordered to the Rio Grande with 4,000 troops. When Mexican forces crossed the river, Taylor defeated them in battles at Palo Alto and Resaca de la Palma. War was declared on May 13, 1846. Taylor then invaded Mexico, and captured Matamoros and Monterrey.

After these victories, Taylor seemed the best choice to

------- IMPORTANT DATES IN TAYLOR'S LIFE -------
1784 (Nov. 24) Born near Barboursville, Va.
1810 (June 21) Married Margaret Mackall Smith.
1812 Defended Fort Harrison against Tecumseh.
1832 Received surrender of Black Hawk.
1847 Defeated Santa Anna in Battle of Buena Vista.
1848 Elected President of the United States.
1850 (July 9) Died in the White House.

TAYLOR, ZACHARY

lead an invading army into the central valley of Mexico. But President James K. Polk, a Democrat, knew that Taylor favored the Whig party. Partly because Polk feared the growth of a popular Whig leader, he named General Winfield Scott to lead the invasion.

On Feb. 22-23, 1847, Taylor's 5,000-man army was attacked by between 16,000 and 20,000 Mexican troops in the Battle of Buena Vista. Taylor's men won a stunning victory over the forces of General Santa Anna. The triumph made Taylor a national hero. See MEXICAN WAR; SANTA ANNA, ANTONIO LÓPEZ DE.

Nomination for President

Whig leaders decided that Taylor could easily win the presidency. Taylor hesitated to enter politics, but the Whigs nominated him anyway. They chose Millard Fillmore, comptroller of New York, for Vice-President. The Democrats nominated Senator Lewis Cass of Mich-

THE WORLD OF PRESIDENT TAYLOR

U.S. population was about 23,300,000 in 1850. Half the 30 states in the Union permitted slavery, and half did not. Neither section could control legislation in Congress.

FREE STATES

SLAVE STATES

WORLD EVENTS
Revolutions swept central Europe in 1848 and 1849. Austria crushed uprisings in Hungary, Sardinia, and Bohemia. Lajos Kossuth, leader of the Hungarian revolt, toured the United States and was hailed as a hero.

Lajos Kossuth

The California Gold Rush began in 1849. Thousands of gold-seekers, or "Forty-Niners," hurried westward by covered wagon, train, and ship.

Overland Mail Service by wagon began in 1850. Mail took about 30 days to travel from Independence, Mo., to Santa Fe and Salt Lake City.

Debates Over Slavery in Congress came close to bringing about a civil war. President Taylor opposed any kind of compromise with the slave states.

The Department of the Interior was created in 1849. President Taylor appointed Thomas Ewing as the first Secretary of the Interior.

UNITED STATES DEPARTMENT OF THE INTERIOR. INDIAN AFFAIRS CENSUS · PATENTS PUBLIC LANDS PENSIONS

Margaret Smith Taylor did not favor her husband's candidacy for President. She took little part in Washington social life, and spent much of the time knitting in her room.

Mary Elizabeth Bliss, the youngest daughter of the Taylors, assumed her mother's duties as First Lady. Her husband, William W. S. Bliss, served as Taylor's private secretary

igan and General William O. Butler of Kentucky.

During the campaign, both Whigs and Democrats avoided the slavery issue. Only the Free Soil party, a group led by former President Martin Van Buren, campaigned on this issue (see FREE SOIL PARTY). Van Buren did not carry a single state, but he drew many votes from Cass. Taylor and Fillmore won by 36 electoral votes. The presidential election of 1848 was the first to be held at the same time in all the states.

Taylor's Administration (1849-1850)

Taylor was inaugurated on March 5, 1849. He would normally have taken office on March 4, but declined to be inaugurated on Sunday. Some historians claim that David R. Atchison, president pro tempore of the Senate, served as acting President on March 4 because the presidency was vacant on that day.

Taylor leaned heavily on the advice of others, because he knew he lacked political experience. Taylor's friends soon learned that anyone could advise him, but

---
TAYLOR'S ELECTION

Place of Nominating Convention	Philadelphia
Ballot on Which Nominated	4th
Democratic Opponent	Lewis Cass
Electoral Vote	163 (Taylor) to 127 (Cass)
Popular Vote	1,360,967 (Taylor) to 1,222,342 (Cass)
Age at Inauguration	64

VICE-PRESIDENT AND CABINET

Vice-President	*Millard Fillmore
Secretary of State	*John M. Clayton
Secretary of the Treasury	William M. Meredith
Secretary of War	George W. Crawford
Attorney General	Reverdy Johnson
Postmaster General	*Jacob Collamer
Secretary of the Navy	William B. Preston
Secretary of the Interior	Thomas Ewing

*Has a separate biography in WORLD BOOK.

no one could influence him to act against his conscience.

Life in the White House. Mrs. Taylor had not favored the idea of her husband running for President. She viewed it as a plot to deprive her of his company. Mrs. Taylor, a semi-invalid, took little part in the White House social life. Hostess duties passed to her daughter Mary Elizabeth, known as Betty. Betty's husband, Colonel William W. S. Bliss, was Taylor's secretary.

The Nicaragua Canal. The acquisition of territory on the Pacific Coast during President James K. Polk's administration revived the dream of a water route across Central America. American businessmen tried to obtain rights to build a canal across Nicaragua. The British were also interested in such a canal. In 1850, the United States and Britain signed the Clayton-Bulwer Treaty, which guaranteed the neutrality of any such canal. See CLAYTON-BULWER TREATY.

Sectional Quarrels. Controversy over the extension of slavery reached a new high in 1849, when California applied for admission to the Union as a free state. Taylor urged the admission of California, and expressed hope that New Mexico would also apply. Southerners angrily demanded the adjustment of other slavery problems before new states were admitted. During the next months, Congress had one of its greatest debates. Southerners threatened secession, and Northerners promised war to preserve the Union.

Many congressional leaders, including Senator Henry Clay of Kentucky, urged some kind of compromise. But Taylor scorned any compromise, and insisted that California be admitted to the Union. Those in favor of compromise eventually won their point, but not until Fillmore had succeeded to the presidency. Congress then adopted a series of laws called the Compromise of 1850. See COMPROMISE OF 1850.

Death. Before the slavery issue could be settled, Taylor became ill and died on July 9, 1850. He was buried in the family cemetery near Louisville, Ky. Mrs. Taylor died on Aug. 14, 1852, and was buried beside her husband.   BRAINERD DYER

Related Articles in WORLD BOOK include:

Davis, Jefferson	President of the United States
Fillmore, Millard	War of 1812
Gold Rush	Whig Party

Outline

I. Early Life
  A. Childhood
  B. Taylor's Family

II. Military Career
  A. Indian Campaigns   B. Mexican War

III. Nomination for President

IV. Taylor's Administration (1849-1850)
  A. Life in the White House   C. Sectional Quarrels
  B. The Nicaragua Canal   D. Death

Questions

How did Taylor become a national hero?

What was one reason that President Polk did not choose Taylor to lead the invasion of Mexico City?

How may Taylor have become interested in the army?

How did President Taylor reply to a Southern threat to secede from the Union?

Why do some historians claim that an acting President served the first day of Taylor's term?

Additional Resources

DYER, BRAINERD. *Zachary Taylor.* Louisiana State Univ. Press, 1946.

HAMILTON, HOLMAN. *Zachary Taylor*. 2 vols. Bobbs, 1941-1951.
SINGLETARY, OTIS A. *The Mexican War*. Univ. of Chicago Press, 1960.

TAYRA, *TY ruh*, is a large member of the weasel family. It lives in tropical forests from Mexico to Argentina. Most tayras have black or dark brown fur, with a white or yellow patch on the chest. The fur on the head gradually turns brown or gray as the animal grows older. An adult tayra weighs about 10 pounds (5 kilograms) and measures about $3\frac{1}{2}$ feet (107 centimeters) long, including a tail 16 inches (41 centimeters) long.

Tayras wander the forests and are active both day and night. They travel alone or in family groups. These graceful animals climb well and can run swiftly.

Tayras eat birds, small mammals, and fruits. The female tayra gives birth to two to four young in a nest she has built in a tree or on the ground.

Scientific Classification. The tayra belongs to the weasel family, Mustelidae. Its scientific name is *Eira barbara*.

JOHN H. KAUFMANN and ARLEEN KAUFMANN

TB. See TUBERCULOSIS.

TBILISI, *T'PIH lih sih* (pop. 1,066,000), is the capital of the Georgian Soviet Socialist Republic, one of the republics of the Soviet Union. The word *Tbilisi* means *warm springs* in the Georgian language. The city was formerly called *Tiflis*, its name in Russian. It lies on the Kura River (see RUSSIA [political map]). Tbilisi is one of the oldest cities in the Soviet Union. Part of the city is modern, and part looks like an ancient Oriental city. The city's chief products are felt, cotton materials, leather goods, and oil. The city also has a steel mill. A railroad links Tbilisi with other parts of the Soviet Union.

THEODORE SHABAD

TCHAIKOVSKY, *chy KAWF skee*, **PETER ILICH** (1840-1893), was the first Russian composer to gain international fame. He was a master of orchestration with a superb talent for blending instrumental sounds and for achieving rousing orchestral effects. He also had a remarkable gift for writing melody.

Tchaikovsky is often described as a composer of music that is basically melancholy. Some of his music is melancholy, especially the tragic last movement of his *Symphony No. 6*. But he also wrote spirited music, as in *Marche Slave* and "1812" overture; lyrical music, as in the symphonic poem *Romeo and Juliet;* lively ballet music, as in the *Nutcracker Suite;* and powerful symphonies.

His Life. Tchaikovsky was born on May 7, 1840, in Votkinsk. He entered a law school in St. Petersburg (now Leningrad) in 1850. From 1862 to 1866, he studied music at the St. Petersburg Conservatory under Anton Rubinstein, a pianist and composer. Tchaikovsky was the first Russian composer to receive systematic training in music fundamentals.

From 1866 to 1877, Tchaikovsky taught at the Moscow Conservatory of Music. He began composing seriously about 1866. At this time, his early emotional sensitivity devel-

Brown Bros.
Peter Tchaikovsky

oped into long periods of depression. Curiously, he wrote some of his most cheerful music during these periods. He was married in 1877, but he and his wife separated within a few weeks. This experience brought him close to a nervous breakdown.

In 1876, Nadezhda von Meck, a wealthy widow, commissioned some works from Tchaikovsky. She admired his music and agreed to support him so he could compose at leisure. She insisted that they never meet, but they exchanged letters for years. Assured of an income, Tchaikovsky left the Moscow Conservatory and concentrated on composing. He traveled widely, and in 1891 took part in the opening of Carnegie Hall in New York City. He died on Nov. 6, 1893.

His Works. Tchaikovsky's six symphonies stand out as landmarks in his artistic development. His first three symphonies are seldom performed today. His fourth, written in 1877, is his first masterpiece in the symphonic form. Tchaikovsky's *Symphony No. 5* (1888) is his finest from the standpoint of formal construction. *Symphony No. 6* (1893) is called the "Pathétique" ("Pathetic"). It departed from the traditional symphonic form by expressing a deeply emotional feeling of tragedy in the final movement. Tchaikovsky's other orchestral works include his *Italian Capriccio* (1880), his famous *Nutcracker Suite*, and four other suites.

Tchaikovsky's *Concerto for Piano and Orchestra No. 1 in B flat minor* (1874-1875) and his *Violin Concerto in D major* (1878) are classics of their types. Tchaikovsky also wrote an important work for violoncello—*Variations on a Rococo Theme for Violoncello and Orchestra* (1876). He composed vocal pieces and works for solo piano, but these are not often played today.

Tchaikovsky's three ballets have become classics. They are *Swan Lake* (1875-1876), *Sleeping Beauty* (1888-1889), and *The Nutcracker* (1892). Tchaikovsky wrote 11 operas, but only *Eugene Onégin* (1877-1878) and *Queen of Spades* (1890) are well known outside of Russia. Both have *librettos* (words) based on works by the Russian poet Alexander Pushkin. *Queen of Spades* is written on a larger scale than *Eugene Onégin*. It is a powerful psychological music drama dominated by the idea that fate rules human beings.

Tchaikovsky has often been described as a "Westerner" among Russian composers. He was the first Russian composer to write polished music in the Western manner and the first to win widespread popularity outside Russia. Some critics tend to see the melancholy strain in Tchaikovsky's music as almost the only trace of his Russian origin. But Tchaikovsky always claimed to be fully Russian in his feelings, and his works contain quotations from Russian folk melodies. He cited Mozart, a Westerner, and Mikhail Glinka, a Russian, as the composers who influenced him the most. Much of Tchaikovsky's work represents a blend of the spirits of these two widely different composers.

MILOŠ VELIMIROVIĆ

Additional Resources

ABRAHAM, GERALD, ed. *The Music of Tchaikovsky*. Norton, 1974.
BROWN, DAVID. *Tchaikovsky: The Early Years, 1840-1874*. Norton, 1979.
STRUTTE, WILSON. *Tchaikovsky: His Life and Times*. Two Continents, 1979.
WARRACK, JOHN H. *Tchaikovsky*. Scribner, 1973.

Tea Council of USA

Shostal

Tea Pluckers on a plantation near Kandy, Sri Lanka, pick leaves from mature tea plants, *left.* The tea plants produce shoots called *flushes,* which consist of two leaves and a bud, *above.* After being picked, the flushes are processed into tea in a nearby factory.

TEA is a beverage made by pouring boiling water over dried tea leaves. It has a yellowish-brown color and a slightly bitter taste. Tea ranks as the most popular drink in more countries than any other beverage.

India leads the world in the total amount of tea used each year—about 575 million pounds (261 million kilograms). But Ireland, Great Britain, and New Zealand, in that order, consume the most tea per person. The Irish use about 8 pounds (3.6 kilograms) of tea per person annually—enough to brew about 1,600 cups of tea for each person. Tea use in the United States is about ¾ pound (0.3 kilogram) per person yearly.

About 4 billion pounds (1.8 billion kilograms) of tea are produced annually. India grows the most—about 1,246,000,000 pounds (565,180,000 kilograms) a year. China is second with 725,320,000 pounds (329,000,000 kilograms). Other tea producers include Bangladesh, Indonesia, Japan, Kenya, Malawi, Russia, Sri Lanka, Turkey, and several other countries.

From Leaf to Cup

The Tea Plant grows in tropical and subtropical climates. The plant, an evergreen, grows quickly at low altitudes where the air is warm. But the finest tea comes from altitudes of 3,000 to 7,000 feet (910 to 2,100 meters). The plant grows more slowly in cool air, adding to its flavor.

Tea plants have small, white, sweet-smelling flowers. Each flower produces three seeds that look like hazelnuts. On a tea estate or in a tea garden where tea plants are grown commercially, workers plant the seeds in a nursery bed. About a year later, when the plants are about 8 inches (20 centimeters) high, they are transplanted to the field. About 3,000 tea plants grow on 1 acre (0.4 hectare) of land.

Wild tea plants grow as high as 30 feet (9 meters). But a commercial tea plant is pruned to keep it from 3 to 4 feet (91 to 120 centimeters) high. The plant matures in three to five years and then produces a *flush* (growth of new shoots). Each shoot consists of two leaves and a bud. At lower altitudes, tea plants may grow a new flush every week. At higher altitudes, a plant needs as long as two weeks to grow a flush. No flushes grow in cold weather.

Workers called *tea pluckers* pick the flushes off the bush by hand. A plucker can harvest about 40 pounds (18 kilograms) of tea leaves a day, enough to make about 10 pounds (4.5 kilograms) of manufactured tea.

Processing Tea. There are three main kinds of tea: (1) black, (2) green, and (3) oolong. They differ in the method used to process the leaves. The processing takes place in a factory on or near the tea estate.

All tea-producing countries manufacture black tea. But most green and oolong tea comes from China, Japan, and Taiwan.

Black Tea. To make black tea, workers first spread the leaves on shelves called *withering racks.* Air is blown over the leaves to remove excess moisture, leaving them soft and flexible. Next, the leaves are crushed between the rollers of a machine to release their flavorful juices. Then, in a *fermenting room,* the tea leaves change chemically under controlled humidity and temperature until they turn coppery in color. Finally, the leaves are dried in ovens and become brownish-black.

Green Tea is made by steaming the leaves in large vats. The steaming prevents the leaves from changing color. The leaves are then crushed in a machine and dried in ovens.

Oolong Tea is made by partially fermenting the leaves. This gives tea leaves a greenish-brown color.

Grades of Tea vary only according to the size of the leaves. The size of a tea leaf has nothing to do with the quality of the tea.

To sort the processed tea leaves by grade, they are passed across screens with different size holes. The largest leaves, selected for packaging as loose tea, are classified—in order of size—as *orange pekoe*, *pekoe*, and *pekoe souchong*. The smaller or broken leaves, generally used in tea bags, are classified as *broken orange pekoe*, *broken orange pekoe fannings*, and *fannings*.

Instant tea is made by brewing tea in large vats and then removing the water by a drying process. Only a powder remains. The powdered tea combines easily with moisture, and so it must be packed under controlled humidity and temperature. People make instant tea at home by simply adding water to the powder.

Teas grown in different countries, or even in different parts of the same country, vary in taste, flavor, and quality. To obtain the best teas, each tea company employs *tea tasters* who select only certain teas for purchase. These teas, after being blended by the company, have a flavor for which the firm is known. Every company sells its blend of tea under its own brand name.

Brewing Tea. Tea is brewed by pouring boiling water over one teaspoon of loose tea, or one tea bag, per cup. To obtain the best flavor, the tea should *steep* (soak) for three to five minutes before being served. People who prefer weak tea can add hot water.

Iced tea, the most popular form of the beverage in the United States, is prepared by first brewing a strong hot tea. For each two glasses, three teaspoons of tea or three tea bags should be used. After steeping for five minutes, the tea is cooled at room temperature and served over ice cubes.

Instant tea requires no brewing. Boiling water poured over a teaspoon of the powder provides a cup of tea.

Iced instant tea is prepared by pouring cold water over the powder and adding ice cubes.

History

According to legend, the use of tea was discovered by Emperor Shen Nung of China about 2737 B.C. The earliest known mention of tea appeared in Chinese literature of about A.D. 350. The custom of tea drinking gradually spread to Japan and other countries of the Orient. Tea was introduced to Europeans about 1600 by merchants who imported it from the Far East. The beverage quickly won wide popularity.

During the 1600's, tea became the national drink of Great Britain. By 1650, it was being imported by the American Colonies. In 1767, the British government placed a tax on the tea being used by the colonists. Colonial resistance to the tax brought about the Boston Tea Party in 1773, which in turn led to the Revolutionary War (see BOSTON TEA PARTY).

The use of iced tea and tea bags began in the United States. Richard Blechynden, an Englishman trying to increase the use of tea in the United States, first served iced tea at the Louisiana Purchase Exposition in St. Louis in 1904. That same year, Thomas Sullivan, a New York City coffee and tea merchant, sent his customers samples of tea leaves in small silk bags instead of the usual tin containers. The customers began to order tea leaves in bags after finding that the drink could be brewed easily with them. Instant tea was developed in the United States and first marketed in 1948.

Scientific Classification. The tea plant is a member of the tea family, *Theaceae*. It is genus *Thea*, species *T. sinensis*.   MARTIN KUSHNER

See also CAFFEINE; INDIA (picture: Tea Pickers); JAPAN (picture: Japanese Agriculture); KENYA (picture: Kenya's Highland); LABRADOR TEA; MATÉ.

Leading Tea-Growing Countries

Tea grown in 1978

India	1,246,000,000 pounds (565,180,000 kilograms)
China	725,320,000 pounds (329,000,000 kilograms)
Sri Lanka	473,994,000 pounds (215,000,100 kilograms)
Japan	238,100,000 pounds (108,000,000 kilograms)
Russia	209,440,000 pounds (95,000,400 kilograms)
Kenya	198,416,000 pounds (89,999,990 kilograms)
Indonesia	160,938,000 pounds (73,000,250 kilograms)
Turkey	127,868,000 pounds (57,999,950 kilograms)
Bangladesh	77,162,000 pounds (35,000,100 kilograms)
Malawi	70,548,000 pounds (32,000,000 kilograms)

Sources: FAO; U.S. Department of Agriculture.

Black Star

Picked Tea Leaves are spread on withering racks to dry. As the first step in making black tea, air is blown over the leaves. The air removes excess moisture, making the leaves soft and pliable.

TEA TAX. See REVOLUTIONARY WAR IN AMERICA (Events Leading to the Revolution).

TEACH, EDWARD. See BLACKBEARD.

TEACHER. See TEACHING; EDUCATION.

TEACHER CORPS is a United States government program designed to improve teacher training and to provide better educational opportunities for children in low-income areas. College graduates who have little or no teaching experience may become interns in the Teacher Corps. Interns practice-teach in schools in poverty areas under the supervision of experienced teachers. They also take advanced courses in such subjects as behavior problems, bilingual education, and teaching the disadvantaged. After two years of training, interns receive a master's degree and a teaching certificate.

The Teacher Corps also provides training for experienced teachers, teacher aides, and other educational personnel in low-income areas. Such training may include special courses and workshops to help the educators make their teaching more effective.

The federal government pays up to 90 per cent of the salaries for interns and experienced teachers in the Teacher Corps. The local school system pays the rest. The Teacher Corps was created by the Higher Education Act of 1965 and is administered by the Department of Education.   Critically reviewed by the TEACHER CORPS

TEACHERS, AMERICAN FEDERATION OF. See AMERICAN FEDERATION OF TEACHERS.

TEACHERS COLLEGE, COLUMBIA UNIVERSITY, is the graduate school of education at Columbia University in New York City. Teachers College prepares men and women for professional service at every level of education.

Teachers College offers programs in all phases of teaching, guidance, curricular planning, and administration for the training of educational personnel. It provides advanced work in psychology, philosophy, and other fields to help students understand the educational process. The college also prepares students for professional careers not directly related to education, such as nursing supervision. It conducts research on problems of education and provides field services to schools throughout the United States. Teachers College also sponsors many international activities in education.

Organization. Teachers College is financially independent, with its own charter, board of trustees, and president. It forms a division of Columbia University by formal agreement between the trustees of the college and the trustees of the university. Under this agreement, faculty members at the college are also members of the Columbia University faculty, and university courses are open to students of Teachers College. Degrees earned at the college are granted through the university.

Many research and service activities at Teachers College are conducted through various institutes and special projects. These activities concern such things as the needs of handicapped children, higher education, the philosophy and politics of education, and curriculum development. Teachers College also conducts technical assistance programs in Afghanistan and Nigeria.

History. Teachers College was founded in 1887 as the New York College for the Training of Teachers. Sponsored by the Industrial Education Association, it prepared teachers in various fields, particularly home economics and industrial arts. The college greatly expanded its curriculum under the leadership of Nicholas Murray Butler, who served as president from 1887 to 1891, and Walter L. Hervey, the president from 1891 to 1897. In 1892, the New York State Regents granted the college a permanent charter. In 1898, Teachers College became part of Columbia University.

The college became a world leader in educational research and experimentation during the administrations of James E. Russell, its dean from 1897 to 1927, and William F. Russell, the dean from 1927 to 1949 and president from 1949 to 1954. These men—father and son—emphasized research and experimentation to advance knowledge about educational goals and processes and to improve teaching practices in schools, colleges, and other academic institutions. As a result of their efforts, many important educational developments were pioneered at Teachers College. For the enrollment of Teachers College, see UNIVERSITIES AND COLLEGES (table [Columbia University]).   FRANK G. JENNINGS

Teachers College includes Thorndike Hall, *center,* and the buildings in the foreground.

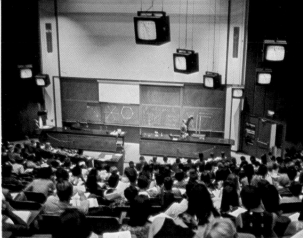

Gene Harris, Meyers Photo-Art

College Professor Giving a Lecture

Jim Collins

WORLD BOOK photo

Elementary-School Teacher Guiding a Student

Kindergarten Teacher Introducing the Alphabet

Teachers at All Levels guide the learning of students in various ways. Sometimes, teachers help students individually. At other times, they instruct an entire group. At still other times, teachers guide students by asking questions or encouraging class discussion.

TEACHING

TEACHING is the process by which a person helps other people learn. It is one of our most important activities. Teaching helps people gain the knowledge and attitudes they need to be responsible citizens, earn a living, and lead a useful, rewarding life. Teaching also provides the chief means of passing knowledge on to the next generation. If there were no teachers, people would have to learn everything by themselves. Few people could learn enough on their own to get along in the world. The world itself would change greatly as humanity lost the knowledge, skills, and ideals inherited from past generations.

Much teaching takes place *informally*—that is, outside school. In the home, for example, parents teach their children everyday skills, as well as values and habits. Businesses and industries often teach their em-

Willard Abraham, the contributor of this article, is Professor of Education and Chairman of the Department of Special Education at Arizona State University.

ployees necessary job skills. But when people speak of teaching, they usually mean *formal teaching*—the kind provided in schools by professional teachers.

More people belong to the teaching profession than to any other. Nearly 22 million men and women throughout the world are professional teachers. The United States has more than 3 million teachers, and Canada has more than 300,000.

The teaching profession has developed mainly since the early 1800's, when the first teacher-training schools began in western Europe. Before then, schoolteachers received little or no special training. Today, most countries require teachers to complete a professional training program and to meet professional standards.

This article deals chiefly with the teaching profession in the United States and Canada. It discusses teaching careers in both countries and current issues in U.S. teaching. For detailed information about the history of teaching, see EDUCATION (History).

A Teacher's Duties

A teacher's job involves four main duties. (1) Teachers must prepare for their classes. (2) They must guide,

55

Jim Collins

Preparing for Class requires thought and effort on a teacher's part. This second-grade teacher is arranging a display of her pupils' art work and poetry in preparation for a class discussion.

WORLD BOOK photo

Teaching Aids, such as the chalkboard and wall map above, help teachers guide learning. Teachers also use such aids as tape recordings, filmstrips, and special television programs.

or assist, the learning of students. (3) They must check student progress. (4) Teachers must set a good example for their students. In carrying out these duties, teachers try to identify and respond to the needs of individual students.

A teacher's main duties also involve a number of related tasks, from keeping attendance records to marking papers. In addition, many teachers take part in school-related activities after school hours and often outside school.

Since the 1950's, science and industry have developed many new devices and techniques for classroom use, including educational television, language laboratories, and other advanced learning aids. Although these *technological* advances may assist the learning process, they have not greatly changed the teacher's basic role in the classroom.

This section deals mainly with the duties of elementary- and secondary-school teachers.

Preparing for Classes. Before each class session, a teacher must do such things as review subject matter, prepare learning activities, and plan special projects. This preparation is often called a *daily lesson plan.* Teachers have guidelines to help them plan their teaching. For example, local school boards usually decide the *curriculum* (courses of study and other learning activities) for students to follow. Many boards involve teachers in curriculum planning.

A state or local school board may also set general learning goals for students. Such goals include the acquiring of certain knowledge and skills and the development of certain values and attitudes (see EDUCATIONAL PSYCHOLOGY [Classifying Learning Goals]). If a school board does not outline these goals, teachers and administrators must decide them. Many teachers involve their students in deciding learning goals. Within the set guidelines, most teachers are free to plan the

kinds of activities they think will help students meet the desired goals.

Guiding the Learning of Students. Most teachers use a variety of methods to guide their students' learning. For example, they sometimes guide students individually and sometimes as a group. But even when dealing with students as a group, a good teacher's basic concern is the individual development of each student. Many teachers believe that students should be given only enough guidance to help them learn to solve problems by themselves.

Teachers have long depended on textbooks to assist learning. Today, many teachers also use *audio-visual materials*, including tape recordings, filmstrips, and television programs (see AUDIO-VISUAL MATERIALS). Some teachers utilize specially designed textbooks or audio-visual materials to give *programmed instruction.* In this method, a subject is broken down into a series of small steps called a *program.* A student must master each step before going on to the next one. Students can thus study at their own pace.

Although teachers generally use a variety of teaching methods and materials, they must suit them to the abilities, age, and needs of their students. Nursery-school teachers, for example, use such instructional materials and methods as toys and games to attract the interest of youngsters. In certain areas, including the poorer sections of large cities, some students may lack the basic communication and study skills they need to progress in school. To help these students acquire the necessary skills, a teacher may decide to use special methods and materials. For example, a teacher of reading in an inner-city school may find it helpful to use textbooks that relate directly to life in the inner city. In all of these cases, a teacher must also take into account the differing needs and abilities of individual students.

WORLD BOOK photo

A Class Test helps teachers check their students' progress. A teacher may use the test results to find out which students need extra help and what kind of help they need.

For more information on how teachers assist learning, see EDUCATION (The Educative Process) and EDUCATIONAL PSYCHOLOGY (Teaching Methods).

Checking Student Progress. Most teachers give written or oral tests to help evaluate the progress of their students. By analyzing the test results of all the students in a group, teachers can discover which students need special help and decide what kind of help they need. By evaluating the performance of the entire group, teachers can judge the effectiveness of their teaching methods and materials.

Most schools group students in various grades according to age. In these schools, teachers use test results to give students specific marks in their courses. *Nongraded* schools do not group students according to age. Instead, students advance in each subject at their own speed. They attend classes with other students who have reached the same level, regardless of age. In most of these schools, teachers give general evaluations rather than specific marks. The evaluations may be written, or a teacher may meet with each student and his or her parents to discuss the student's progress. For more information about school tests and how they are used, see the article TESTING.

Setting a Good Example for Students. Teachers often help students more by their example than they do in any other way. One of the most important ways that teachers set an example is by showing such qualities as patience, understanding, trustworthiness, and attention to work. Students who see these qualities in their teachers may be encouraged to develop similar qualities in themselves. In addition, students are more likely to cooperate with a teacher whom they respect and admire and so are more likely to benefit from the teacher's help.

Other Duties. Teachers often have certain duties after school hours. For example, many teachers act as advisers or sponsors of student groups, such as athletics teams or hobby clubs. Many teachers also serve as student counselors after school hours. Elementary school students ask chiefly for help with minor problems related to their schoolwork or outside activities. But a teacher sometimes faces difficult counseling problems. In high school, for example, some students regularly cut classes or consider dropping out of school altogether. Whenever possible, teachers try to discourage such actions through talks with individual students and their parents.

Most teachers also take part in various professional activities outside school. These activities range from attending teachers' conferences and taking study trips to taking advanced courses in college.

Teaching as a Career

A person who wants to become a teacher should like people and get satisfaction from helping them. It is also important to be well educated and to speak and write effectively. Although the brightest students do not necessarily make the best teachers, most teachers were good students.

Good teaching requires intense work on a personal level. Good teachers take an interest in their students and do all they can to help them. They realize that some students find learning difficult and so require extra patience and encouragement. The best teachers make learning enjoyable. They have a thorough knowledge of the subjects they teach and know how to arouse their students' interest in them.

Teacher-Training Programs. Almost all teacher-training programs in the United States and Canada are offered at general colleges or universities. Most U.S. teacher-training programs consist of three main areas of study: (1) general education, or liberal arts, courses; (2) advanced courses in a major area of study, such as English or mathematics; and (3) professional education courses. Canada's teacher-training programs are similar to those in the United States.

During their first two years in college, teachers-in-training take courses in history, language arts, mathematics, science, and other liberal arts. During their second two years, most students specialize in a particular subject, usually the subject they plan to teach. Also during their second two years, students take such professional education courses as child development, teaching methods, and practice-teaching. In practice-teaching, a student does actual classroom teaching under the guidance of an experienced teacher.

Certification of Teachers. Every state requires public elementary- and secondary-school teachers to obtain a *teaching certificate* before they may teach in the state. The state issues the certificate to persons who meet the state's basic teaching requirements. Some states also require certification to teach in a nursery school, private school, or public junior college. Teachers in four-year colleges and universities do not need a certificate. Instead, they must obtain an advanced degree and demonstrate their teaching ability through satisfactory on-the-job performance.

Almost all states issue separate certificates for elementary- and secondary-school teachers. Every state requires beginning teachers at both levels to be college

TEACHING

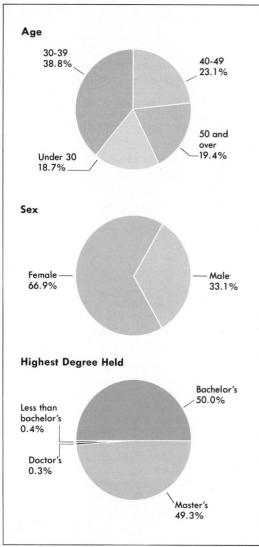

Age

30-39
38.8%

40-49
23.1%

50 and
over
19.4%

Under 30
18.7%

Sex

Female
66.9%

Male
33.1%

Highest Degree Held

Bachelor's
50.0%

Less than
bachelor's
0.4%

Doctor's
0.3%

Master's
49.3%

*Elementary- and secondary-school teachers.
Source: *Public School Teacher, 1980-81,* copyright © 1982 National
Education Association. All Rights Reserved.

basic requirements for a teaching certificate and also be specially trained in their field. *Teachers' aides,* or *paraprofessional teachers,* do not need a professional teaching certificate. They mainly help professional teachers perform such duties as marking test papers and giving students individual guidance.

Most states issue an initial, or provisional, certificate to new teachers who meet the basic teaching requirements. Teachers may apply for an advanced certificate after they have taught a certain number of years. Many states also require additional college courses or a master's degree for advanced certification. A few states issue advanced certificates to new teachers who meet the necessary requirements. Some states issue advanced certificates on a permanent basis. Other states require teachers to renew their advanced certificate every few years. About half the states accept teaching certificates from other states. The rest require teachers from other states to take certain additional courses or to pass a special examination.

Public elementary- and secondary-school teachers in Canada must also have a teaching certificate. Each province issues its own certificates and sets the requirements for them. Most provinces require both elementary- and secondary-school teachers to have a college degree plus, or including, a year or more of teacher-training courses.

Job Opportunities. Schools in the United States and Canada need many thousands of new teachers each year. Teachers who retire or go into other lines of work create most of the openings.

The demand for teachers in the United States varies somewhat by teaching field, grade level, and locality. For example, there is generally a demand for teachers in the fields of mathematics; special education, which is designed for handicapped or gifted children; and vocational education, which prepares students for skilled jobs. There is also a demand for nursery-school teachers, school administrators, guidance counselors, librarians, and psychologists. The United States as a whole has an oversupply of elementary-school teachers

graduates. Teachers at both levels must also have completed a professional training program that prepares them to teach in either elementary or secondary school. In addition, secondary-school teachers must be qualified to teach a particular subject. Many states also require such qualification for elementary-school teachers. Some teachers in special fields earn certificates that allow them to teach at both the elementary level and the secondary level. These fields include art, music, and the education of handicapped children.

Most states issue special certificates for such positions as school principal, school librarian, and guidance counselor. In most cases, applicants must meet the

Milt & Joan Mann

A Teacher-Training Program includes courses in educational theory, *above.* Education students must also do *practice-teaching* —that is, classroom teaching supervised by experienced teachers.

and of secondary-school teachers in such subject areas as English, foreign languages, and social studies. But many small towns and the poor sections of large cities need teachers in these fields.

At one time, almost all elementary-school teachers in the United States were women, and almost all college and university teachers were men. But this situation has been slowly changing. Although women still far outnumber men as elementary-school teachers, men now make up about 15 per cent of the total. At the same time, an increasing number of women have been hired to teach in U.S. colleges and universities, where they now fill about a fourth of the teaching positions. In U.S. secondary schools, teaching jobs are about equally divided between men and women.

Changes in the number of job openings for teachers depend largely on changes in the birth rate. For example, a sharp increase in the U.S. birth rate during the late 1940's led to rising enrollments and a teacher shortage in the 1950's and early 1960's. But the birth rate then dropped sharply, reducing school enrollments. As a result, many qualified college graduates could not find teaching jobs in the late 1960's and the 1970's.

Employment Practices. In most public school districts, the local school board is responsible for hiring teachers. Most boards sign a contract with every teacher they hire. In the contract, the board agrees to pay a certain salary for the teacher's services. The contract covers a specified period of time, after which a new contract must be signed. In many school districts, a teachers' union or other professional organization also signs a *master contract* with the school board. This contract covers not only the teachers who belong to the organization but also all other teachers in the district, including any new teachers the school board hires. Before signing the contract, the organization tries to obtain from the board the highest salaries possible and other benefits for the teachers. The master contract is good for only a certain period of time. A new contract is then signed, after the teachers' organization and the board have again agreed to its terms.

Most colleges and universities in the United States and Canada grant teachers *tenure*—that is, they automatically renew a teacher's contract after a trial period of satisfactory service. Most school districts in the two countries also grant tenure to public-school teachers. A number of states have laws that prohibit school boards from dismissing tenured teachers except in proven cases of inefficiency or misconduct. In states without such laws, school boards can dismiss teachers when their contracts expire.

Rewards of Teaching. One of a teacher's greatest rewards is to see his or her students succeed at their studies and develop into productive, responsible citizens. Nearly every teacher has this opportunity.

The salaries of U.S. teachers vary from district to district and from state to state. In the late 1970's, the national average was about $15,000 a year for elementary- and secondary-school teachers. Annual salaries averaged about $17,200 in junior colleges and about $17,850 in four-year colleges and universities. During the late 1970's and early 1980's, public elementary- and secondary-school teachers in Canada averaged

Photophile

A Teachers' Aide, *right,* helps a professional teacher with certain duties, such as keeping class records. Unlike professional teachers, teachers' aides do not need a teaching certificate.

about $22,500 yearly, and university teachers earned about $32,500 a year.

In most U.S. school districts, teachers receive pay raises according to a *salary schedule.* The schedule grants salary increases for each additional year or other period of service and for additional professional training. Teachers' organizations generally seek to raise scheduled salaries when they work out a new master contract with a school board.

Other U.S. school districts use either a *merit pay system* or a *differentiated staffing system* to grant pay increases. The merit pay system bases raises mainly on how well teachers teach rather than on their experience and additional training. The system thus requires a method of teacher evaluation. The differentiated staffing system divides the teaching positions in a school into various levels according to the amount of responsibility they involve. Teachers receive raises mainly by being promoted to a higher level.

Some school districts and many colleges and universities grant teachers a *sabbatical,* or *professional, leave* after a certain number of years of service. Many sabbaticals consist of a semester's leave of absence with full pay. Teachers are expected to use a sabbatical to further their professional growth.

Continuing Education. All teachers are expected to continue their professional growth throughout their career. Many teachers use their vacation time to take advanced college courses or to attend conventions for teachers in their field. Many school districts provide *in-service* training for teachers. Such training may include conferences and workshops after school hours or special reading materials to be studied at home. A variety of journals and other publications help teachers keep informed about developments in their field.

Teachers' Organizations. In the United States, teachers may join a number of professional organizations. The National Education Association of the United States (NEA) has the largest membership of teachers of any U.S. educational organization. It has branches in every state and in many cities and towns. The NEA works chiefly to raise educational standards and to improve the pay and working conditions of teachers. The American Federation of Teachers (AFT) is a national teachers' union that works mainly to improve teachers' salaries and working conditions. Hundreds of local teachers' unions throughout the United States are associated with the AFT. In the mid-1970's, the NEA and AFT discussed joining to form one organization.

Many U.S. teachers' organizations concentrate on a particular field, such as English, mathematics, or special education. For example, the National Council of Teachers of English is an organization for English teachers at all school levels. The National Catholic Educational Association offers membership to teachers and administrators in Roman Catholic schools. Student Action for Education, formerly the Future Teachers of America, is open to high school students interested in becoming teachers.

Canada has a number of large provincial and local teachers' organizations and unions with goals similar to those of the NEA and AFT. The Canadian Education Association is a small but important national organization that works to improve the quality of education throughout Canada.

Current Issues in U.S. Teaching

Teachers' strikes became common during the 1960's and 1970's. Teachers struck for various reasons, but most often for higher pay and better working conditions.

People have reacted in various ways to the pay demands of teachers. Some people doubt the right of teachers to strike for any reason. Other people feel that educational costs are already too high and that pay raises for teachers will drive such costs even higher. In many communities, voters have turned down tax in-

Chicago Sun-Times

Teachers' Strikes became common in many U.S. communities during the 1960's and 1970's. In most cases, teachers struck for higher pay and better working conditions.

creases for education, including raises for teachers.

The debate over teachers' pay has led to several other issues concerning teachers. Two of the most important issues deal with (1) the effectiveness of teaching and (2) the effectiveness of teacher training.

The Effectiveness of Teaching. During the 1960's and 1970's, many taxpayers urged that teachers be required to improve the quality of their teaching before being granted pay raises. As a result, cost-control systems called *accountability* have gained much public favor in the field of education. These systems were originally designed to hold workers in business and industry responsible for meeting production goals. In education, accountability systems hold teachers responsible for their students' level of achievement. The systems try to ensure that a certain amount of learning results from a certain level of expenditure.

By the mid-1970's, more than 25 states had passed laws setting up educational accountability systems. In many other states, state education agencies or local school districts had established such systems. The various systems differ somewhat, but most require a method of teacher evaluation. Some methods of evaluating teachers require the testing of students to see if they have achieved the desired learning goals. Other methods require the evaluation of teachers by administrators or supervisors. In most accountability systems, a teacher who continually receives a poor evaluation faces dismissal.

Many teachers oppose accountability. They argue that some of the most important results of teaching are difficult to measure. Such results include the acquiring of various values and attitudes and the development of certain mental skills. In addition, accountability systems indirectly result in the loss of tenure. Without a system of tenure, administrators can refuse to renew the contracts of teachers whose work they consider unsatisfactory. But many teachers consider tenure a right to which they are entitled.

The Effectiveness of Teacher Training. Many people have complained that teacher-training programs concentrate too heavily on educational theory. They propose, instead, a *competency-based*, or *performance-based*, program. Such a program would develop specific teaching skills, or *competencies*. These competencies might include the ability to make decisions, provide leadership, and deal with disciplinary problems. To acquire such skills, teachers-in-training would spend more time gaining actual teaching experience and less time attending lectures.

By the early 1970's, a number of teacher-training programs were experimenting with competency-based training. To complete such a program, education students must master the particular skills required by the program. They do so in most cases by working with groups of elementary or high school students. The students' achievements supposedly reflect the student teachers' degree of skill. In the mid-1970's, Texas and Washington approved granting teaching certificates to persons who have completed a competency-based program. Other states plan similar moves.

Some educators believe that competency-based programs concentrate so heavily on teaching methods that they neglect to train future teachers adequately in the subjects they plan to teach. Critics also argue that teachers who have mastered the required competencies might be just as effective had they mastered other teaching methods.   WILLARD ABRAHAM

Related Articles. See EDUCATION with its list of *Related Articles*. See also the following articles:

Questions

What are the four main duties of teachers?
What is a *teaching certificate?* Who must have one?
Why do teachers give tests?
Of what three main areas of study do most teacher-training programs consist?
What are some characteristics of a good teacher?
How do teachers continue their professional growth throughout their career?
Why were many qualified college graduates unable to find teaching jobs in the United States during the late 1960's and early 1970's?
What two national organizations work to improve the pay and working conditions of U.S. teachers?
What is *tenure?* A *sabbatical leave?*
What is an *accountability* system in education?

Additional Resources

ASHTON-WARNER, SYLVIA. *Teacher.* Simon & Schuster, 1971.
BARZUN, JACQUES. *Teacher in America.* Liberty Press, 1981. First pub. in 1945.
HENTOFF, NAT. *Does Anybody Give a Damn?* Knopf, 1977. Examines the problems of teaching in inner-city schools.
HIGHET, GILBERT. *The Immortal Profession: The Joys of Teaching and Learning.* Weybright & Talley, 1976.
POSTMAN, NEIL. *Teaching as a Conserving Activity.* Delacorte, 1979.

Xerox Learning Systems

Teaching Machines use various methods to present information. The above device gives a recorded explanation while the student studies a diagram. The machine then assigns a problem.

TEACHING MACHINE is a device that presents instructional material to students and requires that they respond to it. Immediately after a student responds to a question or requests additional material, the machine tells whether the answer was correct or provides the information. Unlike television and motion pictures, which also may present educational material, teaching machines require active participation by the student. The student may push a button, type on a keyboard, or write on paper in the machine. Teaching machines are used in schools and in business and industry. Some provide instruction at home.

The educational material in a teaching machine is called a *program.* The first teaching machines were testing machines, and their programs were tests. In the 1920's, the American psychologist Sidney L. Pressey designed a mechanical testing device that asked multiple-choice questions, one at a time. The student answered each question by pressing a lever. The machine did not present a new question until the correct lever had been pressed. Students prepared for the tests by studying with a teacher. But they also learned from the tests because they could correct errors immediately.

Modern teaching machines use a technique developed by B. F. Skinner, another American psychologist. During the 1950's, Skinner investigated the learning process. He found that people efficiently learn complicated behavior if they receive an immediate reward for each step toward that behavior. A person using a teaching machine is rewarded by being told that an answer was correct and by going on to new material.

How Teaching Machines Work

Teaching machines are based on the view that a student learns best by working in small steps that gradually increase in difficulty. The program of a teaching

TEACHING MACHINE

machine consists of a carefully planned series of statements and exercises. Each step in the program is called a *frame,* and each frame builds on what the student already knows. The early frames guide the student's thinking so that the learner makes few errors and is rewarded by success. The later frames provide less assistance and present more difficult ideas, and require more sophisticated responses. This method of teaching is called *programmed instruction.*

Kinds of Programs. Teaching machines use *linear programs* and *branching programs.*

A linear program is one in which every student works through the frames in the same order, each at his or her own pace. Each frame gives information and asks the student to supply a word or phrase or to choose among several answers. The machine then gives the correct answer. The table with this article is a linear program.

A branching program is one in which the student's responses determine what frames are presented. The machine gives the student information and then asks a question. If the student answers correctly, the machine presents new material and questions. If the student gives a wrong answer, the machine branches into additional frames that explain the error. If the student's answers show that the material is already known, the machine gives more advanced instruction. Because a branching program is fitted to what each student needs to learn, it allows more adaptation to differences among students than does a linear program.

Subjects of Programs provide a variety of courses for students of all ages. Educators have developed programs to teach English and other languages, mathematics, reading, science, and sports. Training programs have been prepared for use by business, government, and the military. There are even programs to help bridge and chess players improve their skill.

Kinds of Teaching Machines

Teaching machines range from simple cardboard or paper devices to complex electronic equipment. The three major types are (1) programmed texts, (2) mechanical devices, and (3) computers.

Programmed Texts are not actually machines at all. They are books arranged according to the principles of programmed instruction. Each page of the book may present one or more frames of a program. Students work through some programmed texts from beginning to end. Other texts direct students to turn to a certain page, depending on their response to a question.

Mechanical Devices display one frame of a program at a time. The student presses one or more buttons or pulls a lever to bring a new frame into view. The CYCLO-TEACHER® Learning Aid is such a device.

Computers present lessons on a printed sheet, on a screen similar to a television screen, or by audio messages. Students respond by typing answers, touching the screen, or pointing a lighted wand at the screen. Before instruction begins, the computer can test students to determine the best instructional material for each. During the session, it can check a student's progress to determine whether to provide extra help. At the end, the computer can measure the student's achievement and report it to the student. This teaching method is called *computer-assisted instruction* (CAI).

There are three types of computer-assisted instruction: (1) drill-and-practice CAI, (2) tutorial CAI, and (3) dialogue CAI. Drill-and-practice CAI supplements study with a teacher. It gives practice in applying what the teacher has taught. It usually does not introduce new material. Tutorial CAI develops ideas and skills independent of a teacher. Dialogue CAI allows students to make up problems and have the computer show how to solve them. With one system, students carry on a "conversation" with the computer and ask it questions.

The Effects of Teaching Machines

The effects of teaching machines are much like those of tutors working individually with students. A con-

WORLD BOOK photo

A Basic Teaching Machine has windows through which the student reads information and questions. She writes her answer in another space and then moves a lever to see the correct response.

James F. Quinn

Computer-Assisted Instruction takes place at individual teaching machines connected with a computer. The computer puts lessons on the screens, and the students type their answers.

stant exchange occurs between the student and the machine. The machine requires the student to participate. It does not simply present material to be memorized. Like a tutor, the machine makes sure the student understands the material presented at each step before going on. It also gives the student hints and suggestions, as a tutor does. In addition, the student does not have to wait for a final exam to know whether the material has been understood. The machine responds to every answer, so that students are informed of their progress. Also, each student works at his or her own rate. Students who need more time or help can get it. Those who master the subject quickly move on to new lessons.

Some people claim that teaching machines make teaching too mechanized. They argue that the human aspects of teaching are lost by using the devices. Others, however, consider teaching machines as tools that assist teachers, just as other tools assist other workers. The machines give large numbers of students the advantage of individual instruction. They also give a teacher more time to work personally with students.

Educators still need to know what subjects can be taught best by teaching machines. They are seeking ways to measure differences among students so that instruction can be adapted to each one. They also are exploring better ways to break down subjects into units of learning and to guide students through a series of instructional steps. ROBERT GLASER and CHARLES O. TEGGATZ

See also AUDIO-VISUAL MATERIALS; EDUCATIONAL PSYCHOLOGY; SPEED READING.

TEAGARDEN, JACK (1905-1964), was an American trombone player and blues singer. His intense, warm, blues-rooted trombone style was widely imitated. Teagarden was also the first successful nonblack blues singer. His most famous records are "I've Got a Right to Sing the Blues" and "Basin Street Blues." They illustrate his rich, deeply moving vocal style.

Teagarden was born in Vernon, Tex. He was partly American Indian in ancestry. His full name was Weldon John Teagarden. Mainly a self-taught musician, Teagarden went to New York City in 1927 and toured with Ben Pollack's band from 1928 to 1933. He later performed with Paul Whiteman's band and recorded with Benny Goodman. He led his own band from 1939 to 1947, and worked four years with Louis Armstrong. He led small groups after 1951. LEONARD FEATHER

TEAK is a forest tree that comes from southeastern Asia. Its wood is highly valued for shipbuilding and for making furniture. It resembles coarse mahogany. Teakwood is strong and durable and resists water. It takes a high polish and contains an oil that helps it resist insects. The teak tree sometimes grows to a height of 150 feet (46 meters). The leaves often grow 2 feet (61 centimeters) long and 1½ feet (46 centimeters) wide. They yield a purple dye and are also used for thatch and for wrapping material.

Countries which produce teakwood commercially include India, Burma, and Thailand. Teakwood also is grown on plantations in some of these countries.

A tree known as *African teak*, or *African oak*, is also valued for its wood. It is less durable than teakwood.

Scientific Classification. True teak belongs to the vervain family, Verbenaceae. It is *Tectona grandis*. African teak is in the spurge family, Euphorbiaceae. It is *Oldfieldia africana*. K. A. ARMSON

TEAL is a small duck that lives in many parts of the world. The most common teals in North America are the *green-winged*, the *blue-winged*, and the *cinnamon* teals. They are all surface-feeding ducks and never dip more than a short distance beneath the surface for food. They live mostly near ponds, streams, and marshes. Unlike diving birds, they keep their tail feathers completely out of the water when they swim, and can take to the air immediately when frightened. Teals usually breed in Canada and the northern United States and migrate south in winter, often to Mexico.

The *green-winged*, the smallest teal, may reach only 13 to 15 inches (33 to 38 centimeters) in length. The male is gray with a brown head and a speckled breast. Green patches color the wings and the head. The female is more plainly colored. The male makes sharp and mellow whistles. The *blue-winged* teal is 15 or 16 inches (38 or 41 centimeters) long. Except for a blue patch on the front of its wing and a white spot on its face, the male is dull in color. The *cinnamon* teal is about 16 inches (41 centimeters) long. The male has dark cinnamon-red plumage and blue patches on its wings.

Scientific Classification. Teals belong to the genus *Anas* of the family Anatidae. The green-winged teal is *Anas crecca*. The blue-winged teal is *A. discors*. The cinnamon teal is *A. cyanoptera*. JOSEPH J. HICKEY

See also BIRD (picture: Birds of Inland Waters and Marshes); DUCK.

TEAM TEACHING. See EDUCATION (Elementary Education); EDUCATIONAL PSYCHOLOGY (Classifying Teaching Methods).

TEAMSTERS UNION is the largest labor union in the United States. Its official name is INTERNATIONAL BROTHERHOOD OF TEAMSTERS, CHAUFFEURS, WAREHOUSEMEN, AND HELPERS OF AMERICA. The Teamsters also has local unions in Canada and Puerto Rico. Its membership includes truck drivers, chauffeurs, warehouse employees, and helpers; persons who work with automotive vehicles, including salespeople; garage and service-station employees; dairy, brewery, food-processing, and soft-drink plant employees; and industrial workers and airline and public service employees.

The Teamsters is organized primarily through its local unions in the U.S., Canada, and Puerto Rico. It also has joint councils, and an international convention. The major responsibilities of the joint councils include adjusting jurisdictional disputes between local unions, approving or disapproving strikes or boycotts planned by locals, and evaluating wage scales that the locals plan to submit to employers. The convention is the supreme governing body of the union. It meets every five years. Each local's representation at the convention is based on the size of its membership. Only the convention amends the union constitution. It also elects the international officers, including the president, secretary-treasurer, 15 vice presidents, and 3 trustees.

The Teamsters was founded in 1899. It grew rapidly under presidents David Beck and James Hoffa in the 1950's and early 1960's. It was expelled from the AFL-CIO in 1957, after its leaders were accused of unethical practices. Headquarters are at 25 Louisiana Avenue NW, Washington, D.C. 20001. For membership, see LABOR MOVEMENT (table).   GERALD G. SOMERS

See also FITZSIMMONS, FRANK E.; HOFFA, JAMES.

TEAPOT DOME is the name given to one of the most notorious scandals in the administration of President Warren G. Harding. A Senate investigation in 1923, as well as subsequent testimony in court trials, revealed that Secretary of the Interior Albert Fall had persuaded Secretary of the Navy Edwin Denby to transfer government oil reserves at Elk Hills, Calif., and Teapot Dome, Wyo., to the Department of the Interior. Fall then leased the reserves to private oil producers E. L. Doheny and Harry Sinclair. These leases were made without competitive bidding. In both cases, Fall received large sums of money for helping to arrange the transfers—$100,000 from Doheny for Elk Hills and $300,000 from Sinclair for Teapot Dome. Fall resigned in 1923 and joined Sinclair's oil business. Denby resigned in 1924, after Harding had died and Calvin Coolidge had become President. Fall was later convicted of accepting a bribe. See also HARDING, WARREN G. (Government Scandals).   EDWIN C. ROZWENC

Additional Resources

BATES, JAMES LEONARD. *The Origins of Teapot Dome: Progressives, Parties, and Petroleum.* Greenwood, 1978. Reprint of 1963 ed.

NOGGLE, BURL. *Teapot Dome: Oil and Politics in the 1920's.* Greenwood, 1980. Reprint of 1962 ed.

WERNER, MORRIS R., and STARR, JOHN. *Teapot Dome.* Kelley, 1970. Reprint of 1959 ed.

TEAR GAS. See CHEMICAL-BIOLOGICAL-RADIOLOGICAL WARFARE; MACE (gas).

TEARS, *teerz,* are the secretion of the lacrimal glands. The tears continually bathe the *cornea,* the tough outer layer of the eyeball. They help to clear it of foreign particles, such as dust and hairs, and keep it from drying out, which would result in blindness.

Two lacrimal glands, one over each eye, lie behind the eyelid. They pour out their fluid through several small ducts in the underside of the lid. Each time the eyelid blinks, it sucks a little fluid from the glands. When a person feels some emotion such as grief or anger very strongly, the muscles around the lacrimal glands may tighten up and squeeze out the tear fluid. The same thing happens if a person laughs very heartily.

Adapted from *Man in Structure and Function* by Fritz Kahn, by permission of and special arrangement with Alfred A. Knopf, Inc.

TEAR GLANDS AND DUCTS

Glands

Tears flow from glands under the eyelid, over the eye, out through ducts.

After the tears pass across the eyeball, they flow out through two lacrimal ducts that open at the inner corner of each eye. They lead to a lacrimal sac and then to the nasal duct. This duct runs the length of the nose and finally opens into it. Tears flowing through this opening make the nose run when a person cries.

Mostly a salt solution, lacrimal fluid also contains substances that fight bacteria and proteins that help make the eye immune to infection.   GEORGE W. BEADLE

TEASDALE, SARA (1884-1933), an American poet, wrote quiet lyrics noted for their simplicity and purity of form. Her first volume of poetry appeared in 1907. Her *Love Songs* won the Columbia University prize for the best book of poetry published by an American during 1917. *Flame and Shadow* (1920) is probably her best work. She also wrote *Rivers to the Sea* (1915), *Dark of the Moon* (1926), and *Strange Victory* (1933). Teasdale was born in St. Louis.   WILLIAM VAN O'CONNOR

TEASEL, *TEE z'l,* is the name of a group of plants that have one commercially valuable species. This species is the *fuller's teasel, clothier's teasel,* or *clothier's brush,* which comes from southern Europe and is now grown in America. It is used to raise the nap on cloth.

J. Horace McFarland
Teasel Flower Heads

The plant is a thistlelike herb with long, stemless leaves, prickly stems, and stiff bracts surrounding the flower heads. The parts used are the dry flower heads, whose fresh flowers are tubular, and which are colored pale lilac or white. The heads are cut in two and attached to a cylinder which revolves against the cloth. The best heads are used for raising the nap on men's garments. The largest are used for raising the nap on blankets. Small heads are used for fine woolens and broadcloth. No mechanical device has ever been invented that can replace these heads satisfactorily.

Scientific Classification. Teasels belong to the teasel family, *Dipsaceae.* They make up the genus *Dipsacus.* Fuller's teasel is classified as *D. fullonum.*   PAUL C. STANDLEY

TEBALDI, RENATA (1922-   ), an Italian singer, became one of the great operatic stars of her day. Her superb voice is noted for its velvety quality and even scale. Her early lyric roles include Desdemona in *Otello* and Mimi in *La Bohème.* She was able to progress to more dramatic roles, including the title roles in *Aida* and *Tosca,* which require a voice of larger size. She is not especially gifted as an actress, but beauty of tone and her personal appeal brought her success in the United States, especially at the Metropolitan Opera.

Renata Tebaldi was born in Pesaro, Italy. She made her operatic debut in Rovigo as Elena in *Mefistofele* in 1944. She made her debut at the Metropolitan Opera as Desdemona in 1955.   MAX DE SCHAUENSEE

TECHNETIUM, *teck NEE shih um* (chemical symbol, Tc), was the first artificially created element. Its atomic number is 43. The most stable available isotope has a mass number of 99. In 1937, Carlo Perrier and Emilio Segrè isolated technetium in Italy. They produced it by using a cyclotron to bombard a target of molybden-

um with deuterons. They then dissolved the molybdenum target and added many elements as tracers, until they isolated technetium. They proved that the bombardment left one proton in the molybdenum and formed technetium. Scientists first called the element *masurium* and thought that it occurred in nature. The name was changed to technetium, which means *artificial.* Technetium is now obtained as a by-product from atomic fission. Its properties resemble those of manganese and rhenium. Its melting point is 2200° C ($+50°$ C). See also ELEMENT, CHEMICAL.   GLENN T. SEABORG

TECHNICAL ASSISTANCE is a form of foreign aid. Through technical assistance programs, people in developing countries learn skills that help increase production and raise living standards.

There are various forms of technical assistance. Experts from more prosperous countries may set up demonstrations or provide on-the-job training in developing countries. Workers, executives, and engineers from developing countries may go to prosperous countries for training. Technical assistance may be as simple as teaching a farmer to use a plow instead of a forked stick. It may be as involved as showing a government how to keep statistics on its economy.

President Harry S. Truman's Point Four Program of 1949 was an early technical assistance plan (see POINT FOUR PROGRAM). Some private and public agencies gave such aid before 1949. The United Nations and its agencies also offer technical assistance programs.

Technical assistance needs to be linked with *capital funds* (money invested in productive enterprises) in order to make sizable changes in a developing country. But capital funds are often hard to get whether they are in the form of private investment or in the form of foreign aid.   WILLIAM T. R. FOX

See also FOREIGN AID; UNITED NATIONS (Economic and Technical Aid); COLOMBO PLAN; AGENCY FOR INTERNATIONAL DEVELOPMENT; DEVELOPING COUNTRY.

TECHNICAL DRAWING. See MECHANICAL DRAWING.

TECHNICAL SCHOOL. See VOCATIONAL EDUCATION.

TECHNICOLOR is a patented process for making colored motion pictures. Herbert T. Kalmus, a chemical engineer, developed the process about 1917. The process originally involved making three separate negatives of a scene to get a picture that appears to have the colors of a natural object. Technicians separated the colors by a method known as *color subtraction.* Then the negatives were printed on film. A dye process was used to reproduce the colors of nature. The first Technicolor full-length all-color film, *Toll of the Sea,* appeared in theaters in 1923. Since then, hundreds of films have been made in Technicolor.

Technicolor cooperated with the Eastman Kodak Company to produce a simplified color process in the 1930's. This process does not require three separate negatives. It uses a single reversal-process film that has three light-sensitive emulsion layers and a yellow filter film below the upper emulsion. This Kodacolor filter film process saved time and money in meeting the demand for full-color films.   HARRY MUIR KURTZWORTH

TECHNOLOGICAL UNEMPLOYMENT. See UNEMPLOYMENT (Structural Unemployment).

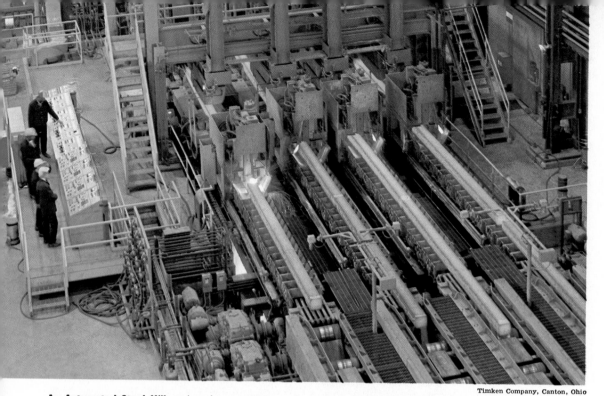

An Automated Steel Mill produces huge steel bars at the touch of a button. The computer-controlled machines that roll the glowing bars are products of modern technology. Other machines and methods will turn the bars into a variety of industrial and household products.

TECHNOLOGY

TECHNOLOGY refers to all the ways people use their inventions and discoveries to satisfy their needs and desires. Ever since people appeared on the earth, they have had to work to obtain food, clothing, and shelter. They have also had to work to satisfy their desire for leisure and comfort. Through the ages, people invented tools, machines, materials, and techniques to make work easier. They also discovered water power, electricity, and other sources of power that increased the rate at which they could work. Technology thus involves the use of tools, machines, materials, techniques, and sources of power to make work easier and more productive.

Many people call the age we live in the *age of technology*. Yet people have always lived in a technological age because they have always had to work to obtain most of life's necessities and many of its pleasures. Technology thus includes the use of both primitive and highly advanced tools and methods of work. But when people speak of technology today, they generally mean *industrial technology*—the technology that helped bring about our modern society.

Industrial technology began about 200 years ago with the development of power-driven machines, the growth of factories, and the mass production of goods.

Melvin Kranzberg, the contributor of this article, is Callaway Professor of the History of Technology at Georgia Institute of Technology and coeditor of Technology in Western Civilization.

As industrial technology advanced, it affected more and more aspects of people's lives. For example, the development of the automobile influenced where people lived and worked and how they spent their leisure time. Radio and television changed entertainment habits, and the telephone revolutionized communication. Today, industrial technology helps people achieve goals that few thought possible a hundred years ago. It gives people the means to conquer hunger and to cure or prevent many diseases. It enables them to transport goods and passengers swiftly and easily to any place on the earth. They can even leave the earth, soar through space, and set foot on the moon.

Science has contributed much to modern technology. But not all technology is based on science, nor is science necessary to all technology. Science attempts to explain how and why things happen. Technology is concerned with making things happen. For example, people made objects of iron for centuries before they learned about the changes that occurred in the structure of the metal during ironmaking. But some modern technologies, such as nuclear power production and space travel, depend heavily on science.

The word *technology* is sometimes used to describe a particular application of industrial technology, such as medical technology or military technology. Each of the various specialized technologies has its own goals and its own tools and techniques for achieving those goals. The engineering profession is responsible for much of today's industrial technology (see ENGINEERING).

Industrial technology enables people to live in greater security and comfort than ever before. But only a small

Assembly Line Production, an important method of technology, increases the amount of goods a worker can produce. Increased productivity provides more goods for more people.

Automobiles, like other inventions of technology, have changed our way of life. The convenience of automobile travel influences where we live and work and how we use our free time.

part of the world's population enjoys the full benefits of modern technology. In addition, nations with advanced technologies have found that certain undesirable side effects, such as air and water pollution, have accompanied technological growth. Technology also enables people to produce more powerful weapons, thus adding to the destructiveness of war.

This article describes technology's benefits and undesirable side effects. It also discusses the problems people face in trying to combat these side effects. The development of technology largely parallels the history of inventions and discoveries, which is traced in the article on INVENTION. Detailed information on the development of technolgy in specific areas can be found in the history sections of such articles as AGRICULTURE, MEDICINE, and TRANSPORTATION.

Benefits of Technology

Technology has helped people gain control over nature and so build a civilized way of life. The first people had little control over nature. They had only simple tools. They did not know how to raise animals or plants and so had to search for wild animals and plants for food. They had no permanent homes. Animal skins were their only protection against the cold. The sun was their only source of light. Then people discovered how to make fire. This discovery helped them gain some control over nature. They could now carry heat and light wherever they went. They next learned to raise animals and crops. The development of farming allowed them to build settlements. It also freed people for work other than producing food. Classes of priests, rulers, craft-

workers, and merchants developed. This division of labor helped make civilization possible.

Through the ages, technology has benefited people in four main ways. First, it has increased their production of goods and services. Second, it has reduced the amount of labor needed to produce goods and services. Third, technology has made labor easier. Fourth, it has given people higher living standards.

Increased Production. Through technology, people have achieved a tremendous increase in the production of goods and services. In the mid-1800's, for example, people and animals were the main source of power on farms in the United States. Farmers labored from dawn to dusk, yet one farmer produced enough food for only about four persons. In the early 1900's, more and more farmers began using tractors and other machines powered by gasoline or electricity. Today, machines do most of the work on U.S. farms. As a result of machinery, fertilizers, and other advances in agricultural technology, one U.S. farmer today produces enough food for 78 persons. Similar developments have occurred in manufacturing, mining, and other industries. Most workers today produce many times more goods than workers did a hundred years ago.

Reduced Labor. Powered machines have increased production. But they have also reduced the amount of labor needed to produce goods and services and so have increased productivity. Increased productivity gives workers more leisure time. In the early 1800's, for example, most factory work was done by hand or hand-operated machines. Workers labored 12 to 16 hours a day, six days a week. Few people received a vacation.

61

Grant Heilman

Farm Machines and other advances in agricultural technology make farm work easier. Such machines and methods also help farmers produce larger and larger amounts of food.

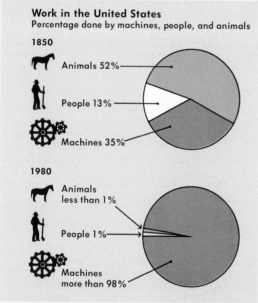

Work in the United States
Percentage done by machines, people, and animals

1850

Animals 52%

People 13%

Machines 35%

1980

Animals less than 1%

People 1%

Machines more than 98%

WORLD BOOK diagram

In 1850, machines did only 35 per cent of U.S. farm and industrial work, while people and animals performed the rest. The charts above show how the 1850 percentages compare with those of today, when machines do over 98 per cent of the work.

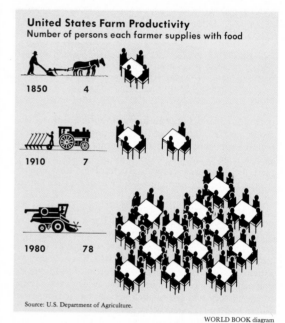

United States Farm Productivity
Number of persons each farmer supplies with food

1850   4

1910   7

1980   78

Source: U.S. Department of Agriculture.

WORLD BOOK diagram

This chart shows the increase in U.S. farm productivity since 1850, when a farmer produced enough food for four persons. Today, a farmer produces enough for 78 persons. Advances in agricultural technology have been largely responsible for the increase.

Today, powered machinery has largely replaced hand labor in factories. Many factories also use mass production techniques. As a result, the amount of labor needed to produce manufactured goods has decreased sharply. Today, most factory employees work only eight hours a day, five days a week. They also receive paid holidays and vacations.

Easier Labor. Technology has enabled people to produce more goods and services with less labor. It has also made labor easier and safer. Coal mining provides an example. In the early 1900's, miners toiled all day with

pick and shovel to produce a few tons of coal. The mines were dark, poorly ventilated, and dangerous. Today, mining is still dangerous. But better lighting and ventilation and improved safety devices have reduced the hazards. The work itself is easier and more productive. Machines perform most of the hard labor. The operator of a coal-mining machine can dig more than 1 short ton (0.9 metric ton) of coal a minute.

Higher Living Standards have resulted from the increased production of goods and services. The industrial nations produce more goods and services than other countries and have the world's highest standard of living. Most people in industrial nations are better fed, clothed, and housed and enjoy a healthier, more comfortable life than any other people in history. Above all, technology has increased human *life expectancy*—the number of years a person can expect to live. Improved public health practices have ended the plagues that once swept through many countries. Better health care and nutrition have also reduced the number of deaths among infants. In 1900, most people born in the United States did not live past the age of 50. Today, Americans live an average of about 73 years (see LIFE EXPECTANCY).

Side Effects of Technology

The advance of technology has benefited people in numerous ways, but it has also created serious problems. These problems have arisen mainly because technologies were put to use without considering the possible harmful side effects. For example, many people welcomed the development of the automobile in the late 1890's and early 1900's. They believed that automobiles would be quieter and less smelly than horses. But as more and more automobiles came into use, the noise of roaring traffic proved more annoying than the clatter of horse hoofs. Automobile exhaust fumes proved worse than the smell of horse manure. The fumes polluted the air with carbon monoxide gas and other impurities and so threatened human health. In addition, automobiles created traffic jams, which often made automobile travel more time-consuming than travel on horseback. The ever-increasing production of automobiles used up iron and other natural resources.

This section discusses four major side effects of technology. They are: (1) environmental pollution, (2) the depletion of natural resources, (3) technological unemployment, and (4) the creation of unsatisfying jobs.

Environmental Pollution ranks as one of the most harmful side effects of industrial technology. Most industrial countries face problems of air, water, soil, and noise pollution. Motor vehicles cause most of the air and noise pollution in these countries. But many other products as well as many processes of technology also pollute the environment. For example, certain insecticides pollute the soil and water and endanger plant and animal life. Factory smoke and wastes also contribute greatly to air and water pollution. In the United States, power plants that burn oil or other fuels to generate electricity add millions of tons of pollutants to the air annually. Junkyards, open-pit mines, logging operations, and freeways detract from the beauty of the natural environment. See the article on ENVIRONMENTAL POLLUTION for a further discussion of technology's harmful environmental effects.

The Depletion of Natural Resources. The rapid advance of technology threatens the supply of resources. For example, the use of electrically powered machinery in the United States and other industrial countries has greatly increased factory production. But at the same time, it has reduced the supply of oil and other fuels used to produce electricity. These fuels cannot be replaced after they are used. As power production increases, the supply of fuels decreases. Since the 1950's, power production has increased so greatly in the United States that the nation began to experience a fuel and power shortage during the 1970's.

Technological Unemployment is a type of unemployment that sometimes results from advances in technology. The most common type of technological unemployment occurs when machines take over workers' jobs. Since the late 1950's, many factories and offices have introduced automatic machines to perform tasks formerly done by workers. The use of such machines, which is called *automation*, has caused some unemployment. But it has not been so severe as some experts predicted. Automation has helped a number of industries expand. As a result, these industries have been able to provide new jobs for displaced workers. But technological unemployment nevertheless remains a threat to workers in many industries. For more information on technological unemployment, see UNEMPLOYMENT (Structural Unemployment).

The Creation of Unsatisfying Jobs. Some tasks required by industrial technology fail to give workers a feeling of accomplishment. For example, most factory workers make only a part of the finished product. As a result, they may lack the feeling of pride in their work that comes from creating an entire product. Many factory jobs also demand concentration. Although factory machines are safer today than in the past, many

---

TECHNOLOGY HAS INCREASED THE SPEED OF TRAVEL

Technology has improved man's methods of transportation and so has enabled him to travel faster than ever before. This chart compares the speeds of common types of public transportation in 1850 with the speeds of common types today.

LAND

1850 ☐ Stagecoach about 9 mph (14 kph)

1975 ▬ Electric rail line (Japan) 130 mph (209 kph)

WATER

1850 ☐ Clipper ship (U.S.) about 23 mph (37 kph)

1975 ▬ Hovercraft (Great Britain) 75 mph (121 kph)

AIR

1850 No means of public air transportation

1975 ▬ Boeing 747 airliner (U.S.) about 600 mph (965 kph)

WORLD BOOK graph

Harmful Effects of Technology include the scarring of once-fertile land by surface, or strip, mining, *left*. Streams fill with mud, the soil becomes acid, and plant and animal life vanish.

are dangerous if not operated with extreme care. The operators must be constantly alert to make sure they are operating their machines properly. But constantly tending a machine or performing the same task again and again can be monotonous as well as demanding.

The Challenge of Technology

Modern technology presents enormous challenges. One of the chief challenges is to combat the undesirable side effects of existing technologies. Another is to prevent possible side effects in the development of new technologies. Still another challenge is to spread technology's benefits to the people of developing countries.

Combating Side Effects. Some of technology's side effects are extremely hard to remedy. For example, it is difficult to make an unsatisfying job satisfying. But automation will continue to free many workers from routine, monotonous jobs. Some of these workers may then face the hardships of unemployment. But with help from industry and government, they can be retrained to fill more highly skilled and possibly more interesting jobs. See AUTOMATION (Automation's Effect on Jobs).

Industries can do much to combat environmental pollution and the depletion of natural resources. One way is by developing substitute technologies for those that produce harmful side effects. Automobile makers, for example, can help curb air pollution by finding a means of purifying automobile exhausts. Manufacturers can help conserve mineral and timber resources by a process called *recycling*. In recycling, raw materials are recovered from waste products and used to make new products (see ENVIRONMENTAL POLLUTION [Recycling]).

Developing a substitute technology can be costly. An industry may need to hire additional experts or invest in expensive equipment. Most industries that develop a substitute technology pass the cost on to buyers in the form of higher prices. Some industries choose not to spend the money to develop a substitute technology. But in many cases, the choice is too serious to be left to industries because the health of an entire community, state, or nation may be affected. In these cases, government agencies make and enforce the decision. For example, many local governments require factories to install pollution control devices.

Substitute technologies may also have side effects. For example, nuclear power plants have several advantages

over fuel-burning plants in producing electricity. Nuclear plants can produce tremendous amounts of electricity using only small amounts of raw materials. In addition, they do not pollute the air as do fuel-burning plants. But nuclear plants, like some fuel-burning plants, release hot water into lakes and rivers. The hot water may cause *thermal pollution*, which harms water plants and animals. But scientists and engineers are working to solve this problem. For example, many nuclear plants have installed *cooling towers*, which use air to cool the hot water they produce.

Preventing Side Effects. Some experts believe that most harmful side effects of technology can be prevented. According to this view, any proposed large-scale technology should be thoroughly tested and then evaluated before it is put into use. Such an evaluation is called a *technology assessment*. The findings of a technology assessment are usually published in a detailed report called an *environmental impact statement* (see ENVIRONMENTAL IMPACT STATEMENT).

The purpose of an assessment is to discover in advance all the possible good and bad effects that a new technology may have on society and the environment. An assessment might show that the benefits of a new technology outweigh any side effects. Or it might show that the side effects would be so harmful that they outweigh any benefits. In 1972, Congress created the Office of Technology Assessment to provide information on the impacts of new technologies.

Some experts doubt the value of technology assessment. They believe that it is not possible to discover all the side effects of a technology before it is put into use. They also fear that technology assessments will block scientific and technological progress.

Spreading the Benefits of Technology. Technology's benefits are limited largely to the industrially developed nations of Europe and North America. But even in these nations, the benefits of technology are not evenly distributed. Many families in the United States, for example, lack all but the bare necessities of life.

The developing nations of the world enjoy few of technology's benefits. Also, the people of these countries want the goods and services that technology has made available to industrialized nations. The transfer of technological knowledge from developed to developing nations is one of today's chief challenges.

Alter Company

A Shredding Machine turns junked automobiles into pieces of scrap for *recycling*. Recycling recovers raw materials from wastes and so helps conserve the resources used by technology.

As technology advances in developing countries, it will probably produce some harmful side effects. Advanced technology will probably also continue to create problems in the industrialized countries. But technological achievements in the past show that people have the intelligence, imagination, and inventive skill to deal with present and future problems created by technology. MELVIN KRANZBERG

Related Articles. See ENGINEERING, INDUSTRY, INVENTION, and MANUFACTURING with their lists of Related Articles. See also the following articles:

Agriculture
Assembly Line
Automation
Building Trade
Careers
Environmental Pollution
Factory

Industrial Revolution
Labor Force
Machine
Machine Tool
Mass Production
Mining

Outline

I. Benefits of Technology
A. Increased Production
B. Reduced Labor
C. Easier Labor
D. Higher Living Standards
II. Side Effects of Technology
A. Environmental Pollution
B. The Depletion of Natural Resources
C. Technological Unemployment
D. The Creation of Unsatisfying Jobs
III. The Challenge of Technology
A. Combating Side Effects
B. Preventing Side Effects
C. Spreading the Benefits of Technology

Questions

In what four main ways has technology aided people?
How does technology differ from science?
What is *technology assessment?* What is its main purpose?
What are four of the major side effects of technology?
Why is less labor needed to manufacture goods today than in the past?
What challenges does modern technology present?

When did industrial technology begin?
What is technological unemployment?
What are some of the ways in which industrial technology has affected people's lives?
Why did many people welcome the development of the automobile in the late 1890's and early 1900's?

Additional Resources

CONGDON, R. J., ed. *Introduction to Appropriate Technology: Toward a Simpler Life-Style.* Rodale, 1977.
KRANZBERG, MELVIN, and PURSELL, C. W., eds. *Technology in Western Civilization.* 2 vols. Oxford, 1967.
SINGER, CHARLES, and others, eds. *A History of Technology.* 7 vols. Oxford, 1954-1978.
SUSSKIND, CHARLES. *Understanding Technology.* Johns Hopkins, 1973.
THRING, MEREDITH W., and BLAKE, ARVIL. *Man, Machines and Tomorrow.* Routledge & Kegan, 1973.

TECHNOLOGY ASSESSMENT, OFFICE OF, is an advisory agency of the United States Congress. The agency, often called OTA, gathers information on the ways that technology can affect people's lives. Many congressional committees ask OTA for studies evaluating the economic, environmental, social, and political effects of legislative decisions that affect uses of technology. The studies may involve a wide range of topics, including communications, energy, food, health, natural resources, transportation, and world trade.

OTA has a congressional board that establishes the policies of the agency. The board consists of six senators and six representatives, plus the OTA director. OTA also has a Technology Assessment Advisory Council that advises the board on technological matters. The council consists of experts in the fields of education, engineering, and science.

Congress established OTA in 1972. The agency began operations in 1974. Critically reviewed by the OFFICE OF TECHNOLOGY ASSESSMENT

TECTONICS

TECTONICS is the study of forces within the earth that form the earth's mountains and ocean basins. Although tectonic forces cannot be explained, earth scientists believe they are produced by heat energy.

The Plate Tectonic Theory. In the 1960's, earth scientists proposed a tectonic theory that included two earlier ideas. These ideas involved *continental drift* and *convection currents* (see CONTINENTAL DRIFT). The new theory led many earth scientists to conclude that the earth's outer shell, called the *lithosphere*, consists of a number of rigid plates. Some of these plates do not follow continental boundaries, and some include both continents and oceans. The lithosphere is about 45 to 95 miles (72 to 153 kilometers) thick and appears to be in continual motion. The lithosphere plates slowly slide on a soft plastic layer of rock called the *asthenosphere*. The plates move in the range of from $\frac{1}{2}$ to 4 inches (1.3 to 10 centimeters) a year.

Tectonic activity seems to occur chiefly along the edges of the plates. If one plate pushes against another, it either crumples and forms mountains or bends toward the earth's *mantle*, the layer beneath the crust and above the *core* (see EARTH [Inside the Earth]). Two plates spreading apart form ocean floors and long underwater mountains called *oceanic ridges*. Major earthquakes and fractures in the earth's crust occur where two plates slide past each other. Such fractures are called *faults*.

Some of the earth's major crustal features occur at the edges of the lithosphere plates. Such features include mountains, ocean floor trenches, oceanic ridges, volcanoes, and volcanic islands that are called *island arcs*.

Tecumseh Threatened William Henry Harrison because Harrison made a treaty that took much of the Indian land. Tecumseh tried to unite all the American Indian tribes in defense of their homelands against the invaders.

Most earth scientists believe convection currents create the power that moves the huge plates. According to this theory, convection currents in the earth's mantle carry molten rock up from the asthenosphere. The rising molten rock adds to the ocean floor at some of the oceanic ridges. Convection currents in the rock carry the newly formed crustal plate away from the ridge as if it were riding on a conveyor belt.

Some scientists do not accept various parts of the convection current theory. Other scientists want proof that convection currents even exist—and that they produce the enormous power needed to move the plates.

Other Theories. Some earth scientists once thought that the earth began as a molten ball and has been cooling ever since. As the earth became cooler, it shrank. The shrinking produced tectonic forces.

Other earth scientists believe that the earth began as a cold mass and was warmed by heat from radioactive material inside the planet. As the earth became hotter, it expanded and created forces that fractured the crust into large blocks. These blocks became the continents, and the regions between the continents became the basins of the oceans.   ALBERT J. RUDMAN

TECUMSEH, *tih KUHM suh* (1765?-1813), was an outstanding leader of the eastern American Indian tribes after the American Revolutionary War. He worked to unite all the American Indian tribes into a single alliance that would defend Indian lands against invasion by white people. Tecumseh means *shooting star* or *meteor*.

Tecumseh, the son of a Shawnee chief, is believed to have been born in the Scioto River Valley, south of Columbus, Ohio. His father and two brothers were killed in battles with the American colonists.

White settlers were rapidly taking the Indian lands, and Tecumseh and his brother, Tenskwatawa, began a crusade to keep Indian lands for the Indians. Tenskwatawa, known as the Shawnee Prophet, led a religious revival (see SHAWNEE PROPHET). Tecumseh, a strong warrior and gifted orator, led in politics and war. He traveled tirelessly from his home in Ohio to almost every tribe east of the Rocky Mountains. He and his brother did much to lead the Indians back to the ways of their forefathers.

Tecumseh condemned a treaty that William Henry Harrison made with the Indians. His action led to the Battle of Tippecanoe in November, 1811. See INDIAN WARS (Other Midwestern Conflicts [1790-1832]).

Tecumseh joined the British armies in the War of 1812 in the hope that the Americans could be defeated. He served with the rank of a brigadier general in command of Indian allies. He was killed while leading his forces in Canada after Commander Oliver H. Perry's victory at Lake Erie (see WAR OF 1812 [Chief Battles of the War]).   E. ADAMSON HOEBEL

TEDDER, ARTHUR WILLIAM (1890-1967), BARON TEDDER OF GLENGUIN, became a marshal of the Royal Air Force of Great Britain in 1945. Tedder served in the Royal Air Force during World War I and World War II. He was named deputy supreme commander to General Dwight D. Eisenhower, the supreme Allied commander, in World War II. He later became deputy supreme commander of the North Atlantic Treaty Organization (NATO) forces in Europe. He was born in Stirlingshire (now Central Region), Scotland.

TEEN AGE. See ADOLESCENT.

TEETH

TEETH are hard, bonelike structures in the upper and lower jaws of human beings and many kinds of animals. They are the hardest parts of the body.

People use their teeth chiefly to chew food. Chewing is the first step in the process of *digestion*. Digestion begins as the teeth chop and grind chunks of food into smaller pieces. As the teeth chew the food, it is mixed with *saliva*, a liquid produced in the mouth. The food becomes a moist pulp, which is easy to swallow. The food is further broken down in the stomach and the small intestine, where it is absorbed by the blood. The blood carries the digested food to all parts of the body. Without teeth, people could not eat foods that must be chewed. They could only swallow soft foods and liquids.

Teeth also play an important part in speech. The teeth and tongue are used together to form many sounds that make up words. To produce the *th* sound, for example, the tip of the tongue is placed against the upper front teeth. A person who lacks these teeth may be unable to make the sound.

Teeth also help support the muscles around the mouth and so contribute to a person's appearance. People who have lost their teeth lack this support. Unless they wear artificial teeth, they may have deep, saggy lines around the mouth.

Like human beings, most animals use their teeth to chew food. They also use their teeth to obtain food. Many animals that eat plants tear off the leaves or stalks of the plants with their teeth. Most meat-eating animals use their teeth to seize and kill prey.

This article chiefly discusses human teeth. The last section of the article describes the differences in the teeth of various kinds of animals.

Kinds of Teeth

Human beings grow two sets of teeth: (1) deciduous teeth and (2) permanent teeth. The individual deciduous teeth appear and fall out gradually early in life. They are replaced, one by one, by the permanent teeth. See the table *Ages at Which Teeth Appear* for the times the various kinds of deciduous and permanent teeth generally appear.

Deciduous and permanent teeth have the same basic structure. Each tooth has a *crown* and one or more *roots*. The crown is the part of the tooth that can be seen in the mouth. The root or roots are covered by the gums. The roots hold the tooth in a socket in the jawbone.

Deciduous Teeth are also called *baby teeth, milk teeth,* or *primary teeth.* They start to form about $7\frac{1}{2}$ months before a baby is born. They begin as oval or round swellings called *buds,* which gradually develop into teeth. When a baby is born, parts of all the deciduous teeth are present deep within the jaws. As the teeth grow, they push through the gums. This process is called *eruption* or *teething.* Babies begin to teethe at about 6 to 9 months of age. Most children have all their deciduous teeth by about 2 years of age.

There are 20 deciduous teeth, 10 in each jaw. They consist of three kinds of teeth: (1) incisors, (2) canines, and (3) molars. Each jaw has 4 incisors, 2 canines, and 4 molars. The incisors and canines are used to bite into food, and the molars to grind food. The positions of these teeth in the mouth are shown in the illustration *Kinds of Teeth.*

The deciduous teeth help the permanent teeth erupt in their normal positions. Most of the permanent teeth form near the roots of the deciduous teeth. When a child is about 3 years old, the roots of various deciduous teeth begin to dissolve slowly. By the time a permanent tooth is ready to erupt, the root of the deciduous tooth has completely dissolved. The crown of the tooth then becomes loose and falls out.

Permanent Teeth, like deciduous teeth, begin to develop before birth. But most of their growth occurs after birth. The permanent teeth begin to erupt after the deciduous teeth start to fall out.

The first permanent teeth appear when a child is about 6 or 7 years old. Between the ages of 6 and 12, a child has some permanent and some deciduous teeth in the mouth. The last permanent teeth erupt when a person is 17 to 21 years old.

There are 32 permanent teeth, 16 in each jaw. They are larger than the deciduous teeth and consist of four kinds of teeth. The four kinds are (1) incisors, (2) canines, (3) premolars, and (4) molars. Each jaw has 4 incisors, 2 canines, 4 premolars, and 6 molars. The following discussion describes the four kinds of permanent teeth. Their positions in the mouth are shown in the illustration *Kinds of Teeth.*

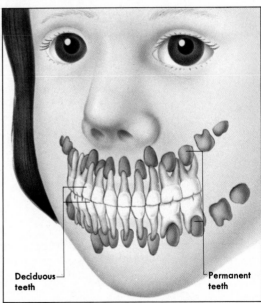

Deciduous teeth

Permanent teeth

WORLD BOOK diagram by Charles Wellek

The Teeth of a Child. By the time a child is about 4 years old, most of the permanent teeth have formed within the jaws near the roots of the deciduous teeth. The deciduous teeth, all of which have erupted by about age 2, will gradually fall out and be replaced, one by one, by the permanent teeth.

John P. Wortel, the contributor of this article, is Assistant Professor of General and Oral Pathology at Loyola University School of Dentistry.

Kinds of Teeth

The illustrations below show the kinds of deciduous and permanent teeth and their positions in the mouth. There are 20 deciduous teeth, 10 in the upper jaw and 10 in the lower jaw. There are 32 permanent teeth, 16 in each jaw.

WORLD BOOK diagrams by Charles Wellek

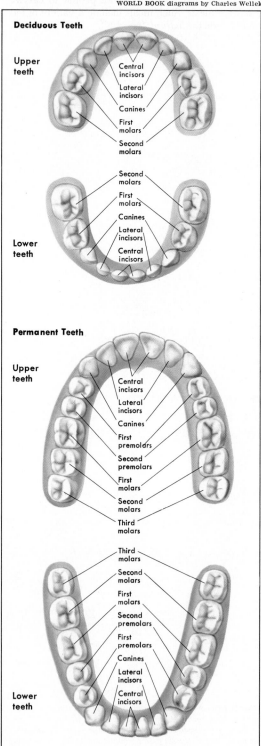

Deciduous Teeth

Upper teeth — Central incisors, Lateral incisors, Canines, First molars, Second molars

Lower teeth — Second molars, First molars, Canines, Lateral incisors, Central incisors

Permanent Teeth

Upper teeth — Central incisors, Lateral incisors, Canines, First premolars, Second premolars, First molars, Second molars, Third molars

Lower teeth — Third molars, Second molars, First molars, Second premolars, First premolars, Canines, Lateral incisors, Central incisors

Ages at Which Teeth Appear*

Deciduous Teeth:	Lower Teeth	Upper Teeth
Central incisors	6 months	7 months
Lateral incisors	7 months	9 months
Canines	16 months	18 months
First molars	12 months	14 months
Second molars	20 months	24 months

Permanent Teeth:	Lower Teeth	Upper Teeth
Central incisors	6-7 years	7-8 years
Lateral incisors	7-8 years	8-9 years
Canines	9-10 years	11-12 years
First premolars	10-12 years	10-11 years
Second premolars	11-12 years	10-12 years
First molars	6-7 years	6-7 years
Second molars	11-13 years	12-13 years
Third molars	17-21 years	17-21 years

*The ages given are approximate. In many cases, individual teeth may erupt at an earlier or later age.

Incisors are the chief biting teeth. They have a sharp, straight cutting edge. In most cases, incisors have one root. The central incisors of the lower jaw are the smallest permanent teeth.

Canines are used with the incisors to bite into food. They are also used to tear off pieces of food. The name for these teeth comes from another word for *dog*—that is, *canine*. The canine teeth resemble a dog's fangs. They have a sharp, pointed edge and one root. Canines are also called *cuspids* or *dogteeth*. The upper canines are sometimes known as *eyeteeth*.

Premolars are used to crush and grind food. They have a broad, lumpy top instead of a sharp biting edge. The small surface lumps are called *cusps*. The cusps enable the teeth to mash pieces of food.

Premolars are sometimes called *bicuspids* because, in most cases, they have two cusps. The prefix *bi* means *two*. The first upper premolars normally have two roots. The other premolars have one root. The premolars erupt in the place of the deciduous molars.

Molars, like premolars, grind food. They are shaped much like premolars but are larger. The various molars normally have three to five cusps and two or three roots.

The permanent molars do not form beneath any of the deciduous teeth. They develop as the jaws grow, which makes space for them. Some adults lack one or more of the third molars, which are commonly called *wisdom teeth*. In many cases, the jaws do not grow large enough to provide space for the wisdom teeth. As a result, the wisdom teeth may become *impacted*—that is, wedged between the jawbone and another tooth. The wisdom teeth must then be removed.

Parts of a Tooth

A tooth consists of four kinds of tissues. They are (1) pulp, (2) dentin, (3) enamel, and (4) cementum. Connective tissue surrounds the root of the tooth. This tissue, called the *periodontal ligament*, holds the root in the socket in the jaw.

Pulp is the innermost layer of a tooth. It consists of connective tissue, blood vessels, and nerves. The blood vessels nourish the tooth. The nerves transmit sensations of pain to the brain.

The pulp has two parts, the *pulp chamber* and the *root canal*. The pulp chamber lies in the crown of the tooth. The root canal lies in the root of the tooth. Blood vessels and nerves enter the root canal through a small hole at the tip of the root. They extend through the root canal and into the pulp chamber.

Dentin is a hard, yellow substance that surrounds the pulp. It makes up most of a tooth. Dentin is harder than bone. It consists mainly of mineral salts and water but also has some living cells.

Enamel overlies the dentin in the crown of the tooth. It forms the outermost covering of the crown. Enamel is the hardest tissue in the body. It enables a tooth to withstand the pressure placed on it during chewing. Enamel consists of mineral salts and a small amount of water. Enamel is white but transparent. The yellow color of the dentin shows through the enamel, and so most teeth appear slightly yellowish.

As a person grows older, small amounts of enamel begin to wear away. This process, called *attrition*, results from the use of the teeth over a long period. As the enamel wears away, the dentin becomes exposed. The teeth may then become increasingly sensitive to hot and cold liquids.

Cementum overlies the dentin in the root of the tooth. In most cases, the cementum and enamel meet where the root ends and the crown begins. Cementum is about as hard as bone. Like dentin and enamel, it consists mainly of mineral salts and water.

Periodontal Ligament consists of small fibers. These fibers extend through the cementum and into the bony socket, which is called the *alveolus*. Besides anchoring the tooth in the alveolus, the periodontal ligament serves as a shock absorber during chewing.

Care of the Teeth and Gums

Most cases of tooth decay and gum disease could be prevented if people took proper care of their teeth and gums. Proper care requires (1) a good diet, (2) cleaning the teeth after eating, and (3) dental checkups.

A Good Diet. Dentists advise people to eat well-balanced meals. Such meals include a variety of foods and provide the *nutrients* (nourishing substances) needed by the teeth and gums. Nutrition experts divide foods into groups to make it easier for people to plan well-balanced meals. According to one system, foods are classified into four groups. Another system lists seven groups. The article NUTRITION describes these food groups. For each group, the article gives the number of daily servings that experts advise people to eat.

Dentists also urge people to eat fewer sugary foods because these foods contribute to tooth decay. Bacteria in the mouth digest sugar and produce an acid as a result. The acid dissolves tooth enamel, forming a cavity.

Foods that have a large amount of sugar include candies, pastries, most breakfast cereals, and sweetened canned fruits. Many people eat sugary foods as snacks. In place of sugary foods, dentists advise people to snack on such foods as fresh fruits and vegetables, cheeses, and nuts. They also recommend that people drink milk or unsweetened fruit and vegetable juices instead of soft drinks and other sugar-sweetened beverages.

Dentists further recommend that children drink water that contains chemical compounds called *fluorides*. Fluorides are absorbed by the enamel as the teeth grow. They help the teeth resist the acid that forms cavities. Some communities have a water supply that naturally contains fluorides. Many other communities add fluorides to the water supply. However, some people oppose *fluoridation* (the addition of fluorides to water supplies). For information on the arguments for and against fluoridation, see FLUORIDATION.

WORLD BOOK diagram by Charles Wellek

Parts of a Tooth

The *crown*, or visible part of a molar tooth, includes projections called *cusps*. The *root* extends into the bone of the jaw. A tissue called *dentin* makes up most of the tooth. A layer of *enamel* covers the dentin of the crown, and *cementum* overlies the dentin of the root. Within the dentin lies the *pulp*, including the *pulp chamber* and the *root canal*, through which blood vessels and nerves enter the tooth. The *periodontal ligament* surrounds the root and holds the tooth in its socket.

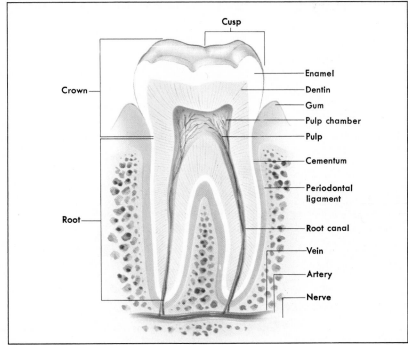

Cusp

Crown

Root

Enamel
Dentin
Gum
Pulp chamber
Pulp
Cementum
Periodontal ligament
Root canal
Vein
Artery
Nerve

TEETH

Fluorides may be applied directly to a child's teeth during a dental checkup. In some cases, dentists prescribe a fluoride substance that children can apply at home. Most dentists also advise children to brush their teeth with a toothpaste that contains fluorides.

Cleaning the Teeth. Dentists advise people to clean their teeth by brushing after every meal and by using *dental floss* once a day. Dental floss is a thin thread that comes in a roll. It is used to clean the areas between teeth and under the gum line. Brushing and flossing remove trapped food particles and *plaque* from the teeth. Plaque is a sticky film that consists of saliva, food particles, and bacteria. The bacteria digest certain foods, particularly sugars, and form an enamel-dissolving acid.

To brush the teeth, you should use a small, soft toothbrush and a toothpaste that contains fluorides. There are several methods of brushing. You should use the one recommended by your dentist. One commonly recommended method is to place the brush against the teeth at a slight angle, with the bristles pointed toward the gums. Brush the upper teeth with a downward, sweeping motion. Brush the lower teeth with an upward, sweeping motion. Clean both the outside and the inside surfaces of the teeth in this way. Use a scrubbing motion to clean the biting surfaces of the premolars and molars. Lastly, brush the tongue to remove food particles and bacteria, which contribute to bad mouth odors. Then rinse the mouth thoroughly. Rinsing with water is just as effective as rinsing with mouthwash.

To floss the teeth, cut a piece of floss about 18 inches (46 centimeters) long from the roll. Wrap one end of the floss around each middle finger. Using the index fingers and thumbs, gently guide the floss between two teeth. Then pull the floss up and down, cleaning the sides of both teeth and the areas around the gum line. Repeat this procedure on all the teeth.

Some people use *disclosing tablets* to determine if any areas of the teeth remain unclean after brushing and flossing. Disclosing tablets contain a red or purple dye. When you chew a tablet, the dye sticks to any unclean areas of the teeth. You can then rebrush and refloss these spots. You can obtain disclosing tablets from your dentist.

Dental Checkups. Dentists advise people to have a dental checkup at least once a year. Children should start going to a dentist after all their deciduous teeth have erupted. Dentists can recognize and treat diseases of the teeth and gums at an early stage, before the diseases cause serious damage. Dentists also provide services that help prevent diseases of the teeth and gums. Many dentists employ a licensed *dental hygienist* to help them in their work.

During a checkup, the dentist looks at the teeth, gums, and other tissues inside the mouth for signs of diseases. The dentist—or the dental hygienist—also X-rays the teeth. X rays can show the location of dental decay that cannot be seen. They also show any abnormal conditions of the jawbones and other tissues that support the teeth. After reviewing the X rays, the dentist may decide to fill cavities or plan other treat-

How to Brush Your Teeth Use a small, soft toothbrush and a toothpaste that contains fluorides. Place the brush against the teeth at a slight angle, with the bristles pointed toward the gums. The illustrations below show one of the brushing methods commonly recommended by dentists.

WORLD BOOK diagrams by Charles Wellek

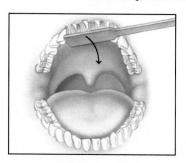

Outside Surfaces of Upper Teeth. Use a downward, sweeping motion.

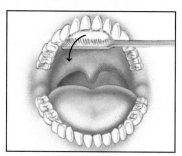

Inside Surfaces of Upper Teeth. Use a downward, sweeping motion.

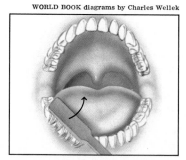

Outside Surfaces of Lower Teeth. Use an upward, sweeping motion.

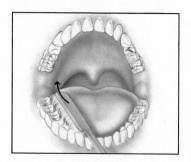

Inside Surfaces of Lower Teeth. Use an upward, sweeping motion.

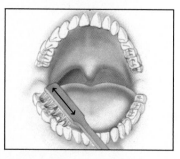

Biting Surfaces of Premolars and Molars. Scrub back and forth.

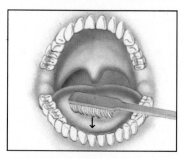

The Tongue. Brush to remove food particles and bacteria.

68b

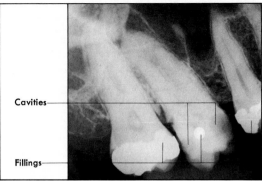

Cavities

Fillings

Patrick D. Toto

An X Ray of the Teeth shows the location of cavities and fillings. Cavities appear as dark spots on the teeth. Fillings show up as distinct white areas.

ment. The dentist or hygienist then cleans the teeth to remove plaque and *calculus*, a hard, yellowish substance formed by the buildup of plaque. Calculus is also called *tartar*. After the teeth have been cleaned, a fluoride substance is applied to help the teeth resist decay. Generally, only children and teen-agers receive applications of fluorides. Lastly, the dentist or hygienist may instruct the patient on how to brush and floss the teeth properly.

Diseases and Defects of the Teeth

Dental decay, also called *caries*, is the most common disease of the teeth. Most people under the age of 35 who lose their teeth do so because of dental decay. A defect in the position of the teeth, called *malocclusion*, is also a common problem among young people. Diseases of the gums and alveolus, called *periodontal diseases*, are the chief dental problem of people over the age of 35. A less common but very severe disease is *oral cancer*, which kills about 8,000 people in the United States each year. The following discussion describes the causes and treatment of (1) dental decay, (2) malocclusion, (3) periodontal diseases, and (4) oral cancer.

Dental Decay is a complex process that involves plaque, bacteria, and food. Saliva produces an invisible film on the teeth. Bacteria and food particles stick to this film, forming plaque. The bacteria digest the *carbohydrates* (sugars and starches) in food and produce an acid. The acid dissolves enamel, causing a cavity. If the cavity is not treated, the decay will progress through the enamel and into the dentin. When the decay reaches the pulp, a toothache results.

The *occlusal* (biting) surfaces of the premolars and molars tend to decay easily because they have many small pits, which trap food. On the other hand, the surfaces of the incisors and canines are smooth. These surfaces do not trap food and so do not decay as easily.

Dentists have several methods of treating dental decay, depending on the severity. The most common methods include (1) filling a cavity, (2) performing root canal therapy, (3) crowning a tooth, and (4) removing and replacing teeth. Before beginning any of these procedures, the dentist usually injects an *anesthetic* (painkilling drug) into the gums near the nerves of the tooth.

Filling a Cavity. To fill a cavity, the dentist first removes the decayed and soft parts of the tooth, using small hand instruments or an electric drill. The dentist

then makes tiny undercuts or ledges in the hole with a high-speed drill. These undercuts help hold the filling, which is not adhesive.

In most cases, dentists fill cavities with *silver amalgam* or gold. Silver amalgam consists of silver and a small amount of copper and tin. To fill the front teeth, dentists sometimes use a plasticlike material that closely resembles the color of natural teeth. But this material is not as hard as silver amalgam or gold, and so it is seldom used to fill the back teeth.

The filling is packed into the hole and allowed to harden slightly. The dentist then carves the filling to restore the original shape of the tooth.

Performing Root Canal Therapy. Root canal therapy is the removal of the pulp of a tooth. It is performed if the pulp has become infected. When decay extends into the pulp, a small sac of pus, called an *abscess*, may form. An abscess can be extremely painful. If it is not treated, infection may spread to other parts of the body.

To perform root canal therapy, the dentist first anesthetizes the area and then drills a hole into the crown of the tooth. The dentist uses small files to reach through the hole and clean out the pulp. After removing the pulp, the dentist fills the empty space, usually with a rubberlike substance called *gutta-percha*. Sometimes,

Filling a Cavity

These illustrations show how a dentist fills a cavity. The dentist usually begins by injecting a drug called an *anesthetic* into the gums near the tooth. The anesthetic prevents the patient from feeling the pain that drilling might produce.

WORLD BOOK diagrams by Charles Wellek

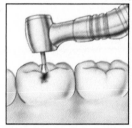

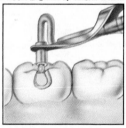

Drilling. The dentist uses a drill to remove decayed and soft parts of the tooth and to form undercuts or ledges that will help hold the filling.

Filling. An instrument is used to place filling material into the hole. Silver amalgam, made from silver, copper, and tin, is a commonly used filling.

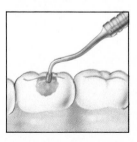

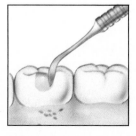

Packing. Using another instrument, the dentist firmly packs the filling into the hole. The filling is then allowed to harden slightly.

Shaping. The dentist carefully carves the filling to restore the original shape of the tooth. Finally, the dentist smooths down any rough edges.

the hole in the crown of the tooth is then filled. But in the majority of cases, the tooth must be fitted with an artificial crown.

Crowning a Tooth. Crowns are toothlike caps that may be made of metal, porcelain, or plastic. They are used when the natural crown of a tooth is so badly damaged that it does not have enough healthy tissue to hold a filling.

To crown a tooth, the dentist first anesthetizes the area and then prepares the natural crown by grinding it down slightly. Next, the dentist covers the prepared tooth and the teeth next to it with a jellylike material. After this material hardens, it is removed from the patient's mouth and serves as an *impression* (mold). The dentist also makes an impression of the teeth in the opposite jaw that press against the prepared tooth and the teeth next to it. The impressions are used to make a plaster reproduction of the prepared tooth and other teeth. Dental technicians then produce a crown, using the plaster reproduction as a model. They must make sure that the crown not only fits the prepared tooth but also fits in place with the other teeth.

Meanwhile, a temporary crown is placed on the tooth. When the permanent crown is ready, the dentist

Crowning a Tooth

A crown is a toothlike cap made of metal, porcelain, or plastic, which is cemented onto a damaged tooth. It is used when a damaged crown does not have enough healthy tissue to hold a filling.

WORLD BOOK diagrams by Charles Wellek

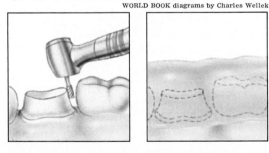

Preparing the Tooth. The dentist uses a drill to remove damaged parts of the tooth and to shape the tooth so that a crown will fit over it.

Making a Mold. The teeth are covered with a gel that forms a mold. Plaster teeth made in this mold serve as models for making the crown.

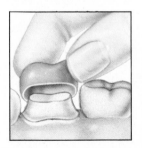

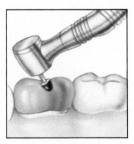

Cementing the Crown. The crown must fit the prepared tooth and also fit in place with the teeth next to it and those in the opposite jaw.

Final Fitting. The dentist may use a small grinding stone to make minor adjustments in the crown so that it will fit properly.

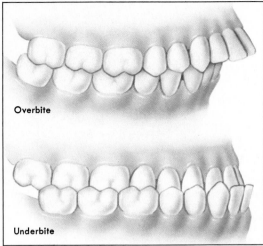

WORLD BOOK diagrams by Charles Wellek

Malocclusion is the failure of the upper and lower teeth to meet properly when a person bites. There are two main kinds of malocclusion, *overbite* and *underbite*. In overbite, the upper front teeth stick out farther than normal over the lower ones. In underbite, the lower front teeth extend in front of the upper ones.

removes the temporary crown and cements the permanent one onto the tooth.

Removing and Replacing Teeth. In severe cases of dental decay, a dentist may remove one or more teeth and replace them with artificial ones. But artificial teeth do not function as well as natural teeth. Dentists therefore remove teeth only if no other method of treatment is considered possible.

To remove a tooth, a dentist first anesthetizes the area. The dentist uses an instrument that resembles a pliers to grip the crown of the tooth and loosen the root from the socket. Both the crown and the root are then removed. After the gums heal, the patient can be fitted with an artificial tooth.

Artificial teeth are made from impressions taken of the patient's mouth. In most cases, the teeth are made of plastic. The most common types of artificial teeth are *bridges*, *partial dentures*, and *full dentures*. Bridges are permanently fixed in the mouth, but partial dentures and full dentures are removable. Bridges are used when only a few teeth are missing. They consist of one or more artificial teeth with a metal or porcelain crown on each side. The crowns fit over the adjoining natural teeth, which must be prepared to hold the crowns. Partial dentures are also used to replace only a few missing teeth. A partial denture has metal clasps that hook around nearby teeth and hold the denture in place. Full dentures are used when all the teeth of one or both jaws are missing. In a full denture, the artificial teeth are attached to a plastic base that fits over the ridge left after the teeth have been removed. In the upper jaw, the plastic base also covers the roof of the mouth.

Malocclusion is the failure of the teeth in the upper and lower jaws to meet properly when a person bites. Normally, the upper front teeth should slightly overlap the lower front teeth. There are two main types of malocclusion, *overbite* and *underbite*. In overbite, the upper front teeth stick out too far over the lower front teeth. This defect is commonly called *buck teeth*. In underbite,

How Braces Work Braces consist of a system of metal bands and wires. The bands are placed around each tooth and connected by wires, *left*. A spring wire is tightened periodically, forcing the irregularly positioned tooth to move. In time, the tooth moves into its correct position, *right*.

WORLD BOOK diagrams by Charles Wellek

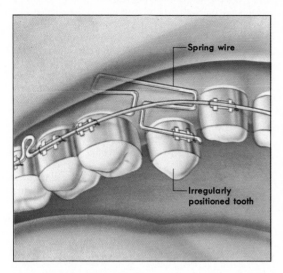

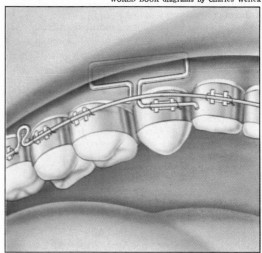

the lower front teeth extend in front of the upper ones. Many people have the correct *occlusion* (bite), but their teeth are crowded.

Malocclusion has various causes. In some cases, a deciduous tooth falls out before a permanent tooth is ready to erupt. The nearby teeth then gradually move into the open space and prevent the permanent tooth from erupting in the correct position. In other cases, the permanent teeth are too large for the jaw and crowd one another. The edges of some teeth may then overlap, or one tooth may grow above another. In still other cases, the jaws do not grow properly.

Malocclusion prevents the teeth from functioning normally when a person chews food. It also may affect the way a person speaks. In addition, malocclusion contributes to the development of dental decay and periodontal diseases, partly because irregularly positioned teeth are hard to clean.

Most cases of malocclusion can be corrected with *orthodontic bands*, commonly called *braces*. Braces consist of metal bands that are placed around each tooth and connected by wires. The wires are tightened periodically to force the teeth to move into the correct position. But the teeth must be moved slowly, and so the treatment may take a year or more. In some cases, one or more teeth must be removed to allow enough space for the others to move into a normal position.

Periodontal Diseases are caused chiefly by the buildup of plaque and calculus between the gums and teeth. The plaque and calculus irritate the gums, causing them to become inflamed. In time, the jawbones may become infected. The best way to prevent plaque from building up under the gum line is by flossing daily. The gums can also become irritated by habitually breathing through the mouth, smoking or chewing tobacco, brushing improperly, or wearing ill-fitting dentures. In addition, irregularly positioned teeth can irritate the gums. There are three main kinds of periodontal diseases: (1) gingivitis, (2) periodontitis, and (3) Vincent's infection.

Gingivitis is an inflammation of the *gingivae* (gums). The gingivae become red and swollen and bleed easily when brushed or prodded. Dentists treat gingivitis by cleaning the teeth and gums to remove plaque and calculus. They also instruct patients on how to brush and floss the teeth and on how to massage the gums. If gingivitis is not treated, it can lead to periodontitis.

Periodontitis, also called *pyorrhea*, is a severe infection of the gingivae, alveolus, and other tissues that support the teeth. The infection gradually destroys the bony walls of the sockets, and the teeth become loose. Periodontitis is difficult to cure. Treatment may involve surgical removal of the damaged tissues and repair of the remaining healthy tissues. Sometimes, loose teeth can be *splinted* (attached) to nearby teeth that are still

Periodontal Diseases

The illustrations below show two kinds of periodontal diseases. In *gingivitis*, calculus builds up between gums and teeth, causing the gums to become inflamed. Gingivitis may lead to *periodontitis*, an infection that gradually destroys the bony socket.

WORLD BOOK diagrams by Charles Wellek

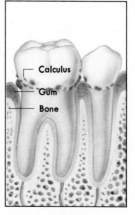

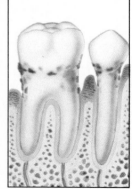

Gingivitis   **Periodontitis**

TEETH

firm. But in many cases, the loose teeth must be removed and replaced by artificial ones.

Vincent's Infection, also called *trench mouth*, is a painful infection of the gingivae. The gums become red and swollen and bleed easily. The mouth has an extremely bad odor, and the victim may develop a fever. To treat Vincent's infection, a dentist cleans the teeth and gums thoroughly and instructs the patient on mouth care. In most cases, the dentist also prescribes antibiotics to combat the infection.

Oral Cancer is a disease that destroys the tissues of the mouth and may spread to other parts of the body. Scientists do not know for certain what causes oral cancer. But many factors can contribute to its development. For example, people who smoke or chew tobacco, drink excessive amounts of alcoholic beverages, or wear ill-fitting dentures increase the risk of developing oral cancer.

Oral cancer may be painless and unnoticeable in its early stages. The first symptom may be a small sore in the mouth that does not heal. To test for cancer, a dentist removes some tissue from the sore. The tissue is examined under a microscope to determine if it is cancerous. Oral cancer may be treated with drugs, radiation, or surgery.

Teeth of Animals

Many kinds of animals have teeth. However, birds, toads, turtles, and some types of insects and whales do not have teeth.

Cats, dogs, and most other mammals have *heterodont teeth*—that is, they have at least two types of teeth, which have different uses. For example, they may have incisors for biting into food and molars for crushing or grinding food.

The teeth of various kinds of mammals differ in shape and size, depending chiefly on what the animals eat. For example, plant-eating mammals, such as elephants, giraffes, and sheep, have unusually broad, flat molars. They use the molars to chew and mash plants. Meat-eating mammals, such as lions, tigers, and wolves, have long, pointed canines. They use the canines to rip and tear the bodies of their prey.

Some mammals have teeth that grow continuously. The tusks of elephants are actually incisors that have become very long. The tusks have an open pulp, which enables them to keep growing. Beavers, rats, and other rodents also have teeth that grow continuously. But most of the growth is worn down by continual use of the teeth, and so the teeth do not lengthen greatly.

Unlike most mammals, many fish and most reptiles have *homodont teeth*—that is, all their teeth are about the same size and shape and have only one use. In general, animals that have homodont teeth use their teeth to catch prey. Fish and reptiles lose and replace their teeth continuously.

Snakes have teeth that curve back toward the throat. Snakes swallow their prey whole and use their teeth to pull the prey back into the throat. In poisonous snakes, certain teeth have a canal or a groove, through which poison can be ejected. The poison comes from glands in the roof of the mouth. JOHN P. WORTEL

Some Animal Teeth Animal teeth vary in size and shape. Most mammals have *heterodont teeth*, which consist of two or more types: incisors and canines for biting and tearing food, and molars for crushing it. Most reptiles and many fish have *homodont teeth*, a single type that generally is used to catch prey.

WORLD BOOK diagrams by Patricia J. Wynne

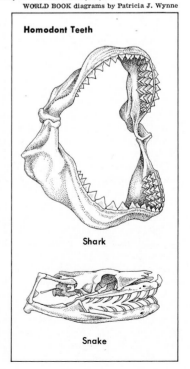

Heterodont Teeth

Lion

Incisors

Molars   Canines

Molars

Incisors

Elephant

Molars   Incisors

Bison

Homodont Teeth

Shark

Snake

Related Articles in WORLD BOOK include:

HUMAN TEETH

Abscess	Mouth
Dental Hygiene	Orthodontics
Dentistry	Periodontitis
Digestion (From Mouth	Races, Human (picture:
to Stomach)	The Upper Front Teeth)
Fluoridation	Saliva
Fluorine	Toothpaste and Toothpowder
Mastication	Trench Mouth

ANIMAL TEETH

Animal (Jaws and	Hog (Teeth)
Teeth)	Horse (Teeth)
Beaver (Teeth)	Insect (Mouth Parts)
Cat (The Body of a Cat)	Lion (The Body of a Lion)
Cattle (Teeth)	Mammal (What
Dog (Body Structure)	Mammals Eat)
Elephant (Tusks	Rodent
and Teeth)	Ruminant
Fish (Digestive System)	Shark (Teeth and Scales)
Hippopotamus	Snake (Skeleton)
(The Body of a River	Whale (picture: Toothed
Hippopotamus)	Whales)

Outline

I. Kinds of Teeth
  A. Deciduous Teeth
  B. Permanent Teeth
II. Parts of a Tooth
  A. Pulp
  B. Dentin
  C. Enamel
  D. Cementum
  E. Periodontal Ligament
III. Care of the Teeth and Gums
  A. A Good Diet
  B. Cleaning the Teeth
  C. Dental Checkups
IV. Diseases and Defects of the Teeth
  A. Dental Decay
  B. Malocclusion
  C. Periodontal Diseases
  D. Oral Cancer
V. Teeth of Animals

Questions

How often should the teeth be brushed?

What are the incisors and canines used for? The molars and premolars?

What are the four kinds of tissues that make up a tooth?

When should children start going to a dentist?

What are some of the causes of malocclusion?

When does dental decay result in a toothache?

How does eating sugary foods contribute to dental decay?

What is dental floss used for?

What does the periodontal ligament do?

What is the chief cause of periodontal diseases?

Additional Resources

Level I
BARR, GEORGE. *Young Scientist and Dentist.* McGraw, 1970. Explains the technical aspects of dentistry.
LANTNER, MINNA, and BENDER, GERALD. *Understanding Dentistry.* Beacon Press, 1969.

Level II
GOLDBERG, HYMAN J. V., and others. *Your Mouth Is Your Business: The Dentists' Guide to Better Health.* Appleton, 1980.
GUERINI, VINCENZO. *History of Dentistry from the Most Ancient Times Until the End of the Eighteenth Century.* Longwood, 1977.
HOLT, ROBERT LAWRENCE. *Straight Teeth: Orthodontics and Dental Care for Everyone.* Morrow, 1980.

MARSHALL, HOWARD B. *How to Save Your Teeth: The Preventive Approach.* Everest House, 1980.
WOODFORDE, JOHN. *The Strange Story of False Teeth.* Universe Books, 1970.

TEGU, *tuh YOO,* or TEJU, is the common name for a few species of South American lizards. They are large, strong, and swift. They burrow in sand or under rocks, and eat small animals such as insects. Tegus hatch their young from eggs. The largest tegus are over 3 feet (91 centimeters) long. Tegus are bluish-black with crosswise yellow stripes above. Their underparts are yellowish.

Scientific Classification. Tegus belong to the New World lizard family, *Teiidae.*   CLIFFORD H. POPE

TEGUCIGALPA, *tuh GOO suh GAL puh* (pop. 267,754), is the capital of Honduras. The city's Indian name means *Silver Hill.* It lies on a fertile plain along the Choluteca River and is about 78 miles (126 kilometers) from the Gulf of Fonseca, an arm of the Pacific. For location, see HONDURAS (map). Mountains surround the city. Tegucigalpa is the center of a well-populated and rich farming and mining area. Important buildings include the cathedral and the National University. See also HONDURAS (picture).   ROLLIN S. ATWOOD

TEHERAN, *teh uh RAHN* (pop. 4,716,000), also spelled *Tehran,* is the capital of Iran and the second largest city in the Middle East. Only Cairo, the capital of Egypt, has more people. Teheran is Iran's cultural, economic, and political center. It lies in northern Iran, at the foot of the Elburz Mountains (see IRAN [map]).

The City. Teheran is one of the most modern cities in the Middle East. Large parts of it have been built or rebuilt since the 1920's. The city has many wide boulevards, which are lined with tall, modern buildings of

Marge Kathan

Teheran, the capital of Iran, is one of the most modern cities in the Middle East. The main street of downtown Teheran, *above,* is lined by office and government buildings and fashionable shops.

Western-style architecture. The major business and government buildings and most of Teheran's fashionable shops are near the center of the city. In the same area is an old business section where merchants sell fabrics, jewelry, and other handmade products at a bazaar that is hundreds of years old.

Most of Teheran's middle-class residents live in apartment buildings. Large numbers of poor people live in run-down apartments and houses in the southern part of Teheran. Many wealthy people live in large, beautiful houses north of the city.

Teheran has many parks and theaters. Its museums include the Archaeological and Ethnological museums and the Golestan Palace, which feature many treasures from Iran's past. The city has several universities, the largest of which is the University of Teheran.

Economy. The Iranian government employs many of Teheran's people. The city's industries include banking, construction, and petroleum processing. Teheran manufactures bricks, cigarettes, textiles, and other products.

Buses and taxis provide public transportation in Teheran. An international airport lies west of the city.

History. People probably lived on the site of what is now Teheran at least 3,000 years ago. Teheran was a small town until the 1200's, when it began to grow. The city became the capital of Iran in 1788.

During the 1920's, many of Teheran's old buildings were torn down and replaced by new ones. The city's population has increased from about 1,800,000 in 1960 to more than 4,700,000. This rapid growth caused such problems as a housing shortage, pollution, and traffic jams. In the 1970's, the government began a number of construction projects to provide more residential and office buildings in Teheran. Much of the construction stopped in 1979, after revolutionaries took control of Iran's government. Manufacturing and other economic activities in the city decreased after the revolution (see IRAN [Recent Events]). MALCOLM C. PECK

TEHERAN CONFERENCE, held in 1943 in Teheran, Iran, was the first meeting of the leaders of the United States, Great Britain, and Russia. U.S. President Franklin D. Roosevelt, British Prime Minister Winston Churchill, and Russian Premier Joseph Stalin held meetings that lasted from November 28 to December 1.

At this conference, the three Allied nations bound themselves together to crush the military might of Germany. The Declaration of Teheran stated, in part, that the three Allied nations "shall work together in the war and in the peace." It also stated the desire to build "a world of democratic nations." But even before the end of World War II, Soviet leaders began betraying the Teheran agreements. By 1945, Russia began setting up dictatorships in Europe and Asia. PAYSON S. WILD

TEHRAN. See TEHERAN.

TEHUANTEPEC, *tay wahn tay PEK*, **ISTHMUS OF,** forms the narrowest part of Mexico. It lies between the Bay of Campeche and the Gulf of Tehuantepec, and includes parts of the states of Veracruz and Oaxaca. For location, see MEXICO (physical map). The isthmus has large petroleum and sulfur deposits. It measures 130 miles (209 kilometers) wide at its narrowest point. Most of the land is tropical lowland. Foothills of the Sierra Madre mountains rise in the south. JOHN A. CROW

TEILHARD DE CHARDIN, PIERRE (1881-1955), was a French *paleontologist* (expert in fossils). He helped discover Peking man, an early type of human being. Teilhard's greatest fame, however, rests on a theory that claims to unify cosmic evolution and Christianity.

Teilhard entered the Jesuit order in 1899 and was ordained a priest in 1911. He lectured for a time at the Catholic Institute in Paris. His theory of evolution in relation to the Catholic doctrine of original sin in his lectures was considered unorthodox. As a result, church authorities forbade him to continue teaching in Paris. Teilhard then lived in China from 1923 to 1946, where he was a consultant to the National Geological Survey. He began his fossil research in 1923. Teilhard wrote extensively while in China, but most of his writings were controversial and were not published until after his death.

According to Teilhard, "Evolution is a general condition to which all theories, all hypotheses, all systems must bow and which they must satisfy if they are to be thinkable and true." He placed humanity at the center of the universe and Christianity at the center of human history. Some theologians welcome Teilhard's extreme optimism as a balance to the fear and discouragement in the world. His best-known works include *The Phenomenon of Man* and *The Divine Milieu.* JOHN A. HARDON

TEJU. See TEGU.

TEKTITE is a glassy stone that may look like a teardrop, ball, disk, rod, dumbbell, or button. A few tektites are blocklike in appearance. Many tektites are nutsized, but some are microscopic. Tektites are black, green, or amber, and they usually have grooved or pitted surfaces.

Some scientists think that tektites were formed when giant meteorites crashed into deposits of sandstone and other sedimentary rock on the earth's surface. Fragments of such rocks were melted by the heat of the impact and scattered over great distances. They solidified in flight and fell back to the earth as tektites. Other scientists have developed an entirely different theory about tektites. They believe tektites are the remains of lava masses that were hurled to the earth by volcanoes on the moon from 750,000 to 35 million years ago. The liquefied rock materials that were ejected during the violent eruptions solidified into stony glass on the way to the earth. JOHN A. O'KEEFE

TEL AVIV-YAFO, *TEHL uh VEEV YAH foh* (pop. 367,600; met. area pop. 1,180,700), is the largest city of Israel and the nation's chief commercial and industrial center. It is one of the most modern cities in the Middle East. Tel Aviv-Yafo lies on the eastern shore of the Mediterranean Sea. For location, see ISRAEL (map).

The heart of Tel Aviv-Yafo is a major downtown intersection called Dizengoff Circle. Fashionable shops and sidewalk cafes line the nearby streets. The 37-story Shalom Tower stands in the center of the city's financial district, several blocks south of Dizengoff Circle. It is the tallest building in Israel. The southwestern section of the city was formerly a separate town called *Jaffa* (*Yafo* in Hebrew). Jaffa, an ancient port area that dates back to Biblical times, has many historic sites that have been restored by archaeologists. Jaffa also has many art galleries, cafes, restaurants, and nightclubs. Most of the people of Tel Aviv-Yafo live in apartment buildings.

Israel Press & Photo Agency

Israel's Tallest Building, the Shalom Tower, stands at the end of a busy street in Tel Aviv-Yafo. The skyscraper has business offices, shops, a department store, and a restaurant.

Cultural attractions in Tel Aviv-Yafo include the Museum Haaretz and the Tel Aviv Museum. Tel Aviv University is one of the city's several institutions of higher learning. Bar Ilan University is in Ramat Gan, a suburb.

Tel Aviv-Yafo is the center of Israel's chief manufacturing district. About half the nation's business companies are in the area. Their products include building materials, chemicals, clothing, electronic equipment, machine tools, and processed foods. The city is also the nation's leading center for such activities as banking, publishing, and trade. Israel's political parties have their headquarters in Tel Aviv-Yafo.

In 1909, Jewish immigrants from Europe founded Tel Aviv northeast of Jaffa. Tel Aviv was administered as part of Jaffa at first, but it became a separate town in 1921. Tel Aviv grew rapidly as Jewish immigrants poured in, mainly from Europe. It became Israel's first capital when the nation was established in 1948. The capital was moved to Jerusalem in 1949, but the Israeli Ministry of Defense and many foreign embassies remained in Tel Aviv. In 1950, Tel Aviv and Jaffa merged to form Tel Aviv-Yafo.

Tel Aviv-Yafo continued to grow rapidly in the 1950's and early 1960's. Its population reached about 392,100 in 1965 and then began to decline, but the suburban population continued to rise. The rapid growth of the Tel Aviv-Yafo area resulted in such problems as air pollution, slums, and traffic jams. SAUL B. COHEN

See also ISRAEL (picture); JAFFA.

TELECOMMUNICATION is the transmission and reception of messages over long distances. Visual signaling with flags, lamps, or smoke was the earliest form of telecommunication. Today, the term refers to a wide variety of electrical and electronic communication sys-

tems that transmit information throughout the world. Modern telecommunication systems send and receive sound, printed materials, and visual images in a fraction of a second.

Common telecommunication systems include telephones, television sets, and radios. Other kinds of systems are used chiefly in industry. These systems can transmit such information as airline reservations, banking transactions, and stock market reports. Newspapers rely on teletypewriter and telephoto equipment to obtain news stories and photographs from all parts of the world. Communication between space stations and the earth also has been established through telecommunication.

Most telecommunication systems transmit messages by wire, radio, or satellite. Many telegraph messages and telephone conversations, especially local calls, travel over wires that are laid underground in cables. Cables on the ocean floor handle such communications that travel overseas. Television and radio broadcasts are sent through the air by radio waves. Radio waves called *microwaves* transmit television signals over extremely long distances. Microwaves are also used in most long-distance telephone communication. Communications satellites orbiting the earth transmit telephone, television, and other communications signals throughout the world.

There are two methods of telecommunication transmission, *analogue transmission* and *digital transmission*. Analogue transmission uses signals that are exact reproductions of the sound or picture being transmitted. For example, an analogue telephone system transmits an electric current that copies the pattern of sound waves of the speaker's voice. This current travels over wire and is converted back to sound waves in the telephone receiver.

In digital transmission, the signals are converted into a code. In most cases, the code has two elements, such as the dot-dash of Morse code or the on-off flashing of a light. In one type of digital telephone system, the coded signals are transmitted by a rapidly flashing beam of light and are decoded in the receiver. A device called a *laser* produces the light, which travels through thin strands of glass called *optical fibers*.

The light in the system flashes on and off about 45 million times per second. This high rate enables two optical fibers to carry almost 700 telephone conversations at the same time. It would take about 60 copper wires to handle as many conversations. Digital transmission also involves less noise and distortion than an analogue system. Many telecommunication systems are being converted from analogue to digital transmission. SOLOMON J. BUCHSBAUM

Related Articles in WORLD BOOK include:

Cable	Electromagnetic	Radio
Coaxial Cable	Waves	Telegraph
Communication	Electronics	Telemetry
(The Development	Facsimile	Telephone
of Modern	Fiber Optics	Telephoto
Communication;	International	Teletypesetter
pictures)	Telecommunica-	Teletypewriter
Communications	tion Union	Television
Satellite	Microwave	

TELEGRAM. See TELEGRAPH.

TELEGRAPH

TELEGRAPH, *TEL uh graf*, was the first method used to send messages by electricity. At one time, most telegraph messages were sent by tapping out words letter by letter with a telegraph key. The telegraph changed the dots and dashes of the Morse code into electrical impulses and sent them over telegraph wires. For more than 40 years in the 1800's, the telegraph was the fastest means of long-distance communication.

The telephone and other methods of communication have replaced the telegraph for some purposes. But the telegraph still is important. Telegraph circuits stretch around the world, over land and water, and by cable under the seas. Businesses depend on the telegraph to get in touch quickly and cheaply with faraway customers and salespeople. Many persons send telegraph messages to friends and relatives on special occasions.

Today, machines called *teleprinters, Teletypes,* or *facsimile machines* are used to send most telegraph messages. The teleprinter has a keyboard that looks much like that of a regular typewriter. The operator sends a message by typing it. A printing device at the receiving end automatically types the message on paper.

The word *telegraph* comes from the Greek words *tele,* which means *afar,* and *graphein,* meaning *to write.* Telegraph messages are called *telegrams* or *wires* if they travel over land circuits. They are called *cablegrams* or *cables* if they go by underwater cables.

Sending a Telegram

A person can send a telegram by telephoning the message to the Central Telephone Bureau of the telegraph company serving his area of the country. There are three such bureaus in the United States. Or a person may go to a local telegraph office and write the message on a form provided there. But most telegrams are sent and received by business firms over direct wires to the telegraph office. The cost of a telegram depends on how quickly it must be delivered, on the number of words to be sent, and on whether it is for delivery within the same state or to another state.

Kinds of Telegrams vary according to the sender's needs. *Fast Telegrams* are transmitted and delivered as soon as possible. A minimum fee is charged for the first 15 words, and an extra fee for each additional word.

Overnight Telegrams are delivered the day after being given to the telegraph office for sending. A minimum rate is charged for the first 100 words, and an extra fee for each additional word.

Personal Opinion Messages are 15-word messages sent to elected federal or state officials at special rates. A person might send such a telegram to a member of Congress, for example, urging support of a certain bill.

Transmitting the Message. A message telephoned to a Central Telephone Bureau is recorded on a *cathode-ray tube,* a device that produces the transmitted message on a screen. After the sender has finished dictating the telegram, an operator at the Central Telephone Bureau depresses a key to transmit the telegram to a computer. The computer instantly routes the message to the circuit serving the point of destination. A message written out at a telegraph office is transmitted on a teleprinter. The operator types the message on a keyboard, and it is then sent to a computer for transmission to the city or town of the receiver.

After reaching the city or town, a telegram may be telephoned or delivered to the receiver. In some cases, a message is sent over a direct wire to a machine in the office of the person receiving the message.

A telegram sent from one area of the United States to another is routed through a computer center at Middletown, Va. The computer center automatically receives telegrams, determines their destinations, and speeds them on their way. The center also serves Canada, Mexico, and overseas locations.

Carrier systems of wire transmission are used for intercity circuits. These systems make it possible to send several hundred messages at the same time over a single pair of wires (see TELEPHONE [How a Telephone Call Travels]). When radio transmission is used, the messages travel by microwave radio beams relayed along a line of towers spaced about 30 miles (48 kilometers) apart.

Special Services. Special telegraph services are available for different purposes. For example, money can be telegraphed by *money order.* The rates are the same as those for a fast or overnight telegram, plus a money-order fee. Flowers, candy, and dolls also may be ordered by wire.

Telegrams are sent and received in picture form by a process called facsimile (see FACSIMILE). Drawings, handwriting, and other kinds of data can also be sent by facsimile. *Wire-Fax* is a public facsimile service available in major cities in the United States.

The telegraph company provides teleprinters and facsimile machines for many business firms and government agencies. This equipment provides a direct link between several plants, factories, or offices so telegrams can be sent or received at any time. A small desk-top facsimile machine called *Desk-Fax* is widely used in offices.

Companies and government agencies also lease various kinds of *private-wire systems.* The largest of these systems, called *Autodin,* handles data for the U.S. Department of Defense. A *bank wire* links large banks in all parts of the United States. Large brokerage firms have private-wire systems to flash stock prices and orders to buy and sell stocks across the nation.

Telex and *TWX* are interconnected two-way dial teleprinter services. Subscribers to either service can con-

Samuel Morse, *left,* developed the first successful telegraph in the United States. He demonstrated his first set, *right,* in 1837. It had an electromagnet that caused a pen to make V-shaped marks on paper. Shortly afterward, Morse developed the Morse Code, a system of sending messages by dots and dashes.

An Early Telegraph used in England, *above,* had two dials with needles and letters. The needles pointed to each letter in the words being sent.

A Later Telegraph, *above,* had a key by which a telegrapher sent dot-dash messages. A sounder above the key clicked out incoming messages.

tact other subscribers by interconnection through the computer center. The two networks together operate 100,000 terminal stations in the United States, Canada, and Mexico.

Mailgram is a communication service developed by Western Union and the U.S. Postal Service. Bills and other messages sent by Mailgram arrive sooner than letters and cost less than telegrams. Mailgrams are sent by Telex or TWX customers from their terminals, or by the general public through the central telephone bureaus. Some can be filed on a magnetic tape produced by a customer's computer. Mailgrams are sent to teleprinter terminals and delivered the day after they are sent.

Development of the Telegraph

The telegraph revolutionized long-distance communication. Until its invention, messengers served as the chief means of communication at a distance. Other means had been tried, but they were poorly suited to widespread use. Some primitive tribes used fires to signal from hill to hill. In the 1790's, Claude Chappe, a French inventor, established a system of *visual telegraphs* or *semaphores* that relayed messages across France.

The development of an efficient long-distance telegraph waited for discoveries in electricity. In 1820, Hans Christian Oersted (1777-1851) of Denmark found that an electric current can produce a magnetic field that will turn a compass needle. In 1825, William Sturgeon (1783-1850) of England invented the electromagnet. Using these discoveries, three men developed successful telegraphs. These were the physicists William F. Cooke (1806-1879) and Charles Wheatstone (1802-1875), working together in England, and American painter and inventor Samuel F. B. Morse (1791-1872).

Cooke-Wheatstone Telegraph. Cooke and Wheatstone patented a telegraph that worked by electromagnetism in 1837. Their receiving instrument had five or six vertical magnetic needles mounted on a dial on which the letters of the alphabet were printed. A separate wire and coil that served as an electromagnet controlled each needle. A sending device sent an electric current through the wires, producing a magnetic field in the coils. As each letter was sent, the magnetic field caused a needle to point to that letter on the dial. A two-needle model was also developed. The Cooke-Wheatstone telegraph was used in Great Britain until 1870.

The Morse Telegraph. Morse became interested in telegraphy in 1832. Returning to the United States from Europe, he heard a fellow traveler's account of experiments then underway in Europe. Morse completed his first telegraphic device in 1836. Then, he learned about an improved electromagnet developed by the American physicist Joseph Henry. Morse discovered that he could send a signal much farther with it. On Sept. 2, 1837, he sent signals over 1,700 feet (518 meters) of wire. His receiving instrument was an electromagnet that caused a pen to make V-shaped marks on a strip of paper moved by a clock mechanism. A message could be sent by varying the marks to form a code.

Shortly after Morse sent his first message, he made two big improvements. He developed a relay device and the dot-dash code that became known as the Morse code. With the relay devices installed in a telegraph line, messages could be relayed over any desired distance. Morse also developed a system for *embossing,* or marking, his dot-dash code on a strip of paper.

In 1838, Morse's assistant, Alfred Vail, redesigned the telegraph. He also suggested that a sounder be used as the receiving instrument. As finally developed, the Morse telegraph worked much like an electric doorbell. The sending device consisted of a switch, called a *key,* that corresponded to a doorbell button. When pressed, the key completed the telegraph circuit and allowed current to flow to a receiving sounder. In the sounder, the current caused an electromagnet to attract a bar so that it made a clicking noise. When the key was released, it broke the circuit so that no current flowed. This caused the electromagnet in the sounder to lose its magnetism, and a spring pulled the bar back to a neutral position. In this way the code was "keyed and sounded."

Morse patented his invention in 1840, but failed to interest investors in his new device. Then, in 1843, Congress appropriated $30,000 to build a test line between Washington, D.C., and Baltimore, Md. On May 24, 1844, Morse sat at a sending device in the Supreme Court chamber of the Capitol and tapped out the Biblical phrase, "What hath God wrought!" (Numbers 23:23). In Baltimore, Vail received the message and sent it back to Washington. Later that year, Morse's telegraph flashed the news to Washington that the Democratic National Convention, meeting in Baltimore, had nominated James K. Polk for President.

TELEGRAPH

This was one of the first important uses of the telegraph in the United States. Newspapers began to use Morse's invention almost at once, and columns of "telegraph news" appeared. Later, cooperative news-gathering agencies were formed to help share the cost of telegraphed news among many newspapers.

Coast to Coast. Expansion of telegraph lines took place rapidly. By 1846, New York City was linked with Washington, D.C. A few years later, lines connected many other cities. By 1851, over 50 telegraph companies were operating in the United States. On April 4, 1856, 12 of the companies were combined into the Western Union Telegraph Company. This marked the beginning of a unified service for the United States. See WESTERN UNION TELEGRAPH COMPANY.

When the Civil War split the United States in 1861, an intense demand developed for the rapid transmission of news. The U.S. government also needed good communications with the West. In 1861, Western Union extended its telegraph line from Omaha, Nebr., to California. The eastern and western work crews met in Salt Lake City, Utah, on Oct. 24, 1861. That day, Stephen J. Field, chief justice of California, sent the first transcontinental message to President Abraham Lincoln. The message declared California's loyalty to the Union. The transcontinental telegraph ended the pony express, which had operated only about 19 months (see PONY EXPRESS).

Across the Atlantic. The next big development was the laying of a successful transatlantic telegraph cable. The first attempt had failed in 1857 when the cable broke. After three more failures, the *Great Eastern*, the largest ship then afloat, laid the first successful cable in 1866. Credit for the success belonged largely to two men, Cyrus W. Field, an American business promoter, and Lord Kelvin, an English physicist. See CABLE (Development of Undersea Cables).

Faster and Better Service. In 1868, the first practical stock ticker was invented (see STOCK TICKER). Various systems were also developed for sending many messages over one wire. The *duplex system*, which could send two messages over one wire at the same time, went into operation in the United States in 1872. Two years later, Thomas A. Edison developed the *quadruplex system* for sending four messages at the same time. In 1875, Émile Baudot (1845-1903), a French telegrapher, developed a *multiplex system* that could send five messages at once. In 1915, Western Union started using a multiplex system capable of sending eight messages at one time.

Several devices that sent and received messages in printed form, rather than in code, were also developed in the late 1800's and early 1900's. So were methods of sending messages by means of holes punched in paper tape. The multiplex system used a punched-tape method of sending. Starting in 1927, teleprinters were generally adopted. In 1935, the first facsimile telegraph system went into operation between New York City and Buffalo, N.Y.

The Telegraph Industry Today has millions of miles or kilometers of land wire circuits and ocean-cable circuits in operation throughout the world. Extensive systems of microwave-radio circuits also serve the United States and Canada. Because one circuit may provide separate channels for many messages to be sent at the same time, there are actually many additional *channel miles* of telegraph circuits in operation. For example, the

Making a Simple Telegraph Set

Two-way communication can be achieved with two telegraph sets. Each set includes a key, a sounder, and a battery. The key of one set is connected to the sounder of the other. Directions for making a set are given below.

1. The Base of the Set is a flat piece of wood that holds the sounder. First, nail together the wood base, one of the smaller wood blocks, and the T-shaped piece of tin, as shown.

2. The Sounder. Hammer two steel nails into one end of the base. Wind a piece of insulated wire around the nails—about 30 turns for each—to form coils. Connect the coils to the battery with one end of the wire. Leave the other end loose to connect the coils to the key. Hammer a bent aluminum nail next to, but not touching, the T-shaped piece of tin.

3. The Key is the thin strip of metal mounted on one of the small blocks. Push two thumbtacks halfway through the key. Scrape the insulating material from one end of the wire attached to the sounder coils. Wrap the bare wire around the tacks and press down.

4. Bend the Key upward about half an inch from the block. Press the third thumbtack under the raised end. Take a piece of wire and scrape the insulating material from each end. Connect the tack to the battery with the wire. The key should touch the tack when pressed and spring up when released.

5. Touching the Key to the Tack causes electric current to flow through the circuit. Electromagnets pull the metal T on the base down, making a clicking sound. When the key is released, the T springs up and strikes the bent nail, making another clicking sound. These sounds form the dots and dashes of the telegraph code.

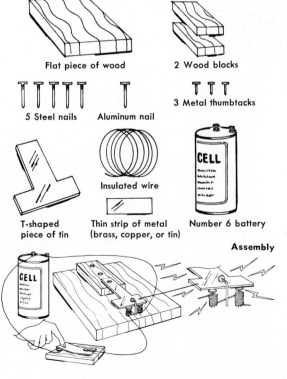

Materials

Flat piece of wood

2 Wood blocks

5 Steel nails   Aluminum nail

3 Metal thumbtacks

Insulated wire

CELL

T-shaped piece of tin

Thin strip of metal (brass, copper, or tin)

Number 6 battery

Assembly

CELL

approximately 1 million miles (1.6 million kilometers) of telegraph circuits in the United States provide about 17 million channel miles (27 million kilometers) of communication circuits. Reports, charts, graphs, weather maps, time signals, and many other types of information flow over these circuits in addition to messages. Leased private-wire systems that are designed for the needs of individual businesses account for a growing share of the telegraph operations in the United States.

In 1979, the Federal Communications Commission voted to end the monopoly over telegraph service that Western Union had held since 1943. This action opened the way for other companies to enter the telegraph business in the United States. In Canada, the telegraph systems are partly privately owned and partly government owned. In most other major countries, the governments own the telegraph systems. EDWIN EMERY

Critically reviewed by WESTERN UNION TELEGRAPH COMPANY

Related Articles. See the Communication sections of the various country articles. Other related articles in WORLD BOOK include:

BIOGRAPHIES

Cornell, Ezra	Kelvin, Lord
Edison, Thomas A.	Morse, Samuel F. B.
Gray, Elisha	Pupin, Michael I.
Henry, Joseph	Wheatstone, Sir Charles

OTHER RELATED ARTICLES

Cable	Morse Code
Common Carrier	Radio (History)
Communication	Radiogram
Electromagnet	Stock Ticker
Facsimile	Telephone
Federal Communications Commission	Teletypewriter
International Telecommunication Union	Western Union Telegraph Company

Outline

I. **Sending a Telegram**
   A. Kinds of Telegrams
   B. Transmitting the Message
   C. Special Services

II. **Development of the Telegraph**

Questions

When is a telegraph message called a *telegram?* A *cablegram?*

What is a *fast telegram?* An *overnight telegram?*

What kind of telegraph system sends telegrams in picture form?

Who developed the telegraph system that used magnetic needles to point out letters on a dial?

What part of the telegraph system developed by Samuel F. B. Morse works like a doorbell button?

What was one of the first important uses of the Morse telegraph?

Where was the first transcontinental telegraph line in the United States completed?

What was the advantage of the *multiplex system* of telegraphy?

What is a teleprinter? How is it used?

What special kinds of messages can be telegraphed?

Additional Resources

COOK, CHERI. *Telephone and Telegraph.* New Readers Press, 1975.

MATH, IRWIN. *Morse, Marconi and You: Understanding and Building Telegraph, Telephone, and Radio Sets.* Scribner, 1979.

WELLS, ROBERT. *Messages, Men and Miles: Electronic Communications, How They Work.* Prentice-Hall, 1959.

TELEGRAPH HILL. See SAN FRANCISCO.

TELEGRAPH PLANT is an herb about 4 feet (1.2 meters) high. It is native to tropical Asia, and grows in greenhouses in many parts of the world. If the plant, or especially its leaves, is touched, the leaves quickly droop downward, like the arms of a railroad semaphore signal. The plant received its common name from these leaf movements. It bears small purple flowers. The seed pods are jointed and can be separated easily.

Scientific Classification. The telegraph plant belongs to the pea family, *Leguminosae.* It is genus *Desmodium,* species *D. motorium.* GEORGE H. M. LAWRENCE

TELEMACHUS. See MENTOR; ODYSSEY; ULYSSES.

TELEMETRY, *tuh LEHM uh tree,* means *measuring at a distance.* Scientists and engineers use telemetry in many ways. Scientists send weather balloons as high as 20 or 30 miles (32 or 48 kilometers) into the air to measure the air temperature, pressure, and humidity above the earth. Radios attached to the balloons relay this information back to the earth.

Telemetry also helps people explore outer space. Rockets and spacecraft send information about their own performance and conditions in outer space to scientists and engineers on the earth. On manned flights, telemetry systems provide data on astronauts' physical condition by reporting their pulse rate, blood pressure, and temperature. To save space and weight, special miniature equipment is used in spacecraft.

Telemetry systems have three parts. One part is the measuring instrument. In temperature measurement, the measuring instrument is an electrical thermometer. The second part is the transmission link. In most systems, this part consists of signals sent along wires or through space by radio. The third part is an *indicator* that changes the signals into readings at the receiving station. These readings are usually recorded on a strip of paper or magnetic tape. IRA M. FREEMAN

TELEOLOGY. See MECHANIST PHILOSOPHY.

TELEOST. See FISH (Modern Bony Fish).

TELEPATHY, *tuh LEHP uh thee,* is the communication of thoughts, feelings, or knowledge from one person to another without the use of the senses of hearing, sight, smell, taste, or touch. Telepathy is sometimes called *mind reading* or *thought transference.* An example of telepathy would be if one person thought of something specific, such as "12 plus 12 equal 24," and another person stated or wrote the thought correctly. But to be telepathic, the performance would have to be repeated and could not be explainable in any other way.

Some scientists believe that neither distance nor time affects telepathy. Thus, a person's thoughts might be received by another person who is far away. Some scientists also believe that a person may know in advance the thoughts, feelings, or knowledge that another person will have at a later time. If true, this would be an example of *precognitive telepathy.*

Telepathy is considered a major form of *extrasensory perception (ESP),* an awareness of something without the use of the known senses. Telepathy is under scientific investigation, and whether it exists is still an open question. WILLIAM M. SMITH

See also EXTRASENSORY PERCEPTION; CLAIRVOYANCE; MIND READING; PARAPSYCHOLOGY; PSYCHICAL RESEARCH.

WORLD BOOK photo

An Automatic Telephone Answering Device records messages and gives tape-recorded information to callers.

Motorola (WORLD BOOK photo)

A Car Phone enables motorists to make and receive calls. Many airplanes, ships, and trains also have mobile telephone units.

Porta-TelTM (WORLD BOOK photo)

A Special Teletypewriter Attachment, called a *TTY*, enables a deaf person to send and receive messages by telephone.

Bell Federal Savings (WORLD BOOK photo)

A Telephone Switchboard connects the phones within an office or building to one another and to outside lines.

TELEPHONE

TELEPHONE is an instrument that sends and receives sound, usually by means of electricity. Telephones provide the commonest method of talking to people at a distance. In just a few seconds, you can telephone a friend on the next block or in another part of the country. Almost as quickly, you can call a person nearly anywhere in the world. The word *telephone* comes from two Greek words, *tele*, meaning *far*, and *phone*, meaning *sound*.

The telephone is one of our most valuable means of communication. A telephone call may cost only a few cents. But in an emergency, a telephone call can swiftly help bring a doctor, the police, or firefighters. People can save time by phoning their grocer or pharmacist. Business people can phone their customers who are far away.

A telephone call can be made from almost anywhere. You can call from your home or from a phone booth in a store. Such telephones are connected to each other by wires that carry sound by electric current. *Radiotelephones* are used in cars, trucks, ships, trains, and airplanes. Radiotelephones carry sound by means of radio waves and are not directly connected to each other by wires.

Alexander Graham Bell invented the telephone in Boston in 1876. Today, about 425 million telephones serve people all over the world. The United States uses approximately two-fifths of this total amount, about 162 million telephones. Japan ranks second with about 51 million telephones, and Great Britain is third with 23 million.

Kinds of Telephones

Engineers have designed different kinds of telephones for different uses. The most familiar type of telephone is the *desk telephone*. It stands on a desk, a table, or a shelf. A *wall telephone* can be a handy space-saver or it may be used where a desk phone would not be convenient.

Telephones in some offices have push buttons, with which a person can make, receive, hold, or transfer calls from two or more lines. The user can make a call to an *extension telephone* or on an *outside line*. An extension telephone is another phone connected to a telephone with the same number. An outside line connects a phone to any other phone with a different number. An *intercom telephone* in a home or office enables the user to talk to someone in another room as well as to make outside calls.

A person who makes or receives many calls might use a phone called a *Call Director*. Some Call Director phones can control more than 100 outside and extension lines at one time. Each line is controlled by a button. Another kind of phone, a *speakerphone*, has a microphone and a loudspeaker. Several people in the room can participate in the conversation.

A device called an *automatic dialer* saves time for a person who dials the same numbers frequently. One type of automatic dialer has a prepunched plastic card for each of these numbers. The caller puts a card into a slot on the phone, then presses a bar to dial the number.

Other automatic dialers use magnetic tape or electronic devices to store numbers.

Regular Telephone Services

A person can make three kinds of telephone calls—*local*, *long distance*, and *overseas*. Over 90 per cent of all calls in the United States are local calls.

Local Service includes various types. One type allows the customer to make an unlimited number of calls for a fixed charge. Another type of local service costs a basic amount for a set number of calls, plus an added amount for each additional call. Extended Area Calling permits local service dialing to nearby areas for a set rate.

Long Distance Service includes *station-to-station calls* and *person-to-person calls*. In a station-to-station call, the charge begins as soon as the telephone is answered. In a person-to-person call, the charge does not begin until a specific person or extension is reached. However, a station-to-station call costs less than a person-to-person call. The cost of both types of calls also depends on the distance called, the number of minutes talked, and the time and the day of the call. Day, evening, and night rates vary on all out-of-state calls and most long distance calls within states.

In the past, a telephone user could make a long distance call only through an operator. Today nearly 99 per cent of the phones in the United States and Canada are equipped for Direct Distance Dialing (DDD). The two countries are divided into about 120 areas, each identified by a three-digit area code. For a call outside his or her own area, a person first dials the area code, then the seven-digit local telephone number.

Overseas Service. A person in the United States can make a phone call to about 220 other countries and territories. Most overseas calls are made through a local or an international operator. In some areas, a person can dial directly overseas. Most overseas calls are transmitted by undersea cables or by communications satellites. A few are sent by radio waves. Telephone calls can be made to ships at sea by means of *high seas telephone service*, which uses radio waves.

Special Telephone Services

Private Lines Services are used by organizations that send many messages between two or more places. For example, a company might receive daily reports from branch offices throughout the country. The company has private lines to each branch.

A number of special services are provided by private telephone lines. Typewritten messages can be sent over a private line by an instrument called a *teletypewriter* (see TELETYPEWRITER). A similar device, called a *teletypesetter*, receives messages over a line and sets them in type automatically (see TELETYPESETTER). Private telephone lines also are used to link radio and television stations into one large network. Drawings, photographs, and similar information can then be sent to each of the stations. Computers also send vast quantities of information over private telephone lines.

Answering Services give and take phone messages for persons who are away from their office or home. Some answering services inform a person that he or she has a message by beeping a signaling device carried by the person. An automatic answering device is an instrument that answers the phone automatically, gives recorded information to callers, and records messages.

Mobile Telephone Service provides two-way radio communication for travelers on land, on water, or in the air. In the United States, many automobiles, trucks, trains, ships, and airplanes have mobile phone units.

Conference Calls enable three or more persons anywhere in the world to talk together at the same time over the regular telephone network.

How a Telephone Works

When a person speaks into a telephone, sound waves created by the person's voice enter the mouthpiece. An electric current carries the sound to the telephone of the person being spoken to. A telephone has two main parts: (1) the *transmitter* and (2) the *receiver*.

The Transmitter of a telephone serves as a sensitive "electric ear." It lies behind the mouthpiece of the phone. Like the human ear, the transmitter has an "eardrum." The eardrum of the telephone is a thin, round metal disk called a *diaphragm*. When a person talks into the telephone, the sound waves strike the diaphragm and make it vibrate. It vibrates at various speeds, depending on the variations in air pressure caused by the varying tones of the speaker's voice.

Behind the diaphragm lies a small cup filled with tiny grains of carbon. The diaphragm presses against

How to Make a Simple Telephone Set You can make a private telephone line with some string and two empty tin cans. First, cut off the tops of the cans and punch a small hole in the bottom of each can. Next, thread the ends of the string through the holes and tie a knot inside each can. Then, you and a friend each take a can and move apart, keeping the string straight and tight. Speak into the open end of your can. Your voice travels along the string and can be heard by your friend through the open end of the other can.

WORLD BOOK illustration by Jack Hagen

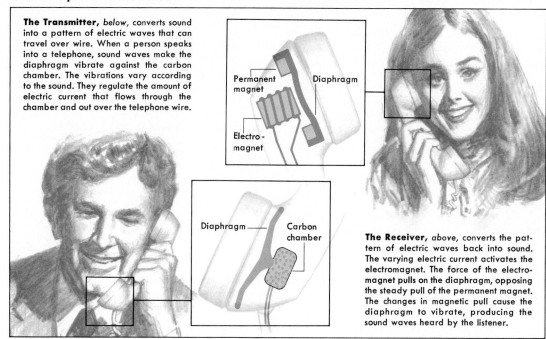

The Transmitter, *below,* converts sound into a pattern of electric waves that can travel over wire. When a person speaks into a telephone, sound waves make the diaphragm vibrate against the carbon chamber. The vibrations vary according to the sound. They regulate the amount of electric current that flows through the chamber and out over the telephone wire.

Permanent magnet

Diaphragm

Electro-magnet

Diaphragm

Carbon chamber

The Receiver, *above,* converts the pattern of electric waves back into sound. The varying electric current activates the electromagnet. The force of the electromagnet pulls on the diaphragm, opposing the steady pull of the permanent magnet. The changes in magnetic pull cause the diaphragm to vibrate, producing the sound waves heard by the listener.

WORLD BOOK illustration by Jack Hagen

these carbon grains. Low voltage electric current travels through the grains. This current comes from batteries at the telephone company. The pressure on the carbon grains varies as sound waves make the diaphragm vibrate. A loud sound causes the sound waves to push hard on the diaphragm. In turn, the diaphragm presses the grains tightly together. This action makes it easier for the electric current to travel through, and a large amount of electricity flows through the grains. When the sound is soft, the sound waves push lightly on the diaphragm. In turn, the diaphragm puts only a light pressure on the carbon grains. The grains are pressed together loosely. This makes it harder for the electric current to pass through them, and less current flows through the grains.

Thus, the pattern of the sound waves determines the pressure on the diaphragm. This pressure, in turn, regulates the pressure on the carbon grains. The crowded or loose grains cause the electric current to become stronger or weaker. The current copies the pattern of the sound waves and travels over a telephone wire to the receiver of another telephone.

The Receiver serves as an "electric mouth." Like a human voice, it has "vocal cords." The vocal cords of the receiver are a diaphragm. Two magnets cause the diaphragm to vibrate. One of the magnets is a *permanent magnet* that provides a steady pull on the diaphragm. The other magnet is an *electromagnet.* It consists of a piece of iron with a coil of wire wound around it. When an electric current passes through the coil, the iron core becomes magnetized and it pulls on the diaphragm, opposing the pull of the permanent magnet. The pull of the electromagnet varies between strong and weak, depending on variations in the current. The changes in magnetic pull cause the diaphragm to vibrate.

The electric current that activates the electromagnet is sent by the transmitter of another telephone. The electric current becomes stronger or weaker according to the sound waves "heard" by the transmitter. Thus, the diaphragm in the receiver vibrates according to the speaker's voice. As the diaphragm moves in and out, it pulls and pushes the air in front of it. The pressure on the air sets up sound waves that are nearly the same as the ones sent into the transmitter. The sound waves strike the ear of the listener, and the listener hears the words of the speaker.

How a Telephone Call Travels

Telephone lines crisscross the United States and connect millions of telephones in a vast network. Most telephone lines consist of copper wires. Many long distance calls travel by radio systems. In the United States, almost all telephone wires are bound together in cables. Some cables have more than 4,000 wires.

Lines for Local Calls. When you make a local telephone call, the call travels over wires or by radio to a central office. There, switching equipment connects your telephone to the phone you are calling. The switching process is discussed in a later section of this article, *How a Telephone Call Is Made.*

Long Distance Lines. The same kind of cables used for local calls could be used for long distance calls. At great distances, however, the electric signals in the wire would become too weak. To overcome this problem, long distance lines are equipped with *repeaters* (amplifiers) that strengthen the electric current through such devices as electron tubes and transistors.

A long distance call would be very expensive if only one call could be transmitted on a pair of wires at a time. Engineers have developed ways to send many messages on the same pair. A process called *carrier trans-*

mission enables two pairs of wires to carry as many as 96 conversations at the same time. Each electric current carrying a conversation travels at a different *frequency* (rate of vibration). Electronic filters at each end of the line sort out the conversations.

Coaxial cables make it possible to send even more messages along the same route. A coaxial cable consists of up to 22 *coaxial conductors*—copper tubes about as big around as a pencil—that work on the carrier transmission principle. A pair of tubes can carry up to 13,200 telephone conversations. See COAXIAL CABLE.

Wires and cables both must be strung on telephone poles or placed underground. To reduce the cost of long distance phoning, telephone companies use radio relay systems that send telephone calls by radio waves.

Radio relay systems use superhigh frequency radio waves called *microwaves* (see MICROWAVE). Unlike radio broadcasting waves, microwaves do not follow the curve of the earth. They travel mostly in straight paths. Microwaves are concentrated in a narrow beam like that of a searchlight. They are focused from one relay station to another. The stations are about 30 miles (48 kilometers) apart. Each has antennas to transmit and receive microwaves. A microwave route can carry almost 36,000 telephone conversations.

The *over-the-horizon* radio relay system sends microwaves beyond the horizon. It uses powerful relay stations up to 200 miles (320 kilometers) apart. The stations send microwaves aimed at the horizon by means of antennas the size of outdoor motion-picture screens. Much microwave energy is lost in space. But enough scatters downward and carries the radio signals to the next station, much as the headlights of a car shine over a hill without being directly seen. Over-the-horizon systems operate between Florida and Nassau, Florida and Cuba, Japan and Korea in the Pacific, and Tortola and Trinidad in the Caribbean. Systems also serve Alaska and military bases in the Arctic.

How a Telephone Call Is Made

Before you can talk to another person on a telephone, the two telephones must be *switched* (connected). A pair of wires extends from each phone to switching equipment in the central office. Large cities have many central offices, all linked together by trunk cables. A *telephone exchange* designates the local area served by one or more central offices. Every telephone number has a prefix that stands for its central office. In the past, all prefixes were combinations of letters and numbers. For example, in the telephone number "AB 7-6452," the prefix "AB 7" means the "ABerdeen 7 central office." Today, most areas have all-numeral telephone numbers, such as "257-6452." The prefix "257" stands for the "257 central office." Many more central office codes are possible with the all-number system than with the use of letters.

There are two main types of switching—*automatic* and *manual*. In automatic switching, used with dial and push-button phones, special equipment makes the connections. In manual switching, a telephone operator makes connections by hand on a switchboard.

Automatic Switching. More than 99 per cent of the telephones in the United States are dial or push-button operated and switched automatically. The dialing equipment goes into action as soon as the phone is lifted. An electric signal flashes over the telephone line to the switching equipment in the central office. A humming sound called the *dial tone* tells the caller that the equipment is ready to handle a call. In a dial phone, the dial returns to its starting position after each letter or number has been dialed. As the dial returns, an electric switch inside the phone opens and closes—once for number 1; twice for 2, A, B, or C; and so on. Each time the switch opens and closes, an electric signal goes to the switching equipment. A push-button phone works in a similar way. However, musical tones, rather than an electric switch, create the electric signal in push-button phones.

Telephone companies use three chief types of automatic switching: (1) step-by-step switching, (2) crossbar switching, and (3) electronic switching. Step-by-step and crossbar are older systems that operate by means of

How Telephones Are Connected

A pair of wires extends from each subscriber's phone to equipment in a *central office*. Central offices are linked by *trunk cables*—either directly or by alternate routes through *tandem offices*.

WORLD BOOK diagrams

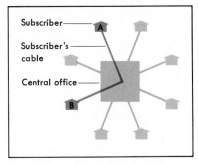

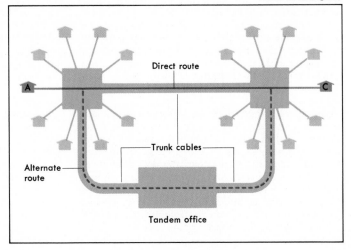

A Telephone Call between subscriber A and subscriber B, *above*, is simply *switched* (connected) by equipment in the central office that serves them both. However, a call between subscribers A and C, *right*, must travel along a trunk cable because they are served by different central offices.

electro-mechanical switches and relays. An electronic switching system (ESS) uses tiny electronic, rather than mechanical, devices. ESS, which was introduced in 1965, is rapidly replacing other switching systems because it provides greater efficiency and speed. For example, an ESS central office can handle more than 200,000 calls per hour. A typical crossbar system can carry fewer than 10,000 calls an hour.

Step-by-Step Switching, which was developed in the late 1800's, is common in small communities. In a step-by-step switching system, a call travels through a series of mechanical switches. Each switch has a vertical rod with a horizontal metal blade called a *contact arm*. Electromagnets move the arm up and down the rod and rotate it horizontally. Sets of *terminals* (electric contacts) are stacked one above the other within reach of the contact arm. The arm moves to a terminal in response to the electric signal created by the dialing of a number. When the arm touches the terminal, the call is connected to a second switch. This process is repeated for each number that is dialed until the connection is made to the telephone of the person being called.

Crossbar Switching, first used in 1938, makes connections faster than step-by-step switching. The crossbar system can be used in both large and small communities. It is fast because it uses a switch that moves only slightly. The switch has a rectangular frame with sets of horizontal and vertical bars. These bars operate electric contacts that are only $\frac{1}{100}$ inch (0.25 millimeter) apart. Electromagnets turn a horizontal bar and then a vertical bar to bring the contacts together in a split second.

Electronic Switching works much like a huge computer. It operates by means of transistors, integrated circuits, and other miniature electronic devices. ESS has three major parts—the *central control*, the *memory*, and the *switching network*.

The central control directs all operations of the system. The memory consists of two sections that store information—the *program store* and the *call store*. The program store contains the exact instructions for all operations. The call store keeps track of which telephones are in use and what paths are available for connecting calls. The switching network provides thousands of paths on which calls can travel.

To make a connection between two telephones, the ESS central control selects a path based on information provided by the memory sections. It sends electrical commands to the proper switch contacts, causing them to close and complete the circuit. The entire switching process takes approximately 25-thousandths of a second.

In addition to speed, ESS provides several special features. For example, it enables callers to abbreviate frequently called numbers to just two, rather than the usual seven, digits. It also allows customers to have their incoming calls temporarily forwarded to a number where they can be reached. Conference calls are also easy to arrange with ESS. Any change in the telephone service that a customer receives requires only a simple change of information in the program store, rather than the alteration of wiring and switches that is necessary in other systems.

Manual Switching is used in only a few small communities without dial telephones. A pair of wires from each phone connects with a switchboard. Each pair of wires has its own *jack*, a hole in the board into which the operator can insert a metal plug. The plugs are attached to the switchboard by a wire cord.

When a person lifts the phone to make a call, a light goes on at the caller's jack. The operator inserts an *answering plug* into the jack and the caller gives the operator the number of the person being called. The operator then puts a *calling plug* into the jack of the person being called and rings the phone. When the person answers, the electric circuit is completed.

The Telephone Industry

In the United States, private companies own and operate the telephone systems. However, the Federal Communications Commission (FCC), an agency of the United States government, regulates rates and services for interstate telephone communications. Public utility commissions regulate telephone rates in the states.

The American Telephone and Telegraph Company (AT&T), a private corporation, is the largest communications company in the world. It heads the Bell System, which manages the nation's long-distance telephone network. The Bell System also includes Western Electric Company, which manufactures telephone equipment and supplies; and Bell Laboratories, a research organization.

In 1974, the United States government filed a lawsuit against AT&T, charging the company with hindering competition in the telephone industry. The lawsuit sought to break up the Bell System. At the time, the Bell System also included 22 local telephone operating companies. These companies operated about 80 per cent of the telephones in the United States. The rest of the phones were served by about 1,600 independent telephone companies.

In 1982, the government and AT&T agreed to settle the lawsuit. Under the terms of the settlement, the local telephone companies would become independent. AT&T would then be allowed to enter the unregulated computer services and information-processing businesses. Previously, AT&T had been prohibited from engaging in any businesses that were not regulated by the government.

In Other Countries, the government, as well as private companies, owns and operates the telephone systems. In West Germany, for example, a branch of the federal government provides telephone service for the entire nation. The central government also owns and operates the phone systems in Peru, Spain, Sweden, and Venezuela. Private companies provide all the telephone service in Italy. In Canada, the Bell Telephone Company of Canada, a private corporation, operates more than half the nation's telephones. Other private companies, government agencies, and cooperative businesses operate the rest. Other countries with some privately owned systems include Denmark, Finland, Portugal, and the Philippines.

History

Bell's Invention. Alexander Graham Bell, a Scotsman who came to the United States in 1871, invented the telephone. Bell was a teacher of the deaf in Boston.

How an Electronic Switching System (ESS) Works

WORLD BOOK diagram

The Memory is the information storage unit of an ESS central office. Its *program store* contains the instructions for the system's operations. The *call store* keeps track of calls in progress and of the paths that are available to connect calls.

The Central Control in an ESS office directs all operations based on information provided by the memory. To connect a subscriber's telephone to another phone, the central control selects the best path available through the switching network.

The Switching Network provides thousands of paths on which telephone calls can travel. Electrical commands from the central control cause certain switch contacts in the network to close. The electric circuit between two telephones is then completed.

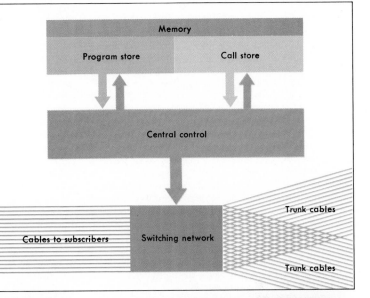

Memory

Program store

Call store

Central control

Cables to subscribers

Switching network

Trunk cables

Trunk cables

The Call Store includes electronic devices called *circuit packs.* A circuit pack, *above,* stores data about which telephones are being used, plus other temporary conditions in the system.

The Program Store provides the permanent information needed to operate and maintain the system. The data is electronically coded on *memory cards,* such as the one shown above.

The Central Control's Computer, *above,* receives information from the program store and call store. It also sends commands to the switching network and regulates all other ESS operations.

Illinois Bell (WORLD BOOK photos)

The Electric Circuits that connect telephone calls travel through the switching network. The worker shown above is testing the line equipment linking a subscriber's phone to the network.

83

TELEPHONE

At night, he experimented with a *harmonic telegraph*, a device for sending several telegraph messages at once over one wire. Bell developed the idea of the telephone in 1874, but he continued his experiments with the harmonic telegraph.

On June 2, 1875, one of the metal reeds of the harmonic telegraph stuck. Bell's assistant, Thomas A. Watson, snapped the reed to loosen it. Bell, who was in another room, heard the sound in his receiver. He realized that the vibrations of the reed had caused variations of electric current. In turn, the electric current had reproduced the same variations in the receiver he was using.

On March 10, 1876, Bell finally succeeded in speaking words over a telephone. He was about to test a new transmitter. In another room, Watson waited for the test message. Suddenly, Bell spilled some acid from a battery on his clothes. He cried out: "Mr. Watson, come here. I want you!"

Watson rushed into the room, shouting: "Mr. Bell, I heard every word you said—distinctly!" Bell had invented the first successful telephone.

In June 1876, Bell exhibited his telephone at the Centennial Exposition in Philadelphia. Scientists praised his work. But the public showed little interest until early in 1877, when Bell gave many demonstrations with his telephone.

Early Telephones. In August 1876, Bell received the first one-way long distance call. This call came over an 8-mile (13-kilometer) line he had built between Brantford, Ont., and Paris, Ont. In October 1876, Bell and Watson held the first two-way long distance telephone conversation. They spoke between Boston and Cambridge, Mass., a distance of 2 miles (3 kilometers). In 1877, Roswell C. Downer, a banker, installed the first commercial telephone line. It extended 3 miles (5 kilometers) between Downer's home in Somerville, Mass., and his bank in Boston.

Also in 1877, E. T. Holmes, the owner of a burglar alarm system, began operating the first switchboard. It connected four banks and a factory in Boston. At night,

the switchboard served as a burglar alarm. The first telephones used no switchboards. A pair of iron wires connected each pair of phones. One person called another by pushing a knob on the telephone. This caused a hammer to make a thumping sound that went over the telephone line to the other phone. As more telephones came into use, each was connected to all the other phones. More than 1,000 connections were required to link only 50 telephones. Switchboards solved this problem by bringing together the wires from all telephones in an area.

The Bell System. Bell, Watson, Gardiner G. Hubbard, and Thomas Sanders formed the Bell Telephone Company in 1877. Hubbard was Bell's father-in-law, and Sanders was the father of one of Bell's pupils. They had helped pay for Bell's experiments.

In 1878, the first telephone exchange opened in New Haven, Conn. It had 21 customers. Soon many other exchanges opened throughout the United States and Canada.

Also in 1878, the Western Union Telegraph Company entered the telephone business. Western Union used transmitters developed by Thomas A. Edison, the great American inventor. Its receivers had been developed by Elisha Gray, another American inventor. The Bell company met the competition by using the improved transmitters of Emile Berliner, an American, and Francis J. Blake, an Englishman.

In September 1878, the Bell company sued Western Union to protect Bell's telephone patents. Western Union claimed that Gray, not Bell, had invented the telephone. But Gray had filed his patent a few hours after Bell had applied for his first patent on Feb. 14, 1876. The United States Patent Office had issued Bell his patent on March 7, 1876. During the lawsuit, in 1879, the Bell Telephone Company was reorganized as the National Bell Telephone Company. That same year, Western Union acknowledged Bell's patents and agreed to stay out of the telephone business. The Western Union case was the first of more than 600 lawsuits over Bell's patents. Many persons claimed to have invented the telephone. In 1888, the Supreme Court of the United States upheld Bell's patents.

Historical Pictures Service, Chicago

Illinois Bell (WORLD BOOK photo)

Telephone Operators connected almost all calls manually through a switchboard until the early 1900's. The picture at the left shows the central telephone exchange of New York City about 1900. Today, operators assist callers when necessary, *right*. But almost all calls are switched automatically.

The Development of the Telephone

The First Telephone was this device, invented in 1876 by Alexander Graham Bell.

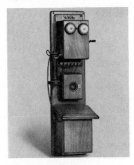

An 1882 Wall Phone had a hand-held receiver and a crank to signal the operator.

A Dial Telephone, such as this 1919 model, required complex switching equipment.

The 1928 Desk Telephone combined the receiver and the transmitter in a handset unit.

The "300" Model desk phone, introduced in 1937, contained a bell in its base.

The Colored Telephone of 1954 gained widespread popularity as a decorative item.

The "Trimline" Telephone of 1968 featured push buttons on the handset.

American Telephone & Telegraph Company

A Touch-A-Matic Phone of 1973 dialed a number at the push of a button.

In 1880, the American Bell Telephone Company was formed. It combined the National Bell Telephone Company and the telephone activities of Western Union. The first commercial long distance line opened in 1881. This line extended 45 miles (72 kilometers) between Boston and Providence, R.I. A 292-mile (470-kilometer) commercial line between New York City and Boston opened in 1884. The following year, the American Telephone and Telegraph Company (A.T.&T.) was organized to operate long distance lines. In 1899, A.T.&T. took over American Bell and became the parent company of the Bell System.

Telephone Improvements. Almon B. Strowger, an American inventor, patented an automatic step-by-step switching system in 1891. The first commercial switchboard based on his patent opened in La Porte, Ind., in 1892. The caller pressed buttons to get the number, then turned a crank to ring the phone. Also in 1892, telephone service began between New York City and Chicago.

In 1896, the first dial telephones went into operation in Milwaukee. The American scientist Lee De Forest patented the electron tube in 1907, and it was adapted as an amplifier in 1912. Transcontinental telephone service began between New York City and San Francisco in 1915. Transatlantic radio-telephone service between New York City and London began in 1927. The first long distance coaxial cable linked New York City and Philadelphia in 1936.

In 1947, the transistor was invented by scientists of Bell Telephone Laboratories, the Bell System research organization. This electronic device is smaller than the electron tube and requires less power. Undersea telephone cables between the United States and Europe began operating in 1956. A cable between the U.S. mainland and Hawaii began operating in 1957, and a cable between Japan and the United States began in 1964. In 1961, Bell scientists developed the first continuously operating *laser*, a device that amplifies light. A light beam from a laser can carry many more phone calls than wires or radio waves can. See LASER (In Communications).

In 1960, the United States began launching communications satellites. The first, *Echo*, was a huge, shiny balloon that simply reflected radio signals from one ground station to another. *Telstar* and *Relay* satellites used electronic equipment to amplify the signals. The *Syncom* satellites were put in orbits about 22,300 miles (35,890 kilometers) above the equator. At this height, a satellite remains above one spot on the earth so it is always in position for use. The first commercial communications satellite, *Early Bird*, was launched in 1965. The *Early Bird* satellite hovers above the Atlantic Ocean, and provides 240 two-way telephone circuits between Europe and the United States. See COMMUNICATIONS SATELLITE (Kinds of Communications Satellites).

Recent Developments. In 1970, International Direct Distance Dialing (IDDD) began operating between New York and London. IDDD, which now serves several cities throughout the world, enables people to dial overseas directly. In 1976, engineers began testing a *fiber optics system* for transmitting local calls. This system uses bundles of extremely fine glass fibers to carry calls on a laser beam (see FIBER OPTICS). In the 1970's, experiments also were begun on electronic telephones. Electronic phones would be easier to produce and would give better performance than electric ones.

During the late 1960's and the 1970's several decisions were made by the Federal Communications

Commission that may lead to greater competition in the U.S. telephone industry. In several cases, the FCC voted to permit independent communications companies to provide private long distance services. In another case, the FCC ruled that people could purchase and install their own telephones and other equipment. Previously, all phone equipment was leased to users by telephone companies for a fee.

In 1982, the U.S. government and AT&T settled a lawsuit in which the government had charged the company with anticompetitive practices. AT&T agreed to give up ownership of its local telephone operating companies in return for being allowed to enter the computer services and information-processing businesses.

Career Opportunities

About a million men and women work in the U.S. telephone industry. They work in offices, in factories that make equipment, and in research laboratories. Telephone operators are perhaps the best-known telephone employees. Telephone companies also employ secretaries, clerks, and sales and service representatives. Skilled workers install and maintain telephones. Engineers prepare plans for switching equipment and transmission systems. Physicists and mathematicians work on research and development.   BARRY R. CAMPBELL

Related Articles in WORLD BOOK include:

BIOGRAPHIES

Outline

Questions

Who invented the telephone?
What were the first words spoken over the telephone?
Who was Thomas A. Watson? Almon B. Strowger?
Where was the first telephone line installed?
What is a *conference call? Carrier transmission?*
When was the first dial telephone used? Where was it used?
What country has the most telephones?
How are satellites used in telephone communication?
Where is the phone greeting "Pronto" used?
What are the two main parts of a telephone?

Additional Resources

BOETTINGER, HENRY M. *The Telephone Book: Bell, Watson, Vail and American Life, 1876-1976.* Riverwood, 1976.
BROOKS, JOHN. *Telephone: The First Hundred Years.* Harper, 1976.
DE SOLA POOL, ITHIEL. *The Social Impact of the Telephone.* MIT Press, 1981.
MATH, IRWIN. *Morse, Marconi and You.* Scribner, 1979. For younger readers.
ZIM, HERBERT S., and SKELLY, J. R. *Telephone Systems.* Morrow, 1971. For younger readers.

TELEPHOTO is a way of sending pictures by wire or radio. The process is also known as *Wirephoto*. A scanning light at the sending station *scans* (passes back and forth over) a picture. The light reflected from the picture is converted into an electric current by a photoelectric cell (see ELECTRIC EYE).

At the receiving station, the electric current is converted into a light beam. The light beam then hits a film or photographic paper in proportion to the strength of the current. The picture is reproduced because the film or paper is sensitive to light.

After development, the photographic film may be used for contact printing or conventional enlarging. It may also be retransmitted by wire or radio. Telephoto differs from the system called *facsimile*, which reproduces pictures by passing an electric current through chemically treated paper (see FACSIMILE).

American news services operate nationwide telephoto networks. The Associated Press opened the first network in 1935.   EARL F. ENGLISH

TELEPROMPTER. See TELEVISION (Talent; picture: Production Preparations).

TELESCOPE is an instrument which *magnifies* (makes larger) objects which are seen at a great distance, such as the heavenly bodies. This instrument has made it possible to see, study, and photograph many of the heavenly bodies which were formerly unknown. It has opened new worlds in astronomy.

Most historians think the first telescope was made in 1608 by a Dutch optician called Hans Lippershey. Before this time, even as far back as the 1200's, scientists experimented with magnifying lenses. Lippershey was refused a patent for his instrument. After hearing of Lippershey's invention, Galileo, the Italian astronomer, in 1609 built his first telescope. It was a crude instrument. In fact, the most powerful instrument that Galileo built magnified objects only 33 times. Furthermore, it was possible to see only a small field area, less than one-fourth of the diameter of the moon, with this telescope. Nevertheless, Galileo made some outstanding discoveries. He was able to see the rings of Saturn, four of the satellites of Jupiter, and the mountains and craters on the moon. Today, the simple principle of the Galilean telescope is used only in opera glasses, where the field of vision is small and the objects do not have to be magnified greatly.

The simplest type of telescope used by astronomers

is called the *refracting* telescope. This telescope consists of a long, heavy tube. At one end of the tube is a small *ocular* (eyepiece) consisting of two lenses. It is that part of the telescope through which the image is seen and by which the image is magnified. At the other end of the telescope is a large, convex lens which may be as large as 40 inches (102 centimeters) in diameter. This lens is called the *objective*, or *object lens*, and is the lens which gathers the light. The objective and the eyepiece are so placed in the tube that it is possible to change the distance between them, thus making it possible to focus the instrument. When light from an object strikes the objective, the light rays are bent by the lens until they come to a bright point, known as the *focal point*. A small representation of the object called an *image* is formed at the focus. As the light passes through the eyepiece, the image is enlarged and seen as though it were very near. But, as the light goes through the objective, it is bent so that the image appears upside down. That is the way it is seen through the eyepiece. This means that when a celestial object is seen through a telescope, it appears upside down.

Some telescopes are used to observe objects on the earth. This type of telescope has two double-convex lenses that are placed between the objective and the eyepiece. This causes the rays of light to cross, and finally form an image that is right side up.

A refracting telescope must have an *achromatic* objective lens in order to magnify all colors equally. Such a lens is made from several pieces of glass.

The second type of telescope used by astronomers is the *reflecting* telescope. It uses a mirror as the objective, instead of a glass lens. Since it is possible to build larger reflecting telescopes than the refracting type, and since these have greater light-gathering power, it is possible to see or photograph fainter objects.

One of the first reflecting telescopes was built by Sir Isaac Newton. This type is known as the *Newtonian*

telescope. It consists of a heavy tube. One end of the tube is open. At the other end is the objective, which is a large mirror. The eyepiece is located at the side of the tube at a 90-degree angle with the tube. Near the open end of the tube, there is a tiny mirror that is set at a 45-degree angle. As the light waves enter the tube, they are reflected by the large mirror to the small mirror, which reflects the image into the eyepiece.

Another type of reflecting telescope is the *Cassegrainian* type, which was invented by N. Cassegrain of France. In this telescope, the objective is located behind a small mirror. The eyepiece is set behind the objective. The objective is a large mirror that has a small opening in the middle. As the light waves strike the objective, they are reflected back to the small mirror. Then they are passed through the tiny opening to the eyepiece, which magnifies the image.

The number of times an object is magnified by a telescope can be determined by knowing the *focal length* of the objective and of the eyepiece. As mentioned earlier, when light from an object falls upon the objective, light rays are bent until they come to the focal point. The distance between the center of the lens and the focal point is known as the *focal length*. The magnification (m) of a telescope can be found by dividing the focal length of the objective (f_1) by the focal length of the eyepiece (f_2). The formula for finding the magnification is:

$$m = \frac{f_1}{f_2}$$

The largest refracting telescope in the world is at Yerkes Observatory at Williams Bay, Wis. The object lens of the telescope has a diameter of 40 inches (102 centimeters). The tube is 63 feet (19 meters) long. One of the largest reflecting telescopes in the world is the Hale telescope, dedicated in 1948 at the Palomar Observatory in California. This telescope has a reflecting

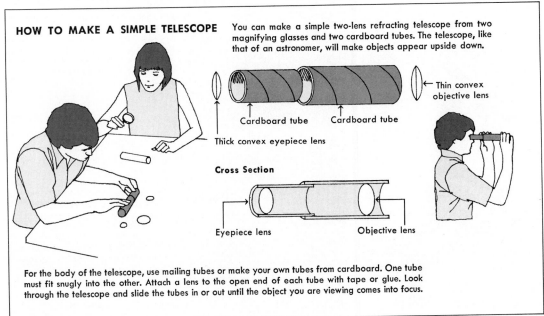

HOW TO MAKE A SIMPLE TELESCOPE   You can make a simple two-lens refracting telescope from two magnifying glasses and two cardboard tubes. The telescope, like that of an astronomer, will make objects appear upside down.

Thin convex objective lens

Cardboard tube   Cardboard tube

Thick convex eyepiece lens

Cross Section

Eyepiece lens   Objective lens

For the body of the telescope, use mailing tubes or make your own tubes from cardboard. One tube must fit snugly into the other. Attach a lens to the open end of each tube with tape or glue. Look through the telescope and slide the tubes in or out until the object you are viewing comes into focus.

WORLD BOOK diagrams

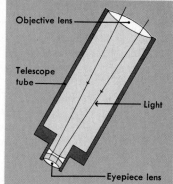

A Refracting Telescope is a tube with lenses at each end. Light enters the telescope through an objective lens at one end of the tube. This lens *refracts* (bends) the light toward the eyepiece at the other end of the tube. A lens in the eyepiece bends the light further and forms an enlarged image of the light source.

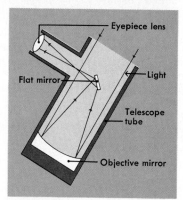

A Newtonian Reflecting Telescope uses a curved mirror instead of a lens as its objective. The mirror gathers light and focuses it on a flat mirror suspended in the center of the telescope tube. The flat mirror reflects the light through a hole in the side of the telescope tube to the eyepiece lens.

Cave Optical Co.

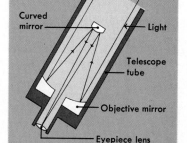

WORLD BOOK diagrams

A Cassegrainian Reflecting Telescope has a curved mirror with a hole in its center as the objective. Light gathered by the mirror is reflected to a smaller curved mirror suspended above the objective. The small mirror focuses the light through the hole in the objective mirror and into the eyepiece lens below it.

A Schmidt-Cassegrainian Telescope resembles a Cassegrainian telescope, but it has a correcting plate in front of the objective mirror. This plate is a lens that corrects irregularities in the image formed by the mirror. The lens and mirror combination can give a sharp picture of a larger area of the sky than other telescopes can.

Edmund Scientific Co.

Astronomers Use Telescopes to observe celestial objects and events. Most of their work is done with large telescopes at observatories. Away from the observatory, they use small portable telescopes. The astronomers shown above went to Africa to photograph an eclipse of the sun. Solar eclipses occur rarely and may be seen from the earth at only a few places.

Owen Franken, Camera 5

mirror 200 inches (508 centimeters) in diameter (see AsTRONOMY [picture: Edwin Hubble]).

In 1931, Bernhard Schmidt, a German optician, invented a combination refractor-reflector telescope. Ordinary telescopes can observe only small areas of the sky. But the Schmidt telescope can actually photograph large areas of the sky. It has a thin specially shaped lens at the end of a tube. At the other end is a spherical mirror, which reflects the image near the middle of the tube. The photographic film is placed where the image forms. Palomar Observatory has the largest Schmidt telescope. The lens is 48 inches (122 centimeters) wide and the mirror is 72 inches (183 centimeters). The McMath solar telescope at Kitt Peak National Observatory was completed in 1963. It is used to photograph and study the sun, solar flares, and sunspots (see KITT PEAK NATIONAL OBSERVATORY).

The Radio Telescope, developed after World War II, is a giant "eye" that sees by radio waves emitted by celestial bodies. The "mirror" of a radio telescope is a huge saucer-shaped radio reflector. The radio telescope has a number of advantages over the optical telescope: (1) it can tune in on stars and galaxies that give off no light at all, or only faint light, not visible to an optical telescope; (2) it can penetrate the clouds of cosmic dust and gas that fill vast regions of space; and (3) it can be used in any kind of weather because radio waves travel through the clouds in the earth's atmosphere.   FRANK D. DRAKE

Related Articles in WORLD BOOK include:

Astronomy	Galileo	World, History of
(Observing with	Lens	(picture: Tele
Telescopes;	Observatory	scopes Used
pictures)	Radio Telescope	by Galileo)
Binoculars		

Additional Resources

ASIMOV, ISAAC. *Eyes on the Universe: A History of the Telescope.* Houghton, 1975.

HOWARD, NEALE E. *The Telescope Handbook and Star Atlas.* Rev. ed. Harper, 1975.

PAUL, HENRY E. *Telescopes for Skygazing.* 3rd ed. Watson-Guptill, 1976.

TELETYPESETTER (TTS) is an electrical machine somewhat like a teletypewriter (see TELETYPEWRITER). It sends typewriter copy over long distances and at the same time it punches holes in a paper tape. When this tape is fed into a typesetting machine, the machine automatically sets the copy in type which is used to print a newspaper. In other words, by using TTS a newspaper does not have to pay a worker to operate the keyboard of a linotype machine. This makes it less expensive to print a newspaper. The leading news wire services began using TTS to send news reports to newspapers in the early 1950's.   EARL F. ENGLISH

TELETYPEWRITER is an electromechanical typewriter that transmits impulses over a wire to a receiver which prints a message. As the typist strikes each key on the transmitter, it activates a certain combination of electrical impulses that makes a similar letter arm react at the receiving end. Teletypewriter machines are often connected in series, and many receivers in different parts of the world can be run from one transmitter at the same time. News agencies send articles to newspapers by teletypewriter. A similar machine, the stock-market ticker, sends financial news to many points.

Weather reports are sent by teletypewriter. Weather-observing stations type reports in a letter code to save time. As the codes are typed, weather forecasters throughout the country can read identical information, and issue forecasts accordingly.   EARL F. ENGLISH

Sports Events

Learning and Fun for Children

The Latest News

Musical Variety Shows

Television is sometimes called "the device that brings the world into the home." TV provides millions of home viewers with a wide variety of entertainment, information, and special events. The pictures on this and the following page show some examples of television's far-reaching coverage.

TELEVISION

TELEVISION, or TV, is one of humanity's most important means of communication. It brings pictures and sounds from around the world into millions of homes. People with a television set can sit in their house and watch the President make a speech or visit a foreign country. They can see a war being fought and watch government leaders try to bring about peace. Through television, home viewers can see and learn about people, places, and things in faraway lands. TV even takes viewers out of this world with coverage of America's astronauts as the astronauts explore outer space.

In addition to all these things, television brings its viewers a steady stream of programs that are designed to entertain. In fact, TV provides many more entertainment programs than any other kind. The programs include action-packed dramas; light comedies; soap operas; sporting events; cartoon, quiz, and variety shows; and motion pictures.

About 77 million homes in the United States—or 98 per cent of all the country's homes—have at least one television set. On the average, a television set is in use in each home for about 6½ hours each day. Thus,

The contributors of this article are Sig Mickelson, Executive Director of the Center for Communication at San Diego State University; and Herbert Zettl, Professor of Broadcast Communication Arts at San Francisco State University and author of Television Production Handbook.

television has an important influence on how people spend their time, as well as on what they see and learn.

Because of its great popularity, television has become a major way to reach people with advertising messages. Most television stations carry hundreds of commercials each day. In 1972, about $8 billion was spent on television advertising in the United States. The use of television advertising has greatly changed the process of getting elected to public office in the United States. Before TV, candidates relied chiefly on public appearances to urge people to vote for them. Today, most candidates for high office reach many more people through TV than they reach in person.

The name *television* comes from the Greek word *tele*, meaning *far*, and the Latin word *videre*, meaning *to see*. Thus, *television* means *to see far*. Most pictures and sounds received by a television set are beamed from a television station on electronic signals called *electromagnetic waves*. The television set changes these waves back into pictures and sounds.

Many scientists contributed to the development of television, and no one person can be called its inventor. Experiments leading to the invention of TV began in the 1800's, but progress was slow. Television as we know it today was not developed until the 1920's, and it had little importance in communication until the late 1940's. But during one 10-year period—the 1950's—it became part of most households in the United States. Since then, television has gained importance in most other countries. In addition, many organizations, including businesses, hospitals, and schools, now use television for their own special purposes.

Government Hearings

The Watergate Investigation; Fred Ward, Black Star

Astronaut Aldrin reaches the moon; NASA

Space Exploration

"Roots"; Warner Bros. Television Distribution, Inc.

Historical Drama

TELEVISION/*Television in the Home*

About 77 million homes in the United States—or 98 per cent of the total—have at least one television set. Half of all American homes have two or more TV's. Altogether, there are about 156 million sets in the United States. On the average, a television set is in use in each home for about 6½ hours a day.

About three-fourths of the nearly 1,000 television stations that broadcast in the United States are *commercial stations*. The rest are *public stations*. Commercial stations are those that sell advertising time to pay for their operating costs and to make a profit. Public stations are nonprofit organizations that rely on business, government, and public contributions to pay for their operating costs. The programming of commercial and public stations differs greatly.

Commercial Television. Commercial television stations broadcast many more entertainment programs than any other kind. These shows include light dramas called *situation comedies;* action-packed dramas about cowboys, detectives, doctors, and lawyers; variety shows featuring comedians, dancers, and singers; and movies, including some made expressly for television. They also include daytime quiz shows and *soap operas* (melodramatic plays), and cartoons and other children's shows.

Another kind of commercial television program is the *documentary*. A documentary is a dramatic, but nonfictional, presentation of information. Some television documentaries entertain as well as inform. These include travel programs about people, animals, and things in faraway places. TV also presents documentaries with little entertainment content, such as studies of alcoholism, drug abuse, poverty, and racial prejudice.

Commercial television stations broadcast many *discussion*, or *talk*, shows. On these shows, a host interviews people from many walks of life—including athletes, authors, movie and television stars, and politicians.

Commercial television stations cover almost every kind of sports event—from baseball and football to table tennis and skydiving. Every four years, TV brings its viewers the colorful Olympic Games—often from halfway around the world.

All commercial stations broadcast brief summaries of local, national, and international news every day. Also, stations often interrupt their regular program schedules to present extended coverage of special events, such as space shots, political conventions, and important presidential activities.

Advertising makes up an important part of commercial television. Television commercials appear between and during most programs. The vast majority of the commercials urge viewers to buy some kind of product—from dog food and hair spray, to cars and insurance policies. At election time, many political candidates buy advertising time on television to ask people to vote for them. A small percentage of TV advertising provides a *public service*. Public service ads include messages that tell people to drive carefully and follow other safety rules. They also include announcements about local community activities.

Commercial television attracts huge audiences.

85

Often, more than 50 million persons tune in to a top entertainment show or sporting event. About 50 million persons watch a television newscast daily. Thus, it must be assumed that large numbers of people like what commercial television offers. Even so, many persons criticize its coverage. They say that commercial TV shows too many programs designed only to entertain, and not enough programs that inform, educate, or provide cultural enrichment. The critics also claim that much of the entertainment is of poor quality because it aims at the largest possible audience. They criticize television newscasts for being too brief to provide the real meaning of news stories.

The persons responsible for deciding what appears on commercial television disagree with these criticisms. They point out that commercial TV can stay in business only by selling much advertising time at high prices. To do this, the programs must attract large numbers of viewers. Statistics show that many more people watch popular shows and brief news reports than watch more sophisticated shows and in-depth news reports.

Public Television. Because public television stations do not rely on advertising to stay in business, they do not have to attract huge audiences. Their programming focuses chiefly on educational and cultural subjects.

Public stations broadcast educational programs on a wide range of subjects, from literature and physics to cooking and yoga. In some cases, viewers can earn college credits by passing tests based on what the programs teach. Some educational programs on public TV take much the same form as classroom instruction. But others use a more entertaining approach. Examples include "Sesame Street" and "The Electric Company," two lively, yet educational, children's shows.

Public television stations offer many programs that combine entertainment and cultural enrichment. They telecast such things as plays by leading dramatists, ballets and symphonies, and surveys of art and history. Such television shows draw up to 2 million viewers—a small audience by commercial TV standards, but a much larger one than ever attended a theater or concert hall.

Many public television stations do not carry regular newscasts. But public TV often presents in-depth discussions of news developments by leading journalists and others who deal closely with current events.

TELEVISION / *Specialized Uses*

Television has many uses other than broadcasting to the home. Schools, businesses, hospitals, and many other organizations use TV for special purposes.

Most of TV's specialized uses involve *closed-circuit television.* That is, the signals are sent—by way of wires—to only certain television sets. Broadcasting, on the other hand, is a form of *open-circuit television.* This means the signals can be received by all sets within the area the signals can reach.

Schools. Many classrooms have TV sets that receive specially prepared lessons by way of closed-circuit television. In addition, some schools show open-circuit broadcasts of lessons and such special events as government hearings and presidential press conferences.

Businesses and Hospitals make extensive use of television. Many companies instruct new employees and conduct nationwide sales meetings through prerecorded television programs. Sometimes, television cameras are placed in hospital operating rooms to give medical students a close-up view of actual operations.

Security and Surveillance. Many banks focus TV cameras on customers so that guards can watch for attempted robberies. Television cameras in jails make it possible for one guard to watch many prisoners at once. United States and Russian satellites that are equipped with TV cameras circle the earth. The cameras on these satellites can detect such military operations as troop build-ups and shifts. Satellite cameras also take pictures of weather patterns that help meteorologists make forecasts.

Video Entertainment Systems became popular during the late 1970's. *Videotape recorders* (*VTR's*) enable users to tape television programs on blank video cassettes and play them back later. A VTR is attached to the user's TV set. Manufacturers also produce a wide variety of prerecorded video cassettes that contain such material as concerts, motion pictures, and sports events. See TAPE RECORDER (Videotape).

Other systems use prerecorded *video disks*, which resemble phonograph records. The pictures and sounds on the disks are transmitted by a special video-disk player to an attached TV set.

Electronic games that work through a television set appeal to many people. *Video game* attachments convert a TV screen into a game board. Each player operates controls that move electronic dots, lines, and other images that appear on the screen. See GAME (picture).

Rush-Presbyterian-St. Luke's Medical Center;
WORLD BOOK photo by Stephen Feldman
Closed-Circuit Television enables hospital personnel to monitor the condition of many patients at the same time.

A Television Production involves achieving an appearance of naturalness amid much activity. Viewers of "The Tonight Show" see Johnny Carson and Ed McMahon chatting in a relaxed atmosphere, above. But off camera, many production workers are doing vital jobs that require split-second timing.

The *production* (putting together) of a television program is an extremely complicated process. A program requires careful planning, much preparation, and the combined efforts of many workers with artistic and technical skills.

Most television productions take place in television studios. But TV production companies also create shows in movie studios, on city streets, in stadiums, in deserts and jungles, and even under water. Broadcasters telecast some programs *live* (as they happen). But most TV programs—including almost all entertainment shows—are prerecorded, and then telecast at a later time. The recording may be done on videotape or on film.

Many prerecorded programs are produced from beginning to end, in the manner of a stage play. But television production companies also use the *piecemeal approach* of the motion-picture industry. In this approach, each scene is recorded separately, and *spliced* (connected together) later.

The first two parts of this section—*Planning and Preparation* and *Putting a Show on the Air*—trace the development of an entertainment program produced

The photographs in this section were taken for WORLD BOOK *at the production facilities of NBC-TV's "The Tonight Show Starring Johnny Carson" by John Hamilton, Globe Photos.*

straight through in a television studio and recorded on videotape. But much of the information under these headings applies to all TV productions. The last part of this section describes the differences involved in other production methods.

Planning and Preparation

The planning of television shows begins in the programming department of the networks and stations that broadcast programs. Members of these departments decide what programs their companies will telecast. Networks and stations produce many programs themselves. Independent producers create others, and sell them to networks and stations. In either case, once a programming department approves an idea for a program, a *producer* takes full responsibility for its production.

The Producer usually begins his work by obtaining a script and choosing a director. Sometimes—especially for uncomplicated shows—the producer writes the script himself. He may also serve as his own director—in which case he is called a *producer-director*. But more often, the producer assigns the script-writing job to a professional writer or team of writers, and the directing job to a professional director. The producer and director select the *talent* (actors, actresses, or other people who will appear on the show). The producer

87

also chooses the production specialists needed to produce the show. These persons may include an art director, a costume designer, and a composer. In addition, the producer works closely with the director throughout the production process.

Writers prepare the scripts for television programs. A television script is a written account of what is to be said and done during the program. The amount of detail a script contains varies, depending on the program. A talk show script, for example, may include only the host's opening remarks, some of the key questions to ask his guests, and directions for any special acts that may take place during the show. During most of the show, the host and his guests carry on *adlibbed* (unplanned) conversations. A script for a television drama, on the other hand, includes every word to be spoken by the actors and actresses. It also describes the actions they are to perform.

The Director. As soon as the writers complete the script, the director reads it and tries to visualize how he can translate it into an actual television program. He gets ideas about how the characters should speak, move, and generally behave. He decides what camera shots will be needed to create the effects he visualizes. Sometimes, the director has an artist prepare a *storyboard* (a series of drawings) that shows how key parts of the program will look.

Production Specialists. The producer and director call on many production specialists to help prepare for the program. An *art director* and artists and craftsmen who work with him design and build the show's scenery. A *costume designer* creates or obtains costumes needed for the production. A *property manager*, or *prop man*, gets special items called *props* for the show. These items include furniture, vases of flowers, and guns. Specialists in technical work also play a key role in the production

process. They advise the producer and director on what kinds of cameras, microphones, and lights will be needed. A *production manager*, or *production coordinator*, sees to it that all the required equipment is available when needed.

Talent is a technical term for all the persons who appear on television programs. A talent may be a *performer*, or an *actor* or *actress*. A talent who appears as himself on television is a performer. A talent who plays someone else is an actor or actress. Television performers include newscasters, sports announcers, and talk show hosts. The people who play roles in TV dramas and situation comedies are actors and actresses.

Selection of talent ranks among the key steps in the planning of a television program. The producer and director do this important job. If a talent is a big star, he may get television roles because of his fame and proven ability. But usually, a talent must *audition* (try out) for the parts he wants to play. During an audition, the director and producer may ask the talent to *take a screen test* (perform in front of a camera).

A talent who earns a job gets a script so he can study his lines. An actor or actress may have less than a week to learn the lines for a one-hour drama. Those who perform on TV's daily soap operas have only a few hours each day to memorize their lines.

Some television productions make use of *cue cards* to help the talent with their lines. A cue card is a large piece of cardboard or similar material with writing on it. The writing may be a key word or phrase, or an entire passage from a script. An off-camera stagehand holds the card up so the talent can see it.

The *Teleprompter* is another aid sometimes used in television productions. A Teleprompter is a mechanical device that contains a roll of paper with words from a script printed on it. The roll moves continuously,

Planning for a TV Program begins long before the telecast. For example, the "Tonight Show" producer, *at desk above*, and his assistants schedule guest appearances weeks in advance.

Production Preparations may include setting up a *Teleprompter*, a device that shows parts of a script. The Teleprompter above shows lines of a commercial Ed McMahon will read.

Rehearsals are the practice sessions of TV productions. During dress rehearsal for a "Tonight Show" comedy routine, *left,* the director (*holding script*) goes over the skit with Carson and other cast members. At right, guest singer James Brown runs through his songs with members of the band.

giving the talent a line-by-line view of the script. Television performers who deliver commercials, news stories, and speeches often use a Teleprompter.

Composers and Musicians. Most television programs include music. A producer and director may decide they need an original musical composition for their show. If so, the producer hires a composer. The composer meets with the producer and director to discuss the theme, mood, and *climaxes* (dramatic high points) of the program. The composer bases his composition on what he learns about the show. Often, producers and directors decide to use existing music for their programs. To do so, they must get permission from the holder of the copyright on the music, and pay him a fee.

The producer hires musicians and a conductor to perform the music. For prerecorded shows, the musicians often record the music after the actual program is produced. Then, technicians combine the music with the rest of the program.

Rehearsals are practice sessions for television shows. Most TV productions require at least one rehearsal. Complicated productions often require many more.

During a rehearsal, the talent—under the director's guidance—practice their lines and their actions. The director also directs the actions of the cameraman and other off-camera workers.

Rehearsal for a dramatic production may begin with a *script reading.* Then, the director may call for a *dry run* (rehearsal without equipment or costumes). Many dry runs take place in a *rehearsal room.* This room has lines on the floor that indicate where such things as doors, chairs, and tables will be during the actual production. A director may watch a dry run through a *director's viewfinder.* This device resembles the viewfinder on a still camera. It enables the director to get an idea of how scenes will appear on television.

Finally, the director calls for a *dress rehearsal,* or *camera rehearsal,* in the studio. The goal of a dress rehearsal is to achieve a performance that is the same as the final production will be. In fact, directors sometimes record both the dress rehearsal and the actual production. In reviewing both recordings, the director may decide that parts of the dress rehearsal came out better than the actual production. He may then substitute the parts of the dress rehearsal he likes for the corresponding parts of the actual production.

Television rehearsals stress the importance of split-second timing. A theater drama may run as much as five minutes more than its planned time. But a television show must be timed exactly. A show cannot run even a few seconds past its planned time, because that time is set aside for the next program.

Putting a Show on the Air

When the time comes to tape a program, everything needed for the process is brought together in a television studio. Workmen put the scenery and props in place in the studio. Other workmen put floodlights and spotlights in place. Technicians turn these lights off and on and brighten and dim them during the production to achieve the desired effect for various scenes. Often, a single televised scene requires as many as 20 different lighting instruments. One or more microphones are put in place. Workmen bring television cameras—usually at least two and sometimes four or five—into the studio. The persons responsible for the technical parts of the show's production get ready in the *control room.* This room lies off to the side of the place where the telecast occurs.

Some studios have rows of seats, very much like a theater. Visitors can come to these *audience areas* and watch shows being produced.

Putting a Show on the Air requires the skills of many behind-the-scenes workers. A "Tonight Show" audio engineer controls the program's sounds at an audio console, *left*. Monitors, *right*, show all the scenes the studio cameras are photographing. The director decides which scenes go on the air.

Before the show begins, makeup men apply makeup to the talent who will appear on the show. Makeup helps people look natural on camera. The talent put on special costumes, if the show calls for such costumes. Finally, they come into the studio and perform the production before the cameras.

The Cameras used to *shoot* (photograph) the production are big, heavy instruments. They are mounted on devices that have wheels so the cameramen can move them around the studio to change the direction of their shots. Many cameras can be lowered and raised mechanically to change the vertical angles. In addition, all broadcast cameras have a lens that allows the cameraman to vary televised scenes without moving the camera. This device is called a *zoom lens*. By pressing a button or turning a handle, the cameraman causes adjustments in the lens. These adjustments enable the cameraman to gradually change a scene from a close-up of a talent's face to a long-range view of an entire scene. *Zooming* (moving in and out on scenes) is a widely used television production technique.

A broadcasting camera also has a *viewfinder* (tiny television set) on it. The viewfinder shows the cameraman the exact scene his camera is photographing.

Microphones. Most studio TV productions involve the use of one or more *boom microphones*. A boom microphone is attached to a *boom* (long metal arm). A worker called the *boom operator* uses mechanical devices to move the microphone above and in front of the person speaking. For dramatic productions, it is essential that the microphone be kept out of camera view. Imagine a dramatic scene in which an actor lies exhausted in a hot desert, crying for help. If suddenly the boom microphone that hangs above him dropped into camera view, the scene would look ridiculous. Sometimes, television makes use of *hidden microphones*—either in addition to,

or in place of, boom microphones. Such microphones may be hidden in or behind scenery or props.

Talk shows and other nondramatic productions may use boom microphones. But they also use microphones that viewers can see. These include *desk microphones*, which stand on desks or tables in front of performers; and *hand microphones*, which performers hold. Another kind of microphone, the *lavalier*, is hung around a performer's neck or attached to his clothing. It may be in camera view, or hidden in the clothing.

The Control Room. During a television program, scenes from each of the studio's cameras will appear on the viewer's screen. Pictures from other video sources, including filmed commercials and slides that show titles, will also be seen. The job of determining which scenes appear when is done in the control room. A program may also include sounds from several sources. Technicians in the *audio control* section of the control room regulate the program's sounds. In addition, engineers operate equipment that keeps up the quality of the pictures and sounds.

The control room has several *monitors* (television sets). Each monitor shows the scenes from a different camera or other video source. The director watches the monitors when choosing which scenes to put on the air. The picture that is on the air at any given time appears on a monitor called the *master*, or *line, monitor*.

An important piece of equipment in the control room is the *switcher*. This instrument has many buttons, including buttons for controlling each studio camera and each other picture source. On command from the director, a technician called the *technical director* (T.D.) presses buttons to change the televised scene. If the director wants the scene being photographed by camera number 1 to be shown, he tells the technical director to press the button for camera number 1. To change to camera number 2, the T.D. presses button number 2, and so on. This switching process goes on throughout the program. But it is done so smoothly that viewers hardly realize it is happening.

The switcher also has levers. By moving levers in various ways, the T.D. can combine scenes from two or more cameras or other video sources. Such combinations are called *special effects*. They include the *dissolve*, the *super*, the *wipe*, and *matting*, or *keying*.

The *dissolve* is a gradual change from one picture to another in which the two pictures overlap briefly. A dissolve can take place slowly or rapidly, depending on how fast the T.D. moves the levers. Directors use the dissolve to move smoothly from scene to scene and, sometimes, to indicate a passage of time.

The *super*, or *superimposition*, is the blending together of two scenes. Television often uses this device to show dream scenes. One camera shows a close-up of the face of the sleeping person, and the other shows the scene about which the person is dreaming.

A *wipe* is a special effect in which one picture seems to push another picture off the screen. A wipe that is stopped halfway is called a *split screen*. TV productions use the split-screen technique to show scenes from two different locations at the same time. Other common wipes include the *circle* and the *diamond*, in which the second picture appears on the screen as an expanding circle or diamond.

The *matting*, or *keying*, technique is used to show titles and other objects over a scene. The letters of the titles come from a title card, title slide, or electronic letter-making machine. The picture on which the letters appear comes from a studio camera, or film or tape.

The switcher also enables television broadcasters to *cut* (switch instantly) from the program to filmed commercials, and back again.

The sound inputs of a television program are controlled by an instrument called an *audio console*. An *audio engineer* operates this instrument. He pushes buttons and moves levers to choose and mix together various audio inputs. For example, a scene of two persons sitting in an automobile might require the audio engineer to mix the sounds of the persons' conversation with recorded sounds of the automobile engine, outside traffic, and mood music. The audio engineer also controls the volume of sounds.

Taping the Program. The program produced in the studio and control room is immediately recorded on a videotape machine. This machine stands in or near a special part of the television studio called *master control*. The director reviews the finished tape, and tape editors correct any major errors in it. Then, the tape is stored until the time the program is scheduled for broadcasting. For technical information on videotape, see *Videotape Recording* later in this article.

Master Control is the electronic nerve center of a television station. Much of the electronic equipment that helps create television pictures is located there. A program goes from master control by cable or microwave to the transmitter. Then, the transmitter sends it on its way to the viewers. Master control also has equipment for switching from program to program. The pro-grams include those that originate at the station, at network headquarters, and at remote locations.

Other Production Methods

A television production can differ from the method just described in four chief ways. (1) Television producers put some programs together piecemeal rather than straight through. (2) They create many programs with film cameras rather than with TV cameras. (3) They telecast many programs live instead of recording them first. (4) They create programs in locations away from studios. Such programs are called *remote telecasts*.

The Piecemeal Approach involves recording a program on videotape or film scene-by-scene with *stopdowns* (stops) between scenes. Each recorded scene is called a *take*. After each take, the director can play back the tape or film and judge its merits. If he likes the take, he goes on to another one. If he does not like it, he can call for a *retake* (shoot the scene over again). The piecemeal approach also allows directors to shoot scenes out of order. If, for example, the first and last scenes of a TV play happen in the same location, the director may shoot them one right after the other. Upon completion, film or tape editors splice all the scenes together in their proper order to create a continuous story.

Filming Television Programs. Film cameras can be carried around and operated more easily than can television cameras. As a result, many television producers use film cameras to create programs that take place at several locations. For example, television news programs, which report on widely scattered events, use film cameras. Programs shot at faraway locations usually use film. In addition, motion-picture studios create many entertainment programs with film cameras (see MOTION PICTURE [How a Motion Picture Is Made]).

After cameramen film a program, broadcasters telecast it from a telecine unit. For technical information, see *Telecine* later in this article.

Live Telecasts include coverage of political conventions, speeches by the President, and sports events. The part of newscasts in which the announcers speak are also live. But most of the news scenes shown on these programs come from film or videotape recordings.

Broadcasters usually videotape live programs at the same time as they telecast them. This allows them to rerun all or parts of a show at a later time. For example, videotaped highlights of a live telecast of a speech by the President are often shown later on newscasts. Videotapes of live sports events allow sportscasters to rerun and analyze key plays immediately after they happen. This process is called *instant replay*.

Remote Telecasts. Almost all remote telecasts are broadcast live. They include telecasts of sports events and political conventions. Producers of these programs use regular-sized television cameras. But they also use cameras small enough to be carried around. These *hand-held cameras* help TV crews cover the huge area of a sports field or convention hall. Broadcasters park a *remote truck* near the place of the telecast. This truck contains control room and master control equipment needed to create TV signals. The signals travel by microwave or wire from the truck to the transmitter.

The enormous public interest in TV programs in the United States has created a huge television industry in a short time. In 1946, there were only six television stations in the United States. Today, the country has nearly 1,000 stations.

The number of TV stations accounts for only part of television's impact on the American economy. The manufacture and sales of television sets and broadcasting equipment became big businesses because of the rise of television. In addition, broadcasting, manufacturing, and sales created thousands of new jobs.

The National Networks. About 80 per cent of all commercial television stations in the United States are *affiliates* of one of three national networks. That is, they agree to carry programs provided by the networks. The national television networks are those of the American Broadcasting Companies (ABC), CBS Inc., and the National Broadcasting Company (NBC). The networks create some of their programs and buy others from independent producers.

An affiliate agrees to carry programs provided by a network. The network pays the affiliate for carrying the programs. Sponsors, in turn, pay the networks for showing their commercials on the stations.

A network's success depends on its ability to select programs that attract large audiences. The bigger a program's audience, the more money sponsors will pay for the right to show commercials on it. For top-rated shows, sponsors pay from about $75,000 to $200,000 for one minute of commercial time.

The persons who choose a network's programs know that certain shows, such as championship sports contests and appearances by famous entertainers, will usually attract huge audiences. But they choose most programs on the basis of their own intuition, or "educated guesses."

After a network program goes on the air, the network and sponsors keep close watch on its *ratings*. Ratings are the results of surveys that supposedly show how many people watch various programs. The Nielsen Survey,

conducted by the A. C. Nielsen Company, ranks as the most important survey. The company arrives at its ratings by determining what programs 1,200 American families watch. The viewing habits of these families supposedly reflect the habits of the entire nation. Networks usually cancel programs that get low ratings. They sometimes do so after only a few showings of a program.

Local Commercial Stations. About 730 local commercial stations operate in the United States. About 80 per cent of them are affiliates of the three national networks. The rest operate independently.

An affiliate carries many hours of network programs daily. But in 1971, the Federal Communications Commission (FCC)—which regulates broadcasting in the United States—limited the amount of network programming affiliates can carry during *prime time*. Prime time refers to the evening hours, when television programs draw the largest audience. The FCC ruled that local stations in the nation's 50 largest television markets cannot broadcast more than 3 hours of network programs during prime time. This ruling was designed to force the stations to offer a wider variety of programs—especially programs of local interest—during the prime-time period.

The nonnetwork programs of affiliates and the programs of independent stations come from several sources. The stations fill some of their time with shows they produce themselves, especially local newscasts. They also telecast interview, discussion, and other kinds of programs of local interest. Both affiliates and independent stations show programs produced by organizations called *syndicates*, films from motion-picture distributors, and reruns of old network shows. The local stations sell commercial time to advertisers to pay for the cost of their programs and to make a profit.

Public Stations. More than 250 public television stations operate in the United States. They create many of the programs they show and buy programs from independent producers. Often, a program created by one public station is carried by many other stations. An agency called Public Broadcasting Service (PBS) serves as a distributor of locally produced public television programs.

Public stations are nonprofit organizations, but they need money to cover their production and operating costs. The largest part of a station's funds come from viewer contributions. A viewer who contributes to a public television station becomes a member of the station. Businesses and foundations also help support public television. Local and state taxes help support many public stations. In addition, stations get funds from the Corporation for Public Broadcasting (CPB).

CPB, created by Congress in 1967, gets most of its funds from the federal government. CPB encourages public stations to serve the needs of their local communities through grants for programming and technical facilities. It also finances the production of programs distributed by PBS and sets policies for a national public broadcasting service.

Cable Television Systems bring television to the home by means of cables rather than through the air.

Number of Television Sets in Use

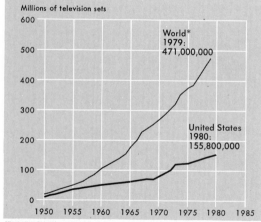

Millions of television sets

World*
1979:
471,000,000

United States
1980:
155,800,000

*Excluding China for most years.
Sources: *Statistical Yearbook,* 1981 and earlier years, UN and UNESCO; *Television Factbook,* 1980 and earlier years, Television Digest, Inc.; *World Communications,* UNESCO.

These systems are also known as *Community Antenna Television* (CATV) because the cables are connected to a powerful antenna that serves a large area.

Cable television, which began in the early 1950's, is one of the fastest-growing parts of the television industry. Originally, its only purpose was to bring network and local station programs to places that either cannot receive TV signals through the air, or can receive them only with much interference. Such places include isolated communities, mountain valleys, extremely hilly regions, and areas with heavy concentrations of tall buildings, such as New York City.

Improved reception of regular television programs still ranks as the main purpose of cable television. But since the 1960's, people have begun to use it for other purposes. A single cable system can carry as many as 60 TV signals. Thus, a cable system can transmit regular network television programs and also provide a wide variety of special features. Some cable systems offer adult education classes; continuous news, weather, and stock market reports; programming from distant independent TV stations; first-run motion pictures; and special sporting events. In many communities, channels are set aside for coverage of such local activities as city council and school board meetings.

Today, there are about 4,000 cable television systems in the United States. Some of these systems provide TV to about 170,000 homes. Others serve fewer than 100 homes. Altogether, cable TV serves about 14 million homes in about 10,000 communities in the nation.

Cable television has great economic potential despite the high cost of installing cable systems. Many operators charge an installation fee. Subscribers to all cable systems pay a monthly service charge, which averages about $6 nationwide. Operators can also create their own programming and sell advertising time to sponsors. Some operators also use their systems for *pay-television*.

Pay-Television. Ever since television broadcasting began, there have been business people who wanted to set up *pay-television systems*—also called *subscription television*. Under such a system, viewers pay a fee to see certain programs in their homes. The Federal Communications Commission has consistently opposed attempts to make programs that are part of *free* (regular) television part of pay-TV systems. But promoters of pay-TV believe it is possible to gain subscribers by offering programs that are not available on free TV, such as first-run motion pictures, live telecasts of theater plays, and certain sporting events.

In the past, attempts to establish pay-TV systems met with little success. However, since the late 1960's, pay-TV promoters have made progress in selling program packages to subscribers of cable television systems. Pay systems that use the airwaves for broadcasting programs also have grown increasingly popular. Such systems send out scrambled TV signals. Subscribers can view the pay-TV programs by attaching to their television set a device that unscrambles the signals.

Related Industries. The spectacular growth of television broadcasting caused a similar growth in other industries. In 1946, manufacturers in the United States turned out only 56,000 television sets, and the American

Leading Countries in Number of TV Sets

Country	Number of Sets	Sets Per 1,000 Persons
United States	155,800,000	688
Russia	80,000,000	303
Japan	28,000,000	245
Great Britain	22,000,000	394
West Germany	20,672,000	337
France	15,609,000	292
Brazil	15,000,000	126
Italy	13,170,000	231
Canada	11,040,000	466
Spain	9,424,000	253

Sources: *Statistical Yearbook, 1981*, UNESCO; *Television Factbook, 1980*, Television Digest, Inc.

people spent about $1 million for sets. Today, manufacturers produce more than 15 million sets a year, and people spend about $4 billion yearly on sets. Set sales have improved the business of many retail stores, including radio and phonograph shops, department stores, and appliance stores. Also, TV repair shops have sprung up throughout the country.

Television broadcasting requires much expensive equipment, including cameras, control boards, and transmitters. The manufacture of such equipment has become a multimillion-dollar industry.

The huge demand for television commercials has created a boom in the advertising industry. About 20 per cent of all the money now spent on advertising in the United States goes to television commercials.

Television Awards are presented each year by a number of organizations. The best-known awards, the *Emmys*, are given by the Academy of Television Arts and Sciences and by the National Academy of Television Arts and Sciences. The two academies recognize achievements of the preceding year in various fields of the TV industry. Some local chapters of the National Academy also present Emmys for local programming.

Careers in Television. The television industry has opened up thousands of job opportunities in a variety of fields. The industry needs such workers as writers, producers, directors, camera operators, engineers, electronic technicians, stagehands, lighting specialists, graphic artists, and set designers to help produce television shows. Actors, actresses, and performers are needed to appear in them. TV news departments provide a variety of jobs for journalists. TV broadcasting also creates many jobs for specialists in management, market research, and advertising.

The television industry also employs workers in technical fields outside of broadcasting. Scientists and engineers are needed to design television equipment. Factory workers manufacture television sets and other TV equipment. Technicians service home receivers.

Almost all careers in television require special training. Many colleges and universities have departments that train students in most nontechnical broadcasting careers. Journalism schools teach courses in broadcast, as well as printed-media, journalism. Technological institutes and engineering departments of colleges offer training in technical areas of television. Information on television careers is available from the National Association of Broadcasters, 1771 N Street NW, Washington, D.C. 20036.

Television ranks as one of the major influences on life in the United States. Some people even call it the most important single influence of all. The *Television Industry* section of this article discusses TV's enormous impact on the American economy. This section deals with some of television's many effects on people and on *institutions* (established parts of society).

Effects on Learning. Home television contributes greatly to what its viewers learn. It provides, on a small scale, *formal* or "classroom" *instruction*. For example, on certain TV programs teachers instruct viewers in such things as foreign languages, literature, mathematics, and science. But television is much more important for the *informal learning* it provides through its noninstructional programs. Informal learning is all the things a person learns through new experiences.

No communication system has ever provided so many people with as wide a range of new experiences as television does. Without leaving their homes, television viewers can watch political figures perform important functions, and see how people of far-off lands look and live. Television takes viewers to deserts, jungles, and the ocean floor, and shows the kinds of animals and plants that live there. A TV viewer can see how a famous actor performs the role of Hamlet, and get an idea of how top comedians draw laughter. Television shows its viewers what real-life tragedy is like, as when it covers the victims of war, natural disasters, and poverty. It also captures moments of great triumph, such as when astronauts first set foot on the moon. The total effect of television's many offerings has been an enrichment of the public's experience far beyond what was possible before the age of television.

Not all of television's effects on learning are generally accepted as "good," however. For example, many television programs include scenes that show violence. Many people believe these scenes may cause viewers —especially children—to act violently themselves. In 1969, a research group sponsored by the U.S. government studied TV's effect on children. The researchers suggested that TV violence might influence children who have violent tendencies to act violently. They also said they could reach no definite conclusion about the effect of TV violence on the vast majority of children. For information on how the TV industry has dealt with violence on television, see the section of this article on *Television Today.*

Effects on Material Expectations. Television programs and commercials often show people who lead more glamorous lives and have more material possessions than most viewers. Many social scientists believe such episodes raise the *material expectations* of viewers. That is, they cause viewers to wish they were better off materially. Such a desire can be helpful. For example, it can cause people to work harder so they can afford more of the things they want. But social scientists believe raised material expectations can also be harmful. The expectations can cause people to become so dissatisfied with their lives that unhappiness results.

Some sociologists believe that television's effect on material expectations even contributes to violence. They say that violent acts of poor minority-group members may be partly, and indirectly, caused by television. These people—the theory says—continually see on television how much better off other people are in comparison to them. This may stir up anger in the viewers, and thus contribute to violent behavior.

Effects on Institutions. Television has brought about major changes in several American institutions, including politics, the motion-picture and radio industries, and professional sports. TV's effect on advertising, another institution, is discussed earlier in this article.

Politics. Every election year, thousands of political candidates use television in their campaigns. They buy commercial time to urge voters to support them. They also appear on interviews to answer questions about their views. Many candidates now reach more voters through a single television appearance than through all the in-person campaigning they do.

Television has led to a unique kind of political campaigning—the *spot announcement*. Spot announcements are political messages that last from 10 to 90 seconds. These brief messages rank as the most widely used form of political advertising on television. They contrast sharply with the long political speeches that are typical of traditional, in-person campaigning.

Television does much to promote interest in politics and political issues. But political advertising on TV also draws criticism. Critics say spot announcements are too short to allow candidates to discuss issues. Instead, candidates use the time to present oversimplified statements to win support or attack their opponents. Critics also claim that, because television time is so expensive, TV campaigning gives unfair advantage to the candidates with the most money. Another complaint about television campaigning is that it leads to the "selling" of candidates through advertising methods similar to those used to sell products.

Motion Pictures and Radio. From the 1920's through the 1940's, motion pictures and radio ranked as the chief forms of entertainment for millions of Americans. Large numbers of people went to the movies at least once a week. They listened to comedies, dramas, and other entertainment programs on the radio almost every night. The rise of television in the 1950's caused a sharp decline in motion-picture attendance. Ever since, the motion-picture industry has faced economic problems (see MOTION PICTURE [Postwar American Movies; Motion Pictures Today]). Radio entertainment changed completely after TV became part of American life. Almost every radio entertainment program went off the air. Recorded music replaced these shows as the chief kind of radio entertainment (see RADIO [History]).

Professional Sports have long attracted millions of spectators yearly. But many more millions now watch the events on television. Television networks and stations pay team owners large amounts of money for the right to televise games. These funds, in turn, help owners pay the high salaries of today's professional athletes. Television also helps increase the popularity of sports. For example, professional football had a limited following when its games began appearing on TV in the 1950's. But largely because of television, professional football's popularity has soared.

A person looking directly at a scene sees the entire view all at once. But television cannot send a picture of an entire scene all at once. It can send only one tiny part of the picture, followed by another tiny part, until it has sent the complete picture. A television camera divides a picture into several hundred thousand tiny parts by a process called *scanning*. As the camera scans the picture, it creates electronic signals from each part of the picture.

A television set uses these signals in re-creating the picture on its screen. The scanning process puts the picture back together again piece by piece. A person looking at the screen of a TV set does not realize this is happening. The scanning process works so quickly that the viewer sees only a complete picture.

Sending television pictures and sounds involves three basic steps. (1) The light and sound waves from the scene being televised must be changed into electronic signals. (2) These signals must be transmitted to the television receiver. (3) The receiver must unscramble the signals and change them back into copies of the light and sound waves that came from the original scene.

Creating Television Signals

A television signal begins when light from the scene being televised enters a television camera. The camera changes the light into electronic signals. At the same time, a microphone picks up the sounds from the scene and changes them into electronic signals. Television engineers call the signals from a camera *video* and the signals from a microphone *audio*.

This section describes how a TV camera creates video signals. It also explains how video signals are produced by *telecine* (television film) and videotape. TV audio signals are created in the same way as radio signals. For information on this process, see RADIO.

The video signals broadcast by most television stations are *compatible color signals*. These signals produce a color picture when received on a color set. The same signals also produce a black-and-white picture on a black-and-white set.

Color television uses the three *primary colors of light*—red, blue, and green—to produce full-color pictures. The proper mixture of these three colors can produce any color of light. For example, a mixture of red and green light produces yellow light. Equal amounts of red, blue, and green light produce white light. See COLOR.

The Television Camera. In producing a compatible color signal, the TV camera must: (1) capture the image of the scene being telecast; (2) create video signals from the image; and (3) encode the color signals for transmission. To perform these tasks, a television camera uses a lens, a system of mirrors, camera tubes, and complex electronic circuits. All the electronic circuits used by the camera are not inside it. They would make the camera too bulky and heavy. Instead, many of the camera circuits are located elsewhere in the TV station and connected to it by wires.

Capturing the Image. The lens gathers the *image* (picture) of the scene in front of the camera. Like the lenses in other cameras and the human eye, the TV lens *focuses* (collects and bends) the light from the scene to form a sharp image. This image contains all the colors of the scene. But to produce color signals, the camera must split the full-color image into three separate images—one for each primary color.

The camera uses two *dichroic mirrors* to split the image into the primary colors. The first mirror reflects the blue image and allows red and green light to pass through it. The second mirror reflects the red image, leaving only the green image. Other mirrors within the camera reflect each of the images to a separate camera tube.

Creating the Video Signals. A camera tube changes the light image into video signals. A black-and-white camera has only one camera tube. Color cameras have at least three such tubes—one for each primary color. These tubes create a separate video signal for each primary color. Some color cameras have a fourth tube that produces a black-and-white signal. The tubes in most color cameras are *Plumbicon tubes,* an improved version of a tube called the *vidicon*. For simplicity, this section describes the working of one vidicon tube.

A vidicon tube has a glass *faceplate* at its front end. In back of the faceplate is a transparent coating called the *signal plate*. A second plate, called the *target*, lies behind the signal plate. The target consists of a layer of *photoconductive material* that conducts electricity when exposed to light. At the rear of the tube is a device called an *electron gun.*

Light from the image reaches the target after passing through the faceplate and the signal plate. The light causes negatively charged particles called *electrons* in the photoconductive material to move toward the signal plate. This movement leaves the back of the target with a positive electric charge. The strength of the positive charge on any area of the target corresponds to the brightness of the light shining on that area. The brighter the light, the higher the positive charge. The camera tube thus changes the light image gathered by the lens into an identical electric image of positive charges on the back of the target.

The electron gun shoots a beam of electrons across the back of the target. The beam moves across the target in an orderly pattern called a *scanning pattern*. As the beam moves across the target, it strikes areas with different amounts of positive charge. Areas of the target that have the strongest charge attract the most electrons from the beam. This occurs because particles of unlike electric charge attract each other. Other areas of the target attract fewer electrons. The electrons from the beam move through the target and cause an electric current to flow in the signal plate. The voltage of this current changes from moment to moment, depending on whether the beam is striking a bright or dim part of the image. This changing voltage is the video signal from that camera tube.

The electron gun scans the target much as a person reads—from left to right, top to bottom. But unlike the way a person reads, the electron beam skips every other line on the target. After the beam scans the top line, it quickly snaps back to the left. Then, it scans the third line, fifth line, and so on. When the beam reaches the bottom of the target, it snaps back and

95

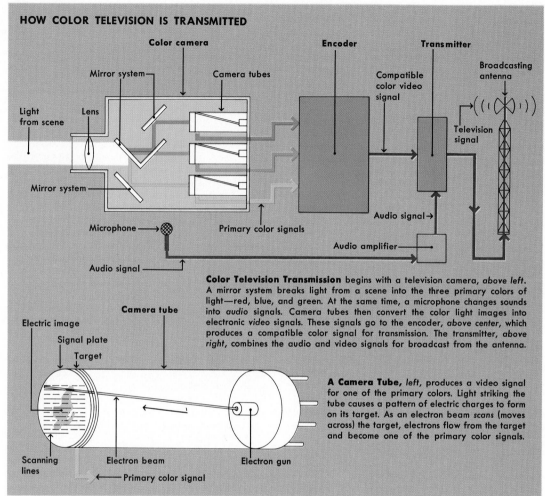

HOW COLOR TELEVISION IS TRANSMITTED

Color camera
Encoder
Transmitter

Mirror system
Camera tubes
Compatible color video signal
Broadcasting antenna

Light from scene
Lens
Television signal

Mirror system

Microphone
Primary color signals
Audio signal→

Audio signal
Audio amplifier

Color Television Transmission begins with a television camera, *above left*. A mirror system breaks light from a scene into the three primary colors of light—red, blue, and green. At the same time, a microphone changes sounds into *audio* signals. Camera tubes then convert the color light images into electronic *video* signals. These signals go to the encoder, *above center*, which produces a compatible color signal for transmission. The transmitter, *above right*, combines the audio and video signals for broadcast from the antenna.

Camera tube

Electric image
Signal plate
Target

A Camera Tube, *left*, produces a video signal for one of the primary colors. Light striking the tube causes a pattern of electric charges to form on its target. As an electron beam *scans* (moves across) the target, electrons flow from the target and become one of the primary color signals.

Scanning lines
Electron beam
Electron gun
Primary color signal

WORLD BOOK diagram by Mas Nakagawa

then scans line two, line four, line six, and so on.

The scanning pattern of TV cameras in the United States is made up of 525 lines ($262\frac{1}{2}$ odd-numbered and $262\frac{1}{2}$ even-numbered lines). The beam completes the scanning of one *field* each time it scans $262\frac{1}{2}$ lines. Two fields make up a complete television picture, called a *frame*. The electron beam moves with such extreme speed that it scans a line in $\frac{1}{15,750}$ of a second and produces 30 complete frames in a second. This speed is fast enough so the television picture does not flicker and it shows moving objects smoothly.

Each of the three vidicon tubes converts its particular primary color to a video signal by means of the scanning process. Wires carry the signals to electronic circuits in the camera that *amplify* (strengthen) them. The three signals then go to the *encoder*.

Encoding the Color Signals. At the encoder, the three video signals are combined with other signals to produce a compatible color signal. The first step in this process involves combining the three video signals into two color-coded signals and a black-and-white signal.

The two color-coded signals are called *chrominance signals* and the black-and-white signal is called a *luminance signal*. A circuit in the encoder, called the *matrix*, performs this function.

Another circuit in the encoder, the *adder*, combines the chrominance and luminance signals and, in the process, adds a *color burst* and a *synchronization signal*. The color burst enables a color TV set to separate the color information in the chrominance signals. This information, along with the luminance signal, produces a full-color picture on the TV screen. The synchronization signal locks the receiving set into the same scanning pattern as that used by the camera.

Telecine (pronounced *TEHL ih SIHN ee*) is motion-picture or still film shown on television. A TV station uses a combination of a film projector and a small television camera to create a video signal from telecine. The projector is aimed directly at the television camera, which converts the light images into a video signal by the method just described. A typical telecine unit has two motion-picture projectors and one or two slide

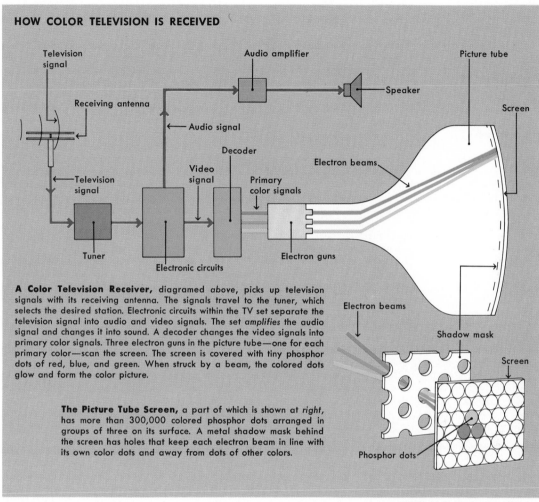

HOW COLOR TELEVISION IS RECEIVED

A Color Television Receiver, diagramed *above*, picks up television signals with its receiving antenna. The signals travel to the tuner, which selects the desired station. Electronic circuits within the TV set separate the television signal into audio and video signals. The set *amplifies* the audio signal and changes it into sound. A decoder changes the video signals into primary color signals. Three electron guns in the picture tube—one for each primary color—scan the screen. The screen is covered with tiny phosphor dots of red, blue, and green. When struck by a beam, the colored dots glow and form the color picture.

The Picture Tube Screen, a part of which is shown at *right*, has more than 300,000 colored phosphor dots arranged in groups of three on its surface. A metal shadow mask behind the screen has holes that keep each electron beam in line with its own color dots and away from dots of other colors.

WORLD BOOK diagram by Mas Nakagawa

projectors set up around one camera. The projectors and camera together are often called a *film chain*.

Videotape Recording stores television pictures and sounds as magnetic impulses on tape. Unlike film, which must be developed before showing, a videotape can be played over the air immediately.

Videotape recorders used by TV stations record the video signals crosswise in the center of a strip of magnetic tape 2 inches (5 centimeters) wide. Sound and control signals are recorded along the tape's edge.

Transmitting Television Signals

Most television signals are broadcast through the air. Engineers at a television station use a device called a transmitter to produce a TV signal from separate audio and video signals. The signal is then carried by wire to an antenna and broadcast. The signal is called an *electromagnetic wave*. Such waves can travel through the air at the speed of light, about 186,282 miles (299,792 kilometers) per second. But the signal can be received clearly only up to a distance of about 150 miles (241 kilometers). To send TV signals farther, other means of transmitting must be used. These include coaxial cable, microwaves, and satellites.

Broadcasting. Before a television signal is broadcast, the transmitter boosts its *frequency* (rate of vibration). A TV signal needs a high frequency to carry the picture information through the air. The transmitter amplifies the signal so it has enough power to reach a large area.

The transmitter increases the frequency of both the video and audio signals by a process called *modulation*. High-frequency electromagnetic waves, called *carrier waves*, are first generated by the transmitter. The transmitter uses the video signal to vary the *amplitude* (strength) of the carrier waves to produce the video part of the TV signal. This process is called *amplitude modulation* (AM). The video signal is then amplified to a power of 1,000 to 100,000 watts.

The transmitter uses the audio signals to modulate another carrier wave, which becomes the audio part of the television signal. This process, called *frequency modulation* (FM), shifts the frequency of this carrier wave slightly. The transmitter then combines the modulated video and audio carrier waves to form the television signal.

A wire called the *transmission line* carries the television signal to the transmitting antenna, which releases the signal into the air. Television stations erect their antennas on high buildings or towers so the signal can reach as far as possible. The maximum range of most TV signals is from 75 to 150 miles (121 to 241 kilometers), depending on the antenna design and transmitting power.

Television stations in the same area transmit on different frequencies so their signals do not interfere with one another. The group of frequencies over which one station broadcasts is known as a *channel*.

A total of 68 channels are available for television broadcasting in the United States. These channels are divided into two groups. Channels numbered 2 through 13 are called *very high frequency* (VHF) channels. VHF refers to signals with a frequency between either *54 megahertz* (54,000,000 vibrations per second) and 72 megahertz, 76 and 88 megahertz, or 174 and 216 megahertz. Channels numbered 14 through 69 are called *ultrahigh frequency* (UHF) channels. UHF signals have a frequency between 470 and 806 megahertz.

Coaxial Cable is used to carry television signals for long distances or to areas that have difficulty receiving signals. The television networks often send programs to their affiliated stations throughout the country through coaxial cables. The affiliates then broadcast the programs to their viewers. Cable television systems use coaxial cables to carry signals to the homes of persons who subscribe to the service.

Microwaves are electromagnetic waves, similar to television signals. Tall relay towers spaced about 30 miles (48 kilometers) apart across the country carry programs from the networks to affiliate stations on these waves. Equipment in a tower automatically receives, amplifies, and then retransmits the microwave signal to the next tower. The affiliate stations must change the microwave signals back into TV signals before they can be received by an ordinary television set.

Satellites carry television signals between stations where cables or microwave towers cannot be built. For example, satellites relay signals across oceans and connect stations on different continents. Satellites work like relay towers in space. They receive coded television signals from a special earth station, amplify them, and send them on to another earth station. The two stations may be thousands of miles or kilometers apart.

Receiving Television Signals

The television signal from a transmitter is fed into a home television set through a *receiving antenna* or *aerial*. The set uses the signal to make copies of the pictures and sounds from the televised scene. In reproducing the television program, a TV set uses a tuner, amplifiers and separators, and a picture tube.

Receiving Antenna. A good antenna collects a strong enough television signal for the receiver to produce a picture. The type of antenna needed depends on the distance between it and the transmitting antenna. A simple *dipole* (rabbit ear) antenna collects enough signal within a few miles or kilometers of the transmitter. At greater distances, a more elaborate antenna mounted on the roof may be needed. The best reception results when the antenna is pointed toward the desired station. Some antennas can be rotated by remote control to align them with widely separated stations.

Tuner. Signals from the antenna are fed into the set's tuner. The tuner selects only the signal from the station the viewer wants to receive. It shuts out all others. Most TV sets have two tuning knobs. One knob selects the VHF channels, 2 through 13, and the other knob selects the UHF channels, 14 through 69.

Amplifiers and Separators. From the tuner, the television signal goes to a group of complicated electronic circuits in the set. These circuits amplify the signal and separate the audio and video portions of it. The audio signals are changed into sound waves by the speaker. The video signals go to the *picture tube*, or *kinescope*, where they re-create the picture.

A color set has circuits that use the color burst to separate the video signal into the two chrominance signals and the luminance signal. Another group of circuits, called the *decoder* or *matrix*, transforms these signals into red, blue, and green signals that duplicate the signals from the three camera tubes. These signals then go to the picture tube.

The Picture Tube transforms the video signals into patterns of light that duplicate the scene in front of the camera. One end of the picture tube is rectangular and nearly flat. This end forms the screen of the TV set. Inside the set, the picture tube tapers to a narrow neck. The neck of a color picture tube holds three electron guns—one each for the red, blue, and green signals. A black-and-white tube has only one electron gun.

Each electron gun in a color picture tube shoots a separate beam of electrons at the screen. Each beam scans the screen just as the beam in each camera tube scanned its target. The synchronization signal, which is a part of the video signal, ensures that the picture tube's scanning pattern follows exactly the pattern used by the camera. The beams must be in step with each other in order to produce a picture.

The screen of most color tubes is coated with more than 300,000 tiny phosphor dots. The dots are grouped in triangular arrangements of three dots each—one red, one blue, and one green. These dots glow with their respective color when struck by an electron beam. A metal plate perforated with thousands of tiny holes lies about $\frac{1}{2}$ inch (13 millimeters) behind the screen of a color tube. It is called the *shadow mask*. Its holes keep the beams from hitting any color dots but their own.

The amount of light given off by the dots depends on the strength of the beam at the instant it strikes them. Since the strength of the beam is controlled by the video signal from the camera, the dots are bright where the scene is bright and dark where it is dark. When the set shows a color program, the three colored dots blend together in the viewer's mind to produce all the colors in the original scene (see EYE [How We See]). The dots produce only differing amounts of white light when showing a black-and-white program.

The Federal Communications Commission (FCC) regulates television—and also radio—broadcasting in the United States. An agency of the federal government, the FCC issues broadcasting licenses to stations and assigns frequencies the stations must broadcast on. These regulations are needed to maintain order in the airwaves. If anyone who wanted to were allowed to broadcast and use any frequency, signals would interfere with each other and make broadcasting impossible.

The FCC also regulates broadcasting in other ways. It cannot censor programs, but it sets standards for broadcasters. The FCC has the power to take away, or refuse to renew, a station's license if the station violates the standards too much. One of the most important FCC standards requires stations to provide public services and programs designed to meet the needs of their local communities. The FCC also insists that stations present all points of view when dealing with controversial subjects. In addition, it expects stations to avoid obscenity and pornography in their programs. The FCC and another government agency, the Federal Trade Commission (FTC), evaluate truthfulness in television advertising.

Congress can also regulate broadcasting. For example, it passed a law prohibiting cigarette advertising on television. The law was based on the government's conclusion that cigarette smoking is harmful to health. In 1973, Congress called for a change in the *blackout* policy of the National Football League (NFL). Under this policy, NFL games were not televised in areas where they were played. Congress ruled that games could not be blacked out if all the seats offered were sold 72 hours before game time. The law expired in 1975, but the NFL agreed to continue the policy while Congress acted on new legislation.

Broadcasters and Regulations. Broadcasters generally oppose government regulations. They say regulations that affect programming interfere with their rights to freedom of expression. The FCC and most members of Congress disagree. They claim that because the airwaves are public property, the government must create regulations that serve the public's interest.

Television broadcasting developed more slowly in other parts of the world than it did in the United States. Throughout the 1950's, there were more television sets in the United States than in all other countries combined. But beginning about 1960, a television boom began in many nations. The United States still has more TV sets than any other country, but it no longer has more than all other countries combined. Today, there are about 156 million sets in the United States, and about 315 million sets elsewhere.

Television programs now reach almost every part of the world that has electricity. Television programming varies from one country to another. But in all nations, the programs provide entertainment, cultural enrichment, education, news, and special events.

The government of every country regulates broadcasters in some ways. But in general, democratic governments—such as those of Australia, Canada, Great Britain, and New Zealand—allow broadcasters much freedom. Communist and other undemocratic governments tightly control broadcasting. They use TV as a tool to promote the government's beliefs and policies.

Canada. The Canadian people own about 11 million television sets, or about 466 for every 1,000 persons. The only major country with a higher ratio is the United States, which has about 688 television sets for every 1,000 persons.

The Canadian Broadcasting Company (CBC), a publicly owned corporation, operates about 100 television stations in Canada. About 300 stations are privately owned. Most Canadian people speak English, but many speak French. Therefore, some Canadian stations broadcast in English, and some in French. Most Canadians live in the southern part of the country, close to the United States. As a result, large numbers of Canada's television viewers can receive programs from U.S. stations, as well as from their own stations.

Europe. World War II and the economic problems that followed it slowed the development of television in Europe. But since the 1960's, television has grown at a rapid rate in Western Europe. Four West European nations each have over 10 million sets and rank among the world's leading nations in the number of sets. These countries are Great Britain, West Germany, France, and Italy.

People in the Communist countries of Eastern Europe have fewer television sets and other luxury items than do people in the West. Russia, the region's most developed country, has about 80 million TV sets. It ranks second to the United States in the total number of sets. Russia has about 303 sets per 1,000 persons.

Asia. Japan has about 28 million television sets—about 5 times more than any other Asian nation. Japan ranks third, after the United States and Russia, in total number of sets. Television is still a small industry in much of Asia. But the industry is growing rapidly in some countries, including Israel, Kuwait, and South Korea.

Africa has fewer television sets than any other continent except Antarctica. In South Africa, the African nation with the most TV's, there are only about 69 sets for every 1,000 persons. About half of the African nations have fewer than 5 sets per 1,000 persons.

Australia and New Zealand have thriving television industries. Australia has about 383 TV sets per 1,000 persons, and New Zealand has about 278 per 1,000 persons, high figures by world standards. But the countries have small populations, and neither ranks among the leaders in total sets.

Latin America. Television is more widespread in Latin America than in Africa and much of Asia. But Latin America lags behind Europe and North America. Brazil has more television sets than any other Latin-American country. Mexico and Argentina rank next.

Early Development. Many scientists contributed to the development of television, and no one person can be called its inventor. Television became possible in the 1800's, when people learned how to send communication signals through the air as electromagnetic waves. This process is called *radio communication.* For details on its development, see RADIO (History).

The first radio operators sent code signals through the air. By the early 1900's, operators could transmit words. Meanwhile, many scientists had conducted experiments involving the transmission of pictures. As early as 1884, Paul Gottlieb Nipkow of Germany had invented a scanning device that sent pictures short distances. His system worked mechanically, rather than electronically as television does. In 1922, Philo T. Farnsworth of the United States developed an electronic scanning system. In 1926, John Logie Baird, a Scottish engineer, invented a television system that used infrared rays to take pictures in the dark. Vladimir K. Zworykin, a Russian-born American scientist, invented the *iconoscope* and the *kinescope* in 1923. The iconoscope was the first television camera tube suitable for broadcasting. The kinescope is the picture tube used in TV receivers. Zworykin demonstrated the first completely electronic, practical television system in 1929.

The Start of Broadcasting. Many experimental telecasts took place during the late 1920's and the 1930's. The British Broadcasting Corporation (BBC) in Great Britain, and CBS and NBC in the United States were leaders in experimental telecasts. World War II and the economic problems that followed the war caused Great Britain to abandon television experiments. The United States moved far ahead of the rest of the world in television broadcasting.

In 1936, the Radio Corporation of America (now RCA Corporation), which owns NBC, installed television receivers in 150 homes in the New York City area. NBC's New York station began experimental telecasts to these homes. A cartoon of Felix the Cat was its first program. NBC established the first regular TV

Important Dates in Television

1800's People learned how to send communication signals through the air as electromagnetic waves.

1929 Vladimir K. Zworykin demonstrated the first practical television system.

1939 NBC made the first regular telecasts in the U.S.

1946 A television boom began. It resulted in making television part of most American homes by 1960.

1951 The first coast-to-coast telecast showed President Harry S. Truman opening the Japanese Peace Treaty Conference in San Francisco.

1953 Color telecasts began.

1954 Television covered the Army-McCarthy hearings.

1960 Presidential candidates John F. Kennedy and Richard M. Nixon debated on TV before a nationwide audience.

1965 Television programs were relayed between the United States and Europe by way of *Early Bird,* the first commercial communications satellite.

1967 Congress established the Corporation for Public Broadcasting to help finance public TV stations.

1969 TV viewers saw the first moon landing by astronauts.

1973 Television covered the Watergate hearings.

1974 A nationwide television audience watched President Richard M. Nixon's resignation speech.

1978 About 1 billion persons in 40 countries—probably the largest audience in the history of television—watched the inaugural mass of Pope John Paul II.

broadcasts in the United States in 1939. The United States entered World War II in 1941. Television broadcasting was suspended until after the war ended in 1945.

The Television Boom. The national networks—all based in New York City—resumed broadcasting shortly after the war. At first, their telecasts reached only the Eastern Seaboard between Boston and Washington, D.C. But by 1951, they extended coast-to-coast. TV stations sprang up throughout the country. Entertainment, news, special events, and sports contests replaced the simple, largely experimental, prewar shows.

The American people became fascinated with the

RCA

An Experimental Telecast of the late 1920's showed a statue of the comic strip character Felix the Cat.

Culver

Milton Berle became the first big TV star. His zany comedy show drew a huge audience during the early 1950's.

CBS

"The $64,000 Question" was one of several television quiz shows of the 1950's that offered valuable prizes to contestants.

TV Coverage of the Army-McCarthy Hearings of 1954 brought a major event of American history into millions of homes. The dramatic hearings included charges by U.S. Senator Joseph R. McCarthy, *center above,* that the Army was "coddling Communists."

Wide World

idea of having so wide a range of visual events available in their homes. The demand for TV sets became enormous. In 1945, there were probably fewer than 10,000 sets in the country. This figure soared to about 6 million in 1950, and to almost 60 million by 1960. In TV's early days, people who had no set often visited friends who had one just to watch television. Also, many stores placed television sets in windows, and crowds gathered on the sidewalk to watch programs.

Early Programs. Milton Berle became the first television entertainer to attract a huge, nationwide audience. His show, "The Texaco Star Theater," was filled with zany comedy routines. It ran from 1948 to 1956, and often attracted 80 per cent of the total television audience. "I Love Lucy," starring Lucille Ball, went on the air in 1951. This early situation comedy also attracted a huge following. Other highly popular early entertainment programs included Ed Sullivan's variety show, "The Toast of the Town"; professional wrestling matches; and quiz shows that offered prizes of thousands of dollars. A major scandal hit television in 1959,

when it was learned that quiz show producers had helped some contestants answer questions.

Coverage of special events did much to widen television's appeal. In 1951, TV broadcast the Kefauver hearings, in which U.S. Senator Estes Kefauver and his Senate committee questioned alleged mobsters about organized crime. In 1954, television covered the famous Army-McCarthy hearings. Viewers watched spellbound as Senator Joseph R. McCarthy accused the United States Army of "coddling Communists," and the Army charged McCarthy's staff with "improper conduct." The hearings reached a dramatic high point when Joseph Welch, a soft-spoken lawyer for the Army, and the outspoken McCarthy clashed in an emotion-filled argument (see McCARTHY, JOSEPH R.).

The 1960's opened with a milestone of television broadcasting. During the fall of 1960, presidential candidates John F. Kennedy and Richard M. Nixon faced each other and the nation in a series of television debates. It marked the first time presidential candidates debated on television. Many persons believe the debates made an important contribution to Kennedy's victory in the 1960 election.

Popular entertainment remained the major part of television's coverage during the 1960's. But TV also reflected the turmoil that marked American life. President Kennedy was assassinated on Nov. 22, 1963. Two days later, millions of viewers witnessed one of the most startling scenes ever shown on television. In full view of TV cameras, Jack Ruby shot and killed accused Kennedy assassin Lee Harvey Oswald as policemen were taking Oswald from one jail to another.

From the mid-1960's on, television regularly brought viewers battle scenes from the Vietnam War. The conflict was sometimes called "the first war to be fought on television." Television viewers also watched war protesters demonstrate—sometimes violently—and witnessed bitter debates over the war policy of the United States. Civil rights protests by blacks and other minority groups also became part of television coverage. Violence

United Press Int.

Vietnam War Scenes appeared on TV in the 1960's. They brought the horrors of war into millions of homes.

CBS

"All in the Family" became a hit show during the 1970's. The program combined comedy with the treatment of controversial topics.

WORLD BOOK photo by Steve Hale

Videotape Recorders became popular in the 1970's. They enable people to record TV shows on tape.

sometimes occurred during the civil rights protests.

Technological Advances made during the 1950's and 1960's helped improve the physical quality of telecasts. In TV's early days, most screens measured 7 or 10 inches (18 or 25 centimeters) diagonally. Today, 21- and 25-inch (53- and 64-centimeter) screens are common. In the 1970's, manufacturers introduced *projection television systems*, which beam programs onto a screen as large as 7 feet (2 meters) measured diagonally.

Improvements in broadcasting and receiving equipment provide much clearer pictures than were available in the past. In early days, all programs were telecast in black and white. Color television began in 1953, and today most programs are telecast in color. More than half of all American households now have a color set.

At first, most telecasts were live productions or programs made from film. The film took time to develop. Also, the equipment and techniques used produced pictures and sounds of poor quality. Videotaping of programs began in the mid-1950's, and became a major production method. Videotapes can be played back immediately after taping. They produce good quality pictures and sounds, and allow flexibility in program scheduling. Later, scientists developed equipment and techniques that improved the quality of filmed shows.

Early Bird, the first commercial communications satellite, was launched in 1965. Satellites made worldwide television broadcasting possible. Today, viewers can see events such as the inaugural Mass of a pope in Rome or the Olympic Games from Asia and Europe as they happen. Satellites are also used to distribute programs nationwide to public television stations and to cable TV systems.

Television Today continues to be a source of entertainment more than anything else. But it also carries on its role of providing coverage of important events. For example, in 1973 networks canceled many regular programs to cover the Watergate hearings—a U.S. Senate investigation of charges of illegal campaign practices during the 1972 election (see WATERGATE).

Through the years, television broadcasters generally avoided controversial themes, such as abortion, alcoholism, divorce, drug abuse, political satire, racial prejudice, and sex. They feared that such themes would result in a loss of viewers. However, beginning in the late 1960's, broadcasters found that they could deal with controversial themes and still attract large audiences. The comedy show "Laugh-In" included many jokes about sex and much political satire. But it became the top-rated show of the late 1960's. "All in the Family," a situation comedy satirizing prejudice, gained top ratings in the early 1970's. Such popular dramatic programs as "Family," "Little House on the Prairie," and "The Waltons" dealt with many moral and ethical problems. The success of such shows encouraged broadcasters to cover a wide range of topics.

Many people believe, however, that television has gone too far in its presentation of controversial themes. The amount of violence and sex on TV have especially drawn a great deal of criticism. In 1975, the national networks adopted a policy prohibiting the broadcasting of programs considered unsuitable for children during the early evening hours. But the next year, a federal court declared this "family hour" policy unconstitutional. The court said the government had pressured the broadcasters into starting the policy and so had violated their rights of free speech. But the court ruled that the networks could continue the policy voluntarily.

In the late 1970's, broadcasters presented an increasing number of made-for-TV movies, serialized dramas called *miniseries*, and other special programs. The most popular such presentation was "Roots," an eight-part drama tracing the history of an American black family from slavery to freedom.

During the early 1980's, subscriptions to cable television and pay-television systems increased dramatically. Video entertainment systems, including videotape recorders, videodisc players, and video games, also gained in popularity.   SIG MICKELSON and HERBERT ZETTL

TELEVISION/*Study Aids*

Related Articles in WORLD BOOK include:

BIOGRAPHIES

Baird, John L.	Hertz, Heinrich R.
Berton, Pierre	Jenkins, Charles F.
Cronkite, Walter	McLuhan, Marshall
De Forest, Lee	Murrow, Edward R.
Farnsworth, Philo T.	Zworykin, Vladimir K.

EQUIPMENT AND PHYSICAL PRINCIPLES

Antenna	Microphone
Coaxial Cable	Microwave
Communications Satellite	Radio
Electromagnetism	Speaker
Electron Gun	Tape Recorder
Electronics	Transistor
Frequency Modulation	Ultrahigh Frequency Wave
Image Orthicon	Very High Frequency Wave

OTHER RELATED ARTICLES

Advertising	CBS Inc.
American Broadcasting	Federal Communications
Companies	Commission
British Broadcasting	Medicine (with pictures)
Corporation	National Broadcasting
Canadian Broadcasting	Company
Corporation	RCA Corporation

Outline

I. Television in the Home
  A. Commercial Television   B. Public Television
II. Specialized Uses
  A. Schools   D. Video Entertain-
  B. Businesses and Hospitals   ment Systems
  C. Security and Surveillance
III. Producing Television Programs
  A. Planning and   B. Putting a Show on the Air
     Preparation   C. Other Production Methods
IV. The Television Industry
  A. The National Networks   E. Pay-Television
  B. Local Commercial Stations   F. Related Industries
  C. Public Stations   G. Television Awards
  D. Cable Television Systems   H. Careers
V. Effects of Television
  A. Effects on Learning   C. Effects on Institutions
  B. Effects on Material Expectations
VI. How Television Works
  A. Creating Television Signals

B. Transmitting Television Signals
C. Receiving Television Signals
VII. Government Regulations
VIII. Television in Other Lands
  A. Canada   D. Africa
  B. Europe   E. Australia and New Zealand
  C. Asia   F. Latin America
IX. History

Questions

What is the role of electromagnetic waves in television?
How does television affect our lives?
What is a dissolve? A super? A wipe?
How did Vladimir K. Zworykin contribute to the development of television?
Who was the first major television entertainer?
What career opportunities are available in television?
What are the methods of transmitting TV programs?
What are some criticisms of television?
What are some specialized uses of television?

Reading and Study Guide

See *Television* in the RESEARCH GUIDE/INDEX, Volume 22, for a *Reading and Study Guide*.

Additional Resources

Level I
GREENFIELD, JEFF. *Television: The First Fifty Years*. Abrams, 1977.
JONES, EURFRON G. *Television Magic*. Viking, 1978. Explains TV production and technology, with experiments to conduct at home.
POLK, LEE, and LESHAN, EDA. *The Incredible Television Machine*. Macmillan, 1977. Examines controversies over TV programming.

Level II
BARNOUW, ERIK. *Tube of Plenty: The Evolution of American Television*. Oxford, 1975.
BROWN, LESTER. *The New York Times Encyclopedia of Television*. Times Books, 1977.
UTZ, PETER. *Video User's Handbook*. Rev. ed. Prentice-Hall, 1980. An amateur's guide to TV electronics.

TELEX. See TELEGRAPH (Special Services).

TELFORD, THOMAS (1757-1834), a noted Scottish civil engineer, devised improved methods of road construction. The Telford method of using large flat stones for road foundations is named after him. Telford engineered bridges, canals, harbors, docks, and waterways. He built the Menai Strait suspension bridge which connects the Island of Anglesey and the mainland of Gwynedd County in Wales, and the Ellesmere Canal, connecting the Mersey, Severn, and Dee rivers in England. He also engineered the Caledonian Canal in Scotland. He was born in Eskdale, Scotland.   ROBERT W. ABBETT

TELL, WILLIAM, was a legendary hero of Switzerland. His story, though not verified by history, represents the spirit of the Swiss movement for independence from the Austrian Hapsburgs in the 1300's. According to legend, Tell was a man of tremendous strength and the most skilled marksman in the whole *canton* (state) of Uri. The Austrian bailiff, Gessler, had ordered all Swiss to bow to a hat he had set up on a pole in the main square of Altdorf. When Tell refused to bow, he was arrested. Gessler knew of Tell's skill with the crossbow and promised to let him go free if Tell could shoot an apple off his own son's head. Tell hit the apple and then said if he had hurt his son, he would have killed Gessler. Gessler had him seized and chained.

While Tell was being taken across a lake in Gessler's boat, a storm broke loose. Gessler ordered Tell untied to help steer the boat safely to the shore. Tell es-

Bettmann Archive

William Tell was a legendary Swiss patriot. The character is known for shooting an apple off his son's head with a crossbow.

caped to the shore and shot an arrow through the tyrant's heart. This act led to a revolt by the Swiss, in which Tell played a leading role. This popular tale is the basis of Johann Friedrich von Schiller's drama *William Tell* (1804). Gioacchino Rossini wrote the opera *William Tell* (1829).   ARTHUR M. SELVI

TELLER. See BANK (Careers in Banking).

TELLER, EDWARD (1908-   ), an outstanding American atomic scientist, is often called the *father of the hydrogen bomb*. His work in nuclear physics led to the development of the H-bomb in 1952.

Teller was born on Jan. 15, 1908, in Budapest, Hungary. He received his doctor's degree in physics from the University of Leipzig, Germany, in 1932. He joined the wartime atomic bomb project in 1941. He worked with the Los Alamos (N. Mex.) National Laboratory until 1952. Then he joined what is now the Lawrence Livermore Laboratory, a research facility at Livermore, Calif., dedicated to designing nuclear weapons. Teller also served as professor of physics at the University of California from 1953 to 1975. He was director of the Livermore laboratory from 1958 to 1960 and associate director from 1972 to 1975.   IRA M. FREEMAN

TELLER, HENRY MOORE (1830-1914), of Colorado, served five terms in the United States Senate. Teller was elected to the Senate as a Republican in 1876. He resigned in 1882 to become Secretary of the Interior. He again won election to the Senate in 1885, and was reelected in 1891. In 1896, he withdrew from the Republican party because its platform called for a monetary system based on the gold standard. Teller favored the free coinage of silver because it would benefit Colorado, a leading silver-producing state. He was elected to the Senate as a Silver Republican party candidate in 1897. In 1903, he was reelected as a Democrat. Teller was born in Allegany County, New York.   MICHAEL McGIFFERT

TELLURIUM, *teh LOO ree uhm*, is a silvery-white semi-metallic element related to sulfur and selenium.

TELSTAR

Franz Müller von Reichenstein, of Romania, discovered it in 1782. Tellurium occurs in the earth's crust in about 2 parts per billion. It is generally obtained as a by-product of copper and lead refining. Industry uses tellurium to improve the machining quality of metal products. It is also used to color glass and ceramics. Tellurium is important in thermoelectric devices.

Tellurium has the symbol Te. The atomic number of Tellurium is 52, and its atomic weight is 127.60. It dissolves in acids and melts at a temperature of about 450° C (842° F.).   J. GORDON PARR

TELSTAR. See COMMUNICATIONS SATELLITE (Kinds); TELEPHONE (Telephone Improvements).

TEMPERA. See PAINTING (Tempera; pictures).

TEMPERANCE is a term for moderation in all activities, especially eating and drinking. It can also refer to the practice of not drinking alcohol at all.

Related Articles in WORLD BOOK include:

Alcoholics Anonymous	Nation, Carry A. M.
American Council	Prohibition
on Alcohol Problems	Woman's Christian
Anthony, Susan B.	Temperance Union

TEMPERANCE UNION, WOMAN'S CHRISTIAN. See WOMAN'S CHRISTIAN TEMPERANCE UNION.

TEMPERATE ZONE. See ZONE.

TEMPERATURE is how hot or cold something is as measured on a particular scale. The concept of temperature is closely related to the flow of heat between two connected objects of different temperatures. Heat always flows from the hotter object to the cooler one.

Instruments that measure temperature are called *thermometers*. A scale marked on the thermometer indicates each level of "hotness." The two most common temperature scales used on thermometers are *Fahrenheit* and *Celsius*. Temperatures on all scales are based on the *International Practice Temperature Scale of 1968* (see THERMOMETER [Temperature Scales]).

Scientists often speak of *thermodynamic temperature*, a fundamental physical quality completely independent of the properties of a substance. The unit of thermodynamic temperature is the *kelvin*, indicated by K. This unit was agreed upon by scientists from many nations. All temperatures are based on their position above or below 273.16 K, a temperature called the *triple point of water*. At this temperature, water, ice, and water vapor all exist together. In common practice, a temperature is actually expressed in terms of its difference from the melting point of ice. Under one atmosphere of pressure, ice melts at a temperature 0.01 K lower than the triple point of water (see ATMOSPHERE).

Temperature does not seem to have an upper limit. Scientists believe the temperature at the center of the sun is about 15 million degrees Celsius (27 million degrees Fahrenheit). However, the interior of any star larger than the sun is probably much hotter. On the other hand, there does seem to be a lower limit to temperature. This theoretical limit, called *absolute zero*, has a value of −273.15° C or −459.67° F. At this temperature, the molecules and atoms of a substance have the least possible energy.   HARMON H. PLUMB

Related Articles in WORLD BOOK include:

Absolute Zero	Boiling Point	Cryogenics
Air	Climate	Freezing Point

Heat
Melting Point
Pyrometry

Specific Heat
Sun (The Sun's Heat)
Weather

TEMPERATURE, BODY. Body temperature is a measurement of the heat in an animal's body. The body of an animal generates heat by burning food. But the animal also loses heat to—or gains heat from—its environment.

Birds and mammals, including human beings, are *warm-blooded animals*. Their body temperature almost always stays fairly constant, regardless of the temperature of their environment. The body of a warm-blooded animal balances the amount of heat it exchanges with the environment with the amount it produces by burning food. Nearly all other animals are *cold-blooded animals*. Their body cannot balance this heat exchange so accurately. As a result, their body temperature tends to vary with the temperature of their environment.

When taken orally, the average body temperature of a healthy, resting adult human being is 98.6° F. (37.0° C). Physicians consider a temperature within 1° F. (0.5° C) of this figure normal. A higher temperature may indicate a fever (see FEVER). A lower temperature may be a sign of old age or of certain illnesses.

Warm-Blooded Animals make various physical and behavioral adjustments to regulate their heat exchange with the environment. In cold surroundings, they increase the production of body heat and decrease the amount of heat lost to the environment. In hot surroundings, they do just the opposite. A part of the brain called the *hypothalamus* controls these adjustments. Certain nerves in the skin and deep within the body send messages to the hypothalamus. The hypothalamus compares the temperatures of these areas with that of the brain. It triggers the necessary responses by nerves and glands to keep a normal body temperature.

Even with the various controls, the body temperature of a warm-blooded animal does not remain entirely constant. It changes slightly throughout the day. In a healthy human being, for example, the body temperature is lowest in the morning and then rises until late afternoon. It falls again during sleep. Strenuous activity can raise the body temperature. In cold surroundings, the temperature of the skin and limbs may drop far below the temperature deep within the body.

Each species of warm-blooded animal has its own normal body temperature. Each species also functions best when the temperature of its surroundings remains within a certain range. This range varies greatly from species to species, depending on such factors as the thickness of fur and the rate at which its body burns food. Some warm-blooded animals hibernate. During hibernation, their body temperature drops almost to the temperature of their environment. See HIBERNATION.

Cold-Blooded Animals lack the precise temperature regulation abilities that characterize warm-blooded creatures. However, many cold-blooded animals can exercise some physical and behavioral control over body temperature. Reptiles, for example, can alter the amount of heat their body absorbs from the sun by changing their skin color. Moreover, many reptiles alternately warm themselves in the sun and cool themselves in the shade, thereby maintaining a fairly constant body temperature throughout the day.   JAMES EDWARD HEATH

See also WARM-BLOODED ANIMAL; COLD-BLOODED ANIMAL; HYPOTHERMIA.

Milt and Joan Mann

The Hall of the Great Buddha in Nara, Japan, is the world's largest wooden building. The temple has a bronze statue of Buddha that stands more than 50 feet (15 meters) high.

TEMPERING is a process of hardening glass and metals, especially steel. Steel can be made very hard and strong by tempering. First, the steel is heated to a high temperature. Next, it is *quenched* (cooled rapidly) by plunging it into water, oil, or other liquid. Then, it is heated again to a temperature lower than that used before quenching it, and is allowed to cool slowly.

Tempering changes the internal structure of the steel. Different uses of steel require different properties, such as varying degrees of hardness, strength, and toughness. To obtain those properties, the structure of steel is changed by tempering it at various temperatures.

Thin films of iron oxide form on steel that is being heated in the tempering process. Those films have different colors, known as *temper colors*, which vary with the tempering temperature.

Glass is tempered in a somewhat similar way. It is heated until it becomes almost soft, then chilled by blasts of air or by plunging it into oil or other liquids. Glass which has been tempered may be up to five times as hard as ordinary glass. It may be used to hammer nails into wood. A sheet of tempered glass can be struck by a hammer without breaking.   Joel S. Hirschhorn

See also Annealing.

TEMPLARS, KNIGHTS. See Knights Templars.

TEMPLE is a building used for worship. Temples have been built since earliest times and in many parts of the world. Most temples are built to honor a god or many gods, and sometimes a temple is considered the home of the god. People have always decorated their temples in the most beautiful way they could. The temple is usually one of the finest buildings in a community.

Many temples contain statues or pictures of the god who is worshiped. An altar may stand inside or in front of the temple. Priests usually conduct the services.

The Bible tells about the beautiful Temple of Solomon in Jerusalem where the Jews worshiped their God. Jesus taught in the Second Temple, rebuilt by Herod.

The ancient Egyptians built large temples with courts and porticoes. Some of these temples are still standing. The Babylonians and Assyrians built temples on platforms, and sometimes beside or on top of great, high towers. The most outstanding temples in the world are those of the ancient Greeks. The finest of these is the Parthenon. Greek temples usually had rows of columns around the outside. The Romans also built magnificent temples, some copied from the Greeks.

In America, the Aztec, the Maya, and the Inca built large temples before Columbus arrived. Remains of these temples still stand in Mexico, Guatemala, and Peru. The Mayan and Aztec temples were built on high pyramids (see Maya [picture: The Ruins of Tikal]).

Temples are found throughout Asia. Carved stone figures usually cover the temples of India. Many-storied towers called *pagodas* often serve as temples in India.

A famous temple is that of the Mormons at Salt Lake City, Utah (see Mormons [picture: Mormon Temple]). Jewish houses of worship are sometimes referred to as temples. Some fraternal orders also call their meeting houses temples.   Carl K. Hersey

Related Articles in World Book include:

Abu Simbel,	Greece, Ancient	Parthenon
Temples of	(pictures)	Sculpture
Altar	Indonesia	(picture:
Angkor	(picture)	Kailasanatha
Architecture	Pagoda	Temple)
(pictures)	Pantheon	Tabernacle
Bangkok (picture)		

TEMPLE, HENRY JOHN. See Palmerston, Viscount.

TEMPLE, SHIRLEY (1928-   ), was the most popular child motion-picture star of the 1930's. She made her movie debut at the age of 3 and became a star in the 1934 film musical *Stand Up and Cheer*. Shirley Temple made about 25 movies during the 1930's, including *Little Miss Marker* (1934), *The Little Colonel* (1935), *The Littlest Rebel* (1935), and *Dimples* (1936). She played teen-age roles in many movies during the 1940's, but these films were not as popular as her earlier pictures.

Shirley Temple retired from motion pictures in 1949. She married Charles A. Black in 1950. In 1969, President Richard M. Nixon appointed her a U.S. representative to the United Nations General Assembly. In 1974, President Gerald R. Ford named her the United States ambassador to Ghana. She was chief of protocol in the Department of State in 1976 and 1977. She was the first woman to hold that post. She was born in Santa Monica, Calif.   Harriet Van Horne

Scene from *Just Around the Corner* (1938); Bettmann Archive
Shirley Temple, a child motion-picture star of the 1930's, appeared in several films with dancer Bill Robinson, *above*.

TEMPLE OF ARTEMIS. See Seven Wonders of the World.

TEMPLE OF SOLOMON. See Solomon; Jerusalem (History).

TEMPLE OF ZEUS. See Olympia.

TEMPLES OF ABU SIMBEL. See Abu Simbel, Temples of.

TEMPO means the rate of speed with which music is to be played or sung. It comes from the Latin *tempus*, meaning *time*. Such words as *lento* (slow), *andante* (moderate), and *allegro* (fast) describe the tempo of music.

TEMPORAL BONES. See Head.

TEN COMMANDMENTS are Biblical rules that state the basic religious and moral ideals of Judaism and Christianity. The commandments are also called the *Decalogue*, from two Greek words meaning *ten words*.

Gouache painting on vellum (A.D. 840) by an unknown artist from the Moutier-Grandval Bible; British Museum, London
The Ten Commandments, according to the Bible, were given from God to the Israelite leader Moses on Mount Sinai. In the top scene above, Moses receives the commandments from the hand of God. Below, Moses reads the commandments to Joshua, his lieutenant, *holding a staff,* and the other Israelites.

The Ten Commandments appear twice in the Old Testament—in Exodus 20: 2-17 and in Deuteronomy 5: 6-21. The two versions differ slightly. The first group of commandments deals with duties toward God, and the second group concerns relations among persons. There are three ways of numbering the individual commandments. In the King James Version of Exodus, the Ten Commandments basically consist of 11 sentences. They are:

1. I am the Lord thy God.
2. Thou shalt have no other gods before me.
3. Thou shalt not make unto thee any graven image, or any likeness of any thing that is in heaven above, or that is in the earth beneath, or that is in the water under the earth. . . .
4. Thou shalt not take the name of the Lord thy God in vain. . . .
5. Remember the sabbath day, to keep it holy. . . .
6. Honor thy father and thy mother.
7. Thou shalt not kill.
8. Thou shalt not commit adultery.
9. Thou shalt not steal.
10. Thou shalt not bear false witness against thy neighbor.
11. Thou shalt not covet thy neighbor's house, thou shalt not covet thy neighbor's wife, nor his manservant, nor his maidservant, nor his ox, nor his ass, nor any thing that is thy neighbor's.

In the Old Testament, the Ten Commandments appear as conditions of a *covenant* (agreement) between God and His chosen people, the Israelites. The Old Testament tells that the finger of God wrote the commandments on two stone tablets given to Moses on Mount Sinai. As Moses came down from the mountain, he saw the Israelites worshiping a golden calf. Enraged at the idol worship, Moses smashed the tablets. But at God's command, he carved the commandments into other stone tablets. The Israelites kept the tablets in a wooden ark (see ARK OF THE COVENANT).

By the A.D. 200's, Christian teachers believed that God had stamped the commandments on the conscience of every human being, even before the laws were engraved on stone. Beginning in the A.D. 400's, everyone who became a Christian memorized the Ten Commandments. By the A.D. 800's, the laws had become a central part of church education. By the 1200's, the leading Christian scholars regarded them as principles of a universal natural law that governed human conduct. Protestant reformers of the 1500's included the decalogue in their catechisms.   WILLIAM A. CLEBSCH

See also MOSES.

TEN LOST TRIBES. See JEWS (Invasions and Conquests).

TENANT, in law, is a person who holds or possesses lands or buildings by any kind of title. In popular speech, a tenant is a person who has the right to occupy and use lands or buildings which belong to another person, known as the landlord. A *lease* (written agreement), signed by both owner and tenant, states the terms and period of time.

The relation of landlord and tenant had its origin in the feudal system of the Middle Ages. Some of the feudal obligations still survive in the present laws. The rights and duties of the *lessor* (landlord) and *lessee* (tenant) are generally defined in detail by the written lease. The terms of a lease bind the heirs, successors, or administrators of both tenant and landlord.

A *tenant at will* occupies property for an indefinite period, which may be ended at any time by either landlord or tenant. A tenant at will is entitled to a notice of removal. If there are crops growing on the land, the tenant may harvest them when they are ready.

A *tenant at sufferance* occupies property without the express consent of the owner or after the term of possession has expired. The tenant may be put off the property at any time by the landlord.   WILLIAM TUCKER DEAN

See also EVICTION; JOINT TENANCY; LEASE.

TENANT FARMING is raising crops and livestock on rented land. Farmers who rent all the land they use are called *tenants*. Those who rent only part of the land they farm are called *part owners* or *part tenants*.

The landlord usually supplies all the land and buildings, while the tenant contributes the labor. A tenant may pay fixed cash rent or may share the crops or the livestock with the landlord. Tenants who share only the crops with the landlord are sometimes called *sharecroppers*. In the early 1970's, 13 per cent of all farmers in the United States were tenants.   MARSHALL HARRIS

See also ASIA (Farm Organization); SHARECROPPER; UNITED STATES, HISTORY OF THE (1870-1916 [The War-Torn South]).

TENDERFOOT. See BOY SCOUTS (Scouting).

TENDON, *TEHN duhn,* or SINEW, *SIHN yoo,* is a strong white cord that attaches muscles to bones or car-

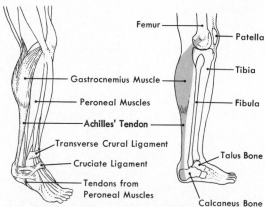

Femur — Patella — Tibia — Gastrocnemius Muscle — Peroneal Muscles — Achilles' Tendon — Fibula — Transverse Crural Ligament — Cruciate Ligament — Talus Bone — Tendons from Peroneal Muscles — Calcaneus Bone

tilage. Muscles move bones by pulling on tendons. The tendons consist of tough fibers twined spirally, as in rope. Some are round, others long or flat. One end of a tendon arises from the end of a muscle. The other end is woven into the substance of a bone. The tendon slides up and down inside a sheath of fibrous tissue, as an arm moves in a coat sleeve. A cut tendon can be *sutured* (sewed) together. It heals from the tendon sheath within six weeks.   MARSHALL R. URIST

See also ACHILLES' TENDON; HAND; HUMAN BODY (picture: Ligaments and Tendons); MUSCLE (Skeletal Muscles); KNEE.

TENEMENT is the legal name for any house built to hold two or more families. But the word *tenement* is generally used to describe the shabby houses occupied by many of the poor people of a city. People allow certain sections in many large cities to decline because building regulations are not strict enough or are ignored. As property values increase, causing taxes to soar, owners divide older houses into tenements that usually hold many families. New buildings are often built cheaply and with little thought for safety or health. Many have small, dark, and unsanitary rooms. Sometimes several families live crowded together in one small apartment. The worst districts are called *slums*.

TENERIFE. See CANARY ISLANDS.

TENG HSIAO-P' ING. See DENG XIAOPING.

TENNENT is the family name of two brothers, American clergymen. They were leaders in the "Great Awakening" religious revival in America (see GREAT AWAKENING). Their father, William Tennent, Sr. (1673-1746), founded the "Log College" near Philadelphia.

Gilbert Tennent (1703-1764), a Presbyterian pastor and a revivalist, aroused both fervent support and bitter opposition. Crowds flocked to hear him during a New England tour in 1740 and 1741. His sermon on "The Danger of an Unconverted Ministry" in 1740 was a cause of the division of the Presbyterian Synod in 1741. As pastor of the Second Presbyterian Church in Philadelphia, he helped reunite the synod in 1758. He was born in Ireland.

William Tennent, Jr. (1705-1777), is remembered for an unusual trance into which he fell as a young man. He appeared to be dead and was prepared for burial. He spoke of having seen heavenly glories when he recovered. He later became an esteemed Presbyterian pastor. He was born in Ireland.   LEFFERTS A. LOETSCHER

Memphis, in West Tennessee, Overlooks the Mississippi.

Black Angus Cattle on Middle Tennessee Farm.

TENNESSEE

THE VOLUNTEER STATE

The contributors of this article are J. Milton Henry, Professor of History at Austin Peay State University; Jewell A. Phelps, Professor Emeritus of Geography at George Peabody College for Teachers of Vanderbilt University in Nashville; and John Seigenthaler, Publisher of The Tennessean *of Nashville.*

Tennessee (blue) ranks 34th in size among all the states, and 8th in size among the Southern States (gray).

TENNESSEE is one of the states that link the North and the South. Life in West and Middle Tennessee resembles life in the Deep South. East Tennessee is similar to parts of the North. Even during the Civil War, Tennessee loyalties were divided between the North and the South. Tennessee was the last Confederate state to leave the Union, and the first to return.

The lonely pioneer, wearing a coonskin cap and carrying a trusty flintlock rifle, is a symbol of Tennessee's great past. But a better symbol of Tennessee's present and future is the nuclear physicist working in an Oak Ridge laboratory, or the engineer designing a new dam for the Tennessee Valley Authority. Like people throughout the United States, Tennesseans today work in business offices and factories as well as on farms.

Tennessee stretches all the way from North Carolina, one of the easternmost states, to Arkansas, one of the westernmost states in the South. At its eastern boundaries, Tennessee starts high in the mountains. The land becomes lower toward the west and gradually slopes until it reaches the banks of the Mississippi River. Tennessee's fertile soil and abundant mineral deposits make it a rich agricultural and mining state. But manufacturing is Tennessee's chief source of income and jobs.

Knoxville Chamber of Commerce

The Great Smoky Mountains Stretch Across East Tennessee.

Indians once roamed Tennessee's mountains and forests. Early explorers passed through the region, and people from Europe fought to decide who would own it. Pioneers crossed the mountains to settle in the wilderness. It was the pioneers who brought with them the spirit of independence and daring that has become a part of Tennessee's history. The pioneers formed their own governments in this region before any other independent governments existed in North America. In 1796, Tennessee became the 16th state in the Union. Such Tennesseans as John Sevier in the Revolutionary War, Andrew Jackson in the War of 1812, and Alvin C. York in World War I established a Tennessee military tradition of honor and bravery.

More Civil War battles were fought in Tennessee than in any other state except Virginia. Three Presidents of the United States—Andrew Jackson, James K. Polk, and Andrew Johnson—all distinguished themselves in Tennessee. Two great heroes of the Texas Revolution, Davy Crockett and Sam Houston, grew up in Tennessee, and served its people.

The name *Tennessee* comes from *Tanasie*, the name of a Cherokee village in the region. Tennessee is sometimes called the *Big Bend State*, because of the sudden bend in the Tennessee River that makes it flow through the state twice. However, Tennessee is usually called the *Volunteer State* because of its outstanding military traditions.

Nashville is the capital of Tennessee. Memphis is the state's largest city.

Facts in Brief

Capital: Nashville.

Government: *Congress*—U.S. senators, 2; U.S. representatives, 9. *Electoral Votes*—11. *State Legislature*—senators, 33; representatives, 99. *Counties*—95.

Area: 42,244 sq. mi. (109,411 km²), including 916 sq. mi. (2,372 km²) of inland water; 34th in size among the states. *Greatest Distances*—east-west, 480 mi. (772 km); north-south, 115 mi. (185 km).

Elevation: *Highest*—Clingmans Dome, 6,643 ft. (2,025 m) above sea level. *Lowest*—182 ft. (55 m) above sea level in Shelby County.

Population: *1980 Census*—4,590,750; 17th among the states; density, 109 persons per sq. mi. (42 per km²); distribution, 59 per cent urban, 41 per cent rural. *1970 Census*—3,926,018.

Chief Products: *Agriculture*—soybeans, beef cattle, milk, hogs, tobacco. *Manufacturing*—chemicals; food products; nonelectric machinery; electric machinery and equipment; clothing; fabricated metal products; transportation equipment. *Mining*—coal, stone, zinc.

Statehood: June 1, 1796, the 16th state.

State Abbreviations: Tenn. (traditional); TN (postal).

State Motto: *Agriculture and Commerce.*

State Songs: "My Homeland, Tennessee." Words by Nell Grayson Taylor; music by Roy Lamont Smith. "My Tennessee." Words and music by Francis Hannah Tranum. "Rocky Top." Words and music by Boudleaux and Felice Bryant. "The Tennessee Waltz." Words by Pee Wee King; music by Redd Stewart. "When It's Iris Time in Tennessee." Words and music by Willa Mae Ward.

Tennessee Conservation Dept.

Tennessee Conservation Dept.

The Governor's Mansion near Nashville was once a private residence. The state bought the building and grounds in 1949.

Inside the Governor's Mansion, the entrance hall has a marble floor and a graceful staircase.

TENNESSEE/Government

Constitution. Tennesseans have kept the same Constitution since 1870. The state had two earlier constitutions. The first constitution was adopted in 1796, the year Tennessee achieved statehood, and the second was adopted in 1834.

Either the state legislature or a constitutional convention can propose amendments to the Constitution. In the legislature, a proposed amendment first needs the approval of a majority of both houses. Then, during the next regular legislative session, it must be approved by two-thirds of both houses. Finally, a majority of persons voting in an election for governor must approve the amendment.

Constitutional conventions cannot be held more often than once every six years. They may be called by a majority of the legislators with the approval of a majority of voters. Amendments proposed by a constitutional convention must be approved by a majority of voters.

Executive. Tennessee's governor holds office for a four-year term and may serve any number of terms, but not more than two in a row. The governor receives $68,226 a year. The speaker of the state Senate has the title of lieutenant governor and is next in line after the governor. For a list of Tennessee's governors, see the *History* section of this article.

The governor appoints the heads of Tennessee's 14 chief administrative departments. These department heads make up the cabinet. But the governor does not have the power to appoint the state's four top administrative officers.

The legislature chooses the secretary of state, who serves a four-year term, and both the state treasurer and the state comptroller of the treasury, who serve for two years. The state Supreme Court selects the attorney general to serve an eight-year term. The voters elect the three members of the Public Service Commission. This board regulates intrastate carriers and privately owned utility companies.

Legislature, called the *General Assembly*, consists of a 33-member Senate and a 99-member House of Representatives. Senators serve four-year terms and house members serve two-year terms, beginning on the day they are elected. They are elected from legislative districts.

The Assembly meets in odd-numbered years on the first Tuesday in January for a 15-day organizational session. The regular session begins on the fourth Tuesday in February. Regular sessions are limited to 90 legislative days. Special sessions may be called by the governor or by two-thirds of the members of each house.

Courts. The highest court in Tennessee is the state Supreme Court. It has a chief justice and four associate justices, elected by the voters for eight-year terms. The Tennessee court of appeals has nine judges. It hears civil cases that have been transferred from lower courts. This court may serve as a complete body or in three separate divisions. The court of criminal appeals has seven judges. It hears appeals from criminal trial courts.

Tennessee has 25 judicial circuits and 12 of them have criminal courts. Circuit courts have jurisdiction over any matters for which no other court exists in the circuit. Other trial courts are *chancery* (equity) courts, juvenile and domestic relations courts, county courts of monthly sessions, and general sessions courts. All judges in Tennessee are elected for eight-year terms.

Local Government. A county court of quarterly sessions governs most of Tennessee's 95 counties. This court consists of from 10 to 50 justices of the peace, and is presided over by a county judge or a county chairman. The court meets four times a year to perform such functions as setting taxes and authorizing bond issues. A few counties have established county commissions to govern them. All counties have such officials as the sheriff, tax assessor, trustee, register, and court clerk.

Any of Tennessee's about 330 incorporated cities and towns may, by popular vote, adopt *home rule*. That is, a city may vote to frame and operate its own charter instead of remaining under the control of the state legislature. But only about 10 cities have adopted home rule since the Constitution made it available in 1953. About 200 cities have a mayor-council government. Other cities use either the council-manager or commissioner

The State Seal

The State Flag

Symbols of Tennessee. The plow, the sheaf of wheat, and the cotton plant on the seal represent agriculture. The river boat symbolizes commerce. The Roman numerals show that Tennessee was the 16th state of the Union. The date 1796 is the year the first state constitution was approved. The seal was adopted in 1801. On the flag, the three stars stand for East, Middle, and West Tennessee. The circle represents unity. The flag was adopted in 1905.

Flag and bird illustrations courtesy of Eli Lilly and Company

system. Nashville has combined city and county governments into one government, called *Metro*. This unit is governed by a mayor and a city council.

Taxation. A sales and use tax, and a tax on gasoline and motor fuels, each account for about 22 per cent of the state government's income. Other taxes include an income tax on investments; corporation income taxes; taxes on tobacco, alcoholic beverages, and inheritance; a gross receipts tax; and license fees. More than a third of the state's income comes from federal grants and other U.S. government programs.

Politics. Tennessee has been a Democratic stronghold for most of its history. During the 1960's, however, Republicans made strong gains in the state legislature. In 1966, Howard H. Baker, Jr., became the first Republican elected to the U.S. Senate from Tennessee since the 1860's. Republicans won the governorship in 1970 and 1978. By the end of the 1970's, Tennessee had become a two-party state.

In presidential elections, Republicans have carried Tennessee nine times. For a record of the state's electoral votes, see ELECTORAL COLLEGE (table).

The State Bird
Mockingbird

The State Capitol overlooks Nashville, Tennessee's capital since 1826. Nashville was also the capital from 1812 to 1817. Other capitals were Knoxville (1792-1812, 1817) and Murfreesboro (1818-1826).

Tennessee Conservation Dept.

The State Flower
Iris

The State Tree
Tulip Poplar

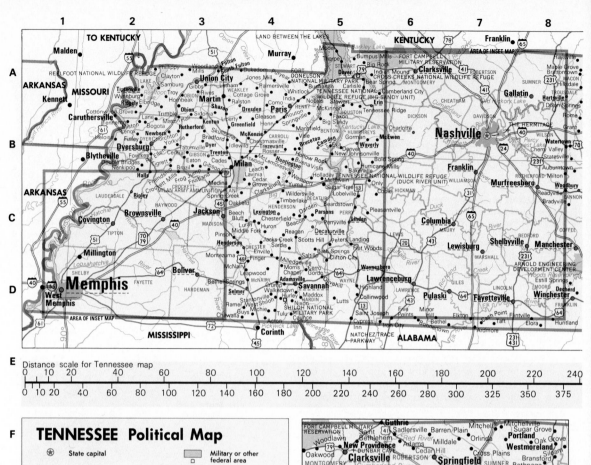

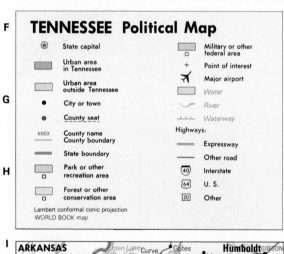

TENNESSEE Political Map

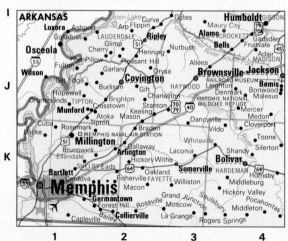

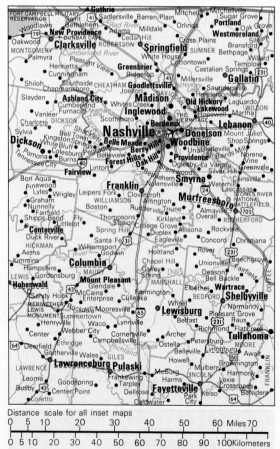

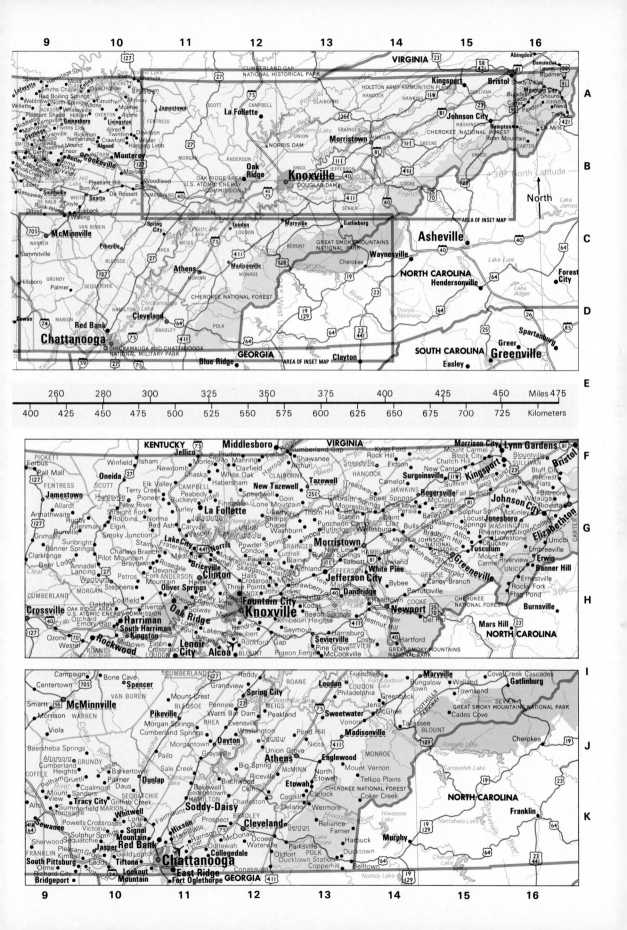

Tennessee Map Index

Jacks Creek ... C 4
Jacksboro ... 1,620. °G 11
Jackson ... 49,131. °C 3
Jamestown ... 2,364. °A 11
Jasper ... 2,633. °K 10
Jefferson City .5,612. .H 13
Jellico ... 2,798. .F 11
Jena ... I 14
Joelton ... G 6
John Sevier ... H 12
Johnson City 39,753. .A 16
Johnson City
Southeast* ... A 15
Jones Mill ... A 4
Jonesboro ... 2,829. °G 16
Joppa ... G 13
Karns* ... B 12
Keeling ... J 2
Kelso ... K 8
Kempville ... A 9
Kenton ... 1,551. .B 3
Kimball ... 1,220. .K 10
Kimberlin Heights ... H 12
Kimmins ... I 5
Kingsport ... 32,027. .A 15
Kingsport North* ... A 15
Kingston ... 4,441. °I 10
Kingston
Springs ... 1,017. .H 6
Kirkland ... I 7
Knoxville ... 183,139. °B 12
Kodak ... H 13
Kyles Ford ... F 14
Laager* ... D 9
Laconia ... K 3
Ladds ... K 10
Lafayette ... 3,808. °A 9
La Follette ... 8,176. .A 12
La Grange ... 185. .K 3
Lake City ... 2,335. .G 11
Lake Hills-Murray
Hills* ... D 10
Lakeland* ... 612. .D 1
Lakemont ... I 12
Lakesite* ... 651. .D 10
Lakewood ... 2,325. .G 7
Lancaster ... B 9
Lancing ... H 10
Lane ... B 2
Lascassas ... H 8
Latham ... A 4
Laurel Bloomery ... A 16
La Vergne ... 5,495. .H 7
Lavinia ... B 4
Lawrenceburg10,175. °D 6
Leach ... B 4
Leapwood ... D 4
Lebanon ... 11,872. °G 8
Leighton ... J 4
Leipers Fork ... H 6
Lenoir City ... 5,446. .I 11
Lenox ... B 2
Leoma ... K 5
Lewisburg ... 8,760. °C 7
Lexie Crossroads ... K 8
Lexington ... 5,934. °C 4
Liberty ... B 4
Liberty ... 365. .B 9
Liberty Hill ... G 13
Limestone ... G 15
Linden ... 1,087. °C 5
Linton ... H 6
Littlelot ... I 5
Livingston ... 3,372. °A 10
Lobelville ... 993. .C 5
Locke ... K 1
Locust Springs ... G 15
Lone Mountain ... G 13
Lone Oak ... K 10
Long Island ... F 16
Lookout
Mountain ... 1,886. .K 11
Loretto ... 1,612. .K 5
Loudon ... 3,940. °C 12
Louisville ... I 11
Lovell ... H 11
Lowland ... G 14
Lupton City ... K 11
Luray ... C 4
Luttrell ... 962. .G 12
Lutts ... D 5
Lyles ... H 5
Lynchburg ... 668. °K 8
Lynn Gardens ... F 16
Lynnville ... 383. .J 6
Macon ... K 2
Maddox ... D 4
Madison ... G 7
Madisonville ... 2,884. °C 12
Malesus ... J 4
Manchester ... 7,250. °C 8
Manring ... F 12
Mansfield ... B 4
Maple Grove ... A 8
Martha ... G 8
Martin ... 8,898. .A 3
Maryville ... 17,480. °C 12
Mascot ... H 12
Mason ... 471. .J 2
Mason Hall ... B 3
Maury City ... 989. .I 3
Mayland ... B 10
Maynardville ... 924. °G 12
McBurg ... K 7
McCains ... J 6
McCloud ... G 14
McCookville ... I 13
McDonald ... K 12
McEwen ... 1,352. .B 6
McGhee ... J 14
McIlwain ... B 5
McKenzie ... 5,405. .B 4
McKinley ... G 16
McKinnon ... A 5
McLemoresville .311. .B 4
McMinnville .10,683. °C 9
McNairy ... D 4
Medford ... G 11
Medina ... 687. .C 3
Medon ... 162. .J 4
Memphis ... 646,356. °D 1
Mercer ... J 4
Michie ... 530. .D 4
Middle Fork ... C 4
Middleburg ... K 4
Middleton ... 596. .K 4
Midtown ... I 10
Midway ... A 10
Milan ... 8,083. .B 3
Milldale ... F 7
Milledgeville ... 392. .D 4
Millersville ... G 7
Milligan College ... G 16
Millington ... 20,236. .D 1
Milton ... B 8
Minor Hill ... 564. .D 6
Miston ... B 2
Mitchell ... F 7
Mitchellville ... 209. .F 7
Model ... A 5
Mohawk Crossroad ... G 14
Monoville ... B 9
Monroe ... A 10
Monteagle ... 1,126. .K 9
Monterey ... 2,610. .B 10
Montezuma ... C 4
Mooresburg ... G 14
Mooresville ... J 6
Morgan Springs ... J 11
Morgantown ... J 11
Morley ... F 11
Morris Chapel ... D 4
Morrison ... 587. .J 9
Morrison City ... F 15
Morristown ... 19,683. °B 14
Moscow ... 499. .K 3
Mosheim ... 1,539. .G 15
Moss ... A 9
Mount Carmel 3,764. .F 15
Mount Carmel ... G 16
Mount Crest ... I 11
Mount Juliet .2,879. .G 7
Mount Olive ... H 12
Mount
Pleasant ... 3,375. J 6
Mount Vernon ... J 13
Mount View ... K 9
Mountain City 2,125. °A 16
Mulberry ... K 8
Munford ... 1,587. .J 1
Murfreesboro 32,845. °B 8
Nankipoo ... B 2
Nashville ... 455,651. °B 7
Netherland ... B 10
Neubert ... H 12
Neva ... A 16
New Canton ... F 15
New Hope* ... 681. .D 9
New
Johnsonville .1,824. .B 5
New Line ... G 13
New Market ... 1,216. .H 13
New Middleton ... B 9
New Providence ... F 5
New River ... G 10
New Tazewell .1,677. .F 13
Newbern ... 2,794. .B 3
Newcomb ... F 11
Newport ... 7,580. °H 14
Niota ... 765. .J 13
Nixon ... D 4
Nobles ... A 5
Nolensville ... H 7
Norene ... H 8
Norma ... G 10
Normandy ... 118. .J 8
Norris ... 1,374. .G 11
North Etowah ... K 13
North Springs ... A 9
Norwood ... H 11
Nunnelly ... I 5
Nutbush ... I 3
Oak Grove ... F 8
Oak Hill ... 4,609. .H 7
Oak Ridge ... 27,662. .B 12
Oakdale ... 323. .H 10
Oakfield ... C 3
Oakland ... 472. .K 2
Oakwood ... F 5
Obion ... 1,282. .A 3
Ocoee ... K 12
Oglesby ... H 7
Old Hickory ... G 7
Oldfort ... K 12
Olivehill ... D 5
Oliver Springs 3,659. .H 11
Oneida ... 3,029. .F 10
Only ... B 5
Ooltewah ... K 11
Orebank* ... A 15
Orlinda ... 382. .F 7
Orme ... 181. .K 9
Orysa ... J 2
Ostella ... J 7
Overall ... I 8
Ozone ... I 9
Pailo ... J 11
Pall Mall ... F 9
Palmer ... 1,027. .D 9
Palmersville ... A 4
Palmyra ... G 5
Pandora ... A 16
Paris ... 10,728. °A 4
Park City ... K 7
Parksville ... K 13
Parrottsville ... 118. .H 14
Parsons ... 2,422. .C 5
Paulette ... G 12
Peabody ... G 11
Peakland ... J 12
Pegram ... 1,081. .H 6
Pelham ... K 9
Pennine ... I 12
Perryville ... C 5
Persia ... G 14
Peters Landing ... C 5
Petersburg ... 681. .J 7
Petros ... H 10
Philadelphia ... 507. .I 13
Phillippy ... A 2
Pigeon Forge .1,822. .I 13
Pikeville ... 2,085. °C 10
Pilot Mountain ... G 10
Pine Grove ... I 13
Pinewood ... H 5
Piney Flats ... F 16
Pinson ... C 3
Pioneer ... G 11
Piperton* ... 746. .D 2
Pittman Center* 488. .C 13
Pleasant Grove ... K 10
Pleasant Grove ... J 7
Pleasant Hill ... 371. .J 2
Pleasant Hill ... B 10
Pleasant Shade ... A 9
Pleasant View ... G 6
Pleasantville ... C 5
Pocahontas ... K 4
Pomona ... H 5
Pomona ... B 10
Portland ... 4,030. .F 7
Powder Springs ... G 12
Powell ... H 12
Powells
Crossroads ... 918. .K 10
Prospect ... K 12
Providence ... H 7
Pruden ... F 12
Pulaski ... 7,184. °D 7
Puncheon Camp ... G 13
Puryear ... 624. .A 4
Quebeck ... C 9
Ralston ... A 3
Ramer ... 429. .D 4
Raus ... J 8
Readyville ... C 8
Reagan ... C 4
Red Ash ... G 11
Red Bank ... 13,297. .D 10
Red Boiling
Springs ... 1,173. .A 9
Reedtown ... H 14
Reliance ... K 13
Rheatown ... G 15
Riceville ... J 12
Richard City ... 87. .K 9
Richland ... H 13
Richmond ... J 7
Rickman ... B 10
Riddleton ... A 9
Ridgely ... 1,932. .A 2
Ridgeside* ... 417. .D 10
Ridgetop ... 1,225. .G 7
Riovista ... G 16
Ripley ... 6,366. °C 2
Riverview ... H 16
Rives ... 386. .A 3
Roan Mountain ... B 16
Robbins ... G 10
Rock Hill ... F 14
Rock Island ... C 9
Rockdale ... J 5
Rockford ... 567. .I 12
Rockvale ... I 7
Rockwood ... 5,767. .I 10
Rocky Fork ... H 16
Roddy ... I 12
Ro Ellen ... B 2
Rogers Springs ... K 4
Rogersville ... 4,368. °G 14
Rome ... B 8
Rosedale ... H 11
Rosemark ... K 2
Rosser ... B 4
Rossville ... 379. .K 2
Routon ... B 4
Rover ... I 7
Rudderville ... I 7
Rugby ... G 10
Russellville ... G 14
Rutherford ... 1,378. .B 3
Rutledge ... 1,058. °G 13
Sadie ... A 16
Sadlersville ... F 6
St. Bethlehem ... F 5
St. Clair ... G 14
St. Joseph ... 897. .D 6
Sale Creek ... J 11
Saltillo ... 434. .D 4
Samburg ... 465. .A 2
Sanders ... K 9
Sandy Hook ... J 5
Santa Fe ... I 6
Sardis ... 301. .C 4
Saulsbury ... 156. .K 3
Saundersville ... G 7
Savannah ... 6,992. °D 4
Scotts Hill ... 668. .C 4
Scottsboro ... G 6
Selmer ... 3,979. °D 4
Sequatchie ... K 10
Sevierville ... 4,566. °I 13
Sewanee ... K 9
Seymour ... H 12
Shacklett ... H 6
Shady Valley ... A 16
Sharon ... 1,134. .B 3
Sharps Chapel ... G 12
Shawanee ... F 13
Shelbyville ... 13,530. °C 8
Sherwood ... K 9
Shiloh ... G 5
Shipps Bend ... I 5
Shooks Gap ... H 12
Shop Springs ... H 8
Shouns ... A 16
Sidonia ... B 3
Signal
Mountain ... 5,818. .K 10
Silerton ... 100. .K 4
Siloam ... F 8
Silver Hill ... H 8
Skaggston ... H 12
Skullbone ... B 3
Slayden ... 69. .G 5
Smartt ... I 9
Smiths Chapel ... A 9
Smithville ... 3,839. °B 9
Smoky Junction ... G 11
Smyrna ... 8,839. .H 7
Sneedville ... 1,110. °F 14
Soddy-Daisy ... 8,388. .K 11
Solway ... H 11
Somerville ... 2,264. °K 3
South
Carthage* ... 1,004. .B 9
South Cleveland* ... D 10
South Clinton* ... B 12
South Fulton ... 2,735. .A 3
South Harriman ... I 10
South
Pittsburg ... 3,636. .K 9
Southside ... G 5
Sparta ... 4,864. °B 10
Spear Springs ... G 14
Speedwell ... G 12
Spencer ... 1,126. °I 10
Spivey ... A 9
Spring City ... 1,951. .C 11
Spring Creek ... C 4
Spring Hill ... 989. .I 6
Springfield ... 10,814. °F 6
Springville ... B 5
Stainville ... G 11
Stanton ... 540. .J 3
Stantonville ... 271. .D 4
Statesville ... B 8
Stephens ... H 10
Stewart ... A 5
Strawberry Plains ... H 13
Sugar Grove ... F 8
Sugar Tree ... C 5
Sullivan Gardens ... F 15
Sulphur Springs ... K 10
Sulphur Springs ... G 16
Summerfield ... K 9
Summertown ... J 5
Summitville ... C 9
Sunbright ... G 10
Surgoinsville .1,536. .F 15
Sweetwater ... 4,725. .J 13
Sylvia ... G 5
Taft ... D 7
Talbott ... G 13
Tallassee ... J 14
Tarpley ... K 6
Tatumville ... B 3
Tazewell ... 2,090. °F 13
Tellico Plains ... 698. .J 14
Templow ... G 8
Tennemo ... B 2
Tennessee City ... H 5
Tennessee
Ridge ... 1,325. .A 5
Terry Creek ... G 11
Tharpe ... A 5
Thompsons Station ... I 6
Thorn Hill ... G 13
Three Points ... H 12
Tiftona ... K 10
Tigrett ... B 3
Timberlake ... C 4
Timothy ... A 10
Tipton ... J 1
Tiptonville ... 2,438. °A 2
Toone ... 355. .K 4
Townsend ... 351. .I 15
Tracy City ... 1,356. .K 9
Trade ... A 16
Treadway ... G 14
Trenton ... 4,601. °B 3
Trentville ... H 12
Trezevant ... 921. .B 4
Trimble ... 722. .B 3
Triune ... I 7
Troy ... 1,093. .A 3
Tullahoma ... 15,800. .J 8
Tulu ... D 4
Turley ... G 11
Tusculum ... 1,242. .G 15
Twinton ... B 10
Tyner ... K 11
Una ... H 7
Unicoi ... G 16
Union City ... 10,436. °A 3
Union Grove ... J 12
Unionville ... I 7
Vale ... B 4
Valley View ... H 11
Vanleer ... 401. .G 5
Vasper ... G 11
Victoria ... K 10
Vildo ... K 3
Vine ... H 8
Viola ... 149. .J 9
Vonore ... 528. .J 14
Waco ... J 6
Walden* ... 1,293. .D 10
Wales ... K 6
Walkertown ... D 4
Walkertown ... G 15
Walland ... I 15
Walling ... C 9
Wartburg ... 761. °H 10
Wartrace ... 540. .J 8
Washburn ... G 13
Washington ... J 12
Watauga ... 376. .G 16
Waterhill ... H 8
Watertown ... 1,300. .B 8
Waterville ... K 12
Watts Bar Dam ... J 12
Waverly ... 4,405. °B 5
Waynesboro ... 2,109. °D 5
Webber City ... J 5
Webbtown ... A 9
West Shiloh ... D 4
Westel ... I 10
Westmoreland 1,754. .F 8
Westport ... B 4
Wetmore ... K 13
Wheel ... J 7
White Bluff ... 2,055. .H 5
White House .2,225. .F 7
White Oak ... F 11
White Pine ... 1,900. .H 14
Whitehaven* ... D 1
Whites Creek ... G 7
Whitesburg ... G 14
Whiteville ... 1,270. .K 3
Whitleyville ... A 9
Whitlock ... A 4
Whitwell ... 1,783. .K 10
Wilder ... B 10
Wildersville ... C 4
Willard ... G 8
Willette ... A 9
Williamsport ... I 6
Williston ... 395. .K 3
Winchester ... 5,821. °D 8
Winfield ... F 10
Woodbine ... H 7
Woodbury ... 2,160. °C 8
Woodland Mills .526. .A 3
Woodlawn ... F 5
Woodlawn ... B 10
Wrigley ... H 5
Wynnburg ... A 2
Yorkville ... 272. .B 3
Yuma ... B 4

*Does not appear on map; key shows general location.
°County seat.

Source: 1980 census. Places without population figures are unincorporated areas.

A. Witman, Black Star

The Traditional Life of Tennessee is symbolized by the *Grand Ole Opry* radio program, which features country and western music. The program has been on the air since 1925. It is broadcast from Opryland, an entertainment center near Nashville.

The 1980 U.S. census reported that Tennessee had 4,590,750 persons. This figure showed a population increase of 17 per cent over the 1970 census figure, 3,926,018.

About three-fifths of the people of Tennessee live in urban areas, and about two-fifths live in rural areas. About 62 out of 100 live in the six metropolitan areas that lie chiefly within the state (see METROPOLITAN AREA). These are, in order of population, Nashville-Davidson, Memphis, Knoxville, Chattanooga, Johnson City-Kingsport-Bristol, Va., and Clarksville-Hopkinsville, Ky. For the populations of all of these metropolitan areas, see the *Index* to the political map of Tennessee.

Memphis is the state's largest city, followed by Nashville, Knoxville, and Chattanooga. Each of these cities has over 100,000 persons. The fifth largest city is Clarksville with about 55,000 persons. Seven other cities have populations of 25,000 or more. See the articles on Tennessee cities listed in the *Related Articles* at the end of this article.

About 99 out of every 100 Tennesseans were born in the United States. About 16 out of every 100 Tennesseans are blacks, a lower percentage than in most southern states. About 40 per cent of the blacks in Tennessee live in Shelby County. Memphis is the county seat of Shelby County.

Baptists are the largest religious group in the state. Other leading church groups in Tennessee, in order of membership size, include Churches of Christ, Methodist, Presbyterian, and Church of the Nazarene.

POPULATION

Persons per sq. mi.		Persons per km²
More than 100		More than 40
50 to 100		20 to 40
25 to 50		10 to 20
Less than 25		Less than 10

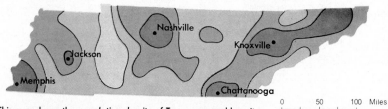

This map shows the *population density* of Tennessee, and how it varies in different parts of the state. Population density means the average number of persons who live in a given area.

0 50 100 Miles
0 50 100 150 Kilometers

WORLD BOOK map

Tennessee Eastman Company

Firestone

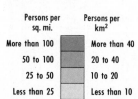

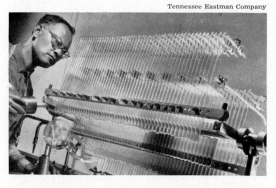

Life in Tennessee Today is reflected in the faces of a chemist in Kingsport, *above*, and workers in a tire factory in Memphis, *right*. As in many other states, the people of Tennessee are moving from country to city and from farm to factory.

Schools. Education in Tennessee began with privately owned schools, usually controlled by churches. Samuel Doak, a Presbyterian minister, started the first school in about 1780. Public schools for children of the poor were established in the early 1800's. In 1873, free education was made available to all children.

The governor appoints a commissioner of education to a four-year term. The commissioner heads the state department of education and the state board of education. The governor serves as a member of the board, and appoints the other 12 members to nine-year terms. Children between the ages of 7 and 16 must attend school. For the number of students and teachers in Tennessee, see EDUCATION (table).

Libraries. The state's first public library was opened in Nashville in 1813. Today, Tennessee has about 230 public libraries. The State Library and Archives in Nashville specializes in collections of Tennessee history, literature, and biography, and state and federal documents. It also operates bookmobiles. The Joint Universities Libraries in Nashville and the University of Tennessee Library in Knoxville have the largest collections in the state.

Museums. The War Memorial Building in Nashville houses the state museum. This museum displays many collections of the Tennessee Historical Society. The Cumberland Museum and Science Center in Nashville features exhibits on natural history and has an art gallery and a planetarium. The Museum of Appalachia in Norris features exhibits on early American life. The Memphis Pink Palace Museum has exhibits on the history of the mid-South.

Cossitt-Goodwyn Library, a branch of the Memphis Public Library, owns a fine collection of books on business, science, and technology.

Memphis Chamber of Commerce

University of Tennessee's Ayres Hall stands on the campus at Knoxville.

Knoxville Chamber of Commerce

UNIVERSITIES AND COLLEGES

Tennessee has 39 universities and colleges accredited by the Southern Association of Colleges and Schools. For enrollments and further information, see UNIVERSITIES AND COLLEGES (table).

Name	Location	Founded	Name	Location	Founded
Austin Peay State University	Clarksville	1927	Maryville College	Maryville	1819
Belmont College	Nashville	1951	Meharry Medical College	Nashville	1876
Bethel College	McKenzie	1842	Memphis Academy of Arts	Memphis	1940
Bryan College	Dayton	1930	Memphis State University	Memphis	1915
Carson-Newman College	Jefferson City	1851	Middle Tennessee		
Christian Brothers College	Memphis	1854	State University	Murfreesboro	1911
Covenant College	Lookout Mountain	1955	Milligan College	Milligan College	1867
David Lipscomb College	Nashville	1891	Scarritt College		
East Tennessee			for Christian Workers	Nashville	1892
State University	Johnson City	1909	South, University of the	Sewanee	1860
Fisk University	Nashville	1865	Southern College of Optometry	Memphis	1932
Freed-Hardeman College	Henderson	1869	Southern Missionary College	Collegedale	1892
Harding University—Harding			Southwestern at Memphis	Memphis	1848
Graduate School of Religion	Memphis	1959	Tennessee, University of	*	*
Johnson Bible College	Knoxville	1893	Tennessee State University	Nashville	1912
King College	Bristol	1867	Tennessee Technological		
Knoxville College	Knoxville	1875	University	Cookeville	1915
Lambuth College	Jackson	1843	Tennessee Wesleyan College	Athens	1857
Lane College	Jackson	1882	Trevecca Nazarene College	Nashville	1942
Lee College	Cleveland	1968	Tusculum College	Greeneville	1794
LeMoyne-Owen College	Memphis	1870	Union University	Jackson	1825
Lincoln Memorial University	Harrogate	1897	Vanderbilt University	Nashville	1873

*For campuses and founding dates, see UNIVERSITIES AND COLLEGES (table).

TENNESSEE/*A Visitor's Guide*

Rugged mountains and thick forests in eastern and central Tennessee provide recreation for hunters, campers, and sightseers. The majestic beauty of Great Smoky Mountains National Park attracts several million visitors a year. Tennessee's beautiful lakes and rivers offer excellent fishing, swimming, and boating. Students of American history delight in the state's many sites of historic interest and importance.

Shostal

Shiloh National Military Park Near Savannah

U.S. Department of Energy

Science and Energy Museum, Oak Ridge

Places to Visit

Following are brief descriptions of some of Tennessee's many interesting places to visit.

American Museum of Science and Energy, at Oak Ridge, features exhibits on energy, including displays on the peaceful uses of nuclear energy.

Blount Mansion, at Knoxville, is the restored home of William Blount, the only governor of Tennessee during territorial days. The mansion was built in 1792.

Fontaine House, in Memphis, is a stately mansion built in 1871 by Amos Woodruff, a prominent businessman. The house features elegant Oriental rugs, crystal chandeliers, and Carrara marble mantels.

Grand Ole Opry House, near Nashville, features weekly performances of country and western music. The music center is at Opryland, an entertainment park.

Lookout Mountain rises 2,146 feet (654 meters) above sea level at the Moccasin Bend of the Tennessee River near Chattanooga. There, Union forces won an important victory in the "Battle Above the Clouds" in November, 1863.

Railroad Museum, at Jackson, is in the restored home of Casey Jones, the railroad hero of the famous folk ballad that describes his fatal ride.

The Hermitage, the home of President Andrew Jackson, is about 10 miles (16 kilometers) east of downtown Nashville. It was first built in 1819, and rebuilt in 1835. Jackson and his wife are buried on the grounds.

The Parthenon, built for the 1897 Tennessee Centennial at Nashville, is the world's only reproduction of the ancient temple at Athens, Greece. It has casts of the Elgin Marbles, sculptures from the original Parthenon.

National Parks, Forests, and Historic Sites. Almost half of the Great Smoky Mountains National Park lies in Tennessee. The rest of the park is in North Carolina.

The Hermitage in Nashville

Fred Bond, Alpha

Memphis Cotton Carnival

Memphis Cotton Carnival Association

The Parthenon in Nashville

Shostal

Annual Events

The Cotton Carnival in Memphis is Tennessee's largest and most colorful yearly event. The carnival, which is held for nine days in May, is called "The Nation's Party in the Land of Cotton." The festivities include a river pageant, grand parade, concerts, and horse shows.

Other annual events in Tennessee include:

January-March: Grand National Field Trials for Bird Dogs in Grand Junction (February); Valleydale 500 Stock Car Race in Bristol (March).

April-June: Mule Day in Columbia (April); Dogwood Arts Festival in Knoxville (April); Spring Wildflower Pilgrimage in Gatlinburg (April); World's Largest Fish Fry in Paris (April); Memphis in May Celebration (throughout May); Bays Mountain Park Spring Festival in Kingsport (May); Appalachian Music Days in Bristol (May); East Tennessee Strawberry Festival in Dayton (May); Iroquois Steeplechase in Nashville (May); Spring Music and Crafts Festival in Rugby (May); Museum of Appalachia Spring Festival in Norris (May); International Country Music Fan Fair in Nashville (June); Dulcimer Convention in Cosby (June); Country Music Days in Elizabethton (June); Rhododendron Festival in Roan Mountain (June).

Tennessee and North Carolina also share the Cherokee National Forest. For its area, see NATIONAL FOREST (table). The Andrew Johnson National Historic Site is located at Greeneville.

The state has several national military parks, including the Chickamauga and Chattanooga, which Tennessee shares with Georgia; Fort Donelson, near Dover; and Shiloh, near Savannah. Tennessee's three national cemeteries include Fort Donelson, Shiloh, and Stones River. The Cumberland Gap National Historical Park lies in the area where Kentucky, Virginia, and Tennessee meet.

State Parks and Forests. Tennessee maintains 51 state parks and 15 state forests. For information on the state parks in Tennessee, write to Director of State Parks, Department of Conservation, 2611 West End Avenue, Nashville, Tenn. 37203.

Tennessee Walking Horse Celebration in Shelbyville

Calvert Phelps, Shelbyville, Tenn.

July-September: Frontier Days in Lynchburg (July); Old Time Fiddlers' Jamboree in Smithville (July); Rugby Pilgrimage in Rugby (August); International Grand Championship Walking Horse Show in Murfreesboro (August); International Banana Festival in South Fulton (August); Tennessee Walking Horse National Celebration in Shelbyville (August-September); Folk Festival of the Smokies in Cosby (September); TVA Agriculture and Industrial Fair in Knoxville (September); Tennessee State Fair in Nashville (September).

October-December: National Storytelling Festival in Jonesboro (October); Autumn Gold Festival in Coker Creek (October); Oktoberfest in Memphis (October); Fall Color Cruise and Folk Festival in Chattanooga (October); The Twelve Days of Christmas in Gatlinburg (December).

Tower on Clingmans Dome, the Great Smoky Mountains

U.S. Department of the Interior

Land Regions. Tennessee has seven main land regions. These are, from east to west: (1) the Blue Ridge; (2) the Appalachian Ridge and Valley; (3) the Appalachian Plateau; (4) the Highland Rim; (5) the Nashville Basin; (6) the Gulf Coastal Plain; and (7) the Mississippi Alluvial Plain.

The Blue Ridge region skirts the entire eastern edge of Tennessee. The region's elevation averages 5,000 feet (1,500 meters), the highest in the state. Clingmans Dome, the state's tallest peak, rises to 6,643 feet (2,025 meters). Several mountain ranges dot the region. They include the Bald, Chilhowee, Great Smoky, Holston, Iron, Roan, Stone, and Unicoi mountains. Rolling lowlands lie within the mountains. The region has a great deal of timber and some minerals.

The Appalachian Ridge and Valley Region stretches westward from the mountainous Blue Ridge for about 55 miles (89 kilometers). This region has fertile farm country in valleys that lie between parallel wooded ridges. The broad valleys and narrow ridges in the eastern part make up an area called the *Great Valley*. *The Appalachian Plateau*, or *Cumberland Plateau*, lies west of the Ridge and Valley Region. There, the land rises in rocky cliffs that range from 1,500 to 1,800 feet (457 to 549 meters) high. The plateau region consists of flat-topped mountains and V-shaped valleys. Most of Tennessee's coal comes from this region. From Lookout Mountain, in the southern part of the region, visitors can see seven states.

The Highland Rim is an elevated plain that surrounds the Nashville Basin. Steep slopes reach from the Rim to the Basin below. In the east, underground streams leave hollowed-out caves in the rocks that lie beneath the surface of the region.

The Nashville Basin lies within the Highland Rim. Most of the Basin drains toward the northwest. The Basin has rich farming areas where cattle graze in fertile pastures, and farms produce bumper crops. The region also has some of the nation's richest phosphate deposits.

The Gulf Coastal Plain is part of an important land region that begins at the Gulf of Mexico and extends northward as far as southern Illinois. In Tennessee, the Plain has two parts. A hilly strip of land about 10 miles (16 kilometers) wide runs along the west bank of the Tennessee River. The other part slopes toward the Mississippi River, ending in a steep bluff that overlooks the Mississippi lowlands.

The Mississippi Alluvial Plain lies along the western edge of the state. It is also part of a larger land region that starts at the Gulf of Mexico. This flat strip along the Mississippi River averages less than 300 feet (91 meters) above sea level. It is the lowest part of the state and is sometimes called *The Mississippi Bottoms*. Farmers raise cotton and other field crops in this region of the Mississippi River.

Rivers and Lakes. Three large river systems—the Mississippi, Cumberland, and Tennessee—drain the

Phosphate Mines in Middle Tennessee rank among the largest U.S. producers of phosphate rocks.

Tom Hollyman, Photo Researchers, Inc.

Land Regions of Tennessee

MISSISSIPPI ALLUVIAL PLAIN

GULF COASTAL PLAIN

HIGHLAND RIM

NASHVILLE BASIN

APPALACHIAN PLATEAU

APPALACHIAN RIDGE AND VALLEY REGION

BLUE RIDGE

Cumberland R.

Tennessee R.

Mississippi R.

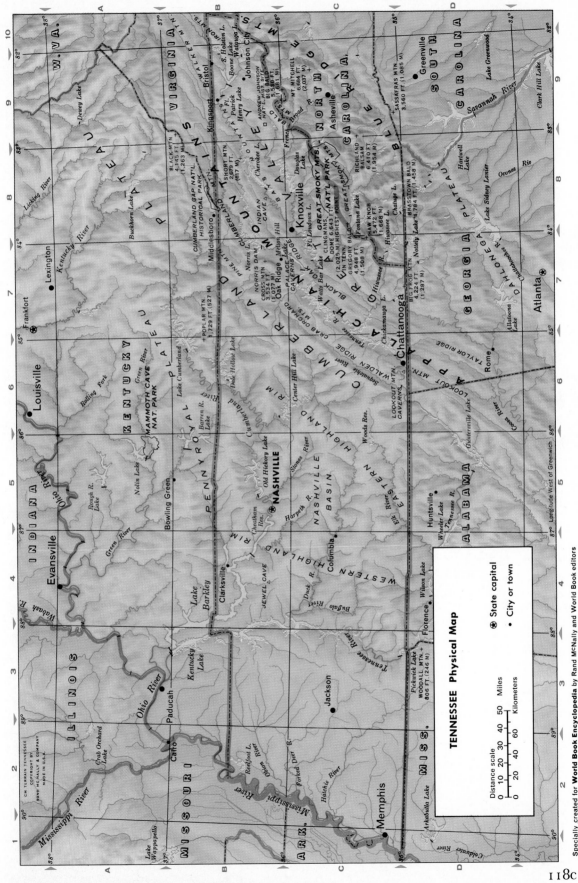

TENNESSEE Physical Map

⊛ State capital

• City or town

Distance scale

Miles 0 10 20 30 40 50

Kilometers 0 20 40 60

Specially created for **World Book Encyclopedia** by Rand McNally and World Book editors

118c

TENNESSEE

state. The Mississippi drains most of West Tennessee. Its largest tributaries in Tennessee include the Forked Deer, Hatchie, Loosahatchie, Obion, and Wolf rivers. The Cumberland and Tennessee drain most of the rest of the state. They rise in the Appalachian Mountains and join the Ohio River. Principal branches of the Tennessee include the Big Sandy, Buffalo, Clinch, Duck, Elk, French Broad, Hiwassee, Holston, Little Tennessee, Powell, and Sequatchie rivers. Tributaries of the Cumberland in Tennessee include the Caney Fork, Harpeth, and Stones rivers.

Since 1933, the Tennessee Valley Authority (TVA) and the U.S. Army Corps of Engineers have built many dams along the Cumberland and Tennessee rivers and their tributaries. Artificial lakes formed by these dams have more than doubled the inland water area of Tennessee. The largest of these man-made lakes is Kentucky Lake. Others include Boone, Cherokee, Chickamauga, Douglas, Fort Loudoun, Fort Patrick Henry, Norris, Pickwick, Watauga, and Watts Bar reservoirs. These lakes are often called the *Great Lakes of the South.*

Reelfoot Lake in northwestern Tennessee lies in a depression made by an earthquake in the early 1800's. The lake is one of many that dot the low, flat lands called *The Mississippi Bottoms* along the Mississippi River.

Lookout Mountain towers 2,146 feet (654 meters) above the city of Chattanooga and overlooks the Tennessee River. The flat-topped mountain is in the southern part of the Appalachian Plateau, or Cumberland Plateau, region of the state.

Gatlinburg nestles in a valley surrounded by the wooded peaks of the Great Smoky Mountains. The mountains form part of the Blue Ridge region.

SEASONAL TEMPERATURES

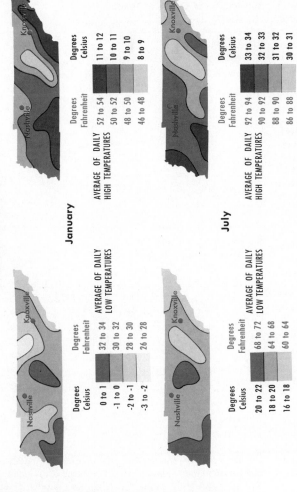

January

AVERAGE OF DAILY LOW TEMPERATURES

Degrees Fahrenheit	Degrees Celsius
32 to 34	0 to 1
30 to 32	-1 to 0
28 to 30	-2 to -1
26 to 28	-3 to -2

AVERAGE OF DAILY HIGH TEMPERATURES

Degrees Fahrenheit	Degrees Celsius
52 to 54	11 to 12
50 to 52	10 to 11
48 to 50	9 to 10
46 to 48	8 to 9

July

AVERAGE OF DAILY LOW TEMPERATURES

Degrees Fahrenheit	Degrees Celsius
68 to 72	20 to 22
64 to 68	18 to 20
60 to 64	16 to 18

AVERAGE OF DAILY HIGH TEMPERATURES

Degrees Fahrenheit	Degrees Celsius
92 to 94	33 to 34
90 to 92	32 to 33
88 to 90	31 to 32
86 to 88	30 to 31

AVERAGE MONTHLY WEATHER

KNOXVILLE

	Temperatures F° High	Low	C° High	Low	Days of Rain or Snow
JAN.	50	31	10	-1	13
FEB.	53	32	12	0	12
MAR.	61	38	16	3	13
APR.	71	47	22	8	11
MAY	79	56	26	13	12
JUNE	87	65	31	18	12
JULY	89	68	32	20	12
AUG.	88	66	31	19	11
SEPT.	84	61	29	16	8
OCT.	73	48	23	9	7
NOV.	59	38	15	3	9
DEC.	50	32	10	0	12

NASHVILLE

	Temperatures F° High	Low	C° High	Low	Days of Rain or Snow
JAN.	49	31	9	-1	12
FEB.	52	33	11	1	11
MAR.	60	40	16	4	12
APR.	71	49	22	9	11
MAY	79	57	14	14	10
JUNE	88	66	31	19	10
JULY	91	69	33	21	10
AUG.	89	68	32	20	9
SEPT.	85	62	29	17	8
OCT.	74	50	23	10	7
NOV.	59	39	15	4	9
DEC.	50	33	10	1	11

Fred H. Ragsdale, FPG

Norris Dam on the Clinch River controls floods, provides electric power, and forms Norris Lake, a vacation playground. It helps protect the fertile lands of the Appalachian Ridge and Valley Region.

TENNESSEE/*Climate*

Most of Tennessee has a humid, temperate climate. Temperatures rarely go above 100° F. (38° C) or below 10° F. (−12° C). The lowlands and plains in West Tennessee generally remain warmer than the mountainous eastern regions. Average temperatures in the west range from 40° F. (4° C) in January to 79° F. (26° C) in July. The east averages 37° F. (3° C) in January and 71° F. (22° C) in July. Tennessee's lowest recorded temperature, −32° F. (−36° C), occurred on Dec. 30, 1917, at Mountain City in the northeast. Its highest recorded temperature, 113° F. (45° C), occurred on July 29 and Aug. 9, 1930, at Perryville in the west. Eastern Tennessee averages about 10 inches (25 centimeters) of snow a year, while the west averages 4 to 6 inches (10 to 15 centimeters). Most of the state averages about 50 inches (130 centimeters) of *precipitation* (rain, melted snow, and other forms of moisture) a year. The growing season lasts 150 to 210 days in the east and 180 to 230 days in the west.

AVERAGE YEARLY PRECIPITATION
(Rain, Melted Snow and Other Moisture)

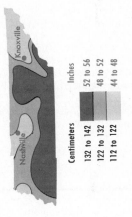

Centimeters	Inches
132 to 142	52 to 56
122 to 132	48 to 52
112 to 122	44 to 48

0   50   100 Miles
0 50 100 Kilometers

WORLD BOOK maps

Each of Tennessee's major industries touches most parts of the state. But there are certain regional patterns. Manufacturing centers around Memphis, Nashville, Chattanooga, and Knoxville. Large factories are also located in smaller eastern industrial cities, such as Kingsport and Johnson City. Most of the more prosperous farms are in the western half of Tennessee. Mining occurs chiefly in the eastern and central portions of the state. Each year, millions of tourists visit Tennessee. They spend about $2¼ billion.

Natural Resources. Tennessee's fertile soil, thick forests, temperate climate, vast water supply, and abundant minerals make the state rich in natural resources.

Minerals. Tennessee has a large variety of minerals. East Tennessee has large deposits of fluorite, marble, pyrite, and zinc. Middle Tennessee contains rich stores of limestone, phosphate rock, and zinc. The Appalachian Plateau has large coal deposits and some oil and gas. Ball clay and lignite are found in West Tennessee. The state also has barite, copper, sand and gravel, and other minerals.

Soil. The most fertile soils lie in the Appalachian Ridge and Valley Region, the Nashville Basin, and the Mississippi Alluvial Plain. A sandy soil covers the mountain coves in the Blue Ridge Region. A clay loam formed from weathered limestone covers the valley floors in the Ridge and Valley Region. The Appalachian Plateau and most of the Highland Rim have poor soil. A loam soil, formed from rich soluble limestone, covers the Nashville Basin. The Gulf Coastal Plain has light soils that can be made to produce well. Fertile sand, silt, and clay soil covers the Mississippi Alluvial Plain.

Plant and Animal Life. Forests cover about 13 million acres (5,260,000 hectares), about half the state. Tennessee's most important trees include the hickory, shortleaf pine, red and white oaks, and yellow poplar. Other common trees include ash, cherry, elm, sycamore, maple, and walnut. Azaleas, mountain laurel, rhododendron, and other shrubs cover the mountain slopes. The passionflower and iris grow throughout the state. Common wild flowers include the dragonroot, hop clover, spring beauty, and yellow jasmine.

Tennessee's mountains, forests, and waters abound with wild game. Hunters seek bears, deer, ducks, wild turkeys, and other game. Bass, crappie, trout, and walleyed pike are caught in the lakes and streams. Savage wild hogs roam remote parts of the Tennessee hills. Beavers, muskrats, rabbits, raccoons, and skunks live in the fields and forests. Common songbirds in Tennessee include the mockingbird, robin, and wood thrush.

Manufacturing accounts for about 85 per cent of the value of goods produced in Tennessee. The state's manufactured goods have a *value added by manufacture* of about $14 billion a year. This figure represents the value created in products by the industries, not counting such costs as materials, supplies, and fuels. Chief manufacturing industries, in order of importance, are (1) chemicals, (2) food products, (3) nonelectric machinery, and (4) electric machinery and equipment.

Chemicals. Tennessee ranks among the leading states in the production of chemicals. This industry has a value added of about $2,433,700,000 yearly, or about

Production of Goods in Tennessee

Total annual value of goods produced—$16,451,917,000

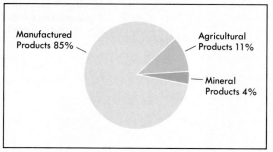

Manufactured Products 85%

Agricultural Products 11%

Mineral Products 4%

Percentages are based on farm income and value of mineral production in 1979 and on value added by manufacture in 1978.
Sources: U.S. government publications, 1980-1981.

Employment in Tennessee

Total number of persons employed — 1,835,500

		Number of Employees
Manufacturing	🧍🧍🧍🧍🧍🧍🧍🧍🧍🧍	504,600
Wholesale & Retail Trade	🧍🧍🧍🧍🧍🧍🧍🧍	376,600
Government	🧍🧍🧍🧍🧍🧍	314,700
Community, Social, & Personal Services	🧍🧍🧍🧍🧍	288,400
Agriculture	🧍🧍	101,000
Transportation & Public Utilities	🧍🧍	85,600
Finance, Insurance, & Real Estate	🧍🧍	78,000
Construction	🧍🧍	76,800
Mining	🧍	9,800

Sources: *Employment and Earnings,* May 1981, U.S. Bureau of Labor Statistics; *Farm Labor,* February 1981, U.S. Department of Agriculture. Figures are for 1980.

17 per cent of the state's manufacturing income. Industrial plants, located in various parts of the state, manufacture such important chemical products as agricultural chemicals, industrial chemicals, paints, pharmaceuticals, plastics, and soaps.

Food Products have a value added of about $1,409,800,000 a year. The state's largest stockyards are in Chattanooga and Memphis. Meat-packing plants operate in Chattanooga, Clarksville, Johnson City, Knoxville, Memphis, Nashville, and Union City. Tennessee has several centers that freeze and can fruits and vegetables. Memphis has large shortening plants.

Nonelectric Machinery has an annual value added of about $1,195,400,000. The industry's chief centers of production are Chattanooga and Memphis. Its leading products include refrigeration and heating equipment, general industrial machinery, and farm machinery.

Electric Machinery and Equipment has an annual value added of about $1,143,900,000. Factories throughout the state make household appliances, welding equipment, and motors and generators.

Other Leading Industries in Tennessee, in order of value, produce clothing; fabricated metal products; transportation equipment; and rubber and plastics products. Tennessee industries also manufacture paper products, primary metals, and printed materials.

East Tennessee plants produce aluminum in Alcoa and metallic manganese in Rockwood. In the middle of the state, Nashville factories make aircraft parts and river barges. A refinery in Clarksville processes zinc ores. In the west, Memphis manufacturers produce aircraft parts and structural steel. CHILDCRAFT— THE HOW AND WHY LIBRARY is printed in Kingsport. The state also has a flourishing music publishing industry. Centered in Nashville, the industry specializes in country, folk, and western music.

Tennessee's textile industry is centered in the eastern part of the state, in Chattanooga, Cleveland, Clinton, Harriman, Knoxville, Lenoir City, Morristown, and other cities. Many textile manufacturers make blankets and hosiery. Bemis and Memphis, in western Tennessee, have cotton mills.

Agriculture supplies about 11 per cent of the value of goods produced, with a yearly income of about $1¾ billion. Farmland covers about 14 million acres (6 million hectares), or about half the state. Tennessee's 92,000 farms average about 148 acres (60 hectares) in size.

Livestock accounts for about 54 per cent of the income received from farm products, with a yearly income of about $955 million. Tennessee is one of the South's leading dairy states. Farmers in most parts of the state raise beef cattle, dairy cattle, and hogs. Other livestock products in Tennessee are *broilers* (chickens between 9 and 12 weeks old) and eggs. The Nashville Basin is the home of the famous Tennessee Walking Horse (see HORSE [Saddle Horses; color picture]). Most of Tennessee's sheep come from there.

Soybeans, Tennessee's largest cash crop, have an annual income of about $432 million. Tennessee is a leading soybean state, with an annual production of about 57 million bushels. Most of this crop comes from western Tennessee.

Tobacco is the second largest cash crop, with an income of about $156 million yearly. Tennessee ranks high among the states in the production of burley tobacco. Most of this tobacco comes from the central and eastern parts of the state. Farms in northern Tennessee produce fire-cured tobacco, which is cured with heat and smoke rather than with air.

Corn is Tennessee's third most valuable crop, with an annual production of about 51 million bushels and an annual income of about $53 million. The crop is grown on farms in most parts of the state. Farmers feed most of the corn to livestock.

Other Crops grown in Tennessee include cotton, hay, and wheat. Tennessee is a leader among the states in cotton production. Many farmers grow hay for livestock. Eastern and central area farmers grow wheat.

Tomatoes and snap beans earn the largest income among the *truck crops* (vegetables grown for market). Truck farmers also grow cabbage, potatoes, and sweet potatoes. Tennessee farmers raise valuable crops of apples, peaches, and strawberries. Other important agricultural products include cottonseed, forest products, and greenhouse and nursery products.

Mining has a production value of about $568 million a year, or about 4 per cent of the value of goods produced. Coal accounts for the greatest income from mining. Stone ranks second and zinc ranks third.

Mines that produce *bituminous* (soft) coal operate in 16 eastern counties and yield about 9 million short tons (8 million metric tons) a year. Blount, Grainger, and Union counties in the northeast are marble producers. About 65 counties, mainly in eastern and central Tennessee, produce limestone.

Tennessee is a leading producer of zinc, most of which comes from Jefferson, Knox, and Smith counties. Tennessee is also a leading producer of phosphate rock. Miners dig most of the phosphate rock in Giles, Hickman, Maury, and Williamson counties in the central portion of the state. Tennessee is the only Southern state that mines copper. All of Tennessee's copper comes from sulfide ores mined in Polk County. These ores support a large sulfuric-acid industry, and also yield some gold, iron, silver, and zinc.

Ball clays and other high-grade ceramic and pottery clays, mined in the northwestern section, support an important ceramics industry. Quality glass sands come from Benton County. Pits in about 40 counties produce sand and gravel.

Electric Power. The Tennessee Valley Authority (TVA) generates almost all the state's electric power.

Farm, Mineral, and Forest Products

This map shows where the state's leading farm, mineral, and forest products are produced. The major urban areas (shown on the map in red) are the state's important manufacturing centers.

0	25	50	75	100	Miles
0	50	100		150	Kilometers

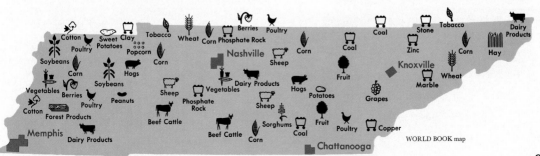

WORLD BOOK map

The TVA produces more power than any other system in the country, and distributes it to local electric power systems (see TENNESSEE VALLEY AUTHORITY). More than three-fourths of the state's power comes from steam-generating plants that burn coal. Hydroelectric plants generate the rest of the state's power.

Transportation. Tennessee faced many problems in building its transportation systems. Many bridges and tunnels had to be built through hilly and mountainous areas. This raised the costs of railroad and highway construction. Between about 1800 and 1860, private companies built turnpikes and collected tolls to maintain them. In 1913, the legislature authorized counties to issue bonds for highway construction. Tennessee now has about 80,000 miles (130,000 kilometers) of highways and roads, nearly all surfaced.

Tennessee has about 125 airports. Railroads operate on about 5,800 miles (9,330 kilometers) of track in the state. About 10 rail lines provide freight services, and

---

TENNESSEE / History

Indian Days. The earliest known people in what is now Tennessee were Indians now known as the Mound Builders. They settled the area about a thousand years ago. The Mound Builders used mounds to support their temples and chiefs' houses. When the first white explorers came to the area, they saw some of the early Cherokee and Chickasaw peoples still building mounds. See MOUND BUILDERS.

The Cherokee claimed Middle Tennessee as their hunting ground. The Chickamauga Indians, a branch of the Cherokee, lived near the present site of Chattanooga. The Chickasaw occupied West Tennessee.

Exploration. In 1540, a party of Spanish explorers led by Hernando de Soto raided some Indian villages in the valley of the Tennessee River. Moving westward, De Soto became the first European to reach the Mississippi River. He came upon it in 1541. He then left the Tennessee region. No other explorers entered the region until 1673, when James Needham and Gabriel Arthur of England explored the Tennessee River Valley. That same year, Louis Joliet of Canada and Father Jacques Marquette of France sailed down the Mississippi River. In 1682, Robert Cavelier, Sieur de la Salle, claimed the entire Mississippi Valley for France. He built Fort Prud'homme on the Chickasaw Bluffs. But the post was so isolated that the French soon had to abandon it. French settlers began moving into the Mississippi Valley, which they called *New France*. In 1714, Charles Charleville set up a French trading post at French Lick, near what is now Nashville.

France, Spain, and Great Britain all claimed the Tennessee region. All three countries competed for the trade and for the friendship of the Indians. The dispute eventually became a contest between the British and the French. Finally, the French and Indian War broke out between British and French settlers in 1754. The British settlers outnumbered the French by about 20 to 1, but the French won decisive victories during the early years of the war. After nine bloody years, however, the

HISTORIC TENNESSEE

Shiloh

The Battle of Shiloh in 1862 ended in a victory for the North when Confederate troops tried to stop a Union advance on Corinth, Miss. The Confederates lost over 10,000 men, including General Albert Sidney Johnston. The Union lost more than 13,000 men.

1795   1849   1767   1845   1808   1875
JAMES KNOX POLK   ANDREW JACKSON   ANDREW JOHNSON
OF   OF   OF
MECKLENBURG COUNTY   UNION COUNTY   WAKE COUNTY
PRESIDENT   PRESIDENT   PRESIDENT
1845–1849   1829–1837   1865–1869

N.C. State Adv. Div.

Three U.S. Presidents lived in Tennessee: Andrew Jackson, James K. Polk, and Andrew Johnson.

United Daughters of the Confederacy was organized at Nashville in 1894 by widows, wives, mothers, and sisters of Confederate veterans of the Civil War.

passenger trains link Memphis and Nashville to other cities. Barges float along the Cumberland, Mississippi, and Tennessee rivers. Memphis ranks as one of the busiest inland ports on the Mississippi River.

Communication. Tennessee has about 120 newspapers, of which about 30 are dailies. George Roulstone established the state's first newspaper, the *Knoxville Gazette*, in 1791. Newspapers with the largest daily circulations include the *Chattanooga News-Free Press*, *The Chattanooga Times*, *The Knoxville Journal*, *The Knoxville News-Sentinel*, *The* (Memphis) *Commercial Appeal*, the *Memphis Press-Scimitar*, the *Nashville Banner*, and *The* (Nashville) *Tennessean*. About 160 periodicals are also published in the state.

Tennessee's first radio station, WNAV, began broadcasting at Knoxville in 1922. The first television station, WMCT-TV, started operations at Memphis in 1948. Today, Tennessee has about 255 radio stations and over 20 television stations.

British won out. And in 1763, by the Treaty of Paris, the French surrendered to the British all claim to lands east of the Mississippi.

Early Settlement. By 1769, permanent settlers lived in the Tennessee region. New settlers began to come into the area from Virginia and North Carolina.

The Tennessee region belonged to the British colony of North Carolina. But vast, rugged mountains separated settlers in Tennessee from the protection of the mother colony. In 1772, a group of settlers established law and order in the wilderness by forming their own government, the Watauga Association. They drew up one of the first written constitutions in North America. See WATAUGA ASSOCIATION.

A group called the Transylvania Company bought a large area of present-day Tennessee and Kentucky from the Cherokee in 1775. Daniel Boone, working for the company, blazed a trail from Virginia across the mountains at Cumberland Gap to open this land to settlement. Boone's trail, the famous Wilderness Road, became the main route to the new settlements.

Territorial Years. In 1779, two groups of pioneers, led by James Robertson and John Donelson, pushed far into the wilds and settled around the Big Salt Lick on the Cumberland River. They built Fort Nashborough (later Nashville), which formed the center of the Middle Tennessee settlements. These pioneers drew up an agreement called the Cumberland Compact. It established representative government for all settlers, and created a court system to enforce its provisions.

In 1780, during the Revolutionary War, John Sevier led a group of pioneers from the Tennessee region across the Great Smoky Mountains into South Carolina. These men helped American forces win a victory over the British at the Battle of Kings Mountain on October 7.

Meanwhile, the settlers and Indians were trying to drive each other out of the Tennessee region. The settlers appealed for help to North Carolina. But help did not come. In 1784, three counties in East Tennessee revolted against North Carolina and formed the independent State of Franklin. They made John Sevier, the hero of Kings Mountain, their governor. North Carolina

Oak Ridge, called the "Atomic Bomb City," was begun in 1942. The city and its nuclear bomb factory were kept almost a complete secret until after World War II.

Davy Crockett, a colorful scout and frontiersman, won fame for his tall tales and funny stories. He served Tennessee in Congress from 1827 to 1831, and from 1833 to 1835.

John Sevier, Tennessee's first governor, served six terms. He also was the first governor of the State of Franklin, now a part of Tennessee. Franklin broke away from North Carolina in 1784. It was an independent state until 1788.

Tennessee Valley Authority, established in 1933, built over 20 dams in the river valley to furnish electric power and control floods.

The Watauga Association was formed in 1772 by Tennessee's first settlers to provide government along the Watauga River. The pioneers drew up one of the first written constitutions in North America.

regained control of the area in 1788 (see FRANKLIN, STATE OF). In 1789, North Carolina gave the Tennessee region to the United States. The federal government made it into a new territory, and called it The Territory of the United States South of the River Ohio. William Blount became the first and only governor of this territory.

The Chickasaw owned nearly all West Tennessee until 1818, when they ceded their land to the federal government. But the Cherokee still held a large area in Middle Tennessee, and a smaller tract south of the Little Tennessee and Sequatchie rivers in the east.

Statehood. On Feb. 6, 1796, Tennessee adopted a constitution in preparation for statehood. It became the 16th state in the Union on June 1. Tennesseans elected John Sevier as their first governor. The new state had a population of about 77,000, and was the first state to be created out of government territory.

Negro slaves toiled on West and Middle Tennessee farms before the Civil War. But most farmers in the eastern part of the state did not own slaves. Free Negroes could vote in Tennessee until a new constitution, adopted in 1834, took that right away from them.

Building the State. Three men who became Presidents of the United States played key roles in the development of Tennessee. They were Andrew Jackson, James K. Polk, and Andrew Johnson.

Andrew Jackson helped draw up the state's first constitution in 1796. He later held office as a United States representative and senator from Tennessee. He also served as a justice of the Tennessee supreme court. During the War of 1812, Jackson led his Tennessee troops to victory against the Creek Indians, who were allies of the British. He became a national hero by leading U.S. forces in an overwhelming defeat of the British Army at the Battle of New Orleans. Tennessee supported Jackson when he ran unsuccessfully for the presidency in 1824, and when he was elected in 1828.

James K. Polk was a close friend and supporter of Andrew Jackson. Polk served Tennessee for two years in the state legislature, for 14 years in the U.S. House of Representatives, and for a two-year term as governor.

Andrew Johnson fought for the rights of the poor. As a state senator, he courageously tried to reduce the voting power of the powerful slave owners. Johnson served as a U.S. representative, as governor of Tennessee, and as a U.S. senator. Although he did not oppose slavery, he believed strongly in the Union. Johnson pleaded with the people of Tennessee to remain in the Union after other Southern States had already seceded.

Many Tennesseans were in favor of staying in the Union. But when President Abraham Lincoln did not show these people his support, feelings in favor of seceding grew stronger in Tennessee. On June 8, 1861, about two months after the Civil War broke out, more than two-thirds of the people voted to join the Confederacy. Tennessee was the last state to secede from the Union. Andrew Johnson was the only Southern Senator who did not secede with his state.

The Civil War. The people of Tennessee were divided in their sympathies between the North and the South. Most Union sympathy came from the eastern part of the state. Confederate forces moved into that region and held it captive for a good part of the war.

In 1862, the war spread across the state's middle and western regions. Union forces under General Ulysses S. Grant moved along the Tennessee River to Pittsburg Landing. There, one of the bloodiest battles of the war took place. It was called the Battle of Shiloh, after a church that stood on the battlefield. Despite enormous losses, Union troops won an important victory at Shiloh. Federal control of West Tennessee was established in 1862. President Lincoln appointed Andrew Johnson the military governor of Tennessee.

In late November, 1863, Grant attacked the Confederate positions around Chattanooga. During the first day of fighting, Union General Joseph Hooker drove Confederate forces from Lookout Mountain in the "Battle Above the Clouds." Union forces captured Chattanooga after three days of fighting.

In 1864, General William T. Sherman's troops marched from Chattanooga into Georgia and captured Atlanta. In Tennessee, Confederate forces under General John B. Hood tried to draw Sherman back by attacking Franklin and Nashville. But General George H. Thomas defeated Hood's army at Nashville.

The Republican Party nominated Andrew Johnson to run for Vice-President under President Lincoln in the 1864 election. They won the election. But on April 14, 1865, President Lincoln was assassinated. Andrew Johnson was inaugurated as President on April 15, 1865. He declared the rebellion in Tennessee at an end on June 13. But a strong group in Congress tried to

Discovery, one of two murals painted by Dean Cornwell for the State Office Building in Nashville, shows highlights of the state's early history. At the far left, LaSalle claims the territory for France. In the center, John Sevier leads minutemen to defeat the British during the Revolutionary War. At lower right, William Blount, the territorial governor, settles land claims with the Chickasaw and Cherokee Indians.

block Tennessee's readmission to the Union. On July 24, 1866, after considerable debate, Tennessee became the first Confederate state to be readmitted.

Reconstruction. The years following the Civil War were tragic ones for the people of Tennessee. The war had left much of the state in ruin and had left thousands of persons homeless. Husbands and fathers, brothers and sons, lay dead on the battlefields.

A group of Northern sympathizers, called *Radical Republicans*, gained control of the Tennessee government after the war. This group included the governor and most of the state legislature. They imposed severe measures on those who had followed the Confederate cause. They gave blacks the right to vote, but they took voting privileges away from a number of Confederate sympathizers. Most of these Radical Republicans were voted out of office in 1869. A more sympathetic legislature adopted a new constitution in 1870. This constitution reduced the power of the governor, set limits on legislative sessions, and extended the right to vote to all male citizens 21 or older.

Tennessee's plantations in Middle and West Tennessee were divided into smaller farms. Farmers had to plant their own cotton and other crops. Progress was slow on the farms. Some farmers had depended on slaves.

It took nearly 40 years for Tennessee's farms to recover from the war. But during that same period the manufacturing and mining industries grew. This growth created more jobs and speeded the state's recovery.

Disease swept across the state during the 1870's. One of the worst yellow fever epidemics in U.S. history hit Memphis in 1878, killing about 5,200 of its 19,600 residents. Memphis lost its city charter after this disaster, and did not regain the charter until 1893.

Poor management of state funds in Tennessee banks left the state deeply in debt after the Civil War. In 1890, the Tennessee Banking Association began a campaign to reform the banking system. Finally, in 1913, a new state banking department was established to protect the public against bank mismanagement, fraud, and harmful speculation.

The Early 1900's saw Tennessee in a period of change. The state's economy had gradually begun to shift from agricultural to industrial. New and better highways and railroads spread across the state. People began to move away from the farms and into the cities. By the mid-1930's, manufacturing was beginning to overtake farming as Tennessee's leading industry.

World attention suddenly focused on Dayton, Tenn., in 1925. John T. Scopes, a high school teacher, had defied a state law by teaching Darwin's theory of evo-

---
IMPORTANT DATES IN TENNESSEE

1540 Hernando de Soto of Spain led the first white expedition into the Tennessee region.

1673 James Needham and Gabriel Arthur of England, and Louis Joliet of Canada and Father Jacques Marquette of France explored the region.

1682 Robert Cavelier, Sieur de la Salle, claimed the Mississippi River Valley for France.

1714 Charles Charleville set up a French trading post near the present site of Nashville.

1763 France surrendered to Great Britain all claim to lands east of the Mississippi River.

1772 The Watauga Association drew up one of the first written constitutions in North America.

1780 Nashville settlers signed the Cumberland Compact.

1784 Three counties established the separate State of Franklin.

1796 Tennessee became the 16th state on June 1.

1818 The Chickasaw Indians sold all their land east of the Mississippi River to the U.S. government.

1838 The Cherokee were forced out of Tennessee.

1861 Tennessee became the last state to secede from the Union, on June 8.

1866 Tennessee became the first state to be readmitted to the Union, on July 24.

1870 A new constitution gave all male citizens 21 or older the right to vote.

1878 One of the worst yellow fever epidemics in U.S. history killed about 5,200 of the 19,600 persons in Memphis.

1925 John Scopes was convicted for teaching evolution in a Tennessee public school.

1933 Congress created the Tennessee Valley Authority.

1942 The federal government began building the atomic energy center at Oak Ridge.

1953 Tennessee voters approved eight amendments to the state constitution.

1962 The U.S. Supreme Court ruled, in a Tennessee case, that federal courts could challenge legislative apportionment.

1970 Winfield Dunn became the first Republican in 50 years to be elected governor of Tennessee.

Dean Cornwell Murals, Tennessee Conservation Dept.

Development, the second of the history murals, traces Tennessee's growth. At the far left, pioneers settle the state. Andrew Jackson dominates the center of the mural as he watches the state and the nation grow. In the center is Nathan Bedford Forrest, Confederate cavalry hero. At the right, James Knox Polk lifts his arms during a speech, and Andrew Johnson holds a book to show his interest in developing a public school system.

lution in his classroom. The state brought Scopes to trial. William Jennings Bryan was prosecuting attorney. Clarence Darrow defended Scopes. The trial aroused an enormous controversy. Scopes lost the trial and was fined $100. Over 30 years later, the legislature repealed the law under which Scopes had been convicted.

In 1933, the federal government established the Tennessee Valley Authority (TVA) to conserve and develop the resources of the Tennessee River Valley.

The Mid-1900's. In 1942, the federal government began to build an atomic energy plant in Oak Ridge. Scientists there worked on the development of the atomic bomb during World War II (1939-1945).

After the war, Tennessee continued to shift from an agricultural to an industrial economy. The TVA built more dams and steam plants to control floods, provide plentiful water supplies, and furnish cheap electric power. These facilities and the state's large labor force attracted new industries to Tennessee. Recreational areas built near lakes and waterways and in the mountains drew many tourists. A multimillion-dollar music industry grew up in Nashville, which became the nation's second largest recording center. The industry had its beginning in the Grand Ole Opry, a radio program featuring country and western music.

Tennessee's political life changed after the war, as many veterans became active in politics. This helped cause a revolt in the 1948 state elections against control by Memphis political boss E. H. Crump. In the elections, Crump began to lose power for the first time in 30 years as Estes Kefauver won a seat in the U.S. Senate. Kefauver had run an anti-Crump campaign.

A constitutional convention was held in 1953, the state's first since 1870. Voters approved all eight amendments proposed by the convention. The amendments extended the governor's term from two to four years but prohibited him from serving two successive terms.

During the 1950's, the Republican Party began to grow in the state. In 1966, Republicans won their first statewide office in Tennessee since 1920 with the election of Howard H. Baker, Jr., to the Senate. By 1969, they made up half the state's House of Representatives.

Political control in Tennessee shifted from rural to urban areas. The shift resulted from an increase in city populations and from a ruling by the Supreme Court of the United States. In 1962, the Supreme Court ruled in *Baker v. Carr*, a Tennessee case, that federal courts

have legal power over state legislative apportionment. In 1964, a federal court ordered Tennessee to redraw its legislative districts. The state did so in 1965, giving equal representation according to population.

Most social change in the state concerned school desegregation. Tennessee's Constitution made it illegal for Negro and white children to attend the same schools. But in 1954, the U.S. Supreme Court ruled that compulsory segregation in public schools was illegal. Desegregation of state-supported schools began in 1956 in Clinton. State officials sent National Guardsmen to enforce the order. Since 1956, there has been gradual desegregation of Tennessee schools.

On April 4, 1968, civil rights leader Martin Luther King, Jr., was murdered in Memphis. He had gone there to lead protests for striking garbage workers.

THE GOVERNORS OF TENNESSEE

	Party	Term
John Sevier	*Dem.-Rep.	1796-1801
Archibald Roane	Dem.-Rep.	1801-1803
John Sevier	Dem.-Rep.	1803-1809
Willie Blount	Dem.-Rep.	1809-1815
Joseph McMinn	Dem.-Rep.	1815-1821
William Carroll	Dem.-Rep.	1821-1827
Sam Houston	Dem.-Rep.	1827-1829
William Hall	Democratic	1829
William Carroll	Democratic	1829-1835
Newton Cannon	Whig	1835-1839
James K. Polk	Democratic	1839-1841
James C. Jones	Whig	1841-1845
Aaron V. Brown	Democratic	1845-1847
Neill S. Brown	Whig	1847-1849
William Trousdale	Democratic	1849-1851
William B. Campbell	Whig	1851-1853
Andrew Johnson	Democratic	1853-1857
Isham G. Harris	Democratic	1857-1862
Andrew Johnson (Military Governor)	Democratic	1862-1865
William G. Brownlow	**Whig-Rep.	1865-1869
DeWitt Clinton Senter	Whig-Rep.	1869-1871
John C. Brown	†Whig-Dem.	1871-1875
James D. Porter	Democratic	1875-1879
Albert S. Marks	Democratic	1879-1881
Alvin Hawkins	Republican	1881-1883
William B. Bate	Democratic	1883-1887
Robert Love Taylor	Democratic	1887-1891
John P. Buchanan	Democratic	1891-1893
Peter Turney	Democratic	1893-1897
Robert Love Taylor	Democratic	1897-1899
Benton McMillin	Democratic	1899-1903
James B. Frazier	Democratic	1903-1905
John I. Cox	Democratic	1905-1907
Malcolm R. Patterson	Democratic	1907-1911
Ben W. Hooper	Republican	1911-1915
Tom C. Rye	Democratic	1915-1919
A. H. Roberts	Democratic	1919-1921
Alfred A. Taylor	Republican	1921-1923
Austin Peay	Democratic	1923-1927
Henry H. Horton	Democratic	1927-1933
Hill McAlister	Democratic	1933-1937
Gordon Browning	Democratic	1937-1939
Prentice Cooper	Democratic	1939-1945
Jim McCord	Democratic	1945-1949
Gordon Browning	Democratic	1949-1953
Frank G. Clement	Democratic	1953-1959
Buford Ellington	Democratic	1959-1963
Frank G. Clement	Democratic	1963-1967
Buford Ellington	Democratic	1967-1971
Winfield Dunn	Republican	1971-1975
Leonard Ray Blanton	Democratic	1975-1979
Lamar Alexander	Republican	1979-

*Democratic-Republican   **Whig-Republican   †Whig-Democratic

Bull Run Steam Plant, at the TVA Melton Hill Dam on the Clinch River, helps supply electric power for East Tennessee.

Tennessee Valley Authority

James Earl Ray, an escaped convict, pleaded guilty to the crime and was sentenced to 99 years in prison. King's assassination in their state made many Tennesseans aware of the need to solve racial problems.

Tennessee Today. In 1974, the Tennessee legislature passed a *sunshine law* that allows the public to attend local and state government meetings. In 1978, the people approved an amendment to the state constitution that limits the growth of spending by the state government.

To increase its job opportunities, Tennessee is trying to attract new industry. But as more industry comes to

the state, air pollution and water pollution increase. Despite the new industry, the living standard of the people in the Appalachian region of eastern Tennessee remains low.

In 1982, a world's fair held in Knoxville helped promote tourism in Tennessee. Knoxville renovated 70 acres (28 hectares) of its downtown area to make room for the event.

J. Milton Henry, Jewell A. Phelps, and John Seigenthaler

TENNESSEE/Study Aids

Related Articles in World Book include:

BIOGRAPHIES

Baker, Howard Henry, Jr.	Jackson, Andrew
Bell, John	Johnson, Andrew
Blount, William	Kefauver, Estes
Crockett, David	Polk, James K.
Davis, Samuel	Ross, John
Driver, William	Sequoya
Forrest, Nathan B.	Sevier, John
Houston, Samuel	White, Hugh L.
Hull, Cordell	York, Alvin C.

CITIES

Chattanooga   Knoxville   Memphis   Nashville

HISTORY

Civil War	Tennessee Valley Authority
Franklin, State of	Watauga Association
Natchez Trace	Westward Movement

PHYSICAL FEATURES

Blue Ridge Mountains	Great Smoky Mountains
Clingmans Dome	Mississippi River
Cumberland Gap	Reelfoot Lake
Cumberland Mountains	Tennessee River
Cumberland River	

OTHER RELATED ARTICLES

Great Smoky Mountains National Park
Oak Ridge National Laboratory

Outline

I. Government
   A. Constitution   D. Courts   F. Taxation
   B. Executive   E. Local Gov-   G. Politics
   C. Legislature   ernment
II. People
III. Education
   A. Schools   B. Libraries   C. Museums
IV. A Visitor's Guide
   A. Places to Visit
   B. Annual Events
V. The Land
   A. Land Regions
   B. Rivers and Lakes
VI. Climate
VII. Economy
   A. Natural Resources
   B. Manufacturing
   C. Agriculture
   D. Mining
   E. Electric Power
   F. Transportation
   G. Communication
VIII. History

Questions

When and why did the people in the Tennessee region form the State of Franklin?

What are the leading minerals found in Tennessee?

Which three U.S. Presidents influenced Tennessee's development?

From what peak in Tennessee is it possible to see seven states?

Why did Memphis lose its city charter during the late 1870's?

How does the way of life in East Tennessee differ from that in West and Middle Tennessee?

How can Tennessee's constitution be amended?

How is most of the electric power in Tennessee generated?

How did the Tennessee region come under British control in the 1700's?

How has the inland water area of Tennessee been doubled since 1933?

Additional Resources

Level I

BAILEY, BERNADINE. *Picture Book of Tennessee.* Rev. ed. Whitman, 1974.

CALDWELL, MARY F. *Tennessee: The Volunteer State.* Childrens Press, 1968.

CARPENTER, ALLAN. Rev. ed. *Tennessee.* Childrens Press, 1979.

FRADIN, DENNIS B. *Tennessee in Words and Pictures.* Childrens Press, 1980.

SCHELL, EDWARD. *Tennessee.* Graphic Arts Center, 1979.

WEST, EMMY, and GOVAN, C. N. *Danger Downriver.* Viking, 1972. Fiction. Slave and Indian life in the early 1800's.

Level II

BERGERON, PAUL H. *Paths of the Past: Tennessee, 1770-1970.* Univ. of Tennessee Press, 1979.

CLARK, JOE. *Tennessee Hill Folk.* Vanderbilt Univ. Press, 1972.

CONNELLY, THOMAS L. *Civil War Tennessee: Battles and Leaders.* Univ. of Tennessee Press, 1979.

CORLEW, ROBERT E. *Tennessee: A Short History.* 2nd ed. Univ. of Tennessee Press, 1981.

DYKEMAN, WILMA. *Tennessee: A Bicentennial History.* Norton, 1975.

DYKEMAN, WILMA, and STOKELY, JIM. *Highland Homeland: The People of the Great Smokies.* U.S. National Park Service, 1978.

GREENE, LEE S., and others. *Government in Tennessee.* 4th ed. Univ. of Tennessee Press, 1982.

JONES, BILLY M., ed. *Heroes of Tennessee.* Memphis State Univ. Press, 1979.

LAMON, LESTER C. *Blacks in Tennessee, 1791-1970.* Univ. of Tennessee Press, 1981.

LUTHER, EDWARD T. *Our Restless Earth: The Geological Regions of Tennessee.* Univ. of Tennessee Press, 1977.

SATZ, RONALD N. *Tennessee's Indian Peoples: From White Contact to Removal, 1540-1840.* Univ. of Tennessee Press, 1978.

123

TENNESSEE, UNIVERSITY OF

TENNESSEE, UNIVERSITY OF, is a coeducational, state-supported institution. Its largest campus is in Knoxville. It also has campuses in Chattanooga, Martin, and Memphis. The university grants bachelor's, master's, and doctor's degrees.

The Knoxville campus includes colleges of agriculture, business administration, communications, education, engineering, home economics, law, liberal arts, nursing, and veterinary medicine; and a graduate school. The campus is the headquarters for the university's statewide programs of agricultural research and extension, continuing education, and public service.

The Chattanooga and Martin campuses also offer a wide variety of programs, including business administration, education, engineering, and liberal arts. In Memphis, the university's Center for the Health Sciences has colleges of basic medical sciences, community and allied health professions, dentistry, medicine, nursing, and pharmacy, and a graduate school of medical sciences.

The university also operates research facilities. The main agricultural experiment station is in Knoxville. Other facilities conduct studies in business and economics, engineering, the environment, health sciences, transportation, and water resources.

The university was founded in 1794 as Blount College, and received its present name in 1879. For the enrollment of the University of Tennessee, see UNIVERSITIES AND COLLEGES (table).

Critically reviewed by the UNIVERSITY OF TENNESSEE

TENNESSEE RIVER is the largest tributary of the Ohio River. It begins at Knoxville, Tenn., where the Holston and French Broad rivers meet, and flows southwest through Tennessee and Alabama. Then the river curves northward. It flows back into Tennessee and northwest across Kentucky. At Paducah, Ky., it empties into the Ohio River. The Tennessee River drains an area of about 41,000 square miles (106,000 square kilometers).

Development of the river's water power to generate electricity began in 1913 with the construction of Hales Bar Dam, near Chattanooga, Tenn. Nickajack Dam replaced Hales Bar Dam in 1968. Wilson Dam, near Muscle Shoals, Ala., began generating electricity in 1925. In 1933, the Tennessee Valley Authority began a series of dams that converted the river into a chain of narrow lakes. The river's 650-mile (1,046-kilometer) course is now navigable.   E. WILLARD MILLER

TENNESSEE VALLEY AUTHORITY (TVA) is a federal corporation that works to develop the natural resources of the Tennessee Valley. Congress created TVA in 1933 and gave it the overall goal of conserving the resources of the valley region. Congress also directed TVA to speed the region's economic development and, in case of war, to use the valley's resources for national defense.

Beginning in colonial times, the valley's forests had been cut down for lumber or to clear the land for farming and mining. The roots of trees and shrubs had held the soil in place and absorbed moisture. But when the forests were removed, the water ran off the land, carrying the topsoil with it. Farming became impossible, and flooding rivers caused loss of life and property.

Through the years, TVA has built dams to control floods, create electric power, and deepen rivers for shipping. It has planted new forests and preserved existing ones, and it has developed cheap fertilizers.

The Valley. The Tennessee Valley covers 40,910 square miles (105,956 square kilometers). The valley includes parts of Tennessee, Kentucky, Virginia, North Carolina, Georgia, Alabama, and Mississippi. The land varies from peaks 1 mile (1.6 kilometers) high in the Great Smoky Mountains to the low, muddy plains near the mouth of the Tennessee River. The valley has rich deposits of coal, copper, gravel, iron, limestone, manganese, marble, sand, and zinc.

The achievements of the TVA program have been spread far outside the valley. Power from TVA dams and steam plants reaches homes, farms, factories, stores, and mines in an area of about 80,000 square miles (210,000 square kilometers). Phosphate fertilizers developed and improved under the TVA program have been tested and demonstrated in more than half the states of the United States.

The Dams. Fifty-one dams on the Tennessee River and its branches work as a single system, making this one of the most effectively controlled waterways in the world. TVA built most of the larger dams. It also bought several dams from private companies. The agency directs the storage and release of water and the generation of power at 13 dams owned by the Aluminum Company of America. TVA also buys power from seven dams of the Cumberland River system, operated by the U.S. Army Corps of Engineers.

The dams are of two general types. On the main stream of the Tennessee River, long dams were built,

TVA

The TVA's Paradise Steam Plant can generate 2,558,200 kilowatts of electricity, more than any other fuel-powered plant.

Norris Dam on the Clinch River is 265 feet (81 meters) high and 1,860 feet (567 meters) long. Its reservoir stores over 2½ million acre-feet (3.1 billion cubic meters) of water.

TVA

making a continuous chain of lakes from Paducah, Ky., to Knoxville, Tenn. Each of these dams has a lock by which towboats and barges may be raised or lowered from one lake level to another.

On the branches of the Tennessee, high dams create great water reservoirs between the hills and mountains. The highest of these dams is Fontana Dam, 480 feet (146 meters) high, on the Little Tennessee River.

TVA dams on the Tennessee River itself are Chickamauga, Fort Loudoun, Guntersville, Kentucky, Nickajack, Pickwick Landing, Watts Bar, Wheeler, and Wilson. Kentucky Dam, the largest, measures 8,422 feet (2,567 meters) long and 206 feet (63 meters) high. The dam creates a lake about 185 miles (298 kilometers) long.

Dams on branches of the Tennessee are Santeetlah on the Cheoah; Melton Hill and Norris on the Clinch; Bear Creek, Cedar Cliff, and East Fork on the East Fork of the Tuckasegee; Tims Ford on the Elk; Douglas on the French Broad; Apalachia, Chatuge, Hiwassee, and Mission on the Hiwassee; Cherokee on the Holston; Calderwood, Cheoah, Chilhowee, Fontana, and Tellico on the Little Tennessee; Nantahala on the Nantahala; Nolichucky on the Nolichucky; Nottely on the Nottely; Ocoee 1, 2, and 3 on the Ocoee; Queens Creek on Queens Creek; Boone, Fort Patrick Henry, and South Holston on the South Fork of the Holston; Blue Ridge on the Toccoa; Thorpe on the Tuckasegee; Watauga and Wilbur on the Watauga; Tuckasegee on the West Fork of the Tuckasegee; and Wolf Creek on Wolf Creek. Cumberland Valley dams in the TVA system are Center Hill and Great Falls on the Caney Fork; Barkley, Cheatham, Old Hickory, and Wolf Creek on

the Cumberland; Dale Hollow on the Obey; and J. Percy Priest on the Stones.

Electric Power. The TVA region uses more than 100 billion kilowatt-hours of electricity a year, about 65 times as much power as it used in 1933. During TVA's early years, dams generated much of its power. But as the demand for electricity increased, the agency had to find other power sources. In the early 1970's, water power supplied less than a fifth of the electricity generated in the TVA system. The rest came from large steam plants that generated power from coal. Several newly built nuclear power plants were scheduled to begin operating during the 1970's.

By 1970, about half the coal used by TVA to generate power came from strip mines. Strip mining, a method of surface mining, usually scars the landscape, pollutes rivers, and destroys valuable timber. TVA had been criticized for buying coal from strip mines. As a result, all TVA coal contracts since 1965 have required strip mine operators to reclaim any damaged land.

Almost all farms in the region have electricity. TVA was designed to provide abundant power for the region at the lowest possible rates. Household users of TVA power pay slightly more than half as much per kilowatt-hour as do consumers on the average in the United States. About 160 local electric power companies distribute TVA power to consumers.

River Shipping. The Tennessee River provides a 650-mile (1,046-kilometer) route for boats of 9-foot (2.7-meter) draft. It connects with the inland waterway system (see INLAND WATERWAY). In the early 1970's,

Tennessee Valley Authority (TVA)

TVA provides electric power, flood control, water recreation, and navigable waterways in Tennessee and the surrounding states. TVA also builds and operates power plants and dams and directs the operation of Alcoa and Corps of Engineers dams.

▨ Tennessee River watershed	—	TVA dam
▪ Coal-fired power plant	— E	Corps of Engineers dam
▫ Nuclear power plant	— A	Alcoa dam

Distance scale

0   50   100   150   200 Miles
0   50   100   150   200   250   300 Kilometers

WORLD BOOK map

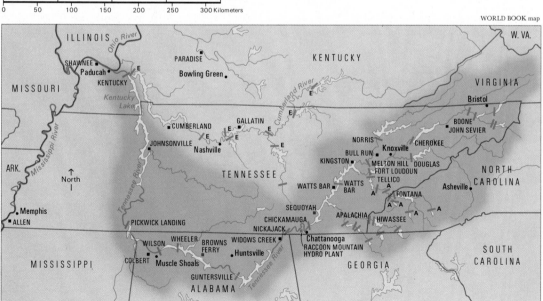

barges on this system carried about 25 million short tons (23 million metric tons) of freight yearly.

Flood Control. The reservoirs behind the dams provide about 15 million acre-feet (19 billion cubic meters) of storage space. During the flood season, which starts about January 1, the storage of water helps control floods in the Tennessee and lower Mississippi and Ohio basins. During drier months, stored water is released to maintain the level of the river.

Other Activities. The TVA chemical facilities at Muscle Shoals are operated as a national laboratory for research and experimental production of fertilizers. This laboratory improved the electric-furnace smelting of phosphate rock to produce elemental phosphorus.

TVA has provided more than 1,300,000,000 seedlings and has reforested more than 1,300,000 acres (526,-000 hectares). Its foresters work with states, counties, and other organizations to promote better forest management. This program includes selective cutting and protection against fire and overgrazing. Woodlands cover more than half the valley region.

The beautiful lakes created by damming the Tennessee River and its branches provide many recreational opportunities. States, counties, cities, and private organizations have developed many parks and other facilities. TVA itself developed the huge Land Between the Lakes recreational area between Kentucky Lake and Lake Barkley in Kentucky and Tennessee.

History. Congress established the Tennessee Valley Authority after about 15 years of debate on how to use the government's two nitrate plants and Wilson Dam at Muscle Shoals, Ala. These projects, built under the National Defense Act of 1916, had not been finished in time for use during World War I. The TVA Act transferred them from the War Department to TVA.

The new corporation represented a great change in national policy. Previously, responsibility for various projects in the valley had been divided among the Departments of Agriculture, the Army, and the Interior. The TVA Act recognized that all conservation problems were related. It gave one agency the responsibility of improving all types of conservation and development of resources.

The creation of TVA became a highly controversial issue and remained so for many years. Private power companies strongly opposed government production of electric power. State and local agencies in the Tennessee Valley feared that TVA would take over their functions. Political opponents of President Franklin D. Roosevelt's New Deal used the issue of the TVA's creation to embarrass him.

TVA pays no federal income taxes, but it pays more than $80 million a year in dividends and repayments to the U.S. Treasury. It also makes payments to states and counties in place of taxes.

A board of three members directs TVA. The President appoints them to nine-year terms with the consent of the Senate, and they report to him.   JOHN R. MOORE

Related Articles in WORLD BOOK include:

Kentucky Lake	Turbine (picture: Kaplan-
Muscle Shoals	Type Wheels)
Norris, George W.	Willkie, Wendell L.
Tennessee River	Wolf Creek Dam

Additional Resources

CALLAHAN, NORTH. *TVA: Bridge Over Troubled Waters*. Barnes, 1980.

HUBBARD, PRESTON J. *Origins of the TVA*. Vanderbilt, 1961.

MOORE, JOHN R., ed. *The Economic Impact of TVA*. Univ. of Tennessee Press, 1967.

MORGAN, ARTHUR E. *The Making of the TVA*. Pemberton, 1974. Written by the first chairman of the board of the Tennessee Valley Authority.

TENNESSEE WALKING HORSE. See HORSE (Saddle Horses; color picture).

TENNESSEE WESLEYAN COLLEGE. See UNIVERSITIES AND COLLEGES (table).

TENNIEL, *TEN yul,* **SIR JOHN** (1820-1914), an English cartoonist and book illustrator, illustrated Lewis Carroll's *Alice's Adventures in Wonderland* (1865) and *Through the Looking-Glass* (1871). He also became famous for his political cartoons in *Punch*, a magazine for which he worked for about 50 years after 1850. His work was admired for its originality, dignity, and excellent technique. Tenniel and other artists of his time helped Great Britain keep leadership in the field of book illustration. He was born in London. NORMAN L. RICE

See also LITERATURE FOR CHILDREN (The Rise of Illustration; picture: Through the Looking-Glass); CARROLL, LEWIS (The *Alice* Books).

Macmillan & Co., Ltd.; Radio Times Hulton Picture Library

Sir John Tenniel, *above,* became famous as the illustrator of Lewis Carroll's *Alice's Adventures in Wonderland.* His drawing of the mad tea party, *left,* expressed comic dignity.

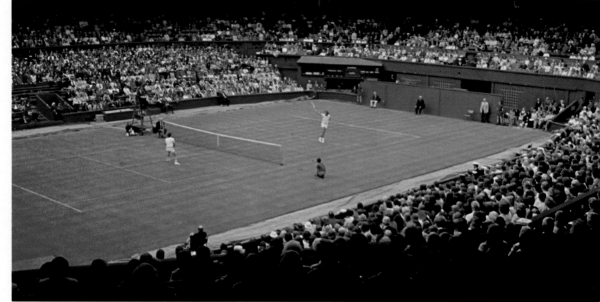

Important Tennis Tournaments attract thousands of fans who come to watch the world's finest players compete against each other. The tournament held each summer in Wimbledon, England, *above*, ranks as the unofficial world championship for men and women players.

TENNIS

TENNIS is a game in which opposing players—one or two on each side—use rackets to hit a ball back and forth over a net. The game is played on a flat surface called a *court*. Each player tries to score points by hitting the ball so that the opposing player or players cannot return it over the net and inside the court.

Tennis may be played indoors or outdoors. If two persons play, the game is called *singles*. If four persons play, it is called *doubles*. In most singles and doubles matches, men play men and women play women. In *mixed doubles*, a man and a woman play on each side.

Millions of people throughout the world play tennis for exercise and recreation. They play on courts in public parks and in private tennis clubs. Players of almost any age can enjoy the sport. The United States Tennis Association (USTA), which governs American tennis, sponsors national tournaments for players as young as 12 and as old as 75.

Professional tennis players travel throughout the world to compete in tournaments that offer thousands of dollars in prize money. Many countries enter men's and women's teams that compete for international trophies. The most famous trophy is the Davis Cup, which represents the world's men's team championship.

Tennis ranks as one of the world's most popular spectator sports as well as a favorite participant sport. Thousands of fans attend the many tennis tournaments held each year. Millions more watch important matches on television.

Margaret Smith Court, the contributor of this article, won more major tennis titles than any other player in the history of the sport.

Tennis as it is played today developed in England during the late 1800's. The game quickly spread to the United States and other countries. By 1900, tennis had become a major international sport.

The Court and Equipment

The Court is a rectangle divided into halves by a net stretched across the middle. The net measures 3 feet (91 centimeters) high at the center and $3\frac{1}{2}$ feet (107 centimeters) high at the side posts that support it. The court is 78 feet (23.7 meters) long. Almost all courts are marked off so that both singles and doubles games can be played on them. The singles court measures 27 feet (8.2 meters) wide. The doubles court is $4\frac{1}{2}$ feet (1.37 meters) wider on each side. Various lines divide the singles and doubles court into sections. For the names of these lines and the sizes and names of the sections, see the diagram of a court in this article.

For many years, major tennis tournaments were played on grass courts. In fact, the early name for the sport was *lawn tennis*. But grass courts cost much to maintain, and so nearly all of them have been replaced by other surfaces.

The most popular surfaces for outdoor courts are asphalt, clay, and concrete. Most indoor courts have a carpet-type surface laid over concrete or plywood. Several manufacturers have developed surfaces made of synthetic materials. Many of these surfaces can be laid on either indoor or outdoor courts.

Tennis Balls are hollow. They are made of rubber and covered with a felt fabric woven of Dacron, nylon, and wool. A tennis ball must have a diameter of more than $2\frac{1}{2}$ inches (6.35 centimeters) but less than $2\frac{5}{8}$ inches (6.67 centimeters). It must weigh more than 2 ounces (56.7 grams) but less than $2\frac{1}{16}$ ounces (58.6 grams). Balls used in tournaments may be either white or yellow. Manufacturers also make balls in other colors for nontournament play.

Tennis Rackets. No rules govern the size and weight of a tennis racket, and so the models of various manufacturers differ slightly. But nearly all rackets measure 27 inches (68 centimeters) long. Most men choose a racket that weighs about 14 ounces (397 grams). Most women select one that weighs about 13 ounces (369 grams). In general, young players use a racket that

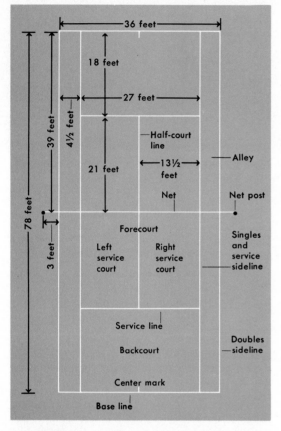

A Tennis Court is a rectangle divided into halves by a net. Various white lines further divide the court into sections.

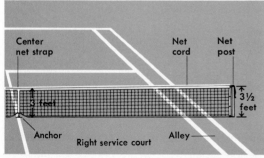

WORLD BOOK diagrams

The Net is suspended across the court by a cable or cord. Two posts, one outside each doubles sideline, support the net. A narrow strap in the middle holds the net tight.

weighs about 9 ounces (255 grams). Almost all racket frames are made of steel, wood, or a metal alloy. The striking surface is a net of tightly strung catgut or nylon strings (see CATGUT).

Tennis Clothes should fit comfortably so that a player can move freely. During the late 1800's and early 1900's, men players wore long-sleeved shirts and trousers, and women wore ankle-length dresses. Such bulky clothing limited a player's movements. Today, men wear short-sleeved shirts and shorts. Women wear minidresses or blouses and short skirts.

Shoes are perhaps the most important item in a player's wardrobe. Tennis shoes are designed specially for the sport. They are made of cloth and have rubber soles and no heels. The shoes help keep players from slipping and do not damage the court.

How Tennis Is Played

Before they begin to play tennis, the players must decide who serves first and which end of the court each player or team will defend. Most players make these decisions by means of a racket "toss." For example, they may use the manufacturer's markings on one side of a racket handle as "heads" and on the other side as "tails." One player stands the racket upright on the frame and spins it. The opposing player or team calls which side will land face up. If the call is correct, the player or team may either (1) choose to serve or receive first or (2) decide which end of the court to defend.

The court diagram in this article locates the various lines and playing areas discussed in this section.

Scoring. Tennis is scored in terms of points, games, and sets. A player or doubles team scores a *point* when the opposing side fails to return the ball properly or

---

TERMS USED IN TENNIS

Ace, or *service ace* is a point scored by a server when the receiver is unable to touch a legal serve.

Deuce is a tie score after 6 points in a game or 10 games in a set.

Fault is called when a player serves into the net or outside the receiver's service court. A server commits a *foot fault* by stepping over the base line or changing position by walking or running before hitting the ball during a service. A server who makes two faults in a row commits a *double fault* and loses a point.

Game is the next highest unit of scoring after a point. To win a game, a player must score four points and lead by at least two points.

Ground Stroke is any shot that a player uses after the ball bounces once on the court.

Let is a serve that hits the net and drops into the proper service court. A let does not count and is replayed.

Lob is a shot hit high into the air. It is intended to land behind an opponent, forcing the player to retreat from the net.

Love is the scoring term for zero.

Overhead Smash is a hard swing at an opponent's shot from above the head.

Set is the highest unit of scoring in a match. To win a set, a player or team must win six games and lead by at least two games unless a tie breaker is played.

Tie Breaker is a play-off of a certain number of points to decide the winner of a set. Most tie breakers are played after the game score reaches 6-6.

Volley is any shot made by hitting the ball before it bounces on the court.

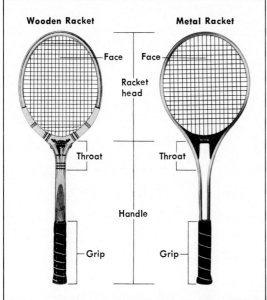

Wooden Racket　　　　　Metal Racket

Face　　Face

Racket
head

Throat　　　Throat

Handle

Grip　　　　Grip

Dunlop Sports Company; AMF/Head Division

Tennis Rackets have frames made of wood, *left*, or metal, *right*. The striking surface consists of a net of tightly strung nylon or catgut strings. The grip has a leather covering.

commits an error. To win a *game*, one side must score four points and lead by at least two points. The first point is called *15;* the second, *30;* the third, *40;* and the fourth, *game point.* A score of zero is called *love.* Historians are not certain how this scoring system began.

The server's score is always given first. For example, if the serving side leads three points to one, the score is *40-15.* If the receiving side wins the first two points, the score is *love-30.* If both sides win three points, the score is *40-40,* which is called *deuce.* To win a deuce game, one side must lead by two points. The first point scored after deuce is called the *advantage* or *ad.* If the side with the advantage loses the next point, the game returns to deuce.

To win a *set,* one side must win six games and lead by at least two games. If the game score is 5-5—a deuce set—play continues until one side has a two-game margin. In some tournaments, if the score reaches 6-6, a *tie breaker* is played. It consists of a play-off of a certain number of points. The side that wins the tie breaker wins the set by a score of 7-6.

In most competitions, the first side to win two sets wins the tennis *match.* In some men's tournaments, the first side to win three sets takes the match.

The Serve, or *service,* puts the ball into play at the start of each game and after each point is scored. The server must toss the ball into the air and hit it before it strikes the ground. The ball must then travel into the service court diagonally opposite. The server begins each game by serving from the right side of the court. The serve then alternates between the left and right sides following each point. The server must serve from behind the base line but may stand anywhere between the center mark and the singles sideline.

In a singles match, a player serves until a game is completed. Then the receiver becomes the server. The players continue to alternate serves after each game. In a doubles match, the serve also changes sides after each game. But in addition, the members of each team alternate serves. If a team serves odd-numbered games, for example, one member would serve the first game, the other the third game, and so on. In both singles and doubles matches, the opposing players change ends of the court after the first, third, and all following odd-numbered games.

If a serve lands in the net or outside the receiver's service court, the server has committed a *fault.* A server commits a *foot fault* by stepping on or over the base line or changing position by running or walking before hitting the ball. A player who commits a fault or foot fault gets a second serve. But if this serve fails through a fault or foot fault, the player has committed a *double fault* and loses the point. If the ball hits the top of the net and drops into the proper service court, the serve is called a *let* and is replayed. A let is also called if a player serves before the receiver is ready.

A powerful, accurate serve can help a player win easy points. A player can serve an *ace,* which is a legal serve that the receiver is unable to touch. Even if the receiver manages to return a serve, the return may be so weak the server can easily hit a winning shot.

Receivers may stand anywhere on their end of the court during the service. A receiver often takes a position based on knowledge of an opponent's serve. If the server has a very fast serve, for example, the receiver will stand far back to allow enough time to sight the ball for the return shot.

The Ball in Play. After the serve, the receiver must hit the ball on the first bounce and return it over the net. The ball must land in the area bounded by the base line and the singles sidelines or, in team play, the doubles sidelines. A shot that lands on a sideline or base line is in play. A shot that hits the net and drops into the opposing court is also in play. After the ball has been served and returned, it may be hit either on the fly, which is called a *volley,* or after the first bounce, which is called a *ground stroke.* The players continue to *rally* (hit the ball back and forth) until one side scores a point. During play, a player or team wins a point if the opposing side (1) hits the ball into the net, (2) hits the ball outside the court, or (3) allows a ball to bounce twice.

Players may use a variety of ground strokes and volleys. The basic shots are the *forehand drive* and the *backhand drive.* Right-handed players hit a forehand drive on the right, or racket, side of the body. They hit a backhand drive by reaching across the body to the left side. Left-handed players hit a forehand drive on the left side and a backhand drive on the right.

To force an opponent away from the net, a player may hit a *lob*—a high shot deep into the opponent's court. The opponent must retreat from the net to reach the ball. If the lob is not hit deep enough, however, the opponent may reply with an *overhead smash.* This shot is made by hitting the ball from above the head. A smash often is so powerful that it cannot be returned.

By hitting the ball in a certain way, a player can

The Grip is the way in which a player holds the racket. Most players use a grip called the *Continental grip* to serve and a form of the *Eastern grip* to hit forehand and backhand drives. In each grip, the player places the palm and fingers on the handle as shown at the right.

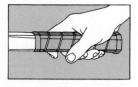

Continental Serve　　　**Eastern Forehand**　　　**Eastern Backhand**

WORLD BOOK illustrations by James Curran

The Serve. (1) The player, *right,* points his racket toward the net and places one foot comfortably behind the other. (2 and 3) He then tosses the ball into the air with his thumb and first two fingers and starts his backswing. (4) He next moves the racket back until it is behind him and pointing toward the ground. (5) The player then hits the ball with his arm fully extended and the ball slightly in front of him. (6) He ends the stroke with a strong follow-through.

1　　2　　3　　4　　5　　6

The Forehand Drive. (1) The player, *right,* stands behind the spot where the ball will bounce. (2 and 3) She pivots her body and starts her backswing as the ball strikes the court. (4) As the ball bounces, she begins to bring the racket forward. (5) She hits the ball when it reaches a height between her knee and waist, keeping the racket parallel to the court. (6) Finally, she shifts her weight to her front foot while following through after hitting the shot.

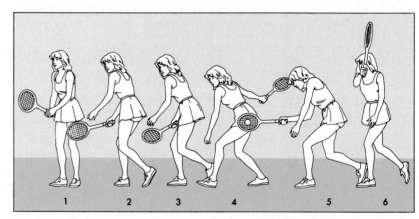

1　　2　　3　　4　　5　　6

The Backhand Drive. (1) The player, *right,* holds the grip with one hand and lightly grasps the throat of the racket with the other hand. (2) As he sights the ball, he turns his shoulder toward the net, pivots, and begins his backswing. (3) He ends the backswing with the racket behind him. (4 and 5) He then swings the racket forward, hip high and parallel to the court, and strikes the ball while it is still rising. (6) He follows through to complete the stroke.

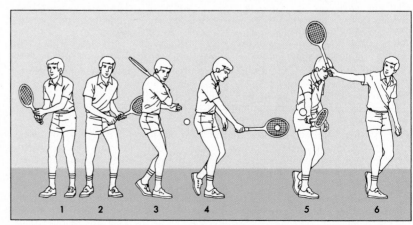

1　　2　　3　　4　　5　　6

give a shot *topspin* or *underspin*. Spin causes the ball to react in such a way that it is difficult to return. A lob hit with topspin will dart toward the rear of the court after it lands. A shot hit with underspin barely clears the net and stays low after it bounces.

Officials. In most tennis matches, the players themselves act as officials and keep their own score. But in an important tournament, many officials may be used. The chief official is the tournament referee, who has charge of the entire tournament. On the court, the top official is the umpire. The umpire sits on a high chair alongside center court and announces the score to the crowd. The umpire also supervises as many as 13 linesmen. These officials are stationed at various spots around the court. They determine whether a ball has been served legally and whether shots are *good* (inside the court) or *out* (outside the court).

Organized Tennis

Amateur Tennis. Most of the world's tennis players are amateurs. They play for enjoyment and exercise and receive no pay. Many of them play in small organized interclub competitions, chiefly on weekends. High schools and colleges also sponsor tennis teams as part of their athletics programs.

The International Tennis Federation (ITF) governs tennis throughout the world. The ITF consists of the national tennis associations of about 100 countries. These associations include the U.S. Tennis Association, the Canadian Lawn Tennis Association, the Lawn Tennis Association of Australia, and the Lawn Tennis Association of Great Britain.

Professional Tennis. For many years, nearly all the world's leading tournament players were amateurs. Professional tennis first became widely accepted in the late 1960's, and today all the top players are professionals. Professionals play tennis for money, or they are paid for coaching or teaching the game.

Both men and women professionals have formed organizations to represent them and supervise their tournaments. Men professional players established the Association of Tennis Professionals in 1972. The same year, women professionals formed the Women's Tennis Association.

Tennis Tournaments. Only amateurs could play in major tournaments before 1968. That year, the member countries of the ITF voted to allow amateurs and professionals to compete in the same tournaments. These events became known as *open* tournaments. Today, almost all major tournaments are open.

The most important tournaments for individual players are the national championships of Great Britain, the United States, Australia, and France. The British meet, popularly called the Wimbledon, is the most highly regarded of the world's major championships. Together, the four championships make up the *grand slam*. Only four players have won all four in the same year. Don Budge of the United States won the grand slam in 1938. Rod Laver of Australia did it twice, in 1962 and 1969. Maureen Connolly of the United States won the grand slam in 1953, and Margaret Smith Court of Australia won it in 1970.

A number of organizations sponsor tournaments just for professional players. The leading male professionals play in a series of tournaments, called the Grand Prix Circuit, held throughout the world. Other tournaments are held for lower ranking players. Women professionals also compete in a series of tournaments.

Most amateur and professional tournaments use a system called *seeding* to prevent the top players from meeting each other in an early round. The best player would be seeded number one; the next best, number two; and so on. Players are seeded according to their records and reputations. In most tournaments, eight players are seeded. The matches are arranged so that seeded players do not face each other until the quarterfinal round, unless unseeded players defeat them.

Several tournaments are held for international team trophies. The best-known trophy is the Davis Cup, donated in 1900 by Dwight Davis, an American player. Competition for the cup takes place every year for teams of men players from any eligible nation. The teams meet in a series, called a *tie*, consisting of one doubles and four singles matches. For the winners of the trophy, see the article DAVIS CUP.

American and Australian men compete for the World Cup each year. The event began in 1970 and is held in Hartford, Conn. The competition consists of five singles and two doubles.

In 1923, Hazel Hotchkiss Wightman, an American player, donated the Wightman Cup as a trophy for competition between British and American women's teams. The annual Wightman Cup tournament consists of five singles and two doubles. In 1963, the ITF established the Federation Cup for teams of women representing member nations. Each round in the Federation Cup elimination tournament consists of two singles and one doubles.

History

Beginnings. Most historians agree that the French originated tennis during the 1100's or 1200's. The French called it *jeu de paume*, meaning *game of the palm*. The players batted the ball back and forth over a net with the palm of their hand.

Major Walter Clopton Wingfield of England is generally considered the father of modern tennis. In 1873, he introduced a version of the game closely resembling the modern sport. In 1874, he patented tennis equipment and rules for playing on grass courts. Wingfield called the game *sphairistike*, the Greek word for *playing ball*. But the name was soon replaced by *lawn tennis*. Some historians feel that Major Harry Gem of England should share credit as the sport's founder. Gem played a form of tennis in the 1860's.

Tennis soon replaced croquet as England's most popular outdoor sport. In 1877, the All England Croquet Club changed its name to the All England Croquet and Lawn Tennis Club. Also in 1877, the club sponsored the first major tennis tournament at its headquarters in Wimbledon, a suburb of London. This tournament has become the unofficial world championship for men's and women's singles and doubles.

The Spread of Tennis. Mary Ewing Outerbridge, an American sportswoman, introduced tennis into the United States. In 1874, she purchased tennis equipment from British army officers in Bermuda. Outerbridge used the equipment to set up the first U.S. tennis court. The court was on the grounds of the Staten Island Cricket and Baseball Club in New York City.

The United States National Lawn Tennis Association (now the United States Tennis Association) was established in 1881. That same year, the association sponsored the first U.S. men's championship tournament in Newport, R.I.

In 1900, the American player Dwight Davis donated the Davis Cup to be awarded annually to the country that wins the world's men's championship. The trophy became recognized as the top prize in international team tennis.

Many of the greatest stars in tennis history played during the 1920's. But the period was dominated by Bill Tilden, an American who is generally considered the sport's finest player. Tilden won the U.S. singles title every year from 1920 through 1925 and again in

1929. He also won the Wimbledon title three times.

The top women players in the 1920's were Suzanne Lenglen of France and Helen Wills (later Helen Wills Moody) of the United States. Lenglen won six Wimbledon and six French championships. Helen Wills Moody won eight Wimbledon championships and seven U.S. titles.

Perhaps the outstanding individual player of the 1930's was Don Budge of the United States. In 1938, he became the first player to win the grand slam.

The Mid-1900's. Until the 1950's, France, Great Britain, and the United States produced almost all the world's major players. Then Australia became the leading country in men's competition. From 1950 through 1967, Australian teams won the Davis Cup 15 times. Such players as Roy Emerson, Lew Hoad, Rod Laver, John Newcombe, Ken Rosewall, Frank Sedgman, and Fred Stolle helped Australia maintain its top position in international men's tennis.

Bettmann Archive   United Press Int.   *Chicago Sun-Times*

Great Women Players include, *from left to right,* Hazel Hotchkiss Wightman and Helen Wills Moody of the United States and Margaret Smith Court of Australia. Wightman starred in the early 1900's, and Moody during the 1920's and 1930's. Court won many titles in the 1960's and 1970's.

United Press Int.

Great Men Players include, *from left to right,* Bill Tilden and Don Budge of the United States and Rod Laver of Australia. Tilden dominated international competition throughout the 1920's. Budge starred in the late 1930's, and Laver was the world's leading player during the 1960's.

All-England (Wimbledon) Championships

The All-England Championships are held annually in the London suburb of Wimbledon. Men's competition began in 1877, and women's competition in 1884. This table lists the Wimbledon singles champions since 1920.

Men's Singles

Year	Winner	Country
1920	Bill Tilden	United States
1921	Bill Tilden	United States
1922	Gerald Patterson	Australia
1923	Bill Johnston	United States
1924	Jean Borotra	France
1925	René Lacoste	France
1926	Jean Borotra	France
1927	Henri Cochet	France
1928	René Lacoste	France
1929	Henri Cochet	France
1930	Bill Tilden	United States
1931	Sid Wood	United States
1932	Ellsworth Vines	United States
1933	Jack Crawford	Australia
1934	Fred Perry	Great Britain
1935	Fred Perry	Great Britain
1936	Fred Perry	Great Britain
1937	Don Budge	United States
1938	Don Budge	United States
1939	Bobby Riggs	United States
1940-45	No competition	
1946	Yvon Petra	France
1947	Jack Kramer	United States
1948	Bob Falkenburg	United States
1949	Ted Schroeder	United States
1950	Budge Patty	United States
1951	Dick Savitt	United States
1952	Frank Sedgman	Australia
1953	Vic Seixas	United States
1954	Jaroslav Drobny	Egypt
1955	Tony Trabert	United States
1956	Lew Hoad	Australia
1957	Lew Hoad	Australia
1958	Ashley Cooper	Australia
1959	Alex Olmedo	United States
1960	Neale Fraser	Australia
1961	Rod Laver	Australia
1962	Rod Laver	Australia
1963	Chuck McKinley	United States
1964	Roy Emerson	Australia
1965	Roy Emerson	Australia
1966	Manuel Santana	Spain
1967	John Newcombe	Australia
1968	Rod Laver	Australia
1969	Rod Laver	Australia
1970	John Newcombe	Australia
1971	John Newcombe	Australia
1972	Stan Smith	United States
1973	Jan Kodes	Czechoslovakia
1974	Jimmy Connors	United States
1975	Arthur Ashe	United States
1976	Bjorn Borg	Sweden
1977	Bjorn Borg	Sweden
1978	Bjorn Borg	Sweden
1979	Bjorn Borg	Sweden
1980	Bjorn Borg	Sweden
1981	John McEnroe	United States
1982	Jimmy Connors	United States

Women's Singles

Year	Winner	Country
1920	Suzanne Lenglen	France
1921	Suzanne Lenglen	France
1922	Suzanne Lenglen	France
1923	Suzanne Lenglen	France
1924	Kitty McKane	Great Britain
1925	Suzanne Lenglen	France
1926	Kitty McKane Godfree	Great Britain
1927	Helen Wills	United States
1928	Helen Wills	United States
1929	Helen Wills	United States
1930	Helen Wills Moody	United States
1931	Cilly Aussem	Germany
1932	Helen Wills Moody	United States
1933	Helen Wills Moody	United States
1934	Dorothy Round	Great Britain
1935	Helen Wills Moody	United States
1936	Helen Hull Jacobs	United States
1937	Dorothy Round	Great Britain
1938	Helen Wills Moody	United States
1939	Alice Marble	United States
1940-45	No competition	
1946	Pauline Betz	United States
1947	Margaret Osborne	United States
1948	Louise Brough	United States
1949	Louise Brough	United States
1950	Louise Brough	United States
1951	Doris Hart	United States
1952	Maureen Connolly	United States
1953	Maureen Connolly	United States
1954	Maureen Connolly	United States
1955	Louise Brough	United States
1956	Shirley Fry	United States
1957	Althea Gibson	United States
1958	Althea Gibson	United States
1959	Maria Bueno	Brazil
1960	Maria Bueno	Brazil
1961	Angela Mortimer	Great Britain
1962	Karen Hantze Susman	United States
1963	Margaret Smith	Australia
1964	Maria Bueno	Brazil
1965	Margaret Smith	Australia
1966	Billie Jean King	United States
1967	Billie Jean King	United States
1968	Billie Jean King	United States
1969	Ann Haydon Jones	Great Britain
1970	Margaret Smith Court	Australia
1971	Evonne Goolagong	Australia
1972	Billie Jean King	United States
1973	Billie Jean King	United States
1974	Chris Evert	United States
1975	Billie Jean King	United States
1976	Chris Evert	United States
1977	Virginia Wade	Great Britain
1978	Martina Navratilova	United States
1979	Martina Navratilova	United States
1980	Evonne Goolagong	Australia
1981	Chris Evert Lloyd	United States
1982	Martina Navratilova	United States

United States Championships

The United States Championships are held annually in Flushing Meadows, N.Y. Men's competition began in 1881, and women's competition in 1887. This table lists the U.S. singles champions since 1920.

Men's Singles

Year	Winner	Country
1920	Bill Tilden	United States
1921	Bill Tilden	United States
1922	Bill Tilden	United States
1923	Bill Tilden	United States
1924	Bill Tilden	United States
1925	Bill Tilden	United States
1926	René Lacoste	France
1927	René Lacoste	France
1928	Henri Cochet	France
1929	Bill Tilden	United States
1930	John Doeg	United States
1931	Ellsworth Vines	United States
1932	Ellsworth Vines	United States
1933	Fred Perry	Great Britain
1934	Fred Perry	Great Britain
1935	Wilmer Allison	United States
1936	Fred Perry	Great Britain
1937	Don Budge	United States
1938	Don Budge	United States
1939	Bobby Riggs	United States
1940	Don McNeill	United States
1941	Bobby Riggs	United States
1942	Ted Schroeder	United States
1943	Joe Hunt	United States
1944	Frank Parker	United States
1945	Frank Parker	United States
1946	Jack Kramer	United States
1947	Jack Kramer	United States
1948	Pancho Gonzales	United States
1949	Pancho Gonzales	United States
1950	Art Larsen	United States
1951	Frank Sedgman	Australia
1952	Frank Sedgman	Australia
1953	Tony Trabert	United States
1954	Vic Seixas	United States
1955	Tony Trabert	United States
1956	Ken Rosewall	Australia
1957	Mal Anderson	Australia
1958	Ashley Cooper	Australia
1959	Neale Fraser	Australia
1960	Neale Fraser	Australia
1961	Roy Emerson	Australia
1962	Rod Laver	Australia
1963	Rafael Osuna	Mexico
1964	Roy Emerson	Australia
1965	Manuel Santana	Spain
1966	Fred Stolle	Australia
1967	John Newcombe	Australia
1968	Arthur Ashe	United States
1969	Rod Laver	Australia
1970	Ken Rosewall	Australia
1971	Stan Smith	United States
1972	Ilie Nastase	Romania
1973	John Newcombe	Australia
1974	Jimmy Connors	United States
1975	Manuel Orantes	Spain
1976	Jimmy Connors	United States
1977	Guillermo Vilas	Argentina
1978	Jimmy Connors	United States
1979	John McEnroe	United States
1980	John McEnroe	United States
1981	John McEnroe	United States
1982	Jimmy Connors	United States

Women's Singles

Year	Winner	Country
1920	Molla Bjurstedt Mallory	United States
1921	Molla Bjurstedt Mallory	United States
1922	Molla Bjurstedt Mallory	United States
1923	Helen Wills	United States
1924	Helen Wills	United States
1925	Helen Wills	United States
1926	Molla Bjurstedt Mallory	United States
1927	Helen Wills	United States
1928	Helen Wills	United States
1929	Helen Wills	United States
1930	Betty Nuthall	Great Britain
1931	Helen Wills Moody	United States
1932	Helen Hull Jacobs	United States
1933	Helen Hull Jacobs	United States
1934	Helen Hull Jacobs	United States
1935	Helen Hull Jacobs	United States
1936	Alice Marble	United States
1937	Anita Lizana	Chile
1938	Alice Marble	United States
1939	Alice Marble	United States
1940	Alice Marble	United States
1941	Sarah Palfrey Cooke	United States
1942	Pauline Betz	United States
1943	Pauline Betz	United States
1944	Pauline Betz	United States
1945	Sarah Palfrey Cooke	United States
1946	Pauline Betz	United States
1947	Louise Brough	United States
1948	Margaret Osborne duPont	United States
1949	Margaret Osborne duPont	United States
1950	Margaret Osborne duPont	United States
1951	Maureen Connolly	United States
1952	Maureen Connolly	United States
1953	Maureen Connolly	United States
1954	Doris Hart	United States
1955	Doris Hart	United States
1956	Shirley Fry	United States
1957	Althea Gibson	United States
1958	Althea Gibson	United States
1959	Maria Bueno	Brazil
1960	Darlene Hard	United States
1961	Darlene Hard	United States
1962	Margaret Smith	Australia
1963	Maria Bueno	Brazil
1964	Maria Bueno	Brazil
1965	Margaret Smith	Australia
1966	Maria Bueno	Brazil
1967	Billie Jean King	United States
1968	Virginia Wade	Great Britain
1969	Margaret Smith Court	Australia
1970	Margaret Smith Court	Australia
1971	Billie Jean King	United States
1972	Billie Jean King	United States
1973	Margaret Smith Court	Australia
1974	Billie Jean King	United States
1975	Chris Evert	United States
1976	Chris Evert	United States
1977	Chris Evert	United States
1978	Chris Evert	United States
1979	Tracy Austin	United States
1980	Chris Evert Lloyd	United States
1981	Tracy Austin	United States
1982	Chris Evert Lloyd	United States

Modern Tennis Stars include Chris Evert of the United States, *above*, and Bjorn Borg of Sweden, *below*. Both first won international fame while in their teens.

Daniel S. Baliotti, Focus on Sports

During the 1940's and 1950's, several American players achieved worldwide success. The most notable included Pancho Gonzales, Jack Kramer, Frank Parker, Ted Schroeder, and Tony Trabert.

The United States provided most of the top women stars from the mid-1940's through the mid-1960's. They included Louise Brough, Maureen Connolly, Margaret Osborne duPont, and Doris Hart. Connolly was probably the greatest woman player of this period. In 1953, she became the first woman to win the grand slam.

Althea Gibson of the United States became the first important black tennis player. She won the U.S. and Wimbledon titles in 1957 and 1958. In the late 1960's, Arthur Ashe of the United States became the first black male tennis star. In 1968, he won the U.S. singles championship.

Laver ranked as the top male star of the 1960's. The Australian became the only player to win the grand slam twice, in 1962 as an amateur and in 1969 as a professional. Other leading male players of the 1960's included Manuel Santana of Spain and Stan Smith of the United States. In the 1960's, Margaret Smith (later Margaret Smith Court) became the first Australian woman to win the U.S. and Wimbledon singles titles. She won the grand slam in 1970. Maria Bueno of Brazil and Billie Jean King of the United States also ranked as important players of the period.

Tennis Today. International tennis has largely been a professional sport since 1968. During the late 1970's, professionals competed for more than $12 million in prize money annually, and several of the leading players earned over $350,000 a year.

Television played an important role in increasing the popularity of tennis in the 1970's. Major tourna-ments were televised to many countries. TV networks also sponsored their own tournaments and matches.

Several highly publicized matches were arranged largely for TV audiences. In 1973, Bobby Riggs, a top-ranked U.S. player of the late 1930's and 1940's, defeated Margaret Smith Court in a televised "battle of the sexes." Later that year, Riggs played Billie Jean King in the Houston Astrodome before 30,472 spectators, the largest crowd ever to watch a tennis match. Millions more watched on TV as King defeated Riggs.

The Davis Cup became a center of political dispute in the 1970's. In 1974, South Africa won the cup by forfeit from India. The Indian government refused to allow its team to play because of South Africa's *apartheid* (racial separation) policies. The Davis Cup had already lost some of its importance because many professionals refused to play for their countries. These players claimed that the many weeks of cup play-offs would force them to miss too many tournaments. In 1981, Davis Cup competition was changed to attract more top players. It was compressed into a shorter period of time and the prize money was increased.

By the mid-1970's, a new generation of players had begun to dominate tennis. The most successful young men included Jimmy Connors, Vitas Gerulaitis, John McEnroe, and Roscoe Tanner of the United States; Bjorn Borg of Sweden; Guillermo Vilas of Argentina; and Ivan Lendl of Czechoslovakia. Leading women players of the 1970's and 1980's included Tracy Austin, Chris Evert, and Andrea Jaeger of the United States; Evonne Goolagong and Wendy Turnbull of Australia; the Czech-born Martina Navratilova; Virginia Wade of England; and Hana Mandlikova of Czechoslovakia.

In 1980, Borg won the men's singles championship at Wimbledon for the fifth consecutive year. No one else has ever won this title more than three straight times in the history of modern tennis.   MARGARET SMITH COURT

Outline

I. The Court and Equipment
    A. The Court
    B. Tennis Balls
    C. Tennis Rackets
    D. Tennis Clothes

II. How Tennis Is Played
    A. Scoring
    B. The Serve
    C. The Ball in Play
    D. Officials

III. Organized Tennis
    A. Amateur Tennis
    B. Professional Tennis
    C. Tennis Tournaments

IV. History

Questions

What is an open tournament?
How does a player hit a backhand drive?
What is a *tie breaker?*
Why have almost all grass courts been replaced by other surfaces?
What is a *fault?* A *double fault?*
Who were the only players to win the grand slam?
When would a player hit a smash?
What is the Davis Cup? The Wightman Cup?
Where are the All-England Championships and the United States Championships held?
Who is generally considered the father of modern tennis?

Additional Resources

BENJAMIN, DAVID A. *Competitive Tennis: A Guide for Parents and Young Players.* Harper, 1979.

BRADEN, VIC, and BURNS, WILLIAM. *Teaching Children Tennis the Vic Braden Way.* Little, Brown, 1980.

KING, BILLIE JEAN, and others. *How To Play Mixed Doubles.* Simon & Schuster, 1980.

UNITED STATES TENNIS ASSOCIATION. *Official Encyclopedia of Tennis.* Rev. ed. Harper, 1981.

TENNYSON, LORD (1809-1892), ALFRED, BARON OF ALDWORTH AND FARRINGFORD, was one of the most important English poets of the 1800's. He succeeded William Wordsworth as poet laureate in 1850. Tennyson earned his position in literature because of the remarkable range of his natural talents and his dedication throughout his long career to perfecting his art. Tennyson stands today both as a great national poet and as one of the supreme craftsmen in the English language.

Oil portrait by M. Armault, National Portrait Gallery, London

Lord Tennyson

His Life. Tennyson was born on Aug. 6, 1809, in Somersby, Lincolnshire. His father was *rector* (clergyman in charge) of the parish there. The lonely marshes of eastern England supplied the setting for many of his finest poems.

Tennyson entered Cambridge University in 1828, but he never received a degree. At Cambridge, he joined "The Apostles," a society of undergraduates that included several men who later became intellectual leaders of the age. Tennyson's most intimate friend in this circle was Arthur Henry Hallam. Hallam's sudden death in 1833 was the crucial event in the poet's otherwise uneventful life. Tennyson expressed his grief and sense of loss in his great *elegy* (poem mourning someone's death) *In Memoriam* (1850).

Tennyson ranked as the most popular British poet of the Victorian era, but he avoided public life. He married in 1850 and lived quietly in his country homes at Farringford on the Isle of Wight and Aldworth in Surrey. Tennyson's long list of works showed his consistent inspiration and creative vitality, beginning with *Poems, Chiefly Lyrical* (1830) and extending to *The Death of Oenone and Other Poems*, published after his death more than 60 years later. He was awarded the title of Baron Tennyson in 1883 by Queen Victoria. He died on Oct. 6, 1892, and was buried in the Poets' Corner of Westminster Abbey.

His Poems. Tennyson's influential place in the intellectual life of his age comes largely from his concern with the vital issues confronting Victorian England. He reveals his sense of political responsibility in such patriotic verses as "Ode on the Death of the Duke of Wellington" and his famous "The Charge of the Light Brigade," which was inspired by an incident in the Crimean War (see BALAKLAVA, BATTLE OF). *Maud*, a narrative in the form of separate lyrics, describes the withering effect of the materialistic spirit of his day on a sensitive young lover.

Tennyson's accurate and concrete descriptions of nature reflect his informed interest in science. The stars, for example, suggest to the unhappy speaker in *Maud*:

> A sad astrology, the boundless plan
> That makes you tyrants in your iron skies,
> Innumerable, pitiless, passionless eyes,
> Cold fires, yet with power to burn and brand
> His nothingness into man.

Tennyson's philosophic masterpiece, *In Memoriam*, is composed of 133 individual poems. The work traces the anguished but triumphant efforts of the author to conquer the religious doubt that was common at that time. These doubts arose partly because of current theories about evolution. The people of Tennyson's day, torn between faith and doubt, gained consolation from the poem's affirmation

> That men may rise on stepping-stones
> Of their dead selves to higher things.

Perhaps no English poet had a more acute ear for fine shades of poetic expression or a greater range of verse style than Tennyson. His exquisite lyrics perfectly express emotions and experiences shared by all people. Among the most moving of these are many of the sections from *In Memoriam*, as well as "Break, Break, Break" and "Tears, Idle Tears." Following the author's wishes, "Crossing the Bar," the noble address to death, always ends collections of his poems.

Tennyson's most characteristic form of poetry was the idyll, a poem about country life developed by the ancient Greeks. These poems often take the form of dramatic *reveries* (daydreams) spoken by mythical figures. They tell a story, but depend primarily on the creation of mood through the power of richly described settings, as in "The Lotos-Eaters." The speakers commonly fall into two groups: the lovelorn maidens of "Mariana," "The Lady of Shalott," and "Oenone"; and the aged heroes and prophets of "Ulysses," "Tithonus," "Tiresias," and "Merlin and the Gleam."

Tennyson's lifelong fascination with King Arthur and his knights led to his most ambitious work, *Idylls of the King*. It is a series of 12 narrative poems that he published with constant revisions between 1842 and 1885. The work has an *allegorical* (symbolic) side, suggested by the *epilogue* (closing) to Queen Victoria, with its invitation to:

> accept this old imperfect tale
> New-old, and shadowing Sense at war with Soul,
> Ideal manhood closed in real man . . .

Nevertheless, the poem is most likely to move a modern audience as the story of King Arthur's vision of the perfect state. This vision was tragically betrayed by the inability of the king's followers to live up to his heroic ideals.
E. D. H. JOHNSON

See also GALAHAD, SIR; JANUARY (Quotations); POETRY (Image and Picture).

Additional Resources

BUCKLEY, JEROME. *Tennyson: The Growth of a Poet.* Harvard, 1974. Reprint of 1960 ed.

MARTIN, ROBERT. *Tennyson: The Unquiet Heart.* Oxford, 1980.

RICKS, CHRISTOPHER. *Tennyson.* Macmillan, 1972.

TENNYSON, HALLAM. *Alfred, Lord Tennyson—A Memoir by His Son.* 2 vols. Longwood, 1977. Reprint of 1897 ed.

TENOCHTITLAN. See Aztec (introduction; History); Indian, American (Indians of Middle America; picture: The Aztec Capital); Cuauhtémoc.

TENOR is the highest of the adult male voices. Its normal range is about two octaves, from one octave above middle C to one octave below. There are two kinds of tenor voices, *lyric* and *dramatic*. The lyric voice is light and high, with a strong upward range. The dramatic voice is a rich, powerful voice with a more powerful lower range than the lyric voice.   Raymond Kendall

See also Opera (The Singers).

TENPINS. See Bowling.

TENSE is a feature of verbs that indicates the time of an action. There are three divisions of time—present, past, and future. Within these divisions, English has six tenses—present, past, future, present perfect, past perfect, and future perfect.

Only two forms of English verbs can express time by themselves. These are the simple present, as in *She sees*, and the simple past, as in *She saw*. All other forms are phrases that include *helping verbs*, also called *auxiliaries*. Such forms combine helping verbs with the simple present (*see*), the present participle (*seeing*), or the past participle (*seen*). The following list shows all six tenses:

Present	She sees.
Past	She saw.
Future	She will see.
Present perfect	She has seen.
Past perfect	She had seen.
Future perfect	She will have seen.

These tenses are written in the active voice and indicative mood. For a complete list of the tenses for all forms of a verb, see Conjugation.

The *progressive* forms of a verb indicate that an action is in progress at a particular time—for example, *She is seeing the picture for the first time*. The emphatic forms provide emphasis, as in *She does see*. However, this form is more commonly used to ask questions, such as *Does she see?* It is also used to make negative statements, such as *She does not see*.

The Perfect Tenses express time relationships other than simple present, past, and future. The present perfect expresses an action that belongs to the past but touches the present: *Until now, we have seen Paris three times*. The past perfect expresses an action completed at some past time: *In 1945, we had seen Paris only once*. The future perfect expresses an action to be completed at some future time: *By next year, we will have seen Paris for the fourth time*.

Perfect tenses sometimes express special kinds of action. For example, *We keep seeing ugly billboards* shows repeated action. *We used to see better times than we do now* expresses past continuing action. *We go on seeing what we want to see* shows present continuing action. *We are about to see an amazing feat* expresses action to come.

Future Time is expressed by the auxiliaries *will* and *shall*. Current usage no longer distinguishes between the two, but *shall* is rapidly disappearing from use. Future time is also indicated by the present tense plus an adverbial expression: *He sails tomorrow*. In addition, future time can be expressed by other forms:

> He is sailing tomorrow.
> He is to sail tomorrow.
> He is going to sail tomorrow.

Tenses in Clauses. The tense of a verb in the main clause of a sentence affects the tense of any verb in a subordinate clause. If the main verb is in the present tense, for example, any of the six tenses may be used in the subordinate clause:

> I think you are healthy.
> I think you were healthy.
> I think you will be healthy.
> I think you have been healthy.
> I think you had been healthy.
> I think you will have been healthy.

If the main verb is in the past tense, the selection of tenses becomes smaller:

> I thought you were healthy.
> I thought you had been healthy.
> I thought you would be healthy.
> I thought you could be healthy.

If the main verb is in the future tense, all past forms are eliminated:

> I will think because I am hopeful.
> I will think because I will be hopeful.

HOW VERB TENSES ARE USED

He will fall. — FUTURE

He falls. — PRESENT

He fell. — PAST

I will think because I have been hopeful.
I will think because I will have been hopeful.

Literary Uses of Tense. Many writers, especially historians and storytellers, use the present tense to tell about the past. This technique, called the *historical present*, provides a quality of vividness and immediacy. In addition, the present tense is often used to describe any published work—for example, *The story of* Alice in Wonderland *includes many fantastic characters and incidents.*

Tenses follow natural sequences, depending on the wishes of the author. A writer generally chooses a tense and maintains it unless a change seems desirable. For example, an author might want to discuss the working conditions in a particular industry. The writer could begin by describing conditions in past years, then follow with an account of present conditions, and end with ideas about developments in the future. The tenses would reflect these changes.   WILLIAM F. IRMSCHER

See also VERB.

TENSILE STRENGTH. See COHESION.

TENSILE STRESS. See STRENGTH OF MATERIALS (How Materials React to Force).

TENSKWATAWA. See SHAWNEE PROPHET.

TENT is a portable shelter that many campers use for protection against the weather and insects. Most tents consist of a wooden or metal frame with a covering and floor made of canvas, nylon, or some other fabric.

Tents are manufactured in a variety of sizes and styles. They range from small models for one person to large cabin tents for as many as six adults. Extremely large tents are used for such group activities as carnivals, circuses, and church meetings. This article discusses camping tents.

Kinds of Tents. There are more than half a million styles and sizes of camping tents. However, most of them are variations of one of three basic types: (1) A-frame tents, (2) umbrella tents, and (3) wall tents.

A-frame tents rise to a point at the top and resemble the letter *A*. One or two persons can sleep in these small, lightweight tents, which are ideal for backpack trips. Most mountaineering tents designed for year-round camping are A-frame shelters.

Umbrella tents are larger and heavier than A-frame tents. An umbrella tent has slightly slanted walls and a pyramid-shaped top. Some models have a center pole that decreases the space inside the tent, but newer ones lack this pole. Umbrella tents have sleeping space for four to six persons. They are sturdy shelters that can withstand high winds.

Wall tents resemble small houses. These shelters have vertical walls and an A-frame roof. They provide more sleeping and standing room than A-frame or umbrella tents but are harder to pitch. One kind of wall tent, the *cabin tent*, offers the highest degree of camping comfort. Its spacious interior and high walls allow more room for standing, walking, and sleeping than any other kind of tent.

Wall tents and most umbrella tents are too large and heavy to carry in a backpack. They are used mainly by campers who drive to campsites.

Most tents of all kinds are made of canvas or nylon. Canvas tents weigh much more but are less likely to leak. Most nylon tents are specially treated to prevent leakage. However, this treatment also seals moisture

Some Kinds of Tents

Tents are manufactured in many sizes and styles. They range from small shelters for one or two persons to larger tents that can hold six adults. Some popular kinds of tents are shown below.

WORLD BOOK illustrations by David Cunningham

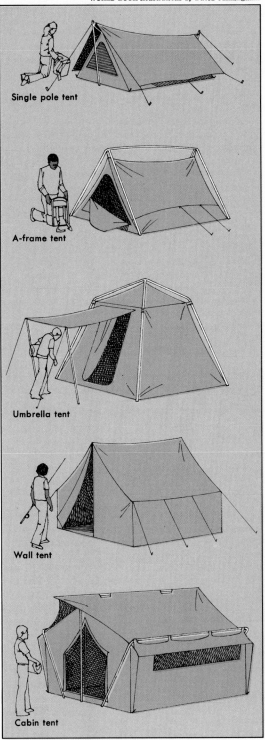

Single pole tent

A-frame tent

Umbrella tent

Wall tent

Cabin tent

inside the tent and may cause the interior to become damp. Some nylon tents have a canvas roof that lets moisture escape. Others have a roof with an untreated nylon layer through which moisture can pass, plus a treated nylon covering that keeps rain out.

All tents provide some type of ventilation and protection against rain and insects. Cabin tents have large windows and a door, and smaller tents have vents and a door flap. In most tents, these openings are covered with netting that keeps insects out. Many tents have flaps that can be closed over the windows during a storm, and some have a storm flap that can be put over the entire tent.

Pitching a Tent. Before setting up camp, campers should find a suitable spot to pitch their tent. The ideal campsite lies on high, level ground near trees and has firewood and fresh water nearby. Camping on high ground helps prevent the tent from being flooded during a storm. If a tent is pitched on low ground, a shallow trench should be dug around it to keep water out. A tent should not be pitched near trees with dead branches that could break off easily in high winds.

In most cases, the first step in pitching a tent is to spread out the floor and secure it to the ground with stakes. The stakes are driven into the ground through small loops along the bottom edge of the tent. The pitching procedure then varies according to the design of the tent. If the tent has an interior frame, the frame is erected and the fabric draped over it. A tent with an exterior frame has hangers to which the fabric is attached. The fabric should be stretched enough to eliminate large wrinkles, but not so tightly that it will rip.

Wall tents and some A-frame tents are staked with ropes called *guy lines*. The guy lines of a wall tent are staked several feet from the tent. They are strung through holes along the top edges of the walls. Some A-frame tents have a guy line attached to the top of the tent at each end. Guy lines can be adjusted to assure the proper shape of the tent and tightness of the fabric.

Caring for a Tent. A tent that receives proper care will provide years of use. The most important points in caring for a tent are to keep it as clean and dry as possible. Dirt, insects, and leaves should be wiped off the shelter each time it is taken down. If the tent is wet, it should be pitched and dried as soon as possible to avoid mildew and discoloration. After a camping trip, a tent should be thoroughly cleaned and dried before storage. Canvas and nylon tents can be washed in a mild detergent. In addition, poles and stakes should not be packed with the tent fabric because they could puncture it.   SAMUEL R. THORESON

See also CAMPING.

TENT CATERPILLAR is the larva of certain moths that damage trees. They get their name because they spin a loose, white web that looks like a tent. This web envelops tree twigs and is the home for a group of caterpillars.

In midsummer, the female moth lays brown egg masses on tree twigs. The eggs hatch the following spring. After feeding for about six weeks, the larvae enter the *pupa stage* in which they spin silky cocoons

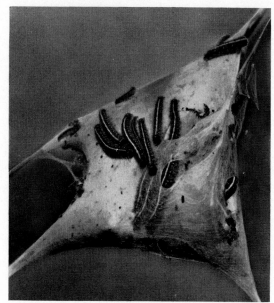

Davey Tree Expert Co.
Eastern Tent Caterpillars and Their Tentlike Nest

around themselves. After three weeks, they emerge as full-grown moths, mate, lay their eggs, and die.

Tent caterpillars damage trees because they eat the leaves. A nest of caterpillars has been known to eat most of the leaves on a single tree. The *eastern tent caterpillar* lives in tents in fruit and shade trees. It has a yellow line along its back. The *forest tent caterpillar* lives in forest trees but it does not build a tent. It has a row of yellow spots along its back. Both species are black and hairy with blue spots on the sides. Both kinds live in eastern and central North America. Other species are found in the West.

Tent caterpillars can be controlled by collecting the egg masses in winter, and by burning the larvae in their tents in spring. Spraying with lead arsenate gives effective control over large areas.

Scientific Classification. Tent caterpillars are members of the tent caterpillar family, *Lasiocampidae*. They are in the genus *Malacosoma*.   ALEXANDER B. KLOTS

TENTACLE, *TEN tuh k'l*, is a slender leg or arm of certain animals. Tentacles are ordinarily used for protection or as feelers. Sea anemones and octopuses use tentacles to capture food. See also COELENTERATE; OCTOPUS (picture); JELLYFISH (with pictures); ANIMAL (picture); MOLLUSK (Univalves; Octopuses and Squids).

TENURE OF OFFICE ACT was passed by Congress in 1867 over the veto of President Andrew Johnson. From the time the United States government was founded, the custom had been to permit the President to dismiss presidential appointees at will. But discord arose between President Johnson and Congress on questions of Reconstruction after the Civil War. Congress passed the Tenure of Office Act for fear that Johnson might use his powers of dismissal to upset the congressional plan of reconstruction. The act in effect required the Senate's consent to the dismissal of any official whose appointment had required its consent.

The law was clearly contrary to American tradition,

and Johnson believed it to be unconstitutional. In 1868, to test this point, Johnson removed Edwin M. Stanton from the office of secretary of war, a course of action which led to the President's impeachment. Johnson was not convicted, however, and the reason for the law ceased to exist. The Tenure of Office Act was repealed in 1887.

An act passed in 1821 also bore the name *Tenure of Office Act*. It limited the terms of many appointive officers to four years, and is said to have laid the foundation for the spoils system.   JOHN DONALD HICKS

See also JOHNSON, ANDREW (Increased Tension).

TENZING NORGAY. See MOUNT EVEREST.

TEOTIHUACÁN. See CITY (picture); MEXICO (picture).

TEPEE, *TEE pee,* or TIPI, was the type of tent most commonly used by the Plains tribes of North American Indians. A tepee was made by stretching a buffalo-skin covering over poles. The poles were arranged in the shape of a cone. At the top, the ends of the poles crossed and stuck out of the covering. Two flap "ears" were opened at the top to let out smoke from the campfire. The tent was pegged to the ground all around the bottom. The front had a slit partly closed with wooden pins to form an entrance.   RUTH M. UNDERHILL

See also INDIAN, AMERICAN (pictures); TENT; WIGWAM.

TEPHRA. See VOLCANO (Rock Fragments; Kinds of Volcanoes).

TEQUILA. See ALCOHOLIC BEVERAGE (Other Distilled Beverages).

TERBIUM, *TUR bee um* (chemical symbol, Tb), is one of the rare-earth metals. Its atomic number is 65, and its atomic weight is 158.924. Swedish scientist Carl Mosander first discovered terbium in 1843. Georges Urbain of France first isolated it in an almost pure form in 1905. Terbium is best separated from the other rare earths by ion-exchange processes. Since 1953, many kilogram-size quantities of high purity have been separated in this way. Terbium resembles silver in appearance. It melts at about 1360° C and boils at about 3041° C. Chemists believe that terbium has a valence of 3 in most compounds. The dark-brown oxide (Tb_4O_7) becomes the white oxide (Tb_2O_3) when heated in a stream of hydrogen. Terbium salts are white with a slight pink cast.   FRANK H. SPEDDING

See also ELEMENT, CHEMICAL; RARE EARTH.

TEREDO. See SHIPWORM (Scientific Classification).

TEREK RIVER. See CASPIAN SEA.

TERENCE (195?-159? B.C.) was a Roman comic playwright. His plays are essentially Latin versions of Greek plots, more refined than those of Plautus and marked by pure style, careful construction, and fine characterization. All six of his comedies survive. They are *The Woman of Andros, The Self-Tormentor, The Eunuch, Phormio, The Mother-in-Law,* and *The Brothers. The Brothers* is a thoughtful comedy about two brothers, a country man and a city man. Each brings up one of the sons of the country brother. The country man is strict and the city man is permissive. The resulting idea, that education must pay attention to human nature, perhaps reflects Terence's own experience.

Terence was born Publius Terentius Afer in Carthage. He came to Rome as a slave in the household of a senator who educated and freed him.   NORMAN T. PRATT

TERESA, MOTHER (1910-   ), is a Roman Catholic nun who received the 1979 Nobel peace prize for her work with the poor. She is known as the *saint of the gutters.* In 1950, Mother Teresa founded a religious order in Calcutta, India, called the Missionaries of Charity. The order provides food for the needy and operates hospitals, schools, orphanages, youth centers, and shelters for lepers and the dying poor. It has branches in about 50 Indian cities and about 30 other countries.

Wide World
Mother Teresa

Mother Teresa, whose original name was Agnes Gonxha Bojaxhiu, was born in what is now Skopje, Yugoslavia. In 1928, she joined a religious order, which sent her to India. She took the name Teresa after joining the order. A few years later, she began teaching in Calcutta. In 1948, the Catholic Church granted her permission to leave her convent and work among the city's poor people. She became an Indian citizen that year.

In addition to the Nobel peace prize, Mother Teresa has received other awards for her work with the needy. These awards include the Pope John XXIII peace prize in 1971 and India's Jawaharlal Nehru award for international understanding in 1972.   JAMES McGOVERN

Additional Resources

DOIG, DESMOND. *Mother Teresa: Her People and Her Work.* Harper, 1976.

GONZALEZ-BALADO, JOSÉ LUIS. *Always the Poor: Mother Teresa, Her Life and Message.* Liguori, 1980.

MUGGERIDGE, MALCOLM. *Something Beautiful for God: Mother Teresa of Calcutta.* Harper, 1971.

SERROU, ROBERT. *Teresa of Calcutta: A Pictorial Biography.* McGraw, 1980.

TERESHKOVA, *ter ESH kaw vuh,* **VALENTINA VLADIMIROVA** (1937-   ), of Russia, became the first woman to travel in space. She made 45 revolutions around the earth in a 70-hour and 50-minute space flight that lasted from June 16 to June 19, 1963. Russian cosmonaut Valery F. Bykovsky was in orbit at the same time. He was launched almost two days before Tereshkova. Russian officials said the two spaceships came within 3 miles (5 kilometers) of each other during the flight. They said the dual flight was conducted for "simultaneous observation of the reactions of a man and woman flying in space."

Tereshkova orbited the earth once every 88 minutes. The *apogee* (highest point) in her orbit carried her about 130 miles (209 kilometers) above the earth. The *perigee* (lowest

Sovfoto
Valentina Tereshkova

135

point) was about 108 miles (174 kilometers) above the earth. Tereshkova said she operated her space ship by manual controls.

Russian officials said Tereshkova parachuted from her spaceship after re-entering the earth's atmosphere. She landed about 380 miles (612 kilometers) northeast of Karaganda, Kazakhstan, an industrial center in central Asia.

Tereshkova, the first space traveler with no experience as a test pilot, became interested in parachuting as a hobby. She made more than 125 jumps before volunteering for space flight training school. She also received training as an airplane pilot.

Tereshkova was born on March 6, 1937. Her father, a tractor driver, was killed during World War II. Her mother worked for several years in a textile mill. Tereshkova went to work in a textile mill when she was 18 years old. She became an active member of the Young Communist League while at the mill. In November, 1963, she married cosmonaut Andrian G. Nikolayev. A baby girl was born to them the next year.   WILLIAM J. CROMIE

See also ASTRONAUT (The Cosmonauts; picture).

TERMAN, LEWIS MADISON (1877-1956), an American psychologist, revised the French Binet-Simon Intelligence Tests for use with English-speaking students. The revised tests became known as the Stanford-Binet Intelligence Tests (see INTELLIGENCE QUOTIENT). He was especially interested in gifted children. He studied the personality and behavior of 1,500 bright children at the average age of 11. Terman's study, published as *The Gifted Child* (1947), helped correct the popular misconception of the bright child as queer or abnormal. Terman was born in Johnson County, Indiana.

TERMINAL MORAINE. See MORAINE; GLACIER (How Glaciers Shape the Land).

TERMITE, *TUR mite,* is the common name of a group of insects that live in communities somewhat as ants do. They have long been known as *white ants.* This name is incorrect, for termites are like ants only in their habits of living together and in their small size. Actually termites are more closely related to cockroaches and grasshoppers than to ants. Their mouth parts, simple feelers, thick waists, primitive wings, and other features resemble those of cockroaches. Ants have thin waists, elbowed feelers, and highly specialized wings. Termites stand near the bottom of the scale of insect life. Ants are near the top.

Life and Habits. There are three *castes* (classes) in most termite colonies. Some reproduce, others are workers, and still others are soldiers. The highest is the *royal* or *reproductive* caste. This is made up of fully developed, or perfect, males and females. Of all the termites, these most closely resemble other insects. They are dark colored and have eyes, fairly hard body walls, and fully developed wings. Each colony of termites is founded by a pair of reproductives, which become the king and queen of the colony. Other and less completely developed kings and queens often develop in old colonies. In every mature colony, also, there develops an annual crop of young winged reproductives that leave the parent nest, mate, and set out to found new colonies. They use their delicate, membranous wings for but one

short flight. The young reproductives break their wings off immediately afterward and just before they seek mates.

The *worker* caste consists of small, blind, wingless termites with pale or whitish soft bodies. Only the heads and feet of the workers are covered with a hard protective material. The workers are the most numerous individuals in a colony. They do all the work. They enlarge the nest, search for food and water for the colony, and make tunnels.

The *soldiers,* which are also wingless and blind, are larger than the workers. They have enormous hard heads, powerful jaws, and strong legs. Their bodies are soft and weak. The sole duty of the soldiers is to defend the colony against attack, principally against ants. The soldiers are strangely unable to care for themselves. They must be fed and groomed by the workers.

All termite castes contain both sexes, and the kings live as long as the queens. In wasp, ant, and bee colonies, *drones* (males) appear only in the reproductive caste and live for only a short time.

Termite eggs and newly hatched young appear to be alike in all the castes. Why some young develop into workers and others into soldiers or reproductives has not been entirely settled. With certain termites it seems development is governed by substances called *hormones* that are contained in skin secretions produced by the reproductives and soldiers. The workers lick off the hormones as they groom the reproductives and soldiers. Hormones are also given with food to the entire colony of termites.

Termites live most abundantly in warm regions, notably in Africa, Australia, and the Amazon regions. Some termites build huge mounds of bits of soil mixed with saliva. These nests may be 20 feet (6 meters) high. The inside of the mound is divided into numerous chambers and galleries. In the center is a closed-in cell, where the king and queen are kept as prisoners. In the cell, the female undergoes an extraordinary change. Her body swells until it is large enough to hold many thousand eggs. The queen lays the eggs at the rate of several thousand a day. The workers carry the eggs away to specially constructed cells. There the workers take care of the *larvae* (young) of the termites as they hatch from the eggs.

Termites digest wood, paper, and other material con-

Hugh Spencer

Termites live in colonies where each *caste* (class) has a certain job. The supplementary queen, *left,* leaves the colony to mate, then sets up a new colony. The termite soldier, *center,* has a large, strong head. His only job is to defend the colony against attack. The worker termite, *right,* is small with a soft body. He gathers the food and does all the work of the colony.

Buffalo Museum of Science

A Section of a Termite Nest may be home for millions of insects. The termite nest is made out of wood particles that are cemented together and then divided into individual chambers.

taining cellulose, with the aid of protozoa in their bodies. They do much damage in tunneling through the woodwork of houses, destroy books and furniture, and do great damage to sugar cane and orange trees. In tropical forests, where these insects occur in large numbers, railroad builders must import cast-iron or steel ties at great expense because the termites destroy wooden ties. Termites are also considered a serious pest in many parts of the United States because they damage houses and other wooden structures.

Kinds of Termites. About 2,000 different species of termites are known. Only two species live in Europe. About 40 species live in North America. Though they do not build large mound nests, they do much damage by tunneling through fence posts, trees, timbers of wooden buildings, bridges, trestles, and other structures. In houses, they eat cloth, books, and paper. A few kinds attack and destroy living plants. Experts have estimated that termites cause as much property damage each year in the United States as fire does.

Termites in the United States fall into three groups, according to their habits. The *subterranean termites*, the smallest but most destructive, nest underground. They extend their burrows for considerable distances into wooden structures. The *damp-wood termites* live only in very moist wood. These termites cause trouble only on the Pacific Coast. The *dry-wood termites* need little moisture. They are destructive in the Southwest. Damp-wood and dry-wood termites have no true worker caste.

Termite Control. The United States Department of Agriculture recommends the use of stone, brick, or concrete for foundations of bridges and trestles, and for support posts of buildings. Where timber has to be used, it should be treated with creosote or other insecticide applied in large tanks under pressure, to make sure it

penetrates the wood deeply. Most termites will die if their supply of moisture is cut off.

Scientific Classification. Termites make up the order *Isoptera*. This order includes the families *Mastotermitidae*, *Holotermitidae*, *Kalotermitidae*, *Rhinotermitidae*, and *Termitidae*. The family *Rhinotermitidae* includes the most important genus in the order. This is genus *Reticulitermes*, which has 10 species of subterranean termites that cover the entire country. Genus *Reticulitermes*, species *flavipes* is distributed widely in the East and Southwest. *R. hesperus* occurs chiefly from British Columbia to Lower California.   DALE W. JENKINS

TERN, *turn*, is a subfamily of sea birds related to gulls. Terns are famous for their powers of flight. About 35 or more kinds of terns are found in different parts of the world. Fourteen kinds are native to North America. Most of them live along seacoasts, rivers, and lakes, rather than in the open sea. The *sooty tern* and some others often range far from land.

Terns have long, pointed bills and webbed feet. Their pointed wings can carry them through the air swiftly and for long distances. Their swift, graceful flight has given them the name *sea swallow*. They live mainly on small fish. They seize the fish by darting quickly into the water from the air, with the bill pointing down.

Great colonies of terns inhabit islands during the nesting season. Usually, the nests are slightly hollowed-out places in the ground. Sometimes, the terns lay eggs on bare rock or sand. Some make nests of seaweed. The *love tern* lays its single egg on a hollow place on a small branch, or on a rock ledge with no nest whatever. One parent then holds the egg in place until it hatches.

One of the largest kinds is the *Caspian tern*, a handsome bird 21 inches (53 centimeters) long. It has a shining black crest, and pearl-gray back and wings. The smallest is the *least tern*, 9 inches (23 centimeters) long. Large numbers of the beautiful *common tern* live on the Atlantic Coast of North America. Once hunters almost killed off this species in seeking its eggs and plumes. This type of tern is now protected by law and is increasing in numbers. It has light, pearl-gray feathers, with a white tail and throat. It is about 15 inches (38 centimeters) long. The common tern lays three or four eggs, which vary in color from whitish to brownish and are thickly spotted with brown and lavender. The tern usually seen on inland marshes and lakes is the *black tern*. Other types include *gull-billed*, *royal*, and *arctic terns*. The arctic tern flies farther in its migration than any

Allan D. Cruickshank, National Audubon Society

The Least Tern Has Gray Feathers and a Yellow Bill.

other bird known. Some arctic terns travel 22,000 miles (35,400 kilometers) in a year, from the Arctic Circle to the Antarctic Circle and back. See ARCTIC TERN.

Scientific Classification. Terns are in the gull family, *Laridae* and make up the subfamily *Sterninae.* Most of them are genus *Sterna.* Terns in the *Sterna* genus include the common tern, species *hirundo;* the sooty tern, *S. fuscata;* the arctic tern, *S. paradisaea.* The Caspian tern is genus *Hydroprogne,* species *caspia.* The royal tern is genus *Thalasseus,* species *maximus.* The gull-billed tern is genus *Gelochelidon,* species *nilotica.* The fairy, or love, tern is genus *Gygis,* species *alba.* The black tern is genus *Chlidonias,* species *niger.* ALEXANDER WETMORE

TERPSICHORE. See MUSES.

TERRA is the symbol of the earth in Roman mythology. She is called Gaea in Greek mythology. *Terra* is a Latin word meaning *earth.* Terra arose from Chaos, and Heaven (Uranus) arose from Terra. Terra was the solid ground and had only a vague personality. She was later replaced in worship by other earth goddesses who had more definite personalities. Terra is frequently represented in art and poetical works. See also MYTHOLOGY (The Creation Myth). JAMES F. CRONIN

TERRA COTTA, *TEHR uh KAHT uh,* is an Italian term for a type of hard, durable earthenware. It is made from clay of a superior quality. Terra cotta is used for pottery, garden vases, tiles, flowerpots, monuments, fountains, chimney pieces, and other objects. It is usually red or cream-colored, but can be made in almost any color.

Terra cotta has been known since ancient times. The Greeks and Romans used it for roof tiles, gutters, statues, vases, and other articles. In Italy, Luca Della Robbia founded a famous workshop in Florence for terra-cotta sculpture during the Renaissance. EUGENE F. BUNKER, JR.

See also DELLA ROBBIA.

Enameled sculpture (early 1500's) by Andrea della Robbia; Metropolitan Museum of Art, New York City
Terra-Cotta Sculpture

TERRA NOVA NATIONAL PARK. See CANADA (National Parks).

TERRACING. See CONSERVATION (Soil Conservation); INDIAN, AMERICAN (picture: Farmers Cut Terraces).

TERRAMYCIN, *TEHR uh MY sihn,* is a drug that fights disease. It is an extract of a bacterium called *Streptomyces rimosus.* Terramycin was isolated in 1950 by scientists working in the United States. It was found in a culture of common soil bacteria. Terramycin is effective against many diseases, including pneumonia, whooping cough, bronchitis, sinusitis, and amebic dysentery. It is related to the drugs streptomycin, Aureomycin, and Chloromycetin, a group of drugs that are called *antibiotics.* See also ANTIBIOTIC. KENNETH B. RAPER

TERRAPIN, *TEHR uh pihn.* Certain fresh-water or tidewater turtles are often called terrapins. The common U.S. terrapins are the diamondback terrapins. The terrapin eats crabs, snails, and other water animals, as well as green plants. The female is the larger animal, with a lower shell that may measure over 7 inches (18 centimeters). Terrapins live along the Gulf and Atlantic coasts, but not north of Massachusetts.

Scientific Classification. The turtles commonly known as terrapins belong to the class *Reptilia.* They are in the common turtle family, *Emydidae.* CLIFFORD H. POPE

TERRARIUM, *tuh RAIR ee uhm,* is the name for a small indoor garden enclosed in a transparent container. Its name comes from the Latin word, *terra,* meaning *earth.* Such a garden may contain small plants in an interesting arrangement. Small land animals may also be kept in a terrarium. Tiny figures, bridges, and paths may be added. Terrariums may be made in covered glass or plastic containers of various sizes and shapes.

Prepare a terrarium by placing a layer of small

HOW TO MAKE A TERRARIUM

A terrarium can be made by placing pebbles, charcoal, and a soil mixture in a transparent container. Then add such plants as ferns and ivy, which grow well in a warm, humid atmosphere.

WORLD BOOK illustration by James Teason

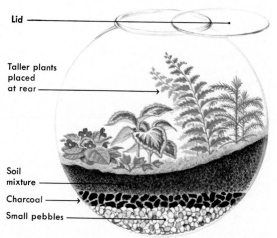

Lid

Taller plants placed at rear

Soil mixture

Charcoal

Small pebbles

pebbles on the bottom of the container for drainage. Add broken charcoal to keep the terrarium sweet. Then add commercial potting soil or a mixture made up of equal parts of garden loam, fresh-water sand, and peat moss or thoroughly rotted leaf mold. Put in the soil mixture carefully, handful by handful. Then moisten it thoroughly, but do not make it muddy. Clean the sides of the container before setting in the plants.

Plant ferns and small evergreen seedlings for the taller plants of the terrarium. Also use ivy, moss, and lichens. For a grasslike, or carpet, effect, plant partridge berry. Place each of the plants carefully in the soil with enough space between plants to allow for growth.

Set the completed terrarium in a light place, but not where sun will strike it. With the container closed, such a balanced terrarium preserves temperature and moisture inside. Open the lid if the container clouds with moisture.   WILLIAM C. BEAVER

TERRE HAUTE, *TER uh HOHT,* Ind. (pop. 61,125; met. area pop. 176,583), is the manufacturing and coal-shipping center of the Wabash Valley. *Terre Haute* is French for *high land.* The city received this name because it stands above the high-water line on the east bank of the Wabash River. Terre Haute is about 175 miles (282 kilometers) south of Chicago, and about 75 miles (121 kilometers) southwest of Indianapolis, the capital of Indiana. For location, see INDIANA (political map).

The city is the home of Indiana State University and the Rose-Hulman Institute of Technology, an engineering college for men. Theodore Dreiser, the novelist, his brother Paul Dresser, author of the song "On the Banks of the Wabash," and Eugene Debs, the Socialist leader, were natives of Terre Haute. The poet Max Ehrmann lived in Terre Haute. The federal government has established a model penitentiary, operated under the honor system, southwest of Terre Haute.

Industry and Trade. Soft-coal fields and oil wells surround Terre Haute. Many coal-mining companies have offices in the city. About 130 factories make such products as heating boilers, steel plates, glass bottles, brick, tile, paints and varnishes, commercial solvents, liquor, canned foods, cartons, and baking powder. The city has air, rail, and highway transportation.

History. General William Henry Harrison built Fort Harrison in 1811, north of the present Terre Haute. During the War of 1812, Captain Zachary Taylor, who later became President, defended Fort Harrison. Terre Haute was founded in 1816 on the site of an old Indian and French fur-trading village. The town became the seat of government of Vigo County in 1818. For some time, people from the East came to the area by way of the Ohio River and then overland. After 1840, settlers came over the National Road. Development of the coal fields near Terre Haute began about 1875. The cheap fuel supply attracted industry to Terre Haute. It was incorporated as a city in 1853, and has a mayor-council form of government.   PAUL E. MILLION, JR.

TERRELL, MARY CHURCH (1863-1954), joined the struggle to gain equal rights for black people in the United States in the 1890's. Mrs. Terrell remained active in the movement until she died at the age of 90.

Mary Church Terrell was born in Memphis, Tenn. Her father was a former slave who became a millionaire

Collection of Phyllis T. Langston
Mary Church Terrell

through real estate and other business transactions. Mary graduated from Oberlin College in 1884, and then settled in Washington, D.C. She became a member of the Washington school board in 1895, and helped found the National Association of Colored Women in 1896. Through most of her career, she advised government leaders on racial problems. In 1953, Mrs. Terrell headed a committee that won a court suit to end racial discrimination in Washington hotels, restaurants, buses, and other public accommodations.   C. ERIC LINCOLN

TERRIER is the name of a group of breeds of dogs. The name comes from the Latin word *terra,* meaning *earth,* because these breeds were once used to drive game out of holes, or burrows, in the ground. Most of these dogs originally came from England.

Some terriers have long hair and others have short. Their sizes vary. They are fearless watchdogs and usually have gay, playful dispositions.

The 22 terrier breeds recognized by the American Kennel Club are the *Airedale, American Staffordshire terrier, Australian terrier, Bedlington terrier, border terrier, bull terrier, cairn terrier, Dandie Dinmont terrier, fox terrier, Irish terrier, Kerry blue terrier, lakeland terrier, Manchester terrier, miniature schnauzer, Norwich terrier, Scottish terrier, Sealyham terrier, Skye terrier, soft-coated wheaten terrier, Staffordshire bull terrier, Welsh terrier,* and *West Highland white terrier.* Four other breeds are called terriers. But they are not members of the terrier group. The *Boston terrier* and the *Tibetan terrier* are classed as nonsporting dogs. The *Silky terrier* and the *Yorkshire terrier* are toy dogs. All of the terrier breeds have separate articles in WORLD BOOK.   JOSEPHINE Z. RINE

See also DOG (table; color pictures: Terriers).

TERRITORIAL AFFAIRS. See INTERIOR, DEPARTMENT OF THE.

TERRITORIAL COURTS are the United States courts in Guam and the Virgin Islands. Unlike federal courts in the United States, they have jurisdiction over both local and federal cases. Territorial court judges serve either four- or eight-year terms.

See also COURT (Federal Courts).

TERRITORIAL WATERS are areas of the ocean where a nation has *sovereign rights.* These rights include control of fishing, navigation, and shipping, as well as the use of the ocean's natural resources.

A nation's territorial waters include its *internal waters* and its *territorial sea.* Internal waters include lakes, rivers, and the waters within such coastal areas as bays and gulfs. A country's territorial sea lies beyond its coast or the boundary of its internal waters. Nations have more authority over their internal waters than their territorial seas. The main difference between the two areas is that ships of other countries can freely cross territorial seas in peacetime.

Various nations have set different outer limits for

their territorial sea. Most of the approximately 120 coastal nations have a limit of 12 or fewer nautical miles. A nautical mile equals about 1.2 statute miles or 1.9 kilometers. The United States has a limit of 3 nautical miles. A few nations claim a limit of as much as 200 nautical miles. Many countries prohibit foreigners from fishing in their territorial sea. Many nations also claim exclusive fishing and other rights in an area called the *exclusive economic zone*, which extends 200 nautical miles from shore.

Many disagreements between governments have occurred about the extent and use of territorial waters. The United Nations sponsored a series of conferences to draw up an international treaty governing many uses of the ocean. Meetings took place in 1958 and 1960, and several additional sessions were held in the 1970's without reaching an agreement.   WILLIAM T. BURKE

See also HIGH SEAS.

TERRITORIALITY is a form of animal behavior in which an individual animal or a group claims a certain area as its own. Such animals also defend the territory against other members of their species. Some animals hold long-term claims on large territories that they use as sources of food. Other species become territorial only during their breeding season, when they defend a small nesting area. Territoriality is most common among birds, fish, and lizards. Some species of amphibians and mammals also claim territories. Only a few kinds of invertebrates do so.

Animals claim territories in different ways. Songbirds establish their areas by vigorous singing. Many kinds of mammals signal their territorial claims by leaving scents, such as that of urine or of secretions from special glands.

Various species also differ in how they defend their territories. Male fur seals fight intensely throughout the breeding season. Some fish push against each other until one retreats. But most animals rarely engage in physical combat. Instead, they make threatening movements to ward off intruders. For example, fiddler crabs signal their territorial rights by waving their large claw. The color of some fish brightens when they are in their own territory. Their color fades rapidly if they swim away from the area.

Territoriality serves different purposes among different kinds of animals. It may protect a female from males other than her mate. Or it might provide a male and a female a good nest site and a feeding area large enough to support their young. Among many species, individual animals without a territory do not breed. Thus, territoriality may prevent the population from becoming too large for the environment.   JOHN A. WIENS

See also ANIMAL (Animal Homes; Communication); MAMMAL (Territoriality).

TERRITORY is a region controlled by a federal government that does not have equal status with the federal states. In such countries as the United States, Canada, Australia, Mexico, and Brazil, the federal government sets up governments for the territories. They are not considered equal to the member states or provinces of the union, because the territories do not have representation in the national government. The territories may or may not be on the road toward self-government and complete equality with the other members of the union.

In the United States

The United States has four main territories and dependencies: American Samoa, Guam, the Virgin Islands, and various Pacific islands. It also governs three island areas in the Pacific Ocean under a United Nations trusteeship. For many years, the United States had many more outlying territories. Two of them, Alaska and Hawaii, became states. One, the Philippines, became an independent country. Another, Puerto Rico, became a commonwealth. See PHILIPPINES (History); PUERTO RICO (Government).

Territorial government is an older institution than the United States Constitution. In 1787, under the Articles of Confederation, Congress passed the Northwest Ordinance, setting up the first American territory, the Northwest Territory (see NORTHWEST TERRITORY). This action set the pattern for congressional action in governing territories and providing for their eventual statehood. The United States Constitution, also written in 1787, provides that "new States may be admitted by the Congress into this Union." Accordingly, Congress has full control over the admission of territories. It decides when a territory is ready for statehood, and the conditions for its admission. All but 19 states—the original 13 and six others—were once territories.

Up to 1867, Congress always set up territories in mainland areas on the frontiers of the United States. Alaska, bought in 1867, was the first area not directly connected with the rest of the states. Gradually, the United States gained other distant territories, most of them after the Spanish-American War. These new territories presented special problems: they were far away, and their peoples had little or no experience of democratic self-government. It did not seem wise to extend to these peoples the protection of all the provisions of the Constitution, especially those on judicial procedures.

As a result, in the Insular Cases of 1901, the Supreme Court drew a distinction between *incorporated* and *unincorporated* territories. It held that all rights guaranteed by the Constitution applied in incorporated territories. In unincorporated ones, only fundamental rights applied, as distinguished from formal or procedural rights such as the right to trial by jury. Congress has the power to decide whether a territory has incorporated or unincorporated status. Incorporated territories are on the road to statehood. Unincorporated territories are not. A third class of territories includes *wholly unorganized and unincorporated* dependencies, controlled by officials in the executive branch, rather than by Congress.

The territories have no regular representatives in Congress. Until it became a state, Hawaii elected one delegate to the House of Representatives. The delegate could serve on committees and take part in debates, but could not vote. Puerto Rico sends delegates with full voting powers to national political conventions of the Republican and Democratic parties.

American Territorial Government

Alaska and Hawaii were the last fully incorporated territories of the United States. Unincorporated territories include the Virgin Islands and Guam. Unorganized and unincorporated dependencies include American Samoa, Wake Island, and other Pacific islands.

The Virgin Islands, purchased from Denmark in 1917, have a considerable measure of home rule. The people elect their own governor and legislature. But Congress can disallow acts passed in the Virgin Islands. The people do not take part in presidential elections. See VIRGIN ISLANDS.

Guam, acquired from Spain in 1898, has a government structure similar to that of the Virgin Islands. It was governed by the Department of the Navy from 1898 to 1950, when officials of the Department of the Interior took over. See GUAM.

American Samoa, ruled by the United States since 1900, is a dependency controlled by the Department of the Interior. The people are regarded as *nationals*, but not citizens, of the United States. See SAMOA.

Pacific Islands, including Wake and several others, are governed by the Department of the Interior. They are for the most part so small that they have virtually no need for civil government. See PACIFIC ISLANDS.

Trust Territory of the Pacific Islands includes islands taken from Japan during and after World War II. The Department of the Interior administers the trust, although some islands are under Navy control. The trust operates under an agreement between the United States and the UN. See PACIFIC ISLANDS, TRUST TERRITORY OF THE; UNITED NATIONS (The Trusteeship Council).

Territories in Canada

Canada has two territories, each governed by a commissioner appointed by the federal government. Each territory elects a representative to the House of Commons in Ottawa.

Northwest Territories, made up of three districts, is governed by a commissioner and a 15-member council. The people elect all the council members. See NORTHWEST TERRITORIES (Government).

Yukon Territory has a commissioner and a 12-member council. The people elect the council members. The commissioner serves for an indefinite term. See YUKON TERRITORY (Government). DAVID FELLMAN

See also AUSTRALIA (Government); CANADA, GOVERNMENT OF; ENCLAVE; TRUST TERRITORY.

TERROR, REIGN OF. See FRENCH REVOLUTION (The Reign of Terror).

TERRORISM is the use or threat of violence to produce fear in people and weaken their resistance. Common acts of terrorism include airplane hijacking, assassination, bombing, kidnapping, and murder. Political terrorism is used to gain or keep power.

Most terrorism has been conducted by government leaders who have wanted to preserve or increase their power. They have used violence and fear to maintain their authority and to eliminate their opposition. During the 1930's, for example, the dictators Adolf Hitler of Germany, Benito Mussolini of Italy, and Joseph Stalin of Russia used terrorism for these purposes.

Terrorism has also been practiced by political movements against established governments. Some revolutionary organizations have used violence and terror to try to overthrow a government. Some underground organizations have used terrorism to force governments to change certain policies. Guerrilla warfare often includes terrorism. Guerrillas are roving bands of fighters who make sudden attacks and then disappear. During the 1970's, Arab guerrillas terrorized Israel with bombings, kidnappings, and murders. They hoped to force Israel to yield to Arab demands and also to make Western nations reduce their support of Israel. In return, Israeli forces attacked Arab territories to reduce the guerrillas' support.

Terrorism frequently results in counterterrorism. The Irish and the British have used terrorism against each other since England first conquered and occupied Ireland in the 1500's. Roman Catholics and Protestants in Northern Ireland have also used terrorism against each other, especially after Ireland was divided into two countries in 1920.

The word *terrorism* first appeared during the French Revolution (1789-1799). The French leader Maximilien Robespierre adopted a policy of violence and fear to defend the revolutionary government against its enemies. E. V. WALTER

See also ANARCHISM; FRENCH REVOLUTION (The Reign of Terror); NORTHERN IRELAND (History); STALIN, JOSEPH (Rule by Terror).

TERRY, ELLEN ALICIA (1848-1928), was considered the greatest actress on the English stage for almost 50 years. Her famous roles included such Shakespearean heroines as Portia in *The Merchant of Venice*, Desdemona in *Othello*, Juliet in *Romeo and Juliet*, and Lady Macbeth in *Macbeth*. In 1867 she appeared as Sir Henry Irving's leading lady. This association continued for 24 years.

Terry was born in Coventry, England. She toured the United States eight times.

Folger Shakespeare Library
Ellen Terry

RICHARD MOODY

TERRY CLOTH is a cotton fabric woven with loops on the surface that help absorb water. It is woven with one tight and one loose set of warp yarn. A filling yarn woven in between the two sets is pulled into loops. Terry cloth is often called Turkish toweling and chiefly used for towels, bathrobes, sweaters, and swim suits.

TERTIARIES. See FRANCISCANS.

TERTIARY PERIOD. See EARTH (table: Outline of Earth History).

TESCHEN, TREATY OF. See SUCCESSION WARS (The War of the Bavarian Succession).

TESLA, NIKOLA (1856-1943), an electrical engineer, invented the alternating-current induction motor. While still a student, he began to devise a motor free of the inconvenience of the commutator. Tesla invented a motor with coils arranged so that when alternating current energized them, the resulting magnetic field rotated at a predetermined speed. See ELECTRIC MOTOR.

Tesla patented the rotating field motor in 1888. He introduced it at a time when advocates of alternating current were seeking such a motor. He sold it to George Westinghouse, who introduced it in his company.

Tesla made advances in the fields of high voltage and frequency apparatus. He invented the Tesla coil, a system of arc lighting, a generator for high-frequency currents, a system of wireless transmission, and a high-potential magnifying transmitter.

Tesla was born in Smiljan, Austria-Hungary (now in Yugoslavia). He received a technical education at a school in Graz and at the University of Prague. He moved to France and came to the United States in 1884. After 1900, Tesla engaged in independent research in his laboratory. ROBERT P. MULTHAUF

TEST. See TESTING; DRUG (Testing with People).

TEST ACT. Certain religious laws passed by the English Parliament were known as Test Acts. The laws were intended to keep persons who were not members of the Church of England from holding public office. One of the most important test acts was the Corporation Act of 1661, which stated that all judges must declare complete allegiance to the king and must receive communion according to the Church of England. The Test Act of 1673 made the same provisions for all other holders of public office. All test acts in Great Britain were finally repealed in 1828. J. SALWYN SCHAPIRO

TEST BAN TREATY. See KENNEDY, JOHN FITZGERALD (Disarmament).

TEST PILOT is a flier who tests new types of aircraft to find out if they are safe. When a new aircraft is designed, engineers subject it to many tests on the ground. But the test pilot is the first to fly the craft. He subjects it to greater than normal stresses and strains, even risking his life, to be sure the plane is safe. The pilot keeps records of the plane's performance and notes any flaws. He then reports his findings to the designers. If his report is favorable, the craft is ready for further development and production. If he finds defects, it must undergo further tests and changes. See AIRPLANE (Design and Testing).

Most test pilots are graduate engineers, who know what to expect from a plane's design and can anticipate possible flaws. Test pilots have thousands of hours of flying experience. They must also be able to think and act calmly and quickly in the face of great danger. Most test pilots also attend a military test pilot school. The U.S. Air Force has a test pilot school at Edwards Air Force Base in California. The U.S. Navy trains test pilots at Patuxent River Naval Test Center in Maryland.

Many of the United States astronauts and Russian cosmonauts were test pilots. Other famous test pilots include Scott Crossfield and Bob White, who tested the X-15 rocket ship, and Charles E. Yeager, the first man to fly faster than the speed of sound. Earlier test pilots include Wilbur and Orville Wright, Charles A. Lindbergh, James Doolittle, Alexander de Seversky, and Wiley Post. WILBERT H. RUENHECK

TESTATOR. See WILL.

TESTES. See REPRODUCTION (The Male Reproductive System; diagram).

TESTIMONIAL. See ADVERTISING (Testimonials).

TESTIMONY. See WITNESS.

TESTING, in education and psychology, is an attempt to measure a person's knowledge, intelligence, or other characteristics in a systematic way. There are many types of tests. Teachers give tests to discover the learning abilities of their students. They also give tests to see how well students have learned a particular subject. Some tests help men and women choose a vocation, and other tests help them understand their own personality.

Standardized Tests

Most printed tests taken by students and others are *standardized*. A test has been standardized after it has been used, revised, and used again until it shows consistent results. Firms that prepare standardized tests include information with them on how to give and score each test. The results of one person's performance may be compared with those of many others who have taken the same test. Most teachers also use *nonstandardized* tests that they make up themselves.

The quality of a test can be measured by three major standards: (1) validity, (2) reliability, and (3) practicality.

Validity reflects how well a test measures what it is intended to measure. For example, a test of reading comprehension could lose validity if it allows too little time for taking the test. It might actually measure reading speed rather than comprehension.

Reliability refers to the uniformity of results achieved by the test. To establish reliability, a test may be given to the same group several times. If very similar results are obtained each time, the test may be considered highly reliable.

Practicality involves the cost and convenience of the test. If a test requires too much expense or effort, it may be impractical. It also may be impractical if the results are too difficult to interpret.

Kinds of Tests

Most tests are designed to measure one of several characteristics: (1) learning ability, (2) learning achievement, (3) aptitude and interest, or (4) personality.

Tests of Learning Ability attempt to predict how well an individual will perform in a situation requiring intellectual ability. These tests are sometimes called *intelligence tests, mental ability tests, academic aptitude tests,* or *scholastic aptitude tests*.

A learning ability test consists of a standard set of tasks or questions. It enables a student to demonstrate the skills he has learned throughout his life, both in and out of school. Tests of learning ability do not measure how "bright" a person is. Educators use the terms *intelligence* and *mental ability* simply to describe a person's ability to solve certain kinds of problems typically involved in schoolwork. These terms do not reflect a person's ability in all areas. See INTELLIGENCE; INTELLIGENCE QUOTIENT.

Achievement Tests try to measure how much an individual has learned about a particular subject, rather than his general ability for learning. Schools use achievement tests more than any other kind of test. Throughout elementary school, high school, and college, most teachers rely on such tests when rating a student's progress.

Many teachers prepare achievement tests that closely follow their own method of instruction. They also use standardized achievement tests. These tests are available on many subjects or topics, including division of

Learning Ability Tests measure intellectual skills that an individual has learned from many sources, including his home, school, and community. These tests are used to estimate a student's capacity for learning. They can help teachers instruct a student better, and direct him toward kinds of learning that best suit his abilities.

The shading on the map at right is used to indicate
(A) population density
(B) percentage of total labor force in agriculture
(C) per capita income
(D) death rate per thousand of population

Achievement Tests measure information, skills, and ideas that are learned in a short time and are taught in schools. These tests are used to determine whether a student has learned what a teacher has tried to teach him. One kind of social science test, *right*, requires a student to use his knowledge of interpreting maps, as well as his understanding of geography and economics.

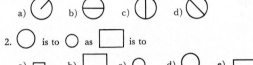

High
Medium
Low

Educational Testing Service

fractions, American history before 1776, and chemical equations. Some schools ask students to take standardized achievement tests, as well as scholastic ability tests, for admission or placement.

There are two types of achievement tests—*norm-referenced* and *criterion-referenced*. In norm-referenced tests, each person's performance is compared with those of others who took the test. A student who answers some questions incorrectly would still rank high if most other students answered a larger number of questions incorrectly. In criterion-referenced tests, on the other hand, each person's performance is compared with a predetermined standard or criterion. For example, a teacher might decide that 90 per cent of the questions on a test must be answered correctly for a student to earn a passing grade.

Aptitude and Interest Tests reveal an individual's talents or preferences for certain activities. A person who likes to tinker with machinery would probably score higher on a test of mechanical aptitude than on one in an activity he dislikes. Such a person has an aptitude for mechanical work—and at least a fairly good chance of succeeding at it.

Interest tests are also known as *interest inventories*. In them, a person indicates his preference among large groups of activities, ideas, and circumstances. One of these tests might ask, "Would you rather fix a broken clock, keep a set of accounts, or paint a picture?" Most individuals prefer certain types of activities over others. The pattern of answers reveals the strength of a person's interest in various fields.

Personality Tests attempt to measure an individual's

143

personal traits scientifically. Some standardized personality tests consist of lists of personal questions requiring yes or no answers. The answers can be analyzed for various characteristics. For example, a person might score high in *social introversion*, which would indicate a strong preference for being alone. Such a person might find scientific research more satisfying as a career than teaching science in a classroom.

Another type of personality test, the *projective test*, requires individuals to tell what certain images mean to them. In a Rorschach test, for example, a person describes what he or she sees in a number of standardized inkblots. A trained counselor can often recognize psychological tendencies in these descriptions. Psychologists use personality tests as clues for further study of an individual. They do not regard them as conclusive evidence about the individual's personality.

Most personality tests are less reliable and less valid than the other kinds of tests discussed in this article. Some people have criticized their use as an invasion of privacy.

How to Take a Test

Knowing how to take tests does not increase anyone's learning ability or achievement. But it does help a person avoid losing points unnecessarily. Experts in testing offer the following suggestions:

1. Get all the experience you can in taking tests. The ability to take tests improves with practice.

2. Cramming before a test is better than no study at all. But a careful review spread over several days is better than cramming.

3. Be sure you understand the directions at the beginning of a test. You may get a lower score than you deserve because you failed to follow certain instructions.

4. Answer the questions that are easy for you, and then go back to the hard ones.

5. If there is no penalty for guessing, put down an answer for every question. If there is a penalty, you may still gain points by guessing some answers. On a multiple-choice question, for example, you may know enough about the subject to eliminate one or more answers. If so, your chance of guessing the correct answer improves considerably.

Interpreting Test Scores

There are several points to keep in mind about test scores. First, a test reflects only a sample of a person's skill or knowledge of a subject. A test score cannot reveal everything about an individual. It can tell only how well the person performed on one particular test on one particular day.

Second, a score on a standardized test simply compares one person's performance with the performance of others. Such a comparison may provide useful information if all the people taking the test are alike in some important way. Most standardized tests give scores for persons of the same age or in the same grade.

Third, every test score is an estimate rather than a precise measurement. To remind people of this, some scores are reported as bands rather than as a single number. The bands show the range in which a person's actual ability probably lies.

Testing often has far-reaching effects, and so it receives much attention from educators and social scientists. Criticism has been directed both at the limitations of tests and at their influence.

Some educators believe that multiple-choice tests penalize a student who has an expert knowledge of a subject. Such a student may see flaws in the answer generally accepted as correct. Other critics say that standardized tests discriminate against disadvantaged and minority groups. These students may be unfamiliar with words, terms, and concepts used in the tests. To give these students an equal chance, educators have tried to prepare *culture-fair* or *culture-free* tests. Such tests might consist of pictures, symbols, and nonsense syllables that are equally unfamiliar to everyone taking the test. This type of test reduces the influence of cultural background on performance. Tests that use no words at all are called *nonverbal tests*.

The general effect of testing on education has also caused concern. Standardized tests sometimes lag behind educational thought and practice. If tests do not measure the content of new programs, they may fail to encourage educational progress.

Many educators believe there is at least some truth in criticisms of tests. But they also know that testing is necessary in teaching. Tests can determine whether one method of teaching works better than another. Tests also tell a teacher what help a student needs most. No better way has been found to determine how much students have learned, what they seem able to learn, and how quickly they might learn it.   RICHARD M. WOLF

Related Articles in WORLD BOOK include:

College Entrance Examination	National Assessment of
Competency-Based Education	Educational Progress
Educational Psychology	Personality
(Testing and Evaluation)	Study

Additional Resources

CRONBACH, LEE J. *Essentials of Psychological Testing.* 3rd ed. Harper, 1970.

FEDER, BERNARD. *The Complete Guide to Taking Tests.* Prentice-Hall, 1979.

POPHAM, W. JAMES. *Modern Educational Measurement.* Prentice-Hall, 1981.

THORNDIKE, ROBERT L., and HAGEN, ELIZABETH. *Measurement and Evaluation in Psychology and Education.* 4th ed. Wiley, 1977.

TETANUS, *TET uh nus,* is a serious disease that affects muscles. It is also called *lockjaw* because severe *spasms* (violent muscle contractions) of the jaw muscles make it hard for the victim to open his mouth.

Tetanus is caused by *toxins* (poisons) produced by bacteria called *tetanus bacilli.* These germs thrive in dust and dirt, and need no air to live. They get into the body through breaks in the skin. Any dirt in a wound may contain tetanus germs. The germs grow quickly if no air gets to the wound.

Symptoms of tetanus usually start from five days to five weeks after infection. The victim feels depressed, has headaches, and soon has trouble opening the mouth or swallowing. After a while, all of the body muscles tighten, and spasms may interfere with breathing. If not treated, the victim may die from exhaustion.

Tetanus can be prevented. All wounds should be cleaned thoroughly. Persons may be immunized against infection with injections of *tetanus toxoid,* a substance made from specially treated toxins of the bacillus.

But if tetanus develops, doctors treat the disease with antitoxin injections. JOHN A. BIGLER

See also KITASATO, SHIBASABURO.

TETANY, *TEHT uh nee,* is a disorder that is characterized by periodic spasms of the muscles. Sometimes fine, fluttering tremors accompany the muscle spasms. Often the person's fingers and toes tingle or feel numb. Then the spasms may move up the arms and into the other parts of the body. When the larynx muscles are affected, breathing is noisy and difficult. LOUIS D. BOSHES

TETON, GRAND. See GRAND TETON NATIONAL PARK.

TETON RANGE, *TEE tuhn,* is a rugged group of 10 Rocky Mountain peaks south of Yellowstone National Park in western Wyoming. The highest peak is Grand Teton (13,770 feet, or 4,197 meters). The range forms part of Grand Teton National Park. See also WYOMING (pictures). JOHN H. GARLAND

TETRA, FLAME. See FLAME TETRA.

TETRAETHYL LEAD is an ingredient added to gasoline to improve the performance of engines. It is called an *antiknock additive* because it reduces the "knocking" or "pinging" sound that an engine makes. An engine knocks if the gasoline in its cylinders begins burning too soon or if it burns too fast. The same conditions that cause knocking also reduce an engine's power and can damage the engine. A small amount of tetraethyl lead in the gasoline corrects these conditions.

The premium grade of automobile gasoline is often called *ethyl* because of its tetraethyl lead content. But both premium and regular gasolines usually contain tetraethyl lead. An engine that burns *leaded* gasoline (gasoline containing tetraethyl lead) gives off an exhaust that includes chemical compounds containing lead. These compounds pollute the air. To reduce lead pollution, oil companies make *low-lead* and *unleaded* gasolines. These fuels contain a larger proportion of gasoline ingredients that resist knocking. As a result, the amount of tetraethyl lead needed in these gasolines is reduced or eliminated. W. M. LANGDON

See also GASOLINE; OCTANE NUMBER.

TETRAHEDRON, *TEHT ruh HEE druhn,* in geometry, is a *regular pyramid* whose sides consist of four equilateral triangles. See PYRAMID.

TETRAZZINI, *teh truh ZEE nee,* **LUISA** (1871-1940), an Italian operatic soprano, was noted for her remarkable vocal agility in coloratura roles. She first appeared in the United States in 1904 in San Francisco. Miss Tetrazzini sang with the Manhattan and Metropolitan opera companies of New York City. She was born and educated in Florence, Italy. SCOTT GOLDTHWAITE

TETZEL, JOHANN (1465-1519), was a Dominican monk who sold papal indulgences in Germany in 1517. He declared that anyone who bought an indulgence could choose a soul to be freed from purgatory. Tetzel's claim led Martin Luther to draw up his Ninety-Five Theses in protest (see LUTHER, MARTIN). Tetzel's action thus brought about the Protestant Reformation. Germans accused Tetzel of telling possible buyers of indulgences:

> When the coin in the coffer rings,
> A soul from purgatory springs.

Many Catholics criticized Tetzel for his vulgar conduct. He defended himself vigorously but clumsily.

Tetzel was born in Pirna, in what is now East Ger-

many. In 1503, he began his long career of selling indulgences. RICHARD MARIUS

TEUTOBURG FOREST, BATTLE OF. See ARMY (table: Famous Land Battles).

TEUTONIC KNIGHTS was the name of an organization of German crusaders that arose in central Europe during the 1100's. The Teutonic Knights were organized for service in the Holy Land. They modeled their organization after two earlier crusading orders, the Knights Templars and the Knights Hospitalers (see KNIGHTS TEMPLARS; KNIGHTS OF SAINT JOHN).

In the 1200's, the Teutonic Knights shifted their activities to central Europe, where they tried to convert and control the people of what became Prussia, Lithuania, Latvia, and Estonia. Their power and influence spread throughout central and eastern Europe. In the 1300's, they lost much of their power, and finally the Poles and Lithuanians overthrew them. In 1525, the Grand Master, Albert of Hohenzollern, embraced Protestantism, and changed the Order from a religious to a civil organization. In 1618, the Order's territory passed to the Hohenzollern Elector of Brandenburg. BRYCE LYON

See also LATVIA (History); LITHUANIA (History).

TEUTONIC LANGUAGES. See TEUTONS.

TEUTONS, *TOO tuhnz,* is a name sometimes given to the Germanic peoples. The term comes from the *Teutones,* or *Teutoni,* who, with the Cimbri, were the first "Germans" to threaten the power of ancient Rome. With their neighbors, the Ambrones, the Teutones left their homeland around the mouth of the Elbe River in the 100's B.C. In Gaul, they allied themselves with the Cimbri. The Roman general Gaius Marius routed them at Aquae Sextiae (Aix) in 102 B.C.

Later, the Teutones mixed with other early groups that wandered through Europe. They eventually gave their name to a whole group of *Teutonic languages.* These languages included the Scandinavian and Germanic tongues, and Low German (Dutch and Flemish) of Belgium and The Netherlands. WILLIAM C. BARK

TEWKESBURY, *TOOKS behr ee,* is an ancient town in Gloucestershire, England. It is the chief town in the district of Tewkesbury, which has a population of 80,815. It was the site of a Roman encampment in early times. One of the last battles of the Wars of the Roses took place at Tewkesbury (see WARS OF THE ROSES).

TEXARKANA, *TEHK sahr KAN uh,* is the name of twin cities that lie across the boundary between Texas and Arkansas, about 25 miles (40 kilometers) north of the Louisiana border. Texarkana, Tex., has a population of 31,271. Texarkana, Ark., has a population of 21,459. The cities have separate mayors and councils, but operate as a unit in trade, industry, and general civic matters. They form a metropolitan area with a population of 127,019.

Broad Street, the main street of the business district, crosses the state line downtown. The United States Post Office, which lies across the boundary, is called the Texarkana, Ark.-Tex., post office. The name Texarkana comes from the first syllable of Texas, the first two of Arkansas, and the last two of Louisiana. Manufactures include mobile homes, clay products, tires, tank cars, pickles, and fertilizers. The area also has woodworking and creosoting plants. H. BAILEY CARROLL

Landscape of West Texas shows the lonely mesas and sage-brush of the desert area known as the Trans-Pecos region.

TEXAS THE LONE STAR STATE

TEXAS is the second largest state in the United States. It has a greater area than Illinois, Indiana, Iowa, Michigan, and Wisconsin combined. Texas is more than 220 times as large as Rhode Island, the smallest state. Only Alaska is larger than Texas. But Texas has about 37 times as many people as Alaska.

The frontier cowboy with his 10-gallon hat has long

The contributors of this article are Joe B. Frantz, Director of the Texas State Historical Association; Walter B. Moore, former Editor of the Texas Almanac; and George W. Schlesselman, Former Head of the Geography Department, Texas A & M University.

been a symbol of Texas. But the Texan of today is just as likely to be a worker in an oil field or a scientist in a laboratory. Or today's Texan might be an engineer in a chemical plant, a computer operator in a bank, or a musician in a symphony orchestra. Cowboys still ride across the plains driving great herds of cattle. And cowboy boots and hats make up part of the everyday dress of Texans in all walks of life. But Texans also have a new hero, the astronaut. During the 1960's, the state became the permanent home of the people at the newest frontier—the frontier of space.

The land of Texas has helped make the state rich. Vast plains and rolling hills provide fertile soil and rich

Capital: Austin.

Government: *Congress*—U.S. senators, 2; U.S. representatives, 27. *Electoral Votes*—29. *State Legislature*—senators, 31; representatives, 150. *Counties*—254.

Area: 267,336 sq. mi. (692,397 km²), including 5,204 sq. mi. (13,478 km²) of inland water but excluding 7 sq. mi. (18 km²) of Gulf of Mexico coastal water; 2nd in size among the states. *Greatest Distances*—north-south, 801 mi. (1,289 km); east-west, 773 mi. (1,244 km). *Coastline*—367 mi. (591 km).

Elevation: *Highest*—Guadalupe Peak, 8,751 ft. (2,667 m) above sea level. *Lowest*—sea level, along the Gulf of Mexico.

Population: *1980 Census*—14,228,383; 3rd among the states; density, 53 persons per sq. mi. (20 persons per km²); distribution, 80 per cent urban, 20 per cent rural. *1970 Census*—11,198,655.

Chief Products: *Agriculture*—beef cattle, cotton. *Fishing Industry*—shrimp. *Manufacturing*—chemicals, petroleum and coal products, nonelectric machinery, food products, fabricated metal products, electric and electronic equipment, transportation equipment. *Mining*—petroleum, natural gas, natural gas liquids.

Statehood: Dec. 29, 1845, the 28th state.

State Abbreviations: Tex. (traditional); TX (postal).

State Motto: *Friendship.*

State Song: "Texas, Our Texas." Words by Gladys Yoakum Wright and William J. Marsh; music by William J. Marsh.

Rozumalski, Black Star

Large Petroleum Refinery at Baytown, Tex., produces chemicals. Petroleum is the most valuable of all Texas minerals.

Texas (blue) ranks second in size among all the states, and is the largest of the Southwestern States (gray).

grasslands. Beneath the plains lie some of the world's great storehouses of petroleum and other vital minerals. Texas leads the country in the production of cattle, cotton, sheep, and wool. It has more farms and farmed area than any other state. Texas also produces more natural gas and oil than any other state. But manufacturing has replaced agriculture and mining as the chief source of income. Chemical plants and other factories have taken over from cattle and oil wells as the state's leading source of wealth.

Many colorful people have played important roles in Texas history. Spanish adventurers began exploring the region about 450 years ago. Texas received its name from their pronunciation of the Indian word *Tejas* (friends or allies). The Tejas formed a group of united Indian tribes that lived in what is now the northeastern part of the state. Texas was part of Mexico when the first Americans settled there in 1821. In 1836, Davy

Crockett, Jim Bowie, and other famous heroes died at the Alamo fighting for freedom from Mexico. Sam Houston led the Texans to final victory against the Mexicans. His battle cry was "Remember the Alamo!" For nearly 10 years, Texas was an independent republic. After Texas became a state in 1845, the settlers fought Indians for many years to protect their families and homes.

Texas is called the *Lone Star State* because of the single star on its flag. Through the years, the flags of six nations have flown over Texas. Besides the United States, these nations were Spain, France, Mexico, the Republic of Texas, and the Confederate States of America.

Austin is the capital of Texas, and Houston is the largest city. For the relationship of Texas to other states in its region, see the article on the SOUTHWESTERN STATES.

Constitution of Texas was adopted in 1876. The state had four earlier constitutions—those adopted in 1845, 1861, 1866, and 1869. An amendment to the constitution must first be approved by two-thirds of the members of each house of the state legislature. Then, the amendment must get the approval of a majority of the voters in a statewide election.

Executive. The governor of Texas holds office for a four-year term and can serve an unlimited number of terms. The governor receives a yearly salary of $71,400. For a list of all the governors of Texas, see the *History* section of this article.

The governor has the power to appoint two of the top state officials—the secretary of state and the adjutant general. All others are elected, most to four-year terms. These officials include the lieutenant governor, attorney general, commissioner of agriculture, commissioner of the general land office, comptroller, and treasurer.

The voters also elect the three members of the Texas Railroad Commission. This important group controls the state's production of petroleum. It does this by deciding how much oil the Texas petroleum industry can pump from the earth each year.

Legislature consists of a Senate of 31 members and a House of Representatives of 150 members. Voters in each of the 31 senatorial districts elect one senator to a four-year term. Voters in each of the 150 representative districts elect one member of the House of Representatives to a two-year term. Both houses meet in odd-numbered years on the second Tuesday in January. By law, regular sessions are limited to 140 calendar days. Special sessions can last only 30 days.

Courts. The highest civil court in Texas is the Supreme Court. It has a chief justice and eight associate justices. The highest criminal court is the Court of Criminal Appeals. This court has nine judges, including a presiding judge. Members of both of these courts are elected to six-year terms.

Each of the 14 supreme judicial districts in Texas has a court of civil appeals. Eleven of these courts have one chief justice and one associate justice each. Each of the remaining courts has one chief justice and five associate justices. Justices for the courts of civil appeals are elected for six-year terms.

The chief trial courts are the district courts. The voters of each judicial district elect a district judge to a four-year term. Other trial courts include the county, corporation, justice of the peace, and criminal district courts. The voters elect judges of all these courts, except the corporation courts, to four-year terms. Most corporation court judges are appointed to two-year terms.

Local Government. Texas has 254 counties—more than any other state. Each one is governed by a county commissioners court made up of the county judge and four commissioners. This court performs such administrative duties as adopting the county budget and setting the county tax rate. County judges are elected to four-year terms. The commissioners are elected to four-year terms from each of four commissioner precincts in a county. Other county officials include the assessor-collector of taxes, county attorney, sheriff, and treasurer.

Texas has about 1,000 incorporated cities, towns, and villages. More than 200 cities have *home rule*. That is, they have adopted their own city charters. The Texas Constitution permits all cities with populations of more than 5,000 to adopt home rule. About 180 home-rule cities use either the council-manager or the commission-manager form of government. The rest have the mayor-council system. Towns with populations of 5,000 or fewer are incorporated under general law.

Taxation. Taxes and licenses bring in about two-thirds of the state's income. A retail sales tax on all items except food and medicine accounts for about a fourth of the state's revenue. About a tenth comes from a production and regulation tax on gas, petroleum, sulfur, and other minerals. Other sources of tax revenues include a corporation-franchise tax and a tax on motor-fuel use. Almost all the remaining income comes

The Cowboy, a life-size bronze statue by Constance Whitney Warren, is on the Capitol grounds. It honors the Texas cowboy.

The Governor's Mansion, with its six stately pillars and lacy balcony, was built in 1856. It stands southwest of the Capitol.

Texas Highway Department; Texas Game and Fish Commission

The State Seal

Symbols of Texas. The single star on both the seal and the flag gives Texas its nickname—the *Lone Star State*. The front side of the present seal was adopted in 1846. The oak branch on the left symbolizes strength, and the olive branch on the right represents peace. The reverse side of the seal was adopted in 1961. It shows a shield with symbols of the Texan war for independence from Mexico surrounded by the six flags that have flown over Texas. The flag was adopted in 1839. The blue stands for loyalty, the white represents strength, and the red is for bravery.

The State Flag

Flag, bird, and flower illustrations courtesy of Eli Lilly and Company

from federal grants and other United States programs.

Politics. The Democratic Party has controlled Texas politics throughout most of the state's history. In 1978, William P. Clements became the first Republican to be elected governor since 1869. Most of the major state and local political contests in Texas are waged in primaries for the Democratic nomination.

In presidential elections, only four Republicans have won Texas' electoral votes—Herbert Hoover in 1932, Dwight D. Eisenhower in 1952 and 1956, Richard M. Nixon in 1972, and Ronald Reagan in 1980. Two United States Presidents were born in Texas. Eisenhower was born in Denison, and Lyndon B. Johnson was born near Stonewall. For Texas' electoral votes and voting record in presidential elections, see ELECTORAL COLLEGE (table).

The State Capitol, in Austin, was completed in 1888. Austin has been Texas' capital since 1845. Temporary capitals during the Texas Revolution (1835-1836) were San Felipe de Austin, Washington-on-the-Brazos, Harrisburg, Galveston Island, Velasco, and Columbia. Other capitals were Houston (1837-1840), Austin (1840-1842), and Washington-on-the-Brazos (1842-1845).

Texas Highway Department

The State Bird
Mockingbird

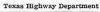

The State Flower
Bluebonnet

The State Tree
Pecan

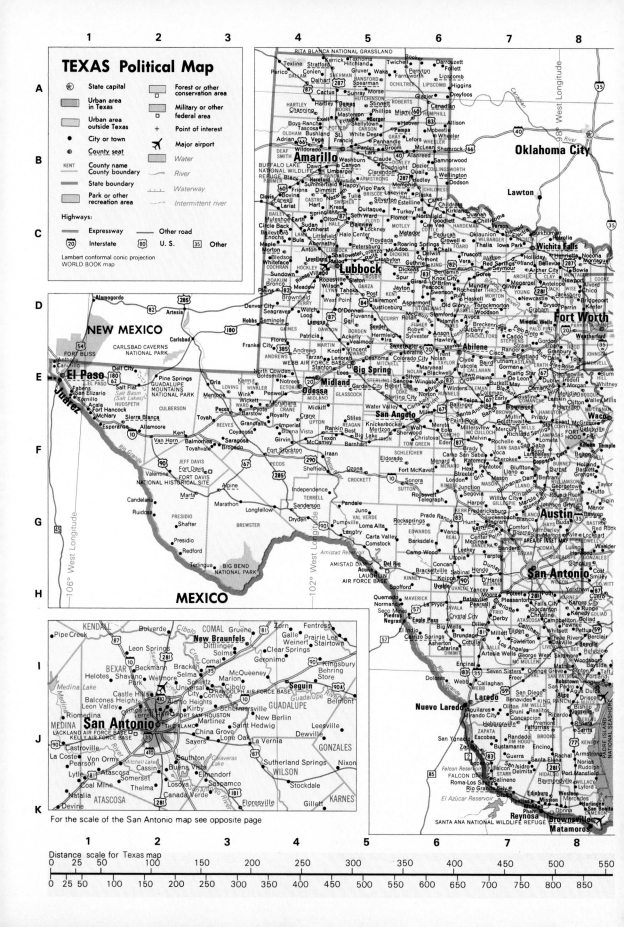

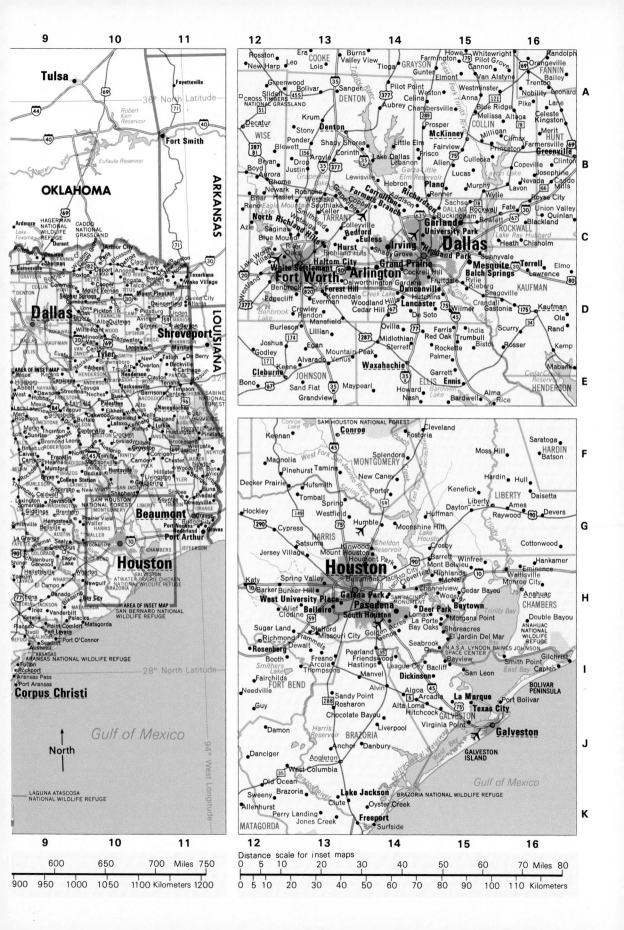

Texas Map Index

Population

14,228,383 .. Census .. 1980
11,198,655 ... " ... 1970
9,579,677 ... " ... 1960
7,711,194 ... " ... 1950
6,414,824 ... " ... 1940
5,824,715 ... " ... 1930
4,663,228 ... " ... 1920
3,896,542 ... " ... 1910
3,048,710 ... " ... 1900
2,235,527 ... " ... 1890
1,591,749 ... " ... 1880
818,579 ... " ... 1870
604,215 ... " ... 1860
212,592 ... " ... 1850

Metropolitan Areas

Abilene ... 139,192
Amarillo ... 173,699
Austin ... 536,450
Beaumont-
Port Arthur-
Orange ... 375,497
Brownsville-Harlingen-
San Benito ... 209,680
Bryan-College
Station ... 93,588
Corpus Christi ... 326,228
Dallas-Fort
Worth ... 2,974,878
El Paso ... 479,899
Galveston-
Texas City ... 195,940
Houston ... 2,905,350
Killeen-Temple ... 214,656
Laredo ... 99,258
Longview-
Marshall ... 151,752
Lubbock ... 211,651
McAllen-Pharr-
Edinburg ... 283,229
Midland ... 82,636
Odessa ... 115,374
San Angelo ... 84,784
San Antonio ... 1,071,954
Sherman-
Denison ... 89,796
Texarkana-Texar-
kana (Ark.) ... 127,019
(75,301 in Tex.;
51,718 in Ark.)
Tyler ... 128,366
Victoria ... 68,807
Waco ... 170,755
Wichita Falls ... 411,313

Counties

Anderson ... 38,381 .. E 10
Andrews ... 13,323 .. E 4
Angelina ... 64,172 .. F 11
Aransas ... 14,260 .. I 9
Archer ... 7,266 .. D 7
Armstrong ... 1,994 .. B 5
Atascosa ... 25,055 .. H 7
Austin ... 17,726 .. G 9
Bailey ... 8,168 .. C 4
Bandera ... 7,084 .. G 7
Bastrop ... 24,726 .. G 8
Baylor ... 4,919 .. C 7
Bee ... 26,030 .. I 8
Bell ... 157,889 .. F 8
Bexar ... 988,800 .. G 7
Blanco ... 4,681 .. G 7
Borden ... 859 .. D 5
Bosque ... 13,401 .. E 8
Bowie ... 75,301 .. D 11
Brazoria ... 169,587 .. H 10
Brazos ... 93,588 .. F 9
Brewster ... 7,573 .. G 3
Briscoe ... 2,579 .. B 5
Brooks ... 8,428 .. J 8
Brown ... 33,057 .. E 7
Burleson ... 12,313 .. F 9
Burnet ... 17,803 .. F 8
Caldwell ... 23,637 .. G 8
Calhoun ... 19,574 .. I 9
Callahan ... 10,992 .. E 7
Cameron ... 209,680 .. K 8
Camp ... 9,275 .. D 10
Carson ... 6,672 .. B 5
Cass ... 29,430 .. D 11
Castro ... 10,556 .. C 4
Chambers ... 18,538 .. G 11
Cherokee ... 38,127 .. E 10
Childress ... 6,950 .. B 6
Clay ... 9,582 .. D 8
Cochran ... 4,825 .. C 4
Coke ... 3,196 .. E 5
Coleman ... 10,439 .. E 7
Collin ... 144,490 .. D 9
Collingsworth ... 4,648 .. B 6
Colorado ... 18,823 .. G 9
Comal ... 36,446 .. G 8
Comanche ... 12,617 .. E 7
Concho ... 2,915 .. F 6
Cooke ... 27,656 .. D 8
Coryell ... 56,767 .. F 8
Cottle ... 2,947 .. C 6
Crane ... 4,600 .. E 4
Crockett ... 4,608 .. F 5
Crosby ... 8,859 .. D 5
Culberson ... 3,315 .. E 2
Dallam ... 6,531 .. A 4
Dallas ... 1,556,549 .. D 9
Dawson ... 16,148 .. D 4
Deaf Smith ... 21,165 .. B 4
Delta ... 4,839 .. D 10
Denton ... 143,126 .. D 9
De Witt ... 18,903 .. H 8
Dickens ... 3,539 .. C 5
Dimmit ... 11,367 .. I 6
Donley ... 4,075 .. B 5
Duval ... 12,517 .. I 7
Eastland ... 19,480 .. E 7
Ector ... 115,374 .. E 4
Edwards ... 2,033 .. G 6
Ellis ... 59,743 .. E 9
El Paso ... 479,899 .. E 1
Erath ... 22,560 .. E 8
Falls ... 17,946 .. F 9
Fannin ... 24,285 .. C 9
Fayette ... 18,832 .. G 9
Fisher ... 5,891 .. D 6
Floyd ... 9,834 .. C 5
Foard ... 2,158 .. C 6
Fort Bend ... 130,846 .. G 10
Franklin ... 6,893 .. D 10
Freestone ... 14,830 .. E 9
Frio ... 13,785 .. H 7
Gaines ... 13,150 .. D 4
Galveston ... 195,940 .. H 10
Garza ... 5,336 .. D 5
Gillespie ... 13,532 .. G 7
Glasscock ... 1,304 .. E 5
Goliad ... 5,193 .. H 8
Gonzales ... 16,883 .. G 8
Gray ... 26,386 .. B 5
Grayson ... 89,796 .. D 9
Gregg ... 99,487 .. D 11
Grimes ... 13,580 .. F 9
Guadalupe ... 46,708 .. G 8
Hale ... 37,592 .. C 5
Hall ... 5,594 .. B 6
Hamilton ... 8,297 .. E 8
Hansford ... 6,209 .. A 5
Hardeman ... 6,368 .. C 6
Hardin ... 40,721 .. G 11
Harris ... 2,409,544 .. G 10
Harrison ... 52,265 .. D 11
Hartley ... 3,987 .. A 4
Haskell ... 7,725 .. D 6
Hays ... 40,594 .. G 8
Hemphill ... 5,304 .. A 6
Henderson ... 42,606 .. E 10
Hidalgo ... 283,229 .. J 8
Hill ... 25,024 .. E 8
Hockley ... 23,230 .. C 4
Hood ... 17,714 .. E 8
Hopkins ... 25,247 .. D 10
Houston ... 22,299 .. F 10
Howard ... 33,142 .. E 5
Hudspeth ... 2,728 .. E 1
Hunt ... 55,248 .. D 9
Hutchinson ... 26,304 .. A 5
Irion ... 1,386 .. F 5
Jack ... 7,408 .. D 8
Jackson ... 13,352 .. H 9
Jasper ... 30,781 .. F 11
Jeff Davis ... 1,647 .. F 2
Jefferson ... 250,938 .. G 11
Jim Hogg ... 5,168 .. J 7
Jim Wells ... 36,498 .. J 7
Johnson ... 67,649 .. E 8
Jones ... 17,268 .. D 6
Karnes ... 13,593 .. H 8
Kaufman ... 39,015 .. E 9
Kendall ... 10,635 .. G 7
Kenedy ... 543 .. J 8
Kent ... 1,145 .. D 5
Kerr ... 28,780 .. G 6
Kimble ... 4,063 .. F 6
King ... 425 .. C 6
Kinney ... 2,279 .. H 6
Kleberg ... 33,358 .. J 8
Knox ... 5,329 .. C 6
Lamar ... 42,156 .. D 10
Lamb ... 18,669 .. C 4
Lampasas ... 12,005 .. F 8
La Salle ... 5,514 .. I 7
Lavaca ... 19,004 .. H 9
Lee ... 10,952 .. G 9
Leon ... 9,594 .. F 10
Liberty ... 47,088 .. G 10
Limestone ... 20,224 .. F 9
Lipscomb ... 3,766 .. A 6
Live Oak ... 9,606 .. I 8
Llano ... 10,144 .. F 7
Loving ... 91 .. E 3
Lubbock ... 211,651 .. C 5
Lynn ... 8,605 .. D 4
Madison ... 10,649 .. F 9
Marion ... 10,360 .. D 11
Martin ... 4,684 .. E 4
Mason ... 3,683 .. F 7
Matagorda ... 37,828 .. H 10
Maverick ... 31,398 .. H 6
McCulloch ... 8,735 .. F 7
McLennan ... 170,755 .. E 8
McMullen ... 789 .. I 7
Medina ... 23,164 .. H 7
Menard ... 2,346 .. F 6
Midland ... 82,636 .. E 4
Milam ... 22,732 .. F 9
Mills ... 4,477 .. F 7
Mitchell ... 9,088 .. E 5
Montague ... 17,410 .. D 8
Montgomery ... 128,487 .. G 10
Moore ... 16,575 .. A 5
Morris ... 14,629 .. D 11
Motley ... 1,950 .. C 5
Nacogdoches ... 46,786 .. E 11
Navarro ... 35,323 .. E 9
Newton ... 13,254 .. F 11
Nolan ... 17,359 .. E 6
Nueces ... 268,215 .. I 8
Ochiltree ... 9,588 .. A 5
Oldham ... 2,283 .. B 4
Orange ... 83,838 .. G 11
Palo Pinto ... 24,062 .. D 7
Panola ... 20,724 .. E 11
Parker ... 44,609 .. D 8
Parmer ... 11,038 .. B 4
Pecos ... 14,618 .. F 4
Polk ... 24,407 .. F 10
Potter ... 98,637 .. B 5
Presidio ... 5,188 .. G 2
Rains ... 4,839 .. D 10
Randall ... 75,062 .. B 5
Reagan ... 4,135 .. F 5
Real ... 2,469 .. G 6
Red River ... 16,101 .. D 10
Reeves ... 15,801 .. F 3
Refugio ... 9,289 .. I 9
Roberts ... 1,187 .. A 5
Robertson ... 14,653 .. F 9
Rockwall ... 14,528 .. D 9
Runnels ... 11,872 .. E 6
Rusk ... 41,382 .. E 11
Sabine ... 8,702 .. F 11
San Augustine ... 8,785 .. F 11
San Jacinto ... 11,434 .. F 10
San Patricio ... 58,013 .. I 8
San Saba ... 5,693 .. F 7
Schleicher ... 2,820 .. F 6
Scurry ... 18,192 .. D 5
Shackelford ... 3,915 .. D 7
Shelby ... 23,084 .. E 11
Sherman ... 3,174 .. A 5
Smith ... 128,366 .. E 10
Somervell ... 4,154 .. E 8
Starr ... 27,266 .. J 7
Stephens ... 9,926 .. D 7
Sterling ... 1,206 .. E 5
Stonewall ... 2,406 .. D 6
Sutton ... 5,130 .. G 6
Swisher ... 9,723 .. C 5
Tarrant ... 860,880 .. D 8
Taylor ... 110,932 .. E 6
Terrell ... 1,595 .. G 4
Terry ... 14,581 .. D 4
Throckmorton ... 2,053 .. D 7
Titus ... 21,442 .. D 10
Tom Green ... 84,784 .. F 6
Travis ... 419,335 .. G 8
Trinity ... 9,450 .. F 10
Tyler ... 16,223 .. F 11
Upshur ... 28,595 .. D 10
Upton ... 4,619 .. F 4
Uvalde ... 22,441 .. H 6
Val Verde ... 35,910 .. G 5
Van Zandt ... 31,426 .. E 10
Victoria ... 68,807 .. H 9
Walker ... 41,789 .. F 10
Waller ... 19,798 .. G 10
Ward ... 13,976 .. E 3
Washington ... 21,998 .. G 9
Webb ... 99,258 .. I 7
Wharton ... 40,242 .. H 9
Wheeler ... 7,137 .. B 6
Wichita ... 121,082 .. C 7
Wilbarger ... 15,931 .. C 7
Willacy ... 17,495 .. K 8
Williamson ... 76,521 .. F 8
Wilson ... 16,756 .. H 8
Winkler ... 9,944 .. E 3
Wise ... 26,575 .. D 8
Wood ... 24,697 .. D 10
Yoakum ... 8,299 .. D 4
Young ... 19,001 .. D 7
Zapata ... 6,628 .. J 7
Zavala ... 11,666 .. H 6

Cities, Towns, and Villages

Abernathy ... 2,904 .. C 5
Abilene ... 98,315 .. °E 6
Addison ... 5,553 .. C 14
Agua Dulce ... 934 .. I 8
Alamo* ... 5,831 .. K 8
Alamo Heights ... 6,252 .. J 2
Albany ... 2,450 .. °D 7
Aldine* ... 12,623 .. G 10
Aledo* ... 1,027 .. D 8
Alice ... 20,961 .. °I 8
Allen ... 8,314 .. B 15
Alpine ... 5,465 .. °G 3
Alto ... 1,203 .. E 10
Alton* ... 2,732 .. K 8
Alvarado ... 2,701 .. E 13
Alvin ... 16,515 .. I 14
Alvord ... 874 .. D 8
Amarillo ... 149,230 .. °B 5
Ames ... 1,155 .. G 16
Amherst ... 971 .. C 4
Anahuac ... 1,840 .. °H 16
Anderson ... °G 9
Andrews ... 11,061 .. °E 4
Angleton ... 13,929 .. °J 13
Anna ... 855 .. A 15
Anson ... 2,831 .. °D 6
Anthony ... 2,640 .. E 1
Anton ... 1,180 .. C 4
Aransas Pass ... 7,173 .. I 9
Archer City ... 1,862 .. °C 7
Argyle ... 1,111 .. B 13
Arlington ... 160,123 .. C 13
Arp ... 939 .. E 10
Asherton ... 1,574 .. I 6
Aspermont ... 1,357 .. °D 6
Athens ... 10,197 .. °E 10
Atlanta ... 6,272 .. D 11
Aubrey ... 948 .. A 14
Austin ... 345,496 .. °G 7
Azle ... 5,822 .. C 12
Bacliff ... 4,851 .. I 15
Baird ... 1,696 .. °E 7
Balch
Springs ... 13,746 .. D 15
Balcones
Heights ... 2,853 .. J 2
Ballinger ... 4,207 .. °E 6
Bandera ... 947 .. °G 7
Bangs ... 1,716 .. E 7
Barrett* ... 3,183 .. G 10
Bartlett ... 1,567 .. F 8
Bastrop ... 3,789 .. °G 8
Bay City ... 17,837 .. °H 10
Baytown ... 56,923 .. H 15
Beaumont ... 118,102 .. °G 11
Beckville ... 945 .. E 11
Bedford ... 20,821 .. C 13
Beeville ... 14,574 .. °I 8
Bellaire ... 14,950 .. H 13
Bellmead* ... 7,569 .. E 8
Bellville ... 2,860 .. °G 9
Belton ... 10,660 .. °F 8
Benavides ... 1,978 .. I 7
Benbrook ... 13,579 .. D 12
Benjamin ... 257 .. °C 6
Bertram ... 824 .. F 8
Beverly Hills* ... 2,083 .. E 8
Bevil Oaks* ... 1,306 .. G 11
Big Lake ... 3,404 .. °F 5
Big Sandy* ... 1,258 .. E 10
Big Spring ... 24,804 .. °E 5
Big Wells ... 939 .. H 6
Bishop ... 3,706 .. I 8
Blanco ... 1,179 .. G 7
Blossom ... 1,487 .. C 10
Blue Mound ... 2,169 .. C 13
Boerne ... 3,229 .. °G 7
Bogata ... 1,508 .. D 10
Bonham ... 7,338 .. °C 9
Booker ... 1,219 .. A 6
Borger ... 15,837 .. A 5
Boston ... °D 11
Bovina ... 1,499 .. B 4
Bowie ... 5,610 .. C 8
Boyd ... 889 .. B 12
Brackettville ... 1,676 .. °H 6
Brady ... 5,969 .. °F 7
Brazoria ... 3,025 .. K 13
Breckenridge ... 6,921 .. °D 7
Bremond ... 1,025 .. F 9
Brenham ... 10,966 .. °G 9
Briar ... 1,810 .. B 12
Bridge City ... 7,667 .. G 11
Bridgeport ... 3,737 .. D 8
Bronte ... 983 .. E 6
Brookshire ... 2,175 .. G 10
Brookside* ... 1,453 .. G 10
Brownfield ... 10,387 .. °D 4
Brownsville ... 84,997 .. °K 8
Brownwood ... 19,203 .. °E 7
Bruceville-Eddy* 1,038 .. F 8
Bryan ... 44,337 .. °F 9
Buffalo ... 1,507 .. F 9
Bunker Hill ... 3,750 .. H 13
Burkburnett ... 10,668 .. C 7
Burleson ... 11,734 .. D 13
Burnet ... 3,410 .. °F 8
Cactus ... 898 .. A 5
Caddo Mills ... 1,060 .. B 16
Caldwell ... 2,953 .. °G 9
Calvert ... 1,732 .. F 9
Cameron ... 5,721 .. °F 9
Canadian ... 3,491 .. °A 6
Canton ... 2,845 .. °E 10
Canyon ... 10,724 .. °B 5
Carrizo
Springs ... 6,886 .. °I 6
Carrollton ... 40,591 .. C 14
Carthage ... 6,447 .. °E 11
Castle Hills ... 4,773 .. I 2
Castroville ... 1,821 .. J 1
Cedar Hill ... 6,849 .. D 14
Cedar Park* ... 3,474 .. G 8
Celina ... 1,520 .. A 14
Center ... 5,827 .. °E 11
Centerville ... 799 .. °F 10
Champion* ... 14,692 .. G 10
Chandler* ... 1,308 .. E 10
Channelview ... 17,471 .. H 14
Channing ... 304 .. °A 4
Charlotte ... 1,443 .. H 7
Chico ... 890 .. D 8
Childress ... 5,817 .. °C 6
Chillicothe ... 1,052 .. C 7
China* ... 1,351 .. G 11
Cisco ... 4,517 .. E 7
Clarendon ... 2,220 .. °B 5
Clarksville ... 4,917 .. °C 10
Claude ... 1,112 .. °B 5
Clear Lake
Shores* ... 755 .. H 10
Cleburne ... 19,218 .. °E 12
Cleveland ... 5,977 .. F 14
Clifton ... 3,063 .. E 8
Clint* ... 1,314 .. E 1
Cloverleaf ... 17,317 .. H 14
Clute ... 9,577 .. K 13
Clyde ... 2,562 .. E 7
Coahoma ... 1,069 .. E 5
Cockrell Hill ... 3,262 .. C 14
Coldspring ... 569 .. °F 10
Coleman ... 5,960 .. °E 7
College
Station ... 37,272 .. F 9
Colleyville ... 6,700 .. C 13
Colorado City ... 5,405 .. °E 5
Columbus ... 3,923 .. °G 9
Comanche ... 4,075 .. °E 7
Combes* ... 1,441 .. K 8
Comfort ... 1,226 .. G 7
Commerce ... 8,136 .. D 9
Conroe ... 18,034 .. °F 13
Converse ... 4,907 .. I 3
Cooper ... 2,338 .. °D 10
Coppell ... 3,826 .. C 14
Copperas
Cove ... 19,469 .. F 8
Corinth ... 1,264 .. B 14
Corpus
Christi ... 231,999 .. °I 8
Corrigan ... 1,770 .. F 11
Corsicana ... 21,712 .. °E 9
Cotulla ... 3,912 .. °I 7
Crandall ... 831 .. D 16
Crane ... 3,622 .. °F 4
Crockett ... 7,405 .. °F 10
Crosbyton ... 2,289 .. °C 5
Cross Plains ... 1,240 .. E 7
Crowell ... 1,509 .. °C 6
Crowley ... 5,852 .. D 13
Crystal City ... 8,334 .. °H 6
Cuero ... 7,124 .. °H 8
Daingerfield ... 3,030 .. °D 11
Daisetta ... 1,177 .. G 16
Dalhart ... 6,854 .. °A 4
Dallas ... 904,078 .. °D 9
Dalworthington
Gardens ... 1,100 .. D 13
Danbury* ... 1,357 .. H 10
Dawson ... 747 .. E 9
Dayton ... 4,908 .. G 15
Decatur ... 4,104 .. °A 12
Deer Park ... 22,648 .. H 14
De Kalb ... 2,217 .. C 11
De Leon ... 2,478 .. E 7
Del Rio ... 30,034 .. °H 5
Denison ... 23,884 .. C 9
Denton ... 48,063 .. °B 13
Denver City ... 4,704 .. D 4
De Soto ... 15,538 .. D 14
Detroit ... 805 .. C 10
Devine ... 3,756 .. K 1
Diboll ... 5,227 .. F 10
Dickens ... 409 .. °C 5
Dickinson ... 7,505 .. I 15
Dilley ... 2,579 .. H 7
Dimmitt ... 5,019 .. °B 4
Donna ... 9,952 .. K 8
Dublin ... 2,723 .. E 7
Dumas ... 12,194 .. °A 5
Duncanville ... 27,781 .. D 14
Eagle Lake ... 3,921 .. G 9
Eagle Pass ... 21,407 .. °H 6
Early ... 2,313 .. E 7
Earth ... 1,512 .. C 4
Eastland ... 3,747 .. °E 7
Edcouch* ... 3,092 .. K 8
Eden ... 1,294 .. F 6
Edgecliff ... 2,695 .. D 13
Edgewood* ... 1,413 .. D 10
Edinburg ... 24,075 .. °K 8
Edna ... 5,650 .. °H 9
El Campo ... 10,462 .. H 9
Eldorado ... 2,061 .. °F 6
Electra ... 3,755 .. C 7
Elgin ... 4,535 .. G 8
Elkhart ... 1,317 .. E 10
El Lago* ... 3,129 .. G 10
El Paso ... 425,259 .. °E 1
Elsa* ... 5,061 .. K 8
Emory ... 813 .. °D 10
Ennis ... 12,110 .. E 15
Euless ... 24,002 .. C 13
Everman ... 5,387 .. D 13
Fabens ... 4,285 .. E 1
Fairfield ... 3,505 .. °E 9
Fairview ... 893 .. B 15
Falfurrias ... 6,103 .. °J 8
Farmers
Branch ... 24,863 .. C 14
Farmersville ... 2,360 .. B 16
Farwell ... 1,354 .. °C 4
Ferris ... 2,228 .. D 15
Flatonia* ... 1,070 .. G 8
Florence* ... 744 .. F 8
Floresville ... 4,381 .. °K 3
Flower
Mound* ... 4,402 .. D 9
Floydada ... 4,193 .. °C 5
Forest Hill ... 11,684 .. D 13
Forney* ... 2,483 .. E 9
Fort Bliss* ... 12,687 .. E 1
Fort Davis ... °F 3
Fort Hood ... 31,250 .. F 8
Fort Stockton ... 8,688 .. °F 4
Fort Worth ... 385,141 .. °D 8
Franklin ... 1,349 .. °F 9
Frankston ... 1,255 .. E 10
Fredericksburg ... 6,412 .. °G 7
Freeport ... 13,444 .. K 14
Freer ... 3,213 .. I 7
Friendswood ... 10,719 .. I 14
Friona ... 3,809 .. B 4
Frisco ... 3,420 .. B 14
Fritch ... 2,299 .. A 5
Fuller Springs* ... 1,470 .. F 11

Gail		°D 5
Gainesville	14,081	°C 9
Galena Park	9,879	H 14
Galveston	61,902	°J 15
Ganado	1,770	H 9
Garden City		°E 5
Garland	138,857	C 15
Garrison	1,059	E 11
Gatesville	6,260	°F 8
George West	2,627	°I 8
Georgetown	9,468	°F 8
Giddings	3,950	°G 9
Gilmer	5,167	°D 10
Gladewater	6,548	D 10
Glenn Heights*	1,033	E 9
Glen Rose	2,075	°E 8
Goldthwaite	1,783	°F 7
Goliad	1,990	°H 8
Gonzales	7,152	°H 8
Gorman	1,258	E 7
Graham	9,055	°D 7
Granbury	3,332	°E 8
Grand Prairie	71,462	C 14
Grand Saline*	2,709	D 10
Grandview	1,205	E 13
Granger	1,236	F 8
Grapeland	1,634	F 10
Grapevine	11,801	C 13
Greenville	22,161	°B 16
Gregory*	2,739	I 8
Griffing Park*	1,802	G 11
Groesbeck	3,373	°F 9
Groom	736	B 5
Groves	17,090	G 11
Groveton	1,262	°F 10
Grulla	1,442	K 7
Gruver	1,216	A 5
Gun Barrel City*	2,118	E 9
Gunter	849	A 15
Guthrie		°C 6
Hale Center	2,297	C 5
Hallettsville	2,865	°H 9
Hallsville*	1,556	E 11
Haltom City	29,014	C 13
Hamilton	3,189	°E 8
Hamlin	3,248	D 6
Hardin	779	F 16
Harker Heights*	7,345	F 8
Harlingen	43,543	K 8
Hart	1,008	C 4
Haskell	3,782	°D 6
Hawkins*	1,302	D 10
Hearne	5,418	F 9
Heath	1,459	C 16
Hebbronville	4,684	°J 7
Hedwig Village*	2,506	H 13
Hemphill	1,353	°F 11
Hempstead	3,456	°G 10
Henderson	11,473	°E 10
Henrietta	3,149	°C 8
Hereford	15,853	°B 4
Hewitt*	5,247	F 8
Hickory Creek*	1,422	D 9
Hico	1,375	E 8
Hidalgo*	2,288	K 8
Hidalgo Park, see Las Milpas [-Hidalgo Park]		
Highland Park	8,909	C 14
Highland Village*	3,246	D 9
Highlands*	6,467	G 10
Hill County Village*	972	G 7
Hillcrest*	771	H 10
Hillsboro	7,397	°E 9
Hitchcock	6,655	J 15
Holland	863	F 8
Holliday	1,349	C 7
Hollywood Park*	3,231	H 8
Hondo	6,057	°H 7
Honey Grove	1,973	C 10
Hooks	2,507	D 11
Houston	1,594,086	°G 10
Howe	2,072	A 15
Hubbard	1,676	E 9
Hudson*	1,659	F 11
Hughes Springs*	2,196	D 11
Humble	6,729	G 14
Hunters Creek Village*	4,215	H 13
Huntington	1,672	F 11
Huntsville	23,936	°F 10
Hurst	31,420	C 13
Hutchins	2,996	D 15
Idalou	2,348	C 5
Ingleside*	5,436	I 9
Iowa Park	6,184	C 7
Iraan	1,358	F 4
Irving	109,943	C 14
Italy*	1,306	E 9
Itasca	1,600	E 9
Jacinto City	8,953	H 14
Jacksboro	4,000	°D 8
Jacksonville	12,264	E 10
Jasper	6,959	°F 11
Jayton	638	°D 6
Jefferson	2,643	°D 11
Jersey Village	4,084	H 13
Joaquin	917	E 11
Johnson City	872	°G 7
Jones Creek	2,634	K 13
Joshua	1,470	E 12
Jourdanton	2,743	°H 7
Junction	2,593	°G 6
Justin	920	B 13
Karnes City	3,296	°H 8
Katy	5,660	H 12
Kaufman	4,658	°D 16
Keene	3,013	E 13
Keller	4,143	C 13
Kemah*	1,304	H 11
Kemp*	1,035	E 16
Kenedy	4,356	H 8
Kenefick	763	G 15
Kennedale	2,594	D 13
Kerens	1,582	E 9
Kermit	8,015	°E 3
Kerrville	15,276	°G 7
Kilgore*	10,968	E 11
Killeen	46,296	F 8
Kingsland	2,241	F 7
Kingsville	28,808	°J 8
Kingwood*	16,261	G 10
Kirby	6,385	J 2
Kirbyville	1,972	F 11
Knox City	1,546	D 6
Kountze	2,716	°G 11
Kress	783	C 5
Krum	917	A 13
Kyle	2,093	G 8
La Coste	862	J 1
Lackland Air Force Base	14,459	J 2
Lacy-Lakeview	2,752	E 9
La Feria*	3,495	K 8
La Grange	3,768	°G 9
La Joya*	2,018	K 7
Lake Dallas	3,177	B 14
Lake Jackson	19,102	K 13
Lake Worth Village	4,394	C 12
Lakeport*	835	E 11
Lakeside*	957	D 8
Lakeway*	790	G 8
La Marque	15,372	I 15
Lamesa	11,790	°D 4
Lampasas	6,165	°F 8
Lancaster	14,807	D 15
La Porte	14,062	H 15
La Pryor	1,257	H 6
Laredo	91,449	°J 7
Las Milpas [-Hidalgo Park]*	3,039	K 8
Laughlin Air Force Base	2,994	H 5
La Villa*	1,442	K 8
League City	16,578	I 14
Leakey	468	°G 6
Leander*	2,179	F 8
Lefors	829	B 6
Leon Valley	8,951	J 2
Leonard	1,421	A 16
Levelland	13,809	°C 4
Lewisville	24,273	B 14
Lexington	1,065	G 9
Liberty	7,945	°G 15
Liberty City*	1,121	D 10
Lindale*	2,180	E 10
Linden	2,443	°D 11
Lipscomb		°A 6
Little Elm	926	B 14
Little River-Academy*	1,155	F 8
Littlefield	7,409	°C 4
Live Oak*	8,183	H 9
Livingston	4,928	°F 10
Llano	3,071	°F 7
Lockhart	7,953	°G 8
Lockney	2,334	C 5
Lomax	2,991	H 15
Lone Star*	2,036	D 11
Longview	62,762	°E 11
Loraine	929	E 6
Lorenzo	1,394	C 5
Los Fresnos*	2,173	K 8
Lott	865	F 9
Lubbock	173,979	°C 5
Lucas	1,371	B 15
Lufkin	28,562	°F 11
Luling	5,039	G 8
Lumberton*	2,480	G 11
Lyford	1,618	K 8
Lytle	1,920	K 1
Mabank	1,443	E 16
Madisonville	3,660	°F 10
Magnolia	867	F 12
Malakoff	2,082	E 9
Manor	1,044	G 8
Mansfield	8,092	D 13
Manvel	3,549	I 14
Marble Falls	3,252	F 8
Marfa	2,466	°G 3
Marlin	7,099	°F 9
Marshall	24,921	°D 11
Mart	2,324	E 9
Mason	2,153	°F 7
Matador	1,052	°C 5
Mathis	5,667	I 8
Maud	1,059	D 11
McAllen	67,042	K 8
McCamey	2,436	F 4
McGregor	4,513	F 8
McKinney	16,249	°B 15
McLean	1,160	B 6
McQueeney	1,332	I 4
Memphis	3,352	°B 6
Menard	1,697	°F 6
Mentone		°E 3
Mercedes	11,851	K 8
Meridian	1,330	°E 8
Merkel	2,493	E 6
Mertzon	687	°F 5
Mesquite	67,053	C 15
Mexia	7,094	E 9
Miami	813	°A 6
Midland	70,525	°E 4
Midlothian	3,219	D 14
Mineola	4,346	D 10
Mineral Wells	14,468	D 8
Mission	22,589	K 8
Missouri City	24,533	I 13
Monahans	8,397	°E 4
Mont Belvieu	1,730	H 15
Montague	1,253	°C 8
Moody*	1,385	F 8
Morgan's Point Resort*	1,082	F 8
Morton	2,674	°C 4
Moulton*	1,009	H 9
Mount Pleasant	11,003	°D 10
Mount Vernon	2,025	°D 10
Muenster*	1,408	D 8
Muleshoe	4,842	°C 4
Munday	1,738	D 6
Murphy	1,150	B 15
Nacogdoches	27,149	°E 11
Naples*	1,908	D 11
Nash*	2,022	D 11
Nassau Bay*	4,526	G 10
Natalia	1,264	K 1
Navasota	5,971	G 9
Nederland	16,855	G 11
Needville	1,417	I 12
New Boston	4,628	D 11
New Braunfels	22,402	°I 3
New London	942	E 10
New Waverly	824	F 10
Newton	1,620	°F 11
Nixon	2,008	J 5
Nocona	2,992	C 8
Nolanville*	1,308	F 8
North Richland Hills	30,592	C 13
North San Pedro*	2,553	I 8
Northcrest*	1,944	F 8
O'Donnell	1,200	D 5
Oak Ridge North*	2,504	G 10
Odem*	2,363	I 8
Odessa	90,027	°E 4
Old River-Winfree*	1,058	G 11
Olmos Park	2,069	J 2
Olney	4,060	D 7
Olton	2,235	C 4
Orange	23,628	°G 11
Orange Grove	1,212	I 8
Ore City*	1,050	D 11
Overton	2,430	E 10
Ovilla	1,067	D 14
Oyster Creek	1,473	K 14
Ozona	3,766	°F 5
Paducah	2,216	°C 6
Paint Rock	256	°F 6
Palacios	4,667	H 9
Palestine	15,948	°E 10
Palmer	1,187	E 15
Palo Pinto		°D 7
Pampa	21,396	°B 5
Panhandle	2,226	°B 5
Panorama Village*	1,186	G 10
Pantego*	2,431	D 8
Paris	25,498	°C 10
Parker*	1,098	D 9
Pasadena	112,560	H 14
Patton*	1,050	G 10
Pearland	13,248	I 14
Pearsall	7,383	°H 7
Pecos	12,855	°E 3
Perryton	7,991	°A 6
Petersburg	1,633	C 5
Petrolia	755	C 8
Pharr	21,381	K 8
Phillips	1,729	A 5
Pilot Point	2,211	A 14
Pinehurst	3,055	F 12
Pineland	1,111	F 11
Piney Point Village*	2,958	H 13
Pittsburg	4,245	°D 10
Plains	1,457	°D 4
Plainview	22,187	°C 5
Plano	72,331	B 15
Pleasanton	6,346	H 7
Point Comfort	1,125	H 9
Port Aransas	1,968	I 9
Port Arthur	61,195	G 11
Port Isabel*	3,769	K 9
Port Lavaca	10,911	°H 9
Port Neches	13,944	G 11
Port O'Connor	1,031	I 9
Portland	12,023	I 8
Post	3,961	°D 5
Post Oak Bend City	878	D 9
Poteet	3,086	H 7
Poth	1,461	H 8
Pottsboro	895	C 9
Prairie View	3,993	G 10
Premont	2,984	J 8
Presidio	1,723	G 2
Primera*	1,380	K 8
Princeton	3,408	B 15
Quanah	3,890	°C 6
Queen City	1,748	D 11
Quinlan	1,002	C 16
Quitman	1,893	°D 10
Ralls	2,422	C 5
Ranger	3,142	E 7
Rankin	1,216	°F 4
Raymondville	9,493	°K 8
Red Oak	1,882	D 14
Refugio	3,898	°I 8
Reno*	1,059	C 10
Reno	1,174	C 12
Richardson	72,496	C 15
Richland Hills	7,977	C 13
Richmond	9,692	°I 12
Richwood*	2,591	H 10
Rio Grande City	8,930	°K 7
Rio Hondo*	1,673	K 8
Rising Star	1,204	E 7
River Oaks	6,890	C 12
Roanoke	910	B 13
Robert Lee	1,202	°E 6
Robinson	6,074	F 9
Robstown	12,100	I 8
Roby	814	°D 6
Rockdale	5,611	F 9
Rockport	3,686	°I 9
Rocksprings	1,317	°G 6
Rockwall	5,939	°C 16
Rogers*	1,242	F 8
Rollingwood*	1,027	G 8
Roma-Los Saenz	3,384	K 7
Roman Forest*	929	G 10
Roscoe*	1,628	E 6
Rosebud	2,076	F 9
Rosenberg	17,995	I 12
Rotan	2,284	D 6
Round Rock	11,812	G 8
Rowlett	7,522	C 15
Royse City	1,566	B 16
Rule	1,015	D 6
Runge	1,244	H 8
Rusk	4,681	°E 10
Sabinal	1,827	H 6
Sachse	1,640	C 15
Saginaw	5,736	C 13
St. Jo*	1,071	D 8
San Angelo	73,240	°F 6
San Antonio	785,410	°H 7
San Augustine	2,930	°E 11
San Benito	17,988	K 8
San Diego	5,255	°I 8
San Elizario	1,548	E 1
San Juan*	7,608	K 8
San Leon	1,745	I 15
San Marcos	23,420	°G 8
San Saba	2,336	°F 7
Sanderson	1,241	°G 4
Sanger	2,574	A 13
Sansom Park Village*	3,921	D 8
Santa Anna	1,535	E 7
Santa Fe*	5,413	H 10
Santa Rosa*	1,889	K 8
Sarita		°J 8
Savoy*	855	C 9
Schertz	7,262	I 3
Schulenburg	2,469	G 9
Seabrook	4,670	I 15
Seadrift	1,277	I 9
Seagoville	7,304	D 15
Seagraves	2,596	D 4
Sealy	3,875	G 9
Seguin	17,854	°I 4
Seminole	6,080	°D 4
Seth Ward	1,186	C 5
Seymour	3,657	°C 7
Shady Shores	813	B 14
Shallowater	1,932	C 4
Shamrock	2,834	B 6
Shavano Park	1,448	I 2
Shenandoah*	1,793	G 10
Shepherd	1,674	G 10
Sherman	30,413	°C 9
Shiner	2,213	H 9
Shoreacres	1,260	H 15
Sierra Blanca		°F 1
Silsbee	7,684	G 11
Silverton	918	°C 5
Sinton	6,044	°I 8
Skellytown	899	A 5
Slaton	6,804	D 5
Smithville	3,470	G 9
Snyder	12,705	°D 5
Somerset	1,102	K 1
Somerville	1,814	G 9
Sonora	3,856	°F 6
Sour Lake*	1,807	G 11
South Houston	13,293	H 14
South Padre Island*	791	K 8
Southlake	2,808	C 13
Southside Place*	1,366	H 13
Spearman	3,413	°A 5
Spring Valley	3,353	H 13
Springtown	1,658	D 8
Spur	1,690	D 5
Stafford	4,755	H 13
Stamford	4,542	D 6
Stanton	2,314	°E 5
Stephenville	11,881	°E 8
Sterling City	915	°E 5
Stinnett	2,222	°A 5
Stockdale	1,265	K 4
Stratford	1,917	°A 4
Sudan	1,091	C 4
Sugar Land	8,826	I 13
Sulphur Springs	12,804	°D 10
Sundown	1,511	D 4
Sunnyvale	1,404	C 15
Sunray	1,952	A 5
Sunset Valley*	733	G 8
Sweeny	3,538	K 12
Sweetwater	12,242	°E 6
Taft	3,686	I 8
Tahoka	3,262	°D 5
Talco	751	D 10
Tatum	1,339	E 11
Taylor	10,619	F 8
Taylor Lake Village*	3,669	G 10
Teague	3,390	E 9
Temple	42,483	F 8
Tenaha	1,005	E 11
Terrell	13,225	C 16
Terrell Hills	4,644	J 2
Texarkana	31,271	D 11
Texas City	41,403	I 15
The Colony*	11,586	D 9
The Woodlands*	8,443	G 10
Thorndale	1,300	F 9
Three Rivers	2,133	I 8
Throckmorton	1,174	°D 7
Tilden		°I 7
Timpson	1,164	E 11
Tomball	3,996	G 13
Tool*	1,591	E 9
Trinidad*	1,130	E 9
Trinity	2,452	F 10
Troup	1,911	E 10
Troy*	1,353	F 8
Tulia	5,033	°B 5
Tye*	1,394	E 6
Tyler	70,508	E 10
Universal City	10,720	I 2
University Park	22,254	C 14
Uvalde	14,178	°H 6
Valley Mills	1,236	E 8
Van	1,881	D 10
Van Alstyne	1,860	A 15
Van Horn	2,772	°F 2
Vega	900	°B 4
Vernon	12,695	°C 7
Victoria	50,695	°H 9
Vidor*	12,117	G 12
Waco	101,261	°E 8
Waelder	942	G 8
Wake Village	3,865	D 11
Waller	1,241	G 10
Wallis*	1,138	G 9
Waskom*	1,821	E 11
Watauga	10,284	C 13
Waxahachie	14,624	°E 14
Weatherford	12,049	°D 8
Webster*	2,168	I 14
Weimar	2,096	G 9
Wellington	3,043	°B 6
Wells	926	F 10
Weslaco	19,331	K 8
West	2,485	E 9
West Columbia	4,109	J 13
West Lake Hills*	1,927	G 8
West Orange*	4,610	G 12
West University Place	12,010	H 13
Westworth*	3,651	D 8
Wharton	9,033	°H 9
Wheeler	1,584	°B 6
White Deer	1,210	B 5
White Oak*	4,415	E 11
White Settlement	13,508	C 12
Whitehouse*	2,172	E 10
Whitesboro*	3,197	C 9
Whitewright	1,760	A 16
Whitney	1,631	E 8
Wichita Falls	94,201	°C 7
Willis*	1,674	F 13
Willow Park*	1,113	D 8
Wills Point	2,631	D 9
Wilmer	2,367	D 15
Windcrest*	5,332	G 7
Wink	1,182	E 3
Winnsboro*	3,458	D 10
Winters	3,061	E 6
Wolfe City*	1,594	D 10
Wolfforth*	1,701	D 5
Woodsboro	1,974	I 8
Woodville	2,821	°F 11
Woodway*	7,091	E 8
Wortham*	1,187	E 9
Wylie	3,152	B 15
Yoakum	6,148	H 9
Yorktown	2,498	H 8
Zapata	3,831	°J 7

*Does not appear on map; key shows general location.
°County seat.
Source: 1980 census. Places without population figures are unincorporated areas.

The 1980 United States census reported that Texas had 14,228,383 persons. The state's population increased 27 per cent over the 1970 census figure, 11,198,-655.

About four-fifths of the people of Texas live in urban areas. Almost half live in the metropolitan areas of Dallas-Fort Worth, Houston, and San Antonio. In all, Texas has 26 metropolitan areas (see METROPOLITAN AREA). For the population of these areas, see the *Index* to the political map of Texas.

Texas has 15 cities with more than 100,000 persons. Houston is the largest city, followed by Dallas, San Antonio, El Paso, Fort Worth, Austin, and Corpus Christi. See the separate articles on the cities of Texas listed in the *Related Articles* at the end of this article.

About 97 of every 100 Texans, including large numbers of Texas-born Mexicans, were born in the United States. Most Texans born elsewhere are Mexicans who work on farms and in factories in the state's southern and southwestern regions. Some Mexicans who live in the Rio Grande Valley speak Spanish and know only a few words of English. Many non-Mexicans who live in other sections of Texas where Mexicans have settled, especially in the San Antonio area, speak Spanish.

The Roman Catholic Church is the largest single religious group in Texas, but there are more Protestants than Roman Catholics. Protestant groups, in order of size, include Baptists, Methodists, members of the Churches of Christ, Disciples of Christ, Presbyterians, and Episcopalians.

Population

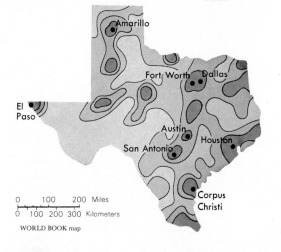

This map shows the *population density* of Texas, and how it varies in different parts of the state. Population density means the average number of people who live in a given area.

Persons per sq. mi.	Persons per km²
More than 48	More than 19
24 to 48	9 to 19
8 to 24	3 to 9
Less than 8	Less than 3

0   100   200 Miles
0 100 200 300 Kilometers

WORLD BOOK map

Cowboys exchange greetings "backstage" at a rodeo. Rugged, weather-beaten cowboys work on Texas ranches.

William H. Burkett, Alpha

Sam Pierson, *Houston Chronicle*

Courtesy El Paso Public Schools

Space Engineers help test a space suit they designed at the Lyndon B. Johnson Space Center at Houston.

Dallas Chamber of Commerce

Dallas Skyscrapers are the headquarters of many of Texas' leading business enterprises.

El Paso Schoolchildren recite the Pledge of Allegiance to the United States flag. Texas has many citizens of Mexican ancestry.

University of Texas

The University of Texas Campus in Austin includes the East Mall Fountain and the 27-story Main Building Tower.

Schools. Texas had only a few public schools when it gained independence in 1836. Mexico had refused to establish a good public school system with English-speaking teachers. Teachers conducted classes only in Spanish. This was a major reason why American settlers objected to Mexican rule. In 1854, Texas established a school system for the entire state.

The Texas Education Agency supervises the public school system. It consists of the commissioner of education, the state board of education, and the state department of education. The board of education has 27 elected members. It appoints the commissioner, with the approval of the Texas senate, to a four-year term. Texas law requires children between the ages of 7 and 17 to attend school. For the number of students and teachers in Texas, see EDUCATION (table).

Libraries. Texas has about 380 public libraries and many college and special libraries. The Texas State Library, established in Austin in 1839 by the Republic of Texas, is Texas' oldest library. Mirabeau B. Lamar Library, at the University of Texas in Austin, is the largest library. It has over $3\frac{1}{2}$ million books.

The Eugene C. Barker Texas History Center, at the University of Texas in Austin, has the largest collection of material written about Texas. The Lyndon B. Johnson Library, also at the University of Texas campus in Austin, houses the papers and mementos of the nation's 36th President. The Armstrong Browning Library, at Baylor University in Waco, has the world's largest collection of material by and about the English poet Robert Browning.

Museums. Collections at the Museum of Fine Arts of Houston include jewelry from ancient Greece and Spanish sculptures of the 1400's. The museum also has works by Frederic Remington, the famous painter of the old West. The Dallas Museum of Fine Arts has a collection of American paintings. The Kimbell Art Museum in Fort Worth displays paintings by European masters.

The Witte Memorial Museum in San Antonio has exhibits on Texas anthropology, art, history, natural history, stamps and coins, and transportation. Other museums include the Texas Hall of State in Dallas, the Sam Houston Memorial Museum in Huntsville, and the Art Museum of South Texas in Corpus Christi.

Universities and Colleges

Texas has 59 universities and colleges accredited by the Southern Association of Colleges and Schools. For further information, see UNIVERSITIES AND COLLEGES (table).

Name	Location	Founded	Name	Location	Founded
Abilene Christian College	Abilene	1906	Our Lady of the Lake University		
American Technological University	Killeen	1973	of San Antonio	San Antonio	1896
Angelo State University	San Angelo	1965	Pan American University	Edinburg	1948
Austin College	Sherman	1849	Paul Quinn College	Waco	1940
Austin Presbyterian			Rice University	Houston	1891
Theological Seminary	Austin	1902	St. Edward's University	Austin	1881
Baylor College of Dentistry	Dallas	1905	St. Mary's University	San Antonio	1852
Baylor College of Medicine	Houston	1969	St. Thomas, University of	Houston	1947
Baylor University	Waco	1845	Sam Houston State University	Huntsville	1879
Bishop College	Dallas	1881	South Texas, University System of	*	*
Concordia Lutheran College	Austin	1926	Southern Methodist University	Dallas	1911
Dallas, University of	Irving	1956	Southwest Texas		
Dallas Baptist College	Dallas	1969	State University	San Marcos	1899
Dallas Theological Seminary	Dallas	1925	Southwestern Adventist College	Keene	1968
East Texas Baptist College	Marshall	1912	Southwestern Baptist Theological		
East Texas State University	*	*	Seminary	Fort Worth	1908
Gulf-Coast Bible College	Houston	1953	Southwestern University	Georgetown	1840
Hardin-Simmons University	Abilene	1891	Stephen F. Austin State University	Nacogdoches	1923
Houston, University of	*	*	Sul Ross State University	Alpine	1917
Houston Baptist University	Houston	1963	Texas, University of	*	*
Howard Payne University	Brownwood	1889	Texas A&M University System	*	*
Huston-Tillotson College	Austin	1877	Texas Christian University	Fort Worth	1873
Incarnate Word College	San Antonio	1881	Texas College	Tyler	1894
Jarvis Christian College	Hawkins	1938	Texas Lutheran College	Seguin	1891
Lamar University	Beaumont	1923	Texas Southern University	Houston	1947
LeTourneau College	Longview	1946	Texas Tech University	Lubbock	1923
Lubbock Christian College	Lubbock	1972	Texas Wesleyan College	Fort Worth	1891
Mary Hardin-Baylor,			Texas Woman's University	Denton	1901
University of	Belton	1845	Trinity University	San Antonio	1869
McMurry College	Abilene	1923	Wayland Baptist College	Plainview	1908
Midwestern State University	Wichita Falls	1922	West Texas State University	Canyon	1910
North Texas State University	Denton	1890	Wiley College	Marshall	1873

*For campuses and founding dates, see UNIVERSITIES AND COLLEGES (table).

TEXAS / A Visitor's Guide

Some of the most popular resort centers in Texas are on the Gulf Coast. Sandy beaches stretch along most of the coast, making it ideal for bathing and boating. Many deep-sea fishing enthusiasts sail from the coastal cities of Aransas Pass, Corpus Christi, and Galveston. They catch marlin, sailfish, and tarpon in the Gulf of Mexico. In northeast Texas, rolling timberlands provide many recreational areas. The region's rivers and lakes offer fine fishing. Central and west Texas are popular deer-hunting sites.

Visitor Center, Lyndon B. Johnson Space Center
Texas Highway Department

Fred H. Ragsdale, Publix
Mission San Jose

PLACES TO VISIT

Following are brief descriptions of some of Texas' many interesting places to visit.

The Alamo, a low, gray chapel of an old Spanish mission, stands in downtown San Antonio. A famous battle was fought there in 1836 during the Texas Revolution.

Aquarena Springs, at Spring Lake in San Marcos, features large springs that form the beginning of the San Marcos River. The attractions include glass-bottom boats, a re-created frontier village, and mission ruins.

Astroworld, in Houston, is one of the largest amusement and entertainment centers in the Southwest. Its attractions include a 300-foot (91-meter) observation tower. The Astrodome stadium is nearby.

Fair Park, in Dallas, covers about 200 acres (81 hectares) and is the home of the State Fair of Texas. The park includes the Cotton Bowl stadium, the Health and Science Museum, the State Music Hall, an amusement park, recreational areas, livestock exhibition buildings, an aquarium, the Hall of State, the Museum of Natural History, the Museum of Fine Arts, the Museum of Natural Resources, and the Dallas Garden Center.

La Villita, in San Antonio, is a restoration and reconstruction of a little city of early Texas days. The

Big Bend National Park
Fred H. Ragsdale, Publix

The Alamo, San Antonio
Texas Highway Dept.

State Fair of Texas
Big Tex, Symbol of the State Fair

Frente, Texas Highway Dept.
Rodeo at Stamford

community shows the influence of Spanish culture, and has a museum and arts-and-crafts shops.

Lyndon B. Johnson Library, in Austin, contains more than 30 million documents dealing with U.S. domestic policies and foreign relations. The library's collection also includes gifts that Johnson received while he was President.

Lyndon B. Johnson Space Center, in Houston, is the headquarters for all manned spacecraft projects of the National Aeronautics and Space Administration (NASA). A visitors' center displays spacecraft equipment and shows films about space flights and moon landings. See LYNDON B. JOHNSON SPACE CENTER.

Mission San Jose, in San Antonio, is considered the most beautiful Texas mission. Established in 1720, the church is one of the marvels of Spanish architecture in North America. The mission is a national historic site and a state park.

Padre Island National Seashore extends about 80 miles (130 kilometers) along the Texas coast on Padre Island. It includes dunes and beaches. Congress established the seashore in 1962.

San Jacinto Monument is 22 miles (35 kilometers) east of downtown Houston. It honors the Texans who fought in the Battle of San Jacinto, in which Texas won independence from Mexico. The memorial monument, one of the tallest in the world, rises 570 feet (174 meters).

A star that weighs 220 short tons (200 metric tons) rests at the top. The monument was built between 1936 and 1939 at a cost of $1½ million. The battleship *Texas*, a veteran of World Wars I and II, is moored near the monument in the Houston Ship Channel.

Six Flags Over Texas is an amusement park in Arlington. The park features the history of Texas under the flags of Spain, France, Mexico, the Republic of Texas, the Confederacy, and the United States.

Texas Memorial Museum, in Austin, has exhibits from Texas botany, geology, history, and zoology, as well as many historical records and documents.

National Parks and Forests. Texas has two national parks. Big Bend National Park lies within the great bend of the Rio Grande. Guadalupe Mountains National Park, authorized in 1966, lies in Culberson and Hudspeth counties. See BIG BEND NATIONAL PARK; GUADALUPE MOUNTAINS NATIONAL PARK.

The state's four national forests are in east Texas. Sabine National Forest is the largest. The other national forests are Angelina, Davy Crockett, and Sam Houston. For the area and chief features of each national forest, see NATIONAL FOREST (table).

State Parks. Texas began its state park system during the 1920's, and now has about 90 state parks. For information on the parks, write to Director, Texas State Parks and Wildlife Department, Austin, Tex. 78711.

ANNUAL EVENTS

Texas has more than 500 fairs, festivals, and expositions each year—more than any other state in the nation. The greatest event is probably the State Fair of Texas, held in Dallas for 16 days in October. Nearly 3 million persons visit the State Fair of Texas every year, making it the largest annual fair held in the United States.

Other annual events in Texas include the following.

January-March: Texas Citrus Festival in Mission (January or February); Southwestern Exposition and Fat Stock Show in Fort Worth (January or February); Charro Days Festival in Brownsville (February); San Antonio Stock Show and Rodeo (February); Houston Livestock Show and Rodeo Exposition (February-March); Texas Independence Day (March 2).

April-June: Fiesta San Antonio in San Antonio (April); Jefferson Historical Pilgrimage in Jefferson (April and May); Buccaneer Days in Corpus Christi (April or May); Texas State Arts and Crafts Fair in Kerrville (Memorial Day weekend); Watermelon Thump in Luling (June).

July-September: Texas Cowboy Reunion and Rodeo in Stamford (July); Aqua Festival in Austin (August); Texas Folklife Festival in San Antonio (August); Four States Fair in Texarkana (September); Rice Festival in Bay City (September or October).

October-December: East Texas Yamboree in Gilmer (October); Texas Rose Festival in Tyler (October); Cowboys' Christmas Ball in Anson (December); Southwestern Sun Carnival in El Paso (late December).

Grant Heilman

Cotton, One of Texas' Chief Crops, thrives in the north-central region. Texas raises more cotton than any other state.

TEXAS/The Land

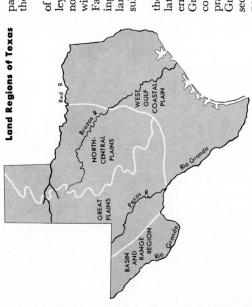

Land Regions of Texas

Land Regions. Texas has four main land regions. These are, from east to west: (1) the West Gulf Coastal Plain, (2) the North-Central Plains, (3) the Great Plains, and (4) the Basin and Range Region.

The West Gulf Coastal Plain of Texas is part of the fertile lowland that lies along the entire Gulf Coast of the United States. In Texas, the plain is from 150 to 350 miles (241 to 563 kilometers) wide. It ranges in elevation from sea level to about 300 feet (91 meters) above sea level. A subtropical region extends along a large

part of the coast. Hardwood trees and rice grow near the streams in this area of Texas.

The southernmost part of the coastal plain consists of the fertile valley of the lower Rio Grande. This valley is famous for its winter vegetables and fruits. The northeastern part of the plain is a rolling timberland, with thick forests of cypress, pine, and other trees. Farmers use the sandy soils of the plain for mixed farming, fruit growing, and cattle grazing. The region has large deposits of coal, natural gas, petroleum, salt, and sulfur.

The North-Central Plains lie west of the forest belt of the coastal plain. This region has the most thickly populated areas and the best farmland in Texas. The eastern part of the plains includes the fertile Black and Grand prairies. There, deep soils produce large crops of cotton and small grains. Hills break the surface of the prairies, and their elevation increases as they meet the Great Plains to the west. Thick grasses make the hilly section an important grazing region. It also has rich petroleum deposits.

The Great Plains reach westward from the North-Central Plains into New Mexico. They form part of the series of treeless plains that extends northward through the western United States into Canada. The Great Plains of Texas rise from an altitude of about 700 feet (213 meters) above sea level in the east to over 4,000 feet (1,200 meters) above sea level in the west. The Texas Panhandle makes up a major part of the plains. It is the northwestern part of the state that juts northward between Oklahoma and New Mexico. Much of this area is on a high plateau. The Panhandle produces more wheat than any other area of Texas. The plateau also has one of the richest petroleum and natural-gas fields

in the United States. Other minerals of the plains include building stones and salt.

The part of the Great Plains that lies along the border of Texas and New Mexico is called the *Llano Estacado* (Staked Plain) or the *High Plains*. This vast region is a high, level area where little rain falls and no trees grow. The area is so dry that people did not settle there until the late 1800's. Irrigation and dry-farming methods have made it one of the state's richest farming regions (see DRY FARMING).

The Edwards Plateau forms the southern part of the Great Plains. Herds of cattle, goats, and sheep feed on the mesquite shrubs and grasses that cover the plateau. A region of hills and streams lies east of the plateau.

The Basin and Range Region, commonly called the *Trans-Pecos Region,* makes up the westernmost part of Texas. It includes high, partly dry plains that are crossed by *spurs* (extensions) of the Rocky Mountains.

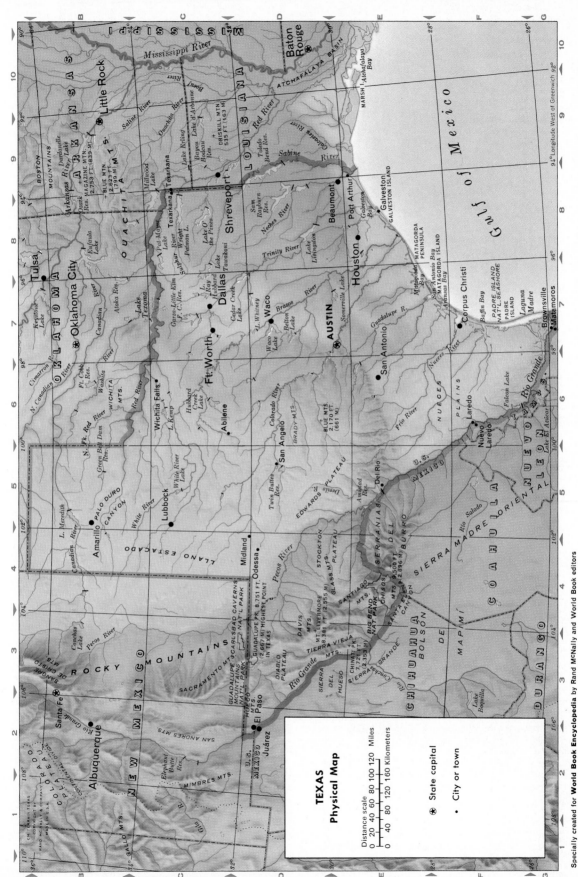

TEXAS
Physical Map

Distance scale

0 20 40 60 80 100 120 Miles

0 40 80 120 160 Kilometers

⊛ State capital

• City or town

Specially created for **World Book Encyclopedia** by Rand McNally and World Book editors

Cattle on the Great Plains thrive where mesquite and many kinds of grasses grow.

Guadalupe Mountains, in the Basin and Range Region of western Texas, include 8,751-foot (2,667-meter) Guadalupe Peak, the highest point in the state.

Padre Island Sand Dunes are at the edge of the coastal plain. The island, a sand bar 100 miles (160 kilometers) long, and others help protect the coast from damage by waves.

TEXAS

The peaks that do not form continuous ranges are called *lost mountains*. Farmers use the level sections mainly for raising cattle. Many beautiful mountain gorges are along the upper Rio Grande, which forms the region's western border. One of the most spectacular gorges is the Grand Canyon of Santa Elena, near Marathon. Minerals of the Basin and Range Region include copper, iron, lead, mercury, and silver.

Coastline. A series of narrow sand bars, enclosing shallow lagoons, lies along the Texas coast. These sand bars help protect the coast from ocean storms and tidal waves. Padre Island, the largest sand bar, is about 100 miles (160 kilometers) long. Other large sand bars include the islands of Galveston, Matagorda, and St. Joseph.

Twenty-eight man-made ports are located on the Texas coast. They were once filled by *silt* (particles of earth) left by the many streams emptying into the Gulf of Mexico. Only small vessels could use them. By removing the silt and deepening the harbors, engineers built 13 deepwater ports and 15 ports for barges and small ships.

The general coastline of Texas is 367 miles (591 kilometers) long along the Gulf. The tidal shoreline, including bays, offshore islands, and river mouths, is 3,359 miles (5,406 kilometers) long.

Mountains. Texas' highest mountains rise in the Basin and Range Region. The chief ranges include the Chisos, Davis, and Guadalupe mountains. The main peak of the Guadalupe Mountains, 8,751-foot (2,667-meter) Guadalupe Peak, is the highest point in Texas.

Rivers and Lakes. The Rio Grande, Texas' largest river, is one of the longest and most historic rivers in North America. For 1,241 miles (1,997 kilometers), it forms the boundary between the United States and Mexico (see RIO GRANDE). Other Texas rivers include the Brazos, Colorado, Guadalupe, Neches, Nueces, Pecos, Red, Sabine, San Antonio, and Trinity.

Most of the state's rivers flow southeastward into the Gulf of Mexico. But the Canadian River drains into the Arkansas River, and the Pecos flows into the Rio Grande. The Red River and its branches empty into the Mississippi River. In the dry western parts of Texas, many streams have water only after a rainstorm.

Texas has thousands of lakes that have been made or enlarged by man. Most of these lakes were created as part of the state's many programs for generating hydroelectric power, irrigating farmlands, and storing water. The largest man-made lake is Lake Texoma, which extends into Oklahoma. This 225-square-mile (583-square-kilometer) reservoir was created by Denison Dam, which crosses the Red River. Other man-made lakes include Falcon and Amistad reservoirs, which lie partly in Mexico, and Belton, Buchanan, Eagle Mountain, and Travis lakes.

Many salt-water lakes and ponds lie in the High Plains, in the Basin and Range Region, and near the mouth of the Rio Grande. The largest include La Sal Vieja, Sal del Rey, and Salt Lake.

TEXAS / Climate

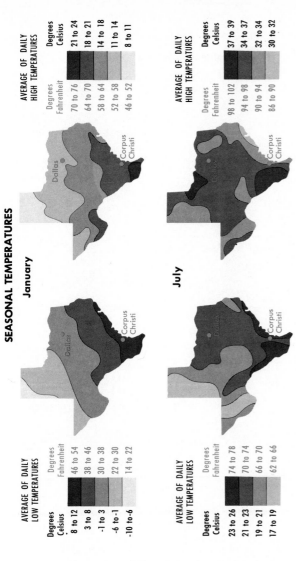

January

AVERAGE OF DAILY LOW TEMPERATURES

Degrees Celsius	Degrees Fahrenheit
8 to 12	46 to 54
3 to 8	38 to 46
-1 to 3	30 to 38
-6 to -1	22 to 30
-10 to -6	14 to 22

AVERAGE OF DAILY HIGH TEMPERATURES

Degrees Fahrenheit	Degrees Celsius
70 to 76	21 to 24
64 to 70	18 to 21
58 to 64	14 to 18
52 to 58	11 to 14
46 to 52	8 to 11

July

AVERAGE OF DAILY LOW TEMPERATURES

Degrees Celsius	Degrees Fahrenheit
23 to 26	74 to 78
21 to 23	70 to 74
19 to 21	66 to 70
17 to 19	62 to 66

AVERAGE OF DAILY HIGH TEMPERATURES

Degrees Fahrenheit	Degrees Celsius
98 to 102	37 to 39
94 to 98	34 to 37
90 to 94	32 to 34
86 to 90	30 to 32

AVERAGE YEARLY PRECIPITATION
(Rain, Melted Snow and Other Moisture)

Centimeters	Inches
122 to 163	48 to 64
81 to 122	32 to 48
41 to 81	16 to 32
0 to 41	0 to 16

```
0   100  200  300  400  Miles
0   200      400      600  Kilometers
```

WORLD BOOK maps

AVERAGE MONTHLY WEATHER

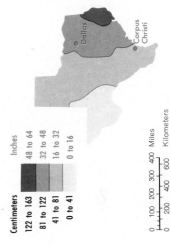

CORPUS CHRISTI

	Temperatures F°		C°		Days of Rain or Snow
	High	Low	High	Low	
JAN.	66	47	19	8	8
FEB.	70	51	21	11	7
MAR.	75	56	24	13	6
APR.	80	63	27	17	5
MAY	86	69	30	21	6
JUNE	90	74	32	23	5
JULY	93	75	34	24	4
AUG.	93	75	34	24	5
SEPT.	89	72	32	22	8
OCT.	84	65	29	18	6
NOV.	75	55	24	13	6
DEC.	68	49	20	9	6

DALLAS

	Temperatures F°		C°		Days of Rain or Snow
	High	Low	High	Low	
JAN.	55	36	13	2	8
FEB.	60	40	16	4	8
MAR.	68	47	20	8	7
APR.	77	56	25	13	9
MAY	84	64	29	18	9
JUNE	92	72	33	22	6
JULY	95	76	35	24	5
AUG.	96	76	36	24	5
SEPT.	89	69	32	21	6
OCT.	80	58	27	14	6
NOV.	66	45	19	7	7
DEC.	58	39	14	4	6

The climate of Texas ranges from subtropical in the lower Rio Grande Valley to moderately temperate in the northwest. The lower Rio Grande Valley is the warmest region of the state. It has an average January temperature of 60° F. (16° C), and an average July temperature of 85° F. (29° C). The coldest area is the Panhandle, in the northwest. It has an average January temperature of 35° F. (2° C), and an average July reading of 79° F. (26° C). Texas' lowest temperature, −23° F. (−31° C), was recorded at Tulia on Feb. 12, 1899, and at Seminole on Feb. 8, 1933. The record high was 120° F. (49° C), at Seymour on Aug. 12, 1936.

Along the Gulf of Mexico, the coast has a warm, damp climate. There, winds from the Gulf reduce the heat of summer and the cold of winter. Central Texas has a mild climate that makes it a popular resort area the year around. In the northeast, the weather is damp and cool. The northwest sometimes has long, cold winters. The west has a dry, cool climate.

Rainfall in Texas decreases from east to west. East Texas averages 46 inches (117 centimeters) of *precipitation* (rain, snow, sleet, and other forms of moisture) a year. Parts of west Texas average only 12 inches (30 centimeters) a year. Port Arthur, in the southeastern part of the state, gets about 45 more inches (114 centimeters) of rain a year than El Paso, in the far west. Along the coast, most of the rain falls in autumn. Northwest Texas gets most of its rain in spring.

Sleet, winds, and heavy rain from the north occasionally sweep across the state in the winter. Strong winds often blow throughout the Great Plains. During periods of drought, these winds carry away the soil. Snow seldom falls in the south-central and central regions. But the High Plains have an average of more than 24 inches (61 centimeters) of snow a year.

160a

A north-south line, drawn across Texas just west of Dallas, would divide the state into two great economic regions. The eastern section has most of the state's large, industrial cities. This section also includes cotton and rice farms, pine forests, and pecan groves. The western section, which also has cotton, forms part of the great oil, wheat, and cattle country of the Southwestern States.

Natural Resources. The great natural wealth of Texas includes large mineral deposits, especially petroleum and natural gas. In addition, the state has fertile soils, thick forests and grasses, and a plentiful supply of fish and game.

Minerals. Texas is one of the world's great petroleum storehouses. About 9 billion barrels of petroleum lie beneath the Texas plains. The state's known petroleum deposits account for about a third of the country's known supply. The Panhandle natural-gas field takes in almost all of five northwestern counties. It is one of the largest known natural-gas reservoirs in the world. The Panhandle also has the greatest known helium supply in the United States.

Other mineral resources of Texas include large sulfur deposits in the West Gulf Coastal Plain and the Basin and Range Region. Underground salt deposits occur in the Gulf Coastal Plain and in western Texas. Surface deposits are found in southern and western Texas. The state also has lignite coal deposits, totaling about 3 billion short tons (2.7 billion metric tons). Layers of rock containing beds of lignite cover about 75,000 square miles (194,000 square kilometers), extending from Laredo to Texarkana. Iron ore occurs in the northeast.

Limestone occurs in a broad belt extending from the Red River to the Rio Grande, and across north-central Texas. Gypsum deposits lie in the North-Central Plains and the Basin and Range Region. Gravel and silica sand are plentiful in many areas of Texas. The largest asphalt deposits in the state are near Uvalde. Potash occurs in a great bed of rock salt in the Basin and Range Region. Mercury, molybdenum, titanium, tungsten, and uranium are found in the southwest part of the state. Texas also has deposits of basalt, fluorspar, fuller's earth and other clays, granite, lead, marble, mica, sandstone, tin, and zinc.

Soil. Texas has about 700 types of soil, in which farmers can grow a great variety of crops. A narrow belt along the Gulf Coast has marshy soils, mixed with clays. Rich soils lie along the banks of rivers throughout the state. Large sections of the interior of the West Gulf Coastal Plain have soils composed of sands and clays. Rich, heavy, blackland clays make up a belt in the eastern interior of the plain. The prairie regions of the North-Central Plains have soils of clays, limestone, and sands. The Great Plains include clays, clay loam, and sandy loam soils. The Basin and Range Region has rough, stony mountain soils.

Forests cover about 23 million acres (9.3 million hectares), or about 14 per cent of the state. Commercially valuable forests, mostly pines and hardwoods, grow on about 12½ million acres (5.1 million hectares). Other forests cover about 10½ million acres (4.3 million hec-

Production of Goods in Texas

Total annual value of goods produced—$69,775,385,000

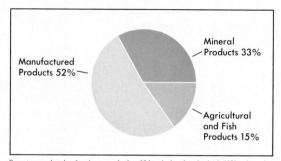

Percentages are based on farm income and value of fish and mineral production in 1979 and on value added by manufacture in 1978. Fish products are less than 1 per cent.

Sources: U.S. government publications, 1980-1981.

Employment in Texas

Total number of persons employed—6,084,800

		Number of Employees
Wholesale & Retail Trade	𝕏𝕏𝕏𝕏𝕏𝕏𝕏𝕏𝕏𝕏	1,429,300
Manufacturing	𝕏𝕏𝕏𝕏𝕏𝕏𝕏𝕏	1,048,900
Community, Social, & Personal Services	𝕏𝕏𝕏𝕏𝕏𝕏𝕏	1,017,600
Government	𝕏𝕏𝕏𝕏𝕏𝕏𝕏	998,100
Construction	𝕏𝕏𝕏	428,600
Transportation & Public Utilities	𝕏𝕏𝕏	366,000
Finance, Insurance, & Real Estate	𝕏𝕏𝕏	336,600
Mining	𝕏𝕏	236,700
Agriculture	𝕏𝕏	223,000

Sources: *Employment and Earnings*, May 1981, U.S. Bureau of Labor Statistics; *Farm Labor*, February 1981, U.S. Department of Agriculture. Figures are for 1980.

tares). More than 225 kinds of trees grow in Texas. The most valuable trees commercially are gums, oaks, and pines. Other common Texas trees include cat's-claw, cypress, elm, hackberry, juniper, mesquite, mountain cedar, native pecan, and redberry.

Plant and Animal Life. Texas plant life includes more than 500 kinds of grasses, such as bluestem, buffalo grass, curly mesquite, grama, and side oats. More than 4,000 kinds of wild flowers grow in the state. They include asters, daisies, goldenrod, and sunflowers. The bluebonnet, the official state flower, blooms in erect clusters of blue, bonnet-shaped flowers with white-streaked upper petals. Several varieties of cactuses grow in the dry Basin and Range Region.

Much wildlife is found in the eastern forests and on the western plains. Landowners in these regions earn millions of dollars a year selling hunting leases to sportsmen. Deer, pronghorn, and wild turkeys are the chief game animals of the state. The most common freshwater fish include bass, catfish, and sunfish. Crabs, menhaden, oysters, and shrimp thrive in the Gulf of Mexico.

Manufacturing accounts for about 52 per cent of the value of goods produced in Texas. Goods manufactured there have a *value added by manufacture* of about $36 billion a year. This figure represents the value created in products by Texas' industries, not counting such costs as materials, supplies, and fuel. This income makes Texas a leader among the states in manufacturing. Texas' chief manufactured products, in order of importance, are: (1) chemicals, (2) nonelectric machinery, (3) petroleum and coal products, and (4) food products.

Chemicals have an annual value added of about $7\frac{3}{4}$ billion and account for about a fifth of the manufacturing income. Texas ranks first among the states as a chemical manufacturer. Important chemical products include benzene, ethylene, fertilizers, propylene, and sulfuric acid. The Texas chemical industry is located chiefly in cities along the Gulf Coast.

Nonelectric Machinery has an annual value added of about $5 billion. It accounts for about a seventh of the state's manufacturing income. The industry's major products include construction machinery, oil-field machinery, and refrigeration and heating machinery. The industry also produces pumps and pumping equipment and farm machinery. Chief centers of production include the Dallas-Fort Worth area, Houston, Lubbock, Odessa, and San Antonio.

Petroleum and Coal Products have a value added of about $4 billion a year. Texas stands first among the states in oil refining. About 80 petroleum refineries operate throughout the state. The largest are along the Gulf Coast in Baytown, Beaumont, Houston, Port Arthur, and other port cities.

Food Products have a value added of about $3\frac{1}{2}$ billion yearly. Beverages are the leading food product made in Texas. Meat products rank second. The Panhandle-Southern High Plains area is a center of the state's meat-packing industry, with large plants in Friona, Hereford, and Plainview. Texas is a leading state in the cleaning and polishing of rice. Other food products that are processed in Texas include bakery products, dairy products, and grain mill products, such as flour, livestock feed, and pet food.

Other Leading Industries in Texas, in order of value, produce fabricated metal products; electric machinery and equipment; transportation equipment; primary metals; stone, clay, and glass products; and printed materials. Other important products made in Texas include clothing, instruments, lumber and wood products, paper products, and rubber and plastics products.

Mining. Texas leads the states in value of mineral production, largely because of oil. Mining accounts for about 33 per cent of the value of goods produced in Texas, or about $23 billion a year.

Petroleum is the most valuable Texas mineral, earning about $12\frac{3}{4}$ billion a year. The state produces about 1 billion barrels of crude oil annually and ranks first among the states in oil production. Its oil wells account for about one-third of the nation's oil production.

Drillers first discovered oil in Texas near Nacogdoches in 1866. Large-scale production began with the opening of the Spindletop field near Beaumont in 1901. For several years, the Spindletop and other Gulf Coast fields formed the center of the Texas oil industry. Later, large fields were opened in the Panhandle, the Pecos Valley, and central, east, and north Texas. The greatest

oil discovery in Texas occurred in 1930, when drillers brought in the famous East Texas oil field. This field was for a time the largest in the world.

Natural Gas, the second most valuable Texas mineral, has an annual value of about $8\frac{3}{4}$ billion. About two-fifths of all the natural gas produced in the United States comes from Texas. The state supplies about $7\frac{1}{4}$ trillion cubic feet (205 billion cubic meters) a year. Gas and natural gas liquids occur in all the oil-producing regions. Pipelines carry gas from Texas as far as Chicago and into Mexico.

Other Minerals. Texas furnishes about half the country's supply of sulfur and is second among the states in salt production. Texas provides all the natural graphite and about 90 per cent of the magnesium produced in the United States. Natural gasoline for fuel is made from Texas oil and gas. Helium occurs mixed with the natural gas found in the Panhandle. Valuable quantities of asphalt, fluorspar, fuller's earth and other clays, granite, gypsum, lignite coal, limestone, marble, sand and gravel, and sandstone also come from Texas. The state also produces gemstones, gold, iron ore, magnesium chloride, silver, sodium sulfate, talc, and zinc.

Agriculture. Texas, with a yearly farm income of about $10 billion, is a leading agricultural state. This figure is about 15 per cent of the value of all goods produced there. Texas has about 159,000 farms, more than

Texaco, Inc.

Oil Riggers place a drill to tap one of the rich deposits that make Texas the leading petroleum-producing state.

any other state. They average about 870 acres (352 hectares) in size. Texas farms cover about 138 million acres (56 million hectares), the greatest farming acreage of any state in the country. Of this total, about 7 million acres (3 million hectares) are irrigated. Most of the irrigated farmlands lie in the Rio Grande and Pecos valleys, near Lubbock, and along the coast.

Beef Cattle are Texas' largest source of farm income, providing about $4¾ billion a year. Texas winters are usually so mild that cattle can graze outdoors all year around. As a result, Texans can raise cattle more cheaply than northern farmers. Texas leads the states in number of beef cattle, with about 13 million.

The United States range-cattle industry began in Texas with long-horned cattle. The ancestors of these *Texas Longhorns* had been brought by early Spaniards and later settlers. After the Civil War, cattlemen drove cattle to Kansas and Missouri for shipment by railroad to northern and eastern markets. The most widely used cattle trails were the Chisholm Trail and the Western Trail. The Chisholm Trail ran from the Mexican border to Abilene, Kans. The Western Trail connected west Texas and Dodge City, Kans. The colorful cattle-drive period ended during the 1880's with the coming of railroads and the fencing of public lands.

Purebred cattle, such as the Aberdeen-Angus, Hereford, and Shorthorn breeds, gradually replaced the Longhorns. During the early 1900's, the white-faced Herefords became the most popular breed in Texas. Ranchers bred Shorthorns with Brahman cattle from India and produced a breed unaffected by heat and insects. This breed, the Santa Gertrudis, was the first beef cattle variety developed in the United States.

Cotton is Texas' leading crop and the second-ranking farm product. It has an annual value of about $1¼ billion. More cotton grows in Texas than in any other state. It thrives best on the coastal plain and on the central and northern prairies. Irrigated cotton grows in the Rio Grande Valley. Jared Groce, who is sometimes called the *Father of Texas Agriculture*, and other early settlers introduced commercial cotton growing. They planted cotton in the fertile valley of the Brazos River during the early 1820's. Today, Texas farmers produce about 5½ million bales of cotton a year. These bales weigh a total of about 2⅔ billion pounds (1.2 billion kilograms).

Sorghum Grain is the second most valuable crop, with an annual value of about $416 million. Texas farmers produce 243 million bushels of sorghum grain a year. Texas and Kansas rank as the leading states in sorghum grain production. Sorghum grain can be raised on the dry plains and prairies because it can survive drought. It is used chiefly for livestock feed.

Poultry and Dairy Products. Texas ranks high in the production of *broilers* (chickens from 9 to 12 weeks old), eggs, and turkeys. The state has about 405,000 head of dairy cattle.

Other Crops. Texas stands high among the states in the production of rice, which thrives along the Gulf Coast. Wheat is also an important crop. Other chief crops in the state include corn, cottonseed, hay, oats, peanuts, soybeans, sugar beets, and sugar cane.

Vegetables. Texas is an important producer of vegetables. Farmers grow large crops in the lower Rio Grande Valley and around Corpus Christi, Jacksonville, Laredo, San Antonio, and Tyler. The chief truck crops include cabbage, cantaloupes, carrots, cucumbers, lettuce, onions, peppers, potatoes, and watermelons (see TRUCK FARMING).

Fruits. Irrigation has made the lower Rio Grande Valley one of the country's finest fruit belts. Trainloads of grapefruit, oranges, and other citrus fruits travel from valley orchards to northern markets. Texas ranks high in the production of oranges and grapefruit. Farmers in the state also grow many peaches. Other fruits include apples, plums, and strawberries. Blackberries come from east Texas.

Nuts and Honey. Texas is a leader in pecan and peanut production. Pecan trees grow along streams throughout most of the state, except in the Great Plains and the Basin and Range Region. Many farmers have large groves of various kinds of pecan trees. Farms in the eastern and central areas produce excellent crops of peanuts. Many Texas farmers also keep colonies of bees, which produce much honey.

Horses, Sheep, and Other Livestock. Texas ranchers raise saddle and race horses, cow ponies, polo ponies, and work horses. Texas raises more sheep than any other state—about 2,400,000 a year. It also produces the most wool—about 19 million pounds (8.6 million kilograms) yearly. Almost all the mohair clipped in the United States comes from Texas goats. Most of them belong to the Angora breed. Most of the goats and sheep graze on the rich grasses of the Edwards Plateau. Farmers throughout the state raise hogs.

Fishing Industry. Texas has an annual fish catch valued at about $160 million. It is a leader among the states in shrimp production. The average yearly catch of shrimp in Texas totals about 75 million pounds (34 million kilograms). The fish catch also includes black drum, crabs, flounder, oysters, red snapper, red drum, and sea trout.

Electric Power. Texas ranks first in the nation in electric power production. The state has about 144 electric-power plants and stations. About 80 per cent of the electric power is produced by plants that burn gas. Most of the rest is produced by plants that burn coal or oil. Less than 1 per cent is produced by a few hydroelectric stations.

Transportation. Several famous trails crossed the Texas wilderness in the early days. During the period of Spanish rule, many of these trails served as transportation routes for missionaries and explorers in the Southwest.

Aviation. About 30 airlines serve Texas, and the state has about 1,300 airports. The largest serve Dallas-Fort Worth and Houston. The airports at Houston and Brownsville are major stops on air routes between the United States and Latin America.

Railroads in Texas operate on about 13,300 miles (21,400 kilometers) of track, more than in any other state. About 30 rail lines provide freight service in the state, and passenger trains link about 20 Texas cities to other cities.

Roads and Highways. Texas has about 260,000 miles (418,000 kilometers) of roads and highways, about 80 per cent of which are surfaced. About 3,000 miles (4,800

FARM, MINERAL, AND FOREST PRODUCTS

This map shows the areas where the state's leading farm, mineral, and forest products are produced. The major urban areas (shown in red) are the state's important manufacturing centers.

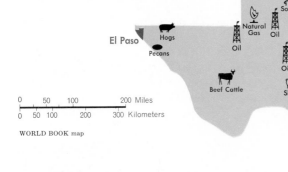

0   50   100   200 Miles
0 50 100   200   300 Kilometers

WORLD BOOK map

kilometers) of the interstate highway system cross Texas. Seven United States highways in the state connect with roads in Mexico.

Shipping. Texas has 15 deepwater ports along the Gulf of Mexico. Houston is the busiest port. It also is one of the chief cotton-shipping centers in the country. The other deepwater ports are Bay City, Beaumont, Brownsville, Corpus Christi, Freeport, Galveston, Harbor Island, Orange, Point Comfort, Port Arthur, Port Isabel, Port Mansfield, Sabine Pass, and Texas City. Fifteen shallow ports also lie along the coast. These shallow ports handle barges, fishing vessels, and other shallow-draft vessels.

Waterways. The Gulf Intracoastal Waterway runs the length of the Texas coast from Brownsville to Orange. Boats from the state's 15 shallow ports use the waterway, which connects with the Mississippi River at New Orleans. See GULF INTRACOASTAL WATERWAY.

Communication. José Álvarez de Toledo, a Mexican, printed Texas' first newspaper, *Gaceta de Texas*, in Nacogdoches in 1813. Today, Texas publishers issue about 110 daily newspapers and over 500 weeklies. Newspapers with the largest circulations include the *Dallas News*, *Dallas Times Herald*, *Fort Worth Star-Telegram*, *Houston Chronicle*, *Houston Post*, *San Antonio Express*, and *San Antonio Light*. Texas publishers also issue about 465 magazines. The *Texas Almanac*, containing information about Texas, has been published since 1857.

Texas' first radio station, WRR, began in Dallas in 1920. The first television station, WBAP-TV (now KXAS-TV), started in Fort Worth in 1948. Texas has about 515 radio stations. It also has about 60 TV stations.

Port of Houston

Port of Houston ranks as one of the world's leading seaports although it lies 51 miles (82 kilometers) from the Gulf of Mexico. Ocean vessels use the Houston Ship Channel to reach the busy port.

HISTORIC TEXAS

The First Capitol of the Republic of Texas stood at Washington-on-the-Brazos, where Texas declared its independence from Mexico in 1836.

The Lone Star has been the symbol of Texas since the days of the early pioneers.

Texas Longhorns were driven northward on the Chisholm Trail to Kansas, from 1867 to about 1885.

Camels were brought into Texas in 1856 to transport supplies to army posts in desert areas of the Southwest.

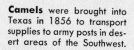

Independent Republic. Texas, Hawaii, and Vermont are the only states that were once independent republics.

Dallas

President Kennedy was assassinated in Dallas on Nov. 22, 1963.

AUSTIN ★

The Lucas Well at Spindletop ran wild for nine days when it began operating in 1901.

Coronado marched across western Texas in 1541 in his famous search for the fabled Seven Cities of Cibola.

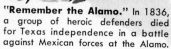
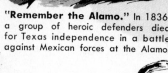

"Remember the Alamo." In 1836, a group of heroic defenders died for Texas independence in a battle against Mexican forces at the Alamo.

King Ranch Brand

The King Ranch is the largest ranch in Texas. It covers 823,403 acres (333,219 hectares), an area about the size of Rhode Island. Captain Richard King started the ranch in 1853.

Lyndon B. Johnson
born near Stonewall

Dwight D. Eisenhower
born in Denison

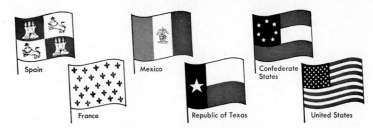

Six Flags Have Flown Over Texas

Spain   Mexico   Confederate States

France   Republic of Texas   United States

TEXAS/*History*

Indian Days. When the first Europeans arrived, about 30,000 Indians lived in what is now Texas. The largest group was the Caddo Indians, in the eastern part of the region. These Indians lived in permanent homes and were farmers. Some of the Caddo tribes, including the Nacogdoches, Nasoni, and Neche, formed a league called the *Hasinai Confederacy.* The Arkokisa, Attacapa, Karankawa, and other smaller tribes lived along the coast. The Coahuiltecan Indians occupied

---
IMPORTANT DATES IN TEXAS

1519 Alonso Álvarez de Piñeda of Spain mapped the Texas coast.

1528 Álvar Núñez Cabeza de Vaca and three other survivors of a shipwrecked Spanish expedition landed on the Texas coast and later explored parts of the region.

1541 Francisco Vásquez de Coronado traveled across part of west Texas.

1542 Hernando de Soto's expedition explored part of northeast Texas.

1682 Spanish missionaries built the first two missions in Texas, near present-day El Paso.

1685 Robert Cavelier, Sieur de la Salle, founded Fort Saint Louis, a French settlement, on the Texas coast.

1690 A Franciscan friar established the first mission in east Texas.

1718 The Spaniards established a mission and a fort on the site of present-day San Antonio.

1821 Texas became part of the new Empire of Mexico. The first colony of Americans settled in Texas under the sponsorship of Stephen F. Austin.

1835 The Texas Revolution began.

1836 Texas declared its independence from Mexico. The Alamo fell to Mexican forces. Sam Houston defeated the Mexicans in the Battle of San Jacinto. Texas became the independent Republic of Texas.

1845 Texas became the 28th state on December 29.

1861 Texas seceded from the Union and joined the Confederate States of America.

1870 Congress readmitted Texas to the Union.

1901 Oilmen discovered the great Spindletop field.

1925 Texas became the second state to have a woman governor—Mrs. Miriam A. Ferguson.

1936 The Texas Centennial Exposition celebrated a hundred years of independence.

1947 A ship explosion in Texas City harbor killed about 500 persons and injured about 3,000.

1953 Congress restored Texas tidelands to the state.

1957 Texas' first toll highway opened, connecting Dallas and Fort Worth.

1962 Construction began on the Manned Spacecraft Center at Houston.

1963 President John F. Kennedy was assassinated in Dallas. Lyndon B. Johnson of Texas was sworn in as the 36th President at Dallas Love Field Airport.

1964 The Manned Spacecraft Center near Houston became the permanent headquarters of the U.S. astronauts.

1973 The Manned Spacecraft Center was renamed the Lyndon B. Johnson Space Center.

---

south Texas. Warlike Lipan Apaches lived on the Edwards Plateau in the west. Comanche and Tonkawa Indians roamed the North-Central Plains.

Spanish Exploration. Spanish adventurers, for "glory, God, and gold," began exploring Texas during the early 1500's. In 1519, the Spanish governor of Jamaica sent Alonso Álvarez de Piñeda to explore the Gulf Coast from Florida to Mexico. Piñeda mapped the coastline. Most historians believe he and his followers were the first white men in Texas. In 1528, a Spanish expedition that planned to explore the southern United States was shipwrecked on the Texas coast. Álvar Núñez Cabeza de Vaca, a leader of the expedition, and three companions traveled among the Indians. For eight years, they gradually made their way westward. They finally reached a Spanish settlement in Mexico near the Pacific Coast. The men brought to Mexico City stories of cities of great wealth that supposedly lay north of their westward route.

The Spaniards sent many expeditions to look for these golden cities, called the *Seven Cities of Cibola.* In 1540, Francisco Vásquez de Coronado led a party north from Mexico. He passed through Texas in 1541. But Coronado found only the grass-house villages of the Plains Indians and the adobe huts of the Pueblo Indians. In 1542, some members of an expedition originally led by Hernando de Soto entered northeast Texas after their leader died. They reached the vicinity of present-day Texarkana. Spain based its claims to Texas on these and other explorations, and on missions that Spanish friars built later. Franciscan missionaries built Texas' first two missions in 1682, near the present site of El Paso.

French Exploration in Texas began in 1685. That year, Robert Cavelier, Sieur de la Salle, landed at Matagorda Bay. He had intended to establish a colony at the mouth of the Mississippi River. Perhaps a storm on the Gulf of Mexico drove him to Texas. La Salle established a colony, Fort Saint Louis, inland, and made expeditions westward in search of gold and silver. One of La Salle's men killed him in a quarrel in 1687. Disease and Indians killed off the rest, and Fort Saint Louis was destroyed by the Indians.

La Salle's explorations in Texas alarmed the Spaniards. In 1689, an expedition led by Alonso de León set out from Mexico to destroy Fort Saint Louis. The party found the ruins of the fort and then traveled eastward as far as the Neches River. In 1690, a Franciscan friar with De León's expedition established the first mission in east Texas, San Francisco de los Tejas. It stood near the present-day town of Weches.

The Mission Period. By 1731, Spain had sent more than 90 expeditions into what is now Texas. Spain also had established missions throughout central, east, and southwest Texas. The Spaniards built forts near some

Social Life in Early Texas reflected the culture of Spain and Mexico. This painting by Theodore Gentilz shows pioneers dancing the fandango, a lively Spanish dance.

missions to protect them from Indians. In 1718, they built the fort of San Antonio de Bexar to guard the mission of San Antonio de Valero. This mission and fort stood on the site of present-day San Antonio. They were about halfway between the Spanish missions in east Texas and the Spanish *presidios* (forts) in northern Mexico. In 1772, San Antonio became the seat of Spanish government in Texas. Spanish colonization of Texas proceeded slowly. The region had only about 7,000 white settlers in 1793, after more than a hundred years of missionary effort.

President Thomas Jefferson of the United States purchased the Louisiana Territory from France in 1803. The United States then claimed all territory as far south as the Rio Grande on the basis of earlier French claims. In 1819, a treaty fixed the southwestern boundaries of the Louisiana Territory at the Sabine and Red rivers.

Mexico broke away from Spain in 1821, and Texas became part of the new Empire of Mexico. Mexico became a republic in 1824.

American Settlement. In 1820, Moses Austin, a Missouri banker, asked Spanish officials in San Antonio to let him establish a colony of Americans in Texas. The Spanish government granted his request, but Austin died before he could organize the colony. His son, Stephen F. Austin, carried out the plan and brought 300 families to Texas. In 1821, Austin's group made its first settlements at Washington-on-the-Brazos and Columbus in southeast Texas. Austin arrived later and officially established the colony in 1822. It grew rapidly. In 1823, Austin laid out San Felipe de Austin in present-day Austin County as the colony's seat of government. Mexico soon issued new land grants to Austin, and he extended the boundaries of his colony.

Other Americans also received land grants from Mexico to establish colonies. The Mexicans called these American colonizers *empresarios*. The empresarios founded many colonies in Texas during the 1820's. From 1821 to 1836, the number of settlers grew to between 25,000 and 30,000. Almost all were Americans.

Mexican officials became alarmed by the increasing number of settlers from the United States. In 1830, they halted American immigration to Texas. From then on, relations between the American settlers and Mexican officials grew steadily worse. In 1834, General Antonio López de Santa Anna, a Mexican politician and soldier, overthrew Mexico's constitutional government and made himself dictator. The next year, the American colonists in Texas revolted against Mexico.

The Texas Revolution. After a few battles with Mexican soldiers, Texas leaders met at San Felipe de Austin on Nov. 3, 1835. They organized a temporary government. Texas troops, led by Colonel Benjamin Milam, attacked San Antonio. The Mexicans there surrendered on December 11. The fall of San Antonio alarmed Santa Anna. He assembled a large army and marched on San Antonio. Texan rebels in the city withdrew behind the walls of the Alamo, the chapel of an old Spanish mission. Santa Anna's forces attacked the Alamo from Feb. 23 to March 6, 1836, when it finally fell. All its defenders, including Jim Bowie, Davy Crockett, and William B. Travis, were killed in the battle. Texas leaders met at Washington-on-the-Brazos on March 2. They issued a declaration of independence from Mexico. The Texans chose David G. Burnet as temporary president and Sam Houston as commander of the army. See ALAMO.

After the fall of the Alamo, Santa Anna moved swiftly to put down the revolution. He ordered more than 330 Texas prisoners shot to death at Goliad on March 27. But the Texans continued to fight, inspired by the battle cries of "Remember the Alamo" and "Remember Goliad." In April, after a long retreat, the smaller army of Sam Houston camped near Santa Anna's forces. On April 21, the Texans took the overconfident Mexicans by surprise. They captured Santa Anna and crushed his army in the Battle of San Jacinto. The victory ended the war, and guaranteed Texas independence. See SAN JACINTO, BATTLE OF.

The Republic of Texas faced serious problems. It had no money, and raiding Indians and Mexicans threatened its people. In the new republic's first national election, Texans chose Sam Houston as president. They also voted to join the United States. But the great powers of Europe, especially France and Great Britain, wanted Texas to remain independent. They feared that the United States would gain control of the Southwest. The Southern States wanted Texas to join the Union. But the North objected because Texas allowed slavery.

During Texas' 10 years as an independent republic, its population increased rapidly. Most of the people farmed for a living. In 1839, Texans passed the first homestead exemption act, which many states later adopted. This law prevented farms from being seized for payment of debts.

Statehood and Early Progress. In 1844, the U.S. Senate defeated a treaty to annex Texas to the United States. The treaty failed to win the approval of two-thirds of the senators voting. Texas finally joined the Union on Dec. 29, 1845. It became the 28th state by a joint resolution of both houses of Congress. Passage of the resolution required the votes of only a majority of the members present in each house.

The statehood agreement provided that Texas could keep its public lands and that it would pay its own public debts. The federal government would settle all boundary disputes with other countries. J. Pinckney Henderson, a Democrat, became the first governor of the state.

After Texas joined the Union, Mexico ended diplomatic relations with the United States. Disputes arose over the boundary between Texas and Mexico. The Mexican War between the United States and Mexico began in 1846. Mexico surrendered in 1848. In the Treaty of Guadalupe Hidalgo, Mexico gave up all claims to Texas and other southwestern lands. See GUADALUPE HIDALGO, TREATY OF; MEXICAN WAR.

Texas claimed much of the southwestern region that Mexico turned over to the United States. In 1850, the federal government agreed to pay the state $10,000,000 for its claims. Texas used part of this money to pay its public debts. Settlers continued to flock to the state. During the 1850's, pioneers pushed the frontier westward, and Texas organized 89 new counties. Northeast Texas and the region east of Waco and Fort Worth attracted the largest number of settlers.

The Civil War and Reconstruction. Texas *seceded* (withdrew) from the Union and joined the Confederate States of America in March, 1861. The state seceded in spite of strong Union feeling in some sections of Texas. Governor Sam Houston refused to take an oath to support the constitution of the Confederate States. As a result, he was put out of office. More than 50,000 Texans fought on the side of the Confederacy during the Civil War (1861-1865). Texas also furnished the Confederacy with great amounts of supplies. The Union navy blockaded the Texas coast and occupied Galveston for a short time. The last battle of the Civil War was fought at Palmito Hill, near the mouth of the Rio Grande, on May 13, 1865. The soldiers had not heard that the war had ended on April 9.

After the war, Northern sympathizers called *Radicals* rose to power in Texas state politics. Lawlessness gripped the state as racial violence broke out and the Ku-Klux Klan became powerful (see KU-KLUX KLAN). During the Reconstruction period, Texas was ruled by a military government, an appointed governor, and three governors elected by the Radicals. Congress readmitted Texas to the Union on March 30, 1870. Reconstruction ended in the state with the inauguration of Democratic Governor Richard Coke in 1874. See RECONSTRUCTION.

Conquering the Frontier. In the mid-1860's, Texans began cattle drives to railroad centers in Kansas and Missouri. The cattle drives continued during the 1870's and 1880's. Indian raids slowed the settlement of the western part of the state. The tribes were subdued by 1880, and cattlemen began to occupy the Panhandle and the western plains. Railroads crossed Texas in the 1880's, ending the cattle drives and aiding settlement. Pioneers followed the railroads west and began farming the western regions of the state. The Texas Rangers, organized in 1835, helped protect the far western settlers from bandits such as Sam Bass. During the 1890's, the state legislature passed various business-reform laws, preventing some price and trade abuses by the railroads and other large corporations.

The Early 1900's. Between 1900 and 1920, Texas increased its railroad mileage and built a road system. The state also developed irrigation and farming on land previously used for raising livestock.

Texas Rangers patrolled the frontiers, protecting the pioneers from attacks by hostile Indians and bandits.

Tom Lea, courtesy King Ranch

The state's great oil and gas industries began in 1901 with the discovery of the Spindletop oil field near Beaumont. To develop the mineral resources, Texans built great refineries and other manufacturing plants. They deepened coastal harbors to help ship their oil and other products. The annual value of manufactured goods more than doubled between 1900 and 1910. Between 1900 and 1920, many Texans became city workers, and the number of cities and towns doubled. By 1920, a third of the people lived in cities. After the United States entered World War I in 1917, the government set up many military training camps in Texas.

During the early 1920's, Governor Pat M. Neff made important improvements in education and prisons. He also led the movement for a state park system. In 1925, Texas became the second state, after Wyoming, to have a woman governor. She was Mrs. Miriam A. "Ma" Ferguson. Her husband, James E. Ferguson, had previously been governor.

Great highway construction took place in Texas during the 1920's and 1930's. New legislation helped ease hardships during the depression and droughts of the 1930's. This legislation included the establishment of old-age pensions and special relief programs. In 1936, the Texas Centennial Exposition at Dallas celebrated a hundred years of independence. In 1937, the Greater Texas and Pan American Exposition was held in Dallas. It aimed at encouraging trade with other nations of the Western Hemisphere.

The Mid-1900's. During World War II (1939-1945), more than a million U.S. servicemen trained in Texas military camps. Lieutenant Audie Murphy of Farmersville won fame as the most decorated U.S. soldier of World War II.

After the war, manufacturing expanded rapidly in

The Lyndon B. Johnson Space Center, at Houston, serves as headquarters for government projects for manned space travel.

Texas. The aerospace, chemical, and electronics industries built many facilities in the state. Thousands of Texans moved from rural areas to cities to find jobs in new factories, and the state began to shift from a rural, farm economy to an urban, industrial economy.

Texas suffered one of its greatest disasters on April 16, 1947, when a French ship loaded with chemicals blew

The Governors of Texas

	Party	Term
J. Pinckney Henderson	Democratic	1846-1847
George T. Wood	Democratic	1847-1849
P. Hansborough Bell	Democratic	1849-1853
Elisha M. Pease	Democratic	1853-1857
Hardin R. Runnels	Democratic	1857-1859
Sam Houston	Independent	1859-1861
Francis R. Lubbock	Democratic	1861-1863
Pendleton Murrah	Democratic	1863-1865
Under Federal Military Rule		1865
Andrew J. Hamilton	Conservative	1865-1866
James W. Throckmorton	Conservative	1866-1867
Elisha M. Pease	Republican	1867-1869
Under Federal Military Rule		1869-1870
Edmund J. Davis	Republican	1870-1874
Richard Coke	Democratic	1874-1876
Richard B. Hubbard	Democratic	1876-1879
Oran M. Roberts	Democratic	1879-1883
John Ireland	Democratic	1883-1887
Lawrence S. Ross	Democratic	1887-1891
James S. Hogg	Democratic	1891-1895
Charles A. Culberson	Democratic	1895-1899
Joseph D. Sayers	Democratic	1899-1903
S. W. T. Lanham	Democratic	1903-1907
Thomas M. Campbell	Democratic	1907-1911
Oscar B. Colquitt	Democratic	1911-1915
James E. Ferguson	Democratic	1915-1917
William P. Hobby	Democratic	1917-1921
Pat M. Neff	Democratic	1921-1925
Miriam A. Ferguson	Democratic	1925-1927
Dan Moody	Democratic	1927-1931
Ross Sterling	Democratic	1931-1933
Miriam A. Ferguson	Democratic	1933-1935
James V. Allred	Democratic	1935-1939
W. Lee O'Daniel	Democratic	1939-1941
Coke R. Stevenson	Democratic	1941-1947
Beauford H. Jester	Democratic	1947-1949
Allan Shivers	Democratic	1949-1957
Price Daniel	Democratic	1957-1963
John B. Connally	Democratic	1963-1969
Preston Smith	Democratic	1969-1973
Dolph Briscoe	Democratic	1973-1979
William P. Clements	Republican	1979-1983
Mark White	Democratic	1983-

up in the harbor at Texas City. The explosion killed about 500 persons, injured about 3,000, and caused about $70 million in damage.

In 1950, the Supreme Court of the United States ruled that Texas had lost ownership of its oil-rich *tidelands* (submerged offshore lands) when it entered the Union in 1845. The ruling meant that the U.S. government owned the oil beneath the tidewaters. After a dispute in Congress, President Dwight D. Eisenhower signed a bill in 1953 that restored the tidelands to Texas.

Like many other states, Texas faced racial problems in the 1950's and 1960's. The state had separate public schools for blacks and whites. In 1954, the U.S. Supreme Court ruled that compulsory segregation in public schools was unconstitutional. By the late 1960's, most school districts in Texas had been integrated.

Texas took a leading role in the U.S. space program during the 1960's. In 1962, the National Aeronautics and Space Administration (NASA) began building a Manned Spacecraft Center near Houston. The center became the headquarters of the U.S. piloted spacecraft program in 1964. In 1969, scientists and engineers at the center directed the Apollo 11 flight, in which astronauts made the first landing on the moon.

Texas also gained in national political importance during the 1960's. Rapid population growth made it a key state in national elections. In 1963, Lyndon B. Johnson of Texas became the first Southern President since the Civil War. Johnson became President on Nov. 22, 1963, after an assassin had killed President John F. Kennedy and wounded Texas Governor John B. Connally in Dallas. Vice-President Johnson was sworn in as the 36th President aboard the presidential plane at Love Field in Dallas. Lee Harvey Oswald was accused of shooting President Kennedy. Two days after Kennedy's death, Jack Ruby, a Dallas nightclub owner, killed Oswald.

Texas Today is continuing the industrial expansion and urban growth that began after World War II. The number of factories and plants has more than doubled since 1945. More Texans now work in manufacturing than in farming and mining combined. About four-fifths of the people live in urban areas. Texas has 26 metropolitan areas—more than any other state.

The Manned Spacecraft Center was renamed the Lyndon B. Johnson Space Center in 1973. It has made southeastern Texas a major center for space research. Besides NASA, several corporations design and test space equipment there. Universities conduct research in space medicine and other fields. In 1977, Houston annexed the area next to the space center.

One of the state's major challenges is to raise the living standards of large numbers of Texans who have not shared in the state's prosperity. Texas ranks 6th among the states in total personal income, but it is 33rd in *per capita* (per person) income.

The Republican Party gained strength in Texas during the 1970's. In 1972, Richard M. Nixon became only the third Republican presidential candidate to win Texas' electoral votes. Ronald Reagan became the fourth in 1980. In 1978, William P. Clements became the first Republican to be elected governor since 1869. In 1982, Clements lost his bid for re-election to Democratic candidate Mark White.

JOE B. FRANTZ, WALTER B. MOORE, and GEORGE W. SCHLESSELMAN

Related Articles in WORLD BOOK include:

BIOGRAPHIES

Austin (family)
Bass, Sam
Bean, Judge Roy
Bentsen, Lloyd M., Jr.
Bush, George H. W.
Bowie, James
Connally, John B.
Cortina, Juan
   Nepomuceno
Crockett, David
Dies, Martin
Dobie, J. Frank
Eisenhower, Dwight D.
Garner, John N.

Gutiérrez, José Angel
Hobby, Oveta C.
House, Edward M.
Houston, Samuel
Johnson, Lyndon B.
Jordan, Barbara C.
Long, Jane
Maverick, Samuel A.
Murphy, Audie
Rayburn, Sam
Travis, William B.
Tyler, John
Wright, James Claude, Jr.

CITIES

Amarillo
Austin
Beaumont
Brownsville
Corpus Christi

Dallas
El Paso
Fort Worth
Galveston
Houston

Lubbock
San Antonio
Waco
Wichita Falls

HISTORY

Alamo
Flag (pictures: Flags in American History [Texas Flags])
Guadalupe Hidalgo, Treaty of
Jefferson, State of
Mexican War (Background of the War)
Mission Life in America
San Jacinto, Battle of
Texas Rangers
Western Frontier Life
Westward Movement (The Southwest)

PHYSICAL FEATURES

Big Bend National Park
Brazos River
Colorado River
Dust Bowl
Guadalupe Mountains
   National Park

Gulf of Mexico
Lake Texoma
Padre Island
Pecos River
Red River
Rio Grande

OTHER RELATED ARTICLES

Alibates Flint Quarries
   National Monument
Corpus Christi Naval
   Air Station
Fort Bliss
Fort Hood
Fort Sam Houston

Gulf Intracoastal Waterway
Gulf of Mexico
Lyndon B. Johnson Space
   Center
Petroleum (picture:
   The First Gusher)
Randolph Air Force Base

Outline

I. Government
  A. Constitution
  B. Executive
  C. Legislature
  D. Courts
  E. Local Government
  F. Taxation
  G. Politics
II. People
III. Education
  A. Schools
  B. Libraries
  C. Museums
IV. A Visitor's Guide
  A. Places to Visit
  B. Annual Events
V. The Land
  A. Land Regions

  B. Coastline
  C. Mountains
  D. Rivers and Lakes
VI. Climate
VII. Economy
  A. Natural Resources
  B. Manufacturing
  C. Mining
  D. Agriculture
  E. Fishing Industry
  F. Electric Power
  G. Transportation
  H. Communication
VIII. History

Questions

How did Texas win independence from Mexico?

What are the two major differences between the two great economic regions of east and west Texas?

What is Texas' most valuable crop?

Who established the first colony of Americans in Texas? When?

Which six nations have flown flags over Texas?

Why was Governor Sam Houston put out of office during the Civil War?

What was the source of the name *Texas?*

What role does Texas play in the United States space program?

Which two minerals have helped make Texas rich?

Which political party has controlled Texas politics throughout most of the state's history?

Additional Resources

Level I

ADLER, LARRY. *The Texas Rangers.* McKay, 1979.

BEATTY, PATRICIA. *A Long Way to Whiskey Creek.* Morrow, 1971. *Billy Bedamned, Long Gone By.* 1977. Both books are fiction.

CARPENTER, ALLAN. *Texas.* Rev. ed. Childrens Press, 1979.

FRADIN, DENNIS B. *Texas in Words and Pictures.* Childrens Press, 1981.

LAWSON, DON. *The United States in the Mexican War.* Harper, 1976.

MAHER, RAMONA. *The Glory Horse: A Story of the Battle of San Jacinto, and Texas in 1836.* Coward, 1974. Fiction.

McCAGUE, JAMES. *When Cowboys Rode the Chisholm Trail.* Garrard, 1969.

Level II

ALLEN, JOHN HOUGHTON. *Southwest.* Univ. of New Mexico Press, 1952. Fiction.

ANDERSON, JAMES E., and others. *Texas Politics: An Introduction.* 3rd ed. Harper, 1979.

CONNOR, SEYMOUR V. *Texas: A History.* AHM, 1971.

DOBIE, J. FRANK. *Longhorns.* Little, Brown, 1941. *Mustangs.* 1952. *Cow People.* 1964.

FEHRENBACH, THEODORE R. *Lone Star: A History of Texas and the Texans.* Macmillan, 1968.

FRANTZ, JOE B. *Texas: A Bicentennial History.* Norton, 1976.

GRAVES, JOHN. *Landscapes of Texas: Photographs from "Texas Highways" Magazine.* Texas A&M Univ. Press, 1980.

The Handbook of Texas. Ed. by WALTER P. WEBB, and others. 3 vols. Texas State Historical Assn., 1952-1976.

HORGAN, PAUL. *Great River: The Rio Grande in North American History.* Rev. ed. Holt, 1960.

PRESLEY, JAMES. *A Saga of Wealth: The Rise of the Texas Oilmen.* Putnam, 1978.

RICHARDSON, RUPERT N., and others. *Texas: The Lone Star State.* 4th ed. Prentice-Hall, 1981.

SAMORA, JULIAN, and others. *Gunpowder Justice: A Reassessment of the Texas Rangers.* Notre Dame, 1979.

TARPLEY, FRED. *1,001 Texas Place Names.* Univ. of Texas Press, 1980.

WOOSTER, RALPH A., and CALVERT, R. A., eds. *Texas Vistas: Selections from the "Southwestern Historical Quarterly."* Texas State Historical Assn., 1980.

TEXAS, UNIVERSITY OF, is a coeducational, state-supported system of higher education. It consists of seven general academic institutions and five health-related institutions. The system's administrative offices are in Austin. Each unit has its own president. A chancellor and deputy chancellor head the entire system.

University of Texas at Austin grants bachelor's, master's, and doctor's degrees. It has colleges of arts and sciences, business administration, education, engineering, fine arts, and pharmacy; and schools of architecture and communication. Its graduate schools include business, law, library science, public affairs, and social work. Classes and research are also conducted at two branches, the McDonald Observatory at Mount Locke and the Marine Science Institute at Galveston and Port Aransas. The Austin campus library contains about $3\frac{1}{2}$ million volumes, including many manuscripts, rare books, and special collections. The Lyndon B. Johnson Library opened in 1971 on the campus. The university was organized in 1881.

University of Texas at Arlington has schools of business administration, engineering, liberal arts, and science; and a graduate school. It grants bachelor's, master's, and doctor's degrees. It opened as a junior college in 1895, and became a four-year college in 1959. It was called Arlington State College until 1967, when it received its present name.

University of Texas at Dallas, located in the Dallas suburb of Richardson, has colleges of business and public administration, humanities, natural science, and social science. The school offers two-year, upper-level programs that lead to the bachelor's degree, and graduate programs that lead to master's and doctor's degrees. The campus was established in 1969.

University of Texas at El Paso was called Texas Western College from 1949 until 1967. It has schools of business administration, education, engineering, liberal arts, and science; and a graduate school. It grants bachelor's, master's, and doctor's degrees. It opened in 1913 as the Texas School of Mines and Metallurgy.

University of Texas of the Permian Basin, in Odessa, accepts only juniors, seniors, and graduate students. It was established in 1969.

University of Texas at San Antonio grants bachelor's and master's degrees. It includes the Institute of Texan Cultures. The campus was established in 1969.

University of Texas at Tyler offers two-year upper-level programs that lead to the bachelor's degree, and graduate programs that lead to the master's degree. It opened in 1971 as Texas Eastern University and became part of the University of Texas system in 1979.

Health-Related Institutions in the system are the three health science centers at Dallas, Houston, and San Antonio; the Medical Branch at Galveston; and the University of Texas System Cancer Center, which has facilities in Houston and near Smithville.

For enrollments, see UNIVERSITIES AND COLLEGES (table). Critically reviewed by the UNIVERSITY OF TEXAS

TEXAS A&I UNIVERSITY. See UNIVERSITIES AND COLLEGES (table).

TEXAS A&M UNIVERSITY SYSTEM consists of four coeducational state universities in Texas. It also includes six agencies that provide service to the state.

Its administrative offices are in College Station, Tex. The agencies in the system are the Texas Agricultural Experiment Station, Texas Agricultural Extension Service, Texas Engineering Experiment Station, Texas Engineering Extension Service, Texas Forest Service, and Texas Transportation Institute.

Texas A&M University, in College Station, is the oldest public institution of higher education in Texas. It was founded as the Agricultural and Mechanical College of Texas in 1871, and the first classes were held in 1876. In 1963, the school's name was changed to Texas A&M University. The university has colleges of agriculture, architecture and environmental design, business administration, education, engineering, geosciences, liberal arts, medicine, science, and veterinary medicine. It has a full graduate program.

Prairie View A&M University is in Prairie View. It has colleges of agriculture, arts and sciences, education, engineering, home economics, industrial education and technology, and nursing. Courses lead to bachelor's and master's degrees. It was founded in 1879.

Tarleton State University, in Stephenville, has schools of agriculture and business, arts and sciences, and education. Courses lead to bachelor's and master's degrees. The institution was founded in 1899.

Texas A&M University at Galveston includes the Texas Maritime College, the Coastal Zone Laboratory, and the Moody College of Marine Technology. It was founded in Galveston in 1971 as Moody College, and it received its present name in 1979. Courses lead to bachelor's degrees in marine biology, marine engineering, marine sciences, marine transportation, maritime administration, and maritime systems engineering. The Texas Maritime College's program includes training on the ship *Texas Clipper.* Students who successfully complete the program qualify as officers in the United States merchant marine or as ensigns in the United States Naval Reserve.

For enrollments, see UNIVERSITIES AND COLLEGES (table). Critically reviewed by the TEXAS A&M UNIVERSITY SYSTEM

TEXAS ANNEXATION. See UNITED STATES, HISTORY OF THE (Manifest Destiny; map).

TEXAS CHRISTIAN UNIVERSITY is a private coeducational school in Fort Worth, Tex. It is related to the Disciples of Christ. The university has a college of arts and sciences, a college of nursing, and an evening college. It also has a divinity school, a graduate school, and schools of business, education, and fine arts.

Courses at Texas Christian lead to bachelor's, master's, and doctor's degrees. The university offers several special programs. These include an honors program, a ranch management program, and foreign study programs in Europe and Mexico. The university operates a speech and hearing clinic and a school for children with learning disabilities. Texas Christian University was founded in 1873. For the school's enrollment, see UNIVERSITIES AND COLLEGES (table). JAMES MATTOX MOUDY

TEXAS FEVER. See CATTLE TICK.

TEXAS MEMORIAL MUSEUM. See TEXAS (Places to Visit).

TEXAS RANGERS are special police officers of the state of Texas. They serve under the authority of the State Department of Public Safety. One noted Ranger summarized their qualities in these words: "The Texas Rangers can ride like a Mexican, trail like an Indian,

Texas Rangers are the state police of Texas. In their crime laboratory, *left,* specially trained Rangers analyze bloodstains, fingerprints, and other evidence connected with crimes.

shoot like a Tennessean, and fight like a very devil." The Rangers have a tradition of individualism, resourcefulness, self-reliance, and politeness. They often "get their man" with quick thinking rather than by force. The Rangers wear no official uniforms. They furnish their own clothing. The state provides weapons and transportation. But Rangers may carry their own weapons, and they ride their own horses.

Early Days. The Rangers were originally a band of mounted riflemen. Early in the 1800's, Stephen F. Austin formed bands of "rangers" to protect American settlers along the Brazos River from Indian warriors and Mexican bandits. The Texas general council in 1835 formally organized the Rangers and assigned them the sole task of defending the frontier against Indians. One company of 25 men patrolled east of the Trinity River, another between the Trinity and the Brazos, and a third between the Brazos and the Colorado River. This was a large assignment. The Spaniards and Mexicans had never succeeded in controlling the Plains tribes.

The Rangers adopted the practices of their enemies in order to keep the peace. The Comanche Indians, with their cunning, speed, and courage, set the pattern of Plains warfare. The Rangers learned the Indian skills of horsemanship, woodcraft, and direction finding. They were excellent marksmen, and adopted the revolving six-shooter as their standard weapon. They always carried rifles, lariats, and bowie knives.

After Texas gained its independence in 1836, it faced a Mexican and Indian danger on a 1,000-mile (1,600-kilometer) frontier. With a population of about 400,000, it could not afford a standing army. Texas required a fighting force that was small and inexpensive, available in time of need but inactive when not needed. The Texas Rangers, without uniforms, drill, or regular pay, met these requirements. They served as a mobile and efficient frontier defense organization.

After Texas joined the Union in 1845, the Rangers continued to play a major role in frontier defense. Dur-

ing the Mexican War (1846-1848), they performed valuable service as scouts and guerrilla fighters with the American armies in Mexico. When the federal government established forts along the Texas frontier and garrisoned them with regular troops, Texans still placed their faith in the Rangers. Sam Houston once said in the U.S. Senate: "Give us 1,000 Rangers, and we will be responsible for the defense of our frontier . . . We ask no regular troops; withdraw them if you please. I ask this not through any unkindness to them, but because they have not the efficiency for frontier service."

Later History. During the Reconstruction period that followed the Civil War, Texas suffered from lawlessness, murder, and Indian raids. In 1874, 450 Texas Rangers received commissions as peace officers. They continued to fight the Comanche along the northern border and Mexican cattle thieves along the Rio Grande. They also tracked down murderers, smugglers, bank and train robbers, and mine bandits. Within 10 years, they restored peace and quiet to the interior of Texas. In 1917 and 1918, they succeeded in clearing the rocky Big Bend region of outlaws. Since then, the Rangers have been greatly reduced in number.   NORMAN A. GRAEBNER

Additional Resources

DAVIS, JOHN L. *The Texas Rangers: Their First 150 Years.* Univ. of Texas Institute of Texan Cultures, 1975.
STERLING, WILLIAM W. *Trails and Trials of a Texas Ranger.* Univ. of Oklahoma Press, 1969.
WEBB, WALTER PRESCOTT. *The Texas Rangers: A Century of Frontier Defense.* Rev. ed. Univ. of Texas Press, 1965.

TEXAS SOUTHERN UNIVERSITY. See UNIVERSITIES AND COLLEGES (table).

TEXAS TECH UNIVERSITY. See UNIVERSITIES AND COLLEGES (table).

TEXAS WOMAN'S UNIVERSITY. See UNIVERSITIES AND COLLEGES (table).

TEXOMA, LAKE. See LAKE TEXOMA.

TEXTBOOK. See PUBLISHING (Books); BOOK (Publishing Books).

Able Fire Equipment, Inc.; Arrow Co.; Beacon Mfg. Co.; E. Virginia Kemper & Assoc.; Stroheim & Romann (WORLD BOOK photo)

A Wide Variety of Textile Products—from carpeting, clothing, and towels to fire hoses, typewriter ribbons, and umbrellas—helps meet the needs of people throughout the world.

TEXTILE

TEXTILE has traditionally meant a woven fabric. The term comes from the Latin word *texere*, meaning *to weave*. Many fabrics are still made by weaving yarn on a loom. But today, all other types of fabrics are also considered textiles. They include knitted goods, felts, laces, nets, and braids. The textile industry also refers to the fibers and yarns that are used in making fabrics as textiles.

Textile mills produce an incredible variety of fabrics. They turn out huge rolls of soft cotton, warm wool, strong nylon, and other fabrics. The mills produce these textiles in every color imaginable and in countless patterns. The largest share of all textile production goes to garment manufacturers to be made into ready-to-wear clothing. The second-largest share is used to make such household products as draperies, blankets, sheets, and towels. In the United States, the textile industry manufactures about 25 billion square yards (21 billion square meters) of fabric a year. About 70 per cent of this output is used in making clothing and household goods.

Textiles are also used in thousands of other products. These products include basketball nets, boat sails, bookbindings, conveyor belts, fire hoses, flags, insulation materials, mailbags, parachutes, typewriter ribbons, and umbrellas. Automobile manufacturers use fabrics in the carpeting, upholstery, tires, and brake linings of cars. Hospitals use such textile products as adhesive tape,

D. S. Hamby, the contributor of this article, is Dean of the School of Textiles at North Carolina State University.

bandages, and surgical thread. Surgeons replace diseased heart arteries with arteries knitted or woven from textile fibers.

Most textiles are produced by twisting fibers into yarns and then knitting or weaving the yarns into a fabric. This method of making cloth has been used for thousands of years. But throughout most of that time, workers did the twisting, knitting, or weaving largely by hand. With today's modern machinery, textile mills can manufacture as much fabric in a few seconds as it once took workers weeks to produce by hand.

Sources of Textile Fibers

Fibers are the raw materials for all fabrics. Some fibers occur in nature as fine strands that can be twisted into yarns. These *natural fibers* come from plants, animals, and minerals. Most natural fibers used for textile production measure $\frac{1}{2}$ to 8 inches (1.3 to 20 centimeters) or longer. Such short fibers are called *staple fibers*.

For most of history, people had only natural fibers to use in making cloth. But modern science has learned how to produce fibers by chemical and technical means. Today, these manufactured fibers account for more than two-thirds of the fibers processed by U.S. textile mills. Unlike most natural fibers, manufactured fibers are produced in long, continuous lengths called *filaments*. Many manufactured fibers also have certain qualities superior to those of natural fibers. For example, they may be stronger or more elastic.

Natural Fibers. Plants provide more textile fibers than do animals or minerals. In fact, one plant, cotton, accounts for about 95 per cent of the natural fibers used in the United States. Cotton fibers produce soft, absorbent fabrics that are widely used for clothing, sheets,

168

Manufactured Fibers

Fiber	Trade Names	Characteristics	Uses
Acetate	Acele, Celaperm, Estron	Resists mildew, shrinking, stains, and stretching	Clothing; draperies; upholstery
Acrylic	Acrilan, Creslan, Orlon, Zefran	Soft; resists mildew, sunlight, and wrinkling	Blankets; carpeting; clothing; upholstery
Aramid	Kevlar, Nomex	Resists heat, chemicals, and stretching	Rope
Glass	Beta, Fiberglas, PPG, Vitron	Resists chemicals, flames, mildew, moisture, and sunlight	Draperies; electrical insulation; ironing board covers
Metallic	Brunsmet, Chromeflex, Fairtex, Lurex, Metlon	Resists insects, mildew, and tarnishing	Decorative trim for bedspreads, tablecloths, and upholstery
Modacrylic	Dynel, Elura, Verel	Soft; resists chemicals, flames, and wrinkling	Artificial furs; blankets; carpeting; wigs
Nylon	Antron, Cumuloft, Enkaloft, Qiana	Strong; elastic; easy to launder; dries quickly; retains shape	Carpeting; hosiery; lingerie; parachutes; upholstery
Olefin	DLP, Herculon, Marvess, Vectra	Lightweight; resists insects, mildew, moisture, and sunlight	Automobile seat covers; filters; indoor-outdoor carpeting
Polyester	Dacron, Encron, Fortrel, Kodel	Resists wrinkling; easy to launder; dries quickly	Blankets; carpeting; clothing; fire hose; sewing thread
Rayon	Avril, Fibro	Absorbent; easy to launder; dyes easily	Carpeting; clothing; draperies; upholstery
Rubber (synthetic)	Contro, Lactron, Lastex	Strong; elastic; repels moisture	Mattresses; support hose; swimwear; underwear
Saran	Rovana, Velon	Resists acids, insects, mildew, moisture, and stains	Draperies; outdoor furniture; rainwear; upholstery
Spandex	Glospan, Lycra, Numa	Elastic; lightweight; resists sunlight and perspiration	Fitted sheets; slipcovers; support hose; swimwear; underwear
Triacetate	Arnel	Resists shrinking, stains, and wrinkling; dries quickly	Draperies; sportswear; blended with other fibers

and towels. Fibers of the flax plant are made into linen. The strength and beauty of linen have made it a popular fabric for fine tablecloths, napkins, and handkerchiefs. Fibers of the jute plant can be woven into burlap. Burlap is used for sacks and as backing for rugs and carpets.

The main animal fiber used for textiles is wool. Another animal fiber, silk, produces one of the most luxurious fabrics. Sheep supply most of the wool, but members of the camel family and certain breeds of goats also furnish wool. Wool provides warm, comfortable fabrics for dresses, suits, and sweaters. Silk comes from cocoons spun by silkworms. Workers unwind the cocoons to obtain long, natural filaments. Fabrics made from silk fibers have great luster and softness and can be dyed brilliant colors. Silk is especially popular for scarfs and neckties.

The only natural mineral fiber used for textiles is asbestos, which comes from several varieties of rocks. Asbestos will not burn, though it melts at extremely high temperatures. Manufacturers use it in making brake linings, insulating wire, and fire-retardant hose.

Manufactured Fibers. Most man-made fibers are manufactured from *wood pulp*, cotton *linters*, or *petrochemicals*. Wood pulp comes from trees and the waste products of the lumber industry. Linters are the short fibers remaining on the cottonseeds after the longer fibers have been removed by the cotton gin. Petrochemicals are chemicals made from crude oil and natural gas.

The fibers made from wood pulp and linters are rayon, acetate, and triacetate. Rayon and acetate are widely used for clothing, draperies, and upholstery. Rayon produces absorbent fabrics that dye easily. Fabrics of acetate resist shrinking and stretching. Triacetate has the desirable qualities of acetate and also resists wrinkling, making it especially popular for sportswear.

The chief fibers manufactured from petrochemicals include nylon, polyester, acrylic, and olefin. Nylon has exceptional strength, wears well, and is easy to launder. It is popular for hosiery, women's underwear, and other clothing and for carpeting and upholstery. Such products as conveyor belts and fire hoses are also made of nylon. Polyester resists wrinkling and is widely used in permanent press clothing. Acrylic fibers produce soft, bulky, lightweight fabrics popular for blankets, carpeting, and children's snowsuits. Olefin cleans easily, dries quickly, and resists mildew. It is widely used for indoor-outdoor carpeting.

Other manufactured fibers include those made from glass and metals. Fabrics of glass fibers are used for insulation and to make boat hulls, molded products, and flame-resistant fabrics. Metallic fibers—chiefly aluminum, gold, and silver—provide decorative yarns for bedspreads, evening gowns, and tablecloths.

Kinds of Fabrics

About 90 per cent of all fabrics produced in the United States are made by weaving or knitting. The

168a

rest are made by other processes. In producing fabrics by the various processes, textile mills may use yarns finer than sewing thread or as heavy as rug yarn.

Woven Fabrics are made of two sets of yarns—a lengthwise set called the *warp* and a crosswise set called the *filling* or *weft*. The warp yarns are threaded into a loom through a series of frames called *harnesses*. During the cloth-making process, the harnesses raise some warp yarns and lower others. This action creates a space, or *shed*, between the yarns. A device called a *shuttle* carries the filling through the shed and so forms the crosswise yarns of the fabric. The pattern in which the harnesses are raised and lowered for each pass of the shuttle determines the kind of weave. There are three basic patterns: (1) the plain weave, (2) the twill weave, and (3) the satin weave.

The Plain Weave is the simplest and most common pattern. In this weave, the crosswise filling passes over one warp yarn and under the next alternately across the width of the fabric. The weave produces long-lasting, flat-textured cloth used in making such products as bedsheets, dresses, and upholstery. Plain-woven fabrics include gingham, percale, and taffeta.

The Twill Weave has a pattern of raised diagonal lines. The filling crosses over and then under two, three, or four warp yarns at a time, with each row following the same pattern. However, each row's pattern begins slightly to the right or left of the pattern in the previous row. This technique creates the diagonal lines. The twill weave produces strong, tightly woven cloth used in coats, sportswear, and work clothes. Popular twill fabrics include denim and gabardine.

The Satin Weave is the least common pattern. The filling may span as many as 12 warp yarns. The weave produces soft, luxurious cloth, but it may snag easily. Satin-weave fabrics are made into such products as draperies and formal clothes. Common satin weaves include damask and satin.

Knitted Fabrics are made from a single yarn or a set of yarns. In making cloth, a knitting machine forms loops in the yarn and links them to one another by means of needles. The finished fabric consists of crosswise rows of loops, called *courses*, and lengthwise rows of loops, called *wales*. This looped structure makes knitted fabrics more elastic than woven cloth. Garment manufacturers use knitted fabrics in producing comfortable, lightweight clothing that resists wrinkling. Textile mills manufacture knit goods by two basic methods: (1) weft knitting and (2) warp knitting.

Weft Knitting is done with single lengths of yarn, which a knitting machine forms into the crosswise courses one row at a time. The loops of each course are pulled through the loops of the previous course. This process forms the wales at the same time. Weft knits can be made in the shape of a tube or as flat pieces of cloth.

Most weft-knitted fabrics are used in making hosiery, sweaters, and underwear. These fabrics are knitted in three basic stitches. In the *plain*, or *jersey*, *stitch*, the tops of the loops stand out on the face of the cloth, and the bottoms of the loops stand out on the back. The *purl stitch* produces crosswise ridges on both sides of the fabric. The *rib stitch* makes cloth with lengthwise ribs on the front and back. Another stitch, the *double knit*, produces a heavier, more tightly constructed fabric than do the other stitches. Double-knit dresses, men's suits, and sportswear are highly popular because of their wrinkle resistance.

Warp Knitting requires hundreds of yarns fed as a sheet to a knitting machine. A separate needle for each yarn forms the wales of the fabric. At the same time, the needles interloop the wales crosswise and so form the yarns into a fabric. Almost all warp knits are produced in flat pieces.

Warp-knitted fabrics are tightly constructed and thus do not stretch as much as weft knits. In warp knits, the loops stand out on the face of the cloth, and the connecting yarns stand out on the back. Common warp-knitted fabrics include tricot and raschel. Tricot knits are lightweight fabrics that are widely used in making bedsheets, blouses, dresses, and women's underwear. Raschel knits are heavier fabrics and are used for a variety of products, including blankets, carpeting, men's suits, and swimwear.

Other Fabrics include tufted fabrics, nets and laces, braids, and felt. None of these fabrics is woven. However, the textile industry produces another class of fabrics specifically called nonwoven fabrics.

Tufted Fabrics are used in about 90 per cent of the carpeting produced in the United States. Such fabrics

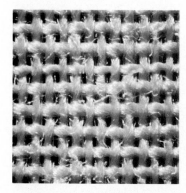

A Woven Fabric consists of two sets of yarns. The yarns are crossed over and under each other to form cloth.

A Knitted Fabric has a single yarn or a set of yarns. Loops are made in the yarn and linked together, forming cloth.

WORLD BOOK *photos*

Felt is made chiefly from fibers of wool, fur, or animal hair. The fibers are matted together by moist heat and pressure.

consist of cut or uncut loops of yarn that have been punched through a backing material.

Nets and Laces, which are called *open-mesh fabrics*, have wide spaces between the yarns. These fabrics can be produced on certain kinds of knitting machines. Netting is used for curtains, fishing nets, hammocks, and tennis nets. Laces have delicate designs and are popular as trim for clothing.

Braids consist of three or more interlaced yarns. Braided fabrics are used for such narrow items as ribbons and shoelaces.

Felt is chiefly produced from fibers of wool, fur, or animal hair. The fibers are matted together by moist heat and pressure. Felt is used in making billiard table covers, hats, and padding.

Nonwoven Fabrics include *needle-punched fabrics* and fabrics produced by a process called *bonding*. Needle-punched fabrics, or *needle felts*, consist of fibers that have been tangled together by means of hooked needles. Such fabrics look like felt and are used in making blankets, indoor-outdoor carpeting, and insulation. Fabrics produced by bonding are made by joining fibers with adhesives. Many of these fabrics are made into items that are used only once, such as disposable diapers and surgical gowns.

How Fabrics Are Produced

Designing a Fabric. Most fabric designers work for companies that manufacture fibers, fabrics, or clothing. Designers create new patterns and color combinations and decide what fibers and methods of construction to use in various fabrics. They must know enough about textile production to realize whether their ideas can be converted into actual products. Fabrics must also be designed so that they can be produced economically on standard textile machinery, such as looms, knitting machines, and tufting machines. In addition, a design has to appeal to a great many consumers for the fabric to be profitable.

Making the Yarn. Yarn can be manufactured in various ways. Fiber companies may take filaments—that is, long, continuous fibers—and draw 15 to 100 of them together to make *multifilament* yarn. Or they may use a single filament to make *monofilament* yarn. Some filament yarns, including those made from nylon and polyester, can be *heat-set* to form *stretch yarns*. In one method of heat-setting, manufacturers tightly twist the yarn and heat it. After the yarn is untwisted, it tends to snap back like a spring. Such yarn is used in double-knit and stretch-woven fabrics. Other treatments can be applied to filament yarns to give them a bulky texture.

Filaments may also be cut into staple, or short, lengths that measure 1 to 3 inches (2.5 to 7.6 centimeters) long. Staple fibers cut from filaments produce yarn that is softer than filament yarn and not as lustrous. Yarn producers can also mix together natural fibers and manufactured fibers of staple length to form *blended yarns*. These yarns have the characteristics of each of the fibers used in their construction. For example, yarn produced from cotton and polyester is absorbent because of the cotton and wrinkle resistant because of the polyester.

Yarn made from natural fibers or manufactured fibers of staple length is called *staple yarn* or *spun yarn*. All staple yarns are manufactured in much the same

Designing a Fabric requires not only artistic ability but also knowledge of fibers and textile machinery. Designers must know whether their ideas can be converted into actual products.

way, whether they are blended or consist of only one kind of fiber. The fibers arrive at the mill in bales, which workers feed into a series of *opening machines*. These machines break up the large masses of fibers, remove some of the trash, and mix the fibers together. A *carding machine* then removes smaller impurities and some of the exceptionally short fibers and arranges the remaining fibers into a loose rope called a *sliver*. Next, as many as eight slivers at a time are drawn together into another sliver. This sliver is then formed into a thin strand called a *roving*. The roving is twisted on a *spinning frame* to form yarn. Some spinning frames produce yarn directly from slivers. Different kinds of fibers may be blended when the bales are opened, when the slivers are drawn together, or when the roving is spun.

After the yarn has been manufactured, it is wound onto large spools. Sometimes, two or more strands of yarn are twisted together for added strength. Each strand of such heavier yarn is referred to as a *ply*. Three-ply yarn, for example, consists of three strands of yarn. After the yarn has been spooled, it is ready to be woven or knitted.

Making the Fabric begins when workers place the spools of yarn on a rack called a *creel*. The creel feeds the yarns onto a *beam* (roller) that is placed on a loom or a knitting machine. For a discussion of how looms and knitting machines make cloth, see the previous section, *Kinds of Fabrics*.

Manufacturers produce woven and knitted fabrics in various lengths, depending on the orders of their customers. Woven fabrics made for clothing manufacturers are usually produced in widths of 36 to 60 inches (91 to 152 centimeters). Most woven *narrow goods*, which are used for such products as gauze bandages and labels, measure $\frac{1}{2}$ to 3 inches (1.3 to 7.6 centimeters) wide.

In general, a knitting mill specializes in one of four kinds of products—fabric; hosiery; underwear; or such outerwear as dresses, shirts, slacks, and sweaters. Most fabric produced in widths of 80 to 168 inches (200 to 427 centimeters) is sold to clothing manufacturers. Fab-

Society for Visual Education Inc.
(Burt Munk Productions)

Making Yarn involves processing fibers through various machines. A carding machine, *above*, straightens the fibers and arranges them into a loose rope called a *sliver*. The slivers are coiled into cans and fed into a spinning frame, *right*, which twists them into yarn.

Burlington Industries, Inc.

rics made in the shape of tubes are used for the bodies of sport shirts and of T-shirts. Such cloth can also be cut and sewed together like flat-knitted fabrics to make garments.

Finishing the Fabric. Fabrics that come directly from a loom or knitting machine are called *gray goods*. This term does not refer to the color of the cloth. It merely means that the fabric has not received any finishing treatments and so is unsuitable for most purposes. Gray goods are also called *greige* (pronounced *gray*).

Almost all gray goods are washed to remove dirt, grease, and other unwanted substances. Many fabrics are also bleached to whiten them or to prepare them for dyeing or printing. Cotton fabrics may be treated with caustic soda before dyeing. This process, called *mercerizing*, swells the cotton fibers and thus increases the strength and luster of the cloth.

Some gray goods are made from dyed yarn. Such cloth may have brilliant colors and highly detailed designs. But most textiles are dyed a single color after the yarn has been made into cloth. Dyeing machines pull the fabric through a dyebath or force the dye into the cloth by means of pressure.

Designs are printed on fabrics by three chief methods. *Roller printing* uses rollers that have designs deeply engraved on their surface. Dye is applied to the raised areas and then transferred onto the cloth by the rollers. *Screen printing* is similar to using a stencil to form a design. Dye is pressed onto the cloth through a pattern on a screen. *Rotary screen printing* uses porous rollers that

J. P. Stevens & Co., Inc.

J. Alex Langley, DPI

Weaving on a Jacquard loom, *above*, produces fabric with complex patterns for such items as towels and upholstery. Punched cards and other attachments guide the yarn to weave the design.

Knitting on a circular knitting machine, *right*, produces fabric for hosiery, underwear, and many other garments. A device at the bottom of the machine rolls up the fabric as it is knitted.

fit inside cylindrical screens. The rollers hold the dye and force it into the cloth through patterns on the screens. In another process, called *heat transfer printing* the design is printed on paper with special ink and then ironed onto the fabric. When the paper is peeled off, it leaves the design on the cloth. Some fabrics are dyed and then printed.

After the cloth has been dyed or printed, it may be dried and stretched on a machine called a *tenter frame*. Fabrics made from heat-set fibers may also be treated by this device to help the cloth resist shrinking and wrinkling. A patented process called *Sanforizing* preshrinks cloth to prevent it from shrinking or stretching more than 1 per cent in home laundering. Other finishing treatments help fabrics resist bacteria, fading, flames, mildew, moths, stains, static, and water.

The final step in manufacturing cloth is ironing it between heavy rollers, a process called *calendering*. The fabrics are then rolled onto bolts for shipment to clothing makers and other customers.

The Textile Industry

In the United States, the textile industry consists of about 5,500 companies that operate more than 7,000 plants. Many of these companies perform every step in the manufacturing process, from making the yarn to finishing the fabric. But some manufacturers specialize in only one operation. For example, a textile mill may produce cloth with yarn it buys from one company and then sell the fabric to another firm for finishing.

Textile producers use over 11 billion pounds (5 billion kilograms) of fibers yearly. Sales of the textile industry total over $36 billion a year. The largest textile companies, in order of sales, include Burlington Industries, Incorporated; J. P. Stevens & Company, Incorporated; West-Point Pepperell, Incorporated; and Springs Mills, Incorporated.

The textile industry employs about a million persons. Specialized workers include cloth inspectors, designers, dyeing supervisors, and loom technicians. Closely related industries, such as companies that manufacture fibers, clothing, and textile machinery, employ about $2\frac{1}{2}$ million persons. Two labor unions—the Amalgamated Clothing and Textile Workers Union (ACTWU) and the International Ladies' Garment Workers' Union (ILGWU)—represent over a fourth of the workers in the textile and related industries.

The U.S. government requires the textile industry to observe certain federal laws designed to protect consumers and give them information about the textiles they buy. The Wool Products Labeling Act of 1939 provides that all garments made of wool have a label telling the amount and kind of wool used. The Textile Fiber Products Identification Act of 1958 covers all other fibers. It requires that all clothing and most home furnishings have a label showing the fiber content by percentage. The Flammable Fabrics Act of 1953 prohibits the sale of fabrics that burn rapidly.

The Federal Trade Commission (FTC) and the Consumer Product Safety Commission (CPSC) are the government agencies chiefly responsible for enforcing the consumer protection laws. These agencies may also issue regulations of their own. Since July 1972, the FTC has required that all clothing be labeled with instructions regarding cleaning, ironing, and bleaching.

Burlington Industries, Inc.

Dyeing Processes may be used either to color fibers and yarns before they are made into cloth or to color the fabric itself. In *package dyeing, above,* tubes of yarn are dyed in large vats.

Burlington Industries, Inc.

Printing produces fabrics with beautiful designs and a variety of colors. In *rotary screen printing, above,* the dye is forced through patterns on cylindrical screens that fit around rollers.

TEXTILE

Weaving with a Hand Loom is still a major way of making cloth in many developing countries. This woman in Guatemala weaves a colorful fabric by an age-old method.

In Canada, about 1,180 textile mills sell more than $3 billion worth of goods annually. Canada's textile industry employs about 100,000 workers. Another 100,000 persons work for clothing manufacturers. About a fourth of all the workers belong to local unions of the ACTWU and the ILGWU.

Canada's Textile Labeling Act requires a label on all clothing to show the fiber content by percentage. The Department of Consumer and Corporate Affairs en-

forces the law. Labeling garments with instructions for their care is voluntary in Canada.

In Other Countries. Almost every country has a textile industry. In Japan and the countries of Western Europe, textile production is highly industrialized and centered on manufactured fibers. For example, England, Italy, Switzerland, and West Germany are leading exporters of textile machinery and manufactured fibers. Textile production is also highly mechanized in East Germany, Poland, Russia, and other Eastern European countries. But natural fibers have greater importance in these countries than in most Western nations.

In some developing nations, such as India and Pakistan, millions of workers still weave fabrics of cotton, silk, and other natural fibers in their homes. As the economies of developing countries advance, however, textile manufacturing often becomes one of the first industries to be mechanized. Textile production provides many jobs that can be filled by unskilled and semiskilled workers. It also supplies a nation's people with clothing, one of the basic human needs.

History

Prehistoric and Ancient Times. No one knows when people first made textiles. The earliest evidence of woolen textiles dates from about 6000 B.C. This evidence comes from what is now southern Turkey. Bits of linen from Egypt indicate that people there wove flax about 5000 B.C. Archaeologists have found Egyptian mummies from the 2500's B.C. wrapped in linen as well made as that produced today. By 3000 B.C., cotton was grown in the Indus River Valley in what are now Pakistan and western India. Cotton may also have been used for textiles in the Americas by this time. The Chinese began to cultivate silkworms about 2700 B.C. They developed special looms for silk filaments.

The ancient Greeks used chiefly woolen textiles. They also used some linen. In the 300's B.C., Alexander the Great's army brought cotton goods from India to Europe. The ancient Romans developed an enormous

Leading Textile-Producing States and Provinces

Value added by manufacture

North Carolina	$4,605,900,000
South Carolina	$2,699,800,000
Georgia	$2,579,700,000
Virginia	$922,000,000
Pennsylvania	$900,800,000
Alabama	$745,500,000
Quebec	$728,900,000
Ontario	$719,600,000
New York	$663,000,000
Massachusetts	$594,300,000

Sources: U.S. Bureau of the Census; Statistics Canada.
Figures are for 1978.

Leading Textile-Producing Countries

Value added by manufacture

Country	Value
United States	$21,277,600,000
Russia	$16,394,700,000
Japan	$14,375,800,000
West Germany	$6,866,600,000
Poland	$6,394,700,000
Italy	$5,677,500,000
Great Britain	$5,067,200,000
France	$4,985,600,000
Brazil	$3,178,500,000
South Korea	$2,332,600,000

Source: Statistical Office of the UN.
Figures are for 1978.

trade in textiles. They imported woolens from Britain, Gaul, and Spain; linen from Egypt; cottons from India; and silks from China and Persia.

During the Middle Ages, which lasted from the A.D. 400's to the early 1500's, the textile industry gradually developed in Europe. The production of woolens centered in England; northern Italy; and Flanders, a region that now covers parts of present-day Belgium, France, and The Netherlands. As the textile industry expanded, production techniques improved, which stimulated further growth. The spinning wheel came into use by the 1200's. Meanwhile, Italy had become the silk center of Europe. The invention of a machine to unwind silk from cocoons led to further expansion of Italy's silk industry. France established a thriving silk industry in the 1400's.

In the large towns of Europe, associations of weavers and other craftsmen regulated textile production. These associations, called *guilds,* established prices and standards of quality for all products made by their members. But the *domestic system* produced most textiles during the Middle Ages. Under the domestic system, merchants delivered raw materials to workers in their homes in rural areas. Later, the merchants collected the work and paid for it by the piece.

The Industrial Revolution. Important developments in textile production continued after the Middle Ages. For example, an English clergyman named William Lee invented a machine for knitting hosiery in 1589. During the 1600's, textile workers in The Netherlands developed improved methods of dyeing and finishing cloth. But the greatest advances in the textile industry occurred during the Industrial Revolution, which began in England in the 1700's. In fact, the Industrial Revolution was largely a "textile revolution" created by a flood of English inventions that enormously increased the production of yarns and fabrics.

In 1733, John Kay, an engineer, invented the *flying shuttle.* This device enabled weavers to pass the filling through the warp yarns mechanically instead of by hand. About 1764, a weaver named James Hargreaves invented the *spinning jenny,* the first machine that could spin more than one yarn at a time. In 1769, Richard

Arkwright, a former barber, patented the *water frame,* a spinning machine that ran on water power. A weaver named Samuel Crompton introduced the *spinning mule* in 1779. This machine combined the features of the spinning jenny and the water frame and gradually replaced them both. Edmund Cartwright, an Anglican clergyman, patented the first power loom in 1785.

In the United States, the New England region became the center of the textile industry. In 1790, an English textile worker named Samuel Slater built the first successful water-powered machines for spinning cotton in the United States. The machines were installed in a mill in Pawtucket, R.I. The production of cotton textiles in New England grew rapidly after the American inventor Eli Whitney developed the cotton gin in 1793. Before Whitney's invention, workers had to remove cotton fibers from the seed by hand. This slow process could not meet the textile mills' demand for cotton. The cotton gin separated the fibers far faster than workers could by hand. As a result, textile mills received ever-increasing supplies of cotton.

The Age of Modern Textiles began in 1884, when Hilaire Chardonnet, a French chemist, developed the first practical manufactured fiber. This fiber, now known as rayon, was first produced in the United States in 1910 under the name *artificial silk.* An American chemist named Wallace H. Carothers developed nylon in 1935. During the 1940's and 1950's, polyester, acrylic, and several other manufactured fibers were introduced.

In the 1960's, textile companies began making double-knit fabrics of textured polyester yarns. These fabrics were lighter in weight and more comfortable than double knits made of other materials. As a result, the popularity of knits greatly increased.

Today, new manufacturing processes and devices have made the textile industry one of the most modern of all industries. For example, knitting machines controlled by computers now produce fabrics with highly complex patterns at tremendous speeds. Many textile firms also use high-speed looms that have many tiny shuttles called *darts* instead of a single shuttle. Other looms weave with no shuttles at all. A jet of water or air carries the filling through the warp up to 1,000 times a minute, about four times faster than a shuttle works on a standard loom.   D. S. HAMBY

Culver
New Textile Machinery of the 1800's greatly increased fabric production. In textile mills like the one above, women operated looms powered by steam engines or water wheels.

Related Articles in WORLD BOOK include:

BIOGRAPHIES

Arkwright, Sir Richard   Hargreaves, James
Chardonnet, Hilaire   Jacquard, Joseph Marie
Crompton, Samuel   Slater, Samuel

TEXTILES

See the articles on clothing materials listed in the *Related Articles* of the CLOTHING article. See also the following:

Braiding   Cambric   Flax   Tapestry
Burlap   Fiber   Oilcloth   Twill

TREATMENTS AND PROCESSES

Batik   Knitting   Spinning Jenny
Bleaching   Knitting Machine   Tie Dyeing
Dye   Mercerizing   Waterproofing
Embroidery   Spinning   Weaving

TEXTILE ENGINEERING

Outline

I. **Sources of Textile Fibers**
  A. Natural Fibers
  B. Manufactured Fibers
II. **Kinds of Fabrics**
  A. Woven Fabrics
  B. Knitted Fabrics
  C. Other Fabrics
III. **How Fabrics Are Produced**
  A. Designing a Fabric
  B. Making the Yarn
  C. Making the Fabric
  D. Finishing the Fabric
IV. **The Textile Industry**
  A. In the United States
  B. In Canada
  C. In Other Countries
V. **History**

Questions

What two methods of making cloth account for about 90 per cent of all fabrics produced in the United States?
What was the first practical manufactured fiber?
Which industry consumes the largest share of all textile production?
What was the *domestic system?*
How are most carpeting fabrics made in the United States?
What are *gray goods?*
What is the most important natural fiber?
From what substances are most manufactured fibers produced?
How must clothing be labeled in the United States and Canada?
What is *blended yarn? Staple yarn?*

TEXTILE ENGINEERING. See ENGINEERING (table: Specialized Engineering Fields).

TEXTURE. See INTERIOR DECORATION (Pattern and Texture; Choosing Patterns and Textures).

TEZEL, JOHANN. See TETZEL, JOHANN.

TFM. See LAMPREY.

THACKERAY, WILLIAM MAKEPEACE (1811-1863), was one of the great novelists of the English Victorian Age. His *Vanity Fair* is one of the finest and best-known novels in English literature. Thackeray wrote in a colorful, lively style, with a simple vocabulary and clearly structured sentences. These qualities, combined with his honest view of life, give him an important place in the history of realistic literature.

Early Career. Thackeray was born in Calcutta, India. In 1817, he was sent to England to live with relatives and begin his education. He later looked back on his school years with mingled affection and dislike. Said Thackeray, "I have the same recollection of Greek in youth that I have of castor oil." He entered Trinity College, Cambridge University, in 1829. No great scholar, he left after a year and a half to travel abroad.

Thackeray had trouble finding a career. He studied law for a short time, and went to art school in Paris. Meanwhile, he had spent his inheritance, losing part of it to professional gamblers. To make a modest living, he turned to writing book reviews, stories, and satirical sketches for magazines.

In 1836, Thackeray married Isabella Shawe. She became mentally ill following the birth of their third daughter in 1840. This tragedy affected Thackeray's natural good humor, making him lonely and depressed. But he needed money more than ever, and he continued turning out articles and stories.

Most of Thackeray's early writings were humorous, and were published under such ridiculous pen names as Michael Angelo Titmarsh. In 1848, he published *The Book of Snobs*, a collection of his magazine writings.

Later Career. Thackeray ensured his fame with *Vanity Fair* (1847-1848), probably his best novel. Like most of his books, it was first published in monthly parts. The novel traces the fortunes of upper-middle-class Londoners of the early 1800's.

Thackeray called *Vanity Fair* "a novel without a hero," in keeping with his belief that most people are a mixture of the heroic and the ridiculous. He knew that men and women are complex, and he avoided oversimplifying them. He wrote with affection about kind and gentle Amelia Sedley. But he also called Amelia "a silly little thing." Becky Sharp, more clearly the "heroine," is selfish, cunning, and cynical. Becky is never bitter, however, and readers enjoy seeing her good-naturedly defeat people who are even less admirable than she.

The novel *Pendennis* (1848-1850) is partly autobiographical. It has the mellow, reflective quality that colors much of Thackeray's writing.

Henry Esmond (1852) is set in England in the early 1700's, a period that Thackeray loved. The book describes the loves and adventures of Esmond, who narrates the book. Henry is also only "part hero." Although well meaning, he is given to pious moralizing, which sometimes makes him a most unheroic bore.

The Newcomes (1853-1855) is the complex story of three generations of the Newcome family. Ethel Newcome is one of Thackeray's finest characters. She has gentleness and sympathy, but also intelligence and spirit. Thackeray's later novels show the diminished energy of an author who was ill and tired.

Thackeray's View of Life. Thackeray disliked people who were unduly impressed by birth and rank. His skillful ridicule of snobs and hypocrites is even evident amid the broad humor of his early works. His realistic temperament enabled him to see and satirize inconsistencies in life. He once said of one of his characters that he "failed somehow in spite of a mediocrity which ought to have ensured any man a success." Thackeray knew that rogues sometimes do well while the innocent suffer, and that virtuous people can be dull and rascals lively. Such ironic twists in Thackeray's books were misunderstood by some people, who accused him of being cynical.

Others complained that Thackeray's writings were sentimental. For example, he seemed to admire womanhood as an abstract ideal. When he wrote about young ladies who were gentle and affectionate but perhaps not very bright, he sometimes fell into a style of adoration. But his deep honesty made him show, at the same time, how these sentimental people were often stupid and dull. His critics often fail to see that Thackeray really hated cruelty and greed, and admired goodness and warm-heartedness.   JOHN W. DODDS

THADDAEUS. See JUDE, SAINT.

The Boats of Merchants and Shoppers jam a canal in Bangkok, Thailand's capital and largest city. This traditional "floating market" is one of the city's most picturesque features.

Rus Arnold

THAILAND

THAILAND, *TY land,* is a country in Southeast Asia. It is a wet, tropical land with many rivers, forests, and mountains. The people of Thailand are called *Thai.* Most of them live in villages and farm the land. But many villagers move to Thailand's cities each year, and so the urban areas are growing rapidly. Bangkok is the capital and largest city.

Thailand is the only nation in Southeast Asia that has never been ruled by a Western power. Local peoples established the first Thai nation in A.D. 1238. The country was called Siam from 1782 to 1939, when it became known as Thailand. Its name in the Thai language is *Muang Thai,* which means *Land of the Free.*

Government

National Government. Thailand is a constitutional monarchy. The nation's Constitution of 1978 provides for a monarch, a prime minister, and a legislature called the National Assembly. Until 1980, only males could serve as monarch. But a law passed that year allows either males or females to hold the office.

Thailand's monarch has an advisory role as chief of state, but the prime minister actually heads the nation's government. The National Assembly nominates the prime minister, who is then formally appointed by the monarch. The prime minister selects a cabinet, called the Council of Ministers, which may have a maximum of 44 members.

The National Assembly consists of a Senate of 225 members and a House of Representatives with 301 members. The senators are selected by the prime minister with the approval of the monarch and may be replaced

Facts in Brief

Capital: Bangkok.

Official Language: Thai.

Official Name: Muang Thai (Land of the Free).

Form of Government: Constitutional monarchy.

Area: 198,457 sq. mi. (514,000 km²). *Greatest Distances—* north-south, 1,100 mi. (1,770 km); east-west, 480 mi. (772 km). *Coastline—*1,635 mi. (2,631 km).

Elevation: *Highest—*Inthanon Mountain, 8,514 ft. (2,595 m). *Lowest—*sea level.

Population: *Estimated 1983 Population—*50,027,000; distribution, 86 per cent rural, 14 per cent urban; density, 251 persons per sq. mi. (97 per km²). *1979 Census—* 46,113,756. *Estimated 1988 Population—*56,601,000.

Chief Products: *Agriculture—*rice, cassava, corn, cotton, rubber, sugar cane, tobacco. *Manufacturing—*automobiles, cement, drugs, electronic equipment, food products, paper, plywood, textiles. *Forestry and Fishing—*teak, bamboo, rattan, anchovies, mackerel, shellfish. *Mining—*tin, bauxite, iron ore, lead, manganese, natural gas, precious stones, tungsten.

National Anthem: "Pleng Chart" ("National Anthem of Thailand").

Money: *Basic Unit—*baht. For its value in U.S. dollars, see MONEY (table: Exchange Rates).

Herbert P. Phillips, the contributor of this article, is Professor of Anthropology at the University of California, Berkeley, and the author of Thai Peasant Personality.

175

THAILAND

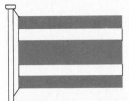

Thailand's Flag was adopted in 1917. The red represents the nation; the white, purity; and the blue, the monarchy.

The Coat of Arms, adopted in 1910, features the *garuda,* a mythical birdlike creature in the Buddhist religion.

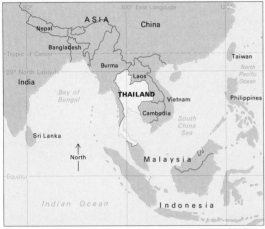

WORLD BOOK map

Thailand, a country in Southeast Asia, lies mostly on the Asian mainland. Southern Thailand extends along the Malay Peninsula.

at any time. The representatives are elected by the people to four-year terms.

Local Government. Thailand is divided into 72 provinces, which, in turn, are divided into 576 districts. Each province has a governor, and every district has a district officer. All these officials are appointed by the minister of the interior. Thailand also has more than 5,300 smaller divisions called *communes,* which consist of a total of almost 50,000 villages. The people of each village elect their own headman. The headmen then choose a *kamnan* from among themselves to serve as the chief administrator of their commune. Every city in Thailand is governed by a mayor and a council, both elected by the people.

Politics. In most cases, a Thai political party comes into power through an election or by a *coup* (sudden revolt) against the ruling party. Thailand has several major political parties and a number of smaller parties. Citizens who are at least 18 years old may vote if they can read and write in Thai.

Courts. The Supreme Court, called the *Sarn Dika,* is the highest court in Thailand. It consists of a chief justice and 21 judges. The Court of Appeals, the second highest court, reviews decisions made by lower courts. All judges of the Supreme Court, and all head judges of the other courts, are appointed by the monarch on the advice of the prime minister.

The Armed Forces of Thailand consist of an army, a navy, an air force, a national police force, and a village defense corps. The forces have a total membership of more than 200,000. Men from 21 to 30 years old may be drafted for at least two years of military duty.

The People

Population and Ancestry. Thailand has approximately 50 million people. About 86 per cent of the Thai live in rural areas. More than 5 million people make their homes in Bangkok.

The majority of the Thai are descendants of Thai-speaking peoples who migrated from southern China between the time period of the A.D. 100's and 900's. Chinese people make up the second largest population group. Most of the rest of the people are immigrants—or decendants of immigrants—from Burma, Cambodia, Malaysia, or Vietnam. The population also includes some European, Indian, and Japanese people—most of whom live in Bangkok. Small groups of peoples who follow tribal ways of life live in the country's northern mountains.

Way of Life. More than 75 per cent of Thailand's people make their living by farming. Large numbers of Thai also work in the fishing, lumbering, and mining industries. In the cities, many have jobs in factories. The nation's Chinese work mainly in commerce.

Most Thai live in villages that range in size from a few hundred to a few thousand people. The villagers raise almost all their own food, including corn, fruit, rice, and *cassava*—a tropical plant used in making tapioca. Every village has a school and a *wat* (Buddhist temple), which serves as the religious and social center of the community. The people enjoy village fairs, harvest celebrations, and other festive occasions.

Maurice G. G. Harvey, Alan Hutchison Library Ltd.

Modern Stores and Offices line the busy streets of the main business districts of Bangkok. The city is Thailand's chief commercial, cultural, and industrial center.

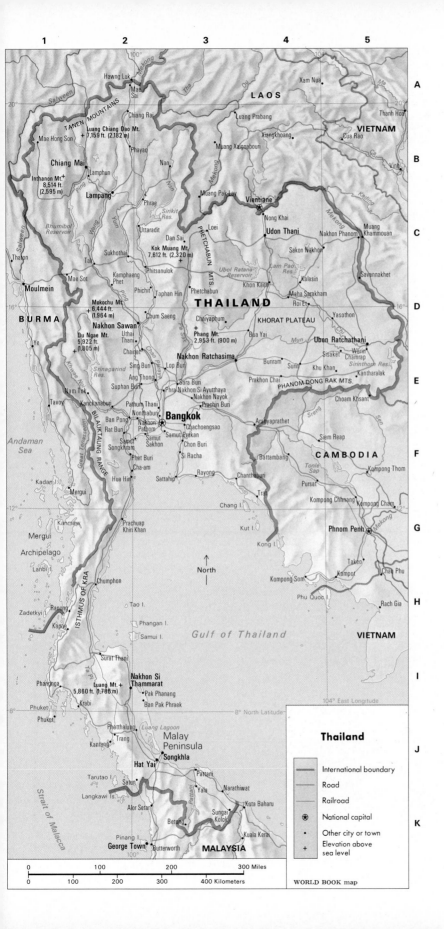

Cities and Towns

Ban Pak Phrat	22,625	.I 2
Ban Pong	25,047	.E 2
Bangkok	5,153,902	.E 2
Buriram	25,899	.E 4
Chachoeng-		
sao	37,931	.F 3
Chaiyaphum	20,932	.D 3
Chanthaburi	30,242	.F 3
Chiang Mai	100,146	.B 2
Chiang Rai	40,641	.A 2
Chon Buri	50,070	.F 2
Hat Yai	98,091	.J 2
Hua Hin	30,415	.F 2
Kalasin	22,152	.D 4
Kamphaeng		
Phet	20,200	.D 2
Kanchanaburi	29,502	.E 2
Khon Kaen	94,019	.D 4
Lampang	43,112	.B 2
Lop Buri	36,928	.E 2
Mae Sot	18,719	.C 1
Maha		
Sarakham	32,989	.D 4
Nakon		
Pathom	45,242	.E 2
Nakon		
Phanom	33,237	.C 5
Nakon		
Ratchasima	88,876	.E 3
Nakon Sawan	88,687	.D 2
Nakon Si		
Thammarat	66,558	.I 2
Nan	22,564	.B 3
Narathiwat	32,146	.K 3
Nong Khai	25,032	.C 4
Nonthaburi	30,940	.E 2
Pattani	32,020	.J 3
Phatthalung	29,948	.J 2
Phayao	24,400	.B 2
Phetchabun	23,763	.D 3
Phet Buri	34,597	.F 2
Phichit	18,675	.D 2
Phitsanulok	73,240	.C 2
Phra Nakon Si		
Ayutthaya	51,628	.E 2
Phrae	19,872	.B 2
Phuket	45,155	.J 1
Prachin		
Buri	20,330	.E 3
Rat Buri	43,316	.F 2
Rayong	37,305	.F 3
Roi Et	31,223	.D 4
Sakon		
Nakhon	24,491	.C 4
Samut		
Prakan	48,960	.F 2
Samut		
Sakhon	47,697	.F 2
Samut		
Songkhram	30,419	.F 2
Sara Buri	46,251	.E 3
Si Racha	21,651	.F 3
Sisaket	19,823	.E 5
Songkhla	72,326	.J 2
Sukhothai	21,931	.C 2
Sungi		
Kolok	21,917	.K 3
Suphan Buri	22,903	.E 2
Surat Thani	35,678	.I 2
Surin	33,737	.E 4
Tak	20,039	.C 2
Trang	44,102	.J 2
Ubon		
Ratchathani	48,537	.D 5
Udon Thani	81,060	.C 4
Uttaradit	33,311	.C 2
Warin		
Chamrap	29,586	.E 5
Yala	49,283	.J 3
Yasothon	19,007	.D 5

Physical Features

Andaman Sea	.F 1
Bilauktaung Range	.F 2
Chang Island	.G 3
Chao Phraya (river)	.E 2
Chi (river)	.D 5
Du Ngae Mountain	.E 1
Gulf of Thailand	.H 3
Inthanon Mountain	.B 1
Isthmus of Kra	.H 1
Khorat Plateau	.D 4
Khwae Noi (river)	.E 1
Kok Muang Mountain	.C 3
Kut Island	.G 4
Luang Chiang Dao	
Mountain	.B 1
Luaog Lagoon	.J 2
Mekong (river)	.C 4
Mokochu Mountain	.D 2
Mun (river)	.D 4
Nan (river)	.B 3
Pa Sak (river)	.D 3
Phang Mountain	.D 3
Phangan Island	.H 2
Phanom Dong	
Rak Mountains	.E 4
Phetchabun	
Mountains	.C 3
Phuket Island	.I 1
Ping (river)	.B 1
Samui Island	.H 2
Ta Pi (river)	.I 2
Tamur Mountains	.A 2
Tao Island	.H 2
Wang (river)	.C 2
Yom (river)	.C 2

Source: 1980 census.

176a

Middle-Class Housing in Thailand consists mainly of small, neat, single-family dwellings. The houses at the left are in a suburb of Bangkok.

Since the early 1960's, large numbers of Thai—especially young people—have moved from rural areas to cities in search of jobs and educational opportunities. The rapid growth of Thailand's cities has led to unemployment, crowded living conditions, and other serious problems.

The women of Thailand have more freedom than those of many other Asian nations. Numerous Thai women have jobs in business, education, government, and medicine.

Most urban Thai people wear Western-style clothing. In rural areas, many people—both males and females—wear the traditional *panung*, a colorful cotton or silk garment. A panung, which consists of a piece of cloth, is wrapped tightly around the body. A male's panung extends from the hips to the ankles, and a female's from above the chest to the ankles. For pictures of other Thai clothing, see CLOTHING (Traditional Costumes).

Housing. Most Thai villagers live in houses of wood or thatch that stand along rivers and canals. The homes are built on stilts to raise them above the ground for protection against flooding. Families use the area under their house as a shelter for farm animals. A high roof of tile or thatch helps keep the interior cool.

In the cities, many people live in small wooden or stucco houses. A number of the Chinese own shops and live in apartments above them. Some wealthy Thai have beautiful mansions. Poor communities in Thai cities consist either of slums or of housing projects built by the government.

Food. Thai people eat rice with almost every meal. Favorite foods served with rice include *curries* (spicy stews) and salads of meat, fish, and vegetables. The Thai take great pride in their *cuisine* (style of cooking and preparing food). Some communities are famous for their special dishes, and people often travel long distances just to taste these specialties.

Recreation. The Thai enjoy such sports as soccer and *Thai-style boxing*, in which opponents fight with both their hands and feet. In another popular sport, called

Thai-Style Boxing, in which opponents use their feet as well as their hands, is a popular sport throughout Thailand.

Buddhist Monks are dwarfed by a statue that guards the Temple of the Emerald Buddha in Bangkok.

Thai Classical Dancers act out traditional stories with religious themes. Jewels and embroidery decorate their costumes.

176b

takraw, the players try to keep a wicker ball in the air by using their heads, legs, and feet. Many Thai play *mak ruk*, a type of chess. Favorite forms of recreation involving gambling include cockfights and fish fights, in which male Siamese fighting fish attack each other in jars (see FIGHTING FISH). Card games and betting on the national lottery are also popular.

Languages. About 90 per cent of Thailand's people speak Thai, the official language. Thai has four main regional dialects. The dialect of central Thailand is the most common form of the language. A small number of Thai speak Malay and various dialects of Chinese. Many of the nation's secondary schools teach English, but few of the nation's people actually use it.

Religion. More than 95 per cent of the Thai people are Buddhists. They are members of the Therevada school of Buddhism (see BUDDHISM [Buddhist Schools]). According to custom, men over the age of 20 are expected to serve in the Buddhist monkhood for at least a few months, and more than 40 per cent of them actually do. Most of the Chinese in Thailand practice Confucianism, and the majority of the Malays are Muslims. Hinduism is the main religion among the Indians of Thailand. Most of the Europeans, as well as some of the Chinese and Vietnamese, belong to a Christian faith.

Education. More than 80 per cent of Thailand's people can read and write. The Thai government operates free elementary schools throughout the country, and all children are required by law to attend school for at least four years. However, most of Thailand's high schools are privately owned and charge tuition. Only about 10 per cent of the people have graduated from high school. Thailand has 14 universities, 43 teachers colleges, and 179 vocational schools. But only about 1 per cent of the people are university or teachers college graduates.

The Arts in Thailand are greatly influenced by Buddhism. The image of Buddha appears in many Thai paintings and sculptures. The nation's Buddhist temples rank among the best examples of Thai architecture, which combines traditional and modern styles.

Thai literature is divided into two groups, *wannakhadi* and *wannakam*. Wannakhadi consist of classical dramas and epic poems that were originally written and performed for royalty. Wannakam consist of novels, poems, and short stories about modern Thailand. Most of these works center on the problems and pleasures of everyday life.

The Land

Thailand covers 198,457 square miles (514,000 square kilometers). The country has four main land regions: (1) the Northern Mountains, (2) the Khorat Plateau, (3) the Central Plain, and (4) the Southern Peninsula.

The Northern Mountains occupy northwest Thailand and extend along the country's western border to the Malay Peninsula. They are covered by thick forests of evergreen and teak trees, which provide valuable timber. The mountains include Inthanon Mountain, the tallest peak, which rises 8,514 feet (2,595 meters) above sea level.

Many streams flow south from the mountains to the Gulf of Thailand. These streams deposit mud and sand

along their banks and help make the soil fertile. Farmers grow rice in the narrow mountain valleys. The region has deposits of copper, iron, and lead.

The Khorat Plateau, which lies in the northeastern part of Thailand, makes up about 30 per cent of the country's land area. It is also the country's most heavily populated region. The plateau is bordered by mountains on the south and west and by the Mekong River on the north and east.

Most of the plateau has sandy soil that holds little moisture. The Mekong, Chi, and Mun rivers provide irrigation water for the farming that takes place there. Rice is the principal crop.

The Central Plain extends between the foothills of the Northern Mountains region and the Gulf of Thailand. The fertile soil of the Central Plain enables farmers to raise more rice there than anywhere else in Thailand. Four rivers—the Nan, Ping, Wang, and Yom—unite in the northern part of the plain and become the Chao Phraya River, which is the country's chief transportation route.

The Southern Peninsula, which forms part of the Malay Peninsula, consists mainly of jungle, with some mountains and rolling hills. Many streams flow through the narrow valleys and flood small coastal plains. In the northern part of this region, Thailand and Burma share the Malay Peninsula. There, only a narrow strip of land belongs to Thailand.

The southern part of the region occupies the entire width of the Malay Peninsula. This mountainous area has fertile soil, and rubber trees thrive there. It also has large deposits of tin.

Animal Life. Thailand's forest and jungle areas abound with boars, crocodiles, deer, tigers, and such poisonous snakes as banded kraits and cobras—including king cobras. In the past, many elephants

Edward S. Ross

The Northern Mountains Region includes Thailand's highest peak, 8,514-foot (2,595-meter) Inthanon Mountain, *background*. In the foreground is a dwelling of the region's Meo people.

© Stephanie Colasanti

In Thailand's Teak Forests, elephants haul heavy logs to rivers to be floated downstream to sawmills. Strong and durable, teak is used mainly for shipbuilding and making fine furniture.

Charles Marden Fitch

Tin Mining contributes greatly to Thailand's foreign trade. Most of the country's tin mines, including the one shown here, are in the mountains of the Southern Peninsula region.

lived in the wild in Thailand. However, today most of the country's elephants have been domesticated. They serve as beasts of burden.

Climate

Thailand has a tropical climate. Most of the country has three seasons—a hot dry spring, a hot wet summer, and a mild winter. Bangkok has an average temperature of 62° F. (17° C) in January and 98° F. (37° C) in May. The Northern Mountains region is cooler, with temperatures averaging 32° F. (0° C) in January and 90° F. (32° C) in May.

From July to December, winds called *monsoons* cause heavy rains throughout Thailand. The Southern Peninsula region receives an average of about 100 inches (254 centimeters) of rain yearly. Bangkok has an average annual rainfall of 55 inches (140 centimeters).

Economy

Thailand has a developing economy that depends mainly on agriculture and manufacturing. More than 75 per cent of the nation's workers make their living by farming, compared with only about 7 per cent in manufacturing. However, manufactured agricultural products contribute about equally to the Thai economy. Large numbers of people have jobs in the fishing, forestry, and mining industries, and many work in commerce, government, and tourism. The economy operates as a free enterprise system, though the government sets prices for such important goods as rice and gasoline.

Agriculture. Thai farmers cultivate about 25 per cent of the nation's land, mostly to grow rice. Other leading crops include cassava, corn, cotton, rubber, sugar cane, and tobacco. Thailand also produces bananas, coconuts, pineapples, silk, soybeans, and *jute*, a fiber plant used in making rope. Farms in Thailand average about 6 acres (2 hectares), and more than 75 per cent of the farmers own their land.

Manufacturing has become increasingly important in Thailand since 1960. The nation's leading industries produce cement, food products, paper, plywood, and textiles. Many international companies operate factories

in the Bangkok area. These plants assemble automobiles and electronic equipment, and manufacture drugs and other products.

Forestry and Fishing. Forests cover about 60 per cent of Thailand. Teak is the chief forest product. Elephants move the heavy teak logs to rivers, and the timber is floated downstream to lumber mills for sawing and shipping. Other important forest products include bamboo and *rattan*, a tough, stringy material that comes from the stems of certain palm trees.

Anchovies, mackerel, and such shellfish as crabs and shrimp are caught in Thailand's rivers and coastal waters. Most Thai farmers raise fish and shellfish in ponds that they build on their property.

Mining. Tin is Thailand's most important mineral, and the nation ranks among the world's leading tin producers. Mines in Thailand also provide large amounts of bauxite, iron ore, lead, manganese, precious stones, and tungsten. Natural gas is obtained from deposits in the Gulf of Thailand.

Foreign Trade. Thailand's chief exports include rice, rubber, tapioca products, teak, and tin. The Thai also export corn, sugar, and tobacco. The nation imports such products as chemicals, fuels, and machinery. Thailand trades mainly with Japan, the United States, and China.

Transportation in Thailand ranks among the best in Southeast Asia. The country has about 8,100 miles (13,000 kilometers) of paved roads and more than 2,400 miles (3,800 kilometers) of railroad track. Rivers and canals in Thailand provide local transportation for passengers and cargo. Bangkok is the country's largest and busiest port.

Four international airports provide daily flights between Thailand and other Asian nations, various European countries, and Australia. Local airlines serve the nation's major cities.

Communication. Thailand has approximately 50 daily newspapers, about 20 of which are published in Bangkok. Most of the newspapers are published in Thai, and the rest in Chinese or English. Telegraph and telephone systems link the principal cities. The nation

176d

has 4 major television networks and more than 200 radio stations. The government owns and operates all the TV and radio stations.

History

Early Days. People have lived in what is now Thailand for more than 5,000 years. Archaeological evidence indicates that people in what is now the northeastern Thai village of Non Nok Tha grew rice for food more than 5,000 years ago. The evidence is the world's first known record of the cultivation of rice—the most widely eaten of all human foods. The ancestors of most present-day Thai probably moved into the region from southern China between the time period of the A.D. 100's and 900's. They established many settlements, and in 1238, the Thai formed the first Thai nation. They named it *Sukothai*, which means *Dawn of Happiness*. King Ramkhamhaeng, one of the early rulers of Sukothai, invented the Thai alphabet. Sukothai expanded and prospered and, by 1350, occupied most of what became Thailand.

Invasions and Wars. In 1350, a group of Thai people established the kingdom and the city of Ayutthaya in what is now the central region of Thailand. By the late 1300's, Sukothai had declined in importance. The Ayutthaya kingdom absorbed it. The city of Ayutthaya served as the Thai capital from the mid-1300's to the mid-1700's. During that period, the kingdom of Ayutthaya fought numerous wars with the Malays to the south, the Burmese to the west, and the Khmer of Cambodia to the east. In 1431, Thai forces invaded Cambodia and captured its capital, Angkor.

European Contact for the Thai began when Portuguese traders came to Ayutthaya in the early 1500's. During the 1600's, Spain, England, France, Japan, and The Netherlands also established trade there. The Thai granted some nations—including France, England, and The Netherlands—*rights of extraterritoriality*. These rights allowed the people of the foreign nations to live in Ayutthaya under the laws of their own countries (see EXTRATERRITORIALITY).

During the late 1600's, many young Thai began going to schools in Europe, where they learned Western ideas and customs. At the same time, European powers began to interfere in Ayutthaya's internal affairs. This interference angered the Thai. They forced all Europeans to leave the country, canceled the extraterritorial rights of some of the European nations, and resisted any contact with Western nations.

A New Dynasty. Burmese troops invaded Ayutthaya in 1767 and destroyed the capital. But Thai forces, led by General Phyra Taksin, soon drove the Burmese out of the country. Taksin became king and established a new capital at Thonburi.

In 1782, General Phyra Chakri replaced Taksin as king. Chakri took the title Rama I and established the Chakri dynasty, which still reigns in Thailand. In 1782, the nation's name was changed to Siam and the Thai capital was moved from Thonburi across the Chao Phraya River to Bangkok.

King Mongkut (Rama IV), who ruled from 1851 to 1868, was one of Siam's most influential monarchs. He employed advisers from Western nations and encouraged his people to study Western languages and modern science. Mongkut also resumed trade relations with France, Great Britain, and other countries, and granted them extraterritorial rights.

King Chulalongkorn (Rama V), Mongkut's son, continued the social reforms started by his father. During his reign, from 1873 to 1910, Chulalongkorn abolished slavery in Siam, reorganized the government, and established a public education system designed to serve all the nation's children.

World War I and World War II. During World War I (1914-1918), Siam supported France and Great Britain against Germany and Austria-Hungary. Some Thai soldiers fought in Europe. In return for Siam's help in the war, France and Great Britain gave up their rights of extraterritoriality.

In 1932, a group of Thai who had been educated in France revolted against King Prajadhipok (Rama VII). They forced him to change the government from an absolute monarchy to a constitutional monarchy. In 1935, Prajadhipok gave up the throne in favor of his 10-year-old nephew, Ananda Mahidol (Rama VIII). A *regency* (group of temporary rulers) governed the country for the young king. Some members of the government were military officials, and others were civilians. The civilians held control at first, but the military officers took over in 1938. The country's name was changed to Thailand in 1939.

In 1940, during World War II, Thailand demanded the return of land that King Chulalongkorn had given French Indochina before World War I. Japan supported Thailand's demand and forced Indochina to return the land. In 1941, Japan invaded Thailand. The Thai resisted for a few hours but then signed a treaty of alliance with Japan. That same year, the Japanese attacked the United States military bases at Pearl Harbor in Hawaii, and the United States went to war against Japan. Thailand declared war on the United States and Great Britain in 1942. During the war, a Free Thai Movement worked against the Japanese within Thailand.

After World War II. Field Marshal Pibul Songgram, who had served as prime minister during the Japanese occupation, ruled Thailand from 1946 to 1957. He was overthrown by Field Marshal Sarit Thanarat, who ruled the country until his death in 1963. Sarit brought widespread economic development to Thailand and strengthened the nation's ties with the United States. His successor, Field Marshal Thanom Kittikachorn, continued these policies. Thanom permitted the United States to build air bases in Thailand. In 1965, during the Vietnam War, United States forces began using the air bases to attack Communist forces in Vietnam, Cambodia, and Laos. Thailand also sent troops to Vietnam to fight on the side of South Vietnam and the United States.

In 1967, Thailand, Indonesia, Malaysia, the Philippines, and Singapore formed the Association of Southeast Asian Nations (ASEAN). This organization promotes economic, cultural, and social cooperation among its members.

In 1973, university students in Thailand led a civilian revolt against the Thai government. For the next three years, Thailand had a series of democratically elected governments. This democratic period ended in October

THAILAND

1976 after conservative groups attacked radical students at Thammasat University in Bangkok. About 40 persons died in the fighting, and thousands of others were arrested. Military leaders then took control of the government again.

Thailand Today is one of the most prosperous nations in Southeast Asia, but it faces many serious problems. Some Malay Muslims in southern Thailand want to establish an independent nation, and they started to revolt against the Thai government in the late 1960's. Communist forces in the northeast areas of Thailand are a constant threat to the government.

Since 1975, after the end of the Vietnam War, thousands of refugees have moved to Thailand from Cambodia, Laos, and Vietnam. The Thai government provides the refugees with food, clothing, and shelter—a considerable drain on the nation's economy. In addition, continued conflicts between Vietnamese and Cambodians near Thailand's borders represent a constant threat to the peace and security of the nation.   HERBERT P. PHILLIPS

Related Articles in WORLD BOOK include:

Asia (pictures: A Buddhist Monk; River Transportation)	Mekong River
Association of Southeast Asian Nations	Rice (graph)
	Rubber (graph)
Bangkok	Southeast Asia Treaty Organization
Buddhism	Teak
Clothing (pictures: Clothing for Work; Religious Clothing)	Tin (graph)

Outline

I. **Government**
  A. National Government
  B. Local Government
  C. Politics
  D. Courts
  E. The Armed Forces
II. **The People**
  A. Population and Ancestry
  B. Way of Life
  C. Housing
  D. Food
  E. Recreation
  F. Languages
  G. Religion
  H. Education
  I. The Arts
III. **The Land**
  A. The Northern Mountains
  B. The Khorat Plateau
  C. The Central Plain
  D. The Southern Peninsula
  E. Animal Life
IV. **Climate**
V. **Economy**
  A. Agriculture
  B. Manufacturing
  C. Forestry and Fishing
  D. Mining
  E. Foreign Trade
  F. Transportation
  G. Communication
VI. **History**

Questions

How does Buddhism influence the arts in Thailand?
What are some popular Thai dishes?
How did King Mongkut help promote the culture of Thailand?
How do elephants serve the Thai lumber industry?
What was the first Thai nation? When was it formed?
What is a *wat*? A *panung*? A *kamnan*?
What is Thailand's major rice-producing area?
How does Thai-style boxing differ from other boxing?
What is Thailand's principal crop? Chief mineral?
What is Thailand's name in Thai? What does it mean in English?

Additional Resources

AMERICAN UNIVERSITY. *Thailand: A Country Study.* 5th ed. U.S. Government Printing Office, 1981.
Fodor's Japan and East Asia. McKay, 1974. Includes description and travel information on Thailand.
MOLE, ROBERT L. *Thai Values and Behavior Patterns.* Tuttle, 1973.
SMITH, HAROLD E. *Historical and Cultural Dictionary of Thailand.* Scarecrow, 1976.

THALASSEMIA, *THAL uh SEE mee uh,* is a hereditary blood disease that causes anemia. It occurs chiefly among children whose ancestors came from the area near the Mediterranean Sea. It also afflicts black Americans and some Asian and Middle Eastern peoples.

The bodies of children with thalassemia do not produce enough *hemoglobin,* a pigment that gives red blood cells their color. Hemoglobin also carries oxygen to body tissues. A shortage of hemoglobin deprives the victim's organs of the oxygen they need. Symptoms of thalassemia are present at birth or appear about six months later. They include pale skin, tiredness, irritability, poor appetite, and retarded growth. The child develops an enlarged heart, liver, and spleen. The disease also deforms and weakens certain bones, especially those in the face.

The severest form of the disease is *thalassemia major,* or *Cooley's anemia.* It occurs in children who inherit the hemoglobin defect from both parents. Many victims of thalassemia major die in infancy, and almost all die by early adulthood. A milder form, *thalassemia intermedia,* occurs in children who inherit a severe form of the defect from one parent or a mild form from both. It is not fatal in most cases. People who inherit the defect from only one parent usually get *thalassemia minor.* Such individuals are called *carriers* of the disease because they do not have its symptoms but may pass it on to their children.

Thalassemia cannot be cured, but it can be treated by blood transfusions given every three to six weeks. This treatment relieves the symptoms, but it causes excess iron to build up in the heart, pancreas, and other organs. The deposits of iron often lead to diabetes and heart failure. Researchers are working to develop drugs and techniques to remove the iron deposits from the body.   DOMINICK SABATINO

THALER. See DOLLAR.

THALES, *THAY leez* (625?-546? B.C.), was the earliest known Greek philosopher. He was born in Miletus in Asia Minor. All that is known about Thales and his thought came from brief and scattered reports by later historians and philosophers.

According to the Greek philosopher Aristotle, Thales was the first philosopher to attempt to discover the underlying material source of all things. Aristotle wrote that Thales believed that this substance was water. He also reported that Thales believed that magnets have souls because of their ability to move iron.

Thales was perhaps the first individual to bring a philosophic and scientific approach to subjects that had previously been given mythological and supernatural explanations. He was the first to use reasoning and observation in attempting to answer questions about human beings and the universe. Thales may therefore be considered the founder of the philosophical and scientific tradition in the Western world. S. MARC COHEN

See also PRE-SOCRATIC PHILOSOPHY (Early Pre-Socratic Philosophers).

THALIA. See GRACES; MUSES.

THALIDOMIDE. See DRUG (Testing with People).

THALLIUM is a soft, bluish-gray metallic element that looks like lead. Most thallium comes from iron pyrites, in which traces of the element occur as an impurity. It also occurs in the minerals crookesite, hutchinsonite, and lorandite. Sir William Crookes, an English chemist and physicist, discovered thallium in 1861.

Thallium has an atomic number of 81 and an atomic weight of 204.37. Its chemical symbol is Tl. Thallium melts at $303.5°$ C and boils at $1457°$ $(+10°)$ C. At $20°$ C, it has a density of 11.85 grams per cubic centimeter (see DENSITY).

Thallium and its compounds have various uses. A radioactive isotope of the element, Tl-201, is useful for diagnosing certain types of heart disease. The compound thallium sulfate ($Tl_2[SO_4]_3$) is widely used in ant and rat poisons. Thallium bromide (TlBr), thallium iodide (TlI), and thallium sulfide (Tl_2S_3) undergo changes when exposed to infrared radiation, and so they are used in devices for detecting and measuring such radiant energy. ALAN DAVISON

See also ELEMENT, CHEMICAL (tables).

THALLOPHYTE, *THAL oh fyte*, is a plant in the subkingdom *Thallophyta*. This group includes the more primitive plants. They may consist of only one cell, or of many cells. But they do not have complex organs such as roots, stems, and leaves. Thallophytes include *algae*, or pond scums and seaweeds; *fungi*, or molds and mushrooms; and *bacteria*. See also ALGAE; BACTERIA; FUNGI; PLANT (table: A Classification). GEORGE B. CUMMINS

THAMES, *tehmz*, **RIVER,** is the most famous and most important river in England. It is also the longest river entirely within England. The Severn, partly in England and partly in Wales, is longer. The Thames flows 215 miles (346 kilometers) from the Cotswold Hills in south-central England to southeastern England, where it empties into the North Sea. The river serves as a major English trade route. For location, see GREAT BRITAIN (terrain map).

A number of cities lie along the River Thames, including Oxford, Reading, Kingston upon Thames, London, Tilbury, and Southend-on-Sea. The river winds through the center of London, passing such famous buildings as the Houses of Parliament and the Tower of London. The Thames measures about 5 miles (8 kilometers) wide at its mouth on the North Sea. The sea creates tides, which affect the lower part of the Thames.

London owes its origin and much of its importance to the Thames. In London, industries were established on the banks of the river and the city became England's most important trading port. The London docks were built on the river in the 1800's. But in the 1900's, most of the shipping activity was moved from London to Tilbury. Oil refineries stand at the mouth of the river. Part of the lower Thames has been *dredged* (deepened by digging up the river bottom) to allow large ships to sail inland from the North Sea. ADRIAN ROBINSON

See also GREAT BRITAIN (picture: The Houses of Parliament).

THAMES RIVER, BATTLE OF. See WAR OF 1812 (Chief Battles of the War); HARRISON, WILLIAM H. (Army Commander); INDIANA (Territorial Days).

THANE, *thayn*, is an Anglo-Saxon title which was used for many years in early England. The word thane had many meanings. At various times it meant servant, attendant, retainer, or official. Early England had a system of thanehood which was similar to the later system of knighthood. Thanehood was open to freemen, not of noble birth, who fulfilled the following conditions: gaining control of a certain amount of land, making three sea voyages, or doing military service.

A thane of ordinary standing received a manor from the lord he served. In time, a successful thane might become an *earl* (member of the higher nobility). In wartime, royal thanes formed the king's personal bodyguard. The title has not been used since the reign of William the Conqueror. ROBERT S. HOYT

THANKSGIVING DAY. In the United States and Canada, a day is set aside each year as Thanksgiving Day. On this day, people give thanks with feasting and prayer for the blessings they may have received during the year. The first Thanksgiving Days were harvest festivals, or days for thanking God for plentiful crops. For this reason the holiday still takes place late in the fall, after the crops have been gathered. For thousands of years people in many lands have held harvest festivals. The American Thanksgiving Day probably grew out of the harvest-home celebrations of England.

In the United States, Thanksgiving is usually a family day, celebrated with big dinners and joyous reunions. The very mention of Thanksgiving often calls

The Thames River flows through the heart of London, past many famous landmarks. Tower Bridge, *background,* is one of 15 London bridges that span the Thames.

Thanksgiving, a Painting by the American Artist Doris E. Lee, Shows Women Preparing Thanksgiving Dinner.

up memories of kitchens and pantries crowded with good things to eat. Thanksgiving is also a time for serious religious thinking, church services, and prayer.

One of the first Thanksgiving observances in America was entirely religious and did not involve feasting. On Dec. 4, 1619, 39 English settlers arrived at Berkeley Plantation, on the James River near what is now Charles City, Va. The group's charter required that the day of arrival be observed yearly as a day of thanksgiving to God.

The First New England Thanksgiving was celebrated less than a year after the Plymouth colonists had settled in the new land. The first dreadful winter in Massachusetts had killed nearly half of the members of the colony. But new hope grew up in the summer of 1621. The corn harvest brought rejoicing. Governor William Bradford decreed that a three-day feast be held. A Thanksgiving Day for the purpose of prayer as well as celebration was decreed by Governor Bradford for July 30, 1623.

The women of the colony spent many days preparing for the feast. The children helped by turning roasts on spits in front of open fires. Indians brought wild turkeys and *venison* (deer meat). The men of the colony brought geese, ducks, and fish. The women served the meat and fish with journey cake, corn meal bread with nuts, and succotash. Everyone ate outdoors at big tables.

Later Thanksgiving Days in the United States. The custom of Thanksgiving Day spread from Plymouth to other New England colonies. During the Revolutionary War, eight special days of thanks were observed for

victories and for being saved from dangers. In 1789, President George Washington issued a general proclamation naming November 26 a day of national thanksgiving. In the same year, the Protestant Episcopal Church announced that the first Thursday in November would be a regular yearly day for giving thanks.

For many years there was no regular national Thanksgiving Day in the United States. Some of the states had a yearly Thanksgiving holiday, and others did not. But by 1830 New York had an official state Thanksgiving Day, and other Northern States soon followed its example. Virginia was the first Southern state to adopt the custom. It proclaimed a Thanksgiving Day in 1855.

Mrs. Sarah Josepha Hale, the editor of *Godey's Lady's Book*, worked many years to promote the idea of a national Thanksgiving Day. Then President Lincoln proclaimed the last Thursday in November 1863, as "a day of thanksgiving and praise to our beneficent Father." See HALE, SARAH JOSEPHA.

Each year afterward, for 75 years, the President of the United States formally proclaimed that Thanksgiving Day should be celebrated on the last Thursday of November. But in 1939, President Roosevelt set it one week earlier. He wanted to help business by lengthening the shopping period before Christmas. Congress finally ruled that after 1941 the fourth Thursday of November would be observed as Thanksgiving Day and would be a legal federal holiday.

Thanksgiving Day in Canada is celebrated in much the same way as in the United States. It was formerly celebrated on the last Monday in October. But, in 1957, the Canadian government proclaimed the second Monday in October for the holiday.　ELIZABETH HOUGH SECHRIST

Additional Resources

BARTH, EDNA. *Turkeys, Pilgrims and Indian Corn: The Story of Thanksgiving Symbols.* Houghton, 1975.
JUPO, FRANK. *The Thanksgiving Book.* Dodd, 1980.
LUCKHARDT, MILDRED C. comp. *Thanksgiving Feast and Festival.* Abingdon, 1966.
SECHRIST, ELIZABETH HOUGH, and WOOLSEY, JANETTE. *It's Time for Thanksgiving.* Macrae Smith, 1957.

THANT, *thahnt,* **U,** *oo* (1909-1974), a Burmese diplomat, served as secretary-general of the United Nations (UN) from 1962 to 1971. He had become acting secretary-general in 1961, filling the unexpired term of the late Dag Hammarskjöld. U Thant had only one name, as do most Burmese. *U,* a title of respect, has a meaning similar to *Mister.*

U Thant was born in Pantanaw, Burma, and attended University College in Rangoon. From 1928 to 1947, U Thant taught school and worked as a journalist. He strongly opposed colonialism. In 1947, he became Burma's press director. He was named director of broadcasting in 1948. In 1957, U Thant became chairman of the Burmese UN delegation.

See also UNITED NATIONS (picture).

THAR DESERT, or **INDIAN DESERT,** stretches northwest of the Aravalli Range in India across Rajasthan to the Indus River plain in Pakistan. The Punjab region forms its northern limits. For location, see INDIA (physical map). The Thar Desert covers 74,000 square miles (192,000 square kilometers). Less than 10 inches (25 centimeters) of rain falls there annually. The few people raise some sheep where the soil has enough water for grass. However, large irrigation projects have been started in the Thar Desert.　PHILLIPS TALBOT

THARP, TWYLA (1941-　　), is an American dancer and *choreographer* (composer of dances). Her works feature a wide variety of movements from many types of dance, including ballet, various social dances, and tap-dancing. Tharp combines these movements to create dances filled with clever gestures and abrupt, unexpected changes in motion. Her choreography seems spontaneous, but actually it is carefully planned.

During the 1960's, Tharp created dances to be performed without music. But beginning with *Eight Jelly Rolls* (1971), she has used a wide variety of music to accompany her works. For example, *As Time Goes By* (1973) is performed to music by the Austrian composer Joseph Haydn. *Deuce Coupe* (1973 and 1974) is danced to the rock music of the Beach Boys. *Sue's Leg* (1975) has an accompaniment of music by the American jazz pianist and composer Fats Waller.

Tharp was born in Portland, Ind. She joined the Paul Taylor Dance Company in 1963. Tharp formed her own dance company in 1965, but she has also composed dances for other companies. In addition, she created the choreography for the motion picture *Hair* (1979).　DIANNE L. WOODRUFF

THATCHER, MARGARET HILDA (1925-　　), became prime minister of Great Britain in 1979. She is the first woman ever to hold the office. Thatcher became prime minister after the Conservative Party—which she heads—defeated the Labour Party in a parliamentary general election. A strong opponent of the La-

bour Party's socialist policies, Thatcher has worked to reduce government control over Britain's economy during her term. She has faced such problems as high inflation and unemployment rates.

Thatcher was born Margaret Hilda Roberts in Grantham, Lincolnshire, England. She married Denis Thatcher, a London business executive, in 1951. She received a degree in chemistry from Oxford University, and worked as a research chemist in the early 1950's. She also studied law. In 1953, she became an attorney specializing in tax law. Thatcher was elected to the House of Commons in 1959. She was secretary of state for education and science from 1970 to 1974. In 1975, she became the first woman to head a British political party, when she was elected leader of the Conservative Party by the party's members of Parliament.　RICHARD ROSE

THAYENDANEGEA. See BRANT, JOSEPH.

THAYER, SYLVANUS (1785-1872), was an American Army officer who became known as father of West Point. From 1817 to 1833, Colonel Thayer served as superintendent of the United States Military Academy at West Point. His long service allowed him to impress his professional standards and his ideas of duty, honor, and loyalty on several generations of cadets. He was born in Braintree, Mass.　H. A. DEWEERD

Wide World
Margaret Thatcher

Martha Swope

A Twyla Tharp Dance, *When We Were Very Young,* dramatizes a woman's search for fulfillment. The dancers use a wide variety of movement to express the work's emotions.

Van Bucher, Photo Researchers

The Bright Lights of Broadway Symbolize the Theater in the United States.

THEATER

THEATER is an art form in which a series of events, usually a written play, is acted out by performers who impersonate the characters. It generally takes place in an auditorium before an audience.

Opening night—or any other night—in a theater is an exciting event, whether in a Broadway playhouse or a high school auditorium. Part of the excitement takes place in front of the stage where the audience waits eagerly for the performance. But the excitement is perhaps even greater backstage. There, the people involved in a play wait to see whether the audience approves of the result of weeks or even months of hard work.

The word *theater* comes from the Greek word *theatron*, meaning *a place for seeing*. In this sense, the word still refers to a building in which plays are performed. However, theater in a broader sense includes all aspects of play production. Theater also refers to a part of human culture that began in primitive times.

Although theater is not the same as *drama*, the words are often used interchangeably. Drama refers to the script of a play—the written work that is used as the basis for theatrical performances. Some critics believe that a play is not really a play until it has been per-

formed in a theater for an audience. Others argue that the script is only a blueprint that the director and other interpretive artists use as the basis for performance.

The theater is perhaps the most complex of the arts because it requires so many kinds of artists for its creation. These specialists include the playwright, performers, director, scene designer, costumer, and lighting designer. For many productions, musicians and a *choreographer* (dance composer) are needed. The theater is sometimes called a *mixed art* because it combines the script of the playwright, the scenic background of the architect and painter, and the speech and movement of the actors and actresses.

In the earliest theatrical performances, all artistic functions were performed by the dramatist, who acted in his own plays. Gradually, specialists developed and the various theater arts took shape. The actor and the playwright gained recognition first, probably because each needed the other to bring his art to life.

In the modern theater, a director is needed to settle differences between performers over such matters as interpretation of lines and movements on stage. The director also plans most of the stage action and coordinates it with the scenic background, costumes, lights, sound effects, music, dancing, and other elements.

This article describes how the theater arts are used to create a play. For a discussion of the history of written drama and theater practices, see DRAMA.

The contributors of this article are Oscar G. Brockett, Ashbel Smith Professor of Drama at the University of Texas, and Lenyth Brockett, a former copywriter for the Indiana University Press.

Every theater building has three basic parts: (1) the auditorium, (2) the stage, and (3) work areas.

The Auditorium is where the audience sits. In the broadest sense, it also includes such facilities as the box office, lobby, entrances and exits, rest rooms, and refreshment stands.

A well-designed auditorium allows every person in the audience to see and hear without strain. It also permits the spectators to reach and leave their seats easily. The interior is decorated in a pleasing fashion that does not distract attention from the stage. Auditoriums may be large or small, and they vary in their basic characteristics. The seats are either all on the main floor, or on the main floor and in one or more balconies. The audience watches the action of the play from one, two, three, or all four sides. The distance between the closest spectators and the stage varies greatly from one auditorium to another.

The Stage. Three basic types of stages are used in today's theater: (1) the proscenium stage, (2) the open or platform stage, and (3) the theater-in-the-round or arena stage. Each of these types creates a different relationship between the actors and the audience, and each requires certain adjustments in play production.

The *proscenium stage* is designed to be viewed only from the front. It is sometimes called a "picture frame" stage, because the opening through which the audience sees the action forms a frame for the actors and scenery.

This frame is called a *proscenium arch*. Normally, the plays are performed behind it.

A proscenium stage has a curtain that is generally used to conceal or reveal the stage. The curtain may be closed to permit changes in scenery, to indicate the passage of time, or to mark the act or scene divisions of a play. Scenery can be placed on three sides of the stage. The actors enter or leave the stage by way of the *wings* (sides) or the back, depending on the location of doors or other openings in the set.

Most proscenium stages are farther from the audience than are open or arena stages. An orchestra pit or a forestage area may be between the seats and the acting area behind the proscenium arch. The scenery is created in three dimensions, but is viewed only from the front.

Most *open stages* have seats arranged around three sides of a raised platform that extends into the auditorium. The purpose of the open stage is to bring audience and performers closer together than the proscenium stage can.

Because the audience sits on three sides of an open stage, little scenery can be used. Often, there is no curtain. An open stage has a limited capacity for realistic effects, but it is well suited for productions written for a theater with a large acting platform. Such plays include many by Shakespeare. The scenery, as well as the acting and other elements, must be planned so they can be seen from three sides at the same time. Large units of

A Proscenium Stage permits the audience to see a play only from the front. Plays are usually performed behind a frame called the *proscenium arch*, which encloses the stage area.

Auditorium Theatre, Chicago (*Chicago Sun-Times*)

Mark Taper Forum, Los Angeles (Center Theatre Group, Los Angeles)

scenery can be used only at the back of the stage, or the audience's view will be blocked.

A *theater-in-the-round* has no stage as such. The actors perform in an open space at floor level in the middle of the auditorium. The audience sits in seats arranged in bleacher fashion around all four sides of the acting area. Most theaters-in-the-round can seat only about 200 persons. As a result, the actors and audience have a close relationship. The spectators sit near enough to see fine shadings of the performers' expressions and gestures.

A limited kind and amount of scenery can be used in a theater-in-the-round. Because the audience sits on all four sides of the acting area, scenery must be low enough to allow the area to be seen from every angle. Most of these theaters do not have curtains, and so scene changes must be made either in darkness or in view of the audience. Pieces of scenery are moved through the aisles of the auditorium. Since the scenery is seen at close view, it must be built with great attention to detail. The performers turn frequently so that each part of the audience can see them from the front as much as possible.

Work Areas in a fully equipped theater include shops to make costumes and scenery, rehearsal and dressing rooms, storage space, lighting booths, and office space. Only such huge theaters as the Metropolitan Opera House have all these facilities. Most professional theaters do not have equipment to build scenery, and many nonprofessional groups work in limited space.

An Open Stage extends into the auditorium on three sides. This stage permits a close relationship between audience and performers, but limits large set pieces to the rear of the stage.

A Theater-in-the-Round is an open area in the auditorium, with the audience sitting on all four sides. The actors must adjust their performances so the entire audience can see and hear.

Production of Shakespeare's *The Taming of the Shrew*.
George de Vincent, courtesy Arena Stage, Washington, D.C.

In the modern theater, the director is responsible for the artistic effectiveness of the production as a whole. He or she decides how the script is interpreted and coordinates the efforts of all the other artists. The director ordinarily has five major duties: (1) analyzing the play and determining the interpretation; (2) working with the playwright, technicians, and designers of scenery, lighting, and costumes in planning the production; (3) casting the performers; (4) supervising rehearsals; and (5) coordinating each element of the final production.

Interpreting the Script. The director must be thoroughly familiar with the play in order to cast and rehearse the performers intelligently and guide the various designers. He or she studies the play's construction, noting its pattern of preparation, complications, crisis, and resolution. The director also examines the devices the author uses to tell the story and to build suspense. For this analysis, the play may be divided into short scenes separated by the entrance or exit of characters. Then the function of each scene is examined. Why do the characters behave as they do? What is the predominant mood? How is each scene related to those before and after it?

The director must understand each character as it functions in the play and what is demanded of the performer who will play the role. The director learns each character's physical characteristics, personality, emotional range, and vocal qualities. The scenic, costume, and lighting requirements must be visualized. The mood of the setting, its arrangement for the flow of action, and its suitability as background for the characters and events must also be pictured. The director also may study the background of the author and the period of the play.

Problems of interpretation vary according to whether the play is historical, a revival of a recent Broadway success, or an original drama. In producing historical plays, the director encounters special problems. Changes may be required in the script to make sure the play will be understood by a modern audience. The director might modernize the language or cut speeches or entire scenes. The director also might try to make a play more meaningful to modern audiences by changing its time and place. For example, *Hamlet* has been costumed in modern dress. Perhaps the director will change the emphasis of a play to give a new interpretation to a character. Shylock in *The Merchant of Venice* was played as a comic character during the 1600's, but most modern productions emphasize his pathetic aspects.

When working with a recent play, the director may be able to obtain a detailed account of how the original production was staged. In producing a new play, the director works directly with the playwright, suggesting changes and cuts. This process of rewriting may continue throughout the rehearsal period.

Working with the Designers. Before beginning rehearsals, the director discusses the interpretation of the play with the scenic, costume, and lighting designers. These experts make suggestions about design, and the director may make specific requests. For example, doors may be needed at particular places on the stage.

The director makes sure that the proposed settings reflect the action, mood, theme, characters, and period of the play. The settings also must be functional in terms of the performers' movements.

Casting. One of the director's first tasks is to select the performers for all the roles in the play. An open tryout may be held, to which anyone may come. In the professional theater, however, many more performers seek work than are needed, and so closed or invitational tryouts are almost always used. Invitations to try out for parts are sent only to performers who are known to the director, producer, or playwright.

Performers trying out for a role may be given the play to read before the tryout. Perhaps they will be asked to read material they have never seen before. Some directors ask performers to memorize and act scenes from various plays. Others ask them to prepare pantomimes, or to respond to directions given during the tryout.

Many factors determine the final casting. Some roles demand specific physical or vocal characterizations. The director also considers the emotional range demanded in a role, and casts each part with the other parts in mind. Directors seek performers who are suited to their roles and who combine with others to make up a balanced and varied cast.

Rehearsing. During rehearsals, the director has three major concerns: (1) stage picture; (2) movements, gestures, and facial expressions; and (3) voice and speech.

Casting a Broadway Play, *above,* may take place in a hotel ballroom. At a rehearsal, *below,* of Arthur Miller's play *After the Fall,* actor Jason Robards, *left,* Miller, *center,* and director Elia Kazan, *standing,* discuss the meaning of a scene.

Inge Morath, Magnum

To achieve a proper *stage picture*, the director makes sure that each moment of the performance presents an image that communicates silently with the audience. Each stage picture should have a center of interest and should express the dominant emotional tone and the relationships among the characters. The director's chief task is to focus the audience's attention on the important elements—usually one or two characters who are most important at the moment. This is done by manipulating the positions of the performers in relation to the audience and to each other. The stage picture is also strongly affected by the setting, costumes, and lighting.

The director uses *movement* to blend one stage picture into another, and to create a sense of flow and development. It is one of a director's most powerful tools. Movement must always be appropriate for the characters, situation, mood, and type of play. For example, surprise and anger tend to cause people to move closer together, but disgust and fear usually move people apart. *Gestures* and *facial expressions* supplement the effects of movement. Most problems of *voice* and *speech* are worked out by the performers, but the director makes sure that they speak clearly and expressively.

Most early rehearsals take place in a rehearsal room rather than on a stage. Chalk lines indicate the floor plan, and only basic furniture and props are used. Directors rarely have as much time as they would like for rehearsals. They carefully prepare their schedule to make the best possible use of the performers' time.

Most rehearsal schedules include the following steps, each of which takes from 5 to 10 rehearsals. First, the director and performers read and study the play. Then the director *blocks* the action. That is, he or she arranges the broad pattern of the performers' movements. Then detailed work begins on characterization, line readings, stage action, changes in mood, and blending

the performers into a unit. Finally, in dress rehearsals, the director combines all elements of production.

The Director's Assistants include a rehearsal secretary, assistant director, and stage manager. The secretary sits near the director during rehearsals and takes notes. This job may be combined with that of the assistant director, who may rehearse certain scenes, coach performers, or act as a go-between for the director and designers. In the professional theater, the stage manager organizes tryouts. He or she attends all rehearsals, and records changes in dialogue and blocking in a master copy of the script. Later, during performances, the stage manager is in charge backstage.

Blocking a Play, *above*, establishes the movements of the actors during the performance of each scene. Director Elia Kazan describes how he wants the performers to arrange their movements during one scene. A dress rehearsal, *below*, is the final step before a play opens before a paying audience.

Inge Morath, Magnum

Performers are among the few artists who cannot separate their means of expression from themselves. They create with their own bodies and voices, and their own psychological and mental qualities. Often it is difficult to separate talent and creativity from the performer's personality. But acting is an art, and, as with any art, natural ability, study, and practice are essential.

Body and Voice. Performers need a flexible, disciplined, and expressive body. They must be able to use their bodies to represent a wide range of attitudes and reactions. They may be aided by courses in stage movement, dancing, fencing, and acrobatics, and by participating in sports that demand physical control and coordination. Dancing and fencing are particularly useful because they provide grace and body control. There are more opportunities for performers with these skills.

The same requirements of flexibility, control, and expressiveness apply to the voice as to the body. Performers learn how to breathe properly, to achieve variety in vocal rhythm and tone, and to make themselves heard and understood. They also learn dialects. Training in oral reading, acting, and singing is helpful. However, most performers require years of practice to change their voices significantly so they can speak higher, lower, louder, or softer—and still be understood.

Observation and Imagination. To portray a role well, performers should know about human emotions, attitudes, and *motivations* (reasons for behavior). They must be able to express these elements so they can be understood by an audience. A good performer develops the habit of observing others and remembering how they behave. If an actor takes the role of an old man, for example, he may prepare by observing how old men walk, stand, and sit. He also learns how different people react to such emotions as happiness, grief, and fear.

Performers may try to develop *emotion memory*, so that in portraying a role they can recall how they felt in a similar situation. They thus learn to know others through knowing themselves, and they portray others partly by using their knowledge of themselves.

Concentration is particularly important for performers. They must be able to involve themselves in an imagined situation and shut out all distractions. Their goal is to give a performance that creates the illusion of something happening for the first time. To do so, they concentrate on listening to other performers in the play and responding appropriately.

Systems of Acting. No matter how well trained performers are, they cannot use their skills effectively without some consistent working method. Performers should try as many approaches to acting as possible, and choose the one they consider to be most successful.

The differences among systems of acting are often described in terms of two extremes: *mechanical-external* and *psychological-internal*. The two differ on the question of whether a performer must be emotionally moved to act convincingly. Supporters of the external system argue that emotion may interfere with good acting.

Performers Develop Their Imaginations at the Actors Studio in New York City. The students in this class are doing exercises in relaxation and in working with imaginary objects to stimulate the growth of their imaginations and emotions. Studio director Lee Strasberg stands in the center.

WORLD BOOK photo by Dan Budnick

Creating a Role, students at the Actors Studio explain their intentions after doing a scene from a dramatization of a portion of Fyodor Dostoevsky's novel *Poor Folk*. This class helps the students analyze their roles to find the best method of expressing their desired characterizations.

They believe the performer should merely try to create the external signs of emotions. Supporters of the internal system claim that only through feeling can performers project themselves into a character and situation. This system is sometimes called the Stanislavski method, for the Russian director Konstantin Stanislavski.

Creating a Role. Performers must solve several specific problems every time they play a new role. These problems include (1) analyzing the role, (2) movement and gesture, (3) vocal characterization, (4) conservation and build, and (5) ensemble playing.

Analyzing the role starts with a study of the play as a whole. Then performers concentrate on their own parts. First they analyze the various aspects of characterization—a character's appearance, occupation, social and economic status, basic attitudes, and general personality. They then examine the character's goals and behavior, both in the play as a whole and in individual scenes. Finally, they study how their role is related to the other characters and to the structure of the play. If the play takes place during an earlier time, performers may study the period and setting. They not only analyze their role independently, but also adjust their interpretation to that of the director.

Movement and gesture are the ways in which the performer portrays the character's walk, posture, gestures, and bodily attitudes. Although the director plans the broad pattern of movement, the performer fills in many details. The performer works to understand the purpose or emotional reason behind each movement so he or she can perform every action "in character."

Vocal characterization refers to the character's general vocal qualities. Performers decide what qualities are desirable, and adjust their voices accordingly. One character may require a high-pitched voice. Another may have a soft, soothing voice. The performer also notes the demands of each scene. Some scenes are relaxed, and others are emotionally high keyed. A change within a scene can be clarified by appropriate vocal patterns. For example, growing tension can be denoted by raised pitch, greater volume, and faster tempo.

Conservation and build include the ways performers conserve their powers and heighten the role to a climax. Every play builds in intensity and suspense, and every performance should also grow. The need to sustain and build a part is most important in highly emotional roles. If performers begin at an emotional pitch that is too intense, they soon may not be able to build the intensity any further. The rest of the performance will seem monotonous. They must pace themselves so the performance grows in strength and interest.

Ensemble playing is the sense of artistic unity that results from the cooperative efforts of the entire cast. No acting performance is fully effective unless it is integrated with all the other performances. Ensemble playing results when every performer adjusts to the needs of the play, and remains aware of the methods, strengths, and weaknesses of the other performers.

Scene design has two basic purposes—to aid the audience's understanding, and to express the distinctive qualities of a play. To aid understanding, the stage setting may define the time and place of the action, and help establish characterizations. The set creates an appropriate mood and expresses the play's dominant elements through design and color. The set also suggests the type of play, such as comedy or tragedy, and emphasizes the drama's most important ideas.

The Scene Designer begins a job by studying the play as a whole. He or she then analyzes its scenic demands. Consideration must be given to the number, size, and kinds of sets needed; their physical arrangement; the period, place, and social and economic background; and the type and style of the play. The designer also may do research to learn about typical manners and customs, decorative details, architectural forms, furnishings, and building materials of the period.

The designer meets with the director to discuss the requirements of the sets, where entrances and exits should be located, and how furnishings should be arranged. The designer also learns how much money can be spent and what type of stage will be used.

Next, the designer makes preliminary sketches of the set and discusses them with the director. Before the designs receive final approval, the designer draws them in perspective and in color. Floor plans are made of each set, and three-dimensional scale models may be built to show how each set will look. The designer also makes a series of working drawings that show how each set will be built. In the professional theater, where scenery is built by a scenic studio, every detail of construction, assembly, and painting must be indicated. In the nonprofessional theater, where the designer often supervises construction, fewer drawings are needed.

Kinds of Scenery. The designer uses several basic scenic units when building sets. Most of these units may be classified as *standing* or *hanging*.

The basic standing unit is the *flat*. A flat is a rectangular wooden frame over which canvas or muslin is stretched, providing a lightweight structure. Flats vary in size from 8 to 16 feet (2.4 to 4.9 meters) high

WORLD BOOK photo by Vories Fisher

Flats Are Basic Pieces in set construction. They are made of high-quality lumber and most are covered with cotton or muslin. Flats are often lashed together to create the walls of a room.

Sketch and model for George Farquhar's *The Recruiting Officer* at the Goodman Theatre, Chicago (WORLD BOOK photos by Vories Fisher)

Designing a Production begins with a sketch of each set, *above*. The designer then may make a model for each set, *right*, to show how the pieces of scenery will look on stage. After the director and designer agree on the designs, construction begins.

and 1 to 6 feet (30 to 180 centimeters) wide. A plain flat has no openings. A door flat, window flat, fireplace flat, and arch flat all have appropriate openings. Other standing units include door and window frames, fireplaces, platforms, steps and staircases, rocks and built-up ground, tree trunks, and columns. A *ground row* is a low flat with a shaped edge that gives the appearance of distant hills or rows of buildings.

Hanging units include *ceilings, borders, drops, drapes, curtains, scrims,* and *cycloramas.* Most ceilings are made from two large rectangular flats hinged together. They are suspended above the set, and lowered to rest on the tops of flats representing walls. In most exterior settings, borders are substituted for ceilings. Borders are short curtains of black cloth or painted canvas hung parallel to the front of the stage. They may be shaped and painted to resemble such objects as trees.

Large pieces of canvas called drops usually extend the full width of the stage. They are attached at the top and bottom to lengths of wood called *battens.* The canvas can be painted to represent any scene. Most drapes or curtains are hung in a series parallel to the proscenium on each side of the stage to conceal off-stage space. A scrim is a curtain of gauze used for special effects. It appears transparent when lighted from the back, but opaque when lighted from the front. A cyclorama is a continuous tightly stretched curtain suspended on a U-shaped batten. It encloses the stage on three sides. Most cycloramas are neutral in color, but can be made any color by lighting. A cyclorama is often used to represent the sky.

Changing Scenery. After scenery has been built, it is assembled on stage. A one-set show can be set up permanently. However, a multiple-set production re-

Set Construction, *above,* may be done in the theater's own shop or by an outside studio. Generally, each piece is designed so stagehands can move it easily during a performance.

Technical Rehearsals, *below,* let the director and the various designers see how the sets, costumes, and lighting of a play look under conditions of an actual performance.

Photos of *The Recruiting Officer* at the Goodman Theatre by Vories Fisher

quires careful planning so that individual units can be set up and dismantled quickly and quietly during each performance.

When scenery is changed by hand, each part is moved by one or more stagehands to a prearranged place offstage. New settings are then assembled onstage. Another common method of changing scenery is called *flying*. Suspended units overhead are raised and lowered as needed on the stage. Flying is generally used only for drops, curtains, borders, ceilings, cycloramas, or small flats.

Rolling platforms called *wagons* are often used to change scenery. Scenery is placed on the wagons, which can be rolled on or off stage. One kind of wagon is called a *jackknife*. It has a platform approximately as wide as the proscenium and attached to the stage floor at one place. It can be rotated on or off stage, much as a jackknife opens and closes.

Scenery can also be changed by means of *revolving stages* or *elevator stages*, but both are expensive and complex, and few theaters have them. A revolving stage has a large circle of the stage floor mounted on a central supporting pivot that can be rotated. Several settings can be erected at one time and moved into view as needed by turning the stage. An elevator stage has sections of the stage floor that can be lowered to the basement of the theater. There, scenery can be changed while another set is being used.

Properties and Decorations are added to the set after the scenery has been assembled. Properties are often divided into two categories. *Set props*, such as sofas, function as part of the design or are attached to the set. *Hand props*, such as guns, are used by the actors. Decorations include such items as pictures and drapes.

Elevator Stages permit a set to be assembled on a separate stage, which is lowered or raised into place. Only large theaters such as the Metropolitan Opera, *below*, can afford these stages.

Flying Scenic Units such as the backdrop, *above*, are suspended backstage, ready to be lowered into place. The banks of lights below the backdrop have been lowered for cleaning.

WORLD BOOK photos by Donald Stebbing

Lighting Methods. Lighting designers analyze a play for its dramatic values and then for its lighting needs. They note everything in the script concerning light. There might be such changes in intensity as a sunrise or lamps being lit. Perhaps variations in light are needed for various parts of the setting. The script may note the direction from which light enters the set, such as moonlight through a window. Colored light can suggest moonlight, sunlight, or firelight. Other special lighting effects include lightning.

The designers pay particular attention to mood because lighting helps establish stage atmosphere. They must understand the style of the play. For realistic drama, they will probably make the light come from specific sources. They will make sure there is a credible reason for each lighting change. In a nonrealistic play, lighting can be unmotivated.

The lighting designer confers extensively with the scene designer and the director. In the professional theater, he or she makes sketches showing how the stage will look when lighted. In most nonprofessional productions, the lighting designer and the director reach general agreement about lighting. Little can be done until the theater is available and the scenery is in place.

Lighting for the stage is divided into (1) specific illumination, (2) general illumination, and (3) special effects. *Specific illumination* concentrates on a limited area. It is used principally for lighting the acting areas, which require strong emphasis. *General illumination* is used to light the sets and background elements, and to blend the lighting of acting areas. It is also used to provide a gradual change between brilliantly lighted acting areas and less intense lighting on the background. *Special effects* refer to a variety of lighting techniques and instruments. Typical examples include projections of clouds and stars, fires, and rainbows.

In planning the lighting, the designer draws a *lighting plot* on a floor plan showing the entire stage, including the setting. A separate lighting plot is usually needed for each set, as well as a plot showing the lighting for all the sets at the same time. An *instrument schedule* provides a summary of all the technical information needed to set up the lights for a play. This schedule lists lighting instruments, mounting positions, areas to be lighted, color filters, and other technical data.

There are several types of lighting instruments. A *spotlight* illuminates a limited portion of the stage with a concentrated beam of light. Spotlights range in power from 100 to 10,000 watts. They have reflectors to increase their brightness, and lenses to give light a specific type of edge, either sharp or soft. Special frames enable the lighting designer to vary the color.

A *striplight* consists of a series of lamps set in a narrow, roughly rectangular trough. Striplights vary in length, wattage, and use. They can be divided into several categories. *Footlights* light the stage from the front. *Borderlights* are hung overhead to spread light to the set or background. Striplights may be placed on the floor or elsewhere to light a cyclorama or scenic units.

Many instruments are used to create special effects. Various kinds of projectors are among the most useful. An entire scenic background can be projected on a screen or on a cyclorama. Some projectors have rotating disks to create the effect of movement, as in clouds.

All lighting includes some method of controlling the light. A *control board* or *switchboard* permits some instruments to be used at maximum brightness while others are off or dimmed. A control board also allows the control of color by mixing the light from several instruments. *Dimmers* permit a gradual increase or decrease in the intensity of light. An *electronic control board* enables the lighting designer to preset all changes in lighting intensity for an entire production.

WORLD BOOK photos by Vories Fisher

A Lighting Control Board, *left,* enables one technician to control all lighting changes from a single location. The lighting designer records lighting changes on a special cue sheet, *right.* The designer holds a gelatin, or *gel,* a thin, transparent colored sheet used to change colors on the stage lights.

Lighting Establishes the Mood of a Play. Dylan Thomas' *Under Milk Wood* takes place during a 24-hour period. This play usually has a single simple set, but proper lighting can indicate the time of day. The picture above shows sunrise, and the one below shows late afternoon.

Sound Production. Sound makes its greatest contribution when designed as a unit and carefully integrated into the production as a whole. Sound includes music, noises of no recognizable origin, and such realistic effects as thunder. In the professional theater, sound produced electrically is considered part of the stage lighting. Sound produced mechanically is regarded as a stage property.

Sound performs two basic functions: (1) to establish mood and style, and (2) to help tell the story. Music and abstract sound help indicate the proper atmosphere for each scene. Such realistic sounds as rainfall or a distant foghorn also contribute to mood. Sound helps tell the story through gunshots, ringing doorbells, and other realistic noises that either prepare the audience for onstage action or indicate action supposedly occurring offstage.

Sound is classified as *live* or *recorded*. Live sound is created fresh for each performance, and includes doorbells and telephones. Recorded sound includes noises made by a passing train and the sounds of a crowd offstage.

Costume Design shares the same broad purposes as scene design. It aids the audience's understanding and expresses the play's distinctive qualities. Costumes help identify the period and country in which the action takes place, and establish such specific locations as a farm. They suggest time of day, season, occasion, and information about the characters—ages, occupations, personalities, and social and economic status.

Costumes can also clarify the relationships among characters. For example, the warring sides in many Shakespearean history plays are identified by contrasting color schemes. Costumes also express the overall mood of the play, its style, and the emotional tone of individual scenes.

The costume designer studies the script in much the same manner as the actor does. The designs, like the actor's or actress's performance, express the characters and the play as a whole. The costumer uses line, mass, color, texture, and ornaments to create a visual equivalent of the dramatic action.

The costumer confers with the director, scenic designer, lighting designer, and principal performers to make sure his or her ideas fit the interpretation of the play. Like the scene designer, the costumer records ideas in color sketches. The sketches, usually accompanied by samples of material, are given to the director for approval. The costumer also makes a chart indicating what each character wears in each scene.

Costume Design begins with a sketch of the proposed costume, *above.* Samples of the material are usually attached. The costume must be fitted correctly, *below left,* so the performer can move freely and comfortably. The costume shown in these pictures is worn by a fortuneteller, *below right,* in George Farquhar's *The Recruiting Officer,* a comedy of the early 1700's.

WORLD BOOK photos by Vories Fisher

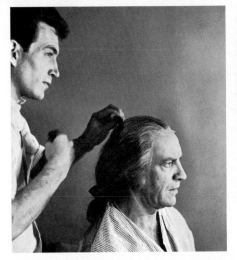

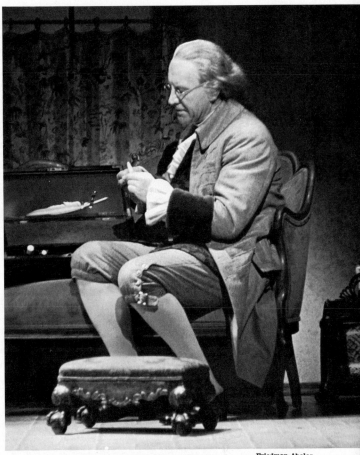

Friedman-Abeles

Makeup Helps Establish Characterization. For a role as Benjamin Franklin, actor Robert Preston applies his makeup, *upper left,* and receives the aid of a hairdresser in fitting his wig, *left.* Through the combination of costume and makeup, Preston on stage, *above,* closely resembles Franklin.

Costumes may be made new, assembled from an existing wardrobe, borrowed, or rented. In the professional theater, a professional costume house makes costumes to order. Nonprofessional theaters borrow costumes or rent them from a costume rental agency. Many permanent theater organizations, both professional and nonprofessional, make their own costumes. Most maintain a wardrobe of items from past shows.

The *dress parade* shows the performers separately and in groups under lights similar to those used during performances. The director and all the designers attend. The dress parade allows any necessary changes to be made during the rehearsal period. After performances begin, a wardrobe attendant works backstage and supervises costume changes, repairs, and adjustments.

Makeup Techniques. Makeup is important in establishing characterization. The appearance of the face indicates the character's age, health, and race. The face also can suggest a general occupation and basic personality. Makeup serves the additional purpose of restoring the face's color and form, which may be affected by the stage lighting or distance from the audience.

For a *straight makeup*, the performer's appearance is not changed significantly. In a *character makeup*, it is changed greatly. The makeup may age the face; make it fat, thin, smooth, or wrinkled; or emphasize some peculiar facial characteristic.

Makeup effects can be achieved in two basic ways: (1) by painting, or (2) by using plastic pieces. Painting involves applying color, line, and shadow to the face or body. All makeup has some painted effects. Plastic makeup devices include beards, wigs, false noses, and warts or scars. Changing the shape of the nose with nose putty, and adding a beard and bushy eyebrows, alters a performer's features more than painting alone.

Traditionally, makeup has been considered the performer's responsibility, though it also concerns the costumer. In the professional theater, performers are responsible for their own makeup, but they consult specialists for help with problems. In many nonprofessional theaters, makeup is considered part of the costumer's duties. Sometimes the director is responsible.

Friedman-Abeles

Broadway Musical Comedy has been called the major contribution of the United States to modern theater. *Hello, Dolly!*, with such stars as Pearl Bailey, *above*, was a hit musical of the 1960's.

Today, more groups than ever before are producing plays in the United States. Most of these groups are nonprofessional, and the process of theatrical production varies from one organization to another. However, the operation of the professional theater is basic for all theatrical organizations.

Broadway in New York City is the best-known center of the professional theater in the United States. But resident professional companies exist in many other U.S. cities. Several of these companies have contributed plays and musicals to Broadway.

The starting point for most theatrical productions, professional or nonprofessional, is the playwright's script. Good scripts are in great demand, but playwrights—unless well established—almost always have difficulty getting their plays performed. If they want a professional production, they must first find a producer. The producer has the overall responsibility of the entire show. He or she acquires the play, hires a director, rents a theater, and raises the money needed to finance the show. The producer may be either one person or a group of people.

A producer who is interested in a script may take an *option* on it. That is, he or she pays the playwright for exclusive production rights to the play for a certain period of time. An option does not guarantee production. A play may be placed under option many times without being produced. If the producer decides to present the play, a contract is drawn up specifying the amount of the author's *royalty* (share of the profits). The contract also states the extent of the producer's control over the play. For example, the contract may require the playwright to be available for consultation and possible rewriting during the rehearsal period. Most contracts do not legally require playwrights to make changes in the script. But in most cases, they are under pressure to do so. Negotiations with producers can become so complex that most playwrights hire literary agents to represent them.

A producer who takes an option on a play then sets out to raise money to stage it. The cost of producing a play on Broadway has become increasingly high. In the mid-1970's, plays with one set cost about $200,000. Many musicals cost at least $1 million and had to run for more than a year to repay their investment. Few individuals can invest this much money, and so most producers seek funds from many people or groups. Investors may be influenced by the reputation of the playwright, director, or star of the show.

After raising the money to finance the play, the producer negotiates contracts with everyone involved in the production. In the Broadway theater, a producer deals with unions representing various employees. These employees include not only the director, actors, actresses, and designers, but also stagehands, musicians, dancers, and box office personnel.

Following the rehearsal period, many plays intended for Broadway are presented first in one or more theaters

188h

outside New York City, such as in Boston or Washington, D.C. The audience reaction and the reviews by local critics may lead to changes in the play. Since the 1960's, out-of-town tryouts often have been replaced by a series of preview performances on Broadway. Tickets are sold, in many cases at reduced prices, but the critics do not write reviews until after the official opening-night performance.

The final step in the production of a play—and the most vital from a dollars-and-cents standpoint—is opening night on Broadway. Drama critics from the leading newspapers in New York City, and from radio and television stations in the New York City metropolitan area, review the play immediately. Top magazines print reviews within the next week or two. The reviews, particularly those of the newspapers, greatly influence the commercial success of a play. If all or most of the reviews criticize the play severely, the producer normally will close the show. If the play is the work of a well-known playwright, or has a major star, the advance sale of tickets may save it despite bad reviews.

A play must be a big box-office hit to survive long on Broadway. Many productions close after only a few performances. Some run for years. The "hit" or "flop" pattern has created a situation in which a play must be a great success financially, or it is considered a failure. This pattern has hurt the range of plays offered. Producers limit themselves almost entirely to shows that indicate promise of success or that have been successful elsewhere. As a result, Broadway drama has less richness and variety than it might have. The number of plays presented outside New York City is also affected because only hit shows generally tour.

Each spring, many awards honor outstanding achievements in New York theater for the season that began the previous autumn. Among the best known are

Community Theaters offer many fine productions of serious dramas for audiences outside New York City. Most of these theaters operate on low budgets, using nonprofessional performers

Scene from *The Indian Wants the Bronx* by Israel Horovitz at the Hull House Theater in Chicago (Larry Lowenthal)

the "Tony" awards, named for Antoinette Perry, a producer and director. Since 1947, Tonys have been presented to the best play and musical as well as the best authors, designers, directors, performers, and producers.

Off-Broadway Theater developed in New York City about 1950 from dissatisfaction with conditions on Broadway. The people who founded off-Broadway theaters believed that Broadway was concerned basically with producing safe hit plays rather than works of artistic quality. Off-Broadway theaters tried to assist playwrights, directors, and performers who had been unable to find work in the Broadway theater. Most off-Broadway theaters were located in low-rent areas. Most had poorly equipped stages, limited seating, and few conveniences for the audience. The originality of the script, the creativeness of the performers, and the low cost of production made up for such disadvantages. By the 1960's, however, costs began to increase, and by the 1970's, off-Broadway theater was encountering many of Broadway's problems and had lost most of its vitality.

With the decline of off-Broadway, a movement called *off-off-Broadway* developed in New York City. Off-off-Broadway theaters emphasized extremely inventive plays and staging. Since 1970, these theaters have become a major force in experimental drama. The most important groups include the La Mama Experimental Theatre Company, the American Place Theatre, the Chelsea Theatre Center, and the Public Theatre operated by the New York Shakespeare Festival. As such groups have gained public and critical acceptance, their operations have come to resemble the off-Broadway theaters of the 1950's and 1960's.

Other Professional Theater. During the 1950's, resident acting companies began to be established in cities other than New York City. In the 1960's, with the financial aid of the Ford Foundation and other organizations, these companies increased in number and reputation. By the mid-1970's, about 55 such companies were performing in the United States.

Most resident companies produce a season of plays each year. They present each play for a limited run, rather than for a long engagement. The theaters try to vary their programs with plays of a number of periods and styles. Some directors and performers are employed for the entire season. Others are hired for a single production. Many of these companies receive money from foundations or government agencies. However, few resident companies have any assurance of continuing financial aid and thus they must be cautious about making long-range plans. Several resident theaters have been particularly helpful to writers. These theaters include the Arena Stage in Washington, D.C., and the Long Wharf Theatre in New Haven, Conn.

A number of professional nonprofit companies comparable to off-off-Broadway groups are scattered throughout the United States. These groups are often called *alternative theaters* to distinguish them from more traditional professional resident theaters.

College and High School Theater. Many colleges and universities have theater and drama departments. They produce plays as part of the education of their students,

Scene from *A Flea in Her Ear* by Georges Feydeau, American Conservatory Theatre, San Francisco

Scene from a 1955 production of Gregorio Martínez Sierra's 1911 play, *The Cradle Song*, at the Circle in the Square. Courtesy of the Theatre Collection, N.Y. Public Library at Lincoln Center (Justin Kerr)

Repertory Theater gives audiences an opportunity to see the same performers playing different roles in a variety of works during a single season. Repertory is especially popular in Europe.

Off-Broadway Theater gained a national reputation in the 1950's and 1960's for its productions of experimental plays and works by new playwrights, and for revivals of older plays.

and as a service to the community. The best college theaters have the administrative organization of resident professional companies. Because their purpose is educational, such theaters usually present standard works from earlier periods as well as more recent plays. Many theaters also produce original plays. Occasionally, a professional performer may appear in a production, but all-student casts are customary.

Almost all U.S. high schools have some kind of theater production program, though relatively few offer courses in drama and theater. The production of plays may be assigned to people untrained in the theater, with poor results. But an increasing number of high schools have developed theater programs of excellent quality, supervised by large qualified staffs. Many schools have fine facilities and offer courses in play production, dramatic literature, and related areas.

Community Theater developed between 1900 and 1920. Today, most towns of more than 30,000 persons have a community theater. The community theater not only provides entertainment for local audiences, but also furnishes an outlet for the creative talents of its members.

Many community theaters employ a full-time director who supervises all productions. Many of these theaters are run by volunteers and cannot afford paid personnel. Others pay the director of each production, and also provide fees for the designer and chief technician. Most plays staged by community theaters are recent works. Classics are less frequently presented.

Children's Theater operates within any framework—professional, educational, or community. Its chief characteristic is its intended audience. Only during the 1900's, and primarily since World War II ended in 1945, have programs been developed for child audiences. The plays are performed by adults or children.

Summer Theater usually operates from late June until early September. Summer theater companies have rapidly increased in number since World War II. Most are in resort areas. Some companies are entirely professional, and others have both professional and nonprofessional personnel. Still others are completely nonprofessional. Summer theater is becoming increasingly popular with college drama departments as a supplement to courses offered during the school year.

Most summer theaters present a season of recent plays or musicals. Groups connected with educational institutions often present both classic and commercial shows. A few companies perform a single work for the entire summer. Groups in several states present dramatizations of local history. Other companies perform in *repertory*. That is, the company prepares plays before the season begins and performs them in rotation throughout the summer. Several organizations specialize in the plays of Shakespeare. Occasionally, summer theaters try out new plays for producers who hope to present the plays elsewhere.

Government-Supported Theater, though common in Europe, has not yet gained full acceptance in the United States. Those who favor such support believe it can provide economic stability for theaters and enable them to charge lower ticket prices and present a wider range of plays. Opponents of government support say that it might lead to government control or censorship, thus reducing the freedom to create.

Many theaters today do receive some assistance from government agencies. In 1965, Congress established the National Endowment for the Arts, which makes grants to groups or projects. Most states now have arts councils that make grants to groups within the state. The amount of aid from such sources is still small, however, and is not assured from one year to the next.

Nearly all major cities have theater districts resembling Broadway in organization and appeal. Many productions are commercial enterprises supported by private investment. However, the theaters with the highest reputations are permanent organizations.

Canada, most European countries, and some Asian and African nations, have several government-supported theaters. These *state theaters* are permanent organizations that employ staffs of directors, performers, designers, and others. Many also import performers, directors, and designers for single productions.

A number of theaters operate in government-owned buildings and pay no rent. The government gives them an annual sum of money called a *subsidy*. A subsidy usually does not cover all production costs, but it supplements the income from ticket sales. The subsidy enables a theater to charge lower admission prices and provides protection against financial loss. Most subsidized companies produce a season of plays annually. Each play is performed for a limited time or in rotation with other plays. Some plays are presented at regular intervals through the years.

Canada has two internationally known theater organizations. One, the Stratford Festival in Stratford, Ont., specializes in the plays of Shakespeare. The other, the Shaw Festival in Niagara-on-the-Lake, Ont., features plays by George Bernard Shaw. Montreal is the center of theater in French-speaking Canada. There are major resident companies in such cities as Halifax, N.S.; Toronto, Ont.; and Winnipeg, Man.

England. The British government started to give subsidies to the theater in 1945. The National Theatre, created in 1963, is one of the world's outstanding companies. It succeeded the Old Vic company, one of England's finest troupes from 1914 until it was disbanded in 1963. In 1976, the National Theatre moved into a new theater center built especially for it.

Another subsidized theater, the Royal Shakespeare Company, was created from the organization that produced the Stratford-upon-Avon Shakespeare Festival. Since 1960, it has divided its company between London and the Shakespeare Festival Theatre in Stratford. Another major organization, the English Stage Society, has introduced the works of many new dramatists. Several resident companies in cities outside London receive subsidies from the local governments.

France. The oldest state theater in the world still operating is the Comédie-Française in Paris. It was established in 1680. The Théâtre Nationale Populaire and several other notable French theaters also receive government support. The government has set up state-supported dramatic centers in such cities as Aix-en-Provence, Bourges, Rennes, St. Étienne, Strasbourg, Toulouse, and Tourcoing. The theatrical companies of many of these cities tour neighboring communities. The government also subsidizes touring companies and aids summer drama festivals.

Germany has the most extensive system of state-supported theaters in the world. Many of these theaters date back to the late 1700's. Although the nation has been divided since 1945, East Germany and West Germany have a similar organization of theaters. West Germany has about 200 professional theaters, of which about 175 are state-owned. East Germany has about

Scene from Brecht's *Mother Courage*. Photo Pic,
courtesy *The Drama Review*, New York University

Theater in Germany is heavily supported by the state. The Berliner Ensemble, *above*, of East Berlin is probably the best known. It was founded by playwright Bertolt Brecht in 1949.

Scene from *Twelfth Night*,
Stratford Festival Theatre

Theater in Canada has gained international recognition with the work of the Stratford Festival, *above*, each summer. Quebec has many French-speaking theater groups.

120 companies, all performing in state-owned theaters.

Almost every large German city has drama, opera, and ballet companies. All subsidized companies in a city generally are under one manager appointed by the city or state. All the companies share a staff of directors and designers. Outstanding organizations include the Berliner Ensemble in East Berlin and the Schiller Theater in West Berlin.

Italy. The Italian theater operates differently than that of most European countries. The most important Italian drama companies tour the larger cities of Italy. In addition, about eight resident theaters are subsidized by city or provincial governments. The leading resident theaters are in Genoa, Milan, Rome, and Turin.

Russia. Theater in Russia was widely popular and generously subsidized before World War II. It suffered a severe blow in 1946 when many subsidies were withdrawn and tight censorship was imposed. After Premier Joseph Stalin died in 1953, the government relaxed its censorship and the variety of plays increased greatly. Today, despite state control and ownership, 98 per cent of Russia's theaters receive no direct subsidies and must support themselves from box-office receipts.

The Moscow Art Theater, founded in 1898, is perhaps the most respected company in Russia. It receives generous subsidies. Its company of about 140 actors may be the largest in the world. The Maly Theater and the Mayakovsky Theater are other leading companies. Two newer groups, the Contemporary Theater and the Moscow Theater of Drama and Comedy, have aroused much interest in Moscow. In Leningrad, the Pushkin Theater ranks only slightly below the Moscow Art Theater in reputation. The Gorky Theater is also highly respected.

THEATER/Training for the Theater

There has been much dispute over the proper way to train theater artists. Some argue that these men and women should first get a general liberal arts education, with little or no theater training. Concentrated work in the theater arts would then follow. Those who favor this method believe that liberal arts training is especially valuable for the study of theater and drama, which deal with all aspects of human experience. Others believe a general education is unnecessary, and that professional training should be taken from the beginning. Still others think that liberal arts courses and professional theater training should be combined.

Colleges and Universities. An increasing number of colleges and universities provide some training in the theater arts. However, many do not have such *performance courses* as acting or directing for undergraduates. These schools may offer courses in dramatic literature and theater history, but they leave specialized theatrical training to graduate schools or professional schools.

Other colleges and universities give academic credit for courses in playwriting; acting; directing; scene, costume, and lighting design; technical production; dance; and stage movement. The student must follow a course of study that provides a broad liberal arts education. But a fourth to a third of the course work may be devoted to the theater arts. Schools with a graduate program may offer one to three additional years of intensive training.

Professional Training Programs are now offered by a number of universities. Such programs are also provided by conservatories and studios not connected with universities. Professional training programs normally allow students to spend most of their time on theater courses. Some schools give certificates for the completion of a prescribed program. Some programs offer academic degrees. Other programs do not lead to a certificate or degree. A student may simply enroll in any class for as long as he or she wishes.

Most professional training schools are in or near cities with professional theaters. Some of the best-known programs are operated by the American Conservatory Theater, the California School of the Arts, Carnegie-Mellon University, and Yale University.

Professional training programs give performers intensive training but do not give any guarantee of employment. Many beginning performers seek work in resident or alternative theater companies, but many still go to New York City or Hollywood to find employment. The supply of performers always greatly exceeds the demand, and therefore most find it difficult to follow a career in the theater.   OSCAR G. BROCKETT and LENYTH BROCKETT

THEATER/Study Aids

Outline

Questions

What is a drop? a scrim? a cyclorama?
What is the difference between a proscenium stage and a theater-in-the-round?
What are the two chief systems of acting?
How can costumes help an audience understand a play?
What kinds of sound can be used in a play?
What is the role of the producer in staging a play?
What does the director need to know about a play?
What is the difference between *theater* and *drama?*
What is the oldest state theater in the world still operating?
What is a stage picture?

Reading and Study Guide

See *Theater* in the RESEARCH GUIDE/INDEX, Volume 22, for a *Reading and Study Guide.*

Additional Resources

BROCKETT, OSCAR G. *History of the Theatre.* 3rd ed. Allyn & Bacon, 1977. *The Theatre: An Introduction.* 4th ed. Holt, 1979.
CLURMAN, HAROLD. *On Directing.* Macmillan, 1972.
The Encyclopedia of World Theater: With an Index of Play Titles. Scribner, 1977.
GILLETTE, A. S. and J. MICHAEL. *Stage Scenery: Its Construction and Rigging.* 3rd ed. Harper, 1981.

HEFFNER, HUBERT C., and others. *Modern Theatre Practice: A Handbook of Play Production.* 5th ed. Prentice-Hall, 1973.
KALTER, JOANMARIE. *Actors on Acting: Performing in Theatre and Film Today.* Sterling, 1979.
STERN, LAWRENCE. *School and Community Theater Management: A Handbook for Survival.* Rev. ed. Allyn & Bacon, 1979.
THOMAS, WILLIAM E. *Backstage Broadway: Careers in the Theater.* Simon & Schuster, 1980. For younger readers.

THEBES, *theebz,* is the Greek name of a city in ancient Egypt that served as a capital for many Egyptian kings. Thebes stood near the Nile River, at the site of what is now the city of Luxor (see EGYPT, ANCIENT [map]).

Thebes was an unimportant village until about 2000 B.C., when a Theban prince became king of Egypt. During the Eighteenth Dynasty (1570-1300 B.C.), most Egyptian kings made Thebes their capital, and the Theban god, Amon-Re, became the most important god in Egypt. Some later Egyptian kings made northern cities their capitals, but they continued to build tombs and temples at Thebes. The Romans destroyed Thebes in 29 B.C.

Theban temples still stand at Karnak and Luxor. The ruins of funeral temples of Egyptian kings and queens are across the Nile from Luxor. Tombs lie in cliffs along the river, in the so-called Valley of the Kings (see VALLEY OF THE KINGS).   BARBARA MERTZ

See also CLOTHING (picture: Ancient Egyptians).

THEBES, *theebz,* was an ancient city in Boeotia, a region located in central Greece. At one time, it was the most powerful city-state in all Greece, and the head of the confederacy of cities known as the Boeotian League. The city lay in the southeastern part of Boeotia, about 30 miles (48 kilometers) north of Athens (see GREECE, ANCIENT [color map; map: After the Peloponnesian War]). According to ancient legends, Cadmus, a king of Phoenicia, founded Thebes. The city appears in the Oedipus legends, which are almost as famous as the stories of Troy (see OEDIPUS).

The historical record of Thebes begins about 500 years before the birth of Christ, when the people of Thebes and of Plataea, another ancient Greek city, began to quarrel. Later, Thebes helped the Persians in their invasion of Greece in 480 B.C. Thebes fought frequent wars with Athens. The most important of these was the Peloponnesian War, which began in 431 B.C., when a Theban force attacked Plataea. After this war, the Boeotian League fell to pieces under the tyrannical rule of Sparta. It became important again between 379 and 374 B.C. through the patriotic efforts of Pelopidas. In 371 B.C. the Thebans, led by Epaminondas, won a victory over the Spartans at Leuctra, and thus gained control over Greece.

When Epaminondas died in 362 B.C., Theban control of Greece came to an end. The exhausted Greek states came under the rule of Philip of Macedon and his ambitious son, Alexander the Great. The Thebans revolted against Alexander, and he punished them by destroying their city. Thebes was rebuilt in 316 B.C., and was important under the later Roman Empire. The city flourished as a center of the silk trade during the A.D. 1000's and 1100's. Thebes began to decline when the Turks gained control of the city. The town of Thivai now stands on the site of Thebes.   DONALD W. BRADEEN

See also CADMUS; PELOPIDAS; PINDAR.

THEILER, MAX. See YELLOW FEVER.

THEINE, another name for caffeine. See CAFFEINE.

THEISM is belief in a god or gods. The term comes from the Greek word *theos*, meaning *god*. Theism plays an important role in most religions, but various faiths differ in their teachings about a god or gods. The followers of ancient Greek and Roman religions were *polytheistic*—that is, they worshiped more than one god. Today, the followers of most major religions are *monotheistic*, meaning that they accept only one god.

The words *theism* and *theistic* are used principally in discussing religions that have one god. Such religions include Christianity, Islam, Judaism, and some forms of Hinduism. These faiths stress the existence of an all-knowing, all-powerful god. This god may provide ways of life for human beings to follow and may offer people salvation.

Theism is also a type of philosophical belief. It supports the existence of a god, as opposed to *atheism*, which argues that no god exists. Theism also states that a god exists apart from the world. This concept differs from *pantheism*, the belief that a god exists in all of nature and the universe. NANCY E. AUER FALK

See also ATHEISM; DEISM; GOD; POLYTHEISM; RELIGION (Belief in a Deity).

THEMISTOCLES, *thee MIS toh kleez* (514?-449? B.C.), was an Athenian statesman and soldier in the Persian Wars. He saved Greece by his statesmanship and laid the foundation for Athens' greatness with his naval policy.

Little is known of Themistocles' early life. He began his political career in 490 B.C. after the Battle of Marathon and the retreat of the Persians. Themistocles opposed Aristides, who was then leader of Athens. In 482 B.C., he defeated Aristides in a dispute about what was to be done with the silver from the mines at Laurium. Themistocles had always favored naval expansion, and proposed that Athens increase its fleet. Aristides was banished for opposing this plan, and Themistocles became the political leader of Athens.

Themistocles was certain that the Persians would attack again, but that this time the battle would be decided on the sea. Two years later the Persians returned. They defeated and annihilated the Spartans under Leonidas at Thermopylae. Themistocles then moved the Athenians to Salamis, where he engaged the Persians. He destroyed the Persian fleet and forced the Persians to leave Athens. The following year the allied Greeks completely defeated the Persians at Plataea.

After the war, the Athenians began to fortify their city and the harbor of Piraeus. The Spartans protested but Themistocles held them off with promises until the project was finished. In spite of all that he had accomplished for Athens, the Athenians did not like Themistocles. They believed that he had accepted bribes, and in 471 B.C. they banished him.

Themistocles stayed for a short time in Argos, and then went to Persia. The Persian king warmly received him and gave him an estate in Magnesia, where he remained until his death. RICHARD NELSON FRYE

See also ARISTIDES; GREECE, ANCIENT (The Persian Wars); SALAMIS.

THEOCRACY, *thee AHK ruh see*, is a form of government in which members of the priesthood interpret the laws, and have authority in both civil and religious matters. The word *theocracy* comes from two Greek words, *theos*, which means *God*, and *kratein*, which means *to rule*.

Many ancient peoples believed that their god or gods had handed down laws for their government. The famous Code of Hammurabi was supposed to have been revealed in this way. The most famous theocracy was that of the Israelites, to whom God gave the Law through Moses.

The Puritan government of Massachusetts was called a theocracy. It was conducted for many years on the principle of obedience to divine law, as interpreted by the clergy. HOWARD R. BURKLE

THEOCRITUS, *thee AHK rih tus* (200's B.C.), was a Greek poet who originated *pastoral* (rustic) poetry. He wrote about 30 poems called *idyls*. Usually, they represent shepherds or goatherds (or poets masquerading as shepherds) talking to each other or competing in singing rustic songs on a summer day. Virgil imitated Theocritus in his *Eclogues*. Theocritus also influenced later poets, such as Lord Tennyson and Algernon Swinburne. Theocritus was born either at Syracuse, or on the Greek island of Kós. MOSES HADAS

THEODOLITE, *thee AHD uh lyt*, is an instrument surveyors use to measure angles and directions. It is similar to the more commonly used transit. A theodolite gives more precise readings than a transit gives. Some theodolites permit measurements to closer than one second of arc ($\frac{1}{3600}$ of a degree). Most theodolites are mounted on a *tripod* (three-legged stand). A theodolite has a telescope that permits accurate sighting in any direction. A horizontal plate below the telescope provides readings around the horizon in degrees, and in divisions of degrees called minutes and seconds. A vertical plate and scale, mounted to the left of the telescope, permit vertical readings. B. AUSTIN BARRY

THEODORA, *THEE uh DOH ruh* (A.D. 502?-548), was the wife of Justinian I, Byzantine (East Roman) emperor from 527 to 565. A beautiful and strong-willed woman, Theodora tried to influence Justinian's policies and to use her position to advance her friends and ruin her enemies. In 532, a rebellion in the capital city of Constantinople threatened to overthrow the empire. Theodora persuaded Justinian to stay and defend the city rather than to flee. Justinian crushed the rebels, thus securing his absolute power.

Theodora was probably born on Cyprus, to a poor family. She became an actress before marrying Justinian in 522, and was accused of numerous scandals, but many of them have been disproved. She founded homes for the care of poor girls. WILLIAM G. SINNIGEN

See also JUSTINIAN I.

THEODORE ROOSEVELT NATIONAL PARK is in western North Dakota. The park's outstanding feature is a scenic badlands area along the Little Missouri River. In this area, erosion caused by floods, rain, and wind has carved deep gullies and steep hills into the landscape. The park includes parts of two cattle ranches that were owned by President Theodore Roosevelt when he was a young man. A restored cabin where Roosevelt once lived is a popular tourist attraction on one of the ranches. The area was established as a national memorial park in 1947 and became a national park in 1978. For the park's area, see NATIONAL PARK

System (table: National Parks). For its location, see NORTH DAKOTA (political map).

Critically reviewed by the NATIONAL PARK SERVICE

THEODORIC, *thee AHD oh rik* (A.D. 455?-526), was an *Ostrogoth* (East Goth) king who governed Italy from A.D. 493 until his death. He won control of Italy from the barbarians who had taken it from the Romans 17 years earlier. Although a barbarian himself, Theodoric maintained a Roman form of government and Roman law in Italy. His rule was enlightened, peaceful, and just, and he won the praise of both barbarians and Romans. Theodoric let Romans hold high public office, and respected the senatorial class. He employed such prominent Romans as Boethius and Cassiodorus as his advisers and ministers of state. Theodoric believed in the Arian heresy, which denied the divinity of Christ, but he permitted his subjects to practice orthodox Christianity.

Theodoric was born in Pannonia, which covered parts of what are now Austria, Hungary, and Yugoslavia. He spent several years in Constantinople (now Istanbul, Turkey), the capital of the Byzantine (East Roman) Empire. When his father, Ostrogoth king Theodemir, died in 471, Theodoric became king.

Theodoric alternately found himself an ally, then an enemy of the Byzantine emperors. He was a victim of a Byzantine plan to confuse and weaken barbarians by encouraging rivalries between them and then shifting support from one side to the other. In 489, Byzantine emperor Zeno commissioned Theodoric to attack Odoacer, the barbarian king of Italy. Theodoric defeated Odoacer in 493, then murdered him. Germanic peoples remembered Theodoric in their legends as the heroic Dietrich of Bern.   WILLIAM G. SINNIGEN

THEODOSIUS I, *THEE oh DOH shih us* (A.D. 346-395), was the Roman emperor who prohibited all *pagan* (non-Christian) practices in the Roman Empire. For this, he became known to Christians as *The Great*. However, he was a shortsighted ruler who weakened the empire by creating many new government jobs and by raising taxes. His will divided the empire between his sons Honorius and Arcadius, splitting it permanently into eastern and western empires.

Theodosius was born in Spain. He became a distinguished soldier. In 379, Emperor Gratian made Theodosius co-emperor, responsible for the eastern provinces. The Visigoths had defeated a Roman army in the east in 378. In 382, a treaty between Theodosius and the Visigoths made the Visigoths the first independent barbarian nation within the Roman Empire.

Theodosius became senior co-emperor when Gratian died in 383. Gratian's brother, Valentinian II, became emperor of the western provinces. Valentinian died in 392, and pagans gained control of the western provinces. Theodosius crushed the pagans in 394 and ruled the entire empire until he died.   WILLIAM G. SINNIGEN

THEOLOGY is the study and description of God. It may also be the expression of religious belief. The word *theology* comes from the Greek words *theos* (god) and *logos* (talk). Theology explores a wide range of questions, such as: "Does God exist? What is the nature of God? What is God's relation to the world and to its inhabitants? and How do human beings know or experience God?" Some branches of theology deal with the history of religion or the study of sacred writings. Other branches deal with the defense of religious doctrines

against opposing views or the application of doctrine to daily life.

Approaches to theology vary from one religion to another. They also vary within a religious tradition. For example, some Christian theologians base their understanding of God on such authoritative sources as the Bible and the decrees of church councils. Others explain their understanding of God in terms of philosophy, psychology, or science. In most cases, a theologian's own religious experience plays an important part in his or her theological system.   JERRY A. IRISH

See also GOD; RELIGION.

THEOREM. See GEOMETRY; BINOMIAL THEOREM; PYTHAGOREAN THEOREM.

THEOSOPHY, *thee AHS uh fee*, is a system of philosophic and religious thought. Theosophy is based on claims of a mystic insight into the nature of God and the laws of the universe. The theosophist believes that the truest knowledge comes not through reason or the senses, but through a direct communion of the soul with divine reality.

The term theosophy has been applied specifically to the beliefs and teachings of the Theosophical Society. This society was founded in the United States in 1875 by Madame Elena Petrovna Blavatsky and others. Hindu and Buddhist thought and doctrines have become prominent in theosophy. A characteristic feature is the belief in reincarnation, in accordance with the Hindu doctrine of Karma. This doctrine states that the spirit advances to its goal through a succession of earthly lives, and that the consequences of a person's actions in the present life are reaped by his or her successor on earth in a fresh incarnation.   H. M. KALLEN

See also BESANT, ANNIE WOOD.

THEOTOKOPOULOS, DOMENIKOS. See GRECO, EL.

THERAPSID. See MAMMAL (Ancestors of Mammals).

THERAPY. See CHEMOTHERAPY; DRUG; OCCUPATIONAL THERAPY; PHYSICAL THERAPY; PSYCHOTHERAPY.

THERAVADA. See BUDDHISM (Buddhist Schools).

THEREMIN, *THEHR uh mihn*, is a boxlike musical instrument that resembles a radio receiver. Musical tones are produced by two high-frequency electronic circuits inside the instrument. A player creates music by moving the right hand through the air in front of an antenna projecting from the instrument. The player controls the volume by means of a switch and by moving the left hand over a metal loop on the theremin.

The Russian scientist Lev Theremin invented the instrument and first played it in public in 1920. The theremin is mainly a musical curiosity, but it has been used as a solo instrument. Composers who have written music for the theremin include Bohuslav Martinů and Edgard Varèse.   REINHARD G. PAULY

THERESA, *tuh REE suh*, **SAINT** (1515-1582), also spelled *Teresa*, is a saint of the Roman Catholic Church. She was a Spanish nun, and is today one of the patron saints of Spain.

Saint Theresa was born at Avila in Old Castile. Her study at an Augustinian monastery and her reading of the tales of ancient martyrs inspired her to seek martyrdom for herself. In 1533, she entered a Carmelite convent. The lack of asceticism and severity displeased her, but for many years she made no attempt to bring about reforms. A reading of the *Confessions* of Saint Augustine, combined with the death of her father and certain supernatural visitations, wakened in her a strong spirituality. She began to feel that it was her duty to restore the Carmelite order to the original rigidness of its rule. Accordingly, she withdrew with a few followers in 1562, and set up a new convent to put her ideas into effect. Opposition to her plan was strong, but the Pope approved of the idea. At last, the general of the order asked her to introduce her reforms into other convents. She opened many new convents in Castile and even beyond its boundaries, and accomplished much in her efforts to reform existing Carmelite houses.

Several cities contended for her body after her death at Alba de Tormes, near Salamanca. The power of working miracles was believed to be in her relics, which were carried to various places. She was canonized by Pope Gregory in 1622. Saint Theresa wrote an autobiography and several treatises and letters, all published in 1587. Her feast day is October 15.   FULTON J. SHEEN

THERMAL INVERSION. See AIR POLLUTION (Chief Sources of Air Pollution).

THERMAL POLLUTION. See ENVIRONMENTAL POLLUTION (Water Pollution; picture); WATER POLLUTION (Sources; Effects).

THERMAL SPRINGS. See HOT SPRINGS.

THERMAL UNIT. See HEAT (What Heat Is).

THERMOCOUPLE is an electric device that changes heat into electricity or electricity into heat. A thermocouple is made by twisting the ends of two different kinds of wire, such as iron and copper, together to form a *junction*. The opposite ends are also twisted together to form another junction. If one junction is heated, an ammeter connected to one of the wires between the junctions will show a *thermoelectric* (heat-generated) current flowing. The German physicist T. J. Seebeck discovered this effect in 1821. If a battery instead of an ammeter is connected to the thermocouple, one junction will become hot and the other will become cool. This effect was first noticed by the French physicist J. C. A. Peltier in 1834.

Thermocouples are used as thermometers and to generate electricity. Refrigeration devices have also been made using thermocouples. In a thermocouple used as a thermometer, one of the junctions senses the temperature being measured, and the other junction is kept at a constant temperature. A voltmeter measures the voltage between the two junctions and shows the temperature.   THEODORE KORNEFF

THERMODYNAMICS is the study of heat and work, and of the conversion of energy from one of these forms to the other. Chemists, engineers, physicists, and others apply the laws of thermodynamics. These laws are important in a variety of activities, including designing machines and calculating the loss or gain of energy in chemical reactions.

Thermodynamics is based on two *laws* (principles). These laws are broad conclusions about the nature of energy, drawn from the results of many experiments. The first law of thermodynamics, essentially the law of conservation of energy, can be stated as follows: *The energy going into a system, minus the energy coming out of a system, equals the change in the energy stored in the system.*

Scientists can express stored energy in terms of an object's properties, such as velocity, temperature, pressure, and so on. By measuring changes in these properties, they can make predictions about energy changes going on within the object.

The second law of thermodynamics is: *Heat will, of its own accord, flow only from a hot object to a cold object.* Scientists conclude from the second law that no heat engine can be completely efficient. A *heat engine*, such as a gasoline engine or a turbine, continuously converts heat into work. The second law requires that, even in a perfect engine, only part of the heat supply is converted into work.   CHARLES L. BROWN

See also ENTROPY; HEAT (Thermodynamics); CARNOT, NICOLAS L. S.; CLAUSIUS, RUDOLF J. E.; JOULE, JAMES PRESCOTT; MAYER, JULIUS ROBERT VON.

THERMOGRAPHY, *thur MAHG ruh fee,* is a detection technique that converts invisible heat energy into a visible picture. A device called a *thermograph* is used, and the resulting heat picture is called a *thermogram.* Thermography is used in industry, medicine, and many other fields.

A thermograph looks like a small television camera. It "sees" temperature by sensing heat energy, called *infrared energy.* Infrared energy is radiated naturally by all objects, and hotter objects radiate more than cooler ones. Inside a thermograph, a solid-state detector converts infrared energy into electrical signals. These signals are displayed as pictures on a TV screen. The pictures show different temperature ranges by variations of brightness or color. These variations can be analyzed by scientists.

Industrial uses of thermography include detecting overheated parts in electrical distribution systems and energy losses in manufacturing processes. The technique also is used to find leaks in the insulation of homes and other buildings. In addition, thermography provides a means of inspecting blast furnaces. A weak spot in a furnace wall is hotter than the surrounding areas, and so it appears lighter on a thermogram.

City of Decatur, Ill. (Thermography of Illinois, Inc.)

A Thermogram of a House reveals heat losses. The light areas indicate where heat is escaping. The dotted lines provide a clear view of the house but are not part of the thermogram.

In medicine, thermography can detect temperature variations that reveal arthritis, breast cancer, and blood circulation problems. Physicians first used thermography in 1956 to detect breast cancer.

Military and police forces and firemen use thermography to see in the dark and through smoke. Pollution-control experts sometimes use the technique to determine the distribution of *thermal* (heat) pollution in bodies of water.   CLIFF WARREN

THERMOMETER is an instrument that measures the temperature of gases, liquids, and solids. The action of a thermometer is based on the fact that certain measurable physical characteristics of substances change when the temperature changes. These characteristics include the volume of a liquid and the length of a solid. Another is the *resistance*—that is, the opposition to the flow of electricity—present in an electrical conductor.

There are three principal types of thermometers: (1) liquid-in-glass, (2) deformation-type, and (3) electrical. Many types of thermometers are manufactured as both *digital* thermometers and *disposable* thermometers.

Liquid-in-Glass Thermometers are the best-known type of thermometers. They include those used to determine the temperature in or outside a building, to measure the temperature of the body, and for cooking. Mercury is the most common liquid in these thermometers. Alcohol is used in areas where the temperature frequently drops below the freezing point of mercury ($-39°$ C or $-38°$ F.). The liquid fills a glass bulb, which is connected to a sealed glass tube partially filled with liquid. When the temperature goes up, the volume of the liquid expands and the liquid rises. A temperature scale is on the outside of the thermometer.

Deformation-Type Thermometers change shape as a result of an increase or decrease in temperature. There are two kinds of deformation thermometers, *bimetallic* and *Bourdon tube*. Bimetallic thermometers, the most

common type, consist of two strips of different metals, such as iron and brass. The strips are fastened together from end to end, forming a bar. When the temperature rises, each metal expands at a different rate, which causes the bar to bend. This motion of the bar causes a pointer to move up or down a scale, indicating a temperature change. A type of bimetallic thermometer called a *thermograph* includes a pen that makes a written record of temperature changes.

Bourdon tube thermometers have a curved, flexible metal tube filled with a liquid, such as glycerol or xylene. A rise in temperature makes the liquid expand. The tube straightens out to accommodate the increased volume of liquid. A pen or pointer attached to the end of the tube indicates the temperature.

Electrical Thermometers include *thermocouples* and *resistance thermometers*. Thermocouples, the most widely used type, consist of two wires of different metals. Both ends of the two wires are twisted together to form junctions. One of these junctions, called the *reference junction*, is kept at a constant temperature—usually $0°$ C ($32°$ F.). As the temperature of the other junction changes, a small voltage is generated between the two wires. The voltage is measured by an instrument called a *millivoltmeter*, which may have a temperature scale marked on it. Most thermocouples that measure the temperature of the air have wires made of copper and an alloy called *constantan*. Thermocouples with wires of other metals can measure temperatures up to $2800°$ C ($5072°$ F.). See THERMOCOUPLE.

Resistance thermometers are made of such materials as copper, nickel, or platinum. A temperature change causes a variation in the *electrical resistance* of these metals (see ELECTRIC CIRCUIT [Circuit Mathematics]). The variation is measured and expressed as a temperature value. Scientists use *platinum resistance thermometers* to check the accuracy of all other types of thermome-

Types of Thermometers

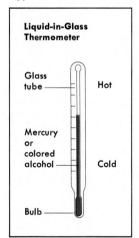

Liquid-in-Glass Thermometer

Glass tube — Hot

Mercury or colored alcohol — Cold

Bulb —

A column of liquid shows the temperature in a liquid-in-glass thermometer. The liquid used in most such thermometers is mercury or colored alcohol.

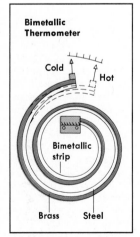

Bimetallic Thermometer

Cold — Hot

Bimetallic strip

Brass   Steel

A bimetallic strip, consisting of two metals, can show temperature. As the temperature changes, the strip bends, indicating the temperature.

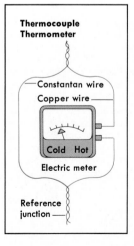

Thermocouple Thermometer

Constantan wire
Copper wire

Cold Hot

Electric meter

Reference junction

An electric voltage from a device called a *thermocouple* can be measured to show the temperature. An electric meter measures the voltage.

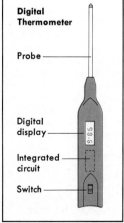

Digital Thermometer

Probe —

Digital display —

Integrated circuit —

Switch —

A digital thermometer has an integrated circuit that changes electric temperature signals into numbers. The numbers appear in a display window.

ters. These extremely reliable thermometers are used to measure temperatures from −259.34° C (−434.81° F.) to 630.74° C (1167.33° F.) on the *International Practical Temperature Scale of 1968*. This scale provides a worldwide reference for temperature values.

Digital Thermometers use electronic circuits and devices to show temperature measurements. These thermometers display the measurements as numbers. Digital thermometers measure temperature by means of a slender device called a *probe*. The probe is made of either a metal, such as copper or platinum, or a *semiconductor* (see SEMICONDUCTOR). Temperature changes cause a large variation in the electrical resistance of these materials. Most semiconductors are more sensitive to temperature changes than are metals.

The probe is connected by wires to an electronic circuit. The circuit receives temperature readings from the probe in the form of electrical signals. The signals are changed into numbers, which appear in a small display window.

Disposable Thermometers are frequently used in homes and medical clinics for measuring body temperature. They are cheaper than regular thermometers to manufacture and to buy. Most disposable thermometers lose their accuracy after a single use, but a few have been designed for repeated use.

Some disposable thermometers are made of materials that melt at certain temperatures. Others use substances called *liquid crystals*, which change appearance at specific temperatures (see LIQUID CRYSTAL).

Temperature Scales. Various manufacturers produce thermometers with a temperature scale in *Fahrenheit*. However, the National Bureau of Standards uses only the *Celsius* and *Kelvin* scales. The bureau is the federal agency that sets measurement standards for science, industry, and commerce in the United States.

On the Fahrenheit scale, 32° F. is the freezing point of water and 212° F. is the boiling point. On the Celsius scale, water freezes at 0° C and boils at 100° C. The Kelvin scale is used for scientific measurement. On this scale, water freezes at 273 K and boils at 373 K. See WEIGHTS AND MEASURES (Temperature).

All temperature scales are based on the International Practical Temperature Scale of 1968. On this scale, temperature is determined by means of six fixed points called *equilibrium states*, which have assigned values. Temperatures are expressed in Celsius and Kelvin units, but may be converted to other scales.

History. The first known thermometer was invented in 1593 by the Italian astronomer Galileo. It was called a *thermoscope* and had only fair accuracy. An accurate thermometer using alcohol was developed in 1641. In 1714, Gabriel D. Fahrenheit, a German physicist, built a mercury thermometer of the type used today.   HARMON H. PLUMB

See also BOLOMETER; PYROMETRY; TEMPERATURE.

THERMONUCLEAR REACTION. See NUCLEAR ENERGY (Nuclear Fusion); SUN (How Long Will the Sun Shine?; How the Sun Produces Energy).

THERMOPLASTIC MATERIALS. See PLASTICS (table).

THERMOPYLAE, *ther MOP ih lee*, was the name of a mountain pass in ancient Greece. The word *Thermopylae* means *Pass of the Hot Springs*. Greek history tells the story of the bravery shown at Thermopylae, where gallant Greek warriors fought against their enemies, the Persians. The ancient pass no longer exists. It is now a wide, marshy plain. But the hot springs remain.

The narrow mountain pass lay between Mount Oeta and the Maliac Gulf. In ancient days, it provided the only way for an army to pass from northern into southern Greece. The pass was only about 50 feet (15 meters) wide, and fairly small forces could defend it.

In 480 B.C., Xerxes led his Persian warriors in an attempted invasion of Greece. The Greek states united to meet the attack. Leonidas, the king of Sparta, led the Greek army of 6,000 men to hold the pass at Thermopylae. The Greek fleet at Artemisium protected the forces of Leonidas from a Persian attack by sea.

For two days, the Greeks held the Persian foe at bay. But on the evening of the second day, a Thessalian traitor named Ephialtes showed Xerxes a new path over the mountains. The Persians crossed and threatened the Greeks from the rear. To save them from death in the pass, Leonidas ordered most of the Greeks to leave. He held off the Persians with a small force of about 300 Spartans and 1,100 other Greeks. But the Persians outflanked him, and killed Leonidas and most of his forces.

In 279 B.C., the invading Gauls tried to enter Greece through the famous pass. The Greeks blocked the enemy for several months. Finally, the Gauls discovered another road over the mountains, but the Greek defenders managed to escape.   THOMAS W. AFRICA

See also GREECE, ANCIENT (The Persian Wars); LEONIDAS I; XERXES (I).

THERMOS BOTTLE. See VACUUM BOTTLE.

THERMOSETTING MATERIALS. See PLASTICS (table: Kinds of Plastics).

THERMOSPHERE is the uppermost region of the earth's atmosphere. It begins at an altitude of about 50 miles (80 kilometers) and continues into space. The thermosphere has only a tiny fraction of the gases that are in the atmosphere. As a result, the atmospheric pressure in the thermosphere is a million or more times as low as the pressure at sea level.

The thermosphere is completely exposed to the sun's radiation. The radiation heats the thin atmosphere of the thermosphere to high temperatures. The temperature increases rapidly from about −135° F. (−93° C) at an altitude of 50 miles (80 kilometers) to more than 2700° F. (1500° C) in the *thermopause*, the upper region of the thermosphere.

Solar radiation, along with cosmic rays, changes the chemical composition of the atmosphere in the thermosphere. From 50 to 60 miles (80 to 97 kilometers) up, oxygen molecules are broken into atoms. Beyond that distance, the thermosphere consists chiefly of helium atoms. The radiation also *ionizes* (charges electrically) atoms in the atmosphere. The region of ionized particles, called the *ionosphere*, extends into the thermosphere.   FRANK SECHRIST

See also AIR; TROPOSPHERE; STRATOSPHERE; MESOSPHERE; IONOSPHERE.

THERMOSTAT, *THUR moh stat*, is a device that helps control the temperature of an indoor area or of an appliance. Thermostats are used in many kinds of equipment, including air conditioners, heaters, electric blankets, ovens, and refrigerators.

A thermostat is set to keep an area or an appliance

at a certain temperature. It measures temperature changes and automatically controls the heating or cooling unit of the equipment being used. For example, the thermostat in a home heating system turns on the furnace if the temperature in the home drops below the desired level. It shuts off the furnace when the temperature reaches that level.

How Thermostats Work. Most metals, liquids, and gases expand when their temperature increases. They contract when their temperature decreases. Some thermostats use such expansion and contraction to measure and control temperature.

Most thermostats used in home heaters and air conditioners have a *bimetallic strip* that "senses" changes in temperature. This thin strip consists of two metals fastened together. When the temperature rises, each metal expands at a different rate, causing the strip to bend. The metals contract unequally when the temperature drops. These actions cause the strip to bend in the opposite direction. The bending action of the bimetallic strip opens or closes the electric circuit that controls heating or cooling equipment. In some thermostats, the bending of the strip tilts a bulb filled with mercury. When the mercury bulb tilts, it completes or breaks the circuit.

Some thermostats use the expansion or contraction of a gas or a liquid to control heating or cooling equipment. Other types use electric devices or infrared detectors that sense temperature changes.

Most thermostats turn heating or cooling equipment completely on or completely off. But some use a method called *proportional control*. These thermostats measure the difference between the actual temperature and the desired temperature. They change the amount of heating or cooling in proportion to this temperature difference. Proportional control thermostats can provide an extremely even temperature. They are used in in-

How a Home Thermostat Works

When the temperature in a room becomes too cold, the bimetallic strip of the thermostat uncoils. This action causes a drop of mercury to close a switch and start the heating system. After the temperature has risen to the desired level, the strip coils up and the mercury opens the switch, shutting off the heat.

WORLD BOOK diagram by Arthur Grebetz

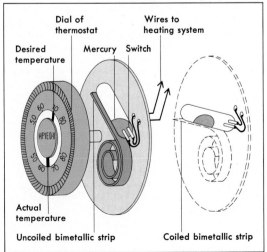

Dial of thermostat

Wires to heating system

Desired temperature

Mercury Switch

Actual temperature

Uncoiled bimetallic strip

Coiled bimetallic strip

dustry and scientific research to control the temperature so that certain chemical processes can take place.

Uses. Thermostats that control air-conditioning and heating systems in houses and other buildings help keep the air comfortable for any activity. Some industries use thermostats to carefully control the temperature needed for manufacturing certain products or for scientific experiments.

Thermostats help keep refrigerators and freezers at the necessary temperature to keep food from spoiling. They control the temperature of household ovens and of industrial furnaces used in making such products as bricks and steel. In homes, thermostats are used in irons, hot water heaters, and heaters for fish tanks.

Thermostats also control the flow of water in automobile cooling systems. The thermostat operates a valve that opens when the water reaches a certain temperature. The open valve allows water to circulate through the radiator and through the water jacket that surrounds the engine.   RICHARD W. HENRY

See also AUTOMATION (Feedback).

THEROPOD. See DINOSAUR (Saurischianis).

THESEUS, *THEE suce,* or *THEE see us,* was a great king of early Athens in Greek mythology. He was the son of King Aegeus and Aethra, a princess of Troezen. Aegeus left Aethra in Troezen and went back to Athens before Theseus was born. The king put his sword and sandals under a large rock and told Aethra that when his son could lift the rock, he should take the sword and sandals and come to him in Athens.

When Theseus was old enough to lift the rock, he set out for Athens. On the way, he killed six brigands and monsters. When he reached Athens, the sorceress Medea, now Aegeus' wife, tried to poison him. But Aegeus recognized Theseus' sword and saved his life.

According to the legend, Athens had to send 14 boys and girls to Crete every year in those days to be eaten by the Minotaur (see MINOTAUR). Theseus decided to go as one of the boys and try to kill the Minotaur. With the help of Ariadne, the daughter of King Minos of Crete, he succeeded, and saved his companions. Ariadne left Crete with him, but Theseus deserted her on the way back to Athens.

He had agreed with Aegeus that his ship would fly white sails if he should come back alive. Otherwise, the black sails with which the ship left Athens would not be changed. In his hurry to return home, Theseus forgot to fly white sails. When Aegeus saw black sails on the returning ship, he killed himself in his sorrow, thinking Theseus had perished. Theseus then became the king of Athens.   JOSEPH FONTENROSE

See also ARIADNE.

THESPIS, a Greek actor and dramatist of the 500's B.C., helped to create drama as we know it. Today, actors are sometimes called *Thespians,* after his name.

Thespis was a real person. However, the ancient Greeks made him a legend and assigned several "firsts" to him. They said he was the first to use a speaker performing a role in dialogue with the choral group. Tragedy seems to have developed from this character-chorus dialogue, so the Greeks concluded that Thespis invented tragedy. The Greeks also credited Thespis with introducing makeup in the form of white lead

THESSALONIANS, EPISTLES TO THE

paint and, later, masks to be worn by performers.

The famous "Parian Marble" tablet records that, in about 534 B.C. in Athens, Thespis became the first to produce a tragedy at the major festival honoring the god Dionysus. Competitions in playwriting were held regularly at the festival after this time.   NORMAN T. PRATT

THESSALONIANS, *THEZ uh LO nee unz,* **EPISTLES TO THE,** the 13th and 14th books of the New Testament, were written by Saint Paul about A.D. 50. Written to Christians in Thessalonica (Salonika, Greece), the first *epistle* (letter) said Christians who had died would meet Christ when He returned to earth just as the living would. It also cautioned against bad conduct and idleness. The second epistle corrected a wrong idea that Christ would return right away. This idea had led some to shun work. The epistle said lazy people should be given no food. These epistles are the earliest writings of the New Testament.   WILLIAM WILSON SLOAN

THESSALY, *THES uh lee,* is a region in northern Greece. It has an area of 5,368 square miles (13,903 square kilometers) and a population of about 660,000 persons. For location, see GREECE (map). Volos and Larisa are Thessaly's largest cities. Three mountains that border the region—Olympus, Pelion, and Ossa—are important in Greek history and legend (see OLYMPUS).

In legend, Thessaly was the home of the great Greek warrior Achilles, and also of Jason, who led the Argonauts in search of the golden fleece. The ancient

WORLD BOOK map
Thessaly is a region in northern Greece. The map at the left shows the location of the region. A map of Thessaly itself appears at the right.

Thessalians were weak militarily because they never banded together. Philip of Macedon conquered Thessaly in 344 B.C. Later, the Romans took Thessaly, and added it to Macedonia in 146 B.C. The Venetians and the Turks controlled Thessaly for hundreds of years. In 1878, by order of the Congress of Berlin, Turkey gave Thessaly to Greece.   NORMAN A. DOENGES

See also GREECE (The Land).

THETIS. See ACHILLES.

THIAMINE. See VITAMIN (Vitamin B); BERIBERI.

THIBAULT, JACQUES A. F. See FRANCE, ANATOLE.

THIERS, *tyair,* **LOUIS ADOLPHE** (1797-1877), was the first president of the Third Republic of France. His 10-volume *History of the French Revolution* (1823-1827) made him famous. He helped place Louis Philippe on the throne of France.

Thiers' political life included terms as foreign minister and president of the council. He also wrote a *History of the Consulate and the Empire* (1845-1862). Emerging from retirement in 1870 during the Franco-Prussian War, he negotiated the peace treaty with Otto von Bismarck, Prussia's chancellor. Thiers then put down the revolt of the Paris Commune, and led the new republic until he resigned in 1873. He was born in Marseille.   FRANCIS J. BOWMAN

See also FRANCO-PRUSSIAN WAR.

THIMONNIER, BARTHÉLEMY. See SEWING MACHINE.

THINKER, THE. See RODIN, AUGUSTE.

THIRA. See VOLCANO (table: Some Famous Volcanoes).

THIRD INTERNATIONAL. See INTERNATIONAL, THE.

THIRD RAIL. See ELECTRIC RAILROAD.

THIRD REICH. See GERMANY (History); REICH.

THIRD REPUBLIC. See FRANCE (History).

THIRD WORLD is a name sometimes given to the economically developing and politically neutral countries of Asia, Africa, and Latin America. These countries are also called *neutral nations* or *nonaligned nations* because they do not regularly support either the First World or the Second World. The First World is said to consist of the United States and other non-Communist industrial nations. The Second World refers to the Soviet Union and the Communist countries of Eastern Europe. Some political experts consider China a Third World country, but others disagree.

The Third World consists of about 120 countries, which have more than half the world's population. Most Third World countries are former colonies of Western European nations and have gained their independence since 1945. Although Third World countries frequently have similar goals, they actually represent different and sometimes opposing political and economic systems.

Most Third World countries have an economy based on agriculture and have developed few industries. Many export raw materials to industrial nations in exchange for manufactured goods. Most Third World countries are poor. About 60 per cent of the people in the Third World live in extreme poverty.

During the 1960's, Third World countries began to use the United Nations (UN) to promote their interests. Today, the Third World has a majority of the votes in the UN General Assembly. Neither the Communist nor the non-Communist bloc can get a resolution adopted without the support of some Third World countries.

Since the mid-1970's, Third World countries increasingly have emphasized their economic problems. They demand financial aid and favorable trade agreements from the industrial countries to redistribute the earth's wealth. They consider the economic differences between developed and developing countries more important than the political differences between Communist and non-Communist ones. For this reason, they prefer the terms *North* for the wealthy nations and *South* for themselves, rather than First, Second, or Third World. Most industrial nations, both Communist and non-Communist, are in the North. Most Third World nations are in the South.

The World Bank, the United Nations Development Program, and other international organizations provide funds for development in the Third World.

But progress has been slow because Third World countries continue to suffer from such problems as rapid population growth and high rates of disease and illiteracy. In addition, richer nations have been unwilling to accept many Third World demands for financial aid and other assistance.   W. SCOTT THOMPSON

See also DEVELOPING COUNTRY.

THIRST is a sensation caused by the body's need for water. The body's *internal environment* (the organs and tissues) needs certain amounts of water and salts to function properly. Too much or too little water, or too much or too little salt, can damage or even kill cells. Therefore, people and animals must control their water intake.

People often describe thirst as a dry feeling in the throat. A lack of sufficient saliva can produce this kind of thirst, even when the internal environment has no need for water. In a similar way, the thirst sensation created by the internal environment's need will disappear briefly if water is drunk and wets the throat. But unless the water reaches the internal environment, thirst will recur after a short time.

The *sensory nerves* in the internal organs are affected by the volume of fluid in the internal environment. These nerves help regulate the amount of water drunk. The internal senses tell how much water and salt are inside and outside the cells of the body (see SENSES). One source of this information is a region of the brain stem called the *hypothalamus*. The hypothalamus is important in maintaining the internal environment. It contains nerve cells that respond to changes in the amount of salt in the blood. The salt concentration of the blood may indicate how much water is in the cells of the body. For example, a decrease in body water produces an increase in the salt concentration in the blood. Thus, the amount of water in the internal environment also affects the amount of water eliminated from the body.   BRUCE P. HALPERN

THIRTEEN COLONIES. See COLONIAL LIFE IN AMERICA; UNITED STATES, HISTORY OF THE.

THIRTEEN-MONTH CALENDAR. See CALENDAR (Calendar Reform).

THIRTEENTH AMENDMENT. See CONSTITUTION OF THE UNITED STATES (Amendment 13).

THIRTY-NINE ARTICLES were a statement of doctrine issued in England in 1563 and approved by Parliament in 1571. The Articles were created to settle religious disputes caused by the Protestant Reformation. The Articles set forth religious positions that all English people were expected to accept. They remain the doctrine of the churches of the Anglican Communion.

The Articles set the Church of England on a middle ground between the Roman Catholic Church and various radical Protestant groups. The Articles condemned several Roman Catholic beliefs and practices, including purgatory, transubstantiation, reverence for saints and relics, indulgences, and the power of the pope. The Articles affirmed the doctrine of predestination—that people are saved solely by God's grace and cannot earn salvation by good deeds. The doctrine of free will was rejected. Contrary to the beliefs of the radicals, the Articles declared that Christians must obey *secular* (nonreligious) governments and could bear arms for the state. The Articles also affirmed infant baptism, rather than adult baptism, which was practiced by the Anabaptists (see ANABAPTISTS).

Some Christians in England, later called Puritans, did not think the Thirty-Nine Articles went far enough in opposing Roman Catholic doctrine. But most of the English people accepted the Articles, and members of the clergy of the Church of England still endorse them today.   RICHARD MARIUS

THIRTY TYRANTS was the name given to the government of Athens after the city was captured by the Spartans in 404 B.C. The men who ruled at this time have also been called simply *The Thirty*. The brilliant Athenian politician Critias led this powerful group. They were appointed to reform the constitution of Athens along conservative lines. But Critias and some of his followers tried to set up a permanent military government. Their reign of terror ended in 403 B.C., when the old democracy was brought back to Athens and the Spartan forces left the city. A group of pretenders who tried to gain control of the Roman Empire around A.D. 260 were also called the Thirty Tyrants.   DONALD KAGAN

THIRTY YEARS' WAR. The Thirty Years' War (1618-1648) was the last of the great religious wars of Europe. This conflict was really a series of wars. It began as a civil war between the Protestants and Roman Catholics in the German states. But before the conflict was over, most of the nations of Europe were involved, and the war had become a general struggle for territory and political power.

Causes of the War. The underlying cause of the war was the old deep-seated hostility between the German Protestants and the German Catholics. The two groups disagreed in their interpretation of the Peace of Augsburg (1555), which had been intended as a settlement of the religious question in Germany. Both groups had violated the peace. In addition, the Peace of Augsburg had recognized only Catholics and Lutherans. There were many Calvinists in southern and central Germany, and they also demanded recognition.

The Bohemian Period (1618-1620). In 1608, the Protestants organized the Evangelical Union. In 1609, the Catholics founded the Holy League. The spark that set off the war came when the Archbishop of Prague ordered a Protestant church destroyed. In anger, the people appealed to Emperor Matthias, who ignored their protests. The Protestants rose in revolt. The event that marked the actual beginning of the Thirty Years' War is known in history as the Defenestration of Prague. (*Defenestration* is from the Latin word *fenestra*, which means *window*.) It was an old Bohemian custom for the people to punish offending officials by throwing them out of a window. The Protestant rebels punished two of their ruler's ministers in this way. Civil war began in Bohemia and spread throughout western Europe.

The Bohemian Protestants removed the Catholic king, Ferdinand, from the throne, and chose the Protestant Frederick, Elector Palatine, in Ferdinand's place. To make matters worse for the Bohemians, Ferdinand was chosen Holy Roman Emperor, which gave him great power. In 1620, his general, Johan Tserclaes, Count of Tilly, decisively defeated the Bohemians in the famous Battle of the White Mountain. This defeat cost the Bohemians their independence. The Protestant rebellion was stamped out, and Catholicism again became the state religion.

THIRTY YEARS' WAR

The Danish Period (1625-1629). After Bohemia was defeated, the other Protestant countries began to realize their danger. The Protestant king of Denmark, Christian IV, aided by several other countries, opposed Ferdinand's forces in Saxony. But the emperor had received unexpected help from the famous general Albrecht Wenzel Eusebius von Wallenstein, who had a great army of hired soldiers and adventurers.

Wallenstein's army, aided by forces of the Holy League under the leadership of General Tilly, defeated the Danish king again and again. Christian IV finally signed the Treaty of Lübeck (1629) and withdrew from Saxony. Meanwhile, the emperor had issued the Edict of Restitution. This document provided that all Church possessions which the Protestants had acquired were to be returned to the Catholics. The Edict was a new source of friction in Germany.

The Swedish Period (1630-1635). The Swedish king, Gustavus Adolphus, known as "the Lion of the North," next entered the war. He had two reasons for this entrance into conflict. He was sincerely devoted to the cause of Protestantism, and he was also ambitious for Sweden, which would be in danger if Emperor Ferdinand became too powerful. So, for the first time, a political issue entered the war.

In 1630, Gustavus Adolphus set sail from Sweden with 13,000 men to relieve the city of Magdeburg, which Tilly was besieging. The Swedish king had the best-trained and best-disciplined army in Europe, but he arrived too late to prevent the capture, looting, and destruction of Magdeburg.

In 1631, the Swedish army defeated Tilly in the Battle of Breitenfeld. In 1632, the Swedish forces were victorious in another important battle, and Tilly was killed in the fighting.

Emperor Ferdinand now called back Wallenstein, whom he had previously dismissed. Another army of recruits was gathered together from many parts of Europe, and placed under Wallenstein's leadership. Ferdinand also made an alliance with Philip IV of Spain. Wallenstein's army met the Swedish forces in the famous Battle of Lützen (1632). The Swedes won, but Gustavus Adolphus was killed in the battle. The Swedes continued the struggle until 1634, when their army was destroyed in the Battle of Nördlingen. The emperor suspected that Wallenstein was negotiating with the Protestants and ordered his arrest. Wallenstein tried to escape, but was assassinated.

The Swedish-French Period (1635-1648). The war now lost its religious character entirely and became purely political. Cardinal Richelieu, who was the real ruler of France, determined to block the growth of Hapsburg power by interfering on the side of the Protestants. The war became a struggle between the French Bourbons and the Austrian Hapsburgs. In 1635, Richelieu sent a French army into Germany, which joined with a new Swedish army. The Protestants and their French allies had excellent leaders, including the French Vicomte de Turenne and Louis II, Prince of Condé. They won a long series of victories, which gave new hope to the Protestants living in Germany.

The Peace of Westphalia (1648). For years the people of Germany had suffered misery and hardships because of the Thirty Years' War. In 1644, the European countries sent representatives to a peace conference. The Catholic and Protestant delegates met separately in two different cities of Westphalia. The negotiations dragged on for four years, until the Peace of Westphalia was finally signed in 1648. By this treaty, France acquired Alsace and Lorraine, Sweden got control of the mouths of the Oder, Elbe, and Weser rivers, and Calvinism was put on an equal footing with Catholicism and Lutheranism.

Results of the War. Germany was in a pitiable condition by the time the war finally ended. Many persons had been killed. Those who survived saw nothing but ruin wherever they looked. Whole cities, villages, and farms had disappeared, and much property had been destroyed. Art, science, trade, and industry declined. It took almost two hundred years for Germany to recover from the effects of the Thirty Years' War. Thousands of persons left Europe, especially Germany, and went to America to build a new life.　　J. SALWYN SCHAPIRO

See also GUSTAVUS (II); RICHELIEU, CARDINAL; WALLENSTEIN, ALBRECHT W. E. VON; TILLY, COUNT OF.

Additional Resources

LANGER, HERBERT. *Thirty Years' War*. Hippocrene, 1980.
MALAND, DAVID. *Europe at War: 1600-1650*. Rowman & Littlefield, 1980.
WEDGWOOD, C. V. *The Thirty Years' War*. Humanities, 1962. First pub. in 1939.

THISBE. See PYRAMUS AND THISBE.

THISTLE, *THIS'l*, is the name given to a group of plants that have sharp spines or prickles. Thistles are often troublesome weeds. They grow in many places throughout the world. The most common thistles are the *Canada thistle*, the *bull thistle*, the *tall thistle*, and the *pasture thistle*. The first two come from Europe, and the last two are native to North America. They grow in pastures and grain and hay fields, and along roads, where the soil is rich. The most troublesome, the Canada thistle, is a perennial. The other three species are biennial.

Thistles have tough, fibrous stems, prickly leaves with many lobes, and soft, silky flowers, usually purple or pinkish-purple in color. The flowers usually grow in round heads that

J. Horace McFarland

The Thistle is a serious pest in grain fields.

form large, downy seed balls after the blossoms wither. The wind scatters the seeds, and this helps the thistles to multiply rapidly. Some kinds have strong roots, and are hard to uproot. Pieces of the roots left in the soil may produce new plants. Thistles are hard to remove from grain fields. Biennial species must be cut down before the flowers bloom. Chlorates, Aminotriazole, or 2,4-D may be used to control them.

A number of plants similar to thistles are sometimes called thistles. Included among these is the *Russian thistle* or *tumbleweed*. This plant has become a serious pest in large areas of North America.

Scientific Classification. Thistles belong to the composite family, *Compositae*. The most important genera include *Silybum, Cirsium, Cnicus,* and *Onopordum*. The Canada thistle is genus *Cirsium*, species *C. arvense*. The bull, or common, thistle is *C. lanceolatum*.   Louis Pyenson

Related Articles in WORLD BOOK include:

Blazing Star	Composite Family
Boneset	Fleabane
Calendula	Sow Thistle
Camomile	Tumbleweed
Canada Thistle	

THISTLE, ORDER OF THE. See KNIGHTHOOD, ORDERS OF.

THIVAI. See THEBES (Greece).

THOMAS, DYLAN, *DIHL uhn* (1914-1953), a Welsh poet, wrote some of the most stirring and passionate verse in modern literature. From the publication of his first book, *Eighteen Poems* (1934), critics recognized him as a brilliant poet. The volume bewildered and fascinated readers with its varied mood and style, alternately ecstatic and morbid, as Thomas revealed his obsessions with death, religion, sex, and the sound of words.

Thomas also revealed his high-spirited love of life in prose and dramatic works. His stories about his youth in Wales were collected in *Portrait of the Artist as a Young Dog* (1940). A group of his early and symbolic stories was published in 1955 as *Adventures in the Skin Trade*. Just before his death, Thomas completed a radio play, *Under Milk Wood*, describing with tender humor a day in the life of a Welsh village.

Atlantic-Little, Brown & Co.
Dylan Thomas

Thomas was born in Swansea, Wales. He gained great popularity through public readings of his works in Great Britain and the United States. Many of his poems are available on records. His drinking and his stormy relationship with his wife Caitlin spread his fame. Thomas died of pneumonia brought on by acute alcoholism while on an American tour.   TIM REYNOLDS

See also THEATER (Lighting and Sound [pictures]).

Additional Resources

FERRIS, PAUL. *Dylan Thomas*. Dial, 1977.
FITZGIBBON, CONSTANTINE. *The Life of Dylan Thomas*. Little, Brown, 1965.
MOYNIHAN, WILLIAM. *The Craft and Art of Dylan Thomas*. Cornell Univ. Press, 1968.
TINDALL, WILLIAM. *A Reader's Guide to Dylan Thomas*. Octagon, 1973. Reprint of 1963 ed.

THOMAS, GEORGE HENRY (1816-1870), was a Union general in the Civil War. Because he held his line at the Battle of Chickamauga, he became known as "the Rock of Chickamauga." He served with the Army of the Cumberland, and succeeded Major General William S. Rosecrans as its commander. Thomas fought at Chattanooga and defeated an invading Confederate army at Nashville. A major general in the regular Army after the war, he died while commanding the Division of the Pacific. He was born in Virginia.   T. HARRY WILLIAMS

See also CIVIL WAR (Tennessee Campaign).

THOMAS, ISAIAH (1749-1831), was the leading printer and publisher in colonial America. He published a Boston newspaper, the *Massachusetts Spy*, which printed strong attacks on the British government.

Thomas was born in Boston and became a printer's apprentice there when he was 7 years old. He began to publish the *Spy* in 1770, when he was 21. In 1775, the British tried to stop the publication of patriot newspapers. Thomas sent his printing equipment by night to Worcester, Mass., about 40 miles (64 kilometers) west of Boston. He arrived there himself a few days later. On the way, he aided Paul Revere in his famous midnight ride and fought at Lexington and Concord in the opening battles of the Revolutionary War.

Thomas later printed books and magazines in addition to his newspaper. He wrote a book, *The History of Printing in America* (1810), which still ranks as an important work on the subject.   WILLIAM MORGAN FOWLER, JR.

See also MOTHER GOOSE.

THOMAS, LOWELL (1892-1981), was an American news commentator and author specializing in world travel. Starting in 1930, he became widely known for his radio broadcasts and motion-picture newsreels. He adapted his travelogue technique to television in 1956. After 1952, he played a major role in developing the three-dimensional motion-picture concept called "Cinerama." He wrote many books on travel, including *With Lawrence in Arabia* (1924), *Kabluk of the Eskimo* (1932), and *Back to Mandalay* (1951). He also wrote *Stand Fast for Freedom* (1940), *Pageant of Life* (1941), and *History As You Heard It* (1957). Thomas was born in Woodington, Ohio.   PAUL MOLLOY

THOMAS, MARTHA CAREY (1857-1935), was an American educator who fought for equal educational opportunities for women. In 1885, she became dean and English professor at Bryn Mawr College, a new women's college in Bryn Mawr, Pa. She served as president from 1894 to 1922 and worked to make Bryn Mawr as good as—or better than—the best men's college. She set up high entrance requirements and a demanding course of study, and she hired outstanding teachers.

Carey Thomas, as she preferred to be known, also worked to gain women the right to vote. She served as president of the National College Equal Suffrage League from 1908 to 1917.

Thomas was born in Baltimore and graduated from Cornell University. She went to Europe for further study because few United States graduate schools would admit a woman. In 1882, she earned a Ph.D. at the University of Zurich in Switzerland.   MIRIAM SCHNEIR

THOMAS, NORMAN MATTOON (1884-1968), an American Socialist leader, was nominated six times for the presidency of the United States by the Socialist Party. His ardent pacifism during World War I (1914-1918) led him into the Socialist Party. He founded the periodical *World Tomorrow* (1918), and became active in the American Civil Liberties Union, an organization devoted to the defense of civil liberties.

During the 1920's, Thomas ran for mayor of New York City, state governor, and senator. He was first nominated for President in 1928, and received his largest popular vote in 1932. At first somewhat sympathetic to the Soviet experiment, by the middle 1930's he vigorously opposed Communism. He tried to keep the United States out of World War II (1939-1945).

Thomas wrote many books and articles advocating "planning" in American economic and social relations. Thomas was born in Marion, Ohio, and graduated from Princeton University and Union Theological Seminary.   RICHARD L. WATSON, JR.

THOMAS, SAINT, called DIDYMUS (The Twin), was one of the better-known disciples of Christ. But there is no record of his having a twin. Thomas was one of the most loyal of the 12 apostles. He was ready to return with Jesus to Jerusalem when he knew that Jesus' life was in danger. He was interested in Jesus' prediction of His death, and wanted to know how he and the others could follow Him. He was called "Doubting Thomas" because he said that he would not believe in Jesus' Resurrection until he could touch the wounds that He carried (John 20: 24, 25). When Jesus allowed him to feel His hands and side, Thomas worshiped Him, saying, "My Lord and my God." He helped the other apostles establish the Church in Jerusalem.

Tradition says he went to India, converted many Indians, and died a martyr there about A.D. 68. His bones were taken to Edessa later and then to Ortona, Italy. His feast day is generally celebrated on December 21. In the Eastern Orthodox Church, it is celebrated on July 3.   FULTON J. SHEEN and MERRILL C. TENNEY

THOMAS, SETH (1785-1859), was an American clock manufacturer. He formed a partnership with two clockmakers, Eli Terry and Silas Hoadley, in 1807, and became skilled at designing and making clocks. Thomas withdrew from the partnership in 1812, and established his own clock factory in Plymouth, Conn. A good businessman, he made a fortune. He built a cotton mill and a brass-rolling and wiremaking factory. Thomas was born in Wolcott, Conn.   JOHN B. McFERRIN

THOMAS À BECKET. See BECKET, SAINT THOMAS À.

THOMAS À KEMPIS (1380?-1471) was a medieval Christian religious writer, and the author of *Imitation of Christ,* one of the most famous devotional books ever written. He was born Thomas Hamerken in Kempen, Germany. In school, he was called *Thomas from Kempen.* This became *Thomas à Kempis.* He was educated in Deventer, The Netherlands, and about 1400 entered the Augustinian monastery of Mount St. Agnes, near Zwolle, The Netherlands. Thomas à Kempis was ordained in 1413. He continued to live in quiet at Mount St. Agnes, and became subprior there in 1425.

Thomas à Kempis wrote *Meditations of Christ's Life, The Soul's Soliloquy,* and *Garden of Roses.* But these works are overshadowed by his *Imitation of Christ.* This has been more widely read by Roman Catholics than any other religious book except the Bible. There is still some doubt as to its authorship. But credit is almost always given to Thomas à Kempis. An existing copy of it in his own hand is not positive proof, because all monks copied good books. *Imitation of Christ* aims to advise all who seek the path to righteousness. Thomas à Kempis finds the root of all good in love, the root of all evil in lack of it. People in every age since have been profoundly moved by the book.   FULTON J. SHEEN

THOMAS AQUINAS, SAINT. See AQUINAS, SAINT THOMAS.

THOMAS JEFFERSON MEMORIAL. See JEFFERSON MEMORIAL.

THOMAS NATURAL SHORTHAND. See SHORTHAND.

THOMPSON, Man. (pop. 17,291), is one of the world's leading centers of nickel production. It lies on the Burntwood River, in north-central Manitoba. For location, see MANITOBA (political map). Thompson is the province's third largest city, after Winnipeg and Brandon.

Thompson was founded in 1956, following the discovery of a huge deposit of nickel ore in the area by the International Nickel Company of Canada, Limited (INCO). The city was named after John F. Thompson, chairman of INCO at that time. The first permanent residents arrived in 1958.

INCO built a huge nickel-producing complex in Thompson. This facility was the first in the world to handle all the processes of nickel production, from mining through refining. Production began in 1961. INCO is Thompson's largest employer.

Thompson is also a government and transportation center for northern Manitoba. Airlines and freight and passenger trains serve the city. Thompson has a mayor-council form of government.   STEPHEN GAUER

THOMPSON, BENJAMIN (1753-1814), COUNT RUMFORD, was an American-born scientist and political figure. He was best known for his observations on the apparent weightlessness of heat (at a time when heat was considered a material substance), and for his role in founding the British Royal Institution in 1800. His work to improve the living conditions of the poor in Munich gained him the title of count in 1791. Thompson was born in Woburn, Mass. He lived in Europe after the Revolutionary War.   ROBERT P. MULTHAUF

See also HEAT (The Caloric Theory of Heat); RANGE (History).

THOMPSON, DAVID (1770-1857), a Canadian geographer and explorer, traveled the Columbia River from its source to its mouth. He explored extensive areas of Canada, and surveyed the northernmost source of the Mississippi River. From 1816 to 1826, he was a surveyor on the U.S.-Canadian boundary.

Thompson was born in Westminster, England, and was apprenticed to the Hudson's Bay Company when he was 14 years old. He worked for the North West Company from 1797 until 1812.   WILLIAM P. BRANDON

THOMPSON, ERNEST SETON. See SETON, ERNEST THOMPSON.

THOMPSON, FRANCIS (1859-1907), was a British poet. A deeply religious Roman Catholic, he wrote some of the best religious poems of his time. His greatest work was the mystical poem "The Hound of Heaven" (1893). Other works include *Poems* (1893), *Sister Songs* (1895), *New Poems* (1897), and *Essay on Shelley* (1909).

Thompson was born in Preston, Lancashire. He intended at first to become a priest, then chose to study medicine. But he was unable to pass the examinations. He settled in London, and began to write poems while living in poverty. He started taking opium, and became addicted to it. He was finally rescued by friends. They helped him publish his poems, and cared for him for the rest of his life.   C. L. CLINE

SIR JOHN SPARROW DAVID THOMPSON

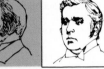

Prime Minister of Canada
1892-1894

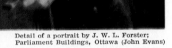

ABBOTT	THOMPSON	BOWELL
1891-1892	1892-1894	1894-1896

THOMPSON, SIR JOHN SPARROW DAVID (1844-1894), served as prime minister of Canada from 1892 until his death two years later. He was the first Nova Scotian to hold that office. Thompson, a Conservative, became prime minister during a period of difficulty for his party following the death of Sir John A. Macdonald. Macdonald, the first prime minister of the Dominion of Canada, had led the party from 1867 until he died in 1891.

Thompson practiced law for several years before he entered politics in 1872. In 1882, he accepted Macdonald's offer of an appointment to the Nova Scotia Supreme Court. Three years later, after some persuasion, Thompson joined Macdonald's Cabinet as minister of justice.

Thompson's honesty and his ability to combine the roles of lawyer and statesman earned wide respect. He gained fame as a skillful diplomat and helped negotiate several international treaties. He also became known for a sarcastic sense of humor that sometimes offended people.

Early Life. John Sparrow David Thompson was born on Nov. 10, 1844, in Halifax, N.S. His father, John Sparrow Thompson, had emigrated from Ireland in 1828. He had settled in Halifax and worked in the Nova Scotian Post Office. In 1829, he married Charlotte Pottinger, a Nova Scotian of Scottish descent.

John, the youngest of five children, went to school in Halifax. He then studied law as a clerk in a legal firm. Thompson was admitted to the Nova Scotia bar in 1865. In 1870, he married Annie Affleck of Halifax. She was a Roman Catholic, and Thompson, a Methodist, converted to Catholicism about a year after their marriage.

Early Political Career. Thompson entered politics in 1872, when Halifax voters elected him as a city alderman. He was elected to the Halifax Board of School Commissioners in 1874 and later served as board chairman. In 1877, the United States government asked Thompson to advise its delegation to the Halifax Fisheries Commission, which met to regulate international fishing rights off the Atlantic Coast. That same year, Conservative Party leaders urged Thompson to run for the Nova Scotia Legislative Assembly from Antigonish. He won the election and soon gained a reputation as an able legislator. In 1878, he became attorney general of Nova Scotia.

Thompson and other members of the legislature had supported reform laws aimed at Nova Scotia municipal government. These laws gave counties powers that had belonged to the provincial government. The new policies caused resentment, and many of the reform legislators were defeated in the election of June, 1882. Thompson, who served as premier of Nova Scotia for less than a month before the election, kept his seat in the legislature. But he had become tired of politics and, in July, accepted appointment by Macdonald to the Supreme Court of Nova Scotia.

Minister of Justice. In the fall of 1885, Macdonald offered Thompson the office of minister of justice in his Cabinet. Thompson did not want to leave the provincial supreme court, but his wife persuaded him to do so. He became minister of justice in September and the next month was elected to the House of Commons from Antigonish, N.S.

Thompson's honesty and legal skill made him one of the most respected members of the government and of the Conservative Party. Macdonald declared that "the

201

best thing I ever invented was Thompson." As minister of justice, Thompson defended some unpopular actions of the Macdonald Administration. One such action involved the execution of Louis Riel, who had led an uprising of Canadian *métis* (people of mixed white and Indian ancestry). Many French Canadians had protested Riel's execution. See RIEL, LOUIS.

In 1887 and 1888, Thompson helped draft a U.S.-Canadian treaty on fishing rights. Queen Victoria knighted him in 1888 for this service. Thompson also directed the revision of the Canadian Criminal Code, which set forth the nation's criminal laws.

Prime Minister. Macdonald died in 1891, and the Conservatives asked Thompson to take over as party leader and as prime minister. Thompson refused because he feared that Protestant Canadians would not accept a Roman Catholic, particularly one who had converted from a Protestant faith. John J. C. Abbott succeeded Macdonald, and Thompson continued as minister of justice.

In 1892, Abbott became ill and resigned as prime minister. The Conservatives again offered Thompson the positions of party leader and prime minister, and this time he accepted. He was sworn in as prime minister on Dec. 5, 1892.

Thompson prevented a controversy involving Roman Catholic schools in Manitoba from becoming a major political issue during his term as prime minister. The controversy arose in 1890, when the Manitoba legislature passed a bill that abolished tax support for the province's Catholic schools. The legislature wanted to make all schools in the province part of the public school system. Catholics in Manitoba demanded that the federal government use its authority to *disallow* (reject) the legislation. Thompson thought the issue was a legal problem and decided to let the courts settle it. The dispute finally ended in 1896, when Prime Minister Wilfrid Laurier helped work out a compromise.

Thompson also worked to bring Newfoundland into the Canadian Dominion. He had almost succeeded at the time of his death. Newfoundland did not join the dominion until 1949.

As prime minister, Thompson continued to use his skill as a diplomat. In 1893, he represented Great Britain at the Bering Sea Convention in Paris. Partly as a result of his arguments, this conference ruled that the United States had to grant Britain fishing rights in the Bering Sea. See BERING SEA CONTROVERSY.

In 1894, Thompson met in London with other British statesmen. They discussed publishing laws, commercial shipping regulations, and other issues involving members of the British Empire. At Windsor Castle, on December 12, Thompson was sworn in as a member of the Imperial Privy Council. This council consisted of leading statesmen of the empire. Immediately after the ceremony, Thompson suffered a heart attack and died within minutes. He was buried in Halifax. P. B. WAITE

THOMPSON, WILLIAM HALE (1869-1944), became a controversial American political leader. Nicknamed "Big Bill," Thompson served as mayor of Chicago from 1915 to 1923 and from 1927 to 1931. His long term in office was largely due to his strict control of an efficient political *machine* (organization). Although a local leader,

Thompson won fame for his stands on national issues. During World War I, he opposed the sending of United States troops to fight against Germany. In 1919, Thompson ran on a "Freedom for Ireland" platform. In his 1927 campaign, he charged that British propaganda was creeping into American textbook treatment of the Revolutionary War in America. Thompson was born in Boston, and moved to Chicago with his parents shortly after his birth. CHARLES FORCEY and LINDA FORCEY

THOMSEN, *TAHM s'n,* **CHRISTIAN JÜRGENSEN** (1788-1865), was a Danish archaeologist. He was one of the first to demonstrate that the vast history of man, before written records began, could be divided into a Stone Age, a Bronze Age, and an Iron Age. His interest in bringing this understanding to the public led him to organize the world's first ethnographical museum, in Copenhagen, in 1846. DAVID B. STOUT

THOMSON, CHARLES (1729-1824), served as secretary of the Continental Congress from 1774 to 1789, the entire period of its existence. As secretary, he signed the copy of the Declaration of Independence that the Congress adopted on July 4, 1776. Born in County Derry, Ireland, Thomson came to America at the age of 10 as an orphan. He became a schoolmaster and then a successful merchant. He published a translation of the Bible in 1808. RICHARD B. MORRIS

THOMSON, CHARLES EDWARD POULETT. See SYDENHAM, BARON.

THOMSON, JAMES (1700-1748), was the most celebrated Scottish poet of the 1700's until Robert Burns. In 1725, he traveled from Scotland to London where he published his masterpiece, *The Seasons* (1726-1730, revised 1744-1746). Thomson broke with the witty artificial poetic style of his day. He turned to nature for his subject matter, and wrote fresh, vivid descriptions of natural scenes in rich blank verse. This style led to the romantic movement later in the 1700's.

Thomson was born in Ednam in the Scottish lowlands. He wrote tragedies, the poem *Liberty* (1735-1736), and an imitation of the poetry of Edmund Spenser, *The Castle of Indolence* (1748). MARTIN C. BATTESTIN

THOMSON, SIR JOSEPH JOHN (1856-1940), a British physicist, received the 1906 Nobel prize in physics for his discovery of the electron. In 1937, his son and pupil, Sir George Paget Thomson (1892-1975), shared the Nobel prize in physics with Clinton Davisson, an American physicist.

Thomson began in 1895 to investigate the mysterious rays which occurred when electricity was passed through a vacuum in a glass tube. Because they seemed to come from the *cathode* (negative electrical pole in the tube), they were called *cathode rays*. No one had succeeded in deflecting them by an electric force. It was assumed that cathode rays were like light waves. Thomson felt that they were really tiny particles of matter (see CATHODE RAYS).

He built a special cathode-ray tube in which the rays passed between charged metal plates inside the glass. The rays became visible as a dot on a fluorescent screen placed inside the tube. By measuring the deflections of the dot, Thomson could determine the ratio of the charge to the mass of the particle (symbolized as e/m). From the direction of their deflection, he decided that they were negatively charged. Because their e/m was always the same, he felt sure that they were a fundamental part of all atoms. These particles were later called *electrons* (see ATOM [diagram: Models of the Atom]; ELECTRON).

Thomson also discovered the first isotopes of the chemical elements, neon 20 and neon 22. This spurred the invention of the mass spectrograph by his pupil, Francis W. Aston (see MASS SPECTROSCOPY).

Thomson was born near Manchester, and was educated at Cambridge. Thomson's experimental work was invaluable to physics. His theoretical model of the atom, however, was discarded in 1911 for that of Ernest Rutherford.   SIDNEY ROSEN

See also ELECTRONICS (picture: The Discoverer of the Electron).

THOMSON, TOM (1877-1917), was a Canadian landscape painter. He was associated with, and greatly influenced, J. E. H. MacDonald, A. Y. Jackson, and the other Canadian artists who, after 1920, called themselves "the Group of Seven."

For eight months of each year, Thomson lived in Algonquin Park, Ont., painting and serving as a ranger. During the winters, Thomson lived in Toronto, where he painted from his sketches the few large pictures that he completed. The pictures portray the beauty and imposing grandeur of the Canadian wilderness. They are characterized by a brilliance of color and a free dashing treatment seldom equaled. His first work to be exhibited, *Northern Lake*, was purchased by the National Art Gallery at Ottawa. Thomson was born near Owen Sound, Ont. He was accidentally drowned in Algonquin Park in 1917.   WILLIAM R. WILLOUGHBY

See also CANADA (The Arts [picture]); GROUP OF SEVEN (picture).

THOMSON, VIRGIL (1896-   ), is an American composer and music critic. He gained international fame for his simple compositions based on early American hymns and folk songs.

Thomson was born in Kansas City, Mo. From 1925 to 1940, he lived in Paris. There, he came under the influence of Erik Satie and other modern French composers. Thomson's *Missa Pro Defunctis* (1960), a religious composition for chorus, shows Satie's influence. In Paris, Thomson and the American writer Gertrude Stein became friends. They collaborated on two operas, *Four Saints in Three Acts* (1928) and *The Mother of Us All* (1947).

Thomson pioneered in writing music for motion pictures. He composed the music for two documentary films about the Great Depression of the 1930's, *The Plow That Broke the Plains* (1936) and *The River* (1937). Thomson won the 1949 Pulitzer prize for his music for the documentary *Louisiana Story* (1948). His other works include such musical portraits as *The Mayor La Guardia Waltzes* (1942) and such descriptive pieces as *The Seine at Night* (1947).

From 1940 to 1954, Thomson served as music critic of the *New York Herald Tribune*. His literary style and insight into modern music made him one of the most respected critics of his time. Thomson wrote several books of music criticism, including *The State of Music* (1939) and *Music, Right and Left* (1951). He also wrote an autobiography, *Virgil Thomson* (1966).   JAMES SYKES

THOMSON, WILLIAM. See KELVIN, LORD.

THOR, the god of thunder and lightning, was the ruler of the sky in Norse mythology. He was the oldest

Oil painting on canvas (1917); National Gallery of Canada

Tom Thomson's *The Jack Pine* is among his brilliant landscapes, showing the beauty of Canada's wilderness.

and most powerful son of Odin, the king of the gods and goddesses. Thor had great strength and was a skilled fighter. His chief weapon was a hammer named Mjollnir, which he threw at his enemies. Mjollnir never missed its mark and always returned to Thor after hitting a target. Thor created lightning whenever he threw Mjollnir, and thunder was the rumbling of his chariot as it moved across the sky. The day Thursday was named for Thor.

Of all the Norse gods, Thor best represented the way of life of the ancient Vikings. For example, the Vikings held great feasts and glorified war. Several myths describe Thor's huge appetite. He once ate an ox and eight salmon and drank three barrels of an alcoholic beverage called mead. Another myth tells of a drinking contest in which Thor tried to drink the sea dry. He failed to do so, but he lowered the level of the sea slightly and thus created the first tides. The gods had several huge drinking horns, and only Thor could consume their entire contents.

Many myths tell of Thor's encounters with the giants, the chief enemies of the gods and goddesses. One story describes his battle with Hrungnir, a giant, who hurled a huge stone at him. Thor threw his hammer, and it shattered the stone in the air and killed Hrungnir.

Someday, according to Norse mythology, the gods and goddesses will fight the giants in a great battle called *Ragnarok*, and the world will be destroyed. Thor and the Midgard Serpent, a vicious snake coiled around the world under the sea, will kill each other during the battle.   C. SCOTT LITTLETON

See also MYTHOLOGY (Teutonic Mythology).

THORACIC DUCT. See LYMPHATIC SYSTEM.

THORAX. See CHEST; INSECT (The Bodies of Insects).

THOREAU, HENRY DAVID (1817-1862), was an American writer who is remembered for his attacks on the social institutions he considered immoral and for his faith in the religious significance of nature. The essay "Civil Disobedience" is his most famous social protest. *Walden*, a study of people in nature, is chiefly responsible for his literary reputation.

Henry David Thoreau by Samuel Rowse. Concord Public Library, Concord, Mass. (The Thoreau Society, Inc.)

Henry David Thoreau

His Life. Thoreau was born in Concord, Mass., on July 12, 1817. Unlike most leading writers of his time, Thoreau came from a family that was neither wealthy nor distinguished. His father made pencils in a small shop. His mother took in boarders.

Thoreau graduated from Harvard College in 1837. He soon met the writer Ralph Waldo Emerson, who encouraged him to write, gave him useful criticism, and later employed him as a gardener and handyman. Emerson also taught Thoreau the philosophy of *transcendentalism*, with its emphasis on mysticism and individualism (see TRANSCENDENTALISM).

Thoreau published only two books during his lifetime, *A Week on the Concord and Merrimack Rivers* (1849) and *Walden*. Many of the books published after Thoreau's death were based on trips he had taken. These books include *Excursions* (1863), *The Maine Woods* (1863), *Cape Cod* (1865), and *A Yankee in Canada* (1866). The books are organized in a loose chronological form that takes the reader through the author's experiences.

His Beliefs and Works. Thoreau believed that people must be free to act according to their own idea of right and wrong, without government interference. In "Civil Disobedience" (1849), he said that people should refuse to obey any government rule they believe is unjust. Thoreau practiced this doctrine of *passive resistance* when, in 1846, he refused to pay poll taxes. He did so to express his opposition to slavery as it became an issue in

Arthur Griffin

Walden Pond, near Concord, Mass., inspired Thoreau's most famous book. He built a one-room cabin near the pond.

the Mexican War. He spent a night in jail because of his refusal.

Thoreau summed up his idea of the role of government in "Civil Disobedience." He wrote, "There will never be a really free and enlightened State until the State comes to recognize the individual as a higher and independent power, from which all its own power and authority are derived, and treats him accordingly." The essay greatly influenced such reformers as Leo Tolstoy of Russia, Mahatma Gandhi of India, and the leaders of the present-day American civil rights movements.

Thoreau called for an end to slavery. He attacked it in the essay "Slavery in Massachusetts" (1854), and defended abolitionist John Brown's raid at Harpers Ferry in "A Plea for John Brown" (1859).

In 1845, Thoreau moved to the shore of Walden Pond near Concord, Mass. He lived there alone from July 4, 1845 to Sept. 6, 1847. *Walden* (1854) records Thoreau's observations of nature there, and tells how he built his house, paid his bills, and spent his time. It also tells about his visitors and reports what he read and thought. On a deeper level, the book is a celebration of people living in harmony with nature.

Thoreau insisted that his trip to Walden Pond was an experiment in simple living, not an idle withdrawal from society. He wrote, "The mass of men lead lives of quiet desperation." He appealed to people to economize, to simplify their lives, and thus to save the time and energy that will allow them "to live deep and suck out all the marrow of life. . . ." JOHN CLENDENNING

Additional Resources

HARDING, WALTER, and MEYER, MICHAEL. *The New Thoreau Handbook.* Rev. ed. New York Univ. Press, 1980.
HOUGH, HENRY BEETLE. *Thoreau of Walden: The Man and His Eventful Life.* Shoe String, 1970. Reprint of 1956 ed.
KRUTCH, JOSEPH WOOD. *Henry David Thoreau.* Morrow, 1974. Reprint of 1948 ed.
NORMAN, CHARLES. *To A Different Drum: The Story of Henry David Thoreau.* Harper, 1954.

THORIUM, a chemical element, is a soft, radioactive metal with a silvery luster. When thorium is bombarded with neutrons, it changes to uranium-233, a nuclear fuel. U-233 is used in bombs and *nuclear reactors* (devices that produce nuclear energy). Thorium is also used in making strong *alloys* (mixtures of metals). In addition, manufacturers use thorium in special photoelectric cells designed to measure ultraviolet light. In the late 1800's, it was used to make mantles for gaslights. The mantles glowed when heated.

Thorium occurs in various minerals, including monazite and thorite. These minerals are mined chiefly in Brazil, India, and South Africa.

Thorium has the chemical symbol Th. The element's atomic number is 90 and its atomic weight is 232.038. Thorium melts at 1750° C and boils at about 4000° C. The Swedish chemist Jöns J. Berzelius discovered thorium in 1828. FRANK C. ANDREWS

See also ELEMENT, CHEMICAL (tables); URANIUM (map); MONAZITE.

THORN, in botany, is a short, hard, sharp-pointed and leafless branch. Thorns develop on many different kinds of plants. Vines such as cat brier, bushes such as blackberries and roses, woody plants such as hawthorns and locusts, and nonwoody and desert plants such as cacti, all have thorns.

THORN APPLE. See Hawthorn; Datura; Jimson Weed.

THORNDIKE, EDWARD LEE (1874-1949), an American educational psychologist, made many contributions to the study of learning, teaching, and mental testing. He invented the puzzle-box to investigate how such animals as cats and dogs solve problems. He found that they tend to repeat those movements which are successful, while other movements drop out. This leads them to a final quick solution.

Thorndike also studied learning in human beings. He found that being right helped the student to retain a correct response, but that being wrong did not seem to eliminate errors. He conducted large-scale statistical studies to show how the study of Latin, mathematics, and other subjects affects the later school performance of students. He was one of the first to devise tests to measure learning and aptitudes.

Thorndike was born in Williamsburg, Mass. He received a Ph.D. from Columbia University, and taught at Teachers College, Columbia University, for 41 years. He developed a method to determine which words are used most often. His data was used as a basis for the Thorndike-Century and the Thorndike-Barnhart school dictionaries. One of his best known books, *Teacher's Word Book* (1921), lists 30,000 words by their frequency of use. His other works include *Mental and Social Measurement* (1904), *The Measurement of Intelligence* (1926), *Fundamentals of Learning* (1932), and *The Psychology of Learning* (1941). B. F. Skinner

THORNTON, MATTHEW (1714?-1803), was a New Hampshire signer of the Declaration of Independence. He served as president of the first New Hampshire Provincial Congress in 1775, and as speaker of the general assembly in 1776. In 1776 and 1778, he was a delegate to the Continental Congress. Thornton was born in Ireland, and came to America about 1718. He practiced medicine in Londonderry. Richard B. Morris

THOROUGHBRED. See Horse (Saddle Horses).

THOROUGHWORT. See Boneset.

THORPE, JIM (1888-1953), was one of the greatest all-around athletes in history. He became an outstanding college and professional football player and won fame as an Olympic track and field champion. Thorpe also played major-league baseball.

In the 1912 Olympic Games, Thorpe became the first athlete to win both the pentathlon and the decathlon (see Track and Field [The Decathlon and the Pentathlon]). But about a month later, Olympic officials took away his medals. Prior to the games, Thorpe had played baseball for a small salary. The Amateur Athletic Union ruled that Thorpe was therefore a professional athlete and ineligible to compete in the Olympic Games.

James Francis Thorpe, an Indian, was born near Prague, Okla. His great-grandfather was Black Hawk, a famous Indian chief. Thorpe began his athletic career at the Carlisle (Pa.) Indian Industrial School. He led the small school to national fame in football. He was an outstanding runner, place kicker, and tackler and won all-America honors in 1911 and 1912.

From 1913 to 1919, Thorpe played six seasons of baseball as an outfielder on three major league teams. He began his professional football career in 1915 and played on seven teams during the next 15 years. Thorpe helped

United Press Int.

Jim Thorpe became one of the first men to be admitted to the National Football Foundation's Hall of Fame in 1951.

establish professional football as a popular sport. In 1920, he became the first president of the American Professional Football Association, now the National Football League. Bob Wolf

Additional Resources

Newcombe, Jack. *The Best of the Athletic Boys: The White Man's Impact on Jim Thorpe.* Doubleday, 1975.
Schoor, Gene. *The Jim Thorpe Story: America's Greatest Athlete.* Messner, 1951. For younger readers.
Wheeler, Robert W. *Jim Thorpe: World's Greatest Athlete.* Rev. ed. Univ. of Oklahoma Press, 1979.

THORVALDSEN, *TOOR vahls'n,* **BERTEL** (1770-1844), also spelled *Thorwaldsen,* a neo-classicist, was Denmark's greatest sculptor. After studying in Copenhagen, he won a scholarship and went to Rome

Sawders

The Lion of Lucerne is a famous Swiss monument based on a model created by Bertel Thorvaldsen. The Swiss sculptor Lukas Ahorn carved the work in 1820 and 1821 to honor Swiss guards who were killed while defending the king of France in 1792.

to complete his training. His first sculpture to attract attention was *Jason with the Golden Fleece*. His best-known work is the *Lion of Lucerne*. His best-loved works are the statues of Christ and the Twelve Apostles.

King Ludwig of Bavaria, one of Thorvaldsen's patrons, chose him to restore the famous early Greek sculptures from the temple of Aeginetum in 1811. This may be what led Thorvaldsen to claim that he had returned to pure Greek sculpture for inspiration, rather than to Graeco-Roman copies that had inspired sculptors before that. Actually, he was influenced little by early Greek art, except in subject matter. Thorvaldsen left a collection of sculptures to found a museum in Copenhagen, where he was born.   MARVIN C. ROSS

See also ADONIS (picture); GANYMEDE (picture); SCULPTURE (picture: A Shepherd Boy).

THOTH, *thohth,* or *toht,* was the ancient Egyptian god of learning, letters, and wisdom. He was the inventor of writing and speech, and the protector of the arts and the scribes. He took care of the libraries and archives, and controlled the science of numbers, weights, and measures. He was believed to have magical powers of healing and was the patron of physicians. Thoth's main center of worship was at Hermopolis Magna in Egypt. The worship of the moon, which Thoth represented, never rivaled that of the sun among the Egyptians. This was in contrast to the great importance attached to the moon in the beliefs of other Oriental peoples such as the Babylonians. Thoth appears in two animal forms. He is portrayed either as an ibis (wading bird) or as a baboon.   I. J. GELB

THOTHMES III. See THUTMOSE III.

THOUGHT AND JUDGMENT. Thinking refers to how people organize and use their past experiences to cope with present situations. Thinking occurs between perceiving a problem and producing a response. For this reason, it is called a *mediating process.* Although thinking cannot be observed directly, psychologists can make assumptions about it by studying the relationship between problem and response.

Mediating processes are considered symbolic because they stand for direct action. Much symbolic activity consists of using words and images. As a result, psychologists who study thinking share interests with researchers who study language.

The word *thought* refers to the mediating process itself. The word *judgment* refers to the response, which usually is in the form of a verbal statement. Suppose you are asked the question, "Which city is more populous—New York City or Philadelphia?" If you reply, "New York City," you have stated a judgment. Between question and judgment occur processes of calling on stored information and organizing it to produce a decision.

Influences on Thought can be divided into four broad areas: (1) intelligence, (2) memory, (3) environmental conditions, and (4) personality.

Intelligence. Intellectual ability determines our understanding of problems and the methods we use to solve them. This ability also determines the speed and accuracy of our performance.

Memory. We use information stored from past experiences to recognize and produce what is required in a particular situation. The circumstances of those experiences influence the selection and organization of responses.

Environmental Conditions. The task, and the demands it makes on us, strongly determine the efficiency of our performance. For example, we are influenced by the difficulty and complexity of the situation, incentives for working, and the degree of stress.

Personality. Certain internal factors also influence our thinking. They include our emotional state, motivation, and attitudes. These conditions determine how strongly aroused we must be to perform well, and the degree to which the task causes anxiety or worry. These factors also determine how effectively we can control or direct our response in relation to the situation.

Autistic and Realistic Thinking. *Autistic* thinking is shaped primarily by our inner feelings, motives, and attitudes. We often use the word *imagination* for this kind of thinking. *Realistic* thinking is directed toward external goals in the environment and coping with any given situation. Logical thinking, problem solving, and using concepts are examples of realistic thinking.

Internal autistic factors and external realistic factors both influence all thinking. But their relative importance varies. Whenever environmental influences are reduced, thinking tends to become more autistic. In dreams, for example, sleep reduces external stimulation. In fantasy, our attention is withdrawn from the environment. When autistic influences do not operate freely, we tend to think more realistically.

Creative Thinking is both autistic and realistic. It is just as much an expression of internal forces as it is coping with a task. The creator allows feelings and images to influence thinking. He or she also copes with a definite medium, such as paint, words, or numbers, and seeks to achieve a definite product.

Psychologists have found that an environment favorable for creative thinking encourages self-expression and provides rewards for originality. Special abilities that characterize creative persons include originality, fluency, and flexibility.

Problem Solving. Some tasks require organizing and/or reorganizing knowledge to arrive at a correct solution. Problem solving involves (1) exploring and manipulating the elements of the problem, (2) searching for meaningful principles that aid in discovering the solution, and (3) adapting available resources in new and different ways.

Concept Attainment. Some tasks require us to use concepts—to classify objects according to a general characteristic or principle, or to learn the correct name for a group of related objects. In performing such tasks, some persons focus on details and have difficulty grouping objects that have something in common. Others look for general information and relate objects to each other because the objects have something in common.

Judgment can be studied by examining the opinion of a person exposed to controversial topics. For example, a man is presented with arguments which create a difference between his opinion and an alternative position. Then his opinion is measured to see how he was influenced. Researchers have found that people tend to reduce differences of opinion. Thus, the man may decide that his own opinion is wrong, and so he expresses agreement with the source of influence. Or he may decide that the source is trying to deceive him. By rejecting the source, the man increases the soundness of his position.   W. Edgar Vinacke

See also Learning; Logic; Prejudice.

THOUSAND AND ONE NIGHTS. See Arabian Nights.

THOUSAND ISLANDS is a group of more than a thousand islands in the Saint Lawrence River. No complete count has ever been made, because some of the islands are only small points of rock above the water. But at least 1,700 islands compose the Thousand Islands group. A few of the islands extend as much as 4 to 5 miles (6 to 8 kilometers) in length. The islands lie in a 40-mile (64-kilometer) stretch of the Saint Lawrence where the river runs from 4 to 7 miles (6 to 11 kilometers) wide as it leaves Lake Ontario. They are formed where the Saint Lawrence flows over the low hills of the Canadian Shield, which extends southeast into New York (see Canadian Shield).

These rocky islands are noted for their beautiful scenery and mild summer climate. Many have popular public summer resorts. Several have luxurious summer homes. Seventeen of the islands are included in Saint Lawrence Islands National Park. The park has been made into a recreational center and game preserve.

The Thousand Islands International Bridge, completed in 1938, spans some of the islands. It consists of two main suspension structures, three smaller bridges, and roadways across two islands. Its total length is about 6½ miles (10.5 kilometers).   John Brian Bird

See also Ontario (picture: Thousand Islands).

THRACE, *thrays,* was the ancient Greek name for a large region in the Balkan Peninsula. It stretched from Macedonia north to the Danube River, and eastward as far as the Black Sea. Under the Romans, Thrace included only the southern half of this region. The mountains of Thrace contained valuable deposits of gold and silver. Its broad plains were used for farming and for raising horses and cattle. Some historians believe that Greece owes the foundation of its music, its mythology, and its philosophy to the people of early Thrace.

The people of Thrace were savage Indo-Europeans who liked warfare and looting. Their rulers acted like kings. Greek trading cities occupied the coast of Thrace in early days. The Greeks established the cities with the consent of Thracian kings. Persians conquered this coast in the time of Darius (558?-486 B.C.). Later it belonged to the Athenian state and then to Macedonia. Philip II conquered all of Thrace, and the region was held by his son, Alexander the Great. Thrace later became a province of the Roman Empire.

The most important Greek cities of Thrace were Abdera, Sestos, and Byzantium. Ancient Byzantium was the foundation of the modern city of Istanbul (Constantinople). The fall of Constantinople in 1453 brought all Thrace under Turkish rule.

After the Russo-Turkish War of 1877-1878, northern Thrace became known as Eastern Rumelia and was united with Bulgaria in 1885. Greece took western Thrace during World War I. Turkey and Bulgaria control the rest of the region. German troops overran Greek Thrace in 1941, but it was given back to Greece after World War II. Greek Thrace includes the departments of Evros and Rhodope. Turkish Thrace corresponds to Turkey in Europe.   Donald W. Bradeen

See also Philippi.

THRASHER. See Brown Thrasher.

THREAD is a fine cord. It is used chiefly to join two or more pieces of material or to sew an object to a piece of fabric. Thread is made of such fibers as cotton, flax, nylon, polyester, rayon, silk, or other textile material. The many uses of thread include sewing clothing, mending tears, and attaching buttons.

Most thread is made by spinning many fibers into a single yarn. Several yarns are then twisted tightly together to form thread. Each yarn, called a *ply,* adds strength and thickness to the thread. Some thread consists of only a single yarn.

Thread is made from three kinds of fibers: (1) plant, (2) animal, and (3) manufactured. Plant and animal fibers are called *natural fibers.* Almost all natural fibers grow in short lengths known as *staple.* For example, cotton staple measures from ½ inch to 1⅛ inches (1.3 to 3.5 centimeters) long or longer. Cotton ranks as the most widely used natural fiber for making thread. Manufactured fibers, such as nylon and polyester, are produced in long, continuous strands called *filaments.* Silk is the only natural fiber that begins as filament. Silk fibers average from 1,000 to 1,300 yards (914 to 1,189 meters) long.

Most natural and manufactured thread goes through some kind of chemical treatment that improves its quality. One such process, called *mercerization,* treats cotton thread in a saltlike solution. This treatment strengthens the thread and gives it a silky finish. Most thread is also bleached or dyed before being packaged.

Making Thread from Natural Fibers. Natural fibers, such as cotton or flax, are first cleaned. Then they are straightened and further cleaned in a process called *carding.* The next step, called *combing,* smoothes the staple and removes some of the exceptionally short fibers. The combed fibers pass between sets of powerful rollers, which draw many pieces of loosely joined staple into continuous strands of increased strength. The strands are then spun into yarn and wound on bobbins. Next, several yarns are *plied* (twisted together) to form thread.

Making Thread from Manufactured Fibers involves few steps. Filaments need little preliminary processing because they are specifically produced to be made into thread. A single filament can be used as *monofilament*

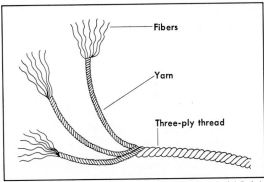

WORLD BOOK diagram by Art Grebetz

Thread consists of many fibers that have been spun into yarns. The yarns are *plied* (twisted together) to form thread.

How Thread Is Made
Thread may be made from natural or manufactured fibers. After preliminary processing, the fibers are drawn into strands, spun into yarn, and plied. Most thread is dyed or bleached before packaging.

WORLD BOOK diagrams by Art Grebetz

Natural Fibers used in making thread include cotton and flax. The carding and combing processes straighten the fibers and smooth them into a sheet before drawing begins.

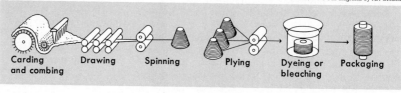

Carding and combing — Drawing — Spinning — Plying — Dyeing or bleaching — Packaging

Manufactured Fibers, such as nylon and polyester, are made in long continuous strands called *filaments*. To make thread, the filaments are cut into fiber-sized pieces before drawing.

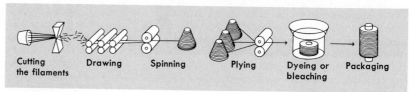

Cutting the filaments — Drawing — Spinning — Plying — Dyeing or bleaching — Packaging

thread, or many filaments may be twisted together to form *multifilament thread.* Filaments may also be cut into staple lengths, which are drawn into strands and then spun into yarn and plied. This process produces a softer thread than that made directly from filaments.

One type of manufactured thread, called *core thread,* combines the qualities of two kinds of fibers. An example of such a thread is a blend of cotton and polyester. This thread is made by combining a core of multifilament polyester with a protective cotton *wrap.* The resulting strand is plied with two or more similar strands. This process gives the thread the smoothness of cotton and the strength of polyester. Core threads can be sewn on a machine faster than other manufactured thread without heating up and breaking. Core threads are ideal for sewing such textiles as knits, permanent-press fabrics, and fabrics that are made from two or more kinds of fibers.   RICHARD JAMES DeMASSE

See also SPINNING.

THREADWORM. See PINWORM.

THREE-DAY MEASLES. See GERMAN MEASLES.

THREE-DIMENSIONAL PICTURE. See HOLOGRAM; STEREOSCOPE; also the Trans-Vision three-dimensional color pictures with the HUMAN BODY article.

THREE MILE ISLAND. See NUCLEAR ENERGY (The Future of Nuclear Energy).

THREE-MILE LIMIT. See TERRITORIAL WATERS; RIGHT OF SEARCH.

THREE WISE MEN. See MAGI.

THRESHER. See SHIPWRECK (table).

THRESHING MACHINE is a machine that farmers once used to *thresh* (separate) kernels of grain from stalks. The machine also *winnowed* (blew) the husks from the kernels. Threshing machines were developed in the mid-

1800's. Before then, farmers had threshed and winnowed by hand, a hard, slow task. The first practical threshing machines enabled farmers to process grain about 30 times as fast as they could by hand. Since the 1930's, combines have replaced most threshing machines (see COMBINE).

Modern threshing machines were based on a type designed in the 1830's by two brothers, Hiram and John Pitts of Winthrop, Me. Horses walking on a treadmill produced power for early threshers. A revolving cylinder knocked the kernels off the stalks, and a fan blew away the husks. The machine was stationary during operation. It cost so much that a group of farmers bought one thresher and shared it in harvesting their crops. By the late 1800's, steam engines powered most threshers. Later, farmers used their tractor motors to power threshing machines.   MELVIN E. LONG

See also AGRICULTURE (picture: Steam-Powered Farm Machinery).

THRIPS are short, slender insects that usually have two pairs of narrow, fringed wings. Thrips are found on all types of vegetation. They destroy plant cells, and spread virus and fungus diseases.

Scientific Classification. Thrips make up the order *Thysanoptera.*

USDA
Thrips

THROAT, *throht,* is a term loosely applied to the part of the neck in front of the backbone. The throat contains structures important in breathing and eating.

Historical Pictures Service, Chicago

Early Threshing Machines, such as the one at the left, were powered by horses walking on a treadmill. The clean kernels poured out of the machine into a bucket, and a conveyor belt carried the stalks away.

It includes the pharynx, the larynx, part of the esophagus, and part of the trachea. A sore throat results when any of these parts becomes inflamed.

When a person breathes, air enters the nose and travels through a passage called the *pharynx*. From the pharynx, it passes into the *larynx* (voice box), then through the *trachea* (windpipe), and into the lungs. Food, on its way from the mouth to the stomach, passes through the pharynx before it enters the *esophagus*, the tube that leads to the stomach. Thus, part of the pharynx is shared by food and air. The routes of food and air cross one another in this passage, and it is possible for food to enter the wrong tube.

Normally, when a person swallows, two actions take place to block off the air passage. The *soft palate* presses against the back of the pharynx, closing the opening to the nose. At the same time, the larynx rises and is covered by the *epiglottis*, a leaf-shaped lid. These actions force the food into its own passage, the esophagus, and muscular waves carry it to the stomach. When a person laughs or talks while swallowing, food may enter the larynx and choke the person until it is removed by coughing.

The largest muscle of the throat is the *sternocleidomastoid*. It moves the head. This muscle looks like a cord in the side of the neck when the head is turned. It runs diagonally across each side of the neck from the breastbone to the skull behind the ear. Smaller muscles in the throat help in the actions of speaking and swallowing.

Large arteries and veins pass through the neck. They carry blood to and away from the face, scalp, and brain. Unconsciousness may result from pressure on the arteries on each side of the trachea.   WILLIAM V. MAYER

Related Articles. See the Trans-Vision three-dimensional picture with HUMAN BODY. See also:

Esophagus	Pharynx
Gargle	Tonsil
Larynx	Windpipe

THROMBOSIS. See BLOOD (Blood Clotting); STROKE.

THROTTLE. See AIRPLANE (Flying an Airplane); CARBURETOR; TURBINE (Turbine Terms).

THRUSH is the name of a group of songbirds that live in most parts of the world. Many of the thrushes are plain brown birds, with whitish and usually spotted breasts. Robins, wheatears, and bluebirds are all thrushes. These birds are migratory. They fly to warmer countries as winter approaches. They live in wooded regions and spend much time on the ground.

The largest and best-known North American type of thrush, except for the American robin, is the *wood thrush.* This bird has bright cinnamon-colored upper parts and spotted white breast and sides. It is noted for its clear, flutelike songs. The wood thrush nests in the eastern United States and southeastern Canada, and winters in Central America. It builds its nest 5 to 20 feet (1.5 to 6 meters) up in a bush or tree. The bird arranges a base of dead leaves and coarse grass, plasters the nest with mud, and lines it with roots or grasses. The female wood thrush lays from three to five greenish-blue eggs.

Other common kinds of North American thrushes are the *veery,* the *hermit thrush,* the *varied thrush,* and *Swainson's thrush.* In Europe, the most common thrushes are the *redbreast,* or *robin;* the *song thrush,* or *mavis;* the *mistle thrush;* the *blackbird;* and the *nightingale.*

Eric Hosking

Allan Cruickshank, NAS

Some Members of the Thrush Family are the European blackbird, *top above,* the wood thrush, *above,* and the veery thrush, *below.* The European blackbird looks like a black robin. The wood thrush has a spotted white breast. The veery thrush, also called Wilson's thrush, is a shy bird found in forests.

Allan Cruickshank, NAS

Scientific Classification. Thrushes belong to the family Turdidae. The wood thrush is *Hylocichla mustelina.* The veery is *Catharus fuscescens;* the hermit thrush is *C. guttatus;* and Swainson's is *C. ustulatus.*   ALBERT WOLFSON

Related Articles in WORLD BOOK include:

Bird (table: State Birds; pictures:	Nightingale
Birds of Inland Waters and	Robin
Marshes; Birds' Eggs)	Stonechat
Bluebird	Veery

THRUSH is a contagious disease of infants. It is sometimes called *parasitic stomatitis, white mouth, oral moniliasis,* and *infantile sore mouth.* Thrush causes the mouth to become sore. It is particularly frequent in weak and undernourished infants. The disease is an infection. It appears in the form of small, roundish, white patches, called *aphthae*, on the lining membrane of the mouth and throat, and also on the tongue. These patches are slightly raised. They cover drops of watery fluid, and contain a fungus growth. When the patches peel off, a raw, red surface is left. As fresh patches continue to appear, the mouth becomes sore. At the start, thrush is usually accompanied by fever, colic, diarrhea, restlessness, no desire for food, and difficulty in swallowing. Preventive treatment requires absolute cleanliness of nipples and nursing bottles, with sterilization of milk and other foods. Physicians treat thrush by swabbing the throat with certain drugs. AUSTIN SMITH

THRUST. See AIRPLANE (Drag and Thrust); JET PROPULSION (How Jet Propulsion Works); SPACE TRAVEL (Space Travel Terms).

THUCYDIDES, *thyoo SID ih deez* (460?-400? B.C.), an Athenian, was the world's first scientific historian. His *History of the Peloponnesian War* covers 21 of the 28 years of this war. Thucydides wrote critically and objectively. He showed much skill in analyzing character, and in showing the relationship between cause and effect in historical events. The history is unfinished, and contains inconsistencies, but it is a dramatic account of stirring events.

Thucydides was born in Athens. In 424 B.C., during the Peloponnesian War, he commanded part of the Athenian fleet. Thucydides failed to relieve the siege of Amphipolis, and was exiled for 20 years. During his exile, he visited all parts of the Greek world, followed the course of the Peloponnesian War, and wrote his history. C. BRADFORD WELLES

THUG is a member of an old society in India, the members of which killed in the name of religion. The term comes from the Hindustani *thag*, meaning a *cheat* or *rascal*. The thugs committed murders and robbed their victims in honor of Kali, the Hindu goddess of destruction and wife of Shiva. The thugs always murdered by strangling. One of their chief principles was not to spill blood. According to legend, the thugs believed that Kali disposed of the bodies by devouring them. But one member of the society pried into Kali's actions. So the angry goddess condemned them to bury their victims in the future. The local Indian and British governments tried many times to stop *thuggee*—the practice of the thugs. In 1831, the British began a drive to end the evil and it is now almost wiped out. In America today, a holdup man or a hired slugger is sometimes called a thug. GEORGE NOEL MAYHEW

THULE, *THYOO lee*, is a settlement in northwestern Greenland on the coast of Hayes Peninsula. For location, see GREENLAND (map). When the U.S. Air Force established a long-range bomber base at Thule in 1951, the 300 Eskimos living there moved to other parts of Greenland. Today, about 1,760 Danish and American civilians and air force personnel live there. See also ULTIMA THULE.

THULIUM, *THYOO lee um* (chemical symbol, Tm), is one of the rare-earth elements. Its atomic number is 69. Its atomic weight is 168.934. The name comes from *Thule*, the Latin word for the northernmost part of the inhabitable world. The Swedish scientist Per Cleve first discovered thulium in 1879. Thulium occurs with other rare earths in the minerals gadolinite, euxenite, xenotime, and others. It is best separated from the other rare earths by ion-exchange processes. It melts at 1545° C, and boils at 1727° C. Portable X-ray units use radioactive thulium. Such units require no electrical equipment, and need to be recharged with thulium only once every few months. See also ELEMENT, CHEMICAL (tables); RARE EARTH. FRANK H. SPEDDING

THUMB. See HAND.

THUMB, TOM. See STRATTON, CHARLES S.; BARNUM, PHINEAS T.

THUN, LAKE OF. See LAKE OF THUN.

THUNDER. Primitive man thought that thunder was the sound of the gods roaring in anger when they were displeased with the people of the earth. Today, we know that the sound of thunder is caused by the violent expansion of air that has been heated by lightning.

Air is heated instantly when an electrical charge of lightning passes through it. The heat causes the molecules of air to expand, or fly out, in all directions. As the molecules seek more room, they collide violently with layers of cool air, and set up a great air wave which has the sound of thunder.

Thunder has many different sounds. The deep, rumbling roar of thunder is caused by the air wave set up by the part of the lightning trunk that is farthest away.

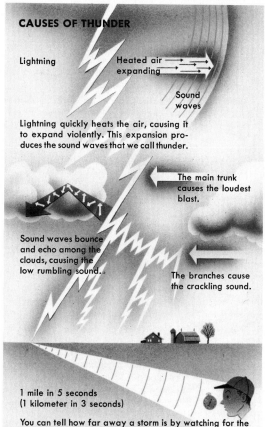

CAUSES OF THUNDER

Lightning

Heated air expanding

Sound waves

Lightning quickly heats the air, causing it to expand violently. This expansion produces the sound waves that we call thunder.

The main trunk causes the loudest blast.

Sound waves bounce and echo among the clouds, causing the low rumbling sound.

The branches cause the crackling sound.

1 mile in 5 seconds
(1 kilometer in 3 seconds)

You can tell how far away a storm is by watching for the jagged streak of lightning. Then count off seconds until the thunder noise reaches you. Thunder travels 1 mile in 5 seconds (1 kilometer in 3 seconds). If it takes 15 seconds, you know the storm is 3 miles (5 kilometers) away.

The sharp crackle of thunder is set up when the large trunk of lightning forks out into many branches. The loud crash of thunder is caused by the lightning's main trunk. The sound of thunder reaches us after we have seen the lightning. That is because light travels 186,282 miles (299,792 kilometers) per second—or almost instantly, while sound travels at a rate of only about 1,100 feet (335 meters) per second. WALTER J. SAUCIER

See also LIGHTNING; JUPITER; THOR; ZEUS.

THUNDER BAY, Ont. (pop. 111,476; met. area pop. 119,253), is a city on the northwest shore of Lake Superior. Its excellent harbor makes it an important shipping center. Thunder Bay was formed in 1970 by the merger of the cities of Fort William and Port Arthur and the townships of McIntyre and Neebing. For location, see ONTARIO (political map).

Trade and Industry. Thunder Bay is an international port. It is the shipping center for much of the wheat raised in western Canada and for many other products. Huge ocean-going ships travel between Thunder Bay and the Atlantic Ocean by way of the Great Lakes and the Saint Lawrence Seaway.

The city's industries produce airplanes, automobile wheels, buses, elevator equipment, and ships. Thunder Bay has breweries, lumber and paper mills, and an oil refinery. Grain elevators in the city can store more than 100 million bushels (2.7 billion kilograms).

Education and Recreation. Thunder Bay is the home of Lakehead University, five public libraries, and a museum. The city has curling rinks, golf courses, hockey rinks, ski areas, swimming pools, and tennis courts.

History. In 1678 and 1717, the French built forts at what later became Fort William. After 1805, Fort William served as a headquarters for the fur traders of the North West Company. Fort William was incorporated as a city in 1907. Port Arthur was founded about 1870. The community was incorporated as a city in 1907. Both Fort William and Port Arthur grew in importance as ports after the Saint Lawrence Seaway opened in 1959. Thunder Bay has a mayor-council form of government. D. M. L. FARR

THUNDER PLANT. See HOUSELEEK.

THUNDERSTORM. See CLOUD (Storms); HAIL.

THURBER, JAMES (1894-1961), was a celebrated American humorist. He became famous both for his comic writings and his cartoonlike drawings.

Thurber's works describe the anxieties of the average individual in modern society. He wrote chiefly about oversensitive, dissatisfied men who feel trapped by the complications of the modern world. The men in his stories are frustrated by their domineering wives and rebellious children. They often fear such machines as automobiles and dread the pressures of their jobs. They try to escape from their problems through alcohol or daydreams. Thurber's short story "The Secret Life of Walter Mitty," for example, portrays a man who finds relief from his nagging wife through daydreams. In his dreams, Mitty always plays the role of the fearless hero.

Many of Thurber's works include cartoons of frightened men, menacing women, wicked children, and sad dogs. Many of his stories, essays, and drawings appear in such collections as *The Middle-Aged Man on the Flying Trapeze* (1935) and *The Thurber Carnival* (1945). He wrote his first book, *Is Sex Necessary?* (1929), with E. B. White and co-authored a play, *The Male Animal* (1940),

THURMOND, STROM

Illustration by the author from *The Thurber Carnival* by James Thurber, published by Harper and Row. © 1945 James Thurber, renewed 1973 Helen W. Thurber and Rosemary Thurber Sauers. Originally printed in *The New Yorker* magazine.

A Thurber Cartoon illustrates one of his favorite subjects, a timid middle-aged man married to a domineering woman.

with Elliott Nugent. Thurber also wrote an autobiography, *My Life and Hard Times* (1933). Much of his work first appeared in *The New Yorker* magazine. He wrote about Harold Ross, the first editor of *The New Yorker*, in *The Years With Ross* (1959). James Grover Thurber was born in Columbus, Ohio. He was blind for the last 15 years of his life. JOSEPH N. RIDDEL

Additional Resources

BERNSTEIN, BURTON. *Thurber: A Biography.* Dodd, 1975.
HOLMES, CHARLES S. *The Clocks of Columbus: The Literary Career of James Thurber.* Atheneum, 1972.
MORSBERGER, ROBERT E. *James Thurber.* Twayne, 1964. Combines biography with literary criticism.

THURMAN, ALLEN GRANBERRY (1813-1895), was the Democratic candidate for Vice-President of the United States in 1888. He and President Grover Cleveland lost to Republicans Benjamin Harrison and Levi P. Morton. Thurman served as a U.S. senator from Ohio from 1869 to 1881. He was chief justice of the Ohio Supreme Court from 1854 to 1856, and served in the U.S. House of Representatives from 1845 to 1847. He was born in Lynchburg, Va. IRVING G. WILLIAMS

THURMOND, STROM (1902-   ), a U.S. senator from South Carolina, is known for his strong support of states' rights. In 1981, he became chairman of the Senate's powerful Judiciary Committee.

Thurmond withdrew from the Democratic Party in 1964 and became a Republican. In 1948, he also left the Democratic Party to run as the States' Rights Democratic (*Dixiecrat*) candidate for President (see DIXIECRAT PARTY). He carried four states and received 39 electoral votes. Thurmond disagreed with the Democratic Party's position on many issues. He felt that the federal government was taking over many duties and powers that rightfully belonged to state and local governments. He opposed federal civil rights legislation and federal welfare programs supported by many Democrats.

Thurmond served as governor of South Carolina from

1947 to 1951. He was elected to the U.S. Senate in 1954 as a write-in candidate. James Strom Thurmond was born in Edgefield, S.C. He graduated from Clemson College.   ERNEST M. LANDER, JR.

THURSDAY is the fifth day of the week. The ancient Norsemen considered the day sacred to Thor, the Teutonic god of thunder. The name means *Thor's day.* This is probably a translation of the Latin *dies Jovis,* meaning *Jove's day,* for Jove, or Jupiter, the Roman god of thunder. In the United States, Thanksgiving Day is on the fourth Thursday in November. See also THOR; WEEK.   GRACE HUMPHREY

THURSTONE, LOUIS LEON (1887-1955), an American psychologist, made original contributions to the development and analysis of psychological tests. He developed the centroid method of factor analysis to find the basic dimensions underlying ability and personality scores. He developed a method for measuring attitudes. He wrote the books *Primary Mental Abilities* (1938) and *Multiple Factor Analysis* (1947). Thurstone was born in Chicago.   KENNETH E. CLARK

THUTMOSE III, *thoot MOH suh* (reigned about 1490-1436 B.C.), ranks among the greatest of all the kings of ancient Egypt. He is also known as THOTHMES III. Thutmose succeeded his father, Thutmose II, but was kept in the background by his stepmother, Queen Hatshepsut. After Hatshepsut died, Thutmose III ordered her name erased from monuments and statues.

Thutmose III became a brilliant general and also a capable administrator. By his well-planned campaigns, mainly in Palestine and Syria, he greatly expanded Egypt's imperial boundaries. The rich booty and many captives taken in his wars provided the means and labor for extensive building operations in Egypt. He greatly enlarged the vast temple at Karnak. Its walls still bear the hieroglyphic records of his wars, long lists of captured cities in Asia and Africa, and pictures of plants and animals collected on his campaigns. Thutmose erected granite *obelisks* (giant stone pillars) in Karnak and Heliopolis. The two he erected at Heliopolis are now known as *Cleopatra's Needles.* One stands in Central Park in New York City, and one on the Thames Embankment in London.   LEONARD H. LESKO

See also EGYPT, ANCIENT (The Early New Kingdom).

THYME, *time,* is a fragrant garden herb. An oil in the leaves and stems causes its scent. The drug thymol is prepared from this oil. The plant grows from 6 to 8 inches (15 to 20 centimeters) high, and has square, hairy stems, narrow leaves, and small lilac or purplish flowers, borne in separate whorls. It grows well in dry places and poor soils. A variety known as *creeping thyme,* with woody, branching stems, makes an excellent cover for rocks and waste places.

Scientific Classification. Thyme belongs to the mint family, *Labiatae.* Common or garden thyme is genus *Thymus,* species *T. vulgaris.* Creeping thyme, or mother-of-thyme, is *T. serpyllum.*   HAROLD NORMAN MOLDENKE

THYMUS is a flat, pinkish-gray organ that plays an important part in the immune system of the body. It is located high in the chest cavity behind the breastbone and extends into the lower neck below the thyroid gland.

The thymus aids in the development of white blood

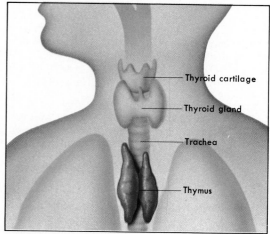

WORLD BOOK diagram by Charles Wellek

The Thymus is in the upper chest, behind the breastbone. It aids in the formation of white blood cells called *lymphocytes,* which protect the body from disease.

cells called *lymphocytes,* which help the body fight disease. There are two kinds of lymphocytes, both of which are formed from cells in the bone marrow. Some lymphocytes, called *B cells,* probably mature in the bone marrow itself (see IMMUNITY [Immune Responses]). The *B* stands for *bone marrow derived.* The other lymphocytes travel to the thymus, where they are changed into *T cells.* The *T* stands for *thymus derived.* The thymus produces a substance called *thymosin,* which scientists believe plays an important part in the change into T cells.

The T cells leave the thymus and inhabit the blood, lymph nodes, and spleen. There, the T cells attack certain bacteria, cancer cells, fungi, viruses, and other harmful organisms. T cells are sometimes called "killer cells" because of their ability to find and destroy such organisms.

When a person is born, the thymus weighs about $\frac{1}{2}$ ounce (15 grams). By the age of 12, it has grown to about twice its original size. At that time, the lymph nodes and the spleen take over the task of producing lymphocytes. The thymus then begins to shrink and produces fewer T cells. By adulthood, the organ has shrunk so much that it may be hard to distinguish from the fatty tissue that surrounds it.

Disease or injury may require the removal of the thymus. The loss of the thymus has little effect in an adult. But in a person under 12 years old, removal of the thymus may lead to difficulties in growing properly and in developing immunities.   DON H. NELSON

THYROID CARTILAGE. See LARYNX.

THYROID GLAND is an *endocrine* (ductless) gland in the neck. It has two *lobes* (parts), one on each side of the windpipe. It is well supplied with blood vessels.

The thyroid gland takes up iodine from the blood. When the iodine combines with other chemicals in the gland, *thyroxine,* an important hormone, is formed (see HORMONE). The thyroid stores thyroxine in an inactive form. However, when the body needs thyroxine, it is released directly into the blood vessels that run through the gland. The blood stream then carries the hormone all over the body to the body cells. In the cells, thyrox-

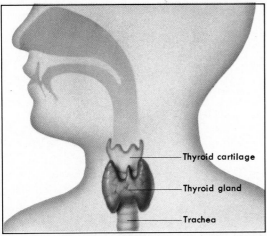

The Thyroid Gland is in the neck. This gland produces and stores a hormone called *thyroxine*, which is essential for mental development and physical growth.

WORLD BOOK diagram by Charles Wellek

ine is changed into several more active hormones that regulate the rate at which the cells change oxygen and food into heat and energy. The thyroid produces another hormone, *triiodothyronine*, which is similar in structure and effect to thyroxine. Both hormones are necessary for body growth and mental development.

The thyroid also produces a hormone called *calcitonin*. This hormone causes calcium present in the blood to become deposited in bone. Calcitonin works together with parathormone, a hormone secreted by the parathyroid glands, to control the amount of calcium in the blood (see PARATHYROID GLAND).

Underactive Thyroid. When the thyroid gland is not active enough, a condition known as *hypothyroidism* develops. In adults this is called *myxedema*. In persons with myxedema, everything slows down. They lose vigor of mind and body. Their skin grows thick and coarse, and they may gain weight. Hypothyroidism that begins in infancy results in a condition called *cretinism* (see CRETINISM). Children with cretinism are called *cretins*. Their bodies do not grow the way they should. Their minds cannot grow, either. Because of this, the mind of such a child may never develop beyond the level of a 5-year-old child.

Overactive Thyroid. Sometimes the thyroid gland produces too much thyroxine. This may be because the gland cells are overactive. Or it may be because the gland has increased in size so that too many cells are producing thyroxine. In either case, too much of the hormone is produced for the body to handle normally and a condition known as *hyperthyroidism* results. Hyperthyroidism causes extreme nervousness, increases heart action, and disturbs the metabolism of the body (see METABOLISM).

Goiter is an enlarged thyroid gland. It may be accompanied by either hypothyroidism or hyperthyroidism. Goiters develop when there is not enough iodine supplied to the body for the thyroid to function properly. People formerly developed goiters when they lived in areas of the world where neither land nor water supplied iodine for the body's use. The lack of iodine in food can be remedied by eating iodized salt. See GOITER.

Treatment of Thyroid Conditions. Doctors are able to treat hypothyroidism by giving a person proper amounts of thyroid hormone, usually in the form of pills. In treating hyperthyroidism, surgeons remove part of the overactive gland. Thyroid surgery was first performed by Emil Theodor Kocher, a Swiss professor of surgery.

Radioactive iodine is sometimes used to decrease thyroid gland activity. This special kind of iodine is removed from the blood as is any other iodine, but it slows down the gland's activity.   THEODORE B. SCHWARTZ

Related Articles in WORLD BOOK include:

Gland	Human Body (diagram)
Goiter	Iodine
Hormone	Kocher, Emil Theodor

THYROXINE. See THYROID GLAND.

THYRSUS. See INFLORESCENCE.

THYSANOPTERA. See INSECT (table); THRIPS.

THYSANURA. See INSECT (table).

TIAHUANACO INDIANS. See BOLIVIA (History).

TIBER RIVER, *TY buhr*, is the third largest river in Italy. Only the Po and the Adige are larger. The Tiber rises in the Apennine Mountains in central Italy, 4,160 feet (1,268 meters) above sea level. The river flows for about 245 miles (394 kilometers), first through the Sabine Mountains, a range of the Apennines, then through Rome and into the Tyrrhenian Sea (see ITALY [physical map]). The Tiber flows into the sea through branches at Ostia and Fiumicino. The Tiber has often overflowed its banks. Flood embankments have been built at Rome.   SHEPARD B. CLOUGH

TIBERIAS, LAKE. See SEA OF GALILEE.

TIBERIUS, *TY BEER ee uhs* (42 B.C.-A.D. 37), was the emperor of Rome during the life of Jesus Christ. His full name was Tiberius Claudius Nero. The second emperor of Rome, Tiberius succeeded his stepfather, Emperor Augustus.

Tiberius became a successful army commander for Augustus. The emperor forced Tiberius to divorce his wife and marry his stepsister—Augustus' daughter, Julia. But Tiberius and Julia were unhappy, and he left her and went to live on the island of Rhodes.

By A.D. 4, both of Augustus' grandsons and Tiberius' brother, Drusus Claudius, had died. Augustus then recalled Tiberius to Rome and made Tiberius his heir and successor. When Augustus died in A.D. 14, Tiberius was proclaimed emperor.

Tiberius was a fine administrator. He carefully supervised tax collections and balanced the budget. He chose efficient governors for the provinces of Rome and maintained friendly relations with the neighboring kingdoms of Parthia and Armenia.

When Germanicus, a possible successor to Tiberius, died, his widow accused Tiberius of causing his death. Because of difficulties with the Senate, Tiberius retired to the island of Capri. He named Sejanus, captain of his personal guard, to govern Rome.

Tiberius became unpopular during his last years because of his poor relations with the Senate and opposition to the gladiator games. But he left a peaceful and prosperous empire to his heir Caligula, a descendant of Augustus.   MARY FRANCIS GYLES

See also CALIGULA.

TIBET

Legend:
- ⊛ **Capital**
- • Other City or Town
- —— Road
- ┿┿ Rail Line
- ▲ MOUNTAIN
- ～ River

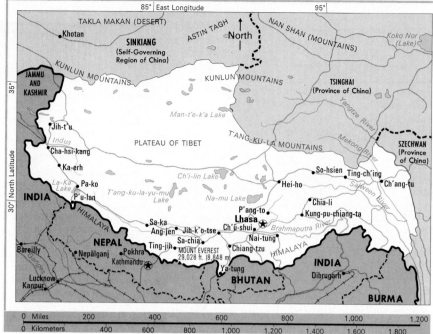

WORLD BOOK map

TIBET, *tih BET*, is a remote land in south-central Asia. It is often called the *Roof of the World*. Its snow-covered mountains and wind-swept plateaus are the highest in the world. The world's highest mountain, Mount Everest, towers along the southern mountain wall of Tibet. Climbers first scaled Mount Everest in 1953. Ka-erh in western Tibet, over 15,000 feet (4,570 meters) high, is believed to be the highest town in the world. Valley bottoms in Tibet are higher than the mountains of most countries. Lhasa is Tibet's capital.

Today, Tibet is a part of China. However, for many years Tibet was independent. Its mountain ranges isolated it from other regions. The Tibetans are sometimes called the *hermit people*. They follow a primitive way of life. Tibet is traditionally a *theocracy* (religious kingdom). Buddhist monks, called lamas, had a strong voice in the rule of Tibet before the Communists took control.

The Land and Its Resources. Tibet covers 463,323 square miles (1,200,000 square kilometers). The land is a high, cold plateau in the heart of Asia. High mountain walls border the land on all sides. Bhutan, Burma, India, and Nepal lie to the south.

Parts of the country have never been explored. In the southern part of the Tibetan plateau, the snowy Himalayas rise higher than any other mountain chain in the world. Mount Everest (29,028 feet, or 8,848 meters) is in the Himalayas. The Ta-Hsüeh Mountains on the eastern border rise over 25,250 feet (7,696 meters). On the north and northwest, the peaks of the Kunlun range rise

Theodore H. E. Chen, the contributor of this article, is Professor Emeritus of Education and Asian Studies at the University of Southern California, and the author of The Chinese Communist Regime: Documents and Commentary.

almost as high. Tibet has an average elevation of 16,000 feet (4,880 meters) above sea level.

Large parts of Tibet are a dreary waste of gravel, rock, and sand. Tibet has hundreds of lakes, but most of them have barren shores. Many also have a large salt content. Some of the great rivers of Asia rise in the mountains of Tibet. These include the Brahmaputra, Indus, Mekong, Salween, and Yangtze rivers.

Tibet has long produced small amounts of borax, gold, and salt. In 1957, geologists discovered rich deposits of coal, gypsum, iron ore, manganese, and oil in the T'ang-ku-la Mountains in the northeast. Dense forests lie in the eastern and southern parts of the country. Most of the land is not farmed. The soil is too poor and the climate is too cold for extensive agriculture.

Climate. Much of Tibet has less than 10 inches (25 centimeters) of rain annually. The Himalayas shut out moisture-bearing winds from India. Sudden blizzards and snowstorms are common. Violent winds sweep Tibet at all seasons. January temperatures average 24° F. (−4° C). July temperatures average 58° F. (14° C).

The People and Their Work. No one knows just how many people live in Tibet. Estimates vary, but about 2 million is commonly accepted as the correct population figure for Tibet. Most of the people live in southern Tibet, an area where there is some farming.

The Tibetans are a branch of the Mongoloid race. They speak dialects related to the Burmese languages. The people are short and sturdy. They engage in heavy physical labor. Most married people have only one spouse. Only the wealthy can afford polygamy (see POLYGAMY). Sometimes several brothers share the same wife and work together to support the family.

Tibet's population consists of nomads, farmers, town people, nobility, and clergy. The nomads are shepherds and herdsmen who roam about in the northern uplands. They live in tents of yak hair. Once a year they come to the lower levels to sell their produce and buy necessities.

Before the Communists seized Tibet, the nobility and clergy governed the region and owned the land. Nobles lived on the estates, and the farmers were their servants. The Communist government broke up the large estates and took property from the wealthy. The Communists have also introduced reforms designed to break the power of the nobility and clergy. The religious emphasis of life has been greatly decreased.

Tibetan homes have stone or brick walls and flat roofs. Houses rarely have more than two floors. But homes built for the wealthy have three or four. The ground floor is used to house animals.

Barley is the chief crop in Tibet, and barley flour is the main food. The Tibetans mix the barley flour with barley beer. They eat two meals each day. Chinese tea is the chief beverage in Tibet. The Tibetans flavor the tea with salt, soda, and yak butter. Milk forms a large part of the diet. The wealthy people drink yak milk, and the poor drink goat milk.

The Tibetan dress for men and women consists of a long robe with long sleeves and a high collar. The wealthy people wear silk robes, and the poor people wear cloth. Rich Tibetans ride on mules and horses, but many of the poor people walk from place to place. Two highways from China to Tibet were built in 1954.

The yak, a sort of hairy buffalo, serves many purposes in Tibet. It provides butter, cloth, cheese, meat, milk, and transportation. It is also used as a beast of burden. Its hair is used for tents, and its hide for shoe leather and boats. See YAK.

The Tibetans celebrate their New Year in early spring. The festivities last for about three weeks. During the festival, the people devote themselves to dancing, music, eating and drinking, and prayer.

Cloth weaving and carpetmaking are household industries in Tibet. Wool is the chief export. Other exports include furs, mules, musk, and ponies.

Religion and Culture. Tibetans are intensely religious. People turn prayer wheels and recite prayers on the streets. Religious rites are an important phase of life. The festivals are religious in character. Nobles have chapels or shrines in their homes.

Tibet's religion is a branch of Buddhism called *Lamaism.* The religion recognizes two Grand Lamas. The Panchen Lama is regarded as the leading spiritual authority in Tibet. The Dalai (High) Lama is looked on as the ruler of the country, and also a spiritual leader. Tibetans regard both Grand Lamas as Buddha, born again. When the Dalai or Panchen Lama dies, his spirit is thought to enter the body of a baby boy. Monks search the country for a boy born about the same time or after the death of the lama. The boy thus selected becomes his successor. The Communists ended the authority of the Dalai Lama and Panchen Lama after they took control of Tibet.

About one-fifth of the people are *lamas* (monks). Many Tibetans become lamas because it is hard to support a family in Tibet. The lamas live together in *lamaseries* (monasteries). Tibet's three largest lamaseries are in Lhasa. They house more than 20,000 lamas.

Eastfoto

The Palace of the Dalai Lama, *above, overlooks Tibet's capital city, Lhasa. The Tibetan actors, foreground, were celebrating the opening of two new highways.*

The lamaseries are supported by government subsidies and private donations. The lamaseries own large amounts of land. There are several different sects of Lamaism. Some permit lamas to marry. The chief sect is the Yellow Hat, headed by the Dalai Lama.

Many monks engage in agriculture and handicraft. The lamaseries are also centers of education and art. Tibetan art reflects Chinese and Indian influences, and presents Buddhist themes.

Cities. Lhasa is the political and religious center of Tibet. The Potala, the private monastery of the Dalai Lama, is the most impressive landmark in Lhasa. It is a grand castlelike structure with gold roofs and more than 1,000 rooms. It houses from 200 to 300 monks, and has numerous art treasures. See LHASA.

The Panchen Lama's monastery stands near Jih-k'a-tse. Other cities include Chiang-tzu and Ya-tung.

History and Government. During the A.D. 600's, Tibet became a powerful kingdom. Buddhism and handwriting were introduced from India, and Lhasa was founded. The Mongols invaded Tibet in the late 1200's. The Dalai Lama became the civil authority and ruler of Tibet in the 1600's. In the early 1700's, Tibet fell under the control of China. A British mission arrived in Lhasa in 1904. The British and Tibetans signed a treaty, setting up trading posts in Tibet.

Tibet remained in Chinese hands until after the Chinese Revolution in 1911. Even after 1911, China claimed Tibet as an area within the Chinese domain. In the 1920's, rivalry grew between the Dalai and Panchen lamas over political affairs. The Panchen Lama fled to China with his court. He remained there until his death in 1937. The 10th Panchen Lama was enthroned in China in 1944. The 13th Dalai Lama died in 1933. According to custom, a baby boy was chosen as his successor. In 1940, a six-year-old peasant boy became the 14th Dalai Lama.

In late 1950, Chinese Communist forces invaded Tibet. The Dalai Lama fled. He returned after about eight months and set up a temporary capital near the Indian border. He was promised control of internal affairs. The Chinese were to control foreign affairs and defense. The Panchen Lama was to assume his role as the Tibetan spiritual leader. In May, 1951, the Communists announced the signing of an agreement in which Tibet surrendered its sovereignty to the Chinese Communist government. However, the Tibetans kept their right to regional self-government. The agreement promised no immediate change in the political system of Tibet, and guaranteed the Tibetans freedom of religious belief.

China continued to tighten its control over Tibet during the late 1950's and the 1960's. The Preparatory Committee for the Autonomous Region of Tibet was started in 1956. The committee was founded to establish Tibet as an *autonomous* (self-governing) region within China. The Chinese appointed the Dalai Lama to head the committee, and they appointed the Panchen Lama to act as the committee's vice-chairman.

Tibetans rioted against the Communists in 1956. The people continued to resist Chinese control, and large-scale fighting broke out in 1959. The Dalai Lama fled to India in that year, and the Chinese Communists made the Panchen Lama the head of the Preparatory Committee. But the Chinese removed the Panchen Lama from power in 1964. In 1965, the Communists made Tibet an autonomous region within China. But in 1967, the Chinese Army took control of the radio stations, newspapers, state banks, and the security bureau. Although autonomous in name, Tibet remained under the strict control of China.   THEODORE H. E. CHEN

Related Articles in WORLD BOOK include:

TIBETAN TERRIER is a breed of dog that originated in Tibet, where Buddhist monks raised it in monasteries. The Tibetans once believed these dogs were holy, and monks gave them to important persons to bring good luck.

Tibetan terriers stand from 14 to 16 inches (36 to 41 centimeters) high and resemble miniature Old English sheep dogs. They have a thick, shaggy coat that may be black, cream, gold, gray, or white, or a combination of those colors. The Tibetan terrier has a fluffy tail that curls over the dog's back.   JOAN MCDONALD BREARLEY

TIBIA. See LEG.

TIC is a nerve ailment, often resulting from fatigue, which causes muscles to jerk tight for a short time and then relax, tighten again, and again relax. A tic usually affects only the face, although it may spread to the neck and arms. A tic of the right side of the face will draw the right eye, the nose, and the right corner of the mouth toward each other.

See also NEURALGIA.

TICINO RIVER. See SWITZERLAND (Rivers); ITALY (physical map).

TICK is the name of a small animal which is related to mites, spiders, and scorpions. The tick is oval in shape. It is a parasite, which means that it lives on other animals. Ticks and mites cause various diseases in people and domestic animals. Ticks often carry certain disease germs in their bodies and transfer these to the blood of their victims. Sometimes the bites of ticks are poisonous. Cases of paralysis are known to have followed their attacks. But such effects are not common.

Ticks and mites look much alike in body structure, but ticks are the larger. Ticks look somewhat like insects but are not. Most kinds of ticks can be seen without a magnifying glass. They live only on animal fluids. But some of the mites feed on plant juices and tissues, and on plant products.

The bodies of these tiny animals seem to be all in one piece. But some of them have a groove between the stomach and the front part of the body. The head of a tick is a movable part at the front end of the body. They draw the blood of their victims through a beak. The beak has strong teeth which are bent backward. These teeth help the parasites cling tightly to their host. Adult ticks have eight legs which stick out on the sides like those of a crab.

The tick lays eggs in dead leaves or other ground rubbish. They produce flat, six-legged larvae. These larvae alight on passing animals from grass stalks and shrubs. As they gorge on the blood of these animals, they swell up. Then, they cease to eat and begin to *molt* (shed their outer covering). After this, they become eight-legged nymphs. Another molting follows, and then the nymphs are adults. In some types of ticks, the larvae and nymphs drop to the ground to undergo each change of form.

While the various kinds of ticks have special names, such as *chicken, cattle, dog,* or *sheep* tick, few of them are

Louise Van der Meid, T.F.H. Publications

The Tibetan Terrier Has a Heavy Coat of Long Hair.

J. C. Allen & Son; USDA

Ticks Are Parasites that suck the blood of animals and human beings. The tick's body is swollen with blood after it has eaten, *above left*. The underside of the body of a fully fed female tick is shown, *above right*. Female ticks lay up to 5,000 eggs at one time, *right*.

limited to one kind. Many which attack animals also annoy human beings. Eight species are pests on cattle in the United States. Only one of these, the Texas fever tick, is of major importance.

Spotted-fever ticks transmit *Rocky Mountain spotted fever*, a disease of humans. The disease was once thought to be limited to the Rocky Mountains, but has been found along the Atlantic Coast. It causes a few deaths each year. The common English sheep tick infests dogs and cattle. This and related species live in America.

Wood ticks often trouble persons walking and camping in the woods. If this pest is pulled out forcibly, the toothed beak often will break off and remain inside the flesh and may cause a festering sore. To remove a wood tick, cover it with petroleum jelly or a heavy oil, such as mineral oil, salad oil, or machine oil. Wait about a half hour and then carefully remove the tick using tweezers. Wash the affected area of the skin thoroughly with soap and water.

Scientific Classification. Ticks belong to the class of *arachnids*. Together with mites, they make up the order *Acarina*. Spotted-fever ticks are genus *Dermacentor*, species *D. andersoni*. EDWARD A. CHAPIN

See also MITE; TICK FEVER; ROCKY MOUNTAIN SPOTTED FEVER.

TICK FEVER is a name for several different diseases carried by the bite of ticks. They include Rocky Mountain spotted fever, relapsing fever, and Texas fever. Texas fever is a disease of cattle. These diseases are infections by different microbes, which enter the body through the tick bite. See also RELAPSING FEVER; ROCKY MOUNTAIN SPOTTED FEVER.

TICKBIRD is a popular name for the *ani*, a bird in the cuckoo family. Anis often perch on the backs of cattle to search for ticks. There are two kinds of tickbirds, the *groove-billed ani* and the *smooth-billed ani*. They are found in pastures and orchards in the southern United States and Central and South America.

Tickbirds are about 12 inches (30 centimeters) long. Their black feathers have a touch of purple or green. They have unusually thick beaks. Two or three female birds often share one large nest. They stack their pale blue eggs in layers separated by leaves.

Scientific Classification. Tickbirds are in the cuckoo family, *Cuculidae*. The smooth-billed ani is *Crotophaga ani;* the groove-billed, *C. sulcirostris*. GEORGE E. HUDSON

TICKING is a cotton fabric used chiefly for mattress covers and pillow cases. It is woven very closely of stout yarn so that feathers, straw, or other fillings for bedding cannot pass through. Fancy damask ticking is woven of mercerized cotton combined with rayon yarn.

TICKNOR, GEORGE (1791-1871), an American scholar, became noted for his learned work, *History of Spanish Literature* (1849). It aroused great interest in Spanish literature in the 1800's. Ticknor was born in Boston. He served as professor of French, Spanish, and belles-lettres at Harvard College from 1819 to 1835. Ticknor wrote a biography of William Prescott, the historian, in 1864. He was also one of the founders of the Boston Public Library. Ticknor was graduated from Dartmouth College in 1807. MERLE CURTI

TICKSEED. See COREOPSIS.

TICONDEROGA, BATTLE OF. See FORT TICONDEROGA; ALLEN, ETHAN.

TIDAL WAVE is a destructive wave that sweeps in from the ocean like a huge tide. Tidal waves are not related to true tides (see TIDE). Many scientists call these waves *tsunami*, the Japanese word for *storm wave*.

Destructive tidal waves are caused by undersea earthquakes, called *seaquakes*, or by hurricanes far out in the ocean. Scientists using seismographs are able to predict almost exactly when a tidal wave will arrive at a given seacoast. For example, they know that an earthquake off the Aleutians may cause a tidal wave that will hit the coast of Hawaii. If seismographs in Hawaii show that an earthquake has occurred off the Aleutians, the forecaster calculates the number of minutes that it took for the earth tremor to reach Hawaii. It will then take about the same number of hours for the tidal wave to hit Hawaii. The reason for this is that earthquake tremors travel at speeds of 350 miles (563 kilometers) per minute or more, while the tidal wave travels 400 to 500 miles (640 to 800 kilometers) per hour. The exact speed depends on the depth of the water.

In 1755, a tidal wave 50 feet (15 meters) high wrecked Lisbon, Portugal. In 1900, Galveston, Texas, suffered great damage from a tidal wave caused by hurricanes at sea. In 1946, a tidal wave severely damaged Hilo, Hawaii. In 1970, a cyclone and tidal wave struck East Pakistan (now Bangladesh), killing about 200,000 persons. WAYNE V. BURT

See also KRAKATOA; SEICHE.

Nova Scotia Information Service

Tides in the Bay of Fundy sometimes rise and fall more than 50 feet (15 meters). Large ships that dock there at high tide may be left high and dry when the tide goes out. A ship docked at Windsor, N.S., rests on wooden planks at low tide, *above.* Cables hold the ship upright.

TIDE is the rise and fall of ocean waters, on a definite time schedule. Tides regulate the day for the people who live along the seacoasts of the world. The tide is more important than any clock to the boy who swims along the wharves when the tide is "in" and digs clams on the uncovered tidal flats when the tide is "out." The tide is the morning and evening whistle of the working day to the fisherman who needs high water to leave or enter his harbor.

All bodies of water, large or small, are subject to the tide-producing forces of sun and moon. But it is only where oceans and continents meet that tides are great enough to be noticed. In the inland bodies of water the regular rise and fall of the tide is so small that it is completely masked by changes in level due to wind and weather. Lake Superior, for example, has a tide that rises and falls only about 2 inches (5 centimeters).

Great harbors and seaports make use of the tides in many ways. The tidal currents help to sweep out the main channels and keep them deep. Ocean liners and cargo steamers use high tide to pass shallow harbor entrances, for at that time there is deep water to float them. Tides help to keep harbors clean and healthful. They pick up waste material from the coastlines and carry it to deep water where it settles to the bottom.

Tides also occur on land and in the atmosphere, but they are much harder to observe than ocean tides. Land and atmospheric tides can only be detected by highly-sensitive scientific instruments.

Tides Follow the Moon in its apparent motion around the earth. The tides rise and fall twice in the time between two rising moons, about 24 hours and 50 minutes. The time between two rising moons is determined by two motions: (1) the rotation of the earth on its axis, and (2) the revolution of the moon around the earth. As the earth turns on its axis, the moon appears to sweep across the sky once a day. But relative to the sun, the moon revolves around the earth once in about $29\frac{1}{2}$ days. Therefore, the moon moves about 12° around the earth each day. Between risings of the moon, the earth makes a complete rotation and then turns this additional 12°. The extra 12° of turning takes about 50 minutes.

Men have known for thousands of years that the moon has some relationship to the tides. Before the year A.D. 100, the Roman naturalist Pliny wrote of the moon's influence on the tides. But the physical laws of tides were not worked out until after the English scientist Sir Isaac Newton discovered the law of gravitation in the 1600's.

The moon's gravity pulls the water nearest the moon slightly away from the solid part of the earth. At the same time, the moon pulls the solid earth slightly away from the water on the opposite side of the earth. In this way, the moon's gravity produces two bulges on the ocean. These bulges are the positions of high tide.

As the earth turns on its axis, the land and water rotate together. But one tidal bulge always stays under the moon, and the other tidal bulge always stays on the opposite side of the earth. Therefore, the earth's rotation brings a high tide to most places on the ocean about twice a day. The two high tides at a given place do not usually rise equally high, because the centers of the tidal bulges usually lie on opposite sides of the

CAUSES OF OCEAN TIDES

Tides in the ocean are caused mainly by the pull of the moon on the earth. The moon's gravity pulls up the water directly below the moon, forming a high tide there. High tide also occurs on the other side of the earth, because the moon pulls the solid earth away from the water. As the earth turns, high tide occurs at each place on the ocean twice a day.

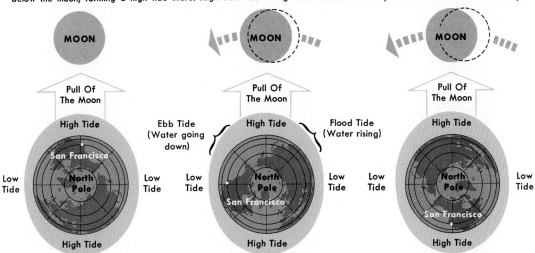

High Tide occurs directly below the moon and on the opposite side of the earth. When the earth is in the position shown *above*, San Francisco has a high tide.

As the Earth Turns, the tides rise and fall at each place on the ocean. About 6 hours and 13 minutes after high tide, San Francisco has a low tide, *above*.

The Next High Tide at San Francisco occurs about 12 hours and 25 minutes after the first. The earth has turned 186° in this time. The moon has moved 6°.

SPRING TIDES

Spring tides result when the pull of the sun combines with the pull of the moon to produce tides that are higher than normal. Spring tides occur about twice a month near the times of the full and new moons. The moon then lies either between the earth and the sun, as shown *below*, or on the opposite side of the earth from the sun.

NEAP TIDES

Neap tides result when the pull of the sun is at right angles to the pull of the moon. Neap tides do not rise as high as normal tides. They occur about twice each month, when the moon is near its first and third quarters. At these times, the moon is either on the side of the earth shown *below*, or on the opposite side of the earth.

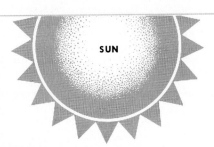

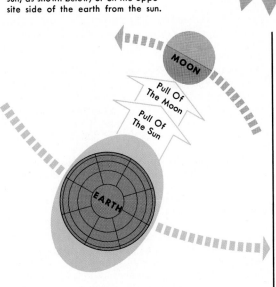

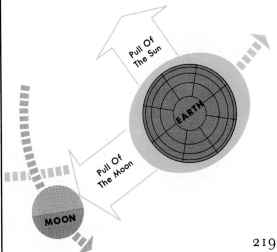

equator. The centers are located there instead of on the equator because the moon is usually located either north or south of the plane of the equator.

Both the sun and the moon exert a pull on the earth called *gravitation*. The force of this pull depends on the body's *mass* (amount of matter) and on the distance of the body from the earth. The force is proportional to the mass of the body. Therefore, if the body's mass could be doubled, the body would exert twice as much force on the earth. The force is inversely proportional to the *square of the distance* (the distance multiplied by itself) between the body and the earth. Therefore, if the distance of the body from the earth could be doubled, the body would exert only one-fourth as much force on the earth.

The sun and the moon pull harder on the side of the earth nearest them than they do on the center of the earth, because the center is farther away. It is this difference in pull that produces the tides. The difference is inversely proportional to the *cube of the distance* (the distance multiplied twice by itself) between the body and the earth. Therefore, if the distance of a body from the earth could be doubled, the body would exert only one-eighth as much tide-producing force on the earth.

The sun has about 27 million times as much mass as the moon. Therefore, if the sun and the moon were the same distance from the earth, the sun would exert about 27 million times as much tide-producing force as the moon. But the sun is about 390 times as far from the earth as the moon. So the tide-producing force of the sun is only 46 per cent as great as that produced by the moon. As a result, the tides caused by the sun are only 46 per cent as high as those caused by the moon. The tides caused by the sun and by the moon combine to produce the tides seen along the seacoast.

Differences in the coastline and in the channels of the sea bottom may make a difference in the times that the tide wave hits the different ports along the same coastline. The governments of most seacoast nations print tide tables showing the times of the tides for the whole year at main ports of the country. Ships are brought to the entrance of a port when the tide is high enough to carry them and is on the flood to help them in. Ship captains use tide tables just as railroad passengers use timetables, and tide tables are even more dependable—for tide times never change their regular pattern.

High Tides and Low Tides. One tide acts very much like another. From its lowest point, the water rises gradually for about six hours, until it reaches *high tide* (high water). Then it begins to fall, continuing for about six hours until it reaches *low tide* (low water). The cycle then begins again. The difference between high water and low water is called the *range* of the tide. As the water rises and falls, it moves toward and away from the coast. This movement of the water is called the *tidal current*. When the water moves toward the coast or inland, it is the *flood current*. When it flows seaward, it is called the *ebb current*.

The range of the tide differs from day to day according to the position of the sun and the moon. When the moon and the sun are pulling along the same line, as they do at full moon and new moon, the tide rises higher than usual and is called a *spring tide*. When the sun and moon pull at right angles, as when the moon is in its first and third quarters, the tide does not rise as high as usual and is called a *neap tide*.

The formation of the seacoast itself also makes a great difference in the range of the tide. In funnel-shaped estuaries and bays, the range may be very high. In the Bay of Fundy, the difference between high and low tide is sometimes more than 50 feet (15 meters). Here, the tide rushes into the Petitcodiac River in a *bore* (high wall) that may rise as high as 4 feet (1.2 meters).

The shape, size, and depth of seas or oceans make differences in the way the tide acts. For example, the Atlantic Ocean has tides that flow and ebb regularly twice a day. But some Pacific islands have *mixed tides*, such as two high tides daily, with only a little ebb between, and then a very low tide. At Saint Michael, Alaska, and certain places along the Gulf of Mexico, there is only a *daily tide*—one high tide and one low tide each day. The Mediterranean Sea has little tide.

Tides in the Air are similar to those in the ocean. At the earth's surface, the speed of these tides, called *lunar winds*, is about $\frac{1}{20}$ mile (0.08 kilometer) per hour. Although they are too low to be felt, scientists detect them by studying variations in weather statistics. High and low tides in the air come twice daily. There also are high stages that are equivalent to the ocean's spring tide. Lunar winds blow eastward in the morning and westward in the evening.   ROBERT O. REID

See also BAY OF FUNDY; BORE; OCEAN (The Tides); SEA LEVEL; SEASHORE; TIDAL WAVE.

TIE. See RAILROAD (The Rails and Crossties).

TIE, in music, is a curved line which connects two notes of the same pitch. The tone is held for the time value of the two notes.

TIE DYEING is a method of dyeing cloth to produce a design or pattern. Parts of the material are bunched together and tied tightly with cord or string. When the dye is applied to the cloth, those sections which are tied do not receive the dye, thus creating a pattern.

TIEN SHAN, *tih EN SHAHN,* is a mountain system in central Asia. It runs for nearly 1,500 miles (2,410 kilometers) northeast from The Pamirs (see PAMIRS, THE). Tien Shan, or Tian Shan, means *Heavenly Mountains.* The system is the highest mountain system north of Tibet. Pobeda Peak, the highest peak, rises 24,406 feet (7,439 meters) above sea level. Rivers flow north from Tien Shan into Russia, and south into China's Takla Makan desert. The system includes some of the world's largest glaciers. Roads follow passes through Tien Shan. For location, see RUSSIA (physical map).   J. E. SPENCER

See also CHINA (The Land [The Sinkiang-Mongolian Uplands]).

TIENTSIN, *tin tsin* (pop. 4,280,000), is a trading center located in northern China. In 1860, the Chinese opened the city and its port to foreign trade. Nine countries received *concessions* (tracts of land). All these have now been given back to China.

Tientsin is 85 miles (137 kilometers) southeast of Peking, near the mouth of the winding Hai River (see CHINA [political map]). Chinese emperors did not allow foreign merchants to live in Peking, the rich capital. So traders who wanted to sell goods to Peking settled in Tientsin. As a result, Tientsin became an important center of foreign trade. Railroads connect Tientsin with

Peking, Nan-ching, Shanghai, and the cities of Manchuria. Tientsin lies at the northern end of the Grand Canal, a water route that leads to the southern part of China.

Tientsin has few large industries. The most important industries there are cotton mills. The city has two universities. Fighting between Japan and China in 1937 badly damaged Tientsin. Japan then held the city until World War II ended in 1945. In 1976, an earthquake struck Tientsin, Peking, and the area around the cities. About 650,000 people died in the disaster and property damage was extensive. THEODORE H. E. CHEN

TIEPOLO, *TYEH poh loh,* **GIOVANNI BATTISTA** (1696-1770), was the last important Italian painter of the Venetian group. He began as an admirer of Paolo Veronese, but he soon developed a grand, colorful mural style that became popular in Europe during the 1700's. His mural decorations show many active figures painted in gay pastel colors and spaced freely in vast, airy settings. His painting *Allegory of the Marriage of Frederick Barbarossa and Beatrice of Burgundy* is reproduced in color in the PAINTING article.

Tiepolo was born in Venice. After 1750, he worked mainly in Germany and Spain. His works include decorations for the archbishop's palace in Würzburg, Germany, and the Royal Palace in Madrid. Some of Tiepolo's small oil sketches for his large murals are displayed in the Metropolitan Museum of Art in New York City. ROBERT O. PARKS

See also PAINTING (Painting as Decoration).

TIERRA DEL FUEGO, *tih EHR ah DEL foo AY goh,* or *TYER rah del FWAY goh,* is the name of a group of islands lying off the extreme southern tip of South America. The name *Tierra del Fuego* means *Land of Fire.* In 1520, Ferdinand Magellan named the region when he sighted large fires blazing along the shore. He was trying to find a passage to the Pacific. The Indians who lived there usually kept many fires burning to warm themselves.

The islands cover 26,872 square miles (69,598 square kilometers). The Strait of Magellan separates them from the mainland. The largest island, also called Tierra del Fuego, covers 19,280 square miles (49,935 square kilometers). The city of Ushuaia, the world's southernmost seat of government, lies on this island. The islanders are called *Fuegians.* The population of Tierra del Fuego is about 19,500.

Argentina owns the eastern part of Tierra del Fuego island, while Chile controls the western part. In 1948, an Italian settlement was made in the Argentine section. Each country also owns several of the smaller islands. Chile controls the Strait of Magellan, and maintains a naval base on Navarino Island. Cape Horn is at the southern tip of the islands. ARTHUR P. WHITAKER

See also CAPE HORN; CLOTHING (introduction); ONA INDIANS.

TIFFANY, *TIHF uh nee,* is the family name of an American jewelry merchant and his son, an artist.

Charles Lewis Tiffany (1812-1902) was a dealer in precious stones. His reputation as a jeweler became so great that his name now stands for the highest quality in jewelry. He was born in Killingly, Conn. Tiffany went to New York City in 1837, and opened a small notions store. Soon he was specializing in jewelry, glassware, and china. Later he imported European crown jewels.

Tierra del Fuego is a group of islands at the southern tip of South America. The islands are divided between Argentina and Chile.

WORLD BOOK map

He also set up factories to make some of the products he sold. JOHN B. McFERRIN

Louis Comfort Tiffany (1848-1933) became known for the development of *Tiffany Favrile glass.* He started his first factory in 1875, and with colored glass made vases, cigarette boxes, lampshades, and tiles for walls and floors. He established the Louis Comfort Tiffany Foundation in 1919. Tiffany was born in New York City. He studied with American artist George Inness and also in Paris. Tiffany served as the art director of the Tiffany Studios and as president of the Tiffany Company. EDWIN L. FULWIDER

TIFLIS. See TBILISI.

TIGER is the largest member of the cat family. People admire the tiger for its strength and beauty, but they fear it because it has been known to kill and eat human beings. Yet almost all wild tigers avoid people. Probably only 3 or 4 of every 1,000 tigers ever eat people, and some of these are sick or wounded animals that can no longer hunt large prey.

Wild tigers are found only in Asia. Until the 1800's, many lived throughout most of the southern half of the continent. Tigers still live in some of this area, but only a few are left. People have greatly reduced the number of tigers by hunting them and by clearing the forests in which they lived. Today, wildlife experts consider the tiger an endangered species.

Tigers can live in almost any climate. They need only shade, water, and prey. They are found in the hot rain forests of Malaya, the dry thorn woods of India, and the cold, snowy spruce forests of Manchuria. They also live in oak woods, tall grasslands, swamps, and marshes. Tigers prefer to be in the shadows and seldom go into open country as lions do. Many tigers also live in zoos. In the past, wild tigers were captured for zoos. Today, enough tigers for zoos are born in captivity.

Ylla, Rapho Guillumette

The Tiger's Coloration helps conceal the animal in its natural surroundings. This female tiger could easily go unseen because her stripes blend with the tall grasses.

The Body of a Tiger. Adult male tigers weigh about 420 pounds (191 kilograms) and are 9 feet (2.7 meters) long, including a 3-foot (0.9-meter) tail. Tigresses weigh about 300 pounds (136 kilograms) and are 8 feet (2.4 meters) long. The tiger's coat ranges from brownish-yellow to orange-red and is marked by black stripes. The stripes vary greatly in length, width, and spacing. The fur on the throat, belly, and insides of the legs is whitish. Many tigers have a ruff of hair around the sides of the head, but the hair is not so long as the mane of lions. The tigers of Manchuria, where the winters are bitter cold, have long, shaggy, winter coats.

The tiger looks different from the lion because of its stripes and more colorful coat. But the two animals have similar bodies. In fact, tigers and lions have mated in zoos. The offspring are called *tiglons*, *tigons*, or *ligers*.

How a Tiger Hunts. Tigers prefer large prey, such as deer, antelope, wild oxen, and wild pigs. Some tigers attack elephant calves. They also eat small prey, such as peafowl, monkeys, tortoises, and frogs. Tigers especially like porcupines, but their quills may stick in a tiger's body and cause painful wounds. In parts of Asia, some tigers prey on domestic cattle and buffalo because hunters have reduced the number of wildlife.

The tiger usually hunts at night, wandering over animal trails and along stream beds. A tiger depends on its sharp eyes and keen ears, but it may also use its sense of smell. The tiger, waiting in cover, rushes at its prey in a series of bounds. Using its sharp claws, the tiger grasps the victim by the rump or side and pulls it to the ground. The tiger's teeth are well suited both for holding prey and for tearing off chunks of meat.

Tigers are extremely swift for short distances and can leap nearly 30 feet (9 meters). But if a tiger fails to catch its prey quickly, it usually will give up because it soon tires. As long as a week may go by without a successful hunt. After a kill, the tiger drags the *carcass* (dead body) to thick cover, preferably near water. The muscles of the tiger's neck, shoulders, and forelegs are very powerful. A tiger may drag the body of a 500-pound (230-kilogram) young water buffalo ¼ mile (0.4 kilometer). The tiger stays near the carcass until it has eaten everything except the bones and stomach. A tiger may eat 50 pounds (23 kilograms) of meat in a night. A long drink and a nap often follow a meal.

Tigers are good swimmers and may swim across rivers or from one island to another in search of prey. On hot days, they may go into the water to cool off. Tigers can climb trees, but they do not usually do so.

The Life of a Tiger. Adult tigers usually live alone, but they are not unfriendly. Two tigers may meet on

_____ FACTS IN BRIEF _____

Names: *Male*, tiger; *female*, tigress; *young*, cub.

Gestation Period: 98 to 109 days.

Number of Newborn: 1 to 6, usually 2 or 3.

Length of Life: Up to 20 years.

Where Found: Chiefly in Bangladesh, India, Nepal, and Southeast Asia, including Sumatra; also a few in China, Iran, Java, and Korea, and along the Siberian-Manchurian border.

Scientific Classification: Tigers belong to the class *Mammalia* and the order *Carnivora*. They are in the cat family, *Felidae*, and the genus *Panthera*. All tigers are of the same species, *P. tigris*.

Marc & Evelyne Bernheim, Rapho Guillumette

The Male Tiger has heavier patches of fur around its face than the female. This male is taking a dip on a hot day.

THE SKELETON OF A TIGER

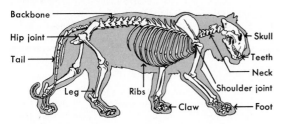

Backbone
Hip joint
Tail
Leg
Ribs
Claw
Skull
Teeth
Neck
Shoulder joint
Foot

TIGER TRACKS

Front feet
Hind feet

WORLD BOOK diagram

WHERE TIGERS LIVE

The black areas in the map below show the parts of the world where tigers are found. Most tigers live in southern Asia.

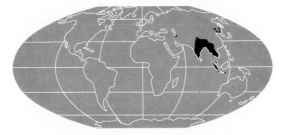

their nightly rounds, rub heads together in greeting, and then part. Several tigers may share a kill.

Many adult males claim a territory as their own and keep other males out. The territory may cover from 25 to 250 square miles (65 to 647 square kilometers) or more, depending on the amount of prey available. The tiger marks a path with urine and with fluids from glands at the base of the tail. The scent lets other tigers know that the territory is occupied. A male may share his area with one or several females, each wandering alone but aware of one another. Tigers communicate by many sounds, including a roar that can be heard for 2 miles (3 kilometers) or more.

A tigress can bear her first cubs when she is $3\frac{1}{2}$ to 4 years old. The cubs are helpless and weigh about 3 pounds (1.4 kilograms) at birth. Tiger cubs, like kittens, are playful. But their life is hazardous, and about half die before they are a year old. The cubs cannot kill enough for themselves until they are more than a year old. Even then, they cannot kill a large animal. The mother may teach her cubs how to kill by providing a live animal for them to attack. Cubs become independent when about 2 years old.   GEORGE B. SCHALLER

See also ANIMAL (Animals of the Tropical Forests [color picture]); LION; SABER-TOOTHED CAT.

TIGER, TASMANIAN. See TASMANIAN TIGER.

TIGER CAT is another name for the moderate-sized wildcats of Africa and the Americas. See MARGAY; OCELOT; SERVAL.

TIGER LILY is a tall garden flower that originally grew in eastern Asia. It received its name because it has reddish-orange flowers splashed with black. People in China, Japan, and Korea serve tiger lily bulbs as food.

The stem of the tiger lily is greenish-purple or dark brown, and many grow from 5 to 6 feet (1.5 to 1.8 meters) tall. Tiny black bulblets appear where the long, spear-shaped leaves join the stalk. The bulblets finally drop off, producing new plants.

Tiger lilies grow best in bright sunlight, in a loose, fertile soil. They can stand cold weather but need some protection in winter. The bulbs should be planted about 4 inches (10 centimeters) in the ground, with a little sand or gravel under each. After being planted, tiger lilies bloom from year to year with little care.

Scientific Classification. The tiger lily belongs to the lily family, *Liliaceae*. It is classified as genus *Lilium*, species *L. tigrinum*.   ALFRED C. HOTTES

TIGLATH-PILESER, *TIHG lath pih LEE zuhr*, was the name of three kings of Assyria, an ancient land in what is now northern Iraq.

Tiglath-pileser I (reigned 1115-1077 B.C.) expanded Assyrian power by military victories. He conquered lands as far north as what is now Turkey, as far east as the Zagros Mountains in what is now Iran, and as far west as the Mediterranean Sea. To avenge a Babylonian raid on his territory, he captured the city of Babylon in what is now Iraq, but spared its temples. He compiled a library of clay tablets that still exists.

Tiglath-pileser II (reigned 967-935 B.C.) is relatively unknown. But scholars believe his reign was a stable one, because it lasted so long.

Tiglath-pileser III (reigned 744-727 B.C.) conquered parts of what are now Turkey, Iraq, and Syria. He founded the Assyrian Empire, which ruled this region for more than 100 years. When he defeated Babylonia in 729 B.C., Tiglath-pileser made himself Babylonian king under the name *Pulu*.   JACOB J. FINKELSTEIN

TIGLON. See LION (Cubs).

TIGRIS RIVER rises north of Diyarbakir in eastern Turkey. For location, see IRAQ (map). The river winds southeast for about 1,150 miles (1,851 kilometers) through Iraq. Then it joins the Euphrates River in Al Qurnah, Iraq, about 120 miles (193 kilometers) from the Persian Gulf, to form the Shatt al Arab. Steamers can use the Tigris River to within 30 miles (48 kilometers) of Mosul. Only rafts can use the upper Tigris. Boats generally have trouble sailing on much of the river, because of clay and sand bars. Many tributaries flow into the Tigris from the east.

Archaeologists believe that writers of the Bible placed the Garden of Eden somewhere in the Tigris-Euphrates Valley. The story of Noah's Ark indicates it may have rested on one of the heights northeast of the valley. The great ancient civilizations of Sumer and Babylonia developed in the southern part of the Tigris-Euphrates basin. The ruins of Nineveh, capital of Assyria, lie on the left bank of the Tigris, opposite the modern town of Mosul in northern Iraq. Baghdad, capital of modern Iraq, was built on the Tigris in the A.D. 700's. It was the capital of the great Abbasid Caliphate of Arab history.   CHRISTINA PHELPS HARRIS

TIHAMAH. See SAUDI ARABIA (The Western Highlands; terrain map); YEMEN (SANA), the section on *Land*.

TIJUANA, *tee WAH nah* (pop. 411,643; met. area pop. 535,535), is a city in the Mexican state of Baja California Norte. It lies on the U.S.-Mexican border, 16 miles (26 kilometers) south of downtown San Diego, Calif. (see MEXICO [political map]). Tourists from the United States spend millions of dollars each year in Tijuana. They visit nightclubs, shops, and restaurants, and attend bullfights and horse races there. Tijuana's streets and buildings resemble those of many U.S. towns. They lack much of the Spanish charm common to cities of central Mexico.

In 1900, Tijuana was a small village of 242 people. A booming tourist trade since 1940 caused the city to grow rapidly.   ROBERT C. WEST

TIKHONOV, *TEE khuhn uhf,* **NIKOLAY ALEKSANDROVICH** (1905-   ), became premier of the Soviet Union in 1980. As premier—officially chairman of the Council of Ministers—Tikhonov is chief administrator of the Soviet government.

However, Leonid I. Brezhnev, the Soviet president and Communist Party leader, is actually the most powerful person in the government of the Soviet Union.

Tikhonov was born in Kharkov. He earned an engineering degree at a technical school in Dnepropetrovsk and worked as an engineer and plant manager in factories. Tikhonov

Sven Simon/Katherine Young
Nikolay A. Tikhonov

joined the Communist Party in 1940. Beginning in 1950, he held various industrial management positions in government. From 1957 to 1960, he headed the Dnepropetrovsk economic council. During the 1960's and 1970's, Tikhonov rose through the ranks of the Soviet government's Council of Ministers. He became a full member of the powerful Politburo of the Communist Party in 1979.   JOHN A. ARMSTRONG

TILDEN, BILL (1893-1953), was the United States men's singles tennis champion from 1920 to 1925, and in 1929. He was the first American to win the Wimbledon, England, championship. He won it in 1920, 1921, and 1930. He led the United States team in winning the Davis Cup from 1920 to 1926. Tall and slender, Tilden was known for his powerful forehand and serve. Tilden left amateur tennis competition in 1930, and became a professional player for 10 years. William Tatem Tilden, Jr., was born in Philadelphia.   PAT HARMON

TILDEN, SAMUEL JONES (1814-1886), an American lawyer, became famous as the leader of the attack on the "Tweed Ring" of New York City. This group of politicians, led by William Tweed, had stolen millions of dollars through city improvement schemes (see TWEED, WILLIAM M.).

Tilden was born in New Lebanon, N.Y., and studied at Yale University and was admitted to the bar in 1841. He practiced law in New York City. Tilden was elected as a Democrat to the New York state assembly in 1845. He was active in the faction of Democrats who were called "Barnburners," and in the Free Soil movement. He became governor of New York in 1875, and in 1876 was nominated by the Democrats as their candidate for President. Although he received a majority of the popular votes, the electoral vote was in doubt. Congress created an electoral commission to pass upon the disputed votes. The commission decided in favor of the Republican nominee, Rutherford B. Hayes, who was declared elected by a margin of one electoral vote (see ELECTORAL COMMISSION). Tilden left $6 million, half of which was used to found the New York City Public Library.   W. B. HESSELTINE

TILE. All the several kinds of clay tile are made in much the same way. Thin sheets of clay are pressed, molded, and baked in kilns in the same process as is used for making brick. The tile may be left in its rough state. It may also be given a smooth surface, called *glazing*, by throwing salt into the kiln or by treating the clay with a chemical wash.

Tile pipe is used for sewage-disposal systems and for draining fields of excess water. A continuous tile line is formed by fitting together short sections, each of which has one end enlarged to form a bell into which the small end of the next section fits. Drain tiles are generally laid with uncemented butt ends through which the drainage water may seep. Sewer pipes are laid with tight cement joints.

Finer grades of clay are used in making tiles for roofs, for walls, and for floors. Roofing tiles are made in various shapes and colors. Hollow clay tile blocks are used in load-bearing walls and partitions.

Home builders use decorative tiles for interior floors and walls. They obtain artistic effects by using tiles of different colors. Mosaics are small, unglazed tiles combined to form a design in colors. White and colored glazed tiles are popular for the walls of kitchens and bathrooms. *Encaustic tiling* is the trade name for decorative tiles used in such a way that there is a background of one color and a pattern of another, contrasting color.

Floor tiles are made of rubber, linoleum, terrazzo, cork, asphalt, plastic, and terra cotta and other ceramics. Acoustic ceiling tiles are made of asbestos, cork granules, wood fiber, and mineral fiber. GEORGE W. WASHA

See also CLAY; TERRA COTTA.

TILEFISH are deep-sea fish that live along the New England coast. The tilefish is the most colorfully decorated ocean fish in northern waters. The upper parts

WORLD BOOK illustration by James Teason
The Tilefish Lives Along the Coast of New England.

of the side are a bluish or olive-green color, blending into yellow or rose on the lower part. The head is reddish and is pure white below. The upper sides are thickly dotted with small yellow spots. Large tilefish are about 3 feet (91 centimeters) long and weigh about 30 pounds (14 kilograms) or more. Tilefish feed chiefly on crabs and other fish. They can be caught on trawl lines and hand lines, with any kind of bait.

Scientific Classification. The tilefish belongs to the tilefish family, *Branchiostegidae.* It is genus *Lopholatilus,* species *L. chamaeleonticeps.*   LEONARD P. SCHULTZ

TILL EULENSPIEGEL. See EULENSPIEGEL, TILL.

TILLER. See SAILING (Hull).

TILLEY, SIR SAMUEL LEONARD (1818-1896), served as premier of the Canadian colony of New Brunswick from 1861 to 1865. He represented New Brunswick at three conferences at which the delegates agreed on the terms of a Canadian union. These conferences were the Charlottetown and Quebec conferences of 1864 and the London Conference of 1866. The delegates became known as the Fathers of Confederation.

In the mid-1860's, many New Brunswickers opposed a plan for confederation because they feared they would lose various political rights. Tilley helped persuade New Brunswick to join the Dominion of Canada by assuring them that the larger provinces would not control the smaller ones.

In 1867, Tilley became minister of customs in the Cabinet of Sir John A. Macdonald, the first prime minister of Canada. Tilley was promoted to minister of finance in 1873 and held that office under Macdonald again from 1878 to 1885. Tilley prepared a program to develop Canadian industries by putting a tariff on many imported products. This program was called the National Policy. Tilley was knighted in 1879. He was born in Gagetown, N. B.   C. M. WALLACE

TILLICH, PAUL (1886-1965), a German-American theologian, left Germany when Hitler came to power in 1933. He became a professor at Union Theological

Seminary in New York, and then in 1955, at Harvard University. He began teaching at the Divinity School of the University of Chicago in 1962. His works include *The Protestant Era* (1948), *Shaking of the Foundations* (1948), *The Courage To Be* (1952), the three-volume *Systematic Theology* (1951-1963), *Morality and Beyond* (1963), and *The Eternal Now* (1963).

Born in Starzeddel, Prussia, Tillich became a minister of the Evangelical Lutheran Church in 1912. Tillich taught in Germany from 1919 to 1933.   L. J. TRINTERUD

TILLMAN, BENJAMIN RYAN. See SOUTH CAROLINA (Industrial Growth).

TILLY, COUNT OF (1559-1632), JOHAN TSERCLAES, was a leading Roman Catholic general during the Thirty Years' War, a struggle between European Catholics and Protestants. Tilly devoted his life to trying to restore the influence of Roman Catholicism in central Europe.

When the Thirty Years' War broke out in 1618, Tilly took command of the Catholic Holy League. He won important early victories over both the Bohemians and Danes. But he was defeated at the Battle of Breitenfeld by King Gustavus Adolphus of Sweden in 1631. Tilly then raised a new army to oppose the advancing Protestants. He was wounded during a battle with Swedish forces along the Lech River in Germany, and died soon afterward in Ingolstadt, Germany.

Tilly was born in Gembloux, Belgium. In 1843, a statue of him was placed in the Hall of Generals in Munich.   THEODORE S. HAMEROW

See also THIRTY YEARS' WAR.

TILSIT, PEACE OF. See FREDERICK WILLIAM (III).

TIMBER. See FOREST PRODUCTS; FORESTRY.

TIMBER LINE. See FOREST (Mountain Evergreen Forests).

TIMBUKTU, *tihm BUK too,* officially TOMBOUCTOU, *TAWNG BOOK TOO* (pop. 9,000), is a small trading town in central Mali. From the 1200's to the 1500's, it was one of the richest commercial cities of Africa and a center of Muslim learning.

Timbuktu was founded about 1100. It lies near the southern edge of the Sahara, about 8 miles (13 kilometers) from the Niger River (see MALI [map]). Timbuktu came to be known as the "meeting point of camel and canoe." Goods from North Africa were exchanged there for products from the forests and grasslands of West Africa. Camel caravans from North Africa carried salt, cloth, copper, cowrie shells that were used as money, dates and figs, and metal manufactures to Timbuktu. The merchants of Timbuktu traded gold, ivory, kola nuts, and slaves—all from the south. A school in Timbuktu became a center of scholarship in history, law, and Islam, the Muslim religion.

Timbuktu's location left it open to attack, and control of the city changed hands many times. It has been controlled by the Mali Empire, the Songhai Empire, Tuareg nomads, Morocco, the Tukulor Empire, and then by France from 1893 to 1960. Since the 1600's, Timbuktu has declined in both importance and population. Many of its mud and brick buildings have crumbled or lie half-buried in the shifting sands. But the arrival of the camel caravans from the northern salt mines is still an important event.   LEO SPITZER

TIME is one of the deepest mysteries known to man. No one can say exactly what it is. Yet, the ability to measure time makes man's way of life possible. Most of his activities involve groups of people acting together in the same place at the same time. People could not do this if they did not all measure time in the same way.

One way of thinking about time is to imagine a world without time. This timeless world would be at a standstill. But if some kind of change took place, that timeless world would be different "now" than it was "before." The period—no matter how brief—between "before" and "now" indicates that time must have passed. Thus, time and change are related because the passing of time depends on changes taking place. In the real world, changes never stop happening. Some changes seem to happen only once, like the falling of a particular leaf. Other changes happen over and over again, like the breaking of waves against the shore.

Any change that takes place again and again stands out from other changes. The rising and setting of the sun are examples of this kind of change. The first people to keep time probably counted such natural repeating events and used them to keep track of events that did not repeat. Later, man made clocks to imitate the regularity of natural events. When man began to count repeating events, he began to measure time.

Measuring Time

Units of Time Measurement. For early peoples, the only changes that were truly regular—that is, repeated themselves evenly—were the motions of objects in the sky. The most obvious of these changes was the alternate daylight and darkness, caused by the rising and setting of the sun. Each of these cycles of the sun came to be called a *day*.

Another regular change in the sky was the change in the visible shape of the moon. Each cycle of the moon's changing shape takes about $29\frac{1}{2}$ days, or a *month*.

The cycle of the seasons gave man an even longer unit of time. By watching the stars just before dawn or after sunset, man saw that the sun moved slowly eastward among them. The sun made a full circle around the sky in one cycle of the seasons. This cycle takes about $365\frac{1}{4}$ days, or a *year*.

For hundreds of years, people tried to fit days and months evenly into a year or a period of several years. But no system worked perfectly. Today, the calendar is based entirely on the year. Even though the year is divided into 12 so-called months, the months have no relation to the actual cycle of the moon. See CALENDAR.

There is no regular change in the sky that lasts seven days, as does the *week*. The seven-day week came from the Jewish custom of observing a *Sabbath* (day of rest) every seventh day.

The division of a day into 24 *hours*, an hour into 60 *minutes*, and a minute into 60 *seconds* probably came indirectly from the ancient Babylonians. Babylonian astronomers and astrologers divided the imaginary circular path of the sun into 12 equal parts. Then they divided the periods of daylight and darkness into 12 parts each, resulting in a 24-hour day.

The Babylonians also divided the circle into 360 parts called *degrees*. Other ancient astronomers further divided each degree into 60 minutes. Later, clocks became accurate enough to need smaller units than the hour. Clockmakers, following the astronomers' division of the degree, divided the hour into 60 minutes and the minute into 60 seconds. In this way, the face of a clock could easily show hours, minutes, and seconds. A clock face has 12 divisions. Each of these divisions equals one hour for the hour hand, five minutes for the minute hand, and five seconds for the second hand.

Some clock faces are divided into 24 hours. On such a clock, 9 A.M. would be shown as 0900 and 3 P.M. would be 1500. This system avoids confusion between the morning and evening hours.

Measuring Time by the Sun. Directly above every spot on the earth, an imaginary curved line called the *celestial meridian* passes through the sky. As the earth rotates on its axis, the sun crosses every celestial meridian once each day. When the sun crosses the celestial meridian above a particular place, the time there is noon. Twelve hours later, the time at that place is midnight. The period from one midnight to the next is called a *solar day*. The length of a solar day varies because of the tilt of the earth's axis, the oval shape of its orbit, and its changing speed along the orbit.

To make all solar days the same length, astronomers do not measure solar time with the *apparent* (real) sun. Instead, they use an imaginary *mean* (average) sun that moves at a steady speed around the sky. *Mean solar noon* occurs when the mean sun crosses the celestial meridian above a particular place. The time between one mean solar noon and the next is always the same. Thus, all *mean solar days* are the same length.

Measuring Time by the Stars. Astronomers also measure time by the earth's rotation in relation to the stars. This time is called *sidereal time*. Each day, as the earth rotates on its axis, an imaginary point among the stars called the *vernal equinox* crosses the celestial meridian above every place on the earth. The time when this happens is *sidereal noon*.

The time between one sidereal noon and the next is one *sidereal day*. A sidereal day is shorter than a mean solar day by 3 minutes and 56 seconds.

Devices That Measure Time. The *sundial* was one of man's earliest devices for measuring time. But a sundial can work only in uncloudy daylight. Early man also used ropes with knots tied at regular intervals or candles marked with regularly spaced lines. When burned, such devices measured time. An *hourglass* or *sandglass* tells time by means of sand trickling through a narrow opening. A *water clock*, or *clepsydra*, measures time by allowing water to drip slowly from one marked container into another. By the 1700's, man had developed accurate clocks and watches that told time to the minute. Modern electronic and atomic clocks can tell time far more accurately.

Time Zones

Local and Standard Time. Clocks in various parts of the world do not all show the same time. Suppose they all did show the same time—3 P.M., for example. At that time, people in some countries would see the sun rise, and people in other lands would see it high in the sky. In still other countries, the sun could not be seen because 3 P.M. would occur at night. Instead, clocks everywhere show 12 o'clock at midday, regardless of their location.

Every place on the earth that is east or west of another place has noon at a different time. The time at any particular place is called the *local time* of that place. At noon local time in one town, the time might be 11 A.M. in another place west of the town or 1 P.M. in a place to the east. The local time in the other places depends on how far east or west they are from the town.

If every community used a different time, travelers would be confused and many other problems would be created. To avoid all such problems, *standard time zones* were established. These zones were set up so there would be a difference of one hour between a place on the

eastern edge of a time zone and a place on the western edge if each were on its own local time. But under the time zone system, each of these places is not on its own local time. The local time at the *meridian* (line) of longitude that runs through the center of the zone is used by all places within the zone. Thus, time throughout the zone is the same.

Time Zones in the United States and Canada. The United States and Canada lie within eight standard time zones. Each of these zones uses a time one hour different from its neighboring zones. The hours are earlier to the west of each zone and later to the east. The boundaries between the zones are irregular so that neighboring communities can have the same time.

The United States has not always had standard time zones. Every locality once set its own time by the sun. Various railroads tried to make their schedules simpler

Standard Time Zones in the United States and Canada

The United States and Canada each have six standard time zones. Western Alaska uses the Bering time zone, not shown on this map. Hawaii and central Alaska are in the same time zone. Each major time zone differs from its neighboring zones by one hour. The zone boundaries are irregular so that places near the edge of a zone can have the same time.

WORLD BOOK map

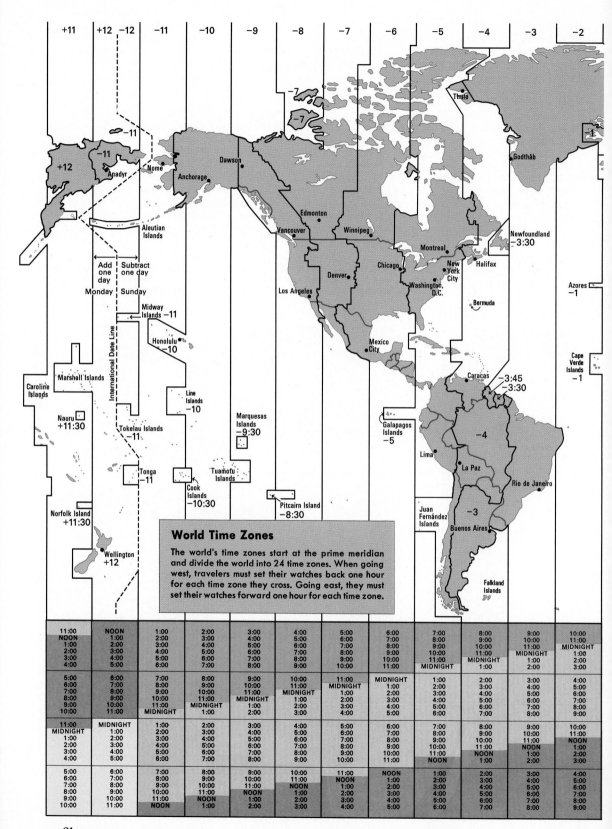

World Time Zones

The world's time zones start at the prime meridian and divide the world into 24 time zones. When going west, travelers must set their watches back one hour for each time zone they cross. Going east, they must set their watches forward one hour for each time zone.

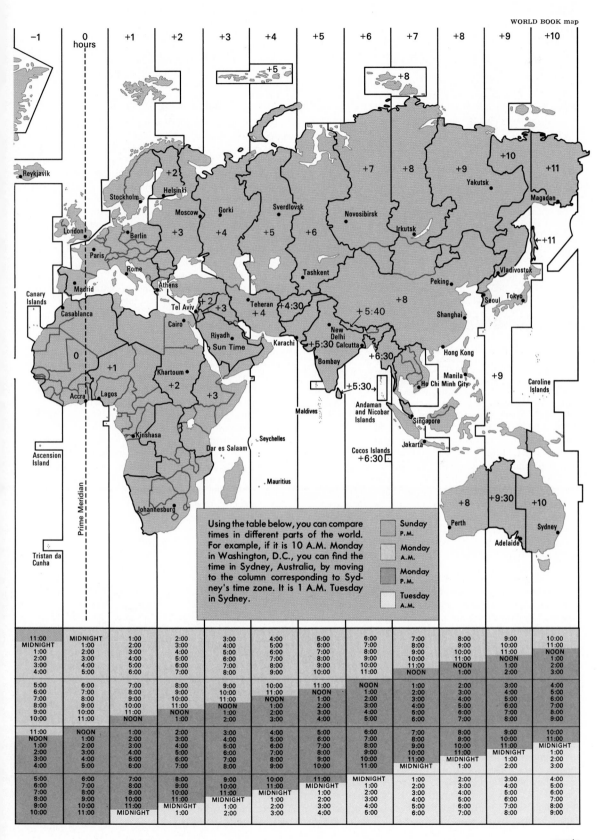

Using the table below, you can compare times in different parts of the world. For example, if it is 10 A.M. Monday in Washington, D.C., you can find the time in Sydney, Australia, by moving to the column corresponding to Sydney's time zone. It is 1 A.M. Tuesday in Sydney.

Sunday P.M.
Monday A.M.
Monday P.M.
Tuesday A.M.

−1	0 hours	+1	+2	+3	+4	+5	+6	+7	+8	+9	+10
11:00	MIDNIGHT	1:00	2:00	3:00	4:00	5:00	6:00	7:00	8:00	9:00	10:00
MIDNIGHT	1:00	2:00	3:00	4:00	5:00	6:00	7:00	8:00	9:00	10:00	11:00
1:00	2:00	3:00	4:00	5:00	6:00	7:00	8:00	9:00	10:00	11:00	NOON
2:00	3:00	4:00	5:00	6:00	7:00	8:00	9:00	10:00	11:00	NOON	1:00
3:00	4:00	5:00	6:00	7:00	8:00	9:00	10:00	11:00	NOON	1:00	2:00
4:00	5:00	6:00	7:00	8:00	9:00	10:00	11:00	NOON	1:00	2:00	3:00
5:00	6:00	7:00	8:00	9:00	10:00	11:00	NOON	1:00	2:00	3:00	4:00
6:00	7:00	8:00	9:00	10:00	11:00	NOON	1:00	2:00	3:00	4:00	5:00
7:00	8:00	9:00	10:00	11:00	NOON	1:00	2:00	3:00	4:00	5:00	6:00
8:00	9:00	10:00	11:00	NOON	1:00	2:00	3:00	4:00	5:00	6:00	7:00
9:00	10:00	11:00	NOON	1:00	2:00	3:00	4:00	5:00	6:00	7:00	8:00
10:00	11:00	NOON	1:00	2:00	3:00	4:00	5:00	6:00	7:00	8:00	9:00
11:00	NOON	1:00	2:00	3:00	4:00	5:00	6:00	7:00	8:00	9:00	10:00
NOON	1:00	2:00	3:00	4:00	5:00	6:00	7:00	8:00	9:00	10:00	11:00
1:00	2:00	3:00	4:00	5:00	6:00	7:00	8:00	9:00	10:00	11:00	MIDNIGHT
2:00	3:00	4:00	5:00	6:00	7:00	8:00	9:00	10:00	11:00	MIDNIGHT	1:00
3:00	4:00	5:00	6:00	7:00	8:00	9:00	10:00	11:00	MIDNIGHT	1:00	2:00
4:00	5:00	6:00	7:00	8:00	9:00	10:00	11:00	MIDNIGHT	1:00	2:00	3:00
5:00	6:00	7:00	8:00	9:00	10:00	11:00	MIDNIGHT	1:00	2:00	3:00	4:00
6:00	7:00	8:00	9:00	10:00	11:00	MIDNIGHT	1:00	2:00	3:00	4:00	5:00
7:00	8:00	9:00	10:00	11:00	MIDNIGHT	1:00	2:00	3:00	4:00	5:00	6:00
8:00	9:00	10:00	11:00	MIDNIGHT	1:00	2:00	3:00	4:00	5:00	6:00	7:00
9:00	10:00	11:00	MIDNIGHT	1:00	2:00	3:00	4:00	5:00	6:00	7:00	8:00
10:00	11:00	MIDNIGHT	1:00	2:00	3:00	4:00	5:00	6:00	7:00	8:00	9:00

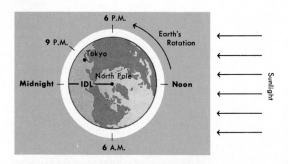

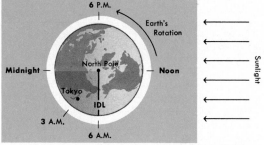

WORLD BOOK diagram

The Time and Date at any place on the earth change as the earth rotates on its axis in relation to the sun. When the International Date Line (IDL) is on the opposite side of the earth from the sun, *top diagram*, it is midnight there and 9 P.M. in Tokyo. At this instant, every place on the earth has the same date. Six hours later, *bottom diagram*, as the earth continues to rotate, it is 6 A.M. at the IDL. A new day, *shown in red*, has begun in the area between the IDL and midnight. Now the time in Tokyo is 3 A.M.

by establishing *railroad time* along sections of their routes. But in 1883, there were still about 100 different railroad times. That year, all the railroads divided the United States into four standard time zones.

Each zone is centered on a meridian of longitude 15° apart. In the United States and Canada, the Eastern Time Zone is centered on the 75° west meridian, and the Central Time Zone on the 90° west meridian. The Mountain Time Zone is centered on the 105° west meridian, and the Pacific Time Zone on the 120° west meridian.

The central meridians of the other U.S. and Canadian time zones are 60° west for the Atlantic Time Zone, 135° west for the Yukon Time Zone, and 150° west for the Alaska-Hawaii Time Zone. Western Alaska uses Bering Standard Time, which is centered on the 165° west meridian.

Worldwide Time Zones were established in 1884. The meridian of longitude passing through the Greenwich Observatory in England was chosen as the starting point for the world's time zones. The Greenwich meridian is often called the *prime meridian*. The mean solar time at Greenwich is called *Greenwich Mean Time* (GMT) or *Greenwich Civil Time* (GCT). Astronomers call it *Universal Time* (UT).

An international conference in 1884 set up 12 time zones west of Greenwich and 12 to the east. These zones divide the world into 23 full zones and two half zones. The 12th zone east and the 12th zone west are each half a zone wide. They lie next to each other and are separated by an imaginary line called the *Interna-

tional Date Line (IDL). The IDL is halfway around the world from Greenwich. A traveler crossing this line while headed west, toward China, loses a day. If he crosses it traveling eastward, he gains a day.

A few places do not use standard time zones. For example, the polar regions have weeks of sunlight or darkness. These regions use GMT.

Scientific Ideas About Time

Physical Time. Scientists think of time as a fundamental quantity that can be measured. Other fundamental quantities include length and mass. The noted physicist Albert Einstein realized that measurements of these quantities are affected by *relative motion* (motion between two objects). Because of his work, time became popularly known as the *fourth dimension*. See RELATIVITY (Special Theory); FOURTH DIMENSION.

Many physicists have considered the possibility that, under certain circumstances, time might flow backwards. But experiments have not supported this idea. Some scientists are considering whether time might have more than one dimension.

Biological Time. The activities of many plants and animals are timed to the cycle of day and night. These natural rhythms are called *circadian rhythms*. The most obvious example is the sleep cycle.

Many plants and animals are sensitive to other natural time cycles. Certain plants do not start their next step of growth until daylight each day lasts a certain time. Some sea animals time their activities to the changing tides. These creatures even seem to know such times away from their home waters.

Geological Time. Geologists have found clues in the earth's crust that indicate how many billions of years ago it was formed. One of these indicators is the element uranium. Uranium changes slowly into the element lead by means of radioactive decay. By measuring the amount of lead in a sample of uranium ore, scientists can estimate when the rock was formed.

A second clue to geological time is radioactive carbon. This form of carbon is absorbed by every living plant and animal. The rate of the carbon's decay can help a geologist estimate how long ago the plant or animal died. See RADIOCARBON.   ERIC D. CARLSON

Related Articles. See CALENDAR and CLOCK with their lists of Related Articles. Other Related Articles include:

Biological Clock	Ship (Nautical Terms [Ship's
Daylight Saving	Bell])
Greenwich Meridian	Sidereal Time
International Date Line	Standard Time
Meridian	Time Capsule
Naval Observatory	Weights and Measures
Radiogeology	

TIME AND MOTION STUDY. See TAYLOR, F. W.

TIME BILL. See BILL OF EXCHANGE.

TIME CAPSULE is a sealed receptacle containing items to give future ages a record of a particular civilization. A huge time capsule was placed under the administration building of Oglethorpe College (now Oglethorpe University) in Atlanta, Ga., in 1940. It is not to be opened until A.D. 8113. It contains microfilms, miniature models, and motion pictures dealing with all phases of life. The vault's location has been recorded in libraries, universities, and temples in various countries. Time capsules were also buried at the New York World's fairs of 1939-1940 and 1964-1965.

TIME LOCK. This type of combination lock cannot be opened before a certain hour to which the lock has been set. There are two general types of time locks. The first kind is used mainly in bank vaults. This lock is set to a certain hour. At that hour, but at no other time, the lock can be opened by dialing the combination.

The second type of time lock is called a time-recording lock. It has several keys. When the lock is opened, it registers the number of the key and the time that the lock was opened.   E. A. FESSENDEN

TIME ZONE. See TIME (Time Zones; map).

TIMED-RELEASE MEDICINE. See MICROENCAPSULATION.

TIMES SQUARE. See NEW YORK CITY (Manhattan; picture: Times Square in the 1930's).

TIMOR is an island in Southeast Asia. For location, see ASIA (political map). Timor covers 11,965 square miles (30,990 square kilometers) and has a population of about 1,356,486.

The western half of Timor has been part of Indonesia since that country was formed in 1949. The eastern half became a territory of Portugal in the 1500's. In 1975, Timorese people there demanded independence from Portugal. Fighting broke out among groups of Timorese who wanted to control the territory, and the Portuguese rulers left eastern Timor. In 1976, Indonesia claimed eastern Timor and sent troops there. Since then, fighting has occurred off and on between the troops and Timorese guerrillas. The fighting caused a sharp decline in farm production. Food shortages resulted, and many people in eastern Timor died from starvation or suffered from malnutrition.   JUSTUS M. VAN DER KROEF

TIMOTHY was one of the friends of Saint Paul. He was probably born in Lystra, in Asia Minor. His father was Greek and his mother was Jewish (Acts 16:1, II Timothy 1:5). He is thought to have converted to Christianity when Paul made his first missionary journey and talked with him. Timothy joined Paul on his second journey and is said to have been his trusted friend and companion until Paul's death. Later, he took Paul's place as bishop of the church at Ephesus. It is believed he died as a martyr, about A.D. 100.

The First and Second Epistles to Timothy and the Epistle to Titus are known as the Pastoral Epistles. This is because they contain advice to pastors concerning church government, church officers, teaching, and Christian faithfulness and endurance. Critics debate whether or not Paul wrote these epistles. Some believe that a later author wrote them, using Paul's ideas. The epistles may have been written between A.D. 90 and 110, or even later.   FREDERICK C. GRANT

TIMOTHY is a valuable grass crop that farmers raise for hay. It ranks as the most important hay grass cultivated in North America. Timothy is widely grown in the United States and Canada. The plant was named in honor of Timothy Hanson, who is said to have introduced the grass into the Carolinas about 1720. It is also called *herd's-grass*. The English call it *cat's-tail*.

Timothy is a perennial, cool-season plant. It grows in tufts 1½ to 3½ feet (46 to 107 centimeters) high. The slender stems bear round spikes of tiny, tightly packed flowers. Timothy is often grown in the United States and Canada in rotation with oats and other grains.

Timothy usually does not last long when cattle or other animals graze on it continually. It is not considered a satisfactory pasture grass unless it is mixed with hardier grasses. Most timothy is harvested as hay.

New York ranks as the leading state in the production of timothy hay, and Minnesota leads in the production of commercial timothy seed. Canada produces large amounts of both hay and seed.

Scientific Classification. Timothy is a member of the grass family, *Gramineae*. It is classified as genus *Phleum*, species *P. pratense.*   ROY G. WIGGANS

See also GRASS (with picture).

TIMPANI. See DRUM.

TIMPANOGOS CAVE NATIONAL MONUMENT is in northern Utah. It contains limestone caverns with hundreds of stalactites, stalagmites, and helictites in varied colors. The cavern has passageways that lead back into Mount Timpanogos, highest peak in the Wasatch Range. The monument was established in 1922. For area, see NATIONAL PARK SYSTEM (table: National Monuments).

TIMUR THE LAME. See TAMERLANE.

TIN is a white metallic element that people have used since ancient times. The earliest known use of tin occurred about 3500 B.C. in the city of Ur in southern Mesopotamia (now Iraq). The people of Ur made articles from bronze, an alloy of tin and copper. Today, tin is used chiefly in the production of *tin plate*. Tin plate consists of steel coated on both sides with an extremely thin film of tin. Most tin plate is made into tin cans for packaging food and other products.

Tin has the chemical symbol Sn. Its atomic number is 50, and its atomic weight is 118.69. At 20° C, tin has a density of 7.29 grams per cubic centimeter (see DENSITY). The difference between its melting point, 231.9° C, and its boiling point, 2270° C, is one of the widest of any metal. Tin is also very *malleable*—that is, it can easily be formed into complex shapes. These and other properties of tin enable it to be used in the manufacture of an extremely wide variety of products.

Uses. The coating on tin cans protects the steel in the cans from rust and provides an attractive ap-

How Tin Is Used

Tin's unusual chemical and physical properties enable it to be used in a wide variety of products for the home and industry.
WORLD BOOK illustration by David Cunningham

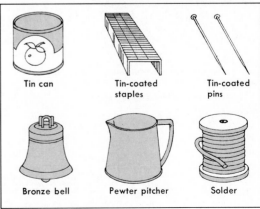

Tin can

Tin-coated staples

Tin-coated pins

Bronze bell

Pewter pitcher

Solder

TIN

Ewing Galloway

Tin Ore from an open-pit mine in Zaire rides up a 300-foot (91-meter) conveyor belt to a plant where the ore is crushed.

pearance. Tin also prevents the weak acids in food from damaging the inside of the cans. See TIN CAN.

Tin coatings also protect many other items. Most paper clips, safety pins, straight pins, and staples are made of steel or brass coated with tin. Many food-preparation containers and utensils have tin coatings.

The second most important use of tin is in *solders*, which are alloys used to join metal surfaces. Solders made primarily of tin and lead are called *soft solders* and melt at relatively low temperatures. Other important

Leading Tin-Mining Countries*

Tons of tin concentrates mined in 1977

Malaysia
64,710 short tons (58,700 metric tons)

Bolivia
33,950 short tons (30,800 metric tons)

Indonesia
27,670 short tons (25,100 metric tons)

Thailand
26,680 short tons (24,200 metric tons)

Australia
11,800 short tons (10,700 metric tons)

Brazil
7,060 short tons (6,400 metric tons)

Great Britain
4,300 short tons (3,900 metric tons)

*The International Tin Council does not report production for China and Russia. *Minerals Yearbook, 1977*, U.S. Bureau of Mines, estimates output for Russia at 36,400 short tons (33,000 metric tons) and for China at 22,000 short tons (20,000 metric tons).
Source: International Tin Council, London, in *Statistical Yearbook, 1978*, UN.

tin alloys include bronze and pewter. See SOLDER; BRONZE; PEWTER.

The malleability of tin enables manufacturers to make tin into extremely thin foil. One use for such foil is as a moistureproof wrapping. *Terneplate* is iron coated with an alloy of lead and tin. Sheets or strips of terneplate are used for roofing and in making such products as fuel tanks and fire extinguishers.

Manufacturers improve the properties of various metals by adding small amounts of tin. For example, cast iron that contains only 0.1 per cent tin is much more durable and easier to work with than ordinary cast iron. Many other products, including bearings, dental fillings, and printing alloys, also contain small amounts of tin, which improves their properties.

Tin combines with other elements to form a great number of useful compounds. Many toothpastes contain *stannous fluoride*, which is a compound of tin and fluorine that helps prevent tooth decay. Certain compounds that contain tin and carbon are used as pesticides.

Where Tin Is Found. Tin makes up only about 0.001 per cent of the earth's crust. As a result, the amount of tin mined annually is very small compared with other common metals. Most known deposits of tin are in the Southern Hemisphere. The United States has none large enough to mine.

The principal tin ore is a compound of tin and oxygen called *cassiterite* (see CASSITERITE). Some tin ores contain sulfur and small amounts of such other metals as copper, iron, and lead. Tin deposits sometimes occur as narrow veins that run through granite. Most tin ore, however, is found in plains, where flowing water has deposited bits of eroded granite and ore.

Malaysia is the world's leading producer of tin. Other important tin-producing countries include Australia, Bolivia, Brazil, China, Great Britain, Indonesia, Nigeria, Russia, Thailand, and Zaire.

Refining Tin. Processors produce tin by heating cassiterite with coal and limestone in a special furnace. After this process, called *smelting*, the processors refine the tin—usually to a purity of 99.8 per cent. For details on refining, see METALLURGY (Extractive Metallurgy). Most pure tin is cast into *ingots* (bars) that weigh about 100 pounds (45 kilograms).   PAUL E. DAVIS

See also GEORGE TOWN.

TIN CAN is a container used for packaging, transporting, and marketing hundreds of food and nonfood items for home and industry. Most tin cans are made of steel covered with a thin coat of tin. But millions of cans contain no tin at all and many are made entirely of aluminum. The first tin cans were handmade and sealed with solder. Today, manufacturers make and seal them on a series of machines called a *can line* that produce more than 500 a minute. The shape, size, and construction of cans differ to meet the specific need of the product they contain. But cylindrical cans are most commonly used. Many tin cans have enamel on the inside to prevent discoloration of the food. Perishable foods are preserved by heating the sealed can. In 1963, an Ohio man received a patent on a "tab-opening" tin can. The user opens the can by pulling off a strip of aluminum on top. In the 1960's, steel companies began making *thin tin* for tin cans. It is thinner and lighter than the usual tin plate used in tin cans. The U.S. produces over 62 billion tin cans a year. See also CANNING (Tin Cans). WILLIAM C. STOLK

TIN PAN ALLEY. See POPULAR MUSIC (The 1900's).

TINBERGEN, JAN (1903-   ), a Dutch economist, shared the first Nobel prize in economics with Ragnar Frisch of Norway in 1969. Tinbergen and Frisch received the award for their work on the development of mathematical models used in *econometrics* (mathematical analysis of economic activity).

Tinbergen was born in The Hague and graduated from the University of Leiden. In 1933, he became a professor at the Netherlands School of Economics in Rotterdam. From 1936 to 1938, Tinbergen worked with the League of Nations and developed the first econometric model of a national economy. He also served with the Dutch government's Central Bureau of Statistics and its Central Planning Bureau. In 1955, Tinbergen became an adviser to other governments and international organizations. He became chairman of the United Nations Committee for Development Planning in 1965. LEONARD S. SILK

TINBERGEN, NIKOLAAS (1907-   ), is a Dutch-born zoologist who studies how the behavior of animals is adapted to their environment. He also investigates the evolution of this behavior over millions of years by comparing the actions of various species. Tinbergen shared the 1973 Nobel prize for physiology or medicine with Austrian naturalists Konrad Lorenz and Karl von Frisch. They received the award for their studies of animal behavior. Tinbergen has worked with birds, butterflies, fish, wasps, and other animals in their natural surroundings. His best-known research concerns the social behavior of gulls.

Tinbergen, the brother of the economist Jan Tinbergen, was born in The Hague. He earned a doctorate from Leiden University in The Netherlands in 1932. Tinbergen joined the faculty of Oxford University in England in 1949 and became a British citizen in 1955.

Tinbergen's *The Study of Instinct* (1951) summarized scientific knowledge of animal behavior. He also wrote *The Herring Gull's World* (1953) and *Curious Naturalists* (1958). JOHN A. WIENS

TINCTURE. See HERALDRY.

TINIAN, *TEE nee AHN,* or *TIN ih AN,* is an island in the Mariana group in the western Pacific Ocean. It lies about 1,500 miles (2,410 kilometers) southeast of Tokyo. Tinian covers about 41 square miles (106 square kilometers). High cliffs line the coast. The interior is flat. Tinian is governed by the United States as part of the United Nations Pacific Islands Trust Territory. The Spanish discovered Tinian in 1521 and turned it into a game preserve. Germany bought Tinian from Spain in 1899. The Japanese captured it during World War I, and the island was colonized by nearly 15,000 Japanese. U.S. troops captured Tinian during World War II. The airplanes that dropped atomic bombs on Japan took off from Tinian. It has about 700 persons. See also MARIANA ISLANDS. EDWIN H. BRYAN, JR.

TINT. See COLOR (The Color Triangle).

TINTORETTO, *tihn tuh REH toh* (1518-1594), was a Venetian painter during the late Italian Renaissance. He became a leading artist of the period for the churches and wealthy families of Venice.

Tintoretto created works noted for their dramatic action. His paintings show the influence of the rich colors used by Titian and the vigorous, muscular forms drawn by Michelangelo. Tintoretto achieved a unique style through exaggeration. He sometimes distorted the proportions of his figures for dramatic effect. The figures move wildly through deep space and changing light.

Tintoretto planned his compositions by placing wax or clay figures in a box—like actors on the stage of a theater—and using candles for lighting effects. He studied these arrangements and drew sketches before beginning to paint.

The theatrical character of Tintoretto's paintings can be seen in one of his most famous works, *Saint Mark Rescuing a Slave* (1548), which appears in the PAINTING article. The figures bend, gesture, and turn. Tintoretto achieved dramatic contrast by spotlighting some forms with intense color and painting others in softer tones and shadows.

Tintoretto's real name was Jacopo Robusti. He was nicknamed *Il Tintoretto,* which means *the little dyer,* because his father was a dyer. Scholars believe Tintoretto taught himself to paint. He opened his first studio at the age of 21. ROBERT F. REIFF

See also MOSES (picture).

TIP AND TIPPING. A tip, or gratuity, is a sum of money given to people for services received from them. The amount of a tip varies. It may be a percentage of the amount of a bill, as in tips given to waiters and barbers. But a tip is also paid when no bill is rendered, as to coatroom attendants.

Tipping was originally a sign of liberality by a wealthy person. It grew into a custom of paying extra to ensure good service, and has developed into a complicated system. Some persons earn more income from tips than from regular salary.

TIPI. See TEPEE.

TIPPECANOE, BATTLE OF. See INDIAN WARS (Other Midwestern Conflicts).

"TIPPECANOE AND TYLER TOO." See HARRISON, WILLIAM HENRY.

TIPPERARY (pop. 4,631) is a town in southern Ireland. It lies on the Ara River, in an area that has many dairy farms. For location, see IRELAND (map).

Tipperary serves as a market town and a processing center for dairy products. It is also a shopping center for the people of the area.

Tipperary was founded in the late 1100's. It developed as a small town that surrounded a castle built by Prince John (later King John) of England. The name Tipperary is known in many parts of the world because of the song "It's a Long, Long Way to Tipperary." This tune was a favorite marching song of Allied troops during World War I (1914-1918). DESMOND A. GILLMOR

TIPPLE. See WEST VIRGINIA (picture: Coal Mining).

TIRANË, *tee RAH nuh* (pop. 175,000), is the capital of Albania. It is also spelled TIRANA. It lies about 20 miles (32 kilometers) from the Adriatic Sea (see ALBANIA [map]). The city was founded in the early 1600's. Most of the people are Muslims, and part of Tiranë looks like an ancient Islamic city. Many buildings were built after 1920 when Tiranë became the capital. Since 1957, it has had a university and several research institutes. Tiranë has food processing, soap making, and textile industries. WAYNE S. VUCINICH

Goodyear Tire & Rubber Co.

Many Types of Tires are made for today's automobiles. The side view of a standard bias belted tire is shown above with the front views of, *left to right,* a standard bias belted tire, a radial ply tire, a snow tire, and a low profile tire. Tread patterns differ for various types of tires.

TIRE is a covering for the outer rim of a wheel. Most tires are made of rubber and are *pneumatic* (filled with compressed air). They are used on airplanes, automobiles, bicycles, buses, motorcycles, tractors, trucks, and other kinds of vehicles. Some rubber tires, such as those used on many wagons and wheelbarrows, are solid rubber.

The main feature of rubber tires is their ability to absorb the shock and strain created by bumps in the road. Tires help provide a comfortable ride and help protect many kinds of cargoes. The air in a rubber tire supports the weight of a vehicle.

Another important feature of rubber tires is their ability to grip the road. The face of a tire, called the *tread,* has many deep grooves. These grooves, and many smaller grooves called *sipes,* make up the *tread pattern.* The tread provides the traction that enables the wheels to grip the road. The tire body consists of the rubber *side walls* (sides) and the *casing.* The casing is made up of

two or more layers of rubberized cord fabric. Each layer is called a *ply.*

How Tires Are Made

Preliminary Operations. Before an automobile tire can be manufactured, several operations must be performed. They include mixing the rubber with sulfur and other chemicals, coating cord fabric with rubber, and cutting the rubberized fabric into strips. All these operations are performed by machines.

A machine called a *Banbury machine* mixes the rubber with the chemicals. The sulfur and other chemicals strengthen the rubber and increase its resistance to wear. The rubber comes from the machine in the form of sheets.

Cord fabric is made of nylon, polyester, or rayon. A *calendering machine* coats it with the rubber sheeting. The triple rollers of this machine squeeze the cords and the rubber together, producing a rubberized fabric. A

Parts of a Tire

The parts of a tire, shown below in cross-section, are assembled by hand, one by one. Starting with the inner liner, a worker *builds* (makes) the tire on a slowly turning *drum* (roller). Later, the process of *vulcanization* shapes the tire, seals the parts together, and molds the tread pattern of grooves and sipes into the tread.

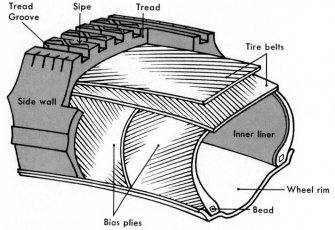

Tread Groove
Sipe
Tread
Tire belts
Side wall
Inner liner
Wheel rim
Bead
Bias plies

Tire Belts improve traction by putting as much tread as possible on the road, as shown in the diagram below. Belted tires eliminate the stretching that occurs in nonbelted tires at high speeds or on turns.

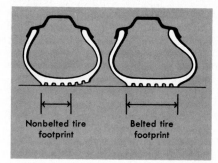

Nonbelted tire footprint

Belted tire footprint

cutting machine then slices the rubberized cord fabric into strips.

Building a Tire. A tire is *built* (made) by hand on a slowly rotating roller called a *drum*. The drum has the same diameter as the wheel on which the tire will be used. As the drum turns, a worker called a *tire builder* wraps an *inner liner* around the drum. The inner liner consists of a band of soft rubber that makes the casing airtight.

The tire builder then wraps the rubberized cord fabric around the drum, ply by ply. Most automobile tires have two plies and two *belts* of fabric between the plies and the tread. The belts are made of steel; such manufactured fibers as aramid, fiberglass, or rayon; or some other material that resists stretching.

After putting on the plies, the tire builder adds two *beads*. Each bead consists of several steel wire strands that have been wound together into a hoop and covered with hard rubber. A bead is put on the outside of the tire on each side. It is inserted at the point where the tire will come into contact with the rim of the wheel. The two ends of each ply are wrapped around the bead, securing the bead to the tire. The beads, in turn, clamp the tire to the rim of the wheel when the tire is filled with air.

Next, the builder adds the side walls, the belts, and the tread. The various parts of the tire are then united by a set of rollers in a process called *stitching*.

The *green* (uncured) tire is now ready to be *vulcanized*. The vulcanization process makes a rubber product strong, hard, and elastic. The tire is taken off the drum and placed in a *curing press*. The press contains a large air bag and a mold that has the sipes and large grooves of the desired tread pattern in it. The press operates like a giant waffle iron. It is closed, heat is applied, and the air bag is filled with steam. The steam presses the tire against the mold. The air bag and the mold squeeze and press the tire into its final shape, complete with tread. See RUBBER (Vulcanization).

Retreading Tires. After the original tread pattern has worn down, a tire—if it is in good condition—can be *retreaded*, or *recapped*. First, a machine rubs away the old tread. Then a worker applies new tread rubber and puts the tire into a mold. The new tread and tread pattern are then vulcanized to the old tire.

Types of Tires and Tread Patterns

There are three basic kinds of automobile tires: (1) *bias;* (2) *bias belted;* and (3) *radial,* or *radial-ply.*

Bias Tires are built with the cord fabric running diagonally—that is, on the bias—from one rim to the other. Each ply is added so that its cords run at an angle opposite to the angle of the cords below it.

As a vehicle moves, the plies of its tires rub against each other and against the tread in an action called *flexing and squirming.* This action produces inner heat, one of the major causes of tire wear. Extreme heat can separate the tread or split the plies.

Bias Belted Tires are made in the same way as bias tires, but belts are placed between the plies and the tread. The belts help prevent punctures and fight tread squirm.

Radial Tires are built with the cord fabric running straight across the tire from one rim to the other. All radial tires are belted. The combination of radial ply and belting produces a tire that has longer tread life than either bias or bias belted tires. Radial tires give longer wear because they have less flex and squirm than bias ply tires.

Low Profile Tires were used on many high-performance cars of the 1970's. They are available as bias, bias belted, or radial tires. Low profile tires look pudgier than regular tires. They are wider (from side wall to side wall) than they are high (from tread to wheel rim). Low profile tires put more tread into contact with the road than do regular bias, bias belted, or radial tires. This additional tread creates a wider *footprint* (track), which provides greater traction. The added traction can give

Tire Size Comparison The size of a car's tires depends on the type and weight of the vehicle as well as the size of its wheels. Almost all new automobiles have standard tires. Some cars, including many high-performance cars of the 1970's, use low profile or ultra-low profile tires.

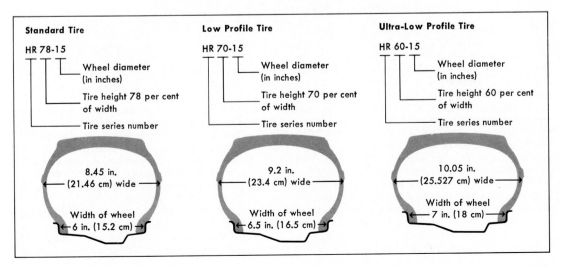

Standard Tire	Low Profile Tire	Ultra-Low Profile Tire
HR 78-15	HR 70-15	HR 60-15
Wheel diameter (in inches)	Wheel diameter (in inches)	Wheel diameter (in inches)
Tire height 78 per cent of width	Tire height 70 per cent of width	Tire height 60 per cent of width
Tire series number	Tire series number	Tire series number
8.45 in. (21.46 cm) wide	9.2 in. (23.4 cm) wide	10.05 in. (25.527 cm) wide
Width of wheel 6 in. (15.2 cm)	Width of wheel 6.5 in. (16.5 cm)	Width of wheel 7 in. (18 cm)

a driver more control of a car at high speeds and around curves than standard tires give.

Tire Tread Patterns are designed for a variety of special purposes. For example, *snow tires* have a tread with extra-deep grooves. This tread bites into snow and mud, providing exceptional traction. A snow tire is not so effective on ice and hard-packed snow, because even the deep grooves cannot gain traction. *Studded snow tires* have metal spikes called *studs*, which stick out of the tire like small, sharp fingernails. They dig into ice, providing added traction. Some states of the United States have banned these tires because studies have shown that studs can damage road surfaces. In the 1970's, manufacturers developed snow tires that get good traction without studs. They introduced other tires designed for use in any kind of weather. Special tread patterns are also made for the tires of racing cars, trucks, and various kinds of construction, farming, and military vehicles.

History

The pneumatic tire was invented in 1845 by Robert W. Thomson, a Scottish engineer. At that time, most vehicles had wooden wheels and steel tires. The steel tires preserved the wood and wore well. Thomson's tires gave a smoother ride but were not strong enough. In 1870, the first solid rubber tires appeared in England. They were used on automobiles, bicycles, and buggies.

John B. Dunlop, a Scottish veterinarian, improved on Thomson's invention in 1888. Dunlop developed air-filled rubber tubes for his son's tricycle. These pneumatic tires provided a smoother ride and made pedaling easier than tires of solid rubber. Bike manufacturers in Europe and the United States soon began to use them.

Pneumatic tires appeared on automobiles in 1895. Like bicycle tires, they were single air-filled tubes. But as automobiles became heavier and were driven faster, the single tube tires could not hold enough air pressure for more than a short time. In the early 1900's, two-part tires were developed. They consisted of a casing and an *inner tube*, a flexible rubber tube that fit inside the casing and held the air. The inner tube held from 55 to 75 pounds per square inch (3.9 to 5.3 kilograms per square centimeter) of air pressure. These tires were called *high-pressure tires*.

Then tire manufacturers learned that less air in the tires would not only support the weight of an automobile, but also add comfort to the ride. In 1922, *low-pressure tires*, or *balloon tires*, were introduced. They held from 30 to 32 pounds per square inch (2.1 to 2.2 kilograms per square centimeter) of air pressure.

The tubeless tire was introduced in 1948. Its casing was made airtight by an inner liner. A tubeless tire seals itself to the rim of a wheel by a band of soft rubber on the inner surface of the tire. Since 1954, most new cars have been equipped with tubeless tires. In 1966, the U.S. Congress passed the National Traffic and Motor Vehicle Safety Act. The act called for a system of grading automobile tires according to their heat resistance, traction, and tread wear qualities. The government required manufacturers to begin labeling tires with performance grades in 1979.

In the 1970's, manufacturers stepped up research into the development of new types of tires that would eliminate the need for spare tires in automobiles. The companies developed thin, "temporary use" spare tires that are much lighter than standard tires and take up less space in the trunk of a car. They also introduced tires that would seal themselves if punctured and experimented with tires that would work even when flat.

Critically reviewed by THE GOODYEAR TIRE & RUBBER COMPANY

See also DUNLOP, JOHN B.; FIRESTONE, HARVEY S.; GOODYEAR, CHARLES; RUBBER.

TIROL, another name for TYROL. See TYROL.

TIROS. See SPACE TRAVEL (Artificial Satellites).

TIRPITZ, *TIHR pihts,* **ALFRED VON** (1849-1930), a German statesman and naval officer, was active in building up the German Navy. He was the first naval commander to use torpedo boats in great numbers. From 1897 to 1916, Tirpitz was secretary of state for naval affairs. He became a grand admiral in 1911. Tirpitz was born in Ebenhausen.   GABRIEL A. ALMOND

TIRSO DE MOLINA is the pen name of GABRIEL TÉLLEZ (1584-1648), a Spanish playwright. His masterpiece *The Deceiver of Seville* (1630) introduced the legend of Don Juan in literature (see DON JUAN). Tirso probably wrote nearly 400 plays, of which 86 survive. They include historical and religious dramas, light comedies about palace society, and romantic tragedies. Tirso had a good understanding of psychology and showed greater skill in creating characters than any other Spanish playwright of his time. He also wrote light-hearted tales, *The Gardens of Toledo* (1624); and the more serious *Pleasure with Profit* (1635), a collection of stories, short plays, and verse. Tirso was born in Madrid. He was a friar and an important official in the Order of Mercy. PETER G. EARLE

TISELIUS, ARNE. See NOBEL PRIZES (table: Nobel Prizes for Chemistry—1948).

TISHAH B'AB, *TIHSH ah buh AHV,* is a Jewish fast day on the ninth day of the Hebrew month of Ab. On that day, the Babylonians destroyed the First Temple in Jerusalem in 587 B.C.; the Romans destroyed the Second Temple in A.D. 70; and the Romans crushed a Jewish revolt in 135. Jews observe partial mourning and hold no weddings or celebrations for three weeks before Tishah B'Ab. Many Jews fast throughout the day. The Book of Lamentations is recited in the synagogue.   LEONARD C. MISHKIN

TISIPHONE. See FURIES.

TISQUANTUM. See SQUANTO.

TISSUE is a group of similar cells that work together to perform a particular function in an organism. Groups of tissues, in turn, form the organs of animals and plants.

Animal Tissues are generally divided into four groups: (1) connective tissue, (2) epithelium, (3) muscle, and (4) nervous tissue.

Connective Tissue is composed of cells and an abundant *intercellular material*. In most connective tissue, the intercellular material consists of fibers and a transparent, jellylike *ground substance*. Some connective tissues surround and connect other tissues and organs. Bone and cartilage are connective tissues that support and protect the body. Blood and lymph are connective tissues in which the intercellular material is a fluid.

Epithelium consists of tightly packed cells. The two main types of epithelium are membranes and glands. Epithelial membranes form the outer layer of the skin. They also line such internal body surfaces as those of the digestive tract and of the blood vessels. Glands produce secretions, such as hormones and perspiration.

Muscle is made up of cells that alternately contract and relax. These actions enable the muscles to move parts of the body and to move substances through the body.

Nervous Tissue consists of highly specialized cells that conduct nerve impulses throughout. Nervous tissue enables the body to coordinate many of its functions and to respond to a wide variety of stimuli.

Plant Tissues. The cells of simple plants, such as algae and fungi, are not organized into tissues. Other plants have two major types of tissues, *meristematic* and *permanent*. Meristematic tissues consist of immature cells that divide continuously. The growing tips of roots and shoots are composed of meristematic tissue. Permanent tissues consist of mature cells that have specialized functions. Types of permanent tissues include *epidermis*, *parenchyma*, *xylem*, and *phloem*. Epidermis forms a plant's protective outer covering, and parenchyma stores food. Xylem conducts water from the roots to other parts of a plant, and phloem transports food throughout the plant.   CHARLES G. CRISPENS, JR.

Related Articles in WORLD BOOK include:

Connective Tissue	Life (diagram:	Muscle
Epithelium	Structural Units)	Nervous
Histology	Membrane	System

TISSUE CULTURE is the process of growing plant and animal cells away from the main part of the body. See CARREL, ALEXIS.

TISSUE TRANSPLANT is any tissue or organ transferred from one part of the body to another, or to another person's body. Transplanted tissues and organs replace diseased, damaged, or destroyed body parts. Tissues include whole blood, blood vessels, bones, and corneas. Such major organs as hearts, kidneys, livers, lungs, and pancreases are also transplanted.

Doctors successfully transplant some kinds of tissues fairly often. For example, they use grafts of healthy skin to replace skin destroyed by extensive burns. They remove diseased or damaged corneas from eyes and put healthy ones in their place. Perhaps the best known type of transplant is the blood transfusion.

Doctors also have transplanted such major organs as kidneys and livers from one person's body to another. Such transplants often fail after months or years. Special mechanisms in the body produce *antibodies*, which destroy all strange cells that enter the body. Antibodies are one of the body's most important defenses against germs. Drugs and X rays are used to stop production of antibodies when organs are transplanted. But this procedure deprives the body of its chief means for fighting infection. Scientists are looking for ways to make the body accept transplanted cells and still protect itself against infection. The most successful transplants of whole organs are those between identical twins. The cells of identical twins are so similar that antibodies do not form.

Large-scale research on transplantation started during the late 1940's. Sir Macfarlane Burnet, an Australian scientist, suggested that such transplants were possible. Burnet and Peter B. Medawar, a British scientist, shared the 1960 Nobel prize in physiology or medicine for their work in transplant immunology. In 1954, doctors at Peter Bent Brigham Hospital in Boston performed the

Painting by Willy Stoewer, United Press Int.

The "Unsinkable" *Titanic* was believed to be the safest ship afloat. It sank on its first voyage after striking an iceberg.

first successful kidney transplant. In 1959, doctors at the same hospital performed the first successful kidney transplant between nonidentical twins. A human heart was transplanted for the first time in 1967. A surgical team headed by Christiaan N. Barnard performed the heart transplant at Groote Schuur Hospital in South Africa (see HEART [Performing Heart Transplants]).   JOHN P. MERRILL

Related Articles in WORLD BOOK include:

Barnard, Chris-	Burnet, Sir	Lymphatic System
tiaan N.	Macfarlane	(Rejection of Trans-
Blood	Eye Bank	planted Tissue)
Transfusion	Immunity	Skin Grafting
Bone Bank		

TITAN, a missile. See SPACE TRAVEL (Launch Vehicles); a satellite of Saturn. See SATURN (planet).

TITANIA. See SHAKESPEARE, WILLIAM (*A Midsummer Night's Dream*).

TITANIA, a gem. See TITANIUM.

TITANIC, *ty TAN ihk*, was a British steamer of the White Star line. On the night of April 14-15, 1912, during its first trip from England to New York City, it struck an iceberg and sank. The tragedy occurred about 1,600 miles (2,570 kilometers) northeast of New York City.

The *Titanic* sighted the iceberg just before the crash, but too late to avoid it. Experts had considered the ship unsinkable, but the collision tore a 300-foot (91-meter) gash in its hull. The lifeboats held less than half of the approximately 2,200 persons, and took on mostly women and children. The ship sank in about 2½ hours. The liner *Carpathia* picked up 705 survivors.

The *Titanic* had been the largest ship in the world, 882.5 feet (269 meters) long, with a gross tonnage of 46,328. The British inquiry reported 1,490 dead, the British Board of Trade, 1,503, and a U.S. Senate investigating committee, 1,517.   WALTER LORD

TITANIFEROUS ORE, *TY tuh NIHF uhr uhs,* is an iron ore rich in the metal titanium. It is usually a black, granular mixture of the minerals ilmenite and magnetite. The ore is ground and the minerals are separated with magnets. Titanium is recovered from ilmenite and iron from magnetite.

See also ILMENITE; TITANIUM.

TITANIUM, *ty TAY nee uhm* (chemical symbol, Ti), is a lightweight, silver-gray metal. Its atomic number is 22, and its atomic weight is 47.90. The density of titanium lies between that of aluminum and stainless

TITANIUM

Titanium Metals Corporation of America

Titanium Resists Corrosion better than most metals. This column, made for distilling chemicals, contains 37 short tons (34 metric tons) of titanium.

steel. It melts at 1660° C (±10° C) and boils at 3287° C.

Titanium resists sea-water and sea-air corrosion or rust as well as platinum and better than stainless steel. Many highly corrosive acids and alkalies do not affect titanium. It is *ductile* (it can be drawn into wire). It also has a higher strength-weight ratio than steel. All these qualities make titanium a metal of great importance.

Uses. The first commercial use of titanium was as an oxide to substitute for white lead in paint. Titanium dioxide, or titanium combined with oxygen, is produced as a white pigment that has superior power to cover surfaces in painting. Titanium dioxide is also used in the manufacture of linoleum, rubber, textiles, paper, porcelain enamels, and welding rods. Barium titanate, a compound of barium and titanium, can be used in place of crystals in television and radar sets, microphones, and phonographs. The gem *titania* is made from crystals of titanium oxide. When cut and polished, titania is more brilliant than the diamond, though not quite so hard. Titanium tetrachloride, or titanium combined with chlorine, has been used for smoke screens, and is the starting point for making the metal.

Titanium metal serves as an important alloying element, because it unites with nearly every material except copper and aluminum. It is used principally as an alloy in iron. The armed forces use large amounts of titanium in aircraft and jet engines, because it is strong but light. It also withstands operating temperatures up to about 427° C (800° F.), which makes it useful in many types of machinery. Because of its superior qualities, titanium has a number of potential uses, such as armor plate and propeller blades for ships, steam-turbine blades, surgical instruments, and tools. The transportation industry would use large amounts of titanium in buses, railroad trains, trucks, and automobiles, if the price of titanium could be lowered enough to compete with the price of stainless steel.

Location of Deposits. Titanium ranks as the world's ninth most plentiful element. But the difficulty of processing the metal makes it expensive. Titanium is never found in a pure state. It usually occurs in ilmenite

or rutile. But it may be found in titaniferous magnetite, titanite, and iron (see ILMENITE; RUTILE; TITANIFEROUS ORE).

The leading titanium-producing countries are Australia, Brazil, Canada, Finland, Malaysia, Norway, and the United States. Russia also has large titanium deposits, but production figures are not available. Florida, Idaho, New Jersey, New York, and Virginia are the chief titanium-producing states. Quebec is the only Canadian province that produces the metal.

Discovery and Manufacture. Titanium was discovered by William Gregor of England in 1791, and named by Martin Klaproth of Germany in 1795. It was not until the 1930's, however, that a refining method adaptable to large-scale production was worked out by William Kroll of Luxembourg. The Du Pont Company first produced the metal commercially in 1948. At the present time, production remains low because of the difficulty and expense of separating titanium from the ores with which it is found. The United States manufactures most of the refined metal. Japan and Great Britain also manufacture titanium. Research is being conducted to increase its supply and lower its cost.   JOHN P. MAGOS

TITANS were the first gods in Greek mythology. Most of them represented—in human form—such natural phenomena as the earth, the sky, and the sun. Previously, the universe had existed in a state of emptiness called *Chaos*.

The first Titan was Gaea, the earth. She emerged from Chaos and gave birth to Uranus, the sky. She then married him. Gaea and Uranus had many offspring. The youngest and most important was Cronus, who married Rhea, his sister. Cronus deposed Uranus and became the king of the gods.

Rhea bore Cronus many children, but he swallowed them as soon as they were born to prevent one of them from overthrowing him. Rhea was determined to save Zeus, her youngest son. She tricked Cronus into swallowing a stone wrapped in baby clothes instead. Then she hid Zeus on the island of Crete.

After Zeus grew up, he tricked his father into vomiting up all the offspring. Zeus then led his brothers and sisters in a war against Cronus and overthrew him. Zeus banished Cronus and the Titans who had supported him to Tartarus, an underground region. The defeat of Cronus established Zeus as the supreme ruler of the universe and thus played an important role in the religion of the ancient Greeks.   C. SCOTT LITTLETON

See also MYTHOLOGY (Greek Mythology); ATLAS; CRONUS; PROMETHEUS; TARTARUS; URANUS; ZEUS.

TITHE. The word *tithe* comes from the Anglo-Saxon word *teotha*, which means a *tenth part*. The term usually means a tax of one-tenth laid on the profits of a piece of land. In the Bible, Moses stated the law of tithes to the Jews (Deut. 12: 6). But this law was not a forced tribute. In the Priestly Code (Lev. 27: 30), the tithe became a fixed due.

In the 500's, councils of the Catholic Church began to ordain the payment of taxes. In Charlemagne's time, such payment became state law. In England, tithes were demanded by Pope Adrian I from all lands except those belonging to the Church and the Crown. A *tithe rent* is still charged in a few parishes of the Church of England. In Quebec, Canada, the Roman Catholic Church is supported by tithes. Members of some

churches contribute a tenth of their income to the church.
WILLIAM F. McDONALD

TITHONUS. See AURORA.

TITIAN, *TIH shuhn* (1487?-1576), was a Venetian painter of the Italian Renaissance. During his long career, which lasted about 70 years, he became one of the most influential and successful painters in the history of art.

Titian's works include portraits and paintings of myths and religious scenes. He developed a style that strongly influenced European painting for more than 200 years. Titian used bright colors, applied his paint in bold brushstrokes, and made one color seem to blend into another. His style may be seen in *The Rape of Europa* (1562), which appears in color in the PAINTING article. This style of painting influenced many great artists, including El Greco, Rembrandt, and Peter Paul Rubens.

Titian painted portraits of royalty and aristocrats. He portrayed his subjects as elegant but spirited. Titian skillfully showed the human side of his subjects through facial expressions and gestures. The works of many great portrait painters, including Anton Van Dyck and Diego Velázquez, show his influence.

Titian was born in Pieve di Cadore, near Venice, Italy. His real name was Tiziano Vecellio. Titian moved to Venice as a boy to study painting. He was apprenticed to two artists, the brothers Gentile and Giovanni Bellini. Titian's early works show the influence both of the Bellinis and of his artist friend Giorgione.

About 1515, Titian began to produce masterpieces. Titian's success led most of Europe's leading art patrons to buy and pose for his paintings. His clients included

© Frick Collection, New York City

Titian's Portraits rank among his finest works. The dreamy *Man in a Red Cap* probably was completed in 1516, when Titian was first developing his mature style.

Holy Roman emperors Charles V and Ferdinand I, Pope Paul III, King Francis I of France, King Philip II of Spain, and many of the most important Italian nobles.
ROBERT F. REIFF

See also DRAWING (picture: A Pen-and-Ink Drawing); PAINTING (Venetian Painting).

TITICACA, LAKE. See LAKE TITICACA.

TITLE is a legal term that is often used to describe ownership of property. The term began with transfers of land. A history of the ownership of land is called a *chain of title.*

The term *title* is properly used to describe the way an owner obtains lawful possession of property. It usually refers to a legal document that describes the interest of the owner. Such documents include deeds to real property, a title to an automobile, the patent for an invention, or the copyright held by an author.

A title to property may be acquired in many ways. If a person buys property from another person, or receives it as a gift or through a will, the title is *derivative.* A title is *original* if the property is not obtained from someone else. For example, trappers may capture wild animals and make them their property. Title by *adverse possession* is a title acquired against the consent of the owner. It is obtained by wrongful entry and continuous possession for a time fixed by state law—10 years in most cases. Suppose, for example, that Jones farms Smith's land for over 10 years against Smith's consent, but Smith does not take legal action against Jones for using the land. Jones then has an original title by adverse possession. A title to land can be acquired by *letters patent.* This term refers to a title transferred from the United States government to a private citizen.
ROBERT E. SULLIVAN

See also ABSTRACT; DEED; TORRENS SYSTEM.

TITMOUSE is the name for any of a number of small, hardy birds that have long, soft feathers. Some of these birds are also known as *tits* or *tomtits.* Titmice live in nearly all parts of the world and are related to the nuthatches. Titmice are valuable because they destroy millions of the eggs and larvae of insects. The *chickadee* is the most common North American titmouse. A larger type, the *tufted titmouse,* lives in the eastern United States, south to the Gulf Coast and west to the Great Plains. It is gray, and has a high crest. It may repeat its call of "peto, peto, peto, peto," for hours. The *verdin,* or

Leonard Lee Rue, National Audubon Society

The Tufted Titmouse Has Soft, Fluffy Feathers.

237

goldtit, lives in the Southwest. The *bush tit* is found from Lower California to the Columbia River.

Scientific Classification. Titmice belong to the titmouse family, *Paridae*. The black-capped chickadee is genus *Parus*, species *P. atricapillus;* the tufted titmouse is *P. bicolor*. The verdin is *Auriparus flaviceps*, and the common bush tit is *Psaltriparus minimus.*   ARTHUR A. ALLEN

See also BIRD (picture: Birds of Forests and Woodlands); CHICKADEE.

TITO, *TEE toh,* **JOSIP BROZ** (1892-1980), established a Communist government in Yugoslavia after World War II, and then became the country's ruler. In 1948, he declared Yugoslavia's independence from Russian control. This act set an example that China and some Eastern European Communist nations later followed. Tito was also the first Communist leader to permit his people some economic and social freedom.

Early Life. Tito was born JOSIP BROZ, the son of a peasant family, in Kumrovec, Croatia. Croatia is now part of Yugoslavia, but then it was part of Austria-Hungary. Broz became a metalworker, then was drafted into the Austro-Hungarian Army in 1913. In 1915, during World War I, he was wounded and captured by Russian troops. In 1917, the Communists released him from prison after they had taken power in Russia. He joined the Communist Party.

In 1920, Broz returned to Yugoslavia, which had gained independence after World War I ended in 1918. He helped organize the Yugoslav Communist Party, but it was outlawed and Broz was sent to jail in 1928. He used the name *Tito* to confuse the police after his release in 1934. He later added *Tito* to his real name. He was secretary-general to the Yugoslav Communist Party from 1937 until 1966 when he became party president.

During World War II, Tito organized and led the *Partisans*, guerrillas who fought German troops occupying Yugoslavia. Another resistance group, the anti-Communist *Chetniks*, fought the Partisans, but lost. After the war, Tito ordered Chetnik leader, Draža Mihailovich, executed (see MIHAILOVICH, DRAŽA).

Yugoslav Leader. Tito set up a Communist government in Yugoslavia in 1945, and it was recognized by the United States, Great Britain, and Russia. Tito became prime minister and defense minister. But Russian efforts to control Yugoslavia led to a split between Stalin and Tito. Stalin expelled Yugoslavia from the Soviet bloc in 1948. Tito became the first independent Communist leader. Later, he became a spokesman for nations that refused to take sides in the Cold War.

But Tito kept tight control over the Yugoslav people, and tolerated no opposition. He had his close associate, Milovan Djilas, jailed for criticizing the government. In 1963, Tito made himself president for life. Later, Tito released Djilas, limited the power of the secret police, and en-

United Press Int.
Josip Broz Tito

couraged some economic and political freedom. In 1968, Tito supported Czechoslovakia's liberalization program, and he criticized Russia for sending troops into the country to stop the reforms. In 1971, he became head of a presidential council that was formed to rule Yugoslavia. As chairman, Tito retained much of his power until his death.   WALTER C. CLEMENS, JR.

See also YUGOSLAVIA (History).

Additional Resources

AUTY, PHYLLIS. *Tito: A Biography*. Rev. ed. Penguin, 1974.
DJILAS, MILOVAN. *Tito: The Story From Inside*. Harcourt, 1980.
FRANCHERE, RUTH. *Tito of Yugoslavia*. Macmillan, 1970. For younger readers.
ROBERTS, WALTER R. *Tito, Mihailovic and the Allies, 1941-1945*. Rutgers, 1973.

TITUS, *TY tuhs* (A.D. 41-81), a Roman emperor, was noted for his generosity and his regard for the people's welfare. He was born in Rome, the oldest son of Emperor Vespasian (see VESPASIAN). Titus served in civil and military posts in many parts of the empire. He captured Jerusalem in A.D. 70 after a long siege. Soon after, he was made co-ruler with his father, and succeeded him in 79. The tragic destruction of Pompeii and Herculaneum, when Mount Vesuvius erupted, occurred during the first year of his reign.

The *Arch of Titus* was begun by Vespasian as a triumphal arch for his son's victory at Jerusalem. It was finished in A.D. 81 and is located on the Sacred Way by the Forum of Rome (see ROMAN EMPIRE [color picture: All Roads Led to Rome]).   MARY FRANCIS GYLES

TITUS was a friend of Saint Paul. He was one of the first non-Jewish Christian missionaries. Paul was fond of Titus and mentioned him often in his Epistles. The Epistle to the Galatians tells us that Paul brought Titus to a council at Jerusalem. This council met to decide whether non-Jewish Christians would have to observe the rules of Moses. It is believed that he became bishop of the churches in Crete after Paul died. The Epistle to Titus is the 17th book of the New Testament. It is believed to be one of the letters of Paul and is similar to the Epistles to Timothy.   FREDERICK C. GRANT

TITUS, EPISTLE TO. See TITUS.

TITUS LIVIUS. See LIVY.

TIVOLI GARDENS. See DENMARK (Recreation; picture: Tivoli Gardens).

TIW. See TUESDAY.

TLINGIT INDIANS are a tribe who live in southeastern Alaska. The word *Tlingit* may also be spelled *Tlinkit*.

Before Europeans arrived in Alaska, the Tlingit occupied an area that extends from present-day Ketchikan to what is now Yakutat. They divided the area into 13 territories called *kwans*, also spelled *quans*. Each kwan belonged to a particular group of Tlingit. During most of the year, the groups moved about their kwans and hunted and fished. They hunted deer and seals; caught halibut, salmon, and other fishes; and gathered berries, bird eggs, and clams. During the winter, the Tlingit lived in villages that consisted of large wooden buildings, each of which houses several families. The villages stood empty the rest of the year.

Tlingit society consisted of two groups, the *Raven* and the *Eagle* or *Wolf*. Children belonged to their mother's group. Men and women from the same group were not permitted to marry each other. Tlingit woodworkers carved symbols called *totems* into tall poles. These totem poles represented the history of a family or clan. To raise their standing in the community, wealthy tribesmen tried to outdo one another by hosting feasts called *potlatches*. At the feast, the host gave gifts to his guests.

Today, many Tlingit work in the logging and fishing industries. The tribe's economy has improved as a result of the Alaska Native Claims Settlement Act of 1971. This law called for payment of $962½ million to the Tlingit and other original inhabitants of Alaska. It also provided for the return of more than 40 million acres (16 million hectares) of land to the original Alaskans. The Indians, in turn, agreed to abandon their claims to the rest of the state. The Tlingit established the Sealaska Corporation, an investment firm, to handle their share of the money. Each of the approximately 13,000 Tlingit owns a share in the corporation.   SAM STANLEY

TM. See TRANSCENDENTAL MEDITATION.

TNT is short for trinitrotoluene, one of the most powerful explosives known. TNT is made up of the chemical elements nitrogen, hydrogen, carbon, and oxygen. The chemical formula for TNT is $CH_3C_6H_2(NO_2)_3$. The explosive is made by nitrating the chemical compound toluene. The resulting explosive forms in pale yellow crystals which may darken to brown. These crystals can be handled safely and may even be melted at low heat without igniting. TNT is used alone and in mixtures with other explosives, such as RDX, in plastic bombs. It is chiefly used as the explosive charge for shells and bombs. See also EXPLOSIVE.   JULIUS ROTH

TO KILL A MOCKINGBIRD. See LEE, HARPER.

TOAD is a small animal with powerful back legs that enable it to jump around. Toads grow up in water, but they spend most of their lives on land. Like their close relatives the frogs, toads are amphibians (see AMPHIBIAN). There are about 200 *species* (kinds) of toads, and they are found in most parts of the world. Some toads stay near ponds and streams. Others live in fields.

The Toad's Body. Toads range from 1 to 9 inches (2.5 to 23 centimeters) in length. However, most toads are from 2 to 5 inches (5 to 13 centimeters) long. Toads are similar to frogs but have shorter legs and are generally more clumsy. Most toads have rough warts on their skin.

A toad has a poisonous liquid in its skin, chiefly in bumps just behind the eyes. Some toads also have the

S. C. Bisserot, Bruce Coleman Inc.

The Striped Toad of South America, like most species of toads, has dry, warty skin. Glands in a toad's skin contain a poisonous liquid that the animal releases if attacked.

poison in bumps on their legs and body. A toad lets out the poison when it is attacked. The attacking animal becomes ill, or may even die, if it touches the toad. Toads' poison cannot cause warts on human beings.

The toad has a tongue 1 inch (2.5 centimeters) long attached at the front of the mouth. The tongue has a sticky surface. A toad flips its tongue at its prey in a quick rolling motion. It catches its prey on the sticky surface and draws its tongue back into its mouth. Some scientists believe that the tongue can also be used to grab food without the use of the sticky surface. The tongue moves so fast that it cannot easily be seen.

The Toad's Life. Toads mate in or near water during the spring or summer. The male attracts the female with a mating call. It makes the call by filling a balloonlike part of its throat with air. It then forces the air across its vocal cords, causing them to *vibrate* (move back and forth quickly). The vibration makes the noise. A few kinds of toads do not have a mating call.

Most female toads lay eggs in long, jellylike strings, although some lay their eggs one at a time. They usually spread the eggs over plants in the water. A large toad may lay more than 20,000 eggs, although only a few of the eggs develop into full-grown toads.

Runk/Schoenberger from Grant Heilman

A Fowler's Toad flips out its sticky tongue to capture a cricket. A toad's tongue is attached to the front of its lower jaw. Fowler's toads are found in the Eastern United States.

Alvin E. Staffan

A Male American Toad puffs out its throat to utter a loud, flutelike mating call. The soft-voiced females cannot swell their throat. American toads live in the Eastern United States.

239

TOADFISH

Toad eggs hatch in 2 to 12 days, depending on the species of toad and on water temperature. Tadpoles emerge from the eggs. The change from tadpole to the young toad takes three weeks or longer, also depending on the species and water temperature. Tadpoles develop more quickly in warm water than in cold water. See TADPOLE.

Many young toads stay near the water for a while, feeding and growing. When small toads leave their birthplace, they travel at night and during rains. They do this because they must keep their bodies moist. Some toads never return to a watery place except to breed. Instead, they make their homes in fields or gardens. Rain keeps them moist. During dry summers these toads dig deep into the soil to stay moist. Most toads probably live from 1 to 2 years.

Scientific Classification. Toads make up the toad family, *Bufonidae*. The common American toad is classified as genus *Bufo*, species *B. americanus*.   W. FRANK BLAIR

See also FROG; MIDWIFE TOAD; SURINAM TOAD.

TOADFISH is a scavenger fish that lives on the bottom of tropical and temperate oceans. It has a large head and a short, scaleless body. The toadfish averages 9 to 10 inches (23 to 25 centimeters) in length. The fish may snap up bait so eagerly that sometimes they make a grunting sound.

Scientific Classification. Toadfishes are members of the toadfish family, *Batrachoididae*. They are genus *Opsanus*, species *O. tau*.   LEONARD P. SCHULTZ

TOADFLAX, or BUTTER-AND-EGGS, is a weed with yellow flowers and pale green leaves. It grows in central North America, as far west as the Rocky Moun-

J. Horace McFarland
Toadflax Has Clusters of Yellow, Tube-Shaped Flowers.

tains. The flowers cluster along the upper part of the stem. They are tube-shaped, with the edge cut into an upper and lower lip. The upper lip has two lobes, and the lower lip has three. A thick, orange-colored ridge on the middle lobe covers the mouth of the tube. The weight of a bee looking for nectar forces the mouth of the tube open. Toadflax was brought to America from Europe. It is sometimes grown in gardens.

Scientific Classification. Toadflax is in the figwort family, *Scrophulariaceae*. It is genus *Linaria*, species *L. vulgaris*.   EARL L. CORE

TOADSTOOL. See MUSHROOM.

TOBACCO is a plant whose leaves are used chiefly in making cigarettes and cigars. Other tobacco products include smoking tobacco for pipes, chewing tobacco, and snuff. Inferior grades of tobacco leaves are used in making insecticides and disinfectants. The stalks and stems of the plant serve as an ingredient for some types of fertilizer.

Tobacco ranks as an important crop in more than 60 countries. During the late 1970's, the annual worldwide production of tobacco totaled about 6 million short tons (5 million metric tons). China leads in tobacco production, followed by the United States, India, Brazil, and Russia.

Farmers in the United States harvest about 788,000 short tons (715,000 metric tons) of tobacco annually. Sales of the crop total about $2 billion. North Carolina is the leading tobacco-producing state, followed by Kentucky, South Carolina, Virginia, and Tennessee.

The tobacco industry in the United States produces about 705 billion cigarettes and about $3\frac{1}{2}$ billion cigars yearly. About 160 million pounds (73 million kilograms) of tobacco are manufactured annually for smoking tobacco, chewing tobacco, and snuff. The annual value of tobacco products amounts to about $18\frac{3}{4}$ billion. Most of this income comes from domestic sales of the products.

The taxes on tobacco products provide a major source of revenue for the United States government. Tobacco products are also taxed by all the state governments and some local governments. Taxes on tobacco total about three times the amount that the growers receive for their crops.

Tobacco contains small amounts of nicotine, a substance that acts as a stimulant on the heart and other organs. Nicotine also stimulates the nervous system, causing many people to become addicted to it. Physicians believe these stimulating effects of nicotine help make smoking pleasurable. However, concentrated amounts of nicotine are poisonous. The nicotine that people consume from cigarettes may contribute to the occurrence of heart attacks and stomach ulcers. The tar produced by burning tobacco is thought to be a major cause of lung cancer in smokers. See SMOKING; DRUG ABUSE.

The Tobacco Plant

Cultivated tobacco is an *annual* plant—that is, it lives only one growing season. The plant reaches a height of 4 to 6 feet (1.2 to 1.8 meters). It produces about 20 leaves, which measure from 24 to 30 inches (61 to 76 centimeters) long and 15 to 18 inches (38 to 46 centimeters) wide. The tobacco plant ranges from light green to dark green in color. A vigorous, mature plant can produce a million seeds yearly—enough to plant about 100 acres (40 hectares) of tobacco.

Kinds of Tobacco

In the United States, tobacco is classified into four main groups: (1) air-cured tobacco, (2) fire-cured tobacco, (3) flue-cured tobacco, and (4) cigar leaf tobacco. The first three kinds are classified according to the method used in *curing* (drying) the leaves. More information on these methods appears in the *Curing Tobacco* section. Cigar leaf tobacco is air cured, but it is classified according to its use.

Air-cured tobacco consists of two varieties, light air-cured and dark air-cured. Most cigarettes contain the two major types of light air-cured tobacco, burley and Maryland. Burley tobacco accounts for about 30 per cent of the tobacco production in the United States. Dark air-cured tobacco is used primarily for chewing tobacco and snuff.

Fire-cured tobacco has a distinctive smoky aroma and flavor. It is used to make smoking tobacco, chewing tobacco, snuff, and strong-tasting cigars.

Flue-cured tobacco is also called *bright tobacco* because the curing process turns it yellow to reddish-orange. It accounts for more than 60 per cent of the tobacco produced in the United States. Most flue-cured tobacco is used in cigarettes.

There are three types of cigar leaf tobacco: (1) cigar filler tobacco, (2) cigar binder tobacco, and (3) cigar wrapper tobacco.

Cigar filler tobacco is used in the body of cigars because it has a sweet flavor and burns evenly. Cigar binder tobacco was once used to hold filler tobacco together, but most cigar manufacturers now use *reconstituted tobacco sheets* instead. These sheets are made from coarse or damaged tobacco leaves. Today, cigar binder is used primarily in making chewing tobacco.

Cigar wrapper tobacco is used for the outside cover of cigars. It must have high-quality leaves that are smooth, thin, and uniform in color. To grow leaves with these characteristics, farmers surround the tobacco with a framework covered by cloth. Production of cigar

U.S. Department of Agriculture

Tobacco Is *Cured* (Dried) in a Special Barn before being sent to market. In a modern curing barn, *above*, a furnace heats the air, which fans force through the drying leaves.

wrapper tobacco is difficult and expensive, and many manufacturers use reconstituted tobacco sheets to cover their cigars.

Raising and Marketing Tobacco

Planting and Cultivation. The soil and climate conditions that favor tobacco growth vary according to the kind of tobacco being raised. However, most tobacco grows best in a warm climate and in carefully drained and fertilized soil.

Tobacco seeds are planted in seed beds in late winter or early spring and covered with cloth or plastic. The plants grow 6 to 8 inches (15 to 20 centimeters) tall in 8 to 12 weeks and are then transplanted into the field.

Farmers cultivate the soil several times to keep it loose and to eliminate weeds and grasses. The last cultivation occurs after the plants reach a height of 18 to 24 inches (46 to 61 centimeters).

The upper part of the plant is *topped* (cut off) when it begins to produce flowers. This process allows the remaining leaves to become larger and heavier.

Harvesting Tobacco. Farmers harvest tobacco from 70 to 90 days after it has been transplanted. They use two harvesting methods, called *priming* and *stalk-cutting*.

Priming involves picking the individual tobacco leaves as they ripen. The leaves were once picked by hand, but most farmers now use priming machines. The priming method is used to harvest cigar wrapper, flue-cured, and some cigar filler tobaccos.

Stalk-cutting consists of cutting the entire plant with a hatchetlike tool. The stalks are then placed on sticks and left in the field for a day or two to wilt. Growers use the stalk-cutting method to harvest air-cured, fire-cured, and most cigar leaf tobaccos.

Diseases and Pests. Diseases that attack tobacco include *black shank* and *black root rot*. Many farmers raise newly developed types of tobacco that resist black

WORLD BOOK illustration by James Teason

The Tobacco Plant, *above*, lives for only one growing season. It stands from 4 to 6 feet (1.2 to 1.8 meters) high and ranges in color from light green to dark green. The plant has about 20 leaves and grows light pink flowers.

TOBACCO

shank and various virus diseases. Crop rotation is the most effective way to control black root rot.

Budworms, flea beetles, grasshoppers, and other insects also damage tobacco plants. Farmers use insecticides to control these pests.

Curing Tobacco involves drying the sap from newly harvested leaves. This process produces various chemical changes in tobacco that improve its flavor and aroma. There are three methods of curing tobacco: (1) air curing, (2) fire curing, and (3) flue curing. Each type of tobacco responds most favorably to one of these methods. Curing takes place in curing barns that are built specifically for the method used.

Air curing uses natural weather conditions to dry tobacco. Air-curing barns have ventilators that can be opened and closed to control the temperature and humidity. This process takes from four to eight weeks.

Fire curing dries tobacco with low-burning fires. The smoke gives fire-cured tobacco its distinctive taste and aroma. Farmers regulate the heat, humidity, and ventilation in the curing barns so the leaves will not be scalded. Fire curing takes from three days to six weeks.

Flue curing dries tobacco by heat from *flues* (pipes) connected to furnaces. The temperature is gradually raised from 90° F. (32° C) to 160° F. (71° C) until the leaves and stems are completely dry. The flue-curing method takes about a week.

Marketing Tobacco. Farmers sell tobacco by two major methods, *loose leaf auctions* and *country sales*.

Loose leaf auctions handle about 95 per cent of the tobacco sales in the United States. The term *loose leaf* refers to the practice of displaying and selling tobacco in leaf form rather than packed in containers.

Auction warehouses operate in cities and towns throughout tobacco-growing regions. In the United States, federal inspectors examine tobacco before it is sold and grade it according to government standards.

Buyers from tobacco companies bid on the tobacco, which is usually sold to the highest bidder. The government has *price supports* that guarantee the seller a certain price for tobacco. The government buys the tobacco if bidders do not offer this amount.

Country sales involve the direct sale of tobacco from farmer to buyer outside the auction system. Most cigar leaf tobacco is sold directly. This system is also called *barn-door marketing* because the buyers usually come to the farm to inspect the crop.

Manufacturing Tobacco Products

Freshly cured tobacco has a sharp aroma and bitter taste. Therefore, most tobacco is put into storage and allowed to age before being used in manufacturing tobacco products.

Prior to storage, most tobacco goes through a redrying process, during which it is completely dried and cooled. Manufacturers then restore some water throughout the leaves to ensure uniform moisture content. This practice prevents the leaves from breaking.

Next, tobacco is stored for two or three years in barrel-like containers. During storage, it ages and undergoes a chemical change called *fermentation*. Fermentation gives tobacco a sweeter, milder flavor and aroma and reduces its nicotine content. Tobacco also loses moisture and becomes darker during aging.

Leading Tobacco-Growing States and Provinces

Tobacco grown in 1979

North Carolina	311,000 short tons (282,100 metric tons)
Kentucky	174,000 short tons (157,900 metric tons)
Ontario	116,800 short tons (106,000 metric tons)*
South Carolina	58,900 short tons (53,430 metric tons)
Virginia	56,700 short tons (51,440 metric tons)
Tennessee	52,700 short tons (47,810 metric tons)
Georgia	50,500 short tons (45,810 metric tons)
Maryland	13,200 short tons (11,980 metric tons)
Wisconsin	12,600 short tons (11,430 metric tons)
Florida	11,300 short tons (10,250 metric tons)

*1978, latest available information.
Sources: U.S. Department of Agriculture; Statistics Canada.

Leading Tobacco-Growing Countries

Tobacco grown in 1979

China	1,064,000 short tons (965,000 metric tons)
United States	788,200 short tons (715,000 metric tons)
India	497,100 short tons (451,000 metric tons)
Brazil	439,800 short tons (399,000 metric tons)
Russia	327,400 short tons (297,000 metric tons)
Turkey	266,800 short tons (242,000 metric tons)
Japan	174,200 short tons (158,000 metric tons)
Bulgaria	165,000 short tons (150,000 metric tons)
South Korea	135,600 short tons (123,000 metric tons)
Greece	134,500 short tons (122,000 metric tons)

Source: U.S. Department of Agriculture.

A somewhat different procedure is used to age cigar leaf tobacco, which does not require redrying. Bales of this tobacco are placed in heated rooms or are simply hung up to ferment before storage.

Cigarettes account for about 87 per cent of the tobacco consumed in the United States. The remainder is used in making cigars, smoking tobacco, chewing tobacco, and snuff.

Cigarettes contain blends of burley, Maryland, flue-cured, and imported Turkish tobaccos. Manufacturers add such flavorings as honey, licorice, menthol, and sugar to the blended tobacco. A chemical called *glycerine* is often added to preserve moisture.

Various machines handle the entire process of making and packaging cigarettes. Cigarette-making machines can produce about 4,000 cigarettes a minute.

Cigars consist of about 85 per cent cigar filler, 10 per cent cigar binder, and 5 per cent cigar wrapper tobaccos. Most cigars are made by machines, but the more expensive kinds are hand-rolled.

Most smoking tobacco is used in pipes, but some people smoke it in the form of cigarettes that they roll by hand. For flavor, manufacturers add tonka beans, vanilla leaves, and other substances. Tobacco flavorings are called *saucing compounds.*

Chewing tobacco is made from various types of inferior grade tobacco. Most chewing tobacco is treated with such saucing compounds as honey or licorice.

Snuff consists of a coarsely ground mixture of tobacco leaves and stems that has been pressed into a fine powder. The powder is strained through cloth and flavored with oils and spices.

History

American Indians smoked tobacco in pipes long before Christopher Columbus sailed to the New World in 1492. Columbus brought some tobacco seeds back to Europe, where farmers began to grow the plant for use as a medicine that helped people relax. In 1560, a French diplomat named Jean Nicot—from whom tobacco receives its botanical name, *Nicotiana*—introduced the use of tobacco in France.

Commercial production of tobacco began in North America in 1612, after an English colonist named John Rolfe brought some tobacco seeds from South America to Virginia. The Virginia soil and climate were excellent for tobacco, and it became an important crop there and in other parts of the South.

Most of the tobacco grown in the American Colonies was exported to England until the Revolutionary War began in 1775. Manufacturers in the United States then began to produce smoking tobacco, chewing tobacco, and snuff for domestic use. Cigars were first manufactured in the United States in the early 1800's.

Spaniards and some other Europeans began to smoke hand-rolled cigarettes in the 1600's, but few people in the United States used them until the 1850's. Cigarette smoking became increasingly popular after the first practical cigarette-making machine was invented in the early 1880's.

The use of tobacco products has been a controversial issue for many years. During the 1500's, European physicians declared that tobacco should be used only for medicinal purposes. The Puritans in America considered it a dangerous narcotic. During the 1960's,

Brown & Williamson Tobacco Corporation

During Cigarette Manufacturing, cakes of blended tobacco are cut into slender shreds and inspected for quality, above.

scientists established that smoking tobacco products—especially cigarettes—could cause lung cancer, heart disease, and other illnesses.

Some cigarette manufacturers reacted to the medical findings by reducing the tar and nicotine content of cigarettes. However, doctors state that these measures have not eliminated the dangers of smoking.

Various federal laws have been passed in the United States regarding the sale of tobacco products. Since 1966, manufacturers have been required to include a health warning on all packages and cartons of cigarettes. Another law, which went into effect in 1971, banned radio and television commercials advertising cigarettes. In 1972, manufacturers agreed to include a health warning in all cigarette advertising. Some states have laws that prohibit smoking in various public places.

Scientific Classification. The tobacco plant belongs to the nightshade family, Solanaceae. The major kind is genus *Nicotiana*, species *N. tabacum.*   J. H. SMILEY

Related Articles in WORLD BOOK include:

Cigar	Drug Abuse	Pipe
Cigarette	Filter	Snuff
Colonial Life in	Kentucky (picture)	Virginia
America (Crops)	Nicotine	(picture)

TOBAGO. See TRINIDAD AND TOBAGO.

TOBEY, MARK (1890-1976), was an American artist who painted elaborate linear abstract pictures, often on a small scale. Tobey's delicately colored compositions have dense patterns of lines and small symbols. They have been compared to *calligraphy* (the art of fine handwriting). Tobey used the term *white writing* to describe his style. Tobey developed his calligraphic style after a study trip to the Orient in the 1930's. Later he ordered his images into highly complex groupings of tiny forms. Tobey's paintings were admired by Europeans, who saw in them an American blend of Eastern and Western styles. Tobey was born in Centerville, Wis.   DORE ASHTON

TOBOGGANING, *tuh BAHG uhn ihng,* is the winter sport of coasting on snow or ice by means of toboggans, which are sleds without runners. A toboggan is made of strips of hickory, ash, or maple, with the front ends

Tobogganing is an exciting winter sport. Many people ride toboggans down specially prepared courses called *runs*.

curved back. The strips are fastened together by cross-pieces into one compact unit. The under surface is highly polished. The sled is usually 6 to 8 feet (1.8 to 2.4 meters) long and 1½ feet (46 centimeters) wide. Four persons usually make up a toboggan team. The one at the rear acts as steersman. Tobogganists have attained a speed of 900 yards (823 meters) in 30 seconds, or more than 61 mph (98 kph).

Indian hunters first built toboggans to carry game over the snow. These were made of bark. The Eskimos used to make toboggans of whalebone. Bobsledding, an offshoot of tobogganing, has become a feature of the Winter Olympics. Bobsleds can reach speeds of 90 mph (145 kph). Two-seater and four-seater steel sleds, 9 to 12 feet (2.7 to 3.7 meters) long, are standard. These sleds may weigh as much as 500 pounds (230 kilograms). See also SLED. BOB BEATTIE

TOBRUK, *TOH brook* (pop. 10,445), is a Mediterranean port in Cyrenaica, a province of Libya (see LIBYA [map]). Its name in Arabic is Ṭubruq. It is noted for its fine harbor, one of the best in Africa. After the Italians took over Libya in 1911, they made many improvements in Tobruk, including an airfield and new buildings. Tobruk was the scene of heavy fighting during World War II. A British garrison held out there for months after the Germans had pushed the main body of British troops into Egypt in 1941. In 1942, German forces seized Tobruk, but British troops regained the city the same year. WILLIAM F. McDONALD

TOCANTINS RIVER, *TOH kan TEENS*, flows 1,677 miles (2,699 kilometers) through central and northern Brazil (see BRAZIL [physical map]). The Tocantins is 8 miles (13 kilometers) wide at its mouth. It enters the Pará River about 50 miles (80 kilometers) southwest of Belém. Rapids and cataracts prevent navigation on much of the river, but regular shipping can sail its last 150 miles (241 kilometers). Chief tributaries include the Araguaia, Paraná, Sono, and Manuel Alves rivers.

TOCOPHEROL. See VITAMIN (Vitamin E).

TOCQUEVILLE, *TAWK veel*, or *TAHK vil*, **ALEXIS DE** (1805-1859), a French statesman and political philosopher, became known for his book *Democracy in America* (1835-1840). He wrote it after a visit to the United States in 1831. It ranks as a classic observation of American democracy by a person from another country. His other famous work is *The Old Regime and the French Revolution* (1856). He was born in Verneuil, France, of an aristocratic family. He became active as a liberal in French politics before Napoleon III came to power in 1852. MERLE CURTI

TODA. See INDIA (People).

TODD, LORD (1907-   ), ALEXANDER ROBERTUS TODD, is a Scottish organic chemist and biochemist. He won the 1957 Nobel prize for chemistry. He worked on the structure and synthesis of natural products, including vitamins, phosphorylated compounds, nucleotide enzymes, nucleotides, and coenzymes. Todd was born in Glasgow, and was graduated from the University of Glasgow. He taught at the universities of Edinburgh, Manchester, and Cambridge. HENRY M. LEICESTER

TODD, MARY. See LINCOLN, MARY TODD.

TOE. See FOOT.

TOENAIL. See NAIL.

TOGA, *TOH guh*, was the loose, draped wrap, or outer garment, worn by the citizens of ancient Rome. They wrapped it about the entire body, and allowed it to fall in graceful folds. Originally, both men and women wore the toga. But gradually the women began to wear the *stola* instead. Later, only Roman citizens could wear the toga. They wore it on all formal occasions.

Shape and Size. The Romans changed the shape of the toga and draped it differently from time to time. It became more elaborate with each period. Originally, the shape was probably oblong. But usually the toga was almost as wide as the height of the wearer. It was long enough to go around the body at least twice.

Colors and Styles. Romans used wool fabrics to make togas. The ordinary citizen usually wore a white toga. But colored borders or a different colored material showed the rank or station of the wearer. For example, Roman youths of from 14 to 17 years of age exchanged their purple-bordered togas for all-white togas, called the *toga of manhood*, or the *toga virilis*. Because of its pure white color, they also called it the *toga pura*.

A Roman Toga was worn by Emperor Augustus, *below*.

Magistrates and high priests wore a purple-bordered white toga, called the *toga praetexta*. A candidate for office wore a white toga known as the *toga candida*.

At first, Romans used a richly embroidered purple toga, called the *toga picta*, or *toga palmata*, to honor victors. Later, emperors adopted it as their official dress. During the imperial period, the toga became elaborate and heavy. It required such careful draping that Romans probably wore it only on formal occasions. The toga never proved to be a practical garment, but it gave protection against dampness.

The Romans wore a type of shoe called the *calceus* with their togas. Different styles of shoes showed the rank or station of the wearer. MARY EVANS

See also TUNIC.

Togo

✪	Capital
•	Other City or Town
—	Road
←→	Rail Line
▲	MOUNTAIN
～	River

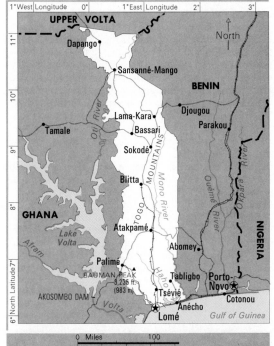

WORLD BOOK map

TOGO is a small country in western Africa. It is about the size of West Virginia, but it has about 1½ times as many people. Togo is long and narrow. It extends about 365 miles (587 kilometers) inland from the Gulf of Guinea, an arm of the Atlantic Ocean. It is only 40 miles (64 kilometers) wide at the coast and 90 miles (145 kilometers) wide at its widest point.

Most of the people of Togo work as farmers. But farm production is small, and many people grow only enough food to feed their families. There are no big factories in Togo. Lomé, which has a population of about 229,-400, is the capital and the only large city. Togo's name in French, the official language, is RÉPUBLIQUE DU TOGO (REPUBLIC OF TOGO). Togo means *behind the sea* in Ewe, the most commonly used language in Togo.

Government. In 1967, army officers led by Lieutenant Colonel Gnassingbe Eyadema overthrew Togo's

Immanuel Wallerstein, the contributor of this article, is Distinguished Professor of Sociology at the State University of New York at Binghamton, and the author of Africa: The Politics of Independence *and* Africa: The Politics of Unity.

civilian government. They suspended the constitution and dissolved the National Assembly (parliament). Eyadema became president and set up a government made up of himself, other army officers, and civilians. In 1969, he created Togo's only legal political party, The Rally of the Togolese People.

Togo is divided into 21 administrative districts. Each is directed by a *chef de circonscription* (district head).

People. The ways of life in Togo reflect the fact that several different groups of people have settled the country. However, the people are similar in physical type, occupation, and religion. Almost all of the people

Facts in Brief

Capital: Lomé.

Official Language: French.

Form of Government: Presidential regime.

Area: 21,622 sq. mi. (56,000 km²). *Greatest Distances—* north-south, 365 mi. (587 km); east-west, 90 mi. (145 km). *Coastline—*40 mi. (64 km).

Population: *Estimated 1983 Population—*2,793,000; distribution, 83 per cent rural, 17 per cent urban; density, 129 persons per sq. mi. (50 persons per km²). *1970 Census—*1,997,109. *Estimated 1988 Population—* 3,114,000.

Chief Products: *Agriculture—*cacao, cassava, coffee, copra, cotton, palm kernels and oil, peanuts. *Mining—* phosphates.

Flag: The flag has five horizontal stripes, three green and two yellow, with a white star on a red square in the upper left corner. Green symbolizes hope and agriculture; yellow, faith; white, purity; and red, charity and fidelity. See FLAG (picture: Flags of Africa).

Money: *Basic Unit—*franc. See MONEY (table).

Farmers in Northern Togo carry live poultry to and from market in cone-shaped baskets that have an airhole in the top.

Marc & Evelyne Bernheim

are black Africans. About four-fifths of the people live in rural areas and work on family-owned farms. Three-fourths of the people practice traditional African religions. But dress, language, and other ways of life differ throughout Togo. The greatest differences are between the south and the north.

The ancestors of the people in southern Togo came from Benin and Ghana. The traditional life of southern Togo is similar to that of those two countries. Many southerners wear a toga, a full-length, loose-fitting garment. Many live in *compounds* (groups of huts inside walls). They speak the Ewe language.

European influence has been greater in the south than in the north. It has affected dress, occupation, and religion. Many southerners wear European-style clothes. Some work for the government and others have small businesses. Most of Togo's 200,000 Christians, mostly Roman Catholics, live in the south.

Northern Togo was settled by people from the West African savanna region, and its way of life is similar to that of Upper Volta and Niger. Northerners live in villages made up of adobe houses with cone-shaped thatched roofs. Most wear a white cotton smock. Many languages are spoken in northern Togo. Most of Togo's 50,000 Muslims live in the north.

Only about 40 of every 100 school-age children in Togo attend primary school. And only 1 out of every 100 children attends secondary school. Togo has only one university, the University of Bénin in Lomé. Many students study abroad, especially in France.

Land. The Togo Mountains divide Togo into two major regions. The mountains stretch from southwest to northeast and cover much of western Togo. Bauman Peak (3,235 feet, or 986 meters) is Togo's highest point.

East and south of the Togo Mountains, the land descends across a sloping plateau to a low, sandy coastal plain. The plateau is covered with tall grass and clumps of hardwood trees. It is drained by the Mono River. The densely populated coastal plain is dotted with swamps, lagoons, and coconut and oil palm forests.

North of the Togo Mountains, the land descends through rolling grasslands to the Upper Volta border. Thorny trees are scattered across the grassland. The Oti River drains the region. Few people live there.

Togo has a hot, humid climate. The temperature averages 81° F. (27° C), and rainfall averages about 40 inches (100 centimeters) a year in the north and 70 inches (180 centimeters) in the south. Rainy seasons last from March to July and September to November in the south, and from April to October in the north.

Economy. Togo is an agricultural country. But good land is scarce, harvests are small, and income is low.

Food crops are the most important farm products. They include cassava, corn, millet, sorghum, and yams. The principal crops raised for export are coffee and cacao. Most of the farms that raise crops for food are owned in common by a group of families. Most of the crops that are sold are raised on small farms owned by individuals. Many Togolese work on these farms as *sharecroppers*. That is, they farm the land and give the landowner part of the receipts in payment for using the land. Fishing is an important coastal industry.

Togo has one of the world's largest phosphate reserves, and phosphate-mining is important to the economy. Bauxite, chromium, and iron deposits have been discovered in Togo, but they have not been developed.

Women of Togo often carry goods on their heads in enamel basins. These women are carrying coconuts still in their husks to the market in Lomé.

Togo has about 300 miles (480 kilometers) of railroads and 2,700 miles (4,350 kilometers) of roads. The chief airport and seaport are at Lomé.

History. Scholars believe that the ancestors of the central mountain peoples were the original inhabitants of Togo. In the 1300's, the Ewe-speaking people began to move into what is now southern Togo and Ghana. Invaders from the north and refugees from wars in Ghana and Dahomey (now Benin) settled in Togo between the 1500's and 1800's.

Portuguese explorers and traders arrived on the coast in the late 1400's. Between the 1600's and 1800's, European slave-traders raided the coast to capture slaves, and Togo became known as the *Coast of Slaves*.

German traders and missionaries went to Togo in the mid-1800's. In 1884, Germany set up a small protectorate on the coast. By 1899, German Togo included what is now Togo and part of what is now Ghana.

British and French troops occupied German Togo in 1914, after World War I began. In 1919, Great Britain gained control of the western one-third of German Togo and France gained control of the eastern two-thirds. In 1922, the League of Nations confirmed a *mandate* (authority to govern) for Great Britain over British Togoland and for France over French Togoland. The United Nations changed the mandates to *trusteeships* (UN authority to govern) in 1946. In 1956, the people of British Togoland voted to join the Gold Coast. When the Gold Coast became independent as Ghana in 1957, it incorporated British Togoland.

After World War II, an independence movement developed in French Togoland. Sylvanus Olympio, leader of the Committee for Togolese Unity Party (CTU), wanted complete independence from France. Nicolas Grunitzky, leader of the Togolese Party for Progress, wanted to remain in the French Union.

In 1956, France made French Togoland a republic within the French Union and gave it internal self-government. France appointed Grunitzky prime minister. The Togolese approved the republic in an election, but the UN refused to accept this method of ending the trusteeship. In a UN-supervised election in 1958, the CTU won control of the legislature and Olympio became prime minister. The UN approved this action. On April 27, 1960, French Togoland became the independent Republic of Togo with Olympio as president.

Rivalry between northerners and southerners has always been important in Togo's politics. In 1963, a group of northern army officers assassinated Olympio, a southerner. They made Grunitzky president. Grunitzky was from the south, but he opposed Olympio and the Committee for Togolese Unity Party. Southern CTU members tried unsuccessfully in 1966 to oust Grunitzky.

Army officers, led by Gnassingbe Eyadema, overthrew Grunitzky's government in January, 1967. They suspended the constitution and set up a government with Eyadema as president. The people endorsed him as president in a vote taken in 1972, and reelected him in 1979.   IMMANUEL WALLERSTEIN

See also LOMÉ.

TOGO, *TOH goh,* **HEIHACHIRO** (1847-1934), was Japan's greatest admiral and naval hero in the 1900's. He achieved fame during the Russo-Japanese War of 1904 and 1905. He commanded the blockade of Port Arthur and then led the Japanese fleet in a spectacular

victory at the Battle of Tsushima, in which almost the entire Russian fleet from the Baltic Sea was destroyed. Togo was born in Kagoshima and studied naval tactics in England.   MARIUS B. JANSEN

TOILET. See PLUMBING.

TOJO, *TOH joh,* **HIDEKI** (1884-1948), was the general who, as premier, led Japan into war with the United States in 1941. He achieved national influence after 1935 as Chief of Staff of the Kwantung Army, the force that guarded Japan's holdings in South Manchuria. There he became one of a group of militarists who objected to democratic developments within Japan.

By provoking "incidents," the militarists tried to commit their home government to decisive steps. In this manner, they engineered the Manchurian Incident of 1931, which inaugurated the train of aggression leading to the Pacific War. Thereafter, young officers also assassinated civilian leaders in Japan. After the collapse of civilian government, military men were named to high political office.

United Press Int.

Hideki Tojo

Tojo rose rapidly during the confusion of the 1930's. In 1940 he became Minister of War. Adolf Hitler seemed to be winning World War II, and Tojo threw his weight behind Hitler and Benito Mussolini and against the democracies. As American embargoes on oil to Japan began to strain the Japanese economy, Tojo insisted that if an agreement with the United States could not be reached, Japan would have to fight. In October, 1941, Tojo succeeded Prince Konoye as premier. When the Washington talks failed to bring results, Tojo decided on war.

Tojo was born the son of a general in Tokyo. His background, training, and interests were exclusively military. Tojo's popularity in Japan was high after the early victories of World War II, but his influence waned as American victories in 1943 and 1944 began to turn the tide. He was forced to resign as premier in 1944 after the fall of Saipan. He was arrested and convicted as a war criminal after Japan's surrender, and was hanged on Dec. 23, 1948.   MARIUS B. JANSEN

See also JAPAN (History).

TOKAMAK. See NUCLEAR ENERGY (Present-Day Research).

TOKELAU, *TOH kuh LOW,* is a territory of New Zealand in the South Pacific Ocean (see Pacific Islands [map]). It consists of the Tokelau Islands, also called the Union Islands. The island group is made up of three atolls—Atafu, Nukunono, and Fakaofo.

About 2,000 Polynesians live in Tokelau, which has an area of 4 square miles (10 square kilometers). Copra is the chief product. The British navigator John Byron, grandfather of the poet Lord Byron, visited the Tokelau Islands in 1765. New Zealand has administered the islands since 1926. Tokelau became a territory of New Zealand in 1949.   EDWIN H. BRYAN, JR.

WORLD BOOK photo by T. Tanuma

Tokyo's Imperial Palace Plaza, *foreground,* adds beauty and charm to the busy downtown section of the city. Tokyo, the world's third largest city, ranks among the most crowded places on earth. But it has many scenic open areas like the plaza.

TOKYO

TOKYO, the capital of Japan, is the third largest city in the world. Only Shanghai and Mexico City have more people. About 8⅓ million persons live in Tokyo. Many countries have fewer people. Tokyo is Japan's main business center as well as the home of the Japanese emperor and the headquarters of the national government. The city's many banks, commercial establishments, and industries help make Japan one of the world's richest nations.

In many ways, Tokyo seems like an American city. It has tall buildings, freeways jammed with traffic, and more neon signs than any other city in the world. Tokyo teen-agers dance to American hit tunes, and the city's restaurants offer everything from hamburgers to the finest European dishes. Many residents of Tokyo go to baseball games and watch movies and television shows from Western countries. But in spite of such outside influences, Japanese tradition remains strong in Tokyo. Many of the people enjoy going to city parks to admire their beautiful cherry trees and lotus blossoms. These and other gorgeous sights in the city reflect the Japa-

This article was critically reviewed by Chie Nakane, Professor and Director of the Institute of Oriental Culture at the University of Tokyo and author of Japanese Society.

nese trait of love of beauty. Large numbers of Tokyo's people take part in dances and parades during the city's many traditional festivals, some of which are hundreds of years old. They visit historic shrines and temples and attend old-style plays and wrestling matches.

Tokyo traces its beginning to 1457, when a powerful warrior built a castle there. It became the Japanese capital in 1868. Tokyo has twice been almost destroyed —by a terrible earthquake in 1923 and by air raids in the early 1940's during World War II.

About 7 per cent of Japan's people live in Tokyo. The city has become so crowded that it has a severe housing shortage. Tokyo's rapid growth has also created other problems, including some of the world's worst pollution and heaviest traffic.

Facts in Brief

Population: *City Proper*—8,349,209. *Metropolitan Area Population*—11,615,069.

Area: *City Proper*—223 sq. mi. (578 km²); *Metropolitan Area* —832 sq. mi. (2,156 km²).

Altitude: 80 ft. (24 m) above sea level.

Climate: *Average Temperature*—January, 39° F. (4° C); July, 76° F. (24° C). *Average Annual Precipitation* (rainfall, melted snow, and other forms of moisture)— 58 in. (147 cm).

Government: *Chief Executive*—governor (4-year term). *Legislature*—126-member assembly (4-year terms).

Founded: 1457.

The city of Tokyo, called the *city proper*, covers 223 square miles (578 square kilometers) and has a population of 8,349,209. The city is part of a large metropolitan area called the *Metropolis of Tokyo*. The Metropolis includes many communities west of the city. It covers 832 square miles (2,156 square kilometers) and has a population of 11,615,069.

The entire metropolitan area operates under the same government. In this way, it differs from most U.S. metropolitan areas, which have completely separate governments for each community within them. Due to its single government, the Metropolis of Tokyo is often considered a single community. But this article describes the city proper and outlying areas separately.

The City Proper is the busiest, most heavily populated part of the Metropolis. It lies at the northwest end of Tokyo Bay on the Kanto Plain, Japan's largest lowland. The city is bordered by the Edo River on the northeast and the Tama River on the south.

The city proper is divided into 23 units called *wards*. The Japanese word for *ward* is *ku*, and so the city proper is called the *ku area*, or the *ward area*. The Imperial Palace, where the emperor lives, stands amid beautiful parklike grounds on high land near the center of the city. Eastward, from the palace to the bay, the land is low and flat. Many of Tokyo's chief business,

commercial, and industrial districts are in these low-lying areas. Part of eastern Tokyo is jammed with office and apartment buildings made of concrete and steel. For a picture of Tokyo's business center, see the start of the CITY article. Tokyo's oldest and poorest residential sections are also in the eastern part of the city.

Much of far eastern Tokyo is filled-in land on what had been part of Tokyo Bay. Some of this land lies below sea level. The low-lying areas are always in danger of floods, especially during heavy rains. Dikes have been built along the waterfront and the river banks. But the filled-in land sinks lower every year, mainly because of the removal of large amounts of ground water for industrial use. The dikes sink along with the land, making flood control difficult.

West of the Imperial Palace, the land becomes hilly. The chief residential sections of the city proper are in the west. The houses include large apartment buildings like those in Western cities and simple one- or two-story wooden buildings, the traditional Japanese houses. Many of the wooden houses are small and plain by Western standards. In some sections, rich families and poor families live in the same neighborhood, and their houses are plain and look much alike. But the western part of the city proper also has luxurious residential sections where the wealthy live.

Tokyo, unlike most other Japanese cities, no longer has large numbers of buildings in the ancient Japanese style that is most familiar to Westerners. This style features low, graceful lines and roofs turned up at the edges. Most of the remaining buildings in this style are religious shrines or temples.

Several well-known districts, each with its own characteristics, lie near the Imperial Palace. The Marunouchi district, an area of tall office buildings southeast of the palace, is Tokyo's business and financial center. The Ginza district lies farther south. It ranks as one of Tokyo's liveliest and most colorful districts and is famous for its stores and nightclubs. The Kanda district, northeast of the palace, is famous for its many bookstores. The Asakusa district, north of Kanda, is one of Tokyo's oldest entertainment sections. It features amusement parks, theaters, and restaurants.

Only main streets in Tokyo have names. Instead of street names, Tokyo addresses give the names of wards and other districts. A ward, called a *ku*, is divided into sections or neighborhoods, each of which has a name. These sections are further divided into *subdivisions* (groups of blocks) called *chome*, which are numbered. Each block in a chome has a number, as does each house in a block. The address *2-7, Yamabuki 1-chome, Shinjuku-ku* stands for *block 2, house 7, subdivision 1 in the Yamabuki section of Shinjuku ward.*

Outlying Areas. In addition to the city proper, the Metropolis of Tokyo includes 26 suburban cities and 1 county area. The suburban cities extend westward from the city proper. The county area, which lies in the westernmost part of the Metropolis, includes several towns and villages as well as farms and forests. Two small island groups in the Pacific Ocean are also part of the Metropolis. They are the Izu Islands and the Bonin Islands. The islands have a few towns and villages.

Tokyo lies on Honshu Island in central Japan. The map below shows the Metropolis of Tokyo which covers the same area as Tokyo Prefecture. Prefectures in Japan are similar to states in the United States. The map shows built-up areas in yellow.

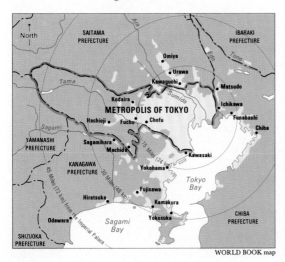

WORLD BOOK map

248a

Tokyo

The map at the right shows central Tokyo and its major landmarks. The map below shows the Metropolis of Tokyo, which includes the city proper and the suburban and county areas. Each area appears on the map in a different color. The red circles show distances from the Imperial Palace.

⎯⎯⎯⎯ Metropolis boundary

– – – Prefecture boundary

⎯⎯⎯ Highway or street

⊢⊢⊢ Rail line

• City or town

▪ Point of interest

City proper

Suburban area

County area

Park or garden

National park

WORLD BOOK maps

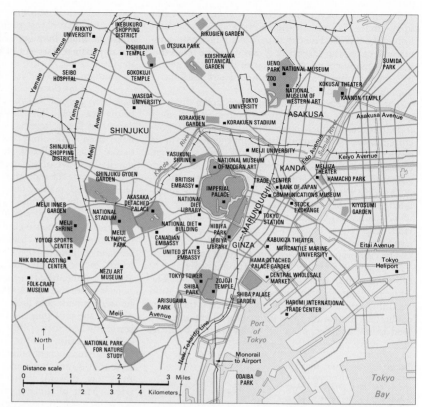

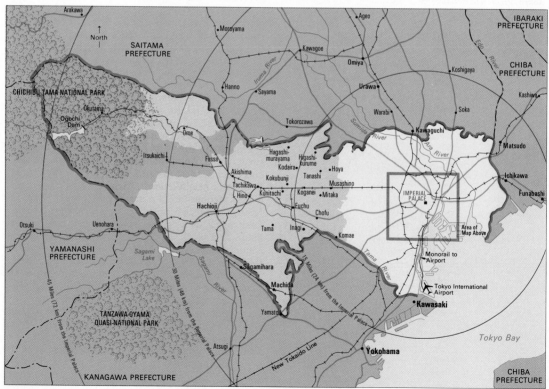

More jobs and educational and cultural opportunities are available in Tokyo than anywhere else in Japan. As a result, the city constantly attracts people—especially the young—from other parts of the country. Between 1960 and 1980, the Metropolis gained nearly 2 million persons. Today, Tokyo proper has an average of about 37,000 persons per square mile (14,000 persons per square kilometer)—nearly twice as many as New York City has.

Housing. Tokyo's soaring population has created a serious housing shortage. In the past, most Tokyo residents lived in small, one- or two-story wooden houses, each with its own yard or garden. As the population grew, many apartment buildings were constructed in the city proper in an attempt to provide housing for all the people. Even so, the housing shortage continued. The shortage of housing and of land in the city proper drove up rents and land prices. Many people—even if they could find housing in the city proper—could not afford to pay for it. As a result, a building boom began in Tokyo's outlying areas during the mid-1900's.

The city government has begun financing the construction of low-rent housing projects. One such project, called Tama New Town, will house 400,000 persons after its completion in the late 1980's. But Tama New Town, like many other Tokyo housing developments, is far from the city proper. Some workers who live in outlying areas spend up to four hours a day traveling to and from their jobs in downtown Tokyo.

Food and Clothing. Many Tokyo residents enjoy traditional Japanese foods. Popular Japanese dishes include *sukiyaki* (beef cooked with vegetables), *tempura* (fish and vegetables fried in batter), and *sushi* (fish and rice prepared in various ways). Western and Chinese foods are also popular in Tokyo.

On the streets and at work, most of the people wear Western-style clothing. Some older people still put on a *kimono* when they get home. The kimono, a traditional Japanese garment of both men and women, is a long robe tied with a sash. Most Tokyo young people wear a kimono only on holidays or other special occasions. Many elementary and some high school students wear uniforms to school. The boys' uniform is a suit with a jacket that fits tightly around the neck. Girls wear skirts and pullover blouses.

Education. The Metropolis of Tokyo has about 1,200 elementary schools, 700 junior high schools, and 400 senior high schools. Most of these schools are in the city proper. Some parts of Tokyo do not have enough schools for the rapidly growing population. But in some old sections that are now largely occupied by businesses, many schoolhouses stand nearly empty.

Tokyo has about 100 four-year colleges and universities and 90 junior colleges. About half of Japan's college students attend these institutions.

Social Problems, such as poverty and crime, exist in Tokyo. But they are not so severe as they are in many other large cities. Because of Tokyo's strong economy, most people can find jobs. In addition, the local and national governments provide aid for people who cannot support themselves. Tokyo's crime rate is much lower than the crime rate in most Western cities. The robbery rate in New York City, for example, is more than 150 times greater than that in Tokyo. Tokyo has no large minority groups, and so the city is not troubled by conflicts that stem from racial or other social differences.

Demonstrations are often held in Tokyo to protest such matters as political and educational policies. They have sometimes resulted in violence.

Sven Samelius from Carl Östman

Life in Tokyo combines the old and the new. Some people, like the woman above, wear the traditional kimono, but most wear Western clothes. Housing in the city includes both old frame houses and modern high-rise apartment buildings, *right*.

Few cities in the world can match Tokyo as a *cosmopolitan* (international) cultural center. Tokyo's art galleries, concert halls, museums, and other cultural institutions reflect the culture of both the East and the West.

The Arts. Many of Japan's finest artists and craftsmen live and work in Tokyo. Some still use the styles and methods of their ancestors to create beautiful paintings on paper or silk and colorful woodblock prints. But many Tokyo artists create paintings and sculptures using Western styles and methods.

Tokyo is the center of Japan's performing arts, such as drama and music. Two traditional types of Japanese drama, *no* and *kabuki*, rank as favorite forms of entertainment in Tokyo. For descriptions of these colorful plays, see DRAMA (Japan). Five professional symphony orchestras that specialize in Western music perform in Tokyo. Other Tokyo musical groups present concerts of traditional music, featuring such Japanese instruments as the three-stringed *samisen*, or *shamisen*, and a kind of harp called a *koto*. Japan's motion-picture industry is also centered in Tokyo. Japanese movies have been praised by audiences throughout the world.

Museums and Libraries. Some of Japan's finest museums and libraries are in Tokyo. The Tokyo National Museum, the largest museum in Japan, has a valuable collection of Asian art objects. The National Museum of Modern Art specializes in works by modern Japanese artists. The National Museum of Western Art houses a large collection of works by Western artists.

Tokyo's public library system includes a central library and more than 70 branch libraries. The National

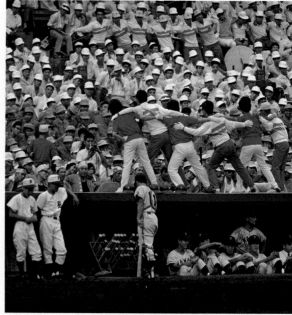

Minoru Aoki, Rapho Guillumette

Sports Events rank among Tokyo's chief forms of entertainment. Many people, like the crowd above, are baseball fans. Many also enjoy sumo wrestling and other ancient Japanese sports.

Diet Library, which is part of the headquarters of Japan's national government, ranks as the country's largest library. It owns about 6 million volumes, and its functions resemble those of the U.S. Library of Congress (see LIBRARY OF CONGRESS).

Entertainment and Recreation. Tokyo offers a wide variety of leisure-time activities. Concerts, motion pictures, and plays attract large audiences. Exhibitions of *judo* and *sumo*, which are Japanese forms of wrestling, rank as favorite sporting events. Western sports, including baseball, bowling, golf, ice skating, tennis, and track and field, are also popular. Baseball is the most popular sport in Tokyo. Home games of the Tokyo Giants professional baseball team and many other sports events are held in the 35,000-seat Korakuen Stadium. Tokyo's largest stadium, the National Stadium, is the site of many important track and field events. It seats about 72,000 spectators.

Tokyo also has many amusement parks and nightclubs. At some of the older Japanese-style restaurants, talented young women called *geishas* entertain patrons with singing, dancing, and conversation.

Most Tokyo families own a television set. Both Japanese programs and American and European programs with Japanese sound tracks appear on Tokyo TV.

Religion. Shinto and Buddhism are the chief religions throughout Japan. Tokyo has hundreds of historic Shinto shrines and Buddhist temples. But most Tokyo residents visit these places of worship only for public festivals or such special occasions as weddings and funerals. Less than 2 per cent of the residents of the Metropolis are Christians.

Toshio Watanabe, DPI

Japan's Performing Arts are centered in Tokyo. Traditional art forms, such as the *no* drama, *above*, are popular. But performances of Western-style drama and music also draw large crowds.

248d

Large numbers of tourists visit Tokyo the year around. In early April, the city's famous cherry trees are in bloom. Autumn in Tokyo usually brings pleasantly mild weather. The city's many festivals are other tourist attractions. These include the exciting parade of Tokyo's firemen on January 6 and the lively festival of the Asakusa Shrine in mid-May.

Tourists can choose from many fine hotels and restaurants in Tokyo. Some of the hotels are built and furnished in Western style. Others are Japanese-style hotels called *ryokan*. They have such traditional features as sliding paper-paneled doors, *tatami* mats that cover the floors, and heavy quilts that serve as beds. Tokyo has an unusually large number of restaurants—more than 60,000. Some of these restaurants specialize in Western or Chinese foods, and others serve only Japanese dishes.

This section of the article describes a few of the interesting places to visit in Tokyo. Other sections discuss additional places of interest.

The Imperial Palace is the home of Japan's emperor. It stands near the center of the city proper and consists of several low buildings and beautiful parklike grounds. Stone walls and a series of wide moats separate it from the rest of the city. The palace is open to the public only two days of the year—January 2 and the emperor's birthday. Thousands of Japanese come to pay their respects to the emperor on these two days.

The National Diet Building, a concrete and granite structure with a tall central tower, stands southwest of the Imperial Palace. It is the meeting place of Japan's *Diet* (parliament) and is open to visitors.

Tokyo Tower, a 1,092-foot (333-meter) steel tower, stands about 1½ miles (2.4 kilometers) south of the Im-

Milt and Joan Mann

The Imperial Palace attracts thousands of visitors on January 2 and the emperor's birthday, when it is open to the public. A family poses for a photograph near the palace grounds, *above*.

perial Palace. The city's tallest structure, Tokyo Tower houses radio and television broadcasting studios and has two observation platforms.

Parks and Gardens of Tokyo attract many visitors. Ueno Park, about 2 miles (3 kilometers) northeast of the palace, is one of the city's most popular parks. Its spring displays of cherry blossoms and summer displays of lotus blossoms are outstanding. The park includes Tokyo's largest concert hall, several museums and art galleries, a zoo, a temple and shrine built during the 1600's, and tombs of Japanese rulers.

Several Japanese-style gardens in Tokyo are open to the public. Korakuen Garden and Rikugien Garden—both a little north of the palace—are two of the oldest and most famous gardens. Many people visit Tokyo's gardens to admire their beautifully landscaped grounds and relax at their teahouses.

Shrines and Temples attract millions of worshipers and tourists yearly. The shrines are Shinto places of worship, and the temples are Buddhist. Meiji Shrine, about 3 miles (5 kilometers) southwest of the Imperial Palace, is one of the best-known shrines in Japan. Many Japanese visit it on New Year's Day, one of the few times when most Japanese women wear traditional dress in public. The Yasukuni Shrine stands northwest of the palace. It is dedicated to Japan's war dead and draws huge crowds of worshipers for special festivals in April and October. Tokyo also has a number of famous Buddhist temples, including the historic Kannon Temple in the Asakusa district. The temple traces its origins to the 600's, though the present buildings were constructed in the 1950's. Colorful souvenir shops line the approach to the temple.

Milt and Joan Mann

At Tokyo's Famous Meiji Shrine, Shinto priests greet visitors with a bow. This and other historic places of worship are among Tokyo's leading tourist attractions.

Tokyo ranks as one of the world's centers of economic activity. Since the end of World War II in 1945, Japan's economy has grown faster than that of any other country. Tokyo has played a major role in this growth. It is the main center of Japan's commercial, financial, and industrial activities and of its transportation industry. About a fourth of Japan's business corporations have their headquarters in the Metropolis. About 15 per cent of all the factories in Japan are also there.

Industry. The Tokyo Metropolis has more than 80,-000 factories. Most of them are small and employ fewer than 20 persons. But some are gigantic plants that have from 10,000 to 20,000 workers. Nearly 1½ million industrial workers hold jobs in the Metropolis.

Tokyo's two leading industries are (1) the manufacture of electrical machinery and (2) publishing and printing. Several huge companies and many small ones in the Metropolis make computers, phonographs, radios, television sets, tape recorders, and other electrical machinery. Many of these products are exported to the United States and other countries. About four of every five Japanese publishing companies have their headquarters in Tokyo. The Tokyo area's newspaper companies publish more than 25 daily papers and sell a total of about 25 million copies daily. Much of the material published in Tokyo is also printed there. Other important products of Tokyo include chemicals, food, furniture, and paper. Several Tokyo companies rank among the 25 largest manufacturing firms in the world.

Finance. Businesses and industries throughout Japan depend on Tokyo banks for loans. The Bank of Japan, the nation's central bank, has its headquarters in Tokyo. Controlled by the national government, it regulates the nation's entire banking system. Tokyo also has many commercial banks. The largest have branches or offices in many Japanese and foreign cities.

The Tokyo Stock Exchange is one of the world's leading stock exchanges. It handles the stocks of over 1,300 Japanese and foreign firms, more than are handled by the New York Stock Exchange.

Trade. Nearly 3,000 companies in the Tokyo Metropolis deal in foreign trade. These firms handle almost half of Japan's export business and more than half its import business. The 40-story Tokyo Trade Center displays Japanese goods for foreign buyers.

About 173,000 wholesale and retail establishments are in the Metropolis. The 41,000 wholesale companies, which sell to buyers throughout Japan, employ more than 600,000 persons. The 132,000 retail stores employ more than 550,000 workers. Most of the retail stores are small shops. But Tokyo has department stores and shopping centers as large and modern as any in the United States.

Transportation. About 2 million motor vehicles are registered in the Metropolis. Most are automobiles. In the mid-1900's, the metropolitan government built a system of freeways to speed traffic through the city. Even so, there are many more motor vehicles than the freeways and streets can handle, and severe traffic jams occur frequently. Automobile exhausts cause such heavy air pollution in Tokyo that policemen often must take oxygen after directing traffic. The metropolitan government is trying to provide more public transportation as a substitute for automobile travel.

© Jerry Cooke

The Tokyo Stock Exchange, *above*, is one of the world's leading stock exchanges. The exchange and the city's many banks help make Tokyo the financial center of Japan.

Organization. The Metropolis of Tokyo is one of Japan's *prefectures*. A prefecture is somewhat like a state of the United States. The government of the Metropolis serves as the government for the prefecture and for the city proper and the rest of the metropolitan area. As a result, it is a large, complicated organization.

The governor of Tokyo Prefecture also serves as the chief government official of the Metropolis of Tokyo. The people of the prefecture elect the governor to a four-year term. Tokyo's chief lawmaking body is the Metropolitan Assembly. It has 126 members, whom the voters elect to four-year terms. Each ward, city, and other community in the Metropolis has at least one representative in the Assembly. The metropolitan government also includes the board of education, the police and fire departments, and many other agencies. Together, they employ more than 220,000 persons.

The wards, cities, towns, and villages of the Metropolis all have some form of local government. Each elects a council and a mayor or other administrator, but the powers of these officials are limited by the metropolitan government. The metropolitan government makes *ordinances* (rules) for all the communities in the Metropolis. It also provides police protection and certain other public services for the entire Metropolis. But it provides some services, including fire protection and sanitation facilities, for the city proper only. Local governments must provide services not supplied by the metropolitan government. They may collect some tax money for these projects, and they receive additional funds from the metropolitan and national governments.

Problems. Tokyo, like cities everywhere, faces enormous problems. The metropolitan government must deal with such problems as a severe housing shortage, air and water pollution, overcrowded streets and highways, and danger from floods and earthquakes. Tokyo's complicated government organization and a shortage of money make solutions to the problems difficult. The metropolitan government has a responsibility to both the national government and the people of the Metropolis. This double responsibility complicates the metropolitan government's work. In addition, much of the tax money collected in the Metropolis goes to the national government. Many Tokyo government officials believe that the national government should make the duties of the metropolitan government simpler and give the Metropolis more control over its finances.

Milt and Joan Mann

The Manufacture of Electrical Machinery ranks as Tokyo's leading industry. Many electrical products made in Tokyo, including tape recorders, *above*, are exported to other countries.

Tokyo's public transportation system is a complicated network of railroad, subway, and bus lines. Railroads extend from the city proper to most outlying areas and to other parts of Japan. Japanese National Railways operates some of the lines, and the rest are privately owned. Tokyo's commuter trains rank among the fastest and most efficient in the world. Nearly 10 million passengers cram aboard them each day and about 3 million use the trains of the city's seven subway lines daily. Employees called *pushers* work at some train stations. Their job involves shoving passengers into crowded trains to make more room (see CITY [picture: Travel in Cities]). One of the world's few successful *monorails* (single-rail trains) carries passengers between central Tokyo and Tokyo International Airport, in the far southern part of the city. Buses carry about 6 million passengers daily.

About 20 major airlines offer scheduled flights between Tokyo International Airport, also called Haneda Airport, and foreign cities. Air travel in and out of Tokyo is heavy, and so a much larger airport had to be built. The New Tokyo International Airport, located about 40 miles (64 kilometers) northeast of central Tokyo was completed in 1973. However, the opening of the airport was delayed because of strong, sometimes violent, protests by nearby residents and others who objected to the airport's presence. The airport opened in 1978.

The Port of Tokyo is not one of Japan's leading ports. Other ports, including those of Kobe and Yokohama, have deeper harbors and therefore can handle larger ships. Much of Tokyo's ocean trade passes through the nearby Port of Yokohama. Railroads, trucks, and barges carry large quantities of freight between the two cities.

Symbols of Tokyo. The flag of the Metropolis of Tokyo, *left*, and the coat of arms, *right*, feature a design made from the *kanji* characters used to write the word *Tokyo*. Kanji are Chinese characters used in the Japanese language. The design also represents the sun casting its rays throughout the city.

Early Development. During most of its history, Tokyo was called *Edo*. The first historical record of a settlement in the area shows that a powerful family named Edo lived there about 1180. The area had military importance because it overlooked both Tokyo Bay and the Kanto Plain. In 1457, a warrior named Ota Dokan built a castle at Edo. Dokan worked in the service of a powerful warrior family, one of several who ruled parts of Japan. He built his castle where the Imperial Palace now stands, and so Tokyo marks 1457 as the year of its beginning. A town named Edo grew up around the castle. But the development that made the town Japan's chief city did not begin until 1590. In that year, a warrior named Tokugawa Ieyasu made Edo his headquarters. In 1603, Ieyasu became *shogun* (military ruler) of Japan, and so Edo became the nation's political center. But Kyoto, a city southwest of Edo and the home of the emperor, remained the official capital. By the early 1800's, Edo had grown into a city of over a million people—more than 15 times larger than New York City at that time. Ieyasu and his descendants ruled as shoguns in Edo until 1867.

Western Influence. During the 1600's and 1700's, Japan kept apart from the rest of the world. The government allowed foreign trading ships to dock only at the port of Nagasaki. It also prohibited the Japanese people from traveling to other countries. In 1853, the U.S. government sent Commodore Matthew C. Perry to open relations with Japan. Perry sailed into Tokyo Bay with four warships and began talks with the Japanese rulers. He returned with more warships the next year and reached a partial agreement with the rulers. Partly as a result of Perry's efforts, Japan signed trade treaties with the United States and other Western countries in 1858. The treaties marked the beginning of modern Western influence in Japan.

Emperor Mutsuhito—also known as the Meiji Emperor—did much to further the Westernization process. Mutsuhito took control of Japan from the shogun in 1867. He transferred the capital from Kyoto to Edo in 1868 and moved into the Edo castle. Edo was renamed *Tokyo*, which means *eastern capital*. After 1868, Japan—and especially Tokyo—rapidly adopted Western styles and inventions. By the late 1800's, Tokyo began to look like a Western city.

Earthquake and Reconstruction. On Sept. 1, 1923, a violent earthquake shook the Tokyo-Yokohama area. Buildings collapsed and fires broke out throughout Tokyo. About 59,000 residents of the city proper died in the disaster, and most of central Tokyo was destroyed. The city was rebuilt during the next 20 years.

At the time of the earthquake, Tokyo consisted of 15 wards in the vicinity of the Imperial Palace. After the tragedy, areas outside the 15 wards began to develop. In 1932, the city took over many of the areas and made them wards, establishing the present ward area.

World War II brought destruction to Tokyo again. American bombers first attacked the city in April, 1942. The heaviest raids took place from March, 1945, until Japan agreed to surrender in August of that year. The bombs destroyed about 97 square miles (251 square kilometers) of Tokyo. More than 250,000 persons were killed or listed as missing. Thousands fled the city. Tokyo's population dropped from about 7,350,000 in 1940 to about 3,500,000 in 1945. In 1943—during the war—Tokyo and communities west of it united to form the Metropolis of Tokyo.

Rebuilding the City. The people of Tokyo began to rebuild their city after the war, but without much planning. Buildings went up wherever there was room. Tokyo's economy began booming a few years after the war. Population growth accompanied economic growth, and the population of the city proper more than doubled between 1945 and 1960. In 1964, Tokyo was host to the summer Olympic Games. In preparation for the games, the city started a construction program that included new freeways and hotels, and the monorail.

Recent Developments. Tokyo's continued growth has made it one of the world's largest cities and has given it a strong economy. But this growth, along with the lack of planning, has helped cause such problems as the housing shortage, pollution, and traffic jams.

In 1969, the metropolitan government started a series of three-year plans to help solve Tokyo's major problems. The plans set annual goals for improving public housing, purifying the polluted air and river water, reducing street noise and traffic jams, and increasing sanitation facilities. Parts of the Metropolis have been set aside for public housing and other community projects. To ease overcrowding, the government encourages the development of new suburban towns. A number of such towns in and around Tokyo Prefecture are growing rapidly.   Critically reviewed by CHIE NAKANE

TOKYO / Study Aids

Related Articles in WORLD BOOK include:

Outline

I. The City
  A. The City Proper   B. Outlying Areas
II. The People
  A. Housing   C. Education
  B. Food and Clothing   D. Social Problems
III. Cultural Life
  A. The Arts   C. Entertainment
  B. Museums   and Recreation
    and Libraries   D. Religion
IV. Visiting Tokyo
V. Economy
  A. Industry   C. Trade
  B. Finance   D. Transportation
VI. Government
  A. Organization   B. Problems
VII. History

Questions

In what ways does Tokyo resemble an American city?
What is the *ward area?*
When was Tokyo made the capital of Japan?
What is the most popular sport in Tokyo?
What makes Tokyo's government unusually complicated?
What kind of clothing do many Tokyo students wear?
What are Tokyo's two leading industries?
How large a part of Japan's population lives in Tokyo?
Why do parts of Tokyo face the danger of flooding?
What are Tokyo's main kinds of public transportation?

ALLINSON, GARY D. *Suburban Tokyo: A Comparative Study in Politics and Social Change.* Univ. of California Press, 1979.

BOARDMAN, GWENN R. *Living in Tokyo.* Nelson, 1970. For younger readers.

KIRKUP, JAMES. *Tokyo.* Dent, 1966. A social, economic, religious, and artistic account of life in Tokyo.

TOKYO ROSE. See WORLD WAR II (Psychological Warfare).

TOLEDO, *toh LEE doh* (pop. 52,988), stands on a high hill 41 miles (66 kilometers) southwest of Madrid, Spain. The Tagus River flows in a deep ravine around the base of the hill. The city is the capital of Toledo province. For location, see SPAIN (political map).

Toledo is a medieval city of narrow, steep, winding streets. There are many historic works of architecture in Toledo, and the Spanish government has declared the entire city a Spanish national monument. Its architecture shows a strong Moorish influence. Houses rise straight up, many of them without windows facing the streets. A magnificent Gothic cathedral dominates the city. Its tower rises 300 feet (91 meters). Beautiful chapels inside contain many fine paintings and statues. El Greco lived in Toledo, and his home is now a museum for some of his paintings.

Toledo has little industry, but is famous for sabers, firearms, Toledo ware (inlaid steel), and textiles. Its founding date is unknown. Arabs destroyed the city in the 700's. Alfonso VI, king of León and Castile, seized Toledo in 1085 and made it his capital. Philip II made Madrid the capital in 1561.   STANLEY G. PAYNE

TOLEDO, *toh LEE doh,* Ohio (pop. 354,635; met. area pop. 791,599), is a leading industrial and transportation center of the state. The city ranks as the largest producer of automotive parts in the United States. Three of the nation's largest glass-manufacturing companies have their headquarters in Toledo, which is often called the *Glass Capital of the World.* Toledo, a major Great Lakes port, lies on both banks of the Maumee River in northwestern Ohio. For location, see OHIO (political map). At Toledo, the river widens into Maumee Bay at the western end of Lake Erie.

The first permanent white settlers in what is now the Toledo area arrived in 1817. The settlers chose the site because of its location on the Maumee River. The city was named for Toledo, Spain, but no one knows why.

Description. Toledo, the county seat of Lucas County, covers about 96 square miles (249 square kilometers). Its business district and most of its homes are west of the Maumee River. Toledo's glass plants lie east of the river. The port is on Maumee Bay.

Institutions of higher education in Toledo include the Medical College of Ohio and the University of Toledo. The Toledo Museum of Art owns one of the largest collections of rare glass objects in the world. Toledo is also the home of the Toledo Symphony Orchestra and the Toledo Opera Association. The Toledo Zoo ranks among the finest zoos in the nation. Several historical monuments lie near the city. They commemorate General Anthony Wayne's victory over Indians in the Battle of Fallen Timbers in 1794 and General William Henry Harrison's victory against the British in the War of 1812.

Economy. The Toledo metropolitan area has more than 1,000 manufacturing plants. They employ about a third of the area's workers. The production of transportation equipment is the chief industrial activity, and Toledo has the world's largest spark plug plant. Other industries, in order of importance, produce glass products, nonelectrical machinery, petroleum and coal products, food products, metal goods, and fabricated metal products. Toledo also is a major producer of scales.

The Port of Toledo handles more than 25 million short tons (23 million metric tons) of cargo annually. The city ranks as one of the world's leading shippers of coal. It also serves as a trading center for the rich agricultural region in northwestern Ohio. Several freight railroads help bring cargo to Toledo for lake shipment. Toledo Express Airport also serves the city.

Government and History. Toledo has a council-manager form of government. The voters elect a mayor and eight other council members, all to two-year terms. The council hires a city manager to carry out its policies.

Erie Indians lived in the Toledo area before white people came there. In 1615, Étienne Brulé, a guide for the French explorer Samuel de Champlain, became the first white man to see the area. In 1817, land speculators established a settlement on the site of Fort Industry, a stockade built about 1795. They called this settlement Port Lawrence. Port Lawrence and the nearby village of Vistula united in 1833 to form Toledo. The community received a city charter in 1837.

The city's growth as a transportation center began in 1836, when railroads first reached Toledo. The Wabash and Erie Canal in Indiana and the Miami and Erie Canal in Ohio began operating during the 1840's. They had a joint outlet in Toledo. The city, with its natural lake port, became an important water gateway to the western United States.

In 1888, Edward Libbey, a glass manufacturer from East Cambridge, Mass., brought skilled workers to the Toledo area and founded the Libbey Glass Company. He was later joined by Michael Owens. The glass industry helped increase the city's population from 3,829 in 1850 to 131,822 in 1900. An automobile plant opened in 1908. By 1930, 290,718 people lived in the city.

During the 1960's, Toledo began several urban renewal programs. One of these programs included the 30-story Owens-Corning Fiberglas Tower, the city's tallest building, which opened in 1969. Toledo's civic plans for the 1970's included the construction of a new municipal courts building. This project was completed in 1976.   WILLIAM ROSENBERG

TOLEDO WAR. See OHIO (Statehood).

TOLERANCE, in human relations, means recognizing and respecting others' views, practices, and beliefs. See CIVIL RIGHTS; FREEDOM OF RELIGION; HUMAN RIGHTS, UNIVERSAL DECLARATION OF.

TOLERATION ACT is a law permitting people to believe in any religion they choose. One famous toleration act, passed by the colony of Maryland in 1649, gave religious liberty to all Christians. The most famous Toleration Act was that of 1689, passed by the English Parliament. It granted religious freedom to the Protestant dissenters from the established Anglican Church. This law did not apply to Roman Catholics, Jews, and

TOLKIEN, J. R. R.

Unitarians. But the dissenters continued to suffer until the 1800's.
J. SALWYN SCHAPIRO

TOLKIEN, J. R. R. (1892-1973), an English author and scholar, wrote a popular series of novels about an imaginary people called *hobbits*. Tolkien introduced the dwarflike hobbits in *The Hobbit* (1937). He continued their story in three related novels called *The Lord of the Rings*. These novels are *The Fellowship of the Ring* (1954), *The Two Towers* (1954), and *The Return of the King* (1955).

Hobbits are industrious and good-natured. They live in a world called Middle-earth, along with elves, goblins, wizards, and human beings. In *The Hobbit*, Bilbo Baggins, a hobbit, discovers a ring that has evil powers. The hero of *The Lord of the Rings* is Frodo Baggins, Bilbo's cousin. After many adventures, Frodo and eight companions destroy the ring so that Sauron, the evil Dark Lord, cannot use it against the hobbits. Many critics have interpreted *The Lord of the Rings* as a symbolic moral or religious story about the battle between good and evil. But Tolkien insisted that he wrote the novels only as fantasies to entertain readers.

In 1917, Tolkien began to write *The Silmarillion*, a history of Middle-earth before the hobbits appeared. He died before completing it, and his son Christopher finished the novel. It was published in 1977. A collection of previously unpublished material about Middle-earth and the legendary island of Númenor appeared in 1980 as *Unfinished Tales*.

John Ronald Reuel Tolkien was born in Bloemfontein, South Africa, of English parents. From 1925 to 1959, he taught at Oxford University in England, where he specialized in medieval languages and literature. He wrote several scholarly works in this field. Tolkien's hobbit stories show the influence of the medieval English, German, and Scandinavian languages and literature.
HARRY OSTER

Additional Resources

CARPENTER, HUMPHREY. *Tolkien: A Biography*. Houghton, 1977.
FONSTAD, KAREN WYNN. *The Atlas of Middle Earth*. Houghton, 1981.
HELMS, RANDEL. *Tolkien's World*. Houghton, 1974.
LOBDELL, JARED, ed. *A Tolkien Compass*. Open Court, 1975.

TOLL ROAD. See TURNPIKE.

TOLMAN, EDWARD CHACE (1886-1959), was an American psychologist known for his theory of how human beings and other animals learn. Tolman rejected the learning theory of John B. Watson and other behavioral psychologists of the time. These psychologists maintained that learning occurs through a random trial-and-error process. Tolman argued that learning is a systematic process guided by goals and expectations. He believed that learners develop what he called *cognitive maps*—that is, mental images of the probable paths to their goals. He explained his theory in a book called *Purposive Behavior in Animals and Men* (1932).

Tolman was born in Newton, Mass. He taught psychology at the University of California at Berkeley from 1918 until his death.
RICHARD M. WOLF

TOLSTOY, ALEXEI NIKOLAEVICH (1882-1945), COUNT TOLSTOY, won great popularity and wealth in Russia as a writer of novels and plays. His name is also

spelled *Tolstoi*. He wrote *Road to Calvary* (1921-1941), a trilogy portraying Russian life during World War I, the 1917 Revolution, and the Civil War; and *Peter I* (1929-1945), an unfinished novel about that czar. Tolstoy was born in the province of Samara (now Kuybyshev). He studied engineering at the Saint Petersburg Technological Institute, but gave up this career for writing. During the Revolution of 1917, Tolstoy fled from Russia, but he returned in 1922. He gave up his title of count and wrote propaganda for Russia. He was a distant relative of Leo Tolstoy.
ERNEST J. SIMMONS

TOLSTOY, LEO NIKOLAEVICH (1828-1910), COUNT TOLSTOY, was one of Russia's most celebrated writers of fiction. His name is also spelled *Tolstoi*. He was also an important moral thinker and a social reformer. Tolstoy wrote *War and Peace*, perhaps the greatest work in Russian realistic fiction, and *Anna Karenina*, one of the great love stories of the world.

His Youth. Tolstoy was born on Sept. 9, 1828 (Aug. 28 by the calendar then in use), on his family estate in the province of Tula. His parents died when he was a boy, and he was brought up by female relatives. He received his early education from foreign tutors, and entered the University of Kazan in 1844. He left school in 1847, and returned to Yasnaya Polyana to manage his estate and continue his education through his own

Count Leo Tolstoy spent long hours at a work table in his country home before he renounced all his wealth and property in 1890 and went to live, work, and write among peasants.

Drawing (1887) by Ilya Repin; Historical Pictures Service

efforts. Dissatisfied with his life there, Tolstoy volunteered in the Russian Army. He fought bravely in the famous siege of Sevastopol in 1855 in the Crimean War.

He retired from the army in 1856. He made two trips to western Europe between 1857 and 1861, and then he settled down at his estate at Yasnaya Polyana. He farmed the land and opened a school for peasant children, whom he taught with great success. Much in advance of his time, Tolstoy believed that teaching should be adapted to the individual needs of the pupil. He was married in 1862, and spent the next 15 years on his estate. He reared a large family and wrote *War and Peace* and *Anna Karenina* there.

New Ideas. As a youth, Tolstoy had often pondered over difficult questions concerning the meaning and purpose of life. At the age of 46, seemingly happy, prosperous, and famous, these questions bothered him so much that he felt he must try to solve them.

He read widely in religious and philosophical books, and talked and corresponded with many wise people for several years. He then believed he had found an explanation to life's meaning in the true significance of Christ's preaching "to resist not evil." Tolstoy believed that every person had the power to understand what is good, and that human beings would justify their lives by striving to do good for themselves and others.

In 1890 Tolstoy, unwilling to own property any longer, left his estate to his wife and nine children. He renounced the copyrights to his writings. His wife then undertook to publish his works. After that he never had a penny of his own.

Tolstoy condemned all violence, gave up tobacco and intoxicating liquors, and became a vegetarian. He dressed simply, worked in the fields with the peasants, made his own boots, and tried to be as self-sufficient as possible. He preached charity and helped others in distress. He insisted that society would become better only when all men and women tried to become more perfect in their personal lives and learned to love each other. His unusual views and principles and his way of life often brought him into conflict with the government and even with his own family.

When he was 82, unhappy in spirit and in his failure to live his life as he thought best, he left his home secretly at night to seek freedom from all worldly cares and to come closer to God. His health broke down a few days later, and on Nov. 22, 1910, Tolstoy died in the tiny railway station at Astapovo. Thousands of people throughout the world mourned his death.

In 1901, the Russian Orthodox Church had excommunicated Tolstoy because of his teachings. When he died, he was denied a religious funeral. He was buried at his estate in Yasnaya Polyana.

His Writing. Tolstoy inspired many people to live by his beliefs. But his success as a reformer came somewhat from his reputation as a writer of fiction.

He began to write when he was quite young. He published his first story, *Childhood*, in 1852. The story is a delightful combination of memoir and fiction, based on his own experiences as a child and those of his family and friends. *Boyhood* (1854) and *Youth* (1857) followed. These stories are admirable, but have less of the charming spontaneity of *Childhood*. During the same period he wrote short stories based on experiences with the Russian forces in the Caucasus. In 1855, Tolstoy wrote

Sevastopol Stories, realistic accounts of the fighting in that city. He brought his first literary period to a close with his highly praised short novel *The Cossacks* (1862). The central character, the refined Olenin, finds much to admire in the almost primitive life of the dashing Cossacks of the Caucasus.

Tolstoy's most famous novels are *War and Peace* and *Anna Karenina*. *War and Peace* was published in installments from 1865 to 1869, and *Anna Karenina* from 1875 to 1877. *War and Peace* is the story of five families seen against the magnificently described background of Napoleon's invasion of Russia in 1812. Numerous other characters appear, from peasants to emperors. All are brought alive through the magic of Tolstoy's writing, which reaches unsurpassed perfection in this novel. *Anna Karenina*, a powerful study of an unhappy woman, is equally impressive, although it does not contain the epic sweep and richness of *War and Peace*.

Tolstoy stopped writing fiction for a time after his religious experience in 1880. He devoted his literary talents largely to books, pamphlets, and articles on religious, moral, and social themes. The best known of these works are *A Confession* (1882), *What I Believe* (1884), *What Then Must We Do?* (1886), and *The Kingdom of God Is Within You* (1894).

He returned eventually to writing fiction. He wrote *The Power of Darkness* (1886), a play; *The Kreutzer Sonata* (1891), and *Resurrection* (1899), both novels; and *The Living Corpse*, a play published after his death. These works reflect the new and rather rigid moral position Tolstoy had assumed, and lack the vitality of his earlier writings.   ERNEST J. SIMMONS

Additional Resources

CHRISTIAN, REGINALD. *Tolstoy: A Critical Introduction.* Cambridge, 1970.

SIMMONS, ERNEST. *Tolstoy.* Routledge & Kegan, 1973.

STEINER, EDWARD. *Tolstoi the Man.* Haskell, 1971. Reprint of 1909 ed.

TOLSTOI, ALEXANDRA. *Tolstoy: A Life of My Father.* Octagon, 1973. Reprint of 1953 ed.

TOLTEC INDIANS, *TAHL tek,* or *TOHL tek,* were the dominant people in the central Mexican highlands from about A.D. 900 to 1200. Their language and way of life influenced the Aztec, who followed them. The Toltec also probably affected the Maya of Yucatán. Buildings at the Mayan city of Chichén Itzá closely resemble Toltec architecture, and may have been built under the Toltec. See MAYA (The Mexican Period).

Aztec legends referred to the Toltec as ancient heroes who brought civilization to Mexico, and who built a majestic capital called Tula, or Tollan, "Place of the Reeds." The word *Toltec* means *people of Tula*. The ruins of the city lie near the present town of Tula, 60 miles (97 kilometers) north of Mexico City.

The ruins of Tula contain several pyramids surmounted by temples, in the usual Mexican fashion. One was the temple of Quetzalcóatl, "The Plumed Serpent," who according to legend, had founded Tula. He was a major god of both the Toltec and the Aztec. Great columns in the form of serpents and human beings supported the roof. Nomadic Mexican tribes gradually overran Tula and the Toltec empire and founded the greater empire of the Aztec.   GORDON F. EKHOLM

TOLUENE

TOLUENE, *TAHL you een*, or METHYL BENZENE (chemical formula $C_6H_5CH_3$), is an aromatic liquid related to benzene. *Aromatic* is a word used to describe a member of the benzene family of chemical compounds. A benzene molecule contains atoms of carbon and hydrogen. These atoms have a closed ring-type structure that is represented as a *hexagon* (six-sided figure). Chemists represent toluene by using the six-sided benzene figure and adding a *methyl* group to it. A methyl group is composed of one carbon and three hydrogen atoms.

Manufacturers make toluene by treating petroleum or distilling coal tar. Chemists use toluene as a raw material to produce other chemicals. For example, they sometimes make benzoic acid from it. Benzoic acid is used as a preservative for foods, beverages, and cosmetics. An antiseptic known as chloramine-T is also made from toluene. Makers of explosives use toluene to make trinitrotoluene, commonly called TNT. Paint manufacturers use toluene as a lacquer solvent. Toluene is also used in the manufacture of many dyes and perfumes. Federal regulations require manufacturers to limit the amount of toluene in the air breathed by workers. Excessive exposure to toluene can damage the skin, the eyes, and the central nervous system.   JAMES S. FRITZ

See also BENZENE; TNT.

TOM SAWYER. See TWAIN, MARK (Novels).

TOM THUMB. See STRATTON, CHARLES SHERWOOD.

TOM THUMB was the name of the first American-built steam locomotive to be operated on a common-carrier railroad. Peter Cooper designed and built it in 1830. It operated on the Baltimore and Ohio Railroad in Baltimore in the summer of 1830. It pulled one of the first passenger trains. See also COOPER, PETER; RAILROAD (Developments in the United States).

TOM-TOM is an African native drum. It is usually beaten with the hands. Jazz bands of the 1920's introduced imitation tom-toms, and today many drummers perform on tom-toms.

TOMAHAWK was a small ax that the Indians of North America used as a tool and a weapon. Most tomahawks measured less than 18 inches (45 centimeters) long and were light enough to be used with one hand. Early tomahawks consisted of a *head* (top part)

made of stone or bone mounted on a wooden handle. Some tomahawks ended in a ball or knob instead of a flat blade. After Europeans arrived in America, the Indians traded with them for iron tomahawk heads.

The Indians used tomahawks to chop wood, to drive stakes into the ground, and for many other purposes. In battle, warriors threw their tomahawks or used them as clubs. Tomahawks also served as hunting weapons.

The Indians used a *pipe tomahawk* in religious ceremonies. This special tomahawk had a pipe bowl on the head and a hollow handle, and it could be smoked as a ceremonial pipe. The Indians decorated pipe tomahawks with feathers or with dyed porcupine quills.

Some people think the expression *bury the hatchet* came from an Indian custom of burying a tomahawk to pledge peace. However, many scholars doubt that the Indians ever had such a custom.   W. ROGER BUFFALOHEAD

TOMATO, *tuh MAY toh* or *tuh MAH toh*, is a plant grown for its smooth, round, juicy fruit. The word *tomato* refers both to the fruit, which people eat, and to the entire plant. The fruit has a slightly acid taste. There are more than 4,000 varieties of tomatoes.

Botanists classify tomatoes as fruits. However, most people consider tomatoes vegetables because fresh tomatoes are used in much the same way as lettuce, onions, cauliflower, and many other vegetables. Fresh tomatoes are eaten raw or cooked and are generally served in salads and other dishes. Most tomatoes grown in the United States are processed for use in making a variety of products. These include catchup, tomato juice, tomato soup, tomato paste, tomato sauce, and canned whole tomatoes. Tomatoes are an important source of vitamins A and C and of certain minerals.

About $54\frac{1}{2}$ million short tons (49.5 million metric tons) of tomatoes are grown throughout the world annually. The United States produces more tomatoes than any other nation, followed by Russia and China. Growers in the United States raise a commercial tomato crop of about $7\frac{1}{2}$ million short tons (6.8 million metric tons) yearly. More than three-fourths of the crop comes from California, but tomatoes are grown in almost every area of the country. Ontario leads the Canadian provinces in tomato production.

The Tomato Plant has a strong smell and has small hairs on its stems. It spreads out while growing and

Some Kinds of Tomahawks

The Indians of North America used many different types of tomahawks. Some ended in a ball or knob, and some in a flat blade. Early tomahawks had stone or bone heads, and later ones were made of iron. Pipe tomahawks had a pipe bowl on the head and a hollow handle, so that they could be smoked.

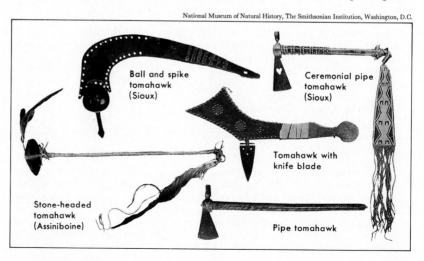

Ball and spike tomahawk (Sioux)

Ceremonial pipe tomahawk (Sioux)

Tomahawk with knife blade

Stone-headed tomahawk (Assiniboine)

Pipe tomahawk

Leading Tomato-Growing States and Provinces

Boxes of tomatoes grown in 1980*

State/Province		Boxes
California	🍅🍅🍅🍅🍅🍅🍅🍅🍅🍅🍅🍅	368,627,000 boxes
Florida	🍅🍅	37,309,000 boxes
Ontario	🍅	24,711,000 boxes
Ohio	🍅	16,034,000 boxes
Indiana	🍅	7,285,000 boxes

*One box equals 32 pounds (14.5 kilograms).
Sources: U.S. Department of Agriculture; Statistics Canada.

produces clusters of small yellow flowers. The flowers develop into fully ripe tomatoes 40 to 75 days after blossoming, depending on the variety. Tomatoes are green at first, but most turn red, orange, or yellow as they ripen.

Tomatoes thrive in fertile, warm, well-drained soil and in locations that receive at least six hours of direct sunlight each day. Tomatoes are a favorite of home gardeners, because they can be grown in nearly any kind of soil. In addition, a large crop requires relatively little space. Many varieties produce 10 to 15 pounds (4.5 to 7 kilograms) of fruit per plant.

Researchers and growers have bred tomatoes to increase the number of fruits per plant and to improve their quality and other features. For example, the leading variety of tomato grown in California, called

VF 145, was developed especially for harvesting by machines. Other types of tomatoes commonly grown in the United States include cherry tomatoes, *Sunray*, and *Big Boy Hybrid*. Another common variety, the *Ponderosa*, sometimes produces tomatoes that weigh more than 3 pounds (1.4 kilograms).

Growing, Harvesting, and Processing. Tomato seeds require 75 to 85 days to develop into mature plants with ripe fruits. In California and other areas that have a long growing season, the seeds can be planted outdoors. They are planted indoors in areas where the growing season is too short for outdoor development. Young tomato plants obtained from the seeds are transplanted outdoors when the seedlings are four to six weeks old. The transplanting takes place about two weeks after the last frost of spring, because tomato plants can be damaged by cold temperatures.

In gardens and greenhouses, most tomato plants are supported with stakes or trellises to keep them from spreading on the ground. Such supports allow the plants to be placed closer together, thus increasing the yield of each unit of land. The supports also help produce a better quality fruit and prevent a disease called *fruit rot* by keeping the fruits off moist ground.

The most common diseases of the tomato are *bacterial wilt*, *fusarium wilt*, and *verticillium wilt* (see WILT). Several kinds of insects and worms, including the tomato fruit worm and various aphids, cutworms, and leaf miners, also attack tomatoes. Plant breeders have developed varieties of the plants that resist a number of diseases and pests. In addition, many growers use chemicals to fight the enemies of tomatoes.

Most tomatoes raised to be eaten fresh are picked by hand, but an increasing number of growers use ma-

WORLD BOOK illustration by Kate Lloyd-Jones, Linden Artists Ltd

Grant Heilman

Tomatoes, *left,* are smooth, round, juicy fruits that grow in almost any soil. They are a favorite of home gardeners and are also widely grown commercially. In the United States, much of the commerical tomato crop is harvested by machine, *above.*

chines to harvest the crop. In the United States, machines harvest most tomatoes grown for processing.

Home gardeners pick tomatoes when they are ripe. Commercially grown tomatoes raised to be eaten fresh are picked before they ripen. Then they are shipped to warehouses in market areas. Unripe tomatoes are less easily damaged while being shipped. Tomatoes ripen in the warehouses.

Tomatoes grown for processing are harvested when ripe. They are then washed and scalded. Scalding loosens the skins and makes peeling easier. After the tomatoes have been peeled, they undergo different processes, depending on the final product. For example, tomatoes may be cooked, strained, or combined with other ingredients. The product is packed into containers, which are heated to destroy harmful bacteria. Finally, the containers are cooled and labeled, and then stored for shipping.

History. Tomatoes originated in South America, and Spanish priests probably brought them to Europe from Mexico in the mid-1500's. People in Spain and Italy then began to grow tomatoes as food. However, many people considered them poisonous because they are related to several poisonous plants. As a result, tomatoes did not become widely accepted as food until the early 1800's. Tomatoes were sometimes called *love apples*, perhaps because of a superstition that eating them made people fall in love.

Scientific Classification. The tomato belongs to the nightshade family, Solanaceae. Its scientific name is *Lycopersicon esculentum.*   WILLIAM L. GEORGE, JR.

TOMB, *toom,* is any chamber in which the dead are buried. Some tombs are cut out of rocks, and others are built above ground. Ancient peoples used tombs to keep the bodies of the dead safe. The Egyptians believed the departed person's spirit visited the burial place. They built the Pyramids, the greatest tombs in the world, for their kings. Many of their tombs were cleverly hidden to keep them safe from robbers (see PYRAMIDS; VALLEY OF THE KINGS).

The Jews cut tombs out of rock. Christ was said to have been placed in a new rock tomb belonging to Joseph of Arimathea. Most Greek tombs were simple, but those in the colonies of Asia Minor were elaborate. The most famous of these was the tomb of Mausolus at Halicarnassus in Caria. The word *mausoleum* comes from the name of this tomb.

The Romans built stately tombs which lined the roads leading to the city, because burial within the city was not allowed. Ruins of Roman tombs still line the Appian Way. The early Christians built tombs in underground rooms called *catacombs* (see CATACOMBS).

Islamic tombs are often large buildings, sometimes with a dome. One of the most famous of these is the Taj Mahal in Agra, India (see TAJ MAHAL).

The Tomb of the Unknown Soldier at Arlington National Cemetery in Virginia, Grant's tomb in New York City, and that of George and Martha Washington at Mount Vernon are perhaps the best known in the United States (see pictures with GRANT, ULYSSES S.; MOUNT VERNON; UNKNOWN SOLDIER).   CARL K. HERSEY

See also CRYPT; FUNERAL CUSTOMS; MEGALITHIC MONUMENTS; SARCOPHAGUS.

TOMBAUGH, CLYDE WILLIAM (1906-   ), is an American astronomer. He discovered Pluto, the ninth planet in our solar system, in 1930 while he was examining some photographic plates with a blink microscope at the Lowell Observatory. Percival Lowell had predicted the general location of Pluto 15 years earlier (see PLUTO). Tombaugh became engaged in ballistics research at White Sands (N.Mex.) Missile Range in 1946. He was born in Streator, Ill.   HELEN WRIGHT

TOMBIGBEE RIVER rises in northeast Mississippi and flows 525 miles (845 kilometers) south to Mobile Bay (see MISSISSIPPI [physical map]). The lower stretch, below the Alabama River junction, is called the *Mobile River* (see MOBILE RIVER). The Tombigbee and Black Warrior, its chief tributary, drain 19,500 square miles (50,505 square kilometers) in Mississippi and Alabama. Locks and dams on the lower Tombigbee and on the Black Warrior provide a navigation channel to Port Birmingham, Ala.   M. W. MYERS

TOMBOUCTOU. See TIMBUKTU.

TOMBSTONE, Ariz. (pop. 1,632), a famous silvermining town of the 1880's, is now a tourist attraction and health center (see ARIZONA [political map]). Tombstone's historic sites include O.K. Corral and Arizona's oldest Protestant church. Tombstone was named by its founder, prospector Ed Schieffelin. Friends told him he would find a tombstone, not a mine, in the area. They feared Indians would kill him. Tombstone was incorporated in 1881.   ALICE B. GOOD

TOMLIN, BRADLEY WALKER (1899-1953), was an American abstract expressionist painter. His best-known works contain strong lines arranged in a rhythmical order that suggest hieroglyphics. They maintain a balance between carefully structured, overlapping forms and such random elements as curving symbols, letters, and numerals. Tomlin's sense of order and his preference for harmonious colors set him slightly apart from most other abstract expressionists. His works are more lyrical and restrained than those of other artists in the movement.

Self-Portrait (1932); collection of the Whitney Museum of American Art, New York City, Gift of Henry Ittleson, Jr.

Bradley Walker Tomlin

Tomlin was born in Syracuse, N.Y. In 1921, he moved to New York City where he earned a living for a time designing magazine covers. From 1925 to the late 1930's, he painted in a moderate realistic style. From 1939 to about 1944, he concentrated on cubistic blends of still-life elements and abstract forms. This style led to the simplification and abstraction of Tomlin's later works. In 1957, the Whitney Museum of American Art presented a definitive exhibition of his works. DORE ASHTON

TOMONAGA, *tow MOW na GA,* **SIN-ITIRO,** *sheen EE chee ROW* (1906-1979), of Japan, shared the 1965 Nobel prize in physics with United States physicists Richard P. Feynman and Julian S. Schwinger. Working independently, the three men developed an improved theory of quantum electrodynamics in the 1940's. *Quantum electrodynamics* is the study of the interaction of electrons and electromagnetic radiation. The theory enables scientists to predict accurately the effects of electrically charged particles on each other in a radiation field. Tomonaga was born in Kyoto, Japan. He was graduated from Kyoto University. Tomonaga served on the faculty of the University of Tsukuba from 1941 to 1969.　　　　　　　　　R. T. ELLICKSON

TOMPKINS, DANIEL D. (1774-1825), served as Vice-President of the United States from 1817 to 1825 under President James Monroe. He was governor of New York from 1807 to 1817. He favored the War of 1812, and defended New York from the British as commander of the state militia.

He was handicapped by inadequate accounting methods during this trying period. During most of the rest of his life, Tompkins fought rumors that he had misappropriated funds entrusted to him as wartime governor. These false charges affected him as Vice-President. He became despondent during his vice-presidency, left Washington for long periods, and wasted his energies defending his character against his critics. Tompkins was born in Fox Meadows (now Scarsdale), N.Y. He served as associate justice of the Supreme Court of New York from 1804 to 1807.　IRVING G. WILLIAMS

See also VICE-PRESIDENT OF THE U.S. (picture).

TON, *tun*, is the name of three different units used to measure weight and capacity. The units are the *long ton*, *short ton*, and *metric ton*. The long and short tons are units most often used in the United States, but the metric ton is used by nearly all other countries. The long ton equals 2,240 pounds (1,016 kilograms), the short ton equals 2,000 pounds (907 kilograms), and the metric ton equals 1,000 kilograms, or 2,204.6 pounds. U.S. custom houses use the long ton in weighing. Coal and iron ore are weighed and sold at the mines by the long ton, and sold by the short ton to customers. See also MEASUREMENT (Measuring Weight); METRIC SYSTEM; WEIGHTS AND MEASURES.　　　　　　　　　　　E. G. STRAUS

TONE, *tohn*, in music, is the sound made by the vibration of a musical instrument or of the human voice. Tones differ in quality, pitch, intensity, and duration. Musicians use the word *tone* to describe the sound of each key on the piano keyboard, symbolized by a *note*. They also use it to describe the intervals on a keyboard. An interval between one white key and the next nearest white or black key, is a *half tone* (also called a *minor tone*). Two half tones (as from C to D on the keyboard) create the interval of a *whole tone* (also called a *major tone*). See also HARMONICS; MUSIC (Tone); SONOMETER; SOUND (Quality).　　　　　　　　RAYMOND KENDALL

TONGA, *TAWNG guh*, is a country made up of about 150 islands in the South Pacific Ocean. The islands lie about 3,000 miles (4,800 kilometers) southwest of Honolulu. The British explorer Captain James Cook, who first visited the islands in 1773, called them the *Friendly Islands*. In 1789, Captain William Bligh and 18 crewmen of the British ship *Bounty* floated through the islands after being cast adrift by mutineers.

Tonga is the only remaining kingdom of Polynesia, one of the three main groups of the Pacific Islands. It became independent in 1970 after being a protectorate of Great Britain since 1900. It is a member of the Commonwealth of Nations.

Most of Tonga's people raise crops for their own use and for export. Most of the people live on Tongatapu,

TONGA

Tonga

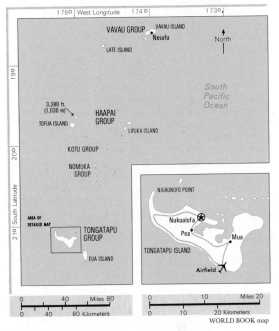

WORLD BOOK map

the largest island. Nukualofa, Tonga's capital and chief port, lies on Tongatapu.

Facts in Brief

Capital: Nukualofa.

Official Language: Tongan.

Official Name: Kingdom of Tonga.

Form of Government: Constitutional monarchy.

Area: 270 sq. mi. (699 km²).

Elevation: *Highest*—Kao, an extinct volcano in the Haapai group, 3,380 ft. (1,030 m) above sea level. *Lowest*—sea level, along the coasts.

Population: *Estimated 1983 Population*—98,000; distribution, 64 per cent rural, 36 per cent urban; density, 363 persons per sq. mi. (140 persons per km²); *1976 Census*—90,085. *Estimated 1988 Population*—99,000.

Chief Products: bananas, copra, sweet potatoes, tapioca.

National Anthem: "'E 'Otua Mafimafi" ("O God Almighty").

Flag: The flag has a red field and a white canton. A red cross in the canton symbolizes the Christian faith of the Tongans. Adopted in 1866. See FLAG (color picture: Flags of Asia and the Pacific).

Money: *Basic Unit*—pa'anga. The pa'anga equals the Australian dollar. See MONEY (table: Exchange Rates [Australia]).

TONGA

Government. Tonga is a constitutional monarchy. The king appoints a premier and a Cabinet to assist him. The Cabinet consists of the premier and six other members. The Legislative Assembly is composed of the Cabinet, seven nobles elected by Tonga's hereditary nobility, and seven commoners elected by the people. Elections take place every three years. Tongans who are at least 21 years old and can read and write may vote.

The Legislative Assembly meets for two or three months a year. When the assembly is not in session, the privy council has the power to make laws. The privy council, headed by the king, consists of the premier, the Cabinet, and the governors of two major island groups —Haapai and Vavau. The Legislative Assembly may change laws passed by the privy council. The king appoints the governors of Haapai and Vavau.

People. Almost all the people of Tonga are Polynesians and are Methodists. Tonga's Constitution prohibits work or recreation on Sunday, and the people follow this law strictly.

The majority of Tongans live in small rural villages and raise crops. The people also fish for such seafood as shark and tuna. Most of the islands have no running water, and many have no electricity.

The law requires all Tongan children from 6 to 14 years old to go to school. Tonga has about 125 elementary schools and 45 high schools. The government operates about 60 per cent of the schools, and the churches direct about 40 per cent. The country's official language is Tongan, but the children also learn English. Tongan schoolchildren enjoy many sports, especially rugby football. The country has no universities, but there is a teacher-training college in Nukualofa. Some Tongans attend universities in Australia, Fiji, and New Zealand.

Land. Tonga is made up of three main island groups —Haapai, Tongatapu, and Vavau. Most of the islands in these groups are coral reefs. Most of Tonga's people live on these islands. A chain of higher, volcanic islands lies west of the coral islands. Some of the volcanoes are active.

Fertile clay soils cover most of Tonga. Strips of sandy soil lie along the coasts. Forests cover about 14 per cent of the land.

Tonga has a warm, wet climate with high humidity. Temperatures average 78° F. (26° C). The average annual rainfall varies from 70 inches (180 centimeters) on Tongatapu to 100 inches (250 centimeters) on some northern islands. Most rain falls from December through March. Cyclones sometimes hit Tonga.

Economy. Tonga, an economically underdeveloped country, has few industries or skilled craftworkers. Fertile soils and a warm climate have made agriculture the basis of the Tongan economy. About three-fourths of the workers are farmers. The government owns all the land. Every male who is 16 or over is entitled to a plot of land, which he rents from the government.

Tongan farmers grow such crops as bananas, breadfruit, sweet potatoes, tapioca, and yams. Tonga's chief exports are bananas and copra. Most exports go to New Zealand. Australia and New Zealand supply most of Tonga's imports, including flour, metal, sugar, textiles, and tobacco.

Tonga has over 200 miles (320 kilometers) of roads, mostly on Tongatapu. Shipping services operate among the many islands. A government-owned shipping service connects Tonga with Australia, New Zealand, and other countries. Neiafu and Nukualofa are Tonga's chief ports. An airport operates at Fuaamotu on Tongatapu. Tonga has no railroads. The government publishes a weekly newspaper in both Tongan and English and operates Tonga's one radio station.

History. The first people to settle in Tonga were Polynesians who probably came from Samoa. Although much of Tonga's early history is based on myths, records of Tongan rulers go back to the A.D. 900's. The early rulers held the hereditary title of *Tu'i Tonga*. The people believed the Tu'i Tonga were sacred representatives of the Tongan gods. About 1470, the ruling Tu'i Tonga gave some governing powers to a nonsacred leader. Through the years, the Tu'i Tonga became only a figurehead. By 1865, after the death of the last Tu'i Tonga, the nonsacred king held all the ruling power.

Qantas Airways

In Nukualofa, the capital and chief port of Tonga, small business offices and shops line the wide streets. Most of the buildings are made of wood, and many of the streets are unpaved.

Two Dutch navigators, Willem Cornelis Schouten and Jakob le Maire, became the first Europeans to visit Tonga. They landed on some of the northern islands in 1616. In 1643, Abel Tasman, a Dutch sea captain, visited Tongatapu and other southern islands.

Methodist missionaries from Great Britain settled in Tonga during the early 1800's and converted most of the people to Christianity. But civil war spread throughout Tonga. One of the most powerful chiefs, Taufa'ahau, united the islands in 1845. He was crowned King George Tupou I, the first monarch of Tonga. Tupou I developed legal codes that became the basis of the Tongan Constitution, which was adopted in 1875.

After Tupou I died in 1893, his great-grandson, George Tupou II, took the throne. Tonga became a protectorate of Great Britain in 1900. Queen Salote succeeded Tupou II in 1918 and ruled until her death in 1965. Salote worked to improve education and health in Tonga. Her son was crowned King Taufa'ahau Toupou IV in 1967.

In 1970, Tonga gained independence from Great Britain. That same year, the nation completed its first five-year development program and began work on a second. With British aid, Tonga is modernizing its agriculture, building wharves and airstrips, and encouraging foreign investment. Through these plans, the government hopes to vary the economy and provide more jobs for Tonga's growing population.

In 1982, a severe cyclone hit Tonga. It killed several people, caused extensive damage to buildings and crops, and left many of the people homeless.　　STUART INDER

TONGUE, *tung,* is the chief organ of taste. It also helps in chewing and swallowing, and plays an important part in forming the sounds of words.

The tongue is made up of many groups of muscles that a person can consciously control. This type of muscle is called *skeletal* muscle. The tongue muscles run in many different directions. They arise from the hyoid bone, and the inner surfaces of the lower jaw and temporal bones. As a result, a person can move the front part of the tongue many different ways. The tongue can move food about, push it between the teeth, roll it into small masses, and thrust it back into the *pharynx* (throat). In swallowing, the tongue presses against the *palate* (roof of the mouth) and also spreads against the sides of the mouth. This action prevents the food from moving in any direction except back into the pharynx.

The tongue is covered with mucous membrane. The under surface of the tongue is smooth. But many *papillae* (small projections) give the tongue a rough surface on the top. Four types of taste buds are found in the papillae that enable us to distinguish between sweet, sour, salty, and bitter tastes (see TASTE). The tip of the tongue is more sensitive to the feeling of touch than any other part of the body (see TOUCH).

The tongue is a highly useful organ to many animals. Frogs and certain kinds of birds use their tongues to catch insects. Hummingbirds use their long, slender tongues to lap up plant nectar. Dogs, cats, and other animals use their tongues for many purposes, such as to lap up water or milk, to clean their fur, or to express affection.　　GORDON FARRELL

See also CHAMELEON; SNAKE (picture); TOAD.

TONIC is a term used for medicines that are supposed to stimulate or "tone up" the body. Tonics were once widely used and could be purchased without a prescription as "patent medicines" (see PATENT MEDICINE). Doctors believe the old idea of a tonic is misleading. They have found no substance that can tone up the en-

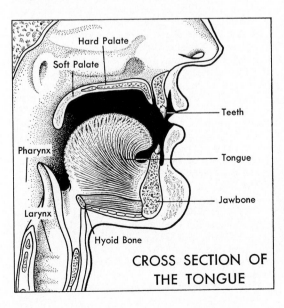

CROSS SECTION OF THE TONGUE

Hard Palate

Soft Palate

Teeth

Pharynx

Tongue

Jawbone

Larynx

Hyoid Bone

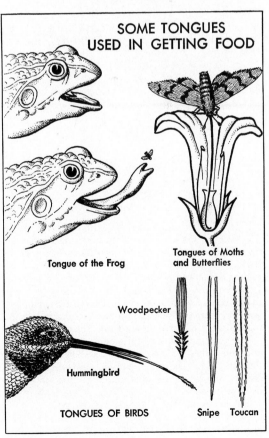

SOME TONGUES USED IN GETTING FOOD

Tongue of the Frog

Tongues of Moths and Butterflies

Woodpecker

Hummingbird

TONGUES OF BIRDS

Snipe　**Toucan**

tire body. They have discovered drugs that can stimulate particular organs and tissues of the body. These drugs must be used carefully, however, and are usually prescribed by doctors. It is now believed that the "lift" or stimulation a tonic gave some people was either imagined or the result of the tonic's alcoholic content. The term *tonic* is also used in many parts of the United States to mean carbonated soft drinks.   SOLOMON GARB

TONKIN. See VIETNAM (History).

TONKIN GULF RESOLUTION. See VIETNAM WAR (The Gulf of Tonkin Incident).

TONNAGE. See SHIP (table: Nautical Measurements).

TONSIL, *TAHN suhl,* is a mass of special tissue, called *lymphoid* tissue, in the throat. Connective tissue and mucous membrane cover it (see TISSUE). Lymphoid tissue forms white blood cells, called *lymphocytes,* the germ fighters in the blood. Because of this, scientists believe that tonsils help destroy harmful bacteria.

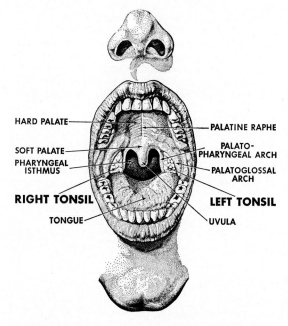

HARD PALATE

SOFT PALATE

PHARYNGEAL ISTHMUS

RIGHT TONSIL

TONGUE

PALATINE RAPHE

PALATO-PHARYNGEAL ARCH

PALATOGLOSSAL ARCH

LEFT TONSIL

UVULA

The throat is surrounded by a ring of tonsil tissue. The *palatine tonsils* are the best known. In human beings, a palatine tonsil can be seen on each side of the back of the mouth just above the throat and below the roof of the mouth. Other tonsils that are not so easily seen are the *lingual tonsils* at the back of the tongue, and the *tubal tonsils* at the entrance of the Eustachian tube (see EUSTACHIAN TUBE). The *pharyngeal tonsils,* commonly called *adenoids,* grow at the back of the nose.

The palatine tonsils of children are larger than those of adults. When badly infected, they may almost block the throat. A common operation, the *tonsillectomy,* is used to remove the palatine tonsils, particularly if they become infected.   WILLIAM V. MAYER

See also ADENOIDS; THROAT; TONSILLITIS.

TONSILLITIS, *TAHN suh LY tihs,* is a painful disease resulting from inflamed tonsils. It is caused by bac-

teria or viruses that infect one or both of the tonsils. Most attacks of tonsillitis occur in persons between the ages of 10 and 40. An attack begins with swelling and pain in the throat and difficulty in swallowing. Fever, headache, backache, stiff neck, and nausea occur in severe cases. Sometimes an *abscess* (collection of pus) forms in the throat.

The treatment for an attack of tonsillitis depends on whether the infection is bacterial or viral. Physicians prescribe antibiotics to cure bacterial infections of the tonsils. Viral infections cannot be treated with antibiotics. Physicians generally recommend bed rest, aspirin, and saltwater gargles to relieve the symptoms of a viral attack of tonsillitis. Some persons suffer from long-lasting or repeated attacks of tonsillitis. Doctors may recommend that the tonsils be removed in such cases. The operation to remove the tonsils is called a *tonsillectomy.* A tonsillectomy is a relatively simple operation.   PAUL R. CANNON

TONSURE, *TAHN shuhr,* is a special type of haircut required of clergymen and monks in some churches. Roman Catholic priests receive the tonsure from their bishops before taking Holy Orders. They do not renew the tonsure. Monks receive the tonsure from their abbots and must keep it constantly renewed.

There are two basic styles of tonsure, with variations from order to order. The *Roman,* or *St. Peter's tonsure,* first used by Christian priests in Rome, leaves a ring of hair around the head to represent the crown of thorns worn by Jesus. The entire head is shaved or clipped close in the *Eastern,* or *St. Paul's tonsure,* practiced in Eastern Orthodox Churches. Scholars are not sure how the tonsure for Christian priests and monks originated. Some think it was intended to show that the person was a servant of Christ, because closely cropped hair was a sign of servitude in early days. Some Hindu priests have their heads completely shaved before taking orders.   R. PIERCE BEAVER and FULTON J. SHEEN

TONTI, *TAHN tih,* **HENRI DE,** also spelled *Tonty,* (1650-1704), was a French explorer who helped open the midwestern part of what is now the United States. He was the companion of Sieur de la Salle in 1682, when they traveled all the way down the Mississippi River to its mouth. Tonti, the son of Italians, was probably born in Paris, France. In 1678 he went to Canada with La Salle, and two years later they traveled together into Illinois. Tonti took command of Fort Crèvecoeur, near the present city of Peoria, Ill. He soon retraced his route toward Canada and met La Salle at Mackinac Island in the spring of 1681.

After exploring the Mississippi Valley, Tonti took charge of Fort St. Louis, a stronghold built at Starved Rock, Ill. This was one of the earliest white settlements in what was to become the United States. Until 1702, Tonti was the leader of the Illinois Indians. Then he joined the French-Canadian explorer Sieur d'Iberville (Pierre le Moyne) in Louisiana.   FRANKLIN L. FORD

See also IBERVILLE, SIEUR D'; LA SALLE, SIEUR DE.

TONTO NATIONAL MONUMENT in southern Arizona contains two pueblo cliff dwellings. Indians who farmed in the Salt River Valley occupied the cliff dwellings during the 1300's. For the area of Tonto National Monument, see NATIONAL PARK SYSTEM (table: National Monuments).

TONY AWARD. See THEATER (Broadway).

TOOL is any instrument that a worker uses to do work. Tools that do their tasks on a machine are called *machine tools* (see MACHINE TOOL). Small *power-driven* tools are similar to both hand tools and machine tools. The two main kinds of tools are *woodworking tools* and *metalworking tools*.

Woodworking Tools. The tools of the carpenter and cabinetmaker include such measuring tools as the *rule* for measuring lengths; the *square* and *protractor* for measuring angles; *compasses* for marking circles and arcs; and *spirit levels* and *plumb lines* for ensuring that carpentry work will be straight and true. *Vises* and *clamps* hold material in place while it is being shaped. Shaping tools include *saws, chisels, planes, files,* and *boring bits.* Woodworkers also use *hammers, hatchets, screw drivers,* and *pliers.* See WOODWORKING.

Metalworking Tools. The work of the machinist and toolmaker ordinarily requires much greater precision than that of the woodworker. For this reason, measuring tools for metalworking must be extremely accurate. Many *micrometers* and *calipers* can measure distances as small as $\frac{1}{10,000}$ inch (0.0025 millimeter). The *hacksaw* used for cutting metal is much thinner and harder than the woodworking saw. Machinists use *taps* and *dies* to cut threads in screws, bolts, and machine parts. Machinists use *wrenches* for repair work and in assembling machinery. Most forming operations on metal parts are done by machine tools such as lathes, milling machines, shapers, and grinders.

History of Tools. Prehistoric people learned that rocks and sticks of certain shapes could help them do things they could not do with their bare hands. They later improved the natural stones they used. They shaped them into knives, hatchets, and hammers, and attached wooden handles to them. Stone-Age people developed a drill for drilling soft stone and wood. Bronze-Age people developed new tools, such as tongs for holding hot objects. Agricultural civilizations later developed new tools such as the hoe and the simple plow. See PREHISTORIC PEOPLE.

After people learned to work iron and steel, they developed newer and more improved tools. Tools became stronger, sharper, and more durable. The development of steam engines, gasoline engines, and electric motors made it possible to replace hand tools with machine tools. Today, much work once done by hand is done by small, power-driven hand tools.　　ARTHUR C. ANSLEY

Related Articles in WORLD BOOK include:

Ax	Machine Tool
Die and Diemaking	Pioneer Life in America
Drilling Tools	(Tools)
Farm and Farming	Plumb Line
Forging	Pneumatic Tool
Hammer	Saw
Indian, American	Steam Hammer
Knife	Trip Hammer
Level	

TOOLMAKING is a craft that makes tools and dies used to make other parts for industry. Toolmakers also specialize in making jigs and fixtures required to hold the metal while it is being shaved, stamped, or drilled. They also make metal molds used in die castings and plastic moldings. Tools used by the toolmaker include lathes, milling machines, grinding machines, and boring machines. However, toolmakers still do much of their work by hand, particularly the finishing touches.

TOOTHPASTE AND TOOTHPOWDER

Metal Stamping requires several kinds of dies to shape, punch, and cut out metal (see DIE AND DIEMAKING). These dies range in size from huge blocks of steel for shaping automobile bodies to tiny precision tools for making watch gears. The dies must be accurate to as little as $\frac{1}{10,000}$ inch (0.0025 millimeter). The die materials must be tough tool steel that can be finished into a smooth, polished surface.

Molds for die castings and plastics are formed from solid blocks of steel. The toolmaker must design the mold or die so that it opens readily and allows the finished part to be removed easily. Jigs and fixtures of many types are used to ensure accurate and uniform drilling, and assembling of the product.

Career Opportunities in toolmaking are many, because toolmaking ranks as one of the most highly skilled crafts in modern industry. Toolmakers must be familiar with many types of machine tools, measuring instruments, and metalworking processes. They serve as apprentices for about four or five years, and are among the highest paid metalworkers.　　ARTHUR C. ANSLEY

See also CAST AND CASTING; MACHINE TOOL; TOOL.

TOOMBS, ROBERT AUGUSTUS (1810-1885), served in the United States Congress before the Civil War and then became Confederate Secretary of State. Toombs did not regain his U.S. citizenship after the war because he refused to swear allegiance to the United States government. He represented Georgia in the House of Representatives from 1845 to 1853 and in the Senate from 1853 to 1861. Toombs served as Secretary of State in the Confederacy in 1861 and as brigadier general of the Army of Northern Virginia from 1861 to 1862. He was born in Wilkes County, Georgia.　　KENNETH COLEMAN

TOOMER, JEAN (1894-1967), was a black American writer. He is best known for *Cane* (1923), a book of poems, short stories, and a novelette about blacks living in the North and the South. *Cane* describes people frustrated by their conflicts with social customs and by psychological conflicts within themselves. The work is noted for its poetic and sensitive descriptions. *Cane* established Toomer as a leading American writer of the 1920's. It inspired authors of the Harlem Renaissance, an important period in black literary history.

Most of Toomer's writings after *Cane* examine philosophical and psychological problems he saw in Americans. He wrote *Essentials* (1931), a collection of thoughts on these problems. Toomer also wrote book reviews, essays, poems, short stories, and a novelette. Some of these writings were collected in *The Wayward and the Seeking,* which was published in 1980 after his death.

Toomer was born in Washington, D.C. His full name was Nathan Eugene Toomer.　　DARWIN T. TURNER

See also AMERICAN LITERATURE (The Harlem Renaissance).

TOOTH. See TEETH.

TOOTH SHELL. See MOLLUSK (Tooth Shells; picture); INDIAN, AMERICAN (Money; picture).

TOOTHACHE TREE. See PRICKLY ASH.

TOOTHBRUSH. See BRUSH; TEETH.

TOOTHPASTE AND TOOTHPOWDER are substances used with a toothbrush to clean teeth. Both contain a mildly abrasive substance, such as finely powdered chalk (calcium carbonate), and a *detergent* (soaplike material). Some sweetening agent other than sugar, and flavoring oils, are included to make the agent taste good. Glycerol or a similar material is added to these basic ingredients to make toothpaste. Some toothpastes contain *stannous fluoride*, a chemical that some scientists believe helps prevent decay.   ROBERT G. KESEL

TOP is the name for a child's toy. Most tops have cylindrical or pear shapes. They are made of wood, metal, or plastic, and usually spin on a metal tip.

Kinds of Tops. The best-known top receives its motion from a string that has been wrapped around it and suddenly pulled. This makes the top spin around and stay erect without being held up. Other tops spin when a center stem is twirled between the thumb and forefinger. *Mechanical* tops receive power to spin from an inside spring that is wound with a key. In *musical* tops, holes, reeds, or whistles inside the top produce sounds when the top spins. Scientists use this spinning force in a type of gyroscopic top that helps stabilize boats and airplanes (see GYROSCOPE).

History of Tops. No one knows exactly when people first began to use tops. But tops have been a popular amusement in China and Japan for hundreds of years. In the 1800's, people in the Orient often became professional top spinners. They made tops do a great variety of tricks, such as jumping steps and walking up an inclined board.

Tops became popular in Europe during the 1700's. In a game called *diabolo*, the player whipped a top into the air. Sometimes the player tried to see how high the top could be sent. Other times, the top was caught in the hand from various bodily positions. Many types of self-winding tops were used in the 1800's. The *bandilor* top unwinds itself while going up an incline, and rewinds as it comes down. The top can be manipulated to wind and unwind itself many times. Tops were among the first toys patented in the United States. The *torpedo* top contained a ball that shot into the air when a paper cap exploded.   PHILIP L. KIRKHAM

TOPAZ, *TOH paz*, is a hard, transparent mineral. It is a compound of aluminum, silica, and fluorine. Gem topaz is valuable. Jewelers call this variety of the stone *precious topaz*. Best-known precious topaz gems range in color from rich yellow to light brown or pinkish red. It is one of the hardest of gem minerals. In the mineral table of hardness, topaz has a rating of 8, which means that a knife cannot cut it, and that topaz will scratch quartz.

The golden precious topaz is a rare variety of the stone. Most of the world's topaz is white or blue. The white and blue crystals of topaz are large, often weighing thousands of carats. For this reason, the value of blue topaz does not depend so much on its size as it does with diamonds and many other precious stones, where the value increases about four times with each doubling of weight. The quality of topaz largely determines its value. Blue topaz is often *irradiated* (exposed to radiation) to deepen and improve its color.

Topaz is found in many parts of the world, especially Brazil, the Ural Mountains of Russia, and the United States. Most precious topaz comes from Brazil.

Blue topaz is often sold as aquamarine, and a variety of brown quartz is widely sold as topaz. This quartz is much softer, less brilliant, and more plentiful than true topaz. Most of it is a variety of amethyst which heat has turned brown. The topaz is the birthstone for November.   FREDERICK H. POUGH

See also CORUNDUM; GEM (color picture); HARDNESS.

TOPEKA, *toh PEE kuh*, Kans. (pop. 115,266; met. area pop. 185,442), is the capital of the state and the seat of Shawnee County. It lies on the Kansas (Kaw) River in the fertile Kaw Valley, about 65 miles (105 kilometers) west of Kansas City (see KANSAS [political map]). The Capitol, the Memorial Building, and the Municipal and City Building stand in the downtown business district. A state office building, covering a square block facing the Capitol, was completed in 1957. Topeka has 46 parks and about 400 miles (640 kilometers) of paved streets. It is an attractive residential city, with wide, tree-lined streets. Forbes Air Force Base is 3 miles (5 kilometers) south of Topeka.

The city is the home of Washburn University of Topeka. The Mulvane Art Center, on the Washburn campus, owns valuable permanent collections of paintings and other art forms. The center displays traveling exhibits during the winter months. The Kansas State Historical Society has a museum of about 50,000 objects and a library of more than 400,000 books and other reference materials. The library includes an almost complete collection of Kansas newspapers since 1875. Topeka is the home of the Menninger Foundation, which conducts psychiatric research, education, and treatment. The foundation also helps operate a psychiatric hospital in Topeka.

Nelson R. Perry
Tops Have Been Popular Toys among children for hundreds of years. The hand-carved, striped tops, *left*, come from Mexico. The Indian top, *upper right*, was made from a hollowed nut. The disklike Eskimo top, *lower right*, was carved out of walrus ivory.

Kansas' Capitol and a statue honoring pioneer women stand in a 10-acre (4-hectare) park in downtown Topeka.

Robert H. Glaze, Artstreet

Industry. Topeka serves as the headquarters for the eastern division of The Atchison, Topeka & Santa Fe Railway Company. The division employs about 3,300 persons in the Topeka area. The city's other industries include flour milling, iron and steel manufacturing, meat packing, printing and publishing, and tire manufacturing. Creamery products are also important. The city lies in a rich dairy-farming area.

History. Nine antislavery settlers founded Topeka in 1854. Topeka received its city charter in 1857, and became the capital of Kansas in 1861. It has a commission form of government.   WILLIAM F. ZORNOW

See also KANSAS (Climate; picture: State Capitol).

TOPELIUS, *too PAY lee UHS*, **ZACHRIS** (1818-1898), was a Finnish short-story writer and poet. His best-known work is *Tales of an Army Surgeon* (1853-1867), a classic of Scandinavian literature. It is a multi-volume series of historical romances that stress the role of common people in Finnish-Swedish history. The stories cover the period from the Thirty Years' War (1618-1648) to the reign of Gustavus III in the late 1700's. Topelius wrote two series of children's stories, *Tales* (1847-1852), and *Readings for Children* (1865-1896). He also wrote sentimental poems, hymns, and a few plays in verse.

Topelius was born near Nykarleby. He edited a Helsinki newspaper, and was professor of history, and then became president of the University of Helsinki. He was a champion of Finnish nationalism, but he wrote in Swedish.   RICHARD B. VOWLES

TOPIARY WORK, *TOH pee EHR ee*, is the art of training and cutting plants into ornamental shapes. It is usually done on shrubs, evergreen trees, and lawns, but decorators make topiary trees from crepe paper and wire. Topiary work was a favorite hobby of the Romans, who made plants grow in geometrical forms such as cubes, cones, and pyramids. Later topiary designs included giraffes, dogs, pigs, and peacocks. Topiary workers also imitated such useful objects as chairs, fountains, and sundials. One design was a long row of trees shaped like elephants, with the trunk of one elephant holding the tail of the one ahead. STEPHEN F. HAMBLIN

TOPOGRAPHY is the natural and artificially created surface features of the land. These include hills, valleys, streams, lakes, bridges, tunnels, roads, and cities. Topography is also the science of making an accurate and detailed drawing of surface features. See also CHART; MAP; PHOTOGRAMMETRY; SURVEYING.

TOPOLOGY, *tuh PAHL uh jee*, is a branch of mathematics that explores certain properties of geometrical figures. The properties are those that do not change when the figures are deformed by bending, stretching, or molding. Topology makes no distinction between a sphere and a cube, because these figures can be deformed or molded into one another. Topology makes a distinction between a sphere and a *torus* (a doughnut-shaped figure) because these cannot be deformed into one another. Topology is often called *rubber-sheet geometry* because its figures can be deformed.

Unlike high school geometry, topology ignores straightness, parallelism, and distance, because deformation can alter them. Instead, topology studies such problems as the number of intersections made by a curve with itself, whether a surface is closed or has boundaries, and whether or not a surface is connected. Topology makes up theorems and tries to prove them, just as high school geometry does.   HOWARD W. EVES

See also GEOMETRY; MATHEMATICS (A Strange Twist).

TOPSOIL is the upper layer of soil. It is usually about 10 inches (25 centimeters) deep. This upper layer gives food to all plants that have short roots, such as small grains and grasses. It is rich in a substance known as humus, which is important to the growth of plants (see HUMUS). Topsoil also contains certain bacteria which are necessary to plant growth. For this reason, people often remove the top layer of large areas of land, and transfer it to gardens. Preservation of the topsoil is one of the most important problems of conservation. Most of the food we eat comes from plants that grow in the fertile topsoil. It takes hundreds of years to make topsoil.

See also CONSERVATION (Soil Conservation); LAWN (Preparing the Soil).

TORAH is the Hebrew name for the *Pentateuch* (first five books of the Bible). See PENTATEUCH.

TORCH is the term used in Great Britain and Commonwealth countries for a flashlight. See FLASHLIGHT.

TORDESILLAS, TREATY OF. See LINE OF DEMARCATION (map).

TORII, *TAWR ee ee*, is a gateway to a Japanese Shinto shrine. It usually has two posts supporting two cross-pieces with ends turned upward. Sometimes the Japanese set up torii in harbors. Some Japanese sailors think that sailing a boat through a torii brings good luck.

See also SHINTO (picture).

TORINO. See TURIN.

TORNADO

National Oceanic and Atmospheric Administration

The Development of a Tornado is shown in the four pictures above. First, a dense, dark cloud forms, *far left*. The second picture shows rotating air at the bottom of the cloud forming into a narrow cloud called a *funnel*. The funnel then extends toward the earth's surface. If the funnel touches the surface, it raises a huge dust cloud, *far right*, and destroys almost everything in its path.

TORNADO is a powerful, twisting wind storm. The winds of a tornado are the most violent winds that occur on the earth. They may whirl around the center of the storm at speeds of more than 300 miles (480 kilometers) per hour. Most tornadoes measure several hundred yards or meters in diameter, and many have caused widespread death and destruction.

A tornado is a rotating funnel cloud that extends downward from a mass of dark clouds. Some funnels do not reach the earth. Other funnels may strike the surface of the earth, withdraw into the dark clouds above, and then dip down and strike the earth again. In the United States, most funnel clouds tend to travel toward the northeast.

The winds of a tornado whirl in a counterclockwise direction in the Northern Hemisphere and clockwise in the Southern Hemisphere. People in some regions call a tornado a *twister* or a *cyclone*. A tornado that occurs over a lake or ocean is called a *waterspout* (see WATER-SPOUT).

Most tornadoes last less than an hour. These storms travel a distance of about 20 miles (32 kilometers) at a speed of 10 to 25 miles (16 to 40 kilometers) per hour. Some tornadoes last several hours and measure up to 1½ miles (2.4 kilometers) in diameter. They may travel 200 miles (322 kilometers) or more at a speed of up to 60 miles (97 kilometers) per hour. Such tornadoes are especially destructive.

Tornadoes occur throughout the world, but mostly in the United States. Those in the United States hit

Where Tornadoes Occur

Tornadoes frequently hit the Midwestern and Southern states. The Western States have few tornadoes. The map shows the number of tornadoes that occurred in each region during a 12-year period.

Less than 10

10-50

50-100

100-200

More than 200

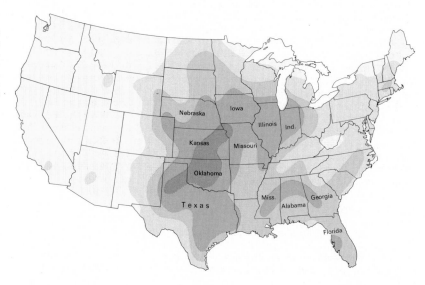

WORLD BOOK map

chiefly in spring and early summer. No one knows how many tornadoes occur yearly because many of the storms occur in thinly populated areas and may not be reported. About 700 tornadoes have been reported annually in the United States since the mid-1950's.

The greatest killer tornado in history roared through Missouri, Illinois, and Indiana on March 18, 1925, and killed 689 persons. This tornado was one of the largest and fastest tornadoes ever recorded. Its path measured about 220 miles (354 kilometers) long and up to a mile (1.6 kilometers) wide. The storm traveled at a speed of about 60 miles (97 kilometers) per hour.

The Story of a Tornado. Most tornadoes in the United States strike the Midwest and the states that border the Gulf of Mexico. Scientists do not know exactly why tornadoes develop.

Most tornadoes form along a *front* (boundary) between cool, dry air from the north and warm, humid air from the Gulf of Mexico. A narrow zone of *cumulonimbus* (thunderstorm) clouds develops along such a front. This zone of clouds, called a *squall line*, produces violent weather. See CLOUD (picture: Some Cumulonimbus Clouds).

The violent weather produced by a squall line results when a mass of warm, humid air rises extremely rapidly. As this air rises, more warm air rushes in to replace it. The inrushing air also rises and, in some cases, begins to rotate. The rotating air then forms into a tornado.

Most tornadoes occur in spring on a hot, humid day in the afternoon or in the early evening. Large thunderclouds appear in the sky, and thunder begins to rumble in the distance. A nearby cloud becomes dark and dense. Rounded masses at the bottom of the cloud start to twist. One of the twisting masses then forms a funnel cloud that gradually extends downward. Heavy rain and some hail begin to fall, and flashes of lightning occur. A hissing sound begins as the funnel cloud extends toward the earth. If the funnel touches the ground, it stirs up dirt and debris. The hissing becomes a loud roar.

The violent, rotating winds of a tornado blow down almost everything in its path. The explosive force of a tornado can demolish a small building. It does so primarily by causing a difference in air pressure between the inside and outside of the building. When a tornado passes over a house, it sucks up air from around the structure. The air pressure outside the house drops suddenly, but the air pressure inside remains the same. As a result, the pressure inside the house is greater than that outside. Because the pressure difference cannot equalize quickly enough, the building explodes outward.

The tremendous lifting force of a tornado results from a powerful updraft of air inside the funnel. Tornadoes have uprooted large trees, overturned railroad cars, and carried such heavy objects as automobiles hundreds of feet or meters.

Protection Against Tornadoes. Scientists of the National Weather Service constantly gather weather information from all parts of the United States. They use radar and other kinds of equipment to forecast and locate tornadoes. If weather conditions indicate that tornadoes or severe thunderstorms may occur, the agency issues an advisory bulletin that is broadcast on television and radio. If a tornado is spotted, the Weather

Wide World

A Tornado Strikes with Terrible Force. Its violent winds can destroy buildings, uproot huge trees, and carry automobiles and other large objects long distances. The demolished houses shown above stood in the path of a tornado.

Service warns communities in the path of the storm. The warning gives the location and size of the tornado and the course the storm is following. Police in the endangered areas may also use sirens to warn the people to take cover.

A storm cellar provides the best protection against a tornado. A basement is the next best place to take shelter. In a basement, people should crouch under a table on the side of the room from which the tornado is approaching. In a building that has no basement, they should lie flat under a table or bed on the ground floor, away from any windows. Some windows should be kept open to reduce the difference in air pressure inside and outside the building and thus help to prevent the building from exploding. Mobile homes that are not anchored should always be vacated if a tornado is approaching. They offer almost no protection and can be easily overturned by a tornado. Outside, people should lie face down in a ditch or ravine if possible. This action would provide protection against flying debris but would not prevent a tornado from lifting a person into its funnel. WAYNE M. WENDLAND

See also CYCLONE; HURRICANE; WEATHER.

TORNE RIVER, *TOHR nuh,* also called the TORNIO RIVER, rises in Lake Torne in northern Sweden and flows eastward through northern Sweden. Then it turns southward, and forms part of the boundary between Sweden and Finland until it empties into the Gulf of Bothnia.

The Finnish people call the part of the river that forms the boundary the Tornio. But in Sweden, the river is called the Torne. The Torne River is more than 250 miles (402 kilometers) long. JOHN H. WUORINEN

TORONTO

TORONTO, *tuh RAHN toh,* is the capital of Ontario and Canada's second largest city. Only Montreal has more people. Toronto lies on the northwest shore of Lake Ontario. It is one of the busiest Canadian ports on the Great Lakes.

Toronto is the chief manufacturing, financial, and communications center of Canada. About a third of Canada's manufacturing industries are within 100 miles (160 kilometers) of the city. The Toronto Stock Exchange ranks first in the nation in daily trading volume. Toronto leads all Canadian cities in printing, publishing, and television and film production. It also ranks as a leading Canadian cultural center. The city has Canada's largest museum and public library system.

During the 1600's and 1700's, Indians used the Toronto area as a *portage* (overland route) between Lake Ontario and Lake Huron. In 1791, John Graves Simcoe became lieutenant governor of the new British province of Upper Canada (now Ontario). He chose the site of present-day Toronto for a new provincial capital to replace Newark, which was then the capital. In 1793, Simcoe established a settlement on the site and named it *York.* In 1834, the town was renamed *Toronto,* a Huron Indian term meaning *meeting place.* During the late 1800's, Toronto began to grow as a center of manufacturing and transportation.

In 1954, the Municipality of Metropolitan Toronto became North America's first metropolitan government federation. The Municipality, commonly called *Metropolitan Toronto,* consisted of Toronto and 12 of its suburbs. The Ontario legislature created the federation to provide a way for Toronto and the suburbs to solve various problems they had in common. In 1967, the 13 members of the federation were merged to form Toronto and 5 boroughs—East York, Etobicoke, North York, Scarborough, and York. In 1979, the borough of North York became a city but remained in the federation. Each of the federation's six units has its own government to handle local needs.

The City

Near the center of Toronto's downtown business district stands the $30-million City Hall, which opened in 1965. This unusual structure consists of two curved office buildings and, between them, the oyster-shaped city council chambers. The three buildings stand in 12-acre (5-hectare) Nathan Phillips Square, named for the mayor who served from 1955 to 1962. Nearby Bay Street is the center of Toronto's financial district.

Toronto Eaton Centre, a huge downtown retail-office complex on Yonge Street, includes Eaton's, Toronto's largest department store. It also has about 300 other stores, a 36-story office building, and a 26-story office building. Downtown Toronto also has several of Canada's tallest buildings. These buildings include Commerce Court West, a 57-story office tower that rises 784 feet (239 meters), and First Bank Tower, a 72-story bank and office tower that is 935 feet (285 meters) high. Even taller is the nearby CN (Canadian National)

Val Sears, the contributor of this article, is a Correspondent on the Toronto Daily Star.

Tower. This concrete shaft rises 1,815 feet (553 meters) and ranks as one of the world's tallest structures. Ontario Place, a recreation center in Toronto's harbor, includes an exhibition area, a marina, and a theater.

The Ontario Parliament Buildings stand at the head of University Avenue in Queen's Park, just north of downtown Toronto. The campus of the University of Toronto lies west of the park.

Toronto itself covers 43 square miles (111 square kilometers). The Municipality of Metropolitan Toronto covers 241 square miles (624 square kilometers). About a fourth of Ontario's people and about a tenth of the Canadian population live in the municipality. The official Toronto metropolitan area, called the Toronto Census Metropolitan Area, occupies 1,401 square miles (3,629 square kilometers).

The People

About 70 per cent of the people of Toronto were born in Canada. Hundreds of thousands of immigrants have settled in the city since World War II ended in 1945. People of English, Irish, and Scottish ancestry make up about half the population. People of Italian descent form another large group. Other groups include those of French, German, Polish, and Ukrainian ancestry.

Roman Catholics form the largest religious group in Toronto. Others, in order of size, include Anglicans, members of the United Church of Canada and of the Eastern Orthodox Churches, Presbyterians, and Jews. The United Church was formed by the union of the Congregational, Methodist, and most Presbyterian churches.

During the 1960's and early 1970's, many immigrants from low-income areas of Canada moved to Toronto. Their arrival strained the city's supply of low-cost public housing. In 1970, the federal, provincial, and federation governments joined in a plan to give financial aid to people with low incomes so they could live in private housing.

Economy

Manufacturing. The Toronto metropolitan area ranks as Canada's chief industrial center. More than 5,700 factories in the area produce over $7 billion worth of goods yearly. About a third of the workers in the metropolitan area have manufacturing jobs. The major

Facts in Brief

Population: *Toronto*—633,318; *Municipality of Metropolitan Toronto*—2,124,291; *Toronto Census Metropolitan Area*—2,803,101.

Area: *Toronto*—43 sq. mi. (111 km²); *Municipality of Metropolitan Toronto*—241 sq. mi. (624 km²); *Toronto Census Metropolitan Area*—1,401 sq. mi. (3,629 km²).

Altitude: 356 ft. (109 m) above sea level.

Climate: *Average Temperature*—January, 24° F. (−4° C); July, 71° F. (22° C). *Average Annual Precipitation* (rainfall, melted snow, and other forms of moisture)—32 in. (81 cm). For the monthly weather in Toronto, see ONTARIO (Climate).

Government: *Toronto*—Mayor-council (3-year terms for the mayor and 22 council members). *Municipality of Metropolitan Toronto*—Metropolitan Council (3-year terms for a chairman and 39 council members).

Founded: Early 1700's. Incorporated as a town in 1793; as a city in 1834.

manufacturing activities are food processing and printing and publishing. Other leading products include clothing; electronics and electrical equipment; and paper, rubber, and wood products.

Finance. Toronto is Canada's leading banking and financial center. More Canadian banks, insurance companies, mining firms, trust companies, and loan companies have headquarters in Toronto than in any other city. Trading at the Toronto Stock Exchange totals millions of dollars daily and nearly $6 billion annually.

Transportation and Communication. Toronto is also a major transportation center. The region's varied prod-

ucts travel to many parts of the world by air and by ship via the St. Lawrence Seaway. Toronto's port handles more than 6 million short tons (5 million metric tons) of cargo a year. Leading railways that serve the city include the Canadian National and the Canadian Pacific. Toronto International Airport, about 15 miles (24 kilometers) northwest of the city, is Canada's busiest airport. The Toronto Island Airport in Lake Ontario has a seaplane base and runways.

The Toronto subway, which opened in 1954, was

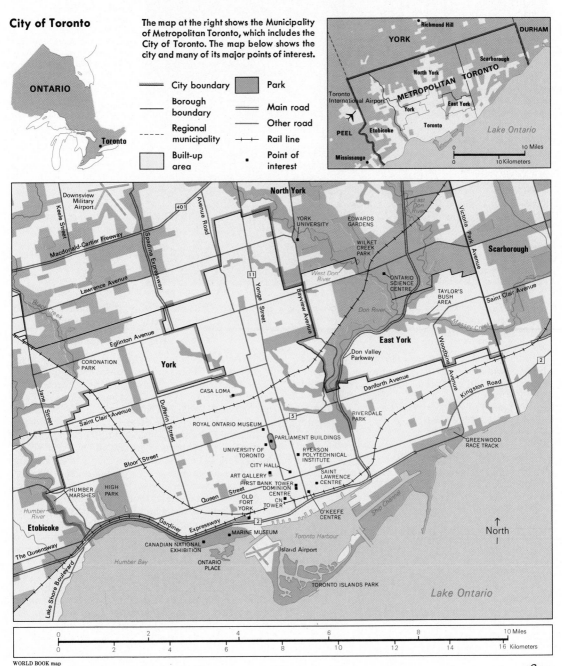

City of Toronto

The map at the right shows the Municipality of Metropolitan Toronto, which includes the City of Toronto. The map below shows the city and many of its major points of interest.

City boundary	Park
Borough boundary	Main road
Regional municipality	Other road
Built-up area	Rail line
	Point of interest

Toronto is Canada's second largest city and its chief center of industry. Toronto landmarks include the modern City Hall, *left.* Toronto's city seal, *above,* bears the city's coat of arms. The Missisauga Indian represents the area's early inhabitants. The Britannia figure indicates Canada's bond with Great Britain. The beaver stands for Toronto's industry and its Canadian identity. The city seal was adopted in 1961.

E. Otto, Miller Services

Canada's first underground rapid transit railway. The first line ran under Yonge Street. Several new rapid transit lines and extensions opened during the 1960's and early 1970's.

Toronto has three daily newspapers, the *Toronto Star*, the *Globe and Mail*, and the *Sun*. The city has about 15 radio stations and 2 television stations. One of Canada's first two TV stations was CBLT, which started broadcasting from Toronto in 1952. The other pioneer television station, CBFT in Montreal, also began operating in 1952.

Education

The public school system of the Municipality of Metropolitan Toronto has over 550 elementary and high schools, with about 400,000 students. About 73,000 children in Toronto attend Roman Catholic schools.

The University of Toronto, founded in 1827, has more than 30,000 students, the largest enrollment of any Canadian university. Other schools include the National Ballet School, the Ontario College of Art, the Royal Conservatory of Music, Ryerson Polytechnical Institute, and York University.

The Toronto Public Library, near the University of Toronto, has more than 750,000 books. It owns the Osborne Collection of early children's books and the John Ross Robertson collection of prints and pictures illustrating Canadian history. The library has about 50 branches serving the city and the five boroughs.

Cultural Life and Recreation

The Arts. The Toronto Symphony Orchestra and the Mendelssohn Choir perform in Massey Hall. The St. Lawrence Centre for the Arts and St. Lawrence Hall present programs by the Canadian Opera Company, the National Ballet of Canada, and a resident professional theater company. The Royal Conservatory of Music, the Canadian Music Centre, and the O'Keefe Centre for the Performing Arts are also in Toronto. The Art Gallery of Ontario owns the country's second largest collection of Canadian paintings. The National Gallery of Canada in Ottawa has the largest.

Museums. The Royal Ontario Museum, Canada's largest, offers exhibits of archaeology, ethnology, mineralogy, and paleontology. It has one of the world's finest collections of Chinese objects. The Marine Museum of Upper Canada shows the development of shipping on the Great Lakes and the St. Lawrence River.

Parks. The Toronto park system covers more than 6,000 acres (2,400 hectares). It includes more than 100 parks. Toronto Islands Park, the city's largest park, occupies 612 acres (248 hectares) in Lake Ontario. The Metro Toronto Zoo lies just northeast of the city.

Sports. The Toronto Maple Leafs of the National Hockey League play their home games in Maple Leaf

Gardens. The Hockey Hall of Fame is in Exhibition Park. The Toronto Argonauts of the Canadian Football League play in Exhibition Stadium. The Toronto Blue Jays of the American League play baseball in Exhibition Stadium.

Other Interesting Places to Visit include:

Casa Loma, about 2 miles (3 kilometers) northwest of downtown Toronto. Sir Henry Pellatt, a Toronto stockbroker, built this 98-room castle in the early 1900's at a cost of about $3 million.

Exhibition Park, on the Toronto lakefront. The Canadian National Exhibition, the world's largest annual fair, is held there from mid-August to Labor Day. The fair features exhibits and sports events.

Old Fort York, near Exhibition Park. This fort, which has been restored, was burned by invading United States forces during the War of 1812.

Ontario Place, on the lakefront near the downtown area, is a cultural and recreational complex. It includes a movie theater and a picnic area.

Ontario Science Centre, 6 miles (10 kilometers) northeast of downtown, consists of three buildings that house nine main exhibit halls.

Government

The chief governing body of Toronto, North York, and the four boroughs is the Metropolitan Council of the Municipality of Metropolitan Toronto. This council provides most of the area's major government services, including ambulance services, highways, police protection, public transportation, urban development, and welfare services. A separate council, the Toronto City Council, handles other services for the city. These services include garbage collection and public health.

The Metropolitan Council consists of 39 members and a chairman. Each of the 39 members is also a member of either a city council or a borough council. The 22 city council candidates and the 17 borough council candidates who receive the most votes in their elections automatically win seats on the Metropolitan Council. Council members, who serve three-year terms, appoint the chairman.

The Toronto City Council has a mayor and 22 other members. The voters elect all these officials to three-year terms. The mayor serves as head of the Executive Committee, which includes four other members of the City Council. This committee is the council's executive branch. However, all council members form its legislative branch.

History

Early Settlement. Iroquois Indians lived in the Toronto area before the first white people arrived. The area lay at the southern end of an Indian trail that ran between Lake Huron and Lake Ontario. During the early 1700's, the French established a mission, a fur-trading post, and a fort opposite the peninsula that helps form Toronto's harbor. In 1759, they burned Fort Toronto—also called Fort Rouillé—to keep the British from seizing it. In 1763, the Treaty of Paris gave all Canada to Great Britain.

In 1787, the Canadian government bought land on the peninsula from the Missisauga Indians. No permanent settlement began until 1793, when John Graves Simcoe chose the site to replace Newark as the capital of the province of Upper Canada (now Ontario). He named the settlement York after the Duke of York.

The 1800's. During the War of 1812, invading United States troops captured and burned York. Largely as a result of this attack, the British burned Washington, D.C. In 1834, York was renamed Toronto and received its city charter. The city had a population of about 10,000. In 1837, William Lyon Mackenzie, a printer who became Toronto's first mayor, led a revolt against the province's British government (see MACKENZIE, WILLIAM L.).

Manufacturing expanded rapidly in Toronto during the late 1800's, when Canada's federal government adopted policies to protect new Canadian industries from American competition. Also during this period, the federal government opened new areas in the western prairies to grain growing and livestock raising. Toronto became the chief banker and market of the West and grew in importance as a railroad center.

The 1900's. The demand for war materials during World War I (1914-1918) and World War II (1939-1945) brought great industrial expansion to the Toronto area. The end of World War II saw a rapid population growth as well. Hundreds of thousands of European immigrants settled in Toronto. The city's population overflowed into 12 suburbs. This growth caused many problems throughout the area, including poor transportation, a housing shortage, and—in some communities—a lack of water. But the city and the suburbs often refused to work together to solve their common problems. Also, some of the suburban governments could not afford to pay for some improvements.

These problems led the Ontario legislature to create the Municipality of Metropolitan Toronto in 1953. The federation of Toronto and 12 of its suburbs came into being on Jan. 1, 1954. The city and the suburbs each had self-government in local matters and sent representatives to a 25-member Metropolitan Council. In 1967, the legislature merged the 13 units into 6—Toronto and the boroughs of East York, Etobicoke, North York, Scarborough, and York. In 1979, the borough of North York became a city but remained in the federation. In 1980, the Metropolitan Council was enlarged to 39 members and a chairman. The council has brought improvement in several fields. For example, it put into operation the first computer-controlled traffic system in the world. The council built public housing for the elderly and moderate rental housing for younger families. It also doubled the area's water supply.

Recent Events. In October, 1968, the Metropolitan Council approved the Metropolitan Waterfront Plan, a renewal program for the Toronto waterfront area. The first part of the plan, construction of Ontario Place, was completed in 1971. The CN Tower, another landmark of the waterfront program, was completed in 1976. It rises 1,815 feet (553 meters) and has a restaurant near the top. The entire waterfront program, including construction of apartments, a hotel, offices, and stores, is expected to be completed in the 1980's.

In the 1970's, construction began on Toronto Eaton Centre, a huge shopping-office complex in downtown Toronto. By 1979, about 300 stores and a 26-story office building had been completed. A 36-story office building was completed in 1981.　　　VAL SEARS

See also ONTARIO (pictures).

TORONTO, UNIVERSITY OF, is Canada's largest university. It is coeducational and supported chiefly by the province of Ontario. The main campus is in downtown Toronto. The university also operates two colleges of arts and science—Erindale and Scarborough —near the city.

The university has 11 undergraduate divisions. The largest division, arts and science, offers more than 1,600 courses. The school of graduate studies consists of over 75 departments, institutes, and other divisions that provide instruction leading to graduate degrees. The university operates more than 50 libraries, with a total of over 4 million volumes. It also administers an astronomical observatory, several research centers, and the University of Toronto Press.

The University of Toronto awards arts and science degrees for three other universities—the University of St. Michael's College, the University of Trinity College, and Victoria University. Three theological colleges —Emmanuel, Knox, and Wycliffe—are also associated with the university, but they grant their own degrees. All six associated institutions are in Toronto.

The university was founded in 1827 as King's College. It received its present name in 1850. For enrollment, see CANADA (table: Universities and Colleges).

Critically reviewed by the UNIVERSITY OF TORONTO

TORPEDO, *tawr PEA doh,* is a self-propelled, cigar-shaped, underwater weapon used to blow up ships. Torpedoes are highly complicated, designed to combat fast-moving warships and merchant ships. Modern torpedoes are difficult to detect and are extremely versatile. They can be launched from submarines, surface vessels, or aircraft. They can even ride piggy-back on a rocket to distant target areas.

Torpedoes vary in size, weight, and mechanical apparatus, according to the purpose for which they are intended. Some are designed for attacking large groups of cargo vessels shielded by warships. Other torpedoes are used in hunting deep-running submarines and aircraft carriers, or in unique battle situations.

How a Torpedo Operates. A conventional torpedo usually has four sections. The *nose* contains acoustic and electronic devices by which the torpedo hunts and pursues an enemy vessel. The *warhead* includes the explosive charge and the mechanism that makes it explode. The *energy* section holds the battery and the electric motor or engine. The *afterbody* houses the control and propulsion units.

Some torpedoes are launched from a tube or rack that points the torpedo toward a target or target area. As the torpedo leaves the launcher, a starting lever in the torpedo puts the energy section into action. At the same time, power flows to the propulsion unit that drives the torpedo forward, and to the control units which stabilize the torpedo. As the torpedo speeds toward the target zone, the explosive mechanism in the warhead automatically becomes armed. Acoustic

University of Toronto

The University of Toronto is Canada's largest university. Its main campus, *above,* lies in downtown Toronto.

A Modern Torpedo carries power, steering, and detonation equipment, as well as a high explosive charge. The hydrophone detects sound vibrations from a target ship's engines, and guides the torpedo to the source of the sound. An air flask supplies oxygen, or air, needed to burn the fuel in the engine. The small engine turns propellers that push the torpedo through the water.

U.S. Navy

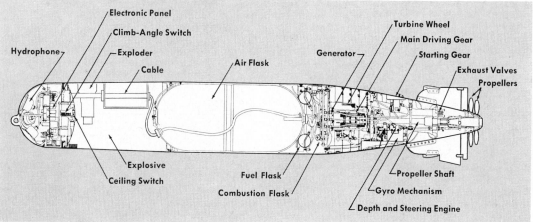

"ears" or hydrophones hunt for the sounds made by the propellers or machinery of a distant ship. When the hydrophones pick up an enemy ship by its noises, the torpedo is within *acquisition range*. At this point, it leaves its hunting course and goes straight to the target. It explodes either *magnetically*, when it nears the ship's hull, or *upon impact*, when it strikes the hull.

A special-purpose torpedo with most of these features can be guided by wire to its target. The torpedo unwinds a reel of wire as it travels to the target area. The attacking ship sends steering signals over the wire, aiming the torpedo at a target at close range.

Another special type is the antisubmarine rocket or *ASROC*. This weapon system detects a submarine at long ranges and quickly computes its course and speed. Then it launches a rocket-propelled ballistic missile containing either an *acoustic-homing*, or sound-detecting, torpedo or a depth charge. The rocket and other parts fall away in the air. In the water, the acoustic-homing device guides the torpedo to its target. A depth charge explodes at a predetermined depth.

On the outside, present-day torpedoes resemble earlier ones. On the inside, the torpedo is vastly different. Modern warfare demands weapons that can operate on a broad scale and that have a high degree of reliability. World War II torpedoes were of simple mechanical or electrical design. They were aimed at surface vessels only, and they ran a straight course. They left a telltale wake of air bubbles behind them, and made a detectable noise as they traveled. These torpedoes could easily be evaded by a maneuvering ship. Today's torpedoes leave no wake behind them, and can track ships making evasive maneuvers.

History. A number of men contributed to the invention of the torpedo. David Bushnell, an American, tried unsuccessfully to blow up British warships with torpedoes in 1776. In the early 1800's, the great American inventor, Robert Fulton, successfully blew up several ships with his torpedo, but there was little interest in it. In 1864, a Captain Luppis of the Austrian Navy took a plan for a torpedo to the famous Scottish engineer, Robert Whitehead. By 1868, Whitehead had developed the first real torpedo. Powered by compressed air, it was completely self-propelled. Today's torpedo designs involve so many fields of science, and are so complicated, that it is not possible to credit the modern torpedo to any one man. PAUL D. STROOP

See also DEPTH CHARGE; GUIDED MISSILE; PT BOAT; SUBMARINE.

TORPEDO, or ELECTRIC RAY, is the name of a particular kind of ray which lives in warm seas. The name of this fish comes from its ability to give off electricity from special glands just behind its head and gills. The body of the fish is flat and broad, and ends in a slender tail. The torpedo uses its strange power to stun small fish and to defend itself. The shock from a full-grown, healthy torpedo is powerful enough to stun a man for a moment. Scientists do not understand exactly how the electric organs in this fish become charged.

Scientific Classification. The torpedo belongs to the electric ray family, *Torpedinidae*. The Atlantic Coast torpedo, also called the *crampfish*, is genus *Torpedo*, species *T. nobiliana*. The Pacific Coast torpedo is classified as *T. californica*. LEONARD P. SCHULTZ

TORPEDO BOAT. See PT BOAT; TORPEDO.

TORQUE, *tawrk*, is the amount of twist that a force exerts on an object. The torque around any *axis* (reference line) is calculated by multiplying this force by the distance between the line of force and the axis. The torque increases as the force moves farther from the axis. For this reason, a wheel turns easier when the force is applied farther from the center. In the English system of measurement, torque is measured in pound-feet. See also FORCE; LEVER. ROBERT L. WEBER

TORQUEMADA, *tawr kay MAH dah*, **TOMÁS DE** (1420-1498), a Roman Catholic priest, was *inquisitor-general* (chief official) of the Spanish Inquisition for 15 years. During that time, 2,000 persons were executed by the Inquisition for *heresy* (beliefs contrary to those of the church).

Torquemada used the Inquisition for both religious and political reasons. He believed punishment of Christian heretics, and non-Christians—chiefly Jews and Muslims—was the only way to achieve political unity in Spain. Torquemada was partly responsible for the royal edict of 1492 that expelled 200,000 Jews from Spain. Many people admired him, but feared his power. King Ferdinand and Queen Isabella of Spain were among his supporters.

Torquemada was born in Valladolid. He became a friar in the Dominican monastery there, and later was prior of the monastery of Santa Cruz, at Segovia, for 22 years. He served as confessor to Isabella after she became queen of Spain. Torquemada became assistant to the inquisitors in 1482, and inquisitor-general for most Spanish lands in 1483. He laid down rules of procedure and established branches of the Inquisition in various cities. He retired to a Dominican monastery at Avila in 1496, but continued to direct the Inquisition until his death. RAYMOND H. SCHMANDT

See also INQUISITION.

TORRENS, LAKE. See LAKE TORRENS.

TORRENS SYSTEM is a system of registering titles to real estate. It is named for Sir Robert Torrens, who introduced it in South Australia in 1858. It has not been widely used in the United States. But nations of the British Commonwealth and Europe have adopted it. The purpose of the system is to make the transfer of real property as simple and safe as the transfer of other property, and to end repeated examination of titles.

A bureau or court of registration, supervised by a registrar, operates the system. An examiner of titles usually works with the registrar. The system substitutes public registration for *conveyancing* (transferring property by deeds and other written documents).

Under the Torrens system, the owner of a piece of land files a petition with the registrar to have his land registered. Searchers make a full inquiry into the title. If they find no flaw, the registrar issues a certificate of title, which a court cannot set aside or overcome. Thereafter, the official certificate of title will always show the state of the title and the person who holds it. If someone later proves to have just claim against the property, an insurance fund pays him. Fees charged for registration maintain the fund.

In the United States, the first Torrens Act was passed by the legislature of Illinois in 1897. From time to time, other states have adopted the system. Since each state has its own system of registering titles, the Torrens acts vary. Few states use this system today.

In Canada. In 1861, Vancouver Island adopted a system of land registration based upon the Torrens system. When Vancouver became a part of British Columbia, in 1866, the entire province continued the system. The provinces of Alberta, Manitoba, Nova Scotia, Ontario, and Saskatchewan also use the Torrens title system.   WILLIAM TUCKER DEAN

TORREÓN, *TAWR reh AWN* (pop. 223,104), is the commercial center of Mexico's reclaimed La Laguna area, the country's chief cotton- and wheat-growing region. It stands beside the Nazas River in a vineyard area of northwestern Mexico. For location, see MEXICO (political map). It has distilleries, textile and flour mills, and silver, zinc, lead, and arsenic smelters. The city was founded in 1887.   JOHN A. CROW

TORRICELLI, *tahr ih SELL ih,* or *tahr ih CHEL ih,* **EVANGELISTA** (1608-1647), was an Italian mathematician and physicist. He became known for his discovery of the principle of the barometer in 1643. He also improved the microscope and telescope. Torricelli was born in Faenza. He followed the great physicist Galileo as professor of philosophy and mathematics at the Florentine Academy and as mathematician to the grand duke of Tuscany. He wrote *Opera Geometrica* (1644). See also BAROMETER; HYDRAULICS (Laws of Hydrodynamics).   CARL T. CHASE

TORRID ZONE. See ZONE.

TORSION. See STRENGTH OF MATERIALS.

TORSION BALANCE is a device for measuring small forces of push or pull. A torsion balance sets an unknown force against the resistance to axial twist in a wire or fiber of small diameter, and measures the twist.

In practice, a torsion balance consists of a fine strand of quartz or sometimes a fine wire of steel or gold. This wire is mounted on a holding mechanism that can be rotated in a horizontal plane, to bring the torsion balance to its zero setting. Suspended from the lower end of the fiber is a horizontal or 45-degree pendulum bearing two balls of a heavy noncorrosive substance, generally gold, lead, or stainless steel. When the force to be measured is permitted to act on these balls, they swing

about, twisting the fiber. A tiny mirror mounted at the junction of fiber and pendulum reflects a beam of light. By noting how much this reflection moves from zero as the force acts, one measures the amount of torsion in dynes or other convenient units. It is necessary to calibrate the instrument first by twisting it with known forces. These tests must be repeated often, because molecular changes in the fiber may occur.

Scientists use torsion balances chiefly in measuring the strength of the earth's gravity. Prospectors for oil and other buried minerals use one form, of rugged construction, where gravity differences denote the presence of a valuable substance.   E. A. FESSENDEN

TORSION BAR SUSPENSION is a method of absorbing shock in automobiles. When a car with coil springs strikes a bump, the coils press closer together and absorb the shock. In torsion suspension, a torsion bar replaces the coils in the front end of the car. A torsion bar is actually a coiled spring that has been straightened. The bar has great elasticity and can withstand the same amount of stress as a spring. But, whereas a spring presses together to absorb shock, a torsion bar is subjected to *torsion* (twisting).

A torsion bar consists of a steel rod attached to an arm from the front wheel. When the car strikes a bump, the torsion bar twists to absorb the shock. Torsion bars take up less room than coil springs.   GEORGE KOETHER

See also AUTOMOBILE (The Suspension System); SHOCK ABSORBER; SPRING (metal).

TORT is a harmful act against a person which gives the person the right to collect money to pay for damage he has suffered. The branch of law that deals with such offenses is called *tort law.* Tort law is concerned mainly with injuries to your person, your reputation, and your property or business. For example, if someone harms your reputation by making false statements about you, you have a right to be paid for damages caused you. Other torts include someone's trespassing on your land or using your idea for a movie script. Most damages that result from a failure to keep a promise or to perform a contract are covered under a branch of law called *contract law.*

A tort may take place even though one person does not intend to harm another person. Many tort cases today result from injuries and damage in automobile acci-

Torsion Bars replace springs in some cars. Twist a piece of hose, *below,* and feel how it twists back. Torsion bars work the same way. When a car wheel hits a bump, *lower left,* it twists the bar. The bar then untwists to help hold the wheel on the road and keep the car level.

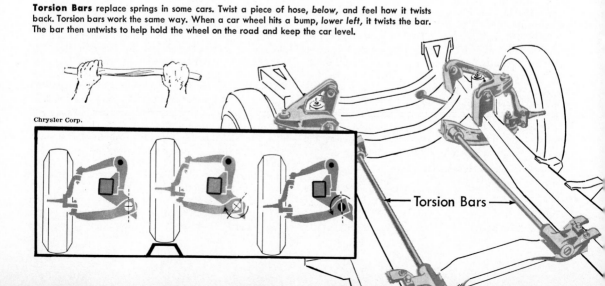

Chrysler Corp.

← Torsion Bars →

dents. The careful use of dynamite may be a tort if someone is injured by the explosion. Also, a tort may be committed by a corporation as well as by a person.

A tort may also be a crime. If someone punches you in the nose, you can be paid for the injury. The state may also punish the person for breaking a criminal law. In tort law, the injured party normally is an individual who sues to recover damages for the harm done. In criminal law, the injured party is the government, which takes legal action to punish the wrongdoer for a crime against the public.　　　　　HARRY KALVEN, JR.

Related Articles in WORLD BOOK include:

Assault and Battery	Negligence	Slander
Damages	Nuisance	Trespass

TORTILLA. See MEXICO (Food; picture: Corn Is Mexico's Chief Food); AZTEC (Food).

TORTOISE, *TAWR tus,* is a turtle that lives only on land. Tortoises have stumpy hind legs like those of an elephant, quite different from the flippers and

Edwin C. Weidlich

The Tortoise has stumpy, clublike legs and feet. When threatened, this lumbering turtle seeks safety inside its high, domed shell.

webbed feet of water turtles. In the United States, tortoises live in the deserts of the Southwest, in dry areas of the Southeast, and in southern Texas. During the winter, they sleep in holes that they dig. They eat plants, and some live more than a hundred years.

The *desert tortoise* lives in California, Nevada, Utah, Arizona, and Mexico. The *Texas tortoise* ranges from San Antonio, Tex., into Mexico. The *gopher tortoise* lives in the southeastern states.

Scientific Classification. The tortoise belongs to the class *Reptilia,* order *Testudinata,* family *Testudinidae.* The desert tortoise is genus *Gopherus,* species *G. agassizi;* the Texas tortoise, *G. berlandieri;* gopher tortoise, *G. polyphemus.*　　　　　CLIFFORD H. POPE

See also TURTLE; ANIMAL (color picture).

TORTOISE SHELL is used in making various objects for ornamentation. It comes from the shell of the hawksbill turtle. See also TURTLE.

TORTUGAS. See DRY TORTUGAS.

TORTURE is the use of physical pain to make persons confess something or to punish them. Great cleverness has been shown in the invention of instruments of torture such as the thumbscrew, scourge, and rack.

Some primitive peoples tortured their captives, but the most elaborate methods of torture were developed by civilized nations in Europe and Asia. The church and the state used torture in the Middle Ages. They made prisoners suffer terrible pain so that they

would give information or change their religious beliefs. Savonarola and John Huss were both tortured before they were killed. Torture was a favorite method of the Inquisition in Spain. In colonial America, torture was practiced during witchcraft trials in Salem, Mass.

In the 1500's, public opinion began to turn against the use of torture. A papal bull in 1816 forbade the practice in Catholic countries. The Fascist governments of the 1900's revived its use on a large scale. In World War II, the Japanese and Germans tortured war prisoners and civilians. During the Korean War, Communist forces used an emotional and mental reconditioning process called *brainwashing.* Many view brainwashing as a modern form of torture. MARVIN E. WOLFGANG

See also BRAINWASHING; PILLORY; RACK; STOCKS.

TORY PARTY was a conservative political party in Great Britain. The term came from a Gaelic word meaning *pursued* or *pursued man,* and was used in the mid-1600's to mean an Irish outlaw. The word was first used in English politics in 1679 to refer to those who wanted James, Duke of York, to succeed to the throne.

Eventually, the Tory party became one of the two chief political parties in Great Britain. The Tories favored maintaining the legal privileges of the Church of England and the powers of the king. Their chief opponents, the Whigs, wanted to increase the power of the people in the House of Commons. After 1832, the name *Conservative* began to replace *Tory.*

During the American Revolutionary War, those colonists who remained loyal to King George III were called Tories.　　　　　JAMES L. GODFREY

See also CONSERVATIVE PARTY; LIBERAL PARTY.

TOSCA. See OPERA (The Opera Repertoire).

TOSCANELLI, PAOLO. See COLUMBUS, CHRISTOPHER (What Columbus Wanted to Do).

TOSCANINI, *TOHS kah NEE nee,* **ARTURO** (1867-1957), was perhaps the most influential symphony orchestra and opera conductor of his time. When Toscanini began his career, standards of musical performance were set by conductors and musicians of the romantic school. The romantics regarded music as a means for expressing their own emotions, ideas, and performance skills. But Toscanini regarded the performer as the servant of the composer. He insisted that an analytic study of the music should form the basis of a performance. In this way, the composer's intentions could best be understood and would dominate the performance. Toscanini's approach became widely accepted in the 1900's.

Wide World

Arturo Toscanini

As a young conductor, Toscanini emphasized the music of Italian composers of his day and the works of such internationally known modern composers as Claude Debussy and Richard Wagner. In later years, his performances stressed the established music of the 1700's and 1800's. Toscanini was especially respected as an interpreter of the works of

TOTALITARIANISM

the composers Ludwig van Beethoven and Giuseppe Verdi.

Toscanini was born in Parma, Italy. He attended the local music conservatory, where he studied cello and piano. Toscanini began his conducting career at the age of 19, when he led a performance of Verdi's opera *Aida* with a traveling Italian opera company in Rio de Janeiro, Brazil. His reputation increased rapidly. In 1898, he became artistic director of La Scala, Milan, the most important opera house in Italy.

Toscanini's American career began in 1908 when he became a conductor of the Metropolitan Opera. He left that position in 1915. From 1921 to 1929, he again was artistic director at La Scala. Toscanini's hatred of Italy's Fascist government led him to return to the United States. From 1929 to 1936, he was principal conductor of the New York Philharmonic Orchestra. From 1937 to 1954, Toscanini directed the National Broadcasting Company Symphony Orchestra, which NBC formed especially for him. He retired at the age of 87.   Robert C. Marsh

TOTALITARIANISM is a form of government in which the state has absolute control over almost every aspect of people's lives. The individual is considered a servant of the state and is allowed almost no freedom of choice or expression.

A totalitarian government is ruled by one political party headed by, in most cases, a dictator. The party sets certain economic and social goals for the state, and it outlaws any activity that could interfere with the achievement of these goals. Most totalitarian governments prohibit such groups as labor unions and trade associations. Religious practices are forbidden unless they promote the policies of the state.

Under a totalitarian system, the government uses terror tactics to suppress individuals or groups who oppose the state. These tactics are carried out by a secret police force and the armed services. The government also uses censorship to silence anyone who criticizes its policies. The media spread government propaganda, and the schools teach students absolute loyalty to the state.

A totalitarian government controls the nation's economy through ownership or management of farmland and industry. Thus, it determines the type and quantity of crops and goods that are produced.

Various totalitarian governments have developed throughout history. In the 1920's and 1930's, however, technological advances in communication and detection systems aided the rise of extreme types of totalitarianism. Totalitarian governments of that period included those of Fascist Italy under Benito Mussolini, Nazi Germany under Adolf Hitler, and Communist Russia under Joseph Stalin. Today, many governments have some totalitarian policies. These governments are especially common in developing nations that are working to build their economies.   Michael Hurst

See also COMMUNISM; FASCISM; GOVERNMENT (Totalitarianism).

Additional Resources

ARCHER, JULES. *Police State: Could It Happen Here?* Harper, 1977. For younger readers.

ARENDT, HANNAH. *The Origins of Totalitarianism.* Harcourt, 1966. Originally pub. in 1958.
BUCHHEIM, HANS. *Totalitarian Rule: Its Nature and Characteristics.* Trans. by Ruth Hein. Wesleyan, 1968.
CURTIS, MICHAEL. *Totalitarianism.* Bobbs, 1979.

TOTEM, *TOH tuhm,* is a symbol for a tribe, clan, or family. The Chippewa, or Ojibwa, Indians first used the term for the animals or birds associated with their clans.

Government of British Columbia

Totem Poles, such as the ones pictured above, were wood carvings made by the Indians of the Northwest Coast.

The clan totem may be a bird, fish, animal, plant, or other natural object. Some groups consider the totem as an ancestor of the clan. A clan may have rules against killing or eating the species to which the totem belongs. Clan members are often known by the name of the totem. Some clans consider the totem holy and pray to it. Totemism, as a form of religion, may have been widespread among black African and American Indian peoples.

Many American Indian tribes, particularly those of the Pacific Northwest, carved the family and clan emblems on totem poles. The tribe held a *potlatch,* or feast, when the totem poles were put up.

Totem poles may be seen in Vancouver and Victoria, B.C.; Seattle, Wash.; in the Field Museum of Natural History in Chicago; and in the American Museum of Natural History in New York City.   Fred Eggan

See also BRITISH COLUMBIA (color pictures); ALASKA (color picture).

Additional Resources

LEACH, EDMUND. *Study of Myth and Totemism.* Methuen, 1968.
SMYLY, JOHN and CAROLYN. *The Totem Poles of Skedans.* Univ. of Minnesota Press, 1976.
WHERRY, JOSEPH L. *The Totem Pole Indians.* Funk & Wagnalls, 1964.

TOUCAN, *TOO kan,* is an unusual-looking bird with an enormous and, in most species, brilliantly colored bill. Toucans live in the tropical and subtropical forests of Central and South America.

The bill of a toucan may be black, blue, brown, green, red, white, yellow, or a combination of colors. Toucans probably use their colorful bill to attract their mates. The toucan's huge bill looks heavy, but it actually weighs little because it contains many air pockets.

There are about 40 kinds of toucans. The largest species, the *toco toucan*, measures about 25 inches (64 centimeters) long. The smallest toucans, called *aracaris* and *toucanets*, grow 13 to 14 inches (33 to 36 centimeters) long. Toucans have a bristly, narrow tongue that resembles a feather. They feed mainly on various small fruits. They sometimes use their bill, which has sawlike edges, to tear off pieces of larger fruits as well.

Most toucans live in small flocks that sleep in hollow trees. When toucans sleep, they turn their head around and place their bill down the center of their back. Then they fold their tail over their head.

Most kinds of toucans mate once a year. They build a nest in a hollow tree, and the female lays from two to four white eggs. The parents take turns sitting on the eggs. The eggs hatch after about 15 days, and the parents care for the young in the nest for about 8 weeks.

Scientific Classification. Toucans belong to the toucan family, *Ramphastidae*. The toco toucan is genus *Ramphastos*, species *R. toco*.   James M. Dolan, Jr.

TOUCH is the sense which gives us notice of contact with an object. It is also called the *tactile sense*. We learn the shape and hardness of objects through this sense. Touching an object can give rise to feelings of warmth, cold, pain, and pressure. Free nerve endings in the tissue give the sense of pain. Touch, warmth, cold, and pain are also called *cutaneous senses*.

Touch was formerly considered one of the five special, or exterior, senses. Now it is considered a common, or

general, sense because the touch organs are found all over the body.

Kinds of Touch Organs. There are several kinds of touch organs, called *tactile corpuscles*, in the skin and mucous membranes. One kind is found near hairs, another in hairless areas, and still another kind in deeper tissues. The sensation occurs when an object comes in contact with the sense organs and presses them out of shape, or touches a nearby hair. Nerves from the organs then carry nerve impulses to the brain.

Touch is more sensitive in some parts of the body than in others. This difference is due to the fact that the end organs for touch are not scattered evenly over the body, but are arranged in clusters. The feeling of pressure is keenest where there are the greatest number of end organs. It is most highly developed on the tip of the tongue, and is poorest on the back of the shoulders. The tips of the fingers and the end of the nose are other sensitive areas.

Measurement. Scientists can easily measure keenness of touch with the *esthesiometer*. This instrument looks like a drawing compass with two needle points. The tip of the tongue can feel both points when they are only 1.1 millimeters apart—about $\frac{1}{25}$ inch. Less-sensitive areas feel only one point at this distance. The back of the shoulders feels the two points as a single one until they are 66 millimeters apart—about 2.6 inches.

The end organs for warmth, cold, and pain are also

Toco Toucan
Ramphastos toco
Found in Guianas and Brazil
(Body length 25 inches, or 64 centimeters)

Emerald Toucanet
Aulacorhynchus prasinus
Found from Mexico to Peru
(Body length 14 inches, or 36 centimeters)

WORLD BOOK illustrations
by Albert Gilbert

Green Aracari
Pteroglossus viridis
Found from Colombia through Brazil
(Body length 13 inches, or 33 centimeters)

269

distributed unevenly. This can be discovered by running a pointed metal instrument over the skin. The instrument is colder than the skin, but it feels cold only at some points. At other points the instrument is simply felt as pressure. Many objects act on several senses at once. For example, a hot iron that touches a person's skin would cause the sensations of pain, heat, and touch.

Scientists know there are several million points on the body that register either cold, heat, pain, or touch. It is possible to map these points for the four cutaneous senses on any area of skin.   W. B. YOUMANS

See also PAIN; INSECT (Touch).

TOUCH FOOTBALL. See FOOTBALL (introduction).

TOUCH-ME-NOT is a yellow wild flower which grows in low, damp land in the eastern and central parts of the United States. Its ruffle-edged petals spread downward from the stem, somewhat like an orchid. Behind the blossom and growing from the base of the petals is a long spur in the form of a hollow tube. It curves inward on the spotted touch-me-not, but spreads outward on the pale touch-me-not. The plant is probably named *touch-me-not* because its seed pods fly open at the slightest touch.

Scientific Classification. The touch-me-not belongs to the balsam family, *Balsaminaceae*. It is genus *Impatiens*. The spotted touch-me-not is *I. biflora;* the pale touch-me-not is *I. pallida*.   MARCUS MAXON

See also FLOWER (picture: Flowers of Woodlands and Forests).

TOULON, *too LAHN* (pop. 181,801; met. area pop. 378,430), France's chief Mediterranean naval base, lies 29 miles (47 kilometers) southeast of Marseille. For loca-

tion, see FRANCE (political map). The docks at Toulon cover almost 800 acres (320 hectares). Its deepwater floating docks accommodate the largest ships. The French Navy destroyed much of its own fleet in the Toulon harbor when the Nazis tried to seize the ships during World War II. The city's chief industries are shipbuilding, lacemaking, fishing, iron and copper manufacturing, petroleum refining, tanning, brewing, and, nearby, the cultivation of grapes. Plants there also produce chemicals, footwear, furniture, clothing, and flour products.   EDWARD W. FOX

TOULON, SIEGE OF. See NAPOLEON I (Early Years).

TOULOUSE, *too LOOZ* (pop. 373,796; met. area pop. 509,939), is 380 miles (612 kilometers) south of Paris. For location, see FRANCE (political map). It carries on trade in grain, wine, tobacco, cannon, vehicles, and farm machinery. Plants in Toulouse manufacture chemical fertilizers, airplanes, hosiery, shoes, glassware, perfumes, and tin cans. Other important industries include flour milling, printing, canning, and paper milling. The university at Toulouse, founded in 1229, is the second oldest in France. Toulouse also has the literary "Academy of Floral Games," founded in 1324. The tomb of St. Thomas Aquinas, the philosopher and theologian, is in Toulouse.   EDWARD W. FOX

See also ROMANESQUE ARCHITECTURE (picture).

TOULOUSE-LAUTREC, *too LOOZ loh TREHK,* **HENRI DE** (1864-1901), was a French painter who also became known for his lithographs and posters. He won fame for his lively pictures of Paris night life and the Paris underworld.

Essentially, Toulouse-Lautrec's paintings are superb line drawings. He was a skilled draftsman and worked hard to give his pictures the appearance of sketches

At the Moulin Rouge (1892), an oil painting, on canvas; The Art Institute of Chicago

Toulouse-Lautrec's Works portray night life in the cafes and music halls of the Paris district called Montmartre. The artist became particularly noted for his skill in capturing the gaiety of the district.

done with little effort. His work shows the influence of Japanese prints and impressionist paintings, especially the works of Edgar Degas (see IMPRESSIONISM). A detail of a water color, *Trapeze Artist at the Medrano Circus*, by Toulouse-Lautrec is reproduced in color in the PAINTING article.

Toulouse-Lautrec lived among the dance halls, nightclubs, restaurants, and theaters of Montmartre, the Paris entertainment district. He immortalized many entertainers, including Jane Avril, May Belfort, Chocolate, La Goulue, and Yvette Guilbert. He portrayed them at work, catching each in a characteristic gesture and then exaggerating it.

Toulouse-Lautrec was born in Albi and moved to Paris with his parents in 1873. When he was 14 years old, he broke both legs in separate accidents. His legs healed but stopped growing, though the rest of his body matured normally. Toulouse-Lautrec's deformed, dwarfish appearance made him extremely sensitive. He sought the company of outcasts and rejects, including prostitutes. But when he painted them, he was neither sentimental nor critical. A museum in Albi has a collection of works by Toulouse-Lautrec. ROBERT F. REIFF

TOUPEE. See WIG.

TOUR DE FRANCE. See BICYCLE RACING; FRANCE (Sports).

TOURACO, *TUR uh KOH,* or TURACO, is any member of a family of African birds that live south of the Sahara. These birds measure from 15 to 30 inches (38 to 76 centimeters) long. Many of them have bright green, red, and violet-blue feathers. Touracos are the only birds that produce a green *pigment* (coloring matter) in their feathers. The green color in other birds results from the reflection of sunlight by the feathers.

Scientists classify touracos into four groups: (1) crested touracos, (2) go-away birds, (3) great blue touracos, and (4) violet plantain-eaters. Most touracos live in pairs or small groups in thick forests, but go-away birds live in dry, open areas.

Anthony Mercieca, NAS

The Red-Crested Touraco and many other forest species of touracos have brightly colored feathers and long tails.

Touracos are weak fliers. They climb and run along tree branches somewhat as squirrels do. Touracos eat fruits and insects and nest chiefly in trees. The females lay two or three white or greenish eggs.

Scientific Classification: Touracos make up the touraco family, *Musophagidae.* The family has 4 genera and about 19 species. JAMES M. DOLAN, JR.

TOURÉ, *too RAY,* **SÉKOU,** *SAY koo* (1922-   ), became Guinea's first president in 1958. Touré has maintained Guinea's neutrality in international politics. He has supported independence movements in Africa, and worked to strengthen ties among African nations.

Touré rose in politics as a trade union leader in French Guinea, then a French territory. He led French Guinea to independence from France in 1958. Touré was born in Faranah. IMMANUEL WALLERSTEIN

TOURMALINE, *TOOR muh lin,* is a hard mineral that is found in deposits of coarse granite, called *pegmatite dikes.* Tourmaline is the gem for October. It is formed in crystals which usually have six sides. It is harder than quartz and scratches glass easily. There are three types, classed according to the mineral oxides which give them their color. There are black, or *iron* tourmalines; brown, or *magnesia* tourmalines; and the *alkali* tourmalines, which range from rich reds through shades of greens and blues. Pink and red gems known as *rubellite* are the most desirable tourmaline gems. Colorless tourmalines are called *achroite.* Blue gems are called *indicolite,* while green ones are known as tourmaline.

Some tourmalines have two or more colors—either sharply distinct or blended—in the same crystal. Often the crystals have a different color when viewed lengthwise than they have across the longest part. This is an important factor in the cutting of gems.

Probably the best and most colorful tourmaline came from Maine, in the region around West Paris. The Ural Mountains, the island of Elba, Brazil, Southwest Africa, Sri Lanka, and Madagascar are all famous for bright-colored tourmalines.

Tourmaline plays an important part in science. When the gem is exposed to heat and pressure, it becomes electrically charged, and is used in electrical instruments. Dark-green transparent tourmaline is one of the few substances known that will absorb some vibrations, or directions, of light. The absorption polarizes the remainder of the light, which then passes through the gem. FREDERICK H. POUGH

See also GEM (color picture); POLARIZED LIGHT.

TOURNAMENT, *TOOR nuh ment,* is a contest of skill. Today, athletes hold tournaments where they show off their skill in games and sports. Series of games lasting several days also are called tournaments. Championships in many sports are decided by tournaments.

In the Middle Ages a tournament was an armed conflict between two groups of knights. A tournament was like actual warfare, except that it was staged as a dramatic performance or show would be. Knights and ladies gathered to watch. The fighters observed rules and fought on horseback. Blood was shed, and often the fighters were killed. Most tournaments were sponsored by a great noble. The knights who took part might represent two countries or two important families. The winners took their opponents' armor and horses or accepted a ransom for them. In the later Middle Ages, tournaments became polite contests. Picturesque ceremonies and words of praise from the ladies became more important than actual fighting. *Jousts* (battles) between individual knights became popular.

Good descriptions of tournaments may be found in romantic novels of the period, such as those of Chrétien de Troyes, and historical records, such as those of Jean Froissart. The most famous tournament in literature is probably the one which is vividly described in *Ivanhoe*, a novel by Sir Walter Scott.   BRYCE LYON

TOURNIQUET, *TUR nuh keht*, is the name for a device used to check bleeding in a wound, or to stop the flow of blood during an amputation. In an emergency, a tourniquet can be made from a stocking, handkerchief, triangular bandage or other piece of cloth, and a short stick. It should be used only when a bleeding wound threatens a person's life, and when the bleeding cannot be controlled by another method (see FIRST AID).

The best way to apply a tourniquet is to place a firm pad over the artery that supplies the wound and tie the tourniquet over the pad. Tie the cloth loosely around the limb, close to the wound but between the wound and the body. Then slip a short stick under the cloth and twist the stick, tightening the tourniquet, until the bleeding is checked. Once a tourniquet is applied, only a doctor should remove it, because the

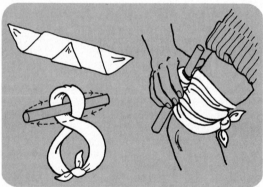

WORLD BOOK diagram

A Tourniquet can be made from a piece of cloth. Wrap it loosely above the wound and tie a knot. Insert a stick under the cloth and twist. As the cloth tightens, the flow of blood will stop.

doctor can check the bleeding by other means. Also, a note stating the time the tourniquet was applied should be tied to the patient.   BENJAMIN F. MILLER

See also BLEEDING.

TOURS, *toor* (pop. 140,686; met. area pop. 245,631), is a historic city and important economic center in western France. It lies in the scenic Loire Valley, along the Loire and Cher rivers (see FRANCE [political map]).

The area around Tours is known for its many old castles. The city's landmarks include the ruins of the Old Basilica of Saint Martin, which was completed in about 470; and the Cathedral of Saint Gatien, which dates from the 1200's. Tours serves as the capital of the *department* (administrative district) of Indre-et-Loire. It is also the commercial and industrial center of the sur-

rounding region. The city's many industries include banking, insurance, and the production of electrical equipment, farm machinery, machine tools, pharmaceuticals, and wine.

Roman soldiers founded the town of Caesarodunum on the site of what is now Tours in the 50's B.C. In 732, Christian Franks, a European people, defeated invading Muslim armies in a great battle that began near Tours and ended near Poitiers (see ARMY [famous Land Battles]). During World War II (1939-1945), German bombing raids heavily damaged parts of Tours. However, the damaged areas were soon rebuilt.   MARK KESSELMAN

TOURS, BATTLE OF. See ARMY (table: Famous Land Battles).

TOUSSAINT L'OUVERTURE, *too SAN loo vehr TYOOR* (1743-1803), Pierre Dominique Toussaint-Bréda, was a black revolutionist and general who became ruler of Haiti. His parents were black slaves. He was a slave himself until he was almost 50 years old. His name, L'Ouverture (The Opening), was taken from a remark by the French governor of Haiti, that "this man finds an opening everywhere," referring to his ability to break through enemy lines.

The island of Haiti was at that time a French colony. After the news of the Revolution in France reached Haiti, various uprisings took place. A slave revolt broke out in 1791, in which Toussaint soon became a leader. The black army first fought against France. But in 1793 the National Convention in

Consulate of Haiti

Toussaint L'Ouverture

France proclaimed freedom for all the slaves. Toussaint then came to the aid of the French against the Spanish and the British, who were fighting the French in Haiti.

In 1799, a civil war broke out between the blacks and the *mulattoes* (half-breeds). Toussaint, as leader of the full-blooded blacks, soon found himself the ruler of the island. He ruled rather wisely, and under him Haiti enjoyed a period of much prosperity.

Meanwhile, in 1802, Napoleon signed the Peace of Amiens, which freed his hands in Europe for a time. He decided to subdue Haiti, and announced the reestablishment of slavery. Toussaint resisted, and Napoleon sent an expedition against him. Toussaint was captured. But he was freed on condition that he would not work against the French again. He was later caught in a plot against the French, and he was taken to France. He died in prison.   DONALD E. WORCESTER

TOWBOAT. See TUGBOAT.

TOWER. In early times, people discovered that in battle those on higher places had the advantage over those below. They also found out that signals traveled farther from high places. Accordingly they built higher places in their walls which came to be called *towers*. Early people who worshiped the sun and stars built towers so that priests could come nearer to the gods.

Later towers were built for ornamental and other purposes. Today, tall buildings are sometimes called towers. Other towers include *campaniles* (bell towers), pagodas, and lighthouses. Lighthouses are built like towers so that the light at the top may be seen from a long distance. The *Pharos of Alexandria* was the most famous lighthouse of ancient times (see ALEXANDRIA).

In the early Middle Ages, bells began to be used to call people to church services. Later, these bells were hung in towers that were close to, or sometimes part of, the church building. Perhaps the most famous bell tower in the world is the campanile of the cathedral at Pisa, Italy, known as the Leaning Tower. Another well-known tower is the campanile of the Cathedral of Saint Mark in Venice. Many bell towers are famous works of architecture. Belfry towers, set in town squares, became common when towns and cities became free from the rule of feudal lords. They were symbols of this new freedom. The town of San Gimignano in Italy is famous for its many towers.

Many Eastern religions use towers as part of their religious buildings. The Muslim mosques have *minarets* (prayer towers). The pagodas of China and India are distinctive towers that reflect the religion of Buddhism.

One of the most famous towers is the 984-foot (300-meter) Eiffel Tower of Paris. It was built for the Paris Exposition of 1889. When built, it was the tallest building in the world. The CN (Canadian National) Tower in Toronto, Ont., is the world's tallest self-supporting tower. It was completed in 1976 and stands 1,815 feet (553 meters) high. CARL K. HERSEY

Related Articles in WORLD BOOK include:

Campanile	Lighthouse	Shot Tower
Eiffel Tower	Minaret	Singing Tower
Leaning Tower of Pisa	Pagoda	Tower of London

TOWER OF BABEL. See BABEL, TOWER OF.

TOWER OF LONDON is a group of stone buildings in the East End of London. It includes an ancient fortress, a dark prison, and a former royal residence. It stands on the north bank of the Thames River.

A shallow *moat* (ditch) and a high stone wall surround this group of buildings. The buildings have great thick walls. The structure is so strong that in former days it could have held off a whole army. The British War Department now uses the buildings chiefly as a showplace and museum. The armor collection in the museum was started by Henry VIII in the 1500's.

The Tower of London holds a leading place in English history. Many famous persons were held prisoner in the damp, dark cells of its prison. Lady Jane Grey came up through the Traitor's Gate on the Thames to be beheaded. The young Edward V and his brother, the Duke of York, were put in the tower after their uncle, Richard III, became king of England in 1483. The boys were never heard of again. Sir Roger Casement, a leader of the Irish Rebellion of 1916, was imprisoned in the tower until his execution.

The Tower of London also houses the royal jewel office. Here the crowns, scepters, and other glittering royal treasures of the English rulers, known as the *regalia*, are closely guarded. Tower of London guards are called *Yeomen Warders* (see YEOMAN). TALBOT HAMLIN

TOWHEE, *TOH hee*, or *TOW hee*, is any of several small North American birds related to the sparrows. The rufous-sided towhee, the most widespread species, lives throughout much of North America, from southern Canada to Mexico. This bird is about 8 inches (20 centimeters) long. Its sides are a chestnut color, and its belly

WORLD BOOK illustration by Trevor Boyer, Linden Artists Ltd.
The Rufous-Sided Towhee Lives Mainly on the Ground.

is white. The head and back are black in males and brown in females. The rufous-sided towhees of western North America have white bars on their wings and white spots on their back.

The rufous-sided towhee makes its home in open woods and bushy fields. It usually builds its nest on the ground, using dead leaves and twigs. There, the female lays two to six whitish eggs with brown speckles. The birds scratch energetically among leaves and grass on the ground, searching for insects, spiders, earthworms, berries, and seeds.

Three other species of towhees—Abert's towhee, the brown towhee, and the green-tailed towhee—are found in the western United States. These birds resemble the rufous-sided towhee in size and habits.

Scientific Classification. Towhees belong to the finch family, *Fringillidae*. The rufous-sided towhee is *Pipilo erythrophthalmus*. HERBERT FRIEDMANN

See also BIRD (picture: Birds' Eggs).

TOWN is a community of closely clustered dwellings and other buildings in which people live and work. It may be large or small. Most of the people in the United States and Canada use the word *town* to refer to a municipal unit which is larger than a village and smaller than a city. In the New England states, the name *town* is given to a minor governmental division known in other parts of the United States as a township. H. F. ALDERFER

Related Articles in WORLD BOOK include:

Boom Town	Local Government	Township
Borough	Town Meeting	Village

TOWN CRIER was a man appointed to make public announcements. He was important in Europe and England before newspapers were common, and was the "walking newspaper" of the American colonies during the 1600's. With his "hear ye, hear ye," he sang out the latest news at every corner, and announced the time of town meetings and other events of public interest. The town crier should not be confused with the colonial night watchman, who walked the streets at night, lantern in hand, calling out the hour. The town crier disappeared when the printing press, newspaper, and other forms of communication came into general use after the 1750's.   ROBERT J. TAYLOR

TOWN MEETING is held once a year by the voters of a town. The first town meetings were held in colonial days. Such a meeting is the purest form of democratic government known, because it is government by the people rather than by their elected representatives.

All citizens 18 years of age or older are free to attend town meetings and express their opinions. At the meetings the township makes its decisions for the year to come. It passes ordinances and discusses township improvements and other business. The town clerk makes and keeps a record of the meeting. The town system is a typical New England institution, but it has been adopted elsewhere.   H. F. ALDERFER

See also VERMONT (picture: A Town Meeting).

TOWN PLANNING. See CITY PLANNING.

TOWNES, CHARLES HARD (1915-   ), is a United States physicist. In 1951, he explained the basic principles that led to the development of the maser. A *maser* is a device that uses the energy of molecules or atoms to amplify radio waves. Townes helped build the first maser in 1953 (see MASER). In 1958, Townes and Arthur L. Schawlow proposed the *laser*, a device for amplifying light waves (see LASER). For his work, Townes shared the 1964 Nobel prize in physics with two Russian scientists who also developed and improved masers.

Townes was born in Greenville, S.C., and was graduated from Furman University. From 1939 to 1947, he was a research physicist at the Bell Telephone Laboratories. Townes taught physics at Columbia University from 1948 to 1961, when he became a professor of physics and provost of the Massachusetts Institute of Technology. In 1967, he became professor of physics at the University of California in Berkeley.   R. T. ELLICKSON

See also BASOV, NIKOLAI; PROKHOROV, ALEXANDER.

TOWNSEND, WILLARD SAXBY (1895-1957), was one of the first black American labor leaders. He improved the wages and working conditions of *redcaps* (railroad baggage porters). Under his leadership, redcaps gained a fixed salary, plus retirement and insurance benefits.

Townsend was born in Cincinnati, Ohio, and began working as a redcap there when he was 19 years old. In 1936, he was elected as the first president of the Auxiliary of Redcaps, a union that belonged to the American Federation of Labor (AFL). In 1937, he was chosen as the first president of an independent union called the International Brotherhood of Redcaps. It became the United Transport Service Employees in 1940 and joined the Congress of Industrial Organizations (CIO) in 1942. Also in 1942, Townsend became the first black member of the CIO executive board. When the AFL and the CIO merged in 1955, he was named a vice-president of the AFL-CIO.

Townsend was a vice-president of the Urban League and an officer of

© *Chicago Sun-Times*
Willard Townsend

the National Association for the Advancement of Colored People (NAACP). He was coauthor of a book, *What the Negro Wants* (1944).   JAMES G. SCOVILLE

TOWNSEND PLAN is an old-age pension plan that was proposed in 1934 by Dr. Francis E. Townsend of Long Beach, Calif. It provided that all citizens of the United States over 60 years of age be paid $200 a month. The funds were to come from a 2 per cent tax on the transfer or sale of goods. Supporters of the Townsend Plan believed that it would stabilize American prosperity, because those receiving pensions would be obligated to spend the money within a month. A modified version of the Townsend Plan was presented to the United States House of Representatives on June 1, 1939, but it was voted down.   ROBERT J. MYERS

TOWNSHEND, VISCOUNT (1674-1738), CHARLES TOWNSHEND, pioneered in improving English agriculture. He retired to a Norfolk estate in 1730 after a successful political career. He then introduced the turnip to English farms, for which he is known as "Turnip" Townshend. He practiced *marling* (fertilization) and *enclosure* (the use of fences). He improved farming by demonstrating the productivity of better cultivation in one of England's poorest farming districts.   C. B. BAKER

TOWNSHEND ACTS. See REVOLUTIONARY WAR IN AMERICA (The Townshend Acts).

TOWNSHIP in the United States is a division of a county. It may be entirely rural, but it may also include one or more cities or towns.

The governing body of a township is generally a board of commissioners, supervisors, or trustees. This body has the power to pass ordinances and resolutions which have the force of law in the township. Administrative affairs of a routine nature are generally handled by a township clerk. In New England, townships are usually called *towns*, and have more elaborate governmental powers.   H. F. ALDERFER

See also LOCAL GOVERNMENT; TOWN.

TOXIC SHOCK SYNDROME, or *TSS*, is a rare disease that most frequently occurs in young women who are having a menstrual period. It can, however, strike men and women of any age. Symptoms include a high temperature, vomiting, diarrhea, low blood pressure, and a sunburnlike rash.

TSS is caused by a bacterium called *Staphylococcus aureus*, which can produce infection anywhere on or inside the body. Scientists do not understand exactly how staphylococcal infections cause TSS. They suspect that the bacteria release a *toxin* (poison) that spreads through the body, probably by way of the bloodstream, and causes TSS.

Fewer than one-thousandth of 1 per cent of all menstruating women are likely to develop TSS each year. Most victims are teen-agers and women in their twenties who use a *tampon*—a roll of absorbent material inserted into the vagina—during the menstrual period. Physicians do not know why women who wear tampons run a greater risk of developing TSS than those who wear sanitary napkins. Public health doctors have not advised women to stop using tampons, but they do recommend that tampon-users recognize the symptoms of TSS. A woman who develops symptoms should remove the tampon and call a doctor immediately.

Physicians treat TSS with antibiotics and with fluids administered through a vein. A female patient not treated with antibiotics may become ill again during her next menstrual period. Most patients recover and have no further problems. However, some lose their hair, fingernails, or toenails about three months after developing TSS. About 4 per cent of toxic shock syndrome cases are fatal.   KATHRYN N. SHANDS

TOXIN, *TAHK sin,* is a poison produced by a living organism. Toxins may cause many diseases and even death. Some toxins remain inside the organism that produces them. They are called *endotoxins.* They cause poisoning only when the organism is broken up and the poison escapes. Other toxins, called *exotoxins,* are secreted into the substance surrounding the organism.

Bacteria (small organisms) that infect the human body may produce toxins that cause such diseases as diphtheria, tetanus (lockjaw), gas gangrene, and scarlet fever. Some bacteria and fungi secrete toxins into the foods in which they grow. Such serious diseases as botulism, ergotism, and alimentary toxic aleukia may result if such food is eaten.

Some tropical fish produce toxins that remain in their bodies. These toxins do not harm the fish, but they can cause illness or death to a person who eats the fish. The venoms of poisonous snakes, spiders, and insects are toxins. Doctors prescribe *antitoxins* to fight toxins. Antitoxins are serums or substances formed in the body to neutralize a toxin.   SOLOMON GARB

See also SERUM; ANTITOXIN; DISEASE (Bacterial Diseases).

TOY. Almost all children enjoy playing with toys. Girls and boys throughout the world like to play with blocks, dolls, puzzles, and miniature houses and automobiles. They have fun building models, flying kites, spinning tops, and operating many other kinds of toys. Youngsters can also make their own toys from such common articles as boxes, cardboard cartons, paper bags, pans, and pieces of wood.

Since ancient times, toys have had an important part in a child's life. They enable boys and girls to have fun

Neil Newton, Miller Services

Puzzles teach children patience in putting things together. Some kinds, such as clock puzzles that show how to tell time, also help youngsters learn various skills.

while learning about the world around them. They also help children learn how to get along with others, prepare for adulthood, and develop special skills.

Toy companies produce hundreds of kinds of toys, most of them for children of various ages. Such toys can be divided into three main groups: (1) toys for babies, (2) toys for preschool youngsters, and (3) toys for young schoolchildren.

Toys for Babies include crib exercisers, rattles, rubber balls, stuffed animals, teething rings, and toys that contain music boxes or chimes. Babies enjoy brightly colored toys that have patterns, make sounds, and are fun to feel. Mirrors and *mobiles* (hanging structures that move) are among a baby's favorite toys.

Toys for Preschool Youngsters. After children learn to stand, walk, and run, their play needs increase greatly. They become interested in colors, places, shapes, sizes, and learning and using language. Push toys help children become sure of themselves in walking and running. Puzzles challenge youngsters to take things apart and put them together again. Wooden or plastic blocks test their skill in building and balancing objects.

Some toys are not only fun but also help a child learn to speak, count, draw, read, tell time, write, and work at a desk or table. Such toys include books, phonograph records, clock puzzles, finger paints, peg desks, letters and numbers, and toy telephones.

Toys for Young Schoolchildren should be closely associated with the world around these girls and boys. Such toys challenge their mental and physical abilities. For example, hobby and model kits can help teach a child care and neatness in putting things together. These kits may also increase a child's interest in handicrafts or help a youngster learn how real airplanes, cars, and ships are made.

A child can learn about clothing and fashions by playing with dolls and doll accessories. Children who like science may spend hours with a chemistry set, a kaleidoscope, a microscope, or a telescope. Youngsters

Vivienne

Stacking Blocks of wood or plastic helps children learn to balance objects and to make many kinds of structures. Youngsters like to use their imagination to arrange blocks into various shapes.

who enjoy music have fun with toy musical instruments. Almost all children like to play with marionettes and hand puppets.

History. Children have played with toys for thousands of years. In ancient Egypt, children enjoyed balls, pull-toys, and toy animals. Children of ancient Greece and Rome had fun with boats, carts, hobbyhorses, hoops, and kites. Tops probably developed hundreds of years ago in China or Japan. During the Middle Ages in Europe, popular toys included puppets and rattles. Some children invented their own toys by imitating the work and following the interests of adults.

Toy manufacturing became an important industry in the United States during the early 1900's. At that time, manufacturers began making many kinds of toys to meet the different interests and needs of children. In 1969, Congress passed the Child Protection and Toy Safety Act. This act enabled the government to prohibit the sale of toys that might be harmful. Such toys may contain poisonous substances, catch fire easily, or have unprotected points or sharp edges. During the 1970's, the U.S. toy industry sold more than $3 billion worth of toys annually. WESLEY E. SHARER

Related Articles in WORLD BOOK include:

Airplane, Model	Kite	Ship, Model
Automobile, Model	Play	Skateboard
Doll	Puppet	Top
Dollhouse	Railroad, Model	Yo-Yo
Kaleidoscope	Rocket, Model	

TOY DOG is the name of a group of small dogs. Many are relatives of larger dogs. For example, the toy poodle is a tiny poodle. Other toys, such as the Chihuahua, are separate breeds. The recognized toy breeds include the affenpinscher, Brussels griffon, Chihuahua, English toy spaniel, Italian greyhound, Japanese chin, Maltese, miniature pinscher, papillon, Pekingese, Pomeranian, pug, shih tzu, silky terrier, and Yorkshire terrier. The WORLD BOOK has separate articles for each of the breeds listed here. JOSEPHINE Z. RINE

See also DOG (color pictures: Toy Dogs).

TOY MANCHESTER TERRIER. See MANCHESTER TERRIER.

TOYNBEE, *TOIN bee,* is the family name of two men, uncle and nephew, who made contributions in the fields of sociology and history.

Arnold Toynbee (1852-1883) was interested in the problems caused by poverty. An enthusiastic social reformer, he lived in a shabby dwelling in Whitechapel, a London slum district. He worked for uplift of the poor, changes in the poor laws, and freedom of work. He urged prevention of waste by an equalization of supply and demand. He thought the church should work for social progress, and taught that imitation of Jesus' life of service to humanity was true Christianity. His best-known book was *The Industrial Revolution,* published in 1884.

Toynbee was born in London, and was educated at Oxford University. His hard work to improve conditions ruined his health. Shortly after his death, Toynbee Hall, the first settlement house in the world, was set up in Whitechapel to help the poor.

Arnold Joseph Toynbee (1889-1975) was a famous historian. His outline of civilizations, *A Study of History,*

was published in 12 volumes from 1934 to 1961. Toynbee divided world history into 26 civilizations, and traced their rise, decline, and fall. He declared that the one hope for the survival of Western civilization lies in a rebirth of the Christian spirit.

Toynbee's original and bold approach to world history, that of "an ancient historian, looking at the Western World from the outside," had a wide appeal. A two-volume abridgment of his great work sold widely in the United States and Europe. His writings include a number of volumes dealing with social-historical problems, such as *Nationality and the War* (1915), *Civilization on Trial* (1948), and *The World and the West* (1953). Toynbee was born in London. He studied at Balliol College, Oxford, and at the British Archaeological School at Athens, Greece. Toynbee became a professor of international history at the University of London in 1925. See also CIVILIZATION (Why Civilizations Rise and Fall). FRANCIS J. BOWMAN

Karsh, Ottawa
Arnold Joseph Toynbee

TRACE ELEMENTS are minerals needed in small amounts by plants, animals, and human beings. Major elements such as iron, carbon, sulfur, oxygen, calcium, hydrogen, and phosphorus are part of the make-up of all living things. The trace elements are also necessary to life. Scientists know the uses of only a few of these minerals. However, scientists do know that they are necessary for the work of certain vital enzymes (see ENZYME).

The trace elements include copper, cobalt, magnesium, manganese, and zinc. The body needs copper so it can use iron to build hemoglobin, an important part of red blood cells. Cobalt, contained in vitamin B_{12}, protects a person against a blood disease called *pernicious anemia*. Only $\frac{1}{15,000,000}$ ounce (0.000002 gram) of this vitamin each day keeps persons with pernicious anemia healthy. Magnesium helps to regulate muscle reaction, and keeps the muscles in good working condition. Plants need magnesium to build chlorophyll, the green color in their leaves and stems. Manganese and zinc are required for the normal action of certain enzymes. Without these two minerals, certain reactions in the body cells would stop. Animals also need manganese and zinc. For example, baby chicks that do not get enough manganese will become crippled. Human beings get all these required trace elements from their food in a balanced diet. SARAH R. RIEDMAN

See also NUTRITION.

TRACERY, in architecture, originally was the framework of light stone bars dividing a large window into smaller areas so that the stained glass could be easily placed and supported. Usually tracery took the form of tall narrow arched divisions below, with circles, cusps, and other shapes filling the upper part of the window. Later, these shapes were used to decorate wall panels, buttresses, vaulting, and furniture, and are still termed *tracery.*

Builders first used tracery in the late 1100's, when

church windows grew too large to be glazed in one unbroken area. From then on, it developed rapidly in delicacy and became a marked feature of nearly all Gothic architecture. The earliest tracery was called *plate* tracery, because the upper circles were pierced through a plate of stone in the upper part of the main window arch. *Geometric* tracery, a complete pattern of thin stone bars, later replaced this pierced "plate." In it, all the openings between the bars are simple geometric forms. Still later, *flowing* and *flamboyant* tracery was used, so called because of its flowing and swaying flamelike shapes. In the late 1300's and the 1400's in England, *perpendicular* tracery was the rule. In this, the vertical bars between the lower openings are carried up the whole height of the window, making small vertical panels.   TALBOT HAMLIN

A. F. Kersting

Tracery is an ornamental pattern for windows and other building elements. It is widely used in Gothic structures.

TRACHEA. See WINDPIPE.

TRACHOMA, *truh KOH muh,* is a contagious eye disease caused by an organism with some characteristics of both viruses and bacteria. Trachoma is relatively rare in the United States because of treatment with antibiotics or sulfonamides. But in Egypt, India, Saudi Arabia, and other developing countries, trachoma is still a major cause of blindness. It affects the *conjunctiva* (membrane of the eyeball and lids) and *cornea,* the window of the eye (see EYE [Parts of the Eye]). Symptoms of acute conjunctivitis develop and the disease may last for years (see CONJUNCTIVITIS). Doctors must report cases of trachoma because the disease spreads easily. People in contagious areas are warned not to use public towels, or rub their eyes with unwashed hands. Severe eye damage by trachoma may require an operation known as *corneal transplantation* (see EYE BANK).   WILLIAM F. HUGHES

TRACK. See RAILROAD (Tracks).

TRACK AND FIELD is a sport in which athletes compete in events that feature running, jumping, and throwing. Track and field meets are held indoors or outdoors, and both men and women compete. *Track events* consist of races over various distances. *Field events* test the athlete's skill at jumping and throwing.

Track and field ranks with soccer as one of the two most popular sports in the world. About 150 nations belong to the International Amateur Athletic Federation (I.A.A.F.), the governing body of track and field. The I.A.A.F. recognizes world records in more than 50 men's and women's events. The table of *World Track and Field Records* that accompanies this article lists most of these events.

The Olympic Games in ancient Greece were the earliest known track and field competition. The first recorded Olympic contest was held in 776 B.C. Today, track and field is an important part of the Summer Olympic Games, held every four years. Annual track and field meets are held at the local, state and provincial, national, and international levels. The teams in

these meets represent elementary schools, high schools, universities and colleges, sports clubs, and nations.

Track Events

Track events consist of four types of races among individual athletes—*running, hurdle, steeplechase,* and *walking*—and team races called *relays.* The distances of all these races are measured in either meters or yards. The I.A.A.F. recognizes world records in metric distances only, except for the mile run.

The athletes race on an oval track. Most outdoor tracks are $\frac{1}{4}$ mile or 400 meters long. Indoor tracks vary in length, but most indoor tracks are shorter than outdoor tracks. Outdoor tracks must be at least 24 feet (7.32 meters) wide, and the most common indoor width is 12 feet (3.66 meters). The tracks are divided into six or eight lanes that measure 4 feet (1.22 meters) wide.

Running Races consist of *sprints, middle-distance races,* and *distance races.* Sprints, sometimes called *dashes,* include all races up to 400 meters or 440 yards long. Middle-distance races cover from 400 meters or 440 yards to 1,500 meters or a mile. Distance races are longer than 1,500 meters or a mile.

Hurdle Races are events in which the runners must jump over obstacles called *hurdles.* Most of these races have 10 hurdles at equal intervals on the track. There are two kinds of hurdle races: intermediate and high. Intermediate hurdles are 36 inches (91 centimeters) high for men and 30 inches (76 centimeters) high for women. Intermediate-hurdle races cover 330 yards in high school and 400 meters or 440 yards elsewhere. Men's high hurdles are 42 inches (106 centimeters) high. They are 39 inches (99 centimeters) in high school. Most men's high-hurdle races cover 60 yards indoors and 110 meters or 120 yards outdoors. Women run a 100-meter high-hurdle race over 33-inch (84-centimeter) hurdles.

The Steeplechase is a 3,000-meter race that involves two kinds of obstacles, hurdles and *water jumps.* The runners must jump over 28 hurdles, each of which is 36 inches high. They also must clear 7 water jumps, each of which consists of a hurdle 36 inches high followed immediately by a water-filled pit 12 feet (3.66 meters) square. The pit is $27\frac{1}{2}$ inches (70 centimeters) deep at the foot of the hurdle and slopes up to the ground level.

Walking Races are events in which athletes walk according to specific rules. Their front foot must touch the ground before their rear foot leaves the ground. While the foot is on the ground, the leg must be straight. Most men's walking races cover distances of 20,000 meters and 50,000 meters. There are world records for these two distances and also for the two-hour walk, in which the winner covers the greatest distance in two hours. Women occasionally compete in walking races, but there are no women's world records.

Relays are run by teams of four runners. The first member of the team runs a certain distance while carrying a baton that measures about 1 foot (30 centimeters) long. He or she then hands the baton to the next member. The second, third, and fourth runners cannot begin their part of the race until they receive the baton. The runners must pass the baton within a zone 22 yards (20 meters) long. If two runners do not exchange the baton within this zone, their team is disqualified.

TRACK AND FIELD

Some Track Events

Sprints include all races up to 400 meters or 440 yards long. The runners begin a sprint from a crouch. Each athlete pushes off from two triangular *starting blocks* to get a fast start.

Marvin Newman, DPI

United Press Int.

Hurdle Races are events in which the runners must jump over fencelike obstacles called *hurdles*. The women shown above are competing in a 100-meter high-hurdle race.

Ed Barnas, DPI

Relays are team races. Each runner on a team covers a certain distance while carrying a *baton*. He or she must give the baton to a teammate before the other athlete continues the race.

The most common relays are run at distances of 400 meters or 440 yards and 1,600 meters or 1 mile. In these relays, all four members of a team run an equal distance. In *medley relays*, the athletes cover different distances. In the *sprint medley*, two members of a team run 220 yards each, another runs 440 yards, and the fourth 880 yards. In the *distance medley*, the team members run distances of 440 yards, 880 yards, $\frac{3}{4}$ mile, and 1 mile.

Field Events

Field events take place in specially prepared areas, usually within the oval track. Field competition consists of four jumping events and four throwing events. The jumps are the (1) long jump, (2) triple jump, (3) high jump, and (4) pole vault. The throwing events are the (1) discus, (2) hammer, (3) javelin, and (4) shot-put. Some high school meets omit the triple jump, hammer, and javelin. Women do not compete in the triple jump, pole vault, or hammer.

Jumping Events. In the long jump and triple jump, the athletes jump as far forward as they can. In the high jump and pole vault, they go as high as possible.

The long jump, once called the *broad jump*, is a single leap. The triple jump, originally called the *hop, step, and jump*, consists of three continuous jumps. The athlete takes off on one foot and lands on that foot. He then jumps again and lands on the other foot. After jumping a third time, he can land on either foot or on both feet.

To begin the long jump and triple jump, the athletes sprint down a runway and leap from a take-off board. If an athlete steps over the board before jumping, the jump does not count. The jumper lands in a pit of sand. The length of a jump is measured from the near edge of the take-off board to the spot where the athlete lands. Each competitor jumps six times if there are eight or fewer contestants. If there are more than eight competitors, each jumps three times. The longest jump wins.

High jumpers and pole vaulters try to propel themselves over a long thin bar that rests on and between two poles. They land in a pit of sawdust or foam rubber, or on an air-inflated pad. If a contestant knocks the bar off the poles, the vault counts as a miss. Each jumper gets three attempts at a certain height. Three consecutive misses at any height eliminate the competitor from the event. The athlete who clears the greatest height wins. In case of a tie, the one with the fewest misses wins.

A high jumper begins with a running start and approaches the bar from any angle. The athlete uses any of a number of jumping styles to clear the bar but must take-off from one foot.

A pole vaulter uses a long fiberglass pole. He begins his jump by sprinting down a runway, carrying the pole almost parallel to the ground. As he nears the end of the runway, he rams the far end of the pole into a wood or metal box imbedded in the ground. The pole bends and then straightens, helping to thrust the athlete into the air. At the peak of his jump, he performs a series of twisting body movements to clear the bar.

Throwing Events require the athletes to toss one of four objects as far as they can. The contestants have six throws in each event if there are eight or fewer competitors. In an event with more than eight competitors, each contestant has three throws. The longest throw wins. Competitors in the discus, hammer, and shot-put all throw from inside a circle. In the javelin, the athlete runs down a runway and throws the javelin before he or she reaches a foul line.

A discus is a platter-shaped object made of metal and wood. The men's discus measures about $8\frac{3}{4}$ inches (221 millimeters) in diameter and weighs at least 4 pounds $6\frac{1}{2}$ ounces (2 kilograms). The women's discus is about $7\frac{1}{4}$ inches (182 millimeters) in diameter and weighs at least 2 pounds 3 ounces (1 kilogram). The athlete grips the discus with one hand, spins around once, and releases it with a sidearm motion.

A hammer is a metal ball attached to one end of a steel wire. A handle is fastened to the other end. The entire hammer weighs 16 pounds (7.26 kilograms). Using both hands, the athlete grasps the handle and spins around three or four times before releasing it.

A javelin is a spear made of metal or wood. The men's javelin measures from 8 feet $6\frac{1}{4}$ inches (2.6 meters) to 8 feet $10\frac{1}{4}$ inches (2.7 meters) long and weighs at least 28 ounces (800 grams). Women throw a javelin that is 7 feet $2\frac{1}{2}$ inches (2.2 meters) to 7 feet $6\frac{1}{2}$ inches (2.3 meters) long and weighs at least 21 ounces (600 grams). The athlete holds the javelin by a cord grip near the center and releases it with an overhand motion.

A shot is a metal ball. Men use a 16-pound shot, and women use one that weighs 8 pounds 13 ounces (4 kilograms). High school athletes use a 12-pound (5.4-kilogram) shot. The competitors hold the shot against their neck. Then they glide across the circle and *put* (push) the shot forward.

The Pentathlon, Decathlon, and Heptathlon

The pentathlon is a men's competition of five events. Each athlete competes in all events in one day. The events are the long jump, javelin throw, 200-meter run, discus throw, and 1,500-meter run, in that order. The contestants earn points based on their performance in each event. The athlete with the most points wins.

The decathlon is a men's competition of 10 events over two days. On the first day, men compete in the 100-meter run, long jump, shot-put, high jump, and 400-meter run, in that order. On the second day, they compete in the 110-meter hurdles, discus throw, pole vault, javelin throw, and 1,500-meter run, in that order.

The heptathlon is a women's contest that consists of seven events over two days. On the first day, women perform in the 100-meter hurdles, shot-put, high jump, and 200-meter run. On the second day they compete in the long jump, javelin throw, and 800-meter run.

Track and Field Meets

Kinds of Meets. Track and field meets range from *dual meets* between two teams to world championships involving teams that represent dozens of nations. Some meets allow men and women to compete as *unattached athletes*, rather than as members of teams.

Dual meets are the most common track and field competition. At the end of the track and field season, many high school and college teams compete in conference or league championship meets. The winners advance to state or national championship meets.

The National Collegiate Athletic Association (NCAA) sponsors an annual championship meet for member col-

Some Field Events

Gerhard E. Gscheidle from Peter Arnold

The Shot-Put is a throwing event in which the athletes *put* (push) a metal ball called a *shot*. They hold the shot against their neck and glide across a circle before releasing it.

Paul J. Sutton, Duomo from DPI

The High Jump requires an athlete to leap over a long thin bar that rests on and between two poles. This jumper is leaping head-first by arching his back and kicking out his legs.

Ingrid Schultheis

The Javelin Throw tests an athlete's ability to toss a javelin after a running start. She or he sprints down a runway to gain momentum and then throws the spear with an overhand motion.

World Track and Field Records

Event	Record	Holder	Country	Date

Men's Records
Running

100 meters	9.95 s.	Jim Hines	United States	Oct. 14, 1968
200 meters	19.72 s.	Pietro Mennea	Italy	Sept. 17, 1979
400 meters	43.86 s.	Lee Evans	United States	Oct. 18, 1968
800 meters	1 min. 41.73 s.	Sebastian Coe	Great Britain	June 10, 1981
1,000 meters	2 min. 12.18 s.	Sebastian Coe	Great Britain	July 11, 1981
1,500 meters	3 min. 31.36 s.	Steve Ovett	Great Britain	Aug. 27, 1980
1 mile	3 min. 47.33 s.	Sebastian Coe	Great Britain	Aug. 28, 1981
2,000 meters	4 min. 51.4 s.	John Walker	New Zealand	June 30, 1976
3,000 meters	7 min. 32.1 s.	Henry Rono	Kenya	June 27, 1978
5,000 meters	13 min. 6.2 s.	Henry Rono	Kenya	Sept. 11, 1981
10,000 meters	27 min. 22.4 s.	Henry Rono	Kenya	June 11, 1978
20,000 meters	57 min. 24.2 s.	Jos Hermens	The Netherlands	May 1, 1976
25,000 meters	1 hr. 13 min. 55.8 s.	Toshihiko Seko	Japan	March 22, 1981
30,000 meters	1 hr. 29 min. 18.8 s.	Toshihiko Seko	Japan	March 22, 1981
1-hour run	13 miles 24 yards (20,944 meters)	Jos Hermens	The Netherlands	May 1, 1976
3,000-meter steeplechase	8 min. 5.4 s.	Henry Rono	Kenya	May 13, 1978

Hurdles

110-meter hurdles	12.93 s.	Renaldo Nehemiah	United States	Aug. 19, 1981
400-meter hurdles	47.13 s.	Edwin Moses	United States	July 3, 1980

Relays

400-meter relay	38.03 s.	U.S. National Team (B. Collins, S. Riddick, C. Wiley, S. Williams)	United States	Sept. 3, 1977
800-meter relay	1 min. 20.26 s.	Univ. of Southern California (J. Andrews, J. Sanford, B. Mullins, C. Edwards)	United States	May 27, 1978
1,600-meter relay	2 min. 56.16 s.	U.S. National Team (V. Matthews, R. Freeman, L. James, L. Evans)	United States	Oct. 20, 1968
3,200-meter relay	7 min. 8.1 s.	Russian National Team (V. Podolyakov, N. Kirov, V. Malozemlin, A. Reshetnyak)	Russia	Aug. 12, 1978
6,000-meter relay	14 min. 38.8 s.	West German National Team (T. Wessinghage, H. Hudak, M. Lederer, K. Fleschen)	West Germany	Aug. 17, 1977

Race Walking

20,000-meter walk	1 hr. 20 min. 6.8 s.	Daniel Bautista	Mexico	Oct. 17, 1979
30,000-meter walk	2 hr. 8 min.	Jose Marin	Spain	Aug. 4, 1979
50,000-meter walk	3 hr. 41 min. 39 s.	Raul Gonzales	Mexico	May 25, 1979
2-hour walk	17 miles 881 yards (28,165 meters)	Jose Marin	Spain	Aug. 4, 1979

Jumping

High jump	7 ft. 8¾ in. (2.36 meters)	Gerd Wessig	East Germany	Aug. 1, 1980
Pole vault	19 ft. ¾ in. (5.81 meters)	Vladimir Polyakov	Russia	June 26, 1981
Long jump	29 ft. 2½ in. (8.90 meters)	Bob Beamon	United States	Oct. 18, 1968
Triple jump	58 ft. 8½ in. (17.89 meters)	Joao Oliveira	Brazil	Oct. 15, 1975

Men's Records (continued)

Throwing

Shot-put . . . . .72 ft. 8 in. (22.15 meters) . . .Udo Beyer . . . . .East Germany . . . . . .July 6, 1978
Discus throw . . . . .233 ft. 5 in. (71.16 meters) . . .Wolfgang Schmidt . . . . .East Germany . . . . . Aug. 9, 1978
Hammer throw . . . . .268 ft. 4 in. (81.80 meters) . . .Yuri Sedykh . . . . .Russia . . . . .July 31, 1980
Javelin throw . . . . .317 ft. 4 in. (96.72 meters) . . .Ferenc Paragi . . . . .Hungary . . . . April 24, 1980

Decathlon

Decathlon . . . . .8,649 points . . .Guido Kratschmer . . . . .West Germany .June 13-14, 1980

Women's Records

Running

100 meters . . . . .10.88 s. . . .Marlies Gohr . . . . East Germany . . . . . .July 1, 1977
200 meters . . . . .21.71 s. . . .Marita Koch . . . . East Germany . . . . June 10, 1979
400 meters . . . . .48.60 s. . . .Marita Koch . . . . East Germany . . . . . . Aug. 4, 1979
800 meters . . . . 1 min. 53.43 s. . . .Nadyezhda Olizaryenko . . . . . . Russia . . . . .July 27, 1980
1,500 meters . . . . 3 min. 52.47 s. . . .Tatyana Kazankina . . . . Russia . . . . Aug. 13, 1980
1 mile . . . . 4 min. 20.89 s. . . .Lyudmila Veselkova . . . . Russia . . . . .Sept. 12, 1981
3,000 meters . . . . 8 min. 27.12 s. . . .Lyudmila Bragina . . . . Russia . . . . Aug. 7, 1976

Hurdles

100-meter hurdles . . . . .12.36 s. . . .Grazyna Rabsztyn . . . . .Poland . . . . June 13, 1980
400-meter hurdles . . . . .54.28 s. . . .Karin Rossley . . . . .East Germany . . . . May 17, 1980

Relays

400-meter relay . . . . .41.60 s. . . .East German National Team . . . .East Germany . . . . . Aug. 1, 1980
(R. Muller, B. Wockel,
I. Auerswald, M. Gohr
800-meter relay . . . . 1 min. 28.15 s. . . .East German National Team . . . .East Germany . . . . . Aug. 9, 1980
(M. Gohr, R. Muller,
B. Wockel, M. Koch)
1,600-meter relay . . . . 3 min. 19.23 s. . . .East German National Team . . . .East Germany . . . . . July 31, 1976
(D. Maletzki, B. Rohde,
E. Streidt, C. Brehmer)
3,200-meter relay . . . . 7 min. 52.3 s. . . .Russian National Team . . . . .Russia . . . . Aug. 16, 1976
(S. Providokhina, V. Gerasimova,
S. Styrkina, T. Kazankina)

Jumping

High Jump . . . . 6 ft. 7 in. (2.01 meters) . . .Sara Simeoni . . . . .Italy . . . . Aug. 4 & 31, 1978
Long Jump . . . . 23 ft. $3\frac{1}{4}$ in. (7.09 meters) . . .Vilma Bardauskiene . . . . .Russia . . . . Aug. 29, 1978

Throwing

Shot-put . . . . 73 ft. 8 in. (22.45 meters) . . .Ilona Slupianek . . . . .East Germany . . . . . May 2, 1980
Discus throw . . . . 235 ft. 7 in. (71.80 meters) . . .Maria Vergova . . . . .Bulgaria . . . . .July 13, 1980
Javelin throw . . . . 235 ft. 10 in. (71.88 meters) . . .Antoaneta Todorova . . . . .Bulgaria . . . . Aug. 15, 1981

Source: *Track and Field News*, Box 296, Los Altos, Calif., April 1982.

leges and universities. The National Association of Intercollegiate Athletics (NAIA) holds a similar meet for its members.

Annual track and field meets are also held for unattached athletes and athletes who represent various sports clubs. These meets are sponsored by the Amateur Athletic Union (AAU) and the United States Track and Field Federation.

Some newspapers and private organizations sponsor *invitational meets*, in which athletes and teams are invited to compete. The best-known invitational meets are held indoors in large cities during the winter.

A relay meet emphasizes relay races rather than individual competition. The Penn Relays, sponsored by the University of Pennsylvania, are the largest annual track and field meet in the world. More than 7,000 athletes enter this meet.

A number of international meets feature athletes from various countries. Some meets are regional, including the European Championships and the Pan American Games. The top international meet is the Summer Olympic Games.   BERT NELSON

Related Articles. See the separate article on OLYMPIC GAMES. See also the following articles:

EVENTS

Cross-Country	Marathon
Decathlon	Pentathlon
Discus Throw	Pole Vault
Hammer Throw	Running
High Jump	Shot-Put
Hurdling	Walking
Javelin	

BIOGRAPHIES

Bannister, Sir Roger	Thorpe, Jim
Owens, Jesse	

Additional Resources

COSTANZA, BETTY. *Women's Track and Field.* Hawthorn, 1978.
DIAGRAM GROUP. *Enjoying Track and Field Sports.* Paddington, 1979. For younger readers.
DOHERTY, J. KENNETH. *Track and Field Omnibook.* 3rd ed. Tafnews, 1980.
SABIN, LOUIS. *Run Faster, Jump Higher, Throw Farther: How to Win at Track and Field.* McKay, 1980.

TRACKING. See SPACE TRAVEL (Communications with the Earth; Artificial Satellites).

TRACTOR is a machine that pulls or pushes a tool or a machine over land. Tractors provide the chief source of power on most farms. They are also used for industrial and military purposes, for logging, highway construction, and snow clearance. Tractors have either gasoline engines or diesel engines (see GASOLINE ENGINE; DIESEL ENGINE).

Parts of a Tractor. The modern tractor has several features that are built-in. They enable the tractor to provide power for other farm machines. These features include the drawbar, a hydraulic system, and a power take-off.

The Drawbar is a device for fastening equipment to the tractor for pulling. The drawbar enables a tractor to pull such equipment as plows, wagons, harrows, combines, and hay balers.

The Hydraulic System controls the working position of implements hitched to or mounted onto the tractor.

An engine-driven hydraulic pump and cylinder provide the power to raise and lower these implements. Many hydraulic systems also have a mechanism that shifts weight from the front to the rear wheels of the tractor. This shift in weight supplies traction for pulling heavy loads.

The Power Take-Off, or *PTO,* provides power for machines that are either mounted on or pulled by the tractor. The coupling device between the PTO and the equipment usually consists of two universal joints, one on each end of a telescoping shaft. The flexible action of the joints and the telescoping action of the shaft allows sharp turning and movement over rough surfaces without harming the power system. The PTO on most tractors can be started or stopped whether the tractor is moving or standing still. The PTO drives the moving parts of mowing machines, hay balers, combines, potato diggers, and spray pumps.

Types of Tractors. There are two types of tractors: the wheel tractor and the tracklayer tractor, known as a *crawler.*

Wheel Tractors make up the majority of farm tractors in the United States. Many farmers use an *all-purpose* tractor because it does a variety of jobs, such as planting, cultivating, and harvesting. It has high rear wheels. It has either one or two small front wheels placed close together or spaced the same as the rear wheels. These enable the tractor to be driven between rows of crops. The smallest wheel tractors weigh about 3,000 pounds (1,400 kilograms), and the largest more than 15,000 pounds (6,800 kilograms). The demand for larger tractors has increased as the average size of farms has increased.

Crawler Tractors are driven on two endless tracks. They are steered by stopping or slowing one of the tracks. Crawler tractors are used for heavy jobs, for land clearing, and for work on soft or rugged land. The

International Harvester

A General-Purpose Tractor performs many jobs on a farm, including plowing, *above.* Such tractors can also pull equipment for planting, fertilizing, and cultivating.

International Harvester

A Lawn and Garden Tractor helps plant saplings, mow grass, and perform other tasks to keep landscaped areas attractive.

Massey-Ferguson Inc.

A Utility Tractor loads manure into a spreader, *above*, and also handles many other light tasks on a farm.

John Deere

A Heavy-Duty Tractor has dual wheels that give it the traction it needs to pull extremely heavy farm equipment, *above*.

WORLD BOOK photo

A Crawler Tractor, sometimes called a *caterpillar tractor*, does such work as moving earth for construction jobs, *above*.

smallest crawlers weigh about 3,800 pounds (1,720 kilograms). The largest of these tractors weigh about 50,000 pounds (22,700 kilograms) or more.

History. Tractors were first used during the 1870's. These tractors, called *traction engines*, were large, four-wheeled machines driven by steam. They could pull as many as 40 plows, but they were too awkward to be practical. Smaller machines with internal-combustion engines soon replaced them. But the new machine had only a kerosene engine mounted on a four-wheeled frame. Later, kerosene or gasoline engines were built into the tractors. These tractors could do almost all the field work, but they were too low to pull a cultivator through crops such as corn and cotton. Then, in the 1920's, the all-purpose tractor was developed.

Early manufacturing companies usually made only one tractor model or size. But modern companies make a complete line. Modern tractors have both speed and power, and are easy to operate. Most have power steering and many have power brakes.   MELVIN E. LONG

See also AGRICULTURE (picture: An Early Gasoline-Powered Tractor); BULLDOZER.

TRACY, SPENCER (1900-1967), was an American motion-picture actor. He became famous for his roles as a strong man of action and conviction in such films as *Bad Day at Black Rock* (1955) and *The Old Man and the Sea* (1958). He also won fame as a sophisticated comedian in several films, including *Woman of the Year* (1942) and *Father of the Bride* (1950). Tracy won Academy Awards for his performances in *Captains Courageous* (1937) and *Boys Town* (1938). He received seven other Academy Award nominations.

Tracy was born in Milwaukee. He appeared in several Broadway plays after making his stage debut in 1922. A 1930 stage role led to a film contract, and he made his movie debut that year in *Up the River. The Power and the Glory* (1933) established him as a major film star. He made over 70 movies, including *State of the Union* (1948), *Adam's Rib* (1949), *Inherit the Wind* (1960), and *Judgment at Nuremberg* (1961).   HARVEY R. DENEROFF

United Press Int.

Spencer Tracy

283

TRADE

TRADE is buying and selling goods and services. Trade takes place because people need and want things that other people produce or services they can perform.

People must have such necessities as food, clothing, and shelter. They also want hundreds of other things that make life convenient and pleasant. They want such goods as cars, books, and television sets. They want such services as haircuts, motion pictures, and bus rides. As individuals, people cannot produce all the goods and services they want. Instead, they receive money for the goods and services they produce that other people want. They use the money to buy the things they want but do not produce.

Trade that takes place within a single country is called *domestic trade*. *International trade* is the exchange of goods and services between nations. It is also called *world trade* or *foreign trade*. For detailed information on international trade, see the WORLD BOOK article INTERNATIONAL TRADE.

Trade has contributed greatly to the advance of civilization. As merchants traveled from region to region, they helped spread civilized ways of life. These traders carried the ideas and inventions of various cultures over the routes of commerce. The mixing of civilized cultures was an important development in world history.

Trade and Specialization

Trade is vital today in such advanced industrial nations as Canada, Japan, the United States, and West Germany. The economic systems of these countries feature a high degree of *specialization*, or *division of labor*.

Specialization means that each worker concentrates on one job, such as being a farmer, mechanic, doctor, or engineer. Factories concentrate on making one product, such as washing machines, canned soup, or shirts. Countries, cities, and regions also concentrate on producing certain goods and services. For example, Australia specializes in raising livestock, and Japan in industrial products. Oregon specializes in producing lumber, Iowa in growing corn, Pittsburgh in steelmaking, Seattle in manufacturing jet airplanes, and Florida in growing oranges.

Specialization makes trade necessary. Because people do not produce everything they need themselves, they become dependent on others. They sell their labor or products for money, and use the money to buy other goods and services that they need.

Trade helps people enjoy a higher standard of living. People can obtain more goods and services at lower cost through specialization and exchange. If workers concentrate on the job they are best fitted to perform, they can produce more than if they try to do several different jobs. If factories specialize, they can use mass-production methods and complicated machines and tools to produce more (see MASS PRODUCTION). If regions specialize, they can take advantage of their most plentiful natural resources. They can build up a supply of skilled labor and specialized *capital* (goods used to produce other goods).

Carrying on Trade

The Use of Money. To make trading easier, people have developed *monetary systems*. Large-scale trade is possible only if money is used as a medium of exchange. Without money, people would have to exchange certain goods and services directly for other goods and services. This system of trade is called *barter*. Using barter, a banana grower who wanted a horse would have to find a horse owner who wanted some bananas. The two traders would then have to agree on how many bananas a horse was worth.

People will accept money for things they want to sell because they know it will be accepted by others in exchange for the things they want to buy. The amount of money exchanged for a particular product is the *price* of that product. The price of something is the value placed on it by those who are buying and selling it. See MONEY (How Money Developed); PRICE.

The Use of Markets. Trade takes place in *markets*. In earlier days, buyers and sellers actually met and bargained with one another at markets. In Europe during

CARRYING ON TRADE

Trade takes place because people need or want the things that other people produce or can do. Various processors and middlemen may treat, prepare, or handle goods as they pass from the producer to the consumer. The illustrations below show some of the steps that take place between the growing of wheat and its enjoyment as toast on the family breakfast table.

Allis-Chalmers Corp.

Farmer Harvesting Wheat

Rie Gaddis Wehrmann

Baker Making Bread

WORLD BOOK photo

Customer Buying Bread

WORLD BOOK photo

Family Eating Toast

the Middle Ages, for example, farmers came to town with their produce on market day. The townspeople shopped around the market and negotiated directly with the seller before buying. Today, most trade is more complicated.

Often, producers and consumers do not deal directly with one another. There are many persons—called *middlemen*—through whom goods pass on their way from producer to consumer.

Two kinds of middlemen are *wholesalers* and *retailers*. Wholesalers buy goods from producers and sell them mainly to other business firms. For example, a wholesaler of vegetables buys large amounts of vegetables from the growers and then sells them to grocers. This kind of trade is called *wholesale trade*. The grocers sell the vegetables to customers who eat them. This type of trade in which merchants sell goods mainly to the final consumer is called *retail trade*. See Marketing.

It is no longer necessary for buyers and sellers to meet face-to-face. Goods and services can be bought and sold by mail, telephone, or teletype. Often, buyers and sellers do not even see the product being traded. They transact their business on the basis of description or sample. For example, cotton, wheat, and many other agricultural products are classified by grade. Buyers know exactly what they will get if they specify a particular grade, such as "Number 2 hard ordinary wheat." A buyer of drapes will usually examine a small *swatch* (sample) of cloth before making a purchase.

The Geographical Extent of Trade varies widely. In some cases, the buyers and sellers are from all parts of the world. Trade in such basic foods and raw materials as coffee, sugar, wheat, copper, oil, and rubber is international in scope. For example, the United States is a leading producer of wheat. It sells large amounts of wheat to India, Pakistan, Japan, Brazil, The Netherlands, and many other countries.

Trade in other products may be conducted on a local, regional, or national basis. For example, the trade in hominy grits is concentrated in the Southern States of the United States. The market for such familiar products as automobiles, clothing, furniture, and television sets is usually national in scope.

In earlier days, local trade was much more important. This was partly because transportation facilities were limited and goods could not be moved on a large scale. Also, perishable food could not be preserved for very long. Perishable items had to be consumed near their place of production. But technological advances have removed these trade barriers. Trains, trucks, airplanes, and pipelines make it possible to move large quantities of goods easily and cheaply. Vegetables, meats, and other perishables can be refrigerated or frozen and shipped to all parts of the world. Even flowers can be flown by jet airplanes to markets great distances away.

Also in earlier days, people's tastes and preferences varied more from one locality to another. Today, mass advertising in magazines and newspapers and on radio and television has persuaded people all over the nation to use the same products. Millions of people drink the same kinds of soft drinks, use the same detergents, drive the same cars, and wear the same kinds of clothes and shoes. Thus, technological advances have created national markets, and nationwide trade has taken the place of much purely local trade.

Trade in the United States is carried out mainly by private persons and businesses. Government plays a less important role than private individuals and groups, and is more important as a buyer than as a seller. The sellers of goods range from such giant businesses as the General Motors Corporation, which sells millions of cars and trucks each year, to small neighborhood shops selling such goods as bakery products, kitchen utensils, or flowers.

Large amounts of goods and services are purchased by

WORLD BOOK photo

Specialization by people makes trade necessary. This lathe operator has great skill at his job, *above.* He sells his labor for pay, and uses the money to buy goods and services that he wants or needs, *below.*

WORLD BOOK photo

individual consumers, who buy such things as dresses, transistor radios, food, and haircuts. Businesses buy the raw materials and capital equipment they need for production from other businesses. The government also buys many goods and services. Its purchases include new highways, missiles, fire trucks, and the services of teachers, police, and members of the armed forces.

The way in which trade is organized and carried on in the United States reflects the nation's economic system. This system is often called *free enterprise, private enterprise,* or *capitalism.* Trade—buying and selling goods and services in the market—is an essential part of a free economy. In the free market, consumers help determine prices and thus what will be produced. Their willingness to pay for what they want indicates to producers what ought to be produced. In the Soviet Union and other countries with *centrally planned economies,* government planners make the basic economic decisions about what will be produced and its price.

The Development of Trade

Early Trade. For thousands of years, families produced most of the things they needed themselves. They grew or hunted their own food, made their own simple tools and utensils, built their own houses, and made their own clothes. Later, people learned that they could have more and better goods and services by specializing and trading with others.

As civilization advanced, exchanges became so common that some individuals did nothing but conduct trade. This class became known as *merchants.* The most famous early land merchants were the Babylonians and, later, the Arabs. These traders traveled on foot or rode donkeys or camels. The Phoenicians were the chief sea traders of ancient times.

Trade became very important during the hundreds of years that the Roman Empire ruled over the known world. Roman ships brought tin from Britain, and slaves, cloth, and gems from the Orient. For more than 500 years after the fall of the Roman Empire in A.D. 476, little international trade took place.

The Expansion of Trade began in the 1100's and 1200's, largely because of increased contacts between people. The crusades encouraged European trade with the Middle East (see CRUSADES). Marco Polo and other European merchants made the long trip to the Far East to trade for Chinese goods (see POLO, MARCO). Italians in Genoa, Pisa, and Venice built great fleets of ships to carry goods from country to country.

A great period of overseas exploration began in the 1400's. Trade routes between Europe and Africa, India, and Southeast Asia were established as a result of the explorations. In the 1500's and 1600's, private groups formed companies, usually with governmental approval, to trade in new areas.

Trade between Europe and America was carried on by the chartered companies that established the earliest American colonies. The colonists sent sugar, molasses, furs, rice, rum, potatoes, tobacco, timber, and cocoa to Europe. In return, they received manufactured articles, luxuries, and slaves. Trade also pushed American frontiers westward. Trading posts sprang up in the wilderness. Many of these posts later grew into cities.

Trade Today has a direct bearing on the lives of most persons. Modern methods of transportation permit trade between all parts of the world. Through specialization, more and better goods and services are produced. Increased production has led to higher incomes, making it possible for people to buy more of these goods and services.   JAMES D. CALDERWOOD

Related Articles in WORLD BOOK. See the trade section of various country articles, such as ITALY (Foreign Trade). See also:

Balance of Payments	Free Trade
Bank	Free Trade Zone
Barter	Fur Trade
Bazaar	Indian, American
Bill of Exchange	(Trade)
Business	Industry
Colonialism	International Trade
Commodity Exchange	Marketing
Common Market	Mercantilism
Contraband	Money
Customs Union	Reciprocal Trade
European Community	Agreement
Exploration	Stock Exchange
Exports and Imports	Tariff
Fair Trade	Trade Association
Fairs and Expositions	Trade Route
Federal Trade Commission	Trading Post

Additional Resources

BARNET, RICHARD J., and MULLER, R. E. *Global Reach: The Powers of the Multinational Corporations.* Jonathan Cape, 1975.

HANDLIN, OSCAR. *The Wealth of the American People: A History of American Affluence.* McGraw, 1975.

Oxford Economic Atlas of the World. 4th ed. Oxford, 1972.

SMITH, ADAM. *An Inquiry into the Nature and Causes of the Wealth of Nations.* Univ. of Chicago Press, 1976. First pub. in 1776.

TRADE, BOARD OF. See COMMODITY EXCHANGE.

TRADE ASSOCIATION is a nonprofit organization that represents a group of business firms in the same country. Businesses join their associations voluntarily and manage them cooperatively. The companies work together to accomplish goals that no single firm could reach by itself.

A trade association may have only a few members, as in the iron- and steelmaking industry. Or it may have thousands of members, as in an association of retail grocers. The size of the membership has little to do with the effectiveness of the association. It is more important that the association include most of the companies in the industry. About 6,000 national, state, and local trade associations operate in the United States.

Trade-association activities include promoting business for the industry; encouraging ethical practices; cooperating with other organizations; holding conventions; and obtaining good relations with the government, the industry's employees, and the general public.

Trade associations sponsor much of the industrial research work in the United States. This research helps improve the quality of goods or services sold by individual firms. Setting industry standardization is another important trade-association activity. By obtaining agreements among firms, the trade association sets standards of size and quality for articles and services.

A trade association acts as a source of information about its industry. It may issue bulletins on business trends and provide statistical information. Some publish magazines which are distributed to the public. Trade associations date back to the *guilds* formed in Europe during the Middle Ages. REUEL W. ELTON

Related Articles in WORLD BOOK include:

Better Business Bureau
Chamber of Commerce
Guild
Iron and Steel Institute, American
Jaycees
National Association of Manufacturers
Railroads, Association of American

TRADE COMMISSION, FEDERAL. See FEDERAL TRADE COMMISSION.

TRADE DISCOUNT. See DISCOUNT.

TRADE EXPANSION ACT. See TARIFF (United States Tariffs).

TRADE PUBLICATION is a periodical devoted to a specific professional, business, industrial, or trade field. Trade journals form an important field of publishing in the United States. Most of them are weekly or monthly magazines, but there are a number of newspaper-style weeklies, as well as some dailies. These publications carry news items and articles designed to help keep the reader informed about the particular trade or industry. VAN ALLEN BRADLEY

See also ADVERTISING (Magazines); MAGAZINE (Kinds).

TRADE ROUTE. Trade routes have always been the means of bringing new goods into the home and community. In early times, the luxuries of the Orient poured into Western Europe. Later, various countries exchanged raw materials and manufactures. Commerce gave rise to great cities along the routes. Trade routes have also increased contacts between peoples and resulted in an exchange of ideas and ways of doing things. Trade routes greatly affected the entire growth of civilization. The returning crusaders brought back to Europe knowledge of the customs and arts of the Muslims. Marco Polo's famous travels revealed knowledge of China and the Mongol Empire.

Early Trade Routes existed among primitive peoples. They expanded greatly as people became more civilized. Early Sumerians traveled by caravans throughout western Asia to the Mediterranean Sea. The Phoenicians traded by water routes connecting Egypt, Greece, Asia Minor, Italy, and the British Isles.

Rich commerce flowed from the Far East to Europe by three major routes. The northern route, or Great Silk Route, cut from China across central Asia to the Caspian and Black seas, ending at Byzantium (now Istanbul). But, as this overland route was expensive and dangerous, much of the silk commerce traveled by the middle route. It passed through the Persian Gulf and Euphrates Valley and ended either on the Black Sea coast or in such Syrian cities as Damascus. The southern route, by water, led from China around the southern tip of India, up the Red Sea, and overland to the Nile and northern Egypt. Merchants used this route to carry spice and pearls from Ceylon; cotton, spices, precious stones, and drugs from India; and cinnamon and incense from Arabia.

Merchants of the Roman Empire carried on a vast amount of trade throughout the then known world. After the fall of the Western Roman Empire, Roman roads were completed and extended. They crossed the Alps, and branched out into Spain, France, and Germany. Water transportation also played a large part in European trading. Early traders shipped goods on the Seine, Rhine, and Danube rivers in Western Europe, and on the Volga and Don in Eastern Europe. Through

such seaports as Bordeaux and Nantes on the Atlantic Ocean, they exchanged the wine, grain, and honey of Gaul for metals from Great Britain, and oil and lead from Spain.

Medieval Routes. Cities trading with the eastern Mediterranean, such as Venice and Genoa, built powerful commercial empires. Ships brought goods from the Far East. Then Italian fleets carried the products to ports in Spain, England, and Flanders. Other goods crossed overland through Italy and across the Alps to France and to German cities along the Rhine and Danube. Merchants of the Hanseatic League bought these goods in Flanders or Germany, and carried them, along with their own products, to England, the Baltic countries, Poland, and Russia.

The Search for New Routes led to a great age of exploration and discovery. During the 1400's, European nations began to search for new routes to the East in order to avoid the expensive tolls and the many hazards of the long journey from the Orient. In addition, Italian city-states had a complete trade monopoly, which resulted in high prices and low profits to northern European merchants.

The voyages of Columbus and other explorers opened people's eyes to a whole new world. Many new all-water trade routes grew up. Nations set up trading companies to govern and control trade. The Portuguese first developed trade between India and the East Indies and Europe. The Spanish, Dutch, French, and English followed. Their commercial empires led to colonial empires.

Today's Trade Routes are almost numberless, and cover the entire world. Highways and networks of railroads cover continents. Airplanes have connected distant points on the globe. Ships carry goods on the world's oceans and waterways.

The United States government lists 30 trade routes over which it believes adequate ship service is essential to the national interest. In some cases, the government gives *subsidies* (grants of money) to shippers for maintaining this service. HAROLD J. HECK

See also EXPLORATION AND DISCOVERY; TRADE; COLONIAL LIFE IN AMERICA (maps: Colonial Trade Routes); COLONIALISM.

TRADE SCHOOL. See VOCATIONAL EDUCATION; SMITH-HUGHES ACT.

TRADE UNION. See LABOR MOVEMENT.

TRADE WIND is a strong wind that blows toward the equator from the northeast or southeast. In the days of sailing ships, sailors depended greatly on trade winds. The paths of these winds were so regular, especially over the oceans, that early navigators named them *trade winds*, which, in the language of that day, meant *course*, or *track*, winds.

The trade winds are part of a great system of winds that blow over the earth. They blow toward the equator from about the 30th parallels of north and south latitude. Differences between the temperature in low latitudes and the temperature in the polar regions cause trade winds. The heating of the air in low latitudes makes it expand and become light. Then it rises. This creates an area of low pressure near the surface. Cooler and heavier air from the polar regions then tends to flow in to fill the area of low pressure. These polar winds do not blow due north or due south, because of the eastward whirling of the earth. Instead, these winds blow from the northeast and from the southeast.

The belt of rising air between the trade winds is a region of mild winds and calms. This region is often called the *doldrums* because it is so calm. Sailing ships of early days were often stranded for many weeks at a time in the doldrums.

Trade winds have a great deal to do with rainfall on land. When trade winds blow against mountain ranges, they are forced upward. As the warm air rises, it cools. Its moisture condenses and falls as rain on the mountain slopes.   JAMES E. MILLER

See also CALMS, REGIONS OF; DOLDRUMS.

TRADEMARK distinguishes the products of one company from those of another. A trademark may consist of a word or words, a phrase, a person's name, a symbol, a picture, or any combination of these identifications. Most trademarks appear on the product, on its container, or in advertisements for the product. A *service mark* identifies the source of a service rather than the source of a product. For example, a utility company may use a service mark to identify the service it offers.

A *strong trademark* consists of a word that has no recognizable meaning, such as Kodak. Strong trademarks receive broad protection from being used by other companies in a manner that is likely to cause confusion, mistake, or deception. *Weak trademarks* consist of a common word, such as Premier, or a word that suggests some characteristic of the product, such as Wet 'n Wash. They receive less protection, unless the public identifies them with a certain manufacturer as a result of wide advertising and long, continuous use.

Trademarks, also called *brand names*, provide an easy way to determine who makes a certain product. They help consumers identify brands they liked in the past so they can purchase them again. A trademark represents the manufacturer's reputation, called *good will*.

Most countries have laws that protect the rights of trademark owners. A firm must establish its rights in each country in which it seeks protection.

In the United States, the first company to use a trademark in commerce has certain rights to that trademark. The firm may prevent others in the same geographic area from using the same trademark or a similar one for related products. But it cannot prevent other firms from using the trademark for unrelated products or in another area where it would not cause confusion.

Trademark rights are not limited in duration, and they are independent of any registration. These rights, which form part of the broader law of unfair competition, protect the good will of the trademark owner. They also protect the public from fraud and deceit. Violation of trademark rights is called *infringement*. An infringing trademark is one that is likely to confuse or deceive consumers because of its similarity to a trademark already in use.

A company may register its trademark in each state in which it uses the trademark. Trademarks also may be registered in the U.S. Patent and Trademark Office in Washington, D.C. Registration of a trademark on the Principal Register in the Patent and Trademark Office serves as notice to everyone of a company's claim of ownership. The owner of a registered trademark may sue for infringement in the federal courts. But a trademark owner does not have to register the trademark to protect it from infringement.

In Other Countries, trademark laws differ from those of the United States. Many governments allow a company to register a trademark before using it. Some require registration before any trademark rights can be enforced.   W. THOMAS HOFSTETTER

TRADER. See TRADING POST; TRADE.

TRADES UNION CONGRESS (TUC) is a national organization of British trade unions. It was founded in the

Trade Winds are strong winds that occur chiefly in the earth's Tropical Zone. They blow steadily toward the equator from both the northeast and the southeast. Trade winds blow mostly over the oceans because the weather there is more uniform than over the continents.

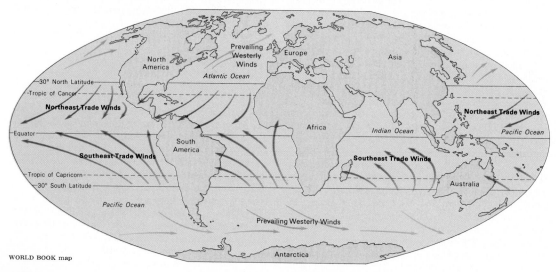

WORLD BOOK map

288

1860's. The TUC is similar to the American Federation of Labor and Congress of Industrial Organizations (AFL-CIO).

TRADING POST is a type of market place where people bring products to sell or to exchange for other goods. In the United States, many posts serve Navajo Indians who live on a large reservation in Arizona, New Mexico, and Utah. At these posts, the Indians sell goods and buy food, clothing, and farm equipment.

In ancient times, trading posts operated in the Near East. Later, Europeans set up trading posts as they explored various parts of the world. At first, before the development of money, traders usually *bartered* with one another—that is, they exchanged items for other items.

The first trading posts in North America were established during the late 1400's in what is now Newfoundland, Canada. By the mid-1800's, trading posts had been set up throughout North America. Indians traded

Detail of an engraving (1876); Hudson's Bay Company, Winnipeg, Canada
Trading Posts of the Mid-1800's, such as the one shown above, served Indians and whites who wanted to exchange goods.

furs and hides to whites for such items as cloth, glass beads, guns, gun powder, liquor, and metal goods.

Private companies and individuals set up many trading posts. The Hudson's Bay Company opened posts along Hudson Bay in Canada after 1670 (see HUDSON'S BAY COMPANY). In 1796, the U.S. government created a system of government trading posts, hoping to keep private traders from cheating the Indians. The government abolished these posts in 1822 because private traders opposed them. Many white traders later opened posts on Indian reservations and charged unfair prices, but the Indians there had nowhere else to buy goods.

Many settlements that grew up around trading posts developed into large U.S. and Canadian cities. These communities included Chicago; Detroit; Kansas City, Mo.; Montreal; and Quebec.   MERWYN S. GARBARINO

TRADING STAMPS are *premiums* or *bonuses* that a retailer gives with a cash purchase of goods. The usual rate is one stamp for every 10¢ spent. The person re-

ceiving the stamps collects them to exchange for some item of value. Trading-stamp companies sell the stamps to retailers. They also *redeem* (exchange) them for various products, such as dishes, toys, or sports equipment. Some states prohibit trading stamps. Thomas Sperry set up the first independent trading-stamp company in 1896. Today, about 100 trading-stamp companies sell and redeem stamps.   JOHN H. FREDERICK

TRADITION is the passing down from generation to generation of ideas, customs, beliefs, and stories. See CULTURE; CUSTOM; FABLE; FOLKLORE; FOLKWAY; LAW; LEGEND; MYTHOLOGY; SUPERSTITION.

TRAFALGAR, *truh FAL guhr,* is a low, sandy cape on Spain's southern coast, at the western entrance to the Strait of Gibraltar. Admiral Horatio Nelson's British fleet defeated a combined French and Spanish fleet there on Oct. 21, 1805, in one of the greatest naval battles in history. The victory gave England undisputed control of the sea. Nelson was wounded and died during the battle.

The battle occurred during Great Britain's war against Napoleon Bonaparte (see NAPOLEON I). Napoleon hoped to draw the British fleet away to the West Indies so his armies could invade England. But Napoleon's admiral, Villeneuve, failed in this, and decided to attack the British fleet with a French and Spanish fleet. His fleet outnumbered Nelson's, 33 ships to 27.

But Nelson surprised the enemy by having his ships cut through the French battle line. The British fleet did not lose a ship in the battle, but it destroyed or captured over half the French and Spanish ships. Trafalgar Square in London was named in memory of Nelson's victory at Trafalgar.   ROBERT B. HOLTMAN

See also LONDON (picture; map); NELSON, HORATIO.

TRAFFIC is the movement of people and goods from one place to another. It is the "life blood" of commerce and industry. This article deals with traffic on streets and highways. For a discussion of other kinds of traffic, see TRANSPORTATION with its list of *Related Articles*.

The United States has about 3,800,000 miles (6,100,000 kilometers) of streets, roads, and highways. Canada has about 470,000 miles (756,000 kilometers). U.S. drivers travel about 1 trillion miles (1.6 trillion kilometers) each year in private and commercial motor vehicles. Passenger cars driven on city streets account for more than two-fifths of this distance. The average passenger car in the United States covers about 9,500 miles (15,300 kilometers) each year.

Traffic Problems

The millions of automobiles in the United States cause many traffic problems. In the morning and evening rush hours, city streets are jammed with automobiles. On holidays and weekends, many highways are too full for comfort or safety. Freeways and expressways are constantly being built to replace the horse-and-buggy-day streets, roads, and highways, to relieve these conditions. The main streets of many small towns are overburdened with through traffic, making it difficult for local people to get to the stores. Bypasses around these towns ease the pressure and help local business. It is hard to find a parking place in the business sections of cities and towns. Parking at the curb is being

Expressways and Traffic Control Devices help move traffic rapidly and safely. Median strips separate traffic going in opposite directions on a Dallas expressway, *left*. Traffic lights and bus lanes help regulate the flow of traffic on a busy Chicago street, *right*.

prohibited in more and more places in order to make additional street space available for traffic. Off-street parking areas are being provided in large numbers.

Improved streetcar and bus service helps relieve congestion when the service is convenient, comfortable, and inexpensive. Better provision for truck loading and unloading at stores, office buildings, and factories eases the problem of truck interference on streets. It also reduces cost of delivery and distribution of goods. More efficient use of existing streets is obtained in several ways. These include: (1) creating one-way streets; (2) changing traffic lanes to one-way operation during hours of heavy traffic; (3) prohibiting curb parking; (4) installing modern coordinated traffic-signal systems, turn controls, and pedestrian controls; and (5) developing through-street systems to move traffic faster.

Traffic Control

In the late 1970's, about 52,000 persons were killed and about 4½ million persons were injured in traffic accidents each year in the United States. Drivers and pedestrians can reduce the number of traffic accidents, injuries, and deaths by watching and obeying traffic control signs, signals, and pavement markings. This is especially true in the relationship between pedestrians and moving vehicle traffic. Special control devices, such as electric signs that tell when to cross streets and highways, are often used to aid pedestrians. These signs operate in conjunction with vehicle traffic signals.

Signals, Signs, and Markings. There is no clear record of who invented or first used traffic control devices. It is generally agreed, however, that automatic traffic signals first appeared in Detroit in the early 1920's. The Wayne County (Michigan) Road Commission developed the use of a white center line for separating driving lanes on highways. Traffic signs date back to the early Roman roads. Today, New York City alone has almost a million traffic signs.

Traffic controls are increasingly necessary for regulating, warning, and guiding both motor vehicle and pedestrian traffic. The law requires signs to indicate how certain traffic regulations apply. Adequate use of warning signs, and well-designed and well-located route markings have great value, too, in helping the orderly flow of traffic. Pavement and curb markings and traffic islands, when properly designed and located, also help guide traffic.

Modern traffic lights are made so that they can be set to change when traffic demands it. In most places, the changes are automatic every so many seconds or minutes. Where there are different amounts of traffic on intersecting highways and streets, the light can be set so that it will remain green longer for the highway or street with the most traffic.

Some traffic lights also are arranged so that the traffic itself will cause them to change. This is done by placing switches or magnets on the roadway. These are called *detectors*. When cars pass over the detectors, the light changes to let the cars go through the intersection. Where there is a great deal of pedestrian cross-traffic but little motor vehicle cross-traffic to change the lights, the signals frequently work from a switch operated by the pedestrian. This permits pedestrians to cross busy streets and highways safely.

Many warning and guide signs are covered with luminous paint, or glass or metal beads or buttons, which reflect beams from headlights. This makes the signs easier to see at night. Traffic lanes, pedestrian crosswalks, turn markings, and warning signs frequently are painted or otherwise marked on street pavements and highway surfaces. Sometimes, various types of reflector buttons or white material are embedded in the surface of the street or highway.

Control devices must be located in the right places or they can cause delay and congestion, and lead persons to disregard them. Good traffic control devices must be based on sound engineering principles. Studies of types and flow of traffic, accidents, speeds, delays, and physical conditions show the exact nature of a traffic difficulty and indicate the particular devices or methods of control that are needed.

Traffic Regulations are the rules of the road governing the actions of pedestrians and drivers on public roads and streets. Regulations should be uniform, so that drivers everywhere will know exactly what actions to take under like conditions. Traffic regulations on a large scale were first adopted in this country in New York City, shortly after 1900. Traffic rules, however, had been used in France and England long before this date.

Parking Meters were first used in Oklahoma City in 1935. The purpose of these traffic-control devices is to measure mechanically time-limit parking regulations. Originally located only at the curb, parking meters now frequently are placed in parking lots. There the parking meters are used either to restrict the length of time that vehicles are allowed to park, or to collect parking fees.

Traffic Police enforce traffic-control measures and regulations, and control traffic emergencies. Development of street and highway facilities and traffic-control plans are the responsibilities of highway or traffic engineers.　　　　　　　　　　　　　Henry A. Barnes

Related Articles in World Book include:

Automobile	Radar (In Controlling Auto-
Bicycle	mobile Speed and Traffic)
Bus (Importance	Roads and Highways
of Buses)	Safety
Police	

TRAFFIC ENGINEERING is a specialized field of civil engineering. It deals with planning streets and highways so that traffic can proceed with a minimum of danger or delay.

TRAGACANTH, *TRAG uh kanth,* is a true gum obtained from various shrubs (Astragalus) of the pulse family. These shrubs grow mainly in Asia Minor, Iran, and Syria. Tragacanth is dull white or yellowish in color, and clear and hornlike in texture. It is usually sold in thin flakes or ribbons which swell into a jellylike mass when soaked in water. The use of tragacanth in pharmacy dates back to Biblical times. Today, it is used in preparing pills, emulsions, and creams. It is also occasionally used in making printing gums for textiles.　　　　　　　　　　　　Charles L. Mantell

TRAGEDY is a form of drama that deals with serious human actions and issues. Tragedy explores questions about morality, the meaning of human existence, relationships between people, and relationships between human beings and their gods. By the end of most tragedies, the main character has died or lost his or her loved ones.

Playwrights have written tragedies throughout the history of drama. The most famous tragedies were written during three periods—the 400's B.C. in Greece,

the late 1500's and early 1600's in England, and the 1600's in France.

The greatest writers of Greek tragedy were Aeschylus, Euripides, and Sophocles. They took most of their plots from Greek mythology. William Shakespeare was the principal tragic dramatist of the English period. His tragedies are noted for their suspenseful plots, insights into human nature, and powerful poetic dialogue. Other leading English playwrights of the period included Christopher Marlowe and John Webster. Jean Racine dominated tragic drama during the French period. His tragic heroes and heroines are victims of violent passions they cannot control. Pierre Corneille was another important French tragic playwright of the 1600's.

Until the 1700's, almost all tragedies dealt with royalty, famous historical figures, or other notable people. Playwrights did not consider the lives of common men and women important enough to provide material for tragedies. After 1700, a number of dramatists wrote *domestic tragedies,* which were plays with middle-class people as heroes and heroines. Perhaps the most important of these playwrights was Gotthold Ephraim Lessing of Germany.

Notable tragedies of the late 1700's and early 1800's were written by Friedrich Hebbel and Friedrich Schiller of Germany and Victor Hugo of France. Most of their works dealt with famous or powerful characters rather than the middle class.

Critics disagree about whether any true tragedies have been written since the late 1800's. Some argue that serious plays of this period lack the moral, philosophical, or religious significance required for genuine tragedy. Other critics believe several playwrights have created works that can be considered tragedies. These playwrights include Georg Büchner of Germany, Henrik Ibsen of Norway, and Arthur Miller and Eugene O'Neill of the United States.　　　Oscar G. Brockett

Each playwright discussed in this article has a separate biography in World Book. See also Drama; Aristotle (Literary Criticism).

TRAGOPAN, *TRAG oh pan,* is the name of a handsome quail-like bird of the pheasant family. It lives in forests high up on the mountain slopes of southern and central Asia. The male bird has a bright-colored *lappet* (loose-hanging skin) on his throat, and a pair of blue, fleshy, erectile horns on each side of his head. Both lappet and horns become enlarged and brilliant during the mating season.

The Brilliantly-Colored Cabot's Tragopan is one of several kinds of handsome Asiatic pheasants.

Tragopans eat insects, leaves, fruits, and seeds. They nest in trees. Their white eggs are slightly speckled with dull lilac. These birds are shy. Hunters usually snare them by driving them slowly toward nooses.

Scientific Classification. The tragopan belongs to the family *Phasianidae* and makes up the genus *Tragopan.* The best known of the five species is *T. satyrus,* the satyr tragopan of the Himalayas. JOSEPH J. HICKEY

TRAIL, B.C. (pop. 9,976), is a smelting and refining center sometimes called *Silver City.* Trail lies on both sides of the Columbia River. For location, see BRITISH COLUMBIA (political map).

Trail's smelting industries, among the largest in the world, produce silver, lead, zinc, gold, cadmium, and antimony. The city also has a large chemical-fertilizer industry. It is a popular winter and summer sports center. The town was established as Trail Creek, and served as an embarkation point for the movement of supplies up the river to frontier posts in the 1880's. It has a mayor-council government. RODERICK HAIG-BROWN

TRAIL OF TEARS. See INDIAN, AMERICAN (The Fall of Indian America [In the United States]); OKLAHOMA (The Indian Nations).

TRAILER is a wheeled vehicle that is pulled by an automobile or truck. Trailers are designed to be used chiefly (1) as temporary living quarters for either recreational travel or camping, or (2) for cargo hauling. *Mobile homes,* on the other hand, are designed to be used for permanent, year-around living (see MOBILE HOME).

Recreational Trailers include *travel trailers* and *camping trailers.* A travel trailer provides a dwelling for people on an automobile, fishing, or hunting trip. Travel trailers can be moved easily and serve as comfortable living quarters. Most travel trailers are sold with furniture and a completely equipped kitchen and bathroom. These trailers range in size from 12 to 35 feet (3.7 to 10.7 meters) long and from 6 to 8 feet (1.8 to 2.4 meters) wide. Popular models are about 7½ feet (2.3 meters) wide.

Camping trailers are smaller and more compact than travel trailers. A camping trailer has collapsible walls of heavy fabric, plastic, or some other material. The trailer folds out into a tentlike structure in which four to eight persons can sleep. Some camping trailers have a kitchen and bathroom.

Hauling Trailers range from 6 to 14 feet (1.8 to 4.3 meters) long, or longer. They are used to carry loads that may be too large to fit in an automobile trunk. They may also be used to transport farm animals to market or to a livestock show. Most hauling trailers look like boxes without tops. Canvas or another material may be spread over the top to protect the load.

Trailers with tops, called *vans,* open from the rear. Some, such as marine vans, used for hauling boats, also open on the sides. Some small vans can be hitched to a car, but large trucks pull most vans. Highway trucks use special trailers to haul various kinds of cargoes, such as automobiles, food, and logs. F. M. RADIGAN

See also RECREATIONAL VEHICLE.

TRAILING ARBUTUS. See ARBUTUS.

TRAILS OF EARLY DAYS. Indian trails served as the earliest roads in the United States. They were little more than footpaths. Pioneers *blazed* (marked) these wilderness trails by making notches on trees that bordered them. At first, people could follow the trails only on foot or on horseback. Wagons and coaches did not come into general use before 1800, because of the lack of hard-surfaced roads.

Thousands of settlers took part in the great westward movement of the 1800's (see WESTWARD MOVEMENT). They needed roads for their wagons, so many new trails appeared. The travelers cut down trees and made mudholes passable by placing logs side by side. They crossed streams at *fords* (shallow places) and set up ferries along rivers. When a region became more settled, people often used gravel or boards to build hard-surfaced roads called *turnpikes.* Construction of these roads was difficult, so the people who built them charged *tolls* (fees) for their use. Many turnpikes were built in the eastern part of the United States.

Overland trails east of the Mississippi River lost their importance after 1840, with the coming of the railroads. But they remained in use in the Far West until railroads came in the 1870's and 1880's. The most important trails in this region included the Oregon Trail and the Santa Fe Trail.

The federal government often helped finance transportation. It aided road building by granting funds, especially when mail or military supplies moved over the route. The U.S. Post Office Department subsidized stagecoach lines which carried passengers, baggage, express, and mail. By 1858, six mail lines, including the Butterfield Overland Mail, served the Pacific Coast. U.S. Army engineers often located or improved western roads used by gold seekers, military detachments, and pioneer settlers. W. TURRENTINE JACKSON

Related Articles. See the Transportation sections of the various state articles, such as OREGON (Transportation). See also the following articles:

EARLY TRAILS

Boston Post Road　　Bozeman Trail　　Braddock's Road

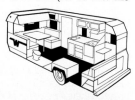

Travel Trailers are popular for family vacations and for fishing and hunting trips. A trailer has a comfortable interior—including a bathroom, kitchen, and other conveniences—and can easily be towed by a car.

Winnebago Industries

SOME TRAILS OF EARLY DAYS

Fort Vancouver
OREGON TRAIL
Missouri River
Sonoma
Sacramento
PONY EXPRESS ROUTE
Salt Lake City
San Francisco
EL CAMINO REAL
SPANISH TRAIL
San Diego
BUTTERFIELD SOUTHERN OVERLAND MAIL
San Antonio
Santa Fe
SANTA FE TRAIL
CHISHOLM TRAIL
MORMON ROUTE
Platte River
Omaha
St. Joseph
Independence
Nauvoo
St. Louis
Nashville
NATCHEZ TRACE
NATCHEZ
Mississippi River
Vandalia
CUMBERLAND ROAD
Cumberland
WILDERNESS ROAD
Boonesborough
Block House
Lancaster
LANCASTER TURNPIKE
Philadelphia
Buffalo
MOHAWK TRAIL
Albany

TRAIN. See ELECTRIC RAILROAD; LOCOMOTIVE; RAILROAD.

TRAINING, MILITARY. See MILITARY TRAINING.

TRAINING SCHOOL. See REFORMATORY.

TRAIT. See HEREDITY (What We Inherit; pictures).

TRAITOR. See TREASON.

TRAJAN, *TRAY jun* (A.D. 53?-117), was a Roman emperor and an important military leader. He expanded the empire by conquest and carried out extensive building programs. He tried to reduce poverty in Italy, and to improve the financial affairs of cities and towns across the empire. Trajan conquered Dacia (now parts of Romania and Hungary) and Arabia, and he won victories in Parthia (now part of Iran). He founded new cities, including Thamugadi in what is now Algeria. Trajan also built bridges and harbors. These included bridges constructed across the Danube River in Dacia and the Tagus River in Spain, and a harbor built at the port of Rome.

Trajan was born Marcus Ulpius Trajanus in Italica, Spain, of Roman parents. His father was a soldier who became governor of an eastern province. Trajan received a military education and won fame in Spain, Syria, and Germany. In A.D. 97, Emperor Nerva

adopted him as his heir and successor. When Emperor Nerva died the next year, Trajan was named emperor.

Trajan's Column, built in the emperor's honor after he conquered Dacia, was dedicated in A.D. 113. The well-preserved column, 100 feet (30 meters) high, stands in Trajan's Forum in Rome. A spiral staircase inside leads to the top. The pedestal and column are covered with carvings portraying the Dacian wars. The ashes of Trajan are said to have been placed in the column, but no trace of them has ever been found. A statue of Trajan once stood on the column, but in 1588 it was replaced by one of Saint Paul.   RAMSAY MacMULLEN

See also ROME (picture: Trajan's Column); SCULPTURE (picture: Trajan's Column [detail]); LIBRARY (Libraries of Papyrus).

TRAJECTORY. See BALLISTICS.

TRAM is the term used in Britain and other Commonwealth countries for a streetcar. See STREETCAR.

TRAMP SHIP. See SHIP (Classification of Cargo Ships).

TRANCE is a term generally used to describe any kind of unnatural sleep or partly conscious state. The term may be used to describe the condition of hypnotized persons, spiritualist mediums, and some persons with mental disorders. In some cases, trances continue for long periods of time, but usually they last only briefly. The word *trance* was first used for conditions in which the soul was believed to have withdrawn for a time from a person's body.

There are no physical signs that always indicate a trance. But in many cases, the pulse and breathing rate slow down. The reflexes may also be affected. Sometimes they disappear entirely. A person in a trance is less responsive to changes in surroundings, and may not know what is happening. The person may appear to be responding to forces not actually present.

The best-known type of trance is probably that of the spiritualist medium who appears to have fallen into a deep sleep, but can still speak and write. Such a trance may be similar to a deep hypnosis, and it may involve hallucinations.   RUSSELL M. CHURCH

See also HYPNOTISM; SUSPENDED ANIMATION.

TRANQUILIZER is a drug that calms a person by acting on the nervous system. Tranquilizers belong to a group of drugs called *depressants*.

There are two types of tranquilizers—*major tranquilizers* and *minor tranquilizers*. Major tranquilizers are used to treat patients with *psychoses* (severe mental illnesses). These tranquilizers are also called *antipsychotic drugs*. Minor tranquilizers are used to treat various emotional problems, particularly anxiety. They are also called *anti-anxiety drugs*.

Major tranquilizers include such drugs as chlorpromazine (commonly known by the trade name Thorazine), fluphenazine, and trifluoperazine. Physicians prescribe these drugs to treat *schizophrenia*, a mental illness that is characterized by illogical, unpredictable thinking. The drugs reduce the patient's confusion and excitement.

Minor tranquilizers include chlordiazepoxide, diazepam, and meprobamate, which are commonly known by the trade names Librium, Valium, and Miltown, respectively. They relax the muscles and reduce tension. Minor tranquilizers are prescribed mainly for the treatment of anxiety. Physicians also use minor tranquilizers to calm children who must undergo surgery. In addition, these drugs are used to treat *delirium tremens*, a disorder that results from alcoholism.

Some tranquilizers have undesirable side effects. For example, meprobamate may cause muscle weakness and general fatigue. Some people become addicted to tranquilizers. In addition, tranquilizers may cause drowsiness, especially if a person drinks alcoholic beverages before or after taking the drugs. A person should not drive a motor vehicle for several hours after taking a tranquilizer.   N. E. SLADEK

See also DEPRESSANT; DRUG (Depressants).

TRANSACTIONAL ANALYSIS is a method of psychotherapy. In this method, therapists treat emotional problems by helping people analyze their relationships in social situations. Such situations are called *transactions*. Eric L. Berne, a Canadian-born psychiatrist, developed the method during the 1960's. Interest in transactional analysis, or TA, was stimulated by two best-selling books—*Games People Play* (1964) by Berne and *I'm OK—You're OK* (1969) by Thomas A. Harris, an American psychiatrist.

Berne regarded the human personality as consisting of three "selves"—the *Child*, the *Parent*, and the *Adult*. According to Berne, any of these "selves" may be in control of a person during a transaction. The Child is dependent, impulsive, fun loving, and creative. The Parent is stern and critical. The Adult is capable of logical thinking. TA is based on the idea that people can learn to use the Adult and begin to think and make decisions for themselves.

Berne thought that transactions can be understood by analyzing *games* in communication. A game is a transaction in which people deceive themselves or others. For example, people who blame their problems on others may be playing a game that Berne called "See What You Made Me Do." Berne believed that people use *scripts*—that is, life plans which they learn in childhood and later feel forced to act out. The games are part of the script.   DAVID L. KRANTZ

TRANS-ALASKA PIPELINE SYSTEM. See PIPELINE (Major Pipelines of the World).

TRANSANTARCTIC MOUNTAINS. See ANTARCTICA (The Continent).

TRANSATLANTIC CABLE. See CABLE.

TRANS-CANADA HIGHWAY stretches about 5,000 miles (8,000 kilometers) across Canada and links the 10 provinces. It runs from St. John's, Nfld., on the Atlantic coast to Victoria, B.C., on the Pacific coast. The toll-free, two-lane highway cost more than $1 billion. It was begun in 1950 and officially opened in 1962.

The all-weather highway made many areas, especially in western Canada, easier to reach and opened them to new economic development. It also has attracted larger numbers of tourists to Canada's national parks. The route goes through Glacier, Mount Revelstoke, and Yoho national parks in British Columbia; Banff in Alberta; and Terra Nova in Newfoundland.

TRANS-CANADA HIGHWAY   The Trans-Canada Highway, shown as a red line on the map, runs from Victoria, B.C., to St. John's, Nfld. It provides a direct and scenic route across all 10 Canadian provinces.

WORLD BOOK map

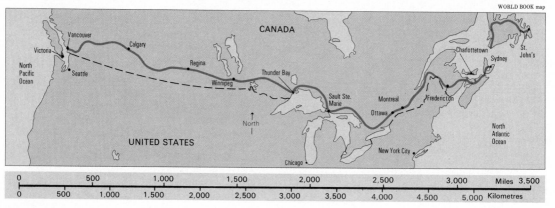

Motorists driving westward along the Trans-Canada Highway travel through the Atlantic Provinces; Montreal, Canada's largest city; Ottawa, the Canadian capital; the upper Great Lakes region; the western prairie wheat fields; and the Rocky Mountains to Vancouver Island. ALLAN R. TURNER

See also BRITISH COLUMBIA (The Land [picture]).

TRANSCAUCASIA. See CAUCASIA.

TRANSCENDENTAL MEDITATION (TM) is a method of relaxing the body that became popular in many countries during the 1970's. It was developed in the 1950's by the Maharishi Mahesh Yogi, a Hindu monk from India. He used the word *transcendental* to describe the process of reaching a state of *pure consciousness*, where the mind is not aware of anything in particular. He declared that people who used this technique became happier and more relaxed and creative. Centers that teach TM operate in many countries, including the United States and Canada. Followers of the Maharishi call TM the Science of Creative Intelligence.

People practice TM by sitting quietly in a comfortable position. They close their eyes and silently repeat their *mantra*, a pleasant-sounding word from the Hindu scriptures. Teachers of TM select a personal, secret mantra for each student. A person who practices TM meditates for 15 to 20 minutes in the morning and evening, before meals.

Scientific studies show that certain bodily changes occur during meditation. For example, the rate of breathing and the amount of oxygen taken in by the body decrease at those times. The blood pressure and the rate of heartbeat also fall while a person meditates. In addition, scientists found that *alpha waves* (brain waves that become prominent when a person is relaxed) increase in intensity during meditation. Psychologists report that many people who practice TM feel less anxious and aggressive than before and can handle stress more easily. Some scientists believe TM causes these changes because people have faith in the method and expect it to help them.

The Maharishi claimed that people cannot meditate effectively without training from a TM teacher and the use of a mantra. However, many scientists declare that other forms of meditation and relaxation can produce the same results as TM. GARY E. SCHWARTZ

Additional Resources

BENSON, HERBERT, and KLIPPER, MIRIAM Z. *The Relaxation Response*. Avon, 1976. Presents an alternative to the TM technique.
BLOOMFIELD, HAROLD H., and others. *TM: Discovering Inner Energy and Overcoming Stress*. Dell, 1975.
RUSSELL, PETER. *The TM Technique: An Introduction to Transcendental Meditation and the Teachings of Maharishi Mahesh Yogi*. Routledge & Kegan, 1976.

TRANSCENDENTALISM was a philosophy that became influential during the late 1700's and 1800's. It was based on the belief that knowledge is not limited to and solely derived from experience and observation. It thus opposed the philosophy of empiricism—that knowledge comes from experience. Transcendentalism also stated that the solution to human problems lies in the free development of individual emotions.

According to transcendentalism, reality exists only in the world of the spirit. What a person observes in the physical world are only appearances, or impermanent

reflections of the world of the spirit. People learn about the physical world through their senses and understanding. But they learn about the world of the spirit through another power, called *reason*. The transcendentalists defined reason as the independent and intuitive capacity to know what is absolutely true.

Elements of transcendentalism can be found in the Neoplatonic philosophy of ancient Greece (see NEOPLATONISM). But the chief source of transcendentalist ideas was the *Critique of Pure Reason* (1781) by the German philosopher Immanuel Kant.

In the United States, transcendentalism became both a philosophy and a literary, religious, and social movement. It began among Unitarians in New England and reached its peak during the 1840's. Ralph Waldo Emerson was the leading American transcendentalist. He taught that the physical world is secondary to the spiritual world. But, said Emerson, the physical world serves humanity by providing useful goods and by making human beings aware of beauty. Emerson believed that people should learn as much as possible through observation and science. But he insisted that they should adjust their lives primarily to the truths seen through reason.

Emerson and his followers believed that human beings find truth within themselves, and so they emphasized self-reliance and individuality. They believed that society is a necessary evil. They argued that to learn what is right, a person must ignore custom and social codes and rely on reason. The transcendentalists believed that the doctrines and organized churches of orthodox Christianity interfered with the personal relationship between a human being and God. They said that individuals should reject the authority of Christianity and gain knowledge of God through reason.

The American transcendentalists never became numerous, but their writings greatly influenced American intellectual history and literature. Besides Emerson, the leading American transcendentalists included Bronson Alcott, Margaret Fuller, Theodore Parker, and Henry David Thoreau. JOHN CLENDENNING

Each person discussed in this article has a biography in WORLD BOOK.

Additional Resources

KOSTER, DONALD N. *Transcendentalism in America*. Twayne, 1975.
MILLER, PERRY G. E., ed. *The Transcendentalists: An Anthology*. Harvard, 1950. *The American Transcendentalists: Their Prose and Poetry*. Johns Hopkins, 1981. Reprint of 1957 ed.

TRANSCONTINENTAL RAILROAD. See RAILROAD (The First Transcontinental Rail Lines; picture: The Meeting of Two Railroads).

TRANSCONTINENTAL TREATY. See ADAMS-ONÍS TREATY.

TRANSDUCER is a device that converts electric waves into mechanical vibrations—or vice-versa. Loudspeakers, microphones, and phonograph pickup cartridges are all transducers. Special *transducer vibrators* make powdered materials flow down chutes. They are also used to compress asphalt pavement. *Sonar transducers* send and receive sound waves in water. *Ultrasonic transducers* generate and detect vibrations above the frequency range of human hearing. They are used to cut hard materials, to clean delicate instruments, to drill oil wells, and to measure the level of liquids in the fuel tanks of space vehicles.

Transducers work in various ways. Many phonograph cartridges use *piezoelectric* materials, which produce a voltage when squeezed. Loudspeakers use electromagnets that vibrate when current flows through them. Some ultrasonic transducers use *magnetostrictive* materials, which contract in a magnetic field.   HENRY H. KOLM

See also ULTRASOUND.

TRANSEXUALISM. See TRANSSEXUALISM.

TRANSFER OF TRAINING. See LEARNING (Efficient Learning).

TRANSFIGURATION was the change in physical appearance that came over Jesus Christ on one occasion during His public ministry. According to the Bible, Jesus took Peter, James, and John up on a mountain, and permitted them to see Him in splendor, with His face shining like the sun, and His garments bright with light. Then the Old Testament figures of Moses and Elias came to talk with Christ. Raphael's altarpiece *The Transfiguration* is said by many to be one of the world's greatest paintings. It now hangs in the Vatican (see RAPHAEL).   FULTON J. SHEEN

TRANSFORMATIONAL GRAMMAR. See CHOMSKY, NOAM.

TRANSFORMER is a device that increases or decreases the voltage of alternating current. Transformers provide a simple, inexpensive way to change such voltage. They enable electric power companies to transmit alternating current easily and efficiently. Transformers also ensure the proper voltage for the circuits of home appliances, lights, industrial machinery, and other electric equipment.

Most transformers consist of two coils of insulated wire. One coil, known as the *primary winding*, is connected to the source of the voltage that is to be changed. This voltage is the *input voltage* of the transformer. The other coil, called the *secondary winding*, supplies the *output voltage* to the desired circuit. In most transformers, the primary and secondary windings are wound around a hollow core made of thin iron or steel sheets. Most cores have the shape of a ring or a square. The two coils are not actually connected to each other.

Transformers work by means of *electromagnetic induction* (see ELECTROMAGNETISM). When the input voltage is applied to the primary winding, it generates alternating current in the coil. As the current flows, it sets up a changing magnetic field in the core of the transformer. When this field cuts across the secondary winding, it produces alternating voltage in the coil. If the secondary winding is connected to a circuit, the output voltage causes alternating current to flow through the circuit.

The ratio between a transformer's output voltage and input voltage equals the ratio of the number of turns in the secondary winding to the number in the primary winding. If E represents the voltage and N stands for the number of turns, then $\dfrac{E \text{ output}}{E \text{ input}} = \dfrac{N \text{ secondary}}{N \text{ primary}}$. The output voltage will be greater than the input voltage in a transformer whose secondary winding has more turns than the primary winding. Such a transformer is called a *step-up transformer*. If the secondary coil has fewer turns than the primary, the output voltage will be less than the input voltage. This type of transformer is called a *step-down transformer*.

In power plants, step-up transformers increase the voltage of the alternating current produced by generators. High voltages make it possible to transmit the current over long distances with only a small loss in power. When the current reaches the area where it will be used, step-down transformers lower the voltage to the level needed by local consumers (see ELECTRIC POWER [Transmitting and Distributing Electric Power]).

Some transformers have special uses. For example, *air-core transformers* and *powdered iron-core transformers* are designed to handle high-frequency alternating currents. *Instrument transformers* are used in measuring extremely large alternating voltages and currents. *Variable transformers* vary the amount of output voltage delivered to a circuit.   DOUGLAS M. LAPP

See also INDUCTION COIL.

TRANSFUSION, BLOOD. See BLOOD TRANSFUSION.

TRANSISTOR is a tiny device used in computers, radios, television sets, and other electronic equipment. Transistors control the flow of electric current in such equipment. A transistor is so small that manufacturers can put many thousands of them on a piece of material no larger than a postage stamp. A single transistor, together with its protective case, is about as large as the eraser on a pencil.

Transistors do the work once done by vacuum tubes. Transistors are smaller and more dependable, and they use far less electricity.

Electronic equipment has been revolutionized by transistors, and almost all such equipment that is made today uses them instead of vacuum tubes. Without transistors, manufacturers could not make pocket calculators or high-speed computers. Battery-operated radios and TV sets would be much larger and cost more to operate. The small size and weight of transistors also led to the development of communications satellites that link continents through telephones and television.

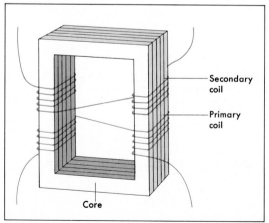

Secondary coil

Primary coil

Core

WORLD BOOK diagram by Arthur Grebetz

A Typical Transformer consists of two coils of wire wound around the sides of a core made of thin iron sheets. The ends of the primary coil are connected to the source of the voltage that is to be changed. The ends of the secondary coil are connected to the circuit to which the electricity is to be transferred.

How Transistors Are Made. Manufacturers make transistors from silicon, which is a solid material called a *semiconductor*. Semiconductors conduct electricity, but not so well as do true conductors, such as copper or iron. The atoms of the semiconductor material used in a transistor must be in the form of crystals.

Transistor manufacturers add small amounts of certain impurities to the crystals of the semiconductor. The impurities control the way electricity flows in the silicon. Some impurities add *free* (extra) electrons to the crystals. Other impurities do not supply the crystal with enough electrons. This lack of electrons causes empty spaces, known as *holes*, in the crystal. A semiconductor material is called *n-type* if it has extra electrons, and *p-type* if it has holes. Electricity flows as a movement of electrons in n-type material and as a movement of holes in p-type material.

Transistors consist of layers of n-type and p-type materials. To make a transistor, manufacturers may *grow* (make) pure crystals and cut them into thin slices. They heat these slices and expose them to impurities to form n-type and p-type layers. They then attach wires to the layers. Finally, the finished transistor is put into a tiny case to protect it.

How Transistors Work. There are two main types of transistors—*junction transistors* and *field effect transistors*. Each works in a different way. But the usefulness of any transistor comes from its ability to control a strong current with a weak voltage. For example, transistors in a public address system *amplify* (strengthen) the weak voltage produced when a person speaks into a microphone. The electricity coming from the transistors is strong enough to operate a loudspeaker, which produces sounds much louder than the person's voice.

Junction Transistors. A junction transistor consists of a thin piece of one type of semiconductor material between two thicker layers of the opposite type. For example, if the middle layer is p-type, the outside layers must be n-type. Such a transistor is an *NPN transistor*. One of the outside layers is called the *emitter*, and the other is known as the *collector*. The middle layer is the *base*. The places where the emitter joins the base and the base joins the collector are called *junctions*.

The layers of an NPN transistor must have the proper voltage connected across them. The voltage of the base must be more positive than that of the emitter. The voltage of the collector, in turn, must be more positive than that of the base. The voltages are supplied by a battery or some other source of direct current.

The emitter supplies electrons. The base pulls these electrons from the emitter because it has a more positive voltage than does the emitter. This movement of electrons creates a flow of electricity through the transistor.

The current passes from the emitter to the collector through the base. Changes in the voltage connected to the base modify the flow of the current by changing the number of electrons in the base. In this way, small changes in the base voltage can cause large changes in the current flowing out of the collector.

Manufacturers also make *PNP junction transistors*. In these devices, the emitter and collector are both a p-type semiconductor material and the base is n-type. A PNP junction transistor works on the same principle as an NPN transistor. But it differs in one respect. The main flow of current in a PNP transistor is con-

Parts of a Transistor

An NPN junction transistor, shown at the lower left, consists of a tiny silicon chip in a protective case. The chip has a layer of one type of material between two layers of the opposite type, as shown in the cross-section drawing at the lower right. Lead wires are attached to each of these layers by metal contacts.

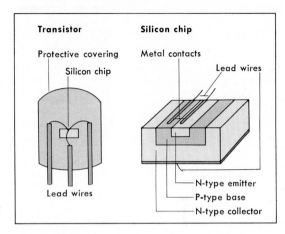

Transistor

Protective covering
Silicon chip

Lead wires

Silicon chip

Metal contacts

Lead wires

N-type emitter
P-type base
N-type collector

How a Transistor Works

The emitter of an NPN transistor has a negative voltage and produces electrons. The collector has a positive voltage and attracts the electrons. A weak current applied to the base enables the electrons to move across the base from the emitter to the collector and create a flow of electricity. The weak base current thus controls the main flow of current through an NPN transistor.

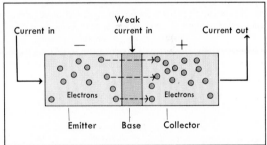

Current in

Weak
current in

Current out

—   +

Electrons   Electrons

Emitter   Base   Collector

WORLD BOOK diagrams by Arthur Grebetz

trolled by altering the number of holes rather than the number of electrons in the base. Also, this type of transistor works properly only if the negative and positive connections to it are the reverse of those of the NPN transistor.

Field Effect Transistors. A field effect transistor has only two layers of semiconductor material, one on top of the other. Electricity flows through one of the layers, called the *channel*. A voltage connected to the other layer, called the *gate*, interferes with the current flowing in the channel. Thus, the voltage connected to the gate controls the strength of the current in the channel. There are two basic varieties of field effect transistors—the *junction field effect transistor* (JFET) and the *metal oxide semiconductor field effect transistor* (MOSFET).

History. Three American physicists—John Bardeen, Walter H. Brattain, and William Shockley—invented

TRANSISTOR RADIO

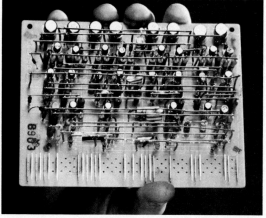

WORLD BOOK photo

Transistor Circuits occupy little space. The transistors on this computer circuit card appear as round objects with white tops.

the transistor in 1947. They shared the 1956 Nobel prize in physics for their work. The first transistor was called a *point-contact transistor*. In 1948, Shockley developed the theory of the junction transistor. Within a few years, junction transistors had replaced the point-contact type. In 1952, Shockley published the theory that led to the field effect transistor.

During the early 1960's, manufacturers developed the technique of making many transistors on a single piece of semiconductor material. This technique led to complete electronic circuits, called *integrated circuits*, on one piece of semiconductor material. In the 1970's, researchers developed larger integrated circuits and reduced the cost of transistors.   RICHARD W. HENRY

Critically reviewed by JOHN ROBINSON PIERCE

See also ELECTRONICS; SEMICONDUCTOR; INTEGRATED CIRCUIT.

Additional Resources

KIVER, MILTON S. *Transistors.* 3rd ed. McGraw, 1962.
LATHAM, DONALD C. *Transistors and Integrated Circuits.* Lippincott, 1966.
MANN, GEORGE B. *ABC's of Transistors.* 3rd ed. Bobbs, 1975.
SANBORN, PAUL. *Fundamentals of Transistors.* Doubleday, 1970.

TRANSISTOR RADIO. See RADIO (diagram: Main Parts of an AM Transistor Radio).

TRANSIT. See SURVEYING.

TRANSIT, in astronomy, is the crossing of one heavenly body over the disk of a larger one, as seen from the earth. Astronomers have studied the transits of Venus and Mercury with much interest. The orbits of these planets are between the sun and the earth's orbit. Mercury passes directly between the sun and earth at intervals from 3 to 13 years. It then appears as a black spot against the sun. Transits of Venus show a circle of light around the dark mass against the sun.

The term *transit* also means the passage of any celestial body, such as sun, moon, planet, or star, across an observer's meridian.   OLIVER J. LEE

See also MERCURY (Phases).

TRANSJORDAN. See JORDAN.

TRANSKEI, *trans KAY* or *trans KY,* is a region within the Republic of South Africa. It is one of the 10 *home-*

lands established by the white South African government for the country's *African* (black) people. The Transkei is the homeland of the Xhosa people.

In 1959, the South African government established a policy of granting independence to the homelands. In 1976, the Transkei became the first homeland to be declared an independent nation by the government. But neither the United Nations (UN) nor the Organization of African Unity (OAU) recognizes the Transkei as independent. Most critics of South Africa claim that the independence was granted to reduce criticism of South Africa's racial segregation policy, called *apartheid.* They believe the Transkei is too dependent on South Africa to be considered truly independent.

The Transkei consists of three separate sections of land in southeastern South Africa. It covers 16,070 square miles (41,620 square kilometers) and has a population of about 1,914,190. Umtata is the largest city of the region and the seat of its government.

Government. The Transkei has a legislature called the National Assembly. It consists of 75 appointed local chiefs and 75 members elected by the people. The Assembly elects a president and a Cabinet.

People. All African citizens of the Transkei are generally called Xhosa. Most of them actually belong to the Xhosa ethnic group. A small percentage of these people are members of related groups that also speak the Xhosa language. About 9,000 whites live in the Transkei, but most of them are citizens of South Africa.

The majority of Xhosa in the Transkei are a rural people, and many live much as their ancestors did. Many Xhosa people still live in cone-shaped huts, tend cattle, and grow crops. Many find it difficult to produce enough food for their own needs.

Less than half of all the Xhosa people live in the Transkei. The others live in white-dominated areas of South Africa, where they work in white-owned indus-

Transkei

The Transkei consists of the three separate areas shown in white on the map below.

⊛   Capital
•   Other city or town
——   Road
------   Rail line

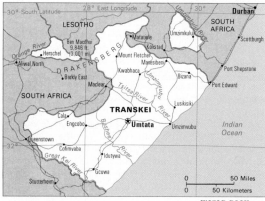

WORLD BOOK map

Ingelore Frank, Sygma

A Rural Area in Transkei includes clusters of small huts along a dirt road. Most of Transkei's people live in rural areas. They grow crops and raise livestock for a living.

Transkei limited self-government in 1963 and declared it independent in 1976. The Transkei claims control of East Griqualand, a small area that lies between its central and eastern sections. But South Africa considers the area its own territory. In 1978, the Transkei broke diplomatic relations with South Africa over the dispute. The diplomatic relations were reestablished in 1980, after South Africa agreed to consider the Transkei's claim.   L. H. GANN

See also APARTHEID; SOUTH AFRICA.

TRANSMIGRATION OF THE SOUL. See REINCARNATION.

TRANSMISSION is a series of parts that transmit power from the engine of a motor vehicle. The power goes from the engine to the *drive shaft*, which carries it to the *final drive*. The power is delivered by the final drive to the vehicle's drive wheels. The transmission, drive shaft, and final drive make up the *drive train* of the vehicle. Automobiles, trucks, buses, bulldozers, and other motor vehicles have drive trains. This article discusses automobile drive trains.

The diagram on this page shows the drive train of what automobile manufacturers call a *conventional car*. Conventional cars have the engine in front and the drive wheels in the rear. The parts of the drive train are arranged differently in cars that have a front-wheel drive or a rear-mounted engine. There are two main kinds of transmissions, *manual* and *automatic*.

What a Transmission Does

The power of an engine consists of *torque* and *speed*. Torque is the twisting force of the engine's crankshaft. Speed refers to the rate of rotation of the crankshaft. The transmission can adjust the proportions of torque and speed that it delivers from the engine to the drive shaft. When it increases the torque, it decreases the speed; and when it increases the speed, it decreases the torque. Thus, the transmission provides the high torque and low speed that a car needs to start moving. It also delivers the low torque and high speed needed for cruising on a highway. The transmission also reverses the torque so a car can back up.

Almost all transmissions vary torque and speed by means of *gears*. A gear is a wheel with projections called *teeth* around the edge. The teeth fit together with the teeth of another gear. Suppose that a small gear with 12 teeth drives a large gear with 24 teeth. The large gear rotates with half the speed, but twice the torque, of the small gear. This relationship is called *reduction*. The amount of reduction is expressed numerically by the *gear ratio*. The gear ratio in the above example is 2 to 1 because the small gear rotates twice for each rotation of the large gear.

Parts of a Drive Train

tries. These Xhosa lost their South African citizenship when the Transkei was declared independent. They became citizens of the Transkei, even though many of them have never been in the region and have no intention of moving there.

Land and Climate. Most of the Transkei consists of rolling grasslands. Elevations range from sea level along the coast to about 9,800 feet (2,990 meters) in the mountains of the northwest. Several rivers in the Transkei have carved out beautiful valleys and canyons.

The Transkei has a mild climate, with rainy summers and dry winters. Temperatures average about 70° F. (21° C) in January and 60° F. (16° C) in July. About three-fourths of the Transkei receives more than 30 inches (76 centimeters) of rain yearly, and no area gets less than 20 inches (51 centimeters).

Economy of the Transkei depends heavily on South Africa. More than 70 per cent of the region's income consists of wages earned by Xhosa who work in South Africa. South Africa also provides about three-fourths of the budget for the Transkeian government.

Farming is the chief economic activity in the Transkei. Farmers grow chiefly corn, and other crops include coffee and tea. The government is working to improve agriculture, but the region has serious problems of overgrazing, soil erosion, and low production. The Transkei produces relatively small amounts of manufactured goods and minerals. But manufacturing and mining have been growing in importance since the mid-1960's. The region has deposits of coal, copper, and nickel.

History. During ancient times, Bushmen and Hottentots lived in what is now the Transkei. By the A.D. 1500's, the Xhosa and other related peoples had migrated into the region. During the 1800's, the Xhosa fought a series of wars, called the Kaffir Wars, against Dutch and British settlers. By 1894, all the Transkei had come under European domination. It became part of South Africa in 1910. South Africa granted the

WORLD BOOK diagram by Richard Fickle

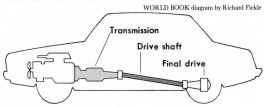

Transmission

Drive shaft

Final drive

TRANSMISSION

The gears in a transmission can be combined in different ways to produce various gear ratios and thus various proportions of torque and speed. The gear ratios are often called simply *gears* or *speeds*. The process of changing from one gear ratio to another is called *shifting gears*.

How a Manual Transmission Works

The driver shifts the gears of a manual transmission by means of a hand-operated lever called a *gearshift*. Most manual transmissions have a neutral position; three, four, or five forward gears; and a reverse gear. The driver puts the transmission into neutral when the engine is being started, or when a car is parked with the engine left running.

To put a car into forward motion, the driver shifts into *first*, or *low gear*. This gear provides the highest torque and the lowest speed. As the car picks up speed, the driver shifts into *second gear*, then into *third gear*, and so on, until the transmission is in the highest gear desired. If extra torque is needed, the driver may *downshift* from a higher gear to a lower one. This situation might occur when the car goes up a steep hill. The reverse gear is used to make the car go backward.

The Clutch. The driver of a car with a manual transmission must operate the *clutch* along with the gearshift. The clutch, which is operated by a pedal, is a device that connects the engine to the transmission. When the driver presses the pedal, the clutch is *disengaged* (disconnected from the engine), and no power is sent to the transmission. When the driver releases the pedal, the clutch is *engaged*, sending power to the transmission. The driver must disengage the clutch when shifting gears.

The clutch consists basically of two disks, the *flywheel* and the *clutch plate*. The flywheel is connected to the crankshaft and turns whenever the engine is running. The clutch plate is connected to the *input shaft*, which leads to the transmission. When the clutch is engaged, springs press the clutch plate against the flywheel. Friction forces the two disks to turn at the same speed. When the clutch is disengaged, the springs are released and the disks separate.

The Gears. Power travels to the transmission through the input shaft. A gear at the end of this shaft drives a gear on another shaft called the *countershaft*. A number of gears of various sizes are mounted on the countershaft. These gears drive other gears on a third shaft, the *output shaft*, which leads to the drive shaft.

The transmission produces various gear ratios by engaging different combinations of gears. Only one combination can be engaged at a time. In a typical three-speed transmission, first gear has a ratio of 3 to 1; second gear, 2 to 1; and third gear, 1 to 1. Some four- and five-speed transmissions have a high-gear ratio of less than 1 to 1. For reverse, an extra gear called an *idler* operates between the countershaft and the output shaft. This extra gear turns the output shaft in the opposite direction of the input shaft, thus making the car go backward.

How a Manual Transmission Works

What Gears Do

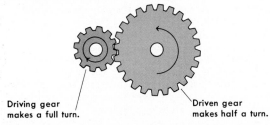

Driving gear makes a full turn.

Driven gear makes half a turn.

Reduction occurs when a small gear drives a large one, *above*. The driving gear makes a full turn for each half turn of the driven gear. Thus, speed is cut in half and torque is doubled.

Parts of a Manual Transmission

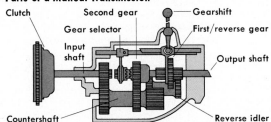

Clutch · Second gear · Gearshift · Gear selector · First/reverse gear · Input shaft · Output shaft · Countershaft · Reverse idler

A manual transmission contains a system of gears controlled by a gearshift. A clutch connects it to the engine. When the transmission is in neutral, *above*, no power is transmitted.

What Happens When Gears Are Shifted

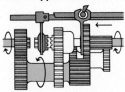

In First, or Low, Gear, the first/reverse gear slides forward and meshes with its mate on the countershaft. Power (green) flows to the output shaft through these gears. The output shaft turns a third as fast as the input shaft.

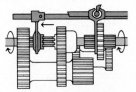

In Third, or high, the gear selector slides forward and connects the output shaft to the input shaft. Power flows directly through the two shafts. No reduction occurs, and the output shaft turns at the same speed as the input shaft.

WORLD BOOK diagrams by Richard Fickle

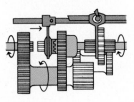

In Second, the gear selector slides back to engage the second gear, which always meshes with its mate on the countershaft. Power flows to the output shaft through these gears. The output shaft turns half as fast as the input shaft.

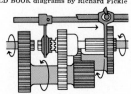

In Reverse, the first/reverse gear slides back and meshes with the reverse idler. The idler, an extra gear, turns the output shaft in the opposite direction of the input shaft, thus making the vehicle go backward.

In early manual transmissions, gears became engaged by sliding along the output shaft until they meshed with their mates on the countershaft. The gears often clashed because they turned at different speeds when they were being meshed. Most modern transmissions overcome this problem by having their forward gears always meshing. When these gears are not engaged, they turn freely on their shaft. They are engaged by a mechanism called a *synchronizer*, which slides against a gear and locks it onto its shaft. The synchronizer forces the gear and the shaft to rotate at the same speed before locking them together.

How an Automatic Transmission Works

An automatic transmission contains special devices that automatically provide various gear ratios as they are needed. Instead of a gearshift, the driver operates a lever called a *selector*.

Most automatic transmissions have selector positions for *park*, *neutral*, *drive*, *low*, and *reverse*. The engine can be started only if the selector is in either the park or neutral position. In park, the drive shaft is locked so that the drive wheels cannot move.

For ordinary driving, the driver moves the selector to the drive position. The transmission starts out in the lowest gear and automatically shifts into higher gears as the car picks up speed. The driver uses the low position of the transmission for going up or down steep hills or driving through snow or mud. When in low, the transmission remains in the lowest gear. Some transmissions have a position between low and drive.

This position prevents the transmission from shifting above second gear. The reverse position makes the car move backward.

The Torque Converter is a device that most automatic transmissions have instead of a clutch. A torque converter delivers power from the engine to the transmission and also increases the torque.

A torque converter resembles a large doughnut sliced in half. One half, called the *pump*, is bolted to the flywheel. The other half, called the *turbine*, is connected to the transmission input shaft. Each half is lined with *vanes* (blades). The pump and the turbine face each other in a case filled with oil. A bladed wheel called a *stator* is between them.

The engine drives the pump. As the pump rotates, it throws oil against the vanes of the turbine. The force of the oil tends to make the turbine rotate and send power to the transmission. After striking the turbine vanes, the oil travels back to the pump, passing through the stator along the way. When the pump turns much faster than the turbine, torque is increased. A complex reaction between the oil and the stator creates the increase in torque.

When the engine is running slowly, the oil may not have enough force to rotate the turbine at all. As a result, the driver can have the transmission in gear and the engine running slowly but can prevent the car from moving by simply applying the brakes lightly. When the driver releases the brakes and presses the accelerator

Parts of an Automatic Transmission

The diagram at the right shows a typical automatic transmission. It contains a *torque converter* rather than the clutch used in a manual transmission. It also has two sets of *planetary gears*. Some automatic transmissions have only one set of these gears. Special devices in the transmission shift the gears automatically.

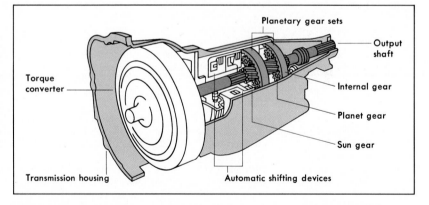

Torque converter

Planetary gear sets

Output shaft

Internal gear

Planet gear

Sun gear

Transmission housing

Automatic shifting devices

How Planetary Gears Work

The parts of a planetary gear set can be held from turning or locked together to achieve a variety of gear ratios. The illustrations at the right show a few possible combinations. In all three cases, the internal gear is driving the other parts of the gear set. The effects can be multiplied by two gear sets arranged in line.

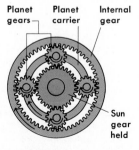

Planet gears   Planet carrier   Internal gear

Sun gear held

Reduction. Sun gear held. Planet gears "walk" around sun gear, causing planet carrier to rotate more slowly than internal gear.

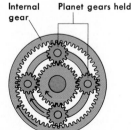

Internal gear   Planet gears held

Direct Drive. Internal gear and planet carrier locked together. Planet gears cannot turn. Entire gear set rotates as a unit.

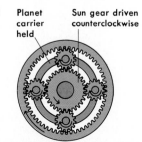

Planet carrier held   Sun gear driven counterclockwise

WORLD BOOK diagrams by Richard Fickle

Reverse. Planet carrier held. Internal gear rotates clockwise. Planet gears turn and act as idlers. Sun gear driven counterclockwise.

pedal, the engine runs faster and so does the pump. The action of the pump increases the force of the oil. This force gradually becomes strong enough to rotate the turbine—and move the car.

The Planetary Gears are a special kind of gears that are part of most automatic transmissions. A set of planetary gears consists of three elements. The first element is a *sun gear*, located in the center. The second element, called a *carrier*, surrounds the sun gear. The carrier holds two, three, or four *planet gears*, which mesh with the sun gear and revolve around it, much as the planets travel around the sun. The third element is an *internal gear*, a ring with teeth on the inside. It surrounds the planet gears and meshes with them.

Any element of a set of planetary gears can be held stationary, or locked to one of the others, to produce different gear ratios. Most automatic transmissions have two sets of planetary gears arranged in line. The gears are shifted by a system of automatic devices inside the transmission. These devices are controlled by the position of the selector, the speed of the car, and other factors.

The Drive Shaft

The drive shaft carries power from the transmission to the final drive. In conventional cars, the drive shaft is a metal tube called the *propeller shaft*.

When a car travels over an uneven surface, its drive wheels and final drive move up and down in relation to the transmission. To allow for this movement, the propeller shaft is fitted with flexible couplings called *universal joints*. These joints have a wristlike action that lets the propeller shaft flex up and down. Without them, the propeller shaft would bend or break as the car traveled over bumpy ground. Most propeller shafts have two universal joints, one at each end. Others have only one.

A car that has its engine and drive wheels at the same end does not need a propeller shaft. A short drive shaft carries the power from the transmission to the final drive. Such a shaft needs no universal joints because the transmission and final drive are bolted together. Universal joints on the axles permit up-and-down motion between the drive wheels and the final drive.

The Final Drive

The final drive transmits power from the drive shaft to axle shafts connected to the drive wheels. In a conventional car, the propeller shaft and the axle are at a right angle to each other. The final drive must carry power through this angle to drive the wheels. In addition to carrying the power to the drive wheels, the final drive divides the torque evenly between those two wheels. The final drive contains two sets of gears: (1) the ring gear and pinion and (2) the differential.

The Ring Gear and Pinion are *bevel gears*—that is, they mesh at a right angle to each other. Thus, they carry power through a right angle to the drive wheels. The ring gear is driven by the pinion, which receives power from the propeller shaft.

In most cars, the ring gear is two to four times as large as the pinion. Therefore, these gears reduce the speed from the propeller shaft and increase the torque.

The reduction in the final drive multiplies the reduction that has already taken place in the transmission. For example, suppose a car has a first-gear ratio of 3 to 1 and a final-drive ratio of 3 to 1. The total reduction is 9 to 1. In other words, when the car is in first gear, the engine crankshaft rotates 9 times for each rotation of the drive wheels.

Some cars have a *transverse* engine, which is mounted across the car and between the drive wheels. In such cars, the power of the engine does not have to be carried through a right angle to the drive wheels. Therefore, the final drive contains ordinary reducing gears rather than a ring gear and pinion.

The Differential is a set of gears that divide the torque evenly between the two drive wheels. The differential also enables one wheel to rotate faster than the other when necessary. For example, when a car goes around a corner, the outside drive wheel travels farther than the inside one. The outside wheel must rotate faster than the inside one to cover the greater distance in the same time.   HOWARD E. CHANA

See also AUTOMOBILE (The Drive Train; illustrations); DIFFERENTIAL; GEAR.

TRANSMITTER. See RADIO (How Radio Works; pictures: Building a Radio Transmitter); TELEPHONE (How a Telephone Works); TELEVISION (Transmitting Television Signals).

TRANSMUTATION OF ELEMENTS is a change of one element into another, caused by nuclear reactions. The atoms of one element are distinguished from the atoms of another by the number of *protons*, or positively charged particles, in their nuclei. An atom becomes another element if the number of protons in its nucleus changes. An atom can alter the number of protons by giving off or taking in atomic particles. When an atom gives off particles, it is said to be *radioactive*. Uranium, radium, thorium, and actinium are naturally radioactive elements.

The atoms of a radioactive element may give off three types of rays: alpha, beta, and gamma rays. The *alpha* ray is actually a stream of particles, each consisting of two protons and two neutrons. Alpha particles are four times as heavy as hydrogen atoms, and each has two units of positive charge. This means that when an atom gives off an alpha particle, the atom becomes lighter in weight and loses two protons, or units of positive charge. The atom now has a different structure and is an atom of a different element. The *beta* ray is a stream of fast-moving *electrons*, or negatively charged particles. These particles have almost no mass. Scientists think that when the nucleus of an atom gives off a beta particle, one neutron in the atom's nucleus decays to form a proton and an electron. The electron is given off as the beta particle, but the proton remains in the nucleus. Thus the charge of the nucleus rises by one unit, but the atom's weight remains the same. This atom, too, becomes an atom of a different element. The *gamma* ray is an electromagnetic wave that simply rearranges the structure of the atom. The charge does not change, and the element remains the same.

For many centuries, alchemists tried to change elements into other elements. Little did they know that all the time nature was changing certain elements into others. In 1919, Ernest Rutherford of New Zealand bombarded nitrogen atoms with alpha rays. Some of the atoms each took in an alpha particle and ejected a proton. This transformed the nucleus from nitrogen into oxygen. It was the first artificially produced nuclear disintegration. Since then, the process popularly known as *atom-smashing* has led to the formation of new elements, such as plutonium. Machines called particle accelerators are used to transmute elements.   RALPH E. LAPP

See also PARTICLE ACCELERATOR; RADIOACTIVITY.

TRANSNATIONAL CORPORATION. See MULTINATIONAL CORPORATION.

TRANSOM is a horizontal crossbar in a building or other structure. The term usually means the top crossbar of the frame of a door or window. In the United States, a narrow window above a door is called a transom. In shipbuilding, transom means the board which supports the stern of the boat.

TRANSPIRATION is the giving off of water by the leaves of a plant. This process is similar to perspiration in animals. Plants give off water chiefly through tiny pores called *stomata* on the surface of the leaves. The amount of water they give off depends somewhat upon how much water the roots of the plant have absorbed. It also depends upon such environmental conditions as sunlight, humidity, winds, and temperature. A plant should not be transplanted in full sunshine because it may lose too much water and wilt before the damaged roots can supply enough water.   WILLIAM C. BEAVER

See also LEAF (Transpiration).

TRANSPLANT, in medicine. See TISSUE TRANSPLANT.

TRANSPLANTING. Some plants have to be started from seed in a protected place, such as a greenhouse,

hotbed, or cold frame. The seeds may be sown in wooden boxes called *flats*, or in seed pans or pots. They are usually sown rather thickly. Then, after they have started to grow, the small seedlings are lifted out, separated, and replanted at uniform distances in other flats or pans. This first transplanting is called *pricking out*.

When the seedlings are large enough, and the weather is warm enough, gardeners transplant them to the garden. Being moved is somewhat of a shock to the plant. Often the gardener breaks off some roots and upsets the balance between the roots and the leaves. Therefore, some of the center or top leaves should be pinched off. Otherwise, they will dry up.

Transplanted plants will resume their growth most quickly if the soil around the roots is not packed. Some air around the roots helps to promote growth. Some plants, such as tomatoes, need more air than others.

If seedlings are grown too rapidly, they become soft and unable to stand the shock of transplanting. Such seedlings must be *hardened* before the gardener transplants them. This is done by gradually exposing them to outdoor temperatures.

See also TREE (Planting the Tree).

TRANSPORT. See AIR FORCE, UNITED STATES (Other Aircraft); AIRPLANE (Airplanes of Today); COAST GUARD, U.S. (picture: Coast Guard Airplanes).

TRANSPORT is the term used in Britain and other Commonwealth countries for transportation. See TRANSPORTATION.

Steps in Transplanting

There are six simple steps to follow in transplanting the seedlings of an annual flowering plant from the seed flat to the flower garden.

Gently lift seedling from flat, *left*, place it in hole, press soil around plant to hold it firm, water it, push soil up around it, and pinch out center.

J. Horace McFarland

@ Alex MacLean, Landslides

Automobiles on an Expressway Interchange

WORLD BOOK photo by Steve Leonard

Passengers Alighting from a Transoceanic Airliner

WORLD BOOK photo by Terry K. McClellan

A Ship Passing Through the Panama Canal

Modern Transportation involves the use of engine-powered vehicles, such as those pictured above and on the next page. Fast, dependable transportation is essential to the economy and way of life in industrially developed countries.

TRANSPORTATION

TRANSPORTATION is the act of moving people or goods from one place to another. Transportation takes people where they need or want to go, and it brings them the goods they need or want. Without transportation, there could be no trade. Without trade, there could be no towns and cities. Towns and cities are traditionally the centers of civilization. Therefore, transportation helps make civilization possible.

Throughout most of history, transportation was extremely slow and difficult. Prehistoric people traveled mainly on foot. They transported goods on their backs or heads or by dragging them along the ground. About 5000 B.C., people began to use animals to haul loads. By 3000 B.C., wagons and sailing vessels had been invented. The use of animals, wagons, and sailing vessels enabled people to transport loads farther and more easily than before. But the speed of transportation improved only slightly over the centuries.

Inventors produced the first engine-powered vehicles

Melvin Kranzberg, the contributor of this article, is Callaway Professor of the History of Technology at Georgia Institute of Technology and coeditor of Technology in Western Civilization.

during the late 1700's and early 1800's. This development marked the beginning of a revolution in transportation that has continued to the present. Today, jet airliners carry travelers nearly as fast as, or faster than, the speed of sound. Trains, trucks, and giant cargo ships haul a steady flow of goods to buyers in almost all parts of the world. Automobiles provide convenient transportation for many millions of people.

Although engine-powered transportation has benefited people in many ways, it has also created problems. For example, it uses great quantities of fuel and so strains the world's energy supplies. Automobiles jam many streets and highways, making travel slow. In addition, their exhaust fumes pollute the air. Such problems are so difficult to solve that governments have become increasingly involved in transportation.

This article discusses the kinds of transportation, the history of their development, and today's systems of engine-powered transportation. The article also discusses the transportation industry and current developments in transportation. Vehicles are also used for recreation, warfare, and space exploration. These uses are described in such articles as AIR FORCE, BALLOON, BOATING, NAVY, and SPACE TRAVEL.

304

Steve McCutcheon

A Snowmobile About to Pull Cargo in the Far North

Photri

A Train Speeding Workers to Their Jobs

Boeing Marine Systems

A Hydrofoil Ferrying Passengers Across a Bay

Photri

School Buses Ready to Take Students Home

TRANSPORTATION / Kinds of Transportation

There are three main kinds of transportation: (1) land, (2) water, and (3) air. Land transportation depends mainly on wheeled vehicles, especially automobiles, trains, and trucks. Ships and boats are the chief water vehicles. Air transportation depends almost entirely on airplanes.

Each kind of transportation can further be classified according to whether the vehicles are engine powered or engineless. Most engine-powered vehicles have gasoline, diesel, or jet engines. The majority of engineless vehicles are powered by the muscles of human beings or animals or by natural forces, such as the wind or flowing water.

Engine-powered transportation has many advantages over engineless transportation. It is quick, convenient, and dependable, and can carry far greater loads. However, such transportation is costly. Most kinds of engine-powered vehicles cost from several thousands to many millions of dollars, depending on the type of vehicle. In most cases, each type of vehicle also requires certain *supporting facilities.* Automobiles require roads. Trains must have tracks. Airplanes require airports. Ships need ports and harbors. All these facilities are expensive to build and maintain. Every form of engine-powered

transportation also requires a source of energy. The combined cost of the vehicles, supporting facilities, and energy makes engine-powered transportation extremely expensive.

Engine-powered vehicles are the chief means of transportation in industrially developed countries, such as the United States, Canada, and most European nations. Engine-powered transportation costs too much to play such an important role in developing countries, which include many African, Asian, and Latin-American nations. Many people in these countries still rely on the kinds of transportation their ancestors used hundreds or thousands of years ago.

Land Transportation is the most common kind of transportation by far. In many cases, it is the only suitable or available transportation.

Engine-Powered Land Transportation. Automobiles, buses, motorcycles, pipelines, snowmobiles, trains, and trucks are the chief engine-powered land vehicles. All these vehicles except pipelines and snowmobiles ride on wheels.

Automobiles, buses, and trucks are the main modern road vehicles. In areas well served by roads, they can provide a variety of transportation services. Automo-

Pack Animals are used to transport goods in many mountainous regions, deserts, and other areas that lack modern roads. In Afghanistan, nomads use camels as beasts of burden, *above top.* In Nepal, Asian oxen called *yaks* carry goods through the high, rugged passes of the Himalaya, *above bottom.*

An Age-Old Method of Transportation is the hauling of goods by people themselves. These women in Burma are carrying bricks on their head to other workers at a construction site.

biles enable people to travel whenever they choose and by the quickest route. Buses carry passengers between and within cities. Trucks can provide door-to-door freight service. In Europe and Japan, many people drive motorcycles to and from work. In the United States, people use motorcycles mainly for recreation.

Unlike road vehicles, trains ride on tracks. As a result, most trains cannot provide door-to-door freight service like trucks or convenient connecting services like buses. But trains can haul far heavier loads than trucks can. They can also carry many more passengers than buses can.

Snowmobiles skim across ice or snow. The vehicles have rotating tracks or skis at the front and a rotating track at the rear. The track or tracks propel the vehicle. People use snowmobiles for transportation mainly in far northern regions that are snow covered during much of the year.

Pipelines, unlike other forms of transportation, do not move. Most pipelines are built across land, but some span rivers or other bodies of water. Pipelines transport chiefly liquids and gases, especially petroleum and natural gas. Engine-powered pumps force the liquid or gas through the pipes.

Engineless Land Transportation. Walking is the most elementary means of transportation. Carrying a load on one's back or head or using animals to carry loads is also elementary. Animals used for this purpose are called *pack animals* or *beasts of burden.* They include camels, donkeys, elephants, horses, llamas, and oxen.

People use pack animals mainly in regions that lack modern roads. Such regions include many deserts, mountainous areas, and jungles.

People use their muscle power to move such wheeled vehicles as carts, bicycles, and pedicabs. A cart is a small box-shaped vehicle with two or four wheels and an open top. A person may either push or pull a cart, whichever is more convenient. Bicycles are two-wheeled vehicles that the rider powers by means of two pedals. Many people in European and Oriental countries ride bicycles to and from work. A pedicab resembles a bicycle but has two rear wheels instead of one. It also has a passenger carriage at the front or rear. Pedicabs are used as taxicabs and even as school buses in some Oriental countries.

Animal-drawn carts and wagons are a major means of transportation in rural areas of developing countries. Carts may be pulled by dogs, donkeys, horses, or oxen. Wagons are large four-wheeled carts that can carry heavy loads. Therefore, they must be pulled by exceptionally strong animals, such as oxen or draft horses.

Water Transportation depends mainly on boats, ships, and rafts. Any small tub-shaped watercraft is classed as a boat. People use boats chiefly on rivers, canals, and lakes. A ship is a large vessel sturdy enough for ocean travel. A raft is a floating platform constructed of such materials as logs or barrels.

Engine-Powered Water Transportation. Nearly all ships and many boats are powered by engines. Most ships specialize in hauling cargo. Cargo ships travel mainly on ocean waters and on bodies of water linked to the ocean, such as the Mediterranean Sea and the Baltic Sea. Some cargo ships operate on large inland waterways, such as the Great Lakes.

Few ships specialize in transporting passengers. However, various types of motorboats carry passengers locally. Some engine-powered boats, especially tugboats, are used in hauling freight. Tugboats have powerful engines that enable them to tow heavily loaded barges. Barges are actually large rafts. Most barges must be pushed or towed. Others have engines and so move under their own power. Barges are used mainly to haul freight along inland waterways.

In general, ships and boats are the slowest engine-powered vehicles. However, engineers have developed two fast-moving water vehicles—*hydrofoils* and *hovercraft*. Hydrofoils skim across the water on skids or runners. Hovercraft, or *air cushion vehicles*, ride above the water on a cushion of air. One or more powerful fans inside the vehicle create the air cushion. Because hydrofoils and hovercraft ride out of the water, they can travel faster than other watercraft of equal horsepower. Most hydrofoils and hovercraft are too small for ocean travel and so are classed as boats. They are used mainly to carry passengers locally. Some larger hydrofoils and hovercraft are used to haul cargo along inland and coastal waters.

Engineless Water Transportation. Engineless water vehicles include dugouts, canoes, rowboats, sailboats, and rafts. People use paddles or oars to propel dugouts, canoes, and rowboats. Sailboats are powered by the wind. Rafts may be propelled by paddles, poles, sails, or water currents.

Broad-bottomed sailboats and rowboats are widely used to haul freight in the Far East. The sailboats are called *junks*, and the rowboats are known as *sampans*.

Large junks have as many as five sails and can carry 100 short tons (91 metric tons) or more. Most sampans haul light cargo. However, many larger sampans have a sail, which enables them to haul heavier loads. In the tropical rain forests of Africa, Asia, and South America, many villagers use dugouts or rafts for transportation along the rivers. Many people of the Pacific Islands use dugouts for travel between islands. Some of the dugouts are equipped with outriggers and sails.

Air Transportation depends almost entirely on engine-powered craft, especially airplanes. Engineless vehicles, such as gliders and hot-air balloons, are used mainly for recreation.

Airplanes provide the world's fastest practical means of transportation. Only spacecraft travel faster, but they are not yet a practical form of transportation. Big airliners routinely fly 500 to 600 miles per hour (mph), or 800 to 970 kilometers per hour (kph). Most private planes and some older airliners are powered by gasoline engines and driven by propellers. Nearly all newer airliners and some private planes have jet engines. *Supersonic* jets fly faster than the speed of sound. These planes travel at about 1,500 mph (2,410 kph). Most airliners chiefly carry passengers. Even the biggest planes can carry only a fraction of the weight that a ship or train can haul. Air freight rates are high as a result. The high cost limits the shipment of goods by air to expensive, lightweight, or perishable cargo. Such goods include electronic equipment and fresh flowers.

Helicopters, like airplanes, are powered by engines. But helicopters are smaller than most airplanes and cannot fly as fast or as far. Nor can they carry as many passengers as airplanes. Helicopters therefore play a secondary role in air transportation. However, they have certain special uses. For example, helicopters are used in rescue work and in fighting forest fires.

TRANSPORTATION/*History*

Prehistoric Times. Transportation developed slowly during prehistoric times, which lasted until about 3000 B.C. Throughout most of the period, people lived by hunting, fishing, and gathering wild plants. They had no beasts of burden, wheeled vehicles, or roads. People traveled on foot and carried their infants and belongings strapped to their backs or heads. Loads too heavy for one person to carry were strapped to a pole and carried by two persons.

In time, prehistoric people learned that they could drag loads along the ground on *sledges*. They made sledges from logs, poles, rawhide, or anything else that could hold a load and be dragged by one or more persons. During late prehistoric times, people began to build sledges with runners. These vehicles slid along the ground more easily than runnerless sledges, especially if the runners were greased. In far northern regions, people built lightweight sledges with runners for use on snow and ice. These vehicles became the first sleds.

By about 8000 B.C., various Middle Eastern peoples had developed agriculture and begun to establish permanent settlements. Trade between settlements then started to develop, which created a need for better means of transportation. The donkey and the ox, which had been *domesticated* (tamed) for farm work, helped meet this need. Between about 5000 and 3500 B.C., people began to use donkeys and oxen as pack animals. Next, they invented harnesses so that the animals could pull sledges. The use of donkeys and oxen as beasts of burden enabled people to transport heavier loads than they could before.

People also began to develop water transportation during prehistoric times. They built rafts of such materials as logs or reeds. Later, prehistoric people learned how to make dugouts and canoes. All these early craft were propelled by paddles or poles and were used on streams and lakes. The craft were too fragile for ocean travel.

The first wheeled vehicles and sailboats appeared near the end of prehistoric times. The wheel was invented about 3500 B.C. The invention probably took place in Mesopotamia, a region of the Middle East. The Egyptians invented sailboats about 3200 B.C. During the following centuries, wheeled vehicles and sailing vessels revolutionized transportation.

The First Great Civilizations arose in Mesopotamia and Egypt between 3500 and 3000 B.C. From these two centers, civilization gradually spread westward along the shores of the Mediterranean Sea. Sailing vessels played a vital role in the spread of civilization. Sea voyagers, for example, transmitted the ideas and inventions of civilized cultures to less developed societies.

The early Mediterranean civilizations flourished from about 3000 to 500 B.C. During this period, improvements in sailing vessels and wheeled vehicles accounted for the chief advances in transportation.

Early Development of Sailing Vessels. By 3000 B.C., the Egyptians had learned to build sailing vessels sturdy enough to put out to sea. Some of these ships ventured onto the Mediterranean and Red seas on short trading missions. Between 2000 and 1000 B.C., other Mediterranean peoples developed bigger and sturdier vessels. By 1000 B.C., the Phoenicians, who lived along the eastern shores of the Mediterranean Sea, had built a large fleet of merchant ships. The Phoenicians sailed the length of the Mediterranean, from their home waters to Spain. They traded everything from pottery to cattle for various other goods at ports along the Mediterranean.

Sea travel remained slow and difficult throughout ancient times. Sailors lacked navigation instruments. As a result, they usually stayed within sight of land. The ships were hard to steer because they had no rudder. Sailors steered their ships by means of one or two oars at the stern. In addition, the ships could not depend entirely on the wind for power. The earliest ships had a single sail, which worked well only when the wind blew from behind. The sail did not work well in sailing against the wind and was useless when there was no wind. Many ships had teams of oarsmen, who rowed the vessels when the wind failed.

Early Development of Wheeled Vehicles. The Mesopotamians built the first known wheeled vehicles about 3500 B.C. But such vehicles were not widely used until after 3000 B.C. The technique of making wheels and wheeled vehicles slowly spread from Mesopotamia. It reached India about 2500 B.C., Europe about 1400 B.C., and China about 1300 B.C.

The first wheeled vehicles were four-wheeled carts. They were pulled by oxen or, after about 3000 B.C., by donkeylike animals called *onagers*. Each wheel on a cart was a wooden disk made from three rectangular boards. To construct a wheel, a wheel maker fastened the boards together edge to edge with wooden braces to make a square. The square was then rounded at the corners to form the disk. The three-piece construction prevented the wheels from being perfectly round. The early carts bumped along at a snail's pace and probably had to be stopped frequently for repairs. The wheelbarrow was not invented until the Middle Ages.

At first, the Mesopotamians used carts mainly as funeral cars. After 3000 B.C., carts drawn by onagers carried Mesopotamian troops into battle. In time, carts were occasionally used to carry passengers and to haul grain, sand, and other goods that were difficult to load

Transportation in Prehistoric Times Nearly all the methods of transporting goods or people during prehistoric times depended on the muscles of either human beings or animals. Some of these methods are pictured below. Similar methods are still used in many parts of the world.

WORLD BOOK illustrations for the *History* section by Robert Addison

onto sledges or pack animals. However, wheeled vehicles could not compete with sledges and pack animals until the design of the wheels was improved.

Wheels continued to be made of three solid pieces of wood until about 2000 B.C. Between 2000 and 1500 B.C., the first spoked wheels appeared. These wheels consisted of a rim, a hub, and spokes. The three parts were constructed separately. Spoked wheels provided smoother riding than solid wooden wheels, and they were lighter and faster. The first spoked wheels were probably made for chariots.

Chariots with spoked wheels were light enough for horses to pull. Horses had been tamed for riding by about 2000 B.C. But they could not be used to pull heavy loads because a suitable harness had not yet been invented. The harnesses then in use pressed against a horse's windpipe. If a horse had to pull too heavy a load, the harness cut off the animal's breathing. However, two or more horses could pull a lightweight chariot easily. Horse-drawn chariots, used chiefly by warriors, became the swiftest vehicles of ancient times.

Ancient Greece. During the 400's B.C., Greece became the chief power in the Mediterranean area. The Greeks expanded the sea trade begun by the Phoenicians. They also pioneered in the building of two-masted vessels and increased the number of sails from one to four.

Greek cargo ships sailed from home with huge jars of olive oil and wine. These products were exchanged for wheat and other grain at various ports on the Mediterranean and Black seas. The grain trade was extremely important to the Greeks. Wheat was the principal food during ancient times, and the Greeks had to import most of their supply. Many Greek grain ships were seized by enemy or pirate vessels. Many others sank in storms. But almost every year, enough ships returned home to prevent famine for another year.

The ancient Greeks developed a highly advanced civilization. Greek merchant ships helped spread Greek civilization westward. As civilization spread, trade and shipping increased. By 400 B.C., about 300 ports lay on the Mediterranean and several thousand trading ships of various countries crisscrossed the sea.

Ancient Rome. From the 100's B.C. to the A.D. 400's, Rome ruled the mightiest empire of ancient times. At its peak, the Roman Empire included all the lands bordering the Mediterranean. It also extended as far north as the British Isles and as far east as the Persian Gulf. To help hold their vast empire together, the Romans built a highly advanced system of roads.

People had built roads long before Roman times. By about 1000 B.C., the Chinese had begun to construct roadways between their major cities. The Persians built a similar road network during the 500's B.C. But most of the early intercity roads were little more than dirt tracks. The Romans constructed the first extensive system of paved roads. The best Roman roads measured 16 to 20 feet (5 to 6 meters) wide and 3 to 6 feet (0.9 to 1.8 meters) thick. They had a base that consisted of several layers of crushed stone and gravel. The roads were paved with stone blocks.

The Romans used their roads chiefly to transport

Vehicles of Ancient Times Wheeled vehicles and sailing vessels were invented during the 3000's B.C. They became the most widely used means of transportation during ancient times. But many people also continued to use earlier forms of transportation, such as pack animals.

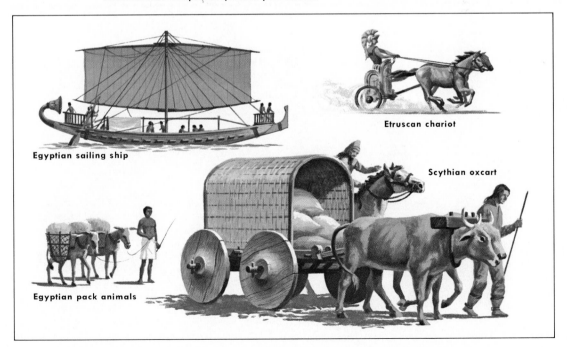

Egyptian sailing ship

Etruscan chariot

Scythian oxcart

Egyptian pack animals

troops and military supplies. But the roads also served as a major communications link between Rome and its provinces. Messengers in horse-drawn carts used the roads to carry government communications. By the A.D. 200's, more than 50,000 miles (80,000 kilometers) of paved roads connected Rome with almost every part of its empire.

During the 400's, Germanic tribes conquered most of the Roman territories in western Europe. The majority of Roman roads fell into ruin during the following centuries. However, a few are still used.

The Romans also built the largest fleet of cargo ships in ancient times. Like the Greeks, the Romans could not survive without sea trade. Roman cargo ships supplied the city of Rome with most of its grain supply.

The Middle Ages, which lasted from the 400's to the 1500's, brought great improvements in land and water transportation. These improvements resulted largely from three remarkable inventions—the rigid horse collar, the iron horseshoe, and the whiffletree. Scholars do not know exactly when or where these devices were invented. But all three had appeared in Europe by the end of the 1000's.

The rigid horse collar appeared about 800. Before this invention came into common use, horses wore a harness that fit across the neck. The harness choked a horse if it pulled a heavy load. The rigid horse collar shifted the weight of a load to a horse's shoulders. Horses collared in this way could pull four or five times as much weight as before.

The iron horseshoe appeared in Europe about 900.

Horses without shoes often suffered from damaged hoofs if they traveled long distances at top speed. Iron shoes protected a horse's hoofs from damage and so enabled the animal to travel farther and faster than it could without them.

The whiffletree, which appeared during the 1000's, made it possible for wagons to be pulled by teams of horses. A whiffletree is a pivoted crossbar at the front of a wagon to which a team's harnesses are fastened. It equalizes the pull of the horses. Without such a device, a wagon may be thrown off balance and may even be overturned.

The invention of the rigid horse collar, iron horseshoe, and whiffletree stimulated overland trade in Europe. They made it possible for horses to pull as much weight as oxen—and for longer distances and at twice the speed.

The increased speeds of horse-drawn vehicles also encouraged greater use of wagons for passenger transportation. But wagon rides were extremely bumpy. Wagon makers tried to correct this problem by building vehicles with *suspension systems,* which provided a certain amount of cushioning against bumps. However, only rich people could afford such vehicles. Most of the people of the Middle Ages traveled on foot or on horseback, just as people had done in the past.

The design and construction of ships improved greatly during the Middle Ages. The triangular *lateen sail* appeared in the 500's. Unlike square sails, which were widely used at the time, lateen sails worked well when ships sailed into the wind. The first ships with

Transportation in Early Modern Times Beginning in the 1400's, Europeans built ships capable of making long ocean voyages. Stagecoaches became widely used in Europe during the late 1600's and early 1700's. In other parts of the world, such as China, people continued to use older forms of transportation.

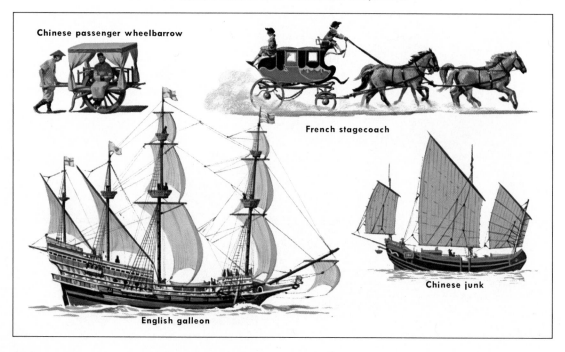

Chinese passenger wheelbarrow

French stagecoach

Chinese junk

English galleon

a rudder rather than steering oars at the stern appeared in Europe about 1300. Rudders could steer much bigger ships than could be steered with oars. During the 1400's, shipbuilders began to produce ships four times as large as any built before. All these ships had a rudder, and most had three masts and three sails.

Several important navigation instruments were also developed during the Middle Ages. One such instrument, called a *mariner's compass*, allowed voyagers to navigate their ships even when the sky was overcast. By the late 1400's, the advances in ship construction and navigation aids helped make long ocean voyages possible.

The Age of Overseas Expansion. During the late 1400's and the 1500's, such European explorers as Christopher Columbus, Ferdinand Magellan, and Sir Francis Drake made great ocean voyages. As a result of these and later voyages, European civilization continued to spread westward—first to North and South America and then to Australia and New Zealand. However, this expansion of European culture took several hundred years. In spite of the improvements in ship construction, ocean travel remained extremely slow.

Overseas trade began to increase rapidly during the 1600's. Shipbuilders launched bigger and bigger cargo vessels to handle the growing trade. The bigger ships had to have more sails, and the added sails helped increase speeds. By the mid-1800's, the fastest merchant ships had as many as 35 sails and traveled at speeds up to 20 knots. These *clipper ships* could sail from New York City, around South America, to San Francisco in three

to four months. The overland journey from New York to California took twice as long.

Development of Inland Transport. By the 1600's, most people used horse-drawn wagons to haul goods locally. But they seldom used wagons for long hauls because of the poor condition of the roads. Until the mid-1800's, horse-drawn boats and barges were the chief means of long-distance inland transport. The animals trudged along the banks of rivers and canals and pulled the vessels with ropes.

Hundreds of canals were built in Europe from the late Middle Ages through the early 1800's. The first major American canal, the Erie Canal, opened in New York in 1825. It connected Albany and Buffalo and provided a vital link in an all-water route between New York City and Great Lakes ports. At that time, the overland journey between Albany and Buffalo took about 20 days. After the Erie Canal opened, horse-drawn barges made the trip in 8 days. The success of the Erie Canal led to a great burst of canal building in the United States. By 1850, the United States had about 4,500 miles (7,240 kilometers) of canals. These waterways carried most of the nation's intercity freight.

During the 1700's, France and England constructed the first well-built paved roads since Roman times. By the mid-1800's, the first major U.S. highway, the National Road, had been completed between Cumberland, Md., and Vandalia, Ill. It was a gravel road and inferior to the best French and English roads of the time. American pioneers traveling west from the Mississippi River crossed a wilderness without roads. They drove

Transportation in the 1800's   The steam engine provided a completely new source of power for transportation during the 1800's. It was used to propel locomotives and paddlewheel boats and ships. However, people also continued to use older sources of power, such as animals and the wind.

Horse-drawn streetcar

Clipper ship

Stern-wheel steamboat

Steam locomotive

Ox-drawn covered wagon

their covered wagons along well-traveled dirt paths, such as the Santa Fe and Oregon trails.

The basic design of wagons and coaches changed little from the late Middle Ages through the 1800's. The first city coach line started in Paris during the 1660's. It was the ancestor of today's mass transit systems. The first long intercity coach line began service between England and Scotland about 1670. The line operated between the cities of London and Edinburgh, a distance of 392 miles (631 kilometers). The coaches were called *stagecoaches* because they traveled in stages, stopping at scheduled places on a route for changes of horses. The first stagecoach lines in the American Colonies began service during the 1730's.

The Steam Age. The invention of the steam engine marked the beginning of the greatest revolution in transportation since the invention of the wheel and the sailboat. British inventors developed the steam engine during the 1700's. In 1807, the first commercially successful steamboat service began in the United States. The first successful steam railroad began service in England in 1825. By the late 1800's, ships powered by steam engines had largely replaced sailing ships on the world's shipping lanes. However, steam-powered trains played the leading role in the transportation revolution.

By the late 1800's, steam locomotives traveled at speeds never imagined possible—up to 60 mph (97 kph) and faster. They could haul loads hundreds of times heavier than a team of horses could pull. By 1900, rail lines had been built throughout Europe and North America and in many parts of Africa, Asia, Australia, and South America. The overland journey by train from New York City to San Francisco took less than a week. In comparison, the trip took weeks or months by stagecoach or covered wagon.

As more and more steamships and steam-powered trains went into service, passenger fares and freight rates dropped. The lower costs encouraged travel, trade, and the growth of cities. In addition, many people became accustomed to fast movement and rapid change. The quickening pace of life created a demand for still faster transportation.

The Beginnings of Modern Transportation. The first electric trains and streetcars appeared in Europe and the United States during the 1880's. In the 1890's, the German engineer Rudolf Diesel invented the engine that was later named after him. In time, diesel engines replaced steam engines on many ships and on most trains. But of all the inventions of the 1800's, the gasoline engine was the one that brought about the most far-reaching changes in transportation.

German inventors built the first gasoline engines during the 1880's and used them to power bicycles. The bicycle had been developed in Europe earlier in the 1800's. During the 1890's, French engineers built the first gasoline-powered vehicles with automobile bodies. The first gasoline-powered buses and trucks were built in Germany during the 1890's. In 1903, two American bicycle makers, Orville and Wilbur Wright, used a gasoline engine to power a small airplane that they had built. The Wright brothers' plane became the

Vehicles of the Early 1900's   By the early 1900's, engine-powered vehicles had revolutionized transportation. Ocean-going steamships, giant airships, electric streetcars, powerful steam trains, and the first mass-produced automobiles were carrying people farther and faster than they had ever traveled before.

Zeppelin airship

Electric streetcar

Steam-powered ocean liner

Transcontinental steam train

Ford Model T

first one to lift a person into the air and fly successfully.

Automobiles became the chief means of passenger transportation in the United States during the 1920's. As the number of automobile owners increased, so did the demand for more and better roads. About 700,000 miles (1,100,000 kilometers) of surfaced streets and highways were built in the United States between 1900 and 1930.

The first commercial airlines began service in Europe in 1919. Airlines began operations in many other parts of the world during the 1920's. By the late 1930's, the world's airlines carried 3½ million passengers annually. All airplanes had propellers and gasoline engines. During the late 1930's, German engineers built the first planes with jet engines. All the early jet aircraft were warplanes. The first jet airliners began service during the 1950's.

The great advances in transportation during the 1900's have brought about enormous changes in people's lives. The development of commercial air travel has made long journeys routine. As a result of improvements in ocean shipping and in refrigeration, goods that were once available only in certain regions are now distributed worldwide. The development of the automobile has led to the growth of sprawling suburbs around big cities. Many suburbanites depend on their cars for shopping and other personal business. They may also use their cars to get to and from work in the central cities. Without this convenient means of private transportation, suburban living would be impractical or impossible for many people.

─────── **Important Dates in Transportation** ───────

c.5000 B.C. People began to use donkeys and oxen as pack animals.

c.3500 B.C. The Mesopotamians built the first wheeled vehicles.

c.3200 B.C. The Egyptians invented sails and produced the first sailboats.

300's B.C.—A.D. 200's The Romans built the first extensive system of paved roads.

c.800 The rigid horse collar appeared in Europe.

1100's Wagon makers in Europe built the first traveling carriages. Carriages with spring suspension systems became known as *coaches* during the 1400's.

1490's Improvements in ship construction helped make long ocean voyages possible.

1660's The first city coach line opened in Paris.

1700's British inventors developed the steam engine.

1807 The first commercially successful steamboat service began in the United States.

1825 The first successful steam railroad began operations in England.

1880's German inventors built the first gasoline engines and used them to power bicycles.

1890's French engineers built the first gasoline-powered vehicles with automobile bodies.

1903 An airplane built by Orville and Wilbur Wright of the United States became the first one to lift a person into the air and fly successfully.

1920's Automobiles became the chief means of passenger transportation in the United States.

1950's The first commercial jet airliners began service.

1970's Declining petroleum reserves throughout the world led to shortages of transportation fuel in the United States and other developed countries.

1976 The first supersonic passenger airliner, the Concorde, began service between Europe and the United States.

Transportation in the 1930's   Most of today's forms of public transportation had taken shape by the 1930's. Railroads were the chief form of intercity public transportation at the time. But intercity bus lines and commercial airlines were beginning to carry more and more passengers. Ferries carried many passengers locally.

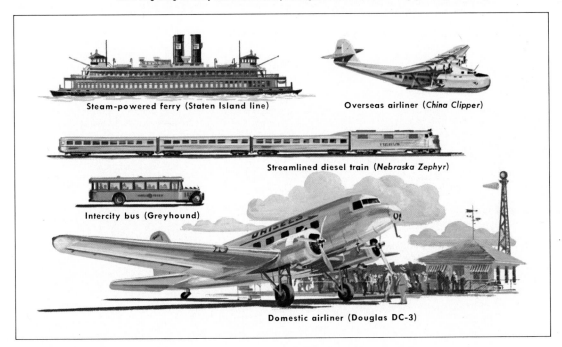

Steam-powered ferry (Staten Island line)

Overseas airliner (*China Clipper*)

Streamlined diesel train (*Nebraska Zephyr*)

Intercity bus (Greyhound)

Domestic airliner (Douglas DC-3)

Before the development of engine-powered vehicles, nearly all transportation involved the shipment of goods. Passenger transportation was relatively uncommon. The development of engine-powered transportation changed this situation dramatically. Today, passenger transportation is an essential part of everyday life in developed countries. Workers in these countries live much farther from their places of employment than workers did in the past. As a result, they need quick, dependable transportation each workday. Many children need transportation to and from school. Families depend on transportation for shopping and other errands. Many people travel long distances on vacations. In the United States today, more money is spent on the various means of passenger transportation than on the shipment of freight.

This section deals mainly with engine-powered passenger and freight transportation in developed countries. In developing countries, many people still rely on age-old transportation methods. For a discussion of these methods, see the section *Kinds of Transportation*.

Passenger Transportation

There are two main types of passenger transportation: (1) private transportation and (2) public transportation. People who use private transportation operate their own vehicles. Those who use public transportation pay to ride on vehicles owned and operated by private companies or the government.

Private Transportation in industrial countries is provided mainly by automobiles, bicycles, motorcycles, and private airplanes. Automobiles are by far the most important means of private transportation.

Most people in the United States travel chiefly by car. Americans use their cars largely for local transportation. But automobiles are also the leading means of travel between U.S. cities. Intercity travel is usually measured in *passenger-miles*. A passenger-mile represents one passenger transported 1 mile (1.6 kilometers). Automobile transportation accounts for about 85 per cent of all the intercity passenger-miles traveled in the United States each year. Travel by motorcycle and travel by private airplane account for less than 1 per cent each.

Automobiles are also the chief means of passenger transportation in Australia, Canada, New Zealand, South Africa, and most of the nations of Western Europe. People in these countries and in the United States own about 85 per cent of the world's automobiles. Americans own by far the largest share—about 40 per cent of the world total. The countries with the most automobiles also have the best road systems. There are about 5 million miles (8 million kilometers) of paved roads throughout the world. More than half of this mileage is in the United States. Most of the rest is in the other countries that have a large number of automobiles.

Highway travel is far less important in developing countries than in developed ones. But a growing number of city dwellers in these countries own a car. The biggest cities have had to build more expressways to handle the ever-increasing flow of auto traffic.

Public Transportation. Any organized passenger service that is available to the general public can be classed as public transportation. There are three main types of public transportation service: (1) urban, (2) intercity, and (3) overseas.

Urban Service. Most large urban areas provide some means of public transportation for people who do not own a car or who prefer to avoid city driving whenever possible. Public transportation in urban areas is called *mass transit*. Mass transit between cities and their suburbs is often called *commuter service*.

Average Speeds of Some Kinds of Passenger Transportation

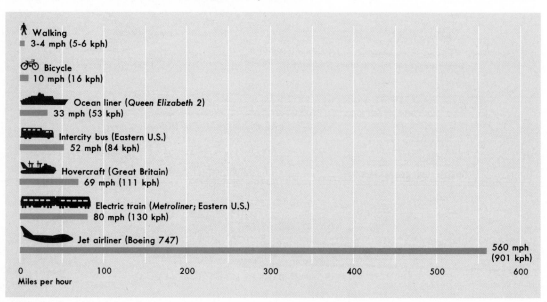

Walking
3-4 mph (5-6 kph)

Bicycle
10 mph (16 kph)

Ocean liner (*Queen Elizabeth 2*)
33 mph (53 kph)

Intercity bus (Eastern U.S.)
52 mph (84 kph)

Hovercraft (Great Britain)
69 mph (111 kph)

Electric train (*Metroliner*; Eastern U.S.)
80 mph (130 kph)

Jet airliner (Boeing 747)
560 mph (901 kph)

0   100   200   300   400   500   600
Miles per hour

Buses are the chief mass transit vehicles. About 950 cities in the United States have a mass transit system. Almost all these systems provide bus service only. However, most of the world's big cities offer rail service in addition to bus service. About 50 cities throughout the world, including 9 U.S. and 2 Canadian cities, have both subway and surface rail lines. Many big cities throughout the world also have elevated trains, which run on tracks above the streets. In addition, a growing number of large cities have a mass transit system that includes *light-rail vehicles*.

A light-rail vehicle is an electrically powered railroad passenger car that runs on tracks at street level. The car gets its power from an electrified third rail or overhead trolley wire. Streetcars are a type of light-rail vehicle. During the late 1800's and early 1900's, streetcars were the chief mass transit vehicles. But most streetcar tracks ran down the middle of the street, and the vehicles interfered with auto traffic. Streetcars have been replaced by buses in nearly every American city where they operated.

Today's light-rail lines differ from streetcar lines mainly in the location of the tracks. Instead of running down the middle of the street, the tracks lie alongside the roadway. This arrangement eliminates interference with automobile traffic. In addition, it speeds up rail service.

Trains are the chief means of public commuter transportation. Many U.S. intercity railroads run commuter trains between big cities and their suburbs. About 75 per cent of all railroad passengers in the United States are commuters.

Intercity Service is provided mainly by airplanes, buses, and trains. Riverboats and ferryboats carry an extremely small share of intercity passengers.

Milt & Joan Mann

Bicycles are an important form of private transportation in various European countries, including The Netherlands, above. Many Europeans ride bicycles to and from work.

© B. Kliewe, ICON

Automobiles are by far the chief means of private transportation in industrial countries. Big cities require large parking lots for the great number of cars driven by workers each day.

Jack Novak, Photri

High-Speed Trains carry much of the intercity passenger traffic in Japan and Western Europe. The sleek, bullet-shaped train above is part of a large fleet of Japanese superexpresses.

Commercial air, bus, and rail transportation account for about 15 per cent of the intercity passenger-miles traveled in the United States each year. Airlines handle the biggest share of this traffic, and railroads the smallest. The airlines' share increases with the length of the trip. In the case of especially long trips, nearly as many Americans travel by air as by automobile. Rail and bus travel are more important in other countries than in the United States. They are the chief modern means of intercity travel in most developing nations. Japan and most Western European countries have many high-speed passenger trains.

High-speed trains can compete with airliners for passengers on runs up to about 500 miles (800 kilometers). Most big airports are on the outskirts of central cities. For short and medium-length flights, the trip to and from the airport may take longer than the flight itself. Trains, on the other hand, take passengers all the way into central cities. Passengers on a high-speed train may thus complete their entire journey in less time than it would take by air.

Overseas Service. The first overseas airlines began operations during the 1930's. But the planes had to stop frequently during a flight for refueling, and the flights were uncomfortable and even hazardous. Most overseas travelers continued to go by ship until the late 1950's, even though it took far longer to sail than to fly. The voyage across the Atlantic Ocean, for example, took four days or more. The first nonstop trans-oceanic airliners appeared during the late 1940's. These propeller-driven planes could carry passengers across the Atlantic safely and comfortably in hours rather than days. As these planes became more common, overseas travel increased. The first transoceanic jet airliners began service during the 1950's, leading to a tremendous increase in overseas air travel.

Today, the great majority of overseas travelers go by plane. Few ocean liners remain in operation. Most of those that do operate make regular runs during the summer and operate as cruise ships during the winter. Cruise ships specialize in taking vacationists to the Caribbean, Mediterranean, and other warm areas.

In 1976, the first supersonic airliner, the Concorde, began service between Europe and the United States. The Concorde travels between New York City and London or Paris—a distance of about 3,500 miles (5,630 kilometers)—in approximately $3\frac{1}{2}$ to 4 hours. However, the Concorde has not been efficient to operate because it uses fuel uneconomically.

Freight Transportation

Pipelines provide the cheapest means of transporting freight. However, their use is largely limited to petroleum and natural gas. The cheapest way to move general cargo is by water. Rail transportation costs about 3 times as much as water transportation, and truck transportation costs about 10 times as much. Air transportation is by far the most expensive way to move freight. It costs nearly 40 times as much as water transportation. As a result, cargo planes usually carry only expensive, lightweight, or perishable merchandise.

The various means of moving cargo are used for both (1) domestic freight and (2) international freight. **Domestic Freight.** Most domestic freight traffic involves the transport of cargo between cities within a country. The cargo is carried by airplanes, barges, pipelines, railroads, ships, and trucks. Freight shipments within cities consist mainly of pickups and deliveries. Trucks carry nearly all such local freight.

Intercity freight traffic is usually measured in *ton-miles*. A ton-mile represents 1 short ton (0.9 metric ton) transported 1 mile (1.6 kilometers). Rail shipments account for about 35 per cent of the ton-miles of freight hauled in the United States yearly. Shipments by truck and by petroleum pipeline account for about 25 per cent each. Barges and ships carry about 14 per cent, and airplanes less than 1 per cent.

Freight transport in other developed countries is

Growth of Intercity Passenger Traffic in the United States

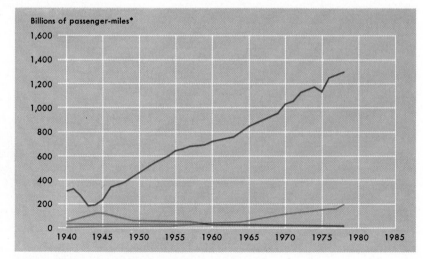

Billions of passenger-miles*

Volume of traffic by type of transportation

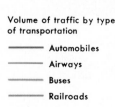

——— Automobiles
——— Airways
——— Buses
——— Railroads

*A passenger-mile is one passenger carried 1 mile (1.6 kilometers).
Source: U.S. Interstate Commerce Commission; Transportation Association of America.

similar to that in the United States. However, railroads carry an even greater share of the intercity traffic in European countries than in the United States. Canal traffic is also greater in Europe.

In many cases, a particular freight shipment must be switched from one type of carrier to one or more other types to reach its destination. For example, many coal shipments travel by train, barge, and truck on their way to the buyer. The movement of freight by more than one method is called *intermodal transport*.

A type of intermodal transport known as *containerization* has become increasingly common since the mid-1900's. Freight is packed into big crates called *containers*. The containers are designed to ride on truck trailers and railroad flatcars. They can easily be transferred between the two types of carriers and to specially designed *container ships*. Containerization is used mainly to transport such goods as machinery and household appliances. The method reduces shipping costs, speeds deliveries, and cuts losses due to breakage. Some domestic freight is containerized. But the method is used mainly in international trade.

International Freight is transported mainly by ships. Many of today's merchant ships are designed to carry containers or a particular kind of cargo, such as petroleum, grain, or iron ore. In numerous cases, the ships require specialized port facilities. Most large ports have been equipped to handle containers. Giant cranes and other lifting devices transfer the containers between container ships and truck trailers or railroad flatcars. Some of the world's busiest seaports specialize in handling oil tanker traffic. These ports have exceptionally deep harbors to accommodate giant tankers. They also have pumping systems and pipelines for loading and unloading the oil.

Some international freight moves by highway, rail, pipeline, inland waterway, or airplane. European countries, especially, depend on these methods in their trade with one another.

Milt & Joan Mann

Intermodal Transport is the movement of freight by more than one method. For example, containers loaded with freight may be transferred from truck trailers to railroad flatcars, *above*.

John Launois, Black Star

Barge Transportation is one of the cheapest ways to haul such cargo as coal, grain, and gravel. These barges are being pushed by a tugboat. Some barges, however, have built-in engines.

Growth of Intercity Freight Traffic in the United States

Volume of traffic by type of transportation

——— Railroads

——— Oil pipelines

——— Trucks

——— Inland waterways

——— Airways

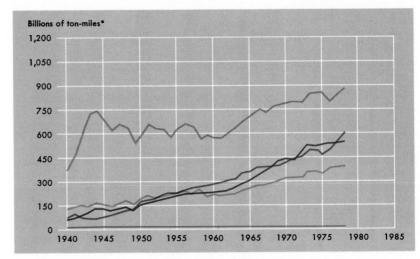

Billions of ton-miles*

*A ton-mile is 1 short ton (0.9 metric ton) carried 1 mile (1.6 kilometers).
Source: U.S. Interstate Commerce Commission; Transportation Association of America.

Transportation is one of the leading industries in the world. Many of the world's biggest industrial firms earn all or much of their income from the sale of equipment or fuel for transportation. The transportation industry employs many millions of people in countries throughout the world. In the United States alone, about 10 per cent of all workers are directly or indirectly involved in providing transportation.

The transportation industry consists of (1) equipment manufacturers, (2) passenger and freight carriers, and (3) related industries. The equipment manufacturers and passenger and freight carriers are the key organizations. However, the related industries play a vital role in transportation by providing fuel and various services and facilities. In addition, governments throughout the world are involved in transportation. The extent of the involvement of governments varies according to the political and economic systems of different countries.

Equipment Manufacturers produce the vehicles on which modern transportation depends. They also supply the equipment needed to operate the vehicles, such as railroad tracks and airplane communications systems. The manufacture of transportation equipment is the second leading manufacturing industry in the United States in terms of *value added by manufacture*. The leader is the nonelectric machinery industry. Value added by manufacture measures the increase in value of raw materials after they become a finished product.

Companies that make automobiles, buses, and trucks are by far the largest producers of transportation equipment. The two leading U.S. producers of such motor vehicles are General Motors Corporation and Ford Motor Company. They rank among the top five manufacturing firms in the world.

Passenger and Freight Carriers include airlines, intercity bus lines, mass transit companies, pipeline companies, railroads, shipping lines, and trucking firms. In most countries, the central government owns and operates all the airlines and railroads and some or all of the intercity bus lines. The United States is the chief exception. Private companies own and operate all the airlines and nearly all the railroads in the United States. Canada has two major airlines and two major railroads. The Canadian government owns and operates one of the airlines and one of the railroads. The other two companies are privately owned and operated. In addition, all of Canada's intercity bus lines are privately owned.

In Communist countries, the central government also owns the intercity bus lines, pipelines, and shipping and trucking lines. In most other countries, including the United States and Canada, these services are provided by privately owned firms, which are subject to various forms of government regulation. In nearly every country, all or most mass transit services are controlled by local governments.

The leading carrier groups in the United States, in order of income, are (1) trucking companies, (2) railroads, (3) airlines, (4) shipping lines, (5) pipeline companies, and (6) intercity bus lines. There are more companies in the trucking group than in any other cate-

Steve McCutcheon

The Trans-Alaska Pipeline, *above,* is part of a vast network of oil pipelines that crisscrosses the United States. Pipeline companies, which transport gas and other products as well as oil, are among the nation's leading freight carriers.

gory. The intercity bus group has the fewest companies.

Related Industries include glass, petroleum, steel, and tire production; road construction; the selling of new and used automobiles; and the servicing of automobiles. Petroleum production is the leading transportation-related industry in terms of value. About half the petroleum processed in the United States is made into fuel for automobiles, airplanes, and other engine-powered vehicles. Of the world's top 10 manufacturing firms, 7 are oil companies. Four of these companies are U.S. firms.

Government and Transportation. Governments are most deeply involved in the transportation industry in countries where all or much of the industry is publicly owned. But even in the United States, where nearly all transportation companies are privately owned, government plays a major role in transportation. This role consists mainly of (1) providing funds for certain transportation facilities and (2) regulating certain aspects of transportation.

Government Funding. Four kinds of transportation facilities in the United States depend almost entirely on public funds. They are (1) air traffic control centers, (2) airports, (3) public roads, and (4) river and harbor facilities. About 85 per cent of the money spent on the four types of facilities is used for the building and upkeep of roads. State and local governments provide most of the funds for airports, roads, and river and harbor facilities. The federal government finances all air traffic control operations. It also helps pay the expenses of Amtrak, a semipublic corporation that operates nearly all the nation's intercity passenger trains.

Mass transit systems in every country depend heavily on government financial support. Few of the systems earn enough from passenger fares to pay all their expenses. Governments must provide whatever additional funds are needed to keep the mass transit systems in operation.

In the United States, the Department of Transportation distributes most of the federal funds for transportation. Most states and a majority of large metropolitan areas have transportation agencies that distribute state and local funds. In Canada, the Canadian Ministry of Transport handles the federal funding of transportation.

Government Regulation deals chiefly with transportation safety and the business practices of transportation companies. Governments throughout the world establish safety rules for the various methods of transportation. In the United States, agencies within the Department of Transportation set and enforce safety standards for the design and manufacture of transportation equipment and for the operation of airplanes and trains. The Canadian Transport Commission sets and enforces such standards in Canada. State, provincial, and local governments regulate traffic safety on roads and waterways under their control.

Several federal agencies regulate the freight rates and other business practices of U.S. transportation companies. The Interstate Commerce Commission oversees the railroad and domestic shipping industries and interstate trucking. The airline industry is regulated by the Civil Aeronautics Board, and the overseas shipping industry by the Federal Maritime Commission. The Federal Energy Regulatory Commission oversees natural gas pipeline companies. It also regulates those oil pipeline companies that provide commercial service. In Canada, the business practices of transportation companies are regulated chiefly by the Canadian Transport Commission.

The airline, railroad, and trucking industries have long been among the most heavily regulated industries in the United States. The federal government began its regulation of these companies to prevent them from charging unfair passenger and freight rates. Regulation also helped protect the companies from unfair competition. However, many people believe that heavy government regulation discouraged the airline and trucking industries from improving their services. These people further believe that both industries would operate more efficiently if they were more competitive. With this end in view, the federal government began to relax some of its controls over the airline and trucking industries during the late 1970's. The federal government has announced plans to remove all economic controls over the airline industry and to disband the Civil Aeronautics Board by 1985.

Since the mid-1900's, governments throughout the world have become increasingly involved in regulating the environmental aspects of transportation. The following section, *Current Developments*, discusses this type of regulation.

Problems of Modern Transportation include (1) traffic safety, (2) declining fuel reserves, (3) environmental problems, and (4) inadequate public transportation. These problems are most severe in countries that depend heavily on automobile transportation.

Traffic Safety. Most types of high-speed, engine-powered transportation involve traffic safety problems. But automobile drivers have an especially poor safety record. In the United States, more people are killed in automobile accidents every year than in all other transportation accidents combined. Most automobile accidents could be prevented if every driver obeyed all traffic laws and all the rules for safe driving.

Airlines have one of the best safety records in the field of transportation. But heavy air traffic at major airports has increased the hazards of commercial flying. When many airliners await clearance to land or take off, airport approaches and runways become dangerously overcrowded. In addition, large airports have a growing amount of private plane traffic, which makes traffic control even more difficult. This problem could largely be eliminated if private planes were prohibited from flying near large commercial airports.

Railroads in the United States are increasingly plagued by train derailments. Worn-out or damaged tracks cause the majority of the derailments. Most railroad companies have track replacement programs. But the companies claim they need federal financial help to replace all their worn-out or damaged tracks.

Declining Fuel Reserves. Gasoline and other fuels made from petroleum supply nearly all the energy for engine-powered transportation. Energy experts warn that the world's supply of petroleum is being used up rapidly. At the current rate of use, the supply may be exhausted by the early 2000's. Developed countries therefore face a difficult problem. On the one hand, they must ensure that their major transportation systems have enough fuel to function normally. On the other hand, these nations must do all they can to conserve fuel. Fuel conservation is necessary not only because of the threat of a serious fuel shortage but also because of the high price of petroleum. Higher petroleum prices result in higher transportation costs, and higher transportation costs drive up the prices of transported goods. During the 1970's, petroleum prices rose sharply, contributing to an increase in the costs of many goods.

Automobiles consume about half the energy used for transportation in the United States. They therefore contribute heavily to the nation's energy supply prob-

Energy Use in Intercity Passenger Transportation

Kind of Vehicle	Number of Passengers	Miles Vehicle Travels per Gallon of Fuel*	Passenger-Miles per Gallon of Fuel*
Diesel Train	720	0.50	360
Bus	47	6.00	282
Standard-Size Automobile	6	18.00	108
Wide-Body Jet Airliner	385	0.14	54

*One mile equals 1.6093 kilometers. One gallon equals 3.7854 liters. A passenger-mile is one passenger carried 1 mile.
Source: *Transit Fact Book*, 1975-1976, American Public Transit Association.

319

lems. To help reduce automobile fuel consumption, the U.S. government sets gasoline-mileage standards for new cars. These standards encourage American automakers to produce smaller, lighter cars, which travel farther per gallon of gasoline than earlier models.

Environmental Problems. Automobiles are the chief cause of traffic congestion in urban areas, and their exhaust fumes contribute heavily to urban air pollution. Many cities plagued by traffic jams and air pollution have taken steps to reduce automobile traffic in their downtown areas. In addition, the U.S. government has established increasingly strict pollution-control standards for new automobiles. These standards require automakers to manufacture cars that give off cleaner exhausts than earlier models.

Inadequate Public Transportation. Except for airline facilities, most public transportation facilities in the United States have been neglected since the 1940's. Today, few of the nation's intercity passenger trains and mass transit systems provide adequate service. Greater use of public transportation would help ease the problems caused by heavy dependence on automobiles. But public transportation must be improved to provide better service before more automobile drivers can be persuaded to use it.

Improvements in Public Transportation chiefly involve expanding and upgrading (1) mass transit service and (2) intercity train service.

Improvements in Mass Transit Service. Most cities today cannot afford to build extensive new mass transit facilities. But many cities are trying to improve their existing facilities. For example, a number of cities have speeded up bus service by reserving certain traffic lanes for buses only. More and more communities provide *paratransit services.* Such services include public car and van pools and subscription bus services. The schedules and routes of paratransit vehicles are arranged to suit the passengers' convenience.

A new type of mass transit facility is the *people mover.* People movers carry passengers along specially constructed guideways in driverless, electrically powered cars. The cars operate automatically. They move along the guideways and stop at designated points to take on and discharge passengers. The U.S. Department of Transportation is helping to finance extensive people-mover systems in the downtown areas of Cleveland, Houston, Jacksonville, and Los Angeles. A number of short-distance people movers are in operation in such places as parks and airports.

Improvements in Intercity Train Service. Most developed countries are trying to improve railroad passenger service along heavily traveled intercity routes. Trains use less energy per passenger than do automobiles, airplanes, and buses. Thus, railroads could help conserve energy if they attracted passengers away from air and highway travel.

The only high-speed passenger trains in the United States are *Metroliners,* which run between New York City and Washington, D.C. They average about 80 mph (130 kph) on their 225-mile (362-kilometer) run. Worn-out tracks and inadequate signal systems prevent most other U.S. intercity trains from traveling as fast.

Orion Press

The Magnetic Levitation Vehicle (MLV) is a high-speed passenger train being developed in Japan, France, and West Germany. A magnetic force holds the vehicle above a guide rail and propels it up to 300 miles (480 kilometers) per hour. Japan hopes to open an MLV line in the early 1980's.

West Virginia University

People Movers are mass transit vehicles that carry passengers along guideways in driverless, electrically powered cars. The cars operate automatically and stop at designated stations.

Amtrak, which operates the *Metroliners*, plans to start similar high-speed service between New York City and Boston. It also has long-range plans to provide such service along heavily traveled routes in other parts of the United States. But before any of these plans can be carried out, the federal government must replace worn-out tracks and modernize signal systems along the routes. Congress has granted the money to make these improvements on the New York City-Boston route. But Amtrak has had great difficulty getting enough federal funding to start high-speed train service on other heavily traveled routes.

Japanese, French, and West German engineers are perfecting a new type of high-speed passenger train called a *magnetic levitation vehicle* (MLV). An MLV track consists of a single guide rail, which the vehicle straddles but does not touch when in motion. MLV's are powered by *linear electric motors*. Magnets on both the motor and the guide rail create a powerful magnetic force. This force holds the vehicle 4 to 6 inches (10 to 15 centimeters) above the guide rail and drives the train forward. MLV's are expected to travel up to 300 mph (480 kph). Japan hopes to open a commercial MLV line by the early 1980's.   MELVIN KRANZBERG

TRANSPORTATION/*Study Aids*

Related Articles in WORLD BOOK. See the *Transportation* section of the state, province, country, and continent articles. See also the following articles:

LAND TRANSPORTATION

Ambulance	Fire Department	Roads and
Amtrak	(Fire Trucks)	Highways
Aqueduct	Jinrikisha	Snowmobile
Automobile	Monorail Railroad	Streetcar
Bridge	Motorcycle	Subway
Bus	Pedicab	Taxicab
Carriage	Petroleum	Tractor
Coach	(Transporting	Travois
Conveyor Belt	Petroleum;	Truck
Electric Railroad	diagram)	Tunnel
Elevated Railroad	Pipeline	Viaduct
Elevator	Railroad	Wagon
Escalator	Recreational Vehicle	Wheel

WATER TRANSPORTATION

Air Cushion Vehicle	Lighthouse	Raft
Barge	Merchant Marine	Ship
Canal	Motorboat	Submarine
Harbor	Port	Tanker

AIR TRANSPORTATION

Airmail	Airport	Aviation	Helicopter
Airplane	Airship	Balloon	

BEASTS OF BURDEN

Camel	Dromedary	Llama	Reindeer
Carabao	Elephant	Mule	Water Buffalo
Donkey	Horse	Ox	Yak

OTHER RELATED ARTICLES

Careers	Exploration	Navigation
(Transportation)	Industrial	Rocket
Coast Guard, U.S.	Revolution	Space Travel
Common Carrier	Interstate	Transportation,
Communication	Commerce	Department of
Containerization	Commission	

Outline

I. Kinds of Transportation
  A. Land Transportation   C. Air Transportation
  B. Water Transportation
II. History
III. Transportation Today
  A. Passenger Transportation   B. Freight Transportation
IV. The Transportation Industry
  A. Equipment Manufacturers
  B. Passenger and Freight Carriers
  C. Related Industries
  D. Government and Transportation

V. Current Developments
  A. Problems of Modern Transportation
  B. Improvements in Public Transportation

Questions

In what countries are automobiles the chief means of passenger transportation?

Why is engine-powered transportation expensive?

Which kinds of transportation facilities in the United States depend almost entirely on government funds?

Who were the first people to build an extensive system of paved roads?

What are the chief mass transit vehicles?

How do pipelines differ from other forms of transportation?

What was the chief means of freight transportation in the United States before the mid-1800's?

Why is the shipment of goods by air limited to expensive, lightweight, or perishable cargo?

Why are most developed countries trying to improve their intercity passenger train service?

What two inventions of late prehistoric times revolutionized transportation during the following centuries?

Reading and Study Guide

See *Transportation* in the RESEARCH GUIDE/INDEX, Volume 22, for a *Reading and Study Guide*.

Additional Resources

Level I

AYLESWORTH, THOMAS G. *Cars, Boats, Trains and Planes of Today and Tomorrow.* Walker, 1975.

GEIL, JOHN J., and JOHNSON, B. S. *Energy and Transportation: Industry and Careers.* Prentice-Hall, 1976.

HELLMAN, HAROLD. *Transportation in the World of the Future.* Rev. ed. Elsevier-Dutton, 1974.

REIT, SEYMOUR. *Sails, Rails and Wings.* Western Publishing, 1978.

ZEHAVI, A. M., ed. *The Complete Junior Encyclopedia of Transportation.* Watts, 1973.

Level II

DUNN, JAMES A. *Miles to Go: European and American Transportation Policies.* MIT Press, 1981.

FARRIS, MARTIN T., and HARDING, FORREST. *Passenger Transportation.* Prentice-Hall, 1976.

REISCHE, DIANA L., ed. *Problems of Mass Transportation.* Wilson, 1970.

SCHAEFFER, K. H., and SCLAR, ELLIOTT. *Access for All: Transportation and Urban Growth.* Penguin, 1975.

TAAFFE, EDWARD J., and GAUTHIER, H. L. *Geography of Transportation.* Prentice-Hall, 1973.

TAYLOR, JOHN W. R., and SWANBOROUGH, F. G. *Civil Aircraft of the World.* Rev. ed. Scribner, 1978.

TRANSPORTATION, DEPARTMENT OF, is an executive department of the United States government. The department develops and promotes national transportation policies and programs. It coordinates programs that provide safe, economical, and efficient transportation on land and sea and in the air. The secretary of transportation, a member of the President's Cabinet, heads the department. Congress established the department in 1966. It began operating in 1967.

Functions. The Department of Transportation includes most of the government agencies and bureaus that administer federal transportation programs. Its chief officials are responsible for coordinating the work of these organizations. The department promotes safety in all methods of transportation. It carries on research and development programs in cooperation with private industry. It conducts studies to identify and solve transportation problems, and to strengthen the weakest parts of the transportation system. It encourages high-quality, low-cost service to the public. The department may recommend to Congress criteria for deciding how to spend federal transportation money.

Organization. The secretary of transportation, who directs the department, is appointed by the President, with the advice and consent of the Senate. Besides directing the department, the secretary serves as the President's chief adviser on transportation matters.

The deputy secretary of transportation is the secretary's chief assistant. The deputy secretary serves as acting secretary in the secretary's absence. The secretary is aided in making decisions by a general counsel and assistant secretaries for administration, budget and programs, governmental affairs, and policy and international affairs.

The Department of Transportation has nine major operating divisions, each headed by an administrator who is responsible directly to the secretary. These divisions are the Federal Aviation Administration, the Federal Highway Administration, the Federal Railroad Administration, the Maritime Administration, the National Highway Traffic Safety Administration, the St. Lawrence Seaway Development Corporation, the United States Coast Guard, the Urban Mass Transportation Administration, and the Research and Special Programs Administration.

The Federal Aviation Administration (FAA) operates air traffic control and navigation systems; certifies civilian pilots, aircraft, and aviation schools; and directs the program of federal aid to airports.

The Federal Highway Administration manages a program that provides financial assistance for states to build highways. The agency's Bureau of Motor Carrier Safety has jurisdiction over the safety performance of motor carriers in interstate or foreign commerce.

The Federal Railroad Administration sets and enforces safety standards for railroads. The agency also conducts research on improved and advanced rail systems, and operates the Alaska Railroad.

The Maritime Administration promotes a strong and efficient United States merchant marine. This fleet consists of more than 4,500 commercial ships.

The National Highway Traffic Safety Administration works to reduce the number of traffic deaths and injuries that occur on the nation's highways. The agency sets standards for vehicle and traffic safety programs.

The St. Lawrence Seaway Development Corporation operates the St. Lawrence Seaway in cooperation with the St. Lawrence Seaway Authority of Canada.

The United States Coast Guard inspects and certifies merchant vessels and licenses civilian sailors. It provides navigational aids, enforces maritime laws, and conducts searches and rescues at sea. In wartime, the Coast Guard becomes an active part of the U.S. Navy.

The Urban Mass Transportation Administration makes federal grants and loans to cities to help provide and improve mass transportation facilities. The administration encourages the planning and establishment of area-wide urban transportation systems.

The Research and Special Programs Administration has responsibility for research and development and for safety regulations, including those covering pipelines and shipping of hazardous materials.

History. The federal government took an active part in transportation long before the Department of Transportation was created. About 100 agencies, bureaus, and divisions have administered federal transportation programs. Since the 1870's, members of both major political parties have tried to consolidate transportation programs under one head. Congress created the Department of Transportation on Oct. 15, 1966.

The department took over several agencies and duties from other executive departments. From the Department of Commerce, it received the Bureau of Public Roads, the Great Lakes Pilotage Administration, the Saint Lawrence Seaway Development Corporation, and the office of the undersecretary for transportation. The Coast Guard was transferred from the Department of the Treasury. The Alaska Railroad was moved from the Department of the Interior. The Federal Aviation Agency, which had been an independent agency, became the Federal Aviation Administration in the new department.

Several agencies that regulate the economic affairs of transportation companies remain outside the department as independent agencies. These include the Federal Maritime Commission and the Interstate Commerce Commission (ICC). However, the safety functions of the ICC were transferred to the department.

Critically reviewed by the DEPARTMENT OF TRANSPORTATION

Related Articles in WORLD BOOK include:

Coast Guard, U.S.
Federal Aviation
  Administration
Federal Highway
  Administration

Flag (picture: Flags
  of the United States
  Government)
Saint Lawrence Seaway De-
  velopment Corporation

Secretaries of Transportation

Name	Took Office	Under President
Alan S. Boyd	1967	Johnson
John A. Volpe	1969	Nixon
Claude S. Brinegar	1973	Nixon, Ford
*William T. Coleman, Jr.	1975	Ford
Brock Adams	1977	Carter
Neil E. Goldschmidt	1979	Carter
Andrew L. Lewis, Jr.	1981	Reagan

*Has a separate biography in WORLD BOOK.

Department of Transportation

Department of Transportation

The Department of Transportation works to develop convenient, economical, and safe transportation throughout the nation. The department's headquarters, *right,* are at 400 Seventh Street SW, Washington, D.C. 20590.

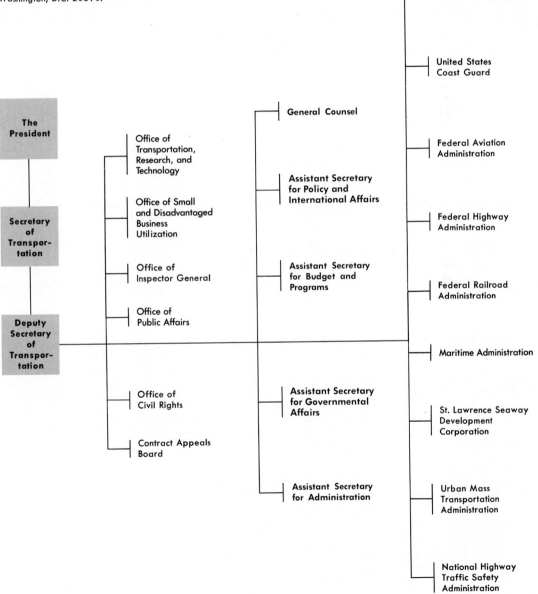

The President

Secretary of Transportation

Deputy Secretary of Transportation

Office of Transportation, Research, and Technology

Office of Small and Disadvantaged Business Utilization

Office of Inspector General

Office of Public Affairs

Office of Civil Rights

Contract Appeals Board

General Counsel

Assistant Secretary for Policy and International Affairs

Assistant Secretary for Budget and Programs

Assistant Secretary for Governmental Affairs

Assistant Secretary for Administration

Research and Special Programs Administration

United States Coast Guard

Federal Aviation Administration

Federal Highway Administration

Federal Railroad Administration

Maritime Administration

St. Lawrence Seaway Development Corporation

Urban Mass Transportation Administration

National Highway Traffic Safety Administration

TRANSPORTATION ACTS. See INTERSTATE COMMERCE COMMISSION.

TRANSSEXUALISM is a condition in which a person who has the anatomy of one sex views himself or herself as a member of the opposite sex. People who view themselves this way are called *transsexuals*. They feel a strong need to act like and be treated as a member of the opposite sex. Transsexualism, also spelled *transexualism*, occurs in more males than females.

Scientists are uncertain about the causes of transsexualism. Some believe that a tendency toward the condition is established before birth. They suspect that hormones within the mother's or the baby's body may affect the sexual development of the unborn child. However, most researchers agree that even if such a tendency exists, a transsexual must have learned to identify with the other sex during early childhood.

Psychotherapy is generally ineffective in treating transsexualism. Some transsexuals seek *reassignment sex-organ surgery* in order to change their external anatomy to that of the opposite sex. Persons considering such surgery are advised to live and dress as a member of the opposite sex for up to two years. By doing so, they confirm that they can succeed as members of the other sex. During this time, they take hormones of the opposite sex in order to change their sexual characteristics. A woman's breasts may also be removed. If a transsexual has adjusted successfully while living as a member of the opposite sex, reassignment sex-organ surgery is performed.　　　　　　　　　　　　　　　JOHN MONEY

TRANS-SIBERIAN RAILROAD was the first railroad built across Siberia, the vast area that makes up most of Asian Russia. When completed, it was the longest railroad in the world. The Trans-Siberian extended more than 5,000 miles (8,000 kilometers) from Yekaterinburg (now Sverdlovsk) and Chelyabinsk in the Ural Mountains to Vladivostok, east of China on the Sea of Japan. It was originally called the Great Siberian Railroad. No railroad in Russia today is officially named the Trans-Siberian Railroad. Today, a train called the Trans-Siberian Express makes the trip from Moscow to Vladivostok in seven days. It runs from Moscow through Kirov to Sverdlovsk, where it joins the original Trans-Siberian Railroad line. It has been electrified between Moscow and Irkutsk.

Construction of the Trans-Siberian marked the beginning of a new era in the development of Siberia. Industries and trade began to develop, and the population grew. The railroad was a valuable Russian asset during the Russo-Japanese War of the early 1900's and World Wars I and II. It was used to transport troops and supplies across Russia's vast territory.

The Trans-Siberian Railroad was built in several sections. It was begun in 1891 and finished in 1916. The section in eastern Siberia, between Vladivostok and Khabarovsk, had been completed about 1897. From 1892 to 1912, other sections were built across western and central Siberia. Between 1897 and 1903, Russia built the Chinese Eastern Railway across Manchuria, in northeast China. This railroad connected Vladivostok with the sections of the Trans-Siberian Railroad in western and central Siberia. By 1904, a continuous railroad stretched from the city of Vladivostok across China and Siberia to the Ural Mountains.

The Russians wanted a railroad route that did not cross China. Therefore, they built a line north of China from Khabarovsk to Kuenga. Completed in 1916, it was the last link in a continuous railroad on Russian soil between Vladivostok and the Ural Mountains. Another railroad led from the Urals west to Moscow. The Trans-Siberian (excluding the Chinese Eastern Railway) cost about $500 million to build.

Since the 1920's, the Trans-Siberian has been connected to other railroads in Russia. The lines along the Trans-Siberian route are part of the railroad network that connects all parts of Russia.　　THEODORE SHABAD

TRANSUBSTANTIATION, *TRAN sub STAN shee AY shun,* is the Roman Catholic belief that bread and wine are changed into the body and blood of Jesus Christ during Mass. The change takes place in the sacrament of *Holy Eucharist* (Communion). The term was defined and adopted at the Council of Trent in the mid-1500's. Although the term *transubstantiation* is peculiarly Roman Catholic, the doctrine it represents is similar to that of the Eastern Orthodox Churches.　　FRANCIS L. FILAS

TRANSURANIUM ELEMENTS, *TRANS yoo RAY nee uhm,* are artificially created elements that are heavier than uranium, which has an atomic number of 92. The known transuranium elements are those with atomic numbers from 93 to 107. They are: neptunium (Np), plutonium (Pu), americium (Am), curium (Cm), berkelium (Bk), californium (Cf), einsteinium (Es), fermium (Fm), mendelevium (Md), nobelium (No), and lawrencium (Lr). Each element has a separate article in WORLD BOOK. Scientists have produced isotopes of most of these elements by nuclear bombardment (see ISOTOPE [Artificial Radioisotopes]). These elements are subject to radioactive decay, and are chemically similar to the rare-earth elements. See also SEABORG, GLENN T.; RADIOACTIVITY; RARE EARTH.　　ROBERT L. THORNTON

TRANSVAAL, *trans VAHL,* is the name of one of the provinces of South Africa. It lies in the northern part of the country. The name *Transvaal* means *beyond the Vaal.* The first Boer settlers in the early 1800's gave this name to the region because it lay beyond the Vaal River. Pretoria is the capital and second largest city of Transvaal. Johannesburg has more people. Pretoria is also the administrative capital of South Africa.

The Transvaal covers 109,621 square miles (283,917 square kilometers). Over three-fourths of the 8,901,054 people are Bantus. Almost 2 million are white.

Wide and generally treeless plains called the *veld* cover most of the Transvaal. Plains in the eastern and southern parts lie as high as 6,000 feet (1,800 meters) above sea level. In the east, the range of mountains known as Drakensberg reaches a height of 8,725 feet (2,659 meters). The Vaal River and its branches water the southwestern Transvaal, a fertile farming area. The *Witwatersrand* (White Waters Ridge), a district in the southern part of the Transvaal, ranks as South Africa's chief industrial area. It has many factories and the world's richest gold mines.　　LEONARD M. THOMPSON

See also BOER WAR; JOHANNESBURG; PRETORIA; SOUTH AFRICA (History; map).

TRANSVERSE ARCH, or METATARSAL ARCH, is one of the two bony arches of the foot. It is located across the ball of the foot, directly behind the toes. It is formed by the heads of the large bones of the feet. When a person walks, the arch spreads. This lets the weight down gently. See also FOOT.

TRANSYLVANIA, TRAN sul VAYN yuh, is a geographical region of Romania near the Hungarian border. It covers an area of about 39,000 square miles (101,000 square kilometers). The majority of its 7½ million people are Romanians. But about 1½ million Magyars, or Hungarians, also live there. The Carpathian Mountains and Transylvanian Alps separate the region from the rest of Romania. See ROMANIA (map).

Transylvania has rich deposits of iron, lead, lignite, manganese, and sulfur. It is also an important source of natural gas. The surrounding mountains are covered with beech and oak trees. Transylvania's high plains make good grazing grounds for cattle and sheep. Its valleys produce large bean, corn, potato, tobacco, rice, and wheat crops. The region's largest city is Cluj.

History. For years, Romania and Hungary quarreled over Transylvania. Magyars conquered the Romanians in the 900's. From 1526 to 1699, Transylvania was part of the Ottoman (Turkish) Empire. It was under Hungarian control from 1699 to 1867, when it once again became part of Hungary. During World War I, Romania joined the Allies after being promised Transylvania. After the war, Transylvania became part of Romania. In August, 1940, Germany and Italy forced Romania to give northern Transylvania to Hungary. After World War II, Transylvania was returned to Romania, and lost its political identity. ALVIN Z. RUBINSTEIN

TRAP-DOOR SPIDER digs a burrow in the ground and covers the entrance with a lid, or trap door. These spiders live in warm climates, including the southern and western United States. They are harmless to man. Some grow more than 1 inch (2.5 centimeters) long.

Trap-door spiders use their burrows for protection and as nests in which to raise young. The burrows are lined with silk. Some burrows are more than 10 inches (25 centimeters) deep and over 1 inch (2.5 centimeters) wide. Some trap-door spiders dig simple, tubelike burrows. Others dig burrows that have a branch tunnel. The branch tunnel, sometimes hidden by a second trap door, serves as an extra hiding place.

The trap doors are made of silk and mud, and are attached to the lining of the burrows by silk hinges. Some trap-door spiders build thin, waferlike doors that cover the burrow entrance loosely. Others construct thick doors, like corks, that fit so snugly into the tunnel entrance they are watertight. Still others build circular folding doors that open in the middle.

Trap-door spiders eat insects, including many kinds that damage valuable plants and flowers. The spider waits behind its door until its prey walks by. Then it quickly opens the door, seizes and poisons its victim, and drags it into the burrow. Trap-door spiders are timid, and the females seldom leave their nests. These spiders are a type of *tarantula* (see TARANTULA).

Scientific Classification. Trap-door spiders make up the trap-door spider family, *Ctenizidae*. The best known trap-door spider in the United States is genus *Bothriocyrtum*, species *B. californicum*. H. K. WALLACE

TRAPEZOID. See QUADRILATERAL.

TRAPPER. See TRAPPING.

TRAPPING is the capture or killing of wild animals in traps. It was one of the first methods by which people obtained animals for food and clothing. Later, people

Trap-Door Spider's Home, *left,* is a silk-lined burrow. The spider makes the trap door, *above,* out of silk and mud, and attaches it to the burrow's lining with silk hinges.

Lee Passmore

The Spider's Silk Egg Sac is spun in the burrow. It contains about 300 white eggs.

began to trap for profit. In North America, many pioneers of the 1700's and 1800's became wealthy by trapping the various fur-bearing animals that roamed the wilderness. They sold the pelts of the animals for use in making fashionable fur garments.

Today, much of the fur supply comes from the manufacture of artificial furs and from farms that raise fur-bearing animals. But many people trap for sport and profit. Popular fur-bearing animals of the United States and Canada include beavers, martens, minks, muskrats, opossums, otters, raccoons, and skunks. Methods of trapping may be found in books at many libraries and in pamphlets published by state agencies.

In some parts of the world, people still trap animals for food and clothing. Some African tribes, for example, trap antelope and monkeys for food. People also trap for other reasons. For example, scientists trap wild animals unharmed to study their habits. Farmers and ranchers use traps to catch such animals as coyotes and foxes, which kill chickens and sheep. These animals that prey on other animals are called *predators*. Many homeowners trap mice, moles, and other pests that ruin lawns or invade cupboards looking for food.

Water color (1858) by Alfred Jacob Miller; Walters Art Gallery, Baltimore, Md.

Beaver Trapping was a profitable occupation for the first white settlers of North America. They used steel traps held in place by a chain and stake. The trappers sold the pelts or traded them for food and other things they needed. Most beaver pelts were made into hats.

Kinds of Traps. There are three main types of traps: (1) arresting traps, (2) enclosing traps, and (3) exterminating traps. Bait can be used in any trap, but it may not be necessary.

Arresting Traps grip animals but do not kill them. The most common kind of arresting trap is the *steel trap*. Manufacturers make steel traps of various sizes and shapes to catch such animals as raccoons and skunks. Steel traps have jaws that operate with a steel spring and grip an animal by the foot or leg. Some steel traps have teeth that can hurt an animal badly if it struggles to get free. Great Britain considers steel traps inhumane and bans them. Some states of the United States forbid steel traps with teeth.

Enclosing Traps hold animals unharmed. A common type is the *box* or *cage* trap. The trapper uses bait to lure an animal into a box trap, and a door then closes and imprisons it. Animal collectors and scientists often use box traps to catch animals for zoos or research. Scientists may trap an animal and tag it so they can follow the creature's movements after freeing it from the trap. Many people use box traps to catch raccoons, squirrels, or other animals in their gardens or homes. They then release the animals in an unpopulated area.

Exterminating Traps grip animals and kill them. They include the *mousetrap* used in many homes and barns. A mousetrap has metal rods that snap shut by means of a coiled spring and break the victim's neck. Another exterminating trap, widely used for catching beavers and muskrats, is the *Conibear*. The metal rods of this trap

Ed Cesar, NAS

Animals Can Be Caught Alive with box traps. This lynx is being pulled from a trap with a looped snare attached to a pole. The animal will then be caged and sent to a zoo.

Kinds of Traps
The type of trap a person uses depends on the kind of animal being trapped and on whether the animal is to be unharmed or killed. Bait can be used in any trap, but it may not be necessary. For example, trapping minks and muskrats seldom requires bait. The trapper simply conceals the traps in areas where the animals live and waits for them to trap themselves.

Enclosing Traps   **Arresting Traps**   **Exterminating Traps**

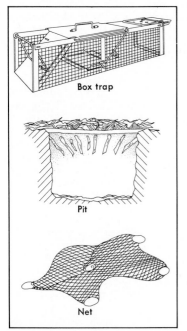

Box trap

Pit

Net

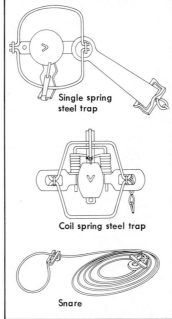

Single spring
steel trap

Coil spring steel trap

Snare

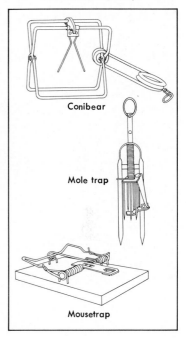

Conibear

Mole trap

Mousetrap

clutch the animal in a "scissors" grip and crush it to death instantly.

Trapping and Wildlife Conservation. Wildlife conservation groups often criticize any trapping that involves killing animals. They fear that certain animals may become extinct if people continue to hunt them.

Some people believe that trapping predators upsets the balance of nature (see BALANCE OF NATURE). They feel that killing predators will in time result in an oversupply of rodents and other animals that predators eat. But others disagree. They point out that when some species of animals become too numerous, the population of predators increases because the predators have a larger food supply.

Through the years, many states have tried to preserve wildlife with various laws, including total bans on the trapping of certain animals. Some states, for example, forbid bear trapping. In the United States, trapping laws vary from state to state. Each state issues trapping licenses and determines where animals may be trapped and during what seasons. State agencies also decide what species may be trapped and set limits on the number of animals that may be trapped at one time.

The federal Endangered Species Act of 1973 forbids the hunting and trapping of any endangered species in the United States. It also prohibits the importation of any endangered species or of products made from any such species. Supporters of this law believe that fewer of these animals will be trapped and hunted in other countries if there is no U.S. market for them. Under the

act, special permits may be issued to exclude animals to be used for research. JOHN W. PETERSON

See also FUR.

TRAPPISTS, *TRAP ihsts,* are monks who belong to a Roman Catholic order called the Order of Cistercians of the Strict Observance. Trappists devote most of their time to prayer and meditation. But they do manual labor several hours a day. They sleep on boards and straw pillows, and observe strict rules of fasting and silence. Trappists follow these strict rules to do penance for sin. The head of a Cistercian monastery in La Trappe, France, reformed the Cistercian order in 1664. The reformed order came to be known as *Trappists,* after the monastery's name. FRANCIS L. FILAS

See also CISTERCIANS.

TRAPSHOOTING is the sport of shooting at saucer-shaped targets called *clay pigeons.* They are sprung into the air from a trap. The pastime began in England about 1830, when wealthy landowners set up much of the hunting land as private preserves. The game was not available to small farmers. The farmers experimented with a substitute sport, first by shooting at small birds which they released from under their hats. Soon they used glass balls, and finally clay pigeons.

Trapshooting came to the United States late in the 1870's. In 1923, the Amateur Trapshooting Association was formed. In singles and doubles, competitors fire at the clay targets with shotguns from a distance of 16 yards (15 meters) behind the trap. In handicap shooting, they stand from 18 to 27 yards (16 to 25 meters) be-

Marvin Christian, *Trap & Field Magazine*

Trapshooters from Many Parts of the World compete in the annual Grand American Tournament, *above*, in Vandalia, Ohio. This event is sponsored by the Amateur Trapshooting Association.

hind the trap, depending on past performances of the individual. JACK O'CONNOR

TRAUMA, *TRAW muh*, in psychiatry, is an unpleasant emotional experience of such intensity that it leaves a lasting impression on the mind. Psychiatrists believe that childhood traumatic experiences sometimes lead to later neurotic symptoms (see NEUROSIS). Emotional experiences take place in everyone's childhood, and certainly have an effect upon the adult personality. The study of such childhood traumas plays an important part in the psychotherapeutic treatment given to the emotionally ill (see PSYCHOTHERAPY).

An injury or a wound is also called a trauma. See TRAUMA CENTER. GEORGE A. ULETT

TRAUMA CENTER is a specialized area of a hospital that treats only persons suffering from *trauma* (serious accidental injury). Some hospitals are devoted entirely to trauma care. In the United States, trauma kills an average of about 110,000 persons annually. From 20 to 50 per cent of these people die because they do not promptly receive suitable medical care.

Trauma centers have specialized equipment and permanent staffs of physicians, nurses, and paramedics who are skilled in emergency lifesaving techniques. Staff members provide first aid at the accident site and rapid transportation by ambulance or helicopter to the center itself. Trauma centers developed from military hospitals that provided such service during the Korean War (1950-1953) and the Vietnam War (1957-1975).

One of the most extensive trauma care systems was established by Illinois in 1971. This statewide system

has four kinds of trauma centers: (1) local, (2) areawide, (3) regional, and (4) specialized. Local centers serve rural areas. After receiving basic treatment in a local trauma unit, the most seriously injured accident victims may be transferred to an areawide, regional, or specialized center. Areawide centers have such facilities as blood banks, intensive-care units, laboratory services, operating rooms, and specialized X-ray units. Regional centers are located within university medical centers. They have highly trained staffs and can provide sophisticated treatment for seriously injured patients. Specialized trauma centers treat such problems as spinal cord injuries and children's trauma.

In 1969, Maryland opened a statewide trauma hospital in Baltimore called the Maryland Institute for Emergency Medical Services. Helicopters pick up accident victims and fly them directly to the institute. In the mid-1970's, several U.S. cities established local trauma centers, and a number of states were considering statewide systems. DAVID R. BOYD

TRAVEL. See AIRPLANE (Airplanes of Today); AUTOMOBILE; BUS; RAILROAD (pictures); SHIP (Passenger Vessels); SPACE TRAVEL; TRANSPORTATION; also the Places to Visit section in WORLD BOOK state and province articles, such as TEXAS (Places to Visit).

TRAVEL AGENCY is a business that helps people plan trips. A travel agency simplifies the job of planning a trip by handling many travel arrangements. It makes reservations for hotel rooms and transportation and arranges sightseeing tours. It supplies customers with applications for passports, which travelers need for foreign travel. A travel agency also provides customers with information on the travel regulations of the United States and other governments. Travel agencies arrange tours for individuals and for groups.

Most of the income of travel agencies comes from commissions paid by airlines, car rental companies, hotels, tour operators, and other businesses that serve travelers. These businesses pay a commission on each reservation that an agency makes or on each ticket it sells. Travelers pay nothing for most services. But agencies may charge a fee for planning individual tours that require much of their time and effort.

Travel agencies operate in most countries of the world. In the mid-1970's, the United States and Canada had more than 10,000 agencies. In Russia and some Eastern European countries, the government owns and runs all travel agencies.

In the mid-1970's, some professional travel agent associations and many individuals in the United States urged Congress to provide for government regulation of travel agencies. They believed such regulation was needed to establish standards of ethical conduct for travel agents. MILTON A. MARKS

TRAVELERS AID is a social service for persons who are in difficulty when traveling or who are newcomers to a community. The service helps nearly 2 million persons each year, including children traveling alone, the elderly, immigrants, runaways, and the unemployed. Travelers Aid provides counseling and helps people obtain clothing, food, jobs or job training, medical aid, shelter, and other assistance.

About 80 local Travelers Aid societies and more than 800 cooperating organizations form a network serving about 3,000 communities in Canada, Mexico, Puerto

Rico, and the United States. Many of these organizations operate service offices in such locations as airports and bus stations. All of these organizations belong to the Travelers Aid Association of America (TAAA). TAAA was founded in 1917. It has headquarters at 701 Lee Street, Des Plaines, Ill. 60016. Critically reviewed by the TRAVELERS AID ASSOCIATION OF AMERICA

TRAVELER'S CHECK is a check that can be used as money or as a letter of credit. Banks and travel agencies issue traveler's checks. The purpose of traveler's checks is to protect the money carried by travelers. People sign the checks when they buy them and again when they spend them.

Marcellus F. Berry, general agent of the American Express Company, originated the system of traveler's checks in 1891. Today people buy millions of dollars' worth of these checks every year.

In the United States, such checks are issued in denominations of $10, $20, $50, and $100. Almost any bank, or any travel or express agency, sells them and adds a small fee. People can redeem them in foreign currencies abroad at the rate of exchange when converted. Thus, travelers bear the risk of exchange fluctuation. If travelers plan to be chiefly in the United Kingdom, they may buy sterling checks to avoid this risk. Traveler's checks are accepted the world over in payment for accommodations or merchandise, or in exchange for currency. JAMES B. LUDTKE

See also LETTER OF CREDIT.

TRAVELLER. See LEE, ROBERT EDWARD (picture).

TRAVERS, MORRIS WILLIAM. See KRYPTON; NEON.

TRAVERS, PAMELA (1906-   ), an Australian writer, is best known for her books about Mary Poppins, a favorite children's character. These works include *Mary Poppins* (1934) and *Mary Poppins Comes Back* (1935). Miss Travers was born of Irish parents in North Queensland, Australia, and began writing stories when she was seven years old. When she was 17, she wrote poetry which was first published in *The Irish Statesman*. From 1923 to 1936, she acted in Shakespearean plays in England. JEAN THOMSON

TRAVERTINE, *TRAV uhr tihn*, or *TRAV uhr teen*, is a dense, closely compacted form of limestone found mostly in banded layers. Most travertine is white or cream colored. It consists mainly of calcium carbonate and has the chemical formula $CaCO_3$. It forms when calcium carbonate separates from water through evaporation. Travertine is often used as decorative building stone because it is easy to cut.

Travertine occurs in areas where limestone is common and where circulating ground water contains calcium carbonate. It often forms around the mouths of hot springs and in streams. Rock formations called *stalactites* and *stalagmites*, which are found in caves, consist chiefly of travertine (see STALACTITE; STALAGMITE).

The word *travertine* comes from an old Roman name for Tivoli, a town in Italy where large deposits of travertine occur. In the United States, travertine forms around the Mammoth Hot Springs in Yellowstone National Park. MARY EMMA WAGNER

TRAVIS, WILLIAM BARRET (1809-1836), was one of the heroes of the Alamo. He commanded the Texas patriots who died defending the Alamo against the Mexicans in 1836. Travis was born near Red Bank, S.C. He taught school and practiced law in Alabama before he

moved to Texas in 1831. Travis also led troops at Anahuac and San Antonio. H. BAILEY CARROLL

See also ALAMO.

TRAVOIS, *trah VOY*, is a device used by American Indians and other peoples for carrying loads. It consists of two poles, a net or platform lashed between, and a harness for hitching the device to a horse or dog. A travois has no wheels. The ends of the poles drag on the ground. FRANKLIN M. RECK

See also TRANSPORTATION (picture: Prehistoric Times).

TRAWL. See FISHING INDUSTRY (Nets).

TREADMILL, *TREHD mihl*, is a wheeled mechanism rotated by people or animals walking on or inside the wheel. A treadmill with an axle is called a *wheel and axle* (see WHEEL AND AXLE). The movement of the wheel turns the axle and any mechanical device to which it is attached.

The ancient Romans used treadmills for such tasks as grinding grain, lifting water out of mines, and powering cranes that hoisted construction materials. People and such animals as cows and horses provided the power for these devices. Treadmills were used for heavy work until the 1700's and 1800's, when they were replaced by steam and hydraulic engines. Today, many people exercise indoors by jogging on a device that resembles a treadmill. Tiny treadwheels provide exercise for hamsters and other small pets in cages. MELVIN KRANZBERG

TREASON, *TREE zuhn*, once meant disloyalty to a sovereign ruler, such as a king. People who criticized the ruler's policies and actions might find themselves convicted of treason. But today, the meaning of treason has changed. The people in a democratic country can criticize the government, and work as freely as they like for the election of a new government. The United States Constitution clearly defines treason as:

"Treason against the United States shall consist only in levying war against them or in adhering to their enemies, giving them aid and comfort." See CONSTITUTION OF THE UNITED STATES (Article III [Section 3]).

This definition protects the right of citizens to oppose the actions of their government in all reasonable ways. Congress determines by law what the penalties shall be for treason against the United States. Many states have laws against treason. Death or life imprisonment is the usual penalty. A person convicted of treason is usually called a *traitor*.

A famous case of treason in modern times is that of Julius and Ethel Rosenberg. The Rosenbergs were convicted under the General Espionage Act of 1917 of supplying Russia with atomic secrets in World War II. During appeals, their lawyers pointed out that Russia was an ally of the U.S. at the time the Rosenbergs passed secrets. But the husband and wife were executed in 1953. Another famous trial for treason in the United States was that of Aaron Burr, the country's third Vice-President. Burr was acquitted. FRED E. INBAU

Related Articles in WORLD BOOK include:

Arnold, Benedict	Quisling, Vidkun
Brown, John	Rosenberg
Burr, Aaron	Sedition
Dreyfus, Alfred	

TREASURE ISLAND. See STEVENSON, ROBERT LOUIS.
TREASURE STATE. See MONTANA.

TREASURY, DEPARTMENT OF THE, is an executive department of the United States government. Among its important jobs are collecting federal taxes and customs duties. It receives all money paid to the government, serves as custodian of the government's revenues, pays federal government expenses, and keeps accounts of government revenues and expenditures.

The Treasury Department prepares all paper money, coins, and federal securities. It also supervises the operation of national banks. Upon authorization from Congress, the department borrows money for the federal government and manages the national debt.

The department makes and carries out policies relating to the international economic, financial, and monetary field. For example, it has responsibilities in U.S. balance of payments problems. It also enforces anti-smuggling laws, prevents counterfeiting, and protects the President and Vice-President.

The Secretary of the Treasury heads the department. The secretary is appointed by the President with the approval of the Senate, and is a member of the President's Cabinet. The secretary advises the President on financial policies and reports to Congress each year on the nation's finances. Chief staff members include a deputy secretary, two undersecretaries, a general counsel, and 10 assistant secretaries.

The department's operating bureaus include:

Bureau of Alcohol, Tobacco, and Firearms supervises the production and distribution of alcohol and tobacco. It also checks the illegal possession and use of firearms and explosives.

Bureau of Engraving and Printing prints money and securities.

Bureau of the Mint manufactures coins. See MINT.

Federal Law Enforcement Training Center trains law enforcement agents of the Treasury Department and other government agencies.

Fiscal Service has two agencies. The Bureau of Government Financial Operations issues checks for most government agencies, records receipts and expenditures of all public funds, and supervises the issue and redemption of U.S. currency. The Bureau of the Public Debt administers and keeps records of the public debt.

Internal Revenue Service assesses and collects taxes imposed by federal law. See INTERNAL REVENUE SERVICE.

Office of the Comptroller of the Currency charters the national banks. It also directs a periodic inspection

Secretaries of the Treasury

Name	Took Office	Under President	Name	Took Office	Under President
* Alexander Hamilton	1789	Washington	William Windom	1881	Garfield, Arthur
* Oliver Wolcott, Jr.	1795	Washington, Adams	Charles J. Folger	1881	Arthur
			Walter Q. Gresham	1884	Arthur
Samuel Dexter	1801	Adams, Jefferson	Hugh McCulloch	1884	Arthur
* Albert Gallatin	1801	Jefferson, Madison	Daniel Manning	1885	Cleveland
			Charles S. Fairchild	1887	Cleveland
George W. Campbell	1814	Madison	William Windom	1889	B. Harrison
Alexander J. Dallas	1814	Madison	Charles Foster	1891	B. Harrison
* William H. Crawford	1816	Madison, Monroe	John G. Carlisle	1893	Cleveland
Richard Rush	1825	J. Q. Adams	Lyman J. Gage	1897	McKinley, T. Roosevelt
Samuel D. Ingham	1829	Jackson			
Louis McLane	1831	Jackson	Leslie M. Shaw	1902	T. Roosevelt
William J. Duane	1833	Jackson	George B. Cortelyou	1907	T. Roosevelt
* Roger B. Taney	1833	Jackson	Franklin MacVeagh	1909	Taft
Levi Woodbury	1834	Jackson, Van Buren	William G. McAdoo	1913	Wilson
			* Carter Glass	1918	Wilson
Thomas Ewing	1841	W. H. Harrison, Tyler	David F. Houston	1920	Wilson
			* Andrew W. Mellon	1921	Harding, Coolidge, Hoover
Walter Forward	1841	Tyler			
John C. Spencer	1843	Tyler	Ogden L. Mills	1932	Hoover
George M. Bibb	1844	Tyler	William H. Woodin	1933	F. D. Roosevelt
Robert J. Walker	1845	Polk	* Henry Morgenthau, Jr.	1934	F. D. Roosevelt, Truman
William M. Meredith	1849	Taylor			
Thomas Corwin	1850	Fillmore	* Frederick M. Vinson	1945	Truman
James Guthrie	1853	Pierce	John W. Snyder	1946	Truman
Howell Cobb	1857	Buchanan	George M. Humphrey	1953	Eisenhower
Philip F. Thomas	1860	Buchanan	Robert B. Anderson	1957	Eisenhower
John A. Dix	1861	Buchanan	Douglas Dillon	1961	Kennedy, L. B. Johnson
* Salmon P. Chase	1861	Lincoln			
* William P. Fessenden	1864	Lincoln	* Henry H. Fowler	1965	L. B. Johnson
Hugh McCulloch	1865	Lincoln, A. Johnson	Joseph W. Barr	1968	L. B. Johnson
			* David M. Kennedy	1969	Nixon
George S. Boutwell	1869	Grant	* John B. Connally	1971	Nixon
William A. Richardson	1873	Grant	George P. Shultz	1972	Nixon
Benjamin H. Bristow	1874	Grant	* William E. Simon	1974	Nixon, Ford
Lot M. Morrill	1876	Grant	W. Michael Blumenthal	1977	Carter
* John Sherman	1877	Hayes	G. William Miller	1979	Carter
			Donald T. Regan	1981	Reagan

*Has a separate biography in WORLD BOOK.

Department of the Treasury

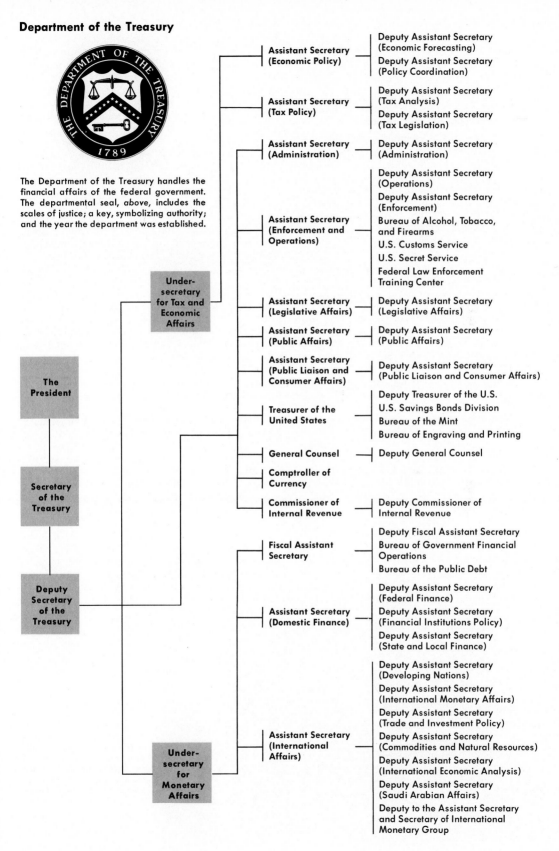

The Department of the Treasury handles the financial affairs of the federal government. The departmental seal, *above*, includes the scales of justice; a key, symbolizing authority; and the year the department was established.

The President

Secretary of the Treasury

Deputy Secretary of the Treasury

Under-secretary for Tax and Economic Affairs

Under-secretary for Monetary Affairs

Assistant Secretary (Economic Policy)
- Deputy Assistant Secretary (Economic Forecasting)
- Deputy Assistant Secretary (Policy Coordination)

Assistant Secretary (Tax Policy)
- Deputy Assistant Secretary (Tax Analysis)
- Deputy Assistant Secretary (Tax Legislation)

Assistant Secretary (Administration)
- Deputy Assistant Secretary (Administration)

Assistant Secretary (Enforcement and Operations)
- Deputy Assistant Secretary (Operations)
- Deputy Assistant Secretary (Enforcement)
- Bureau of Alcohol, Tobacco, and Firearms
- U.S. Customs Service
- U.S. Secret Service
- Federal Law Enforcement Training Center

Assistant Secretary (Legislative Affairs)
- Deputy Assistant Secretary (Legislative Affairs)

Assistant Secretary (Public Affairs)
- Deputy Assistant Secretary (Public Affairs)

Assistant Secretary (Public Liaison and Consumer Affairs)
- Deputy Assistant Secretary (Public Liaison and Consumer Affairs)

Treasurer of the United States
- Deputy Treasurer of the U.S.
- U.S. Savings Bonds Division
- Bureau of the Mint
- Bureau of Engraving and Printing

General Counsel
- Deputy General Counsel

Comptroller of Currency

Commissioner of Internal Revenue
- Deputy Commissioner of Internal Revenue

Fiscal Assistant Secretary
- Deputy Fiscal Assistant Secretary
- Bureau of Government Financial Operations
- Bureau of the Public Debt

Assistant Secretary (Domestic Finance)
- Deputy Assistant Secretary (Federal Finance)
- Deputy Assistant Secretary (Financial Institutions Policy)
- Deputy Assistant Secretary (State and Local Finance)

Assistant Secretary (International Affairs)
- Deputy Assistant Secretary (Developing Nations)
- Deputy Assistant Secretary (International Monetary Affairs)
- Deputy Assistant Secretary (Trade and Investment Policy)
- Deputy Assistant Secretary (Commodities and Natural Resources)
- Deputy Assistant Secretary (International Economic Analysis)
- Deputy Assistant Secretary (Saudi Arabian Affairs)
- Deputy to the Assistant Secretary and Secretary of International Monetary Group

of these banks. See COMPTROLLER OF THE CURRENCY.

United States Customs Service collects duties on imports and prevents illegal entry of goods. See CUSTOMS SERVICE, UNITED STATES.

United States Savings Bonds Division promotes the sale of the savings bonds issued by the United States government. See SAVINGS BOND.

United States Secret Service guards against counterfeiting. It protects the President, the President's family, the Vice-President, and certain other persons. See SECRET SERVICE, U.S.

History. The Department of the Treasury, established on Sept. 2, 1789, was the second executive department created by the first Congress. Alexander Hamilton was the first secretary of the treasury, and his department had five employees. The department now employs about 120,000 persons.

Critically reviewed by the DEPARTMENT OF THE TREASURY

See also FLAG (picture: Flags of the U.S. Government); MINT; MONEY.

TREATY. A treaty is a formal agreement between two or more independent governments. It is usually a written document, but it may be a verbal statement agreed to by representatives of the countries. The history of treaty making goes back many hundreds of years. As early as 3000 B.C., rulers of ancient countries signed treaties with neighboring kingdoms. The treaties served various purposes. Some treaties ended wars, and others settled boundary disputes. But through the history of the world, treaties have played an important part in the relations between countries.

Today only sovereign states are able to make treaties. A sovereign state is one which is free from outside control. For example, Great Britain is a sovereign state because its government is free to make its own decisions. But the British colony of Gibraltar is not free to make its own decisions. It is therefore not a sovereign state, and cannot make its own treaties.

A treaty is much like a contract between private individuals. In both cases, the signing parties promise to do or not do some act. But there are important differences between treaties and contracts. A contract is not binding if one of the parties has forced the other party into agreement. But the use of force does not make a treaty void unless the force is actually used against the government representative who is working out the treaty terms. Unlike a private contract, a treaty does not go into effect until it is *ratified*. For example, a treaty between the United States and Great Britain is not official until it is approved by the United States Senate and by the British Crown.

There are several kinds of international agreements which have the force of treaties. One of these is called a *convention*. This is usually an agreement between states relating to a single topic, such as extradition. A *concordat* is an agreement between the pope and a sovereign state. An agreement between two monarchs on a private matter is not a treaty.

Kinds of Treaties. Treaties may be divided into several classes according to their purposes, although international law recognizes no formal distinctions among treaties. A single treaty may include clauses under several classes. Some of the classes are described below.

Political. A peace treaty is one kind of political treaty. For example, the Treaty of Ghent in 1814 ended the War of 1812. Others deal with alliances between countries and settle disputes. The Clayton-Bulwer Treaty in 1850 gave the United States and Britain equal protection rights in a future canal through Central America.

Commercial. Commercial treaties include agreements on tariffs, navigation, fisheries, and consular services. The Elgin-Marcy Treaty of 1854 between the United States and Canada is an example of a commercial treaty. By this treaty, the United States and Canada agreed to reduce the taxes on goods imported from each other.

Confederation. These treaties set up such international organizations as the Universal Postal Union.

Extradition. These treaties deal with escaped criminals. For example, let us suppose that two countries have signed an extradition treaty. If a criminal from one country flees to the other for safety, the criminal must be returned, or *extradited*, to stand trial for the crime.

Civil Justice. These treaties protect a country's trademarks, copyrights, and patents in foreign countries. Some civil-justice treaties deal with the rights of aliens.

Negotiation. In monarchies, the king or queen usually has the power to make treaties and is represented at negotiations by a diplomatic agent, or *envoy*. For example, in Great Britain neither house of Parliament has any power over treaties. That power is re-

An Indian Treaty was made by Peter Minuit at Fort Amsterdam. Today, this little trading post is the metropolis of New York City. The walls of the old fort are responsible for the name of the world-famous financial center—Wall Street.

The Ratification of the Hay-Pauncefote Treaty, sent by Great Britain to the United States, bears a pendant seal and tassels.

served for the Crown. British dominions, such as Canada and Australia, have the right to make their own treaties.

In republics, the chief executive usually has treaty-making power. This power is often subject to various restrictions. In the United States the President may enter into a treaty with "the advice and consent" of the Senate. Two-thirds of the Senators present must agree to the treaty terms. Separate states in the United States may not make any treaty agreements. The Department of State carries on treaty negotiations. Sometimes the President of the United States enters into an *executive agreement* with a foreign country. This kind of agreement has the force of a treaty in international law, but it does not require Senate approval.

Language Used. Until the 1700's all treaties were written in Latin. Then French became the official language. Today most treaties are written in the various languages of the treaty-making nations.

Enforcement of Treaties. In ancient times a country had to "back up," or guarantee, its treaty promises. One way of doing this was to exchange hostages. Each country which signed the treaty would send one or more important persons to the other countries which had agreed to the treaty. Hostages were held as prisoners. They could be killed if the terms of the treaty were not carried out.

The hostage system has not been used for many years. Today, most countries rely on the good faith of other countries, and on international public opinion. But often these are not enough. Treaties have been violated in the 1900's, just as in earlier times. When World War I broke out, the German government declared that the treaty which protected Belgian neutrality was a "scrap of paper," and invaded Belgium. Under the dictatorship of Adolf Hitler, Germany violated treaties with many other European countries. After World War II, people pinned their hopes for peace on the United Nations, and the recommendations it made for the settlement of international problems which arose.

Termination. Treaties may be ended in many ways. They may end upon the agreement of all parties concerned. Sometimes a treaty clause permits either party to cancel the agreement after due notice. The failure of one country to carry out its part of the agreement may cause the other country or countries to refuse to observe the treaty terms. A treaty becomes void when the physical conditions of the agreement become impossible to fulfill. For example, two countries may agree to the mutual use of a waterway. But if an earthquake makes the waterway unfit for navigation, the treaty is automatically canceled. War nullifies many treaties.

Ecclesiastical Treaties deal with the religious rights of people who are living in a foreign country. Among Western nations, people may worship as freely in foreign lands as in their homelands. In several non-Christian parts of the world, Christian missionaries are permitted by treaty to teach the beliefs of Christianity. In some countries ecclesiastical treaties permit foreign residents to practice their own religions, but forbid them to try to convert others.   TELFORD TAYLOR

Related Articles. The principal treaties among nations are listed in THE WORLD BOOK ENCYCLOPEDIA under their respective titles, such as CLAYTON-BULWER TREATY; GHENT, TREATY OF. See also the following articles:

Arbitration   International Law   Protocol
Extradition   International Relations

TREATY OF 1783. See REVOLUTIONARY WAR IN AMERICA (The Peace Treaty); PARIS, TREATIES OF (Treaty of 1783).

TREATY PORT. Through the years, foreign powers have used different methods to gain trading rights in China. One of these methods was to persuade the Chinese government to open certain Chinese seaports to foreign trade. These cities were known as treaty ports because trade with foreign countries was carried on under treaty agreement at these ports.

In 1842, China entered into a treaty-port agreement with Great Britain. This treaty opened five Chinese ports to British trade. The ports open to Britain were Canton, Amoy, Fu-chou, Ning-po, and Shanghai. Later, China signed treaty-port agreements with many other countries, including the United States, Germany, Russia, and Mexico. By 1894 there were more than 60 treaty ports in China. Most treaty-port agreements were forced upon China by foreign pressure or wars. Treaty ports gave many special privileges to foreign countries. The foreigners who enjoyed privileges in treaty ports could not even be punished under Chinese laws.

In 1912 China began to object to treaty-port agreements. After World War I, Russia gave up its rights in China, and in 1929 Mexico did the same. In 1943 both Great Britain and the United States signed treaties giving up their special rights in China. Today China no longer has treaty ports.   H. F. SCHURMANN

See also AMOY; CANTON; EXTRATERRITORIALITY; FU-CHOU; SHANGHAI.

TREBLE, *TREB'l*, is the upper, or highest, part in choral music of two or more parts. It is often called the *soprano* part, and is sung by women or boys. The treble part in instrumental music is played by such instruments as the violin, flute, clarinet, and oboe. It is also played on the higher keys of the piano or organ, roughly above middle C. *Treble clef* or *G clef* ($\&$) is the sign used to mark the five-line staff from which treble voices or instruments read.   RAYMOND KENDALL

David Muench,

The Magnificent Giant Sequoias of California rank among the world's oldest and largest living things. Some of these trees are thousands of years old and over 200 feet (61 meters) tall.

TREE

TREE is the largest of all plants. The tallest trees grow higher than 30-story buildings. Many trees also live longer than other plants. Some trees live for hundreds or even thousands of years. They are the oldest known living things.

People do not think of trees the way they think of other plants, most of which grow only a short time and

Martin H. Zimmermann, the contributor of this article, is Charles Bullard Professor of Forestry at Harvard University and Director of the Harvard Forest.

then die. People think of trees as if they will live forever. Year after year, large, old trees shade houses and city streets from the sun. Their buds and flowers are a sign of spring each year, and their colorful leaves brighten every autumn.

Trees continue to grow as long as they live. A tree's leaves make food that keeps the tree alive and helps it grow. Where winters are cold, many trees lose their leaves in autumn. Other trees keep their leaves during the winter and so stay green all year long. Trees rest during the winter months. With the coming of spring, they grow new leaves and flowers. The flowers grow into fruits or *cones*, which contain seeds for making new trees. Some tree fruits, such as apples and oranges,

Theodore F. Welch, Van Cleve Photography

Dwarf Trees never reach full size. Some, such as this miniature cypress tree, are deliberately kept small by a special pruning process. But many dwarf trees grow naturally in arctic regions.

WORLD BOOK illustration by James Teason

Coconut

Coconut palm

The Coconut Palm provides wood and other building materials. The tree's nuts provide sweet-tasting milk and meat. Oil from dried coconut meat is used in making such products as margarine and soap.

The World's Largest Living Thing is the General Sherman Tree, a giant sequoia in Sequoia National Park in California. It towers more than 272 feet (83 meters) and has a trunk about 36 feet (11 meters) wide. It probably dates from before 1,000 B.C.

The Traveler's-Tree, which grows in Madagascar, stores up to a pint of water inside the base of each of its long leaf stalks. The tree received its name because it provides thirsty travelers with fresh drinking water.

Traveler's-tree

The Tallest Trees are California's redwoods, which may tower more than 360 feet (110 meters). Australia's eucalyptuses may grow more than 300 feet (91 meters) tall.

The Thickest Tree Trunk is that of a Montezuma bald cypress near Oaxaca, Mexico. Its diameter exceeds 40 feet (12 meters).

The Baobab Tree of Africa is one of the most useful trees. It has a huge trunk, which the people hollow out to store water in or to live in. They eat the tree's leaves, fruit, seeds, and roots and use its parts in many other ways.

Baobab

The Oldest Trees are California's bristlecone pines and giant sequoias. Some bristlecone pines have lived between 4,000 and 5,000 years. The oldest sequoias are about 3,500 years old.

The Banyan Tree of India spreads by growing trunklike roots from its branches. In time, a banyan may cover acres of ground.

The Ombu Tree of Argentina is one of the hardiest trees. It can live with little water and can survive insect attacks, violent storms, and intense heat. The tree's wood is so moist it will not burn and so spongy it cannot be cut down.

Ombu

The Largest Seeds are the nuts of the coco-de-mer, or double coconut palm, of the Seychelles, an island group in the Indian Ocean. A nut may weigh up to 50 pounds (23 kilograms).

taste good. Fruit growers raise large amounts of these fruits for sale. Trees also make new wood each year when the weather turns warmer. Wood is one of the most valuable parts of a tree. Mills and factories use wood to make lumber, paper, and many other products.

A tree differs from other plants in four main ways. 1) Most trees grow at least 15 to 20 feet (4.6 to 6.1 meters) tall. (2) They have one woody stem, which is called a *trunk*. (3) The stem grows at least 3 to 4 inches (8 to 10 centimeters) thick. (4) A tree's stem can stand by itself. All other plants differ from trees in at least one of these ways. For example, no plant with a soft, juicy stem is a tree. Most of these plants, called *herbs*, are much shorter than most trees. *Shrubs*, like trees, have woody stems.

But most shrubs have more than one stem, and none of the stems grows so thick or so tall as a tree trunk. Some jungle *vines* grow several hundred feet or meters long and have a woody stem. But the stems of most vines cannot support themselves. Some huge seaweeds called *kelp* have stems that may grow 200 feet (61 meters) tall, but they cannot stand—or even live—out of water.

There are thousands of kinds of trees. But most trees belong to one of two main groups—the broadleaf trees and the needleleaf trees. These two types of trees grow in Europe, North America, and many other parts of the world. Most other types of trees, such as palms and tree ferns, grow mainly in warm regions.

335

Ted Saylor, FPG

Wood is one of the most useful tree products. This maple log is being checked for size at a lumber mill to see if it can be cut into boards of the desired measurements.

U.S. Dept. of Agriculture

Trees Help Conserve Our Resources. These men are planting trees on sloping land along a highway. The trees' roots will hold the soil in place and help store water in the ground.

For thousands of years, trees have provided man with foods, fibers, and medicines. Above all, they have provided him with wood. Prehistoric man used wood to make his first spear, his first boat, and his first wheel. Throughout history, man has used wood to make tools, construct buildings, and create works of art. He has also used it for fuel. Living trees are as valuable to man as are tree products because they help conserve natural resources.

Wood Products. Each year, loggers cut down millions of trees in the world's forests. Logs from these trees are shipped to sawmills and pulp mills. Sawmills cut the logs into lumber, which the building industry uses for many types of construction work. Manufacturers use lumber to make everything from furniture to baseball bats. Pulp mills break down the logs into wood pulp, the main raw material for making paper. The chemical industry uses wood pulp to make alcohol, plastics, and other products. See FOREST PRODUCTS; LUMBER.

Food Products. People throughout the world eat fruits, nuts, and other tree products. The greatest variety of fruit trees grow in tropical and subtropical regions. These trees produce such fruits as avocados, grapefruits, mangoes, and oranges. A number of these fruits serve as basic foods in some tropical lands. Cooler, temperate regions—such as most of the United States and Europe—have fewer kinds of fruit trees. But several kinds are widely grown. For example, orchards in the United States produce vast amounts of apples, cherries, and peaches. The most important nut tree of warm regions is the coconut palm, which produces coconuts. Nut trees of temperate regions include almonds, pecans, and walnuts. Trees also supply chocolate, coffee, maple syrup, olives, and such spices as cinnamon and cloves. See FRUIT; NUT.

Other Tree Products are used by man in a variety of ways. The rubber tree produces *latex*, a milky fluid used to make natural rubber. Pine trees produce a sticky *resin*, used in making turpentine. The bark of oak and some other trees contains a compound called *tannic acid*. The tanning industry uses this compound to change animal hides into leather. The spongy bark of a type of oak that grows in Mediterranean countries provides cork. Some trees produce substances used as medicines. For example, the bark of the cinchona tree contains *quinine*, which doctors use to treat malaria and other diseases.

Trees in Conservation. Trees help conserve soil and water. In open country, trees act as windbreaks and keep the wind from blowing away topsoil. Their roots prevent soil from being washed away by heavy rains. Tree roots also help store water in the ground. In mountain regions, forests prevent sliding snow from causing avalanches. Forests also provide shelter for wildlife and recreation areas for vacationists. See CONSERVATION.

Trees help preserve the balance of gases in the atmosphere. A tree's leaves absorb carbon dioxide from the air. They also produce oxygen and release it into the atmosphere. These two processes are necessary to man. He could not survive if the air had too much carbon dioxide or too little oxygen.

There are about 20,000 kinds of trees. More than 1,000 kinds grow in the United States. They range from mighty forest trees to fragile ornamentals. The greatest variety of trees grow in wet tropical regions.

Scientists who study plants divide plants with similar characteristics into various groups (see PLANT [Kinds of Plants]). These scientists, called *botanists*, do not put trees in a separate group of plants. Instead, each kind of tree is grouped with other plants that have certain features in common with it. Therefore, a group of plants may include certain trees, certain shrubs or vines, and certain herbs. For example, locust trees, broom plants, and clover all belong to the same *family*. These plants are grouped together because they reproduce in the same way and have similar flowers. On the other hand, some trees that look much alike, such as tree ferns and palms, belong to different groups of plants.

Trees can be divided into six groups according to various features they have in common. These groups are: (1) broadleaf trees; (2) needleleaf trees; (3) palm,

THE SIX MAIN GROUPS OF TREES

Trees can be divided into the six main groups illustrated below. All the trees in each group are similar in appearance and have other features in common.

Silver maple
Fruit — Leaf

Broadleaf Trees are known for their autumn colors, bare winter branches, and spring flowers, which develop into fruits.

Red, or Norway, pine
Needles and cone

Needleleaf Trees have needlelike or scalelike leaves and plain flowers that develop into cones. Most are evergreen.

Royal palm
Fruit

Palms, with pandanus and lily trees, make up a group of mainly tropical trees. Most palms have huge leaves and no branches.

South African cycad
Leaves and cones

Cycad Trees live only in warm, moist regions. They bear heavy cones that may grow 3 feet (91 centimeters) long.

West Indies tree fern
Leaflet and spore cases

Tree Ferns differ from all other trees because they have no flowers, fruits, or seeds. They reproduce by means of *spores*.

Seeds   Ginkgo   Leaf

WORLD BOOK illustrations by James Teason

Ginkgo Trees are a single species. They bear seeds but have neither fruits nor cones. The seeds have an unpleasant odor.

337

pandanus, and lily trees; (4) cycad trees; (5) tree ferns; and (6) ginkgo trees.

Broadleaf Trees are the most numerous and varied of the world's trees. They include ashes, elms, maples, oaks, walnuts, willows, and many other familiar trees of the United States and Canada. They also include most trees of the tropics, such as mahogany trees and mangrove trees.

In addition to their broad, flat leaves, broadleaf trees have other features in common. Almost all broadleaf trees of temperate regions are *deciduous*—that is, they lose their leaves each autumn. A few kinds of broadleaf trees in temperate regions do not lose their leaves in the fall. These broadleaf *evergreens* include the holly trees and live oaks of the Southeastern United States. Some tropical broadleaf trees are deciduous, but most are evergreen. See DECIDUOUS TREE; EVERGREEN.

Foresters call broadleaf trees *hardwoods* because many of these trees, such as beeches, maples, and oaks, have tough, hard wood. Such wood makes excellent furniture. Some broadleaf trees, including basswoods and cottonwoods, have soft, lightweight wood.

Broadleaf trees belong to a large *class* of plants called *angiosperms*. These plants have flowers which develop into *fruits* that completely surround the seeds. Fruits are the seed or seeds of a plant together with the parts in which they are enclosed. Botanists divide angiosperms into two subclasses—*monocotyledons* and *dicotyledons*. Monocotyledons produce seeds with one seed leaf, which is called a *cotyledon* (see COTYLEDON). These plants include palm, pandanus, and lily trees. Dicotyledons produce seeds with two cotyledons. These plants include broadleaf trees. A few kinds of trees that do not have broad, flat leaves also belong to the dicotyledon group. An example is the saguaro cactus of the Southwestern United States, which has prickly spines. See ANGIOSPERM.

Needleleaf Trees include such familiar trees as firs, hemlocks, pines, redwoods, and spruces. There are about 500 species of needleleaf trees. Most of them have narrow, pointed, needlelike leaves. But a few types, such as cedars and junipers, have narrow, scalelike leaves.

Most needleleaf trees are evergreen, though they produce new needles each year. The oldest needles turn yellow or brown and drop, but the youngest needles remain green and do not fall. A few species of needleleaf trees are deciduous. One kind is the larch, which grows in northern forests throughout the world. Another deciduous needleleaf tree is the bald cypress that grows in swamps of the Southeastern United States.

Foresters call needleleaf trees *softwoods* because most of them have softer wood than broadleaf trees have. But the wood of Douglas firs, yews, and some other needleleaf trees is hard.

Needleleaf trees belong to a class of plants called *gymnosperms*. Gymnosperms have extremely plain flowers which produce seeds that are not enclosed. Most gymnosperm trees bear their seeds in cones composed of hard scales. The seeds lie open on the surface of the scales. Botanists call such trees *conifers*. See CONE-BEARING PLANT; GYMNOSPERM.

Most conifers grow north of the equator. They belong to four families—the pine, yew, cypress, and taxodium families. The *pine family* is by far the largest. It includes not only pines, but also such trees as firs, hemlocks, larches, and spruces. Pine trees make up a large *genus* (group of species) within the pine family. Loblolly pines, ponderosa pines, and white pines are a few North American members of this genus. The *yew family* includes such well-known ornamental trees as English yews and Japanese yews. Although yews are classified as conifers, they do not produce cones but cup-shaped "berries." Many members of the *cypress family*, such as

---

TREES OF THE STATES

Bald Cypress Louisiana	**Holly** (American) Delaware	Iowa Maryland (White Oak) New Jersey (Red Oak)	Montana (Ponderosa Pine) North Carolina
Birch New Hampshire (White Birch)	**Horse Chestnut** Ohio (Buckeye)	**Palm** (Sabal) Florida	**Piñon** (Nut Pine) Nevada (Single-Leaf Piñon) New Mexico
Cottonwood Kansas Nebraska Wyoming	**Kentucky Coffeetree** Kentucky **Kukui** Hawaii	**Palmetto** South Carolina	**Redbud** Oklahoma
Dogwood (Flowering) Missouri Virginia (American)	**Magnolia** Mississippi	**Paloverde** Arizona	**Redwood** California (California Redwood)
Douglas Fir Oregon	**Maple** New York (Sugar Maple) Rhode Island Vermont	**Pecan** Texas **Pine**	**Spruce** Alaska (Sitka Spruce) Colorado (Blue Spruce) South Dakota
Elm (American) Massachusetts North Dakota	West Virginia (Sugar Maple) Wisconsin (Sugar Maple)	Alabama (Southern Pine) Arkansas Idaho (Western White Pine)	(Black Hills Spruce) Utah (Blue Spruce)
Hemlock Pennsylvania Washington (Western Hemlock)	**Oak** Connecticut (White Oak) Georgia (Live Oak) Illinois (White Oak)	Maine (White Pine) Michigan (White Pine) Minnesota (Norway, or Red, Pine)	**Tulip Tree** Indiana Tennessee (Tulip Poplar)

Each tree listed in boldface type has a separate article in WORLD BOOK. All state trees are shown in color in the state articles.

Fruit

Spine cluster

WORLD BOOK Illustration by James Teason

The Saguaro, or Giant Cactus, is a tree that has spines instead of leaves. It grows 25 to 50 feet (8 to 15 meters) tall. The saguaro has a thick, woody stem and bears sweet fruit.

Josef Muench

A Prehistoric Log in the Petrified Forest National Park of Arizona turned to stone millions of years ago. Scientists study such *petrified* logs to learn about the ancestors of today's trees.

arborvitae and junipers, have scalelike leaves and give off a spicy fragrance. The *taxodium family* includes bald cypresses and the largest of all trees—the redwoods and giant sequoias.

Two conifer families—the *podocarpus family* and the *araucaria family*—grow mainly south of the equator. Podocarpus trees are tall evergreens with broader leaves than those of most needleleaf trees. The araucaria family includes the Chile pine. This strange-looking tree has snakelike branches covered with sharp, scaly leaves. It is sometimes called the monkey puzzle tree because its sharp leaves make it difficult to climb.

Palm, Pandanus, and Lily Trees belong to the large group of flowering plants called monocotyledons. These trees grow mainly in warm climates. Of the three types of trees in this group, palms are the most important.

There are about 2,500 kinds of palm trees. They range from the coconut palms of tropical islands to the date palms of desert oases. Most palm trees have no branches. The trunk has a crown of enormous leaves that are either feather-shaped or fan-shaped. See PALM.

Unlike most palms, pandanus and lily trees have branches. Each branch has a crown of sword-shaped leaves. Most pandanus trees have tall *stilt roots* that extend into the ground from high on the trunk or branches. Lily trees are closely related to the garden flowers called lilies, and many of the trees have attractive, fragrant flowers. The yucca trees of Mexico and the far Southern United States are lily trees. The best-known yucca is the colorful Joshua tree found in the deserts of the Southwestern United States.

Cycad Trees look much like palm trees. They have a trunk without branches and a crown of long, feathery leaves. But cycads are more closely related to pine trees than to palms. They produce seeds in cones that look

like large pine cones. Millions of years ago, cycads grew in nearly every part of the world. Today, they grow mainly in a few warm, moist sections of Africa, Asia, and Central America. See CYCAD.

Tree Ferns. Ferns are best known as rather short plants with feathery, green *fronds* (leaves). But in the tropics and some areas with mild climates, many relatives of these plants are trees. Tree ferns look much like palm trees, but they belong to a different group of plants. Tree ferns do not have flowers or fruits and so do not reproduce by seeds. They reproduce by means of tiny bodies called *spores*, which develop on the undersides of their fronds. See FERN.

Ginkgo Trees are an extremely old species of tree. Millions of years ago, various kinds of ginkgoes existed. Only one species survives today. The ginkgo, like needleleaf trees, is a gymnosperm. But unlike other gymnosperm trees, the ginkgo has fan-shaped leaves. These leaves look like the fronds of a fern called the *maidenhair*. Ginkgoes are sometimes called *maidenhair trees*. They are natives of Asia, but many are grown in the United States and Europe.

Fossil Trees. About 300 million years ago, there were whole forests of trees unlike most of the trees that grow today. Huge club moss trees and horsetail trees grew along with tree ferns in steaming hot swamps. Over millions of years, the trees and other plant life in the swamps died, became buried, and turned into coal. In other places, buried forests became *petrified* (turned into stone). Coal deposits and petrified forests contain fossils of many trees that died out more than 100 million years ago (see FOSSIL). Two of these extinct trees are the club moss tree and horsetail tree of the coal-forming swamps. The club mosses and horsetails living today are herbs.

339

A tree has three main parts: (1) the trunk and branches; (2) the leaves; and (3) the roots. The branches and leaves together are called the *crown*. The trunk supports the crown and holds it up to the sunlight. Tree ferns, cycads, and most palms have no branches. Their crowns consist only of leaves. The roots of most trees are hidden in the ground, but they may take up as much space as the trunk and crown do above the ground. Other important parts of a tree include the flowers and fruits.

Trunk and Branches give a tree its shape. The trunks of most needleleaf trees grow straight up to the top of the tree. The branches grow out from the trunk. On most needleleaf trees, the branches near the top are shorter than those farther down, which gives the crown a spirelike shape. The trunks of most broadleaf trees do not reach to the top of the tree. Instead, the trunk divides into spreading branches near the base of the

crown, giving the crown a rounded shape. The trunks of a few broadleaf trees, such as black willows and white poplars, sometimes divide so close to the ground that the trees seem to have more than one trunk.

The trunks of broadleaf and needleleaf trees consist of four layers of plant tissue wrapped around one another. These layers, from innermost to outermost, are: (1) the *xylem*, (2) the *cambium*, (3) the *phloem*, and (4) the *cork*. Each layer continues up into the branches and down into the roots.

The xylem is the woody, central part of the trunk. It has tiny pipelines that carry water with a small amount of dissolved minerals from the roots to the leaves. This water is called *sap*. The cambium, which surrounds the xylem, is a thin layer of growing tissue. Its job is to make the trunk, branches, and roots grow thicker. The phloem, also called the *inner bark*, is a layer of soft tissue surrounding the cambium. Like the

PARTS OF A TREE

These diagrams show the three main parts of a tree: (1) the leaves, (2) the trunk and branches, and (3) the roots. The branches and leaves together make up a tree's crown. The diagrams also show the main types of tissue that compose most trees.

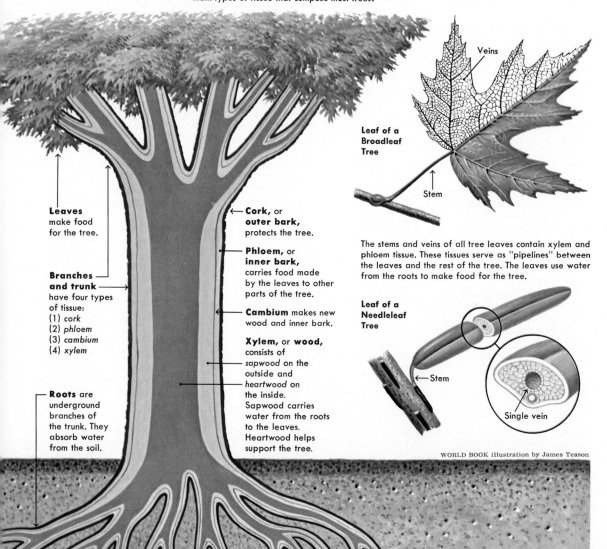

Veins

Leaf of a Broadleaf Tree

Stem

Leaves make food for the tree.

Cork, or **outer bark,** protects the tree.

Phloem, or **inner bark,** carries food made by the leaves to other parts of the tree.

Branches and trunk have four types of tissue:
(1) *cork*
(2) *phloem*
(3) *cambium*
(4) *xylem*

Cambium makes new wood and inner bark.

Xylem, or **wood,** consists of *sapwood* on the outside and *heartwood* on the inside. Sapwood carries water from the roots to the leaves. Heartwood helps support the tree.

Roots are underground branches of the trunk. They absorb water from the soil.

The stems and veins of all tree leaves contain xylem and phloem tissue. These tissues serve as "pipelines" between the leaves and the rest of the tree. The leaves use water from the roots to make food for the tree.

Leaf of a Needleleaf Tree

Stem

Single vein

WORLD BOOK illustration by James Teason

SEEDS OF BROADLEAF AND NEEDLELEAF TREES

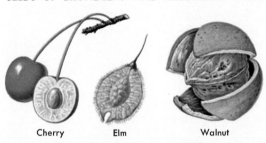

Cherry Elm Walnut

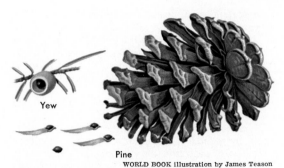

Yew

Pine

WORLD BOOK illustration by James Teason

Seeds of Broadleaf Trees, or *angiosperm seeds,* have protective coverings. The seed and covering together are called a fruit. Cherry and walnut seeds are enclosed in a pit or shell with a fleshy outer covering. Elm seeds have thin, winged coverings.

Seeds of Needleleaf Trees, or *gymnosperm seeds,* do not have protective coverings. The seeds of most needleleaf trees lie in cones and are released after the cones ripen. The yew and a few other coneless needleleaf trees have berrylike seeds.

xylem, it has tiny pipelines. The food made by the leaves moves through the phloem to the other parts of a tree. In palms and tree ferns, the xylem and phloem are not separate layers. Instead, bits of xylem and phloem are connected and form small double pipelines scattered throughout the trunk.

The cork layer is the *outer bark* of a tree. It forms a "skin" of hard, dead tissue that protects the living inner parts from injury. The outer bark stretches to let the trunk and branches grow thicker. The bark of a few kinds of trees, such as beeches and birches, is smooth because it stretches easily. But the bark of most other trees does not stretch so well. As the trunk and branches grow thicker, they push against the bark. It finally cracks and dries and so becomes grooved and rough. Most trees lose old bark from time to time and replace it with a new layer.

Leaves of various species of trees differ greatly in size and shape. Palms have leaves up to 4 feet (1.2 meters) wide and over 20 feet (6 meters) long. The leaves of some needleleaf trees measure less than $\frac{1}{2}$ inch (13 millimeters) long. Some broadleaf trees have *compound leaves,* which are made up of small leaflets.

The main job of the leaves is to make food for the tree. Every leaf has one or more *veins,* which consist of xylem and phloem tissue. The tissue that surrounds the veins contains tiny green bodies called *chloroplasts.* Water from the roots passes through the xylem of the trunk, branches, and leaves to the chloroplasts, which use the water to make food sugar. Only a small amount of the water carried to the leaves is used to make sugar. The leaves lose most of the water to the atmosphere through *transpiration* (evaporation). Like the water and dissolved minerals carried from the roots, the food made by the leaves is also called *sap.* It travels through the phloem of the leaves, branches, and trunk to parts of the tree where it is needed. See SAP.

Almost all leaves are green during the spring and summer. Their color comes from chlorophyll, a green substance in the chloroplasts. Most trees also have reds and yellows in their leaves. But the green conceals the other colors. In late summer and early autumn, the chlorophyll in the leaves of many broadleaf trees breaks down. The leaves then die. But before the leaves drop

to the ground, they reveal their hidden reds and yellows. After the chlorophyll breaks down, the leaves of many trees also develop scarlets and purples. See LEAF (Why a Leaf Turns Color).

Roots are long, underground branches of the trunk. They have the same layers of tissue as the trunk. The roots anchor a tree in the ground and absorb water with dissolved minerals from the soil. The main roots branch out into small roots, which, in turn, branch out into still smaller roots. The main roots of most trees begin to branch out 1 or 2 feet (30 or 61 centimeters) under the ground. Some trees have one main root larger than the others. This root, called a *taproot,* extends straight down 15 feet (5 meters) or more.

A tree develops millions of small roots. Each root grows longer at its tip, which is as small as a thread. As a root tip grows, it pushes its way through particles of soil. Thousands of fine, white *root hairs* grow just back of the root tip. When the tip comes in contact with drops of water in the soil, the root hairs soak up the water and dissolved minerals. The xylem layer of the roots, trunk, and branches then carries this sap to the leaves.

Flowers and Fruits are the means by which all trees except tree ferns reproduce. Tree ferns reproduce by means of spores.

Trees have many kinds of flowers. Some broadleaf trees, such as horse chestnuts and magnolias, produce large, showy flowers. Many other broadleaf trees have small, plain-looking flowers. Needleleaf and ginkgo trees have such small, plain flowers that they are hardly noticeable. A cycad's flowers grow inside the tree's cones and cannot be seen at all. Most palm, pandanus, and lily trees have small flowers that grow in bunches. Many of these are brightly colored and fragrant.

The fruits of some broadleaf trees, such as apples and cherries, have a fleshy outer covering. The fruits of other broadleaf trees, including acorns and beechnuts, are hard nuts. Ashes, elms, and maples have thin, winged fruits. Cycads and most needleleaf trees bear their seeds in cones. Palm, pandanus, and lily trees have a variety of fruits, ranging from nuts to berries. Ginkgo trees do not bear fruits. They produce seeds with a fleshy outer covering.

Most trees begin life as a seed. The young tree that develops from this seed is called a *seedling*. After a tree reaches a height of 6 feet (1.8 meters) or more and its trunk becomes 1 to 2 inches (2.5 to 5 centimeters) thick, it is called a *sapling*. The tree grows taller and its trunk grows thicker every year. The tree continues to grow as long as it lives. Many trees reach a height of more than 100 feet (30 meters). Some old trees have trunks more than 10 feet (3 meters) in diameter.

Trees require enormous quantities of water. A large apple tree in full leaf may absorb as much as 95 gallons (360 liters) of water from the soil every day. Most of the water goes to the leaves. On a sunny summer day, some trees move water up through their trunks at the rate of 3 feet (91 centimeters) per minute. A tree's wood is about half water.

How Seeds Sprout into Trees. A seed contains parts that develop into the trunk and roots of a tree. It also has one or more cotyledons and a supply of plant food. After a seed has left the parent tree, it rests for a while on the ground. Water, air, and sunshine help the seed *germinate* (begin to grow). The part of the seed that develops into the trunk points upward toward the sunlight. As the seed absorbs water, the root part swells and bursts through the seed's shell. As the root grows, it pushes down into the soil. The food stored in the seed nourishes the young tree and helps it grow. Gradually, the root begins to soak up water from the soil. At the same time, the trunk begins to develop leaves.

How Leaves Make Plant Food. As a young leaf develops, it receives sap from the roots. It also absorbs carbon dioxide from the air. The leaf uses the energy of sunlight to change the sap and carbon dioxide into sugar. This process is called *photosynthesis*. The sugar made by the leaves provides food for the trunk,

branches, and roots. During photosynthesis, the leaves also produce oxygen, which they release into the atmosphere. See LEAF (How a Leaf Makes Food).

How Trees Grow Taller. Trees grow taller only at the tips of their trunk and branches. Each year, the tip of the trunk and of each branch develop a *bud*. The bud contains a tiny leafy green stem called a *shoot*. The bud is wrapped in a protective covering of *bud scales*. After a period of rest, the buds swell and open. The shoots that were inside the buds begin to grow and so make the trunk and branches taller. Another type of bud grows on the sides of the trunk and branches. These buds contain a shoot that develops into a leaf-bearing *twig* after the bud opens. As a twig grows larger, it becomes another branch of the tree. Some types of tree buds develop into flowers. Still other types develop into twigs that bear both leaves and flowers. In warm climates, trees produce buds frequently during the year or continue to grow without forming buds. In colder climates, trees produce buds only during the summer. These buds rest through the winter and open after warm weather arrives in spring.

Trees that do not have branches—cycads, most palms, and tree ferns—grow in a somewhat different way. For example, a young palm tree does not grow taller for a number of years. Its short trunk grows thicker and produces more and larger leaves each year. After the trunk and the crown of leaves reach adult size, the tree begins to grow taller. The trunk remains about the same thickness for the rest of the tree's life.

How Trunks and Branches Grow Thicker. The trunk and branches of a broadleaf or needleleaf tree grow thicker as long as the tree lives. The cambium tissue just underneath the inner bark causes this thickening. It uses the sugar manufactured by the leaves to make new

HOW A TREE REVEALS ITS HISTORY

Most trees in temperate regions grow a layer of wood each year. After such a tree has been cut down, the layers can be seen as rings in the trunk. These *annual rings* reveal the tree's life story. The pine log in this drawing has 72 annual rings, showing that the tree lived for 72 years.

Narrow Center Rings indicate that other trees shaded the young tree, depriving it of moisture and sunlight.

Wider Rings on the log's lower side after the 30th year show that the tree was slightly bent in this direction. The tree then began to grow more wood on this side than on the other to keep from falling. Most rings after the 38th year are wider than the center rings. This indicates that many surrounding trees had been removed, giving the tree more moisture and sunlight. Differences in the width of rings after the 38th ring were caused mainly by varying amounts of rainfall from year to year.

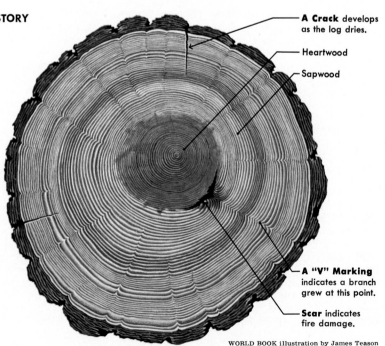

A Crack develops as the log dries.

Heartwood

Sapwood

A "V" Marking indicates a branch grew at this point.

Scar indicates fire damage.

342

HOW MOST TREES REPRODUCE

Most trees reproduce by means of sex organs in their flowers. Pollen from male organs produces sperms, which unite with eggs in female organs. This union, called *fertilization*, produces seeds.

Fruit-Bearing Trees, or *angiosperms*, have flowers with an *ovary*, which becomes the outer part of the fruit.

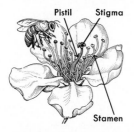

Pistil · Stigma

Stamen

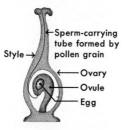

Style

Sperm-carrying tube formed by pollen grain
Ovary
Ovule
Egg

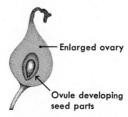

Enlarged ovary

Ovule developing seed parts

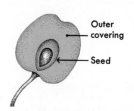

Outer covering

Seed

A Cherry Flower has male *stamens* and a female *pistil*. The top, or *stigma*, of the pistil receives pollen grains from the stamens.

The Pistil has an immature seed, or *ovule*, in an *ovary*. A sperm from a pollen grain moves down the *style* and fertilizes the egg in the ovule.

After Fertilization, the ovule develops into a seed, and the ovary grows larger. The other parts of the pistil and flower wither and die.

The Fruit has an outer covering formed from the ovary. The seed or seeds are inside. A seed contains parts from which a new tree will grow.

Cone-Bearing Trees, or *gymnosperms*, have flowers without an ovary. The flowers develop into cones.

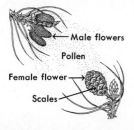

Male flowers
Pollen
Female flower
Scales

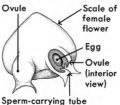

Ovule
Scale of female flower
Egg
Ovule (interior view)
Sperm-carrying tube formed by pollen grain

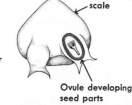

Hardening scale

Ovule developing seed parts

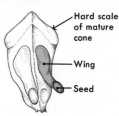

Hard scale of mature cone
Wing
Seed

Pine Flowers are male or female. The wind carries pollen from male flowers to the *scales* of a female flower.

A Scale has two ovules, which are not enclosed in ovaries. Pollen grains enter the ovules and produce sperms.

After Pollination, the scales slowly harden. Fertilization occurs as a sperm in each ovule unites with the egg.

The Seed produced from each fertilized ovule has the parts for a new tree. The seeds develop long wings.

plant tissue. On its outside, the cambium makes new phloem tissue, or inner bark. On its inside, it makes new xylem, or wood.

Wood consists largely of *cellulose*, a tough substance made from sugar. The xylem has two kinds of wood—*sapwood* and *heartwood*. The wood nearest the cambium is the sapwood. It is the living part of the xylem and contains the tiny pipelines that carry sap from the roots to the leaves. In tropical climates, the sapwood grows thicker throughout the year. In cooler climates, the cambium usually makes a new layer of sapwood only early in summer. As a tree grows older, the wood nearest the center dies. This dead wood is the heartwood. It helps support the tree.

In regions where trees make a new layer of wood once a year, the layers form a series of *annual rings*. Each ring represents one year's growth. After such a tree has been cut down, a person can count the annual rings and find out how long the tree lived.

How Trees Reproduce. Most trees reproduce sexually. That is, seeds are produced only after pollen from the male part of a tree flower comes in contact with the female part of a flower. Many trees have flowers with both male and female parts. The pollen from the male part can simply drop onto the female part. Other kinds of trees have separate male and female flowers, which grow on the same tree or on separate trees. The pollen is carried to the female flowers by insects, the wind, or other means. After receiving pollen, a flower develops into a fruit or cone containing one or more seeds. See REPRODUCTION (Plant Reproduction).

When the fruit or cone has ripened, the seeds are ready to leave the tree. The wind scatters the seeds of needleleaf trees. It also scatters the winglike seeds or fruits of such broadleaf trees as ashes, maples, poplars, and willows. Birds, squirrels, and other animals scatter seeds contained in nuts or fleshy fruits. Ocean currents sometimes carry the seeds of coconut palms, mangroves, and a few other trees.

Trees can also reproduce by a process called *vegetative reproduction*. After a tree has been cut down or blown down, the stump may develop green sprouts. In time, one or several of these sprouts can grow into trees. A clump of birches or tulip trees may be produced in this way. The roots of apple trees, aspens, and some other trees sometimes develop shoots called *suckers* that may also grow into trees. Nurserymen often grow trees from *cuttings*—that is, small twigs cut from an older tree. The cuttings are planted in the ground and develop roots.

This section illustrates some of the chief characteristics of 58 North American broadleaf and needleleaf trees. The drawings show the summer and winter appearance, the leaf, the fruit or other seed-bearing structure, and the bark of each species. In some cases, the flower also is shown. The set of drawings for each tree includes information about the tree's native geographic range—that is, the part of North America where the tree is most likely to be found. But a number of the species shown have spread or have been planted outside their native range. The average height of adult trees of each species is given in feet and in meters alongside the illustration of the tree's shape.

The drawings and other information in this section can help in identifying trees. For example, if the leaf and bark of a tree match the leaf and bark of one of the trees shown here, the tree should be fairly easy to identify. Tree guidebooks can provide additional help in identifying trees. Several guidebooks are listed in the *Study Aids* at the end of this article.

Broadleaf Trees

WORLD BOOK illustrations by Donald Moss

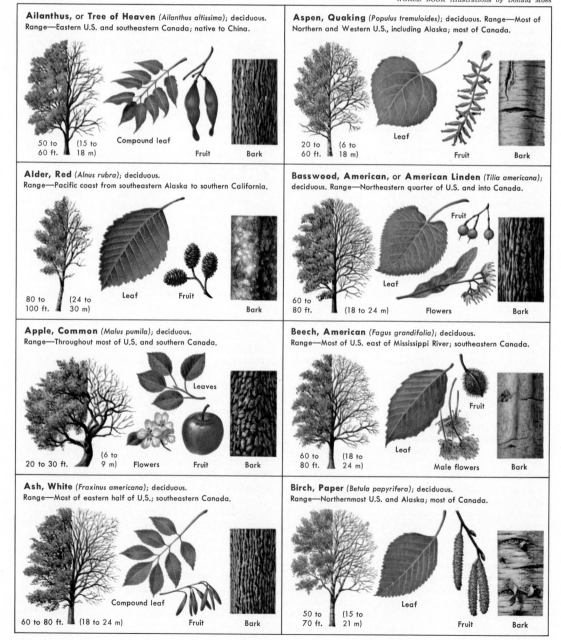

Ailanthus, or Tree of Heaven (*Ailanthus altissima*); deciduous. Range—Eastern U.S. and southeastern Canada; native to China.
50 to 60 ft. (15 to 18 m) — Compound leaf — Fruit — Bark

Aspen, Quaking (*Populus tremuloides*); deciduous. Range—Most of Northern and Western U.S., including Alaska; most of Canada.
20 to 60 ft. (6 to 18 m) — Leaf — Fruit — Bark

Alder, Red (*Alnus rubra*); deciduous. Range—Pacific coast from southeastern Alaska to southern California.
80 to 100 ft. (24 to 30 m) — Leaf — Fruit — Bark

Basswood, American, or American Linden (*Tilia americana*); deciduous. Range—Northeastern quarter of U.S. and into Canada.
60 to 80 ft. (18 to 24 m) — Fruit — Leaf — Flowers — Bark

Apple, Common (*Malus pumila*); deciduous. Range—Throughout most of U.S. and southern Canada.
20 to 30 ft. (6 to 9 m) — Leaves — Flowers — Fruit — Bark

Beech, American (*Fagus grandifolia*); deciduous. Range—Most of U.S. east of Mississippi River; southeastern Canada.
60 to 80 ft. (18 to 24 m) — Fruit — Leaf — Male flowers — Bark

Ash, White (*Fraxinus americana*); deciduous. Range—Most of eastern half of U.S.; southeastern Canada.
60 to 80 ft. (18 to 24 m) — Compound leaf — Fruit — Bark

Birch, Paper (*Betula papyrifera*); deciduous. Range—Northernmost U.S. and Alaska; most of Canada.
50 to 70 ft. (15 to 21 m) — Leaf — Fruit — Bark

Broadleaf Trees

Box Elder, or Ashleaf Maple (*Acer negundo*); deciduous.
Range—Most of U.S. except coastal regions; parts of southern Canada.

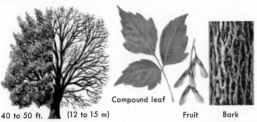

Compound leaf

40 to 50 ft.   (12 to 15 m)   Fruit   Bark

Cottonwood, Eastern (*Populus deltoides*); deciduous.
Range—Most of eastern half of U.S.; parts of southern Canada.

Leaf

80 to 100 ft.   (24 to 30 m)   Fruit and seeds   Bark

Butternut, or White Walnut (*Juglans cinerea*); deciduous. Range—
Northeastern U.S. and into Midwest and South; southeastern Canada.

Compound leaf

40 to 60 ft.
(12 to 18 m)   Fruit   Bark

Dogwood, Flowering (*Cornus florida*); deciduous. Range—Most
of Eastern U.S. and southwestward into Texas; southernmost Ontario.

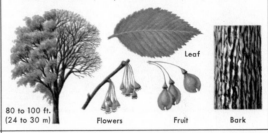

Leaves

20 to 40 ft.   Flower cluster
(6 to 12 m)   with petallike leaves   Fruit   Bark

Catalpa, Northern (*Catalpa speciosa*); deciduous.
Range—Throughout Eastern U.S.; native to central Mississippi Valley.

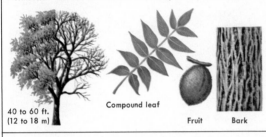

Fruit

30 to   (9 to
60 ft.   18 m)   Flowers   Leaves   Bark

Elm, American (*Ulmus americana*); deciduous. Range—Eastern half
of U.S. and into Canada; many have been destroyed by disease.

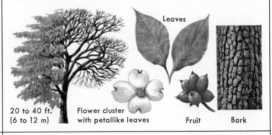

Leaf

80 to 100 ft.
(24 to 30 m)   Flowers   Fruit   Bark

Cherry, Wild, or Common Chokecherry (*Prunus virginiana*);
deciduous. Range—Most of Northern and Western U.S.; southern Canada.

20 to   (6 to
25 ft.   8 m)   Leaf   Fruit   Bark

Hackberry, Eastern (*Celtis occidentalis*); deciduous. Range—Most
of northeastern quarter of U.S.; parts of far southern Canada.

30 to 50 ft.
(9 to 15 m)   Leaf   Fruit   Bark

Chestnut, American (*Castanea dentata*); deciduous. Range—Once
widespread in Eastern U.S., but now nearly wiped out by disease.

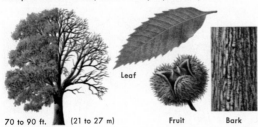

Leaf

70 to 90 ft.   (21 to 27 m)   Fruit   Bark

Hawthorn, Cockspur (*Crataegus crus-galli*); deciduous.
Range—Northeastern U.S. through upper South; southeastern Canada.

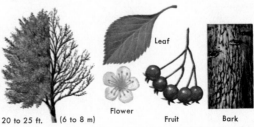

Leaf

20 to 25 ft.   (6 to 8 m)   Flower   Fruit   Bark

Broadleaf Trees

Hickory, Shagbark *(Carya ovata)*; deciduous. Range—Most of eastern half of U.S.; southeastern Canada; northeastern Mexico.

60 to 80 ft. (18 to 24 m)   Compound leaf   Fruit   Bark

Maple, Red *(Acer rubrum)*; deciduous. Range—Most of eastern half of U.S. and northward into Canada.

50 to 70 ft. (15 to 21 m)   Leaf   Fruit   Bark

Holly, American *(Ilex opaca)*; evergreen. Range—Most of southeastern quarter of U.S. and as far north as Massachusetts.

40 to 50 ft. (12 to 15 m)   Leaf   Fruit   Bark

Maple, Sugar *(Acer saccharum)*; deciduous. Range—Northeastern quarter of U.S. and southward into Georgia and northward into Canada

60 to 80 ft. (18 to 24 m)   Leaf   Fruit   Bark

Honey Locust, Common *(Gleditsia triacanthos)*; deciduous. Range—Most of southeastern quarter of U.S. except coastal areas; lower Midwest.

70 to 80 ft. (21 to 24 m)   Compound leaf   Fruit   Bark

Mesquite *(Prosopis juliflora)*; deciduous. Range—Throughout Southwestern U.S. and most of Mexico.

20 to 50 ft. (6 to 15 m)   Compound leaf   Fruit   Bark

Horse Chestnut, European *(Aesculus hippocastanum)*; deciduous. Range—Much of U.S. and southeastern Canada; introduced from Europe.

25 to 60 ft. (8 to 18 m)   Flowers   Compound leaf   Fruit   Bark

Mountain Ash, American *(Sorbus americana)*; deciduous. Range—Southeastern quarter of Canada and into Northern U.S. and Appalachians.

20 to 30 ft. (6 to 9 m)   Compound leaf   Fruit   Bark

Locust, Black *(Robinia pseudoacacia)*; deciduous. Range—Widespread in Eastern U.S.; native to Appalachian and Ozark areas.

40 to 60 ft. (12 to 18 m)   Flowers   Compound leaf   Fruit   Bark

Mulberry, Red *(Morus rubra)*; deciduous. Range—Eastern half of U.S. except upper New England and upper Midwest.

20 to 40 ft. (6 to 12 m)   Leaf   Fruit   Bark

Broadleaf Trees

Oak, California White (*Quercus lobata*); deciduous.
Range—Widespread throughout most of California.

50 to 90 ft. (15 to 27 m)   Leaf   Fruit   Bark

Redbud, Eastern, or **Judas Tree** (*Cercis canadensis*); deciduous.
Range—Most of eastern half of U.S.; southern Ontario; northern Mexico.

20 to 25 ft. (6 to 8 m)   Leaf   Flowers   Fruit   Bark

Oak, Live (*Quercus virginiana*); evergreen.
Range—Atlantic and Gulf coastal plains and northward into central Texas.

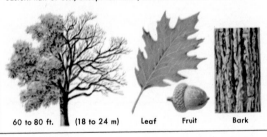

40 to 50 ft. (12 to 15 m)   Leaf   Fruit   Bark

Sassafras (*Sassafras albidum*); deciduous.
Range—Southern U.S. and into parts of Northeast, Midwest, and Southwest.

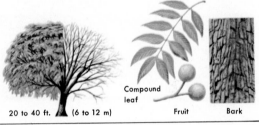

20 to 50 ft. (6 to 15 m)   Leaves   Fruit   Bark

Oak, Northern Red (*Quercus rubra*); deciduous. Range—Most of eastern half of U.S., except far South, and northward into Canada.

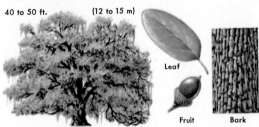

60 to 80 ft. (18 to 24 m)   Leaf   Fruit   Bark

Soapberry, Western (*Sapindus drummondii*); deciduous.
Range—South-central and Southwestern U.S.; northern Mexico.

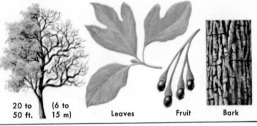

20 to 40 ft. (6 to 12 m)   Compound leaf   Fruit   Bark

Pecan (*Carya illinoensis*); deciduous. Range—Southeastern quarter of U.S., though native only to western portion.

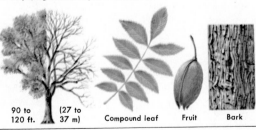

90 to 120 ft. (27 to 37 m)   Compound leaf   Fruit   Bark

Sweet Gum, or **Red Gum** (*Liquidambar styraciflua*); deciduous.
Range—Southern U.S. and surrounding areas; parts of Mexico.

80 to 120 ft. (24 to 37 m)   Leaf   Fruit   Bark

Persimmon, American or **Common** (*Diospyros virginiana*);
deciduous. Range—Southeastern quarter of U.S. and surrounding areas.

30 to 50 ft. (9 to 15 m)   Leaf   Fruit   Bark

Sycamore, American (*Platanus occidentalis*); deciduous. Range—Eastern half of U.S., except far North and far South; southern Ontario.

80 to 120 ft. (24 to 37 m)   Leaf   Fruit   Bark

FAMILIAR BROADLEAF AND NEEDLELEAF TREES OF NORTH AMERICA (continued)

Broadleaf Trees

Tulip Tree, or Yellow Poplar (*Liriodendron tulipifera*); deciduous.
Range—Southern U.S. and into Northeast and Midwest; southern Ontario.

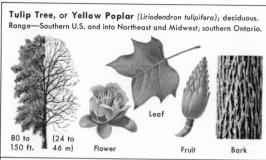

80 to 150 ft. (24 to 46 m) Flower Leaf Fruit Bark

Tupelo, Black, or Black Gum (*Nyssa sylvatica*); deciduous.
Range—Southern U.S. and into Northeast, Midwest, and Southwest.

60 to 80 ft. (18 to 24 m) Leaves Fruit Bark

Walnut, Black (*Juglans nigra*); deciduous. Range—Eastern half of
U.S., except far North and far South; southern Ontario.

50 to 90 ft. (15 to 27 m) Compound leaf Fruit Bark

Willow, Black (*Salix nigra*); deciduous. Range—Most of eastern
half of U.S.; southeastern Canada; parts of Mexico.

30 to 40 ft. (9 to 12 m) Leaf Fruit Bark

Willow, Weeping (*Salix babylonica*); deciduous. Range—Widely
planted in Eastern U.S. and southeastern Canada; native to China.

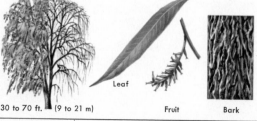

30 to 70 ft. (9 to 21 m) Leaf Fruit Bark

Needleleaf Trees

Arborvitae, American, or Northern White Cedar (*Thuja occidentalis*); evergreen. Range—Southeastern Canada and into Eastern U.S.

30 to 50 ft. (9 to 15 m) Scalelike leaves Cones Bark

Bald Cypress (*Taxodium distichum*); deciduous.
Range—Atlantic and Gulf coastal plains and lower Mississippi Valley.

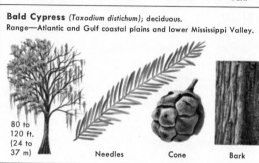

80 to 120 ft. (24 to 37 m) Needles Cone Bark

Cypress, Monterey (*Cupressus macrocarpa*); evergreen.
Range—Monterey County, California.

20 to 70 ft. (6 to 21 m) Scalelike leaves Cone Bark

Douglas Fir (*Pseudotsuga menziesii*); evergreen. Range—Chiefly
Pacific coast and Rocky Mountain regions of U.S. and Canada.

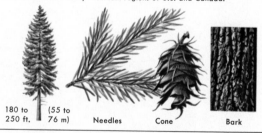

180 to 250 ft. (55 to 76 m) Needles Cone Bark

Fir, Balsam (*Abies balsamea*); evergreen. Range—Most of eastern
Canada and northwestward into Alberta and southward into Eastern U.S.

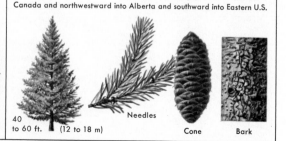

40 to 60 ft. (12 to 18 m) Needles Cone Bark

348

Needleleaf Trees

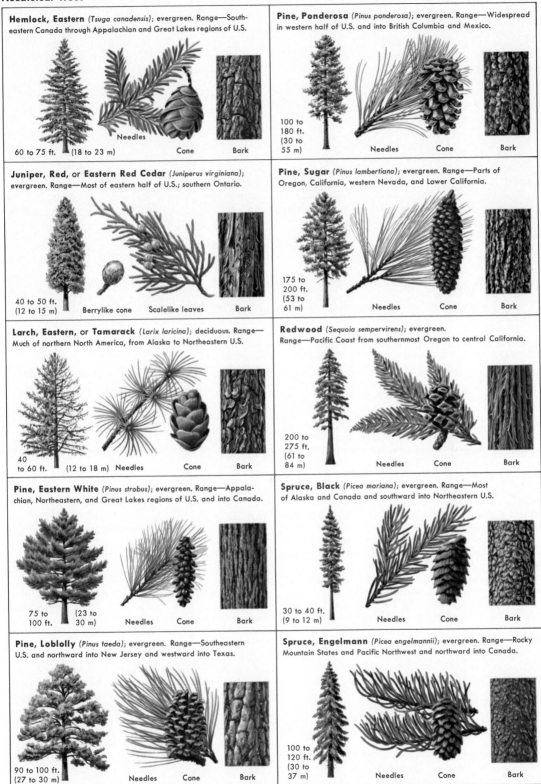

Hemlock, Eastern (*Tsuga canadensis*); evergreen. Range—Southeastern Canada through Appalachian and Great Lakes regions of U.S.

60 to 75 ft. (18 to 23 m) — Needles — Cone — Bark

Juniper, Red, or **Eastern Red Cedar** (*Juniperus virginiana*); evergreen. Range—Most of eastern half of U.S.; southern Ontario.

40 to 50 ft. (12 to 15 m) — Berrylike cone — Scalelike leaves — Bark

Larch, Eastern, or **Tamarack** (*Larix laricina*); deciduous. Range—Much of northern North America, from Alaska to Northeastern U.S.

40 to 60 ft. (12 to 18 m) — Needles — Cone — Bark

Pine, Eastern White (*Pinus strobus*); evergreen. Range—Appalachian, Northeastern, and Great Lakes regions of U.S. and into Canada.

75 to 100 ft. (23 to 30 m) — Needles — Cone — Bark

Pine, Loblolly (*Pinus taeda*); evergreen. Range—Southeastern U.S. and northward into New Jersey and westward into Texas.

90 to 100 ft. (27 to 30 m) — Needles — Cone — Bark

Pine, Ponderosa (*Pinus ponderosa*); evergreen. Range—Widespread in western half of U.S. and into British Columbia and Mexico.

100 to 180 ft. (30 to 55 m) — Needles — Cone — Bark

Pine, Sugar (*Pinus lambertiana*); evergreen. Range—Parts of Oregon, California, western Nevada, and Lower California.

175 to 200 ft. (53 to 61 m) — Needles — Cone — Bark

Redwood (*Sequoia sempervirens*); evergreen. Range—Pacific Coast from southernmost Oregon to central California.

200 to 275 ft. (61 to 84 m) — Needles — Cone — Bark

Spruce, Black (*Picea mariana*); evergreen. Range—Most of Alaska and Canada and southward into Northeastern U.S.

30 to 40 ft. (9 to 12 m) — Needles — Cone — Bark

Spruce, Engelmann (*Picea engelmannii*); evergreen. Range—Rocky Mountain States and Pacific Northwest and northward into Canada.

100 to 120 ft. (30 to 37 m) — Needles — Cone — Bark

Forests of Broadleaf Trees, or *hardwood forests,* grow in many parts of the world. This forest is in Germany. In temperate regions, most broadleaf trees lose their leaves each fall.

TREE / *Trees Around the World*

In some parts of the world, trees grow in thick forests. In other regions, they do not grow at all. To grow, trees need a period of more than two months without frost each year. The few trees that grow in the Arctic never reach full tree size. No trees can grow in the ice and bitter cold of Antarctica. Most trees also need at least 15 to 20 inches (38 to 51 centimeters) of rainfall a year. Only a few trees, such as the Joshua tree and some types of palms, can survive in deserts.

Most broadleaf trees grow best in regions that are warm and moist at least three or four months of the year. Colder, dryer climates are better suited to most needleleaf trees. But some broadleaf trees, such as birches and willows, grow well in cool climates. Some needleleaf trees, including bald cypresses and various types of pines, need fairly warm climates. Palm trees grow in warm areas throughout the world, especially the wet and the dry tropics. Pandanus trees, cycads, and tree ferns grow mainly in the wet tropics and other warm, moist regions. Lily trees also thrive in warm areas, but they do not need so much moisture as do pandanus trees, cycads, and tree ferns.

Different kinds of trees also require different soils. For example, many needleleaf trees grow well in poor, sandy soil. But most broadleaf trees need more fertile soil.

Some trees grow alone or in small groups. Where moisture is scarce, trees may grow only along riverbanks. Tree seeds carried by ocean currents may take root along shorelines. Man plants individual trees in such places as parks and gardens. But most trees by far grow in forests. The world's forest regions consist chiefly of broadleaf and needleleaf trees.

Broadleaf Forests grow in regions that have a fairly long growing season and plentiful rainfall. Every continent except Antarctica has broadleaf forests, which are also called *hardwood forests.* In areas with cold, snowy winters, almost all the trees in broadleaf forests lose their leaves each autumn. In tropical areas, most broadleaf trees are evergreen.

Before the 1800's, splendid broadleaf forests covered much of the Eastern United States. They included such trees as ashes, birches, maples, and oaks. During the 1800's, most of the trees in these forests were cut down to provide lumber and fuel and to make room for farms and cities. Today, only a few parts of the Eastern United States still have large broadleaf forests. Western Europe also had great forests of broadleaf trees, including ashes, beeches, and oaks. But most of these forests have been cut down.

Broadleaf forests made up largely of quaking aspens and balsam poplars cover parts of southern Canada and large areas of southern Siberia. Forests of birches and oaks grow in the central part of European Russia and along the Yellow Sea coast of China and Korea. Southeastern Australia has valuable forests of eucalyptus trees. These broadleaf trees grow nearly as tall as California's needleleaf giants, the redwoods. Some eucalyptuses are more than 300 feet (91 meters) tall. About 600 kinds of eucalyptus trees grow in Australia. Almost all of them are evergreen.

348b

Forests of Needleleaf Trees, or *softwood forests,* cover huge areas in the far north as well as the slopes of such mountain ranges as the Italian Alps, *above.* Most of the trees are evergreen.

In many areas, *mixed forests* of broadleaf and needleleaf trees grow alongside broadleaf or needleleaf forests. Central Canada, the Eastern United States, central and southern Europe, and eastern Asia all have large mixed forests.

Remarkable broadleaf forests grow in tropical regions where the weather is always hot and rain falls regularly every month of the year. In these *tropical rain forests,* many of the trees look alike. They are tall, and many tower more than 150 feet (46 meters). The trees have leathery, dark-green leaves. Because the trees receive plenty of moisture throughout the year, most of them are evergreen. The trees may thus look alike, but they belong to many species. Many palms grow among the broadleaf trees in the tropical rain forests. The largest rain forests are in South and Central America, central Africa, and Southeast Asia.

Needleleaf Forests grow mainly in regions that have long, cold winters. These forests, which are also called *softwood forests,* stretch across Canada, northern Europe, and Siberia. Many firs, larches, and spruces grow in these northern forests, along with a few broadleaf trees, such as birches and willows. Some willows grow even farther north than needleleaf trees do. But they seldom reach more than shrub size. Needleleaf forests also blanket slopes in such mountain ranges as the Alps and Rocky Mountains.

The Canadian needleleaf forests extend southward into the Western United States, where they include many of the world's largest trees. Many California redwoods tower over 300 feet (91 meters). Tall Douglas firs also grow in the Western United States.

A few needleleaf forests grow in warmer regions. For example, the Southeastern United States has large forests of pines, such as loblolly pines and longleaf pines. These forests provide great quantities of wood for lumber and wood pulp.

How Forests Spread. Many forests did not always grow where they are growing now. These forests have spread from other areas. For example, broadleaf forests grow today in parts of the Northeastern United States where only needleleaf forests grew several thousand years ago. The spread of forests from one area to another is called *migration.* The wind helps trees migrate by carrying their seeds beyond the forests. Animals also help spread the seeds. Trees that grow from these seeds produce their own seeds, which may be spread in the same ways. Over hundreds or thousands of years, a particular kind of tree may thus spread to surrounding areas if the climate and soil are suitable.

Several hundred thousand years ago, glaciers moved down across much of North America and Europe. These glaciers caused the forests of needleleaf and broadleaf trees to migrate south. Thousands of years passed, and the ice began to melt. As the glaciers retreated northward, forests of needleleaf trees grew up again on the land that the glaciers had covered. The glaciers moved still farther north, and the climate became warm enough for broadleaf trees. Broadleaf trees usually crowd out needleleaf trees in areas where both grow equally well. As a result, broadleaf forests replaced needleleaf forests in many regions.

Forests can migrate over fairly level land but not across oceans or mountain ranges. Yet similar types of forest trees grow in areas separated by oceans or mountains. For example, the United States has oak trees much like those that grow in Europe. Most scientists believe that many millions of years ago, all the continents were connected. Needleleaf trees developed and spread across much of the earth. Broadleaf trees developed next and also spread. Over millions of years, the continents became separated—along with their trees and other forms of life—by the oceans. Mountain ranges rose up on the continents and separated the trees on each side of the mountains. In time, many of the trees on each continent and on each side of the mountain ranges developed into different species.

How Man Helps Trees Spread. Man has transplanted many species of trees across oceans and mountain ranges. Transplanted trees may grow well in a new region with a climate like that of their native lands. In time, these *introduced species* may spread and become native trees in their new surroundings. A kind of rubber tree that once grew only in Brazil was introduced into the Far East during the late 1800's. Today, whole forests of these trees grow in the Far East. About 100 years ago, Australian eucalyptus trees were planted in California. Today, many thousands of eucalyptuses shade streets and parks in several Western states. Monterey pines originally grew only in a small area of California. They now cover large areas in Australia and other countries south of the equator.

Alan Pitcairn, Grant Heilman

Joshua Trees, such as this one at California's Joshua Tree National Monument, are among the few kinds of trees that can grow in deserts. Most trees need more moisture than deserts provide.

Norman Meyers, Bruce Coleman Inc.

Tropical Rain Forests grow in Uganda, *above*, and in other hot, wet areas of the world. Most of the trees are broadleaf and evergreen. Although they look alike, they belong to many different species.

Homeowners plant various kinds of trees on their property. They plant shade trees for protection from the sun and ornamental trees for beauty. They may also plant trees as windbreaks. Many people enjoy having fruit trees in their yard or garden to provide shade and beauty as well as fruit.

Selecting the Right Tree. To grow well, a tree must be suited to the region where it is planted. Trees from faraway places should be planted only in regions with similar climates. A tree's special characteristics must also be considered. For example, trees with wide-reaching roots should not be planted near houses because the roots may damage drains and foundations.

Trees with full, leafy crowns make the best shade trees. These trees include ashes, basswoods, maples, oaks, and willows, all of which are popular in the Eastern United States. Trees with showy flowers, such as the catalpa and the crab apple, are popular ornamental trees in the Eastern United States. In fairly warm areas west of the Rocky Mountains, such trees as acacias and pepper trees are planted as both shade and ornamental trees. Needleleaf trees are grown as ornamentals in many parts of the United States and Canada. They also make good windbreaks. Various broadleaf trees, including cottonwoods and Lombardy poplars, are also planted as windbreaks. Apple and cherry trees are popular fruit trees in temperate climates. In warm climates, many people grow citrus trees.

Planting the Tree. A tree should be planted where it will have enough room when fully grown. The soil should be fertile and should drain well so that water does not collect and drown the roots.

It takes much time and effort to grow a tree from seed. Most people prefer to buy a tree at a nursery. If a nursery tree is taller than 15 feet (4.6 meters) or if its trunk is thicker than 3 inches (8 centimeters), special transplanting equipment may be needed.

The best time to transplant a tree is when it is resting —that is, in the fall, winter, or early spring. The roots of a deciduous tree can be removed from the ground without a covering of soil. But they must be kept moist while out of the ground. The roots of an evergreen should be dug up with a ball of soil around them. The hole for any new tree should be deep enough to provide room for all the roots below ground level. A small tree may need to be supported by stakes to keep the wind from blowing it over.

Caring for the Tree. A young tree should be kept moderately watered until it is well rooted. It usually takes about a year for a tree to become firmly rooted.

Pruning improves the shape of trees. Cutting off some of a young shade tree's lower buds will keep it from developing many low branches. But enough buds should be left so that the tree has a full, leafy crown. As the tree develops upper branches, more lower branches may be removed. See PRUNING.

Insects and diseases may attack a tree. With normal care, it can overcome most minor attacks. But if a tree fails to develop as many leaves as usual or if the leaves look pale, the tree may require the professional care of a tree surgeon. In some areas, air pollution threatens the health of trees.   MARTIN H. ZIMMERMANN

HOW TO PLANT A TREE

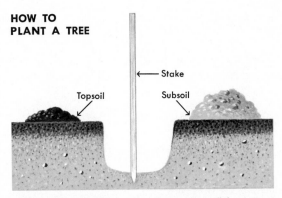

Stake
Topsoil   Subsoil

Digging the Hole. Dig the hole big enough so all the roots can be spread out. Pile the topsoil and subsoil separately. A supporting stake, if needed, can be inserted at this time.

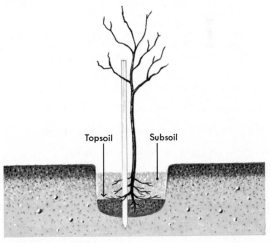

Topsoil   Subsoil

Planting the Tree. Carefully spread out the roots in the hole and cover them with topsoil. Use the subsoil, which is less fertile, to fill the top part of the hole.

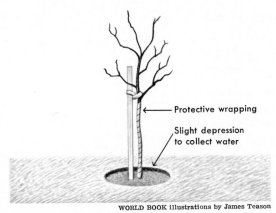

Protective wrapping

Slight depression to collect water

WORLD BOOK illustrations by James Teason

Caring for the Tree. Keep the tree moderately watered during the first year. The trunk may be wrapped in burlap or heavy paper for the first two years to protect it from sunburn and insects.

Trees belong to the subphylum *Pteropsida*, a major grouping within the plant kingdom. The subphylum is divided into three *classes* of plants, according to various characteristics they have in common. The classes, in turn, are divided into *orders*, and the orders into *families*. A few plant families consist largely of trees or shrubs, but some families have no trees at all. This table lists the families with the most species of trees or with one or more outstanding species. The classes, subclasses, orders, and families are arranged in the probable order of their evolutionary development.

CLASS FILICINEAE (ferns)
Order Filicales
Family Cyatheaceae—tree ferns
Family Dicksoniaceae—tree ferns

CLASS GYMNOSPERMAE (cone-bearing and related plants)
Subclass Cycadophytae
Order Cycadales
Family Cycadaceae—cycads
Subclass Coniferophytae
Order Ginkgoales
Family Ginkgoaceae—ginkgo
Order Coniferales
Family Taxaceae—torreyas, yews
Family Podocarpaceae—podocarpuses
Family Pinaceae—deodar cedar, Douglas firs, firs, hemlocks, larches, pines, piñons, spruces
Family Taxodiaceae—bald cypresses, giant sequoia, redwood
Family Cupressaceae—arborvitae, cypresses, junipers, western red cedar
Family Araucariaceae—Chile pine, kauri pine, Paraná pine

CLASS ANGIOSPERMAE (flowering, or fruit-bearing, plants)
Subclass Dicotyledoneae
Order Casuarinales
Family Casuarinaceae—beefwoods, or Australian pines
Order Salicales
Family Salicaceae—aspens, cottonwoods, poplars, willows
Order Myricales
Family Myricaceae—wax myrtles, or bayberries
Order Juglandales
Family Juglandaceae—butternut, hickories, pecan, walnuts
Order Fagales
Family Betulaceae—alders, birches, hazels, hornbeams
Family Fagaceae—beeches, chestnuts, chinquapins, oaks
Order Urticales
Family Ulmaceae—elms, hackberry, planer tree, sugarberry
Family Moraceae—banyan, breadfruit, figs, mulberries, Osage orange
Order Proteales
Family Proteaceae—macadamias, silky oak, silver tree
Order Santalales
Family Santalaceae—sandalwoods
Order Centrospermae
Family Phytolaccaceae—ombu
Order Ranales
Family Magnoliaceae—magnolias, sweet bay, tulip tree
Family Annonaceae—cherimoya, pawpaw, ylang-ylang
Family Myristicaceae—nutmegs
Family Lauraceae—avocado, cinnamon, laurels, sassafras
Order Rhoeadales
Family Moringaceae—horseradish tree
Order Rosales
Family Pittosporaceae—lemonwood, Victoria box
Family Hamamelidaceae—sweet gums, witch hazels
Family Platanaceae—sycamores, or plane trees
Family Rosaceae—almonds, apples, apricots, cherries, crab apples, hawthorns, loquat, medlar, mountain ashes, nectarine, peaches, pears, plums, quinces, serviceberries
Family Leguminosae—acacias, brazilwoods, carob, cassias, honey locusts, laburnums, locusts, logwood, mesquite, mimosa, monkeypod, paloverdes, poincianas, redbuds, rosewoods, tamarind
Order Geraniales
Family Zygophyllaceae—lignum vitae
Family Rutaceae—citruses, hop trees, prickly ashes

Family Simaroubaceae—ailanthus, bitter ashes, bitterbushes
Family Burseraceae—gumbo limbo, Java almond
Family Meliaceae—cedrelas, chinaberry, mahoganies
Family Euphorbiaceae—kukui, manchineel, rubber tree, tung tree
Order Sapindales
Family Anacardiaceae—cashew, mango, pistachio, quebrachos, sumacs
Family Aquifoliaceae—hollies, mountain winterberry, possumhaw
Family Celastraceae—canotia, Eastern wahoo, maytens
Family Aceraceae—box elder, maples
Family Hippocastanaceae—buckeyes, horse chestnut
Family Sapindaceae—butterbough, litchi, soapberries
Order Rhamnales
Family Rhamnaceae—buckthorns, jujubes, raisin tree
Order Malvales
Family Tiliaceae—basswoods, or lindens
Family Bombacaceae—balsa, baobabs, kapok
Family Sterculiaceae—bottle tree, cacao, Chinese parasol tree, kola
Family Theaceae—loblolly bay, mountain stewartia, wild tea
Family Guttiferae—copey, mammee apple, mangosteens
Family Tamaricaceae—tamarisks
Family Caricaceae—papayas
Order Opuntiales
Family Cactaceae—prickly pears, saguaro
Order Myrtales
Family Lythraceae—crape myrtles
Family Lecythidaceae—Brazil nut, cannon-ball tree
Family Rhizophoraceae—dove tree, mangroves
Family Nyssaceae—tupelos
Family Combretaceae—Indian almond, oxhorn bucida
Family Myrtaceae—bay rum tree, bottlebrushes, clove tree, eucalyptuses, guavas, pimento, turpentine tree
Order Umbellales
Family Araliaceae—devil's walkingstick, lancewood
Family Cornaceae—cornelian cherry, dogwoods
Order Ericales
Family Ericaceae—madroñas, mountain laurel, sorrel tree
Order Ebenales
Family Sapotaceae—bumelias, gutta-percha tree, sapodilla
Family Ebenaceae—ebonies, persimmons
Family Styracaceae—epaulette tree, silverbells, snowbells
Order Gentianales
Family Oleaceae—ashes, devilwood, fringe tree, olives
Family Loganiaceae—strychnine trees
Family Apocynaceae—devil tree, frangipani, yellow oleander
Order Tubiflorae
Family Boraginaceae—anaqua, geiger tree, strongbarks
Family Verbenaceae—Florida fiddlewood, teak
Family Bignoniaceae—calabash tree, catalpas, desert willow, jacaranda, royal paulownia, sausage tree
Order Rubiales
Family Rubiaceae—buttonbush, cinchonas, coffee trees
Family Caprifoliaceae—black haw, elders, viburnums
Subclass Monocotyledoneae
Order Pandanales
Family Pandanaceae—pandanuses, or screw pines
Order Palmales
Family Palmae—palmettos, palms
Order Liliales
Family Liliaceae—aloes
Family Agavaceae—dragon tree, Joshua tree, Spanish bayonet
Order Zingiberales
Family Musaceae—traveler's-tree

Related Articles in WORLD BOOK include:

COMMON BROADLEAF TREES

Alder	Cottonwood	Kentucky	Oak
Ash	Elm	Coffeetree	Osage Orange
Aspen	Eucalyptus	Laurel	Poplar
Beech	Gum Tree	Linden	Prickly Ash
Birch	Hackberry	Live Oak	Sorrel Tree
Bitternut	Honey Locust	Locust	Sweet Gum
Box Elder	Horse	Madroña	Sycamore
Catalpa	Chestnut	Maple	Tulip Tree
Chestnut	Ironwood	Myrtle	Willow

COMMON NEEDLELEAF TREES

Arborvitae	Cypress	Juniper	Sequoia
Bristlecone	Douglas Fir	Larch	Spruce
Pine	Fir	Pine	Yew
Cedar	Hemlock	Redwood	

FRUIT TREES

Anchovy Pear	Date and	Litchi	Papaya
Apple	Date Palm	Loquat	Pawpaw
Apricot	Fig	Mango	Peach
Avocado	Grapefruit	Mangosteen	Pear
Breadfruit	Guava	Mulberry	Persimmon
Cherimoya	Kumquat	Nectarine	Plum
Cherry	Lemon	Olive	Pomegranate
Citron	Lime	Orange	Quince
Crab Apple			

EDIBLE-NUT TREES

Almond	Cashew	Hickory	Pistachio Nut
Brazil Nut	Coconut Palm	Pecan	Walnut
Butternut	Hazel	Piñon	

TREES THAT YIELD SPECIAL PRODUCTS

Balsa	Camphor	Cork	Rubber
Bayberry	Carob	Kapok	Sapodilla
Betel	Cinchona	Kola Nut	Sassafras
Brazilwood	Cinnamon	Mesquite	Tallow Tree
Cacao	Clove	Nutmeg	Witch Hazel
Calabash	Coffee	Palm	

ORNAMENTAL TREES

Acacia	Holly	Mimosa	Poinciana
Box	Laburnum	Myrtle	Redbud
Fringe Tree	Magnolia	Pepper Tree	Rhododendron

TROPICAL TREES

Baobab	Mahogany	Mangrove	Tamarind
Jacaranda	Manchineel	Monkeypod Tree	Teak

UNUSUAL TREES

Banyan Tree	Bottle Tree	Ginkgo Tree
Beefwood	Cannon-Ball Tree	Upas
Bo Tree	Cycad	

PARTS OF TREES

Bark	Cell	Fruit	Phloem	Sap	Stem
Bud	Flower	Leaf	Root	Seed	Wood

MAPS

See the plant life maps with the following articles:

Africa	Australia	North America
Asia	Europe	South America

OTHER RELATED ARTICLES

Bonsai	Ecology	Grafting
Cellulose	Environmental Pollution	Lumber
Chlorophyll	Evergreen	Nursery
Conservation	Forest	Plant
Cotyledon	Forest Products	Pruning

Outline

I. The Importance of Trees
  A. Wood Products
  B. Food Products
  C. Other Tree Products
  D. Trees in Conservation

II. Kinds of Trees
  A. Broadleaf Trees
  B. Needleleaf Trees
  C. Palm, Pandanus, and Lily Trees
  D. Cycad Trees
  E. Tree Ferns
  F. Ginkgo Trees
  G. Fossil Trees

III. The Parts of a Tree
  A. Trunk and Branches
  B. Leaves
  C. Roots
  D. Flowers and Fruits

IV. How a Tree Grows
  A. How Seeds Sprout into Trees
  B. How Leaves Make Plant Food
  C. How Trees Grow Taller
  D. How Trunks and Branches Grow Thicker
  E. How Trees Reproduce

V. Familiar Broadleaf and Needleleaf Trees of North America

VI. Trees Around the World
  A. Broadleaf Forests
  B. Needleleaf Forests
  C. How Forests Spread
  D. How Man Helps Trees Spread

VII. Planting and Caring for Trees
  A. Selecting the Right Tree
  B. Planting the Tree
  C. Caring for the Tree

VIII. Scientific Classification of Trees

Questions

What is *sapwood? Heartwood?*
What is the main job of a tree's leaves?
In what climate do most needleleaf forests grow?
What do root hairs do?
How do forests spread?
How do *deciduous* trees differ from *evergreen* trees?
When is the best time of year to transplant a tree?
How do trees help conserve soil and water?
In what four ways do trees differ from all other plants?
How do trees grow taller?

Additional Resources

Level I

COWLE, JERRY. *Discover the Trees.* Sterling, 1977.
DAY, JENIFER W. *What Is a Tree?* Western, 1975.
DOWDEN, ANNE O. *The Blossom on the Bough: A Book of Trees.* Harper, 1975.
GARELICK, MAY, and BRENNER, B. J. *The Tremendous Tree Book.* Four Winds, 1979.
JOHNSON, HUGH. *The International Book of Trees: A Guide and Tribute to the Trees of Our Forests and Gardens.* Simon & Schuster, 1973.
MARI, IELA. *The Tree and the Seasons.* Barron, 1979.
NORRIS, LOUANNE, and SMITH, H. E. *An Oak Tree Dies and a Journey Begins.* Crown, 1979.

Level II

CLAPHAM, ARTHUR R. *The Oxford Book of Trees.* Oxford, 1975.
COLLINGWOOD, GEORGE H., and BRUSH, W. D. *Knowing Your Trees.* Scribner, 1979.
CONSTANTINE, ALBERT, JR. *Know Your Woods.* Rev. ed. Scribner, 1975.
HUDAK, JOSEPH. *Trees for Every Purpose.* McGraw, 1980.
LEATHART, SCOTT. *Trees of the World.* A & W Publishers, 1977.
MENNINGER, EDWIN A. *Fantastic Trees.* Horticultural Books, 1975.
PETRIDES, GEORGE A. *A Field Guide to Trees and Shrubs.* 2nd ed. Houghton, 1973.
PRESTON, RICHARD J., JR. *North American Trees (Exclusive of Mexico and Tropical U.S.): A Handbook Designed for Field Use.* 3rd ed. Iowa State Univ. Press, 1976.

TREE BELT. See SHELTER BELT.

TREE FARMING. A tree farm is a privately owned area used to grow forest crops for a profit. Tree farms range in size from 10 acres (4 hectares) to nearly 1 million acres (400,000 hectares). The American Forest Institute sponsors the national tree-farm program.

The owner of a tree farm must have the land certified by a local forest-practices agency of a forest industry association. The owner must show that the timber will be grown and harvested in such a way that crops can also be grown on the land in the future. The owner must also agree not to harvest more mature timber than can be regrown, and to protect the crop from fire, insects, disease, excessive grazing, and other damage.

The Weyerhaeuser Company originated the first tree farm in 1941 in Montesano, Wash. The company began a tree-management project to plant seedlings and to develop a fire-control system. There are about 32,000 tree farms covering about 77,200,000 acres (31,240,000 hectares).   HARRY E. TROXELL

See also FORESTRY; WASHINGTON (Natural Resources).

TREE FERN. See TREE (Tree Ferns).

TREE FROG, or TREE TOAD, spends much of its life in trees. There are several hundred kinds of tree frogs. They have sticky pads called *adhesive disks* on their feet, and can climb trees and leap through the tree tops. Tree frogs are from less than 1 inch (2.5 centimeters) to about 5 inches (13 centimeters) long. They eat insects. Most tree frogs can change color.

Tree frogs are common in North and South America and Australia. Probably more persons hear them than ever see them. In the early spring and sometimes on mild winter days, *peepers* (a type of tree frog) may be heard near waterways or marshes. Some of them make little high-pitched peeps during their mating seasons.

Other kinds of tree frogs give their call through much of the summer. They may be heard evenings or before rains in woodlands. Male tree frogs do all the calling. When a male calls, its throat swells until it looks like a bubble about to burst. Then it makes the call that is

characteristic of its species. This sound is hard to locate, even though it may be nearby.

Tree frogs may be kept in aquariums or terrariums, and fed chopped earthworms or hamburger. In this way, they will be active through the winter and will not hibernate, as do the frogs that live outdoors.

Scientific Classification. Tree frogs belong to the tree toad family, *Hylidae*. American tree frogs make up the genera *Acris*, *Pseudacris*, and *Hyla*.   W. FRANK BLAIR

See also FROG.

TREE OF HEAVEN. See AILANTHUS.

TREE OF LIFE. See EDEN.

TREE OF WISDOM. See BO TREE.

TREE SHREW is a small, swift-moving mammal that lives in the forests of India, Southeast Asia, and southern China. Tree shrews look and act like small squirrels with long noses. They grow less than 8 inches (20 centimeters) long, not including their tails, and weigh less than 1 pound (0.5 kilogram). Tree shrews dart about in trees and bushes and on the ground. Their food consists mostly of fruits, insects, and worms.

Zoologists disagree on what animals are the tree shrew's closest relatives. Some zoologists believe that tree shrews belong to the order of animals called

A. W. Ambler, NAS

Tree Shrews have keen vision and hearing. Zoologists believe that the ancestors of monkeys resembled these small mammals.

primates, which include monkeys. Tree shrews, like primates, have relatively large brains and eyes. Other zoologists classify tree shrews as members of the order of *insectivores*, which includes shrews and moles. Like insectivores, tree shrews have claws on all their fingers and toes. Primates have at least one nail on each foot. Still other zoologists put tree shrews in an order of their own. Experts do agree that the tree shrew is related to both primates and insectivores.

Scientific Classification. Tree shrews belong to the tree shrew family, *Tupaiidae*. A common species is genus *Tupaia*, species *T. glis*.   NEIL C. TAPPEN

TREE SNAIL. See SNAIL (with picture).

TREE SPARROW. See SPARROW.

TREE SURGERY is the care of trees, chiefly by pruning, bracing, filling hollows, and removing decayed wood. Large operations may call for the skill of a tree surgeon who is an expert in these methods. Present-day tree surgeons also treat cuts and wounds in trees. They spray trees with chemicals to protect them against insects and diseases and they provide the proper fertilizers and moisture conditions for trees.

Trees decay when fungi enter through wounds in the

Hugh Davis

The Giant Tree Frog Has Sticky Pads on Its Feet.

bark, and spread in the wood. An important part of tree surgery is to cover such cuts. Pruning cuts should be painted with shellac, grafting wax, or tree paint. The expert makes a pruning cut flat with the limb or tree trunk, and cuts off stubs of branches. The bark easily grows over the smooth cut. In cutting off large branches, the branch is first cut a distance away from the trunk, then the stub is removed. This method keeps the heavy limb from tearing bark from the tree when it falls.

Removing decayed wood is known as cavity work. It is rather expensive, and often not worth while unless the tree is large and beautiful or has sentimental value. This type of surgery is most successful with sapwood, which is near the surface. Cavities in the heartwood are often large, and weaken the tree. The tree surgeon tries to remove all the decayed wood, and shape the hollow so it will not hold stagnant water. The cut part of the bark and cambium is painted with shellac and the rest of the hollow is coated with a dressing like tar. The tree sometimes looks better if the hollow is filled, but filling does not strengthen the tree. It is often just as well to brace the tree with bolts or cables.

Some types of trees tend to split at the crotches of heavy limbs, especially in winter. A split of this kind can be dangerous. The right way to prevent it is to connect the limbs with a metal rod running through them and bolted at each end. The rod does not injure the tree, for it passes through a very small section of the living cambium. Cables or metal bands around a limb cut through the cambium as the limb grows, and strangle it.   WILLIAM M. HARLOW

See also PRUNING.

TREE TOAD. See TREE FROG.

TREFOIL, *TRE foil,* meaning *three-leaved,* is the name generally applied to various plants having compound leaves with three leaflets, like the clover. It is specifically applied to the lotus group, which belongs to the pea family. Several members of this group are found in the temperate parts of the Northern Hemisphere. *Bird's-foot trefoil* is so called because it bears clusters of pods somewhat resembling a crow's foot. Other *species* (kinds) of trefoil include *marsh bird's-foot,* common in damp meadowland, and *coralgem deervetch,* often planted in California.

Scientific Classification. The trefoils belong to the pea family, *Leguminosae.* They make up the genus *Lotus.* Bird's-foot trefoil is genus *Lotus,* species *L. corniculatus.* The marsh bird's-foot is classified as *L. uliginosus,* and the coralgem deervetch as *L. bertholeti.*   ALFRED C. HOTTES

See also BIRD'S-FOOT TREFOIL.

TREK, THE GREAT. See BOERS.

TRENCH FOOT. See IMMERSION FOOT.

TRENCH MOUTH, or VINCENT'S INFECTION, is a disease which centers in the mouth and throat. It was given the name *trench mouth* during World War I, when thousands of soldiers got it while fighting in the trenches. Doctors are not sure what causes trench mouth, though they think it may be a viral or bacterial infection, or the result of improper diet. Some persons get it without being near anyone who has trench mouth. Others get it soon after being in contact with the disease.

The first symptoms of trench mouth are mouth pains and bad breath. The disease may settle in the gums, which swell and bleed. Or it may center in the tonsils and jaws. A person who has the disease may find it difficult to chew or swallow food. Trench mouth is uncommon among people who have had all their teeth extracted.   J. F. A. McMANUS

TRENT, COUNCIL OF, was a series of conferences held by the Roman Catholic Church in Trent, Italy, between 1545 and 1563. The council attempted to define Catholic beliefs and to counteract Protestant teachings. The council also established many reforms in church practices. Its work became a major force in the Counter Reformation, the renewal movement in the Catholic Church during the 1500's and 1600's (see COUNTER REFORMATION). The doctrines issued by the council have greatly influenced the church ever since.

Pope Paul III called the council in 1542, and it opened on Dec. 13, 1545. The council met during three separate periods, and wars and religious disputes often interrupted its work. During the first period, from 1545 to 1547, the council declared that Scripture and tradition were equally valid sources of the Catholic faith. The council decreed that the church had the sole right to interpret Scripture. Tradition includes the writings of the apostles, the decrees of popes and councils, and the customs practiced by Catholics throughout church history. The council also rejected Protestant views on salvation and sin.

During the second period, from 1551 to 1552, the council defined the nature of the seven sacraments. The council also reaffirmed the doctrine of *transubstantiation,* the belief that bread and wine are changed into the body and blood of Jesus Christ during Communion.

During its final period, from 1562 to 1563, the council defended the granting of *indulgences* (pardons from some of the penalty for sins). It also approved prayers to the saints and defined the sacrifice of the Mass and many other Catholic doctrines. The council passed such reforms as the establishment of seminaries to train priests and the requirement that each bishop live in his own area. Pope Pius IV confirmed all the council's decrees on Jan. 26, 1564, and they became part of Catholic doctrine.   WILLIAM J. COURTENAY

TRENT AFFAIR was a naval incident in the first year of the Civil War. It almost brought England into the conflict on the side of the South. In the fall of 1861, two men representing the Confederacy, James M. Mason and John Slidell, set sail for Europe. Their mission was to enlist the aid of neutral France and England to the Southern cause. Since Northern ships were blockading Southern ports, they boarded a British ship, the *Trent,* in Havana. Charles Wilkes, commander of the U.S.S. *San Jacinto,* stopped the British ship without orders to do so. He took Mason and Slidell prisoner and brought them to Boston. This act violated the principle of freedom of the seas, because England was a neutral nation.

The people of the North rejoiced, but the British government furiously demanded an apology and the immediate release of Mason and Slidell. To back up these demands, it ordered 8,000 troops to Canada. President Abraham Lincoln and Secretary of State William Seward realized that Wilkes was wrong. The United States government ordered the prisoners released, and made a formal apology. Mason and Slidell went on to Europe, but their mission failed.   JOHN DONALD HICKS

See also MASON AND SLIDELL; WILKES, CHARLES.

TRENTON (pop. 92,124; met. area pop. 307,863) is the capital of New Jersey and an important manufacturing center of the state. The city lies in west-central New Jersey, where the Assunpink Creek flows into the Delaware River (see NEW JERSEY [political map]).

In 1679, Quaker farmers led by Mahlon Stacy established the first permanent white settlement in what is now the Trenton area. In 1714, Mahlon Stacy, Jr., sold part of his father's property to William Trent, a merchant who later became chief justice of the New Jersey colony. The community was named *Trent's Town* in 1719, and its name later became *Trenton*.

Description. Trenton, the county seat of Mercer County, covers about 7 square miles (18 square kilometers). The golden dome of the State Capitol rises above the downtown area (see NEW JERSEY [picture: The State Capitol]). The New Jersey Cultural Center is near the capitol. The center consists of the state library and museum, and a planetarium. The Battle Monument, 150 feet (46 meters) high, marks the site of a famous Revolutionary War battle (see REVOLUTIONARY WAR IN AMERICA [Princeton and Trenton]). Other landmarks include the 1719 home of William Trent and the Old Barracks, built in 1758 to house British troops.

Rider College, Trenton State College, and Princeton University are near Trenton. Fort Dix, a large Army post, is also nearby (see FORT DIX).

Economy. About 30 per cent of Trenton's workers are employed by the state government. The city has about 180 factories. Major industries of Trenton manufacture electrical goods, fabricated metal products, machinery, and rubber products. The printing and publishing industry is also important. The city's slogan, *Trenton Makes—The World Takes*, refers to Trenton's history as a manufacturing center.

Government and History. Trenton has a mayor-council form of government. The voters elect the mayor and the seven city council members to four-year terms.

Delaware Indians lived in what is now the Trenton area before the British occupied New Jersey in the 1660's. During colonial times, Trenton became a major stopping place on the stage line between New York City and Philadelphia. George Washington made his famous crossing of the Delaware River near Trenton in December 1776, during the Revolutionary War. Washington's troops defeated the Hessians in the battle that followed (see HESSIANS).

Trenton served as the nation's capital in November and December 1784. It became the capital of New Jersey in 1790 and received a city charter in 1792. During the 1800's, Trenton developed into an industrial and trade center. An increase in river traffic, combined with the construction of railroads, brought great industrial growth to the city. Thousands of factory workers moved to Trenton, and the city's population rose by about 90,000 from 1880 to 1920. By 1920, Trenton was the leading U.S. pottery producer. The city also ranked high in the production of rubber goods, steel, and wire cable.

After 1920, many of Trenton's residents and largest businesses began to move to the suburbs. This relocation continued through the years. Since 1950, the population of Trenton has declined. To reverse this decline,

Warren Kruse, *Trenton Times*

Trenton, N.J., lies on the east bank of the Delaware River. The city served as the U.S. capital for a short time in 1784.

Trenton started a modernization program. In 1974, the city barred traffic from two blocks of its main street and created a pedestrian mall called Trenton Commons. Trenton also began a downtown complex called Capital Place, consisting of office buildings and a shopping center. Most of this project was built during the late 1970's. In 1979, Trenton completed a complex of judicial office buildings.   GEORGE E. AMICK, JR.

See also NEW JERSEY (pictures).

TRENTON, BATTLE OF. See REVOLUTIONARY WAR IN AMERICA (Princeton and Trenton).

TREPANG, *trih PANG*, or BÊCHE-DE-MER, *BESH-duh-MAIR*, is the commercial name of the dried bodies of certain *species* (kinds) of marine animals called *sea cucumbers* (see SEA CUCUMBER). Trepang is used as food in the Far East. Sea cucumbers have soft, wormlike bodies. They vary from a few inches or centimeters to 2 feet (61 centimeters) in length. To prepare the edible species, the inner parts are removed and the bodies are boiled. Then they are soaked in fresh water and smoked or dried in the sun. This preparation produces a rubberlike substance used to thicken and flavor soups.

The chief center of the trepang industry is Ujung Pandang, a seaport of Celebes, in Indonesia. California also has a trepang industry.   ROBERT D. BARNES

TREPHINING, *trih FYN ihng*, is an operation that makes a small opening in the skull. Trephining is also used to remove tissue from the cornea of the eye. The instrument used in trephining is called a *trephine* or *trepan*. It is patterned after a carpenter's bit, and has a small cylinder with cutting teeth on the edge. It has a T-shaped handle and a steel pin that projects below the edge of the cylinder. The steel pin forms an axis, and the cutting edge moves around it.

Trephining is the oldest known surgical operation. Trephine openings have been found in skulls of people who lived thousands of years ago. American Indian tribes practiced trephining. Certain tribes of North Africa and Melanesia still practice it. Ancient peoples used trephining chiefly for magical reasons, but occasionally to remove objects from the brain. WARREN H. COLE

TRESPASS, in law, is unlawful entrance upon the property of another, or injury to the person of another. "No trespassing" signs are seen commonly where owners of groves, private estates, and club grounds desire to protect their property from intrusion. Failure to regard such notices is an unlawful act. False imprisonment and assault and battery are examples of trespass to the person. Trespass makes a person liable to a civil suit for damages. See also ASSAULT AND BATTERY; FALSE IMPRISONMENT; TORT.   FRED E. INBAU

TRESTLE, in engineering, is a structure used to support a roadway over a valley or crossroad. A wooden trestle, made of *bents* (tall posts connected by ties and braces), usually costs less to build than a bridge. In carpentry, a trestle is a beam on legs. It is used to support work. Some tables and drawing boards are supported by a frame called a trestle.   ROBERT G. HENNES

TREVELYAN, *trih VEHL yuhn,* is the family name of two British historians, father and son.

Sir George Otto Trevelyan (1838-1928) became well known for his two-volume biography of his uncle, Lord Thomas Macaulay, *Life and Letters of Lord Macaulay,* published in 1876. His four-volume *The American Revolution* (1899-1912) was very much on the American side. He also wrote two satires, *Horace at the University of Athens* (1861) and *The Ladies in Parliament* (1867). Trevelyan was born at Rothley Temple, Leicestershire. He studied at Harrow School and Trinity College, Cambridge. From 1865 to 1886, he served in Parliament.

Sir George Macaulay Trevelyan (1876-1962), the third son of Sir George Otto Trevelyan, is most famous for two histories of England. The first, *History of England,* was published in 1926. In one volume he tells a clear, direct, and well-balanced story of what England did and how it lived. His three-volume *England Under Queen Anne* was published between 1930 and 1934.

Trevelyan was born at Rothley Temple, Leicestershire. He studied at Harrow School and Trinity College, Cambridge. He was a professor of modern history at Cambridge from 1927 to 1940. He wrote books on Italy, on the Middle Ages, and on social history. He also wrote a biography of his father.   FRANCIS J. BOWMAN

TREVIÑO, ELIZABETH BORTON DE (1904-   ), is an American author. She won the 1966 Newbery medal for *I, Juan de Pareja* (1965). This book is a fictional biography of the black slave of the painter Velázquez. Treviño's other books for children include *A Carpet of Flowers* (1955) and *Nacar, the White Deer* (1963). Her works for adults include the memoirs *My Heart Lies South* (1953) and *Where the Heart Is* (1962); and *The Greek of Toledo* (1959), a novel about the painter El Greco. Treviño was born in Bakersfield, Calif. She graduated from Stanford University.   ELOISE RUE

TREVINO, LEE (1939-   ), is an American golfer. Few people had heard of Trevino before he won the U.S. Open in 1968. But he soon gained fame as one of the most colorful and popular figures in sports. During tournaments, Trevino often traded jokes with his many followers, who became known as "Lee's fleas."

In 1971, Trevino accomplished one of the most re-

Pictorial Parade
Lee Trevino

markable winning streaks in golf history. Within 16 weeks that year, he won five tournaments and finished among the top five money winners in four other tourneys. No other golfer had ever won the U.S., Canadian, and British opens during the same year. Trevino also won the Professional Golfers' Association (PGA) tournament in 1974. Lee Buck Trevino was born in Dallas, Tex.   HERMAN WEISKOPF

TREVITHICK, RICHARD (1771-1833), a British inventor and engineer, designed the first high-pressure steam engine. He also introduced rails into steam transportation, and designed the return-flue boiler and the wheel coupling of early steam locomotives. He improved the early steam engine and used it in Cornish mines. He worked for a time in Peru, but was ruined in the Peruvian revolution of the 1820's and returned to England. He was born in Cornwall.   ROBERT E. SCHOFIELD

See also RAILROAD (Invention of the Locomotive; picture: An Early Locomotive).

TRIACETATE. See TEXTILE (table).

TRIAGE, *tree AHZH,* is a French word that means *choosing* or *sorting.* The word is frequently used to refer to a proposed method of distributing limited food supplies among the world's nations. Under a triage system, nations that were temporarily short of food—but seemed likely to eventually become self-sufficient in food production—would receive help. But those that seemed incapable of ever producing enough food for their people would be left to starve.

Supporters of triage believe we will not be able to produce enough food to keep up with the growing world population. Opponents consider it ruthless and unethical to deliberately deprive the neediest nations of food. Despite fears of a food shortage, the world food supply has so far kept pace with population growth.

The word *triage* was introduced into English during World War I (1914-1918) to describe a system of classifying wounded soldiers. Physicians divided the soldiers into three groups: (1) those too severely wounded to survive, (2) those who would recover even without treatment, and (3) those who would survive only with immediate help. If medical resources were limited, only the third group received treatment.   JEAN MAYER

TRIAL is a method of settling disputes verbally in a court of law. In most cases, the people on each side of the dispute use a lawyer to represent their views, present evidence, and question witnesses. About half the trials held in the United States are jury trials. In the other trials, the defendant chooses to be tried by a judge or a panel of judges instead of a jury.

There are two types of trials, *civil trials* and *criminal trials.* Civil trials settle noncriminal matters, such as contracts, ownership of property, and payment for personal injury. The jury decides who is at fault and how much money must be paid in damages. In a criminal trial, the jury decides the legal guilt or innocence of a person accused of a crime.

A jury trial begins with the selection of the jurors. Then the *prosecutor,* who argues the state's case against the defendant in a criminal trial, and the *defense attorney* make their opening statements to the jury. In a civil trial, one side is represented by the attorney for the *plaintiff* (the person who began the lawsuit). The other side is represented by the defense attorney. In their opening statements, the lawyers for both sides declare what they intend to prove during the trial.

Presenting Evidence. Each lawyer presents evidence to support his or her side of the case. The evidence may include documents, such as letters or receipts; or objects, such as weapons or clothing. In most cases, the evidence consists of testimony given by witnesses who are sworn to tell the truth. Witnesses generally give their testimony in response to questions asked by an attorney. Then the opposing attorney cross-examines the witnesses and attempts to find mistakes in their testimony. A witness who is suspected of deliberately lying may be accused of *perjury*.

The admission of evidence in a trial is governed by certain rules. In general, information is admitted as evidence only if it is (1) relevant, (2) material, and (3) firsthand. Relevant information is related to a question in the case and helps answer the question. Material information helps settle the main issue of the trial. Firsthand information comes from the witness's personal knowledge, not from hearsay.

Following the testimony and cross-examination, the lawyers for each side summarize the case. Then, in a *charge to the jury*, the judge gives instructions concerning the laws that apply to the case.

The judge in each trial decides what evidence will be admitted. He or she may declare a *mistrial* if improper evidence is heard by a jury or if the fairness of a trial is jeopardized in some other way. A mistrial results in a new trial with new jurors. The judge may also hold in *contempt of court* any person who shows disrespect for the court by disrupting a trial. Such a person may be fined or imprisoned, or both.

Reaching a Verdict. The jury is taken to a private room to discuss the case and reach a verdict. In cases that have received much publicity, the jurors may be *sequestered* (isolated) from other people, including their families, throughout the trial. Sequestered jurors may read newspapers and magazines only if articles about the trial have been cut out. Depending on the nature of the trial, the judge may order that the jurors not be allowed to watch television. These restrictions prevent jurors from reading or hearing anything that could influence their opinions about the trial.

In a criminal trial, the prosecutor tries to prove the defendant's guilt "beyond a reasonable doubt," which is the standard required by law. If the jurors do not feel the prosecutor has done so, they must *acquit* the defendant—that is, find him or her not guilty. If the jury finds the defendant guilty, the judge sets a date for sentencing. In a civil trial, the law requires the attorney for the plaintiff to prove the plaintiff's claim by a "fair *preponderance* (the greater weight) of the evidence."

A *hung jury* is one in which the required number of jurors cannot agree on a verdict. A new trial—with new jurors—is then held.

In some trials, the evidence points without question to the defendant's innocence. In such cases, the judge may order the jury to return a *directed verdict* of not guilty. The jury does not discuss a directed verdict. A judge cannot order a guilty verdict.

The Defendant's Rights. The Constitution of the United States guarantees accused people many rights concerning a fair trial. For example, it specifies the right to a jury trial. Other guarantees are included in the Bill of Rights, the first 10 amendments to the Constitution. The first of the guarantees appears in the Fifth Amendment. It ensures by the right of *due process* that each trial will be conducted according to the law.

The Sixth Amendment sets forth the most important rights of a defendant in a criminal trial. These include the right to "a speedy and public trial." The right to a speedy trial means that a person must be tried as soon as possible after being accused. However, the large number of cases awaiting trial may prevent the courts from trying every defendant promptly. Many courts put time limits on criminal prosecution to ensure prompt trials. The right to a public trial means that a defendant cannot be tried in secret. Each trial must be open to observation by the public.

The Constitution states that a criminal trial must be held in the community in which the crime occurred. The Sixth Amendment requires that the jurors be chosen from that community. In some situations, many local residents have formed an opinion about a case, and so the defendant cannot receive a fair trial there. The defense may then request a *change of venue*—that is, a change in the locality of the trial.

The Supreme Court of the United States has issued many decisions that provide additional rights for accused persons. In 1963, for example, the court guaranteed the right to free legal counsel in all felony cases. In 1972, the court extended that right to persons accused of any offense involving a jail sentence.

A defendant who has been tried and convicted can use his or her right to *appeal*. In an appeal, the defendant asks that the case be retried by a higher court called an *appellate court*. Some cases have an automatic right of appeal. In others, the defendant must show some reason for retrying the case, such as the discovery of new evidence. In such cases, the appellate court may refuse to hear the appeal. However, this court must retry the case if the judge feels there has been a violation of federal law or of the defendant's constitutional rights. An appellate court does not use a jury. Lawyers present the appeal by written arguments called *briefs* and by oral arguments.

The United States legal system is based on the belief that a person is considered innocent until proven guilty. But only a small percentage of the legal disputes in the United States are settled by a trial. The defendant pleads guilty in most cases, and so no trial is needed.

Many cases are settled by *plea bargaining*. In this procedure, the prosecuting attorney agrees to dismiss certain charges if the defendant pleads guilty to the remaining ones. The state saves time and money by plea bargaining rather than putting a defendant on trial. Critics of plea bargaining feel that such an arrangement weakens the nation's system of justice. They point out that the defendant's guilt is assumed instead of proven, as it would be in a trial.

History. The Saxons, who lived in England during the Middle Ages, gave accused people a *trial by ordeal* rather than by jury. The defendant was perhaps required to hold a piece of red-hot iron or was deliberately injured in some other way. The Saxons believed that God would heal the accused person's wounds within three days if he or she was innocent. After the Norman Conquest in 1066, two persons fought if they disagreed about a matter. They believed that God would grant victory to the one who was right.

The present trial system in the United States and Canada developed from English *common law* and *equity*. Common law is a group of rulings made by judges on the basis of community customs and previous court decisions. Equity is a set of standards based on broad principles of justice. English colonists brought their legal system with them to North America. JACK M. KRESS

Related Articles in WORLD BOOK include:

Appeal	Judge
Constitution of the	Jury
United States	Law
Contempt	Perjury
Court	Sentence
Due Process of Law	Trial by Combat
Evidence	Witness

TRIAL BY COMBAT, also called TRIAL BY BATTLE or WAGER OF BATTLE, was a way of settling legal disputes in the Middle Ages. Noblemen used it for many years. Trial by combat differed from a fight or duel because people believed that God would interfere and help the righteous person to win. The general procedure was for the accused to fight the accuser. Noblemen sometimes appointed champions to do their fighting for them. Women and priests were generally represented by others. Trial by combat was introduced into England by William the Conqueror. Trial by jury gradually took its place.

Trial by ordeal was another way of determining a person's innocence or guilt during the Middle Ages. In trial by ordeal, a person was subjected to various forms of physical torture. If the injuries healed within three days, the person was considered innocent. BRYCE LYON

See also DIVINATION.

TRIANGLE, in geometry, is a figure that has three sides. The sides meet at three points called *vertices* (one point is a *vertex*). The sides form three angles inside the triangle at the three vertices. If the sides of a triangle are extended beyond the vertices, the angles formed outside the triangle are called *exterior angles*. So the angles inside the triangle are often called *interior angles*.

A *plane triangle* is a triangle that lies on a flat surface. Its sides are straight lines, and the sum of its interior angles always equals 180°. A *spherical triangle* lies on the surface of a sphere (see SPHERE). Its sides are arcs of great circles of the sphere. The sum of its interior angles is always greater than 180° and less than 540°.

Kinds of Triangles

Certain kinds of triangles have special names and important uses in geometry. The ancient Greeks invented most of these special names.

Scalene Triangle is a triangle in which the lengths of none of the sides are equal. None of the angles of a scalene triangle are equal. The name *scalene* comes from a Greek word that means *uneven* or *odd*.

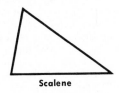

Scalene

Isosceles Triangle is a triangle that has two equal sides. The third side is called the *base*. The interior angle opposite the base is called the *vertex*. The two interior angles opposite the vertex are always equal. The name *isosceles* comes from a Greek word that means *equal legs*.

Equilateral Triangle is a triangle that has three equal sides. An equilateral triangle is also *equiangular*. That is, the triangle's three interior angles are equal. In plane geometry, each interior angle in an equilateral triangle equals 60°.

Acute Triangle is a triangle whose interior angles are all *acute*, or sharp. That is, each interior angle is less than 90°.

Right Triangle is a triangle one of whose interior angles is a right angle. That is, one interior angle equals 90°. The side opposite the right angle is called the *hypotenuse*. The other two sides are called *legs*. On a sphere, a right triangle can have one, two, or three 90° interior angles.

Obtuse Triangle is a triangle one of whose interior angles is *obtuse*, or blunt. That is, one of its interior angles is greater than 90° and less than 180°.

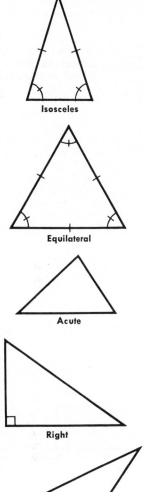

Isosceles

Equilateral

Acute

Right

Obtuse

Constructing a Triangle

In plane geometry, students must often "construct" a triangle. That is, they must draw a triangle to certain specifications, using only compasses and a straightedge. Here is how it is done. Suppose you want to construct a triangle with sides *AB*, *CD*, and *EF*. Draw side *AB* with the straightedge. Set the compasses with the radius *CD*. Using *A* as a center, draw an arc with the compasses. Now set the compasses with the radius *EF*. Using *B* as a center, draw a second arc that cuts the first arc. Draw two straight lines from the intersection

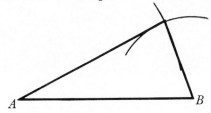

A   *B*

TRIANGLE

of the arcs to *A* and to *B*. The three straight lines form the required triangle.

Finding the Hypotenuse

Suppose you know the lengths of the two legs of a right triangle, but not the length of the hypotenuse. You can find the length of the hypotenuse by using the following formula: $c^2 = a^2 + b^2$. This formula comes from the famous Pythagorean Theorem (see PYTHAGOREAN THEOREM). In the formula, c^2 is the square of the length of the hypotenuse, and a^2 and b^2 are the squares of the two legs (see SQUARE). All you need to do is substitute numbers in the formula and solve it for the missing length. You can find a missing side or angle in any triangle with trigonometry. See TRIGONOMETRY.

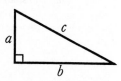

Finding the Area

Here is a formula for finding the area of a triangle:

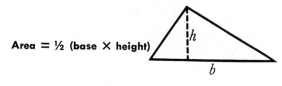

Area = ½ (base × height)

The *height* or *altitude* is the distance from a vertex to an opposite side. The *base* is the length of that opposite side.

See also ANGLE.

TRIANGLE is a percussion instrument often used in modern orchestras, military bands, and children's rhythm bands. It consists of a steel rod bent in the shape of a triangle and open at one end. It usually hangs on a string. The player strikes it with a small spindle-shaped metal bar, producing a clear tone of indefinite pitch. Early triangles had metal rings hanging from the rod to increase the tinkling effect, but these rings were no longer used after the 1700's. KARL GEIRINGER

WORLD BOOK photo, courtesy Chicago Symphony Orchestra
The Triangle is a steel bar bent into a triangular shape and hung from a string. The musician strikes it with an iron rod.

356

TRIANGULAR TRADE. See BLACK AMERICANS (The Slave Trade).

TRIANON, *TREE AH NAWN,* **TREATY OF,** was signed by Hungary and the Western Allies after World War I. The treaty was signed in the gallery of the Grand Trianon, a palace at Versailles, on June 4, 1920. It severely punished Hungary for its part in the war.

The Trianon treaty reduced Hungarian territory from 125,609 square miles (325,326 square kilometers) to 35,184 square miles (91,126 square kilometers). The country's population dropped from about 21 million to about 8 million, and it was left with no seaports. Hungary's bitter complaints against the treaty brought few results.

The Treaty of Trianon forced Hungary to recognize the new boundaries of Austria, Czechoslovakia, Yugoslavia, and Romania. Hungary had to give up its claims to the port of Fiume, and was allowed to keep an army of only 35,000 men. All Hungarian merchant ships had to be surrendered to the Allies. Hungary lost Slovakia, Transylvania, and Croatia to neighboring countries. About 3 million Magyars were separated from their fellow Hungarians. DWIGHT E. LEE

TRIASSIC PERIOD. See EARTH (table: Outline of Earth History).

TRIBE is a term used to describe certain human social groups. Most scholars dislike the term because it lacks a precise meaning and has been applied to many widely different groups. In addition, many of the peoples called tribes consider the term offensive or inaccurate. Most of them prefer such terms as *ethnic group, nation,* or *people.*

The first use of the word *tribe* in English referred to the Hebrews. Until about 1000 B.C., the Hebrews were loosely organized into 12 groups, each of which traced its descent to one of the 12 sons of Jacob. These groups were called the 12 Tribes of Israel. The term *tribe* was soon extended to mean any group of families who traced themselves to a common ancestor.

Beginning in the 1400's, many European nations established colonies in Africa, Asia, and North and South America. The Europeans often described the peoples of those areas as tribes, though the groups varied greatly in their economic, political, and social organization. Some of the so-called tribes consisted of unrelated groups. Others were more accurately called nations. Most Europeans regarded the colonized peoples, whose technology was less advanced than theirs, as primitive. In time, the word *tribe* acquired the broad meaning of "primitive group."

Anthropologists have added other characteristics to the definition of tribe, though different scholars emphasize different features. Many define a tribe as a group with a sense of shared identity and ties of ancestry, customs, language, and territory. Others believe a tribe also must have some form of political organization, such as a means of making decisions for the group and of settling disputes between its members. Some scientists regard only groups without a written language as tribes. Others define a tribal economy as one that produces only enough food and other necessities for members of the group, with little or no surplus. Almost no groups have all these characteristics, though the Tiv of Nigeria and the Zuñi Indians of the United States come close.

Today, many black Africans and other peoples consider the word *tribe* insulting because they believe it implies that they are primitive. Other so-called tribes consider the term inaccurate because they regard themselves as separate groups. For example, the Yoruba, Nigeria's largest ethnic group, are sometimes called a tribe. But they include the Egba, the Ife, the Oyo, and other peoples, each with their own culture and political organization.

On the other hand, several American Indian groups have struggled since the mid-1900's to gain or regain legal status as tribes. These Indians declare that they need tribal status to get the protection and benefits that have been promised them by treaties.

Some scholars also use the term *tribe* to refer to an early stage in the development of political systems, about 10,000 years ago. The tribe came after the family or band and before the appearance of more centralized and specialized governmental systems, such as chiefdoms and kingdoms.   JENNIE KEITH

See also CLAN; ETHNIC GROUP; NATION.

TRIBOROUGH BRIDGE connects three boroughs of New York City, Manhattan, the Bronx, and Queens. This great engineering work is actually a series of bridges forming three steel and concrete arms which form a rough Y in plan. The total length of the three arms is 17½ miles (28.2 kilometers), of which about 3½ miles (5.6 kilometers) consist of bridges and viaducts. The four overwater spans cross the East and Harlem rivers, the Bronx Kills, and Little Hell Gate.

Parts of the structure rest on Wards Island and Randalls Island, in the East River. The suspension span between Wards Island and Queens is the most important arm. It is 1,380 feet (421 meters) long. There is a vertical-lift bridge between Manhattan and Randalls Island.

The Triborough system includes crossings, highways, streets, park and parkway constructions, and 12 land bridges. The Triborough was the first project to give direct connection between the Bronx and Queens. It was opened to traffic on July 11, 1936.   ARCHIBALD BLACK

TRIBUNE, *TRIB yoon,* was an official in ancient Rome. There were two kinds of tribunes, *military tribunes* and *tribunes of the people.*

The first military tribunes were leaders of the soldiers which the various Roman tribes furnished to serve in the army of the republic. There were six tribunes to each *legion* (group of soldiers). They ranked next after the commander in chief. The early tribunes were appointed by *consuls* (chief government officials). Later, the people elected them. During the Roman Empire period, military tribunes lost much of their importance.

Tribunes of the people were officials elected to protect the rights of *plebeians* (commoners). According to one account, the plebeians left Rome in 494 B.C. and refused to return until they were allowed to elect their own defenders. Historians believe that at first there were only two tribunes. Later there were four or five, and then 10. They held office for a term of one year, but could be re-elected. The tribunes could defend citizens against unfair acts by officials. In the Senate, they could veto bills. In their own assembly, they could introduce *plebiscites* (resolutions made by the plebeians). They could not be imprisoned. Tribunes became the most powerful civil officers in the state, although their powers did not extend beyond the city limits of Rome. Largely

because of the work of the tribunes, the plebeians gradually took over many of the political rights which had once belonged only to *patricians* (aristocrats). In 23 B.C., Emperor Augustus received the powers of a tribune. These powers enabled Roman emperors to add civil authority to their military power.

In the A.D. 1300's, an Italian patriot named Cola di Rienzi took the title of tribune when he led the common people in their fight for freedom from the nobles. Those who defend the common people are often called tribunes. See RIENZI, COLA DI.   FRANK C. BOURNE

See also LEGION; ROMAN EMPIRE (The Republic).

TRIBUTARY. See RIVER (Parts of a River).

TRICEPS. See ARM.

TRICHINA, *trih KY nuh,* is a small roundworm that causes the disease *trichinosis.* The worm is a *parasite.* That is, it lives in and feeds on other animals.

The trichina infects human beings and other animals, especially hogs, bears, and rats. Most infections of trichinosis in the United States and Canada result from eating infected pork that has not been cooked enough. Trichinosis in hogs, bears, and rats usually results from eating infected meat and infected garbage.

The *larvae* (early form of the worms) live in microscopic *cysts* (sacs) in the muscles of animals they infect. They usually live in the animal's chest and neck muscles. If an animal infected by the larvae is allowed to live, the cysts eventually harden and the larvae die. But sometimes infected animals are killed for meat. In such cases, the larvae can be killed by thoroughly cooking or freezing the meat. However, if the larvae are not killed and the meat is eaten, the larvae are freed from the cysts during digestion. The larvae attach themselves to the intestine of the person who eats the meat. They become adult worms in about 3 or 4 days. The largest are only about ¼ inch (6 millimeters) long.

The adult females burrow into the wall of the intestine, where they produce large numbers of active larvae. The larvae enter the blood and are carried to many parts of the body. They eventually leave the blood and form new cysts in the muscles.

Some persons carry trichina worms in their bodies for many years and never have severe symptoms. But in other persons, the worms irritate the intestine and cause diarrhea, nausea, and vomiting. When they pass through the blood, fever, headache, and muscular pain

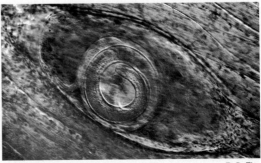

P. S. Tice

A Trichina Cyst forms in the muscle tissue of an infected person. Each cyst measures about 1/50 inch (0.5 millimeter) long.

occur. After they reach the muscles, they cause swelling of the face and other parts and bleeding under the skin. The worms may form their cysts in the *diaphragm* (chief muscle used for breathing) and make breathing painful. The disease is seldom fatal.

The prevention of trichinosis involves several steps. Garbage may carry trichina worms, so it should be cooked before it is fed to hogs. Meat packers should freeze pork to kill any worms the pork may carry. Finally, cooks should be sure the central section of pork is held at a temperature of at least 137° F. (58° C) for 5 minutes or more. The number of trichinosis infections is low in places where these preventive measures are carefully followed.

Scientific Classification. The trichina belongs to the trichina family, *Trichinellidae*. It is genus *Trichinella*, species *T. spiralis*.   J. A. McLEOD

TRICHINOSIS. See TRICHINA.

TRICHOPTERA is an order of insects with soft bodies and hairy wings. Many resemble moths. Insects of this order are often called caddis flies, case flies, and water moths. They live in or near water. They build movable cases, or nests, of sand, gravel, leaves, or plant stems bound together and lined with silk webs. Some weave nets and funnels in water to catch small water creatures for food.

See also INSECT (table).

TRICLINIC SYSTEM. See CRYSTAL.

TRICOLOR, *TRY kul er*, is the French national flag. It has equal red, white, and blue vertical sections. The three colors were first used as a French emblem on July 17, 1789, during the French Revolution. King Louis XVI had come to Paris after the fall of the Bastille. He put a tricolor knot of ribbons on his hat. Red and blue were the official colors of Paris, and white was the color of the royal family. After the royal family was restored to power, it rejected the tricolor. But the tricolor again became the French national flag in 1830. See FRANCE (picture).   ROBERT B. HOLTMAN

TRICUSPID VALVE. See HEART (Parts of the Heart; Right Side).

TRICYCLE is a children's vehicle with two rear wheels and one front wheel. It is propelled by foot pedals. Tricycles were developed about 1870.

TRICYCLE LANDING GEAR. See AIRPLANE (The Landing Gear; diagram: Landing Gears).

TRIDENT. See NEPTUNE (god); POSEIDON.

TRIER, *treer* (pop. 96,787), is the oldest city in Germany. It lies on the Moselle River in the state of Rhineland-Palatinate. Trier is the center of a famous wine district. The city makes leather goods, steel products, and textiles. The city is also an important railroad junction. Trier has a theological seminary, founded in 1773, and a school of *viticulture* (vine cultivation). See GERMANY (political map).

Trier was founded by the Romans, probably around 15 B.C. It was named for the Treveri, a people of ancient Gaul. A number of Roman monuments including an amphitheater, baths, and the celebrated *Porta Nigra* (fortified north gate) stand in the city. Trier's cathedral dates from Roman times, and houses a garment believed to be the seamless coat of Jesus Christ. The city was captured by the Franks in the A.D. 400's. It be-

C. Antonier, Photo Trends

Trieste lies at the north end of the Adriatic Sea. Several countries use its port, which does not tax imported goods.

came part of France in 1801, and was awarded to Prussia by the Congress of Vienna in 1814-1815. The French occupied Trier after World War I. U.S. troops captured the city during World War II.   JAMES K. POLLOCK

TRIESTE. See EXPLORATION (Deep-Sea Exploration; picture: The Bathyscaph *Trieste*).

TRIESTE, *tree EST* or *tree ES tay* (pop. 272,412) is a city in northeastern Italy. Several nations use Trieste's free port, which does not tax imported goods. The city produces clothing, iron and steel, machinery, and paint. Trieste lies at the northern end of the Adriatic Sea. For location, see ITALY (political map).

Trieste was a Roman colony from the 100's B.C. to about A.D. 500. Austria gained control of the area in the late 1300's. Treaties following World War I (1914-1918) gave Trieste to Italy.

In 1946, after World War II, the United Nations (UN) took over Trieste and a large area surrounding the city. The UN set up the Free Territory of Trieste there and divided the total of 293 square miles (759 square kilometers) into two zones. United States and British troops occupied Zone A, which included the city of Trieste and an area to the north. Most of the people of this zone were Italians. Yugoslav forces occupied Zone B, an area south of the city. This zone had a largely Slavic population. In 1954, the city and most of Zone A came under Italian control. Yugoslavia continued to administer Zone B. In 1975, Italy took formal possession of Zone A, and Zone B became part of Yugoslavia.   JOSEPH S. ROUCEK

TRIGONOMETRY, *TRIG uh NAHM uh tree*. How can you measure the height of a mountain that you cannot climb? How can you measure the distance across a river that you cannot cross? Trigonometry, a branch of mathematics, can supply the answers to these questions and to many other questions of the same kind. For example, you can make the unknown height of a mountain part of a triangle. Trigonometry can help you find the unknown part of this triangle. In fact, the word *trigonometry* originally meant *triangle measurement*. Astronomers, navigators, surveyors, and many others use trigonometry. But, today, trigonometry means much more than just the measurement of triangles.

Any triangle has three sides. Mathematicians have

studied the relations between these sides. They can write the relations between sides as *ratios*. That is, they can write the relation of one side to another as one number or quantity divided by another. They call this kind of relation a *trigonometric ratio* or *trigonometric function*. Trigonometry today is the branch of mathematics that deals with the properties and the applications of trigonometric ratios.

On an elementary level, trigonometry deals with triangles lying in a flat surface, or *plane*, and on the surface of a sphere. We can speak of *plane trigonometry* and *spherical trigonometry*. Mathematicians have found that the values of trigonometric ratios have *periods*, or repeat again and again. On an advanced level, trigonometry involves the application of these periods to describing such things as the vibration of a violin string or the motion of a pendulum.

Trigonometry had its origins in ancient times. It grew out of attempts to study and describe the spheres within which the sun, moon, planets, and stars were supposed to move. Two Greek astronomers—Hipparchus of Nicaea (c. 100's B.C.) and Ptolemy (c. A.D. 100's) —made the first important advances in trigonometry. Modern trigonometry developed after the Middle Ages. Regiomontanus, the Latin name of Johann Müller (1436-1476), a German mathematician, published one of the first systematic works on trigonometry. A second German mathematician, Bartholomäus Pitiscus (1561-1613), published the first textbook of trigonometry. Pitiscus' book was the first with the word *trigonometry* in its title.

Measuring Angles

Mathematicians deal with trigonometric ratios in terms of the measure, or size, of angles. For this reason, the notion of an angle has great importance.

In geometry, an angle consists of two lines extending from a point. Trigonometry uses the same definition, but adds that the angle formed by two lines can be measured. In trigonometry, *the measure of an angle corresponds to the amount of rotation required to move a line from the position of one of these lines to the other.*

Look at the angle formed by lines *m* and *n*. The lines meet at point *O*. Line *m* is the *initial*, or beginning, side of an angle. Line *n* is the *terminal*, or ending, side of the angle. You can measure the angle by measuring the rotation from *m* to *n*:

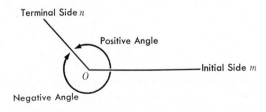

The angle is said to be *positive* if the rotation of side *m* is counterclockwise. The angle is *negative* if the rotation is clockwise.

Now look at a horizontal and a vertical line intersecting at point *O*, as shown in the next diagram. Line *m* issues from point *O* and coincides with the horizontal line. Then line *m* rotates. Suppose line *m* has point *A*

on it. As line *m* rotates, point *A* will trace out part or all of the circumference of a circle. This circle has the radius *OA*. After the rotation, the line *OA* has a new position. The new position is line *OP*. Point *P* corresponds to point *A*. You can see that point *A* and point *P* are the same distance from *O*. The angle *AOP*, as shown in the diagram, is in *standard position*. The amount of rotation determines its size.

What unit can you use to measure an angle? The most logical unit to measure angles comes from the *revolution system*. A revolution means a complete turn around a circle. The revolution system counts the number of revolutions (or fractional parts of revolutions) made by the rotation from the initial to the terminal side of the angle. For example, the angle from the hour hand to the minute hand of a clock at 9 o'clock is $\frac{1}{4}$ of a revolution.

In elementary work, the *sexagesimal* ("sixtieth") *system* is commonly used to measure angles. The *degree* is the unit in this system. In this system, one revolution equals 360 degrees, or 360°. An angle of $\frac{1}{4}$ revolution measures 90°, or one right angle.

In calculus and advanced mathematics, the *radian system* measures angles. In this system, one revolution, or 360°, equals 2π radians. Here is a table comparing the three systems:

Revolutions	Degrees	Radians
1	360°	2π
$\frac{1}{4}$	90°	$\frac{\pi}{2}$
$\frac{1}{6}$	60°	$\frac{\pi}{3}$
$\frac{1}{10}$	36°	$\frac{\pi}{5}$

One radian equals 57.2958°. An angle of one radian is formed by two radiuses of a circle if they mark off an *arc* (portion of a circle) equal to the length of the radius of the circle. See RADIAN.

Trigonometric Ratios

How are trigonometric ratios defined? Look at the angle *AOP* in standard position. The angle comes from

TRIGONOMETRY

rotating OA, a part of the horizontal line, to OP. This rotating line has the length r.

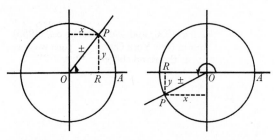

So point P is a positive distance, r, from point O. Point P can be either above or below the horizontal line and either right or left of the vertical line, as shown in the diagram above.

The distance between P and the vertical line is x. This distance is positive when P is located on the right and negative when P is on the left.

The distance between P and the horizontal line is y. This distance is positive when P is above the horizontal line and negative when P is below.

Here are the three most important trigonometric ratios and their names:

$$\frac{y}{r} = \text{the } \textbf{sine} \text{ of } AOP \text{ (or } \textbf{sin } AOP)$$

$$\frac{x}{r} = \text{the } \textbf{cosine} \text{ of } AOP \text{ (or } \textbf{cos } AOP)$$

$$\frac{y}{x} = \text{the } \textbf{tangent} \text{ of } AOP \text{ (or } \textbf{tan } AOP)$$

Here are the other three trigonometric ratios and their names:

$$\frac{x}{y} = \text{the } \textbf{cotangent} \text{ of } AOP \text{ (or } \textbf{cot } AOP)$$

$$\frac{r}{x} = \text{the } \textbf{secant} \text{ of } AOP \text{ (or } \textbf{sec } AOP)$$

$$\frac{r}{y} = \text{the } \textbf{cosecant} \text{ of } AOP \text{ (or } \textbf{csc } AOP)$$

These six ratios do *not* change with the length r, because the corresponding sides of similar triangles are proportional. And an angle may not only be positive or negative, but also its ratios may be positive or negative. Whether a ratio is positive or negative depends on the size of the angle. Tables have been prepared that give the approximate values of the trigonometric functions for an angle of any size. For example, the sine of a 36° angle is 0.5877853.

Some beginners simply try to memorize these trigonometric ratios. But this is often the wrong approach. You should try to see what the ratios mean. Using paper and pencil, you can make diagrams such as the one given above. You can make one diagram for each ratio. Then you can see what each ratio means and how its values change for differently sized angles.

If angle AOP is between 0° and 90°, the sine, cosine,

and tangent become ratios of the actual sides of a right (90°) triangle. Here is another way of describing these ratios:

$$\textbf{sine} \text{ of } AOP = \frac{\text{side opposite the angle}}{\text{hypotenuse}}$$

$$\textbf{cosine} \text{ of } AOP = \frac{\text{side adjacent to the angle}}{\text{hypotenuse}}$$

$$\textbf{tangent} \text{ of } AOP = \frac{\text{side opposite the angle}}{\text{side adjacent to the angle}}$$

The *hypotenuse* is the side opposite the right angle.

Solving Triangles with Trigonometry

A triangle has three sides and three angles. If you know three parts of a triangle, of which one must be a side, you can find the remaining parts with the aid of trigonometric ratios and a table of values.

Solving Right Triangles. Using the diagram given previously, suppose you have a right triangle ORP. Suppose you know angle ROP (the angle opposite side PR) and side OR. To find the missing parts, you can use the ratios for a right triangle. To find PR, you can use the tangent of angle ROP:

$$\textbf{tan } ROP = \frac{PR}{OR}$$

You can find the tangent in a table of values. You know OR. Now you can solve the equation for PR using algebra. See ALGEBRA (Solving Equations).

To find OP, you can use the Pythagorean Theorem (see PYTHAGOREAN THEOREM):

$$OP^2 = OR^2 + PR^2$$

You can also use the cosine of ROP to find OP:

$$\textbf{cos } ROP = \frac{OR}{OP}$$

This gives you the three sides of the triangle. The missing angle OPR (the angle opposite side OR) must equal 90° − angle ROP, because the sum of the angles in any triangle is 180°. You already know angle ROP. Angle ORP was given as a right (90°) angle. Now you know all the parts of the triangle.

Law of Sines. For more general triangles, mathematicians have formulated two general laws, the *Law of Sines* and the *Law of Cosines*. Look at this triangle:

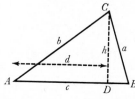

In this triangle, a, b, and c are the lengths of sides of the triangle, and A, B, and C are the corresponding opposite angles.

Here is the Law of Sines:

$$\frac{a}{\textbf{sin } A} = \frac{b}{\textbf{sin } B} = \frac{c}{\textbf{sin } C}$$

Law of Cosines consists of three statements. Using the diagram in column 2 of the previous page, here is one statement:

$$a^2 = b^2 + c^2 - 2bc \cos A$$

The Law of Sines and the Law of Cosines permit you to compute any triangle. In surveying, you can use these laws to measure distances when no direct measurement is possible.

Trigonometry and Physics

An important branch of trigonometry deals with the relation between the size of an angle and the size of its trigonometric ratio. Here is a picture of the relation between an angle and its sine:

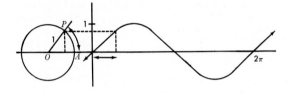

The curve shown above is called a *sine curve* or a *sine wave*.

To understand this curve, imagine two perpendicular lines laid off along the horizontal line. These two lines have intervals of 2π from the intersection of the horizontal and the vertical line. Now look at the circle with the radius 1 located with its center on the horizontal line. Because the circumference of this circle is 2π, the length of the arc from point A to P is the radian measure of the angle that cuts this arc. So the distance of the wave above or below the horizontal line is the same as the distance of point P on the circle (the sine of the angle). And the distance of the wave along the horizontal line is the same as the length along the arc of the circle from A to P (the size of the angle). So the relation between the size of any angle and its sine can be pictured as a wave that continues indefinitely to the right and left. This wave repeats itself every distance of 2π. This repetition in the wave emphasizes the *periodic* nature of the sine relation.

Science, particularly physics, deals with a large number of problems that are periodic in nature. These problems occur in astronomy, mechanics, and in dealing with light, sound, and electricity. A scientist who studies these problems must frequently use the sine wave with special emphasis on its periodic property. For example, the sine wave may be used to study the simple pendulum, a vibrating violin string, a particle of air during the passage of a sound wave, or a particle of earth during an earthquake. Other studies include the tones of musical instruments, the behavior of alternating electric current, and certain problems in radio or television. So trigonometry through its study of sine waves can help science in many ways.   ELBRIDGE P. VANCE

Related Articles in WORLD BOOK include:

Algebra	Mathematics	Surveying
Angle	Navigation	Triangle
Geometry		

TRIGRAPH. See CODES AND CIPHERS (Cryptanalysis).

TRILBY. See DU MAURIER (George Louis).

TRILLING, LIONEL (1905-1975), was an American literary critic and a professor of English at Columbia University. His books include studies of Matthew Arnold and E. M. Forster; a novel, *The Middle of the Journey* (1947); and two collections of essays, *The Liberal Imagination* (1950) and *The Opposing Self* (1955). Trilling was born in New York City.   JAMES WOODRESS

TRILLION is a thousand billion. One trillion is written 1,000,000,000,000. That is, it has 12 zeros. The British trillion is a billion billion, so it has 18 zeros. See also DECIMAL NUMERAL SYSTEM (Larger Numbers).

TRILLIUM, *TRIL ee um*, is a wild flower that grows in damp, wooded places in the United States, Canada, and Asia. There are about 25 kinds. The flowers have three sepals, three petals, and six stamens. Each stem bears one flower and three leaves. Trilliums are often called *wake-robins* because some kinds bloom when the robins return north. The best-known trillium is the *large-flowered trillium.* It grows from New England to the Carolinas and west to Minnesota. The *painted trillium* is the most colorful. Its white flowers have deep pink or purple stripes. It grows from Quebec to Georgia and west as far as Wisconsin and Missouri.

Scientific Classification. Trilliums belong to the lily family, *Liliaceae.* They make up the genus *Trillium.* The large-flowered trillium is *T. grandiflorum;* the painted trillium is *T. undulatum.*   ROBERT W. HOSHAW

See also FLOWER (picture: Flowers of the Woodland).

TRILOBITE, *TRY luh byt*, was a prehistoric sea animal. It lived during the *Paleozoic Era*, which lasted from about 600 million years ago to about 225 million years ago. Trilobites lived in all parts of the world, and scientists have identified more than 4,000 species from fossils. Trilobites were covered by a shell, and most were under

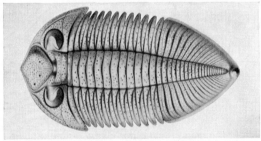

Field Museum of Natural History

Artist's Drawing of a Trilobite

4 inches (10 centimeters) long. Two grooves divided the animal's shell lengthwise into three *lobes* (sections). The name *trilobite* means *three lobes.* Trilobites had three main parts: the head, the thorax, and the tail. The thorax had many segments, each bearing legs. The trilobite breathed through gills on the legs. See also FOSSIL (picture: Fossils of Trilobites).   SAMUEL PAUL WELLES

TRIMETER. See METER (in poetry).

TRINCOMALEE, *TRING koh muh LEE* (pop. 40,000), is a seaport on the northeast coast of Sri Lanka. For location, see SRI LANKA (map). It has an excellent natural harbor. The Portuguese, Dutch, French, and British controlled the city for periods during the 1600's and 1700's. The British captured it in 1795.

Trinidad and Tobago

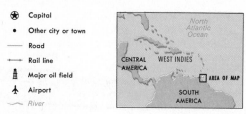

- ⊛ Capital
- • Other city or town
- ─── Road
- ─┼─ Rail line
- 🛢 Major oil field
- ✈ Airport
- ～ River

WORLD BOOK map

TRINIDAD AND TOBAGO is a country that consists of two islands in the West Indies. It lies in the Caribbean Sea, near the northeast coast of South America. Trinidad, the larger island, is 7 miles (11 kilometers) east of Venezuela. Tobago is about 20 miles (32 kilometers) northeast of Trinidad.

Trinidad and Tobago covers 1,980 square miles (5,128 square kilometers) and has a population of about 1,232,000. It is slightly smaller than Delaware but has about twice as many people as that state. Trinidad accounts for about 95 per cent of the country's land area, and approximately 95 per cent of the people live there. Port-of-Spain, on Trinidad, is the nation's capital, largest city, and chief port.

Government. Trinidad and Tobago is a republic. A prime minister, who is the leader of the majority party in Parliament, serves as the head of the government. The prime minister appoints a Cabinet of any number of members for assistance. A president, elected by the Parliament, serves as head of state. The Parliament consists of a 31-member Senate and a 36-member House of Representatives. Leading government officials appoint the senators. The people elect the members of the House of Representatives.

People. More than a third of the nation's people have black African ancestry, and about a third are descendants of people from India. People of mixed European and black African ancestry, plus groups of Europeans and Chinese, make up the rest of the population.

English is the country's official language, but French, Spanish, and Hindi are also spoken. Most of the poorer people speak *Trinidad English*, a form of standard English with French and Spanish influences. About 95 per cent of the people can read and write. The law requires all children from 6 to 12 years old to go to school. Roman Catholics make up the largest religious group, followed by Anglicans and Hindus.

Many people in the country play native musical instruments called *pans*, which are made from empty oil drums. Trinidad is the home of a form of folk music called *calypso* and of the *limbo* dance (see CALYPSO).

Land and Climate. Tropical forests and fertile flatlands cover much of Trinidad. A mountain range extends east and west across the northern area, and hills rise in the central and southern sections. Tobago has a central mountain ridge, and scenic beaches lie along the coast. This island is said to have been the scene of the famous adventure story *Robinson Crusoe*.

Trinidad and Tobago has a warm, moist climate. Temperatures range from 64° F. (18° C) to 92° F. (33° C). The average annual temperature is 78° F. (26° C) on Trinidad and slightly lower on Tobago. The average annual rainfall is about 80 inches (203 centimeters).

Economy of Trinidad and Tobago is based on oil production and refining. The nation produces more than 50 million barrels of crude oil annually and imports about twice as much for refining. Petroleum accounts for about 80 per cent of the country's export income.

Pitch Lake, on Trinidad, is the world's chief source of natural asphalt, a tarlike substance used to make paving materials. This lake provides more than 100,000 short tons (91,000 metric tons) of asphalt yearly.

Other major industries of Trinidad and Tobago include agriculture and tourism. Sugar, the chief export crop, is also used to produce molasses and rum.

Trinidad and Tobago has about 4,000 miles (6,400 kilometers) of roads, and an airport operates on each island. The country has two daily newspapers, a television station, and two major radio stations.

History. Christopher Columbus claimed Trinidad for Spain in 1498, during his third voyage to the New

Facts in Brief

Capital: Port-of-Spain.

Form of Government: Republic.

Official Language: English.

Total Land Area: 1,980 sq. mi. (5,128 km²). *Coastline*—292 mi. (470 km).

Elevation: *Highest*—Mt. Aripo, 3,085 ft. (940 m). *Lowest*—sea level.

Population: *Estimated 1983 Population*—1,232,000; distribution, 51 per cent rural, 49 per cent urban; density, 622 persons per sq. mi. (240 per km²). *1970 Census*—940,719. *Estimated 1988 Population*—1,334,000.

Chief Products: Asphalt, cocoa, oil, sugar.

National Anthem: "Forged from the Love of Liberty."

Flag: A black stripe, bordered by white stripes, runs across a red field from the upper left to the lower right corner. See FLAG (picture: Flags of the Americas).

Money: *Basic Unit*—West Indies dollar. See MONEY (table: Exchange Rates).

362

Port-of-Spain is the chief port of Trinidad and Tobago. Small interisland vessels and large ocean-going ships dock at the busy harbor.

World. Two tribes of American Indians, the Arawak and the Carib, lived there at that time. The Spaniards established a permanent settlement on the island in 1592, but the population did not begin to grow rapidly until 1783. That year, Spain offered land grants in Trinidad to any Roman Catholic settlers who were willing to develop the island's economy. Many planters of French ancestry then went there from Haiti and other nearby islands. They established thriving sugar cane plantations, and the island prospered. The British captured Trinidad in 1797 and ruled it for over 150 years.

A British sea captain named Lawrence Keymis reported seeing Tobago in 1596, and the Dutch settled there in 1632. Great Britain, France, and The Netherlands fought for possession of the island until 1814, when Britain took control of it.

Through the years, thousands of black slaves had been brought from Africa to work on the islands' plantations. Labor shortages occurred after Britain abolished slavery in 1834, and many workers were brought from India.

In 1888, Trinidad and Tobago became one colony under British rule. During the Great Depression of the 1930's, the colony suffered severe economic setbacks. The people then began to demand a greater voice in their government. Britain allowed a gradual increase in self-government during the 1940's and 1950's, and the colony became an independent nation in 1962.

In the early 1970's, black-power supporters protested against widespread unemployment and what they considered social and economic inequality in Trinidad and Tobago. Violent demonstrations broke out, and the government twice declared a state of emergency. Racial tensions eased in the mid-1970's, but unemployment continued to be a major problem in Trinidad and Tobago.   ARCHIBALD W. SINGHAM and NANCY L. SINGHAM

See also PORT-OF-SPAIN.

TRINITROTOLUENE. See TNT.

TRINITY, *TRIN uh tee,* is a term used of God to express the belief that in the one God there are three divine Persons, the Father, the Son, and the Holy Spirit (or Holy Ghost). The idea of trinity is drawn from the teaching of Christ as recorded in the New Testament. Belief in Father, Son, and Holy Spirit was first defined by the earliest general council of churches. This was the First Council of Nicaea in 325. This council declared that the Son is of the same substance as the Father. The East and West branches of the church later disagreed as to how the Holy Spirit proceeds from the other divine Persons. The Eastern Church held that the Son comes from the Father and the Spirit comes from the Father through the Son. The Western Church held that the Spirit comes from Father and Son together. Most Christians believe that Father, Son, and Holy Spirit have equal power and glory. Each has His own activity. The Father creates; the Son saves souls; and the Spirit makes holy.   FULTON J. SHEEN and MERVIN MONROE DEEMS

See also NICENE COUNCILS; ARIANISM.

TRINITY SUNDAY is the Sunday after Pentecost. It was introduced into the church calendar by Pope John XXII (1316-1334) to honor the Trinity of Persons in God. Trinity Sunday ends the main festivals of the church year. In the Episcopal Church, Sundays from then until Advent are called "Sundays after Trinity." The Roman Catholic Church counts the Sundays from Pentecost. The Greek Church does not observe this feast or arrange its calendar in the same way. Roman Catholics must take Holy Communion between the first Sunday of Lent and Trinity Sunday. See also TRINITY; PENTECOST.   ALBERT E. AVEY and FULTON J. SHEEN

TRIODE. See VACUUM TUBE.

TRIP. See LSD.

TRIP HAMMER is a high-speed, power-driven hammer. Machinists use it to shape small forgings, such as edged tools, ornamental ironwork, and small, light machine parts. It gets its name from the way it operates. A *cam* (projection on a wheel) raises it, then loosens its hold on it (*trips*), and suddenly releases the hammer.

The trip hammer is mounted on a pivoted beam. A motor-driven cam revolves on a wheel and raises the hammer. Then, at a certain point in its turning, the cam no longer catches onto the hammer, and stops lifting. Thus, the cam trips, and the hammer falls of its own weight. The power of the blow from a trip hammer cannot be regulated. Its force is due only to its weight and the height from which it falls. The trip hammer differs from the steam hammer, the force of which can be controlled (see STEAM HAMMER).   ARTHUR C. ANSLEY

TRIPARTITE PACT is an agreement entered into by three powers. A well-known tripartite pact in history was the 1940 alliance of Germany, Italy, and Japan. This pact bound the three powers to assist one another in case of attack by a power not yet engaged in the European or Asiatic war. See also TRIPLE ALLIANCE.

TRIPE is the fatty lining of the first and second stomachs of beef animals. "Honeycomb" tripe, taken from the second stomach, is the most tender. Beef tripe is the most common, and should be thick, white, and fat.

Calf tripe is more tender, but little of it is sold. Tripe is easily digested. It is usually prepared by boiling. Canned tripe is cooked in milk and salt.   JOHN C. AYRES

TRIPITIKA. See BUDDHISM (Buddhist Schools).

TRIPLE ALLIANCE was a defense agreement among Austria-Hungary, Germany, and Italy. It lasted from 1882 until World War I. The three nations agreed to help one another in case of attack by two or more great powers. Austria-Hungary and Germany also agreed to help Italy in case of attack by France, and Italy agreed to help Germany if France attacked that nation. The three countries renewed the alliance several times, the last time in 1912.   STEFAN T. POSSONY

See also BISMARCK (Bismarck's Diplomacy); WORLD WAR I (Military Alliances); TRIPARTITE PACT.

TRIPLE ENTENTE, *AHN TAHNT,* means *triple,* or *three-fold, agreement.* When World War I broke out in 1914, the chief powers of Europe were divided into two opposing groups. Germany, Austria-Hungary, and Italy made up the Triple Alliance, while Great Britain, France, and Russia formed the Triple Entente.

The Triple Entente was only an informal grouping when first formed. But between 1912 and 1914, it became an effective diplomatic combination. After the outbreak of war, the Entente Powers signed the Declaration of London, in which each power agreed not to make a separate peace. This act transformed the Triple Entente into a formal union.   DWIGHT E. LEE

See also TRIPLE ALLIANCE; WORLD WAR I (Military Alliances).

TRIPLE JUMP. See TRACK AND FIELD.

TRIPLET, in music, is a group of three notes which, when played, have the value of only two notes of the same kind. A triplet of eighth notes is usually written with the stems joined. But a tie usually connects a triplet of quarter notes.

TRIPLET, in poetry. See POETRY (table: Terms).

TRIPLETS are three children born at the same time of the same mother. One set of triplets is born in about every 9,216 births. *Fraternal* triplets are born from three egg cells. *Identical* triplets are born from one egg cell that divided into three separate eggs. Triplets may also include an identical pair plus a third fraternal child. See also MULTIPLE BIRTH.   GEORGE W. BEADLE

TRIPOLI, Lebanon. See TARABULUS.

TRIPOLI, *TRIP oh lee,* or, in Arabic, TARABULUS (pop. 551,477), is the capital and largest city of Libya. Tripoli is the trading center for a farming region, and it has a fine harbor on the Mediterranean Sea. For location, see LIBYA (map).

Tripoli was technically part of Turkey's Ottoman Empire from the mid-1500's until 1911. But it was controlled by the Barbary pirates during much of this period. Pirate attacks on American ships led to a war between the U.S. and Tripoli in 1801. Italy controlled Tripoli from 1911 until World War II.   LEON CARL BROWN

See also BARBARY STATES; JEFFERSON, THOMAS (War with Tripoli).

TRIPOLI is a light colored substance made chiefly of fine grains of silica. Tripoli is used as a powder for polishing glass, marble, and metals. It is also used to make high grade filters and to give weight and body to paper and paint. Deposits of tripoli are found at the bottom of ponds and bogs. Tripoli also comes from the shells of tiny water plants called *diatoms.* It is called *tripolite* or *diatomaceous earth* when made from diatoms. Tripoli gets its name from Tripoli, Libya, where it was first used.   CECIL J. SCHNEER

TRIPOLITANIA. See LIBYA (History).

TRIPPE, JUAN TERRY (1899-1981), an airline pioneer, founded the Pan American World Airways System in 1927 and directed it until 1968. In 1923, after working for a year in banking, Trippe organized Long Island Airways with seven World War I airplanes. He also helped organize one other airline before he founded Pan American, which became one of the world's largest airlines. He was born in Sea Bright, N.J.   ROBERT B. HOTZ

TRIREME, *TRY reem,* was a large war galley used in ancient times in the Mediterranean Sea. The Corinthians invented it, and other Greeks and the Romans used it later. The name comes from Latin words for *three* and *oar.* The trireme had three *banks* (rows) of oars, one above the other, and a crew of about 200 men. It was steered by long, special steering oars at the stern. At the Battle of Salamis between the Greeks and Persians in 480 B.C., the Greek fleet included many triremes. See also GALLEY; SHIP (picture: Phoenician and Greek Ships).   ROBERT H. BURGESS

TRISTAN AND ISOLDE. See GOTTFRIED VON STRASSBURG; WAGNER, RICHARD (Later Career).

TRISTAN DA CUNHA ISLANDS, *TRISS tan duh KOON yuh,* are a group of British islands in the South Atlantic. They lie about halfway between South America and southern Africa (see ATLANTIC OCEAN [color map]). They include Tristan da Cunha, Gough, Inaccessible, and Nightingale islands. The capital is Edinburgh. The group is a dependency of Saint Helena Island. The islands cover 79 square miles (205 square kilometers) and have a population of about 290.

In 1961, a volcano erupted on Tristan da Cunha Island, and the people living there were moved to Great Britain. But they moved back to the island in 1963 when the island was declared safe.

TRISTRAM SHANDY. See STERNE, LAURENCE.

TRITICALE, *TRIHT uh KAY lee,* is a grain produced by crossbreeding wheat and rye. It has a high nutritional content because it contains more usable protein than either wheat or rye. The triticale plant stands from 18 to 41 inches (45 to 105 centimeters) tall and has 6 to 10 long, narrow leaves. The head consists of many spikelets, each of which holds three to five kernels of grain.

Botanists first crossbred wheat and rye in 1876. This process yielded a hybrid plant that could not produce seeds. In 1937, scientists discovered that treating wheat-rye seedlings with a chemical called *colchicine* made the plants fertile.

The first triticale breeding program was set up in Sweden in the mid-1930's. By the 1950's, many countries, including the United States and Canada, had such programs. These programs have developed many varieties of the grain. Someday, triticale may become an important food in countries not suited for wheat production. Some varieties can grow in cold climates and in sandy or acid soils. Others resist rust better than wheat does and produce a higher yield than rye.

Triticale will probably be used in many countries mainly as an animal feed. Food companies in these

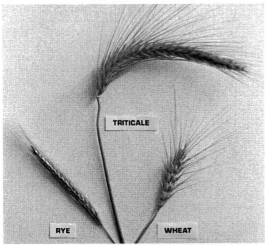

TRITICALE

RYE   WHEAT

Gary Hair, Triticale Industries

Triticale is a hybrid grain produced by crossbreeding rye and wheat. It contains more usable protein than either of the parent plants and grows well in various types of climates and soils.

countries may also use it in the manufacture of flour for bread and cake. In addition, triticale can serve as a pasture crop.

Scientific Classification. Triticale is a member of the grass family, Gramineae. It makes up the genus *Triticosecale*.　　　　　　　　　　　　EDWARD N. LARTER

TRITIUM, *TRIHT ee uhm*, is a hydrogen isotope used in the release of nuclear energy through fusion, as in the hydrogen bomb. It is three times as heavy as ordinary hydrogen. The name *tritium* comes from the Latin *tri*, meaning *three*. Tritium decays to form helium; half the tritium disintegrates in about 12 years.

See also HYDROGEN; HYDROGEN BOMB.

TRITON, *TRY tuhn*, was a sea-god in Greek mythology. He was the son of Poseidon and Amphitrite, and lived with them at the bottom of the sea. He carried a three-pronged spear and a trumpet made of a large twisted sea shell. He stirred up or calmed waves by blowing a trumpet.　　　　　　　　　JAMES F. CRONIN

See also NEPTUNE.

TRIUMPH, in ancient Rome, was the highest honor given to a victorious general. The word *triumph* probably came through the Etruscan language from *thriambos*, a Greek word that means a procession honoring the god Bacchus.

When a victor received a triumph, he entered Rome in a triumphal car drawn by four horses, and proceeded along the *Via Sacra* (Sacred Way) to the capitol. The senators walked at the head of the procession. Behind them came trumpeters, carriages bearing the spoils of war, oxen to be sacrificed, and captives in chains. Then came the general, crowned with laurel, and his children and friends. The general's soldiers were at the end of the procession, cheering and singing as they marched. In a triumph given to honor a naval commander, nautical trophies were carried.

Under the Empire, only the emperor could receive a triumph. A great general might receive a minor celebration called an *ovation*.　　　　　　　　　FRANK C. BOURNE

TRIUMPH, ARCH OF. See ARC DE TRIOMPHE.

TRIUMVIRATE, *try UHM vuhr iht*. In Roman history, a triumvirate was a group of three men who seized control of the government. Rome had two triumvirates. The first was formed in 60 B.C. It was made up of Julius Caesar, Pompey the Great, and Marcus Licinius Crassus. The second triumvirate was formed in 43 B.C., after Brutus and Cassius had murdered Caesar. Its members were Gaius Octavianus (Augustus), Marcus Lepidus, and Mark Antony.

The Roman republican form of government almost disappeared while the triumvirates lasted. Both triumvirates ended in civil war to determine the supremacy of one member of the group. In the first war, Caesar defeated Pompey the Great. In the second civil war, Mark Antony was overcome by Octavianus, who became Emperor Augustus.　　　　　　　　　CHESTER G. STARR

See also ANTONY, MARK; AUGUSTUS; CAESAR, JULIUS; CRASSUS, MARCUS LICINIUS; POMPEY THE GREAT.

TRIVIUM. See EDUCATION (Christian Education in the Middle Ages).

TROBRIAND ISLANDS, *TROH bree ahnd*, make up a small group in the southwestern Pacific. They are part of the nation of Papua New Guinea, and lie about 150 miles (241 kilometers) northeast of the island of New Guinea. For location, see PAPUA NEW GUINEA (map). Kiriwina, the largest island, served as a base for Australian and United States air forces during World War II (1939-1945). The islands cover an area of 210 square miles (544 square kilometers) and have a population of about 13,725. The people are of mixed Melanesian and Polynesian stock. The Trobriand Islands are composed of raised coral limestone. The fertile soil produces good crops. The chief exports are pearls and pearl shells.　　　　　　　　　EDWIN H. BRYAN, JR.

See also MYTHOLOGY (What Myths Are About).

TROCHAIC METER. See POETRY (Metrical Patterns).

TROGLODYTE, *TRAHG luh dyt*, is a Greek word which means *cave dweller*. Ancient Greeks gave the name to certain primitive tribes, who lived in hillside caverns and tunnels. The best known of these people lived along the shores of the Red Sea. They raised cattle and hunted animals, and were sometimes robbers. The Troglodytes were probably of mixed Arabian and Ethiopian stock. They often served as guides on military expeditions of the Greeks.　　　　　　　　　C. BRADFORD WELLES

TROGON, *TROH gahn*, is a family of birds. Trogons live in the warm regions of both the Eastern and the Western hemispheres. The feathers of adult males shine like metal. The underparts of their bodies are colored red, orange, or yellow. The trogon has a short, strong bill. Two of its toes point forward, and two backward. Its feet are small and weak. The female lays two to four white, pale blue, or pale green eggs. The nestlings are naked when hatched. African and Asian trogons feed mostly on insects. American trogons eat fruits and insects. See also QUETZAL.

Scientific Classification. Trogons make up the trogon family, *Trogonidae*. The collared trogon is genus *Trogon*, species *T. collaris*.　　　　RODOLPHE MEYER DE SCHAUENSEE

TROIKA, *TROI kuh*, is a Russian word that means *a group of three*. A light, Russian sleigh that is pulled by three horses is called a troika. The term *troika* was applied to a 1960 Russian plan to have the United

Nations headed by three secretaries-general instead of one. See also COLD WAR (The Troika Proposal).

TROILUS AND CRISEYDE. See CHAUCER, GEOFFREY.

TROJAN HORSE. See TROJAN WAR; MYTHOLOGY (picture).

TROJAN WAR was a conflict in which ancient Greece defeated the city of Troy. The war, which probably took place during the mid-1200's B.C., inspired many leading works of classical literature. Some of the events that occurred during and after the Trojan War became the subject of three great epic poems. These poems are the *Iliad* and the *Odyssey* by the Greek poet Homer and the *Aeneid* by the Roman poet Virgil. The heroes and victims of the war were portrayed in such Greek tragedies as *Agamemnon* by Aeschylus, *Ajax* by Sophocles, and *The Trojan Women* by Euripides.

Scholars know little about the actual Trojan War. Their knowledge of the war comes chiefly from the epics of Homer and Virgil, which are largely fictional. These poetic accounts combine historical facts with material from Greek legends and myths. But archaeologists have found historical evidence in the ruins of Troy and other cities that confirms certain events described by the poets.

The Beginning of the War. According to ancient Greek myths, the Trojan War resulted from an incident at the wedding feast of Peleus, the king of Thessaly, and Thetis, a sea goddess. All the gods and goddesses of Mount Olympus had been invited except Eris, the goddess of discord. Eris was offended and tried to stir up trouble among the guests at the feast. She sent a golden apple inscribed "For the most beautiful." Three goddesses—Hera, Athena, and Aphrodite—each claimed the apple, and a quarrel began. Paris, the son of King Priam of Troy, judged the dispute. He awarded the apple to Aphrodite because she had promised him Helen, the most beautiful woman in the world.

Helen was already married to King Menelaus of Sparta. But when Paris visited her, she fled with him to Troy. Menelaus and his brother, Agamemnon, organized a large Greek expedition against Troy to win Helen back. The Greek army included such heroes as Achilles, Ajax the Greater, Nestor, and Odysseus (Ulysses in Latin).

The Siege of Troy. The Greek army laid siege to Troy for 10 years but could not conquer the city. The *Iliad* describes some of the events that occurred during the last year of the struggle. The war began to go badly for the Greeks after Achilles, their bravest warrior, left the battlefield. Achilles refused to fight because Agamemnon, the Greek commander, had insulted him. The Trojans, led by Hector, drove the Greeks back to their ships. Achilles finally returned to combat after his best friend, Patroclus, had been slain by Hector. Achilles killed Hector to avenge Patroclus' death.

The *Iliad* ends with Hector's burial, and Greek legends relate events that followed. The Trojans received help from their allies, the Ethiopians and an army of women warriors called Amazons. But Achilles enabled the Greeks to defeat their enemies by killing Penthesilea, the queen of the Amazons, and Memnon, the king of the Ethiopians. Paris, aided by the god Apollo, later wounded Achilles fatally.

The Fall of Troy is described in the *Aeneid*. The Greeks built a huge wooden horse, which has become known as the *Trojan horse*, and placed it outside the walls of Troy. Odysseus and some other warriors hid inside the horse while the rest of the Greek army sailed away.

The prophetess Cassandra and the priest Laocoön warned the Trojans against taking the horse into their city. But Sinon, a Greek prisoner, persuaded them that the horse was sacred and would bring the protection of the gods. The Trojans then pulled the horse into Troy. That night, they fell asleep after celebrating their apparent victory. Odysseus and his companions then crept out of the horse and opened the city gates for the rest of their warriors, who had returned from a nearby island.

The Greeks took back Helen, slaughtered almost all the Trojans, and burned Troy. According to the *Aeneid*, the few Trojan survivors included the warrior Aeneas, whose descendants founded Rome.   ROBERT J. LENARDON

Related Articles in WORLD BOOK include:

Achilles	Andromache	Iliad	Paris
Aeneas	Cassandra	Laocoön	Priam
Aeneid	Hector	Menelaus	Troy
Agamemnon	Helen of Troy	Odyssey	Ulysses
Ajax			

Additional Resources

COOLIDGE, OLIVIA. *The Trojan War.* Houghton, 1952.
EDMONDS, I. G. *The Mysteries of Troy.* Elsevier-Nelson, 1977.
GRAVES, ROBERT. *The Siege and Fall of Troy.* Doubleday, 1963.

TROLL. See FAIRY.

TROLLEY. See ELECTRIC RAILROAD; STREETCAR.

TROLLOPE, ANTHONY (1815-1882), was a popular English novelist of the 1800's. He was over 30 years old when he published his first book. But after he started, he wrote with such regularity that his novels and tales fill more than 50 volumes.

Trollope's most famous books are the "Barsetshire Novels." These six stories about life in the imaginary county of Barsetshire, and especially the cathedral city of Barchester, are mildly satirical. But their tone shows Trollope's affectionate tolerance for the weaknesses of his basically generous and well-meaning characters. Trollope had so clear an idea of his creation that he could draw a map of Barsetshire.

The Barsetshire novels are *The Warden* (1855), *Barchester Towers* (1857), *Doctor Thorne* (1858), *Framley Parsonage* (1861), *The Small House at Allington* (1864), and *The Last Chronicle of Barset* (1867). Trollope's other works include social satire novels, such as *The Bertrams* (1859) and *The Way We Live Now* (1875); political novels, such as *The Eustace Diamonds* (1873); and novels of psychological analysis, such as *Cousin Henry* (1879).

Trollope was born in London. In his autobiography, he described his unhappy childhood. His family was poor, and his education was often interrupted by lack of money. Frances Trollope, Anthony's mother, was also a famous writer. She wrote *Domestic Manners of the Americans* (1832) after a visit to the United States. The book sold well, but did not provide enough money to pay the family bills. The Trollopes moved to Bruges, Belgium, to escape their creditors. All his life, Trollope remembered the humiliation of those early years.

Trollope returned to London in 1834. He became a

clerk in the post office, where he worked for many years. He designed the red mail boxes that are still used in England. His last years were happy. He died in London of a stroke brought on, it is said, by over-hearty laughter. JAMES DOUGLAS MERRITT

Additional Resources

BAREHAM, TONY, ed. *Anthony Trollope*. Barnes, 1980. A collection of essays which discusses Trollope's political and social thoughts.
SNOW, C. P. *Trollope: His Life and Art*. Scribner, 1975.
TRACY, ROBERT. *Trollope's Later Novels*. Univ. of California Press, 1978.
TROLLOPE, ANTHONY. *Autobiography*. Pub. in 1883, after his death. Now available in many eds.

TROMBONE is a brass instrument that consists chiefly of an oblong tube expanded into a bell at one end. It is played by blowing into a cup-shaped mouthpiece and vibrating the lips. Most trombones have a long slide. The player changes tones by tightening the lips and by moving the slide back and forth. A *valve trombone* has three valves instead of a slide. The *tenor trombone* is the most popular type of trombone. The *bass trombone* is larger. It has, in addition to the slide, one or two rotary valves for extending the range downward.

WORLD BOOK photo, courtesy Chicago Symphony Orchestra

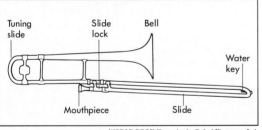

WORLD BOOK illustration by Oxford Illustrators, Ltd.

The Trombone is an important brass instrument in both popular and classical music. It has a long slide attached to a tube. A musician plays different notes by moving the slide back and forth.

A primitive type of trombone was used as early as 1495 in England. The trombone became a part of symphony orchestras during the 1800's. Today, the instrument is popular in concert, marching, and military bands, and in popular music and jazz. JOHN KEIL RICHARDS

TRONA is one of the most important natural soda minerals. It consists of sodium carbonate, sodium bicarbonate, and water and has the chemical formula $Na_2CO_3 \cdot NaHCO_3 \cdot 2H_2O$. Trona is the main source of soda ash, which is used for many purposes, including the manufacture of chemicals, glass, and paper.

Trona is gray or yellowish-white and forms fibrous crystals. It dissolves easily in water, and so it is found at the earth's surface in solid form only in dry regions. Trona also occurs underground and is extracted from *brine* (extremely salty water). The largest pure deposit of trona in the United States lies underground near Green River, Wyo. MARIA LUISA CRAWFORD

See also WYOMING (The Mid-1900's).

TRONDHEIM, *TRAWN haym* (pop. 135,085), is the third largest city in Norway. It lies on the southern shore of Trondheims Fiord, where the Nid River empties into the fiord (see NORWAY [map]).

Trondheim is an important export center for copper and iron ores, pyrites, wood pulp, timber, and fish. The city was founded in A.D. 998 by King Olaf Trygvason. The Nidaros Cathedral, one of the finest Norman Gothic buildings in the world, dates back to A.D. 1070. The modern Technical University of Norway is also in Trondheim. OSCAR SVARLIEN

TROOPER. See POLICE (State Police).

TROPIC BIRD is the name of a bird which flies over tropical waters. It is also called the *boatswain*. The

John Warham, *The Geographical Magazine*, London

A Red-Tailed Tropic Bird and Its Chick, *foreground*

tropic bird dives straight down into the water for fish, as the tern does. But it has long, willowy, middle tail feathers, which the tern does not have (see TERN). The tropic bird's feathers are pure white or pinkish, striped with black on top. The *red-billed tropic bird* lives in the tropical parts of the Atlantic and Pacific oceans. It is pure white, with a coral-red bill, and is nearly 40 inches (100 centimeters) long. Its tail measures about 26 inches (66 centimeters). Other kinds of tropic birds are the *yellow-billed* and the *red-tailed*.

All tropic birds make their nests in holes, in cracks in the rocks, or on the bare sand. The one egg is whitish or brownish, spotted with dark brown. On land, a tropic bird shuffles along on its breast, because it cannot stand. Its voice is harsh and hoarse-sounding.

Scientific Classification. The tropic birds belong to the tropic bird family, *Phaëthontidae*. The red-billed is genus *Phaëthon*, species *P. aethereus;* the yellow-billed, *P. flavirostris;* the red-tailed, *P. rubricauda*. ALEXANDER WETMORE

TROPIC OF CANCER is an imaginary line that traces the northern boundary of the earth's Tropical Zone. It marks the farthest limit north of the equator where the sun can appear directly overhead. The line, which is also known as the *northern circle*, lies 23° 27′ north of the

367

equator. The vertical rays of the sun shine down on the Tropic of Cancer at noon on the day of the summer solstice, which is June 20 or 21.

The Tropic of Cancer passes through many lands with a variety of climates. It crosses the middle part of Mexico, passes between Florida and Cuba, and crosses the Sahara, Arabia, northern India, and southern China. It crosses the Pacific Ocean immediately north of the Hawaiian Islands. The word *Cancer* means *crab* in Latin, and refers to a star constellation. This group of stars is one of the 12 constellations of the zodiac. The position of the Tropic of Cancer on the map was first marked by the fact that it was directly beneath the heavenly constellation of Cancer. The inclination of the earth to the plane of its orbit determines the position of Cancer. When one is on the Tropic of Cancer, the North Star appears at an angle of 23° 27′ above the horizon. SAMUEL N. DICKEN

See also TROPICS; ZONE.

TROPIC OF CAPRICORN is an imaginary line that traces the southern boundary of the earth's Tropical Zone. It marks the farthest limit south of the equator where the sun can appear directly overhead. The Tropic of Capricorn, which lies 23° 27′ south of the equator, is also known as the *southern circle*. The vertical rays of the sun shine down on the Tropic of Capricorn at noon on the day of the winter solstice, which is December 21 or 22.

The Tropic of Capricorn crosses northern Chile and southern Brazil, South Africa, and Madagascar, and passes through the middle part of Australia. The Tropic of Capricorn separates the southern tropics from the South Temperate Belt. The word *Capricorn* comes from the Latin *caper*, meaning *goat*, and *cornu*, meaning *horn*. It refers to a group of stars representing one of the signs of the zodiac, known as Capricorn. The Tropic of Capricorn used to lie directly beneath this constellation. SAMUEL N. DICKEN

See also TROPICS; ZONE.

TROPICAL FISH. Many kinds of fish live in the tropics, but this term is applied particularly to small, brightly colored kinds that breed very rapidly, and are popular for home aquariums. Tropical fish are usually a little smaller than goldfish. About 300 different kinds of tropical fish are kept in aquariums.

Most tropical fish will eat food made from grains, dried shrimp, fish, insects, and salts. Such food can be purchased in any pet shop. Small pieces of shrimp, oyster, crab, canned fish, boiled fish, and other kinds of fish may also be given them, for most tropical fish are carnivorous. Some persons raise small white worms to feed their pet fish. A good rule is to feed only the amount that the fish will clean up promptly, because uneaten food drops to the bottom and decays. This makes the water foul, and it may kill the fish.

A tropical fish aquarium should be covered with a flat pane of glass to control the temperature. This also keeps the fish from leaping out of the aquarium. Water plants should be grown, because they keep the water in better condition and they also produce oxygen for the fish to breathe.

The most common and best-known tropical fish is the *guppy*. It comes from the West Indies and South

America, and is very valuable in its homeland, for it eats great numbers of mosquito larvae. The female guppy is about 1½ inches (3.8 centimeters) long, and the male is even smaller. The female is gray, but the male is brilliantly rainbow-hued.

Guppies breed when they are about three months old, and bear their young alive. Each female guppy produces from 20 to 50 young. The guppy can survive in water at a temperature as low as 55° F. (13° C), but the temperature should be at least 68° F. (20° C).

Other popular tropical fish which bear live young are the *swordtail*, the *platyfish*, and the *black molly*. Some tropical fish that bear their young in eggs are the *barbs*, *danios*, *rasboras*, *characins*, and *cichlids*. The various *labyrinth fishes* are so named because they have a cavity in their head above the gills in which they store air.

Scientific Classification. Live-bearing tropical fish belong to the live bearer family, Poeciliidae. The guppy is *P. reticulata*. The swordtail is *Xiphophorus hellerii*. The platyfish is *Xiphophorus*. The black molly is *Poecilia latipinna*. Barbs, danios, and rasboras belong to the carp and minnow family, Cyprinidae. The barb is *Barbus;* the danio is *Danio;* and the rasbora is *Rasbora*. Each has many popular species. The characins form the characin family, Characinidae and the cichlids form the cichlid family, Cichlidae. CARL L. HUBBS

See also FISH (pictures: Fish of Coral Reefs; Fish of Tropical Fresh Waters); ANGELFISH; FIGHTING FISH; GUPPY; AQUARIUM.

Additional Resources

AXELROD, HERBERT R., and others. *Exotic Tropical Fishes*. Rev. ed. TFH Publications, 1980.
AXELROD, HERBERT R., and VORDERWINKLER, WILLIAM. *Tropical Fish in Your Home*. Harper, 1973.
WALKER, BRAZ. *Tropical Fish Identifier*. Sterling, 1971.

TROPICAL FRUIT. See FRUIT (How Horticulturists Classify Fruits).

TROPICAL PLANT. See TROPICAL RAIN FOREST.

TROPICAL RAIN FOREST is a forest of tall trees in a region of year-round warmth and plentiful rainfall. Almost all these forests lie near the equator. They occupy large regions in Africa, Asia, and Central and South America, and on Pacific islands. The largest tropical rain forest, the Amazonian rain forest, covers about a third of South America. Tropical rain forests stay green throughout the year.

A tropical rain forest has more kinds of trees than any other area in the world. Scientists have counted 179 species in one 8½-acre (3.4-hectare) area in South America. Most forests of this size in the United States have fewer than 7 species of trees. In addition, more species of certain animals—amphibians, birds, insects, mammals, and reptiles—live in tropical rain forests than anywhere else.

The tallest trees of a rain forest may grow as tall as 200 feet (61 meters). The *crowns* (tops) of other trees form a covering of leaves about 100 or 150 feet (30 to 46 meters) above the ground. This covering is called the *upper canopy*. The crowns of smaller trees form one or two *lower canopies*. All the canopies shade the forest floor so that it receives less than 1 per cent as much sunlight as does the upper canopy.

Most areas of the forest floor receive so little light that few bushes, herbs, or flowering plants can grow there. As a result, a person can easily walk through most parts of a tropical rain forest. Areas of dense growth called *jungles* occur within a tropical rain forest in areas where

Alan Band Associates

Squirrel Monkeys, which live only in the tropical rain forests of Central and South America, scamper along tree branches and climbing vines.

Huge Growths Called *Buttresses* extend from the trunk to the roots of many trees in tropical rain forests. The buttresses may help support the trees. Yagua Indians hunt small birds with blowguns in the upper Amazon Valley of South America, *right.*

Loren McIntyre, Woodfin Camp, Inc.

much sunlight reaches the ground. Most jungles grow near broad rivers or in former clearings. See JUNGLE.

The temperature in a rain forest rarely rises above 93° F. (34° C) or drops below 68° F. (20° C). In many cases, the average temperature of the hottest month is only 2° to 5° F. (1° to 3° C) higher than the average temperature of the coldest month. At least 80 inches (200 centimeters) of rain falls yearly in a tropical rain forest. Thundershowers may occur more than 200 days a year. The air beneath the lower canopy is almost always humid.

All tropical rain forests resemble one another. But each of the three largest ones—the American, the

TROPICAL RAIN FORESTS

Tropical rain forests lie chiefly near the equator. These areas receive some of the world's heaviest rainfall.

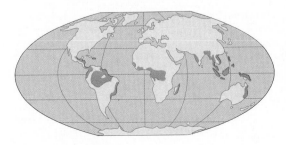

African, and the Asian—has a different group of species of animals and plants. For instance, each rain forest has many species of monkeys, all of which differ from the species of the other two rain forests. For illustrations of rain forests, see PLANT (Where Plants Live) and TREE (Trees Around the World). For illustrations of the animals that live in rain forests, see ANIMAL (Animals of the Tropical Forests).

Plant Life. A tropical rain forest is always green because most of its trees lose old leaves and grow new ones throughout the year. Different kinds of trees bear flowers and fruit at various times of the year. As a result, some kind of tree is in bloom or in fruit at any time of the year. Some short trees bear fruit on the trunk or on large, low branches. Some tall trees bear large fruit on long, drooping, ropelike stalks.

Tropical rain forest trees include some species of great beauty and others that provide fruit, timber, and other useful products. Cassias, dhaks, shellseeds, and tabebuias bear bright-colored flowers. But most rain forest trees have smaller, less noticeable flowers, and the canopy always appears mostly green. Cashews, durians, mangosteens, sapodillas, and many kinds of figs and palms yield fruit. Valuable timber comes from balsas, brazilwoods, lauans, logwoods, mahoganies, and rosewoods. Kapoks bear fruits that contain a fluffy fiber used to stuff life jackets and upholstery. Cinchonas provide the drug quinine.

In a tropical rain forest, many plants grow on tree

branches, where they receive more sunlight than they would on the ground. Such plants, called *air plants*, include ferns, mosses, orchids, and bromeliads. Climbing plants called *lianas* twine around tree trunks and branches. Some of these plants form loops and knots as they grow toward the sunlight. See AIR PLANT.

Several kinds of *strangler* trees grow in rain forests. These trees start life as air plants. But unlike other species of air plants, they develop roots that reach down to the ground. The roots surround the tree on which the strangler lives. In time, the strangler may kill the other tree by depriving it of food, light, and water.

In a tropical rain forest, most plant food is stored in a thin layer of soil near the surface. In this layer, decaying vegetation mixes with the soil and adds food to it. The roots of most rain forest trees remain close to the supply of plant food near the surface. In some species, the roots form large growths called *buttresses* that extend between the roots and the trunk. The buttresses may help keep the trees upright.

Animal Life. A great variety of animals lives in a tropical rain forest. Many of these animals spend their lives in the trees and never descend to the ground. The fruits and nuts of the upper and lower canopy furnish food for bats, gibbons, monkeys, squirrels, parrots, and toucans. Sloths and some monkeys feed on the leaves. Hummingbirds and sunbirds sip nectar from flowers there. Frogs, lizards, and snakes also dwell among the branches. Large birds and large snakes prey on the smaller animals.

Many canopy animals are especially suited to tree-top life. Flying lemurs and flying squirrels glide from tree to tree. Galagos and marmosets jump from branch to branch. Several kinds of anteaters, monkeys, opossums, and porcupines sometimes hang by their tail.

Antelope, deer, hogs, tapirs, and many kinds of rodents roam the forest floor. They feed on roots, seeds, and leaves, and also on fruit that drops to the ground. Chimpanzees, coatis, and several members of the cat family live both on the floor and in the trees.

Ants may be found at all levels in a rain forest. Bees, butterflies, mosquitoes, moths, termites, and spiders are also abundant.

People of the Rain Forests. Few people dwell in tropical rain forests. Most such people clear small areas and plant crops there. They chop down the trees, burn them, and plant seeds among the ashes. But after a few years, the thin layer of soil no longer provides good harvests. The farmers then move elsewhere and begin the process all over again. Such farming, called *shifting cultivation*, can support only a small population.

A few groups of rain forest people practice no agriculture. For example, the Pygmies of the Central African rain forest live by hunting wild animals, gathering wild plants, and occasionally trading with agricultural tribes.   HERBERT G. BAKER

See also the sections on plant and animal life in the articles on AFRICA, ASIA, NORTH AMERICA, and SOUTH AMERICA.

Additional Resources

BATTEN, MARY. *The Tropical Forest: Ants, Ants, Animals and Plants.* Harper, 1973.
EMSLEY, MICHAEL G., and SANDVED, K. B. *Rain Forests and Cloud Forests.* Abrams, 1979.
ROSS, WILDA. *The Rain Forest: What Lives There.* Coward, 1977. For younger readers.

TROPICS are the regions of the earth that lie within about 1,600 miles (2,570 kilometers) north and 1,600 miles south of the equator. Two imaginary lines, the Tropic of Cancer and the Tropic of Capricorn, form the boundaries of the tropics. The Tropic of Cancer is 23° 27′ north of the equator, and the Tropic of Capricorn is 23° 27′ south of the equator. These lines mark the northernmost and southernmost places on the earth where the sun ever shines directly overhead.

Most places in the tropics have warm to hot temperatures the year around. Tropical places are hot because the sun's rays shine almost straight down at noon. Such direct rays shine more intensely and produce higher temperatures than do slanted rays.

The temperature does not change much in the tropics because the amount of daylight does not differ greatly from season to season. At the equator, the sun shines about 12 hours each day of the year. At the edges of the tropics, daylight varies from about $10\frac{1}{2}$ hours a day in winter to about $13\frac{1}{2}$ hours a day in summer. Places at the edges of the tropics have cool periods in winter. Tropical places at high altitudes are cool because the temperature drops about $3\frac{1}{2}$° F. per 1,000 feet (2° C per 300 meters) of elevation.

Many tropical areas have definite rainy and dry seasons. Most places near the equator get much rain during all seasons and are covered by tropical rain forests (see TROPICAL RAIN FOREST). Farther to the north and

The Tropics

The tropics, shown on the map at the right, lie on both sides of the equator. They are bounded by two imaginary lines called the Tropic of Cancer and the Tropic of Capricorn. Most tropical places are warm to hot the year around.

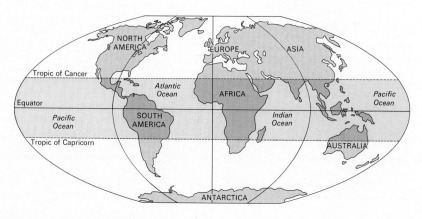

south, one or two short dry seasons occur yearly. Such areas have forests of trees that lose their leaves during these dry seasons. Areas even farther from the equator have one long dry season each year. These areas are covered by *savannas* (grasslands with scattered trees and shrubs). HERBERT G. BAKER

For information on how people live in the tropics, see AFRICA (Ways of Life South of the Sahara); ASIA (Way of Life in Southeast Asia); INDIAN, AMERICAN (Indians of the Tropical Forest); LATIN AMERICA (Way of Life). See also FISH (pictures); JUNGLE; SAVANNA; TROPIC OF CANCER; TROPIC OF CAPRICORN.

TROPISM, *TROH pihz'm,* is a bending movement in living things caused by an outside *stimulus* (signal). For example, sunlight causes plant leaves and stems to bend toward it. A tropism results from differences in the growth rate of various parts of an *organ* (a body structure) when the stimulus is present. The bending usually is slow. For example, some tropisms in plants take from one hour to several days for completion. They occur only in young tissues.

Tropisms are named for the stimulus that causes them. For example, *geotropism* is bending caused by gravity, *phototropism* is bending caused by light, and *hydrotropism* is bending caused by moisture. Tropisms may be *positive* (bending toward the stimulus) or *negative* (bending away from the stimulus). Studies of tropisms led to the discovery of *auxins,* the plant hormones that control growth (see AUXIN). NEAL D. BUFFALOE

TROPOSPHERE, *TROH puh sfihr,* is the layer of the atmosphere closest to the earth. We live in the troposphere, and nearly all the earth's weather—including most clouds, rain, and snow—occurs there. The troposphere extends upward from 6 to 10 miles (10 to 16 kilometers). The *stratosphere* lies above the troposphere, followed by the *mesosphere* and the *thermosphere.*

The temperature of the air in the troposphere drops as the altitude increases. The temperature averages about 60° F. (15° C) at the earth's surface. At the top of the troposphere, called the *tropopause,* the temperature is about −67° F. (−56° C). There, the temperature stops decreasing with altitude. The temperature of the tropopause varies from the equator to the poles. Surprisingly, the tropopause at the poles is nearly 50 degrees Fahrenheit (28 degrees Celsius) warmer than the tropopause at the equator.

The thickness of the troposphere varies from the poles to the equator. At the equator, the tropopause has an altitude of 10 miles (16 kilometers). In the polar regions, it is about 6 miles (10 kilometers) high.

The temperature drop at increasing altitudes in the troposphere plays an important part in changes in the weather. Air in the troposphere can mix because cold, *dense* (heavy) air lies above warmer, less dense air. If something starts air moving upwards, the air continues to rise because it remains warmer and less dense than its surroundings. Likewise, sinking air remains colder than its surroundings and continues to sink. These tropospheric mixings are the major weather systems of the earth. Rising air forms clouds and rain, and sinking air brings fair weather. Such mixing cannot occur in a layer such as the stratosphere that has warm air over cold air. FRANK SECHRIST

See also AIR; STRATOSPHERE; MESOSPHERE; THERMOSPHERE.

TROT. See HORSE (Gaits).

TROTSKY, *TRAHT skee,* **LEON** (1879-1940), also spelled *Trotzky,* was a leader of the Bolshevik revolution in Russia (see BOLSHEVIKS). While Lenin lived, Trotsky was the second most powerful man in Russia. After Lenin's death, Trotsky lost the leadership to Joseph Stalin. Trotsky was later exiled. Until his violent death, he waged a bitter fight against Stalin from abroad. See LENIN, V. I.; STALIN, JOSEPH.

Trotsky was born Lev Davidovich Bronstein in the Ukraine of well-to-do parents. After two years of revolutionary activity as a Social Democrat, he was arrested in 1898. He escaped from Siberian exile in 1902 and went to London, where he met Lenin. He returned to Russia to take an active part in the revolution in 1905.

Trotsky was jailed for his leadership in the Saint Petersburg (now Leningrad) Soviet of 1905. But he escaped in 1907. For 10 years he was a revolutionary writer and editor in western Europe. During World War I, he was expelled from France and Spain, and came to New York, where he received the news of the czar's downfall in 1917. He returned to Russia. With Lenin, he successfully plotted the Bolshevik seizure of power and formation of the Soviet regime in November, 1917. Trotsky became the first Soviet commissar of foreign affairs, and was soon the commissar of war.

United Press Int.

Leon Trotsky

In the civil war of 1918-1920, Trotsky was an efficient organizer of the triumphant Red army. After Lenin's death, many believed that Trotsky would be the new head of the Soviet government, but he was outsmarted by Stalin. Trotsky was expelled from the Communist Party in 1927, and the next year was exiled to Soviet Central Asia. He was deported to Turkey in 1929. He later moved to Norway and then to Mexico.

By 1940, Stalin apparently regretted his "leniency" with Trotsky. His secret police sent an agent to Mexico, and Trotsky was murdered there. Trotsky died on Aug. 21, 1940. ALBERT PARRY

See also RUSSIA (The October Revolution).

Additional Resources

CARMICHAEL, JOEL. *Trotsky: An Appreciation of His Life.* St. Martin's, 1975.
DEUTSCHER, ISAAC. *The Prophet Armed: Trotsky, 1879-1921.* Oxford, 1954. *The Prophet Unarmed: Trotsky, 1921-1929.* 1959. *The Prophet Outcast: Trotsky, 1929-1940.* 1963.
SEGAL, RONALD. *Leon Trotsky: A Biography.* Pantheon, 1980.

TROUBADOUR, *TROO buh door,* was one of a large group of poet-musicians who flourished in southern France from the early 1100's to the late 1200's. The word comes from the Latin *tropare* (to compose). Many scholars believe the troubadours may have modeled their lyric verse on the works of Spanish Arab poets and classical Roman poets such as Ovid.

Troubadours composed their poetry in a Romance

Troubadours were singing poets of southern France who often entertained kings and other royalty with their songs of love. This illustration is taken from a medieval illuminated manuscript.

language called Provençal, or *langue d'oc*. The *canso d'amor* (love song) was one of the most important of the rich and varied poetic forms used by troubadours. In the *canso*, the poet imagines the lady of his desires as the model of virtue, and dedicates his talents to singing her praises. The troubadours' praise of physical love stood in direct contrast to traditional Christian morality. The troubadours' ideal of love and their praise of women influenced many later writers, including Dante and Petrarch.   RICHARD O'GORMAN

See also KNIGHTS AND KNIGHTHOOD (Knighthood in Literature); MINNESINGER; STORYTELLING (The Middle Ages); TROUVÈRE.

TROUGH. See WAVES (Characteristics of Waves).

TROUT is a fish of northern waters which is related to the salmon. Most kinds of trout live in northern lakes and rivers, and those which live in the sea run up the streams to spawn. Trout are important food and game fish. Many fishing enthusiasts say that the trout and the salmon are the best of the game fish. All put up a good fight when hooked. They are very greedy eaters.

Trout thrive in cool, clear waters with a gravelly bottom, where the current is strong and there are rapids and deep pools. The fish spawn in the cold weather of the fall or early spring. The eggs hatch when the temperature of the water rises in the spring. The eggs can be kept on ice and are shipped to all parts of the world. During the winter, the fish may go down the rivers and into the open sea. They often remain for many days in the mouths of rivers or in small bays along the coast.

Scientists divide trout into two main groups: the *true trout* and the *chars*. The true trout belong to the same genus as the Atlantic salmon. The most handsome and active of the trout are the chars.

Chars. The *brook* or *speckled trout* is perhaps the best-known char. This fish was originally found from the Appalachian regions westward to the Great Lakes territory and Minnesota, and in Canada from the Saskatchewan River to Labrador. But brook trout now have been placed in hundreds of lakes and streams of the Upper Mississippi Valley and the Western States.

Brook trout in large bodies of water grow to be about $1\frac{1}{2}$ feet (46 centimeters) long. A brook trout weighing $14\frac{1}{2}$ pounds (6.6 kilograms) has been the world record for years. It was caught in the Nipigon River on the north shore of Lake Superior. But brook trout this large are becoming rare because they are so popular as game fish. Anglers speak of their coloring as the "bloom of the trout." The back is marked with dark olive and black, the sides are spotted with red, and the fins have dark and orange mottlings. The season for catching brook trout is limited in all states.

The native char of the Pacific coastal waters is the *Dolly Varden*, a fish with a slender body and no wavy markings on the back. It has red spots on both back and sides. The larger Dolly Vardens are 2 to 3 feet (61 to 91 centimeters) long and weigh from 5 to 12 pounds (2.3 to 5.4 kilograms). The flesh is as delicious as that of the brook trout. These trout are caught in swift, cold streams, and are game fighters.

The northernmost char is the *arctic char*, found north of Hudson Bay. It is related to both an American species, the *Sunapee trout*, and the *European char*, which swims in the cold lakes and mountain streams of Northern Europe. The Sunapee lives in Sunapee Lake, New Hampshire, and Flood Pond, Maine, which have very cold and clear water. The Sunapee is famous for its beautiful coloring and active, graceful movements.

The *lake trout*, a char, is the largest trout. It is caught in the Great Lakes and large lakes to the north. This trout has many local names. It has small pale-yellow spots all over its body, and a deeply forked tail fin. It often weighs from 15 to 20 pounds (6.8 to 9.1 kilograms), sometimes as much as 100 pounds (45 kilograms). Its tasty flesh makes it one of the most valuable food fishes of the Great Lakes.

True Trout. The most important of the true trout are the *rainbow* trout. Rainbow trout live in the streams and lakes of western North America. They have also been set free in streams in the East, and in other countries. They are brightly colored fish with a brilliant rosy band along each side of the body. Some rainbow trout migrate from fresh water to the sea. They are generally called *steelheads*. The steelheads look quite different because their bodies acquire a steely-blue color. Rainbows are highly prized as game fish and as food. They fight hard and long for their freedom.

The *cutthroat trout* is a black-spotted species like the rainbow trout, but it has a brilliant red streak on each side of the lower jaw. It is found along the northwest coast throughout the Rocky Mountain region. There are many kinds, all good fighters and excellent to eat. The cutthroat trout are also called black-spotted trout, mountain trout, salmon trout, and native trout.

The *golden trout* is the state fish of California. It lives in mountain waters of the Western United States.

True Trout

All true trout, also known as black-spotted trout, have dark markings on a light background. The rainbow trout, *below*, like every true trout of North America, originally lived only in the waters of the western half of the continent.

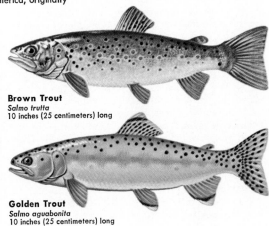

Brown Trout
Salmo trutta
10 inches (25 centimeters) long

Golden Trout
Salmo aguabonita
10 inches (25 centimeters) long

Bill Noel Kleeman, Tom Stack & Assoc.

Chars

Most chars have light markings on a dark background, the opposite of the true trout. Chars also have much smaller scales than do true trout. The scales of some chars, such as the brook trout, *below*, are so small that the skin appears scaleless.

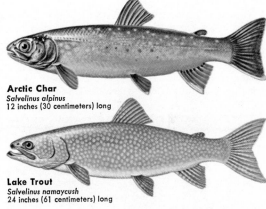

Arctic Char
Salvelinus alpinus
12 inches (30 centimeters) long

Lake Trout
Salvelinus namaycush
24 inches (61 centimeters) long

Treat Davidson, NAS

WORLD BOOK illustrations by James Teason

The *brown trout* is a European fish which has been placed in many streams and lakes in the United States. Some fishermen like it, and others scorn it.

Scientific Classification. The trout belongs to the salmon and trout family, *Salmonidae*. The chars are in the genus *Salvelinus*. The true trout are in the genus *Salmo*. The brook trout is species *Salvelinus fontinalis*. The rainbow trout is species *Salmo gairdneri*.   CARL L. HUBBS

See also FISH (pictures: A Leaping Trout, Fish of Temperate Fresh Waters, How a Fish Develops, How Fish Reproduce).

TROUT LILY. See DOGTOOTH VIOLET.

TROUVÈRE, *troo VAIR*, was one of a group of lyric poets who flourished in northern France from about 1150 to the early 1300's. The word comes from an Old French word meaning *to compose*. The Trouvères composed their poems in an Old French dialect, *langue d'oïl*. They were strongly influenced by the style and subject matter of the troubadours of southern France. Like the troubadours, the trouvères wrote *chansons d'amor* (love songs).   RICHARD O'GORMAN

See also TROUBADOUR.

TROVATORE, IL. See OPERA (*Trovatore, Il*); VERDI, GIUSEPPE.

TROY, also called ILIUM, was an ancient city in Asia Minor (now Turkey) that was made famous in the legends of early Greece. The *Iliad* and the *Odyssey*, epics composed by the Greek poet Homer, and the *Aeneid*, an epic written by the Roman poet Virgil, tell a story about Troy that is probably only partly true. The city's two names come from Ilus, its legendary founder, and Tros, the father of Ilus.

The Legendary Troy was a mighty city ruled by King Priam. The king's son Paris judged a beauty contest between the goddesses Hera, Athena, and Aphrodite. He chose Aphrodite as the winner because she promised

373

to give him the most beautiful woman in the world as his wife. Soon after the contest, Paris visited Menelaus, the king of Sparta. Paris fell in love with Menelaus' wife, Helen, who was known as the most beautiful woman in the world. Paris took Helen to Troy, and thereby angered Menelaus.

The people of the mainland of Greece, called *Achaeans* by Homer, swore revenge on Paris and the people of Troy. The Greeks sent a great naval expedition to Troy. The expedition was led by Agamemnon, Menelaus' brother, and included Achilles, Odysseus, and many other Greek heroes. The Greeks besieged Troy for 10 years. But they could not capture the city, which was protected by high stone walls. Finally, Odysseus ordered workers to build a huge wooden horse, in which some Greek soldiers hid. The rest of the Greeks then pretended to sail away, leaving the horse standing outside the city walls.

The curious Trojans dragged the wooden horse inside the city, though Laocoön, a Trojan priest, warned them not to do so. That night, the Greek soldiers crept out of the horse, opened the city gates, and let the rest of the Greek forces into Troy. The Greeks massacred the people of Troy and looted and burned the city. Only Aeneas, the hero of Virgil's *Aeneid*, and a few other Trojans escaped. Paris was killed in the war, and Helen returned to Menelaus.

The Real Troy. Apart from the legends, little is known about the history of Troy. Archaeologists have learned that Troy was founded in the early Bronze Age, which began about 3000 B.C. in Asia Minor. The city stood on a high point of a fertile plain in what is now northwestern Turkey. It was near the southern end of the *Hellespont*, a strait now called the Dardanelles. Ar-

chaeologists have discovered that nine cities were built on the site of Troy. Each successive city was built on the ruins of the one before it.

The second Troy and the sixth one were especially wealthy cities. The Trojans farmed, bred and raised horses, herded sheep, and produced woolen goods. They traded with the Mycenaeans, who lived in Greece, and with other people who lived along the Aegean coast of Asia Minor.

Scholars know little about the actual Trojan War. Archaeologists have found evidence that the Greeks may have attacked and destroyed Troy in a great expedition similar to the one described in the *Iliad*. However, no one knows the cause of the war. According to Greek legends, Troy fell about 1184 B.C. Many archaeologists think that the seventh city on the site of Troy was the one written about in ancient Greek literature. These scholars believe that the city was destroyed about 1250 B.C.

The Archaeological Troy. The first archaeologist to study Troy was a German named Heinrich Schliemann. Other persons had noted that a small mound about 4 miles (6 kilometers) from the Dardanelles seemed to fit the geographical location of Troy described in the *Iliad*. The mound was called *Hissarlik*. Schliemann began digging there in 1870. He found evidence that several cities had been built on the site over a long period. Near the bottom of the excavation, he discovered the ruins of an ancient city with massive walls, well-built houses, and hidden treasures of gold and silver. Schliemann mistakenly believed this city, which he called Troy II, was the Troy described by Homer.

The German archaeologist Wilhelm Dörpfeld, who had assisted Schliemann, conducted further excavations at Troy in the 1890's. He was the first researcher to recognize that nine cities had stood on the site. Dörpfeld

Detail of *The Burning of Troy* (early 1600's), an oil painting on canvas by an unknown French artist; Blois Museum, France (Lauros, Giraudon)

The Fall of Troy was made famous in legends. Greek soldiers hid in a huge wooden horse, and curious Trojans dragged it into the city. The Greeks later crept out and attacked and burned Troy.

Peter Loud,
Robert Harding Picture Library

The Site of Troy has the remains of nine successive cities. The stone walls above are from Troy VI, destroyed by an earthquake about 1300 B.C. It was probably not the Troy of legend.

believed the sixth was the city of Homer's *Iliad*. This city, called Troy VI, was larger than the earlier ones and was protected by high walls. The houses were large and rectangular and were probably built around a central palace.

In 1932, Carl Blegen, an American scholar from the University of Cincinnati, began a new research expedition at Troy. His study lasted six years and confirmed the findings of Dörpfeld, except that Blegen believed the seventh city was the legendary Troy. According to Blegen, Troy VI represented a major stage in the development of the city, even though it was not the Troy of Greek legends. This stage was marked by the arrival of immigrants who shared many cultural characteristics with the Mycenaeans in Greece. Troy VI was destroyed by an earthquake about 1300 B.C. The next city, which archaeologists called Troy VIIa, had small, crude houses that were crowded together. The city was less prosperous than the earlier Troys. Around 1250 B.C., Troy VIIa was looted and burned. Although Blegen believed that Troy VIIa was the legendary city, archaeologists cannot prove that it was.

From about 1100 B.C. to 700 B.C., no one lived at Troy. Some Greek settlers then established a small village there about 700 B.C. The last city on the site, Troy IX, was built in the late 300's B.C. It was called Ilium by the Greeks and Romans. Ilium lasted about 700 years. It was abandoned about A.D. 400, and remained undisturbed until Schliemann discovered it.   Norman A. Doenges

See also Trojan War with its list of *Related Articles;* Homer; Schliemann, Heinrich.

Additional Resources

Blegen, Carl W. *Troy and the Trojans.* Praeger, 1963.
Edmonds, I. G. *The Mysteries of Troy.* Elsevier-Nelson, 1977.
Schliemann, Heinrich. *Ilios: The City and the Country of the Trojans.* Arno, 1968. Reprint of 1881 ed.

TROY WEIGHT is a standard system used in weighing gold, silver, platinum, and coins. It is also used to weigh jewels, except pearls and diamonds, which are weighed in carats. The name *Troy* comes from *Troyes,* a French town. In the 1300's, Troyes had its own system of weights and measures. In the system of troy weight, the pound contains 12 ounces. The ounce equals 20 pennyweights, and the pennyweight equals 24 grains. The troy pound and the apothecaries' pound both contain 5,760 grains. The pound avoirdupois equals 7,000 grains. The grains in all three systems are equal. The troy pound equals 0.3732 kilogram.   E. G. Straus

See also Pennyweight; Weights and Measures; Apothecaries' Weight; Avoirdupois.

TRUANCY, *TROO uhn see,* refers to the shirking of responsibility. A *truant* is a person who deliberately stays away from duties at school or on a job because the person dislikes the place, the people, or the responsibilities. Truancy laws are designed to help prevent habitual truancy in schools. Truant officers try to persuade

truants that it is to their advantage to attend school regularly.   Paul R. Hanna

TRUCIAL STATES. See United Arab Emirates.

TRUCK is a motor vehicle used to carry freight. Trucks transport a wide variety of cargo. They carry food to grocery stores and gasoline to service stations. Trucks haul manufactured products from factories to stores, and in some cases, to consumers' homes. In fact, trucks help transport nearly everything we eat, wear, and use. Some kinds of trucks are commonly called vans. The British word for truck is *lorry.*

Trucking is one of the most important industries in the United States. The nation spends about $110 billion yearly to transport goods by truck. The United States has more than 30 million trucks. Canada has almost 3 million trucks. Trucking is also important in many other countries.

Trucks vary greatly in size. Some kinds of trucks are smaller than certain automobiles. The largest trucks are *tractor trailers,* which have two main parts. The tractor is the front part of the truck and includes the engine and cab. The trailer is the rear part and holds the cargo. In some Western states, tractor trailers, also called *18-wheelers,* may weigh as much as 120,000 pounds (54,400 kilograms) fully loaded.

Trucks are sturdily built for rugged work. Most trucks have more powerful engines than automobiles have because trucks must carry heavy loads, often over long distances. The engines of large trucks have from about 200 to more than 400 horsepower. In comparison, the engines of automobiles have from about 75 to 225 horsepower. Some trucks have as many as 20 forward driving gears and 10 reverse gears. These gears enable a truck to reach and maintain desired speeds under various conditions through the most efficient use of the engine. For example, certain gears on a truck make it possible for the truck to travel up an icy hill with a huge load. Trucks also have strong brakes and wide tires that grip the road. Many trucks have special devices on the rear wheels to prevent skidding on hills and curves.

Some trucks are powered by diesel fuel. Others operate on gasoline. In the United States, trucks use over 40 billion gallons (151 billion liters) of fuel annually. After the nation experienced periodic fuel shortages during the 1970's, many truck manufacturers and trucking firms began to seek ways to conserve fuel. For example, some manufacturers redesigned the engines of trucks for greater fuel efficiency.

Uses of Trucks

Trucks are a vital part of the transportation system of the United States. They haul about 75 per cent of the nation's industrial products, and carry most of the goods moved short distances.

Trucks are often used in combination with other forms of transportation in a method called *piggybacking.* For example, a loaded trailer can be separated from a truck tractor and moved onto a railroad flatcar. The trailer is then transported to a railroad terminal, where it is reconnected to another truck tractor. The truckdriver then delivers the goods. Truck trailers can also be carried by ship. See Containerization.

WORLD BOOK map

Troy was an ancient city in Asia Minor. Ruins of Troy have yielded historical relics nearly 5,000 years old.

TRUCK

Trucks have a wide variety of industrial, agricultural, and governmental uses. In addition, trucks have certain special uses.

Industrial Uses. Many industries use trucks to haul raw materials to factories and to carry manufactured products to warehouses and stores. Trucks also transport manufactured parts to *assembly plants*, where finished products are made. For example, the parts for a car may be produced at several factories and then trucked to an assembly plant.

Agricultural Uses. Trucks are used to transport almost all fruits, vegetables, and livestock from farms to markets. They thus help make it possible for American supermarkets to offer a wide variety of foods, some of which are grown in distant areas. Farmers can truck perishable crops, such as fruits and vegetables, to market while the foods are fresh. During winter, people in cold areas can eat fresh fruits and vegetables transported from warm areas where the foods are grown.

Farmers also transport other crops, such as hay and various grains, by truck. In addition, they use trucks to haul fertilizer, livestock feed, farm machinery, and other items. Many farm trucks have *power take-off*, a mechanism that provides power for other machines. Farmers use the mechanism to pump water, grind feed, saw wood, and perform other tasks.

Governmental Uses. Federal, state, and city governments in the United States own or lease more than 1¼ million trucks. The federal government uses more trucks than any single industry. Many federal trucks are used to transport mail. The U.S. armed forces use trucks to carry equipment, troops, and weapons. Some huge army trucks even serve as missile launchers. State governments use trucks in the construction and maintenance of bridges, roads, and parks. In cities, police and fire departments require trucks. Trucks are also used to sweep streets, clear away snow, and collect garbage.

Special Uses. Many people use trucks to move their furniture, household goods, and personal belongings from one apartment or house to another. Some large trucks can even be used to move houses. Trucks called *bookmobiles* serve as traveling libraries. Similar trucks transport art exhibits. Trucks carry medical equipment and workers who collect blood from the public and take various kinds of X rays. Trucks used as ambulances have lifesaving equipment and serve as mobile emergency rooms. Some types of *recreational vehicles* are used as temporary mobile homes by people who are camping or traveling (see RECREATIONAL VEHICLE).

Kinds of Trucks

Truck manufacturers build more than 3 million trucks yearly. They produce thousands of kinds of trucks. A large manufacturer may offer customers a choice of nearly 500 designs. Many trucks are equipped with air conditioning and other comforts found in automobiles. The cabs of some tractor trailers have a small bed, in which drivers can sleep during long trips.

Trucks are classified into three main groups, *light*, *medium*, and *heavy*. Heavy trucks are sometimes further categorized as *light heavy* and *heavy heavy*. The groups are based on *gross vehicle weight*, the combined weight of the truck and of the load it carries. Light trucks weigh less than 10,000 pounds (4,500 kilograms). Medium trucks weigh from 10,000 to 20,000 pounds (4,500 to 9,100 kilograms). Light heavy trucks weigh from 20,000 to 26,000 pounds (9,100 to 11,800 kilograms), and heavy heavy trucks weigh more than 26,000 pounds (11,800 kilograms).

Most trucks in the United States are light. Pickups and tow trucks are familiar light trucks. Many of these vehicles have transmissions similar to those in automobiles and can carry a load weighing about 1½ short tons (1.4 metric tons). Most light trucks have gasoline engines. In 1977, some manufacturers began to produce light trucks with diesel engines.

Medium trucks are wider and higher than light trucks and are commonly used as commercial vehicles. They include multistop, or parcel delivery, trucks and bottlers. Multistop trucks are designed so the driver can stand behind the steering wheel and easily step on and off the vehicle. Bottlers have racks to carry bottled goods. Most medium trucks have diesel engines.

Heavy trucks perform a wide variety of rugged tasks. These vehicles include dump trucks and tractor trailers. Dump trucks are designed so the rear of the truck tilts for easy unloading. Tractor trailers have a powerful tractor that pulls a separate trailer with a full set of wheels. Almost all heavy trucks have diesel engines, which convert fuel to energy more efficiently than gasoline engines. Diesel engines enable trucks to haul heavier loads. Heavy trucks have stronger brakes and a better *suspension system* than other kinds of trucks. The suspension system is a set of devices that protect a vehicle from the jolts of travel.

Another way of grouping trucks is according to where they are used. Trucks may be classified as *highway trucks* or *off-the-highway trucks*.

Highway Trucks. The three most popular types of trucks used on the road are panels, pickups, and tractors and semitrailers. A panel is a small, fully enclosed truck. A pickup has an enclosed cab and open-topped cargo compartment. A tractor and semitrailer has a trailer with only rear wheels. The front of the trailer rests on a wheeled extension of the tractor.

Other kinds of highway trucks include flatbed trucks and tank trucks. Flatbed trucks have an enclosed cab and a trailer that consists of a platform with rear wheels. The platform may have brackets along its side so that stakes can be inserted to help hold a load. Such trucks are also called platform or stake trucks. They are used to haul large pieces of equipment and other bulky cargo. Tank trucks have a trailer with a large tank used to carry compressed gas or such liquids as gasoline or milk.

Several kinds of highway trucks are called vans. Light vans are commonly used for recreation. Heavier vans transport furniture or bulky goods. Refrigerated vans called reefers are used to carry perishable food and other products that require cooling.

Off-the-Highway Trucks are built for use on rugged terrain, rather than for highway driving. They are used on construction sites and in lumber camps, mines, oil fields, and quarries. These trucks can haul loads that weigh more than 200 short tons (180 metric tons). The largest truck used in North America is an off-the-highway vehicle that measures 67 feet long and 25½ feet wide (20.4 meters long and 7.77 meters wide). This

Some Kinds of Trucks

Thousands of kinds of trucks perform specialized work. They range from small pickup trucks that carry relatively light loads to huge log carriers with tremendous hauling power. The United States has more than 30 million trucks.

WORLD BOOK illustrations by Robert Keys

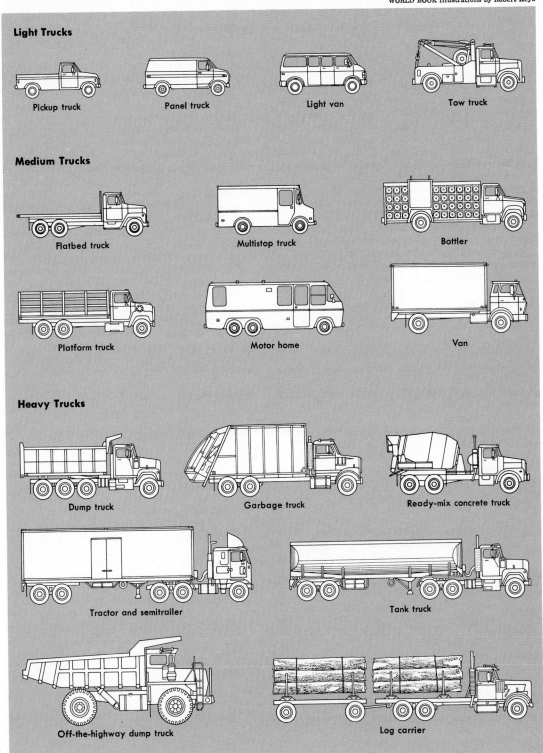

Light Trucks

Pickup truck   Panel truck   Light van   Tow truck

Medium Trucks

Flatbed truck   Multistop truck   Bottler

Platform truck   Motor home   Van

Heavy Trucks

Dump truck   Garbage truck   Ready-mix concrete truck

Tractor and semitrailer   Tank truck

Off-the-highway dump truck   Log carrier

huge truck is used at mining sites and can transport loads weighing 350 short tons (317 metric tons). Some off-the-highway trucks are equipped with earth-moving, hoisting, or pumping machinery. Small electric-powered trucks that are used to carry loads inside factories are also a kind of off-the-highway truck.

The Trucking Industry

The United States has about 17,000 trucking firms, and Canada has more than 4,000. In the United States, truckers provide the only commercial land transportation for most communities without railroad or waterway service. Most U.S. trucking firms are either *local* or *intercity carriers.* Local carriers conduct more than half their business in one metropolitan area. Intercity carriers, also known as *line-haul* or *over-the-road carriers,* work in more than one metropolitan area.

Trucking firms may be (1) private carriers or (2) for-hire carriers. Both kinds of carriers are subject to government regulation.

Private Carriers are businesses that either own or lease trucks and use them to transport their own goods. For example, a chain of supermarkets would use its trucks to deliver food from warehouses to stores. The company makes its profit on the sale of the food, not on the trucking.

For-Hire Carriers are trucking companies that earn profits by transporting the freight of other businesses or of individuals or groups. They operate in local areas, *intrastate* (within one state), and *interstate* (between states).

There are three types of for-hire carriers: (1) common, (2) contract, and (3) exempt. Common carriers are required by law to transport the goods of any shipper who can pay for the service. Such carriers charge set rates, haul specific types of freight, and operate only on certain routes (see COMMON CARRIER). Contract carriers work for a limited number of customers. They agree to deliver only the products of these customers. Exempt carriers transport only special kinds of goods or use their trucks only for specific purposes. Exempt carriers include firms that haul certain agricultural

products or carry newspapers. These carriers are exempt from certain government regulations.

Government Regulation. In the United States, the trucking industry is regulated by federal, state, and local governments. The Interstate Commerce Commission (ICC), a federal agency, has responsibility for common and contract carriers that travel interstate. Intrastate and local carriers are regulated by state and local governments.

The ICC must approve an interstate carrier's rates and routes. It also checks the types of services offered and the kinds of goods carried. The agency assigns unprofitable routes so that truck transportation is available to all communities.

All interstate carriers must obey the safety regulations of the U.S. Department of Transportation (DOT). These rules set standards for certain types of truck equipment, such as lights and brakes. The regulations also govern the operation of trucks. For example, the DOT specifies the number of hours a driver can work without rest. The DOT also regulates the interstate transport of chemicals and other hazardous cargoes.

State governments set limits on the size and weight of trucks that use state roads. The largest trucks allowed to travel on public highways are 65-foot (20-meter) twin trailers, which consist of two short trailers pulled by one tractor. Thirty-two states allow twin trailers on their roads. According to the Federal Highway Act of 1975, trucks that use interstate highways may not weigh more than 80,000 pounds (36,000 kilograms). However, some states have a lower or higher weight limit than the one allowed by federal law.

Trucking firms must pay taxes to use highways. The federal and state governments collect about $9 billion in such taxes annually. The money is used to construct and repair roads.

History

No one knows who manufactured the first truck. But by the mid-1890's, trucks were being made in the United States. By 1904, the trucking industry in the United States had only about 700 trucks. Many of these early trucks were poorly designed and weighed more than the loads they carried. Most were powered by steam or electrical engines. They had solid rubber tires and crude springs, which made traveling over the bumpy roads of the time uncomfortable for the driver and rough on the cargo. Sometimes, a truck was gradually shaken apart during a trip. Nevertheless, the early trucks were more efficient and less costly than the horse-drawn vehicles they replaced.

Such improvements as gasoline engines and air-filled tires were introduced during the early 1900's. These improvements enabled trucks to carry heavier loads at greater speeds. The trucking industry then grew rapidly. Trucks proved especially valuable during World War I (1914-1918). At that time, the railroads were unable to carry all the necessary war supplies to the Atlantic seaports for shipment overseas. Convoys of trucks helped move the supplies.

By 1918, the number of trucks in the United States had risen to about 605,000. During the 1920's, the federal and state governments began building a national system of highways. The improved roads enabled trucks to travel between cities more quickly.

Historical Pictures Service
A Coal Truck, above, was used as early as 1905. Today, trucks carry about 75 per cent of the goods handled by United States shippers and play a major role in the nation's economy.

In 1935, Congress passed the Motor Carrier Act. This law gave the Interstate Commerce Commission authority to regulate the motor carriers and drivers involved in interstate commerce. At the time, many people believed government regulation was necessary to protect shippers and the trucking industry from various abuses that had become common practice. Today, some critics charge that government regulation makes the establishment of new trucking firms difficult and raises shipping costs. Supporters claim that regulation lowers shipping costs, provides trucking services to areas that might not have such services otherwise, and helps keep the industry stable.

Careers

The trucking industry employs over 9 million persons, more than any other private industry in the United States. About 2 million of these workers are drivers. Those who operate tractor trailers must pass a driving test and receive a special state license.

The trucking industry employs many kinds of workers besides drivers. For example, dispatchers are needed to direct trucks to the right destination with the right cargo. Freight handlers and loading-dock and warehouse workers load and unload trucks. Mechanics repair and maintain trucks. Trucking firms require various office workers, such as shipping clerks and computer programmers. Truck manufacturers employ engineers and factory workers. Companies that produce engines, tires, and other parts for trucks also offer employment opportunities.   BENNETT C. WHITLOCK, JR.

See also AUTOMOBILE with its list of Related Articles.

TRUCK FARMING is raising vegetables for market. Truck farmers do not usually need as much land for growing vegetables as they would for grain crops, and truck farms often are simply large gardens. But truck farms in southern Texas often cover large areas.

The terms *truck farm* and *truck garden* mean the same thing. They come from an old use of the word *truck*, which meant *to exchange or barter goods*. People have come to speak of vegetables that are raised for sale as *garden truck*.

Kinds of Truck Farms. In general, there are two kinds of truck farms. Some truck farms are located near cities, and supply the city dwellers with vegetables in season. They often also have greenhouses for growing tomatoes and other vegetables out of season. Such farms usually are small, and raise many different kinds of vegetables. If the farm is close to the city, the farmer may set up a roadside stand to sell the produce.

The other kind of truck farm may be located far from any city. It depends on railroad, truck, or airplane transportation to carry the vegetables to market. Such a farm is usually large, and specializes in growing only one or a few kinds of vegetables. Some of these truck farms are located in warm regions where they can produce certain vegetables in winter months, and ship them to cold northern regions where they are out of season. Examples include the great winter vegetable gardens of southern Florida, southern California, Texas, and Arizona. Other truck farms can be located far from market because they grow a particular vegetable that is in demand throughout the country, and can easily be shipped. Examples include the large onion, head lettuce, and celery farms of Idaho and Utah. Special

conditions of soil and climate needed to grow certain vegetables also may influence the location of truck farms far from market. For example, most of the head lettuce produced in the United States grows in the West and the South, where conditions are most favorable. But the greatest market for this vegetable is in the northeastern part of the country.

How Truck Farms Operate. Many truck farmers ship and market their produce through cooperatives (see COOPERATIVE). This method usually is cheaper and more convenient than for the growers to ship their crops separately. Even a small grower of watermelons could produce enough melons to fill a boxcar. But a grower of lettuce who ships constantly throughout the season might have difficulty getting together an entire carload of the produce for shipment at one time. Therefore, the farmer and other growers ship produce cooperatively, and as a result they get lower freight rates for carload lots.

Truck farming is hard work. Vegetables usually require more constant and careful cultivation than field crops. They are also harder to harvest.

Truck farmers usually rotate their crops every three or four years to keep the soil productive. Land for truck gardening is usually expensive, because it must be rich and fertile and it is often located near big cities.

History. There was little need for truck gardening in the early times, when the United States was largely an agricultural country. In those days most persons could raise their own vegetables in summer and store some of them for the winter. But the growth of large cities brought a great need for truck farming. Persons who live in apartments usually have no place to raise vegetables.

The building of railroads throughout the country gave the truck farmer the freedom to locate in nearly any part of the country that offered good growing conditions and good soil. The railroads also introduced out-of-season vegetables to large numbers of persons. The invention of the refrigerator car made it possible for vegetables to arrive at market nearly as fresh as when they were picked. It also put the more perishable vegetables on city market stands throughout the country during most of the year.

Truck farm products are the second largest food group in the United States in terms of volume and consumption. Only milk and milk products exceed them. The leading truck farming states include California, Florida, Texas, and Wisconsin.   WILLIAM R. VAN DERSAL

TRUDEAU, *TROO doh*, **EDWARD LIVINGSTON** (1848-1915), was a famous pioneer in the antituberculosis movement in the United States. Trudeau himself contracted the disease at the age of 25. He became convinced of the need for adequate sanitariums, and established the Adirondack Cottage Sanitarium at Saranac Lake, N.Y. It later became the Trudeau Sanitarium, which achieved a worldwide reputation.

Trudeau also founded the Saranac Laboratory in 1894, the first research laboratory in the United States for the study of tuberculosis. The Trudeau Sanitarium was closed in 1957 because of the gigantic strides made in antituberculosis therapy. Trudeau was born in New York City. He studied medicine at Columbia College (now Columbia University).   NOAH D. FABRICANT

PIERRE E. TRUDEAU

Prime Minister of Canada
1968-1979
1980-

| PEARSON | TRUDEAU | CLARK | TRUDEAU |
| 1963-1968 | 1968-1979 | 1979-1980 | 1980- |

TRUDEAU, *troo DOH,* **PIERRE ELLIOTT** (1919-   ), served as prime minister of Canada from 1968 to 1979 and became leader of the government again in 1980. He was the third French-Canadian prime minister. Like the first two—Sir Wilfrid Laurier and Louis S. St. Laurent—he was a Liberal.

The energetic and wealthy Trudeau generated great interest among Canadians, particularly the nation's youth. But during the late 1970's, Trudeau's popularity and that of his party declined as Canada's economic problems worsened. The Progressive Conservatives defeated the Liberals in May 1979, and the Conservative leader, Charles Joseph Clark, succeeded Trudeau as prime minister. However, Clark's government fell from power at the end of the year, and Trudeau led the Liberals to an easy victory over the Conservatives in February 1980.

Before his first term as prime minister, Trudeau had worked as a lawyer and law professor. He had had only three years of experience in public office. Trudeau's social life had made him famous. He often wore colorful clothes; drove fast cars; and enjoyed skiing, skin diving, and canoeing.

As prime minister, Trudeau worked to broaden Canada's contacts with other nations and to ease the long-strained relations between English- and French-speaking Canadians. He achieved a personal goal in 1970, when Canada and China agreed to reestablish diplomatic relations. At home, Trudeau faced such problems as rapid inflation, high unemployment, and a movement to make the province of Quebec a separate nation. Trudeau achieved another major goal in 1982, when the Canadian constitution came under complete Canadian control. Previously, constitutional amendments required the British Parliament's approval.

Early Life

Boyhood. Joseph Philippe Pierre Yves Elliott Trudeau was born in Montreal on Oct. 18, 1919. His father's family had gone to Canada from France in the 1600's. His mother's family was descended from British colonists in America who remained loyal to Great Britain at the time of the Revolutionary War in 1775 (see UNITED EMPIRE LOYALISTS). Trudeau, his sister Suzette, and his brother Charles learned to speak French and English with equal ease. Trudeau's father became wealthy as owner of a chain of service stations.

Education. Trudeau grew up in Montreal, where he attended a small Jesuit college, Jean-de-Brébeuf. He received a law degree from the University of Montreal in 1943. While at the University of Montreal, he enlisted in the Canadian Officer Training Corps. He later completed his training with an army reserve unit. In 1945, Trudeau earned a master's degree in political economy at Harvard University. He then studied at the *École des Sciences Politiques* (School of Political Sciences) in Paris and at the London School of Economics.

Paul D. Stevens, the contributor of this article, is Associate Professor of History at York University in Toronto.

His Travels. In 1948, Trudeau set out to tour Europe and Asia. He traveled by motorbike or hitchhiked with a knapsack on his back. First he visited Germany, Austria, and Hungary. Then he traveled through Eastern Europe. In Jerusalem, the Arabs arrested him as an Israeli spy. But he continued on to Pakistan, Afghanistan, India, Burma, Thailand, Indochina, and China. He returned to Canada from China in 1949.

Next, Trudeau worked in the Privy Council office in Ottawa as a junior law clerk. He returned to Montreal in 1951 and began to practice law. In 1960, Trudeau and five other Canadians toured China. They were the first Westerners admitted to China since the Communists conquered the country in 1949. Trudeau became a law professor at the University of Montreal in 1961.

Entry Into Public Life

During the late 1940's and the 1950's, Trudeau became concerned about the political situation in Quebec. The province was controlled by Premier Maurice Duplessis and the Union Nationale Party. Trudeau and a group of youthful liberal friends set out to expose what they saw as dishonesty in the provincial government. They believed this corruption had resulted from government, religious, and business leaders working together to prevent reforms. To express their ideas, Trudeau and his group established the magazine *Cité Libre* (Community of the Free).

Trudeau worked in many ways for reform in Quebec. The most publicized event took place in 1949 when miners went on strike in the town of Asbestos. Premier Duplessis ordered the provincial police to aid the company and the nonunion men it tried to hire during the strike. The strikers blockaded the roads into Asbestos and kept the strikebreakers from entering. Trudeau spent more than three weeks encouraging the strikers and speaking at their rallies. The police and many ministers called him an "outside agitator."

In 1956, Trudeau helped organize *Le Rassemblement* (The Assembly). The group's 600 members worked to explain democracy to the people of Quebec and to persuade them to use it. Trudeau later served as president of the group. In 1960, the people voted the Union Nationale Party out of office.

French Canadians demanded more than democratic reform for Quebec. They had always struggled against what they believed was discrimination by Canada's English-speaking majority. Many French Canadians told of being refused jobs in government and industry because they spoke French. They feared that the French language would disappear in Canada if they were required to use English. They also feared that with the loss of their language they would lose their national identity and their culture and customs. Some demanded full equality. Others called for Quebec to become a separate country. During the early 1960's, demands for separation from Canada became even stronger.

Trudeau favored preserving the French culture in Canada. But he opposed the creation of any country in which nationality was the only major common bond.

Member of Parliament. In 1965, Trudeau decided to enter national politics and run for a seat in the House of Commons as a member of the Federal Liberal Party. He wanted to show French Canadians that they could play a useful role in the federal government. He also wanted to show the people of Quebec that they were better off as part of Canada. In November 1965, he was elected to Parliament from Mont-Royal, a Montreal suburb.

Parliamentary Secretary. In January 1966, Prime Minister Pearson appointed Trudeau as his parliamentary secretary. Trudeau used this position to influence the government's policy on constitutional issues. He wanted the constitution changed to provide a stronger federal government and to promote more cooperation among the provinces. For example, Trudeau believed the wealthy provinces should help support the poorer ones. He favored a tax program that would divide tax money more fairly among the provinces. In March 1966, the government adopted a similar plan.

Minister of Justice. In April 1967, Pearson named Trudeau to the Cabinet as minister of justice and attorney general. In this post, Trudeau introduced legislation to strengthen gun-control laws and to reduce restrictions on abortion, divorce, gambling, and homosexuality. He believed that individuals should be free to do whatever they wished if they did not endanger society as a whole. The government sponsored similar legislation after Trudeau became prime minister.

Prime Minister

In December 1967, Pearson announced his intention to retire. Trudeau was elected leader of the Liberal Party on April 6, 1968, and became prime minister on April 20. He called a general election for June 25, and the voters strongly supported him.

Foreign Affairs. Trudeau wanted to strengthen Canada's independence in world affairs. Early in his term, he changed the nation's defense arrangements and expanded its relations with China and Russia.

New Defense Policy. Trudeau adopted a defense policy that emphasized the protection of Canadian territory. In 1969 and 1970, he withdrew about half of the 9,800 Canadian troops serving with forces of the North Atlantic Treaty Organization (NATO) in Europe.

Foreign Relations. In 1970, Canada and China agreed to reestablish diplomatic relations. These ties had ended when the Communists gained control of China in 1949. The agreement had been one of Trudeau's chief goals. Trudeau visited China in 1973. He traveled to the Soviet Union in May 1971, and Premier Aleksei N. Kosygin of Russia toured Canada five months later. Canadian trade increased with both China and Russia.

─── **IMPORTANT DATES IN TRUDEAU'S LIFE** ───

1919 (Oct. 18) Born in Montreal.
1943 Earned law degree at University of Montreal.
1945 Earned master's degree at Harvard.
1961 Named professor of law at University of Montreal.
1965 Elected to House of Commons.
1966 Named parliamentary secretary to prime minister.
1967 Appointed minister of justice.
1968 Elected leader of Liberal Party and prime minister.
1971 (March 4) Married Margaret Sinclair.
1979 Progressive Conservatives defeated Liberals. Trudeau resigned as prime minister on June 4.
1980 Liberals defeated Progressive Conservatives. Trudeau became prime minister again on March 3.

Wide World

Prime Minister Trudeau escorted Russian Premier Aleksei N. Kosygin, *left,* when the Soviet leader toured Ottawa in 1971. The two men agreed to broaden contacts between Canada and Russia.

The National Scene. As prime minister, Trudeau worked hard to help preserve the French heritage in Canada. For example, he greatly expanded the use of the French language in government services. Trudeau hoped his efforts would strengthen national unity. But relations between English- and French-speaking Canadians remained tense.

Domestic Legislation. Parliament passed several far-reaching bills that were supported by Trudeau. In 1969, Parliament approved the Official Languages Act. This law requires courts and other government agencies to provide service in French in districts where at least 10 per cent of the people speak French. It also requires service in English in districts where at least 10 per cent of the people speak that language. The Election Act, passed in 1970, reduced the minimum voting age in national elections from 21 to 18. In 1971, Parliament extended unemployment insurance benefits to cover nearly all Canadian workers. In 1976, Parliament abolished the death penalty.

The Terrorist Crisis. Terrorism by French-Canadian separatists in October 1970, forced Trudeau to make his most difficult decision as prime minister. Members of the *Front de Libération du Québec* (FLQ), an underground separatist group, kidnapped Pierre Laporte, the labor minister of Quebec, and James R. Cross, the British trade commissioner in Montreal. Trudeau suspended civil liberties and sent thousands of federal troops to Quebec. He invoked Canada's War Measures Act, which permits police to search and arrest without warrants and to deny bail.

Laporte was murdered, and four men were charged with the crime. All the defendants were later sent to prison. The government let Cross's kidnappers go to Cuba in return for his release. Trudeau's firm stand received strong popular support.

The Economy. Inflation became one of Canada's chief problems in 1969. To halt rising prices, Trudeau reduced government spending and eliminated thousands of civil service jobs. These policies contributed to a sharp increase in unemployment in 1970.

Economic conditions in Canada worsened in August 1971, when the United States placed a 10 per cent *surcharge* (extra tax) on many imports. The surcharge affected about a fourth of Canada's exports. In September, unemployment reached 7.1 per cent, the highest level since 1961. To encourage spending and help create jobs, Trudeau ordered cuts in individual and corporation income taxes. He also made available several hundred million dollars in loans for construction projects. The U.S. surcharge was ended in December.

The 1972 Election. Trudeau called a general election for Oct. 30, 1972. He promised to seek new ways to reduce unemployment if he were returned to office. In the election, the Liberal and Conservative parties each won about 110 seats in the House of Commons. Although Trudeau's party failed to win a parliamentary majority, he remained prime minister.

Canada's economy expanded in 1973. But rapidly rising prices for clothing, food, fuel, and shelter caused hardship for many Canadians.

The 1974 Election. On May 8, 1974, the House of Commons passed a motion expressing no-confidence in Trudeau's government. This motion, which forced a new general election, came on a vote concerning Trudeau's proposed budget. It was the first time that a Canadian government was defeated over its budget.

In the election of July 1974, Trudeau led the Liberal Party to victory. The Liberal Party gained a majority in the House of Commons, winning 141 of the 264 seats.

New Economic Policies. The cost of energy continued to rise sharply during the mid-1970's, largely because of increasing Canadian demand for oil and the nation's decreasing petroleum reserves. In 1974, the government adopted a plan to reduce oil exports to the United States and to end them entirely by the early 1980's.

Trudeau was also concerned about the influence of foreign companies on the Canadian economy. In the

Wide World

Trudeau Visited China in 1973 and helped mark the third anniversary of the agreement that reestablished diplomatic relations between Canada and China. Chinese Premier Zhou Enlai, *center,* welcomed Trudeau and Mrs. Trudeau at Peking airport.

mid-1970's, for example, U.S. firms controlled about half of Canada's manufacturing. Trudeau supported establishment of a Federal Investment Review Agency to ensure that foreign investments in Canada serve Canada's best interests. This agency, which was approved by Parliament in 1973, began to operate in 1974.

Inflation continued to soar in 1975. Late that year, the Trudeau Administration set limits on price and wage increases. The controls expired in 1978.

The Separatist Challenge to Canada's national unity became more serious in 1976. The Parti Québécois, a political party that favors the separation of Quebec from Canada, won control of the province's government. Trudeau spoke out strongly against separatism.

The 1979 Election. In March 1979, Trudeau called a general election for May 22. During the campaign, the Conservatives criticized Trudeau and the Liberals for their failure to solve Canada's economic problems. In the election, the Conservatives won 135 seats in the House of Commons, the Liberals won 115, and the remaining 32 seats went to smaller parties. Charles Joseph Clark, the leader of the Conservatives, replaced Trudeau as prime minister. On November 21, Trudeau announced his intention to resign as party leader.

Return to Power. The Liberals planned to select Trudeau's successor in a party convention in March, 1980. But on Dec. 13, 1979, the House of Commons passed a motion of no-confidence in Clark's government. The vote came during consideration of the government's proposed budget, which called for tax increases.

As a result of his government's defeat, Clark called a general election for Feb. 18, 1980. Trudeau led the Liberals in the campaign. He climaxed an amazing political comeback when the Liberals won a majority of the seats in the House of Commons. Trudeau became prime minister again on March 3.

Trudeau's new administration soon faced a serious challenge. The government of Quebec called a vote for May 20 on a proposal to give provincial leaders the authority to negotiate with the federal government for political independence. Trudeau campaigned against the proposal, and the voters of Quebec rejected it.

Trudeau achieved a major goal in 1982 when the British Parliament approved an act giving Canada complete control over the Canadian constitution. The act, called the Constitution Act of 1982, set up a procedure for approving constitutional amendments in Canada instead of in Great Britain. Previously, all amendments required the British Parliament's approval.

Trudeau's Family. On March 4, 1971, Trudeau married Margaret Sinclair, the daughter of a former member of Parliament. The marriage surprised the nation because the couple's romance had received no publicity. The Trudeaus have three children, Justin (1971-   ), Alexandre (1973-   ), and Michel (1975-   ). In 1977, Trudeau and his wife separated. Trudeau received custody of their children.   PAUL D. STEVENS

See also CANADA, HISTORY OF; CLARK, CHARLES JOSEPH; PEARSON, LESTER BOWLES.

Additional Resources

GWYN, RICHARD J., ed. *The Northern Magus: Pierre Trudeau and Canadians.* McClelland (Toronto), 1980.
RADWANSKI, GEORGE. *Trudeau.* Macmillan, 1979.
THORDARSON, BRUCE. *Trudeau and Foreign Policy: A Study in Decision Making.* Oxford, 1972.

TRUFFAUT, *troo FOH,* **FRANÇOIS** (1932-   ), is a leading French motion-picture director. He directed several partly autobiographical films, beginning in 1959 with *The 400 Blows.* The main character, Antoine Doinel, reflects Truffaut's almost delinquent youth. Truffaut continued Antoine's story in *Stolen Kisses* (1968) and *Bed and Board* (1971). Truffaut's *Day for Night* won the 1973 Academy Award as best foreign language film.

Truffaut began his career in the 1950's as a film critic and developed a deep respect for American suspense and action movies. His *Shoot the Piano Player* (1960) resembles an American gangster film. Two other Truffaut movies, *The Bride Wore Black* (1967) and *Mississippi Mermaid* (1969), show the influence of the American director Alfred Hitchcock. Truffaut was born in Paris. His other major motion pictures include *Jules and Jim* (1961) and *The Wild Child* (1970). He also directed a film in English, *Fahrenheit 451* (1966).   ROGER EBERT

TRUFFLE is a fungus that is used as a food and a flavoring. Truffles grow on or near the roots of trees, usually oaks. Most truffles are found from 3 to 12 inches (8 to 30 centimeters) belowground. They vary from $\frac{1}{4}$ to 4 inches (0.6 to 10 centimeters) in diameter. Truffles have a fleshy interior and a round, warty exterior. They may be black, brown, or white.

Truffles grow in several European countries and in the United States. The tastiest ones come from the Périgord region of southwestern France. White truffles found in Italy are also prized. Truffles have a strong odor, and trained dogs and pigs are often used to locate them by the scent. Wild truffles have declined in number, and most attempts to grow the plants commercially have failed. As a result, truffles are an extremely expensive delicacy.

Scientific Classification. Truffles belong to the truffle family of ascomycete fungi, Tuberaceae. The Périgord variety, which is found in France, is classified as *Tuber melanosporum*.   J. B. HANSON

TRUJILLO MOLINA, *troo HEE yoh moh LEE nah,* **RAFAEL LEONIDAS** (1891-1961), was the Dominican Republic's strongman from 1930 to 1961. He rose to power through the Dominican Guard. In 1927, he became its commander in chief. He served as president from 1930 to 1938, and from 1942 to 1952. Even when he was not president, he retained control of his country.

Politically, Trujillo's rule was unusually severe. There were many plots against him, often spurred by exiles. They occurred chiefly after World War II. Trujillo was killed by an assassin on May 30, 1961. He was born at San Cristóbal.   DONALD E. WORCESTER

TRUK ISLANDS, *truhk,* form a large island group in the western Pacific about 1,800 miles (2,900 kilometers) southeast of Manila (see PACIFIC ISLANDS [map]). They are part of the eastern Carolines. About 48 of them lie inside a barrier coral reef that forms a lagoon 40 miles (64 kilometers) wide. About 50 small islets lie along the reef. About 38,000 people live on the islands.

The French navigator Louis Duperrey first explored the islands in 1825. Germany bought the islands from Spain in 1899, but lost them to Japan in World War I. Truk, formerly a great Japanese naval base, is now administered by the United States Trust Territory of the Pacific Islands.   EDWIN H. BRYAN, JR.

HARRY S. TRUMAN

HOOVER
31st President
1929 — 1933

F. D. ROOSEVELT
32nd President
1933 — 1945

TRUMAN, HARRY S. (1884-1972), became President at one of the most critical moments in American history. He had been Vice-President for only 83 days when President Franklin D. Roosevelt died on April 12, 1945. World War II still had to be won. Plans to establish the United Nations organization had just been started.

When Truman became President, he was known mainly for his work as chairman of a wartime Senate investigating committee that had saved millions of dollars in military contracts. The Missouri Democrat met the challenges of his presidency with courage, determination, and imagination. During the first few weeks of his administration, the Allies won victory in Europe. Truman then made one of the most awesome decisions ever considered by one man—to use the powerful new atomic bomb against Japan to end World War II.

Truman faced other great problems throughout his years in the White House. The United States had to reorganize its economy from a wartime to a peacetime basis. Many war-torn countries needed large relief programs. Western nations faced communist subversion and aggression in a Cold War that divided the world. To meet these challenges, Truman's administration created such far-reaching programs as the Truman Doctrine, the Marshall Plan, the Point Four Program, and the North Atlantic Treaty Organization (NATO).

When communist forces from North Korea invaded South Korea in 1950, Truman faced another grave decision. If he sent armed forces to intervene without waiting for United Nations action, he risked war with communist Russia. But if he delayed, help might be too late. Within two days, the President ordered American armed forces to aid South Korea. His action preserved South Korean independence and demonstrated that the United States would support and defend its allies.

Truman's strong personality and fighting spirit won

him loyal friends and bitter enemies. Blunt and outspoken, he often lashed out with strong language at those who opposed him. His opponents said he was too undignified. His friends loved him as a straightforward man of the people.

Early Life

Childhood. Harry S. Truman was born in Lamar, Mo., on May 8, 1884. He was the oldest of the three children of John Anderson Truman and Martha Ellen Young Truman. His parents named him Harry in honor of his uncle, Harrison Young. They chose the middle initial "S." But they gave him no middle name so that both his grandfathers, Solomon Young and Anderson Shippe Truman, could claim that he was named for them.

When Harry was 6 years old, his family moved from a farm near Grandview, Mo., to Independence, Mo. Harry went to elementary school and high school in Independence and attended the First Presbyterian church there. He later joined a Baptist church. He began wearing glasses when he was 8. "I was so carefully cautioned by the eye doctor about breaking my glasses and injuring my eyes," he later wrote, "that I was afraid to join in the rough-and-tumble games in the schoolyard and back lot. My time was spent in reading, and by the time I was 13 or 14 years old I had read all the books in the Independence Public Library and our old Bible three times through." During the summers, Harry, his brother Vivian (1886-1965), and his sister Mary Jane (1889-1978) visited their grandparents' farm near Grandview.

First Jobs. Truman wanted to go to the United States Military Academy at West Point, but his vision was not good enough to meet army standards. After being graduated from high school in 1901, Harry went to work as a timekeeper for a construction crew of the Santa Fe Railroad. Then he worked in the mailing room of the *Kansas City Star.* His next jobs were as a clerk and later as a bookkeeper in two Kansas City banks. He moved to Grandview in 1906, a few years after his grandfather's death, and operated the family farm until 1917.

Soldier. When the United States entered World War I in 1917, Truman helped organize a field artillery regiment. He had joined the Missouri National Guard in 1905. He quickly became a lieutenant, then won promotion to captain while serving in France with the 35th Division. He and a friend, Sergeant Eddie Jacobson, ran the regimental canteen. Truman commanded an artillery battery in the St. Mihiel, Sommedieu, and

---

IMPORTANT DATES IN TRUMAN'S LIFE

1884 (May 8) Born in Lamar, Mo.
1917-1919 Served in the U.S. Army during World War I.
1919 (June 28) Married Elizabeth Virginia Wallace.
1922 Elected judge of Jackson County, Missouri.
1934 Elected to the United States Senate.
1941-1944 Served as chairman of the Truman Committee.
1944 Elected Vice-President of the United States.
1945 (April 12) Became President of the United States.
1948 Elected President of the United States.
1972 (Dec. 26) Died in Kansas City, Mo.

Harris & Ewing

EISENHOWER
34th President
1953 — 1961

KENNEDY
35th President
1961 — 1963

33RD PRESIDENT

OF THE

UNITED STATES

1945-1953

Meuse-Argonne campaigns. He was discharged as a major in 1919, and later rose to colonel in the reserves.

Truman's Family. Six weeks after he returned home, on June 28, 1919, Truman married his childhood sweetheart, Elizabeth "Bess" Virginia Wallace (1885-1982), the daughter of an Independence farmer. They had met at Sunday school when he was about 6 years old and she was about 5. They had one child, Mary Margaret (1924-), whom they called Margaret. She had a brief career as a concert soprano on the stage, radio, and television and later became a successful writer.

Businessman. Later in 1919, Truman and his friend Eddie Jacobson invested their savings in a men's clothing store in Kansas City. They worked hard, keeping the store open from 8 A.M. to 9 P.M., but the business failed during the farm depression that began in 1921. Truman worked about 15 years to pay the store debts.

Political Career

Discouraged by the failure of the store, Truman decided to seek a career in politics. He received help from friends who belonged to the political organization of "Big Tom" Pendergast, the Democratic party boss of Kansas City. Pendergast led one of the largest political machines in the United States. He decided that Truman could win votes because of his farm background, his war record, and his friendly personality.

County Judge. Pendergast supported Truman in his campaign for election as county judge of Jackson County. This post in Missouri resembles that of county commissioner in other states. Truman won the election, and served from 1922 to 1924. He lost the 1924 election because of a split in local Democratic forces. Truman attended the Kansas City School of Law during the mid-1920's, but did not obtain a degree. He served as presiding county judge from 1926 to 1934. During this period, Truman won a reputation for honesty and efficiency. He supervised projects financed by more than $60,000,000 in tax funds and bond issues.

U.S. Senator. In 1934, again with Pendergast's support, Truman was elected to the United States Senate. As a member of the Senate Interstate Commerce Com-

381

Truman's Birthplace was this small frame house in Lamar, Mo. The Truman family moved to Independence when Harry was 6 years old.

"The Bosses." Truman often spoke of his wife Bess as "the boss," and of their daughter Margaret as "the one who bosses her."

mittee, Truman directed an investigation of railroad finances. His staff found damaging evidence about many of Truman's friends in Missouri, but he ordered the investigation completed. Then a government study of the Pendergast political machine disclosed vote frauds and shady financial dealings. Pendergast pleaded guilty to income tax evasion, and he and many of his followers were sent to prison. The scandals did not touch Truman. In 1940, he won re-election to the Senate without help from the tottering Pendergast machine.

The Truman Committee. In 1940, although the United States was not formally involved in World War II, the nation's defense spending rose to huge sums. Truman realized that the defense effort created many opportunities for waste and corruption. He remembered that many committees had investigated military spending after World War I—when they were powerless to recover wasted funds. Truman urged the Senate to set up a committee to investigate defense spending as it occurred. Early in 1941, the Senate established the Committee to Investigate the National Defense Program. Truman was named chairman. The Truman Committee, as the group soon became known, uncovered waste and inefficiency. It saved the government about $1,000,000,000, and greatly speeded war production.

Vice-President. In 1944, many Democratic leaders believed that President Roosevelt would not live through a fourth term in the White House. They realized that the man they chose for Vice-President would probably succeed to the presidency.

The contest for the vice-presidential nomination almost split the party. Many liberals supported Vice-President Henry A. Wallace for renomination. Others favored Supreme Court Justice William O. Douglas. Southern conservatives preferred James F. Byrnes, a former justice of the Court. Roosevelt refused to name a preference. But Robert E. Hannegan, chairman of the party's national convention, supported Truman as a compromise candidate. Truman had a national reputation as a result of his committee investigations. He also had a good voting record as a Senator, and Roosevelt was willing to accept him. Byrnes withdrew, and the

delegates nominated Truman on the second ballot.

Roosevelt and Truman easily defeated their Republican opponents, Governor Thomas E. Dewey of New York and Governor John W. Bricker of Ohio (see ROOSEVELT, FRANKLIN D. [Election of 1944]). As Vice-President, Truman presided over the Senate. His most important act in the 83 days he held this office was to break a Senate tie by voting to continue the lend-lease program (see LEND-LEASE).

First Administration (1945-1949)

Late in the afternoon of April 12, 1945, Truman was suddenly summoned to the White House by telephone. He was taken to Mrs. Eleanor Roosevelt's study, and she stepped forward to meet him. "Harry," she said quietly, "the President is dead." Truman's first words were: "Is there anything I can do for you?" Mrs. Roosevelt replied: "Is there anything *we* can do for *you?* For you are the one in trouble now."

At 7:09 P.M., Truman took the oath of office as President. The next day, while talking to White House newsmen, he said: "Boys, if you ever pray, pray for me now. I don't know whether you fellows ever had a load of hay fall on you, but when they told me yesterday what had happened, I felt like the moon, the stars, and all the planets had fallen on me."

The End of World War II. When Truman became President, Allied armies were winning the war in Germany, and were preparing to invade Japan. Events moved swiftly. Thirteen days after Truman took office, the first United Nations conference met in San Francisco (see SAN FRANCISCO CONFERENCE). Then, on May 7, Germany surrendered. Truman proudly proclaimed May 8 as V-E Day (Victory in Europe Day). It was his 61st birthday.

In July, Truman traveled to Potsdam, Germany, to confer with Prime Minister Winston Churchill of Great Britain and Premier Joseph Stalin of Russia (see POTSDAM CONFERENCE). While in Potsdam, the President received secret word that American scientists had successfully tested an atomic bomb for the first time. On his way home, Truman ordered American fliers to drop an atomic bomb on Japan. The first bomb fell on the city of Hiroshima on August 6. Three days later, a second atomic bomb was dropped on Nagasaki. Japan opened peace negotiations on August 10, and the war ended on August 14. See ATOMIC BOMB (Atomic Explosions); WORLD WAR II (Target Tokyo).

The Fair Deal. Truman wanted to extend Roosevelt's "New Deal" policies. He prepared a program that he called the "Fair Deal," because he thought it would be fair to both rich and poor. In September, 1945, Truman

--------- VICE-PRESIDENT AND CABINET ---------

Vice-President..........	*Alben W. Barkley
Secretary of State.......	*Edward R. Stettinius, Jr.
	*James F. Byrnes (1945)
	*George C. Marshall (1947)
	*Dean G. Acheson (1949)
Secretary of the.........	*Henry Morgenthau, Jr.
Treasury	*Frederick M. Vinson (1945)
	John W. Snyder (1946)
Secretary of War†.......	*Henry L. Stimson
	Robert P. Patterson (1945)
	Kenneth C. Royall (1947)
Secretary of Defense.....	*James V. Forrestal (1947)
	Louis A. Johnson (1949)
	*George C. Marshall (1950)
	Robert A. Lovett (1951)
Attorney General........	Francis Biddle
	*Tom C. Clark (1945)
	J. Howard McGrath (1949)
	James P. McGranery (1952)
Postmaster General......	Frank C. Walker
	Robert E. Hannegan (1945)
	Jesse M. Donaldson (1947)
Secretary of the Navy†...	*James V. Forrestal
Secretary of the Interior..	*Harold L. Ickes
	Julius A. Krug (1946)
	Oscar L. Chapman (1950)
Secretary of Agriculture...	Claude R. Wickard
	Clinton P. Anderson (1945)
	Charles F. Brannan (1948)
Secretary of Commerce...	*Henry A. Wallace
	*Averell Harriman (1946)
	Charles Sawyer (1948)
Secretary of Labor.......	*Frances Perkins
	Lewis B. Schwellenbach (1945)
	Maurice J. Tobin (1948)

*Has a separate biography in WORLD BOOK.
†Reduced to non-Cabinet rank under Secretary of Defense, 1947.

asked Congress for (1) an enlarged social security program; (2) a permanent Fair Employment Practices Commission (FEPC) to protect minority rights; (3) government aid for scientific research; and (4) public power projects on the Arkansas, Columbia, and Missouri rivers.

The Republicans gained control of Congress in the 1946 elections, and blocked most of Truman's domestic measures. Congress did approve Truman's plan to unify the armed forces under a single Secretary of Defense (see DEFENSE, DEPARTMENT OF). A commission was established to study ways of improving government efficiency, and Truman named former President Herbert Hoover to head it (see HOOVER COMMISSION). In 1947, after a long fight, Congress passed the Labor-Management Relations Act, or Taft-Hartley Act, over the President's veto (see TAFT-HARTLEY ACT).

The Truman Doctrine. Soon after World War II, the Cold War developed between Russia and its former allies (see COLD WAR). The communists gained control over one nation after another in eastern Europe. Truman realized that the United States would have to lead in the fight for freedom, spending as much as necessary to strengthen its war-torn allies. In 1946, Congress approved a $3,750,000,000 loan to Great Britain. Then, on March 12, 1947, Truman announced a doctrine of international resistance to communist aggression. The Truman Doctrine guaranteed American aid to any free nation resisting communist propaganda or sabotage.

The Marshall Plan, outlined by Secretary of State George C. Marshall in 1947, extended the Truman Doctrine. It proposed that the war-damaged nations of Europe join in a program of mutual aid for economic recovery, assisted by grants from the United States. Communist nations rejected the plan, but 16 other countries accepted it. See MARSHALL PLAN.

Election of 1948 seemed certain to bring victory to the Republicans. United and confident, they faced a sharply divided Democratic party. The Democratic national convention nominated Truman on the first ballot, and picked Senator Alben W. Barkley of Kentucky for Vice-President. A group of liberal Democrats then

TRUMAN, HARRY S.

The Potsdam Conference. Truman conferred with Sir Winston Churchill of Great Britain and Joseph Stalin of Russia in Germany in July, 1945.

Brisk Morning Walks helped Truman keep fit. Newsmen often had to run to match the President's rapid pace.

The 1948 Election was a great political upset. Truman defeated Republican Thomas E. Dewey. He was delighted when one newspaper prematurely reported that Dewey had won—the outcome many had expected.

United Press Int.

382a

left the party and formed the Progressive party. The Progressives nominated former Vice-President Wallace for President. Another group, made up of Southern Democrats who opposed a strong civil rights program, organized the Dixiecrat party. They nominated Strom Thurmond, then governor of South Carolina. The Republicans again nominated Dewey for President, and chose Governor Earl Warren of California as his running mate. See DIXIECRAT PARTY; PROGRESSIVE PARTY.

Few persons beside Harry Truman himself thought that he could win election to a full term as President. Every public opinion poll predicted that Dewey would win a landslide victory. But, with an extraordinary show of fighting spirit, Truman made the experts look ridiculous. He traveled 31,000 miles (49,900 kilometers) by train in a "whistle-stop" campaign and made more than 350 speeches. He attacked what he termed the "do nothing" Republican Congress, calling it "the worst in my memory." Truman received a warm response with his simple language, earthy humor, and pluck. In one of the biggest upsets in political history, Truman won 28 states, to 16 for Dewey and 4 for Thurmond.

Life in the White House. Early every day—often as early as 5:30 A.M.—Truman arose and went for a brisk walk, always accompanied by Secret Service agents and newsmen. At the White House, Truman often played the piano for visitors, and particularly enjoyed the music of Chopin and Mozart. The Trumans spent most evenings together in a family living room upstairs.

The structural part of the White House had become dangerously weak, and engineers had to make extensive repairs. The rebuilding began late in 1948, and the Trumans moved to Blair House. They lived there until March, 1952. See BLAIR HOUSE; WHITE HOUSE.

On Nov. 1, 1950, two Puerto Rican nationalists tried to invade Blair House and assassinate the President. They killed one Secret Service guard and wounded another. One of the gunmen was killed and the other captured. Truman commented that "A President has to expect those things." He kept all his appointments that day, and took his usual walk the next morning.

Second Administration (1949-1953)

Foreign Affairs. In the spring of 1949, the United States, Canada, Great Britain, France, and eight other nations signed the North Atlantic Treaty, forming the North Atlantic Treaty Organization (NATO). They agreed that an attack on one member would be considered an attack on all. Other countries later joined NATO and helped group their armed forces to defend

------ TRUMAN'S ELECTION ------

Place of Nominating Convention. Philadelphia
Ballot on Which Nominated..... 1st
Republican Opponent......... Thomas E. Dewey
Dixiecrat Opponent........... Strom Thurmond
Progressive Opponent......... Henry A. Wallace
Electoral Vote................. 303 (Truman) to:
189 (Dewey)
39 (Thurmond)
0 (Wallace)
Popular Vote.................. 24,105,695 (Truman) to:
21,969,170 (Dewey)
1,169,021 (Thurmond)
1,156,103 (Wallace)
Age at Inauguration........... 64

THE WORLD OF

WORLD EVENTS

1945 (May 7) The German surrender ended World War II in Europe.
1945 (Aug. 14) Japan surrendered, ending World War II.
1946 Communist leaders began the Cold War with the West.
1947-1948 India, Pakistan, and Ceylon won independence in the British Commonwealth; Burma became a republic.
1948-1949 An Allied airlift supplied blockaded West Berlin.
1948 Israel became a republic in Palestine.
1952 Elizabeth II became Queen of England.

★ ★ ★ ★ ★ ★ ★

The United States Flag had 48 stars throughout Truman's term of office.

UNITED STATES EVENTS

1945 Many wartime economic controls ended.
1946 Congress created the Atomic Energy Commission.
1947 Congress passed the Taft-Hartley Act after the President had vetoed it.
1948 The Marshall Plan began giving economic aid to war-torn countries.
1948-1952 Workmen renovated the White House.
1948 Scientists began using cortisone to treat arthritis.
1949 The United States and its allies set up the North Atlantic Treaty Organization (NATO).
1950 Two Puerto Ricans tried to kill the President.
1951 A Senate committee investigated U.S. crime.
1951 Truman relieved General Douglas MacArthur as UN commander in Korea.
1951 Americans saw the first nationwide telecast.

western Europe. General Dwight D. Eisenhower served as the first supreme commander of NATO forces. See NORTH ATLANTIC TREATY ORGANIZATION.

In his inaugural address, Truman called for "a bold new program for making the benefits of our scientific advances and industrial progress available for the improvement and growth of underdeveloped areas." In 1950, Congress approved $25,000,000 for the first part of this Point Four Program (see POINT FOUR PROGRAM). Late in 1951, Truman asked Congress to set up a new foreign aid program for communist-threatened countries in Southeast Asia. Congress established the Mutual Security Administration to strengthen military defenses in many countries. Truman changed the emphasis of foreign aid from economic help to mutual security. He believed that if the nation's allies were strong, America would be strengthened, too. See FOREIGN AID.

The Korean War began on June 25, 1950, when communist forces from North Korea invaded South Korea.

PRESIDENT TRUMAN

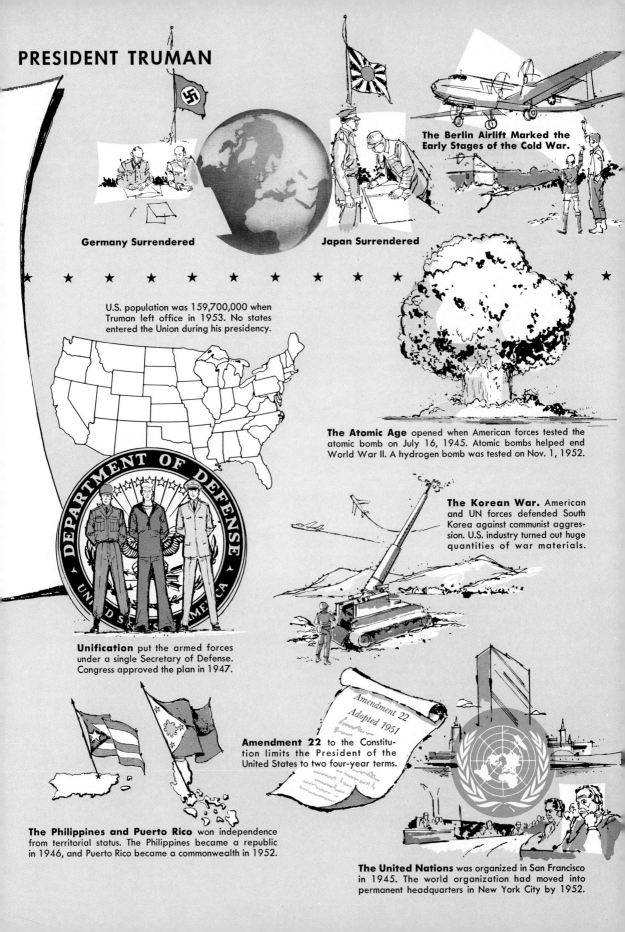

Germany Surrendered

Japan Surrendered

The Berlin Airlift Marked the Early Stages of the Cold War.

U.S. population was 159,700,000 when Truman left office in 1953. No states entered the Union during his presidency.

The Atomic Age opened when American forces tested the atomic bomb on July 16, 1945. Atomic bombs helped end World War II. A hydrogen bomb was tested on Nov. 1, 1952.

The Korean War. American and UN forces defended South Korea against communist aggression. U.S. industry turned out huge quantities of war materials.

Unification put the armed forces under a single Secretary of Defense. Congress approved the plan in 1947.

Amendment 22
Adopted 1951

Amendment 22 to the Constitution limits the President of the United States to two four-year terms.

The Philippines and Puerto Rico won independence from territorial status. The Philippines became a republic in 1946, and Puerto Rico became a commonwealth in 1952.

The United Nations was organized in San Francisco in 1945. The world organization had moved into permanent headquarters in New York City by 1952.

The United Nations demanded that North Korea withdraw. Truman decided to intervene to save South Korea's independence. On June 27, he announced that he had sent U.S. planes and ships to help South Korea. Congress cheered the announcement. That same day, the UN approved sending troops of other nations to join South Korean and American units. Truman ordered ground forces to South Korea on June 30. He later said that sending U.S. troops to South Korea—and thus taking the risk of starting World War III—was the hardest decision of his political career.

General Douglas MacArthur commanded all UN forces in Korea. His troops brought most of Korea under UN control by October, 1950. But later that month, Chinese communist troops joined the North Koreans. Truman recognized the urgency of the situation and put the United States on a semiwar basis. MacArthur wanted to attack Chinese communist bases in Manchuria. But Truman believed that the fighting must be confined to Korea, and not be allowed to spread into a possible global war. Truman became angry when MacArthur made several public statements criticizing this policy. In April, 1951, Truman dismissed MacArthur, creating a nationwide furor. See KOREAN WAR.

Problems at Home. The voters had elected a Democratic Congress in 1948. It soon proved almost as uncooperative in domestic affairs as the preceding Republican Congress had been. Southern Democrats joined conservative Republicans to defeat most of the President's domestic proposals. The Democrats lost strength in the 1950 congressional elections.

Charges of communist infiltration into the federal government added to the President's concerns. Truman set up a federal board to investigate the loyalty of government employees, and the Department of Justice prosecuted leaders of the American Communist Party. A House committee investigated charges that communists worked for the Department of State. The trials of Alger Hiss and Ethel and Julius Rosenberg revealed that spies had stolen secret information and given it to Russian agents (see HISS, ALGER; ROSENBERG). Senator Joseph R. McCarthy of Wisconsin also accused the Department of State of employing communists.

Campaign of 1952. On March 29, 1952, Truman announced that he would not seek reelection. "I have served my country long, and I think efficiently and honestly," he said. "I do not feel that it is my duty to spend another four years in the White House." Instead, he campaigned for the Democratic candidate, Governor

Highlights of Truman's Administration

1945 (May 7) Germany surrendered to the Allies.
1945 (July 16) The first atomic bomb was tested.
1945 (Aug. 14) Japan's surrender ended World War II.
1945 (Oct. 24) The United Nations was founded.
1947 (May 15) Congress approved the Truman Doctrine.
1947 (June) Congress passed the Taft-Hartley Act over Truman's veto.
1947 (July) Congress unified the U.S. armed forces.
1948 (April 2) Congress approved the Marshall Plan.
1949 (April 4) The United States and 11 other nations set up the North Atlantic Treaty Organization (NATO).
1950 (June 27) The United States sent forces to defend South Korea against Communist aggression.

Adlai E. Stevenson of Illinois, who lost to Dwight D. Eisenhower.

Elder Statesman

Truman left office on Jan. 20, 1953, and retired to his home in Independence. He published the two volumes of his memoirs, *Year of Decisions* in 1955 and *Years of Trial and Hope* in 1956. Truman also continued his active interest in politics and in the Democratic party.

After Truman left the White House, his friends collected funds to build the Harry S. Truman Library in Independence. The library holds Truman's papers and souvenirs. It opened in 1957. See MISSOURI (Places to Visit; picture: Harry S. Truman Library in Independence).

Truman became ill late in 1972 and entered the hospital on December 5 suffering from severe lung congestion. He died on December 26. He was buried in Independence in the Truman Library courtyard. ALLAN NEVINS

Related Articles in WORLD BOOK include:

Atomic Bomb	President of the
Cold War	United States
Defense, Department of	Roosevelt, Franklin Delano
Dewey, Thomas E.	San Francisco Conference
Dixiecrat Party	United Nations
Foreign Aid	Vice-President of the
Hoover Commission	United States
Marshall Plan	Wallace, Henry Agard
Point Four Program	World War II
Potsdam Conference	

Outline

I. Early Life
   A. Childhood
   B. First Jobs
   C. Soldier
   D. Truman's Family
   E. Businessman

II. Political Career
   A. County Judge
   B. U.S. Senator
   C. The Truman Committee
   D. Vice-President

III. First Administration (1945-1949)
   A. The End of World War II
   B. The Fair Deal
   C. The Truman Doctrine
   D. The Marshall Plan
   E. Election of 1948
   F. Life in the White House

IV. Second Administration (1949-1953)
   A. Foreign Affairs
   B. The Korean War
   C. Problems at Home
   D. Campaign of 1952

V. Elder Statesman

Questions

Why did Truman call his program "the Fair Deal"?
Where did Truman meet his future wife?
What was the Truman Doctrine?
How did Truman win an upset victory in 1948?
What awesome decision did Truman make to end World War II?
Why did Truman dismiss General MacArthur in Korea?
What did the Truman Committee accomplish?
Why did some Democrats feel that Truman would make a good vice-presidential nominee in 1944?
How did Truman fight communism at home?
Why was the Democratic vice-presidential nomination especially important in 1944?

Reading and Study Guide

See *Truman, Harry S.*, in the RESEARCH GUIDE/INDEX, Volume 22, for a *Reading and Study Guide*.

Additional Resources

DONOVAN, ROBERT J. *Conflict and Crisis: The Presidency of Harry S. Truman, 1945-1948.* Norton, 1977.

MILLER, MERLE. *Plain Speaking: An Oral Biography of Harry S. Truman*. Putnam, 1974.
ROBBINS, JHAN. *Bess and Harry: An American Love Story*. Putnam, 1980.
ROSS, IRWIN. *The Loneliest Campaign: The Truman Victory of 1948*. Greenwood, 1977. Reprint of 1968 ed.
TRUMAN, HARRY S. *Memoirs*. 2 vols. Doubleday, 1955-1956.
TRUMAN, MARGARET. *Harry S. Truman*. Morrow, 1972.

TRUMAN DOCTRINE. See TRUMAN, HARRY S.; COLD WAR (The Containment Policy).

TRUMBULL is the family name of an American colonial governor and his son, an American painter.

Jonathan Trumbull (1710-1785) was governor of Connecticut in the Revolutionary period. He was the only prewar colonial governor who suppported the patriots. Trumbull supplied the Continental Army with food, clothing, and munitions. This task kept him in close touch with General George Washington (see BROTHER JONATHAN).

Trumbull was born in Lebanon, Conn. He built up a business with Britain, which failed just before war began. The experience helped him later in supplying the patriots. He served in the legislature and as deputy governor before holding office as governor from 1769 to 1784. In 1872, his statue was placed in the Capitol in Washington, D.C.   ROBERT J. TAYLOR

John Trumbull (1756-1843) is best known for his small, dramatic paintings of Revolutionary War scenes. Thomas Jefferson, James Madison, and John Adams helped him select his historical subjects. From 1789 to 1794, Trumbull made portraits of the individuals he intended to include in the scenes. He later copied the portraits into his compositions.

Trumbull was born in Lebanon, Conn. In 1784, he studied historical painting under Benjamin West in London. In 1817, he received a commission to paint four large murals of Revolutionary War subjects in the Rotunda of the U.S. Capitol. The remaining years of his life were disappointing, partly because of his failing eyesight and quarrelsome disposition.   EDWARD H. DWIGHT

See also DECLARATION OF INDEPENDENCE (picture); HAMILTON, ALEXANDER (picture); HESSIANS (picture); REVOLUTIONARY WAR IN AMERICA (picture).

TRUMBULL, LYMAN (1813-1896), was an American political leader. He strongly opposed slavery. As a U.S. senator, he supported President Abraham Lincoln during the Civil War, and helped frame Amendment 13 to the U.S. Constitution, which abolished slavery. Trumbull guided Amendment 14, guaranteeing the rights of blacks, through Congress. He voted against conviction during President Andrew Johnson's impeachment in 1868.

Trumbull was born in Colchester, Conn., and moved to Illinois in 1837. He served in public office as a Democrat, a Republican, and a Liberal Republican. He served on the Illinois Supreme Court from 1849 to 1854 and in the U.S. Senate from 1855 to 1873. After leaving the Senate, Trumbull was active in Illinois politics as a Democrat and then as a Populist.   FRANK L. KLEMENT

TRUMPET is a popular brass instrument in bands and orchestras. A player produces tones by blowing into a cup-shaped mouthpiece and vibrating the lips. The player changes notes by fingering the instrument's three valves and changing lip tension. The largest part of the trumpet consists of a curved tube. Most trumpets used in modern bands are pitched in the key of B flat and have

WORLD BOOK photo courtesy Chicago Symphony Orchestra.

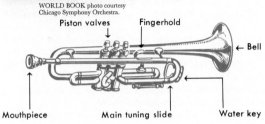

The Trumpet has three piston valves. A trumpet player can produce all notes of the scale by pressing the valves in various combinations.

Piston valves — Fingerhold — ← Bell
Mouthpiece — Main tuning slide — Water key

a tube $4\frac{1}{2}$ feet (1.4 meters) long. In addition to such trumpets, orchestras also use ones with shorter tubes and pitched in other keys. The small diameter and cylindrical shape of its tube give the trumpet its brilliant, powerful sound.

Trumpets date back to about 1200 B.C. The valve trumpet was developed in 1813.   JOHN KEIL RICHARDS

TRUMPET CREEPER. See BIGNONIA.

TRUNDLE BED. See COLONIAL LIFE IN AMERICA (Furnishings).

TRUNK. See TREE (The Parts of a Tree).

TRUSS. See BRIDGE.

TRUST is a term which usually means a combination of business firms that controls all or most of an industry. Some business firms form trusts to reduce or eliminate price competition. They set a higher price for their goods or services than they would get if they competed with one another. Some companies establish trusts to divide markets or reduce competition in other ways. Some trusts are formed to increase efficiency or to gain other advantages not directly related to competition.

The term *trust* has a more limited meaning in the field of law and in many historical writings. It refers to an arrangement in which stockholders of several corporations transfer their voting power to a single group of representatives called *trustees*. In the United States, this kind of trust is now illegal.

Kinds of Trusts

Trusts occur in various forms. A trust may consist of separately controlled firms linked by an agreement or of formerly independent firms combined under common control.

Separately Controlled Firms can form trusts through an informal, unwritten arrangement called a *gentleman's agreement* or through such formal arrangements as *cartels*, *patent pools*, and *trade associations*. Some of these forms are prohibited under U.S. law. For example, American firms may not enter a gentleman's agreement to follow *price leadership*. Under price leadership, competing firms agree to take one firm as a guide in raising or lowering prices, thus eliminating price competition.

A cartel is an association formed among producers in an industry to raise the selling price of their product by limiting the supply. The cartel also assigns each member a share of the market or a certain sales territory. Cartels within the United States are illegal. Under certain conditions, however, U.S. firms may lawfully join an international cartel to export goods.

A patent pool is an agreement between companies to share patents covering a particular product or manufacturing process. The firms thus discourage newcomers from entering the industry. Federal laws regulate patent pools in the United States.

A trade association is a nonprofit organization formed by firms within an industry to promote business for the industry. Trade associations also set standards and provide information about the industry. However, they sometimes reduce competition by pressuring their members to conform to certain price policies.

Firms Under Common Control include *voting trusts, holding companies, interlocking directorates,* and companies formed by *mergers.* In a voting trust, the stockholders of competing companies transfer control to trustees. The trustees elect a board of directors, who then run all the companies as a single firm. The stockholders receive *trust certificates,* which entitle them to share in the profits. U.S. law prohibits voting trusts.

A holding company is a firm that has bought enough stock in other companies to direct their activities. Many holding companies control firms that are supposedly competing with one another. Holding companies that reduce competition are illegal in most states of the United States, but some states have legalized them.

An interlocking directorate is an arrangement in which the same person sits on the board of directors of two or more companies. U.S. law prohibits interlocking directorates among competing firms of a certain size that engage in interstate or foreign trade.

A merger is the joining of two or more firms to form a single company. Mergers that might lessen competition are strictly controlled by U.S. law.

The Effects of Trusts

People disagree about the effects of trusts. Many economists—and many people in general—believe that competition is desirable. It encourages producers to hold prices down, operate efficiently, and keep the quality of their products high. According to these people, trusts harm consumers by reducing competition.

Some people, however, believe certain types or degrees of competition are harmful. They wish to avoid cutthroat competition, in which companies sell at a loss to force one another out of business. Such competition prevents companies from predicting prices and makes long-term planning and investment difficult. In addition, workers lose their jobs if cutthroat competition drives their employers out of business. Because of such problems, some people would prefer that firms maintain stable, reasonable prices. The firms would then compete to offer new products and higher quality products instead of lower prices. According to this view, trusts are desirable because they can contribute to price stability.

Many people believe trusts benefit consumers in ways not related to competition. In many industries, for example, a large firm can produce the same output more cheaply than several smaller firms. When a company

grows through a merger or other means, its *fixed costs* per unit may fall. Fixed costs are expenses, such as heating costs and property taxes, that vary little with the quantity produced. Lower fixed costs per unit and other advantages available only to large companies are called *economies of scale.* In many cases, producers pass on the savings to consumers in the form of lower prices. Some experts also believe that trusts promote industrial progress because large companies can afford to sponsor more research and development.

History

During the late 1800's, competitors in several major industries in the United States formed large trusts. The trusts cut prices to force the remaining competitors out of business. Then they limited production and raised prices. A public outcry against such practices led to the passage of the Sherman Antitrust Act in 1890. The act outlaws any contract, combination, or conspiracy in restraint of trade. It also forbids any attempt to create a monopoly.

In 1914, Congress passed two laws to support the Sherman Antitrust Act. The Clayton Antitrust Act outlaws certain anticompetitive mergers and business practices. The Federal Trade Commission Act established the Federal Trade Commission (FTC), a federal agency that works to protect competition. In 1950, Congress passed the Celler-Kefauver Act to tighten the Clayton Act's control over mergers.   ROBERT A. SOLO

Related Articles in WORLD BOOK include:

Antitrust Laws	Holding Company
Cartel	Monopoly and
Conglomerate	Competition
Federal Trade Commission	

TRUST ESTATE. See TRUST FUND.

TRUST FUND is money or other property managed by one person or group for the benefit of another person or group. Other terms for a trust fund include *corpus, principal,* and *trust estate.* The arrangement under which a trust fund is managed is called a *trust.*

In some cases, the property in a trust fund is taxed less heavily than property owned without such an arrangement. As a result, many people establish trust funds to reduce their taxes. Others create trust funds for the benefit of children or other people who cannot manage property themselves. Some people use trust funds to take advantage of an individual's or institution's special skill in managing property.

How a Trust Fund Works. Most trust funds involve three parties: a *trustor,* a *trustee,* and a *beneficiary.* In some cases, the trustor is also the trustee or the beneficiary. The trustor, also called the *settlor* or *donor,* creates a trust fund by giving property to a trustee. The trustee holds or invests the fund for the good of the beneficiary. The trustee may have charge of the fund for a few years or for more than a lifetime, depending on the terms of the trust. After the trust has *terminated* (ended), the trustee distributes the property as directed in the terms of the trust.

Any sane adult may serve as a trustee. However, most trust funds are handled by *trust departments* of banks or by businesses called *trust companies.* In most cases, the fee for the trustee's services is set by an agreement between the trustor and trustee. Trustees must keep accounts of all trust funds they hold, invest, or distribute. In addition, they must follow the trustor's wishes concerning investment of the fund. If the trust does not indicate the trustor's wishes concerning investment, the trustee must follow guidelines set by state laws. A trustee must make good any losses that result from wrongful use of a trust fund.

Beneficiaries receive income from trust funds according to a variety of arrangements. For example, some beneficiaries periodically receive income earned by the trust fund. Other beneficiaries must wait and receive the accumulated income from the fund when they reach a certain age. Some beneficiaries receive payments from the trust fund until they reach a certain age, when they take possession of the fund themselves.

Kinds of Trusts. A trust that operates during the trustor's life is called a *living* or *inter vivos trust*. A trust established by a will is called a *testamentary trust*. A *revocable trust* can be changed or abolished by the trustor. A trustor who gives up all rights to the trust fund creates an *irrevocable trust*.

Trusts established for the benefit of churches, colleges, or other nonprofit organizations are *charitable trusts*. *Life insurance trusts* are created to receive the proceeds of insurance policies on the life of the trustor.

Courts occasionally create *constructive trusts* to protect property. For example, a person who has property that belongs to another may be named *constructive trustee* of that property. Such an arrangement protects the property and ensures that it will be returned to the rightful owner.   T. BRYAN UNDERWOOD, JR.

TRUST TERRITORY refers to an area administered by a country under the supervision of the United Nations (UN) Trusteeship Council. In the mid-1970's, there was only one trust territory—the Trust Territory of the Pacific Islands, administered by the United States. See PACIFIC ISLANDS, TRUST TERRITORY OF THE.

The administering country has complete authority over the government of a trust territory. It administers the territory under an agreement with the UN according to principles set down in the UN Charter.

A total of 11 trust territories were established after World War II. They included Somaliland, a former Italian colony, and 10 of the 11 former mandates of the League of Nations (see MANDATED TERRITORY). The 11th mandate, Namibia (South West Africa), remained under South Africa's control. Of the 11 trust territories, 10 either have become independent or have voted to become a part of other nations (see UNITED NATIONS [The Trusteeship Council]).   WILLIAM T. R. FOX

TRUSTEE. See TRUST FUND.

TRUSTEESHIP COUNCIL. See UNITED NATIONS (The Trusteeship Council).

TRUTH, SOJOURNER (1797?-1883), was the name used by Isabella Baumfree, one of the best-known American abolitionists of her day. She was the first black woman orator to speak out against slavery. She traveled widely through New England and the Midwest on speaking tours. Her deep voice, quick wit, and inspiring faith helped spread her fame.

Baumfree was born a slave in Ulster County, New York. She became free in 1828 under a New York law that banned slavery. In 1843, she experienced what she regarded as a command from God to preach. She took the name Sojourner Truth and began lecturing in New York. Her early speeches were based on the belief

TRYON, WILLIAM

that people best show their love for God by their love and active concern for others. She soon began directing her speeches toward the abolition of slavery.

Chicago Historical Society
Sojourner Truth

In 1864, she visited President Abraham Lincoln in the White House. She stayed in Washington, D.C., and worked to improve living conditions for blacks there. She also helped find jobs and homes for slaves who had escaped from the South to Washington. During the 1870's, she promoted a plan under which the federal government was to set aside undeveloped lands in the West as farms for blacks. But the plan won no government support.   OTEY M. SCRUGGS

Additional Resources

BENNETT, LERONE. *Pioneers in Protest*. Johnson, 1968.
ORTIZ, VICTORIA. *Sojourner Truth*. Harper, 1974.
PAULI, HERTHA. *Her Name Was Sojourner Truth*. Avon, 1976. Reprint of 1962 ed.

TRUTH IN LENDING ACT. See CONSUMERISM (THE RIGHT TO INFORMATION); USURY.

TRUTH SERUM. See SODIUM PENTOTHAL.

TRUTH TABLE is a method of showing logical relationships. Truth tables are used by computer engineers, logicians, and others who reason by symbolic logic.

To understand truth tables, we must first understand some ideas of logic. A basic declarative sentence is a *proposition* if its meaning can be classified as true or false. For example, the sentences *"The door is open."* and *"The light bulb is not burned out."* are propositions.

A limited number of propositions when combined may form a *propositional function*. For example, the two propositions above may be combined into the propositional function *"The light in the refrigerator will be on if the door is open and the light bulb is not burned out."* The truth or falsity of a propositional function depends on the truth or falsity of each of the basic propositions and the way the function relates them.

The truth table corresponding to the above propositional function would look like this:

Basic Propositions		Propositional Function
Door Open	Bulb Not Burned Out	Light On
false	false	false
false	true	false
true	false	false
true	true	true

A truth table lists all possible combinations of true and false values that can be assigned to the basic propositions. The table is then completed by indicating the truth or falsity of the propositional function for each entry.   TAYLOR L. BOOTH

TRYON, WILLIAM. See NORTH CAROLINA (Places to Visit [Tryon Palace]; Revolution and Independence).

TRYPANOSOME

TRYPANOSOME, *TRIP uh noh SOHM*, is a microscopic one-celled animal. It is a parasite in the blood and spinal fluid of human beings and other vertebrates. Some trypanosomes are parasites in plants. One kind causes African sleeping sickness. Others cause Chagas' disease and nagana, an African disease of animals. A trypanosome is long and thin, with a whiplike extension at one end called a *flagellum*. It also has a thin waving membrane down the length of its body. Many trypanosomes spend part of their lives inside certain insects.

Scientific Classification. Trypanosomes are in the family *Trypanosomidae*. One that causes sleeping sickness is genus *Trypanosoma*, species *T. gambiense*. RALPH BUCHSBAUM

See also TSETSE FLY; SLEEPING SICKNESS.

TSAR. See CZAR.

TSCHAIKOWSKY, PETER ILICH. See TCHAIKOVSKY, PETER ILICH.

TSERCLAES, JOHAN. See TILLY, COUNT OF.

TSETSE FLY, *TSET see*, is a two-winged fly of Africa. It carries the animal parasites that cause African sleeping sickness. These parasites are called *trypanosomes*.

There are about 20 kinds of tsetse flies. Most of them attack people. The flies look somewhat like ordinary houseflies, but they are larger and fold their wings flat over their backs in such a way that the wings do not stick out at an angle, as they do on houseflies. The tsetse fly has a long *proboscis* (beak) which it uses to pierce the skin of its victim. The fly sucks the blood of mammals. As it sucks the blood, it infects its victim.

The tsetse fly transmits a deadly disease called *nagana* to cattle and horses. Sleeping sickness and nagana are spread in much the same way as malaria. The fly bites an animal or person already infected, picks up the germs, and infects the next person it bites.

The flies usually cannot infect people or animals until the germs have lived in their bodies for several days and have passed

Walter Petana

A Tsetse Fly

through the stomach to their salivary glands. But then, for at least 96 days, the flies can transmit the parasites to anyone they bite.

Tsetse flies breed slowly. The female fly does not lay eggs and it produces only one larva at a time. The larva is nourished during its growing period inside the body of the parent. When the larva is full-grown, it is deposited on the ground, and it becomes a pupa.

Both male and female flies are active bloodsuckers. They are harmful chiefly along lake shores or river banks, making parts of Africa uninhabitable. In some regions, insecticide sprays control tsetse fly populations. Other successful control programs use radiation to sterilize male flies, making them unable to reproduce. Drugs that protect cattle from nagana are also used. However, political unrest has hampered tsetse fly control efforts in many parts of Africa.

Scientific Classification. The tsetse fly belongs to the tsetse fly family, *Glossinidae*. The most dangerous fly is genus *Glossina*, species *G. palpalis*. *G. morsitans* carries Rhodesian sleeping sickness. DALE W. JENKINS

See also SLEEPING SICKNESS; TRYPANOSOME.

TSHOMBE, MOISE. See ZAIRE (History).

TSIMSHIAN INDIANS, *TSIM shih un*, were a wealthy group of Pacific Coast Indians. They were also called Chimmesyan Indians. The Tsimshian lived in many small villages along the Nass and Skeena rivers in what is now British Columbia. The Tsimshian were the only Indians of the northern Northwest Coast to have tribal chiefs.

The Tsimshian lived by fishing, hunting, and gathering wild plants. Salmon was one of the most important foods in their diet. Their houses of large cedar beams and planks sometimes held seven to ten families, ruled by a house chief. Wealthy chiefs had slaves and servants. Each person had a place in a social class. Secret societies were also important. The Tsimshian made ocean-going canoes, totem poles, masks, rattles, boxes, and small objects of wood, bone, and ivory.

During the 1900's, the Tsimshian Indians rapidly adopted the customs of white people. But many persons in British Columbia still speak the Tsimshian Indian language. MELVILLE JACOBS

TSUNAMI. See TIDAL WAVE.

TSUSHIMA, BATTLE OF. See NAVY (Famous Sea Battles).

TU FU. See CHINESE LITERATURE (Poetry).

TUAMOTU ISLANDS, *TOO ah MO too*, are an island group in the South Pacific, about 3,000 miles (4,800 kilometers) southeast of Honolulu. For location, see PACIFIC ISLANDS (color map). The Tuamotu group is made up of 75 atolls and reef islands. The islands stretch across almost a thousand miles of water, and have dangerous sunken reefs. They cover an area of about 308 square miles (798 square kilometers), and have a population of about 6,700. Polynesians live on the islands. Pearls and copra are the chief sources of income.

In 1606, the Spanish navigator Pedro de Queirós discovered the archipelago. A native king ruled the islands until 1881, when France annexed them. They are governed from Papeete, Tahiti. France began using Mururoa atoll, in the Tuamotu group, as a nuclear bomb test area in 1965. EDWIN H. BRYAN, JR.

TUAREGS. See BERBERS; AFRICA (People).

TUATARA. See REPTILE; ANIMAL (color picture: Ways of Life).

TUBA, or BASS HORN, is the largest of the cupped-mouthpiece brass instruments. It also has the lowest pitch. Musicians use it mostly in bands, but sometimes they also use it in orchestras. The brass *basses*, as they are called, come in different shapes, but are usually circular in design. One kind is upright, with the bell turned either upward or forward. The helicon and sousaphone models have bell joints of various shapes. They rest on the player's shoulder. Basses, as used in a band, supply the lowest harmonic part. They also are often used in music that is heavily rhythmic. Sometimes they carry bass melodies. CHARLES B. RIGHTER

TUBAL-CAIN was a metalsmith of ancient times. He appears in many stories and legends and is often called the father of all workers in brass and iron.

TUBE. See ELECTRONICS (Electron Tubes); TELEVISION (Amplifiers and Separators; The Picture Tube); VACUUM TUBE.

TUBE. See LONDON (Transportation); SUBWAY.

TUBE FOOT. See ANIMAL (How Animals Move About); ECHINODERM; STARFISH (with picture).

TUBER is the thick, enlarged part of a stem that grows underground. The potato is the best example of the tuber. The tuber stores the food, usually starch, for the plant. It has small scalelike leaves and tiny buds known as *eyes*. These eyes sprout new plants, which obtain their food from the tuber until their own roots and leaves are formed. The Jerusalem artichoke is another example of a tuber. See also ARTICHOKE; POTATO.   WILLIAM C. BEAVER

TUBERCULOSIS, *too* BUR *kyuh* LOH *sihs,* is a serious infectious disease that attacks primarily the lungs but can also affect almost any part of the body. Tuberculosis once ranked among the world's worst killers. Today, it remains a major health threat in many developing nations. Tuberculosis is also called *TB* and *consumption.*

Tuberculosis attacks people of all ages. At one time, most victims of the disease died from it. Physicians now use drugs to prevent or treat tuberculosis, and nearly everyone who receives proper treatment recovers. The disease also afflicts animals, especially such domestic animals as cattle, hogs, and poultry.

Tuberculosis is caused by bacteria called *tubercle bacilli.* The tubercle bacillus, a microscopic, rod-shaped organism, was discovered in 1882 by the German physician Robert Koch (see KOCH, ROBERT). Tubercle bacilli need oxygen to live, and they cannot move under their own power. These germs cannot reproduce outside the body of a human being or an animal unless they are grown in a laboratory.

A person who is infected by tuberculosis germs may not get the disease. In most cases, the invading bacteria are soon killed or made harmless by the body's natural defenses. Years later, the infection may develop into tuberculosis disease. But millions of infected people carry tubercle bacilli in their bodies for many years and never get the disease.

In almost all cases, people get a tuberculosis infection by inhaling tubercle bacilli that are floating on droplets of moisture in the air. Infection may occur if the bacteria are inhaled over a period of time, not just once. The germs are expelled into the air when a person with tuberculosis coughs or sneezes. The bacteria also enter the body through contaminated food. For example, the bacteria may be in milk from a tubercular cow. Such an infection occurs very rarely in countries where the milk is pasteurized and the cows are tested for tuberculosis.

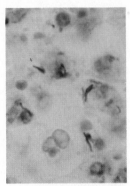

John R. Dainauskas, M.D.

Tuberculosis Germs appear as short, red rods in diseased lung tissue, *above.* This photograph magnifies the tissue 200 times.

How Tuberculosis Affects the Body

The lungs have several defenses against invading bacteria. One of their best defenses is a layer of mucus that lines the largest of the countless tubes of the lungs (see LUNG). Almost all the tubercle bacilli that are inhaled into the lungs get stuck in this mucus. The mucous layer constantly moves upward. It carries the trapped germs into the throat, where they are swallowed harmlessly or spat out. Sometimes, however, a few bacilli are inhaled into the deepest and smallest lung tubes, which have no mucus. There, they may thrive and cause infection.

The Infection activates other natural defenses against the bacilli. White blood cells engulf and kill many of the invading germs. Other defending cells surround groups of the bacteria and form hard *tubercles* (lumps) around them. The word *tuberculosis* comes from *tubercle.* The bacteria may remain alive inside a tubercle, but they are inactive and harmless.

The first invasion of the germs, followed by the formation of tubercles, is called a *primary infection.* Most people who get a primary infection are not aware of it because the condition rarely produces symptoms. In some cases, however, it causes such symptoms as fever, nausea, and a rash.

The Disease may develop at any time after a primary tubercular infection. It occurs immediately in many

WORLD BOOK photo, courtesy Chicago Symphony Orchestra

Mouthpiece

Slide pull ring

Bell →

Coiled tubing →

Piston valves

The Tuba has a lower pitch than any other brass instrument. The musician presses the piston valves to produce notes. *Tuba* is also the general name for such instruments as the sousaphone.

389

How Tuberculosis Develops

Most cases of tuberculosis begin with an infection deep in the lung, *left*. The top series of drawings below shows how invading bacteria called *tubercle bacilli* cause a primary infection. The bottom drawings illustrate how tuberculosis can later develop from the primary infection.

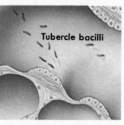

Tubercle bacilli

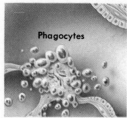

Phagocytes

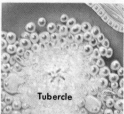

Tubercle

Tubercle Bacilli in the air are inhaled deep into the tiniest tubes of the lung at the start of a primary infection.

Phagocytes, a type of white blood cell, attack the invading bacilli. These cells kill many of the invaders.

Other Defending Cells trap the remaining bacilli inside hard lumps called *tubercles.* The trapped bacilli are harmless.

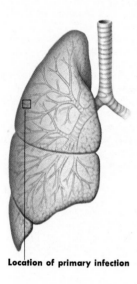

Location of primary infection

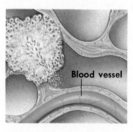

Blood vessel

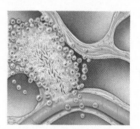

The Bacilli Break Out of the tubercles if the body's defenses weaken. This action marks the start of tuberculosis.

The Bacilli Multiply and invade surrounding tissue. Phagocytes and other defenses unsuccessfully attack the bacilli.

Multiplying Bacilli break through the lung tube wall and penetrate a blood vessel. They then spread through the body.

infants and other people who have a low resistance to tubercle bacilli. But in most cases, the disease does not develop unless the body's natural defenses have been weakened by another illness or by some other cause. If the defenses are weakened, the tubercles break open and release the bacilli, which multiply and spread. Young people who are infected after infancy may lose some resistance to tuberculosis during adolescence.

Tuberculosis that attacks the lungs is the most common form of the disease and is called *pulmonary tuberculosis.* As the bacteria multiply, they invade the surrounding lung tissue. White blood cells and other body defenses again fight the bacilli. Many germs and defending cells die in the battle. The dead matter forms a soft, cheeselike material. This material eventually becomes liquid and is coughed up, leaving a cavity in the lung.

The first symptom of pulmonary tuberculosis may be prolonged coughing. Many victims think they have only a lasting cold. Later, they lose considerable weight. They also have a fever in the afternoon and perspire heavily at night. Eventually, they begin to cough up blood. By then, the disease is well advanced.

The battle between the bacilli and the body's defenses may continue for several years. The victim, if not treated, gradually becomes increasingly ill. Additional cavities form in the lungs, and the germs spread to other parts of the body.

Tubercle bacilli may invade many parts of the body besides the lungs, including the bones, brain, joints, kidneys, lymph glands, and skin. Symptoms vary, depending on the organ involved.

Diagnosing Tuberculosis

Physicians use several methods to diagnose tuberculosis, including skin tests, X-ray examinations, and laboratory tests. In most cases, all these methods are used to confirm a diagnosis of the disease.

Skin Tests show whether a person has a tuberculosis infection, but they do not necessarily indicate the disease. Several weeks after a primary infection, the body develops an allergy to the proteins in the bacilli. These proteins are called *tuberculins.* Skin tests are based on this allergic reaction.

The most reliable skin test for tuberculosis is the Mantoux test. In this test, a small amount of tuberculin is injected just below the skin. Two to four days later, a lump forms at the site of the injection. A positive test results in a lump at least 10 millimeters (0.39 inch) wide. This large lump indicates the presence of infection. A lump 4 millimeters (0.16 inch) wide or less is negative. It indicates no infection. A lump from 4 to 10 millimeters wide is an uncertain reaction. Other skin tests are less reliable, but easier to perform, than the Mantoux test. They are often used to test large groups of people.

X-Ray Examinations may reveal cavities, tubercles, or other signs of tuberculosis in the lungs. Such tests were once the main method of diagnosing tuberculosis. Physicians no longer take X rays to diagnose tuberculosis unless a skin test has shown a positive reaction.

Laboratory Tests are normally the final step in diagnosing tuberculosis. The most common test involves examination of the patient's *sputum*, the mucus and other material that is coughed up. The doctor examines the sputum under a microscope to learn if it contains any tubercle bacilli. The physician may also let the germs grow in a test tube. This procedure helps distinguish tubercle bacilli from similar bacteria.

Treating Tuberculosis

The first effective treatment for tuberculosis was provided by health resorts called *sanitariums*. They were developed during the later 1800's by physicians in Europe and the United States. At a sanitarium, tuberculosis patients received bed rest, fresh air, and mild exercise. They also were isolated and thus kept from infecting other people. Sanitarium treatment helped many people overcome the disease. However, most of them had to spend months or even years in a sanitarium before they recovered.

Today, almost all tuberculosis patients can be treated successfully with drugs. Isoniazid (INH) ranks as the most effective antituberculosis drug. Other effective drugs include ethambutol, para-amino salicylic acid (PAS), rifampin, and streptomycin. The drugs stop the bacteria from multiplying and allow the body's natural defenses to work against the disease.

Doctors normally prescribe two or more drugs at a time because tuberculosis germs may become resistant to only one medication. Depending on which drugs are used, the patient takes the medications daily or twice a week for nine months to two years. However, hospitalization is not required in most cases, and normal daily activities can be followed while taking the drugs.

Surgery was sometimes used in sanitariums to collapse a diseased lung so that it no longer functioned. Doctors still perform surgery in some cases, but they remove the afflicted part of a tubercular lung rather than collapse the lung. The remaining part continues to function normally.

Preventing Tuberculosis

The drug isoniazid prevents most tuberculosis infections from developing into the disease. Doctors often prescribe isoniazid for people who have a positive skin test. They also give the drug to a child who lives with someone who has tuberculosis, even if the youngster has a negative skin test.

A vaccine called *BCG* (*Bacillus Calmette-Guérin*) has been used in many parts of the world in an effort to prevent tuberculosis. However, physicians have long recognized that the vaccine does not work for everyone. Some studies suggest that BCG is ineffective among certain populations. Physicians in the United States seldom prescribe BCG because tuberculosis occurs infrequently in the United States.

Treatment and preventive action have greatly reduced the number of tuberculosis cases in the developed countries, including the United States. But the disease remains a major problem in a number of developing nations, especially those in Africa. Drugs for tuberculosis are not readily available in those countries. During the 1970's, the United States had about 30,000 new cases of tuberculosis and about 3,000 deaths from the disease annually. Throughout the world, the disease killed about 142,000 persons each year.   LEWIS B. CLAYTON

See also AMERICAN LUNG ASSOCIATION; SCROFULA; TRUDEAU, EDWARD L.; VETERINARY MEDICINE.

Additional Resources

DOWLING, HARRY F. *Fighting Infection: Conquests of the Twentieth Century.* Harvard, 1977.
DUBOS, RENÉ JULES, and PORTER, JEAN. *White Plague: Tuberculosis, Man, and Society.* Little, Brown, 1952.
WAKSMAN, SELMAN A. *The Conquest of Tuberculosis.* Univ. of California Press, 1964.

TUBEROSE, *TOOB rohz,* is a plant of the agave family. It grows wild in tropical America and Asia. It is also raised for use in perfumes and toilet preparations in central Europe, southern Africa, and in North Carolina and New Jersey. The tuberose has a heavy, almost sickening, odor. Its slender stem springs from a tubelike rootstock, and often grows 3 feet (91 centimeters) high. The stem of the tuberose bears waxy-white blossoms and has eight sword-shaped leaves. The tuberose is named for the shape of its rootstock, not for its resemblance to a tube-shaped rose. The tuberose is not a rose.

J. Horace McFarland
Tuberose Blossoms

Scientific Classification: The tuberose belongs to the agave family, *Agavaceae*. It is genus *Polianthes*, species *P. tuberosa.*   DONALD WYMAN

TUBMAN, HARRIET

TUBMAN, HARRIET (1820?-1913), was a black American whose daring rescues helped hundreds of slaves escape to freedom. She became the most famous leader of the *underground railroad*, which aided slaves fleeing to the free states or to Canada (see UNDERGROUND RAILROAD). Blacks called her Moses, after the Biblical figure who led the Jews from Egypt.

Tubman was born a slave in Bucktown, Md., near Cambridge. Her name was Araminta Ross, but as a child, she became known by her mother's name, Harriet. Her father taught her a knowledge of the woods that later helped her in her rescue missions. When Harriet was 13, she interfered with a supervisor to save another slave from punishment. The enraged supervisor fractured Harriet's skull with a 2-pound (0.9-kilogram) weight. She recovered but suffered blackouts for the rest of her life. She married John Tubman, a freed slave, in 1844.

Harriet Tubman es-

Library of Congress
Harriet Tubman

TUBMAN, WILLIAM V. S.

caped from slavery in 1849 and went to Philadelphia via the underground railroad, without her husband. She then vowed to return to Maryland and help other slaves escape. Tubman made her first trip back shortly after Congress passed the Fugitive Slave Act of 1850. This law made it a crime to help a runaway slave. Tubman returned 18 more times during the 1850's and helped about 300 slaves escape.

During one rescue, Tubman sensed that pursuers were close behind, and so she and the fugitives boarded a southbound train to avoid suspicion. On another mission, she had just bought some live chickens in Bucktown when she saw her former master walking towards her. She let the chickens go and chased after them before he could recognize her. In 1857, Tubman led her parents to freedom in Auburn, N.Y.

Tubman never was caught and never lost a slave on any of her 19 rescue trips. She carried a gun and threatened to kill anyone who tried to turn back. Rewards for her capture once totaled about $40,000.

In the late 1850's, Tubman met with the radical abolitionist John Brown, who told her of his plan to free the slaves (see Brown, John). She considered Brown the true liberator of her race. Soon afterward, Tubman also became active in the women's rights movement in New England and New York.

During the Civil War (1861-1865), Tubman served as a nurse, scout, and spy for the Union Army in South Carolina. During one military campaign, she helped free more than 750 slaves.

After the war, Tubman returned to Auburn, where she helped raise money for black schools. The author Sarah H. Bradford wrote *Scenes in the Life of Harriet Tubman* (1869), which described Tubman's work against slavery. In 1908, Tubman established a home in Auburn for elderly and needy blacks. It became known as the Harriet Tubman Home. The people of Auburn erected a plaque in her honor. A U.S. postage stamp bearing her portrait was issued in 1978.   Otey M. Scruggs

Additional Resources

Bradford, Sarah. *Harriet Tubman: The Moses of Her People.* Citadel, 1974. Reprint of 1869 ed.
Conrad, Earl. *Harriet Tubman.* Eriksson, 1970. Reprint of 1943 ed.
Sterling, Dorothy. *Freedom Train.* Doubleday, 1954.

TUBMAN, WILLIAM V. S. (1895-1971), was president of Liberia from 1944 until his death in 1971. Educated in Liberia, he became a lawyer, and later a senator and associate justice of the Liberian Supreme Court. As president, he worked for progress in health, agriculture, and education. Tubman was born in Harper, Liberia. See also Liberia (History).   T. Walter Wallbank

TUCHMAN, *TUHK muhn,* **BARBARA WERTHEIM** (1912-   ), is an American historian who won two Pulitzer prizes for general nonfiction. She received her first Pulitzer in 1963 for *The Guns of August* (1962), which deals with the early phase of World War I (1914-1918). In 1972, Tuchman won a Pulitzer for *Stilwell and the American Experience in China, 1911-1945* (1971). This book centers on the career of the American general Joseph W. Stilwell.

Tuchman was born in New York City. During 1934 and 1935, she worked as a research assistant for the Institute of Pacific Relations. She then became a reporter for the *Nation* magazine and covered the Spanish Civil War (1936-1939). Her first book, *The Lost British Policy: Britain and Spain Since 1700*, was published in 1938. Since the mid-1950's, Tuchman has written a number of historical books on a wide variety of topics. These works include *Bible and Sword: England and Palestine from the Bronze Age to Balfour* (1956), *The Zimmermann Telegram* (1958), *The Proud Tower: A Portrait of the World Before the War, 1890-1914* (1966), *Notes from China* (1972), *A Distant Mirror: The Calamitous Fourteenth Century* (1978), and *Practicing History: Selected Essays* (1981).   Arthur Cyr

Wide World
Barbara Tuchman

TUCKER, RICHARD (1914-1975), was generally considered the outstanding American operatic tenor of his day. The richness of his tone and the high-spirited characteristics of his singing earned him the nickname of the "Jewish Caruso." A devout Orthodox Jew, Tucker was once a *cantor* (singer) in a synagogue.

Tucker was born in Brooklyn. His real name was Reuben Ticker. He made his debut at the Metropolitan Opera in 1945.   Max de Schauensee

TUCSON, *too SAHN,* or *TOO sahn,* Ariz. (pop. 330,-537; met. area pop. 531,263), is a commercial, mining, and research center of the Southwest. It ranks second to Phoenix as the state's largest city. Tucson's warm, dry, sunny climate makes it a popular health and winter resort area. Many retired men and women have settled there. Tucson lies in southern Arizona. For location, see Arizona (political map).

Tucson is the home of the University of Arizona. Museums in the city include the Arizona State Museum and the Arizona Historical Society. The nearby Arizona-Sonora Desert Museum features animals and plants of the Sonora Desert in their natural surroundings. The Kitt Peak National Observatory, southwest of Tucson, is the site of the world's largest solar telescope. A noted landmark in the Tucson area is the San Xavier Mission, called the "White Dove of the Desert."

Over a fourth of the nation's annual production of copper is mined within 50 miles (80 kilometers) of Tucson. Electronics is a growing industry in the city.

Papago and Pima Indians lived in what is now the Tucson area before European explorers arrived there. In 1776, Juan Bautista de Anza established Tucson as a military outpost for the part of the Spanish territory in America that was called New Spain. In 1853, the city became part of the United States as a result of the Gadsden Purchase (see Gadsden Purchase). From 1867 to 1877, it was the capital of the Arizona Territory.

Tucson's population boomed from 1950 to 1965, increasing from 45,454 to 234,600. Many of the new residents had been stationed in the area with the armed services during World War II (1939-1945).

The Tucson Community Center, a $17-million convention and entertainment facility in downtown Tucson, was completed in 1971. La Placita Village opened in 1974. La Placita is a group of office buildings, restaurants, and small shops in a plaza designed to look like a Mexican village. Tucson has continued to grow rapidly since the mid-1960's. By 1980, the city's population had reached 330,537.

Tucson is the seat of Pima County. It has a council-manager form of government. June Johnson Caldwell Martin

TUDOR, HOUSE OF. Tudor is the name of the family that ruled England from 1485 to 1603. The first Tudor ruler was Henry VII. He won his crown at the battle of Bosworth Field, defeating Richard III and ending the Wars of the Roses. Henry claimed the throne through his mother, Margaret Beaufort, a descendant of Edward III. Henry restored order to England after 30 years of civil war, and the nation took its first steps towards becoming one of the major world powers.

His son, Henry VIII, continued his policies. Henry VIII broke all ties between England and the Roman Catholic Church. He was succeeded first by his son, Edward VI, and then in turn by his daughters, Mary I and Elizabeth I. The reigns of Edward and Mary were short and unhappy because of civil unrest, foreign wars, and religious disturbances. Under Elizabeth, however, England once again enjoyed the strong rule typical of the Tudors. At her death in 1603, the crown passed to King James VI of Scotland, the great-grandson of Henry VII's oldest daughter. He was the first Stuart king of England. W. M. Southgate

See also England (History); Henry (VII, VIII).

TUESDAY is the name of the third day of the week. Its name comes from *Tiu*, or *Tiw*, the old Anglo-Saxon form of *Tyr*, name of the Norse god of war. Tyr was the son of Odin, or Woden, for whom Wednesday was named. The French call Tuesday *Mardi*, for Mars, the Roman war god. *Shrove Tuesday*, the day before Lent, was so-called because it was customary to confess and be *shriven* or *shrove* (receive absolution) by a priest. See also Shrove Tuesday; Week. Grace Humphrey

TUFTED TITMOUSE. See Titmouse.

TUGBOAT, also called *Tug* or *Towboat*, is a small boat that is used to move large ships. Tugboats get their power from a steam or diesel engine. Tugboats used in harbors are powerful enough to tow large ocean liners or freighters. They can tow from the front or side, or push from the back. Most tugs are from 65 to 100 feet (20 to 30 meters) long, and are driven by engines with as much as 3,500 horsepower (2,610 kilowatts). The tugboats used on inland lakes and rivers tow or push long lines of barges loaded with heavy cargoes. They have engines of as much as 6,600 horsepower (4,920 kilowatts). Robert H. Burgess

See also Barge (picture).

TUILERIES, *TWEE ler iz,* or *TWEEL REE,* a famous royal palace, stood on the right bank of the river Seine in Paris. During the French Revolution, mobs forced Louis XVI and his family to live there instead of at Versailles. In 1792, the mobs killed Swiss guards who tried to defend the royal family at the Tuileries. For a time, the Convention of the Revolution held its sessions in the Tuileries. Napoleon made it his home, and it served as the royal residence after the Restoration.

Catherine de Médicis began the building of the palace in 1564, but it was not completed until the 1600's. It formed a long, narrow band of buildings with high roofs and dormer windows. At one end it joined the Louvre. The famous Tuileries Gardens covered 75 acres (30 hectares) on the west side of the palace. Supporters of the Commune destroyed most of the palace in 1871, but the garden is still popular. G. Holmes Perkins

TUKE, WILLIAM. See Mental Illness (Humane Treatment).

TULANE UNIVERSITY OF LOUISIANA is a private university in New Orleans. It includes two liberal arts schools—the College of Arts and Sciences for men and H. Sophie Newcomb College for women. Tulane also has coeducational schools of architecture, business administration, continuing education, engineering, graduate studies, law, medicine, public health and tropical medicine, and social work. The university offers a junior-year program of study abroad and special programs in comparative law, Latin-American studies, and public policy. Tulane was founded in 1834 as the Medical College of Louisiana. In 1884, it was renamed in honor of Paul Tulane, a New Orleans merchant who gave the university its first endowment. For enrollment, see Universities and Colleges (table).

Critically reviewed by Tulane University of Louisiana

TULAREMIA, *too luh REE mih uh,* or Rabbit Fever, is an infectious disease of certain animals that can be carried to people. Tularemia is caused by a microbe, *Pasteurella tularensis*. It was first reported in Tulare County, California, in 1911. Human beings catch this disease by handling infected animals such as squirrels, rabbits, and rats. Sometimes they catch it through insect bites. Tularemia causes a fever that comes and goes, and lasts several weeks. The lymph glands become swollen around the bite, and often form pus. Tularemia should be treated by a physician.

TULIP is a lovely, graceful garden flower which came from southern Europe and Asia. Tulips now grow in many other parts of the world, but we associate them with The Netherlands.

The tulip blooms in the spring. Tulips grow from bulbs, and the leaves and flower stems grow directly out of the bulb. The stem usually grows more than 2 feet (61 centimeters) high. But in some dwarf varieties of the tulip, the stem is only about 3 inches (8 centimeters) tall. The tulip usually develops only one large, bell-shaped flower at the tip of its stem.

Ewing Galloway

Graceful Tulips herald the arrival of spring in many parts of the world.

The flowers may be either single or double. They usually grow erect on the stem. They may be almost any color. Some become streaked with other colors because of virus diseases that affect the plant's color but not its health.

Gardeners usually plant tulip bulbs in autumn. They require a well-drained, loamy soil of average richness.

TULIP TREE

Usually only professional tulip growers or experimenters grow the flowers from seed, because tulip seed does not produce a flowering bulb for three to seven years.

Thousands of varieties of tulips have developed from a few *species* (kinds). Almost all the cultivated kinds of tulips were developed from a tulip of Asia Minor which was brought to Vienna from Constantinople (now Istanbul) in the 1500's. The name *tulip* comes from a Turkish word which means *turban*. The beautiful blossoms look a little like turbans. Popular garden varieties of tulips, differing in shape and blooming dates, include the Darwin, the Cottage, and several fringed varieties.

After the tulip was brought to Europe, it became the most fashionable flower in both England and Holland. Interest in the flower developed into a craze in Holland, called the *tulipomania*, between 1634 and 1637. Individual bulbs sold for huge prices. People invested their money in tulips as American business people might invest in steel or oil. Many persons lost fortunes in the tulip market, and finally the government was forced to regulate the trade in bulbs.

Tulip cultivation is an important industry in The Netherlands today. It is also important around Holland, Mich., and in other parts of the United States. Millions of bulbs are produced every year. Dutch growers produce nearly 2,000 varieties. Many new species were discovered in Turkestan. These species were taken to Europe, and now tulips of all kinds are grown more widely than ever in both Europe and America.

Scientific Classification. Tulips belong to the lily family, *Liliaceae*. The tulip brought to Europe in the 1500's is genus *Tulipa*, species *T. gesneriana*.   GEORGE A. BEACH

See also FLOWER (picture: Garden Perennials [Bulbs]); NETHERLANDS (picture: The Polders); OTTAWA (Annual Events).

TULIP TREE, also called *yellow poplar* and *tulip poplar*, is the tallest broadleaf tree in the eastern United States. In forests, it may grow 200 feet (61 meters) high, and its trunk may be 5 to 10 feet (1.5 to 3 meters) thick at the base. One of the most valuable of the North American hardwoods, it grows from New England southward to Florida and westward to Arkansas. It is the state tree of Indiana, Kentucky, and Tennessee.

The showy yellow blossoms of the tulip tree resemble tulips, and are an important source of nectar for bees. Its leaves are smooth, notched, long-stemmed, and graceful. The *sapwood* (outer wood) is whitish. The *heartwood* (inner wood) is sunshine-yellow to pale-tan. The wood is easily worked, and is used chiefly for furniture, veneer, boxes, and baskets.

Scientific Classification. The tulip tree belongs to the magnolia family, *Magnoliaceae*. This tree is genus *Liriodendron*, species *L. tulipifera*.   T. EWALD MAKI

See also TREE (Familiar Broadleaf and Needleleaf Trees [picture]).

J. Horace McFarland

Tulip Tree Flowers

TULL, JETHRO (1674-1741), an English gentleman farmer, introduced many new farming methods. In his day, farmers sowed the seed by throwing it by hand. Tull regarded this practice as both wasteful and uncertain. So he invented a drill for boring straight rows of holes into which he dropped the seed. He also claimed that farmers could keep their soil fertile by frequent hoeing. His ideas were adopted slowly. He was born in Berkshire, and was educated at St. John's College, Oxford University. Tull traveled in France and Italy to observe farming methods. He wrote *Horse-hoeing Husbandry*, published in 1731.   C. B. BAKER

See also AGRICULTURE (The Invention of New Farm Equipment).

TULLIUS. See SERVIUS TULLIUS.

TULSA, Okla. (pop. 360,919; met. area pop. 689,628), is a major center of the United States petroleum industry. Among the cities of Oklahoma, only Oklahoma City has more people. Tulsa lies on the Arkansas River, about 105 miles (169 kilometers) northeast of Oklahoma City. For location, see OKLAHOMA (political map). Tulsa serves as Oklahoma's main port and is also the state's chief manufacturing center.

During the 1830's, Creek Indians from Tallassee, Ala., settled in what is now the Tulsa area. The Creek named their new village after their former community, but this name in time became shortened to Tulsa. Construction of the first railroad to Tulsa in 1882 brought white settlers to the area. But until 1901, Tulsa remained a small village. That year, the discovery of oil in nearby Red Fork attracted many people to the area. Since then, the petroleum industry has helped make Tulsa one of the fastest-growing U.S. cities.

The City. Tulsa, the county seat of Tulsa County, covers about 180 square miles (466 square kilometers), including 4 square miles (10 square kilometers) of inland water. The Arkansas River divides the city into two parts, the larger of which lies east of the river. Tulsa's metropolitan area covers six entire counties—Creek, Mayes, Osage, Rogers, Tulsa, and Wagoner.

A group of government buildings called the Civic Center forms the heart of downtown Tulsa. These buildings cover eight square blocks and include the city hall, the county courthouse, the main public library, and police headquarters. The Assembly Center, which has exhibit halls and an arena that seats 10,000 persons, also stands in this area. A federal office building is nearby.

More than 98 per cent of Tulsa's people were born in the United States. They are descendants of people of many nationalities. Blacks make up about 8 per cent of the population, and Tulsa has smaller groups of American Indians and Mexican Americans. Baptists form the largest religious group in Tulsa, followed by Methodists and members of the Assembly of God and the Church of Christ.

Economy. Tulsa has almost 1,000 manufacturing plants. The chief industries manufacture fabricated metal products and nonelectric machinery. The city leads the world in the manufacture of industrial heaters and *winches* (hoisting devices). Other Tulsa products include transportation equipment; metals; and clay, glass, and stone products. The city's largest employers include a commercial airline maintenance center and two of the nation's biggest aerospace companies.

Oklahoma's largest oil refinery stands just outside the Tulsa business district. But the city has become more important as an administrative center of the U.S. petroleum industry than as an oil producer. Tulsa serves as a major control center of the industry, including distributors, manufacturers, producers, and research activities.

About 860 oil or oil-related companies maintain offices in the Tulsa area. More than 350 of these firms have headquarters in the city. Tulsa has large data-processing offices, including the credit card centers of several major oil companies. The city also is the national headquarters of the United States Jaycees.

Tulsa became a major port in 1970, after the Mc-Clellan-Kerr Arkansas River Navigation System was extended to Catoosa, 3 miles (5 kilometers) east of the city. This system links Tulsa's port, located near Catoosa on the Verdigris River, to the Mississippi River, the Gulf of Mexico, and the Atlantic Ocean. An industrial area is located near the port. Many airlines use Tulsa International Airport. Freight trains also serve the city.

Education and Cultural Life. Tulsa's public school system includes about 95 elementary schools and 10 high schools, with a total of about 71,000 students. The city also has about 12 parochial and private schools, with about 3,700 students. Colleges in Tulsa include American Christian College, Oral Roberts University, and the University of Tulsa.

The Thomas Gilcrease Institute of American History and Art owns more than 5,000 works of art. This museum features one of the world's finest collections of Indian art and historical documents. It also exhibits the world's largest collections of works by the American painters Thomas Moran, Frederic Remington, and Charles M. Russell. The Philbrook Art Center displays collections of Italian Renaissance paintings and sculpture, Chinese jewelry, and American Indian baskets and pottery.

Two daily newspapers, the *Daily World* and the *Tribune*, serve the city. Tulsa has 3 television stations and 14 radio stations. Its public library has 18 branches in Tulsa County. The Tulsa Civic Ballet, the Tulsa Opera Company, and the Tulsa Philharmonic Orchestra perform at the 2,800-seat Tulsa Performing Arts Center.

Tulsa has about 90 public parks, which cover more than 4,000 acres (1,600 hectares). Mohawk Park, the largest park, occupies 2,817 acres (1,140 hectares). It includes a golf course and a zoo with over 600 animals. The Tulsa Municipal Rose Garden, in Woodward Park, features about 12,000 rose plants. The annual Tulsa State Fair begins in late September at the Tulsa State Fairgrounds. The fairgrounds includes the world's largest livestock display barn and show ring and the Tulsa Exposition Center. The center has the largest continuous area—10½ acres (4.2 hectares)—of any exhibition hall in the world.

Government. Tulsa has a commission form of government. The voters elect a mayor and four commissioners to two-year terms. Each commissioner supervises a department of the city government. Tulsa gets most of its income from a sales tax.

History. Several Indian tribes once hunted in the area that is now Tulsa. During the 1830's, Creek Indians from Tallassee, Ala., settled in the Tulsa area. According to tradition, a Creek named Archie Yahola presided at tribal councils under a huge tree called the Council Oak in 1836. This tree still stands on Cheyenne Avenue in Tulsa.

In 1848, Lewis Perryman, a Creek, opened a village trading post on the Arkansas River. A post office called Tulsa was established at the ranch of his son, George Perryman, in 1879. The village had fewer than 1,000 people in 1882, when the Atlantic and Pacific Railroad—now the St. Louis-San Francisco (Frisco) Railway—was extended from Vinita to the Arkansas River near the present site of downtown Tulsa. Tulsa, or Tulsey Town, as it was sometimes called, became a cattle-shipping terminal. Tulsa was incorporated as a town in

Tulsa's Civic Center includes, *left to right,* the Assembly Center, City Hall, and the Tulsa City-County Library. Tulsa, the second largest city in Oklahoma, is a major administrative center of the nation's petroleum industry.

1898. In 1900, the town had a population of 1,390.

The town grew slowly until 1901, when the discovery of oil at nearby Red Fork attracted large numbers of people to the area. Tulsa became an oil center in 1905, when the large Glenn Pool oil field was opened 15 miles (24 kilometers) southwest. When Oklahoma gained statehood in 1907, Tulsa had a population of 7,298. Tulsa received a city charter in 1908. The oil boom increased the city's population to 72,075 by 1920 and to 141,258 by 1930, and Tulsa became known as the *Oil Capital of the World.*

The number of Tulsans increased to only 142,157 by 1940. But during World War II (1939-1945), workers flocked to Tulsa from rural areas to take factory jobs. The government built a huge bomber airplane factory in the city. By 1945, this plant employed almost 22,000 persons and had become the largest factory in Oklahoma. The increased defense activities helped raise Tulsa's population to 182,740 by 1950. Today, the McDonnell Douglas Corporation and Rockwell International use the plant to manufacture commercial and military aircraft.

During the 1960's, Tulsa completed its Civic Center. In 1970, the completion of the McClellan-Kerr Arkansas River Navigation System made Tulsa a major port. The navigation project, which included construction of many dams and locks, cost $1,200,000,000.

Tulsa's 41-story First National Bank & Trust Company Building was completed in 1973. In 1977, the 50-story Bank of Oklahoma Tower replaced it as Oklahoma's tallest structure. The Bank of Oklahoma Tower forms part of the Williams Center, a project covering nine square blocks in downtown Tulsa. The project includes the $14-million·Tulsa Performing Arts Center, which was completed in 1977. JOHN A. DRUMMOND

For the monthly weather in Tulsa, see OKLAHOMA (Climate). See also OKLAHOMA (pictures).

TULSA, UNIVERSITY OF, is a private coeducational school in Tulsa, Okla. The university has colleges of arts and sciences, business administration, education, engineering and physical sciences, and law. It also has a graduate school and a school of nursing. The University of Tulsa grants bachelor's, master's, and doctor's degrees.

The University of Tulsa was founded in 1894 in Muskogee, Indian Territory. The school, originally known as Henry Kendall College, moved to Tulsa in 1907. It took its present name in 1920. For the enrollment of the University of Tulsa, see UNIVERSITIES AND COLLEGES (table). J. PASCHAL TWYMAN

TUMACACORI NATIONAL MONUMENT is a site at Pima, in southern Arizona. The site has a Catholic mission building commemorating the introduction of Christianity to the region. Father Kino, a Jesuit missionary, visited the area in 1691. The site became a national monument in 1908. For area, see NATIONAL PARK SYSTEM (table: National Monuments).

TUMBLEBUG is the name of a beetle that eats decayed material. People call this type of insect a *scavenger.* The tumblebug, also called *dung beetle,* rolls together a large ball of dung and lays its egg in it. It buries this ball in the ground. The egg develops into a larva which eats the decayed material. The tumblebug gets its name from the fact that it often tumbles as it rolls these large balls of dung. See also SCARAB.

Scientific Classification. Tumblebugs belong to the family *Scarabaeidae.* They may belong to the genera *Canthon, Copris,* or *Phanaeus.* R. E. BLACKWELDER

TUMBLEWEED is the popular name for several plants that grow in the prairie and plains regions of the United

Western Ways

Balls of Tumbleweed bounce along the prairies in the western United States and often pile up against barbed-wire fences.

States. These plants develop rounded tops, and in autumn they wither and break off at the ground level. The dried plants are then carried or tumbled about by the wind, like great, light balls. As they move, they scatter their seeds about over the plains. These plants are considered great pests by farmers and ranchers. Tumbleweeds often pile up against barbed-wire fences or fill small gullies. The common tumbleweeds include the so-called *Russian thistle* and an amaranth. All tumbleweeds are *annuals* (grow from seed to maturity each year).

Scientific Classification. The Russian thistle belongs to the goosefoot family, *Chenopodiaceae.* It is genus *Salsola,* species *S. kali.* The amaranth is of the amaranth family, *Amaranthaceae.* It is *Amaranthus albus.* ARTHUR CRONQUIST

TUMBLING. See ACROBATICS.

TUMBOA. See WELWITSCHIA.

TUMOR, *TOOM er,* is a swelling or abnormal growth of tissues in the body. Tumors are also called *neoplasms.* Some tumors are *benign.* They limit themselves to a certain region and do not spread elsewhere in the body. Once benign tumors are removed, they usually do not grow again. *Malignant tumors* (cancers) that are not completely removed can spread throughout the body, often destroying other tissues in the body (see CANCER [How Cancer Develops]). When cancer arises from the skin, glands, or tissues that line the body cavities, it is called *carcinoma.* Cancer that affects bones and cartilages is called *sarcoma. Leukemia* is cancer of the blood. Only doctors can determine whether a tumor is benign or malignant.

Tumors may grow from any kind of tissue in the body. They may develop in the skin, in muscles, nerves, blood vessels, bones, or any organ. A well-known tumor is the mastoid tumor, which grows over the mastoid process just behind the ear (see MASTOID).

Tumors are often named after the tissue from which they grow. For example, a *lipoma* is made up of *lipid* (fat) tissue. *Gliomas* (nerve-tissue tumors) are made up of *glia,* the peculiar branched cells that support the nerves. *Hematoma* (blood tumor) is one of the best-known tumors. It sometimes occurs as a "black and blue" swelling in the skin.   E. Clinton Texter, Jr.

See also Biopsy; Cancer; Epithelioma; Leukemia; Malignancy; Mole.

TUMPLINE. See Indian, American (Transportation).

TUNA, a fruit. See Prickly Pear.

TUNA, or Tunny, is any of 13 kinds of saltwater fish in the mackerel family. Tuna meat is a popular food in many countries and is sold canned, fresh, and frozen. The tuna is also a leading game fish. The most important commercial types of tuna are the *albacore*, the *skipjack*, and the *yellowfin*.

The largest tuna is the northern bluefin, which measures as long as 10 feet (3 meters) and weighs up to 2,000 pounds (910 kilograms). The smallest tuna is the *frigate*, which grows up to 24 inches (60 centimeters) long and weighs only 10 pounds (4.4 kilograms).

Tuna can swim as fast as 45 miles (72 kilometers) per hour and rank among the swiftest fish. Like most species of fish, the tuna has gills that take oxygen from the water passing over them. But unlike most fish, the tuna cannot pump water over its gills. Therefore, it must swim continuously in order to breathe.

Tuna live in temperate and tropical waters. In summer, they range as far north as Newfoundland and Norway in the Atlantic Ocean, and British Columbia and Northern Japan in the Pacific Ocean. Major tuna fisheries operate off the coast of Japan, the coast of West Africa near the equator, and the west coasts of California and Latin America.

Tuna are caught in three main ways. In *baitfishing*,

Leading Tuna-Fishing Countries

Tons of tuna caught in 1977

Japan	●●●●●●●●●●●●●● 672,000 short tons (610,000 metric tons)
United States	●●●● 245,800 short tons (223,000 metric tons)*
Philippines	●●●◖ 167,600 short tons (152,000 metric tons)
South Korea	●●●◖ 162,000 short tons (147,000 metric tons)
Taiwan	●●● 131,200 short tons (119,000 metric tons)
Spain	●●◖ 108,600 short tons (98,500 metric tons)
France	●● 84,220 short tons (76,400 metric tons)
Indonesia	◖ 36,270 short tons (32,900 metric tons)
Ghana	◖ 31,310 short tons (28,400 metric tons)
Ecuador	◖ 30,900 short tons (28,000 metric tons)

*Includes 61,839 short tons (56,099 metric tons) caught by Puerto Rico. Sources: *Fisheries Yearbook, 1977*, Taiwan; *Yearbook of Fishery Statistics, 1977*, FAO.

crews throw live bait overboard to attract the tuna and then catch them by hook and line. In *longlining*, tuna are caught with a line that measures 75 miles (121 kilometers) long and has as many as 2,000 baited hooks attached. *Purse seining*, a chief method of catching yellowfin tuna, traps fish in large nets called *purse seines*. In the eastern Pacific, fishing crews locate yellowfin tuna by seeking schools of porpoises, which often swim above the fish. Some porpoises are trapped with the tuna and accidentally killed. The United States government limits the killing of porpoises by American boats and requires that nets have escape chutes for porpoises.

Scientific Classification. Tuna belong to the mackerel family, Scombridae. The albacore is *Thunnus alalunga*, the yellowfin is *T. albacares*, and the skipjack is *Katsuwonus pelamis*.   James Joseph

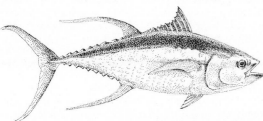

WORLD BOOK illustration by Marion Pahl

Tuna are one of the most important food fish. The yellowfin tuna, *above*, provides light meat for canning. Much of the tuna catch is landed by means of hooks and lines, *below*.

National Oceanic and Atmospheric Administration

See also Fish (picture: Fish of Coastal Waters and the Open Ocean [Bluefin Tuna]); Fishing Industry (Where Fish Are Caught).

TUNDRA is a cold, dry region where trees cannot grow. Most tundras are covered by snow more than half the year. The long, extremely cold winters and short, cool summers prevent the growth of trees in a tundra. But mosses, lichens, grasses, and grasslike plants called *sedges* grow in a tundra, and many kinds of animals live there. There are two kinds of tundras, *Arctic* and *Alpine*.

Arctic tundras lie near the Arctic Ocean. They include Greenland and the northern parts of Alaska, Canada, Europe, and Russia. Most are lowlands with many lakes, but some have mountains. Few people live in Arctic tundras, but some Eskimos live in areas where they can fish and hunt for food (see Eskimo).

Each spring, tundras come to life. Geese, terns, and

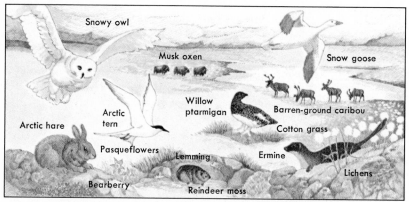

Many Plants and Animals live in the Arctic tundra. Lichens, mosses, and bright flowers cover the ground in summer. Each fall, Arctic hares, ermines, willow ptarmigans, and other tundra animals grow white winter coats. These white coats blend with the snow and help protect the animals from their enemies.

WORLD BOOK illustration by Jean Helmer

other birds fly north to nest. The tundra plants grow rapidly and cover the ground with bright flowers. Caribou, reindeer, and musk oxen graze on these plants, and wolves prey on the grazing animals. Other tundra wildlife includes Arctic foxes and hares, grizzly bears, lemmings, polar bears, and ptarmigans. Seals and walruses live along the coastlines. Arctic char and a few other kinds of fishes live in the lakes and rivers. Mosquitoes, black flies, and other insects thrive.

Summer temperatures in an Arctic tundra range from

Florida State News Bureau

The Tung Tree, above, develops lovely white blossoms in the spring. The tree has large, heart-shaped leaves, and olive-green fruits, below, that drop to the ground in autumn.

Field Museum of Natural History

about 37° to 54° F. (3° to 12° C). The soil remains permanently frozen from 1 to 5 feet (30 to 150 centimeters) below the surface of the ground. This soil, called *permafrost*, prevents water from draining away. As a result, most of the soil stays cold and wet throughout the summer.

Most of the precipitation in Arctic tundras comes from snow, which covers the ground from September to April or May. In the fall, caribou, reindeer, and most Arctic birds migrate south to winter feeding grounds. The other Arctic animals remain active in the tundra throughout the winter.

Arctic tundras have large deposits of coal, natural gas, oil, iron ore, lead, and zinc. The coal, oil, and natural gas can help meet the world's demands for fuel. Special pipelines were designed to transport the oil and gas with the least possible damage to the environment of the tundras.

Alpine tundras are on mountains throughout the world at altitudes where trees cannot grow. Permafrost rarely occurs in Alpine tundras, and most of these regions have well-drained soils. Deer, elk, and various species of mountain goats and sheep graze on Alpine tundras during the summer. Pikas, ptarmigans, woodchucks, and many kinds of insects also live in Alpine tundras. LAWRENCE C. BLISS

See also ARCTIC; BIOME (map); PERMAFROST.

TUNDRA WOLF. See ARCTIC WOLF.

TUNG OIL is an oil that comes from the seed kernels of the tung tree. The tung tree originally grew in the Far East, chiefly in China. Tung oil is also called *China-wood oil, Japanese-wood oil,* or simply *wood oil.* The tree has also been successfully grown in the southern United States. Tung oil is one of the most powerful drying agents. The oil resists acids, alkalis, and alcohols.

Tung oil is widely used in paints, lacquers, varnishes, and printing inks. Paints containing tung oil help seal the underwater surfaces of swimming pools, dams, piers, and boats. Varnishes made with it help insulate wire and metallic surfaces. Tung oil helps some printing inks stick to metal surfaces such as bottle caps. Because of its relatively high cost, tung oil is sometimes replaced with epoxy resins and other synthetics.

Scientific Classification. The tung tree belongs to the spurge family, *Euphorbiaceae.* It is genus *Aleurites,* species *A. fordii.* JOHN R. KOCH

TUNGSTEN, or WOLFRAM, is a hard, silver-white metal, and one of the chemical elements. Tungsten has many uses. It has the highest melting point of all metals, and remains strong at very high temperatures. For these reasons, it is used in equipment that must withstand high temperatures. Tungsten is added to steel to make steel harder, stronger, and more elastic. Tungsten steel tools last longer than ordinary steel tools. Tungsten and carbon form tungsten carbide, an extremely hard substance used in the tips of high-speed cutting tools, and in mining and petroleum drills. *Carboloy* is the General Electric Company's trade name for a form of tungsten carbide.

Tungsten is widely used in the electronics industry. It is made into heating filaments for vacuum tubes used in radios, television sets, and other electronic equipment. It is also used to make filaments for electric lights and contact points for the ignition systems of automobiles. Compounds of tungsten with either calcium or magnesium are *phosphors* (chemicals that give off light). They are used in fluorescent lamps.

Tungsten occurs in nature in the minerals scheelite (calcium tungstate, $CaWO_4$) and wolframite (ferrous-manganous tungstate, [Fe,Mn] WO_4). China and Russia are the leading tungsten-mining countries. In the United States, California and Colorado lead in mining tungsten. Tungsten is prepared from the minerals by first adding sodium hydroxide to convert the insoluble tungsten compounds into a solution of sodium tungstate (Na_2WO_4). Acid is then added to make tungstic trioxide (WO_3) come out of the solution. Tungstic trioxide is heated with hydrogen to form the pure metal.

Tungsten has the chemical symbol W. Its atomic number is 74 and its atomic weight is 183.85. Tungsten melts at $3410°$ C ($\pm 20°$ C) and boils at $5927°$ C. It was discovered in 1783 by two Spanish chemists, Fausto de Elhuyar and his brother Juan José.   ALAN DAVISON

See also ALLOY (Alloys of Iron); ELEMENT, CHEMICAL (tables); WOLFRAMITE; ELECTRIC LIGHT (The Filament).

The Types of Tunics include the Greek, called a *chiton, left,* the Etruscan, *upper right,* and the Phrygian, *lower right.*

Leading Tungsten-Mining Countries

Tons of tungsten mined in 1976

China	9,900 short tons (8,980 metric tons)
Russia	8,800 short tons (7,980 metric tons)
Bolivia	3,400 short tons (3,080 metric tons)
United States	2,900 short tons (2,630 metric tons)
South Korea	2,800 short tons (2,540 metric tons)
Australia	2,700 short tons (2,450 metric tons)
North Korea	2,400 short tons (2,180 metric tons)
Thailand	2,100 short tons (1,910 metric tons)
Canada	1,800 short tons (1,630 metric tons)
Portugal	1,400 short tons (1,270 metric tons)

Source: U.S. Bureau of Mines.

TUNGUSKA METEORITE. See METEOR (Meteorites).

TUNIC, *TOO nihk,* is a loose, short garment, reaching from the neck to some distance above the knee. It is usually fastened at the waist by a belt or girdle. The name comes from the Latin *tunica,* a garment worn by both men and women of ancient Rome. The men covered it with the *toga,* and the women with the *stola.* Greek men and women wore a similar garment called the *chiton.*

Tunic, or *tunicle,* also means a robe worn by a subdeacon of the Roman Catholic and some Episcopal churches during Mass.   MARY EVANS

See also CLOTHING (Ancient Times); TOGA.

TUNICLE. See TUNIC.

TUNING. See RADIO (The Tuner; pictures: Building a Radio Transmitter); TELEVISION (Tuner).

TUNING FORK. A tuning fork is a simple tone-producing, U-shaped metal object. It has a handle on the curved bottom part of the U. A tuning fork is used for tuning musical instruments and for finding the standard pitch.

The tone a tuning fork produces when struck remains always the same and is not subject to changes resulting from moisture and other conditions which often affect the pitch and tone of musical instruments. The forks are made for any note of the scale, but those most often used are for A, B flat, or the C above middle C.

John Shore, George Frideric Handel's trumpeter, invented the tuning fork.   CHARLES B. RIGHTER

TUNIS, *TOO nihs* (pop. 1,000,000), is the capital and largest city of Tunisia. The city lies near the northeastern coast of the country, and is connected with the Mediterranean Sea by a narrow channel. For the location of Tunis, see TUNISIA (map). The ruins of the ancient city of Carthage lie on the edge of Tunis.

The city is the chief commercial, industrial, and transport center of Tunisia. During World War II, Axis forces occupied Tunis from late 1942 until Allied troops captured the city in May, 1943.   LEON CARL BROWN

Tunisia

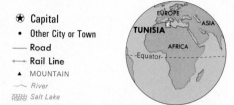

★ Capital
● Other City or Town
──── Road
┼──┼ Rail Line
▲ MOUNTAIN
～～ River
▨▨ Salt Lake

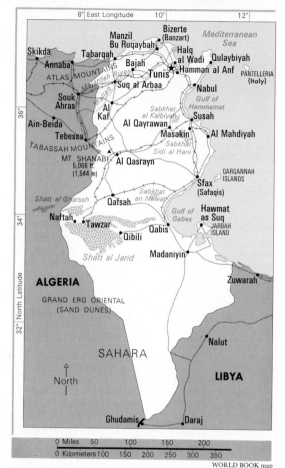

WORLD BOOK map

TUNISIA extends farther north than any other country in Africa. Its northern tip is only 85 miles (137 kilometers) from Sicily, a part of Europe. Both northern and eastern Tunisia border the Mediterranean Sea.

Tunisia is part of the Arab world, the Mediterranean area, and Africa. Almost all Tunisians speak Arabic and follow an Arab way of life. For hundreds of years, trade routes have connected Tunisia to Africa south of the Sahara. France controlled Tunisia from 1881 to

Leon Carl Brown, the contributor of this article, is Professor of Near Eastern History and Civilization at Princeton University, and the coauthor of Tunisia: The Politics of Modernization.

Facts in Brief

Capital: Tunis.

Official Language: Arabic.

Form of Government: Republic. *Head of State*—President.

Area: 63,170 sq. mi. (163,610 km²). *Greatest Distances*—north-south, 485 mi. (781 km); east-west, 235 mi. (378 km). *Coastline*—639 mi. (1,028 km).

Population: *Estimated 1983 Population*—7,083,000; distribution, 52 per cent urban, 48 per cent rural; density, 111 persons per sq. mi. (46 persons per km²). *1975 Census*—5,572,193. *Estimated 1988 Population*—8,092,000.

Chief Products: *Agriculture*—barley, citrus fruit, olives, wheat, wine. *Mining*—iron, lead, lignite, phosphates, zinc. *Forestry*—oak, pine.

Flag: The flag has a large white circle on a red field. A red crescent and star are inside the circle. The red color and the crescent and star design come from the flags of the Ottoman Turks. The crescent and star are emblems of the Muslim religion. See FLAG (color picture: Flags of Africa).

Money: *Basic Unit*—dinar. See MONEY (table).

1956, and the country shows many French influences.

Tunis, a city of about 1 million people, is the capital and the largest city. Tunisia's name in Arabic is AL-JUMHURIYAH AL-TUNUSIYAH (REPUBLIC OF TUNISIA).

Government. Tunisia is a republic headed by a president. Habib Bourguiba, Tunisia's first and only president, has extensive authority. He runs both the government and the Socialist Destour (formerly Neo-Destour) party, the only effective political party in Tunisia. The party carries out the president's policies at all levels of government.

The people elect the president for a five-year term, but the president cannot be re-elected more than three times in a row. The president appoints a Cabinet to assist him. Tunisia has a one-house legislature called the National Assembly. The people elect the 90 members of the National Assembly to five-year terms. All persons who have been citizens for five years and who are 20 or older may vote. The president appoints a governor to head each of Tunisia's 13 provinces.

People. Life in Tunisia is more uniform than it is in most other African and Middle Eastern countries. This uniformity is chiefly due to the people's similarity in language and religion, and to the fact that political and cultural life is centered in one city, Tunis.

Small groups of Europeans, Jews, and Berbers live in Tunisia. But almost all Tunisians are Arabs and Muslims. French culture has influenced several features of Tunisian life, including architecture and food. Many Tunisians speak French as a second language.

About half the people live on farms and in small towns. Rural dwellings include stone houses, mud huts, and tents. Many towns have brick houses with inner courtyards. People in rural areas wear traditional Arab clothing—a turban or skullcap, and a long, loose gown, or a long coatlike garment with long sleeves.

About half the people live in larger towns and cities. Most cities are divided into old and new sections. Narrow streets and covered markets characterize the old sections. Tree-lined avenues and European-style buildings are typical of the new sections. Many people in the cities wear European-style clothes.

400

The government spends more than one-fifth of its budget on education. About 70 per cent of the school-age children attend primary schools. About 20 per cent attend secondary schools. The University of Tunis, the country's only university, was founded in 1960.

Land. The uniformity of Tunisian life is also partly due to the country's geography. Two branches of the Atlas mountain range, which crosses northwestern Africa, extend into Tunisia. In Tunisia, the northern branch is called the Atlas Mountains, and the southern branch, the Tabassah Mountains. But the mountains are low. Few peaks reach more than 2,000 feet (610 meters), and the highest, Mount Shanabi, is just 5,066 feet (1,544 meters) above sea level. Unlike neighboring Algeria and Morocco, Tunisia has no hard-to-reach mountain regions which would cut the people off from the influences of the cities and plains.

Hills and grassland lie between the mountain ranges. Much of Tunisia's wheat is grown in the Majardah River valley in the north. The Majardah is the only river in Tunisia that does not dry up in summer.

From the Tabassah range, the land descends across a plateau to the Sahara in the south and to a coastal plain in the east. The plateau is covered with coarse grass. The people on the plateau raise cattle, sheep, and goats. The southern desert contains great salt lakes and date palm oases.

The fertile coastal plain extends along the east coast from Sfax to Tunis. Cereals, citrus fruits, and olives are grown there. This region also has Tunisia's largest towns and cities.

Tunisia has hot, dry summers and warm, wet winters. The average temperatures are 79° F. (26° C) in summer and 52° F. (11° C) in winter. In the north, most rain falls in winter, but it is irregular and droughts occur every three or four years. There is little rain in the south.

Economy. Tunisia is an agricultural country and about 70 per cent of the working people farm or raise livestock. Wheat, barley, grapes for wine, olives, olive oil, and dates are the chief farm products.

Tunisia is a leading producer of phosphates. The country also mines good quality iron ore. Tunisia's manufacturing is confined mainly to food processing.

Tunisia is not rich in natural resources. Due to poor soil and irregular rainfall, crop yields are far lower than in Europe and the United States. Mineral resources—except for phosphates—are small. Unlike many other Arab countries, Tunisia has not discovered large quantities of oil. But Tunisia has a more balanced economy than many of its neighbors. There is neither a large wealthy class nor a large poor class, and land ownership is not concentrated in the hands of a small minority. The north and east—with their industries and more fertile land—are richer than the dry, less developed south.

The French left Tunisia with an excellent transportation system. There are about 4,500 miles (7,200 kilometers) of paved roads and more than 1,200 miles (1,900 kilometers) of railroads. The chief ports are Tunis, La Goulette, and Sfax.

History. Men and ideas have entered northwest Africa through Tunisia for centuries. The Phoenicians began the Carthaginian Empire in Tunisia about 1100 B.C. According to tradition, the famous city of Carthage was founded near present-day Tunis about 814 B.C. The Romans defeated Carthage in 146 B.C., and ruled Tunisia for the next 600 years. In A.D. 439, European tribesmen called Vandals invaded Tunisia, defeated the Romans, and captured Carthage. They ruled the region for almost 100 years. The Byzantines, from Constantinople (now Istanbul), ousted the Vandals in 534. The Byzantines had loose control over Tunisia when

Marge Kathan

Tunis, the capital and largest city of Tunisia, has many wide boulevards and both old and new buildings. Some people of Tunis wear Western-style clothing, but others prefer Arab dress.

TUNKHANNOCK VIADUCT

Marge Kathan

Tunisian Traders often meet to buy and sell animals. In the above scene at Qibili, in central Tunisia, the men in the foreground are bargaining over the sale of a camel.

Arabs from the Middle East invaded in the mid-600's. The Arab invasion was a turning point in Tunisia's history. Tunisia began to slowly become a part of Arab-Moslem civilization. But in the centuries that followed, it was inclined to cut close political ties with the eastern Arab world. The Ottoman Empire, which was centered in Turkey, won control of Tunisia in 1574. The Ottoman rulers appointed a *bey* (ruler) to govern Tunisia from Tunis. Tunisia was technically part of the Ottoman Empire until 1881, but by the 1800's the beys in Tunis had achieved a large measure of independence.

In 1881, France imposed a protectorate over Tunisia. It controlled Tunisia's financial, foreign, and military affairs, but left the bey some authority in local matters.

A Tunisian independence movement began after World War I, but the most successful movement did not begin until 1934. Habib Bourguiba founded the Neo-Destour (New Constitution) party that year. He led the independence struggle for more than 20 years. France finally granted Tunisia internal self-government in 1955, and full independence in 1956. France kept troops and military bases in Tunisia after independence. In the late 1950's and early 1960's, France, at Tunisia's demand, withdrew its troops and gave up its Tunisian bases.

Tunisia became a republic in 1957, and the people elected Bourguiba president. Bourguiba was re-elected in 1959, 1964, and 1969. His government introduced many social and economic reforms. It gave voting rights to women and set up a national school system.

In late 1969, heavy floods in Tunisia killed about 500 persons. The floods upset important industries and damaged Tunisia's economy.　　　LEON CARL BROWN

Related Articles in WORLD BOOK include:

Arab League	Carthage	Olive
Bourguiba, Habib	Dinar	Tunis

TUNKHANNOCK VIADUCT. See VIADUCT.

402

TUNNEL is an underground passageway. Tunnels are bored through hills and mountains and under rivers, and have helped overcome some of the great natural barriers to land transportation. The building of great tunnels played a major part in the development of the transcontinental railroad systems in the United States during the 1800's.

How Tunnels Are Built

Engineers class tunnels according to the conditions under which they are built. Some tunnels are driven through the hard rock of mountains. Others are dug through soft earth and loose gravel.

Rock Tunnels. Rock offers the greatest resistance to tunneling. But rock has one advantage. It needs no supports for the top and sides of the tunnel. Small pockets are drilled into the rock and filled with charges of high explosives. After the charges are exploded, the pieces of rock are carted out. Five of the world's greatest tunnels, Frejus, Mont Cenis, St. Gotthard Road, St. Gotthard Railroad, and Simplon, all in the Alps, were blasted out of solid rock.

Sometimes, engineers come across a pocket of shattered rock, or a *fault zone*. When this happens, they must construct a special lining. Some very deep mountain tunnels through solid granite often require repair because stress around the granite reduces the size of the hole.

Earth Tunnels. Engineers must take great care in digging tunnels through soft earth, clay, or silt, or under the mud of a river bed, because of the danger of cave-ins. The roof of such a tunnel is held up with a *sheath*, or shell, of timbers or steel until a permanent lining can

be built. Modern tunnels usually have concrete linings.

Digging machines called *moles* have been developed to speed construction. The face of the mole is a revolving disk that cuts into the earth. A conveyor belt carries excavated material to waiting *muck cars*.

In the building of underwater tunnels, the greatest trouble comes from the water that flows in. This becomes a serious problem when the tunnel lies beneath the bed of a stream. Engineers solve the problem by using the compressed-air or the shield system. The two systems are used together where the tunnel is being bored through fairly soft material under rivers.

In the *compressed-air method*, the pressure of incoming water is held back by compressing the air in the end of the tunnel where the work is going on. Since the air pressure inside the tunnel exceeds the water pressure outside, the water is kept out.

The *shield system* takes its name from a steel shield used in the operation. The tunnel shield is a cylinder of steel plate, shaped to form a sharp edge at the front. Jacks operated by water pressure are attached to the inner surface of the cylinder. When power is applied, piston rods on the jacks press against the lining of the tunnel already finished. At the same time, the cutting edge of the cylinder is pushed into the earth yet to be dug. Near the rear end of the cylinder is a partition with openings, which the operator may close at will. As the cylinder is forced ahead, the earth is withdrawn in small amounts through the openings. If the material is soft, it is possible and sometimes necessary to drive the shield forward with the openings closed. The material is then pushed aside as the shield moves ahead. In the rear end

of the shield, sections of cast-iron lining are placed against the tunnel's sides and bolted together to form a tube. As each ring of tube is added, the shield drives ahead, and the operation is repeated.

In another method of river tunneling, machines sink several steel tunnel sections into a trench that has been excavated across the river bed. Divers connect the sections, and pumps remove the water. This method was used on the subway tunnels under the Harlem River and on the railroad tunnel under the Detroit River.

Types of Tunnels

Tunnels are built to provide a flow of water or to permit the movement of vehicles. Underground *conduits* (tunnels) take water to hydroelectric plants or to municipal waterworks. Underground conduits also remove storm water and sewage. These tunnels measure 10 feet (3 meters) or more in diameter. They must be able to withstand heavy water pressures, and are designed to carry away water run-off from the heaviest rainfalls.

Railroad Tunnels. In building the railroad systems of Europe and America, many great engineering feats were performed. The greatest of these was the boring of long tunnels through the hard rock of the Alps and the Rocky Mountains. Such tunnels reduce traveling time and increase the efficiency of trains. The steeper a locomotive must climb, the less weight the locomotive can pull. The steepest grade for railroads is known as a *ruling grade*. It determines the size of the load that a freight train can pull. Tunnels reduce the ruling grade

A Huge Trench Tunnel built like a double-barreled shotgun runs under the Baltimore harbor. The tunnel's underground portion consists of twin-tube sections, each 300 feet (91 meters) long, joined end to end, *left.* The giant sections were assembled on land, then sunk in the river-bed trench. The 7,650-foot (2,332-meter) tunnel is part of a major throughway, *below.* It carries four lanes of traffic, *right.*

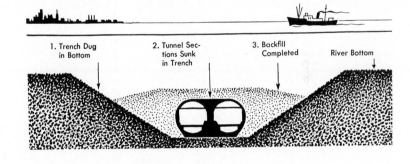

1. Trench Dug in Bottom 2. Tunnel Sections Sunk in Trench 3. Backfill Completed River Bottom

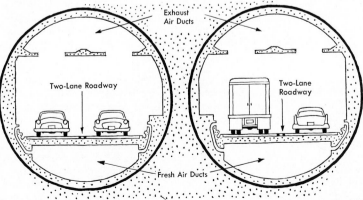

Exhaust Air Ducts

Two-Lane Roadway   Two-Lane Roadway

Fresh Air Ducts

Photographs, *Steelways; Art* work reprinted by permission from *Popular Science Monthly* for October, 1957

and thus allow trains to haul more goods at less cost.

The first important railroad tunnel in North America was cut through the Hoosac Mountains in Massachusetts from 1855 to 1873. The Hoosac Tunnel is 4 miles (6.4 kilometers) long and wide enough for double sets of tracks. The Cascade Tunnel in Washington is 7.8 miles (12.6 kilometers) long. It is the longest U.S. railroad tunnel. The world's longest railroad tunnels are:

Tunnel	Location	Length	
		Miles	Kilometers
Seikan*	Japan	33.5	53.9
Ooshimizu*	Japan	13.8	22.2
Simplon	Italy-Switzerland border	12.3	19.8
Shin Kanmon	Japan	11.6	18.7
Apennine	Italy	11.5	18.5
Rokko	Japan	10.1	16.3
St. Gotthard	Switzerland	9.3	15.0
Lötschberg	Switzerland	9.1	14.6
Hokuriku	Japan	8.6	13.9
Mont Cenis	France-Italy border	8.5	13.7

*Under construction.

New York, London, Berlin, Moscow, Paris, Toronto, and other great cities have underground railroad systems. Although these are subways, part of their construction is properly called tunneling because it was done by boring through the earth. See SUBWAY.

Motor-Traffic Tunnels. The increase in vehicle traffic has brought about the building of many tunnels just for motor traffic. A major problem is to provide enough ventilation to remove exhaust fumes. Traffic engineers must also try to prevent traffic jams in tunnels.

The world's longest automobile tunnel is the 53,-539-foot (16,319-meter) St. Gotthard Road Tunnel in the Alps. It opened in 1980 and runs parallel to the St. Gotthard Tunnel, a railroad tunnel in southern Switzerland. Other automobile tunnels through the Alps include the 42,240-foot (12,875-meter) Frejus Tunnel and the 38,280-foot (11,668-meter) Mont Blanc Tunnel, both of which connect France and Italy.

The Holland tunnels under the Hudson River link New York City and Jersey City. These tunnels, opened in 1927, consist of two tubes 93 feet (28 meters) below the river surface. The north tube is 8,558 feet (2,608 meters) long and the south tube 8,371 feet (2,551 meters). The cast-iron tubes have outside diameters of about 30 feet (9 meters). Each has a two-lane roadway 20 feet (6 meters) wide. The tubes were driven under the river with shields under compressed air, and cost about $48 million. About 20 million vehicles use them each year.

The River Mersey vehicular tunnel, between Liverpool and Birkenhead, England, is the largest circular tube tunnel in the world. The tubes have an outside diameter of 46 feet 3 inches (14.1 meters). The main roadway of the tunnel includes four lanes of traffic and two footwalks. The main section of the River Mersey Tunnel extends for about 2 miles (3 kilometers).

One of the world's longest vehicular tunnels under water is the Brooklyn-Battery Tunnel, opened for traffic in 1950. It links Brooklyn and Manhattan under the New York harbor. It is 9,117 feet (2,779 meters) long. The longest land vehicular tunnel in the U.S. is the 1.7-mile (2.7-kilometer) Eisenhower Memorial Tunnel in Colorado. It is also the world's highest vehicular tun-

nel—11,000 feet (3,400 meters) high. Other famous traffic tunnels are the International Tunnel between Detroit, Mich., and Windsor, Ont., and the Lincoln Tunnel between New York City and Weehawken, N.J.

Tunnels have been proposed for an undersea connection between England and France, under the English Channel. Others have been considered under the entrance to the Mediterranean at Gibraltar and under the Bering Strait between Alaska and Siberia.

Natural forces form many tunnels. Rivers may tunnel out courses underground, and the sea tunnels caves along the coasts. Mammoth Cave in Kentucky was formed by the tunneling of a river.   ROBERT G. HENNES

Related Articles in WORLD BOOK include:

Apennine Tunnel	Queens Midtown Tunnel
Cascade Tunnel	Saint Gotthard Tunnel
Lincoln Tunnel	Simplon Pass and Tunnel
Moffat Tunnel	Subway
Mont Cenis Tunnel	

TUNNEL KILN. See KILN; BRICK (Kilns).

TUNNEY, GENE (1897-1978), defeated Jack Dempsey in 1926 to become world heavyweight boxing champion. He defended the title twice—against Dempsey and Tom Heeney—before he retired in 1928. The second Tunney-Dempsey fight drew a record gate of $2,658,660. See DEMPSEY, JACK.

Tunney was born James Joseph Tunney in New York City. He began boxing in 1915. He won the American light-heavyweight title in 1922 and lost it the same year to Harry Greb, Tunney's only defeat in 76 professional bouts. Tunney's son John served as a United States senator from California from 1971 to 1977.   LYALL SMITH

TUNNY. See TUNA.

TUOLUMNE RIVER. See YOSEMITE NATIONAL PARK (Hetch Hetchy Valley).

TUPAC AMARU. See INDIAN, AMERICAN (After European Contact); PERU (Spanish Conquest and Rule).

TUPELO TREE, *TOO puh loh*, is a large attractive tree that grows about 60 feet (18 meters) high in swamps in the southeastern United States. It has large leaves, and tiny greenish-white flowers from which tupelo honey is made. The fruit of the tree is blue, red, or purple. The tree is also known as the *tupelo gum* tree. Its wood is known as gum. It is widely used for cheap construction. See also BLACK TUPELO; TREE (Familiar Broadleaf and Needleleaf Trees [picture]).

Scientific Classification. Tupelo trees belong to the nyssa family, *Nyssaceae*. The common tupelo is genus *Nyssa*, species *N. aquatica*.   WILLIAM M. HARLOW

TUPÍ-GUARANÍ INDIANS, *too PEE GWAH rah NEE*, formed many different tribes that spoke related languages. These forest Indians lived in eastern South America. Each tribe had a different name, such as Tupinamba or Omagua. Tupí-Guaraní languages served as the basis of the *linguageral* (general language) of Brazil. One of them, Guaraní, is more widely spoken in rural Paraguay than Spanish, the country's official language.

The Tupí-Guaraní were farmers. Manioc, a root crop, provided their main food. They also planted yams, maize, peppers, and cotton. Their villages included from four to six big houses facing a square. Each family had its own partitioned section. Some tribes, especially along the Brazilian coast, were warriors and cannibals. They are now extinct. There are still a few peaceful Tupí-Guaraní tribes in Brazil.   CHARLES WAGLEY

SIR CHARLES TUPPER

Charles Tupper

Prime Minister of Canada
1896

BOWELL
1894-1896

TUPPER
1896

LAURIER
1896-1911

TUPPER, SIR CHARLES (1821-1915), served as prime minister of Canada for about 10 weeks in 1896. He was the oldest person to hold that office. Tupper, whose countrymen called him the Grand Old Man of Canada, was almost 75 when he became prime minister.

Tupper accomplished little as his nation's leader, probably because he held office for such a short time. He worked hard, but with little success, to unite the Conservative Party, which had been badly divided since the death of Prime Minister John A. Macdonald in 1891.

Before Tupper became prime minister, he served in the Nova Scotia legislature and as premier of the province. Tupper helped establish the Dominion of Canada in 1867 and was one of the Fathers of Confederation. He also played an important part in bringing Nova Scotia into the Dominion. Tupper won election to the Canadian House of Commons in 1867. He held several Cabinet positions under Macdonald, who was prime minister from 1867 to 1873 and from 1878 to 1891.

Tupper, a master politician, became known for his ability to gain the cooperation of other public officials. He was a shrewd, unyielding debater and a skilled public speaker. Tupper lacked a sense of humor, but his dignified appearance made his attempts at wit seem funny.

Early Life

Family Background. Charles Tupper was born on July 2, 1821, in Amherst, N.S. He was the oldest of the three sons of Charles Tupper, a Baptist minister, and of Miriam Lockhart Lowe Tupper. Charles attended Horton Academy and Acadia College in Wolfville, N.S. He later studied medicine at the University of Edinburgh in Scotland and earned an M.D. degree in 1843. Tupper then returned to Amherst and entered the prac-

tice of medicine. He helped found the Canadian Medical Association in 1867 and served as its first president.

Tupper's Family. In 1846, Tupper married Frances Amelia Morse, the daughter of the chief clerk of the court in Amherst. The couple had three sons and three daughters. Their second son, Charles H. Tupper, served in the Canadian Parliament from 1882 to 1904 and held Cabinet positions from 1888 to 1896. Tupper's third son, William J. Tupper, served in the Manitoba Legislative Assembly from 1920 to 1922. He also held office as lieutenant governor of Manitoba from 1934 to 1940.

Early Public Career

Entry into Politics. Tupper became well known in Nova Scotia through his successful medical practice. He entered politics in 1855, when he won election to the Nova Scotia legislature as a Conservative representative from Cumberland. He defeated Joseph Howe, the leader of the Liberal Party in Nova Scotia. Howe had been known for his role in persuading Great Britain to grant more control over local affairs to its North American colonies.

The leaders of the Nova Scotia Conservative Party quickly recognized Tupper's political and debating skills. In 1857, he became provincial secretary in the Cabinet of Premier J. W. Johnston of Nova Scotia, a Conservative. The Liberals gained a majority in the legislature and returned to power in 1860, but Tupper won re-election from Cumberland. In addition to serving as a member of the legislature in Halifax, he practiced medicine and served as the city's medical officer. He also was the editor of the *British Colonist*, a Nova Scotia newspaper that supported the Conservative Party. He campaigned to help the Nova Scotia Conservatives defeat the Liberals in 1863, and Johnston became premier again. In 1864, after Johnston left office to become a federal judge, the Conservatives named Tupper leader of the party and premier of Nova Scotia.

Premier. As premier, Tupper worked for government construction of railroads and for a system of nonreligious public schools. Tupper showed great courage when he introduced the School Act of 1864, which established public schools supported by tax funds. This act was unpopular in Nova Scotia.

Tupper also worked to promote a union of the three small maritime colonies—New Brunswick, Nova Scotia, and Prince Edward Island. He believed such a union would strengthen those colonies politically and economically. Talk of Canadian confederation began before Tupper's idea won public acceptance.

Confederation. Tupper represented Nova Scotia at the Charlottetown and Quebec conferences of 1864, which led to Confederation. The Quebec Resolutions, prepared at the Quebec Conference, proposed a union of the colonies of British North America. This union became known as the Dominion of Canada.

Led by Tupper, the Nova Scotia legislature approved the plan for the Canadian confederation. Nova Scotia became an original member of the Dominion when the British Parliament approved the resolutions in 1867. But many Nova Scotians opposed the union. They feared losing the increased independence they had gained in 1848, when Great Britain granted Nova Scotia more control over local affairs. In the 1867 election, the Liberals, led by Howe, opposed Confederation and won control of the Nova Scotia legislature.

Tupper was elected to the Canadian House of Commons in 1867. He was the only Nova Scotian in favor of Confederation whom the province elected to the House of Commons that year.

In 1868, the Nova Scotia legislature voted to repeal the Quebec Resolutions. Howe went to London and presented his anti-Confederation views to the colonial office. Tupper also went to the British capital, arguing that Nova Scotia should not leave the Dominion. The British government refused to let Nova Scotia drop out, and so the province remained in the Dominion.

Tupper persuaded Macdonald, the first prime minister of the Dominion, to offer a Cabinet position to Howe. Tupper then persuaded Howe to accept the post. By helping to bring Howe into the Dominion government, Tupper assisted in ending the anti-Confederation movement in Nova Scotia.

Rise to National Prominence

Federal Offices. After Tupper entered the House of Commons, Macdonald offered him a position in the Cabinet. Tupper refused the offer and advised Macdonald to appoint a Roman Catholic from Nova Scotia instead. Tupper, a Protestant, wanted to ensure the rights of the province's Catholic minority through representation in the national government. Macdonald followed his advice. In 1870, Tupper joined Macdonald's government as president of the Privy Council, a group formed to advise the representative of the British monarch in Canada.

Tupper held various Cabinet positions under Macdonald. He served as minister of inland revenue in 1872, as minister of finance in 1873 and 1874, and as minister of public works in 1878. Queen Victoria of Great Britain knighted Tupper in 1879. From 1879 to 1884, he served as the first minister of railways and canals, one of the most important government positions. Tupper held that office during most of the construction of the Canadian Pacific Railway, Canada's first transcontinental railroad.

Canadian High Commissioner. In 1884, Tupper went to London as Canadian high commissioner to Great Britain. He returned to Canada in 1887 and became minister of finance. In 1888, he returned to London to serve again as high commissioner. In this position, Tupper worked to expand trade between Canada and Great Britain and to increase emigration from Britain to Canada. He also encouraged British investment in Canadian commerce and industry.

Prime Minister

Macdonald died in 1891, three months after the Conservatives won the election that year. Tupper continued to serve as high commissioner in the Conservative governments of Sir John Abbott, Sir John Thompson, and Sir Mackenzie Bowell. Bowell became prime minister after Thompson died in 1894. In 1896, Bowell called Tupper home from London to serve as secretary of state in his Cabinet.

Bowell's poor handling of a government crisis over Manitoba schools led to the resignation of seven members of the Cabinet. Bowell resigned three months later, in April, 1896. The Conservatives called on Tupper to serve as prime minister and lead the party in the June election. Tupper succeeded Bowell as prime minister on April 27, 1896.

Tupper's many years in England had weakened his political strength at home. As prime minister, he faced a divided party and many political problems. The

Nova Scotia Museum, Halifax

Sir Charles Tupper's Home in Halifax, built in 1865, still stands at the corner of Tupper Grove and Armview Avenue.

The Turban of an Iraqi Herdsman

A Bedouin Tribesman's Turban

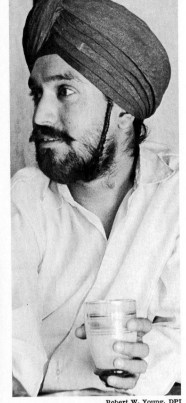

The Turban of a Khyber Pass Guide

A Turban Worn in Pakistan

A Turban of Northwestern India

Manitoba school dispute continued to cause a crisis in the government. This problem had begun when the Manitoba legislature voted in 1890 to abolish the province's French-language Roman Catholic schools. While Tupper was in Bowell's Cabinet, he supported a bill in Parliament to restore the Catholic schools in Manitoba. But the Liberals did not allow a vote on the bill before the election. The Manitoba school dispute became the major issue of the 1896 campaign.

The Liberals won the June election, and Tupper left office on July 8. Wilfrid Laurier, the French-Canadian leader of the Liberal Party, became prime minister. Tupper took over as leader of the Opposition in the House of Commons.

Later Years

Tupper served as Opposition leader until 1900, when he lost the election for his seat in the House. He then retired from public life and moved to Kent, England. Tupper visited Canada a number of times between 1900 and 1908. In 1908, he became a member of the United Kingdom Privy Council, composed of former prime ministers and Cabinet members who advised the British monarch.

Tupper spent much time writing his memoirs, and magazine articles on political issues. He died at his home in Kent on Oct. 30, 1915. Tupper was the last surviving Father of Confederation.   ALAN WILSON

TUPUNGATO, *too poong GAH toh,* is one of the five highest mountains in South America. It towers 22,310 feet (6,800 meters) in the Andes Mountains on the Chile-Argentina boundary. For the location of Tupungato, see CHILE (physical map).

TURACO. See TOURACO.

TURBAN, *TUR bun,* is a headdress. The name comes from the Persian word *dulband,* which means a scarf wound around the head. The first turbans were scarfs which men in the hot countries of the Orient and Middle East wrapped around their heads to provide protection against the sun. Gradually, turbans came to show differences in rank among the men of Oriental countries. A white muslin scarf wound around a small cap on the head was the headdress of the priests of India, and native princes of that country wore showy silk scarfs. At one time, the sultan of Turkey wore a turban that was decorated with three heron feathers and many precious stones. The country's grand vizier wore two heron feathers in his turban, and a turban with one heron feather marked less important officers of Turkey's government. Today, turbans are worn chiefly by the Hindus of India.

TURBINATE BONE, *TUR bih nayt.* There are three *turbinate* bones in the nose. These large, shelflike bones warm the air before it enters the lungs. They may be involved in sinus trouble and the common cold. See also NOSE (with diagram).

TURBINE

General Electric Co.

A Powerful Steam Turbine can generate all the electricity needed by about 1,000,000 people. Rushing steam spins bladed wheels, such as those in this partly-assembled turbine. Turbines were developed from the simple windmill, *upper left,* and water wheel, *lower left.*

TURBINE, *TUR bihn* or *TUR byn*, is a wheel turned by the force of a moving fluid, such as water, steam, or gas. It changes the force of the fluid into energy that can be used for work. Turbines rank among the simplest and most powerful machines. Generators driven by turbines produce electricity to light homes and to run factories. Turbines also drive ocean liners and some airplanes. A water wheel and a windmill are both turbines. So is a pinwheel that spins when you blow on it. The word *turbine* comes from the Latin word *turbo*, meaning that which *spins* or *whirls around*.

A turbine does not create power. It changes the force of moving fluids into *rotary*, or circular, motion. This motion can do useful work. For example, flowing water spins a water wheel below a dam. The water wheel turns a generator that produces electricity, which lights homes and drives machinery. In this way, the energy of the flowing water is put to work. Nuclear power plants also use turbines to produce electricity.

There are three main kinds of turbines: (1) water, (2) steam, and (3) gas. Wind turbines are a fourth kind. But they can be used only in a few regions that have fairly steady winds. Water, steam, and gas turbines generate most of the electric power used today.

How Turbines Work

A paper pinwheel, the simplest kind of turbine, turns when you blow on it. But it does not produce much

———————— TURBINE TERMS ————————

Buckets are the parts of the turbine wheel that the moving fluids push against. They may be shaped like *scoops*, or like *blades* or *vanes* similar to the slats of a Venetian blind or the blades of a propeller.

Casing is the outside shell of a turbine. It holds the flowing fluids against the turbine wheel.

Condenser is a cooling device that changes the exhaust steam from a steam turbine into water.

Exhaust is the part of a turbine where the used fluids come out. The channel for the exhaust water from water turbines is called a *tailrace*.

Nozzles are the parts of the casing that aim moving fluids against rows of buckets. They may look like curved blades or like nozzles of garden hoses.

Rotor is the rotating part of a turbine. It includes the buckets and the shaft on which they are mounted.

Stage is a single wheel of rotor buckets and its fixed ring of nozzles. Most steam and gas turbines have many stages, or sets of bucket wheels and nozzles. A water turbine usually has only one stage.

Throttle is a valve or faucet that controls the flow of fluids into a turbine.

power, because most of the air escapes and does not hit the wheel. You could improve the effectiveness of the pinwheel turbine by enclosing the wheel and your breath so that all the air strikes the wheel. A second pinwheel placed behind the first could use some of the force that remains in the air after it passes the first wheel. Another improvement would be to create a vacuum behind the pinwheels. Then the air would be pulled as well as pushed past the pinwheels, because air and other fluids always rush into a vacuum (see VACUUM).

The efficiency of modern turbines comes from improvements like those described. *Casings* enclose the turbine so that all the flowing fluid strikes the turbine wheel. Steam and gas turbines have many *stages*, or sets of wheels, one behind the other. Each wheel uses part of the energy from the flowing fluids. *Condensers* create a vacuum at the exhaust end of steam turbines. They cool the used steam so that it condenses into water. The water occupies far less space than the steam. This produces a vacuum that sucks steam through the turbine.

Only gasoline and diesel piston engines rival the turbine as power producers. A turbine works more efficiently than a piston engine, because the flowing fluid pushes continuously against the turbine wheel. In a four-cycle piston engine, the exploding fuel pushes against the piston on only one of the piston's four strokes. The turbine is also more efficient than piston engines because of its faster running speed. This makes it possible to deliver more power for its weight and volume. See GASOLINE ENGINE (diagram: How a Four-Stroke Cycle Gasoline Engine Works).

Water Turbines are used to generate electricity at dams and waterfalls. The rim of a water turbine wheel has many metal buckets. Flowing water from a dam or waterfall strikes the buckets. This spins the wheel and the shaft on which it is mounted. The shaft then spins an electric generator that produces electric power.

Water turbines have a big advantage over steam and gas turbines: they do not need fuel to produce steam or burning gases. But they do require a constant flow of water. The water flow may vary with the seasons and the weather. During a drought, it may stop completely.

The power of a water turbine depends on (1) the *volume* (amount) of flowing water, and (2) the *head* (distance that water falls before it strikes the turbine wheel). The head may be only 8 to 10 feet (2.4 to 3 meters) at a dam on a river, or more than 1,000 feet (300 meters) in a mountain region. Lowhead sites usually have water passages built inside the dam to bring water to the turbine. Long pipes called *penstocks* carry water to the turbine at high-head sites. For example, penstocks may

bring water from a mountain lake to a power station in a valley. See DAM.

There are two main kinds of water turbine wheels: (1) impulse and (2) reaction.

Impulse turbine wheels may be mounted on either horizontal or vertical shafts. The *Pelton wheel* is a type of impulse turbine with cup-shaped buckets. From one to as many as six nozzles aim high-speed jets of water against the buckets. The *impulse* (force) of the water striking the buckets turns the wheel. Impulse wheels work best where a small volume of water falls a great distance. See WATER WHEEL.

Reaction turbine wheels are mounted on vertical shafts and are completely under water. They have either spirally curved vanes, called *Francis-type*, or blades like a ship's propeller, called *Kaplan-type*. The *pitch*, or slant, of the blades on Kaplan-type wheels can be changed while the wheel is running. This adjusts the wheel to differing amounts of water flow. The wheels of a reaction turbine are turned by the weight or pressure of the water as well as by its speed of flow. They work best where a large volume of water falls a short distance.

Gates and valves control the flow of water through water turbines. Reaction turbines have movable vanes all around the wheel edge. These vanes look like the shutters of a Venetian blind. They can be opened or closed to adjust the flow of water hitting the wheel. They also act as nozzles to direct the water at the proper angle against the buckets on the rim of the wheel.

Steam Turbines rank among the world's most powerful machines. A million-kilowatt steam turbine turning a generator can supply all the electricity used by about 1 million people. Steam turbines propel huge ships, run various types of pumps, and drive other kinds of machinery. They work like water turbines, but they use high-pressure steam instead of water. The steam enters at one end of the turbine. It expands as it rushes through the turbine, spinning the turbine wheels. Among the first artificially created objects to move faster than sound were the wheels of a steam turbine. Some turbines use mercury vapor instead of steam.

Boilers burn coal, oil, or natural gas to heat water to produce the steam that turns the wheels of steam turbines. Nuclear power plants use nuclear reactors in which heat produced by splitting atoms changes water to steam (see NUCLEAR REACTOR). Steam enters many steam turbines at temperatures up to 1050° F. (566° C). This is almost five times the boiling point of water. At this temperature, the steam may have a pressure up to

HOW TURBINES WORK

Moving fluids turn turbine wheels in two main ways—by reaction or impulse. The *reaction* of water squirting from a lawn sprinkler causes it to rotate. When you blow on a pinwheel, the *impulse* of the air striking the blades makes the wheel spin. All turbine wheels work either by reaction or impulse, or through a combination of the forces.

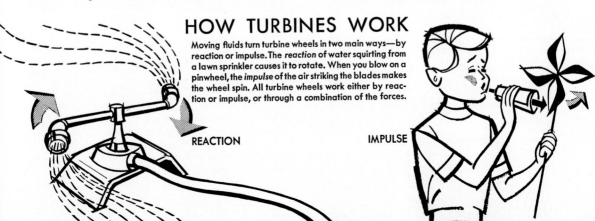

REACTION

IMPULSE

WATER TURBINES

Reaction Water Turbines usually turn generators at dams. The weight, or pressure, of the flowing water turns the turbine wheel. A control gate in the dam, and guide vanes, regulate the water flow.

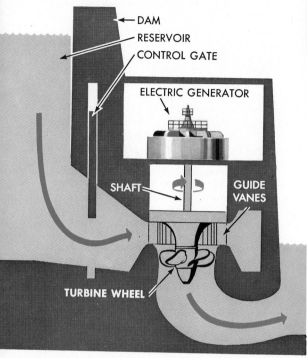

DAM
RESERVOIR
CONTROL GATE

ELECTRIC GENERATOR

SHAFT

GUIDE VANES

TURBINE WHEEL

Impulse Water Turbines such as the *Pelton wheel* work best where water falls a long distance, as from a mountain lake to a valley. The force of the water striking the wheel makes it spin. Long pipes that are called *penstocks* carry the water to the turbine.

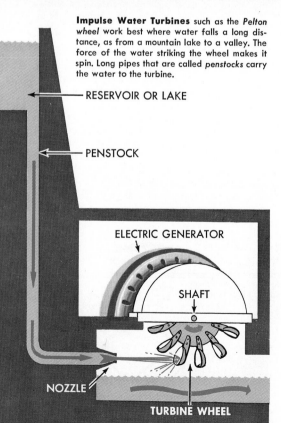

RESERVOIR OR LAKE

PENSTOCK

ELECTRIC GENERATOR

SHAFT

NOZZLE
TURBINE WHEEL

Allis-Chalmers Corp.

Kaplan-Type Wheels, used in reaction water turbines, look like huge propellers. This wheel, installed at a TVA dam in Kentucky, dwarfs the man standing on top of it.

2,000 pounds per square inch (140 kilograms per square centimeter).

Steam rushes into the turbine at 1,000 miles (1,600 kilometers) per hour. It strikes the first wheel, giving it a push, goes on to the next wheel, and then the next. A modern steam turbine has as many as 24 wheels mounted on a horizontal shaft. In front of each wheel is a fixed ring of curved, blade-shaped nozzles fastened to the casing. The nozzles direct the steam to meet the wheels at the proper angle. The steam follows a zigzag path between the nozzles and the turbine wheels.

Steam expands as much as 1,000 times its original volume as it passes through the turbine. Therefore, each succeeding pair of nozzles and wheels must be larger than the last one to make use of all the expanding steam. This gives the steam turbine its typical trumpet-like shape. To obtain just the right effect from the rushing steam, engineers carefully design the blades of each wheel and ring of nozzles. A steam turbine must be built of especially strong steel. It usually runs red-hot 24 hours a day, 7 days a week, for months or even years without stopping.

Steam turbines have impulse-type and reaction-type wheels, just as water turbines do. In an impulse turbine, the shape of the nozzles allows the steam to expand before it hits the blades of the wheels. In a reaction turbine, the steam expands while passing through the blades of the wheel. The expansion and speed of the steam helps push the wheel. Most modern turbines use both types of wheels at different stages along the shaft.

After the spent and expanded steam leaves the last wheel, it goes to the *condenser*. This is a large chamber with a network of pipes through which cooling water flows. The condenser cools the steam into water, which falls to the bottom of the condenser. A pump sends the water back to the boiler to be made into steam again. The condenser creates a vacuum, because the water takes up only about $\frac{1}{30,000}$ of the space of low-pressure steam. The vacuum helps pull more steam through the turbine.

In $\frac{1}{30}$ of a second, the steam travels through the turbine to the condenser. It drops in temperature from 1050° F. (566° C) to less than 100° F. (38° C). The pressure drops from 2,000 pounds to about $\frac{1}{2}$ pound per square inch (140 kilograms to 0.04 kilogram per square centimeter). This is about 4 pounds (0.3 kilogram) less than the air pressure on top of Mount Everest.

Allis-Chalmers Corp.

Cup-Shaped Buckets rim the edge of a Pelton wheel. Nozzles squirt water at the buckets.

STEAM TURBINE

Whirling steam turbines spin the propellers of huge ocean liners, turn electric generators, and run pumps. Steam from a boiler rushes through the turbine, rotating a series of bladed wheels mounted on a long shaft. As the steam leaves the turbine, a condenser cools it and changes it into water. This creates a vacuum that sucks steam through the turbine.

S.S. *United States*, Port Authority of New York and New Jersey

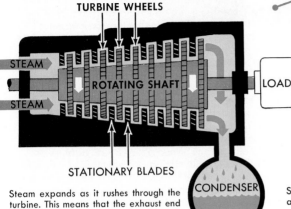

TURBINE WHEELS

STEAM

ROTATING SHAFT

STEAM

LOAD

STATIONARY BLADES

CONDENSER

Steam expands as it rushes through the turbine. This means that the exhaust end must be made larger than the intake end.

TURBINE WHEELS

STEAM

SHAFT

STATIONARY BLADES

Sets of stationary blades fastened to the turbine casing aim the steam at the wheels. These blades guide the steam so that it strikes the wheels at the correct angle. Each wheel has its own set of aiming blades.

Steam-turbine plants usually stand near railroads or other transportation facilities, so that fuel for their boilers can be delivered easily. Some steam-turbine plants burn huge amounts of coal daily. These plants must also be near a good water supply, to obtain cooling water for their condensers. One power station in New York City pumps 3,600,000 short tons (3,270,000 metric tons) of water a day through its condensers. This is more water than all the rest of the city uses daily. In a modern steam turbine plant, for every short ton of coal that is burned, 12 tons of air must be blown into the furnace, 13 tons of combustion gases go up the furnace chimney, and about 10 tons of water must be supplied to the boiler. However, the same water can be

pumped back to the boiler from the condenser and used again and again.

Gas Turbines work much like steam turbines, but use hot gases instead of steam. Any burning fuel produces hot gases such as those you see in the flame of fire. Gas turbines use these hot gases directly, without first using them to heat water into steam. They burn fuels such as oil, kerosene, and natural gas. Engineers hope to use synthetic gases made from coal as a fuel in gas turbines some day.

Gas turbines have three main parts: (1) a compressor, (2) a combustion chamber, and (3) one or more turbine wheels. The *compressor* is a special-type fan that sucks in air and compresses it. The compressed air mixes with

GAS TURBINE

Gas turbines turn electric generators and drive ships and airplanes. They also have been tried experimentally in automobiles. In a gas turbine, a compressor forces air into a combustion chamber where it mixes with fuel. An electric spark ignites the fuel-air mixture, creating hot gases that blast through the turbine.

General Motors Corp.

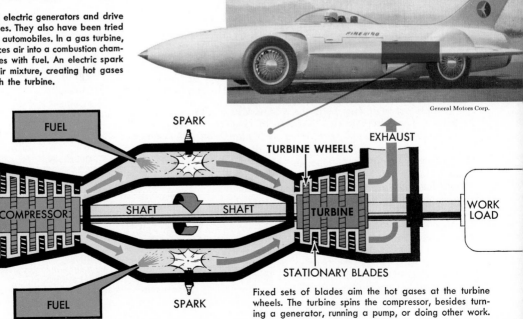

AIR INTAKE

FUEL

SPARK

TURBINE WHEELS

EXHAUST

COMPRESSOR

SHAFT

SHAFT

TURBINE

WORK LOAD

STATIONARY BLADES

FUEL

SPARK

Fixed sets of blades aim the hot gases at the turbine wheels. The turbine spins the compressor, besides turning a generator, running a pump, or doing other work.

the fuel and burns in the *combustion chamber*. The burning gases expand enormously and rush through the turbine, spinning the *turbine wheels*. Part of the rotary power from the turbine wheels drives the air compressor. This compressor is often mounted on the same shaft as the wheels. The rest of the rotary power can turn electric generators, run pumps, or drive ships.

Gas turbines are designed to make use of their hot exhaust gases. For example, a gas turbine used to turn an electric generator has a waste-heat recovery device called a *regenerator*. The regenerator uses heat from the exhaust gases to warm up the high-pressure air from the compressor before it enters the combustion chamber. By preheating the air, the regenerator reduces the amount of fuel needed for the combustion process. Other types of gas turbines, including turbojet and turbofan engines for aircraft, use the energy from exhaust gases for power. The gases are forced out the tailpiece of such turbines at high speed to produce forward thrust. See JET PROPULSION.

Gas turbines run at even hotter temperatures than steam turbines do. Engineers must make gas turbines from metals that keep their strength and shape in heat that would weaken steel. The temperature in many gas turbines is 2,000° F. (1093° C) or higher. The hotter a gas turbine runs, the more efficiently it operates. But a gas turbine works best only when run at from three-fourths of full power to full power. This can be a disadvantage when the turbine is used to propel ships, which often must move slowly. Gas turbines are usually very light and small for the power that they produce. For example, gas turbines that are used on land and in ships produce 3,000 to 30,000 horsepower (2,200 to 22,000 kilowatts), and they have an average weight of from 5 to 15 pounds per horsepower (3 to 9 kilograms per kilowatt).

History

Early Days. Water wheels are so old that no one knows who invented them. The ancient Greeks, Egyptians, and other peoples in the Mediterranean area used water wheels to grind grain and to irrigate crops.

Hero of Alexandria described the first known steam turbine about A.D. 60. It consisted of a small metal globe mounted on a pipe leading from a steam kettle. Steam from the kettle escaped from two pipes fastened to opposite sides of the globe and whirled it around. See JET PROPULSION (picture: The First Jet Engine).

Windmills first came into use in the Middle East in the 900's and in Europe in the 1100's. In the 1600's, people built the first crude gas turbines by mounting fans over a cooking fire to turn roasting meat on a spit. The hot gases from the fire spun the fan. Gears connected the fan to the spit.

These first forms of the turbine worked inefficiently, because much of the flowing fluids escaped around the sides of the turbine wheels. Benoît Fourneyron (1802-1867), a French engineer, developed the first fully successful enclosed water turbine in 1832. It developed 50 horsepower (37 kilowatts) and drove hammers used to forge metal. After Fourneyron's success, engineers soon overcame most of the problems that were involved in building efficient water turbines. By 1855, a Paris water-

works had a turbine that provided 800 horsepower (600 kilowatts).

Carl Gustaf de Laval (1845-1913), a Swedish engineer, built an impulse steam turbine in 1883 to power a cream separator he had invented. One year later, Charles A. Parsons (1854-1931) developed a reaction steam turbine in England. About 1900, Charles G. Curtis (1860-1953), an American inventor, developed the first steam turbine using many sets of wheels. The first big Curtis turbine was installed at an electric-power plant in Chicago in 1903. It ran a generator that produced 5,000 kilowatts of electricity. This Curtis turbine started a revolution in power production. It took up one-tenth as much space as the steam piston engine it replaced, weighed one-eighth as much, cost one-third as much, and used less steam. French and Swiss engineers also did important pioneering work on steam turbines.

Recent Developments include the perfection of the gas turbine during World War II. Gas turbines could not be built until engineers learned how to make metals that could withstand the great heat inside the combustion chamber. Gas turbines are now used in electric-power plants, pipeline pumping stations, and heavy industry. They power ships and experimental cars and trucks. In 1963, the Chrysler Corporation tested 50 gas-turbine powered cars.

Engineers have designed and built steam turbines capable of using steam at pressures of more than 4,500 to 5,000 pounds per square inch (316 to 350 kilograms per square centimeter). Such high-pressure steam enables turbines to produce more power with less fuel. In 1957, the American Gas and Electric Company installed a turbine at its Philo, Ohio, plant that uses steam at a pressure of 4,500 pounds per square inch (316 kilograms per square centimeter) and a temperature of 1150° F. (621° C). This power station can produce a kilowatt-hour of electricity from only about ¾ pound (0.3 kilogram) of coal. The average power plant burns about 1 pound (0.5 kilogram) of fuel to produce one kilowatt-hour of electricity. Engineers also have designed more powerful steam turbines by combining two or more rotors, so that several turbines become in effect one machine.

GLENN B. WARREN

Critically reviewed by J. T. RETTALIATA

Outline

I. **How Turbines Work**
    A. Water Turbines
    B. Steam Turbines
    C. Gas Turbines

II. **History**

Questions

Do turbines create power? Explain your answer.

In what ways can a pinwheel turbine be improved?

What are the two main kinds of water turbines?

What is the purpose of a condenser in a steam turbine?

Why were gas turbines not perfected until as recently as World War II?

What are the parts of a turbine rotor?

What are four basic kinds of turbines?

What serious disadvantage does a gas turbine have when it is used to drive a ship or locomotive?

What are the major uses of turbines?

Who invented the first steam turbine? How did it work?

TURBOFAN. See JET PROPULSION (Turbofan).

TURBOJET. See JET PROPULSION (Turbojet).

TURBOPROP. See JET PROPULSION (Turboprop); TURBINE (Gas Turbines).

TURBOT, *TUR but*, is a large flatfish that lives along the Atlantic Coast of Europe, and in the Mediterranean Sea. From the side it looks almost as round as a basketball. It seldom grows over 2 feet (61 centimeters) long, and usually weighs from 18 to 30 pounds (8 to 14 kilograms). But fishermen sometimes catch 90-pound (41-kilogram) turbot that are 3 feet (91 centimeters) long. The turbot is flat and wide, with a long fin on its top and bottom ridges. Hard, round knobs cover its brown upper surface. Both eyes are on the left side. The turbot lays five to ten million eggs, which float on

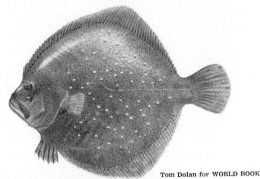

The Flat-Bodied Turbot of Europe's North Atlantic coastal waters has eyes only on one side of its body. When it swims, the eyeless side is on the underside.

Tom Dolan for WORLD BOOK

the surface of the ocean. The young fish that hatch settle to the bottom and live there.

Turbot are valuable commercially and are exported. Turbot became a favorite fish of the English. An American fish, also called turbot, is not a flatfish, and is not related to flounders, as is the European turbot.

Scientific Classification. The European turbot belongs to the family *Psetta*. It is classified as genus *Scophthalmus*, species *S. maximus*.   LEONARD P. SCHULTZ

See also FLATFISH; FLOUNDER.

TURCO. See ZOUAVE.

TURGENEV, *toor GEN yef*, **IVAN SERGEEVICH** (1818-1883), is generally regarded as one of the three greatest Russian novelists. He was the first Russian writer to win wide recognition outside Russia. He published his book *A Sportsman's Sketches* in 1852. These sympathetic tales, largely about the life of peasants, gained a reputation for Turgenev. He added to it with a series of brilliant novels, including *Rudin* (1856), *A Nest of Gentlefolk* (1859), *On the Eve* (1860), *Fathers and Sons* (1862), *Smoke* (1867), and *Virgin Soil* (1877). He wrote the plays *A Month in the Country* (completed in 1850) and *A Provincial Lady* (1851).

Brown Bros.

Ivan Turgenev

He began to publish poems in 1841. His first story, *Andrei Kolosov*, was published in 1844.

An analysis of the works of Ivan Turgenev reveals him as broadly sympathetic to a group in Russia called the "Westerners." They believed that Russia's well-being depended upon its ability to learn from the best of western European culture. His heroes are often frustrated and disillusioned liberals, the so-called "superfluous men" of the time. His heroines, on the other hand, are usually strong-willed and have a powerful sense of duty. Although he wrote realistically, his prose, and especially his descriptions of nature, often contain a beautiful poetic atmosphere.

Turgenev tried to find favor with the liberals of his day, but they criticized him for the politically ineffective heroes in his novels. This criticism mounted to considerable heights over the character Bazarov in *Fathers and Sons*. Turgenev called him a *nihilist*, a man who opposed all tradition and authority (see NIHILISM). Offended by the unfavorable reception, he spent more and more time abroad, and died near Paris in 1883. He was born in Orël. He studied in Moscow, Saint Petersburg, and Berlin.   ERNEST J. SIMMONS

TURGOT, ROBERT. See LOUIS (XVI).

TURIN, *TOO rihn*, or, in Italian, TORINO, *toh REE noh* (pop. 1,172,476), is a city in northern Italy that lies on the Po River. It is the capital of Piedmont, one of Italy's 20 political regions. For location, see ITALY (political map).

Turin is one of the loveliest places in northern Italy. Beautiful parks and botanical gardens stretch along the left bank of the Po. The great church of the Superga stands on a hill near the city. A cable railway runs to the top of the hill. From the hill, travelers enjoy a fine view of Turin. Many beautiful *piazzas* (public squares) provide open space in the city.

Turin is an old city, with a long and interesting history. In 218 B.C. the Carthaginian general, Hannibal, crossed the Alps and captured the city. In A.D. 69 a great fire swept Turin and many buildings burned to

Italian Government Travel Office (E.N.I.T.)

Turin's Piazza San Carlo, a public square, lies in the center of the city. Two large churches—Santa Cristina, *left*, and San Carlo, *right*—face the piazza.

TURK

the ground. From 1861 to 1865, Turin served as the capital of the Kingdom of Italy. The royal palace and park are still famous landmarks.

Educational institutions include several military schools, an observatory, museums, and a science academy. The University of Turin was founded in 1404. The city has a library with a collection of ancient writings.

During World War II, Turin served as an important munitions-manufacturing center for Italy and Germany. Many of the city's factories were destroyed by Allied air raids in 1942 and 1943. But the city recovered from the destruction of the war. Today, Turin has become one of Italy's leading industrial centers. Its chief products include fine silk materials and various kinds of Italian automobiles.　　　　　　　BENJAMIN WEBB WHEELER

See also SHROUD OF TURIN.

TURK. See TURKS.

TURKESTAN, *TUR kuh STAN*, in Turkish, TURKISTAN, a vast geographical region in China and Russia, has no definite boundaries. It stretches from Siberia on the north to Iran, Afghanistan, Pakistan, India, and Tibet on the south. The Mongolian Desert lies to the east, and the Caspian Sea to the west. The name *Turkestan* refers to the Turkish tribes that have lived in this region since as early as the A.D. 500's.

For hundreds of years, Turkestan has linked Europe with eastern Asia. Many ancient trade routes crossed the area. Marco Polo's famous Golden Road went through Turkestan. During World War II, Turkestan provided a route for transporting arms from Russia to China.

Soviet, or Western, Turkestan lies in Russia between the Caspian Sea and the Tien Shan Mountains. The Kazakh, Kirgiz, Tadzhik, Turkmen, and Uzbek Soviet Socialist Republics make up Soviet Turkestan. Flat and sandy in the north and west, the land rises to form mountains in the southeast. Rivers from the mountains flow inward, to disappear in the desert sands. Most of

the people are Muslims, and make their living by farming and raising cattle. Irrigation ditches provide water for the main crops of wheat, rice, millet, oats, and cotton. Chief cities include Alma-Ata, Samarkand, Tashkent, Bukhara, and Ashkhabad.

Chinese, or Eastern, Turkestan, in the heart of Asia, extends east from Soviet Turkestan to the Gobi Desert and Tibet. The rugged Tien Shan ranges on the north, and the Kunlun Mountains, rising over 20,000 feet (6,100 meters) on the south, border the region. Chinese Turkestan, which now forms part of the Chinese province of Sinkiang, has a harsh, dry climate. The people are of Turkish origin, and are called *Uigurs*. They make their living by farming, raising domestic animals, and trading. Most of them are Muslims. Major cities include Urumchi, Kashgar, and Khotan.

Afghan Turkestan is bounded on the north by the Amu Darya (Oxus River), and on the northwest by Soviet Turkestan. Uzbek chiefs ruled the country for a long time before Afghanistan gained possession of it. This part of southern Turkestan forms the Afghan province of Mazar-i-Sharif. Afghan Turkestan's many mountains have rich copper, iron, lead, and gold deposits. The people are chiefly of Persian and Uzbek stock.

History. The known history of Turkestan began about the time of Christ, when much of it belonged to the Chinese Empire. In the 500's, Turkish tribes conquered the rich trading cities of Bukhara and Samarkand. In the 600's, Tibet gained control of eastern Turkestan, but later the Chinese again took the region. Turkish tribes invaded Turkestan in 1073, and the followers of Genghis Khan swept through the land in the 1200's. Bukhara and Samarkand became centers of Muslim culture during the 1300's and 1400's.

Russia began to extend its rule to western Turkestan soon after the Russian conquest of Siberia in the 1600's. During the 1700's, the czars forced Kazakh tribes to recognize their authority. Most of western Turkestan became Russian during the 1800's. The czar's government created the province of Turkestan, and made Tashkent its capital. In 1887, an Anglo-Russian commission established the boundary between Afghanistan and Russian Turkestan.

In 1924, Soviet Turkestan was divided into five separate states. Each national group formed its own government under the communist dictatorship of Russia. The Russian government developed the region's resources. It also built schools, extended irrigation systems, and laid additional railroad lines.

Ancient eastern Turkestan remained under Chinese rule. In the 900's, the Muslim religion began to spread over this entire area. The Muslims made repeated attempts to set up their own government, especially in the 1800's. Chinese Turkestan almost became an independent state from 1872 to 1876, under the kingship of Yakub Beg. But after he died, China regained control. Chinese Turkestan is now governed as a part of the province of Sinkiang. The Chinese Communists barred this part of the world to Western trade after they took over in 1950.　　　　　　　THEODORE SHABAD

Related Articles in WORLD BOOK include:

Aral Sea	Sinkiang	Tashkent
Genghis Khan	Tadzhikistan	Turkmenistan
Kazakhstan	Tartary	Uzbekistan
Kirgiz		

Turkestan Rug Weavers are world-famous for their skill. In the background is one side of the loom upon which the rug is woven.
Sovfoto

Owen Franken, Stock, Boston

Remote Mountain Valleys are a common scene throughout Asian Turkey. The Asian part of Turkey, called *Anatolia* or *Asia Minor,* is about 30 times as large as European Turkey, called *Thrace.*

Ian Berry, Magnum

Historic Istanbul, Turkey's largest city, is famous for its beautiful *mosques* (Islamic houses of worship). This mosque overlooks the Bosporus, part of a Turkish waterway called the *Straits.*

TURKEY

TURKEY is a Middle Eastern nation that lies both in Europe and in Asia. About 3 per cent of the country occupies the easternmost tip of southern Europe, a region called *Thrace.* Istanbul, Turkey's largest city, lies in this region of green, fertile hills and valleys. To the east, the rest of Turkey covers a large, mountainous peninsula called *Anatolia* or *Asia Minor.* Anatolia has several large cities, including the capital city of Ankara, and areas of rich farmland. But much of Anatolia is rocky, barren land.

Turkey is a little larger than Texas, but it has about $3\frac{1}{2}$ times as many people as that state. The country borders Bulgaria on the northwest, Greece on the west, Russia and Iran on the east, and Iraq and Syria on the south. The Black Sea lies to the north, the Aegean Sea to the west, and the Mediterranean Sea to the south.

Three bodies of water—the Bosporus, the Sea of Marmara, and the Dardanelles—separate Anatolia from Thrace. These waters, often called the *Straits,* have had a major role in Turkish history. By its control of the Straits, Turkey can regulate the movement of ships between the Mediterranean Sea and southern Russia on the Black Sea.

About 56 per cent of Turkey's people live on farms or in small villages. The rest live in cities or towns. Nearly all the people are Muslims—that is, they practice the religion of Islam. Turkey is a developing country, and more than half of all its workers are farmers.

Andrew C. Hess, the contributor of this article, is Associate Professor of History at Temple University.

However, Turkey's economy has become increasingly industrialized since the mid-1940's. As a result, manufacturing now contributes about as much to the national income as does agriculture.

Various Asian and European peoples have ruled what is now Turkey since ancient times. During the A.D. 1300's, a group of Muslim Turks called the *Ottomans* began to build a powerful empire that eventually controlled much of the Middle East, southeastern Europe, and northern Africa. The Ottoman Empire ended in 1922. The next year, Turkey became a republic.

Facts in Brief

Capital: Ankara.

Official Language: Turkish.

Official Name: Türkiye Cumhuriyeti (Republic of Turkey).

Area: 301,382 sq. mi. (780,576 km²). *Greatest Distances*—north-south, 465 mi. (748 km); east-west, 1,015 mi. (1,633 km). *Coastline*—2,211 mi. (3,558 km).

Elevation: *Highest*—Ararat, 17,011 ft. (5,185 m). *Lowest*—sea level along the coast.

Population: *Estimated 1983 Population*—48,410,000; distribution, 56 per cent rural, 44 per cent urban; density, 161 persons per sq. mi. (62 per km²). *1980 Census*—45,217,556. *Estimated 1988 Population*—54,239,000.

Chief Products: *Agriculture*—barley, corn, cotton, fruits, potatoes, sugar beets, wheat. *Manufacturing*—fertilizers, iron and steel, machinery and metal products, motor vehicles, processed foods and beverages, pulp and paper products, textiles.

National Anthem: "Istiklâl Marşi" ("Independence March").

Money: *Basic Unit*—lira. One hundred kurus equal one lira. For the lira's value in U.S. dollars, see MONEY (table: Exchange Rates).

413

David Bellak, Jeroboam

Endless Lines of Traffic jam a wide, modern street in downtown Ankara, Turkey's capital. The city has grown into a center of commerce and industry since it became the capital in 1923.

Turkey's Flag was adopted in 1936. The crescent and five-pointed star are traditional symbols of the Islamic religion.

The Coat of Arms, adopted in 1923, bears the nation's official name, Republic of Turkey, in Turkish.

WORLD BOOK map

Turkey is a country in the Middle East. It covers the peninsula of Asia Minor and a small section of southeastern Europe.

Islamic law had strongly influenced Turkish life for nearly 1,000 years. However, Turkey's new republican government introduced sweeping cultural and political reforms that discouraged or outlawed many traditional Islamic practices. Most Turks accepted the reforms. But many others, especially in rural areas, resisted the changes. This conflict over the role of Islam in Turkish life continues to divide the nation.

Government

Turkey is a republic. Its Constitution, adopted in 1961, provided for a parliamentary form of government that included a president, a prime minister and cabinet, and a legislature called the Grand National Assembly. In 1980, military leaders took control of the government and suspended the executive and legislative parts of the Constitution. However, they began plans to create a new Constitution and a new civilian government. This section describes the government as it functioned before the 1980 take-over.

The President is Turkey's head of state, commander in chief of the armed forces, and the presiding officer at cabinet meetings. The president is elected by the Grand National Assembly from among its members to a seven-year term and may not serve two terms in a row. If the president disapproves of any bill passed by the legislature, it is returned. If the legislature then repasses the bill, it becomes law.

The Prime Minister and Cabinet. The prime minister is Turkey's head of government. The president selects the prime minister from among the most influential members of the legislature. The prime minister, in turn, chooses the members of the cabinet, called the Council of Ministers, from the legislature. Cabinet ministers supervise the various government departments. The prime minister must submit a proposed government program and the names of all cabinet ministers to the legislature for a *vote of confidence*. The prime minister and cabinet must resign if at any time the legislature refuses to grant a vote of confidence in their policies.

The Grand National Assembly makes Turkey's laws, ratifies treaties, and has the power to declare war. It consists of two houses, the National Assembly and the Senate of the Republic. The National Assembly, the lower house, has 450 members, all elected by the people to four-year terms. The Senate, the upper house, has 150 members elected by the people and 15 appointed by the president. These members serve six-year terms. Members of the Committee of National Unity, which ruled Turkey in 1960 and 1961, and former presidents serve in the Senate for life.

Court System. Courts throughout Turkey handle commercial disputes, criminal trials, and other cases. The Court of Appeals reviews the decisions of lower courts. The Constitutional Court determines the legality of laws passed by the legislature.

Local Government. Turkey has 67 provinces. Each province has a governor appointed by the president and a council elected by the province's people. Provinces are divided into counties, districts, *municipalities* (communities of 2,000 or more persons), and villages.

Political Parties. Turkey has two major political parties, the Republican People's Party and the Justice

Turkey
Political Map

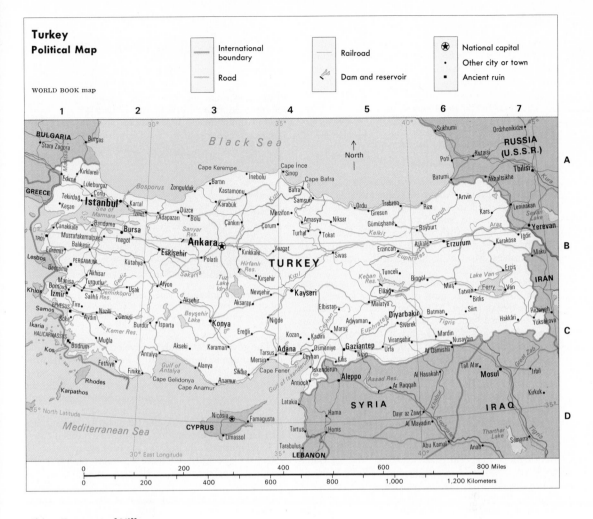

	International boundary
	Road
	Railroad
	Dam and reservoir
⊛	National capital
•	Other city or town
■	Ancient ruin

WORLD BOOK map

Cities, Towns, and Villages

Adana ...475,384
  *541,551 ...C 4
Adapazarı .114,130
  *223,046 ..B 2
Adıyaman .43,782 ..C 5
Adrianople, see Edirne
Afyon ...60,150 ..B 2
Akhisar ...53,357 ..B 1
Aksaray ...45,564 ..C 3
Akşehir ...35,544 ..C 3
Alanya ...18,520 ..C 3
Alaşehir* ..23,243 ..C 2
Alexandretta, see
  İskenderun
Alibeyköyü* 33,387 ..B 2
Amasya ...41,496 ..B 4
Anamur ...21,475 ..D 3
Ankara ..1,701,004
  *1,794,999 ..B 3
Antakya, see Antioch
Antalya ..130,774
  *212,245 ..C 2
Antioch
  (Antakya) 77,518 ..D 4
Artvin ...13,390 ..A 6
Aşkale ...10,817 ..B 6
Aydın ...59,579 ..C 1
Bafra ...34,288 ..A 4
Balıkesir ...99,443 ..B 1
Bandırma .45,752 ..B 1
Bartın ...18,409 ..A 3
Batman ...64,384 ..C 6
Bayburt ...20,156 ..B 6
Bayram-
  paşa* ...157,367 ..A 2
Bergama ..29,749 ..B 1
Bingöl ...22,047 ..B 6
Bitlis ...25,054 ..C 6
Bolu ...32,812 ..B 3

Bolvadin* ..29,218 ..B 2
Bornova ...45,096 ..B 1
Buca* ...70,715 ..C 1
Burdur ...36,633 ..C 2
Bursa ...346,103
  *465,657 ..B 2
Çamdibi* ..42,376 ..B 2
Çanakkale .30,788 ..B 1
Çankırı ...28,512 ..B 3
Çarşamba* .23,973 ..A 4
Ceyhan ...62,909 ..C 4
Çorlu ...40,134 ..A 1
Çorum ...64,852 ..B 4
Denizli ...106,902
  *171,521 ..C 2
Diyarbakır 169,535
  *244,686 ..C 6
Düzce ...32,129 ..B 3
Edirne (Adrian-
  ople) ...63,001 ..A 1
Edremit ...26,110 ..B 1
Elâzığ ...131,415
  *203,417 ..C 5
Elbistan ...26,048 ..C 5
Erciş ...22,351 ..B 7
Ereğli* ...45,992 ..A 3
Ereğli ...50,354 ..C 3
Erzincan ...60,351 ..B 5
Erzurum ..162,973
  *232,428 ..B 6
Esenler* ...49,379 ..A 2
Eskişehir .259,952
  *324,950 ..B 2
Fethiye ...12,700 ..C 2
Gaziantep 300,882
  *372,938 ..C 5
Gebze* ...33,110 ..B 2
Giresun ...38,236 ..B 5
Gölcük* ...33,279 ..B 2

Gültepe* ...44,469 ..C 1
Gümüşhane 11,166 ..B 5
Güngören* .48,593 ..A 2
Hakkâri ...11,735 ..C 7
Iğdır ...29,542 ..B 7
İnegöl ...37,805 ..B 2
İskenderun
  (Alexan-
  dretta) .107,437 ..C 4
İsparta ...62,870 ..C 2
İstanbul .2,547,364
  *3,432,234 ..A 2
İzmir
  (Smyrna) 636,834
  *896,062 ..C 1
İzmit
  (Kocaeli) 165,483
  *267,811 ..B 2
Kadirli ...34,779 ..C 4
Kâğıthane* 164,448 ..A 2
Karabük ...69,182 ..A 3
Karaköse ..35,284 ..B 7
Karaman ..43,759 ..C 3
Kars ...54,892 ..B 7
Kartal ...53,073 ..B 2
Kastamonu 29,993 ..A 3
Kayseri ...207,037
  *326,456 ..C 4
Keşan ...27,088 ..A 1
Kilimli* ..26,649 ..A 3
Kilis ...54,055 ..C 5
Kırıkhan* ..38,118 ..C 4
Kırıkkale .137,874 ..B 3
Kırklareli ..33,265 ..A 1
Kırşehir ...41,415 ..B 4
Kocaeli, see İzmit
Kocasinan* 51,311 ..A 2

Konya 246,727
  *339,203 ..C 3
Kozan ...32,045 ..C 4
Kozlu* ...27,322 ..A 3
Küçükçek-
  mece* ...58,709 ..A 2
Küçükköy* 56,411 ..A 2
Küçükyalı* 30,327 ..A 2
Kütahya ...82,442 ..B 2
Lüleburgaz .32,401 ..A 1
Malatya ...154,505
  *259,504 ..C 5
Maltepe* ..66,343 ..A 2
Manisa ...78,114 ..B 1
Maraş ...135,782
  *232,131 ..C 5
Mardin ...36,629 ..C 6
Mersin ...152,236
  *226,555 ..C 4
Merzifon ..30,801 ..B 4
Muğla ...24,178 ..C 1
Muş ...27,761 ..B 6
Mustafa-
  kemalpaşa 27,706 ..B 2
Nazilli ...52,176 ..C 1
Nevşehir ..30,203 ..C 4
Niğde ...31,844 ..C 4
Niksar ...19,156 ..B 5
Nizip ...36,190 ..C 5
Nusaybin ..23,684 ..C 6
Ödemiş* ...37,364 ..C 1
Ordu ...47,481 ..B 5
Osmaniye ..61,581 ..C 4
Pendik* ...38,384 ..B 2
Polatlı ...35,267 ..B 3
Reyhanlı* ..25,749 ..D 4
Rize ...36,044 ..A 6
Safra* ...47,103 ..A 2

Salihli ...45,514 ..C 1
Samsun ...168,478
  *263,413 ..A 4
Seydişehir* 25,651 ..C 3
Siirt ...35,654 ..C 6
Silifke ...19,257 ..C 3
Silvan* ...29,599 ..C 6
Sinop ...16,098 ..A 4
Sivas ...149,201
  *214,346 ..B 5
Siverek ...40,990 ..C 5
Smyrna, see İzmir
Soğanlık* ..23,304 ..A 2
Söke ...35,407 ..C 1
Soma* ...23,713 ..B 1
Tarsus ...102,186 ..C 4
Tatvan ...29,271 ..C 6
Tekirdağ ..41,257 ..A 1
Tire ...30,694 ..C 1
Tokat ...48,588 ..B 4
Trabzon ...97,210 ..B 5
Tunceli ...11,637 ..B 5
Turgutlu ..47,009 ..B 1
Turhal ...39,170 ..B 4
Umraniye* .38,730 ..A 2
Ünye* ...23,366 ..B 5
Urfa ...132,934
  *191,700 ..C 5
Uşak ...58,578 ..B 2
Uzunköprü* 27,005 ..A 1
Van ...63,663 ..C 7
Viranşehir .26,244 ..C 6
Yakacık* ..25,500 ..C 4
Yalova* ...27,289 ..B 2
Yarımca* ..23,042 ..B 2
Yenibosna* 26,424 ..A 2
Yozgat ...32,501 ..B 4
Zile* ...32,157 ..B 4
Zonguldak .90,221 ..A 3

*Does not appear on map; key shows general location.
*Population of metropolitan area, including suburbs.

Source: 1975 census.

414a

Party. The Republican People's Party supports government guidance of the economy and opposes a return to traditional Islamic practices. The Justice Party works to lessen the government's direction of the economy and to relax the laws against traditional religious customs. Turkey also has several smaller parties.

Armed Forces. About 500,000 men serve in Turkey's army, navy, and air force. Men from 20 to 32 years old may be drafted for 20 months of service.

People

Population and Ancestry. Turkey has a population of about 48,410,000. About 90 per cent of the people are descendants of an Asian people called *Turks*. Turks began to migrate to Anatolia from central Russia and northern Mongolia during the A.D. 900's. Kurds form Turkey's largest minority group, with more than 2 million members. Most of them live in the mountainous regions of the southeast.

Turkey also has several smaller minority groups. Nearly 300,000 Arabs, most of whom are farmers, live near the Syrian border. More than 100,000 Caucasians —people whose ancestors came from the Caucasus Mountains region of Russia—live in the provinces bordering the Black Sea. About 70,000 Greeks and 69,000 Armenians live in the Istanbul area.

Only about 44 per cent of Turkey's people live in cities and towns. However, the number of urban dwellers has increased rapidly since the 1940's. Hundreds of thousands of people have left their farms and villages to seek work in the cities. But the cities do not have enough jobs for all the people. As a result, many Turks have gone abroad to work. Many Turkish citizens are working in such countries as Australia, Belgium, Canada, France, Switzerland, and especially West Germany.

Languages. More than 90 per cent of all Turks speak Turkish, the country's official language. About 6 per cent speak Kurdish. The rest speak Arabic, Greek, or one of the other languages of the minority groups.

John Nicolais, Woodfin Camp, Inc.

A Crowded Street Along the Istanbul Waterfront reflects the rapid growth of Turkish cities since the 1940's. However, about 56 per cent of Turkey's people still live in rural areas.

Owen Franken, Stock, Boston

Education in Turkey has made rapid progress. But the nation still does not have enough schools or teachers. Many children, unlike these youngsters, do not receive a primary education.

The government began to develop the modern Turkish language in the late 1920's. For centuries, the written language was Ottoman Turkish, a complicated language written in Arabic characters. However, the Arabic alphabet had no letters to represent many sounds used in spoken Turkish. In addition, Ottoman Turkish included words and grammar from the Arabic and Persian languages. Ottoman Turkish was so difficult that only scholars and the ruling class learned to read it. In 1928, the government established a new alphabet and eliminated most foreign words from the language. It also ordered a language education program throughout the country and outlawed the use of Ottoman Turkish.

Ways of Life have changed greatly in Turkey since the 1920's, when a new republican government was established. The government set out to make Turkey a modern state and so began a program to sweep away the customs and traditions of centuries.

Since the 1920's, one of the government's major goals has been to change the status of women in Turkish life. Men have dominated Turkish society for hundreds of years. Before the 1920's, women had almost no civil rights. Parents arranged the marriages of their daughters by means of a contract with the groom's family. The bride had little voice in the matter. Women could not vote and had difficulty getting a divorce. During the 1920's, the government outlawed the arrangement of marriages by contract and made it easier for women to get a divorce. It also gave women the right to vote and to receive alimony. Today, women are still generally considered less important and less intelligent than men in Turkey. However, increased educational opportunities and exposure to Western ideas are gradually improving their position.

The government has also tried to bring the Kurds and other tribal people into the mainstream of modern Turkish life. Many Turks, as well as the Kurds, have lived in tribal groups as nomads or in isolated communities for centuries. During the 1920's, the government

David Bellak, Jeroboam

Islamic Rituals, such as group prayer, *above,* play an important part in the daily life of most Turks. About 98 per cent of the people of Turkey are Muslims.

began to force these people to abandon their tribal way of life as a means of modernizing Turkish society. The Kurds revolted against these attempts several times in the 1920's and 1930's. Since then, some Kurds adopted modern Turkish culture while serving in the armed forces or attending school outside areas with large Kurdish populations. However, tribes of Kurds and other Turks still travel across the countryside with their goats and sheep in search of pastures as their ancestors did.

Housing varies throughout Turkey. Turks who live near the Black Sea build thatch-roofed cottages with timber from nearby forests. In rural areas of Thrace and northeastern Anatolia, many people have replaced their old wooden homes with one-story houses of con-

crete blocks. Many villagers in central Anatolia live in flat-roofed houses of sun-dried brick. Stone houses are common in southern and western Anatolia.

Most wealthy Turks live in luxurious concrete block houses on the outskirts of cities or in suburban apartment complexes. Middle-class city dwellers live in old two- and three-story wooden houses or in concrete homes. The rapid growth of industry in the major cities has created a severe housing shortage among workers who moved there from rural areas. As a result, large shantytowns have sprung up at the edges of the cities.

Clothing worn by the people of Turkey changed dramatically during the 1920's. The government discouraged or forbade the wearing of certain garments required by Islamic custom. City dwellers and many rural people then adopted Western clothing styles. However, some Turks in rural areas still cling to Islamic tradition. Only a few men wear the traditional loose-fitting cloak and baggy trousers. But rural women still continue some of the old clothing customs. These women wear a simple blouse and pantaloons. They cover their head and often the lower part of the face with a scarf as a sign of modesty.

Food and Drink. Cracked-wheat bread and a creamy dairy product called *yogurt* are the chief foods of most Turks. Mutton and rice are also favorite foods, but they are expensive and eaten sparingly. Turkish cooks prepare rice with chunks of mutton in grease and olive oil. For special occasions, they combine rice with almonds, meat, pine nuts, and raisins. Turkish cooks are especially famous for their tasty *shish kebab,* which consists of pieces of lamb, tomatoes, peppers, and onions cooked together on a spikelike skewer. A popular dessert is *baklava,* made of thin layers of pastry, honey, and chopped nuts. Favorite beverages include tea, thick coffee flavored with sugar, and a liquor called *raki,* which is made from raisins.

Recreation. Family outings and celebrations are the most common forms of recreation in Turkey. The peo-

LeRoy Woodson

The Kurds of Turkey make up the nation's largest minority group. Most of them, like these women and children, live much as their ancestors did centuries ago. They roam the countryside with their livestock and live in caves and other temporary shelters.

ple also enjoy drinking coffee or tea at a restaurant with a scenic view. Many men spend their leisure time in coffee houses playing the ancient dice game of backgammon. Archery, horseback riding, soccer, and wrestling are popular sports. A Turkish form of wrestling called *greased wrestling* is a favorite event at festivals and wrestling matches. Contestants wear tight leather trousers and cover their bodies with olive oil to make the holds more difficult. The Turkish people also enjoy concerts, movies, stage plays, and operas.

Religion. More than 98 per cent of the Turkish people are Muslims. However, Turkey has no state religion, and the Constitution guarantees religious freedom. The population thus includes many Gregorians, Jews, Roman Catholics, and members of various Eastern Orthodox groups.

One of the most controversial issues in Turkey is whether Turkish society should be organized on a worldly or religious basis. Islamic law provides specific rules for all activities of life—economic, political, and social. In the 1920's, the government made religion a private matter, restricting it to personal morals and behavior. But many Turks strongly objected. Today, the dispute continues over what part Islam should have in Turkish life.

Education. About 65 per cent of Turkey's people 15 years old and older can read and write. The government's greatest challenge in education is in rural areas. The government spends nearly 20 per cent of its budget on public education, and much of this money is used for the education of rural people. But rising costs and a lack of qualified teachers prevent the nation from providing enough schools in rural areas.

Turkish law requires all children to attend a five-year primary school until they graduate or reach the age of 15. However, this law is difficult to enforce. After graduation, students may attend a middle school for three years and then take a state examination. Students who do well on the test may enter a three-year college-preparatory high school called a *lise*. Other middle-school graduates enter a vocational school or find a job. Many lise graduates go on to college. Turkey has about 150 institutions of higher learning. Istanbul University, the oldest and largest university, was founded in 1453. It has more than 35,000 students.

The Arts. Turkey's most important contribution to the arts is in the field of architecture. In Istanbul stands the great-domed cathedral Hagia Sophia, a classic example of Byzantine architecture. It was built in the A.D. 500's, when Turkey was part of the Byzantine Empire. Turkish *mosques* (Islamic houses of worship) were built throughout Anatolia during the 1200's. These structures, with their thin *minarets* (towers), follow the Persian and Arabic style of architecture. Many of Turkey's finest buildings were constructed during the 1400's and the 1500's, when the Ottoman Empire was at its height. A large number were designed by Koca Sinan, who is considered Turkey's greatest architect. His majestic Mosque of Suleiman I in Istanbul is one of the world's most beautiful mosques.

For hundreds of years, Turkish craftworkers have made excellent dishes, bowls, and other objects of ceramics. Richly colored ceramic tiles decorate many mosques and palaces. Turkish weavers have long been famous for their elaborately designed rugs. They made many of the first Oriental rugs used in Europe.

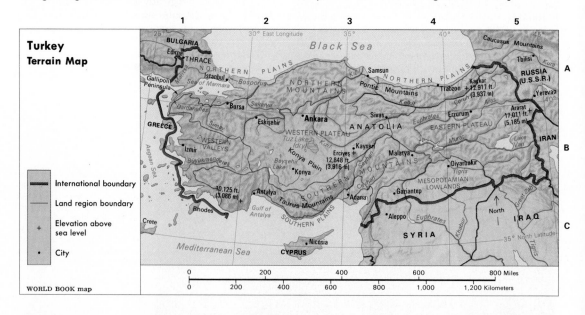

Turkey
Terrain Map

International boundary

Land region boundary

+ Elevation above sea level

• City

WORLD BOOK map

0	200	400	600	800 Miles
0	200	400	600	800	1,000	1,200 Kilometers

Physical Features

Aegean Sea ....B 1	Beyşehir Lake .....B 2	Dardanelles	Kaçkar (Mountain) A 4	Sakarya River ......A 2
Anatolia	Black Sea ....A 3	(Strait) ....A 1	Kelkit River ....A 4	Sea of Marmara ...A 1
(Region) ....B 3	Bosporus	Erciyeş	Kizil River ....A 3	Seyhan River ......B 3
Ararat	(Strait) ....A 2	(Mountain) .....B 3	Konya Plain ......B 2	Simav River ....B 1
(Mountain) ......B 5	Büyükmenderes	Euphrates River ...B 4	Lake Van ....B 5	Taurus Mountains ..C 2
Aras River ....A 5	River ....B 1	Gallipoli	Maritsa River ......A 1	Thrace (Region) ...A 1
	Ceyhan River .....B 3	Peninsula .....A 1	Murat River ....B 4	Tigris River ....B 4
	Çoruh River ....A 4	Gulf of Antalya ....C 2	Pontic Mountains ..A 3	Tuz Lake ....B 2

Most of Turkey's traditional literature is written in the complicated Ottoman Turkish language and deals with religious themes and life during Ottoman rule. Modern Turkish literature centers largely on nationalism, social justice, and folk history. In some works, modern writers include stories from ancient folk dramas about the legendary puppet character Karagöz (Black Eyes). In these folk dramas, the clever Karagöz produces much laughter as he outwits his enemies.

The Land

Turkey covers 301,382 square miles (780,576 square kilometers) in the northwestern part of the Middle East. Much of Thrace and the coastal areas of Anatolia consist of lowlands and green, rolling plains. A broad expanse of dry highlands called the *Anatolian Plateau* stretches across central Anatolia. The plateau is bordered by the Pontic Mountains on the north and the Taurus Mountains on the south.

Turkey has several large saltwater lakes and numerous rivers. But most of the rivers dry up during the country's hot, dry summers. In the spring, many rivers become torrents as waters from the melting snows rush down from the mountains and overflow the riverbanks.

Turkey can be divided into eight land regions. They are (1) the Northern Plains, (2) the Western Valleys, (3) the Southern Plains, (4) the Western Plateau, (5) the Eastern Plateau, (6) the Northern Mountains, (7) the Southern Mountains, and (8) the Mesopotamian Lowlands.

The Northern Plains cover Thrace and extend along the Black Sea coast of Anatolia. Thrace's gently rolling grasslands make it an important farming and grazing region. Along the Black Sea coast, farmers raise corn, fruits, nuts, and tobacco.

The Western Valleys are broad, fertile river valleys along the Aegean Sea coast. The region produces barley, corn, olives, tobacco, and wheat. The value of its crop output exceeds that of any other region.

The Southern Plains are a narrow strip of land along the Mediterranean Sea. A great variety of crops, including cereal grains, citrus fruits, cotton, and olives, grow in the region's rich soil. Farmers must irrigate their fields during the hot, dry summer.

The Western Plateau, a region of highlands and scattered river valleys, extends across central Anatolia. The region receives very little rainfall. Farmers raise barley and wheat in the river valleys and wherever irrigation water is available. Goats, sheep, and other livestock graze on uncultivated land.

The Eastern Plateau is a rugged area of towering mountains and barren plains. It extends from the Western Plateau to Turkey's eastern border. The Taurus and Pontic mountains meet in this region. Ararat, the country's highest point, rises 17,011 feet (5,185 meters) above sea level near the Iranian border. Most of the region's people are nomadic herders.

The Northern Mountains, or Pontic Mountains, rise between the Northern Plains and the Anatolian Plateau. Only a few roads and railroads connect the plateau with the Black Sea.

The Southern Mountains consist of the Taurus Mountains and several smaller ranges on the southern edge of the Anatolian Plateau. These mountains almost completely cut off the plateau from the Mediterranean.

The Mesopotamian Lowlands are fertile plains and river valleys in southeastern Anatolia. Cereal grains and fruits grow well in the region's rich soil.

Climate

The climate differs greatly from one region of Turkey to another. Thrace and the south and west coasts of Anatolia have mild, rainy winters and hot, dry summers. Summer temperatures along the Aegean often

Ian Berry, Magnum

Vast Barren Plains cover much of central Anatolia. The region receives little or no rain during the hot summer, and so few crops can be grown without extensive irrigation. Many of the region's people, like this herdsman, raise sheep or other livestock.

TURKEY

Turkey's Gross National Product

Total gross national product in 1979—$59,506,000,000

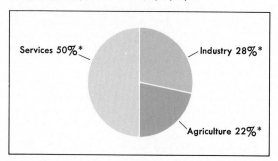

Services 50%*

Industry 28%*

Agriculture 22%*

The gross national product (GNP) is the total value of goods and services produced by a country in a year. The GNP measures a nation's total annual economic performance. It can also be used to compare the economic output and growth of countries.

Production and Workers by Economic Activities

Economic Activities	Per Cent of GDP* Produced	Employed Workers†	
		Number of Persons	Per Cent of Total
Agriculture, Forestry, & Fishing	22	10,452,966	64
Manufacturing	22	1,243,567	8
Community, Social, & Personal Services	16	1,866,002	11
Hotels, Restaurants, & Trade	15	818,644	5
Transportation & Communication	9	512,327	3
Construction	5	447,324	3
Housing	5	—	—
Finance and Insurance	3	176,207	1
Utilities	2	16,401	**
Mining	1	108,506	1
Other	—	677,436	4
Total	100	16,319,380	100

*Based on gross domestic product (GDP). GDP is gross national product adjusted for net income sent abroad or received from abroad.
†Figures are for 1975.
**Less than 1 per cent.
Sources: State Institute of Statistics, Turkey; International Monetary Fund.

rise above 90° F. (32° C). The Black Sea coast has cooler summers, with an average temperature of about 72° F. (22° C). Yearly rainfall averages from 20 to 30 inches (51 to 76 centimeters) along the Aegean and Mediterranean coasts to more than 100 inches (254 centimeters) near the Black Sea.

Northeastern Turkey has mild summers but bitterly cold winters. Temperatures sometimes fall to −40° F. (−40° C). Southeastern Turkey and the interior of Anatolia have cold winters with heavy snowstorms. Summers are hot, windy, and extremely dry.

Economy

Turkey has a developing economy. When the republican government came to power in the 1920's, Turkey was almost entirely an agricultural country. Under government direction, the number of factories increased from 118 in 1923 to more than 1,000 in 1941. Today,

Turkey has over 30,000 factories. But agriculture remains the chief economic activity. It provides jobs for about 67 per cent of the country's workers. However, farm output accounts for only about 27 per cent of the value of all goods and services produced in Turkey. Manufacturing employs only around 8 per cent of all workers, but the value of industrial production about equals that of agricultural output.

The national government owns Turkey's communications systems, railroads, airports, and major utilities. It also controls steel production, the mining industry, the nation's forests, most of the banking system, and about 1 million acres (400,000 hectares) of farmland. However, most farms and small manufacturing and construction companies are privately owned. Since 1963, the government has directed the nation's economic growth through a series of five-year plans.

Agriculture. Turkey's most productive farmlands are in the coastal regions, which have fertile soil and a mild climate. Farmers on the desertlike Anatolian Plateau raise wheat and barley. However, the region often has long droughts that cause serious crop losses.

In most years, Turkey's farmers produce enough food for all the people plus a surplus to sell abroad. About 90 per cent of the cropland is used for grains, especially wheat. Cotton production has increased rapidly since the 1960's and become Turkey's most profitable export. Tobacco, another major export, is grown along the Aegean and Black seas. Other leading crops include barley, corn, fruits, nuts, potatoes, and sugar beets. Sheep, goats, and other livestock make up about 20 per cent of farm output.

Turkey's agricultural productivity is low largely because of insufficient irrigation and a general lack of knowledge about modern farming methods. An unequal distribution of land has been another problem

Malcolm S. Kirk from Peter Arnold

Manufacturing is one of Turkey's chief industries. Most textile workers are employed in modern mills. Others, such as these women, work at home. The women are weaving an Oriental rug.

in Turkey. Many of the nation's farmers own no or very little land. In 1973, the legislature passed a bill that provides for the distribution of 8 million acres (3.2 million hectares) of land to more than 500,000 farmers over a 15-year period.

Manufacturing. Turkey's largest manufacturing industries are the processing of food and beverages and the production of textiles. Other leading manufactured products include fertilizers, iron and steel, machinery and metal products, motor vehicles, and pulp and paper products. Most factories and mills are in and around the large cities of northern and western Turkey. In 1973, the government built the huge Keban Dam on the Euphrates River near Elâziğ. The government hopes that electricity generated by the dam will stimulate industry in eastern Turkey.

Mining. Turkey is rich in mineral resources, but the mining industry is largely undeveloped. The country's most abundant mineral is coking coal, which is used in steelmaking. Turkey is one of the world's largest producers of chromite, the mineral from which chromium is obtained. It also produces and refines about half the petroleum used in the country. Other minerals produced in Turkey include copper; iron ore; and *meerschaum*, a soft, white mineral that is used to make jewelry and tobacco pipes.

Foreign Trade. The government's program to speed Turkey's industrial growth requires the nation to import large quantities of machinery and raw materials. The nation spends more money for these and other imports than it receives for its exports. As a result, Turkey has an *unfavorable balance of trade*. Turkey's chief imports include cereals, chemicals, iron and steel, machinery, mineral fuels, and motor vehicles. Major exports include chromite, cotton, nuts, and tobacco. Turkey's main trading partner is West Germany. Other leading partners include France, Great Britain, Italy, and the United States.

Transportation and Communication. Turkey has about 77,920 miles (125,400 kilometers) of roads, about a fourth of which are paved. The Turkish State Railways, owned and run by the national government, operates about 6,109 miles (9,831 kilometers) of track. The government-owned Turkish Airlines serves about 30 cities in Turkey and several European and Mideastern cities outside the country. Turkey has many fine natural harbors. Istanbul and Izmir are the chief ports.

More than 450 newspapers are published in Turkey. The country has eight radio stations and one television station.

History

The earliest known inhabitants of what is now Turkey were a people called the Hittites. About 2000 B.C., they began to migrate to central Anatolia from Europe or central Asia. During the next several hundred years, they conquered much of Anatolia and parts of Mesopotamia and Syria. By 1500 B.C., the Hittites had created a powerful empire that made them the leading rulers of the Middle East. See HITTITES.

From about 1200 to 500 B.C., large areas of Anatolia fell to the Phrygians, the Lydians, and other peoples. During the same period, the Greeks founded many city-states along Anatolia's Aegean coast. About 500 B.C., the Persian Empire seized control of Anatolia and Thrace. The Persians held control until Alexander the Great of Macedonia crushed their army in 331 B.C. After Alexander's death in 323 B.C., Anatolia became a battleground in the wars among his successors. Small kingdoms rose and fell until 63 B.C., when the Roman general Pompey conquered the region. Anatolia was at peace under Roman rule for nearly 400 years.

In A.D. 330, the Roman emperor Constantine the Great moved the capital from Rome to the ancient town of Byzantium in Thrace. Byzantium was renamed *Constantinople*, meaning *city of Constantine*. In 395, the Roman Empire split into two parts—the East Roman Empire, which included Anatolia and Thrace, and the West Roman Empire. Barbarians conquered the West Roman Empire in the mid-400's. But the East Roman Empire, also called the Byzantine Empire, thrived. Byzantine emperors thus came to rule all of what is now Turkey until the late 1000's. See BYZANTINE EMPIRE.

The Seljuk Turks became one of the first Turkish peoples to rule in Turkey. The Seljuks were Muslims from south-central Russia and northern Mongolia. During the mid-1000's, they conquered Armenia; the Holy Land, or Palestine; and most of Iran. Then they invaded Anatolia. In 1071, the Seljuks destroyed most of the Byzantine power in Anatolia by defeating the Byzantine army in the Battle of Manzikert. They set up an empire with Iconium (now Konya) as the capital. From this point onward, the Christian religion and Greek language of the Byzantine Empire were gradually replaced in Anatolia by Islam and the Turkish language.

In 1095, Christians in western Europe organized a series of military expeditions called the *Crusades* to drive the Turks from the Holy Land (see CRUSADES). During the First Crusade (1096-1099), Christian troops

Ian Berry, Magnum
Hard-Working Turkish Farmers pick cotton by hand in one of the country's many cotton fields. Turkey is a world leader in cotton production, and cotton is the nation's most valuable export.

417

Bettmann Archive

The Conquest of Constantinople by the Turks in 1453 ended the Byzantine Empire, which had ruled in Turkey since the 300's.

defeated the Seljuk Turks in western Anatolia. As a result, the Byzantine Empire recovered about a third of Anatolia. But the crusaders then left the peninsula to fight in the Holy Land. The Seljuk empire thus endured until 1243, when it was invaded by an Asian people known as the Mongols (see MONGOL EMPIRE).

The Rise of the Ottoman Empire. The Mongol Empire was torn by internal struggles and soon fell apart. As a result, the Turks' influence in Anatolia continued to grow. During the 1300's, a group of Turks called the Ottomans began to build a mighty empire. In 1326, they seized the Anatolian city of Bursa, which became their capital. By the late 1300's, the Ottomans had conquered the western two-thirds of Anatolia; most of Thrace; and much of the Balkan Peninsula, including Greece. All that remained of the Byzantine Empire was the area around Constantinople.

In 1453, Ottoman forces led by Muhammad II captured Constantinople, ending the Byzantine Empire. The Turks called the city Istanbul and made it their capital. By 1481, their empire extended from the Danube River in Europe to southern Anatolia.

The Ottoman Empire reached its height in the 1500's. During the reign of Sultan Bayezid II, who ruled from 1481 to 1512, the empire became the leading naval power in the Mediterranean region. Ottoman forces conquered Syria in 1516 and Egypt in 1517. Suleiman I, whom Europeans called the *Magnificent*, ruled from 1520 to 1566. In 1526, his army conquered much of Hungary in the Battle of Mohács. Suleiman also expanded the empire's borders to Yemen on the south, Morocco on the west, and Persia on the east.

The Start of the Ottoman Decline. After the Battle of Mohács, European powers feared that the Turks would overrun Europe. However, European forces successfully defended Vienna, Austria, during a Turkish attack in 1529. In 1571, European fleets defeated the Turkish navy in the Battle of Lepanto, near Greece. The Turks again failed to capture Vienna in 1683.

During the 1700's, the Ottoman Empire continued to weaken. In 1774, the Turks lost a six-year war against Russia and were forced to allow Russian ships to pass

through the Straits—the Turkish waters that link the Black Sea with the Mediterranean. The Turks lost the Crimea, a peninsula in the Black Sea, to Russia in 1783.

"The Sick Man of Europe," as the Ottoman Empire came to be called, lost more territory during the 1800's. In 1821, Greek nationalists revolted against Ottoman rule. France, Great Britain, and Russia sided with the Greeks and sent forces to fight the Turks (see GREECE [History]). The Treaty of Adrianople (Edirne) ended the fighting in 1829. It acknowledged the independence of Greece and gave Russia control of the mouth of the Danube River. The Turks also lost other Balkan territory in a series of wars with Russia (see RUSSO-TURKISH WARS). But European powers forced Russia to give up much of its gains at the Congress of Berlin in 1878. The Ottoman Empire continued to decline, however. It had lost Algeria to France in 1830, and France seized Tunisia in 1881. Great Britain gained Cyprus in 1878 and Egypt in 1882.

Ottoman leaders tried to halt the empire's decline through a reform program. They reorganized the military and improved the educational system. In 1876, Turkey's first constitution was adopted. It provided for representative government and granted the people various freedoms. However, Sultan Abdul-Hamid II, who came to the throne the same year, set the constitution aside and ruled as a dictator. Government policies became increasingly violent, and Abdul-Hamid ruled by the use of fear. Religious persecution began to spread as members of the various religious minorities became revolutionaries.

The Young Turks. During the late 1890's, small groups of Turkish students and military officers who opposed Abdul-Hamid's harsh policies banded together secretly. The most influential group was the Young Turks. In 1908, the Young Turks led an army revolt against Abdul-Hamid and forced him to restore constitutional government. But the sultan soon staged an unsuccessful counterrevolution, and the Young Turks made him give up the throne in 1909. They then ruled the empire through his brother Muhammad V.

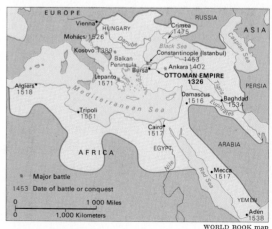

WORLD BOOK map

The Ottoman Empire began during the 1300's as a small state around the city of Bursa. It grew to include much of the Middle East and parts of northern Africa and southeastern Europe.

1500 B.C. The Hittites, the earliest known inhabitants of what is now Turkey, ruled in Anatolia.

63 B.C. The Roman general Pompey conquered Anatolia.

A.D. 330 Constantine the Great moved the capital of the Roman Empire to Byzantium and renamed the town Constantinople.

1071 The Seljuk Turks conquered most of Anatolia by defeating the Byzantine forces in the Battle of Manzikert.

1326 The Ottoman Turks captured Bursa, which marked the beginning of the Ottoman Empire.

1453 The Ottomans captured Constantinople, ending the Byzantine Empire.

1783-1914 The Ottoman Empire lost much of its territory in a series of military defeats.

1908 The Young Turks revolted against the government.

1914-1918 In World War I, the Ottoman Empire allied with Germany and lost much of its remaining territory.

1923 Mustafa Kemal (Atatürk) set up the Republic of Turkey and began a program to modernize the nation.

1947 Turkey received economic and military aid from the United States to resist Russian expansion.

1960 Turkish army units overthrew the government and ruled until free elections were held in 1961.

1974 Turkish forces invaded Cyprus.

1980 Army units again took control of the government.

The Young Turks wanted to restore the greatness of the Ottoman Empire. But many Turkish people no longer cared about the idea of maintaining an empire. In addition, the empire's Christian minorities demanded freedom from Ottoman rule. And so the empire continued to crumble. Soon after the revolution in 1908, Bulgaria declared its independence, and Austria seized Bosnia. Italy took Libya in 1912, and the empire surrendered Crete to Greece in 1913. By 1914, the empire had lost all its European territory except Thrace.

In 1914, the Ottoman Empire entered World War I on the side of Germany and Austria-Hungary in an attempt to regain lost territory. The empire's forces fought well and won some battles. In 1915, British, French, and other Allied troops tried to gain control of the Straits so that aid could be shipped to Russia. Turkey drove back the invaders, dealing the Allies a crushing defeat. However, the Allies won the war in 1918.

After World War I, the Allies set out to break up the Ottoman Empire. Allied troops occupied Istanbul and the Straits. In May 1919, Greek troops, protected by Allied fleets, landed at the Turkish port of Izmir. The Greeks then advanced into the country. The Turks deeply resented the Ottoman government's inability to defend their homeland. Mustafa Kemal, a Turkish military hero, quickly organized a nationalist movement. Under his leadership, a nationalist congress met in Sivas in September to form a new *provisional* (temporary) government. In April 1920, the congress organized the Turkish Grand National Assembly in Ankara and elected Kemal as Assembly president.

In August 1920, the sultan's government signed the harsh Treaty of Sèvres with the Allies (see SÈVRES, TREATY OF). The treaty granted independence to some parts of the empire and gave other parts to various Allied powers. Turkey was reduced to Istanbul and a portion of Anatolia. As a result of the treaty, the sultan's

popularity among the Turks declined further, while the power of Kemal and the nationalists grew. In September 1922, the nationalist forces finally drove the Greeks from Turkey. The Grand National Assembly then abolished the office of sultan, and the Allies agreed to draw up a new peace treaty with the nationalists. The Treaty of Lausanne, signed in 1923, set Turkey's borders about where they are today.

The Republic of Turkey. The Grand National Assembly proclaimed Turkey to be a republic on Oct. 29, 1923, and elected Kemal as president. Kemal and other nationalist leaders believed that the new nation could not survive without sweeping social changes.

During the 1920's and 1930's, the government did away with such Islamic traditions as the Arabic alphabet, Muslim schools, the Islamic legal system, and the wearing of the veil by women and the fez by men. It abolished the religious and civil office of the caliph. It also outlawed *polygyny*, the practice of having more than one wife at the same time. Women received the right to vote and to hold public office. All Turks were required to choose a family name. At the same time, the Grand National Assembly gave Kemal his surname— *Atatürk*, which means *father of the Turks*.

Atatürk held enormous political power. He controlled the Assembly and could appoint and dismiss the prime minister and cabinet without its approval. However, some Turks opposed Atatürk's anti-Islamic policies. The Kurds revolted against them in 1925, but the government put down the uprising.

Atatürk served as Turkey's president until he died in 1938. Ismet Inönü then became president. Under Inönü's leadership, Turkey avoided entering World War II (1939-1945) until February 1945, when Germany's defeat seemed certain. Turkey joined the United Nations (UN) the same year.

After World War II, Russia demanded control of territory in eastern Turkey and the right to build military bases along the Straits. Turkish leaders turned to the Western powers for help. In 1947, U.S. President Harry Truman announced the Truman Doctrine, under

Kemal Atatürk founded the Republic of Turkey in 1923 and was its first president. In an attempt to modernize the nation, he introduced major cultural, political, and economic reforms.

419

which the United States would provide aid to any country threatened by outside forces. The United States gave Turkey millions of dollars in economic and military aid. In return, Turkey allowed the United States to build and operate military bases on Turkish soil.

The Republican People's Party, founded by Atatürk, had governed Turkey since the establishment of the republic. But in 1950, the Democrat Party won a majority in the Grand National Assembly. Celal Bayar became president, and Adnan Menderes became prime minister. Unlike the Republicans, the Democrats encouraged foreign investments and wanted less government control of the economy. But by the late 1950's, a rise in the national debt and restrictions on freedom of speech had made the Democrat government unpopular.

The 1960's. Turkish military forces believed that the Democrat government had strayed too far from Atatürk's political principles. In 1960, army units led by General Cemal Gürsel seized control of the government and set up a provisional government. The military placed many former government leaders on trial. Prime Minister Menderes was hanged. President Bayar was sentenced to life imprisonment but was later released.

In 1961, Turkey's present constitution was adopted. The provisional government then held free national elections. No party won a majority in the legislature. But two members of the Republican People's Party were chosen for the highest offices. Inönü became prime minister, and Gürsel became president. In 1965, the Justice Party won a majority in the legislature, and the party leader, Süleyman Demirel, became prime minister. Gürsel held office until 1966.

The Cyprus Crisis. During the 1960's, Turkey and Greece nearly went to war over the issue of the Mediterranean island of Cyprus. In 1964 and 1967, fighting broke out on Cyprus between the island's Turkish minority and Greek majority. Both Turkey and Greece threatened to intervene before outside peacemakers arranged a settlement. But in 1974, Greek military officers overthrew the president of Cyprus. Turkish troops then invaded the island and captured much territory. The Turks on Cyprus later declared the territory to be an independent state and set up a separate government. However, the Greek Cypriots protested strongly against these measures. Since then, efforts by Turkey, Greece, and Turkish and Greek Cypriots to form a new government for Cyprus have failed. See CYPRUS (History).

Recent Developments. High taxes, inflation, and political unrest have troubled Turkey since the late 1960's. At that time, radical groups of Turks began staging such terrorist acts as bombings, kidnappings, and murders in an attempt to overthrow the government. In the 1970's, deep divisions developed between secular and religious groups. Since the mid-1970's, much fighting has taken place between the two sides. Terrorist acts have continued in the country, and the radicals of the two groups have accused each other of committing the acts.

Control of Turkey's government changed hands many times during the 1970's. In 1971, Prime Minister Demirel resigned under pressure from the military. A series of prime ministers then failed to form a stable government. In 1975, Demirel again became prime minis-

ter. In the late 1970's, the office passed back and forth between Demirel and Bülent Ecevit of the Republican People's Party several times. Demirel became prime minister in November 1979. In 1980, army leaders took control of the government in an effort to halt the civil disorder in Turkey. In 1981, the military established an assembly to draft a new constitution as a step toward civilian rule. The assembly's work on the new constitution continued in 1982.   ANDREW C. HESS

Related Articles in WORLD BOOK include:

BIOGRAPHIES

Abdul-Hamid II	Inönü, Ismet	Muhammad Ali
Atatürk, Kemal	Muhammad II	Suleiman I
Barbarossa		

CITIES AND TOWNS

Ankara	Edirne	Izmir
Antioch	Istanbul	Tarsus

HISTORY

Armenia	Janissaries	Sèvres,
Balkans	Kurdistan	Treaty of
Berlin, Congress of	Ottoman Empire	Sultan
Byzantine Empire	Russo-Turkish	Thrace
Crimean War	Wars	Turks
Cyprus	Seljuks	World War I

PHYSICAL FEATURES

Ararat	Dardanelles	Marmara, Sea of
Bosporus	Euphrates River	

OTHER RELATED ARTICLES

Anatolia	Asia Minor	Middle East

Outline

I. Government
  A. The President
  B. The Prime Minister and Cabinet
  C. The Grand National Assembly
  D. Court System
  E. Local Government
  F. Political Parties
  G. Armed Forces

II. People
  A. Population and Ancestry
  B. Languages
  C. Ways of Life
  D. Housing
  E. Clothing
  F. Food and Drink
  G. Recreation
  H. Religion
  I. Education
  J. The Arts

III. The Land
  A. The Northern Plains
  B. The Western Valleys
  C. The Southern Plains
  D. The Western Plateau
  E. The Eastern Plateau
  F. The Northern Mountains
  G. The Southern Mountains
  H. The Mesopotamian Lowlands

IV. Climate

V. Economy
  A. Agriculture
  B. Manufacturing
  C. Mining
  D. Foreign Trade
  E. Transportation and Communication

VI. History

Questions

What is Turkey's chief economic activity?
Why was a new Turkish language developed?
What are the *Straits?*
How has the role of Turkish women changed since 1900?
Who are the Kurds?
Why is Turkey's agricultural production low?
How did Atatürk's modernization program revolutionize Turkish life during the 1920's?
Who were the Young Turks?
What are the chief foods of most Turks?
What was the Ottoman Empire?

Additional Resources

American University. *Turkey: A Country Study*. 3rd ed. U.S. Government Printing Office, 1980.

Bean, G. E. *Turkey Beyond the Maeander: An Archaeological Guide*. 2nd ed. Norton, 1980.

Hale, William M. *The Political and Economic Development of Modern Turkey*. St. Martin's, 1981.

Kinross, Lord. *The Ottoman Centuries: The Rise and Fall of the Turkish Empire*. Morrow, 1979.

Lewis, Bernard. *The Emergence of Modern Turkey*. 2nd ed. Oxford, 1968.

Spencer, William. *The Land and People of Turkey*. Rev. ed. Harper, 1972. For younger readers.

TURKEY is a large game bird of North America that is related to the pheasants. Biologists know of two kinds of wild turkeys. One is the *ocellated turkey* of Yucatán and Guatemala, a brilliantly colored bird with eyelike spots on its tail. The other is the wild turkey of Mexico and the United States. At one time many wild turkeys lived as far north as Maine and southern Ontario. The wild turkey was a favorite bird of the pioneer hunters.

The adult male turkey is about 4 feet (1.2 meters) long, with a plumage of metallic green, copper, and bronze. The body feathers have black tips. The tail and upper tail feathers of the wild turkey in eastern North America are deep reddish-brown. Those of the Mexican wild turkey have white tips. A long tuft of bristle-like feathers hangs from the center of the male's breast, and his legs have spurs. His head and neck have no feathers. A fleshy growth on the front of the head is called a *snood* or *dewbill*. The turkey has a pouchlike area at the front of his throat, called a *wattle*. Small reddish growths of skin at the base of the throat are called *caruncles*. The female turkey is smaller than the male turkey. Females look duller and few have bristles on the breast. Male turkeys are called *toms*, and females are called *hens*. The name for a young turkey is *poult*.

Wild turkeys gather in small flocks in the forests.

Leading Turkey-Producing States and Provinces

Number of turkeys produced in 1977

Minnesota	🦃🦃🦃🦃🦃🦃🦃🦃🦃🦃🦃
	22,739,000 turkeys
California	🦃🦃🦃🦃🦃🦃🦃🦃🦃
	17,244,000 turkeys
North Carolina	🦃🦃🦃🦃🦃🦃🦃🦃
	16,500,000 turkeys
Arkansas	🦃🦃🦃🦃🦃
	10,258,000 turkeys
Missouri	🦃🦃🦃🦃🦃
	9,846,000 turkeys
Virginia	🦃🦃🦃🦃
	8,694,000 turkeys
Texas	🦃🦃🦃🦃
	8,600,000 turkeys
Ontario	🦃🦃🦃🦃
	7,006,000 turkeys
Iowa	🦃🦃🦃
	6,009,000 turkeys
Wisconsin	🦃🦃🦃
	5,544,000 turkeys

Sources: U.S. Department of Agriculture; Statistics Canada.

Louis C. Williams

Domestic Turkeys have long provided Thanksgiving and Christmas dinner for many families in the United States.

They eat small nuts, seeds, insects, berries, and other small fruits. At night wild turkeys rest in trees. They build their crude nests of dry leaves on the ground. Turkey eggs are about twice as large as ordinary chicken eggs. They have a pale creamy-tan color, speckled with brown.

Domestic Turkey Breeding is an important part of the American poultry industry. Turkey meat is nourishing and delicious.

The wild turkeys of southern Mexico were probably first domesticated, or tamed, by the Mexicans. Spaniards brought tame Mexican turkeys to Europe in 1519, and they reached England in 1524. The Pilgrims brought several to America in 1620.

Seven main varieties of domesticated turkeys live in America. The largest is the *Bronze* turkey. The adult male weighs up to 50 pounds (23 kilograms), and the adult hen up to 16 pounds (7 kilograms). The Bronze turkey has the white tail-feather tips of its wild ancestor. Its feathers are dull black, glossed with red and green on the front, and bronze in the rear.

The White Holland Turkey is not related to European white turkeys. It is thought to be of American origin.

USDA

TURKEY CARVING

Other Varieties include the *Beltsville Small White*, the *Narragansett*, the *White Holland*, the *Bourbon Red*, the *Black*, and the *Slate*. All except the Beltsville Small White are about the same size. Adult males weigh as much as 33 pounds (15 kilograms), and young hens weigh up to 14 pounds (6 kilograms). The Beltsville Small White males weigh up to 23 pounds (10 kilograms) and the young females weigh as little as 11 pounds (5 kilograms). The Beltsville Small White and the White Holland are all white. The Narragansett resembles the Bronze turkey, but does not have the red and green or bronze colors. The Bourbon Red is a brownish-red with white wings. The Black turkey is all black, and the Slate turkey has slate-colored feathers.

Turkeys need much the same care as chickens, but need more space to live in. They are more delicate, especially when young. They are particularly susceptible to cold rains. Young turkeys need more nutrients than young chickens because they grow faster.

The United States turkey-raising industry produces a gross income of about $905 million a year. The business is somewhat seasonal because people buy most turkeys during the winter holiday seasons.

Breeding has improved the meat on the turkey. The domesticated bird develops a larger body than its wild relative, has shorter legs and neck, and also more flesh. Large turkeys are still popular for use in restaurants but are too large for most families to eat at one meal. To solve this problem, the turkey industry has developed boneless turkey roasts and turkey steaks. Food companies make such products as cold cuts and hot dogs from processed turkey meat.

Scientific Classification. The turkey belongs to the turkey family, *Meleagrididae*. The ocellated turkey is genus *Agriocharis*, species *A. ocellata*. The American wild turkey is *Meleagris gallopavo*.   JOHN W. WEST

See also FARM AND FARMING (picture: Poultry Farming); POULTRY (Raising Poultry).

TURKEY CARVING. See MEAT (pictures).

TURKEY RED. See MADDER.

TURKEY RED, a wheat variety. See WHEAT (Early Days in the United States).

TURKEY VULTURE. See BUZZARD.

TURKIC PEOPLES. See RUSSIA (People).

TURKISH BATH is one of the most thorough cleansing baths known. The Turks of medieval times believed in taking hot-air baths to preserve health, and their warriors spread this custom in most of the Middle East and parts of Europe. People in the Western World liked taking such hot-air baths, and they called them *Turkish baths*.

The process of taking such a bath is simple. Bathers wear only bathing clothes, or none at all. They first enter a sweating room which has dry heat in temperatures of about 160° F. (71° C). They then move to a room in which wet steam reaches a temperature of about 128° F. (53° C). The wet steam causes the bathers to perspire freely. The skin is then washed with warm water and soap or salve, and an attendant massages the body muscles. After being completely scrubbed and rubbed, the bathers dry off with a rough cloth or towel. Sometimes the hard skin of the feet is rubbed off with pumice stone. The bathers next take a cold shower or a swim, and then rest until their body temperature returns to normal.

The Turkish bath purifies the body of grease and dirt, and benefits many muscular ills. It is also sometimes used to relieve acute alcoholism. But persons who have heart trouble or a kidney disease should never take a Turkish bath. The *Russian bath* is similar to the Turkish bath, except that only steam is used. The Finns have a system of dry-heat bathing called a *sauna* (see SAUNA).

TURKMENISTAN is a region that makes up the Turkmen Soviet Socialist Republic, one of the 15 republics of the Soviet Union. It lies north of Iran and Afghanistan, east of the Caspian Sea, and mostly west of the Amu Darya River. For location, see RUSSIA (political map). It has an area of 188,456 square miles (488,100 square kilometers), and a population of 2,759,000. Most of Turkmenistan is a desert known as Kara Kum. Crops can be grown only by irrigation. Farming is the chief work. The leading products are cotton, wool, astrakhan (a fur taken from young lambs), a special breed of Turkoman horses, and Karakul sheep. A characteristic part of the Turkmenian national costume is the high wool hat. The most thickly settled region is a strip of hilly country along the southeastern border. Most of the people are Muslims and many belong to wandering Turkish tribes. The capital is Ashkhabad. Turkmenistan became a *republic* (major political division of Russia) in 1925.   GEORGE KISH

See also MERV.

TURKS are Turkic-speaking peoples of Turkey and central Asia. They include the Tartars, the Kirgiz, and other groups that live in the Balkans, Siberia, and Mongolia. Turks make up Russia's largest non-Slavic minority group.

Turks use about 25 Turkic languages that are closely related but differ greatly in pronunciation and vocabulary. Almost all Turks are Muslims.

The ancestors of Turks include the Huns and other nomadic peoples. The Huns controlled central Asia during the A.D. 300's and 400's. In the 1000's, the Seljuk Turks seized Persia (now Iran) and then took over Asia Minor.

The Ottoman Turks appeared in Asia Minor during the late 1200's. By the 1500's, they had created an empire that included much of the Middle East, southeastern Europe, and northern Africa. The Republic of Turkey succeeded the Ottoman Empire in 1923. Since then, the government has abolished many traditional ways of life in Turkey.   JOHN R. KRUEGER

See also KIRGIZ; SELJUKS; TARTARS; TURKEY.

TURKS AND CAICOS ISLANDS are barren, sandy islands that lie in the West Indies, about 90 miles (140 kilometers) north of the Dominican Republic. The two island groups form a British dependency in the Commonwealth of Nations. The main islands are Grand Turk and Salt Cay in the Turks Islands, and South Caicos, East Caicos, Grand or Middle Caicos, North Caicos, Providenciales, and West Caicos in the Caicos Islands. For location, see WEST INDIES (map).

The islands cover a total land area of 166 square miles (430 square kilometers). Many of the 7,000 residents engage in fishing. Lobster is the chief export. The capital and largest city is Grand Turk on the island of Grand Turk. In 1512, the Spanish explorer Juan Ponce de León sighted the islands.

TURKU, *TOOR koo* (pop. 165,004; met. area pop. 235,004), Finland's third largest city, lies on the Baltic Sea, 90 miles (140 kilometers) northwest of Helsinki (see FINLAND [map]). Its port handles lumber and dairy products. Turku has shipyards, steel and lumber mills, and machinery and tobacco plants. It has an ancient cathedral, and Finnish and Swedish universities. Turku was founded in 1157, and was the capital of Finland until 1812.   PEKKA KALEVI HAMALAINEN

TURMERIC, *TUR mer ik,* is a plant which grows in southern Asia. Its fleshy roots are the source of a substance, also called turmeric, which is used mainly for dyeing. These roots are hard and tough. On the outside, they are brownish- or yellowish-green. When they are broken, they show a resinous interior which varies from orange-brown to deep reddish-brown. The roots are ready for the market after being cleaned, boiled for some hours, and then dried in an oven. The yellowish powder which they yield when ground has a strong, aromatic odor and a strong, pungent taste.

Turmeric has been used for hundreds of years as a dye-stuff and as a spice. It is an important ingredient in curry powder and is used to color mustard. It does not yield a fast color, however, as a dyestuff. It has gone out of use as a medicine, but in India people mix it with milk to form a cooling lotion for the skin and eyes. Turmeric is useful in chemistry in making test papers for alkalies. With the addition of alkali, white paper soaked in a tincture of turmeric turns to reddish-brown and, on drying, to violet.

Scientific Classification. Turmeric belongs to the ginger family, *Zingiberaceae.* It is classified as genus *Curcuma,* species *C. longa.*   HAROLD NORMAN MOLDENKE

See also CURRY.

TURNER, FREDERICK JACKSON (1861-1932), an American historian, became famous for a theory set forth in his paper, "The Significance of the Frontier in American History." Turner's theory emphasized the influence of an abundance of free land in strengthening democratic beliefs in the United States. He viewed the frontier, not as a line between east and west, but as a process that changed constantly, depending on the new area's natural resources and the backgrounds and beliefs of the people who moved into it. Turner founded a new school of thought in American history when he read this paper at the World's Columbian Exposition, which was held in Chicago in 1893.

Another work, *The Significance of Sections in American History* (1932), won the Pulitzer prize for history in 1933. Turner also pioneered in using the materials and methods of the geographer, the economist, the sociologist, and the statistician in history. He was born in Portage, Wis., and taught at the University of Wisconsin and Harvard University.   MERLE CURTI

TURNER, J. M. W. (1775-1851), was perhaps the greatest landscape painter in the history of English art. In many oil paintings and water colors, Turner departed from traditional ways of dealing with atmosphere, light, and color. Earlier artists had treated such elements realistically. In Turner's works, forms and outlines seem to dissolve into shimmering mist, steam, or smoke, or into the intense light of bright sky or water. By changing the way artists represented reality, Turner began a process continued by the impressionists and many other artists of the late 1800's and the 1900's.

Joseph Mallord William Turner was born in London. He began art training at the Royal Academy of Arts at the age of 14 and became an accomplished water-colorist. His early style shows the influence of the English artists J. R. Cozens and Thomas Girtin. The young painter was also influenced by the landscapes of the French painters Nicolas Poussin and Claude. Beginning in 1790, Turner exhibited at the Royal Academy. He was elected a member of the academy in 1802.

Turner's early paintings emphasize drama and romance. His oil painting *The Shipwreck* (1805) is an example. Later in his career, Turner stressed atmosphere in his pictures. He traveled widely, producing thousands of water color sketches. In many of these sketches, he experimented with the brilliance of color. During the 1830's and 1840's, Turner painted a series of water color views of Venice that rank among his masterpieces. Turner achieved a colorful, abstract quality in such oil paintings as *The Slave Ship* (1840) and *Rain, Steam, and Speed—The Great Western Railway* (1844). Many of his oil paintings reveal his fascination with the visual effects of fire and water. A famous example, *Burning of the Houses of Parliament* (about 1835), appears in PAINTING (Romanticism).   DOUGLAS K. S. HYLAND

See also RUSKIN, JOHN.

TURNER, NAT (1800-1831), a Negro slave and preacher, led the most famous slave revolt in United States history. In 1831, Turner and from 60 to 70 other slaves killed about 60 whites in Virginia. The victims included the family of Joseph Travis, who was Turner's owner.

More whites died during the rebellion led by Turner than in any other in the nation's history. The Virginia militia captured and hanged about 20 of the slaves, including Turner. In addition, angry whites killed about 100 innocent slaves. The rebellion caused the Southern States to pass strict laws for the control of slaves, especially those who were preachers.

Turner was born on a plantation in Southampton County, Virginia. His parents and grandmother encouraged him to become educated and to fight slavery. Through the years, Turner became the property of several other slave owners. The son of one of his masters taught him to read and write. Turner became known as a forceful preacher who believed that God wanted him to free the slaves. This conviction led to his planning the rebellion.   FRANK OTTO GATELL

Additional Resources

APTHEKER, HERBERT. *Nat Turner's Rebellion: Together With the Full Text of the So-Called "Confessions" of Nat Turner Made in Prison, 1831.* Humanities, 1966. Reprint of 1937 ed.
FONER, ERIC. *Nat Turner.* Prentice-Hall, 1971.

TURNER, ROSCOE (1895-1970), was an American racing pilot and aviation business executive. He won the 300-mile Thompson Trophy race in 1934, 1938, and 1939. He won the Bendix Trophy Race in 1933, and finished second in the London-Melbourne race in 1934. He also set several transcontinental speed records between 1932 and 1934. Turner served as an army pilot in World War I. He became board chairman of his own aviation firm, the Turner Aeronautical Corporation, in 1946. He was born in Corinth, Miss.   ROBERT B. HOTZ

Purple-Top Turnips Are a Favorite of Gardeners.

TURNIP, *TUR nuhp,* is a fast-growing, cool-season vegetable. It belongs to the mustard branch of the cabbage family. The upper part of the root becomes greatly enlarged to form the main part we eat. The leaves can also be eaten, and people in the Southern States use them to make a favorite potherb, or greens. Turnips grow in northern Europe, the United States, and Canada.

No one knows when turnips were first eaten. They were a common food of both the Greeks and the Romans, and have long been a favorite food in England and northern Europe. People have grown them in the United States since early colonial times.

Turnips are easy to grow. They are well suited for home gardens, and the seeds can be sown directly in the rows about two weeks before the last frost of spring. Gardeners thin the plants so they are about 2 inches (5 centimeters) apart in the rows. The crop is ready for harvest in about two months. The fall crop should be sown about two months before the first frost of autumn. This crop can be stored at cool temperatures.

Turnips are often attacked by turnip aphids. These may be controlled by spraying or dusting the plants with nicotine sulfate.

Turnip greens are an excellent food. They are high in vitamins A, B complex, and C. They give flavor to the diet, and bulk, which tends to regulate elimination.

Scientific Classification. The turnip belongs to the mustard family, *Cruciferae.* It is classified as genus *Brassica,* species *B. rapa.*　　　　　　　　ERVIN L. DENISEN

TURNIP, RUSSIAN. See RUTABAGA.
TURNIP, SWEDISH. See RUTABAGA.

TURNPIKE is a road upon which a traveler must pay a fee, or toll, in order to use the highway. These roads were named *turnpikes* because in the early days travelers stopped at turnstiles, or turnpikes, to pay their fares before traveling farther. The first record of tolls being collected was on a Persian military road between Babylon and Syria about 2000 B.C.

Private investors brought the idea of building turnpikes to the United States from England. They formed turnpike companies to build the roads, and operated them for profit. The first turnpike in the United States was built in Virginia in 1785. In 1795, the Lancaster Turnpike Company completed a stone-surfaced road that stretched 62 miles (100 kilometers) between Philadelphia and Lancaster, Pa. The company, chartered in Pennsylvania in April, 1792, built the road at a cost of $465,000. From 1792 to 1810, investors organized 175 turnpike companies in New England. These companies spent over $5 million to build and improve nearly 3,000 miles (4,800 kilometers) of road.

Turnpike companies brought about many improvements in New England roads. They built bridges and surfaced the roads. Stage lines came into wide use as a result of the building of turnpikes. But in spite of the good they did, turnpikes proved to be poor business investments. By 1825 turnpike stocks in the United States were nearly worthless, because the toll fees seldom paid for more than the cost of keeping up the roads.

State and local governments in the United States took over the task of building and maintaining roads. Interest in turnpikes revived during the depression of the 1930's. Several important toll roads were built after World War II, when taxes failed to provide enough money for new highways.　　　　ROBERT G. HENNES

See also PENNSYLVANIA TURNPIKE; ROADS AND HIGHWAYS; TRAILS OF EARLY DAYS.

TURNSOLE. See HELIOTROPE.

TURNSTONE is the name given to two kinds of small shore birds. The name refers to their habit of turning over shells and pebbles with their bills as they look for food. The *ruddy turnstone* nests only in arctic regions. In winter it flies to far southern shores, reaching both coasts of the United States in its migrations. It is about 9 inches (23 centimeters) long, with black, white, and

Turnstones Often Look Under Pebbles for Food.

reddish-brown feathers. The *black turnstone* is slightly larger and lacks the reddish color. It nests along the shores of the Bering Sea to the Sitka district, and winters from southeastern Alaska to Lower California.

Scientific Classification. Turnstones belong to the sandpiper family, *Scolopacidae*. The ruddy turnstone is genus *Arenarius*, species *A. interpres*. The black turnstone is *A. melanocephala*. ALFRED M. BAILEY

TURNTABLE. See PHONOGRAPH.

TURNVEREIN, *TURN vuh ryn*, or TURNER, is a name given to the athletic organizations established by Friedrich Ludwig Jahn in Germany in the early 1800's (see JAHN, FRIEDRICH L.). German immigrants formed the first turnvereins in the United States in Philadelphia and Cincinnati in 1848. Such organizations are usually found in large centers of German population. Membership in turnvereins in the United States is about 20,000. The national organization, The American Turners, has headquarters at 1550 Clinton Ave. North, Rochester, N.Y. 14621.   Critically reviewed by the AMERICAN TURNERS

TURPENTINE is a colorless or yellowish liquid that has a strong odor and is highly flammable. It is used chiefly in making chemical products and synthetic rubber. The chemical products include disinfectants, insecticides, medicines, and perfumes. Turpentine is also used as a thinner in paints and varnishes and for removing paint stains from clothing and the skin. Some turpentine is used in the processing and flavoring of certain foods.

Turpentine is made chiefly from longleaf pines and slash pines, which grow throughout the Southeastern United States. There are three types of turpentine. They are, in order of importance: (1) sulfate turpentine, (2) wood turpentine, and (3) gum turpentine.

Sulfate turpentine accounts for about 85 per cent of the turpentine produced in the United States. It is made from trees as they are converted into pulp. A vapor containing the turpentine forms during the pulping process. When the vapor cools, it becomes a liquid that contains sulfate turpentine.

Wood turpentine is produced from stumps and logs. The wood is gathered and taken to a steam distillation plant. There, it is shredded and mixed with a *solvent*, a chemical that dissolves other substances. The solution is then steamed to collect the turpentine. Wood turpentine makes up about 10 per cent of the turpentine made in the United States.

Gum turpentine is produced by *wounding* (cutting) the bark of living trees. A solution of sulfuric acid is applied to the wound, which measures about $\frac{1}{2}$ inch (1.3 centimeters) wide and $\frac{1}{2}$ inch deep. The acid causes gum to ooze out for as long as four weeks, until the wound closes. The gum is collected in metal cups. The wound is then reopened and a sulfuric acid solution is applied again. This procedure is repeated throughout the gathering period, which lasts from March to October. The gum is taken to a steam distillery where it is made into turpentine. Gum turpentine accounts for about 5 per cent of the turpentine that is produced in the United States.   HARRY E. TROXELL

TURPIN, DICK (1706-1739), was an English robber whose exploits have appeared in English legends and literature. As a youth, he joined a band of thieves who stole farm animals and deer. Later, he worked with Tom King as a highwayman, robbing travelers along the road from London to Oxford. He accidentally killed King while shooting at a constable. Finally, Turpin was arrested in York for stealing horses, was found guilty, and was hanged. William Ainsworth's novel *Rookwood* (1834) described Turpin's famous ride from London to Yorkshire on his horse, Black Bess. The story of this ride was originally told of an earlier highwayman named "Nicks." Richard Turpin was born in Hempstead, Essex, the son of an innkeeper.   KNOX WILSON

TURQUOISE, *TUR koyz*, or *TUR qwoyz*, is an opaque, semiprecious stone in varied shades of green and blue. This gem stone occurs in rock deposits in Turkestan and Asia Minor, and in New Mexico, Colorado, Arizona and Nevada. Its name means *Turkish stone*.

Turquoise consists chiefly of hydrous phosphate of aluminum. Small quantities of iron give it a greenish tint, and the presence of a small amount of copper gives the stone its blue color. The color may fade if it is exposed to strong light or heat, and because turquoise is slightly porous, it may absorb dirt or grease.

Turquoise has been a favorite gem for thousands of years. The Egyptians used it as early as 4000 B.C. In Iran, where fine turquoise has been mined for centuries, it is the national gem. Many of the people of the Orient used the turquoise as a gem and as an amulet to ward off illness and misfortune, and the earliest Mexicans wore turquoise jewelry. The stone is possibly the most widely used of all gem minerals.

Today, people prize most the blue turquoise, but in ancient times green stones were most popular. Persian and Mexican jewelers often used turquoise as an inlay. It was popular in the United States in the 1800's in the form of beads, and today is seen in Indian style jewelry. The turquoise is one of the December birthstones.

Odontolite (bone turquoise) closely resembles turquoise. It is made from fragments of fossil bone colored blue with phosphate of iron. It can be distinguished from turquoise under a microscope.   FREDERICK H. POUGH

See also GEM (color picture).

TURRET is a towerlike structure. In architecture, a turret may be a small circular or square section at the corner of a building. Turrets are also used in warfare. The first military turrets were towers built on wheels to help soldiers in climbing and in battering down the walls of castles and towns. Some of these turrets were as much as 20 stories tall. They held soldiers, siege engines, battering rams, and sometimes even bridges.

Present-day naval and military turrets are heavily armored towers used for mounting and protecting guns fired from inside. They usually are turned by machinery to permit the guns to be fired in any direction. Six-inch and heavier guns are built into turrets in naval vessels. These form the primary batteries of battleships and cruisers. Naval turrets often mount two or three guns in sizes up to 16-inch. The first warship with a revolving gun turret was the *Monitor*, built by John Ericsson in 1862 for use by the Union navy in the American Civil War. Airplanes with turrets were developed during World War II. These turrets revolved by electrical or hydraulic power, and mounted two or four .50-caliber machine guns. They enabled the gunner to track his target without having to resist the pressure of rushing air.   THEODORE ROPP

E. R. Degginger

Clem Haagner, Bruce Coleman Inc.

William M. Stephens, Tom Stack & Associates

Turtles Live in a Variety of Habitats. The painted turtle, *upper left,* makes its home in fresh water. It uses its webbed feet for both swimming and walking. The green turtle, *lower left,* dwells in the sea. It has long, paddlelike flippers. The leopard tortoise, *above,* lives on land. Its stumpy legs and feet are well suited for walking on dry, rough ground.

TURTLE is the only reptile with a shell. Most kinds of turtles can pull their head, legs, and tail into their shell, which serves as a suit of armor. Few other backboned animals have such excellent natural protection.

Turtles, like all reptiles, are cold-blooded—that is, their body temperature stays about the same as the temperature of the surrounding air or water. Turtles cannot be warm and active in cold weather, and so they cannot live in regions that are cold throughout the year. They live almost everywhere else—in deserts, forests, grasslands, lakes, marshes, ponds, rivers, and the sea.

There are about 240 species of turtles, about 50 of which live in North America north of Mexico. Some turtles live only on land, but others spend almost their entire life in the sea. Still other species dwell mainly in fresh water or live about equally on land and in fresh water. Many turtles live their entire life within a few miles or kilometers of where they were hatched. But large numbers of sea turtles migrate thousands of miles or kilometers from their birthplace.

Turtles vary greatly in size. The largest turtle species, the leatherback turtle, grows from 4 to 8 feet (1.2 to 2.4 meters) long. But the common mud turtle measures

Carl H. Ernst, the contributor of this article, is Associate Professor of Biology at George Mason University and coauthor of Turtles of the United States.

only 3 to 5 inches (7.5 to 12.4 centimeters) in length.

Sea turtles, all of which swim rapidly, rank as the fastest turtles. One of these species, the green turtle, can swim for brief periods at a speed of nearly 20 miles (32 kilometers) per hour. On land, many kinds of turtles are slow, lumbering creatures. But some kinds of land turtles can move with surprising speed. For example, the smooth softshell turtle, a fresh-water species of North America, often can outrun a man on level ground.

The first turtles lived more than 185 million years ago. The *Archelon*, a sea turtle of about 25 million years ago, grew about 12 feet (3.7 meters) long. This creature died out, as did many other species. Today, many species of turtles face extinction because man hunts them for food and for their shells. He also destroys their natural homes to make way for cities and farms.

At one time, pet shops throughout the United States sold thousands of painted turtles and red-eared turtles yearly. But medical researchers discovered that many of these turtles carried bacteria that cause *salmonella poisoning*, a serious illness in human beings. In 1975, the U.S. Food and Drug Administration banned the sale of most pet turtles.

The Body of a Turtle

Shell. Most species of turtles can pull their head, legs, and tail into their shell for protection. A few kinds of turtles, particularly sea turtles, cannot withdraw into their shell.

A turtle's shell consists of two layers. The inner layer is made up of bony plates and is actually part of the skeleton. Among most species, the outer layer consists of hard, horny structures called *scutes*, which are formed from skin tissue. Soft-shelled turtles and the leatherback turtle have an outer layer of tough skin rather than scutes. The part of the shell that covers the turtle's back is called the *carapace*, and the part that covers the belly is called the *plastron*. The carapace and the plastron are joined along each side of the body by a bony structure called the *bridge*.

Most turtles that live on land have a high, domed shell. Those that live in water have a flatter, more streamlined shell. Some species of turtles, including Blanding's turtle, box turtles, and mud turtles, have a hinged plastron. These turtles can close the plastron tightly against the carapace after withdrawing into their shell.

The shells of some kinds of turtles are plain black, brown, or dark green. But others have bright green, orange, red, or yellow markings.

Head. The head of most species of turtles is covered by hard scales. Turtles have no teeth, but they have a beak with a hard, sharp edge that they use to cut food. Many turtles have powerful jaws, with which they tear food and capture prey.

Legs and Feet. A turtle's legs and feet vary according to the habitat of the species. Land turtles, particularly tortoises, have heavy, short, clublike legs and feet. Most fresh-water turtles have longer legs and webbed feet. Sea turtles have legs shaped like long paddles, with flippers instead of feet.

William M. Partington, NAS · Hladik, Jacana

Turtles Have a Hard Beak. Among most species, such as the mud turtle, *left*, the beak is not covered. But a soft-shelled turtle, *right*, has fleshy lips that cover its beak.

The hip bones and shoulder bones of the turtles, unlike those of any other animal, are inside the ribcage. This unusual feature enables most kinds of turtles to pull their legs inside their shell. The species that are unable to withdraw their legs cannot do so because the shell is too small.

Senses. Turtles have a well-developed sense of sight and of touch. Scientific experiments indicate that they also have a good sense of smell, at least for nearby objects. Turtles have a middle ear and inner ear, and a *tympanic membrane* (eardrum) forms their outer ear. A turtle can hear low-pitched sounds about as well as a human being can.

The Life of a Turtle

Young. Turtles hatch from eggs, which are fertilized within the female's body. One mating can result in the

The Skeleton of a Land Turtle

Bottom view

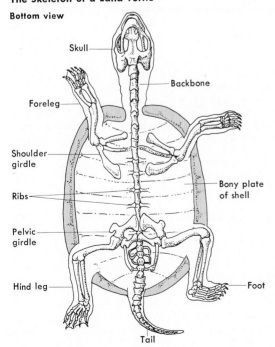

- Skull
- Backbone
- Foreleg
- Shoulder girdle
- Ribs
- Pelvic girdle
- Hind leg
- Bony plate of shell
- Foot
- Tail

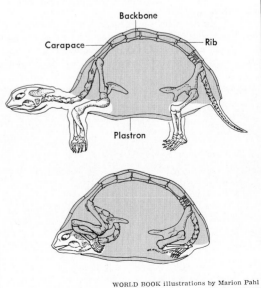

A Turtle's Shell provides excellent protection. Most turtles retract their head by pulling their long, flexible neck straight back in a U-curve. Scales protect the parts of the body exposed at the shell openings.

- Backbone
- Carapace
- Rib
- Plastron

WORLD BOOK illustrations by Marion Pahl

R. R. Pawlowski, Bruce Coleman Inc.

All Turtles Lay Their Eggs on Land. Among most species, the female digs a hole in the ground, lays her eggs and covers them, and then leaves them. The heat of the sun hatches the eggs. The female shown above is one of the side-necked species.

fertilization of all the eggs of a female for several years. Most kinds of turtles lay their eggs between late spring and late autumn, and some lay eggs more than once during this period. For example, a green turtle may lay as many as seven *clutches* (groups) of eggs during one breeding season.

All turtles, including sea and fresh-water species, lay their eggs on land. Among most species, the female digs a hole in the ground with her back feet when ready to lay her eggs. She lays the eggs in the hole and covers them with soil, sand, or rotting plant matter. The number of eggs laid varies. An African pancake tortoise lays only one egg per clutch, but a sea turtle may lay 200 eggs at a time.

The female turtle walks away after covering her eggs and does not return. The warmth of the sun hatches the eggs. Newly hatched turtles must dig their way to the surface of the ground, obtain food, and protect themselves—all on their own.

Many animals prey on turtle eggs and newborn turtles. Various birds and mammals flock to beaches and eat baby sea turtles as they crawl toward the water. Fish attack many others as they enter the sea. Skunks,

Alan Blank, Bruce Coleman Inc.

A Baby Desert Tortoise hatches from its egg after about 100 days. Young turtles have a horny growth on the tip of their beak. This growth, called a *caruncle*, helps break open the shell.

raccoons, and snakes dig up the nests of fresh-water turtles and devour the eggs.

Scientists believe turtles live longer than any other backboned animal. Some box turtles and tortoises have lived more than 100 years. Most of a turtle's growth occurs during the animal's first 5 to 10 years. The turtle continues to grow after reaching this age, but at a much slower rate.

Food. Most kinds of turtles eat both animals and plants. The organisms eaten by a turtle vary among the species. A few kinds of turtles, including green turtles and tortoises, feed almost entirely on plants. Certain fresh-water species, such as map turtles and soft-shelled turtles, eat chiefly animals.

Hibernation. Turtles, like other cold-blooded animals, cannot remain active in cold weather. Species that live in regions with harsh winters must hibernate. Most fresh-water turtles hibernate by burrowing into the warm, muddy bottom of a pond, stream, or other body of water. Land turtles bury themselves in soil or under rotting vegetation.

Some species of turtles survive hot, dry periods by going into a state of limited activity called *estivation*. Estivation somewhat resembles hibernation.

Kinds of Turtles

There are seven main groups of turtles: (1) mud and musk turtles, (2) pond and marsh turtles, (3) sea turtles, (4) side-necked turtles, (5) snapping turtles, (6) soft-shelled turtles, and (7) tortoises.

Mud and Musk Turtles make up a family of 23 fresh-water species. They live in the Western Hemisphere, particularly in Central America. Mud and musk turtles of the United States include the common mud turtle, common musk turtle, razor-backed musk turtle, and yellow mud turtle.

Few mud and musk turtles grow more than 6 inches (15 centimeters) long. But they have large heads and strong jaws, and they may bite. When disturbed, these turtles give off a foul-smelling substance called *musk* from glands in front of their hind legs. The common musk turtle, whose musk has a particularly strong, unpleasant scent, is often called the "stinkpot."

Pond and Marsh Turtles form the largest family of turtles—more than 80 species. Members of this family live in Asia, Europe, North and South America, and northern Africa. Pond and marsh turtles of North America include the box turtle, chicken turtle, diamondback terrapin, map turtle, painted turtle, red-eared turtle, spotted turtle, and wood turtle. Many of these species are brightly colored, with green, red, or yellow markings on their head, legs, and shell. Most pond and marsh turtles found in the United States are small, but some kinds may grow more than a foot (30 centimeters) long. The majority of pond and marsh turtles live in lakes, ponds, rivers, streams, and tidewater areas. A few species, including box turtles and wood turtles, dwell mainly on land.

Sea Turtles. There are at least seven species of sea turtles. Six of them—the green turtle, the flatback, the hawksbill, the loggerhead, the Atlantic ridley, and the Pacific ridley—have bony, scute-covered shells. Most zoologists classify these species into one family. The

Giuseppe Mazza

Leonard Lee Rue, Bruce Coleman Inc.

Box Turtles are well protected by their shell. The *carapace* (upper shell) forms a high dome, *left*. The *plastron* (lower shell) is hinged and can be pulled up against the carapace when the turtle is inside the shell, *above*. The box turtle shown above has its plastron only partly pulled up.

seventh species, the leatherback, forms its own family. Its shell has far fewer bones than that of the other sea turtles and is covered with skin rather than scutes. Sea turtles live in warm seas throughout the world. All except the Australian flatback may be found in the coastal waters of the United States.

Sea turtles rank among the largest species. Even the smallest ones, the ridleys, grow up to 28 inches (70 centimeters) long and weigh nearly 100 pounds (45 kilograms). A leatherback may measure 8 feet (2.4 meters) long and weigh 1,500 pounds (680 kilograms). Sea turtles swim by beating their flippers much as a bird flaps its wings. Other turtles swim with a back-and-forth paddling motion. Sea turtles cannot withdraw into their shell, and so they depend on their size and swimming speed for defense.

Female sea turtles do not normally leave the water except to lay their eggs. Most of the males never return to land after entering the sea as hatchlings. The females often migrate thousands of miles or kilometers to reach their breeding beaches. They drag themselves onto a sandy beach, bury their eggs, and then return to the sea. Female sea turtles are almost completely helpless while they are on land.

Side-Necked Turtles bend their neck sideways when withdrawing their head, instead of pulling straight back into their shell. There are about 50 species of these turtles, which are divided into two families. They live in Africa, Australia, and South America, mainly in areas south of the equator.

Snapping Turtles make up a family of large, freshwater turtles that live only in North America, Central America, and northern South America. There are three species of snappers. The common snapper, which may be found from Canada to Ecuador, grows as long as 19 inches (47 centimeters). The Florida snapping turtle, which lives only in Florida, closely resembles the common snapper. The third species, the alligator snapper,

Jim Teason

The Common Snapping Turtle has a small shell in relation to the rest of its body. The snapper cannot retreat into its shell for protection, and so it depends on its strong jaws for defense.

E. R. Degginger

A Soft-Shelled Turtle has a round, flat shell covered by leathery skin. Most softshells also have paddlelike legs and a long, flexible nose that serves as an underwater breathing tube.

428a

The Galapagos Tortoise ranks as one of the largest land turtles. This huge reptile measures up to 4 feet (1.2 meters) long and may weigh more than 600 pounds (270 kilograms).

Lloyd McCarthy, Tom Stack & Associates

lives in the Central and Southeastern United States. Alligator snappers are the largest turtles of North America, except for sea turtles. An alligator snapper may measure more than 24 inches (60 centimeters) long and weigh over 200 pounds (91 kilograms).

Snapping turtles eat small water animals, such as fish, frogs, insects, snails, and young waterfowl. They also feed on plants, especially algae. Snappers have a large head and strong jaws. They may bite fiercely if disturbed. Snappers have a small shell that does not give much protection, and so they depend on their strong, sharp-edged jaws for defense.

Soft-Shelled Turtles make up a family of 22 species. These fresh-water turtles have a shell covered by smooth skin. They live in Africa, Asia, and North America. Three species of soft-shelled turtles—the smooth softshell, the spiny softshell, and the Florida softshell—live in the continental United States. The Chinese softshell, an Asian species, is found in Hawaii.

Unlike other turtles, softshells have fleshy lips that cover their beak. Most kinds of softshells also have a long, flexible nose that serves as an underwater breathing tube. Most softshells do not grow much longer than a foot (30 centimeters), but some species measure up to 3 feet (91 centimeters) long. A soft-shelled turtle may bite when disturbed, and it can strike with lightning speed.

Tortoises form a family of about 40 species. These land turtles live in Africa, Asia, Europe, North and South America, and on certain ocean islands. The tortoises of the Aldabra Islands and the Galapagos Islands are the world's largest land turtles. These huge reptiles may measure up to 4 feet (1.2 meters) long and may weigh up to 600 pounds (270 kilograms).

Three species of tortoises live in the United States. The desert tortoise makes its home in the dry areas of the Southwest. The gopher tortoise lives in sandy-soiled areas of the Southeast. The Texas tortoise is found living in the scrub forests of southern Texas.

Tortoises live only on land. Most species are slow-moving creatures with a high, domed shell. But the African pancake tortoise has a flat, flexible shell. When in danger, this tortoise runs quickly into a crack in a nearby rock. It then takes a deep breath and inflates its body, wedging itself tightly in the crack.

Turtles and Human Beings

The activities of human beings are a serious threat to the survival of many turtles, and turtle conservation must improve to prevent certain species from becoming extinct. Wildlife experts classify more than 40 kinds of turtles as endangered. These rare turtles include many types of tortoises, most sea turtles, and the box turtle of North America.

People have long used turtle meat and eggs for food and turtle shells as ornaments. The most threatened species include the most economically valuable ones. For example, the green turtle is a popular food in many parts of the world. The use of its meat and eggs by humans has seriously endangered its survival. The hawksbill turtle also has almost been killed off because *tortoise shell*, a substance used in making ornamental objects, comes from its carapace.

Human beings further endanger turtles by poisoning their homes with pollution. In addition, they continually replace forests, swamps, and other natural areas with cities and farms. This action almost ensures the extinction of certain kinds of turtles.

Some governments forbid the capture of rare species of turtles. Turtle preserves have been established in certain areas, and scientists are experimenting with raising valuable species on turtle farms. But zoologists must know more about how turtles live in the wild to save many of the endangered ones.

Scientific Classification. Turtles make up the order Testudines (sometimes called Chelonia) in the class Reptilia and the phylum Chordata.   CARL H. ERNST

See also TERRAPIN; TORTOISE.

TURTLE MOUNTAIN. See ALBERTA (Places to Visit [Frank Slide]; picture).

TURTLE MOUNTAINS. See NORTH DAKOTA (Land Regions).

Eric Hosking

The Turtledove Is a Small, Ash-Gray European Bird.

TURTLEDOVE is a small European dove. The turtledove lives in woods and on farms, and migrates to warm climates in winter. It feeds mainly on small grains and seeds. The turtledove is shy and seldom seen. But its sad, cooing note is often heard in spring. The turtledove may raise two broods of young in a season. The female lays two eggs in a loose nest placed in a low tree, shrub, or hedge. The mourning dove is sometimes wrongly called a turtledove.

Scientific Classification. The turtledove belongs to the pigeon and dove family, *Columbidae*. It is classified as genus *Streptopelia*, species *S. turtur*.   LEONARD W. WING

TUSCALOOSA, *TUS kuh LOO suh*, Ala. (pop. 75,143; met. area pop. 137,473), is an educational and industrial city on the Black Warrior River in western Alabama. It lies 58 miles (93 kilometers) southwest of Birmingham (see ALABAMA [political map]).

Tuscaloosa is a city of broad streets, tree-lined avenues, and beautiful old homes. Because of its many trees, Tuscaloosa is called the *Druid City*. The name comes from a religious sect of ancient Britain whose priests lived in forests. See DRUIDS.

The city is the home of the University of Alabama. Stillman College and several hospitals, including the $4,200,000 Druid City Hospital, are also in Tuscaloosa. Large industrial plants located near the city produce cast-iron pipe, munitions, rubber tires, bricks, lumber, chemicals, and paper and paper bags. Tuscaloosa is also a large market place for the farm products of the region.

The word *Tuscaloosa* comes from two Choctaw Indian words, *tuska* (warrior), and *lusa* (black). Some people believe the city received its name from the Indian chief Tuskalusa who was defeated by Hernando de Soto in 1540. Tuscaloosa, incorporated as a city in 1819, served as Alabama's capital from 1826 to 1846. The capital then shifted to Montgomery, a larger city. Tuscaloosa has a commission form of government, and is the county seat of Tuscaloosa County.   CHARLES G. SUMMERSELL

TUSCAN COLUMN. See COLUMN.

TUSCANY, *TUS kuh nih*, or, in Italian, TOSCANA, is a political region, or state, in Italy. It lies on the western coast of Italy, and north of the city of Rome. Tuscany is made up of nine provinces. It covers an area of 8,877 square miles (22,991 square kilometers), and has a population of 3,502,362. Tuscany is an important agricultural and industrial center. Tuscan straw hats are known all over the world as *Leghorns*. Tuscany has the famous Italian cities of Florence, Pisa, Siena, and Leghorn (Livorno).

Tuscany has long been an important Italian center of art and learning. In early times, the territory was the home of an ancient people known as *Etruscans*. The Italian poets, Dante and Petrarch, used the language of Tuscany for their poems.   BENJAMIN WEBB WHEELER

See also ETRUSCANS; FLORENCE; SIENA.

TUSCARORA INDIANS. See IROQUOIS INDIANS.

TUSK. See ELEPHANT; HOG (Teeth); BOAR, WILD.

TUSKEGEE INSTITUTE is a privately controlled coeducational school in Tuskegee Institute, a part of Tuskegee, Ala. The institute has a college of arts and sciences and schools of applied sciences, education, engineering, nursing, and veterinary medicine. Courses lead to bachelor's and master's degrees.

Tuskegee Institute was established by an act of the Alabama state legislature in 1881. Booker T. Washington opened the school and served as principal and instructor for 33 years. George Washington Carver was one of the institute's best-known instructors. He was associated with the school from 1896 until his death in 1943. The institute's George Washington Carver Foundation conducts research in the natural sciences. The school also maintains a behavioral science research division. In 1974, Congress established the Tuskegee Institute National Historic Site. It includes Booker T. Washington's home, the George Washington Carver Museum, and several student-made buildings. For the enrollment of Tuskegee Institute, see UNIVERSITIES AND COLLEGES (table).   CRITICALLY REVIEWED BY Tuskegee Institute

See also CARVER, GEORGE WASHINGTON; WASHINGTON, BOOKER T.

TUSSAUD, *tuh SOH*, **MARIE GRESHOLTZ** (1760-1850), a Swiss modeler in wax, founded Madame Tussaud's Exhibition in London in 1802. Her descendants still maintain this famous museum of wax figures of prominent people. Some of the characters and scenes in the exhibition were modeled from life by Madame Tussaud and members of her family with remarkable accuracy. Additional figures for the museum are made each year.

Marie Gresholtz was born in Bern, Switzerland, and learned to model in her uncle's museum in Paris. In 1794 she married François Tussaud. During the French Revolution she was suspected of sympathy for the king. She was forced to model heads of the revolutionary leaders, and of victims of the guillotine. She was later imprisoned. When released, she moved to London with one of her two sons.   HELEN E. MARSHALL

TUSSOCK MOTH makes up a family whose caterpillars have *tussocks* (tufts) of hair along the back. These hair tufts are often brightly colored. The caterpillars may also have distinct stripes on the back. The adult moths develop only dull colors.

About 20 kinds of tussock moths live in the United States. The *gypsy moth* and *brown-tail moth* were brought

Larvae, or Caterpillars, of the Tussock Moth

USDA

to the United States from Europe. Their caterpillars have done much damage to New England trees (see BROWN-TAIL MOTH; GYPSY MOTH). The *white-marked moth* is another tussock moth, common in the eastern United States. The female has no wings.

The caterpillars, which are the moth larvae, damage trees by eating the leaves. The caterpillars often destroy whole orchards and forests. One method of fighting the gypsy moth has been to import beetles which eat the caterpillars.

Scientific Classification. The tussock moth belongs to the tussock moth family, *Lymantriidae*. The gypsy moth is genus *Porthetria*, species *P. dispar*. The brown-tail is genus *Euproctis*, species *E. chrysorrhea*.   EDWIN WAY TEALE

TUTANKHAMON, *TOOT ahngk AH mun*, was a king of ancient Egypt from about 1347 to 1339 B.C. His tomb, discovered in 1922 by Howard Carter, an English archaeologist, had not been opened since ancient times and still contained most of its treasures (see CARTER, HOWARD). Its four rooms were filled with objects that had belonged to Tutankhamon. These objects, including the innermost coffin of solid gold, are now part of the collection of the Egyptian Museum in Cairo. The king's body, in another of its threefold nest of coffins, has been restored to his tomb (see EGYPT, ANCIENT [picture: A Gold Mask of King Tutankhamon]).

Tutankhamon was a son-in-law of King Akhenaton. However, some scholars think that Tutankhamon was also the son of Akhenaton and the grandson of King Amenhotep III. Others argue that Tutankhamon and Akhenaton were brothers. Akhenaton had made Aton, the sun's orb, the sole god of Egypt. At first Tutankhamon's name was *Tutankhaton*, meaning *the living image of Aton*, or *the life of Aton is pleasing*. He took the name Tutankhamon when he restored a former state religion to appease the priests of the god Amon. See AKHENATON.

Tutankhamon was a child of eight or nine when he became king, and his unimportant reign continued for only nine years. His aged *vizier* (minister of state), Eye (also spelled Ay or Aye), served as co-regent. Eye was possibly Tutankhamon's other grandfather or a grand-uncle. After Tutankhamon's death, his widow asked the Hittite king Shuppiluliuma to send one of his sons to marry her and share the throne. The king sent Prince Zannanza, but the Egyptians intercepted and killed him. Eye succeeded Tutankhamon as king, and held his funeral in the Valley of the Kings.   LEONARD H. LESKO

Additional Resources

BRACKMAN, ARNOLD. *The Search for the Gold of Tutankhamen.* Reinhold, 1976.

CARTER, HOWARD, and MACE, A. C. *The Tomb of Tut-ankh-amen: Discovered By the Late Earl of Carnarvon and Howard Carter.* 3 vols. Cooper Square, 1963. Reprint of 1922-1933 ed.

HOVING, THOMAS. *Tutankhamen: The Untold Story.* Simon & Schuster, 1978.

TUTUILA. See AMERICAN SAMOA.

TUVA, *TOO vah*, was once a separate country, under the protection of Russia. Before it became part of Russia in 1944, it was known as *Tannu Tuva*. It is now an autonomous republic in Russia. Tuva lies in central Asia, between Siberia and Outer Mongolia. It has an area of 65,830 square miles (170,500 square kilometers), and a population of 266,000. Half of the people are Tuvinians, of Turkish stock. They make their living by raising cattle and other animals. The chief exports are wool and animal hides. The capital of the republic is Kyzyl.

The region was part of Outer Mongolia until 1911. Russia gained increasing control of Tuva and finally annexed it.   THEODORE SHABAD

TUVALU, *too VAH loo* or *TOO vuh LOO*, is a small island country in the South Pacific Ocean. It has a population of only 7,300 and a land area of only 10 square miles (26 square kilometers). Tuvalu ranks second to Vatican City as the world's smallest nation in population. It is the fourth smallest in area, after Vatican City, Monaco, and Nauru.

Tuvalu lies about 2,000 miles (3,200 kilometers) northeast of Australia. For location, see PACIFIC IS-LANDS (map). It consists of nine islands that are spread over about 360 miles (579 kilometers).

Tuvalu, formerly called the Ellice Islands, was ruled by Great Britain from the 1890's to 1978. It became independent in 1978.

Funafuti, a village of about 900 people, is the capital of Tuvalu. The country's basic unit of money is the tala. For a picture of Tuvalu's flag, see FLAG (Flags of Asia and the Pacific).

Government. Tuvalu is a constitutional monarchy and a member of the Commonwealth of Nations (see COMMONWEALTH OF NATIONS). A prime minister, chosen by a legislature of 12 members elected by the people, heads the government. Each island is administered by a council of 6 members. Island courts handle most trials. The High Court of Tuvalu hears appeals.

People. Most of the people of Tuvalu are Polynesians. They live in villages, most of which cluster around a church and a meeting house. Tuvaluan houses have raised foundations, open sides, and thatched roofs. The main foods of the people are bananas, coconuts, fish, and *taro*, a tropical plant with one or more edible root-like stems. The islanders raise pigs and chickens to eat

Schoolchildren in Funafuti, the capital of Tuvalu, play a game near their school. All except one of the islands of Tuvalu have a government-sponsored elementary school.

at feasts. Tuvaluans usually wear light, bright-colored cotton clothing.

The people speak the Tuvaluan language, and many also know English. Both languages are used in official government business. All the islands except one have an elementary school supported by the government. A few Tuvaluans attend a university in Fiji, an island country to the south.

Land and Climate. The nine islands of Tuvalu are, from north to south, Nanumea, Niutao, Nanumanga, Nui, Vaitupu, Nukufetau, Funafuti, Nukulaelae, and Niulakita. Most of the islands are *atolls* (ring-shaped coral reefs) that surround lagoons. The principal trees of Tuvalu are coconut palms and pandanus palms.

Tuvalu has a tropical climate, with daytime temperatures of about 80° F. (27° C). The southern islands receive about 140 inches (356 centimeters) of rain a year. The northern islands are drier.

Economy. Tuvalu has poor soil, few natural resources, almost no manufacturing, and no mining. Coconut palm trees cover much of the country, and the islanders use the coconuts to produce *copra* (dried coconut meat), their chief export (see COPRA). The people grow such crops as bananas and taro for their own use. They also weave baskets and mats for export. Many young islanders work on ocean ships because of a lack of opportunities at home. Tuvalu receives aid from some other countries, including Australia and Great Britain.

History. The first inhabitants of Tuvalu probably came from Samoa hundreds of years ago. In 1568, Álvaro de Mendaña, a Spanish explorer, became the first European to see part of Tuvalu. But the islands remained largely unknown to Europeans until the early 1800's. Europeans called them the Ellice Islands. Great Britain took control of the islands in the 1890's. In 1916, Britain combined the islands with the Gilbert Islands to the north to form the Gilbert and Ellice Islands Colony. In 1975, the two island groups were separated. The Ellice Islands were renamed Tuvalu. Great Britain granted Tuvalu independence on Oct. 1, 1978.   ROBERT LANGDON

TUZIGOOT NATIONAL MONUMENT stands near Clarkdale, in central Arizona. It contains the ruins of three large pueblos believed to have been occupied between A.D. 1000 and A.D. 1400 by ancestors of the Hopi Indians. Beads, pottery, and mosaics found there are now in the Tuzigoot Museum. The monument was established in 1939. For its area, see NATIONAL PARK SYSTEM (table: National Monuments).

TVA. See TENNESSEE VALLEY AUTHORITY.

TWAIN, MARK (1835-1910), was the pen name of SAMUEL LANGHORNE CLEMENS, one of the best and most popular American authors. He is generally considered the greatest humorist in American literature.

Few authors have been as successful as Twain in writing for both children and adults. *The Adventures of Huckleberry Finn*, one of the finest novels in literature, delights readers of all ages. Younger readers especially enjoy *The Adventures of Tom Sawyer* and *The Prince and the Pauper*, while adults best understand and appreciate Twain's travel books, satirical sketches, and the novel *A Connecticut Yankee in King Arthur's Court*.

Mark Twain traveled widely during his lifetime. He went from his boyhood home in Missouri to the East, up and down the Mississippi River from St. Louis to New Orleans, to the Far West and Hawaii, back to the East, to Europe many times, and finally around the world. Wherever he went, he gathered material for his stories. Twain observed and appreciated the comedy in life,

Mark Twain was a great American humorist. A white linen suit and a cigar became his trademarks in public appearances.

The Adventures of Tom Sawyer was the first novel Mark Twain wrote by himself. It contains a famous episode in which Tom tricks friends into whitewashing a fence. The novel, one of Twain's most popular works, led to three later novels about Tom.

BROOKLYN ACADEMY OF MUSIC, FEB. 7th

Tickets at 244 Fulton St. and
172 Montague St.

The Celebrated Jumping Frog of Calaveras County is generally considered Mark Twain's first important short story. This poster advertised one of Twain's lectures. Twain's reputation as a speaker rivaled his popularity as a writer.

but he was often gloomy in his outlook. His writings reflect both of these attitudes.

Mark Twain's Life

Boyhood. Mark Twain was born in Florida, Mo., on Nov. 30, 1835. He moved with his family to Hannibal, Mo., in 1839. Twain later made Hannibal famous when he wrote about it in *Tom Sawyer* under the name St. Petersburg, meaning St. Peter's town or heaven.

Twain's family was poor. The father died when Twain was 11, and the boy left school to become a printer. At first, he worked in Hannibal, principally setting type for his brother Orion's newspaper, the *Journal*. Twain left Hannibal in 1853. He lived in St. Louis, New York City, and Philadelphia, supporting himself by working as a printer. In 1854, he returned to work with Orion, this time in Muscatine and Keokuk, Iowa.

On the Mississippi. In the fall of 1856, Mark Twain moved to Cincinnati. The following spring he boarded a riverboat for New Orleans. He intended to go to South America to seek his fortune collecting coca along the Amazon River. While steaming down the Mississippi, he changed his mind and persuaded Horace Bixby, the pilot of the boat, to teach him to pilot.

Twain was a cub pilot until April, 1859, when he received a license to pilot on the Mississippi between St. Louis and New Orleans. The outbreak of the Civil War in the spring of 1861 closed the Mississippi to commercial traffic and Twain left the river.

Twain's work on the Mississippi was a valuable experience. He later said, "In that brief, sharp schooling, I got personally and familiarly acquainted with about all the different types of human nature. . . ."

On the Frontier. In July, 1861, Twain and Orion set off by stagecoach for Nevada, where Orion had been appointed secretary of the Nevada Territory. Twain tried gold mining in Nevada but failed. He wrote humorous stories of his experiences in the West and signed them "Josh." These stories gained him a job with the Virginia City *Territorial Enterprise* in the summer of 1862. He first signed himself "Mark Twain" in a dispatch to the *Enterprise* on Feb. 2, 1863. The name probably comes from a riverboating term meaning *two fathoms* (a depth of 12 feet, or 3.7 meters).

In May, 1864, Twain left for San Francisco. There, he worked as reporter for *The Morning Call* and wrote for two local magazines. He first came to the attention of Eastern readers when his story "The Celebrated Jumping Frog of Calaveras County" appeared in the New York *Saturday Press* on Nov. 18, 1865. Twain visited the Hawaiian Islands for the Sacramento *Union* in 1866. He sent back both serious and hilarious accounts of his experiences there. He returned to San Francisco, and gave his first public lecture on Oct. 2, 1866. Thus, during his five years in the West, Twain began his two permanent careers, writing and lecturing.

World Fame. Mark Twain's reputation spread rapidly after he returned from a cruise to Europe and the Holy Land in 1867. Humorous accounts of the trip appeared first in letters to newspapers, and later as lectures and as the travel book *The Innocents Abroad*.

On the voyage, Twain met Charles Langdon of Elmira, N.Y. Langdon showed Twain a miniature painting of his sister Olivia. Twain fell in love with Olivia through the picture, and never ceased to idolize her. He met her in December, 1867, and he married her in

February, 1870. They had four children: Langdon, who died in infancy; Susy, Clara, and Jean.

Twain and his wife lived in Hartford, Conn., from 1871 to 1891. There they built one of the most spectacular houses of the day. The porch, staircase, and other parts of the house suggested a Mississippi River steamboat. Twain was kept busy with lectures and frequent trips to Europe. Even so, he wrote his best books during this time. By the 1890's, he had earned more money and fame than his own Tom Sawyer ever dreamed of.

Last Bitter Years. Mark Twain's last 20 years were largely unhappy. Despite his extraordinary sense of humor, Twain had always been basically melancholy and often depressed. He was also torn by contradictory feelings. He shifted between liberal and conservative social beliefs. He wanted to have faith in God, but he basically doubted that God exists. He attacked persons who were too concerned with making money, yet he tried many schemes to increase his own wealth.

Twain invested in dozens of get-rich-quick schemes, almost all of them failures. A national financial crisis of 1893 left him deeply in debt. The income from his books and from a world lecture tour in 1895 and 1896 helped him regain much of his wealth, but his misfortune continued. Susy, his favorite daughter, died while he was on tour. Mrs. Clemens' health, which had never been good, became steadily worse. She died in 1904. The youngest daughter, Jean, died in 1909.

As Twain became embittered by misfortune and weakened by his own declining health, his writings became more bitter and pessimistic. He especially attacked the United States' acquisition of territory through military power. Twain always hoped for moral and social reform, but his hope decreased as he came to believe that people's actions are all guided by a tendency toward selfishness. Twain died on April 21, 1910. He is buried in Elmira.

Mark Twain's Works

Early Works. Twain's early writings consist of humorous sketches, letters, and newspaper accounts. His

Mark Twain Memorial, Hartford, Conn.

Mark Twain's House in Hartford, Conn., was built with profits from his book *The Innocents Abroad*. The Twain family lived in the house from 1871 to 1891. The author wrote his best books during this time, despite a busy schedule of lecturing and traveling.

first humorous story was "The Dandy Frightening the Squatter," which appeared in the magazine *The Carpetbag* on May 1, 1852.

"The Celebrated Jumping Frog of Calaveras County" (1865) is Twain's best early work. In it, Twain retold an old story about a frog being filled with buckshot. But he turned the story into a fine character sketch of frontier types. Aside from this story, however, there is little in his early writing to distinguish it from the work of other newspaper humorists of the day.

Travel Books. Twain's writing began to take on a more polished literary quality in his travel books. *The Innocents Abroad* (1869) deals with his trip to Europe and the Holy Land in 1867; *Roughing It* (1872) with his trip west from 1861 to 1866; and *A Tramp Abroad* (1880) with a walking trip he took in Europe in 1879. Most of *Life on the Mississippi* (1883) is the result of a trip from New Orleans to St. Paul in 1882 and 1883. However, chapters 4 to 17 treat Twain's days as a cub pilot hilariously. These chapters were originally published in *The Atlantic* magazine in 1875 as "Old Times on the Mississippi." In *Following the Equator* (1897), Twain describes his lecture tour of 1895 and 1896.

In all these books, Twain used his travels largely as an excuse for stories, jokes, old legends, bits of descriptions, character sketches, and satirical comments on the life of the time. With the possible exception of *Roughing It*, none of these books holds together well. However, single incidents are often superbly handled.

The following chapter headings from *Following the Equator* show Twain's sarcastic wit in the 1890's: "It could probably be shown by facts and figures that there is no distinctively native criminal class except Congress." "Man is the Only Animal that Blushes. Or needs to." "Pity is for the living, envy is for the dead."

Novels. Twain's novels vary greatly in quality. They range in artistic value from the masterpiece *Huckleberry Finn* to the confusing failure *The American Claimant*.

Twain's first novel was *The Gilded Age* (1873), a satire written with Charles Dudley Warner. The novel tries to capture the frantic life and uncertain values of the period following the Civil War in America. This period has since been called "the Gilded Age."

Tom Sawyer (1876) describes the adventures of an imaginative boy in a small Missouri town before the Civil War. Twain used his own boyhood to create three memorable characters—Tom, Tom's friend Huck Finn, and Injun Joe. The novel contains none of the preaching quality then common in books about boys.

The Prince and the Pauper (1881) resembles the popular sentimental and historical novels of Twain's time. It is a story of Edward VI, a boy who was king of England, and Tom Canty, a poor boy who looked almost exactly like Edward. The novel is an amusing satire of England in the mid-1500's, but most critics today do not consider it one of Twain's best works.

Huckleberry Finn was published in England in 1884 and in the United States in 1885. It deals chiefly with the adventures of the homeless boy Huck and the runaway black slave Jim as they travel down the Mississippi River. Its appeal is due largely to the fact that Huck tells the story. The material is highly concrete, being what a boy would talk about. The language gives the impression of real talk. Most of all, the story achieves unity and dignity through Huck's growing awareness that Jim is a human being, not a piece of property. The first three chapters and the last ten, in which Tom Sawyer is the central character, are primarily low comedy. Many readers find them less appealing than the central section.

A Connecticut Yankee in King Arthur's Court (1889) is a satire on the legends about the days of King Arthur. It describes the adventures of a New England mechanic of the 1800's who is magically transported back to the England of the 500's. The novel combines slapstick comedy with cutting satire on unreasonable human conduct. It shows how scientific and industrial developments can make people insensitive to human suffering.

Twain's last novels include *The American Claimant* (1892), *Tom Sawyer Abroad* (1894), *Pudd'nhead Wilson* (1894), and *Tom Sawyer Detective* (1896). Of these, only *Pudd'nhead Wilson* is considered a major work. The novel concerns a murder trial in Missouri in the 1830's. In the story, Twain returned to the subject of slavery and how it damages the human personality.

The Mysterious Stranger exists only in three incomplete versions. The material is important, however, since it shows Mark Twain trying to use fiction to express his late pessimism about life and the human race. The best-known version deals with a visit by a nephew of Satan to an Austrian village in the 1500's.

Nonfiction. Many of Mark Twain's essays and journalistic works are satirical attacks on current events. Twain also attacked people's false pride in their moral sense and their presumption in considering themselves godlike. In the essay *What Is Man?* (1906) and other works, Twain argued that everything we do is predetermined, and that free choice is therefore an illusion. All our motives, he said, are basically selfish.

Mark Twain's Standing as a Writer

Twain's reputation has risen steadily since his death. Twain's humor amuses the reader but leaves the reader thoughtful. As Twain himself hoped, he has come to be considered more than a humorist. Several serious themes appear throughout Twain's work. For example, he showed the great difference between what people hope to achieve and what they actually achieve. He also showed the difference between ideals and actions.

Twain's satire on America and Americans in the late 1800's is both shrewd and devastating. His comments on human beings and the universe, while often exaggerated, are almost always stimulating. Best of all, in his finest works Twain displayed a sensitivity to character, an ability to make episodes live on the page, and a precision of style. These elements help raise his writing to the level of art. In *Huckleberry Finn*, Twain became the first American to cut through the artificial qualities of the traditional novel and write in a style that gives the impression of real speech. Ernest Hemingway said that modern American literature "begins with *Huckleberry Finn*."

JOHN C. GERBER

See also CONNECTICUT (Places to Visit); MISSOURI (Places to Visit). For a *Reading and Study Guide*, see *Twain, Mark*, in the RESEARCH GUIDE/INDEX, Volume 22.

Additional Resources

GIBSON, WILLIAM M. *Theodore Roosevelt Among the Humorists: W. D. Howells, Mark Twain, and Mr. Dooley.* Univ. of Tennessee Press, 1980. The reaction of Twain to the political and social events of his time.

KAPLAN, JUSTIN. *Mr. Clemens and Mark Twain.* Simon & Schuster, 1966.

TWAIN, MARK. *Mark Twain Speaks for Himself.* Ed. by Paul Fatout. Purdue, 1978.

WAGENKNECHT, EDWARD C. *Mark Twain: The Man and His Work.* 3rd ed. Univ. of Oklahoma Press, 1971.

TWEED is a rough, heavy, hairy, woolen cloth that may contain synthetic fibers. Tweed is usually woven of fibers in two or more colors. Some tweed has a plain weave. Other tweed has a *twill* weave, with raised diagonal lines. A third way of weaving tweed is with the diagonal raised lines of yarn meeting each other to form "V's." This is called *herringbone twill*. In Scotland, where tweed was first woven, *twill* is often pronounced *tweel*, and *tweed* may have developed from this. Some people believe the cloth was named for the River Tweed. Genuine Harris Tweeds are made by hand. They are woven on the islands of the Outer Hebrides—chiefly on Lewis with Harris Island.

The yarns are dyed the colors of the heather in the Hebrides. The dyes are made from plants called *lichens*, which grow on the rocks of the islands. The lichen has an odor, called *cretal smell*, which never leaves the cloth. Rainy weather brings out this smell in a Harris Tweed suit. After the yarn is dyed, the longwise, or *warp*, threads are put on the looms. When the cloth is woven, the weavers have a ceremony called *waulking*, which means *shrinking*. The cloth is soaked in soapy water. The weavers stand around a table and pass the cloth around while each one pounds it and rubs it. As the weavers do this, they sing *waulking songs*. The cloth is then washed and dried and is ready to be made into clothing.

Tweed is a favorite cloth for sports clothing, and men's and women's coats and suits. Some tweeds are made in the United States, but they are usually lighter in weight and softer in texture than the cloth made in Scotland and England.

KENNETH R. FOX

TWEED, RIVER, rises in Borders Region, in Scotland. This stream flows generally eastward to empty into the North Sea at Berwick. Tweed cloth may have been named for the River Tweed.

TWEED, WILLIAM MARCY (1823-1878), was an American political boss who swindled New York City out of millions of dollars. He was born in New York City and received a grammar school education. He entered politics at an early age, and became boss of Tammany Hall. He organized his associates into the *Tweed Ring*, which sponsored schemes for city improvements. Millions went into the pockets of the Tweed Ring.

Thomas Nast exposed these corrupt practices in political cartoons, and many others fought Tweed. Finally in 1871, the Tweed Ring was broken up. Tweed was jailed, but escaped to Spain. In 1876, the Spanish government returned Tweed to the U.S., and he died in prison.

W. B. HESSELTINE

See also NAST, THOMAS; TAMMANY, SOCIETY OF; TILDEN, SAMUEL JONES.

Additional Resources

CALLOW, ALEXANDER B., JR. *The Tweed Ring.* Oxford, 1966.

HERSHKOWITZ, LEO. *Tweed's New York: Another Look*. Doubleday, 1977.

LYNCH, DENIS TILDEN. *Boss Tweed: The Story of a Grim Generation*. Arno, 1974. Reprint of 1927 ed.

MANDELBAUM, SEYMOUR J. *Boss Tweed's New York*. Wiley, 1965.

TWEED RING. See TWEED, WILLIAM MARCY.

TWEEDSMUIR, BARON. See BUCHAN, JOHN.

TWELFTH AMENDMENT. See CONSTITUTION OF THE UNITED STATES (Amendment 12).

TWELFTH NIGHT. See SHAKESPEARE, WILLIAM (*Twelfth Night*).

TWELVE TABLES, LAWS OF THE, were the first written laws of the Romans. The laws were inscribed on 12 tables, or tablets, that were fastened to the speaker's stand in the Roman Forum. They were the basis of private rights of Roman citizens. They dealt with legal procedures, property ownership, building codes, punishments for crime, and marriage customs.

The laws were drawn up in 451 and 450 B.C. by *decemvirs* (members of a council of ten men). The decemvirs based the laws on earlier Roman civil, criminal, and religious customs. The laws applied equally to all Roman citizens, and were written out so the common people could know their legal rights. The original tables were destroyed about 390 B.C. But large parts of them are preserved in works of Roman writers who, like all Roman boys, had learned them by heart. FRANK C. BOURNE

12-TONE MUSIC. See MUSIC (The 1900's); SCHÖNBERG, ARNOLD; BERG, ALBAN.

TWELVE TRIBES. See JACOB; JEWS (Early Days); PALESTINE (Early History and Hebrew Settlement; map).

TWENTIETH AMENDMENT and later amendments to the Constitution. See CONSTITUTION OF THE UNITED STATES (Amendments to the Constitution).

TWILIGHT is the period just before sunrise and the period just after sunset when the light in the sky is soft and mellow. Although the sun is below the horizon, light can be seen because the rays are scattered by molecules of the earth's atmosphere. Morning twilight begins when the sun is about 18 degrees below the horizon and ends when it reaches the horizon. Evening twilight begins when the sun first drops below the horizon and ends when it has sunk about 18 degrees below the horizon.

Twilight lasts the longest time at the North and South poles and the shortest time at the equator. During the six sunless months at the poles, dawn and dusk last a month each. But there is a period during Arctic and Antarctic summers when the sun never sinks below the horizon, and twilight does not occur. Just south of the Arctic, the summer sun never reaches 18 degrees below the horizon, and twilight lasts from sunset to sunrise. At the equator, twilight lasts about an hour, with some seasonal variations. SIDNEY ROSEN

TWILL is the name of a weave which is used in making many kinds of cloth. In twill, the lengthwise threads, known as *warp*, meet the crosswise threads, called *weft*, in such a way as to form diagonal, raised lines on the finished cloth. The lines may be raised either by the warp or the weft yarn. They may be raised only a little or a great deal. Twill weaves can be varied in many ways to produce broken, entwining, figured, or reversing lines. *Cashmere cloth* is a twill made with the weft threads. *Drilling* is a twill made with the warp yarns.

The materials *serge*, *gabardine*, and *cheviot* are twill-weave fabrics. KENNETH R. FOX

TWIN CITIES. See MINNEAPOLIS; SAINT PAUL.

TWINE is tough cord made from the twisted strands of hard leaf fibers, usually those from the sisal or henequen plants. The strands are mixed with abacá to make manila hemp. Twine is manufactured by drawing the raw fibers into slivers, which are combed and spun into twine. String is a type of twine, thinner than a cord and thicker than a thread. ELIZABETH CHESLEY BAITY

See also ABACÁ; SISAL.

TWINFLOWER, or LINNAEA, *lih NE uh*, is a favorite plant in rock gardens. The twinflower is an evergreen plant, which means that it does not shed its leaves in the winter. It has long, woody stems and roundish leaves. The plant's delicate flowers are shaped like bells, and are either pink or white. The flowers have a fragrant odor.

The twinflower, or Linnaea, grows best in moist, loose soil. It is reproduced by planting a cutting of the stem. It is native to Northern Europe, Asia, and North America. The Swedish botanist Carolus Linnaeus gave the plant his own name because it was his favorite among the wild flowers of Sweden.

Scientific Classification. The twinflower belongs to the honeysuckle family, *Caprifoliaceae*. It is classified as genus *Linnaea*, species *L. borealis*. PAUL C. STANDLEY

TWINS are two children born at the same time of the same mother. Twins occur about once in every 96 births. The tendency to have twins is hereditary. There are two general types of twins, *fraternal* and *identical*.

Fraternal Twins may be one boy and one girl. If the twins are of the same sex, they still may be easy to tell apart, because they grow from two different egg cells which happen to have been fertilized at the same time.

Identical Twins are of the same sex. Such twins are born from a single egg cell which separated into two parts early in its development. Each of the parts became one of the twins. They are usually much more difficult to tell apart than fraternal twins. But some identical twins have almost exactly the same characteristics in reverse. The hair of one twin may part on the right, for example, while the other's hair parts naturally on the left. These twins come from a common egg cell which did not separate until it began to develop right- and left-sided characteristics.

Identical twins are sometimes born joined together, usually at the hip, chest, or abdomen. Such twins are called *Siamese*, after Eng and Chang (1811-1874), Chinese twins who were born in Siam. Siamese twins may look different from each other. Sometimes they can be separated by surgery. But if they share a vital organ, surgery is rarely attempted.

Craniopagus Siamese twins are joined at the head. In 1956, surgeons at the National Institutes of Health in Bethesda, Md., separated 4-month-old craniopagus twin girls. Both twins survived and developed into normal adults. GEORGE W. BEADLE

See also MULTIPLE BIRTH.

TWISTER. See TORNADO.

TWO SICILIES, KINGDOM OF THE. See SICILIES, KINGDOM OF THE TWO.

TYCHE. See FORTUNA.

JOHN TYLER

John Tyler (signature)

Oil painting on canvas (1842) by George Peter Alexander Healy; Corcoran Gallery of Art, Washington, D.C.

The United States Flag had 26 stars when Tyler took office.

VAN BUREN
8th President
1837—1841

W. H. HARRISON
9th President
1841

POLK
11th President
1845 — 1849

TAYLOR
12th President
1849 — 1850

10TH PRESIDENT OF THE UNITED STATES 1841-1845

TYLER, JOHN (1790-1862), was the first Vice-President to become President upon the death of a Chief Executive. He succeeded William Henry Harrison, who died a month after taking office. Tyler, a Southern Democrat, had split with his party and had run with Harrison on the Whig party ticket.

As President, Tyler soon became a man without a party. The Whig program clashed with many of Tyler's lifelong beliefs. He vetoed almost every important bill. Angry Whigs tried to impeach him, the first such move against a President. They failed, but the resulting friction destroyed the Whig program.

For more than 75 years after the courteous, soft-spoken Tyler left office, historians dealt harshly with him. President Theodore Roosevelt summed up this opinion when he said: "Tyler has been called a mediocre man, but this is unwarranted flattery. He was a politician of monumental littleness."

Many historians today take a different view. They regard Tyler as a President of exceptional courage and imagination who displayed great devotion to the principles of Thomas Jefferson. He inherited a political situation he had never expected, and could not support. He could not have acted other than the way he did.

Historians also point to Tyler as the man who firmly established the right of the Vice-President to succeed completely to the presidency. When Harrison died, many Whig leaders suggested that Tyler be called only "Acting President." Tyler, with a patience that irritated his enemies even further, took over the presidency in fact as well as in name.

During Tyler's administration, many regions began to show signs of their future importance. Pittsburgh was becoming the home of busy ironworks. Cincinnati boasted of its well-paved streets and its schools that required children from 6 to 10 years old to learn algebra. Texas won its long fight to join the Union. Fighting with the Seminole Indians in Florida ended in 1842. Just two days after he signed the bill approving statehood for Texas, Tyler signed a bill making Florida a state. In New York City, stylish young men turned their shirt collars down and let their chin whiskers grow.

Early Life

John Tyler was born at Greenway estate in Charles City County, Virginia, on March 29, 1790. He was the second son of John and Mary Armistead Tyler. His father served at various times as governor, as speaker of the Virginia House of Delegates, and as a judge.

Young John had a mind of his own. When only 11 years old, he led a revolt against his tyrannical school-

─── **IMPORTANT DATES IN TYLER'S LIFE** ───

1790 (March 29) Born in Charles City County, Virginia.
1813 (March 29) Married Letitia Christian.
1816 Elected to the U.S. House of Representatives.
1825 Elected governor of Virginia.
1827 Elected to the United States Senate.
1840 Elected Vice-President of the United States.
1841 (April 6) Succeeded to the presidency.
1842 Mrs. Letitia Tyler died.
1844 (June 26) Married Julia Gardiner.
1861 Elected to Confederate House of Representatives.
1862 (Jan. 18) Died near Charles City, Va.

436

master, William McMurdo. His father sent him to William and Mary College in 1802. The boy studied hard and became especially interested in political subjects. He relaxed from his studies by writing poetry and playing the violin. John was graduated at the age of 17. He then studied law under his father, and was admitted to the Virginia bar in 1809.

Public and Political Career

State Legislator. At the age of 21, Tyler won election to the Virginia House of Delegates. He became a captain of volunteers when the War of 1812 began. But he resigned and returned to the legislature after a month, because his company had seen no action.

Tyler's Family. On March 29, 1813, Tyler married Letitia Christian (Nov. 12, 1790-Sept. 10, 1842), the daughter of a Virginia planter. They had five daughters and three sons. Mrs. Tyler died during her husband's presidency, and Tyler remarried 22 months later.

Congressman. Tyler ran for a vacant seat in the United States House of Representatives in 1816 and won an easy victory. He then was elected to a full term. In Congress, Tyler fought for a strict interpretation of the Constitution. He opposed any measure that extended the powers of government. Tyler voted against John C. Calhoun's bill for internal improvements because he believed such projects increased federal control. He denounced the Bank of the United States for the same reason (see BANK OF THE UNITED STATES).

Governor and Senator. When Tyler was 31, he ran for the United States Senate but lost. He served briefly as chancellor of William and Mary College, then as governor of Virginia from 1825 to 1827. Tyler was elected to the Senate in 1827, and his convictions on strict interpretation of the Constitution soon put him in an awkward position. He denounced South Carolina's

THE WORLD OF PRESIDENT TYLER

U.S. population was about 20,200,000 in 1845. Florida joined the Union on March 3, 1845, Tyler's last full day in office.

FLORIDA

WORLD EVENTS

1841-42 China opened its ports to world trade.

1843 The Hudson's Bay Company founded Fort Victoria in Canada.

1844 Gustave E. Pasch of Sweden invented the safety match.

1844 The YMCA was organized in London.

China Opened Its Ports

The Oregon Trail opened the way for settlement of the Pacific Northwest. About 1841, settlers began to follow this 2,000-mile (3,200-kilometer) route to Oregon.

Samuel Morse successfully demonstrated his electric telegraph before the members of Congress in 1844.

What hath GOD wrought

Kit Carson and John C. Frémont explored vast parts of the western United States between 1842 and 1844, traveling as far west as California.

The Birthplace of John Tyler still stands on the Greenway estate, which lies about one mile south of Charles City, Va.

Letitia Tyler, the President's first wife, died in 1842.

Julia Gardiner married Tyler during his last year in office.

attempt to nullify acts of Congress, but he also believed that President Andrew Jackson's measures against nullification were illegal (see NULLIFICATION). When the Virginia legislature instructed him to support Jackson, Tyler resigned from the Senate and withdrew from the Democratic party.

Tyler Becomes a Whig. In 1840, the Whig party was a loose coalition of groups with no agreed policies or political beliefs. In hope of luring Southern votes, the Whigs chose Tyler as the vice-presidential running mate of William Henry Harrison. Tyler accepted, believing that the Whigs had dropped their fight for a national bank and protective tariffs. Tyler opposed these measures. The Whigs barnstormed to victory, shouting the slogan "Tippecanoe and Tyler too." Harrison and Tyler defeated President Martin Van Buren by a huge majority. See HARRISON, WILLIAM HENRY.

Tyler's Administration (1841-1845)

Opposition to the Whigs. President Harrison died one month after his inauguration, and Tyler became President on April 6, 1841. He kept all the members of Harrison's Cabinet. Senator Henry Clay, the Whig leader in Congress, quickly submitted a legislative program. It called for a new Bank of the United States and for higher tariffs. Congress passed these bills, and Tyler replied with a sharply worded veto. That night,

---
TYLER'S CABINET

Secretary of State	*Daniel Webster
	Abel P. Upshur (1843)
	*John C. Calhoun (1844)
Secretary of the Treasury	Thomas Ewing
	Walter Forward (1841)
	John C. Spencer (1843)
	George M. Bibb (1844)
Secretary of War	*John Bell
	John C. Spencer (1841)
	James M. Porter (1843)
	William Wilkins (1844)
Attorney General	John J. Crittenden
	Hugh S. Legaré (1841)
	John Nelson (1843)
Postmaster General	Francis Granger
	Charles A. Wickliffe (1841)
Secretary of the Navy	George Edmund Badger
	Abel P. Upshur (1841)
	David Henshaw (1843)
	Thomas W. Gilmer (1844)
	John Y. Mason (1844)

*Has a separate biography in WORLD BOOK.

an armed mob marched to the White House. Hoodlums shouted insults at the President and hurled rocks through the windows. Tyler calmly issued guns to the White House servants and stood firm against the mob. The rioters melted away. When Congress passed a second bank bill, Tyler vetoed it again. He said it included all the abuses of a private banking monopoly.

The Whigs Disown Tyler. Tyler's second veto set off more Whig demonstrations against the President. Mobs burned him in effigy. The entire Cabinet resigned, except for Secretary of State Daniel Webster. Clay, still pushing the Whig program, rushed through a bill to give the states money from public-land sales. Tyler vetoed it. Clay came back with another measure linking distribution of this money with a higher tariff. Tyler vetoed that bill, too. Clay finally gave up and resigned from the Senate.

Attempt at Impeachment. The fight between Tyler and his own party became increasingly bitter. On Jan. 10, 1843, Whigs introduced impeachment resolutions in the House of Representatives. But the charges were so farfetched that even some Whigs sided with the Democrats to defeat the impeachment attempt, 127 to 83.

Tyler's Accomplishments. In 1841, Tyler approved the Pre-Emption Act, which allowed a settler to claim 160 acres of land by building a cabin on the property. This law sped settlement of Illinois, Wisconsin, Minnesota, and Iowa. Tyler brought an end to the Seminole War in Florida in 1842. That same year, a dispute with Great Britain over the boundary between Maine and Canada was settled on terms set up by Webster, who had remained in the Cabinet for this purpose (see WEBSTER-ASHBURTON TREATY). The United States signed a treaty with China in 1844 that opened the Orient to American traders for the first time.

The Annexation of Texas provided the chief issue during the last half of Tyler's term. The Texans had declared their independence from Mexico in 1836, and had petitioned to join the Union. Tyler favored annexation, but Northern Congressmen opposed him because Texas would have been a slave state. Congress did not act until after the election in 1844 of James K. Polk, who supported annexation. With annexation then a certainty, the House and Senate passed a joint resolution admitting Texas. Tyler signed the resolution on March 1, 1845. Two days later, on Tyler's last full day in office, he signed a bill admitting Florida to the Union. Texas formally joined the Union on Dec. 29, 1845, after Tyler had left office.

Life in the White House. Letitia Tyler was suffering from the effects of a paralytic stroke when her husband became President. Her only public appearance in the White House was at the wedding of her daughter, Elizabeth, on Jan. 31, 1842. Mrs. Tyler died on Sept. 10, 1842. Tyler's daughter-in-law, Priscilla Cooper Tyler, served as White House hostess until the spring of 1844. Tyler's daughter, Letitia Tyler Semple, then served as hostess until June of that year.

In 1844, Tyler was cruising on the U.S.S. *Princeton* to watch the firing of a new naval gun. The gun exploded, killing eight persons, including David Gardiner, a former New York state senator. Tyler had been courting Gardiner's daughter Julia (1820-1889), who was also among the guests on the ship. The death of Gardiner brought Tyler and Julia closer together. They were married in New York City on June 26, 1844. Tyler was the first President to be married while in office. Julia Tyler served as First Lady for eight months, and delighted the capital with her brilliant entertaining. President Tyler and his second wife had seven children.

Later Years

Spurned by both Whigs and Democrats, Tyler retired to Sherwood Forest, his estate near Charles City, Va. He lived quietly until just before the Civil War. Then, in February, 1861, he headed a Southern peace mission to Washington seeking a compromise on the issues that threatened the Union. Congress rejected the Southerners' proposals. In April, at a Virginia secession convention, Tyler voted in favor of Virginia leaving the Union. He won election to the Confederate House of Representatives in November, 1861, but died on Jan. 18, 1862, before taking his seat. In 1915, Congress dedicated a monument to Tyler's memory in Hollywood Cemetery, at Richmond, Va., where he is buried beside his second wife.   HUGH RUSSELL FRASER

Questions

Why did Tyler resign from the army?
Why and how did the Whigs desert Tyler?
How did Tyler show independence as a U.S. Senator?
Why did Tyler's second marriage arouse interest?
Why did Daniel Webster remain in Tyler's Cabinet after the other members had resigned?
Why did Tyler oppose the Bank of the United States?

Additional Resources

CHIDSEY, DONALD B. *And Tyler Too.* Nelson, 1978.
CHITWOOD, OLIVER P. *John Tyler: Champion of the Old South.* Russell, 1964. Reprint of 1939 ed. A political biography.
MORGAN, ROBERT J. *A Whig Embattled: The Presidency Under John Tyler.* Univ. of Nebraska Press, 1954.

SEAGER, ROBERT. *And Tyler Too: A Biography of John and Julia Gardiner Tyler.* McGraw, 1963.

TYLER, MOSES COIT (1835-1900), became the first great authority on early American literature. His chief books were the two-volume *A History of American Literature During the Colonial Time, 1607-1765* (1878); and the two-volume *The Literary History of the American Revolution, 1763-1783* (1897). In 1881, at Cornell University, he became the first professor of American history in the United States. He was born at Griswold, Conn.   MERLE CURTI

TYLER, ROYALL (1757-1826), was an American playwright and lawyer. He wrote the satire *The Contrast* (1787), the second American play and the first American comedy to be performed by professional actors. (*The Prince of Parthia* (1767) by Thomas Godfrey was the first American play.) In *The Contrast*, Jonathan, the first of many New England "Yankees" in American drama, gives a description of a playhouse of the 1700's.

Tyler's writing is patriotic and humorous. He wrote five other plays, but only one was performed. Tyler also wrote a novel, *The Algerine Captive* (1797); and a series of satirical letters, *The Yankey in London* (1809).

Tyler was born in Boston, and graduated from Harvard College in 1776. He studied law under John Adams and was an officer during the Revolutionary War. Tyler served as chief justice of the Vermont supreme court from 1807 to 1813.   RICHARD MOODY

TYLER, WAT. See WAT TYLER'S REBELLION.

TYLOR, SIR EDWARD BURNETT (1832-1917), a British anthropologist, is often regarded as the father of anthropology in the English-speaking world. His books stimulated the development of this science. Tylor was born in London. He traveled widely. Although he never studied formally at a university, he was professor of anthropology at Oxford from 1896 to 1909. He wrote *Researches into the Early History of Mankind* (1865) and *Primitive Culture* (1871).   DAVID B. STOUT

See also CULTURE (Characteristics of Culture); MYTHOLOGY (How Myths Began); RELIGION (The Origin of Religion).

TYNDALE, WILLIAM (1492?-1536), was one of England's leaders of the Protestant Reformation. He is famous for his translation of the Bible from Greek into English. In an effort to help enlighten the people, Tyndale translated the New Testament of the Bible, but could not get it published in England. After visiting Martin Luther in 1524, he finally got it printed in Germany and smuggled copies into England.

Tyndale was born on the Welsh border, probably in Gloucestershire. He was ordained a priest and preached in Gloucestershire. Other clergymen suspected him of heresy. Tyndale opposed King Henry VIII's divorce from Catherine of Aragon. He was burned at the stake as a heretic on Oct. 6, 1536.   GEORGE L. MOSSE

See also BIBLE (Early English Translations).

TYNDALL, *TIN dul,* **JOHN** (1820-1893), was a British physicist and natural philosopher. He is best known for his experiments on the scattering of light of different colors by small particles. The bluish appearance of a light beam passing through something like a soap solution is called the *Tyndall effect.* Tyndall was also interested in the biological sciences. In 1876, he described the action of a *Penicillium* mold in slowing the growth of bacteria. This was more than 50 years before Sir Alexander Fleming's chemical work on penicillin.

Tyndall was born in Leighlin Bridge, Ireland. He became director of the Royal Institution in 1867. G. GAMOW

TYPE is a letter, number, or other character used in printing. The words and numbers in all printed materials, including books, magazines, and newspapers, are made from type. There are two chief kinds of type, *metal type* and *photographic type*.

Metal type, or *hot type*, consists of small pieces of metal that have raised letters on top. It is made by machines that force a mixture of molten lead and other metals into *matrices* (molds) of each character.

Photographic type, also called *cold type*, consists of photographic images of letters. It may be produced by several methods, all of which are called *photocomposition*. In one method, printers make a film negative that contains a *font*, a set of all the characters of one style and size. A beam of light is projected through a character on the negative, producing a photographic positive of that character. *Cathode-ray tube photocomposition* is another method of producing type. Detailed instructions for the shape of each character in a font are stored in a computer. Using these instructions, a device called a cathode-ray tube projects beams of electrons that reproduce the character images on a screen. The images are then focused through a lens onto photosensitive paper or film. See PHOTOCOMPOSITION.

Another kind of type, called *dry transfer* or *rub-down type*, is often used to compose only a few words. Each character consists of a thin layer of hardened ink attached to a piece of waxed paper. The ink is simply rubbed onto another piece of paper.

Type is made in many sizes and thousands of styles. Each style of type, or *type face*, has its own characteristics. Some styles of type have bold, heavy lines, and

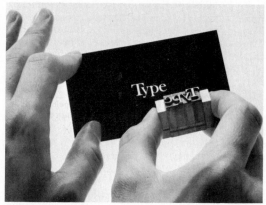

WORLD BOOK photo

Type is used in producing books, magazines, newspapers, and other printed materials. The two chief kinds of type are metal type and photographic type, both of which are shown above.

other type faces have a thin, graceful appearance.

Classes of Type. There are four general classes of type styles: (1) roman, (2) sans-serif, (3) script, and (4) italic.

Roman Types have small finishing strokes called *serifs* that extend from the main strokes of the letters. These types include the most commonly used styles. Printers use roman types for books, magazines, and newspapers. Popular roman styles include Baskerville, Bodoni, Garamond, and Times Roman. The text of WORLD BOOK articles is printed in Baskerville type.

Roman types include a few designs called *black letter* and a few called *uncial*. Black letter designs have highly decorative letters with thick, heavy lines. The first European printing types were black letter. Uncial designs are based on a letter style that was popular from the A.D. 300's to 700's. They were first produced in type in the 1900's. Most uncial letters look like rounded

Classes of Type   Type is made in thousands of styles. These type styles are grouped into four general classes: roman, sans-serif, script, and italic. A few styles of each class are shown below.

WORLD BOOK diagram

Roman

Give me liberty or give me death.
14-point Baskerville

Give me liberty or give me death.
14-point Garamond

Give me liberty or give me death.
14-point Times Roman

Sans-Serif

Give me liberty or give me death.
14-point Futura Medium

Give me liberty or give me death.
14-point Helvetica Medium

Give me liberty or give me death.
14-point Univers Medium

Script

Give me liberty or give me death.
14-point Bank Script

Give me liberty or give me death.
14-point Kaufmann Bold

Give me liberty or give me death.
14-point Brush

Italic

Give me liberty or give me death.
14-point Baskerville Italic

Give me liberty or give me death.
14-point Garamond Italic

Give me liberty or give me death.
14-point Futura Medium Italic

Parts of Letters

This diagram shows the main parts of lower-case letters. Printers measure the distance from the top of an *ascender* to the bottom of a *descender* to determine the point size of type.

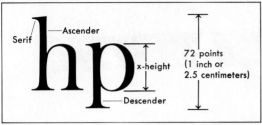

WORLD BOOK diagram

capitals. The first roman-style type similar to the ones used today was perfected about 1470 by a French printer named Nicolas Jenson.

Sans-Serif Types have no serifs. *Sans* is a French word that means *without*. Sans-serif styles are often used for advertisements, headings, and texts. Popular styles of this class include Futura, Helvetica, and Univers. The titles of WORLD BOOK articles are printed in Futura type. William Caslon IV, an English printer, made the first sans-serif type about 1816.

Script Types resemble handwriting. The *lower-case* (small) letters of many script styles are joined together. This class of types is widely used in advertising. Script styles include Bank Script, Brush, and Kaufmann. The first script types were produced in the mid-1500's.

Italic Types have slanted letters that *look like this*. Italics are often used to emphasize a word or a group of words. Most italic types are designed to accompany a roman or sans-serif type. The titles of many books, magazines, and newspapers are printed in italics. This class includes such styles as Baskerville Italic and Futura Italic. Aldus Manutius, a French printer, developed the first italic type in 1490.

Sizes of Type. Printers in some countries, including the United States, Canada, England, and Mexico, use a special scale to measure the size of type and the length

of lines of type. This scale is called the *American Point System*. One *point* on the scale equals 0.013837 inch (0.3514598 millimeter). One inch (2.5 centimeters) equals about 72 points. Printers measure the length of a line of type in *picas*. One pica equals 12 points.

The point size of type refers to the height of the characters. The height of the main part of a small letter is called the *x-height*. Such letters as *a*, *c*, *e*, and *x* have only an x-height, but others have strokes that extend above or below the x-height. Letters with *ascenders* include *b*, *d*, and *f*. Letters with *descenders* include *g*, *j*, and *p*. The point size of any type is the distance from the top of the ascenders to the bottom of the descenders. It may include a slight space above the ascenders or below the descenders.

Metal type ranges in size from 4-point to 120-point. However, most styles are not made in all sizes. The most common sizes include those from 6-point to 72-point. You are now reading 9-point type.

Most photographic type is made in only a few small sizes. A font can be enlarged or reduced to a few other sizes by lenses in the photographic equipment. In cathode-ray tube photocomposition, instructions for enlarging or reducing the type size are stored in the computer.

In some European countries, including France, Germany, and Italy, type is measured by the *Didot point*. This point is slightly larger than the American point.

History. Until the 1400's, most books were produced by people who copied them by hand. About 1440, a German printer named Johannes Gutenberg made the first practical use of *movable type*. Movable type consists of an individual piece of type for each character. It had been invented about 1045 by Pi Sheng, a Chinese printer, but did not become widely used.

For about 400 years, printers *set* (assembled) all type by hand. In the 1880's, Ottmar Mergenthaler, a German instrument maker, invented the *Linotype*. This machine assembled matrices from which whole lines of type were *cast* (molded) as solid slugs. In 1887, an American inventor named Tolbert Lanston developed a machine called the *Monotype*, which cast individual pieces of type and set them into lines. Printers still use the Linotype and Monotype. See LINOTYPE; MONOTYPE.

One of the first commercially practical machines to produce and set photographic type was invented in the 1940's. During the 1950's and 1960's, engineers developed new phototypesetting machines that set type much faster than the earlier kinds. These machines can be linked to computers that handle many tasks formerly performed by people. For example, the computers "tell" the machine how to *justify* (align) lines of type and hyphenate words. Other developments in typesetting included machines that reproduced type characters from computer instructions onto the screen of a cathode-ray tube.   LEONARD F. BAHR

Related Articles. See the WORLD BOOK article on PRINTING for an explanation of how type is used in the printing process. See also the following articles:

Baskerville, John	Electrotyping	Italics
Bodoni,	Goudy, Frederic	Jenson, Nicolas
Giambattista	Gutenberg,	Stereotyping
Book (History)	Johannes	Teletypesetter

TYPE METAL. See ALLOY (Other Alloys).

Some Type Sizes

The most common sizes of type range from 6-point to 72-point. A few of the sizes within this range are shown below.

WORLD BOOK diagram

Type   6-point Baskerville

Type   18-point Baskerville

Type   30-point Baskerville

Type   72-point Baskerville

WORLD BOOK photos

A Typewriter prints when the typist strikes a key, forcing a metal character on an inked ribbon against paper, *above*. The characters on most typewriters are attached to metal levers, *lower left*. Some have the characters on a rotating ball, *lower right*.

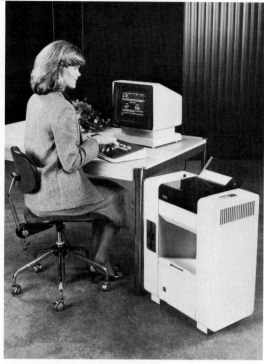

Wang Laboratories

A Word Processor is a machine that allows the typist to revise material quickly and easily without retyping the entire document. Most word processors have televisionlike *display screens*, which show the text as it is typed or edited.

TYPEWRITER is a machine that produces printed letters and figures on paper. People in homes and offices throughout the world use typewriters to write rapidly and neatly. The typewriter ranks as the most widely used kind of business machine.

Kinds of Typewriters. There are four basic kinds of typewriters: (1) manual, (2) electric, (3) electronic, and (4) text editing, usually called *word processing typewriters* or *word processors*. A manual typewriter operates entirely by the power supplied by the typist's hands. An electric typewriter has an electric motor to provide power, and so the typist only needs to touch the keys lightly. Such a typewriter costs more to buy and operate than a manual typewriter, but it is easier to use. It also enables a person to type faster and more neatly.

Manufacturers make portable models of both manual and electric typewriters. The greater compactness and lighter weight of portable typewriters make them popular among students and travelers.

Electronic typewriters resemble electric typewriters but include a tiny computer called a *microprocessor*. The microprocessor enables the typewriter to automatically perform such functions as setting margins and underlining. Most microprocessors in electronic typewriters also have a device called a *memory*. Names, dates, addresses, and other material that a typist frequently repeats can be stored in the memory. When the typist presses the appropriate key, the machine types the stored material automatically.

With word processors, the material the operator types is stored on a magnetic card, tape, or disk. The typist can make corrections by simply typing over an error. The typist can also add, delete, or move individual letters, words, lines, and paragraphs without retyping the entire document. After the operator finishes typing a document, the machine prints it out at the touch of a button. Many word processing units print as many as 600 words per minute—more than eight times the speed of a good typist.

Most word processors have a *display screen*, an electronic screen that shows material as it is typed and changed. Most word processors also include a microprocessor, which enables the machine to handle a variety of complicated tasks. For example, most word processors can sort and merge lists, perform mathematical equations, and transfer information to other word processors and to computers.

Parts of a Typewriter. Most manual, electric, and electronic typewriters have similar basic features. The machine has a keyboard that consists of buttons called *keys*. Each key carries two characters—letters, numbers, punctuation marks, or other symbols. A key forms one end of a lever that has a bar of metal type at the other end. When the typist strikes a key, the type bar rises and hits an inked ribbon or a thin strip of carbon tape. The ribbon or tape is in front of the paper, on which the type bar prints a letter or other character. A hard rubber roll called a *platen* holds the paper in the typewriter. The

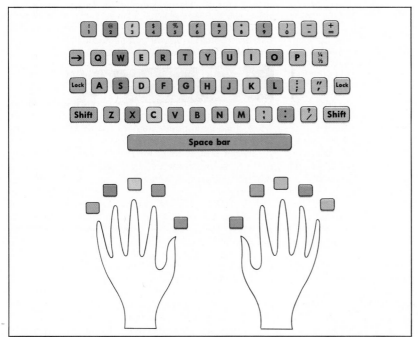

A Typewriter Keyboard has a standard arrangement of keys. The colors in this diagram show which finger is used to strike each key. Either thumb is used for the space bar.

platen automatically moves the paper one space to the left after the typist strikes a key.

Some typewriters do not have type bars. Instead, they have a ball-shaped *font* or *typing element*, a complete set of all the characters. When the typist strikes a key, the ball turns so that the correct character hits the paper. The ball moves along the line being typed, but the platen does not move. The type style or size can easily be changed by replacing the ball.

A warning bell rings when the typist nears the end of a line. A lock prevents any typing past a particular point unless the typist presses the margin-release key. Most typewriters also have such devices as an automatic ribbon reverse, a backspace lever, and a *tabulator*, which enables the machine to quickly list numbers or words in neat columns.

Typewriter manufacturers produce more than 5,000 kinds of keyboards and over 100 type styles. Some keyboards have the letters and symbols of various languages, and others feature special symbols, such as those used in music.

Some typewriters have large type for the partially sighted. Some typewriters for the blind are equipped with special devices that "speak" the characters as they are typed. Others type in braille.

Each letter or other character on most typewriters fills the same amount of space on the paper. But some typewriters feature *proportional spacing*, in which the space taken by each character varies according to its size. Proportional spacing gives letters the appearance of having been printed. Some machines have a *justifier*, a device that provides right-hand margins that are even.

Early Typewriters. A typographer, *left,* built in 1829, was an impractical forerunner of the typewriter. Three Milwaukee inventors designed the first efficient typewriter, *center,* in 1867. They experimented with the machine and made a greatly improved version, *right,* by 1873.

TYPHOID FEVER

History. During the 1700's and 1800's, many inventors in Europe and the United States tried to develop a practical typewriter. Such a machine had to be accurate, easy to use, fast, and inexpensive. In 1867, three inventors from Milwaukee—Carlos Glidden, Christopher L. Sholes, and Samuel W. Soulé—designed the first one. They patented their typewriter in 1868. Sholes continued to experiment and improve the invention. In 1873, E. Remington and Sons, a gun manufacturer, became interested in Sholes's typewriter. The company put the machine on the market in 1874, and other firms soon began to produce typewriters. The first successful portable typewriter appeared in the early 1900's, and electric typewriters came into use during the 1920's.

Through the years, many improvements have been made in the design and operation of typewriters. For example, some electric typewriters, called *self-correcting typewriters*, erase typing errors. They have chemically treated correcting ribbons in addition to typing ribbons. The chemicals cause any incorrect figure to peel off when the typist presses a certain key. The typist then types the correct character in the space that has been left blank. EILEEN FERETIC TUNISON

See also EDISON, THOMAS A. (The Wizard of Menlo Park); GLIDDEN, CARLOS; SHOLES, CHRISTOPHER L.; TELETYPEWRITER.

TYPHOID FEVER, *TIE foid,* is a serious infectious disease caused by the typhoid bacillus. It was once severe among soldiers during wartime, and common in all populated regions. However, as methods of good hygiene and sanitation developed, typhoid fever occurred less often. It is now relatively rare in areas with modern standards of sanitation.

How Typhoid Fever Spreads. Scientists call the typhoid bacillus *Salmonella typhi.* This organism is so tiny it can be seen only under a microscope. It lives and grows in waste materials from human bodies. Persons who eat food or drink water contaminated by this waste can get typhoid fever. Some persons who do not have the disease themselves carry the germs and can infect others. They are called "carriers."

Typhoid fever can be spread in rural areas where seepage from an outdoor toilet may infect the water supply. Also, flies may deposit germs on food or drink.

Symptoms. The illness develops from one to two weeks after the infection occurs. The person becomes feverish, with headache and pain in his back, arms, and legs. Nausea develops, and he loses his appetite. Red spots may appear on his body, usually on the abdomen.

The invading bacteria grow and multiply rapidly in the intestine. They cause changes, chiefly ulcerations, which are often accompanied by hemorrhages (see ULCER). If the ulcerations become severe, they may make holes in the intestine. Sometimes typhoid germs get into the blood stream. Then complications follow. The bone marrow may become infected, or the membrane covering the spinal cord may become infected, causing meningitis (see MENINGITIS). Typhoid fever reaches its height at about the start of the third week. By the fourth week, the intestinal ulcers begin to heal.

Treatment. Cold sponge baths help to control the fever. Large amounts of liquids are given to keep the person from becoming dehydrated. When the person has lost blood because of the intestinal hemorrhages, the doctor will sometimes perform blood transfusions or infusions of blood plasma. The doctor may also prescribe some of the antibiotic drugs (see ANTIBIOTIC). It has been found that chloramphenicol or tetracycline may alter the course of the disease, shortening the period of fever and freeing the person of the disease germs more rapidly.

Prevention. Good personal hygiene and public sanitation are the best measures for preventing the spread of typhoid fever. Sometimes persons must live or work where good conditions cannot be maintained, as in disaster areas. A special vaccine made from killed typhoid germs can protect them for several years. Perhaps one of the most important methods of prevention, but often the most difficult, is to identify and treat the carriers of the disease. H. WORLEY KENDELL

TYPHOON, *ty FOON.* The violent tropical cyclones that sweep over the Pacific Ocean from the Philippine Islands to Japan and the coast of China are called typhoons. Similar storms are called *hurricanes* in the West Indies and the eastern part of the United States. Typhoons are most frequent from July to October. They begin in low latitudes in the North Pacific, move northwest, and then turn northeast. These storms often do great damage in Japan. The western Pacific typhoons cut a storm path 50 to 100 miles (80 to 160 kilometers) wide. They travel slowly, but the violent gusty winds within the circle of the typhoon cause great destruction. See also CYCLONE; HURRICANE. JAMES E. MILLER

TYPHUS, *TIE fuhs,* is any one of a group of important diseases caused by *rickettsias.* These are tiny organisms that look like small bacteria but often behave like viruses (see RICKETTSIA). In human beings, they damage the lining and walls of blood vessels, causing bleeding and skin rashes. Some types of these germs infect animals as well as man. Scientists often call the infected animals "reservoirs" of the disease. Typhus diseases may be transmitted from man to man or from animals to man by lice, fleas, ticks, or mites. The diseases are named for the way they affect the human population (*epidemic typhus*), for the type of reservoir host (*murine,* or *rat, typhus*), or for the *vector,* or carrier (*tick typhus*). In the United States, tick typhus is called Rocky Mountain spotted fever (see ROCKY MOUNTAIN SPOTTED FEVER).

Epidemic Typhus is a serious type of typhus spread by the human body louse. This typhus has been associated with wars throughout history. Crowding, uncleanliness, and human misery during wartime favor the transfer of infected lice from one person to another. Often, more soldiers die of typhus than in combat. Observers estimated that typhus killed more than 3 million people in Russia during the revolutionary period after World War I. Typhus epidemics occurred in North Africa, Yugoslavia, Japan, and Korea during World War II. The disease also was common in many Nazi concentration camps. Scientists estimate that about 25 of every 100 people infected during a typhus epidemic die.

Primary symptoms of all typhus diseases are headache, skin rash, and stupor or delirium. The patient's temperature may rise to more than 104° F. (40° C), remain high for three or four days, and then drop rapidly. Some persons who recover from typhus harbor the live germs in their bodies. Years later these organisms may cause another attack. This makes it possible for immigrants to the United States to have typhus years after their arrival. When typhus recurs in this way it is called *Brill-Zinsser disease*. The disease was named for two American physicians who studied it extensively.

Murine Typhus, also called *endemic typhus*, is a mild form of the disease. It is transmitted to people by the rat flea. Like epidemic typhus, this disease occurs throughout the world, but does not spread as easily or rapidly. It was once a common disease in the southeastern United States. During the 15-year period that ended in 1946, scientists reported about 40,000 cases. But modern methods of treatment have caused a sharp decline in the occurrence of murine typhus.

Treatment. Doctors use antibiotics, particularly the tetracyclines and chloramphenicol, to treat typhus diseases. They also use specially prepared vaccines to prevent the diseases. To control the spread of typhus, particularly during an epidemic, doctors often use DDT and certain other insecticides. They dust people and their clothing with these substances, which kill the insect carriers. THOMAS H. WELLER

See also DDT; VIRUS.

TYPOGRAPHICAL UNION, INTERNATIONAL, is a union of workers in the printing trades affiliated with the American Federation of Labor and Congress of Industrial Organizations. It has about 800 locals in the United States and Canada, organized by crafts.

The union was founded in 1852. At first, its membership covered the entire printing trade. Later, the pressmen, bookbinders, stereotypers, electrotypers, and photoengravers organized unions of their own. The Typographical Union has headquarters at 301 S. Union Boulevard, Colorado Springs, Colo. 80901. The union publishes a monthly magazine called the *Typographical Journal*. WILLIAM R. CLOUD

TYPOLOGY. See ARCHAEOLOGY (Relative Chronology).

TYRANNOSAURUS. See DINOSAUR (Kinds).

TYRANNY. In ancient Greece, the type of government that had authority centered in a single all-powerful ruler was called a *tyranny*. The ruler held the title of *tyrant*; for example, *Dionysius*, tyrant of Syracuse. Today the word *tyranny* means a cruel and despotic government. See also GOVERNMENT (Who Governs?).

TYRE is the British spelling for *tire*. See TIRE.

TYRE, *tire*, was an ancient Phoenician seaport. It stood on the Mediterranean Sea in what is now southern Lebanon. Part of the city stood on the mainland and part on an island across a narrow channel. Tyre was an important shipping port, handling goods from Mesopotamia and Arabia. The city was also noted for the purple dye and fine glass that was manufactured there. The people of Tyre were noted as sailors as well as for their cultural and intellectual activities.

Egypt controlled Tyre before about 1100 B.C. Tyrians carried on trade for the Egyptians with the peoples of Asia Minor and the Aegean Sea. The city enjoyed its greatest prosperity between 1100 and 573 B.C. Part of that time, Tyre was ruled by Assyria, then by Babylonia, and the city was also briefly allied with Israel. Because of its island location, Tyre resisted capture for centuries. Tyrian merchants competed for trade with Greek merchants on the Mediterranean Sea. Tyre founded several trading colonies, including Carthage and Utica on the Mediterranean coast of North Africa

and Gades (now Cádiz, Spain), on the Atlantic Ocean.

In 573 B.C., King Nebuchadnezzar II of Babylonia crushed a 13-year Tyrian revolt. Alexander the Great conquered the city in 332 B.C. and built a road from the mainland to the island, creating a peninsula upon which the present town of Tyre stands (see LEBANON [map]). Tyre later became a part of the Roman and then Byzantine (East Roman) empire. Christian crusaders occupied the city from A.D. 1124 until Muslims captured it in 1291. LOUIS L. ORLIN

See also PHOENICIA.

TYROL, *tih ROHL*, or TIROL. The Tyrol is a beautiful mountainous region in western Austria and northern Italy. Before World War I, the Tyrol was a crownland of Austria. The Treaty of Saint Germain, signed in 1919, divided the region into two parts. Northern Tyrol was given to Austria and Southern Tyrol to Italy.

Austrian Tyrol. The Northern Tyrol has an area of 4,883 square miles (12,647 square kilometers) and a population of about 541,000. It is a scenic country, with beautiful mountains and many rivers. Important rivers include the Inn, the Ziller, the Lech, and the Isar. The Tyrol is a province of Austria. Its capital is Innsbruck, a city in the Inn Valley. See INNSBRUCK.

Italian Tyrol. The part of the Tyrol in Italy is known as *Trentino-Alto Adige*. It extends southward from the southern boundary of Austria to the Italian provinces of Brescia, Verona, and Vicenza. It is about 100 miles (160 kilometers) wide. The Italian Tyrol is divided into the provinces of Bolzano and Trento, which cover 5,256 square miles (13,613 square kilometers). About 849,000 people live in the area. Some 250,000 of them are German-speaking. Between World Wars I and II, the region was called *Venezia Tridentina*.

The Land and Its Resources. The Alps cover most of the Tyrol. The region is much like Switzerland except that it has no large lakes. The Oetztal Alps rise about 12,500 feet (3,810 meters) above sea level. Along the Tyrol's northeastern boundary, the Hohe Tauern mountain chain rises over 12,400 feet (3,780 meters) at Gross Glockner peak. The Kitzbühel Alps form the eastern border, and the Ortler Mountains stretch along the southwestern frontier. Brenner Pass cuts through the

WORLD BOOK map

The Tyrol is a region in Europe that includes part of western Austria and northern Italy. The map at the left shows its location. A map of the region itself appears at the right.

Tyrol at the Austro-Italian border. Adolf Hitler and Benito Mussolini held many meetings at Brenner Pass during World War II.

The Tyrol is a winter playground for the people of many countries. Skiing and tobogganing are favorite sports. The warm summers in the Tyrol attract vacationists and mountain climbers. Mineral springs in the south make the Italian Tyrol a popular health resort. Many people also visit Trento, which is a famous art center.

Forests cover more than half of the Tyrol region, but there are a few scattered farming districts. The Southern Tyrol is famous for its vineyards and fruit orchards. The mountains of Tyrol have some mineral deposits, including zinc, sulfur, coal, iron, and copper.

History. The Romans conquered the Tyrol in 15 B.C. Later, the region fell into the hands of various warring German tribes. In 1363, it became part of Austria. In 1919, the northern part of the Tyrol became a province of the Austrian republic. The Southern Tyrol was given to Italy. The Italians promised political and cultural autonomy to the large German-speaking minority in the Italian Tyrol, but the Fascist government of Italy suppressed all German clubs and newspapers, and forbade the teaching of the German language in the area. During World War II, thousands of German citizens in the Italian Tyrol were moved to Germany. In 1946, in spite of Austrian objections, the Southern Tyrol was again given back to Italy. By an agreement signed with Austria, Italy promised autonomy for German-speaking South Tyroleans. In the late 1950's, these people claimed they had not received autonomy and began fighting for it. A number of border skirmishes occurred between Italians and German-speaking South Tyroleans. Italy and Austria tried to reach an agreement but failed. In 1971, the Southern Tyrol conflict was finally settled after Italy granted the region a large amount of autonomy.   WILLIAM J. McGRATH

See also ALPS; DOLOMITES.

TYROTHRICIN, *TY roh THRY sin*, was one of the first antibiotic drugs. René Dubos discovered it in 1939. It is too poisonous to be used internally, but it is useful in preparing surgical dressings. Tyrothricin is also used in lozenges and nasal sprays for treating mouth, nose, and throat infections. It is produced by the soil bacillus *Bacillus brevis*.   KENNETH B. RAPER

See also ANTIBIOTIC; DUBOS, RENÉ J.

TYRRELL, *TIHR ehl*, **JOSEPH BURR** (1858-1957), was a Canadian geologist, historian, and mining engineer. He conducted studies during several expeditions in northwestern Canada that aided the development of the Canadian mining industry.

Tyrrell was born in Weston, Ont., near Toronto. He graduated from the University of Toronto in 1880 and joined the Geological Survey of Canada in 1881. In 1884, near Drumheller, Alta., Tyrrell discovered the first dinosaur bones ever found in Canada. Shortly afterward, he discovered one of the nation's largest coal deposits nearby.

During 1893 and 1894, Tyrrell traveled from Lake Athabasca across the barren lands of the Northwest Territories to Hudson Bay. During one eight-month period, he covered about 3,200 miles (5,150 kilometers), mostly through wilderness. This expedition included about 900 miles (1,448 kilometers) traveled largely on snowshoes. Tyrrell mapped the region and predicted correctly that the minerals there would greatly increase Canada's wealth.

Tyrrell left the Geological Survey of Canada in 1898 and became a mining engineer and manager. He joined the Kirkland Lake Gold Mining Company in 1924 and served as president of the firm from 1931 until his death. Tyrrell wrote many articles about geology and exploration in Canada and edited the journals of the great land geographer David Thompson.   LEWIS H. THOMAS

TYRRHENIAN SEA, *tuh REE nee uhn*, an arm of the Mediterranean Sea, lies between Italy, Sicily, Sardinia, and Corsica. It has an area of 60,000 square miles (155,399 square kilometers). It is sometimes called the Tuscan Sea, and its Italian name is *Mare Tirreno*. For location, see ITALY (physical map). The Tyrrhenian Sea connects with the Ligurian Sea to the north. The Strait of Messina links it with the Ionian Sea to the south. Principal ports on its shores include Naples and Palermo.

446